PRINCIPLES OF COMMUNICATION ENGINEERING

Principles of Communication Engineering

John M. Wozencraft
Irwin Mark Jacobs

WAVELAND PRESS, INC.
Prospect Heights, Illinois

For information about this book, write or call:
Waveland Press, Inc.
P.O. Box 400
Prospect Heights, Illinois 60070
847/634-0081

1990 reissued by Waveland Press, Inc.

ISBN 0-88133-554-1

Printed in the United States of America

7 6 5

Preface

During recent years a vast body of knowledge central to the problems of communication engineering has accumulated piecemeal in the journal literature. Unfortunately, this work is often couched in advanced mathematical terms, and no over-all synthesis at the level of an introductory textbook has been available. As a result, even at second glance, the disciplines of coding and modulation often appear to be distinct and the abstractions of information theory to be only vaguely connected with the realities of communication system design.

We hope that this book will provide a cohesive introduction to much of this apparently disparate work. We have been motivated by three related objectives. The first is to establish a sound frame of reference for further study in communication, random processes, and information and detection theory. The second is to make the central results and concepts of statistical communication theory accessible and intuitively meaningful to the practicing engineer. The third is to illuminate the engineering significance and application of the theory and to provide a quantitative basis for the compromises of engineering design.

Book content and scope reflect these objectives. The subject matter progresses systematically from elements of probability and random process theory through signal detection and selection, modulation and coding, demodulation and decoding, and engineering compromises. Unity is sought through consistent exploitation of the geometric concepts of Shannon and Kotel'nikov, which place clearly in evidence the interrelations among such phenomena as the incidence of threshold with "twisted" and "sampled and quantized" modulation systems.

The development of the subject matter is almost entirely self-contained and does not demand mathematics more sophisticated than now encountered in an undergraduate electrical engineering curriculum. We presume that the reader has a thorough grasp of Fourier and linear systems theory—that he is able not only to write down but also to evaluate a convolution integral—and that he has been exposed to complex integration. Prior knowledge of linear algebra and probability theory is helpful but not necessary. In those half dozen instances in which theorems must be invoked whose formal proof exceeds the level of the text an effort has been made to make their meaning plausible as well as plain. We also presume that the reader is already well founded in electronic circuits, which we do not discuss.

Although the mathematical level of the book is intentionally constrained, the intellectual level of the subject matter is not. Indeed, although the book begins at a quite elementary level, later chapters treat many topics that lie near the forefront of current communication research and incorporate certain results that have not previously been published. The early chapters are presented in a way that leads naturally into the deeper material of the later chapters, even though a less general presentation might suffice if an open-ended treatment were not desired.

To some extent depth of treatment has been facilitated by new and less formidable derivations of well-known results. To a larger extent, however, it has required restricting consideration to communication models that are mathematically tractable. The premise is that complex ideas are best conveyed in the simplest possible context. Thus the book is primarily concerned with Gaussian channel disturbances and performance bounds obtainable from union arguments. Extension to more general channels and tighter bounds requires additional technique but little that is new in the way of concept.

The selection and treatment of the subject matter reflects our bias as well as our objectives. For example, although coding is not an economically viable solution in many engineering environments, in certain others it appears to be the most attractive solution. We feel in consequence that a communication engineer needs to appreciate the operating characteristics, capabilities, and limitations of coding. An entire chapter is therefore devoted to a study of coding and decoding implementation.

The scope of the book is adequate to span a two-semester sequence of first-year graduate instruction, and the subject matter has been arranged with such a course in mind. A natural division is to cover Chapters 1 to 5 in the first semester and Chapters 6 to 8 in the second. This progression provides a unified and extensive treatment of digital communication before consideration of the mathematical and conceptual issues of continuous modulation, which are inherently more subtle.

The first five chapters may also be used alone as a self-contained one-semester introduction to data communication. An alternative one-semester course comprises Chapters 1 to 4 plus the first half of Chapter 7 and the first two thirds of Chapter 8. The latter sequence has the advantage of including some continuous modulation theory but forfeits the central idea that error-free communication is attainable even when a channel is noisy.

Either one-semester configuration may be used as a senior honors course for undergraduates who are seriously interested in communications; successively revised versions of Chapters 1 to 5 have been taught at the Massachusetts Institute of Technology to seniors by nine different faculty members during the four years of manuscript preparation. On the other hand, Chapter 6 and the last parts of Chapters 7 and 8 seem distinctly graduate in character. Most of the problems at the end of each chapter are relatively deep and many extend the material of the text. We anticipate that instructors teaching undergraduates will wish to supplement these problems with others designed for purposes of drill.

No book is written in a vacuum, but we feel a special debt to our colleagues. The intellectual mainsprings of this work stem from the pioneering research of T. A. Kotel'nikov, C. E. Shannon, R. M. Fano, and P. Elias. To the last three we are indebted not only for their work but also for their inspired teaching, generous counsel, and constant encouragement. Several of the recent refinements and extensions of the theory are attributable to R. G. Gallager. Valuable suggestions were received from W. B. Davenport, W. M. Siebert, B. Reiffen, H. A. Van Trees, D. A. Sakrison, R. S. Kennedy, I. G. Stiglitz, V. R. Algazi, T. S. Huang, A. M. Manders, H. A. Yudkin, and J. E. Savage. In addition, both of us have benefited immeasurably from our association with the M. I. T. Lincoln Laboratory, at which the experimental work discussed in Chapter 6 was performed under the direction of P. Rosen and I. L. Lebow.

Deborah Brunetto, Barbara Johnson, Marilyn Pierce, Elaine Geller, and Louise Juliano typed and retyped the manuscript through innumerable revisions. Helen Thomas generously edited and D. G. Forney, Jr., carefully proofread the final version. Most of the computations were programmed by Martha Aitken.

We are grateful to the Department of the Army and to the National Aeronautics and Space Administration for partial support of the research reported herein. Manuscript preparation was supported in part by a grant made to the Massachusetts Institute of Technology by the Ford Foundation for the purpose of aiding in the improvement of engineering education. Lastly, to our students and associates in the Research Laboratory of Electronics and Department of Electrical Engineering at the Massachusetts Institute of Technology we owe an unrepayable debt for stimulation and opportunity.

J. M. WOZENCRAFT
IRWIN M. JACOBS

Cambridge, Massachusetts
June 1965

Contents

Glossary of Notation

Symbol	Meaning	Typical page reference
	section which may be omitted on a first reading	97
$\triangleq$	defined as	18
$\neq$	not equal to	30
$\approx$	approximately equal to	25
$\sim$	monotonically related to	109
$\gtrsim$	bound which is asymptotically tight	128
$\Rightarrow$	implies, causes	132
$\Leftrightarrow$	if and only if	152
$\rightarrow$	transformed to	111
$\leftrightarrow$	1:1 transformation or identification	8
$8 = 5 + 3 > 5 + 2 = 7;$		
or	sequence of equalities and inequalities	
$8 = 5 + 3$	8 equals 5 + 3	
$> 5 + 2$	5 + 3 is greater than 5 + 2	
$= 7;$	5 + 2 equals 7	185
$\alpha, \beta, \gamma, \xi$	dummy variables (continuous)	
i, j, k, l	indices (integers)	
j	$\sqrt{-1}$	90
$\ln$	natural logarithm	79
$\log_a$	logarithm to base a	286
$\mathcal{S}/\mathcal{N}$	signal-to-noise ratio	240, 588
$\{\ \}$	set of objects	8, 17
$\{A_i\}$	set of events	17
A^c	complement of A	18
$A \cup B$	union of events	18
AB or $A \cap B$	intersection of events	18
$\mathbf{A}$	matrix	192
$\mathbf{A}^T$	matrix transpose	193
$\mathbf{A}^{-1}$	matrix inverse	198
(0)	matrix with all zero elements	161
$\mathbf{z} = (z_1, z_2, \ldots z_N)$	vector	193
$\sum_{i=1}^{N} a_i$	$a_1 + a_2 + \cdots + a_N$	21

Symbol	*Meaning*	*Typical page reference*
$\prod_{i=1}^{N} a_i$	$a_1 a_2 \cdot \cdots \cdot a_N$	71
$\bigcup_{i=1}^{N} A_i$	$A_1 \cup A_2 \cup \cdots \cup A_N$	115
Σ (circled)	addition—block diagram symbol	7
$\otimes$	multiplication—block diagram symbol	228
* (on line)	convolution	72, 91
* (superscript)	complex conjugate	242
$[a, b]$	interval of the real line, $a \leqslant x \leqslant b$	2
$\int_I$	integral over I $\left(= \int_a^b \text{ if } I = [a, b]\right)$	23
$\mathbf{a}$	vector	57
$\lvert a \rvert$	magnitude of a	70
$\lvert \mathbf{a} \rvert$	length of vector	217
$\lvert \mathbf{A} \rvert$	determinant of matrix	199
$\mathbf{a} \cdot \mathbf{b}$	dot product	217, 234, 238
$\mathbf{a} \leqslant \mathbf{b}$	vector inequality	42
$k!$	k factorial, $0! \triangleq 1$	26
$\binom{M}{k} \triangleq \dfrac{M!}{k!\,(M-k)!}$	binomial coefficient	26
N!!	product of alternate terms	362

I

Introduction

Today the world is spanned by a web of electrical circuits that permits near-instantaneous communication over vast distances. This book is concerned with the fundamental principles underlying the engineering of these communication links. In particular, it provides an introduction to what communication technology can, and cannot, accomplish.

1.1 HISTORICAL SKETCH

The development of communication technology has proceeded in step with the development of electrical technology as a whole. Few indeed are the innovations that have not found almost immediate communication application. For example, the demonstration of telegraphy by Joseph Henry in 1832 and by Samuel F. B. Morse in 1838 followed hard on the discovery of electromagnetism by Oersted and Ampère early in the 1820's. Similarly, Hertz's verification late in the 1880's of Maxwell's postulation (1873) predicting the wireless propagation of electromagnetic energy led within 10 years to the radio-telegraph experiments of Marconi and Popov. The invention of the diode by Fleming in 1904 and of the triode amplifier by de Forest in 1906 made possible the rapid development of long-distance telephony, both by radio and wire.

In recent times the coin has often been reversed. The instantaneous success of the telephone, patented by Alexander Graham Bell in 1876, created an insatiable demand for communication which in turn has stimulated innumerable fundamental advances in electrical technology. For instance, the invention of the wave filter by G. A. Campbell[16] in 1917 came in response to the need for transmitting many different conversations simultaneously over a single telephone line.

Communication technology may be broken conveniently into three interacting parts: the signal-processing operations performed, the devices that perform these operations, and the underlying physics. Although it is to the first of these areas that this book is directed, it is important to realize that developments in all three have been mutually reinforcing. Indeed, one impact of a new device has frequently been the uncovering of new signal-processing questions. As an example, the development of the wave filter led naturally into Nyquist's investigation of the properties of bandlimited waveforms.

Communication Theory

Given that it is possible to perform a sequence of signal-processing operations, when is it desirable to do so and what are the advantages and limitations? Such questions and their answers constitute the corpus of what is called communication theory. This theory has assumed increasing importance since the advent of digital computers provided opportunities for signal-processing orders of magnitude subtler and more complex than ever possible before.

The beginnings of communication theory lie in the work of Nyquist,[60] who in 1924 extended unpublished work by J. R. Carson and concluded that the number of resolvable (noninterfering) pulses that can be transmitted per second over a bandlimited channel is proportional to the channel bandwidth. More exactly, Nyquist concluded that the maximum number of pulses resolvable in a T-sec interval with a channel of bandwidth W cps is kTW; here k is a proportionality factor no greater than 2, the exact value of which depends on the pulse waveshape and the particular definition of "bandwidth."

Shortly thereafter, in 1928, Hartley[41] reasoned that Nyquist's result, when coupled with a limitation on the accuracy of signal reception, implied a restriction on the amount of data that can be communicated reliably over a physical channel. Hartley's argument may be summarized as follows. If we assume that (1) the amplitude of a transmitted pulse is confined to the voltage range $[-A, A]$ and (2) the receiver can estimate a transmitted amplitude reliably only to an accuracy of $\pm\Delta$ volts, then, as illustrated in Fig. 1.1, the maximum number of pulse amplitudes distinguishable at the receiver is $(1 + A/\Delta)$. It follows that a sequence of kTW resolvable pulses, each of which can assume any one of $(1 + A/\Delta)$ amplitudes, affords a total of

$$M = \left(1 + \frac{A}{\Delta}\right)^{kTW} \tag{1.1}$$

distinguishable received signals.

As illustrated in Fig. 1.2, an equal number of distinguishable transmitter pulse sequences can be constructed and used to communicate one of M different possible messages reliably in time T. The procedure, indicated in Fig. 1.3, is to associate each distinguishable transmitter sequence

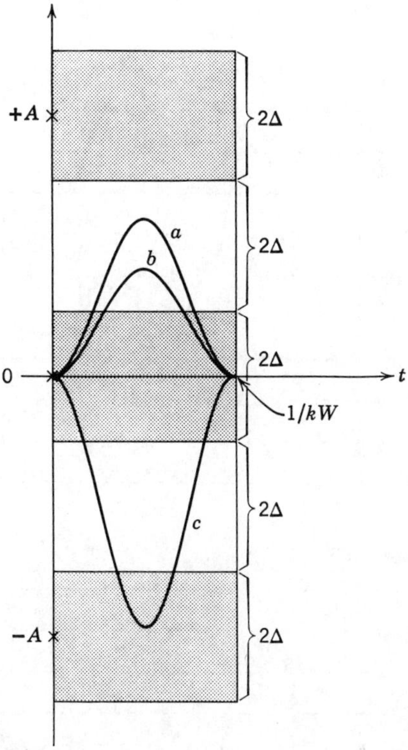

Figure 1.1 Distinguishable receiver amplitudes. Hartley considered received pulse amplitudes to be distinguishable only if they lie in different zones of width 2Δ. Thus pulses a and c are distinguishable but a and b are not. For the case shown, $A/\Delta = 4$ and there are five distinguishable zones.

uniquely with one of the M messages, say $m_0, m_1, \ldots, m_{M-1}$, and to transmit the kth sequence if and only if the actual transmitter input is m_k. Hartley concluded that if we attempt to increase M above the value specified in Eq. 1.1 by transmitting more than kTW pulses or by using pulse amplitude levels less than 2Δ volts apart, the signaling strategy of Fig. 1.2 will break down. The receiver no longer distinguishes reliably between all signal sequences, and communication becomes unsatisfactory.

Hartley's formulation exhibits a simple but somewhat inexact interrelation among the time interval T, the channel bandwidth W, the maximum signal magnitude A, the receiver accuracy Δ, and the allowable number M of message alternatives. Communication theory is intimately concerned with the determination of more precise interrelations of this sort. It is also concerned with maximizing the distinguishability of the transmitted message by appropriate signal processing (waveform design)

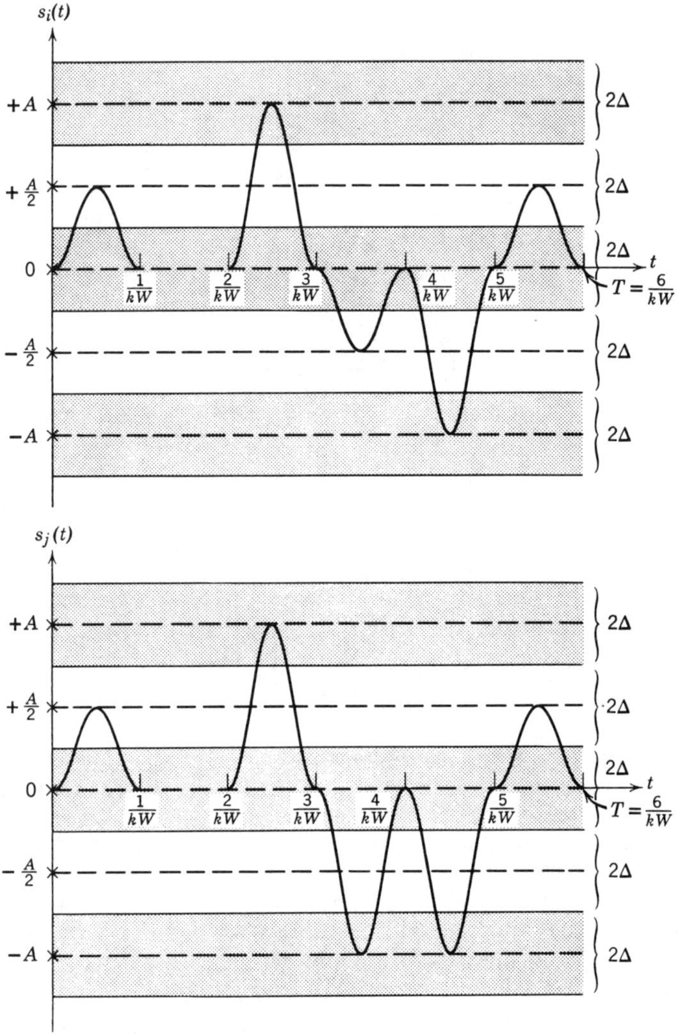

Figure 1.2 Distinguishable transmitter sequences. Two sequences of received pulses are distinguishable if one or more of their constituent pulse amplitudes are distinguishable. The two transmitter sequences $s_i(t)$ and $s_j(t)$ illustrated above lead to distinguishable receiver sequences whenever each pulse amplitude is altered by less than $\pm\Delta$ during propagation and are therefore called distinguishable. We may construct $M = (1 + A/\Delta)^{kTW}$ such sequences by allowing each pulse to assume any one of the $(1 + A/\Delta)$ amplitudes indicated by the dashed lines. (For the case shown, $A/\Delta = 4$, $kTW = 6$, hence $M = 15{,}625$.)

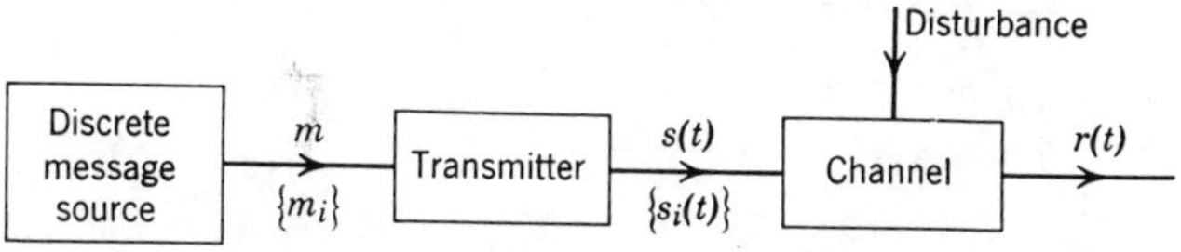

Figure 1.3 Discrete message transmission. There are M messages $\{m_i\}$, and M corresponding signal sequences $\{s_i(t)\}$. The transmitted signal, $s(t)$, is $s_k(t)$ whenever m is m_k.

at the transmitter, with processing the received signal to determine the transmitted message as accurately as possible (or as accurately as is justified economically), and with the complexity of implementing the transmitter and receiver signal processors.

Randomness

The essence of communication is randomness. If a listener knew in advance exactly what a speaker would say, and with what intonation he would say it, there would be no need to listen! Thus communication theory involves the assumption that the transmitter is connected to a random source, the output of which the receiver cannot with certainty predict. Otherwise, no communication problem exists.

Although less obvious, it is also true that there is no communication problem unless the transmitted signal is disturbed during propagation or reception in a random way. By way of example, consider communicating the content of a book chosen at random from the Library of Congress and assume that the alphabet (plus punctuation and numerals) comprises 64 symbols. To each symbol we can assign a six-digit binary number; for instance,

$$
\begin{array}{ll}
a\colon & 0\ 0\ 0\ 0\ 0\ 0 \\
b\colon & 0\ 0\ 0\ 0\ 0\ 1 \\
c\colon & 0\ 0\ 0\ 0\ 1\ 0 \\
\cdot & \\
\cdot & \\
\cdot & \\
9\colon & 1\ 1\ 1\ 1\ 1\ 1.
\end{array}
$$

The total content of the selected volume can then be written as a single long sequence of the binary symbols 0, 1 by allotting the first six digits of the sequence to the first letter of the volume, the next six digits to the second letter, and so forth. Finally, we may interpret the resulting binary sequence as a binary number between zero and one by placing a binary point at the beginning of the sequence, as shown in Fig. 1.4*a*.

We now observe that the entire volume can be designated by a single Nyquist pulse. As indicated in Fig. 1.4*b*, we need only adjust the pulse

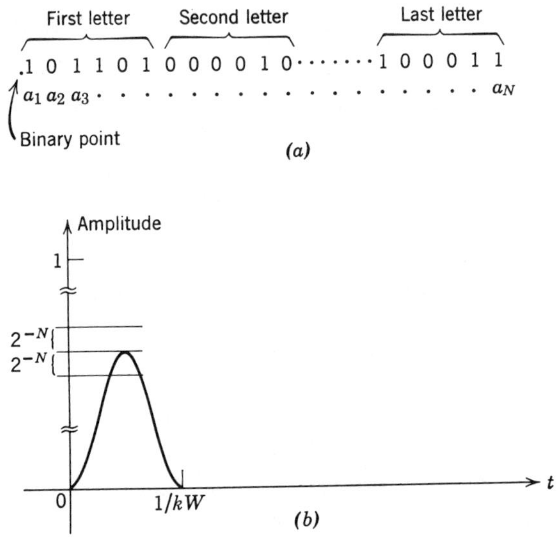

Figure 1.4 (*a*) A message represented by a binary number. If successive binary symbols are denoted $a_1, a_2, \ldots, a_N$, as shown, the value of the number is $a_1 \cdot 2^{-1} + a_2 \cdot 2^{-2} + \cdots + a_N \cdot 2^{-N}$. Here N is six times the total number of letters constituting the message. (*b*) A pulse with amplitude equal to the number representing one of 2^N messages.

amplitude to equal the value of the binary number in Fig. 1.4*a*. Indeed, if the transmitted amplitude could be precisely determined by a receiver, not only a single volume but also the contents of the whole Library of Congress could be communicated in this way by means of a single amplitude value. The procedure, however, is clearly preposterous. Small disturbances, called noise, always preclude either transmitting or receiving with such incredible precision. In Hartley's result, Eq. 1.1, the precision limitation implied by noise is incorporated in the accuracy, or quantization, parameter Δ.

Probabilistic Formulation of the Communication Problem

Although it recognizes the importance of noise, Hartley's conclusion does not account for the empirical fact that any receiver will occasionally estimate a transmitted amplitude incorrectly, regardless of how large a quantization grain Δ is designed into the communication system. The next major advance in communication theory occurred in 1942, when Norbert Wiener[84] ingeniously circumvented this difficulty by adopting a totally different point of view. His approach included the situation illustrated in Fig. 1.5, in which the received signal $r(t)$ is the sum of a

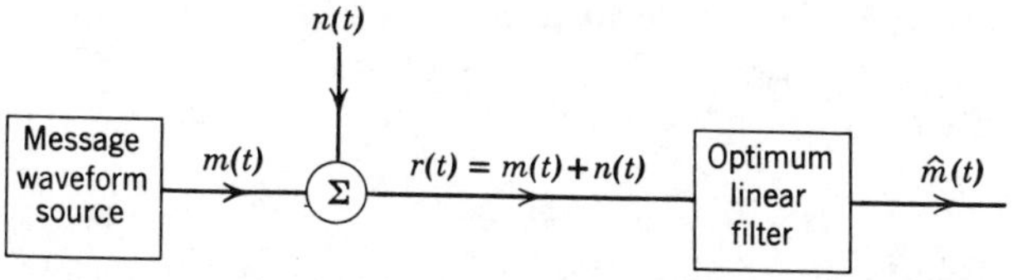

Figure 1.5 A communication problem considered by Wiener. The optimum filter minimizes the average value of the squared error $[m(t) - \hat{m}(t)]^2$, in which $\hat{m}(t)$ denotes the receiver's estimate of $m(t)$.

desired random message waveform $m(t)$ and an unwanted noise waveform $n(t)$. Wiener then solved the optimum linear filtering problem; that is, he determined the linear filter whose output is the best mean-square approximation to $m(t)$ when $r(t)$ is the filter input.

The use of the word "optimum" entered the world of communication engineering primarily in the pioneering work of Wiener. Many problems, however, remained unresolved. In particular, a message waveform $m(t)$—such as speech—is not often transmitted directly; instead, $m(t)$ is used to modulate (control some parameter of) the actual transmitted signal, say $s(t)$, as indicated in Fig. 1.6. Questions related to optimizing the transformation $m(t) \rightarrow s(t)$ and to processing the received signal when this transformation is nonlinear could not be answered until Rice[69] developed a satisfactory representation of the effects of noise, in 1944.

Kotel'nikov[51] addressed himself to these questions in 1947. He succeeded not only in analyzing all modulation systems then in existence but also in stating certain fundamental and unavoidable performance limitations on all possible future modulation and receiver systems. A significant portion of this book is based on Kotel'nikov's methods and results.

Communication theory reached maturity in the work of Shannon[75] in 1948. Previously the intuitively apparent but erroneous concept that noise placed an inescapable restriction on the accuracy of communication had been universally accepted. In sharp contradiction Shannon proved that the transmission effects of noise, constrained bandwidth, and restricted signal magnitude can be incorporated into a parameter, C, called the

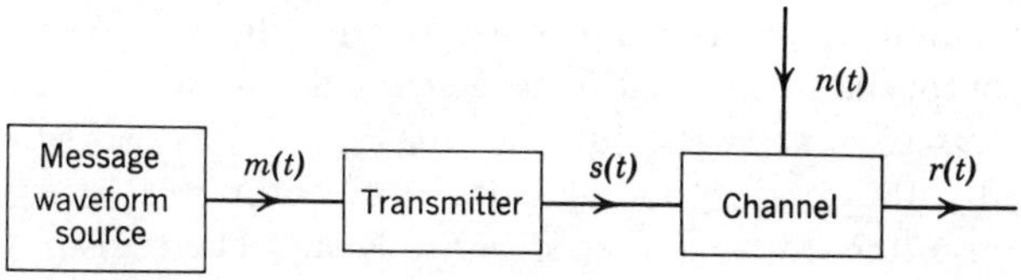

Figure 1.6 The transmitter transforms $m(t)$ into a signal $s(t)$ suitable for propagation over the channel.

channel capacity. The significance of channel capacity is this: provided the number M of message alternatives grows as a function of the signal duration T slowly enough so that

$$M < 2^{CT}, \tag{1.2a}$$

then arbitrarily high communication accuracy can be obtained in principle by choosing T large enough; that is, by using signals that are sufficiently long. Conversely, Shannon also showed that reliable communication is *not* possible—regardless of the signal-processing schemes adopted at transmitter and receiver—whenever

$$M > 2^{CT}. \tag{1.2b}$$

A major fraction of communication research since 1948 and a corresponding fraction of this text have been devoted to extending these results and determining how they may be approximated in engineering practice.

1.2 PLAN OF THE BOOK

A second principal result of Shannon's work has been the recognition that communication is fundamentally a *discrete* process. By this we mean that a receiver can meaningfully distinguish between only a finite number of message alternatives in a finite time. Although proof that the communication process is discrete—apparently even when the ultimate transmitter and receiver are human beings—exceeds the scope of an introductory text, an appreciation of this point of view can be gained by considering how well an accomplished novelist uses a finite alphabet to convey not only meaning but emotion. Indeed, the primary difficulty encountered in extending discrete analysis to voice communication is simply that no adequate criterion has thus far been discovered for describing the subjective equivalence to a listener of many quite different speech waveforms.

Once the fact that a receiver can distinguish meaningfully between only a finite number of message alternatives has been accepted, it follows that no significant loss in communication performance is entailed in restricting the transmitter to sending one of a finite set of signals. The block diagram of such a communication system is illustrated in Fig. 1.7. As in Fig. 1.3, the source output m is assumed to be generated at random from a set of M possible discrete messages, $\{m_i\}$, $i = 0, 1, \ldots, M-1$. Each message is associated with a corresponding signal waveform, $m_i \leftrightarrow s_i(t)$ for all i, and the transmitter sends $s_k(t)$ whenever m is m_k. The transmitted signal then propagates through the channel, and a corrupted version $r(t)$ is delivered to the receiver input.

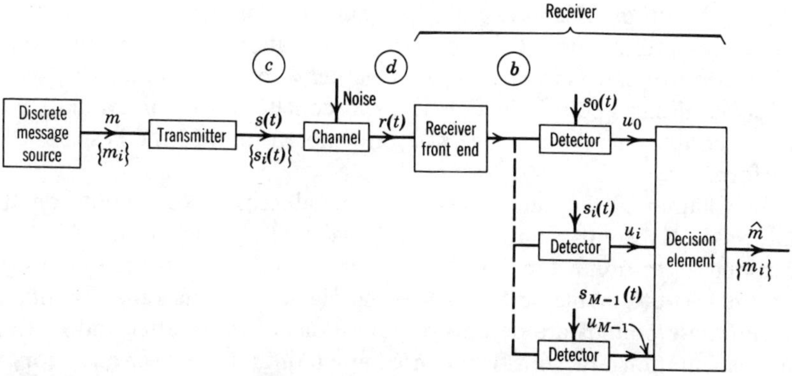

Figure 1.7 Block diagram of a discrete communication system.

The task of the receiver is to produce an estimate, $\hat{m}$, of the message generated by the source. It does this by comparing $r(t)$ against each member of the set of all M signal alternatives $\{s_i(t)\}$, replicas of which we presume are stored in the receiver.

The receiver structure shown in Fig. 1.7 is quite general. The receiver consists of a linear "front end" that compensates for attenuation during propagation, a set of M detectors, and a decision element. Each detector performs one of the comparison operations. In particular, the ith detector compares the received *waveform* $r(t)$ with the ith signal *waveform* $s_i(t)$ and produces a *voltage* value, say, u_i, that is a measure of their similarity. The decision element then determines $\hat{m}$ on the basis of these $\{u_i\}$, $i = 0, 1, \ldots, M-1$. For certain choices of the $\{s_i(t)\}$ a single detector may suffice, in which case the receiver diagram reduces to that shown in Fig. 1.8.

The chapters that follow are organized around these block diagrams. We begin by considering the point labeled a in Fig. 1.8 and by assuming that the entire communication system, with the exception of the decision element, has already been designed. In Chapter 2 we introduce the mathematical tool—probability theory—that is necessary for determining how best to design this element.

Chapter 3 is devoted to extending the concepts of probability theory to the study of random waveforms. In Chapter 4 we consider first the point

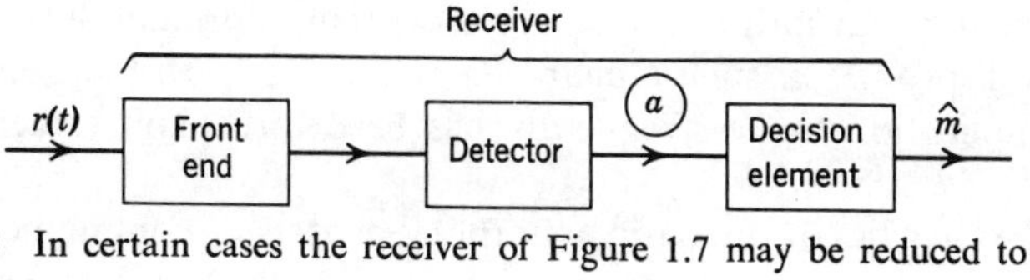

Figure 1.8 In certain cases the receiver of Figure 1.7 may be reduced to the form shown above.

labeled *b* in Fig. 1.7 and exploit the results of Chapters 2 and 3 to determine the optimum detector and decision operations when transmission is disturbed by white Gaussian noise. Chapter 4 continues with a discussion of signal design (point *c* in Fig. 1.7) and concludes with an evaluation of the over-all system when the $\{s_i(t)\}$ are chosen to yield the best possible performance.

In Chapter 5 we study the effects introduced by constraints on the allowable transmitter power and the available channel bandwidth (corresponding to point *d* in Fig. 1.7). In particular, bounds are established on the best attainable performance, and classes of signals that essentially attain these bounds are described. Questions of transmitter and receiver implementation are considered in Chapter 6, and the over-all theory is discussed in relation to a telephone line data communication experiment.

Chapter 7 is concerned with the extension of the preceding results to bandpass channels, to filtered signals, and to nonwhite noise. Certain effects of random scattering during propagation are described and evaluated.

Finally, in Chapter 8 we consider the case in which the output of the random source is a continuous waveform, such as speech, rather than one of a finite set of discrete messages. Conventional modulation systems are evaluated, and their performance is related to that afforded by discrete signaling. The chapter concludes with a determination of the fundamental limitations of continuous modulation and a discussion of the inherent advantage obtainable in a discrete approach to the communication problem.

1.3 THE ROLE OF COMMUNICATION THEORY

It is interesting that ingenious experimentation has often led historically to advances in communication technology far antedating real understanding of the principles involved. For example, frequency modulation (abbreviated FM) came into widespread use soon after Armstrong[3] first appreciated its noise-suppression capability in 1936, even though to this day some aspects of FM noise behavior remain puzzling and are the subject of active research. Moreover, the basic idea of frequency modulation had been devised long before in a misguided attempt to conserve transmission bandwidth and had lain essentially dormant subsequent to Carson's disproof[17] of such a characteristic in 1922. In the past the role of communication theory frequently has been to explain rather than to foretell.

On the other hand, the basic conceptual aspects of communication are now on solid ground, and an extensive body of methodology and results has been accumulated. Although innumerable strides of invention, both theoretical and experimental, remain to be taken, it appears increasingly likely that future advances will germinate within the framework of communication theory. Even when a problem is best approached experimentally, appreciation of the principles underlying communication engineering will provide insight vital to guiding the experiments to be performed.

2

Probability Theory

In our discussion of communication thus far we have emphasized the central role played by the concept of "randomness." If the ultimate receiver knew in advance the message output from the originating source, there would be no need to communicate; and if the propagation of electromagnetic signals were not disturbed by nature, to communicate the message would be no problem. The word "random" means "unpredictable"; on the basis of what we know about the past of a phenomenon, we are unable to predict its future *in detail.* A considerable body of mathematics (calculus, for example) has been developed to treat causal phenomena occurring in the real world. Similarly, mathematical models have been developed that are useful in the study of real-world random phenomena. The objective of Chapters 2 and 3 is to present the mathematical background essential to our further study of communication.

2.1 RANDOMNESS IN THE REAL WORLD

Our inability to predict the detailed future of a random phenomenon may arise either from ignorance or laziness: to the limit of our knowledge, the laws governing a progression of events may be fundamentally random (as in quantum physics); or they may be so complicated and involve such critical dependence on initial conditions (as in coin tossing) that we deem it unprofitable to undertake a detailed analysis.

A pertinent example of randomness is the transmission of radio waves through the ionosphere, illustrated in Fig. 2.1. Radio waves at certain frequencies are refracted as they pass through the ionized gas that constitutes the ionosphere. The degree of refraction depends on the detailed structure of the ionosphere, which depends, in turn, on the amount of ionizing solar radiation, the incidence and velocities of meteors, and on many other factors.

The voltage at the terminals of the receiving antenna is the resultant of a number of waves traveling over a variety of different paths. The

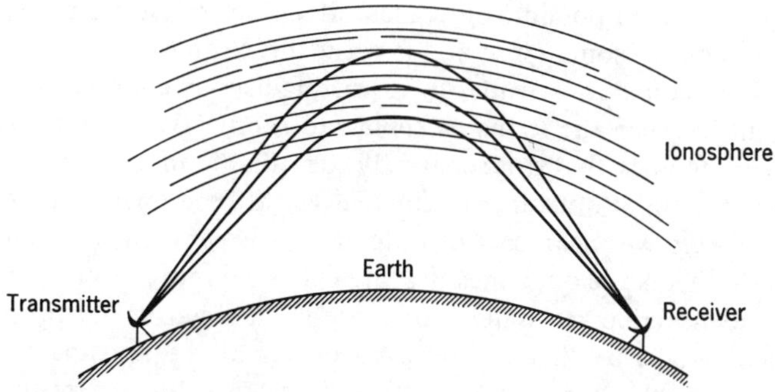

Figure 2.1 Refraction of radio waves by the ionosphere.

attenuation and propagation delay vary from path to path at any given instant of time and vary with time for any given path. The causes of these variations are far too complex to be calculable in detail. Thus the receiving antenna terminal voltage varies in a manner unpredictable in detail. We say it varies randomly.

Although we cannot predict exactly what the antenna output voltage will be, we find experimentally that certain *average properties* do exhibit a reasonable regularity. The received power averaged over seconds does not vary greatly over minutes; the received power averaged over a month does not differ greatly from that averaged over another month characterized by the same solar activity.

This *statistical regularity* of averages is an experimentally verifiable phenomenon in many different situations involving randomly varying quantities. We are therefore motivated to construct a mathematical model adequate for the study of such phenomena. This is the domain of the mathematical field of probability and statistics.

Random Experiments

To avoid confusion, we introduce the following terminology. By an *experiment* in the real world we mean a measurement *procedure* in which all conditions are predetermined to the limit of our ability or interest. We use the word *trial* to mean the making of the measurement. By a *sequence of N independent trials* of an experiment we mean a set of N measurements, in the performance of each of which the discernible conditions are the same.

An experiment is called *random* when the conditions of the measurement are not predetermined with sufficient accuracy and completeness to permit a precise prediction of the result of a trial. Whether an experiment should be considered random depends on the precision with which we wish to distinguish between possible outcomes. If we desire (or are able) to look closely enough, in some sense any experiment is random.

The discussion above leads us to distinguish in connection with an experiment between the terms *outcome* and *result*. By different *outcomes* we mean outcomes that are separately identifiable in an ultimate sense; in general, the set of outcomes in any real-world experiment is infinite. By different *results* we mean sets of outcomes between which we choose to distinguish. Thus the outcomes that are classified into a result share some common identifiable attribute. For example, a result in our propagation experiment might be that the received power at the antenna terminals, averaged over T sec, is between 10 and 15 μw. Such a result clearly embraces an infinitum of different possible received waveforms, or outcomes.

Relative Frequencies

We can now discuss more precisely what we mean by statistical regularity. Let A denote one of the possible results of some experiment and consider a sequence of N independent trials. Denote by $N(A)$ the number of times that result A occurs. The fraction

$$f_N(A) = \frac{N(A)}{N} \tag{2.1}$$

is called the *relative frequency* of the result A. Clearly,

$$0 \leqslant f_N(A) \leqslant 1. \tag{2.2}$$

In Fig. 2.2 we plot $f_N(A)$ versus N for a typical sequence of trials in a coin-tossing experiment, where A denotes the result "Heads." We observe that the relative frequency fluctuates wildly for small N but eventually settles down in the vicinity of $\frac{1}{2}$. This stabilization of the average incidence of Heads in a large sequence of repeated trials is a simple example of statistical regularity. In fact, we are so imbued with the notion that this stability is proper that were it not in evidence we would immediately suspect either the coin or the tosser. We feel intuitively that statistical regularity is a fundamental attribute of nature.

We often denote different results of an experiment by different subscripts; for instance $A_1, A_2, \ldots, A_M$. Results that cannot happen simultaneously in a given trial are called *mutually exclusive*. As a trivial example, in a coin toss the results Heads (say A_1) and Tails (say A_2) are mutually exclusive. For mutually exclusive results it is clear that the

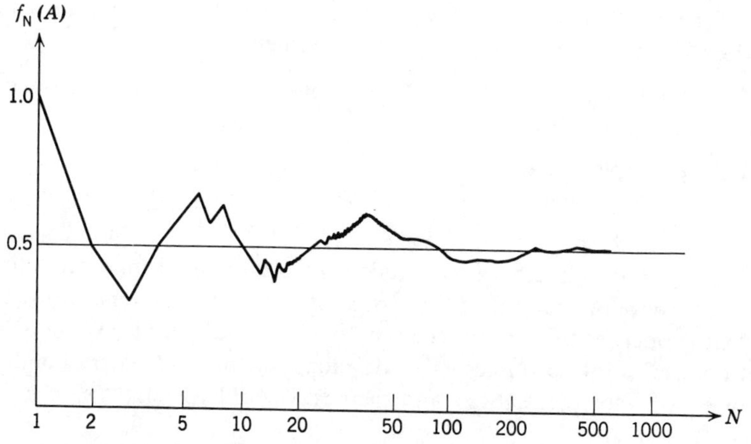

Figure 2.2 Relative frequency in coin tossing. (N is plotted on a logarithmic scale.)

occurrence of the result "either A_i or A_j" satisfies the equality

$$N(A_i \text{ or } A_j) = N(A_i) + N(A_j);$$

hence

$$f_N(A_i \text{ or } A_j) = f_N(A_i) + f_N(A_j). \tag{2.3}$$

Another example is tossing a die, with A_i denoting the result that the ith face shows. The result "odd face shows" is therefore the result "A_1 or A_3 or A_5." Clearly,

$$f_N(A_1 \text{ or } A_3 \text{ or } A_5) = f_N(A_1) + f_N(A_3) + f_N(A_5).$$

For a fair die we expect the relative frequency of each A_i to stabilize about $\frac{1}{6}$. Thus we expect the relative frequency of the result "odd face shows" to stabilize at $\frac{1}{2}$.

2.2 MATHEMATICAL MODEL OF PROBABILITY THEORY

Mathematical models prove useful in predicting the results of experiments in the real world when two conditions are met. First, the pertinent physical entities and their properties must be reflected in the model. Second, the properties of the model must be mathematically consistent and permissive of analysis.

We have seen that real-world random experiments involve three pertinent entities:

1. The set of all possible experimental outcomes.
2. The grouping of these outcomes into classes, called results, between which we wish to distinguish.

3. The relative frequencies with which these classes occur in a long sequence of independent trials of the experiment.

In the mathematical model of probability theory the corresponding abstractions are called:

1. The sample space.
2. The set of events.
3. The probability measure defined on these events.

We begin our discussion by defining these three mathematical entities. We then develop our model by assigning to them mathematically consistent properties that reflect constraints in the real world. We conclude with a series of examples that develops further the correspondence between our abstract entities and their real-world correlatives.

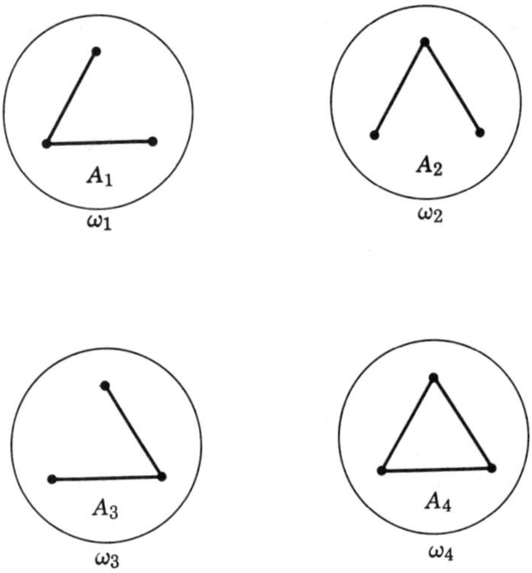

Figure 2.3 A sample space. Each graph A_i is associated with the sample point ω_i, $i = 1, 2, 3, 4$.

Fundamental Definitions

Sample space: a collection of objects. The collection is generally referred to by the symbol Ω. An object in Ω is called a *sample point* and denoted ω. As examples, Ω might consist of

the set of 4 graphs shown in Fig. 2.3,
several points on the real line,
the closed interval [0, 1] of the real line,
all points in a plane,
all time functions $f(t)$ defined for $-\infty < t < \infty$.

The sample space Ω corresponds to the set of all possible outcomes of a real world experiment; each outcome, in turn, corresponds to a sample point.

Event: a set of sample points. We usually label events by capital letters, such as $A, B, \ldots$, or $A_1, A_2, \ldots$. An event is concisely defined by the expression

$$A = \{\omega\text{: some condition on } \omega \text{ is satisfied}\}, \tag{2.4}$$

which is read "the event A is the set of all ω such that some condition on ω is satisfied."† For example, if Ω is the x,y plane and $\rho^2 \triangleq x^2 + y^2$, a possible event is $A = \{\omega\colon \rho < 1\}$. Then A is the set of all points interior to a unit circle centered on the origin. Similarly, if Ω is the set of all time functions, a possible event A is the subset of all time functions such that

$$2 \leqslant \int_{-\infty}^{\infty} f^2(t)\, dt \leqslant 2.5.$$

Since the entire sample space is a set of sample points, Ω itself is always an event.

Events in the mathematical model correspond to results in the real world.

Probability measure: an assignment of real numbers to the events defined on Ω. The probability of an event A is denoted $\mathrm{P}[A]$. The conditions that the assignment must satisfy will be discussed subsequently.

Example 1. If the sample space Ω is the set of 4 graphs shown in Fig. 2.3 and we define the event A_i to be the ith graph (sample point), a possible probability assignment is

$$\mathrm{P}[A_1] = \tfrac{1}{2},$$
$$\mathrm{P}[A_2] = \mathrm{P}[A_3] = \tfrac{1}{4},$$
$$\mathrm{P}[A_4] = 0.$$

Example 2. If Ω is the real line segment $0 \leqslant \omega \leqslant 1$ and we define the events $A_l \triangleq \{\omega\colon 0 < \omega \leqslant l\}$, $l \leqslant 1$, a possible probability assignment is $\mathrm{P}[A_l] = l$.

Example 3. If Ω is the set of all time functions $\{f(t)\}$ and we define the events $A_x \triangleq \{\omega\colon 0 \leqslant f(0) \leqslant x\}$, a possible probability assignment is $\mathrm{P}[A_x] = 1 - e^{-x}$.

The probability assigned to an event corresponds to that value at which we expect the relative frequency of the associated result to stabilize in a long sequence of independent real-world experimental trials.

† Throughout this text, braces are used to denote a set: for example, $\{A_i\}$ denotes the collection of all A_i, $i = 1, 2, \ldots$.

Ancillary Definitions

The definition of a sample space Ω and events such as $A, B, \ldots$ implies the existence of certain other identifiable sets of points.

1. The *complement* of A, denoted A^C, is the event containing all points in Ω but not in A.

$$A^C \triangleq \{\omega: \omega \text{ not in } A\}. \tag{2.5a}$$

2. The *union* of A and B, denoted $A \cup B$, is the event containing all points either in A or B or both.

$$A \cup B \triangleq \{\omega: \omega \text{ in } A \text{ or } B \text{ or both}\}. \tag{2.5b}$$

3. The *intersection* of A and B, denoted AB, is the event containing all points in both A and B,†

$$AB \triangleq \{\omega: \omega \text{ in both } A \text{ and } B\}. \tag{2.5c}$$

4. The event containing no sample points is called the *null event*, denoted $\varnothing$. Thus $\Omega^C = \varnothing$.

5. Two events A and B are called *disjoint* if they contain no common point, that is, if $AB = \varnothing$.

The relations between the operations complementation, union, and intersection are easily visualized geometrically. In Fig. 2.4 the events Ω, A, B, and C are represented by sets of points lying within labeled closed contours. Such drawings are called Venn diagrams. From Fig. 2.4 it is immediately obvious that

$$A \cup A^C = \Omega, \tag{2.6a}$$

$$AA^C = \varnothing = \Omega^C, \tag{2.6b}$$

$$A\Omega = A. \tag{2.6c}$$

Moreover, further study of Fig. 2.4 reveals that

$$(AB)^C = A^C \cup B^C \tag{2.7a}$$

$$(A \cup B)^C = A^C B^C \tag{2.7b}$$

$$A \cup B = (AB^C) \cup (AB) \cup (A^C B), \tag{2.7c}$$

where the three events on the right-hand side of Eq. 2.7c are disjoint.

† Intersection is also denoted $A \cap B$. We use this notation only when necessary for clarity.

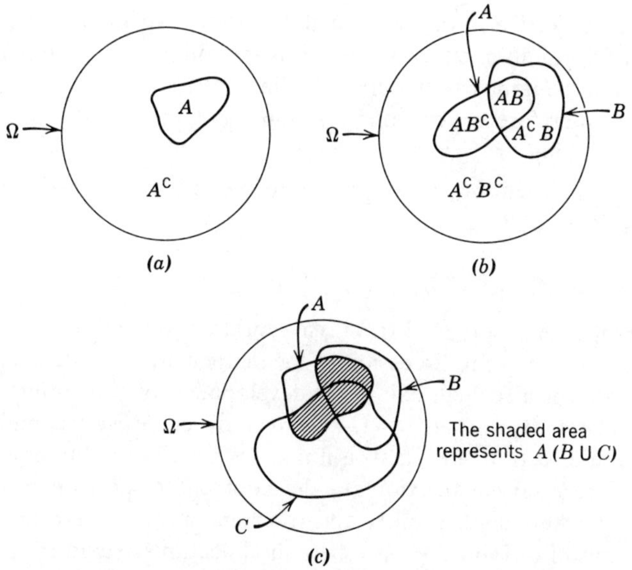

Figure 2.4 Venn diagrams.

A moment's reflection makes it clear that the union and intersection operations are commutative, associative, and distributive. That is to say,

$$\text{commutative} \begin{cases} A \cup B = B \cup A \\ AB = BA \end{cases}$$

$$\text{associative} \begin{cases} A \cup (B \cup C) = (A \cup B) \cup C \\ A(BC) = (AB)C \end{cases}$$

$$\text{distributive} \begin{cases} A(B \cup C) = (AB) \cup (AC) \\ A \cup (BC) = (A \cup B)(A \cup C). \end{cases}$$

Properties

In a long sequence of N independent trials of a random experiment in the real world the results $\{A_i\}$ and the observed frequencies $\{f_N(A_i)\}$ with which these results occur meet certain conditions:

1. The relative frequency $f_N(A_i)$ of every result satisfies the inequalities $0 \leqslant f_N(A_i) \leqslant 1$.
2. Every trial of an experiment has an outcome.
3. If two results A and B are mutually exclusive, then $f_N(A \text{ or } B) = f_N(A) + f_N(B)$.

Since our objective is to use probability theory to predict the results of real-world random experiments, it is reasonable that similar conditions should be imposed on corresponding entities in our mathematical model. We therefore restrict our assignment of probability measure to have the following properties.

I. To every event A_i, a unique number $\mathrm{P}[A_i]$ is assigned such that $0 \leqslant \mathrm{P}[A_i] \leqslant 1$.
II. $\mathrm{P}[\Omega] = 1$.
III. If $AB = \varnothing$, $\mathrm{P}[A \cup B] = \mathrm{P}[A] + \mathrm{P}[B]$.

These properties, motivated from real-world considerations, are all that we require in our present discussion of the mathematical model. They are also adequate for a formal, axiomatic development of probability theory whenever the totality of events on Ω—defined to include every complement, union, and intersection of events—is finite. (When this totality of events is infinite, it is necessary in an axiomatic development to specify carefully the collection of events defined on Ω and to extend property III to include infinite unions of disjoint events. These modifications extend the scope of the theorems derivable from the axioms.)

Properties I to III have several immediate implications. Since $A^{\mathrm{C}}A = \varnothing$, II and III imply that

$$\mathrm{P}[A] + \mathrm{P}[A^{\mathrm{C}}] = 1$$

or

$$\mathrm{P}[A^{\mathrm{C}}] = 1 - \mathrm{P}[A]. \tag{2.8a}$$

In particular, when $A = \Omega$,

$$\mathrm{P}[\varnothing] = 1 - \mathrm{P}[\Omega] = 0. \tag{2.8b}$$

Also, since the events (AB), (AB^{C}), and $(A^{\mathrm{C}}B)$ are disjoint, property III implies that

$$\mathrm{P}[A] = \mathrm{P}[AB] + \mathrm{P}[AB^{\mathrm{C}}]$$

$$\mathrm{P}[B] = \mathrm{P}[AB] + \mathrm{P}[A^{\mathrm{C}}B];$$

hence, from Eq. 2.7c, we have

$$\begin{aligned}\mathrm{P}[A \cup B] &= \mathrm{P}[AB^{\mathrm{C}}] + \mathrm{P}[AB] + \mathrm{P}[A^{\mathrm{C}}B] \\ &= \mathrm{P}[A] + \mathrm{P}[B] - \mathrm{P}[AB],\end{aligned} \tag{2.9}$$

$$\mathrm{P}[A \cup B] \leqslant \mathrm{P}[A] + \mathrm{P}[B]. \tag{2.10}$$

Probability Systems

A sample space, a set of events, and a probability assignment to the events together constitute a *probability system*. The probability assignment must be complete, in the sense that if events A and B are assigned probabilities a probability must also be assigned to the intersection AB and (by Eq. 2.9) to the union $A \cup B$. We now consider two examples that illustrate the assignment of probabilities.

Finite sample spaces. A probability system in which Ω has only a finite number of points, say k, is especially simple. The maximum number of distinct events that can be defined on such a sample space is exactly 2^k, since each of the k points may or may not be included in any particular event. For instance, if Ω consists of the three points ω_1, ω_2, ω_3, the most general set of events can be denoted by the binary sequences

$$\begin{aligned} A_0 &= (000) = \varnothing \qquad & A_4 &= (100) \\ A_1 &= (001) & A_5 &= (101) \\ A_2 &= (010) & A_6 &= (110) \\ A_3 &= (011) & A_7 &= (111) = \Omega; \end{aligned}$$

the convention is to set the ith digit of a k-digit sequence equal to 1 or 0, the choice depending on whether or not the point ω_i is included in the event.

The most general probability assignment for the 2^k possible events can be obtained by associating with each point ω_i in Ω a non-negative number P_i such that

$$\sum_{i=1}^{k} P_i = 1. \tag{2.11a}$$

The probability of an event A is then taken to be the sum of the P_i's of the points it contains. We write

$$\mathrm{P}[A] = \sum_{I} P_i, \tag{2.11b}$$

where I denotes the set of subscripts of sample points constituting A. For example, the probability of the event A_3 defined in the preceding paragraph is $\mathrm{P}[A_3] = P_2 + P_3$. It is evident that probabilities assigned in this way meet the conditions of properties I–III.

Real-line sample spaces. In sample spaces that contain an infinite number of sample points, events and probabilities may be assigned with considerably more freedom than in finite sample spaces. Consider, for example, the case in which the sample space is the real-line interval $\Omega = \{\omega: 0 \leqslant \omega \leqslant 1\}$. A possible probability system, which we have already briefly encountered, results when events are intervals of this line segment, plus unions, intersections, and complements of such intervals. The intervals may include both, one, or either of the end points. A possible probability assignment is then one in which the probability of an event is the sum of the lengths of the disjoint intervals that constitute the event. For example, if the event A illustrated in Fig. 2.5 is defined as

$$A = \{\omega\colon (a_1 < \omega \leqslant a_2) \text{ or } (a_3 \leqslant \omega \leqslant a_4) \text{ or }$$
$$(a_5 \leqslant \omega < a_6) \text{ or } (a_7 < \omega < a_8)\}$$

with

$$0 \leqslant a_i \leqslant a_{i+1} \leqslant 1; \qquad \text{for all } i,$$

then

$$\mathrm{P}[A] = (a_2 - a_1) + (a_4 - a_3) + (a_6 - a_5) + (a_8 - a_7).$$

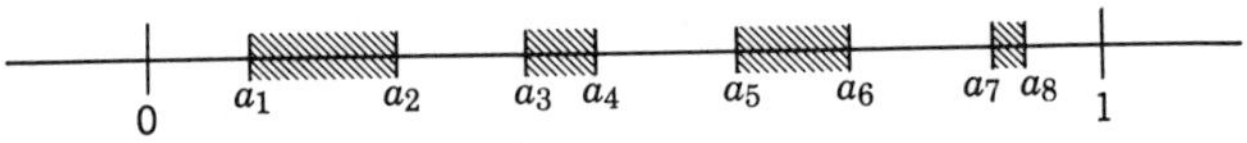

Figure 2.5 An event on the sample space $\Omega = \{\omega\colon\ 0 \leqslant \omega \leqslant 1\}$. The event A is the union of the shaded intervals.

A convenient way to describe the probability system considered above is to write

$$\mathrm{P}[A] = \int_I f(\omega)\, d\omega, \tag{2.12a}$$

where the integration is over the intervals constituting the event A and

$$f(\omega) = \begin{cases} 1; & 0 \leqslant \omega \leqslant 1 \\ 0; & \text{elsewhere.} \end{cases} \tag{2.12b}$$

For the event A defined above and the probability assignment of Eq. 2.12, P[A] is given by the length of the shaded area in Fig. 2.5. It is clear from the figure that this probability system satisfies properties I, II, and III. It is also clear, in contradistinction to the case of a finite sample space, that the most general probability assignment to events is not built up from probabilities assigned to individual sample points. The probability assigned to any point ω by Eq. 2.12 is zero; obviously this conveys no knowledge about the probability assigned to an interval.

The probability assigned to an interval *cannot* be an arbitrary function if properties I to III are to hold. For example, if the probability of an interval A were chosen to be the square of its length, properties I and II would hold for the unit-interval sample space, but property III would not. In particular, if

$$A \triangleq \{\omega\colon a \leqslant \omega \leqslant c\},$$

we would have

$$\mathrm{P}[A] = (c - a)^2. \tag{2.13}$$

Alternatively, however, we can write

$$A = \{\omega : a \leqslant \omega \leqslant b\} \cup \{\omega : b < \omega \leqslant c\}.$$

Since the two events on the right-hand side are disjoint, property III states that

$$\text{P}[A] = (b - a)^2 + (c - b)^2,$$

which is inconsistent with Eq. 2.13. Using two different methods of calculation, we get two different answers for P[A], and therefore the probability assignment is invalid. In assigning probabilities we must be careful to preclude the possibility of inconsistency.

A general probability assignment to intervals on $[-\infty, \infty]$ which is always valid is

$$\text{P}[A] = \int_I f(\omega)\, d\omega, \tag{2.14a}$$

where $f(\omega)$ can be any integrable non-negative function such that

$$\int_{-\infty}^{\infty} f(\omega)\, d\omega = 1 \tag{2.14b}$$

and I is the set of sample points constituting A. Equation 2.14a is analogous to the summation of Eq. 2.11b for finite sample spaces. Examples of appropriate functions $f(\omega)$ are shown in Fig. 2.6.

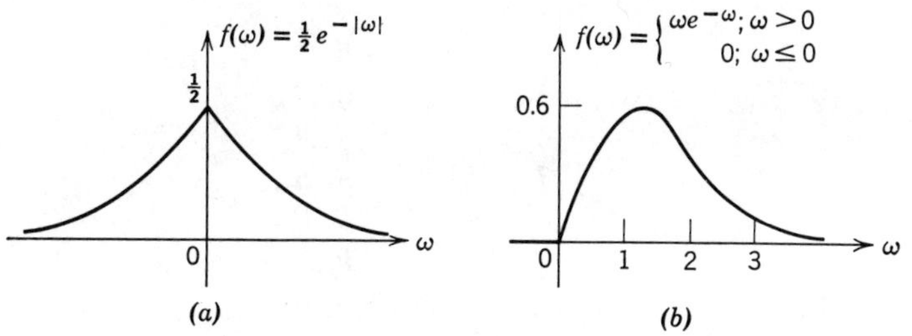

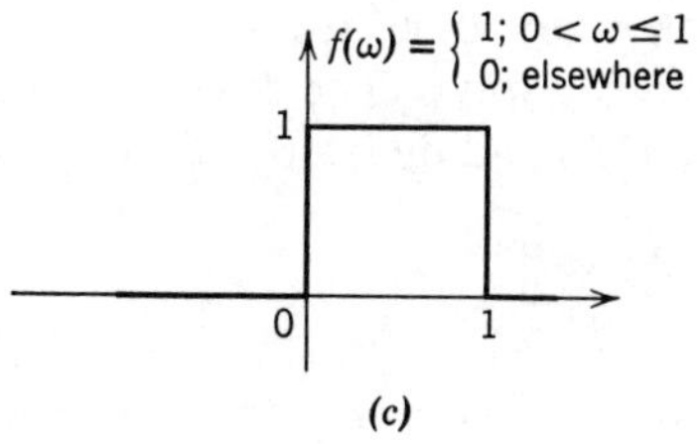

Figure 2.6 Examples of functions for probability assignment to real-line sample spaces.

Relation of the Model to the Real World

The function of a mathematical model in engineering is to permit the prediction, by calculation, of observable results in the real world. The utility of probability theory derives from the fact that it enables us to make precise mathematical statements that mirror the statistical regularity observed in nature. Before we can discuss this mirroring in a meaningful way, however, it is necessary to construct a mathematical model for a *compound experiment*; that is, an experiment which itself consists of a sequence of N independent trials of a simpler experiment. To do so we first consider relative frequency in more detail. Our objective is to discover how to assign probabilities meaningfully in the mathematical model of a compound experiment.

Consider the compound experiment that consists of two independent trials of a simple experiment, one result of which is A. In the compound experiment a set of possible results consists of the four sequences of observations (A, A), (A, B), (B, A), and (B, B), where the first entry denotes the result of the first trial, the second entry denotes the result of the second, and $B \triangleq A^c$. For $N = 10$ independent repetitions of the compound experiment, a typical sequence of results might be

Trial Number	Result	
1	B, B	
2	A, B	✓
3	B, A	
4	B, A	
5	B, B	
6	A, A	✓
7	A, B	✓
8	B, B	
9	B, B	
10	A, B	✓

The relative frequency of a particular compound result, say (A, B), can be calculated in either of the two following ways. The direct method is to count the number of occurrences, $N(A, B)$ and divide by N.

$$f_N(A, B) = \frac{N(A, B)}{N}.$$

An indirect method is to check (as shown) all results that begin with A

and to calculate the fraction of checked results that end with B. We call this fraction the "conditional relative frequency of B on the second trial, given A on the first trial," and denote it $f_N(B \mid A)$. For our example $f_N(B \mid A) = \frac{3}{4}$. Then $f_N(A, B)$ is also given precisely by the alternative expression

$$f_N(A, B) = f_N(A) f_N(B \mid A), \tag{2.15a}$$

where $f_N(A)$ is the relative frequency with which A occurs on the first trial. In our example $f_N(A) = \frac{4}{10}$. Both methods of calculation yield $f_N(A, B) = \frac{3}{10}$.

Although these manipulations appear trivial, the formulation in terms of conditional relative frequency permits us to exploit the fact that the trials in each sequence-of-two are independent. Independence implies that the result of one trial of the simple experiment does not affect the result of another. Thus, when N is sufficiently large, we usually observe that both $f_N(B \mid A)$ and $f_N(B)$ stabilize at the same numerical value. In a long sequence of independent repetitions of pairs of trials we therefore expect that the following approximation to Eq. 2.15a will be valid:

$$f_N(A, B) \approx f_N(A) f_N(B). \tag{2.15b}$$

For instance, in coin tossing we anticipate that the over-all frequency of Tails and the frequency with which Tails follows Heads will both be near $\frac{1}{2}$. Therefore we expect that $f_N(H, T)$ will be near $\frac{1}{4}$ for large N.

Similarly, if a compound experiment consists of M independent trials of a simple experiment, the relative frequency with which the result is any particular sequence such as $(A, B, B, \ldots, A)$ is usually observed to approximate the M-term product of the relative frequencies of the result's constituents:

$$f_N(A, B, B, \ldots, A) \approx f_N(A) f_N(B) f_N(B) \cdots f_N(A). \tag{2.15c}$$

With this background, we can discuss the problem of determining a mathematical model to represent a sequence of M trials of a real-world experiment. Assume that we have already determined a probability system that adequately represents a single trial of the experiment and that our only interests are in some particular event A having probability $\mathrm{P}[A]$ and in the complementary event $B = A^c$. We now construct a new probability system appropriate for modeling the sequence of M independent trials. The sample space of the new system consists of 2^M points, each of which stands for one of the possible sequences of length M constructible from A and B. For example, if $M = 3$, there are eight sample points.

We are guided in assigning probabilities to these 2^M points by a desire that probabilities should act as relative frequencies. Accordingly, in our new system we mirror Eq. 2.15c and *assign to each sequence (sample point) a probability equal to the product of the probabilities of its constituents.* Thus, if $P[A] = p$, which implies $P[B] = 1 - p$, we assign events and probabilities to sample points as shown in Table 2.1 for $M = 3$. In order ultimately to establish a tie between the repeated physical experiment and our mathematical model we also associate with each sample point a number $m(A)$ equal to the fractional number of times A occurs in the corresponding sequence:

$$m(A) \triangleq \frac{M(A)}{M}, \tag{2.16a}$$

where $M(A)$ is the number of A's in a sequence.

Table 2.1 *Probability assignment, $M = 3$*

Sample Point	Event	Probability	$m(A)$
ω_1	AAA	p^3	1
ω_2	AAB	$p^2(1-p)$	$\frac{2}{3}$
ω_3	ABA	$p^2(1-p)$	$\frac{2}{3}$
ω_4	BAA	$p^2(1-p)$	$\frac{2}{3}$
ω_5	BBA	$p(1-p)^2$	$\frac{1}{3}$
ω_6	BAB	$p(1-p)^2$	$\frac{1}{3}$
ω_7	ABB	$p(1-p)^2$	$\frac{1}{3}$
ω_8	BBB	$(1-p)^3$	0

For this example the probability of the event $m(A) = \frac{2}{3}$ is

$$P[m(A) = \tfrac{2}{3}] = P[\{\omega_2, \omega_3, \omega_4\}] = \sum_{i=2}^{4} P[\omega_i] = 3p^2(1 - p).$$

For general M the probability that $m(A) = k/M$ is

$$P\left[m(A) = \frac{k}{M}\right] = \binom{M}{k} p^k(1 - p)^{M-k}; \qquad 0 \leqslant k \leqslant M, \tag{2.16b}$$

where

$$\binom{M}{k} \triangleq \frac{M!}{k!\,(M - k)!}. \tag{2.16c}$$

To show this, we first note that probability $p^k(1 - p)^{M-k}$ is assigned to each sequence that contains exactly k A's. It is well known that there are $\binom{M}{k}$ distinct sequences of k A's and $M-k$ B's. Since each distinct sequence corresponds to a sample point, there must be $\binom{M}{k}$ sample points for which $m(A) = k/M$, each having probability $p^k(1 - p)^{M-k}$. Equation 2.16b then follows immediately from property III.

The probability assignment of Eq. 2.16b is called the *binomial distribution*, and the $\binom{M}{k}$ are the *binomial coefficients*. We check that the binomial probabilities sum to unity (as they must to satisfy property II) by invoking the binomial theorem

$$(a + b)^M = \sum_{k=0}^{M} \binom{M}{k} a^k b^{M-k}, \tag{2.17}$$

and obtain

$$\sum_{k=0}^{M} \mathrm{P}\left[m(A) = \frac{k}{M}\right] = [p + (1 - p)]^M = 1.$$

Plots of $\mathrm{P}\left[m(A) = \frac{k}{M}\right]$ are given in Fig. 2.7 for $M = 16, 100, 400$, and for $p = 0.1$ and 0.5.

Our primary interest is in the probabilistic behavior of $m(A)$ when M is large. For any small number ϵ, let us consider the event

$$\{\omega : |m(A) - p| \geqslant \epsilon\}.$$

Thus

$$\mathrm{P}[|m(A) - p| \geqslant \epsilon] = \sum_{I} \binom{M}{k} p^M (1 - p)^{M-k}, \tag{2.18a}$$

where

$$I = \left\{k : \frac{k}{M} \leqslant p - \epsilon \quad \text{or} \quad \frac{k}{M} \geqslant p + \epsilon\right\}. \tag{2.18b}$$

From Fig. 2.7 it is quite clear that, for any ϵ, this probability tends to zero as M becomes large. Indeed, we shall see later that

$$\mathrm{P}[|m(A) - p| \geqslant \epsilon] \leqslant \frac{p(1 - p)}{M\epsilon^2} \tag{2.19a}$$

and even more strongly that

$$\mathrm{P}[|m(A) - p| \geqslant \epsilon] \leqslant e^{-M\alpha}, \tag{2.19b}$$

where α is a positive number independent of M.

The number $m(A)$ in the mathematical model of a compound experiment has been defined in a manner that makes it directly analogous to relative frequency; we have $f_N(A) \triangleq N(A)/N$ and $m(A) \triangleq M(A)/M$. Equation 2.19 states, in addition, that $m(A)$ exhibits properties that *mirror those of relative frequency in nature*: $m(A)$ is close to the number $\mathrm{P}[A]$ with high probability when M is large, just as $f_N(A)$ almost always stabilizes close to this same number when N is large. Furthermore, the low-probability event that $m(A)$ is very different from $\mathrm{P}[A]$ mirrors atypical results in the real world such as observing the relative frequency of Heads to be close

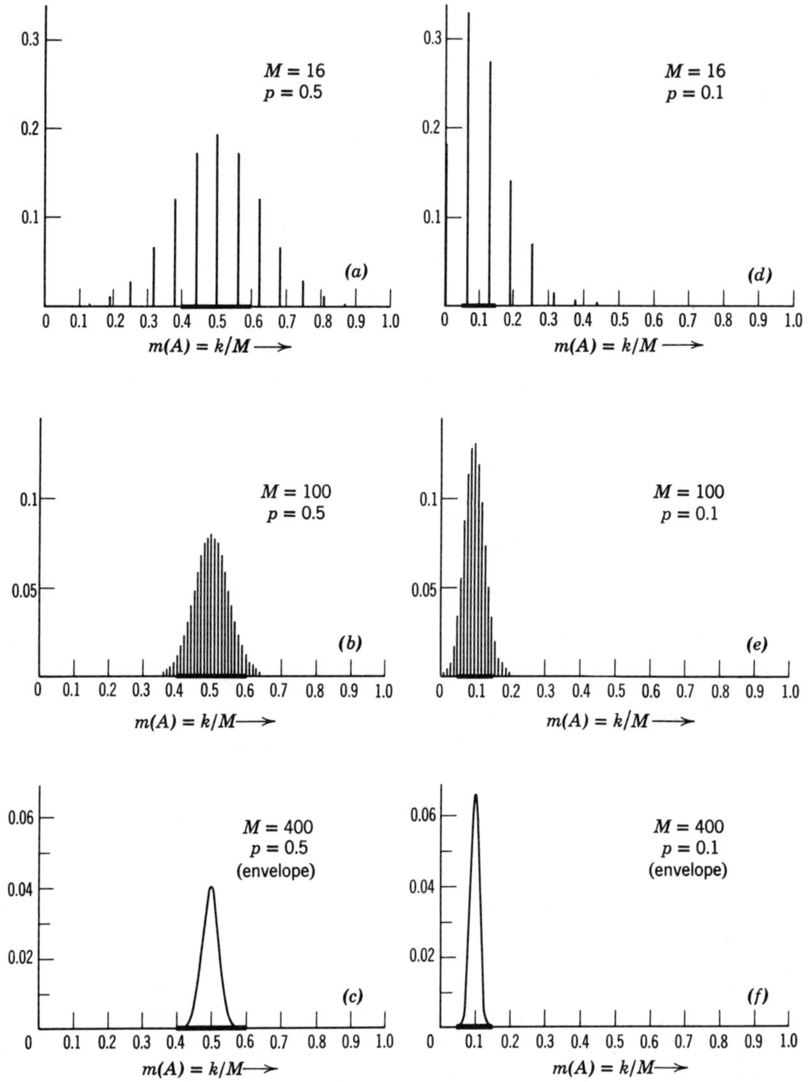

Figure 2.7 Binomial probabilities and behavior of $\mathbf{P}[m(A)]$. The heavy line segment along the horizontal axis indicates the interval $p \pm 0.1$ in (*a*), (*b*), (*c*) and the interval $p \pm 0.05$ in (*d*), (*e*), (*f*).

to unity in a long sequence of independent coin tosses. We say that such sequences are unlikely; the mathematical model says that they are improbable. We connect the model of probability theory with the real world by saying that *we do not expect to observe a particular experimental result if it corresponds to an event of low probability.* Thus in a long sequence of independent trials we expect the measured relative frequency of a result to converge to the probability of the corresponding mathematical event. As in Newtonian mechanics, probability theory is ultimately justified by the fact that it predicts—in this case, the relative frequency—successfully.

Naturally, the success of a mathematical prediction depends not only on the rules used in calculating but also on the accuracy of the original numerical data. For instance, the mass of a mathematical body in mechanics must approximate the mass of the physical body. In application, probabilities are usually assigned initially to fairly simple events; then we proceed to calculate the probabilities of other, more complex, events. Care must be taken that the original assignment is realistic. For example, one objective of communication theory is the design of communication systems that operate over noisy channels with a minimum probability of error. Successful engineering results are obtained only if the mathematical model of the channel adequately reflects the true nature of the disturbance.

In many cases study of the physics underlying a random phenomenon leads to a proper initial probability assignment; we shall see that transistor and vacuum tube noise can be treated in this way. In some cases symmetry provides the starting point; for instance, it is reasonable to assign probability $\frac{1}{2}$ to Heads in coin tossing. In other cases we make recourse to the observation of relative frequencies: life insurance rates are based on mortality experience tables. The unavoidable hazard here, of course, is that the observed frequencies *may not be typical.* In any event, the final test of validity is always whether or not predictions based on the original data are accurate enough to be useful.

Conditional Probability

In dealing with repeated trials of a physical experiment, we have introduced the concept of conditional relative frequency. It is convenient to introduce a corresponding concept into the mathematical model. Given any two events A and B, we define the *conditional probability* $P[A \mid B]$ of an event A as

$$P[A \mid B] \triangleq \frac{P[AB]}{P[B]} \tag{2.20}$$

whenever $P[B] \neq 0$. When $P[A]$ is also nonzero, it follows that

$$P[AB] = P[A \mid B]\, P[B] = P[B \mid A]\, P[A]. \tag{2.21}$$

Since the intersection of B with itself is B,

$$P[B \mid B] = 1. \tag{2.22}$$

Conditional probabilities serve to narrow consideration to a subspace B of a sample space Ω. This can easily be visualized with the help of Fig. 2.8, in which we show a sample space Ω on which several events $\{A_i\}$ are

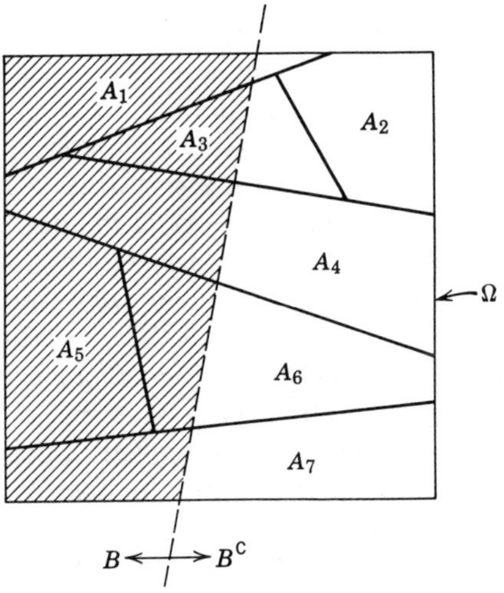

Figure 2.8 Conditioning on an event B.

defined. The shaded area to the left of the dotted line is another event B. It is useful to think of "conditioning" as a means of generating a new probability system from a given one:

1. The new sample space, say Ω', is the original event B.
2. The new events, say $\{A_i'\}$, are the original intersections $\{A_iB\}$.
3. The new probabilities, $\{P[A_i']\}$, are the conditional probabilities $\{P[A_i \mid B]\}$.

This probability assignment to Ω' satisfies the necessary properties.

I. Since $0 \leqslant P[A_iB] \leqslant P[B]$, we have $0 \leqslant P[A_i'] \leqslant 1$.
II. By Eq. 2.22, $P[\Omega'] = P[B \mid B] = 1$.

III. If $A_i'A_j' = \varnothing$, then $(A_iB) \cap (A_jB) = \varnothing$ and

$$\begin{aligned} P[A_i' \cup A_j'] &= P[A_iB \cup A_jB \mid B] \\ &= \frac{P[A_iB \cup A_jB]}{P[B]} \\ &= \frac{P[A_iB] + P[A_jB]}{P[B]} \\ &= P[A_i'] + P[A_j']. \end{aligned}$$

Since conditional probabilities can be considered as ordinary probabilities defined on a new sample space, all statements and theorems about ordinary probabilities also hold true for conditional probabilities. In particular, if the set of intersections $\{A_iB\}$ is disjoint and if

$$\bigcup_{\text{all } i} (A_iB) = B, \tag{2.23a}$$

then

$$P[B] = \sum_{\text{all } i} P[A_iB] = \sum_{\text{all } i} P[B]\, P[A_i \mid B] \tag{2.23b}$$

and

$$1 = \sum_{\text{all } i} P[A_i \mid B]. \tag{2.24}$$

Equation 2.23 is called the *theorem of total probability*. It corresponds to the geometrical axiom that the whole equals the sum of its parts.

Statistical Independence

As interpreted, conditional probability is directly analogous to conditional relative frequency in a physical experiment; in both cases we consider only the subset of possibilities that satisfies the condition. In a long sequence of independent experimental trials we therefore anticipate that a conditional relative frequency will stabilize at the corresponding conditional probability.

If the joint probability† of two events A and B satisfies

$$P[A, B] = P[A]\, P[B], \tag{2.25a}$$

or equivalently

$$P[A \mid B] = P[A], \tag{2.25b}$$

we call the pair of events *statistically independent*. Equation 2.25 mirrors the corresponding approximate relationship for relative frequency with independent trials given by Eq. 2.15b.

† The probability of the intersection AB of two events A and B is frequently written $P[A, B]$, instead of $P[AB]$, and referred to as the probability of the "joint event A and B." The notation arises naturally in modeling a sequence of trials, as in Table 2.1.

A set of k events $\{A_i\}$ is defined as statistically independent if and only if the probability of every intersection of k or fewer events equals the product of the probabilities of the constituents. Thus three events A, B,

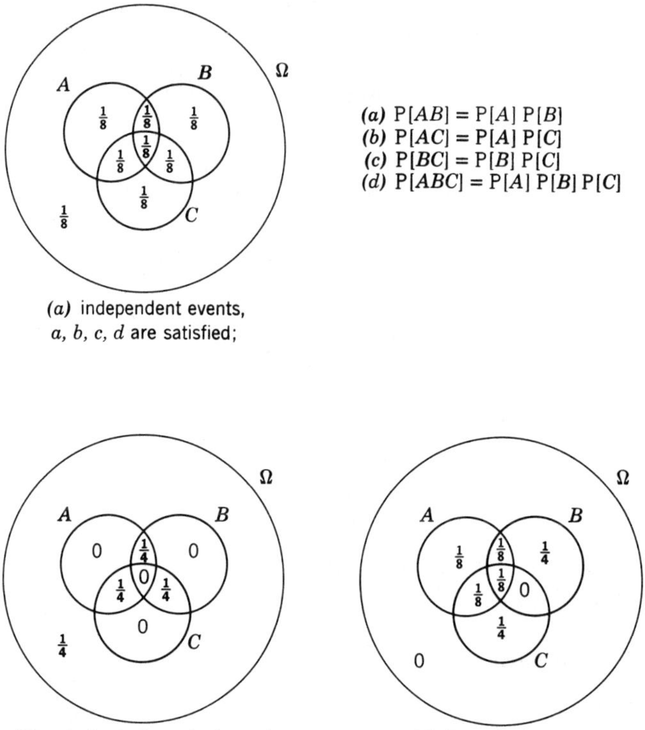

(*a*) independent events, *a*, *b*, *c*, *d* are satisfied; (*b*) pairwise independent events, *a*, *b*, *c* satisfied, *d* not satisfied; (*c*) dependent events, *a*, *b*, *d* satisfied, *c* not satisfied.

Figure 2.9 Independence and dependence of three events.

C are statistically independent when

$$\left.\begin{aligned} P[A, B] &= P[A]\,P[B] \\ P[A, C] &= P[A]\,P[C] \\ P[B, C] &= P[B]\,P[C] \end{aligned}\right\} \tag{2.26}$$

and

$$P[A, B, C] = P[A]\,P[B]\,P[C]. \tag{2.27}$$

No three of these relations necessarily implies the fourth. If only Eq. 2.26 is satisfied, we say that the events are *pairwise independent*. Pairwise independence does not imply complete independence. Various possibilities are given in Fig. 2.9.

An urn problem. The use of conditional probability often simplifies the assignment of probabilities to the joint occurrence of two events. Consider the urn problem, for example, in which we draw two balls at random from an urn containing one black and two red balls. When we draw two balls without replacement, the only possible outcome sequences are (R, R), (R, B), and (B, R). In the mathematical model we employ a subscript to denote the draw. For the first draw we set $\mathrm{P}[R_1] = \frac{2}{3}$, $\mathrm{P}[B_1] = \frac{1}{3}$. For the second draw we set

$$\mathrm{P}[R_2 \mid R_1] = \tfrac{1}{2} \qquad \mathrm{P}[R_2 \mid B_1] = 1$$

$$\mathrm{P}[B_2 \mid R_1] = \tfrac{1}{2} \qquad \mathrm{P}[B_2 \mid B_1] = 0,$$

where the conditioning is on the result of the first draw. Thus

$$\mathrm{P}[R_1, R_2] = \mathrm{P}[R_1]\,\mathrm{P}[R_2 \mid R_1] = \tfrac{1}{3},$$

$$\mathrm{P}[R_1, B_2] = \mathrm{P}[R_1]\,\mathrm{P}[B_2 \mid R_1] = \tfrac{1}{3},$$

$$\mathrm{P}[B_1, R_2] = \mathrm{P}[B_1]\,\mathrm{P}[R_2 \mid B_1] = \tfrac{1}{3}.$$

A communication problem. A second, particularly germane, example of the utility of conditional probability is the following idealized communication problem. Consider a mathematical model of a discrete communication channel having M possible input messages $\{m_i\}$, $0 \leqslant i \leqslant M - 1$, and J possible output symbols $\{r_j\}$, $0 \leqslant j \leqslant J - 1$. For purposes of this example the channel model may be completely described by a set of MJ conditional probabilities, $\{\mathrm{P}[r_j \mid m_i]\}$, that specifies the probability of receiving each output conditioned on each input. For small values of MJ it is convenient to diagram these conditional probabilities (often called "transition probabilities" in a communication context) as shown in Fig. 2.10.

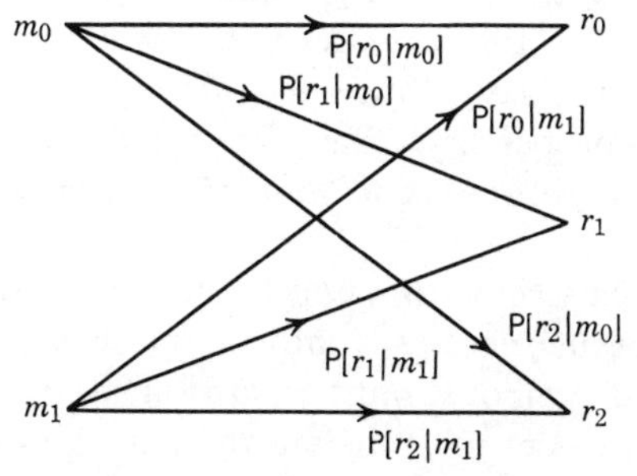

Figure 2.10 Transition probability diagram, $M = 2, J = 3$.

The model introduced above describes an actual communication system such as that diagrammed in Fig. 1.7 when the entire system from source output to decision element input is considered, for purposes of analysis, to be the "channel." Specifically, the model results when there is only one detector (as in Fig. 1.8) and its output (point a) is constrained to assume one of a set of J discrete values. Under these conditions the design of the "receiver" amounts to specification of the decision element.

Assume that we know the set of M probabilities $\{\mathrm{P}[m_i]\}$ with which the input messages occur. These probabilities are called the *a priori* message probabilities (meaning the probabilities before reception). Our problem is to specify a receiver that, on the basis of the symbol r_j received, makes the optimum decision regarding which message m_i was transmitted. We define *optimum* to mean that the probability of deciding correctly, denoted $\mathrm{P}[\mathcal{C}]$, is maximum. In a long sequence of independent transmissions we therefore expect the optimum receiver to decide correctly more often than any nonoptimum receiver.

A single operation of the channel can be described on a sample space Ω comprising MJ sample points ω, each labeled with one of the possible input-output pairs (m_i, r_j). Probabilities are assigned to these points by the equation

$$\mathrm{P}[m_i, r_j] = \mathrm{P}[m_i]\, \mathrm{P}[r_j \mid m_i]. \tag{2.28a}$$

We can then use Eq. 2.23b to calculate such quantities as

$$\mathrm{P}[r_j] = \sum_{i=0}^{M-1} \mathrm{P}[m_i, r_j] \tag{2.28b}$$

and

$$\mathrm{P}[m_i \mid r_j] = \frac{\mathrm{P}[m_i, r_j]}{\mathrm{P}[r_j]}. \tag{2.28c}$$

An example of a typical probability system, with $M = 2$ and $J = 3$, is illustrated in Fig. 2.11.

Before a transmission the a priori probability that any particular input m_i will be transmitted is $\mathrm{P}[m_i]$. After a transmission, given that r_j is received, the probability that m_i was transmitted is $\mathrm{P}[m_i \mid r_j]$, which is called the *a posteriori* probability. *The effect of the transmission is to alter the probability of each possible input from its a priori to its a posteriori value.*

The specification of a receiver amounts to the specification of a mapping from the channel output space $\{r_j\}$ onto the message input space $\{m_i\}$: each possible received symbol r_j must be attributed to one and only one of the possible inputs. Let $\hat{m}(j)$ denote the particular input in the set $\{m_i\}$ to which a receiver attributes r_j. Then the conditional probability

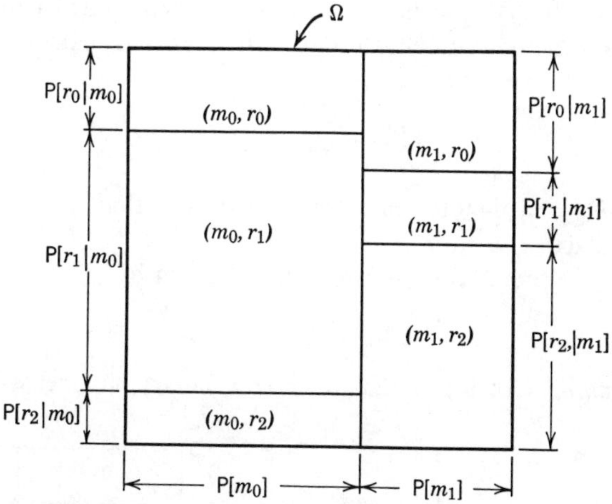

Figure 2.11 Probability system for communication example. The probability of each input-output pair (m_i, r_j) is represented by its area.

$P[\mathcal{C} \mid r_j]$ of a correct decision, given that r_j is received, is just the probability that $\hat{m}(j)$ was in fact transmitted. We write

$$P[\mathcal{C} \mid r_j] = P[\hat{m}(j) \mid r_j]. \tag{2.29}$$

Obviously, $P[\mathcal{C} \mid r_j]$ is maximized by choosing $\hat{m}(j)$ to be that member of $\{m_i\}$ with the largest a posteriori probability. This maximum a posteriori probability *decision rule*, applied independently to each possible received symbol r_j, determines the optimum receiver. If several m_i have the same (maximum) a posteriori probability, r_j can be arbitrarily assigned to any one without loss of optimality.

That this decision rule is optimum becomes clear when we use Eq. 2.29 to compute the unconditioned probability of a correct decision, $P[\mathcal{C}]$.

$$P[\mathcal{C}] = \sum_{j=0}^{J-1} P[\mathcal{C} \mid r_j]\, P[r_j]. \tag{2.30}$$

The positive quantities $P[r_j]$ are independent of the decision rule, and therefore the sum on j is maximized if and only if each of the terms $P[\mathcal{C} \mid r_j]$ is maximum.

It is not necessary to compute the probability $P[r_j]$ in order to determine the optimum mapping $\{\hat{m}(j)\}$ and the resulting probability of error. From Eq. 2.28, m_k has maximum a posteriori probability,

$$P[m_k \mid r_j] \geqslant P[m_i \mid r_j] \quad \text{for all } i \neq k, \tag{2.31a}$$

hence $\hat{m}(j) = m_k$, if and only if

$$P[m_k]\, P[r_j \mid m_k] \geqslant P[m_i]\, P[r_j \mid m_i] \quad \text{for all } i \neq k. \tag{2.31b}$$

Once the set $\{\hat{m}(j)\}$, $j = 0, 1, \ldots, J-1$, is determined from Eq. 2.31b, the probability of correct decision, P[$\mathcal{C}$], can be calculated from the equation

$$\mathrm{P}[\mathcal{C}] = \sum_{j=0}^{J-1} \mathrm{P}[\hat{m}(j), r_j], \tag{2.32a}$$

where $\mathrm{P}[\hat{m}(j), r_j]$ denotes the joint probability that $\hat{m}(j)$ is transmitted and r_j received.

Finally, the probability of error, P[$\mathcal{E}$] is given by

$$\mathrm{P}[\mathcal{E}] = 1 - \mathrm{P}[\mathcal{C}]. \tag{2.32b}$$

An Example. In Fig. 2.12*a* we show a binary channel with two input

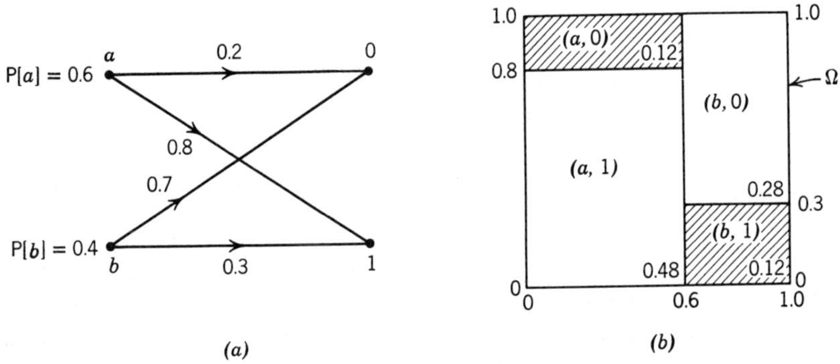

Figure 2.12 A binary communication channel.

symbols $\{a, b\}$ and two output symbols $\{0, 1\}$. The input probabilities are

$$\mathrm{P}[a] = 0.6 \qquad \mathrm{P}[b] = 0.4.$$

The channel transition probabilities are

$$\mathrm{P}[0 \mid a] = 0.2 \qquad \mathrm{P}[0 \mid b] = 0.7$$

$$\mathrm{P}[1 \mid a] = 0.8 \qquad \mathrm{P}[1 \mid b] = 0.3.$$

Thus the probabilities of the four possible input-output pairs, as shown in Fig. 2.12*b*, are

$$\mathrm{P}[a, 0] = \mathrm{P}[a]\,\mathrm{P}[0 \mid a] = 0.6 \times 0.2 = 0.12$$

$$\mathrm{P}[a, 1] = \mathrm{P}[a]\,\mathrm{P}[1 \mid a] = 0.6 \times 0.8 = 0.48$$

$$\mathrm{P}[b, 0] = \mathrm{P}[b]\,\mathrm{P}[0 \mid b] = 0.4 \times 0.7 = 0.28$$

$$\mathrm{P}[b, 1] = \mathrm{P}[b]\,\mathrm{P}[1 \mid b] = 0.4 \times 0.3 = 0.12.$$

Since

$$P[b, 0] > P[a, 0]$$

$$P[a, 1] > P[b, 1],$$

the optimum receiver is specified by the mapping

$$\hat{m}(0) = b$$

$$\hat{m}(1) = a.$$

From Eq. 2.32a,

$$P[\mathcal{C}] = P[b, 0] + P[a, 1] = 0.76$$

and

$$P[\mathcal{E}] = 1 - P[\mathcal{C}] = 0.24.$$

The sample points corresponding to error are shaded in Fig. 2.12*b*.

2.3 RANDOM VARIABLES

In many of the applications of probability theory—one is tempted to say most—real numbers are associated with the points $\{\omega\}$ in a sample space. For example, in discussing the mathematical model for a sequence of M independent trials of an experiment, it was natural to assign to each point ω a number $m(A)$, chosen to equal the fractional occurrence of A in the event sequence associated with ω. Another natural example, when Ω is the real line, is to associate with each point ω the distance from ω to the origin. Equally well, of course, we could associate with ω the square of this distance.

The real number associated with a sample point ω is denoted $x(\omega)$. In the general case, in which Ω is an abstract collection of points, $x(\ )$ may be viewed as a function that maps Ω into the real line: given any point ω, the function $x(\ )$ specifies a finite real number $x(\omega)$. A simple example of such mapping is illustrated in Fig. 2.13. When Ω itself is the

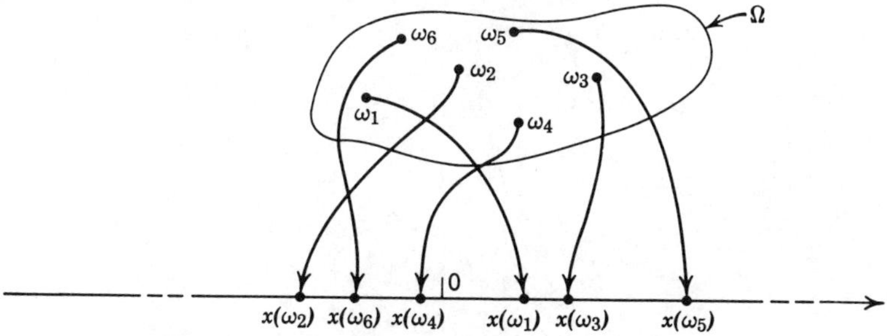

Figure 2.13 A mapping $x(\ )$ from Ω to the real line.

real line, examples might be $x(\omega) = \omega$, $x(\omega) = \omega^2$, or $x(\omega) = \sin \omega$. Hereafter, in referring to functions we often delete empty parentheses and simply write x to denote the function $x(\;\;)$.

Distribution Functions

Once x has been specified, we may inquire into the probability of events such as

$$A = \{\omega: a < x(\omega) \leqslant b\},$$

$$B = \{\omega: x(\omega) = c\},$$

$$C = \{\omega: x(\omega) > d\},$$

and so on. The answer to any such question is readily obtained from

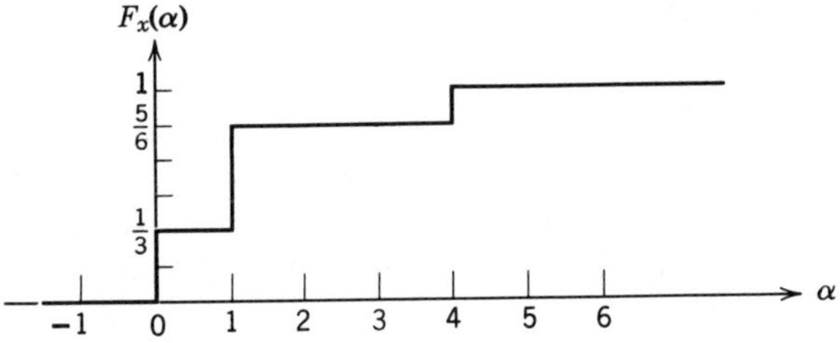

Figure 2.14 An example of a probability distribution function.

knowledge of the probability distribution function, F_x, defined as

$$F_x(\alpha) \triangleq \mathrm{P}[\{\omega: x(\omega) \leqslant \alpha\}]. \tag{2.33}$$

Clearly, F_x is a function from the real line into the interval [0, 1]. For example, if

$$\Omega = \{\omega_1, \omega_2, \omega_3\}$$

$$\mathrm{P}[\omega_1] = \tfrac{1}{3} \qquad \mathrm{P}[\omega_2] = \tfrac{1}{6} \qquad \mathrm{P}[\omega_3] = \tfrac{1}{2}$$

$$x(\omega_1) = 0 \qquad x(\omega_2) = 4 \qquad x(\omega_3) = 1$$

then

$$F_x(\alpha) = \begin{cases} 0 & \text{for } \alpha < 0, \\ \frac{1}{3} & \text{for } 0 \leqslant \alpha < 1, \\ \frac{5}{6} & \text{for } 1 \leqslant \alpha < 4, \\ 1 & \text{for } 4 \leqslant \alpha, \end{cases}$$

as shown in Fig. 2.14.

Functions x for which probability distribution functions can be specified are called *random variables*.† In this text we do not consider functions x for which F_x does not exist. In an axiomatic treatment of probability theory care must be taken to avoid the choice of a function x for which some event $\{\omega: x(\omega) \leqslant a\}$ has not been assigned a probability.

The properties of distribution functions listed below follow directly from the definition of Eq. 2.33.

I. $F_x(\alpha) \geqslant 0; \quad \text{for } -\infty < \alpha < \infty.$

II. $F_x(-\infty) = 0.$

III. $F_x(+\infty) = 1.$

IV. If $a > b, \quad F_x(a) - F_x(b) = \mathrm{P}[\{\omega: b < x(\omega) \leqslant a\}].$

V. If $a > b, \quad F_x(a) \geqslant F_x(b).$

The first three properties follow from the facts that $F_x(\alpha)$ is a probability and $\mathrm{P}[\Omega] = 1$. Properties IV and V follow from the fact that

$$\{\omega: x(\omega) \leqslant b\} \cup \{\omega: b < x(\omega) \leqslant a\} = \{\omega: x(\omega) \leqslant a\}.$$

Another property of distribution functions concerns the nature and significance of discontinuities, such as those illustrated in Fig. 2.14. Consider any positive number ϵ. Since F_x is defined in such a way that $F_x(a - \epsilon)$ does not include the probability, say P_a, of the event $\{\omega: x(\omega) = a\}$, whereas $F_x(a)$ does include this probability, $F_x(\alpha)$ has a discontinuity of magnitude P_a at the point $\alpha = a$ whenever $P_a > 0$. Furthermore, $F_x(a)$ is the value of F_x at the top of this discontinuity. If $P_a = 0$, the height of the discontinuity is zero; that is, there is no discontinuity. The properties of distribution functions are summarized by remarking that F_x increases monotonically from 0 to 1, is continuous on the right, and has a step of size P_a at point a if and only if

$$\mathrm{P}[\{\omega: x(\omega) = a\}] = P_a.$$

We are not restricted to assigning only one real number to each point ω in a sample space. In general, we define many different mappings (functions) from a single sample space Ω into the real line. Then we have a set of coexisting random variables, say $\{x_i\}$, $i = 1, 2, \ldots, k$.

† The nomenclature is somewhat misleading. Actually, a random variable is a well-defined function on the points of a sample space. The terminology comes from the use of random variables as mathematical models for quantities in the real world such as a noise voltage measured at some time t_1.

First consider the case for which k is 2. Once the functions x_1 and x_2 are specified, we may inquire into the probability of *joint events* such as

$$\{\omega: x_1(\omega) \leqslant a_1, x_2(\omega) \leqslant a_2\} \triangleq \{\omega: x_1(\omega) \leqslant a_1\} \cap \{\omega: x_2(\omega) \leqslant a_2\}.$$

In order to answer such questions, it is *not* sufficient to know only the one-dimensional distributions, F_{x_1} and F_{x_2}. All such questions can be

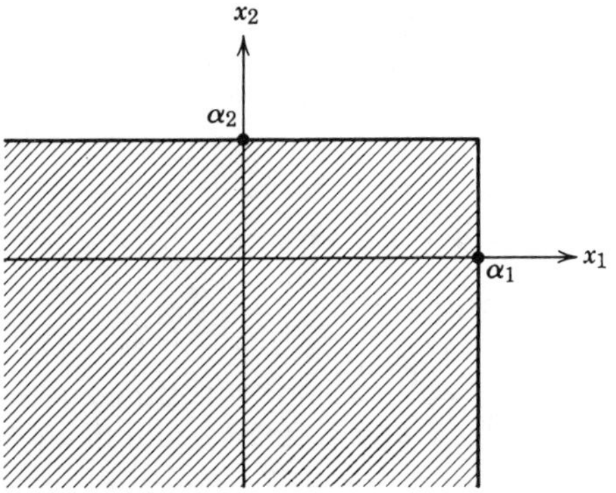

Figure 2.15*a* $F_{x_1,x_2}(\alpha_1, \alpha_2)$ is the probability of the set of all ω for which the point $(x_1(\omega), x_2(\omega))$ falls into the shaded region.

answered, however, through knowledge of the *joint probability distribution* function, F_{x_1,x_2}, defined as

$$F_{x_1,x_2}(\alpha_1, \alpha_2) \triangleq \mathrm{P}[\{\omega: x_1(\omega) \leqslant \alpha_1, x_2(\omega) \leqslant \alpha_2\}]; \quad -\infty < \alpha_1, \alpha_2 < \infty. \tag{2.34}$$

Thus $F_{x_1,x_2}(\alpha_1, \alpha_2)$ is the probability assigned to the set of all points ω in Ω that are associated with the region of the two-dimensional Euclidean space which is shaded in Fig. 2.15*a*.

The properties of joint distribution functions listed below follow directly from the definition of Eq. 2.34.

I. $F_{x_1,x_2}(\alpha_1, \alpha_2) \geqslant 0$; for $-\infty < \alpha_1 < \infty$, $-\infty < \alpha_2 < \infty$.

II. $F_{x_1,x_2}(-\infty, \alpha) = F_{x_1,x_2}(\alpha, -\infty) = 0$; for $-\infty < \alpha < \infty$.

III. $F_{x_1,x_2}(\infty, \infty) = 1$.

IV. $F_{x_1,x_2}(\infty, \alpha) = F_{x_2}(\alpha)$.

V. $F_{x_1,x_2}(\alpha, \infty) = F_{x_1}(\alpha)$.

VI. If $a_1 > b_1$ and $a_2 > b_2$,

$$F_{x_1,x_2}(a_1, a_2) \geqslant F_{x_1,x_2}(a_1, b_2) \geqslant F_{x_1,x_2}(b_1, b_2).$$

Properties I, II, III, and VI are self-evident. Properties IV and V are consequences of the facts that $\{\omega: x(\omega) < \infty\} = \Omega$ for any random variable and the intersection of any event with Ω is the event. In summary, $F_{x_1,x_2}(\alpha_1, \alpha_2)$ is a monotonically increasing function of both arguments,

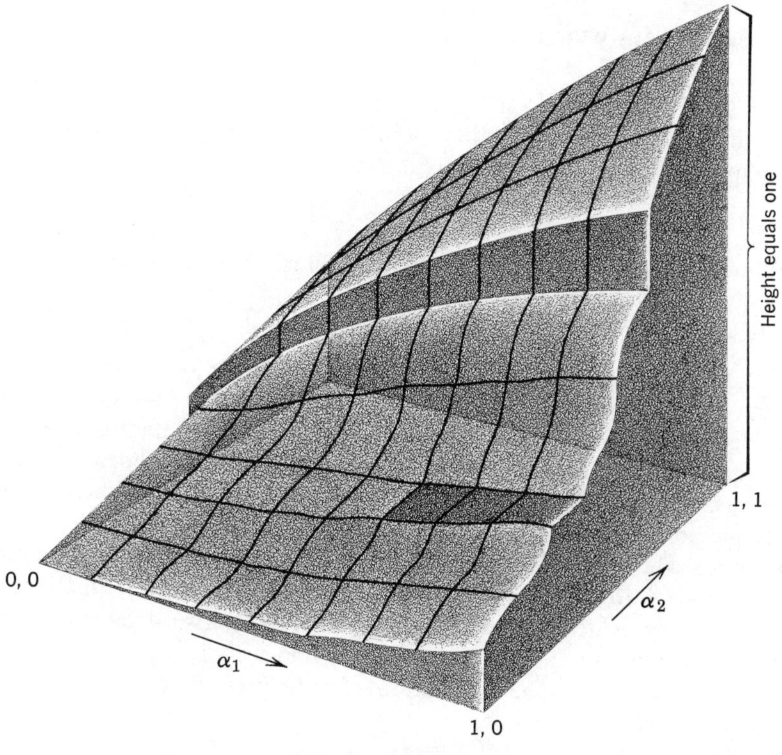

(b)

Figure 2.15b Example of a two-dimensional distribution function, $F_{x_1,x_2}(\alpha_1, \alpha_2)$.

and $0 \leqslant F_{x_1,x_2}(\alpha_1, \alpha_2) \leqslant 1$. An example of a possible distribution function F_{x_1,x_2} is shown in Fig. 2.15b.

When k random variables, $x_1, x_2, \ldots, x_k$, are defined on Ω, it is convenient to adopt a concise notation. Let $\mathbf{x}$ denote the k-tuple $(x_1, x_2, \ldots, x_k)$. We then define the k-dimensional joint probability distribution function $F_{\mathbf{x}}(\boldsymbol{\alpha})$ as

$$F_{\mathbf{x}}(\boldsymbol{\alpha}) \triangleq P[\{\omega: x_1(\omega) \leqslant \alpha_1, x_2(\omega) \leqslant \alpha_2, \ldots, x_k(\omega) \leqslant \alpha_k\}], \tag{2.35}$$

where $\boldsymbol{\alpha} \triangleq (\alpha_1, \alpha_2, \ldots, \alpha_k)$. We refer to $\mathbf{x}$ as a k-dimensional *vector* of random variables or, more simply, as a *random vector*.

Two k-dimensional vectors, say

$$\mathbf{a} \triangleq (a_1, a_2, \ldots, a_k) \tag{2.36a}$$

and

$$\mathbf{b} \triangleq (b_1, b_2, \ldots, b_k), \tag{2.36b}$$

are said to satisfy the relationship

$$\mathbf{a} \leqslant \mathbf{b} \tag{2.36c}$$

if and only if the inequality holds for each pair of corresponding components; that is, if and only if

$$a_i \leqslant b_i; \quad \text{for } i = 1, 2, \ldots, k. \tag{2.36d}$$

With this notation, we can rewrite Eq. 2.35 more concisely as

$$F_{\mathbf{x}}(\boldsymbol{\alpha}) \triangleq \mathrm{P}[\{\omega : \mathbf{x}(\omega) \leqslant \boldsymbol{\alpha}\}]. \tag{2.37}$$

A vector such as $\boldsymbol{\alpha}$ in Eq. 2.37 may be thought of as designating a point in a k-dimensional Euclidean geometry, the coordinates of the point being the components of the vector. Similarly, a random vector $\mathbf{x}$ designates a mapping from the sample space Ω into Euclidean k-space; that is, $\mathbf{x}$ assigns a particular point $\mathbf{x}(\omega)$ in Euclidean k-space to each sample point ω in Ω. The inequality $\mathbf{x} \leqslant \boldsymbol{\alpha}$ defines a region in Euclidean k-space. The number $F_{\mathbf{x}}(\boldsymbol{\alpha})$ is the probability of the set of sample points ω mapped into the region $\mathbf{x} \leqslant \boldsymbol{\alpha}$ by $\mathbf{x}(\omega)$. Distribution functions in k dimensions evidence properties that are straightforward generalizations of those already discussed for one or two dimensions.

As an example of the calculation of joint probabilities, consider the three-dimensional vector

$$\mathbf{x} = (x_1, x_2, x_3),$$

the three functions

$$x_1(\omega) \triangleq \omega,$$

$$x_2(\omega) \triangleq \omega^2,$$

$$x_3(\omega) \triangleq 1 - \omega,$$

and the probability assignment encountered in Eq. 2.12; that is, consider $\Omega = \{\omega : 0 \leqslant \omega \leqslant 1\}$, and the probability assignment given by

$$\mathrm{P}[A] = \int_I f(\omega)\, d\omega = \int_I d\omega,$$

where the integration is over the set of intervals constituting the event A.

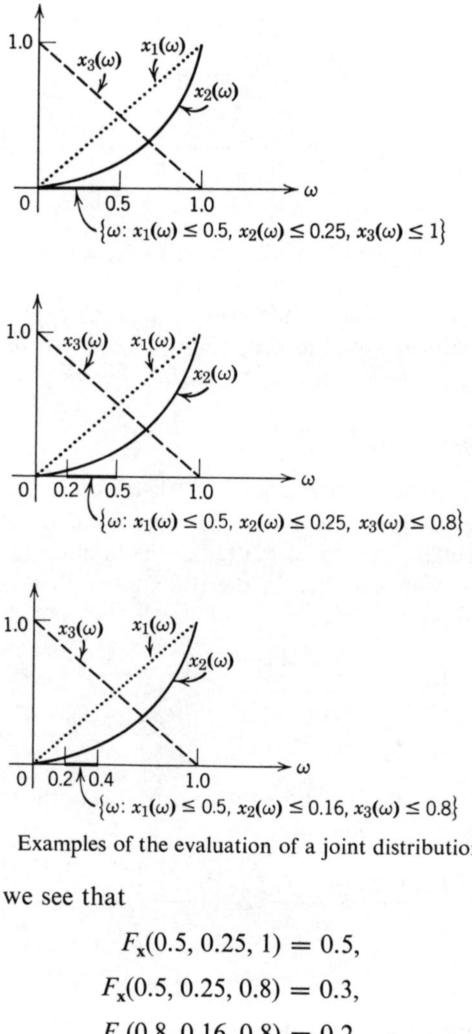

Figure 2.16 Examples of the evaluation of a joint distribution function.

From Fig. 2.16 we see that

$$F_{\mathbf{x}}(0.5, 0.25, 1) = 0.5,$$

$$F_{\mathbf{x}}(0.5, 0.25, 0.8) = 0.3,$$

$$F_{\mathbf{x}}(0.8, 0.16, 0.8) = 0.2.$$

It is evident that the k-dimensional distribution function always provides all information necessary for determining the probability of the set $\{\omega\}$ such that $\mathbf{x}$ lies in any specified region of k-dimensional Euclidean space. But the direct use of $F_{\mathbf{x}}$ is usually inconvenient in computations. For example, from Fig. 2.17 it is clear that for the probability of a rectangular region we have

$$\mathrm{P}[\{\omega: a < x_1(\omega) \leqslant b, c < x_2(\omega) \leqslant d\}] = F_{\mathbf{x}}(b, d) - F_{\mathbf{x}}(b, c) - F_{\mathbf{x}}(a, d) + F_{\mathbf{x}}(a, c).$$

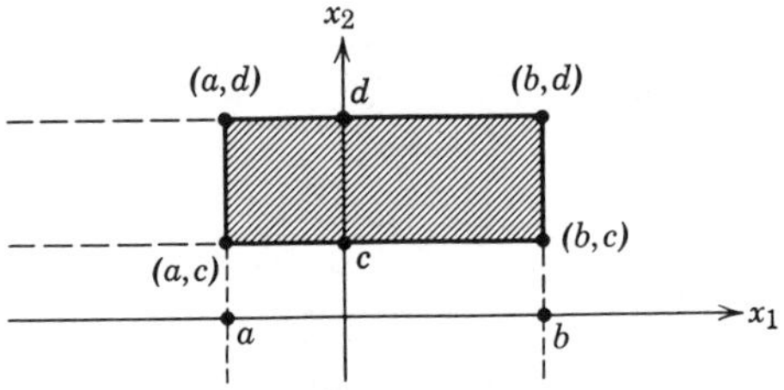

Figure 2.17 Region of plane for which $a < x_1 \leqslant b$, $c < x_2 \leqslant d$.

The probability of even this simple event entails an expression with four terms. In three dimensions the probability of a cubic region entails an expression with eight terms, and so forth.

Density Functions

The notational inconvenience of the distribution function can be avoided by introducing a function called the *probability density function* which permits probabilities to be written in the familiar form of integrals. For the single random variable, x, the probability that x lies in a small interval $[a, a + \Delta]$ is

$$P[\{\omega: a < x \leqslant a + \Delta\}] = F_x(a + \Delta) - F_x(a)$$
$$= \Delta\left[\frac{F_x(a + \Delta) - F_x(a)}{\Delta}\right].$$

If Δ is very small and $F_x(\alpha)$ is differentiable at $\alpha = a$, the term in brackets is approximately

$$\frac{F_x(a + \Delta) - F_x(a)}{\Delta} \approx \left.\frac{dF_x(\alpha)}{d\alpha}\right|_{\alpha=a}; \quad \Delta > 0 \tag{2.38a}$$

and

$$P[\{\omega: a < x \leqslant a + \Delta\}] \approx \Delta\, F_x'(a) \tag{2.38b}$$

in which the prime denotes the derivative of F_x.

Now consider a region, say I, of the real line: any such region may be thought of as the union of a large number of disjoint intervals, each of which has length Δ, as shown in Fig. 2.18. Furthermore, the probability of a union of disjoint events is the sum of their probabilities. If $F_x(\alpha)$ is

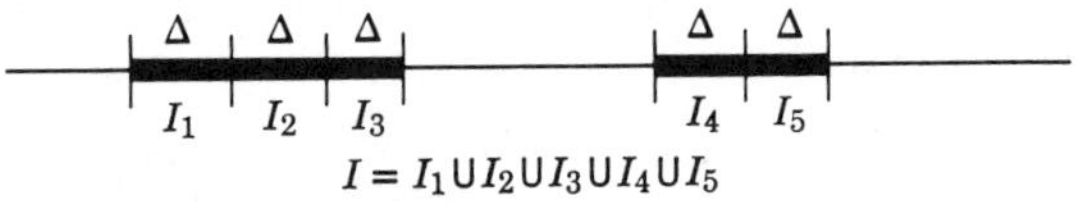

Figure 2.18 Decomposition of a region I into a union of small disjoint intervals.

everywhere differentiable, it follows by taking the limit $\Delta \to 0$ that the probability that x lies in I is

$$P[\{\omega: x(\omega) \text{ in } I\}] = \int_I F_x'(\alpha)\, d\alpha.$$

Whenever it exists, the derivative of F_x is called the *probability density function of* x and given the symbol p_x. Thus

$$P[\{\omega: x(\omega) \text{ in } I\}] = \int_I p_x(\alpha)\, d\alpha, \tag{2.39}$$

where

$$p_x(\alpha) \triangleq \frac{dF_x(\alpha)}{d\alpha}. \tag{2.40a}$$

In order to calculate the probability of an event, we integrate the probability density function over the region defining the event. In particular,

$$F_x(\alpha) = \int_{-\infty}^{\alpha} p_x(\beta)\, d\beta. \tag{2.40b}$$

The class of distribution functions with which we are concerned may fail to have a continuous derivative at a point, say $\alpha = a$, for one of two reasons:

1. The slope of $F_x(\alpha)$ is discontinuous at $\alpha = a$.
2. $F_x(\alpha)$ has a step discontinuity at $\alpha = a$, that is,

$$P[\{\omega: x(\omega) = a\}] = P_a \neq 0.$$

In the first case the problem is one of ambiguity, which is easily resolved by always taking p_x to be the derivative on the right of F_x, as implied by Eq. 2.38a.

In the second case the problem is more fundamental but may be resolved by extending our definition of the probability density function. Consider a distribution function F_x which has a single discontinuity of magnitude P_a at the point $\alpha = a$, as shown in Fig. 2.19. For a region $I = [b, c]$ which includes this point, the contribution to $P[\{\omega: x(\omega) \text{ in } I\}]$ from all small subintervals† of $[b, c]$ except the subinterval $[a - \epsilon, a]$ is

$$\int_b^{a-\epsilon} p_x(\alpha)\, d\alpha + \int_a^c p_x(\alpha)\, d\alpha.$$

† In this section. subintervals such as $[\beta, \gamma]$ include the right end point (γ) but not the left end point (β).

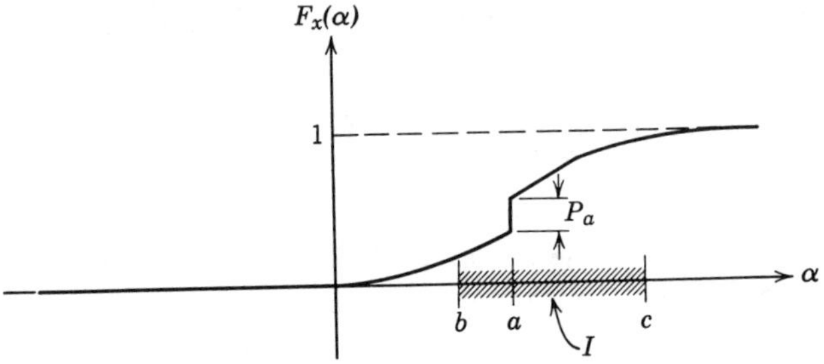

Figure 2.19 A discontinuous probability distribution function.

When ϵ is sufficiently small, the contribution to P[I] of the interval $[a - \epsilon, a]$ is P_a, the magnitude of the discontinuity, and

$$\mathrm{P}[I] \triangleq \mathrm{P}[\{\omega: b < x(\omega) \leqslant c\}] = \int_b^{a-\epsilon} p_x(\alpha)\, d\alpha + P_a + \int_a^c p_x(\alpha)\, d\alpha. \quad (2.41)$$

To reduce Eq. 2.41 to the simple form of Eq. 2.39, we introduce the Dirac impulse notation.† A unit impulse may be visualized as the limiting

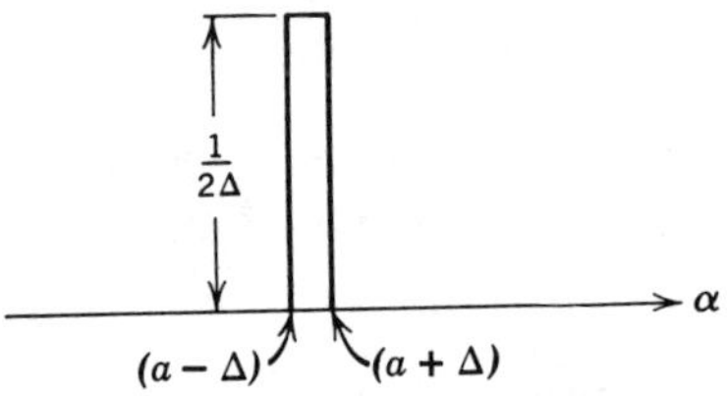

Figure 2.20 The square pulse approaches the unit impulse $\delta(\alpha - a)$ when Δ approaches zero.

form of a positive pulse of unit area as the pulse duration is reduced to zero, as shown in Fig. 2.20. Operationally, a unit impulse at $\alpha = a$, denoted $\delta(\alpha - a)$, is defined by the equation

$$\int_I f(\alpha)\, \delta(\alpha - a)\, d\alpha = \begin{cases} f(a); & \text{if } I \text{ includes point } a \\ 0; & \text{otherwise} \end{cases} \quad (2.42a)$$

for any function f continuous at a. If a is an end point of the interval I and ambiguity is possible, it is desirable to indicate explicitly whether a is in I. This may be accomplished by using an asterisk if a is *not* in I. Thus

$$\int_{-\infty}^{a} f(\alpha)\, \delta(\alpha - a)\, d\alpha = \int_a^{\infty} f(\alpha)\, \delta(\alpha - a)\, d\alpha = f(a), \quad (2.42b)$$

$$\int_{-\infty}^{a^*} f(\alpha)\, \delta(\alpha - a)\, d\alpha = \int_{a^*}^{\infty} f(\alpha)\, \delta(\alpha - a)\, d\alpha = 0. \quad (2.42c)$$

† The impulse is discussed in more detail in reference 62, Appendix 2A.

A trivial implication is that

$$\int_{-\infty}^{a} P_a\, \delta(\alpha - a)\, d\alpha = P_a.$$

If, therefore, we introduce into $p_x(\alpha)$ a term of the form $P_a\, \delta(\alpha - a)$ for each point at which F_x has a discontinuity, we can again write the probability that x lies in I in the simple form

$$\mathrm{P}[\{\omega: x(\omega) \text{ in } I\}] = \int_I p_x(\alpha)\, d\alpha. \tag{2.43}$$

For example, the density function for the distribution considered in Fig. 2.14 is

$$p_x(\alpha) = \tfrac{1}{3}\,\delta(\alpha) + \tfrac{1}{2}\,\delta(\alpha - 1) + \tfrac{1}{6}\,\delta(\alpha - 4),$$

which implies

$$P[\{\omega: x(\omega) \leqslant 1\}] = F_x(1) = \int_{-\infty}^{1} p_x(\alpha)\, d\alpha = \tfrac{1}{3} + \tfrac{1}{2} = \tfrac{5}{6},$$

as it should.

Since any distribution function F_x increases monotonically and $F_x(+\infty) = 1$, any density function must satisfy the properties

$$p_x(\alpha) \geqslant 0; \quad \text{all } \alpha \tag{2.44a}$$

and

$$\int_{-\infty}^{\infty} p_x(\alpha)\, d\alpha = 1. \tag{2.44b}$$

Examples. The following continuous probability density functions are frequently encountered. In each case, the parameter b is a positive constant. The density functions are illustrated in Fig. 2.21.

1. EXPONENTIAL

$$p_x(\alpha) = \begin{cases} \dfrac{1}{b}\, e^{-\alpha/b}; & \alpha \geqslant 0, \\ 0; & \alpha < 0, \end{cases} \tag{2.45a}$$

$$F_x(\alpha) = \begin{cases} 0; & \alpha < 0, \\ 1 - e^{-\alpha/b}; & \alpha \geqslant 0. \end{cases} \tag{2.45b}$$

2. RAYLEIGH

$$p_x(\alpha) = \begin{cases} \dfrac{\alpha}{b}\, e^{-\alpha^2/2b}; & \alpha \geqslant 0, \\ 0; & \alpha < 0, \end{cases} \tag{2.46a}$$

$$F_x(\alpha) = \begin{cases} 0; & \alpha < 0, \\ 1 - e^{-\alpha^2/2b}; & \alpha \geqslant 0. \end{cases} \tag{2.46b}$$

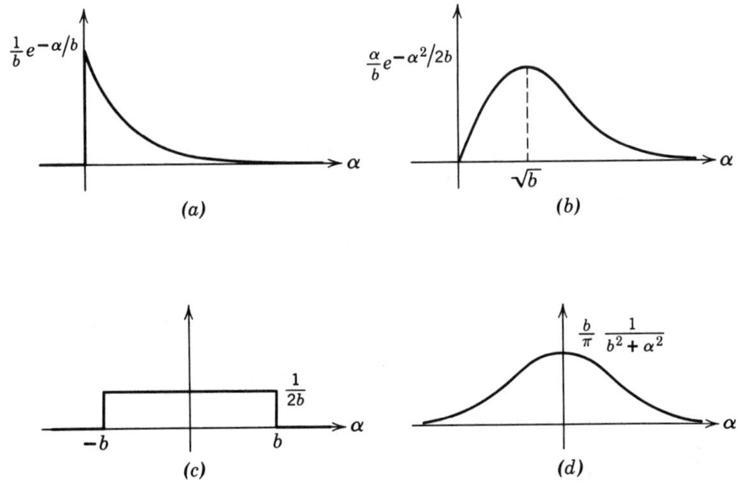

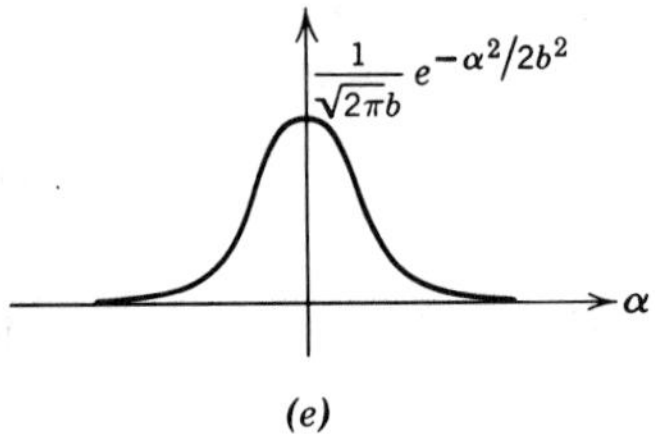

Figure 2.21 Examples of probability density functions: (*a*) the exponential density function; (*b*) the Rayleigh density function; (*c*) the uniform density function; (*d*) the Cauchy density function; (*e*) the Gaussian density function.

3. UNIFORM

$$p_x(\alpha) = \begin{cases} \dfrac{1}{2b}; & -b \leqslant \alpha \leqslant b, \\ 0; & \text{elsewhere,} \end{cases} \tag{2.47a}$$

$$F_x(\alpha) = \begin{cases} 0; & \alpha < -b, \\ \dfrac{1}{2b}(\alpha + b); & -b \leqslant \alpha \leqslant b, \\ 1; & \alpha > b. \end{cases} \tag{2.47b}$$

4. CAUCHY

$$p_x(\alpha) = \frac{b/\pi}{b^2 + \alpha^2}; \qquad -\infty < \alpha < \infty, \tag{2.48a}$$

$$F_x(\alpha) = \frac{1}{2} + \frac{1}{\pi}\tan^{-1}\frac{\alpha}{b}; \qquad -\infty < \alpha < \infty. \tag{2.48b}$$

5. GAUSSIAN

$$p_x(\alpha) = \frac{1}{\sqrt{2\pi}b} e^{-\alpha^2/2b^2}, \tag{2.49a}$$

$$F_x(\alpha) = 1 - Q\left(\frac{\alpha}{b}\right), \tag{2.49b}$$

in which we have defined

$$Q(\alpha) \triangleq \frac{1}{\sqrt{2\pi}} \int_\alpha^\infty e^{-\gamma^2/2} \, d\gamma. \tag{2.50}$$

The function $Q(\alpha)$ is not an elementary integral, but its complement, $1 - Q(\alpha)$, is well-tabulated.[59] It is related to the more familiar error function

$$\operatorname{erf}(\alpha) \triangleq \frac{2}{\sqrt{\pi}} \int_0^\alpha e^{-\gamma^2} \, d\gamma \tag{2.51a}$$

by the equation

$$Q(\alpha) = \frac{1}{2}\left[1 - \operatorname{erf}\left(\frac{\alpha}{\sqrt{2}}\right)\right]. \tag{2.51b}$$

As an illustration of the calculation of probabilities by use of density functions consider the interval $I = [1, 2]$. If the random variable x is exponentially distributed,

$$\begin{aligned} P[\{\omega: x(\omega) \text{ in } I\}] &= \int_I p_x(\alpha) \, d\alpha = \int_1^2 \frac{1}{b} e^{-\alpha/b} \, d\alpha \\ &= (e^{-1/b} - e^{-2/b}). \end{aligned}$$

Two-dimensional density functions. The notational convenience of writing probabilities as integrals is extended to two random variables, say x_1 and x_2, by defining a *joint density function*, p_{x_1,x_2}, in such a way that for any two-dimensional region I we have

$$P[\{\omega: (x_1(\omega), x_2(\omega)) \text{ in } I\}] = \iint_I p_{x_1,x_2}(\alpha_1, \alpha_2) \, d\alpha_1 \, d\alpha_2. \tag{2.52}$$

(The arguments α_1 and α_2 are associated with x_1 and x_2, respectively.) To see how p_{x_1,x_2} must be defined in order that Eq. 2.52 may be valid, let us first consider the small rectangular region shown in Fig. 2.22:

$$[a_1 - \Delta_1 < \alpha_1 \leqslant a_1, \quad a_2 - \Delta_2 < \alpha_2 \leqslant a_2].$$

From Eq. 2.52 we have then

$$\begin{aligned} &P[\{\omega: a_1 - \Delta_1 < x_1(\omega) \leqslant a_1, \quad a_2 - \Delta_2 < x_2(\omega) \leqslant a_2\}] \\ &\quad = F_{x_1,x_2}(a_1, a_2) - F_{x_1,x_2}(a_1, a_2 - \Delta_2) - F_{x_1,x_2}(a_1 - \Delta_1, a_2) \\ &\qquad + F_{x_1,x_2}(a_1 - \Delta_1, a_2 - \Delta_2). \end{aligned} \tag{2.53a}$$

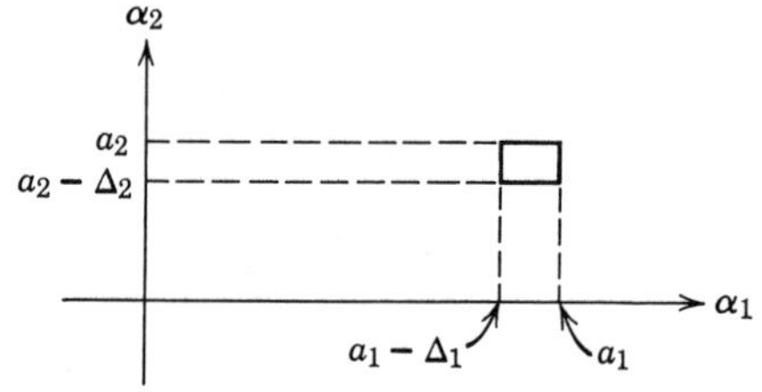

Figure 2.22 A small rectangular region.

The right-hand side of Eq. 2.53a may be rearranged in the form

$$\Delta_1\left[\frac{F_{x_1,x_2}(a_1, a_2) - F_{x_1,x_2}(a_1 - \Delta_1, a_2)}{\Delta_1} - \frac{F_{x_1,x_2}(a_1, a_2 - \Delta_2) - F_{x_1,x_2}(a_1 - \Delta_1, a_2 - \Delta_2)}{\Delta_1}\right].$$

If the partial derivative of F_{x_1,x_2} with respect to α_1 exists, for small Δ_1 this approaches

$$\Delta_1\left[\frac{\partial F_{x_1,x_2}(\alpha_1, a_2)}{\partial \alpha_1} - \frac{\partial F_{x_1,x_2}(\alpha_1, a_2 - \Delta_2)}{\partial \alpha_1}\right]_{\alpha_1=a_1}$$

$$= \Delta_1\Delta_2 \frac{\partial}{\partial \alpha_1}\left[\frac{F_{x_1,x_2}(\alpha_1, a_2) - F_{x_1,x_2}(\alpha_1, a_2 - \Delta_2)}{\Delta_2}\right]_{\alpha_1=a_1}$$

Finally, if $(\partial^2/\partial\alpha_1\,\partial\alpha_2)F_{x_1,x_2}(\alpha_1, \alpha_2)$ exists, for small Δ_2 this in turn approaches

$$\Delta_1\Delta_2 \frac{\partial^2}{\partial\alpha_1\,\partial\alpha_2}[F_{x_1,x_2}(\alpha_1, \alpha_2)]_{\substack{\alpha_1=a_1\\ \alpha_2=a_2}}.$$

Thus, when both Δ_1 and Δ_2 are small, we have

$$P[\{\omega: a_1 - \Delta_1 < x_1(\omega) \leqslant a_1, \quad a_2 - \Delta_2 < x_2(\omega) \leqslant a_2\}]$$
$$\approx \Delta_1\Delta_2 \frac{\partial^2}{\partial\alpha_1,\,\partial\alpha_2}[F_{x_1,x_2}(\alpha_1, \alpha_2)]_{\substack{\alpha_1=a_1\\ \alpha_2=a_2}} \qquad (2.53b)$$

whenever the derivative exists.

Now consider an arbitrary two-dimensional region, say I, in the (α_1, α_2) plane, as shown in Fig. 2.23. The region I may be built up of small disjoint rectangular regions, each having area $\Delta_1\Delta_2$. From probability property III, the probability that $\mathbf{x} = (x_1, x_2)$ lies in I is the sum of the

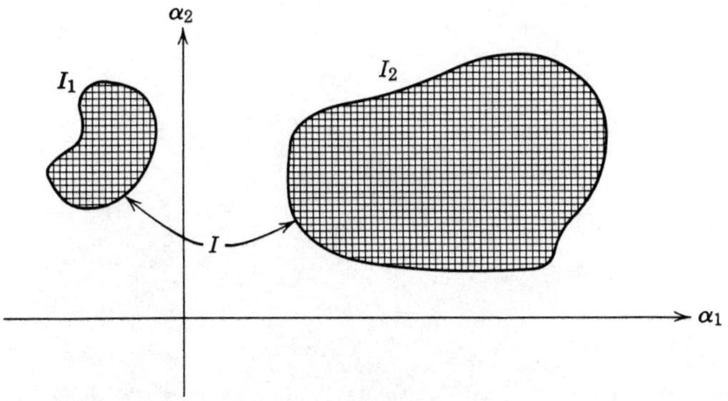

Figure 2.23 Building up the region $I = I_1 \cup I_2$ out of small disjoint rectangular regions.

probabilities that $\mathbf{x}$ lies in these rectangles. Whenever F_{x_1,x_2} is differentiable, in the limit as both Δ_1 and Δ_2 go to zero we have

$$P[\{\omega: \mathbf{x}(\omega) \text{ in } I\}] = \iint_I \frac{\partial^2}{\partial\alpha_1\,\partial\alpha_2} F_{x_1,x_2}(\alpha_1, \alpha_2)\, d\alpha_1\, d\alpha_2. \tag{2.54}$$

Defining

$$p_{x_1,x_2}(\alpha_1, \alpha_2) \triangleq \frac{\partial^2}{\partial\alpha_1\,\partial\alpha_2} F_{x_1,x_2}(\alpha_1, \alpha_2), \tag{2.55}$$

we can write Eq. 2.54 concisely in vector notation as

$$P[\{\omega: x(\omega) \text{ in } I\}] = \int_I p_{\mathbf{x}}(\boldsymbol{\alpha})\, d\boldsymbol{\alpha}, \tag{2.56a}$$

where

$$p_{\mathbf{x}}(\boldsymbol{\alpha}) \triangleq p_{x_1,x_2}(\alpha_1, \alpha_2), \tag{2.56b}$$

$$d\boldsymbol{\alpha} \triangleq d\alpha_1\, d\alpha_2, \tag{2.56c}$$

and the (multiple) integration is over all points $\boldsymbol{\alpha}$ in the two-dimensional region I.

Just as in the one-dimensional case, Eq. 2.55 is inadequate to define the joint probability density function $p_{\mathbf{x}}$ at points where $F_{\mathbf{x}}$ is discontinuous. The difficulty is again resolved by using impulses to account for discontinuities, as illustrated in the examples that follow.

Since any joint distribution function $F_{x_1,x_2}(\alpha_1, \alpha_2)$ is a monotonically increasing function of both α_1 and α_2, it is clear that any joint density function p_{x_1,x_2} must be non-negative at every point (α_1, α_2):

$$p_{x_1,x_2}(\alpha_1, \alpha_2) \geqslant 0; \qquad -\infty < \alpha_1 < \infty, \qquad -\infty < \alpha_2 < \infty. \tag{2.57a}$$

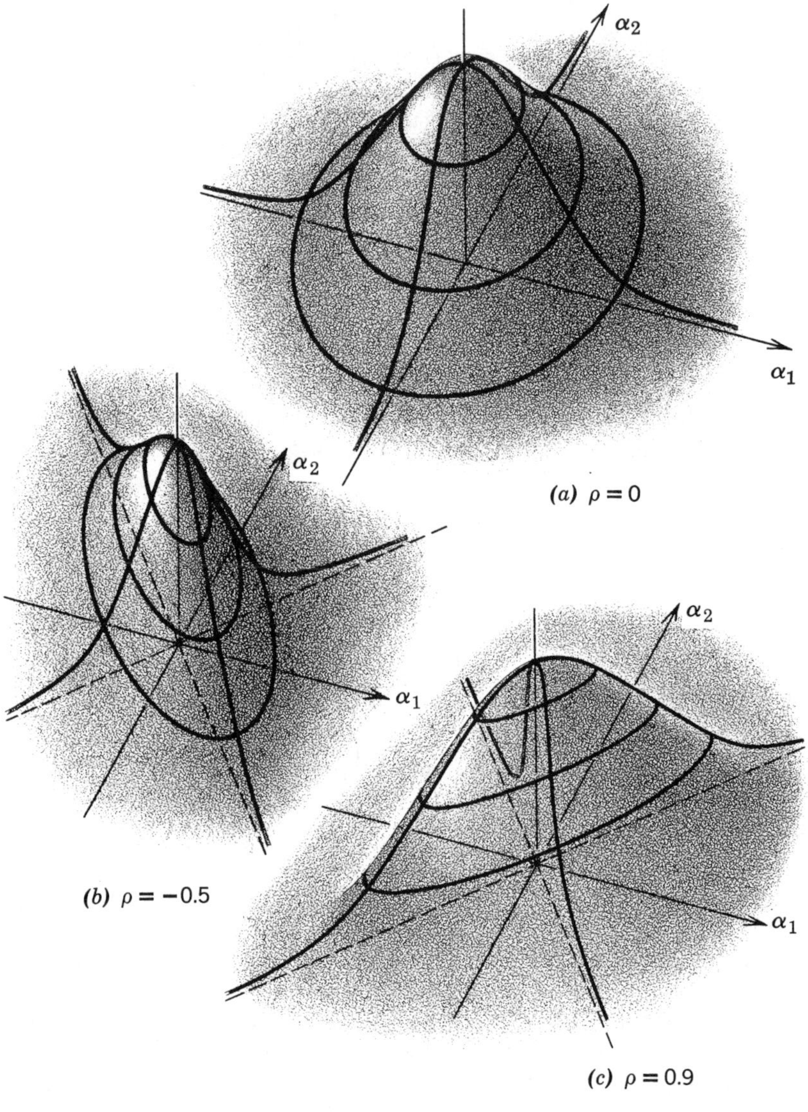

Figure 2.24 Examples of the two-dimensional Gaussian density function.

Also, since $F_{x_1,x_2}(\infty, \infty)$ equals unity, p_{x_1,x_2} must satisfy the equation

$$\int_{-\infty}^{\infty} \int_{-\infty}^{\infty} p_{x_1,x_2}(\alpha_1, \alpha_2)\, d\alpha_1\, d\alpha_2 = 1. \tag{2.57b}$$

Examples. An example of a valid joint density function that is everywhere continuous is the *two-dimensional Gaussian density function,*

$$p_{x_1,x_2}(\alpha_1, \alpha_2) = \frac{1}{2\pi\sqrt{1-\rho^2}} \exp\left[-\frac{(\alpha_1{}^2 - 2\rho\alpha_1\alpha_2 + \alpha_2{}^2)}{2(1-\rho^2)}\right]; \quad -1 < \rho < 1, \tag{2.58}$$

which is illustrated for several values of the parameter ρ in Fig. 2.24.

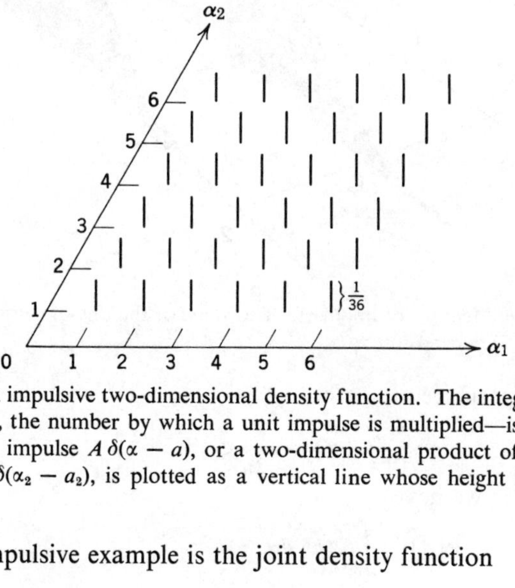

Figure 2.25 An impulsive two-dimensional density function. The integral through an impulse—that is, the number by which a unit impulse is multiplied—is called the impulse *value*. An impulse $A\,\delta(\alpha - a)$, or a two-dimensional product of impulses such as $A\,\delta(\alpha_1 - a_1)\,\delta(\alpha_2 - a_2)$, is plotted as a vertical line whose height is equal to the value A.

A purely impulsive example is the joint density function

$$p_{x_1,x_2}(\alpha_1, \alpha_2) = \sum_{i=1}^{6}\sum_{j=1}^{6} \frac{1}{36}\, \delta(\alpha_1 - i)\, \delta(\alpha_2 - j), \tag{2.59}$$

illustrated in Fig. 2.25. The probability is concentrated at the 36 points (i, j); $1 \leqslant i \leqslant 6$, $1 \leqslant j \leqslant 6$. This density function would be appropriate as a mathematical model for a dice game.

We may also encounter joint density functions that are impulsive in one dimension and continuous in the other. An example is

$$p_{x_1,x_2}(\alpha_1, \alpha_2) = \sum_{i=1}^{2} \frac{1}{2}\, \delta(\alpha_1 - i) \frac{1}{\sqrt{2\pi}} \exp\left[-\frac{(\alpha_2{}^2 - i)^2}{2}\right]. \tag{2.60}$$

As shown in Fig. 2.26, this density function may be visualized as two "fences" of impulses at $\alpha_1 = 1$ and $\alpha_2 = 2$.

For a simple example of the use of a joint density function to calculate a probability, consider the event A defined by

$$A = \{\omega: x_1^2(\omega) + x_2^2(\omega) < c^2\}$$

and the two-dimensional Gaussian density function of Eq. 2.58, with the

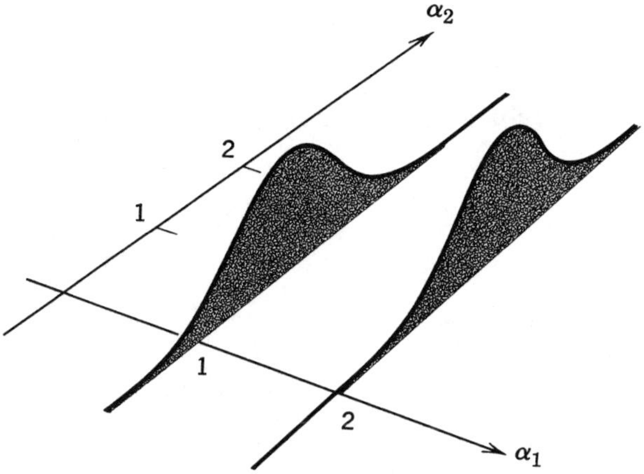

Figure 2.26 Two "fences" of impulses. The value of the one-dimensional impulse at $\alpha_1 = 1$ (or $\alpha_1 = 2$) depends on α_2.

parameter ρ specialized to zero:

$$p_{x_1,x_2}(\alpha_1, \alpha_2) = \frac{1}{2\pi} e^{-(\alpha_1{}^2+\alpha_2{}^2)/2}.$$

From Eq. 2.56a we have

$$\begin{aligned}
\mathrm{P}[A] &= \int_I p_{\mathbf{x}}(\boldsymbol{\alpha})\, d\boldsymbol{\alpha} \\
&= \iint_I p_{x_1,x_2}(\alpha_1, \alpha_2)\, d\alpha_1\, d\alpha_2 \\
&= \iint_I \frac{1}{2\pi} e^{-(\alpha_1{}^2+\alpha_2{}^2)/2}\, d\alpha_1\, d\alpha_2,
\end{aligned}$$

where the region I is the interior of a circle of radius c, centered on the origin of the (α_1, α_2) plane. The integration is easily carried out by making the change of variables

$$r \triangleq \sqrt{\alpha_1{}^2 + \alpha_2{}^2}, \quad \theta \triangleq \tan^{-1}\frac{\alpha_2}{\alpha_1}.$$

Since the differential area in polar coordinates is $r\,dr\,d\theta$, we have

$$\text{P}[A] = \int_0^c \int_0^{2\pi} \frac{1}{2\pi} e^{-r^2/2}\, r\, dr\, d\theta = \int_0^c re^{-r^2/2}\, dr$$

$$= \int_0^{c^2/2} e^{-\beta}\, d\beta = 1 - e^{-c^2/2}. \qquad (2.61)$$

Elimination of a random variable. It often happens in applications that we know a joint density function, say p_{x_1,x_2}, but are interested in the one-dimensional density p_{x_1}, which is easily obtained as follows. From Equation 2.56,

$$F_{x_1,x_2}(\alpha_1, \alpha_2) = \int_{-\infty}^{\alpha_1} \int_{-\infty}^{\alpha_2} p_{x_1,x_2}(\beta_1, \beta_2)\, d\beta_2\, d\beta_1.$$

But it has already been established (property V of joint distribution functions) that

$$F_{x_1}(\alpha_1) = F_{x_1,x_2}(\alpha_1, \infty),$$

hence

$$F_{x_1}(\alpha_1) = \int_{-\infty}^{\alpha_1} \int_{-\infty}^{\infty} p_{x_1,x_2}(\beta_1, \beta_2)\, d\beta_2\, d\beta_1.$$

As usual, we obtain p_{x_1} by differentiating F_{x_1}. Since the derivative of a definite integral with respect to the upper limit is given by

$$\frac{d}{d\alpha} \int_{-\infty}^{\alpha} h(\beta)\, d\beta = \lim_{\Delta \to 0} \left[\frac{\int_{-\infty}^{\alpha} h(\beta)\, d\beta - \int_{-\infty}^{\alpha-\Delta} h(\beta)\, d\beta}{\Delta} \right]$$

$$= \lim_{\Delta \to 0} \left[\frac{h(\alpha)\,\Delta}{\Delta} \right] = h(\alpha) \qquad (2.62)$$

whenever $h(\beta)$ is continuous at $\beta = \alpha$, we have

$$p_{x_1}(\alpha_1) = \frac{d}{d\alpha_1} F_{x_1}(\alpha_1) = \frac{d}{d\alpha_1} \int_{-\infty}^{\alpha_1} \left[\int_{-\infty}^{\infty} p_{x_1,x_2}(\beta_1, \beta_2)\, d\beta_2 \right] d\beta_1$$

$$= \int_{-\infty}^{\infty} p_{x_1,x_2}(\alpha_1, \beta_2)\, d\beta_2. \qquad (2.63)$$

Equation 2.63 is a generalization of the theorem on total probability of Eq. 2.23b.

It may be helpful to think of a two-dimensional joint probability density function $p_{\mathbf{x}}(\boldsymbol{\alpha})$ as analogous to a mass density distributed over a plane, where the total mass is unity. The situation can be visualized with the help of Fig. 2.27. The probability that $\mathbf{x}$ lies in a region I is identified with the total mass located over I, since total mass is also obtained by

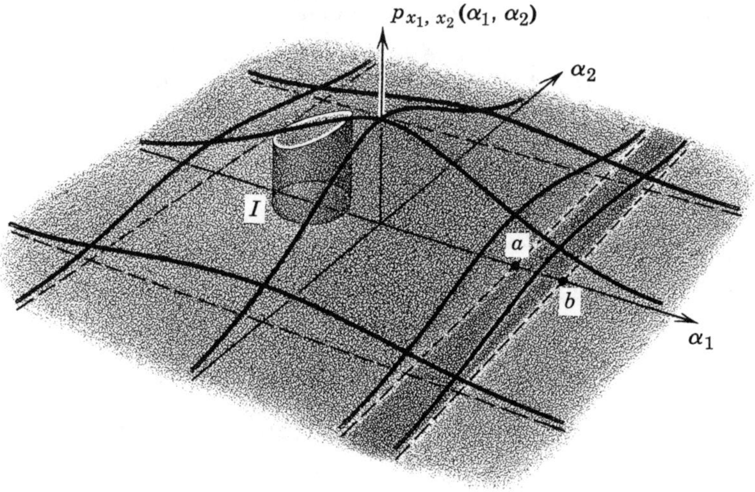

Figure 2.27 A two-dimensional probability density function.

integrating (mass) density. We extend the analogy by noting that integration over one axis of the plane, as in Eq. 2.63, determines the (one-dimensional or "marginal") mass density along the remaining axis. Thus an integral such as $\int_a^b p_{x_1}(\alpha_1)\, d\alpha_1$ corresponds in a two-dimensional problem to determining the total mass over an infinite strip, parallel to the α_2-axis and extending from $a < \alpha_1 \leqslant b$, as shown in Fig. 2.27.

As an example of the calculation of p_{x_1} from p_{x_1,x_2}, consider the two-dimensional Gaussian density function of Eq. 2.58. Then, for a given value of ρ, $|\rho| < 1$,

$$p_{x_1}(\alpha_1) = \int_{-\infty}^{\infty} \frac{1}{2\pi\sqrt{1-\rho^2}} \exp\left[-\frac{(\alpha_1^2 - 2\rho\alpha_1\alpha_2 + \alpha_2^2)}{2(1-\rho^2)}\right] d\alpha_2.$$

The integral is readily evaluated by completing the square in the exponent and letting $\gamma = (\alpha_2 - \rho\alpha_1)/(1 - \rho^2)^{1/2}$:

$$(\alpha_1^2 - 2\rho\alpha_1\alpha_2 + \alpha_2^2) = (\alpha_2 - \rho\alpha_1)^2 + \alpha_1^2(1-\rho^2),$$

$$p_{x_1}(\alpha_1) = \frac{e^{-\alpha_1^2/2}}{\sqrt{2\pi}} \int_{-\infty}^{\infty} \frac{1}{\sqrt{2\pi(1-\rho^2)}} \exp\left[-\frac{(\alpha_2 - \rho\alpha_1)^2}{2(1-\rho^2)}\right] d\alpha_2$$

$$= \frac{e^{-\alpha_1^2/2}}{\sqrt{2\pi}} \int_{-\infty}^{\infty} \frac{1}{\sqrt{2\pi}} e^{-\gamma^2/2}\, d\gamma$$

$$= \frac{1}{\sqrt{2\pi}} e^{-\alpha_1^2/2}. \tag{2.64}$$

Thus x_1 (and also x_2) individually are Gaussianly distributed. For this joint Gaussian case the total probability that $\mathbf{x} = (x_1, x_2)$ lies in the infinite strip in Fig. 2.27 is therefore

$$\int_a^b \int_{-\infty}^{\infty} p_{x_1,x_2}(\alpha_1, \alpha_2)\, d\alpha_2\, d\alpha_1 = \int_a^b \frac{1}{\sqrt{2\pi}} e^{-\alpha_1^2/2}\, d\alpha_1$$

$$= Q(a) - Q(b).$$

The function $Q(\ )$ has been defined in Eq. 2.50.

Multidimensional Density Functions

By analogy with the two-dimensional case, the probability density function of a k-component random vector $\mathbf{x} = (x_1, x_2, \ldots, x_k)$ is defined in such a way that

$$\mathrm{P}[\{\omega\colon \mathbf{x}(\omega) \text{ in } I\}] = \int_I p_{\mathbf{x}}(\boldsymbol{\beta})\, d\boldsymbol{\beta} \tag{2.65}$$

for any k-dimensional region I. In particular, by letting I denote the region $\mathbf{x} \leqslant \boldsymbol{\alpha}$, where

$$\boldsymbol{\alpha} = (\alpha_1, \alpha_2, \ldots, \alpha_k), \tag{2.66a}$$

we have

$$F_{\mathbf{x}}(\boldsymbol{\alpha}) = \mathrm{P}[\{\omega\colon \mathbf{x}(\omega) \leqslant \boldsymbol{\alpha}\}]$$

$$= \int_{-\infty}^{\alpha_k} \cdots \int_{-\infty}^{\alpha_2} \int_{-\infty}^{\alpha_1} p_{\mathbf{x}}(\boldsymbol{\beta})\, d\beta_1\, d\beta_2 \cdots d\beta_k. \tag{2.66b}$$

Differentiating with respect to the limits, we identify

$$p_{\mathbf{x}}(\boldsymbol{\alpha}) = \frac{\partial^k}{\partial \alpha_1\, \partial \alpha_2 \cdots \partial \alpha_k} F_{\mathbf{x}}(\boldsymbol{\alpha}) \tag{2.66c}$$

whenever $F_{\mathbf{x}}(\boldsymbol{\alpha})$ is continuous at the point $\boldsymbol{\alpha}$. At points of discontinuity impulses are introduced into $p_{\mathbf{x}}$ (as in the one- and two-dimensional cases) in such a way that Eq. 2.65 is valid.

As an aid to visualizing the meaning of joint probability density, it is convenient to interpret Eq. 2.65 as stating that *the probability that* $\mathbf{x}$ *lies in a small k-dimensional region of volume* ΔV *containing a point* $\boldsymbol{\alpha} = \mathbf{a}$ *is approximately* $p_{\mathbf{x}}(\mathbf{a})\, \Delta V$ *whenever* $p_{\mathbf{x}}(\boldsymbol{\alpha})$ *is nearly constant over the region.*

In the general k-dimensional case, just as for $k = 2$, unwanted random variables are eliminated by integration: If

$$\mathbf{x} \triangleq (x_1, x_2, \ldots, x_k) \tag{2.67a}$$

$$\mathbf{x}' \triangleq (x_1, x_2, \ldots, x_{i-1}, x_{i+1}, \ldots, x_k), \tag{2.67b}$$

then

$$F_{\mathbf{x}'}(\boldsymbol{\alpha}') \triangleq \mathrm{P}[\{\omega: \mathbf{x}' \leqslant \boldsymbol{\alpha}'\}]$$

$$= \mathrm{P}[\{\omega: \mathbf{x}' \leqslant \boldsymbol{\alpha}', x_i \leqslant \infty\}] \triangleq F_{\mathbf{x}}(\alpha_1, \alpha_2, \ldots, \alpha_{i-1}, \infty, \alpha_{i+1}, \ldots, \alpha_k),$$

where

$$\boldsymbol{\alpha}' = (\alpha_1, \alpha_2, \ldots, \alpha_{i-1}, \alpha_{i+1}, \ldots, \alpha_k). \tag{2.67c}$$

Differentiating with respect to all α_j, $j \neq i$, yields

$$p_{\mathbf{x}'}(\boldsymbol{\alpha}') = \int_{-\infty}^{\infty} p_{\mathbf{x}}(\boldsymbol{\alpha})\, d\alpha_i, \tag{2.67d}$$

which generalizes Eq. 2.63.

Equality of Random Variables

Let x_1 and x_2 denote two random variables defined on a sample space Ω. Two random variables are said to be *equal* if and only if the probability of the set of points ω on which they differ has zero probability; that is, we write

$$x_1 = x_2 \tag{2.68a}$$

if and only if

$$\mathrm{P}[\{\omega: x_1(\omega) \neq x_2(\omega)\}] = 0. \tag{2.68b}$$

In particular, $x_1 = x_2$ if $x_1(\omega) = x_2(\omega)$ for all ω in Ω. Since we do not expect to observe an event of zero probability, we do not make a distinction between $\{\omega: x_1(\omega) \neq x_2(\omega)\} = \varnothing$ and the more general Eq. 2.68b.

Transformation of Variables

Electrical communication involves the generation and processing of random signals: waveforms are transformed by modulation, detection, filtering, and so forth. As a consequence, many of the communication applications of probability theory involve the generation of new random variables by means of transformations applied to given ones. We now consider the calculation of the probability density function for new random variables obtained by certain simple (but important) transformations. We begin by assuming that the density functions of the original random variables do not contain impulses. Impulses are considered separately at the end of this section.

Assume that we are given a random variable x with density p_x. Let y be a new random variable, obtained from x by a real-valued piecewise-differentiable transformation

$$y = f(x). \tag{2.69}$$

By Eq. 2.69 we mean that the number $y(\omega)$ associated with each sample point ω is

$$y(\omega) = f(x(\omega)).$$

One method of obtaining the density function p_y from p_x and Eq. 2.69 is first to express in terms of p_x the probability of the set of sample points $\{\omega: y(\omega) \leqslant \alpha\}$. This gives the probability distribution function of y, F_y, from which p_y can be obtained by differentiation.

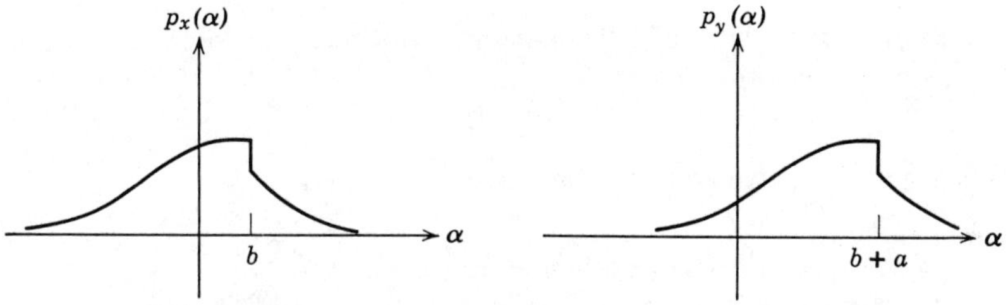

Figure 2.28 The effect of the transformation $y = x + a$.

Transformation by the addition of a constant. Consider as an example the transformation

$$y = x + a$$

in which a is a constant. The set of sample points $\{\omega: y(\omega) \leqslant \alpha\}$ is identically the set $\{\omega: x(\omega) \leqslant \alpha - a\}$. Thus

$$\mathrm{P}[\{\omega: y(\omega) \leqslant \alpha\}] = \mathrm{P}[\{\omega: x(\omega) \leqslant \alpha - a\}]$$

or

$$F_y(\alpha) = F_x(\alpha - a).$$

Differentiating with respect to α, we have

$$p_y(\alpha) = p_x(\alpha - a); \qquad y = x + a. \tag{2.70}$$

The density function p_y is the density p_x translated a units to the right, as shown in Fig. 2.28. For example, if x is Gaussian with density function

$$p_x(\alpha) = \frac{1}{\sqrt{2\pi}} e^{-\alpha^2/2}$$

and $y = x + a$, then

$$p_y(\alpha) = p_x(\alpha - a) = \frac{1}{\sqrt{2\pi}} e^{-(\alpha-a)^2/2}.$$

More generally, if $\mathbf{x}$ is a random vector and $\mathbf{y} = \mathbf{x} + \mathbf{a}$, where $\mathbf{a} \triangleq (a_1, a_2, \ldots, a_k)$ is a constant vector, then

$$F_{\mathbf{y}}(\boldsymbol{\alpha}) = \mathrm{P}[\{\omega: \mathbf{x} + \mathbf{a} \leqslant \boldsymbol{\alpha}\}]$$
$$= \mathrm{P}[\{\omega: \mathbf{x} \leqslant \boldsymbol{\alpha} - \mathbf{a}\}] = F_{\mathbf{x}}(\boldsymbol{\alpha} - \mathbf{a})$$

and

$$p_{\mathbf{y}}(\boldsymbol{\alpha}) = \frac{\partial^k}{\partial \alpha_1 \, \partial \alpha_2 \cdots \partial \alpha_k} F_{\mathbf{x}}(\boldsymbol{\alpha} - \mathbf{a}) = p_{\mathbf{x}}(\boldsymbol{\alpha} - \mathbf{a}); \qquad \mathbf{y} = \mathbf{x} + \mathbf{a}. \tag{2.71}$$

Transformation by multiplication by a constant. A slightly more involved transformation is

$$y = bx.$$

When b is a positive constant, we have

$$\mathrm{P}[\{\omega: y(\omega) \leqslant \alpha\}] = \mathrm{P}\left[\left\{\omega: x(\omega) \leqslant \frac{\alpha}{b}\right\}\right]$$

or

$$F_y(\alpha) = F_x\left(\frac{\alpha}{b}\right),$$

and thus

$$p_y(\alpha) = +\frac{1}{b}\, p_x\left(\frac{\alpha}{b}\right); \qquad y = bx,\ b > 0. \tag{2.72a}$$

On the other hand, when b is negative, we have

$$\mathrm{P}[\{\omega: y(\omega) \leqslant \alpha\}] = \mathrm{P}\left[\left\{\omega: x(\omega) \geqslant \frac{\alpha}{b}\right\}\right]$$

or

$$F_y(\alpha) = 1 - F_x\left(\frac{\alpha}{b}\right),$$

and thus

$$p_y(\alpha) = -\frac{1}{b}\, p_x\left(\frac{\alpha}{b}\right); \qquad y = bx,\ b < 0. \tag{2.72b}$$

Equations 2.72a and b can be combined into the single expression

$$p_y(\alpha) = \frac{1}{|b|}\, p_x\left(\frac{\alpha}{b}\right); \qquad y = bx. \tag{2.73}$$

For example, if x is a Gaussian random variable with density

$$p_x(\alpha) = \frac{1}{\sqrt{2\pi}} e^{-\alpha^2/2}$$

and $y = bx$, $b \neq 0$, then

$$p_y(\alpha) = \frac{1}{|b|} p_x\left(\frac{\alpha}{b}\right) = \frac{1}{\sqrt{2\pi b^2}} e^{-\alpha^2/2b^2}.$$

More general transformations. Identical reasoning is also applicable to transformations that are not one-to-one. Consider, first, the half-wave linear rectifier transformation

$$y = \begin{cases} x; & x \geqslant 0 \\ 0; & x < 0 \end{cases} \tag{2.74a}$$

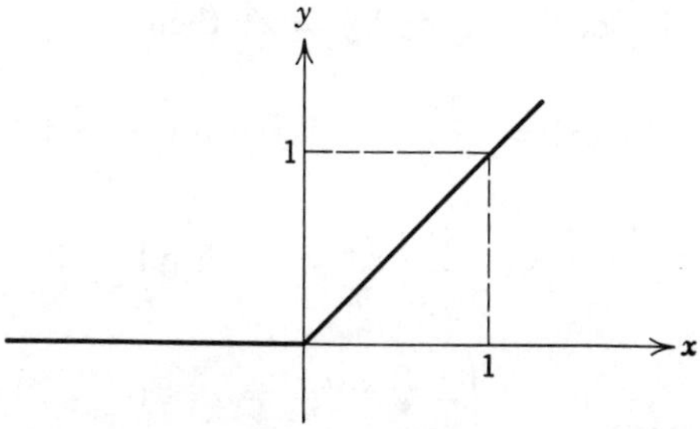

Figure 2.29 The half-wave rectifier transformation.

illustrated in Fig. 2.29. In terms of the input density function p_x, we have

$$P[\{\omega\colon y(\omega) < 0\}] = 0,$$

$$P[\{\omega\colon y(\omega) = 0\}] = \int_{-\infty}^{0} p_x(\beta)\, d\beta \triangleq P_0,$$

$$P[\{\omega\colon 0 < y(\omega) \leqslant \alpha\}] = \int_0^{\alpha} p_x(\beta)\, d\beta.$$

For the half-wave linear rectifier it follows that

$$p_y(\alpha) = P_0\, \delta(\alpha) + u_{-1}(\alpha)\, p_x(\alpha), \tag{2.74b}$$

where $u_{-1}(\alpha)$ is the unit step function

$$u_{-1}(\alpha) = \begin{cases} 1; & \alpha \geqslant 0 \\ 0; & \alpha < 0. \end{cases} \tag{2.74c}$$

A second example is the full-wave quadratic rectifier transformation $y = x^2$. Clearly,

$$F_y(\alpha) \triangleq P[\{\omega\colon y(\omega) \leqslant \alpha\}] = \begin{cases} \displaystyle\int_{-\sqrt{\alpha}}^{+\sqrt{\alpha}} p_x(\beta)\, d\beta = F_x(\sqrt{\alpha}) - F_x(-\sqrt{\alpha}); \\ \qquad\qquad\qquad\qquad \alpha \geqslant 0 \\ 0; \quad \alpha < 0. \end{cases}$$

It follows that

$$p_y(\alpha) = \begin{cases} \dfrac{1}{2\sqrt{\alpha}}\,[p_x(\sqrt{\alpha}) + p_x(-\sqrt{\alpha})]; & \alpha \geqslant 0 \\ 0; & \alpha < 0. \end{cases} \tag{2.75}$$

For instance, if x is a Rayleigh random variable with density

$$p_x(\alpha) = \begin{cases} 0; & \alpha < 0 \\ \dfrac{\alpha}{b}\, e^{-\alpha^2/2b}; & \alpha \geqslant 0 \end{cases}$$

(where b is a positive constant) and $y = x^2$, then

$$\begin{aligned} p_y(\alpha) &= \frac{1}{2\sqrt{\alpha}}\,[p_x(\sqrt{\alpha}) + p_x(-\sqrt{\alpha})]; & \alpha \geqslant 0 \\ &= \frac{1}{2\sqrt{\alpha}}\left(\frac{\sqrt{\alpha}}{b}\, e^{-\alpha/2b} + 0\right); & \alpha \geqslant 0 \\ &= \begin{cases} \dfrac{1}{2b}\, e^{-\alpha/2b}; & \alpha \geqslant 0 \\ 0; & \alpha < 0. \end{cases} \end{aligned}$$

We observe that y is an exponentially distributed random variable.

Iterated transformations. It is sometimes convenient with complicated transformations to apply the above-mentioned techniques in sequence. We illustrate this by the simple example

$$y = bx + a. \tag{2.76a}$$

Define the new random variable $z = bx$. Then $y = z + a$ and

$$p_z(\alpha) = \frac{1}{|b|}\, p_x\!\left(\frac{\alpha}{b}\right)$$

$$p_y(\alpha) = p_z(\alpha - a) = \frac{1}{|b|}\, p_x\!\left(\frac{\alpha - a}{b}\right). \tag{2.76b}$$

For instance, if x is Gaussian with density function

$$p_x(\alpha) = \frac{1}{\sqrt{2\pi}}\, e^{-\alpha^2/2},$$

we have

$$p_y(\alpha) = \frac{1}{\sqrt{2\pi b^2}}\, e^{-(\alpha-a)^2/2b^2}. \tag{2.77}$$

Calculation by change of variables. A more complicated transformation that might be handled by the iterative technique but is more easily carried out by change of variables is given by

$$y = \sqrt{x_1^2 + x_2^2}. \tag{2.78a}$$

Here we may determine p_y from $p_{\mathbf{x}}$ as follows:

$$F_y(\alpha) = \iint\limits_{\beta_1^2+\beta_2^2 \leqslant \alpha^2} p_{\mathbf{x}}(\beta_1, \beta_2)\, d\beta_1\, d\beta_2.$$

Making a change of variables to polar coordinates

$$r = \sqrt{\beta_1^2 + \beta_2^2}; \qquad 0 \leqslant r < \infty$$

$$\theta = \tan^{-1}\frac{\beta_2}{\beta_1}; \qquad 0 \leqslant \theta < 2\pi$$

so that

$$\beta_1 = r\cos\theta,$$

$$\beta_2 = r\sin\theta,$$

$$d\beta_1\, d\beta_2 = r\, dr\, d\theta,$$

we have

$$F_y(\alpha) = \begin{cases} \displaystyle\int_0^{\alpha}\int_0^{2\pi} p_{\mathbf{x}}(r\cos\theta, r\sin\theta)\, r\, dr\, d\theta; & \alpha \geqslant 0 \\ 0; & \alpha < 0 \end{cases}$$

and

$$p_y(\alpha) = \begin{cases} \displaystyle\int_0^{2\pi} \alpha p_{\mathbf{x}}(\alpha\cos\theta, \alpha\sin\theta)\, d\theta; & \alpha \geqslant 0 \\ 0; & \alpha < 0. \end{cases} \tag{2.78b}$$

For example, if

$$p_{\mathbf{x}}(\boldsymbol{\beta}) = \frac{1}{2\pi b^2} e^{-(\beta_1^2+\beta_2^2)/2b^2},$$

then, for $y = \sqrt{x_1^2 + x_2^2}$,

$$p_y(\alpha) = \int_0^{2\pi} \alpha \frac{1}{2\pi b^2} e^{-\alpha^2/2b^2}\, d\theta; \qquad \alpha \geqslant 0$$

$$= \begin{cases} \dfrac{\alpha}{b^2} e^{-\alpha^2/2b^2}; & \alpha \geqslant 0 \\ 0; & \alpha < 0. \end{cases}$$

The resulting random variable y is Rayleigh. This method is further elaborated in Appendix 2A.

Impulsive densities. When $y = f(x)$ and p_x contains impulses, we determine p_y in two parts. The first, resulting from the nonimpulsive component of p_x, is obtained as before; the second, resulting from impulses in p_x, is obtained by the following means. If p_x contains an impulse

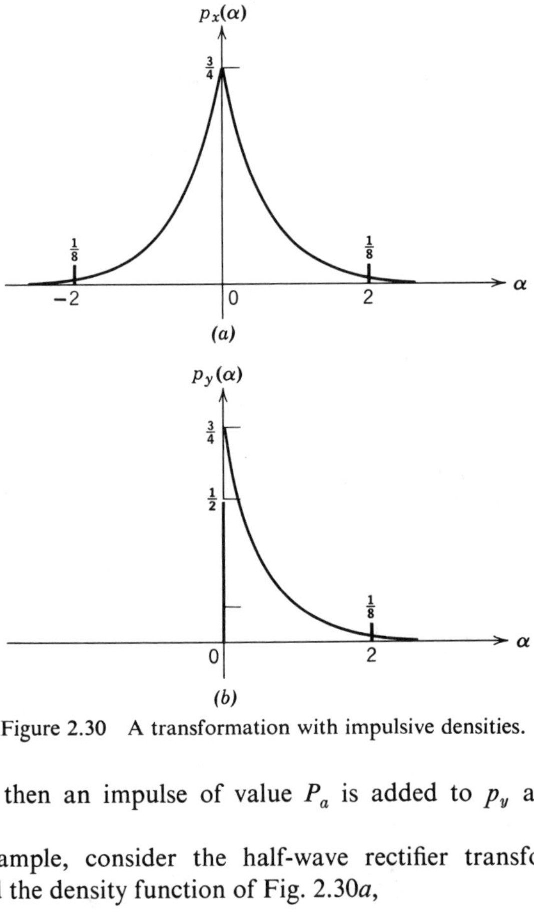

Figure 2.30 A transformation with impulsive densities.

$P_a\,\delta(\alpha - a)$, then an impulse of value P_a is added to p_y at the point $\alpha = f(a)$.

As an example, consider the half-wave rectifier transformation of Fig. 2.29 and the density function of Fig. 2.30a,

$$p_x(\alpha) = \tfrac{1}{8}[\delta(\alpha - 2) + \delta(\alpha + 2)] + \tfrac{3}{4}e^{-2|\alpha|}.$$

From Eq. 2.74b the continuous part of p_x contributes to p_y the terms

$$\tfrac{3}{8}\,\delta(\alpha) + \tfrac{3}{4}\,u_{-1}(\alpha)e^{-2|\alpha|}.$$

The impulse $\frac{1}{8}(\delta - 2)$ in p_x contributes to p_y the impulse $\frac{1}{8}\,\delta(\alpha - 2)$. The impulse $\frac{1}{8}\,\delta(\alpha + 2)$ in p_x contributes to p_y the impulse $\frac{1}{8}\,\delta(\alpha)$. Thus, as shown in Fig. 2.30*b*,

$$p_y(\alpha) = \tfrac{1}{2}\,\delta(\alpha) + \tfrac{1}{8}\,\delta(\alpha - 2) + \tfrac{3}{4}\,u_{-1}(\alpha)e^{-2\alpha}.$$

Conditional Probability Density

Given an event B of nonzero probability, the conditional probability of an event A has been defined as

$$\mathrm{P}[A \mid B] = \frac{\mathrm{P}[A, B]}{\mathrm{P}[B]}.$$

Often events A and B are defined in terms of random variables. For example, let x and y be two random variables defined on a sample space Ω and define the events

$$A = \{\omega\colon a_1 < x_1(\omega) \leqslant b_1\} \qquad (2.79\text{a})$$

$$B = \{\omega\colon a_2 < x_2(\omega) \leqslant b_2\}. \qquad (2.79\text{b})$$

Then, whenever the denominator is nonzero,

$$\mathrm{P}[A \mid B] = \frac{\displaystyle\int_{a_2}^{b_2}\int_{a_1}^{b_1} p_{x_1,x_2}(\alpha, \beta)\, d\alpha\, d\beta}{\displaystyle\int_{a_2}^{b_2} p_{x_2}(\beta)\, d\beta}. \qquad (2.79\text{c})$$

If $b_2 = a_2$, however, and $p_{x_2}(\beta)$ is not impulsive at $\beta = a_2$, the denominator in Eq. 2.79c is zero and the meaning of $\mathrm{P}[A \mid B]$ is not immediately clear.

Before proceeding with the mathematical treatment of this issue, let us consider in more detail the role played by random variables in modeling the real world. A random variable with a continuous density function is an appropriate model for a real-world experiment whenever the outcome may be any real number. The measurement of a noise voltage at some time t_1 furnishes an example. In such a physical experiment there is a fundamental limitation to the accuracy of measurement; we cannot read a voltmeter with infinite precision. Thus "a measured voltage x equals v" actually means that the result of the experiment is a voltage lying in some interval $v - \Delta < x \leqslant v + \Delta$, where Δ is a small positive number reflecting the precision of the voltmeter.

This distinction becomes important when we wish to use the result of such a measurement as a conditioning statement. In order to retain physical verisimilitude, we should introduce into our mathematical formulations a quantity such as Δ. Thus event B in Eq. 2.79 might be

$$\{\omega : v - \Delta < x_2(\omega) \leqslant v + \Delta\},$$

which in general is an event of nonzero probability. Equation 2.79c then becomes

$$P[A \mid B] = \frac{\displaystyle\int_{a_1}^{b_1}\int_{v-\Delta}^{v+\Delta} p_{x_1,x_2}(\alpha, \beta)\, d\beta\, d\alpha}{\displaystyle\int_{v-\Delta}^{v+\Delta} p_{x_2}(\beta)\, d\beta}. \tag{2.80}$$

From a mathematical viewpoint it is inconvenient to carry along the parameter Δ. Whenever the ratio on the right-hand side of Eq. 2.80 is insensitive to the precise value of the (small) quantity Δ, it is simpler to consider the limit as $\Delta \to 0$, even though P[B] may then approach zero. Thus we define the conditional probability of A, given $x_2 = v$, to be this limit and write†

$$P[A \mid x_2 = v] = \lim_{\Delta \to 0} \frac{\displaystyle\int_{a_1}^{b_1}\int_{v-\Delta}^{v+\Delta} p_{x_1,x_2}(\alpha, \beta)\, d\beta\, d\alpha}{\displaystyle\int_{v-\Delta}^{v+\Delta} p_{x_2}(\beta)\, d\beta}. \tag{2.81a}$$

Interchanging the order in Eq. 2.81a, we have

$$P[A \mid x_2 = v] = \int_{a_1}^{b_1} d\alpha \left[\lim_{\Delta \to 0} \frac{\displaystyle\int_{v-\Delta}^{v+\Delta} p_{x_1,x_2}(\alpha, \beta)\, d\beta}{\displaystyle\int_{v-\Delta}^{v+\Delta} p_{x_2}(\beta)\, d\beta} \right]. \tag{2.81b}$$

We note in Eq. 2.81b that the conditional probability that x_1 will lie in the interval $[a_1, b_1]$ is obtained by integrating a non-negative quantity over the interval. Moreover, by Eqs. 2.63 and 2.81a, the integral of this quantity over the entire real line is unity, so that it meets all the requirements of a probability density. Accordingly, we define

$$p_{x_1}(\alpha \mid x_2 = v) \triangleq \lim_{\Delta \to 0} \frac{\displaystyle\int_{v-\Delta}^{v+\Delta} p_{x_1,x_2}(\alpha, \beta)\, d\beta}{\displaystyle\int_{v-\Delta}^{v+\Delta} p_{x_2}(\beta)\, d\beta} \tag{2.82}$$

and call $p_{x_1}(\alpha \mid x_2 = v)$ the *conditional probability density* of x_1, given $x_2 = v$. Equation 2.81b can then be rewritten

$$P[A \mid x_2 = v] = \int_{a_1}^{b_1} p_{x_1}(\alpha \mid x_2 = v)\, d\alpha. \tag{2.83}$$

† Whenever the meaning is unambiguous, we shall henceforth denote events such as $\{\omega : x_2(\omega) = v\}$ by the simpler expression $x_2 = v$.

When the density functions in Eq. 2.82 are continuous at $\beta = v$, the defining equation for the conditional density function simplifies to

$$p_{x_1}(\alpha \mid x_2 = v) = \frac{p_{x_1,x_2}(\alpha, v)}{p_{x_2}(v)} \tag{2.84a}$$

or

$$p_{x_1,x_2}(\alpha, v) = p_{x_1}(\alpha \mid x_2 = v)p_{x_2}(v). \tag{2.84b}$$

Equation 2.83 can still be used when the density functions contain impulses at $\beta = v$; that is, even when there is a finite probability that $x_2 = v$. We then interpret the right-hand side of Eq. 2.84a to be the ratio of the values of corresponding impulses in numerator and denominator. It is evident from Eq. 2.83 that conditional probability density is completely analogous to ordinary one-dimensional density.

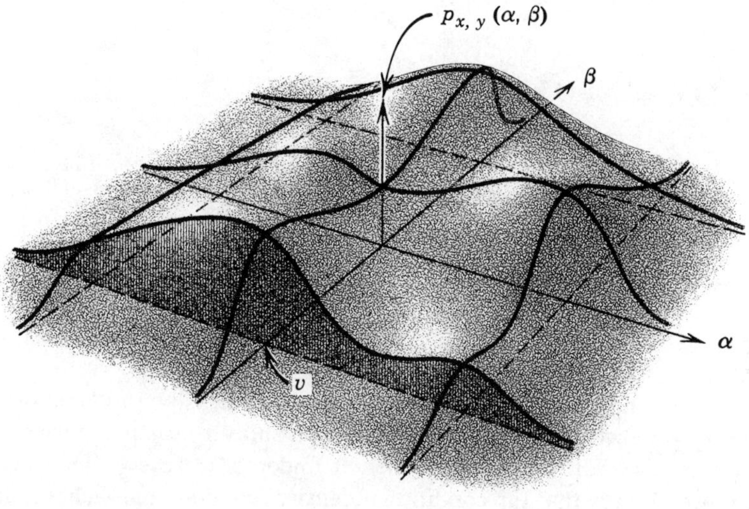

Figure 2.31 A plot of $p_{x,y}(\alpha, \beta)$ illustrating the dependence on v of the shape of $p_x(\alpha \mid y = v)$. There is no dependence only in the special case $p_{x,y}(\alpha, \beta) = p_x(\alpha)\, p_y(\beta)$; see, for example, Fig. 2.27.

The relationships between two-dimensional density functions on the one hand and conditional density functions on the other can be easily visualized graphically. Consider the continuous joint density function shown in Fig. 2.31. The shape as a function of α of the conditional density function $p_{x_1}(\alpha \mid x_2 = v)$ is given by tracing the intersection of the surface $p_{x_1,x_2}(\alpha, \beta)$ with a vertical plane erected on the line $\beta = v$. In general, the shape is different for different values of v. Division by $p_{x_2}(v)$ normalizes the total area under the trace to unity. Given $x_2 = v$, the conditional distribution function of x_1, denoted $F_{x_1}(\alpha \mid x_2 = v)$, is the area under the normalized trace from $-\infty$ to α.

As an example of the definitions, consider the random variables x_1 and x_2 with the Gaussian density function

$$p_{\mathbf{x}}(\alpha_1, \alpha_2) = \frac{1}{2\pi\sqrt{1-\rho^2}} \exp\left[-\frac{\alpha_1^2 - 2\rho\alpha_1\alpha_2 + \alpha_2^2}{2(1-\rho^2)}\right]; \qquad |\rho| < 1.$$

We have determined in Eq. 2.64 that

$$p_{x_1}(\alpha_1) = \int_{-\infty}^{\infty} p_{\mathbf{x}}(\alpha_1, \alpha_2)\, d\alpha_2 = \frac{1}{\sqrt{2\pi}} e^{-\alpha_1^2/2},$$

hence, by symmetry, that

$$p_{x_2}(\alpha_2) = \frac{1}{\sqrt{2\pi}} e^{-\alpha_2^2/2}.$$

Thus

$$\begin{aligned} p_{x_1}(\alpha \mid x_2 = v) &= \frac{p_{x_1,x_2}(\alpha, v)}{p_{x_2}(v)} \\ &= \frac{1}{\sqrt{2\pi(1-\rho^2)}} \exp\left\{-\left[\frac{\alpha^2 - 2\rho\alpha v + v^2}{2(1-\rho^2)} - \frac{v^2}{2}\right]\right\} \\ &= \frac{1}{\sqrt{2\pi(1-\rho^2)}} \exp\left[-\frac{(\alpha - \rho v)^2}{2(1-\rho^2)}\right]. \end{aligned} \qquad (2.85)$$

Given $x_2 = v$, the conditional density function of x_1 has the form of Eq. 2.77 with $a = \rho v$ and $b^2 = 1 - \rho^2$.

When $|\rho|$ approaches unity, the conditional density function of x_1, given $x_2 = v$, becomes very large for $\alpha \approx \rho v$ and very small elsewhere, as shown in Fig. 2.32. Since the integral under $p_{x_1}(\alpha \mid x_2 = v)$ is always unity, we observe that the conditional density function approaches a unit impulse centered on $\pm v$ as $\rho \to \pm 1$.

Applications. The usefulness of the concept of conditional probability density can be demonstrated by two examples. For the first example consider two random variables x and y and the transformation

$$z = x + y.$$

We desire the probability density function of the random variable z.

We have already considered a transformation of the form $z = x + \beta$ when β is a constant and found (Eq. 2.70, with a change of notation)

$$p_z(\gamma) = p_x(\gamma - \beta). \qquad (2.86a)$$

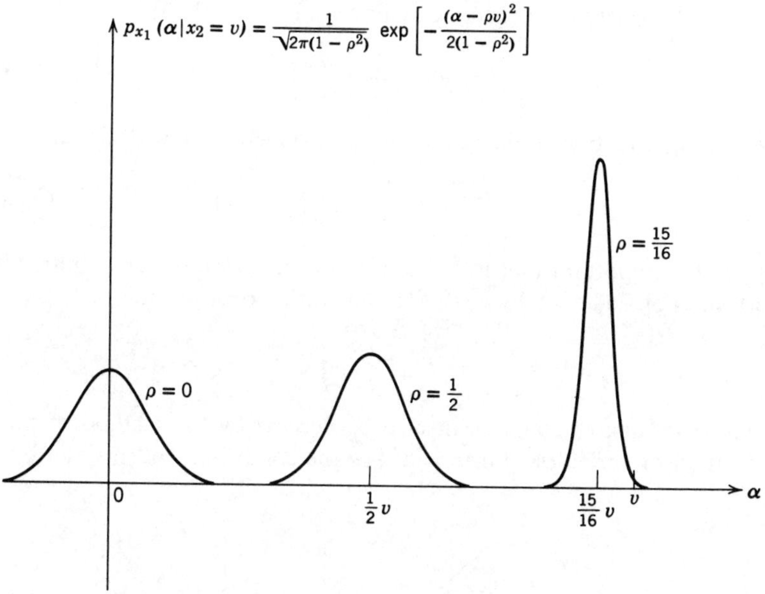

Figure 2.32 The conditional Gaussian density function, $p_{x_1}(\alpha \mid x_2 = v)$ as a function of ρ.

This result can be applied to the present problem by use of conditional probability density. Focus attention on that part of the sample space for which $y(\omega)$ equals β. Over this region $x + y$ is $x + \beta$, and Eq. 2.86a is valid, with the important proviso that we state the condition explicitly. We have

$$p_z(\gamma \mid y = \beta) = p_x(\gamma - \beta \mid y = \beta). \tag{2.86b}$$

The joint density of z and y is obtained by first multiplying both sides of Eq. 2.86b by $p_y(\beta)$,

$$\begin{aligned} p_{z,y}(\gamma, \beta) &= p_z(\gamma \mid y = \beta)\, p_y(\beta) \\ &= p_x(\gamma - \beta \mid y = \beta)\, p_y(\beta) \\ &= p_{x,y}(\gamma - \beta, \beta), \end{aligned}$$

and then integrating out the unwanted variable in accord with Eq. 2.63:

$$p_z(\gamma) = \int_{-\infty}^{\infty} p_{x,y}(\gamma - \beta, \beta)\, d\beta; \qquad z = x + y. \tag{2.87}$$

As a second example, consider the product transformation

$$z = xy.$$

For $z = \beta x$, where β is constant, we have found (Eq. 2.73)

$$p_z(\gamma) = \frac{1}{|\beta|} p_x\left(\frac{\gamma}{\beta}\right). \tag{2.88a}$$

Restricting attention to the region of Ω for which $y(\omega) = \beta$, we have

$$p_z(\gamma \mid y = \beta) = \frac{1}{|\beta|} p_x\left(\frac{\gamma}{\beta} \,\middle|\, y = \beta\right). \tag{2.88b}$$

Again it is important that the condition be stated explicitly. Multiplying both sides of Eq. 2.88b by $p_y(\beta)$ and integrating over β yields

$$p_z(\gamma) = \int_{-\infty}^{\infty} \frac{1}{|\beta|} p_{x,y}\left(\frac{\gamma}{\beta}, \beta\right) d\beta; \qquad z = xy. \tag{2.89}$$

These results, of course, can also be derived by the method of transformation of variables. For $z = x + y$ the condition $z \leqslant \gamma$ is met by all

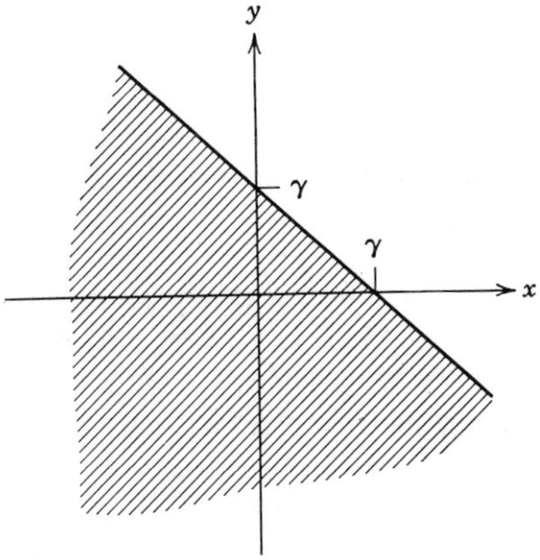

Figure 2.33 The region for which $x + y \leqslant \gamma$.

points in the x, y plane below the line $x + y = \gamma$, as shown in Fig. 2.33. The probability that the point (x, y) will fall in this region is

$$F_z(\gamma) = \int_{-\infty}^{\infty} d\beta \int_{-\infty}^{\gamma-\beta} p_{x,y}(\alpha, \beta)\, d\alpha,$$

and thus

$$p_z(\gamma) = \int_{-\infty}^{\infty} p_{x,y}(\gamma - \beta, \beta)\, d\beta; \qquad z = x + y.$$

Statistical Independence

In the case of random variables the definition of statistical independence is somewhat simpler than in the case of events (see Eqs. 2.26 and 2.27).

We call k random variables $x_1, x_2, \ldots, x_k$ *statistically independent* if and only if the joint density function $p_{\mathbf{x}}$ factors into the product $\prod_{i=1}^{k} p_{x_i}$; that is, if and only if

$$p_{\mathbf{x}}(\boldsymbol{\alpha}) = p_{x_1}(\alpha_1)\, p_{x_2}(\alpha_2) \cdots p_{x_k}(\alpha_k) \qquad \text{for all } \boldsymbol{\alpha}. \tag{2.90}$$

Let $\mathbf{x}$ denote a set of k statistically independent random variables and consider the random vector

$$\mathbf{x}' = (x_1, x_2, \ldots, x_{l-1}, x_{l+1}, \ldots, x_k) \tag{2.91a}$$

obtained by omitting x_l. The joint density function $p_{\mathbf{x}'}$ is given by

$$p_{\mathbf{x}'}(\boldsymbol{\alpha}') = \int_{-\infty}^{\infty} p_{\mathbf{x}}(\boldsymbol{\alpha})\, d\alpha_l = \prod_{\substack{i=1 \\ (i \neq l)}}^{k} p_{x_i}(\alpha_i). \tag{2.91b}$$

We conclude that the components of $\mathbf{x}'$ are also statistically independent. It is readily induced that the statistical independence of a set of random variables guarantees the independence of any subset of them.

If we have a set of k events, say $A_1, A_2, \ldots, A_k$, such that each event A_i is defined in terms of a single corresponding random variable x_i,

$$A_i = \{\omega\colon x_i \text{ in } I_i\}; \qquad i = 1, 2, \ldots, k, \tag{2.92a}$$

then from Eq. 2.90

$$\begin{aligned} \mathrm{P}[A_1, A_2, \ldots, A_k] &= \int_{I_1}\int_{I_2}\cdots\int_{I_k} p_{\mathbf{x}}(\boldsymbol{\alpha})\, d\alpha_1\, d\alpha_2 \cdots d\alpha_k \\ &= \prod_{i=1}^{k} \int_{I_i} p_{x_i}(\alpha_i)\, d\alpha_i = \prod_{i=1}^{k} \mathrm{P}[A_i] \end{aligned} \tag{2.92b}$$

whenever the $\{x_i\}$ are statistically independent.

Similarly, the probability of the intersection of any subset of these events factors into the product of the probabilities of the individual events. Thus the statistical independence of the $\{x_i\}$ implies that the set of events $\{A_1, A_2, \ldots, A_k\}$ is also statistically independent.

An interesting example of statistical independence occurs when each of k random variables is Gaussian:

$$p_{x_i}(\alpha_i) = \frac{1}{\sqrt{2\pi}}\, e^{-\alpha_i^{\,2}/2}; \qquad i = 1, 2, \ldots, k. \tag{2.93a}$$

Then

$$p_{\mathbf{x}}(\boldsymbol{\alpha}) = \prod_{i=1}^{k} p_{x_i}(\alpha_i) = \frac{1}{(2\pi)^{k/2}} \exp\left(-\frac{1}{2}\sum_{i=1}^{k} \alpha_i^{\,2}\right). \tag{2.93b}$$

If in the two-dimensional Gaussian density function of Eq. 2.58 the parameter ρ is set equal to zero, then

$$p_{x_1,x_2}(\alpha_1, \alpha_2) = \frac{1}{2\pi} \exp\left[-\tfrac{1}{2}(\alpha_1^{\,2} + \alpha_1^{\,2})\right]$$

$$= \left(\frac{1}{\sqrt{2\pi}} e^{-\alpha_1^{\,2}/2}\right)\left(\frac{1}{\sqrt{2\pi}} e^{-\alpha_2^{\,2}/2}\right). \tag{2.93c}$$

Thus the condition $\rho = 0$ implies statistical independence. Conversely, for $\rho \neq 0$ the joint density function does not factor and therefore x_1 and x_2 are not independent.

Sums of independent random variables. When random variables are statistically independent, the form of the probability density function of their sum is simplified. For $z = x + y$ we have already obtained the result

$$p_z(\gamma) = \int_{-\infty}^{\infty} p_{x,y}(\gamma - \beta, \beta)\, d\beta.$$

Substituting $p_x p_y$ for $p_{x,y}$ in this equation, we have

$$p_z(\gamma) = \int_{-\infty}^{\infty} p_x(\gamma - \beta)\, p_y(\beta)\, d\beta. \tag{2.94}$$

Equation 2.94 is the *convolution* of p_x and p_y. Using the symbol $*$ to denote convolution, we can write, for statistically independent random variables,

$$p_z = p_x * p_y; \qquad z = x + y.$$

By induction,

$$p_z = p_{x_1} * p_{x_2} * \cdots * p_{x_k}; \qquad z = \sum_{i=1}^{k} x_i, \quad p_{\mathbf{x}} = \prod_{i=1}^{k} p_{x_i}. \tag{2.95}$$

As in the familiar case of signal analysis, it is often easier to calculate a k-fold convolution by means of Fourier transforms. We define the *characteristic function*, denoted by $M_x(\nu)$, of a random variable x to be the Fourier transform of its density function:

$$M_x(\nu) \triangleq \int_{-\infty}^{\infty} p_x(\alpha) e^{j\nu\alpha}\, d\alpha. \tag{2.96}$$

Since

$$|e^{j\nu\alpha}| = 1 \quad \text{and} \quad \int_{-\infty}^{\infty} p_x(\alpha)\, d\alpha = 1,$$

$|M_x(\nu)| \leqslant 1$ and the characteristic function always exists. The density function is regained by the inverse Fourier transform†

$$p_x(\alpha) = \frac{1}{2\pi}\int_{-\infty}^{\infty} M_x(\nu)e^{-j\nu\alpha}\, d\nu. \tag{2.97}$$

It is well known that when functions are convolved their Fourier transforms multiply. This can be shown by evaluating $M_z(\nu)$ with the use of Eq. 2.94:

$$M_z(\nu) \triangleq \int_{-\infty}^{\infty} e^{j\nu\gamma}\, p_z(\gamma)\, d\gamma = \int_{-\infty}^{\infty} e^{j\nu\gamma}\, d\gamma \int_{-\infty}^{\infty} p_x(\gamma - \beta)\, p_y(\beta)\, d\beta$$

$$= \int_{-\infty}^{\infty} e^{j\nu\beta}\, p_y(\beta)\, d\beta \int_{-\infty}^{\infty} e^{j\nu(\gamma-\beta)}\, p_x(\gamma - \beta)\, d\gamma$$

$$= M_y(\nu)\, M_x(\nu).$$

It follows by induction that for k statistically independent random variables

$$M_z(\nu) = \prod_{i=1}^{k} M_{x_i}(\nu); \qquad z = \sum_{i=1}^{k} x_i,\ p_{\mathbf{x}} = \prod_{i=1}^{k} p_{x_i}, \tag{2.98}$$

from which p_z can be calculated by the inverse transformation of Eq. 2.97.

Mixed Probability Expressions

In communication problems we frequently consider a sample space Ω on which some events are defined in terms of random variables or vectors and some are not. We now develop notation for dealing conveniently with such probability systems. Consider two k-dimensional random vectors, $\mathbf{x}$ and $\mathbf{y}$, and arbitrary events B and C defined as

$$B = \{\omega\colon \mathbf{x}(\omega) \text{ in } I_1\}$$

$$C = \{\omega\colon \mathbf{y}(\omega) \text{ in } I_2\},$$

where I_1 and I_2 are regions of k-dimensional space. The following discussion is general and includes the special case $k = 1$. In terms of notation

† When p_x is impulsive we use the transform pair

$$\int_{-\infty}^{\infty} \delta(\alpha)\, e^{j\nu\alpha}\, d\alpha = 1, \qquad \frac{1}{2\pi}\int_{-\infty}^{\infty} e^{-j\nu\alpha}\, d\nu = \delta(\alpha).$$

previously developed we have

$$P[B] = \int_{I_1} p_{\mathbf{x}}(\boldsymbol{\alpha})\, d\boldsymbol{\alpha},$$

$$P[C] = \int_{I_2} p_{\mathbf{y}}(\boldsymbol{\beta})\, d\boldsymbol{\beta},$$

$$P[BC] = \iint_{I_1 I_2} p_{\mathbf{x},\mathbf{y}}(\boldsymbol{\alpha}, \boldsymbol{\beta})\, d\boldsymbol{\alpha}\, d\boldsymbol{\beta}.$$

The new notation introduced below is a consistent extension of that already encountered. Let A be an event of nonzero probability.

1. $p_{\mathbf{x}}(\quad | A)$: The conditional probability of the event B, given the event A, is conveniently written

$$P[B \mid A] = \int_{I_1} p_{\mathbf{x}}(\boldsymbol{\alpha} \mid A)\, d\boldsymbol{\alpha}. \tag{2.99}$$

The function $p_{\mathbf{x}}(\quad | A)$ is called the *conditional density function of* **x**, *given A*.

In common with all quantities conditioned on an event of nonzero probability, $p_{\mathbf{x}}(\quad | A)$ may be regarded as the density function of the random vector **x** under the condition that attention is restricted to those sample points that constitute the event A. In effect, A becomes a new sample space: all theorems and results valid over Ω are also valid over A whenever *all* quantities involved are conditioned on A. Thus conditioning density functions on an event of nonzero probability involves no new ideas, but only augmented notation. For example,

$$P[B, C \mid A] = \iint_{I_1 I_2} p_{\mathbf{x},\mathbf{y}}(\boldsymbol{\alpha}, \boldsymbol{\beta} \mid A)\, d\boldsymbol{\beta}\, d\boldsymbol{\alpha}.$$

2. $p_{\mathbf{x}}(\quad , A)$: The probability of the joint event AB is conveniently written

$$P[AB] = \int_{I_1} p_{\mathbf{x}}(\boldsymbol{\alpha}, A)\, d\boldsymbol{\alpha}.$$

The function $p_{\mathbf{x}}(\quad , A)$ is called the *joint density function of the random variable* **x** *and the event A*.

Since

$$P[AB] = P[A]\, P[B \mid A]$$

$$= \int_{I_1} P[A]\, p_{\mathbf{x}}(\boldsymbol{\alpha} \mid A)\, d\boldsymbol{\alpha},$$

we have the relation

$$p_{\mathbf{x}}(\ \ , A) = \mathrm{P}[A]\, p_{\mathbf{x}}(\ \ \mid A). \tag{2.100}$$

3. $\mathrm{P}[A \mid \mathbf{x} = \mathbf{a}]$: The conditional probability of an event A, conditioned on the event $\mathbf{x} = \mathbf{a}$, is defined analogously to the corresponding one-dimensional definition of Eq. 2.81a:

$$\mathrm{P}[A \mid \mathbf{x} = \mathbf{a}] \triangleq \lim_{\Delta \to 0} \frac{\displaystyle\int_{I_\Delta} p_{\mathbf{x}}(\boldsymbol{\alpha}, A)\, d\boldsymbol{\alpha}}{\displaystyle\int_{I_\Delta} p_{\mathbf{x}}(\boldsymbol{\alpha})\, d\boldsymbol{\alpha}}, \tag{2.101}$$

where

$$I_\Delta = \{\boldsymbol{\alpha} : \mathbf{a} - \boldsymbol{\Delta} < \boldsymbol{\alpha} \leqslant \mathbf{a} + \boldsymbol{\Delta}\}$$

$$\boldsymbol{\Delta} = (\Delta, \Delta, \ldots, \Delta).$$

If the density functions are continuous at $\mathbf{x} = \mathbf{a}$, the limit can be evaluated by noting that as Δ becomes smaller and smaller both the numerator and denominator are given to a better and better approximation by the product of the appropriate density function, evaluated at $\mathbf{x} = \mathbf{a}$, and the volume of I_Δ. Cancelling this volume in numerator and denominator, we obtain in the limit

$$\mathrm{P}[A \mid \mathbf{x} = \mathbf{a}] = \frac{p_{\mathbf{x}}(\mathbf{a}, A)}{p_{\mathbf{x}}(\mathbf{a})}, \tag{2.102a}$$

or

$$\mathrm{P}[A \mid \mathbf{x} = \mathbf{a}] p_{\mathbf{x}}(\mathbf{a}) = p_{\mathbf{x}}(\mathbf{a}, A). \tag{2.102b}$$

Bayes rule. Both Eqs. 2.102b and 2.100 provide expressions for $p_{\mathbf{x}}(\mathbf{a}, A)$. Equating these two expressions yields the useful result

$$p_{\mathbf{x}}(\mathbf{a} \mid A)\, \mathrm{P}[A] = \mathrm{P}[A \mid \mathbf{x} = \mathbf{a}]\, p_{\mathbf{x}}(\mathbf{a}). \tag{2.103a}$$

Equation 2.103a is called the "mixed form" of *Bayes rule*; "mixed" refers to the fact that the probability expressions involve both random variables and events. The two unmixed forms of Bayes rule, from Eqs. 2.21 and 2.84b, are

$$\mathrm{P}[B \mid A]\, \mathrm{P}[A] = \mathrm{P}[A \mid B]\, \mathrm{P}[B] \tag{2.103b}$$

and

$$p_{\mathbf{x}}(\mathbf{a} \mid \mathbf{y} = \mathbf{b})\, p_{\mathbf{y}}(\mathbf{b}) = p_{\mathbf{y}}(\mathbf{b} \mid \mathbf{x} = \mathbf{a})\, p_{\mathbf{x}}(\mathbf{a}). \tag{2.103c}$$

Factoring probability expressions. The use of conditional notation permits us to factor joint probability expressions with considerable freedom. For example, with three random vectors $\mathbf{x}$, $\mathbf{y}$, and $\mathbf{z}$, we can write

$$\begin{aligned} p_{\mathbf{x},\mathbf{y},\mathbf{z}}(\boldsymbol{\alpha}, \boldsymbol{\beta}, \boldsymbol{\gamma}) &= p_{\mathbf{x}}(\boldsymbol{\alpha})\, p_{\mathbf{y}}(\boldsymbol{\beta} \mid \mathbf{x} = \boldsymbol{\alpha})\, p_{\mathbf{z}}(\boldsymbol{\gamma} \mid \mathbf{x} = \boldsymbol{\alpha}, \mathbf{y} = \boldsymbol{\beta}) \\ &= p_{\mathbf{y}}(\boldsymbol{\beta})\, p_{\mathbf{z}}(\boldsymbol{\gamma} \mid \mathbf{y} = \boldsymbol{\beta})\, p_{\mathbf{x}}(\boldsymbol{\alpha} \mid \mathbf{y} = \boldsymbol{\beta}, \mathbf{z} = \boldsymbol{\gamma}), \end{aligned}$$

and so forth. Similarly, mixed expressions can be factored in many different ways such as

$$p_{\mathbf{x},\mathbf{y}}(\boldsymbol{\alpha}, \boldsymbol{\beta}, A, B) = \mathrm{P}[B]\, p_{\mathbf{x}}(\boldsymbol{\alpha} \mid B)\, \mathrm{P}[A \mid \mathbf{x} = \boldsymbol{\alpha}, B]\, p_{\mathbf{y}}(\boldsymbol{\beta} \mid \mathbf{x} = \boldsymbol{\alpha}, A, B).$$

Statistical independence. We have already considered the statistical independence of events and the statistical independence of random variables. The definitions can be extended in an obvious way to more general probability situations.

1. Two random vectors $\mathbf{x}$ and $\mathbf{y}$ are defined to be statistically independent if and only if

$$p_{\mathbf{x},\mathbf{y}} = p_{\mathbf{x}}\, p_{\mathbf{y}}. \tag{2.104a}$$

An event B defined exclusively in terms of $\mathbf{x}$ and an event C defined exclusively in terms of $\mathbf{y}$ are statistically independent,

$$\mathrm{P}[BC] = \mathrm{P}[B]\, \mathrm{P}[C],$$

whenever $\mathbf{x}$ and $\mathbf{y}$ are statistically independent. An alternative expression for the independence of $\mathbf{x}$ and $\mathbf{y}$ is

$$p_{\mathbf{x}}(\quad \mid \mathbf{y} = \boldsymbol{\beta}) = p_{\mathbf{x}}(\quad); \qquad \text{for all } \boldsymbol{\beta}, \tag{2.104b}$$

which we also write in the shortened form, but with identical meaning,

$$p_{\mathbf{x}|\mathbf{y}} = p_{\mathbf{x}}. \tag{2.104c}$$

We observe that specification of $\mathbf{y}$ does not affect the density function of $\mathbf{x}$ when $\mathbf{x}$ and $\mathbf{y}$ are independent.

2. A random vector $\mathbf{x}$ and an event A are defined as statistically independent if and only if

$$p_{\mathbf{x}}(\quad, A) = \mathrm{P}[A]\, p_{\mathbf{x}}(\quad). \tag{2.105}$$

Then any event B defined only in terms of $\mathbf{x}$ is statistically independent of A:

$$\mathrm{P}[BA] = \mathrm{P}[B]\, \mathrm{P}[A].$$

3. Two random vectors $\mathbf{x}$ and $\mathbf{y}$ are defined as statistically independent when conditioned on an event A if and only if

$$p_{\mathbf{x},\mathbf{y}}(\quad \mid A) = p_{\mathbf{x}}(\quad \mid A)\, p_{\mathbf{y}}(\quad \mid A). \tag{2.106}$$

Then any event B defined exclusively in terms of $\mathbf{x}$ and any event C defined exclusively in terms of $\mathbf{y}$ satisfy

$$P[BC \mid A] = P[B \mid A]\, P[C \mid A].$$

One important implication of statistical independence is the following: consider the transformations

$$z_1 = g_1(\mathbf{x}); \qquad z_2 = g_2(\mathbf{y}), \tag{2.107a}$$

where g_1 and g_2 are any two functions mapping the random vectors $\mathbf{x}$ and $\mathbf{y}$ into random variables z_1 and z_2. (As a special case, g_1 and g_2 might be the same function.) We now prove that whenever $\mathbf{x}$ and $\mathbf{y}$ are statistically independent so also are z_1 and z_2. The statement follows from first noting that the events

$$B \triangleq \{\omega: g_1(\mathbf{x}(\omega)) \leqslant \alpha\}$$

and

$$C \triangleq \{\omega: g_2(\mathbf{y}(\omega)) \leqslant \beta\}$$

are statistically independent, since B is defined exclusively in terms of $\mathbf{x}$ and C is defined exclusively in terms of $\mathbf{y}$. But

$$F_{z_1,z_2}(\alpha, \beta) = P[B, C] = P[B]\, P[C] = F_{z_1}(\alpha)\, F_{z_2}(\beta) \tag{2.107b}$$

for any values α and β. Thus the joint density function of the random variables (z_1, z_2), obtained by differentiating F_{z_1,z_2} in Eq. 2.107b, can be factored and the variables are independent. We summarize this result by stating that functions of statistically independent random vectors (or variables) are statistically independent.

A Communication Example

The concepts and notation of conditional probability, which we have seen to be fundamentally the same whether we are dealing with random variables or random vectors, are basic to the formulation of communication theory. We now illustrate many of the essential ideas by considering the idealized one-dimensional communication example illustrated in Fig. 2.34. First suppose that there are two possible messages, that is, $M = 2$. One of these two messages, say m_0 or m_1, is presented to the transmitter input, with a priori probabilities $P[m_0]$ and $P[m_1]$. The transmitter maps the abstract input symbol into a voltage s, say $m_0 \to s_0$ and $m_1 \to s_1$, which is then applied to the channel input. The channel corrupts the transmitted voltage s by the addition of a statistically independent voltage n, which has a density function p_n. Thus the received signal at the channel output is the sum, r, of the random variables s and n.

We wish to find a decision rule for the receiver, that is, a rule for determining whether the receiver output is to be m_0 or m_1, given any value of the received voltage. In particular, we seek the (optimum) decision rule that minimizes the probability of error. The mathematical problem again corresponds to observing the detector output at point a of Fig. 1.8. In contrast to the discrete communication model considered earlier, however, r is now allowed to be any real number rather than being constrained to a discrete set of values.

Suppose the random voltage r equals ρ. As in the discrete communication example on p. 33, the probability of correct decision is maximized by mapping ρ into that message m_i for which the a posteriori probability

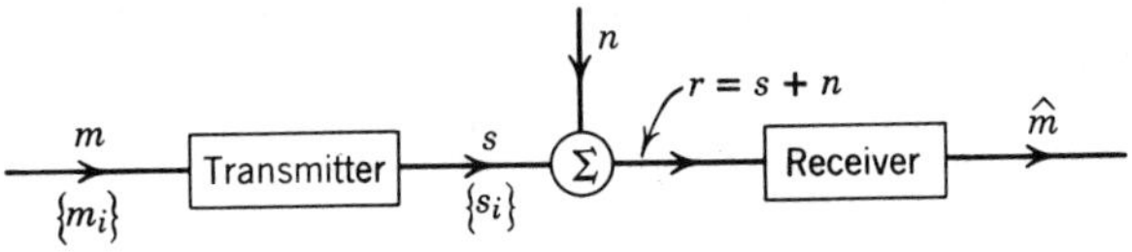

Figure 2.34 A simple communication model. The transmitter input m is one of the set of M messages $\{m_i\}$. The transmitter output s is the corresponding member of the set of M voltages $\{s_i\}$. The receiver output $\hat{m}$ is one of the input set $\{m_i\}$.

is maximum; that is, on observing $r = \rho$, we set the receiver output, say $\hat{m}(\rho)$, equal to m_0 if and only if

$$P[m_0 \mid r = \rho] > P[m_1 \mid r = \rho]. \tag{2.108}$$

We next place Eq. 2.108 in a more convenient form by use of the mixed Bayes rule of Eq. 2.103a. Thus $\hat{m}(\rho) = m_0$ if and only if

$$\frac{p_r(\rho \mid m_0)\, P[m_0]}{p_r(\rho)} > \frac{p_r(\rho \mid m_1)\, P[m_1]}{p_r(\rho)},$$

or, since the denominator is common to both sides of the inequality, if and only if

$$p_r(\rho \mid m_0)\, P[m_0] > p_r(\rho \mid m_1)\, P[m_1]. \tag{2.109}$$

We may proceed by noting that $r = s_i + n$ when the transmitted message is m_i. Thus, conditional on the event that m_i is the message input, r is obtained from n by the addition of the (known) constant s_i. Under this condition $r = \rho$ if and only if $n = \rho - s_i$. Thus, from the section on transformations,

$$p_r(\rho \mid m_i) = p_n(\rho - s_i \mid m_i). \tag{2.110a}$$

Moreover, since the noise is assumed to be independent of the transmitted signal, hence of the message,

$$p_n(\rho - s_i \mid m_i) = p_n(\rho - s_i). \tag{2.110b}$$

It follows that the optimum receiver sets $\hat{m}(\rho) = m_0$ if and only if

$$p_n(\rho - s_0)\, \mathrm{P}[m_0] > p_n(\rho - s_1)\, \mathrm{P}[m_1]. \tag{2.111}$$

The decision rule of Eq. 2.111 may be immediately generalized to include the case $M > 2$. If the possible input messages are $m_0, m_1, \ldots, m_{M-1}$, with corresponding transmitter voltages $s_0, s_1, \ldots, s_{M-1}$ and a priori probabilities $\{\mathrm{P}[m_i]\}$, the optimum receiver again assigns $\hat{m}(\rho)$ as the message with maximum a posteriori probability. It follows immediately from Eq. 2.111 that $\hat{m}(\rho) = m_i$ if and only if

$$p_n(\rho - s_i)\, \mathrm{P}[m_i] > p_n(\rho - s_j)\, \mathrm{P}[m_j]; \qquad j = 0, 1, \ldots, M-1,\ j \neq i. \tag{2.112}$$

If two or more messages have the same a posteriori probability, ρ may be assigned arbitrarily to any one of them without loss of optimality.

The decision rule of Eq. 2.112 cannot be simplified further without introducing a specific noise density function p_n. The Gaussian noise case in which

$$p_n(\alpha) = \frac{1}{\sqrt{2\pi}\sigma} e^{-\alpha^2/2\sigma^2} \tag{2.113}$$

is frequently encountered. The decision rule then becomes: set $\hat{m}(\rho) = m_i$ if and only if

$$\mathrm{P}[m_i]\, e^{-(\rho - s_i)^2/2\sigma^2} > \mathrm{P}[m_j]\, e^{-(\rho - s_j)^2/2\sigma^2}; \qquad j = 0, 1, \ldots, M-1,\ j \neq i. \tag{2.114}$$

This situation is illustrated in Fig. 2.35*a* for $M = 2$. From the figure it is clear that an equivalent rule is then: assign ρ to m_0 if and only if $\rho > a$, where the threshold a is the value of ρ at which the two curves intersect. The location of this threshold, from Eq. 2.114 with $M = 2$, is

$$a = \frac{s_0 + s_1}{2} + \frac{\sigma^2}{s_0 - s_1} \ln \frac{\mathrm{P}[m_1]}{\mathrm{P}[m_0]}. \tag{2.115}$$

The optimum receiver output $\hat{m}(\rho)$ is determined by Eq. 2.112 for any value of M and for any specified noise density function p_n. It is helpful to view the function $\hat{m}(\ )$ as partitioning the space of all possible values of ρ into a set of M disjoint decision regions $\{I_i\}$, $i = 0, 1, \ldots, M-1$. For the case illustrated in Fig. 2.35*a*, I_0 is the interval $a < \rho < \infty$ and I_1 is the interval $-\infty < \rho \leqslant a$. A case with $M = 3$ is shown in Fig. 2.35*b*.

A correct decision results when m_i is the message if and only if the received voltage ρ is in the decision region I_i: letting $\mathcal{C}$ denote a correct decision, we have

$$\mathrm{P}[\mathcal{C} \mid m_i] = \int_{I_i} p_r(\rho \mid m_i)\, d\rho. \tag{2.116}$$

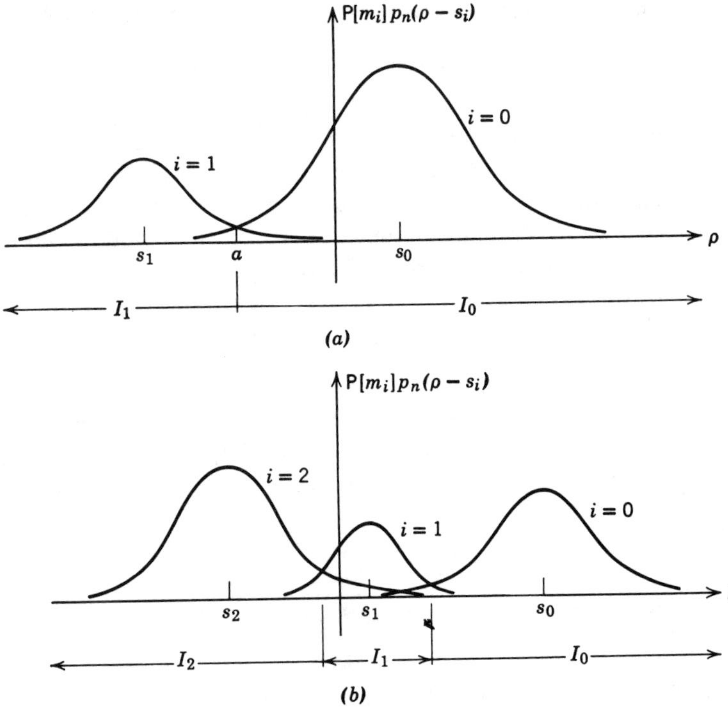

Figure 2.35 The behavior of the aposteriori message probabilities as a function of the received signal value, ρ. (a) $M = 2$, $\mathrm{P}[m_0] > \mathrm{P}[m_1]$; (b) $M = 3$, $\mathrm{P}[m_2] > \mathrm{P}[m_0] > \mathrm{P}[m_1]$.

Since the set of events $\{m_i\}$ are mutually exclusive, it follows from the theorem of total probability that the unconditioned probability of a correct decision is

$$\mathrm{P}[\mathcal{C}] = \sum_{i=0}^{M-1} \mathrm{P}[m_i]\,\mathrm{P}[\mathcal{C} \mid m_i] = \sum_{i=0}^{M-1} \mathrm{P}[m_i] \int_{I_i} p_r(\rho \mid m_i)\, d\rho, \qquad (2.117a)$$

and the unconditioned probability of the event error, denoted $\mathcal{E}$, is

$$\mathrm{P}[\mathcal{E}] = 1 - \mathrm{P}[\mathcal{C}]. \qquad (2.117b)$$

For the two-message case in Fig. 2.35

$$p_r(\rho \mid m_i) = p_n(\rho - s_i) = \frac{1}{\sqrt{2\pi}\sigma} e^{-(\rho - s_i)^2/2\sigma^2}$$

and

$$\mathrm{P}[\mathcal{C}] = \mathrm{P}[m_0] \int_a^{\infty} \frac{1}{\sqrt{2\pi}\sigma} e^{-(\rho - s_0)^2/2\sigma^2}\, d\rho + \mathrm{P}[m_1] \int_{-\infty}^{a} \frac{1}{\sqrt{2\pi}\sigma} e^{-(\rho - s_1)^2/2\sigma^2}\, d\rho.$$

The probability of error is therefore

$$P[\mathcal{E}] = P[m_0]\int_{-\infty}^{a} \frac{1}{\sqrt{2\pi}\sigma} e^{-(\rho-s_0)^2/2\sigma^2}\, d\rho + P[m_1]\int_{a}^{\infty} \frac{1}{\sqrt{2\pi}\sigma} e^{-(\rho-s_1)^2/2\sigma^2}\, d\rho. \qquad (2.118a)$$

Equation 2.118a can be expressed in terms of the function $Q(\ )$ of Eq. 2.50 by making the change of variable $\alpha = (\rho - s_0)/\sigma$ in the first integral and $\beta = (\rho - s_1)/\sigma$ in the second: then

$$P[\mathcal{E}] = P[m_0]\, Q\left(\frac{s_0 - a}{\sigma}\right) + P[m_1]\, Q\left(\frac{a - s_1}{\sigma}\right). \qquad (2.118b)$$

In the particular case of equally likely messages, $P[m_0] = P[m_1] = \frac{1}{2}$, $a = \frac{1}{2}(s_0 + s_1)$ and the error probability is just $Q[(s_0 - s_1)/2\sigma]$.

Input probabilities. Before a transmission occurs, the a priori probability $P[m_i]$ of each message m_i is known at the receiver. When a voltage $r = \rho$ is received, the a posteriori probability of each message m_i at the receiver is $P[m_i \mid r = \rho]$ and the optimum receiver decides in favor of that message for which the a posteriori probability is greatest. The channel permits "communication" by enabling the receiver to make decisions with a smaller probability of error after a transmission than before.

In the absence of a channel, the "optimum receiver" would always decide in favor of that message whose a priori probability was greatest, and the probability of error would be *maximum* if all possible inputs were *equally probable*. A similar statement holds true in general when a channel is available; accurate communication is most difficult to accomplish when the messages are equally likely.[27]

We prove this general statement only for the binary-input, Gaussian noise example. First, note that Eq. 2.115 gives the *optimum* threshold a for arbitrary a priori probabilities $P[m_0]$ and $P[m_1]$; any other choice of threshold, say b, would *increase* the probability of error. In particular, the choice

$$b = \frac{s_0 + s_1}{2} \qquad (2.119a)$$

increases the probability of error over that given by Eq. 2.118 unless, as is the case only when $P[m_0] = P[m_1]$, b is the optimum threshold. Thus the minimum probability of error $P[\mathcal{E}]$ of Eq. 2.118 is bounded by

$$P[\mathcal{E}] \leqslant P[m_0]\int_{-\infty}^{b} \frac{1}{\sqrt{2\pi}\sigma} e^{-(\rho-s_0)^2/2\sigma^2} + P[m_1]\int_{b}^{\infty} \frac{1}{\sqrt{2\pi}\sigma} e^{-(\rho-s_1)^2/2\sigma^2}. \qquad (2.119b)$$

Simplifying, we have

$$P[\mathcal{E}] \leqslant P[m_0]\, Q\left(\frac{s_0 - s_1}{2\sigma}\right) + P[m_1]\, Q\left(\frac{s_0 - s_1}{2\sigma}\right) = Q\left(\frac{s_0 - s_1}{2\sigma}\right). \quad (2.119c)$$

The equality holds only when $P[m_0] = P[m_1]$. Thus the probability of error for equally likely binary inputs provides a strict upper bound on the probability of error for nonequally likely binary inputs and the proof is complete.

Choice of signals. Since equally likely input messages are the most difficult to communicate, the case of uniform a priori probabilities is an interesting one to assume when investigating other aspects of a communication system. For example, let us next consider how the $P[\mathcal{E}]$ in Eq. 2.118 depends on the signal voltages s_0 and s_1 when $P[m_0] = P[m_1] = \frac{1}{2}$. Then the optimum threshold a equals $\frac{1}{2}(s_0 + s_1)$, and the probability of error is given by Eq. 2.119c with the equality.

It is clear from Eq. 2.119c that the probability of error can be forced arbitrarily close to zero by making the difference voltage $(s_0 - s_1)$ sufficiently large. A more interesting (and realistic) situation results when there is a constraint on the magnitude of the largest allowable signal, say

$$|s_i| \leqslant \sqrt{E_b}. \quad (2.120a)$$

Subject to this constraint, it is clear that $(s_0 - s_1)$ is maximized by choosing

$$s_0 = \sqrt{E_b}, \qquad s_1 = -\sqrt{E_b}, \quad (2.120b)$$

which yields

$$P[\mathcal{E}] = Q(\sqrt{E_b/\sigma^2}\,). \quad (2.120c)$$

The minimum attainable error probability then depends only on the ratio E_b/σ^2.

We have remarked that the function $Q(\;)$ is widely tabulated. For large ratios E_b/σ^2, a good approximation to the integral is obtained in the following way. Consider

$$Q(\alpha) \triangleq \int_\alpha^\infty \frac{1}{\sqrt{2\pi}} e^{-\beta^2/2}\, d\beta,$$

and integrate by parts. For $\alpha > 0$ we have

$$\begin{aligned}\sqrt{2\pi}\, Q(\alpha) &= \int_\alpha^\infty \frac{1}{\beta}(\beta e^{-\beta^2/2}\, d\beta)\\ &= \frac{1}{\beta}(-e^{-\beta^2/2})\Big|_\alpha^\infty - \int_\alpha^\infty \frac{1}{\beta^2} e^{-\beta^2/2}\, d\beta\\ &= \frac{1}{\alpha} e^{-\alpha^2/2} - \int_\alpha^\infty \frac{1}{\beta^2} e^{-\beta^2/2}\, d\beta; \qquad \alpha > 0.\end{aligned}$$

Since

$$0 < \int_{\alpha}^{\infty} \frac{1}{\beta^2} e^{-\beta^2/2} \, d\beta < \frac{1}{\alpha^3} \int_{\alpha}^{\infty} \beta e^{-\beta^2/2} \, d\beta = \frac{1}{\alpha^3} e^{-\alpha^2/2},$$

we have the bounds

$$\frac{1}{\sqrt{2\pi}\alpha} e^{-\alpha^2/2}\left(1 - \frac{1}{\alpha^2}\right) < Q(\alpha) < \frac{1}{\sqrt{2\pi}\alpha} e^{-\alpha^2/2}; \qquad \alpha > 0. \tag{2.121}$$

These two bounds are plotted together with $Q(\alpha)$ in Fig. 2.36.

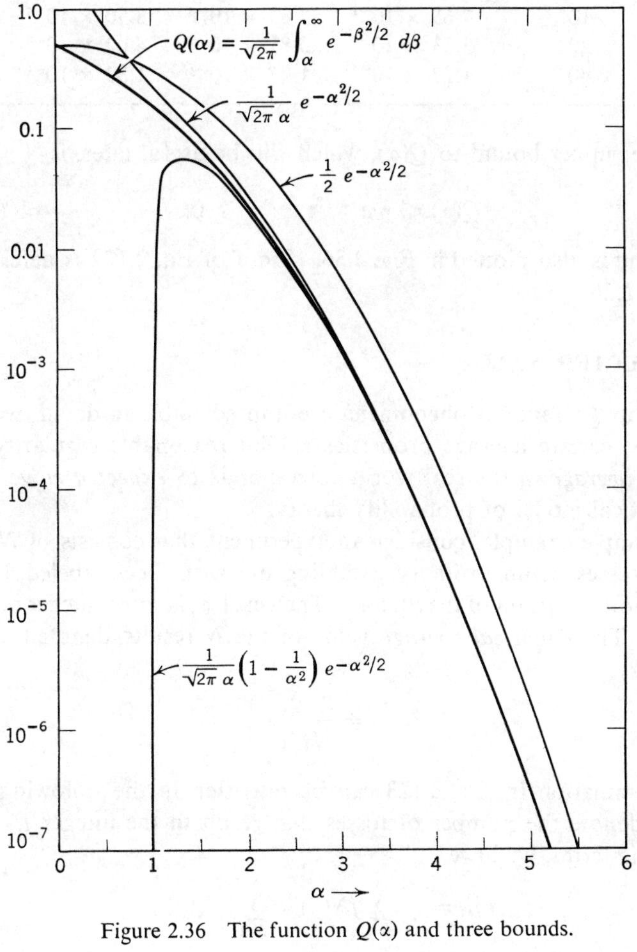

Figure 2.36 The function $Q(\alpha)$ and three bounds.

Substitution of Eq. 2.120c in these bounds yields

$$\frac{1}{\sqrt{2\pi}\sqrt{E_b/\sigma^2}}\, e^{-E_b/2\sigma^2}\left(1-\frac{\sigma^2}{E_b}\right) < \mathrm{P}[\mathcal{E}] < \frac{1}{\sqrt{2\pi}\sqrt{E_b/\sigma^2}}\, e^{-E_b/2\sigma^2}.$$

Thus the probability of error decreases approximately exponentially with increasing E_b/σ^2. Table 2.2 contains some typical values.

Table 2.2 *Binary Error Probability Bounds*

Signal-to-Noise Ratio, E_b/σ^2	Lower Bound	P[$\mathcal{E}$]	Upper Bound
4	2.02×10^{-2}	2.28×10^{-2}	2.70×10^{-2}
10	7.65×10^{-4}	7.83×10^{-4}	8.50×10^{-4}
20	3.83×10^{-6}	3.87×10^{-6}	4.02×10^{-6}
40	1.27×10^{-10}	1.27×10^{-10}	1.30×10^{-10}

Another upper bound to $Q(\alpha)$, which will be useful later, is

$$Q(\alpha) \leqslant \tfrac{1}{2}\, e^{-\alpha^2/2}; \qquad \alpha \geqslant 0. \tag{2.122}$$

This bound is also plotted in Fig. 2.36. Proof of Eq. 2.122 is deferred to Problem 2.26.

2.4 EXPECTED VALUE

Even though random phenomena are unpredictable in detail, we have noted that certain average properties exhibit reasonable regularity. An *empirical average* in the real world corresponds to *expected value* in the mathematical model of probability theory.

As a simple example, consider an experiment that consists of N independent tosses of an ordinary gambling die with faces labeled 1 to 6. Let x_i denote the result of the ith toss. Then each x_i is some integer between 1 and 6. The *empirical average* value of the N results, denoted $\langle x\rangle_{\mathsf{N}}$, is defined as

$$\langle x\rangle_{\mathsf{N}} \triangleq \frac{1}{N}\sum_{i=1}^{N} x_i. \tag{2.123}$$

The summation in Eq. 2.123 can be rewritten in the following way: let $N(j)$ denote the number of tosses that result in the integer j. Then, regrouping terms, we have

$$\langle x\rangle_{\mathsf{N}} = \frac{1}{N}\sum_{j=1}^{6} jN(j) = \sum_{j=1}^{6} j\, f_{\mathsf{N}}(j),$$

where $f_N(j) \triangleq N(j)/N$ is the relative frequency, defined in Eq. 2.1, of the result j.

Since the x_i are random, that is, unpredictable in detail, so also is their empirical average $\langle x \rangle_N$. But when N is large, $f_N(j)$ is almost always observed to stabilize close to some particular number. This number corresponds in the mathematical model to the probability $P[j]$. Thus, for large N, we expect $\langle x \rangle_N$ to stabilize at the number $E[x]$ given by

$$E[x] = \sum_{j=1}^{6} jP[j]. \tag{2.124}$$

We call $E[x]$ the *expected value* of the random variable x.

Equation 2.124 defines the expected value for the particular experiment of tossing a die. More generally, we define the expected value of a random variable x, with density function p_x, as

$$E[x] \triangleq \int_{-\infty}^{\infty} \alpha p_x(\alpha)\, d\alpha. \tag{2.125}$$

Note that Eq. 2.125 reduces to Eq. 2.124 for

$$p_x(\alpha) = \sum_{j=1}^{6} P[j]\, \delta(\alpha - j).$$

We shall see in connection with the weak law of large numbers that the general definition of $E[x]$ retains the property of being the number onto which we expect an empirical average $\langle x \rangle_N$ to *converge*. The expected value of a random variable x is also called its *mean value*, or *expectation*, and is alternatively denoted $\bar{x}$.

The Fundamental Theorem of Expectation

In many cases we need to calculate the expected value of a random variable x that is defined by means of a transformation on a random vector $\mathbf{y}$:

$$x = g(\mathbf{y}), \tag{2.126a}$$

where $g(\ )$ maps every k-dimensional vector into a real number. Although $E[x]$ can be calculated from Eq. 2.125 by first calculating p_x from the joint density $p_{\mathbf{y}}$ and the transformation $x = g(\mathbf{y})$, it is often less laborious to invoke the *theorem of expectation*, which states that

$$\begin{aligned} E[x] &\triangleq \int_{-\infty}^{\infty} \alpha p_x(\alpha)\, d\alpha \\ &= \int_{-\infty}^{\infty}\int_{-\infty}^{\infty} \cdots \int_{-\infty}^{\infty} g(\boldsymbol{\beta})\, p_{\mathbf{y}}(\boldsymbol{\beta})\, d\beta_1\, d\beta_2 \cdots d\beta_k \\ &= \int_{-\infty}^{\infty} g(\boldsymbol{\beta})\, p_{\mathbf{y}}(\boldsymbol{\beta})\, d\boldsymbol{\beta}. \end{aligned} \tag{2.126b}$$

Equation 2.126b can be written still more concisely as

$$\bar{x} = \mathrm{E}[g(\mathbf{y})] = \overline{g(\mathbf{y})}. \tag{2.126c}$$

An intuitive feeling for the validity of Eq. 2.126 can be gained from an outline of its proof. Let us partition the real line (on which x is defined) into a large number of small contiguous disjoint intervals of length Δ, as shown in Fig. 2.37. Let I_i denote the ith interval $[a_i - \Delta/2, a_i + \Delta/2]$. Then

$$\mathrm{P}[x \text{ in } I_i] = \int_{a_i-\Delta/2}^{a_i+\Delta/2} p_x(\alpha)\, d\alpha.$$

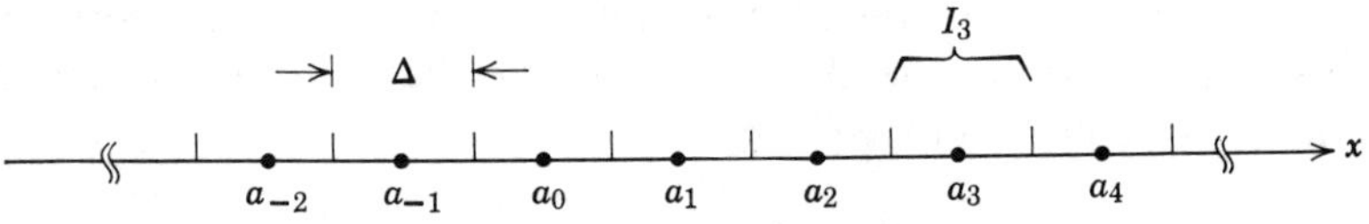

Figure 2.37 Partitioning the real line into contiguous disjoint intervals.

We know that the probability of the event $\{x \text{ in } I_i\}$ can also be written in terms of $p_{\mathbf{y}}$:

$$\mathrm{P}[x \text{ in } I_i] = \int_{B_i} p_{\mathbf{y}}(\boldsymbol{\beta})\, d\boldsymbol{\beta},$$

where

$$B_i = \{\boldsymbol{\beta} : a_i - \Delta/2 < g(\boldsymbol{\beta}) \leqslant a_i + \Delta/2\}.$$

Since by definition the event $\{\boldsymbol{\beta} \text{ in } B_i\}$ implies that $g(\boldsymbol{\beta}) \approx a_i$, we have

$$\int_{a_i-\Delta/2}^{a_i+\Delta/2} \alpha p_x(\alpha)\, d\alpha \approx a_i \int_{a_i-\Delta/2}^{a_i+\Delta/2} p_x(\alpha)\, d\alpha = a_i \,\mathrm{P}[x \text{ in } I_i]$$
$$= a_i \int_{B_i} p_{\mathbf{y}}(\boldsymbol{\beta})\, d\boldsymbol{\beta} \approx \int_{B_i} g(\boldsymbol{\beta})\, p_{\mathbf{y}}(\boldsymbol{\beta})\, d\boldsymbol{\beta},$$

in which the approximations are tight for small Δ. Summing over all i yields

$$\bar{x} \triangleq \int_{-\infty}^{\infty} \alpha\, p_x(\alpha)\, d\alpha = \sum_{i=-\infty}^{\infty} \int_{a_i-\Delta/2}^{a_i+\Delta/2} \alpha\, p_x(\alpha)\, d\alpha$$
$$\approx \sum_{i=-\infty}^{\infty} \int_{B_i} g(\boldsymbol{\beta})\, p_{\mathbf{y}}(\boldsymbol{\beta})\, d\boldsymbol{\beta}$$
$$= \int_{-\infty}^{\infty} g(\boldsymbol{\beta})\, p_{\mathbf{y}}(\boldsymbol{\beta})\, d\boldsymbol{\beta}.$$

Here the last step follows from the fact that the $\{B_i\}$ are disjoint and their union includes all $\boldsymbol{\beta}$ (the function $g(\ \ )$ maps every $\boldsymbol{\beta}$ into some real number). The theorem follows from considering the limit as $\Delta \to 0$.

As an example of the application of the theorem of Eq. 2.126, consider the simple one-dimensional transformation $x = y^2$. From Eqs. 2.125 and 2.75,

$$\begin{aligned} \mathrm{E}[x] &= \int_0^\infty \frac{\alpha}{2\sqrt{\alpha}} \, [p_y(+\sqrt{\alpha}) + p_y(-\sqrt{\alpha})] \, d\alpha \\ &= \int_0^\infty \frac{1}{2} \sqrt{\alpha} \, p_y(+\sqrt{\alpha}) \, d\alpha + \int_0^\infty \frac{1}{2} \sqrt{\alpha} \, p_y(-\sqrt{\alpha}) \, d\alpha. \end{aligned}$$

Let $\beta = +\sqrt{\alpha}$ in the first integral and $\beta = -\sqrt{\alpha}$ in the second. Then

$$\begin{aligned} \mathrm{E}[x] &= \int_0^\infty \beta^2 \, p_y(\beta) \, d\beta - \int_0^{-\infty} \beta^2 \, p_y(\beta) \, d\beta \\ &= \int_{-\infty}^\infty \beta^2 \, p_y(\beta) \, d\beta, \end{aligned}$$

which is in accord with Eq. 2.126b.

We conclude that the expected value of a random variable x is a specific number determined by the mapping $x(\ )$ from Ω into the real line and by the probability assignment to events on Ω. Equation 2.126 states that the value of this number does not depend on whether p_x is described explicitly, or implicitly in terms of $p_{\mathbf{y}}$ and the transformation $g(\mathbf{y})$.

Linearity. One of the most important properties of expectation is linearity. Let x and y be two random variables and consider the linear transformation

$$z = ax + by.$$

The expected value of the new random variable z follows from Eq. 2.126.

$$\begin{aligned} \mathrm{E}[z] &= \int_{-\infty}^\infty \int_{-\infty}^\infty (a\alpha + b\beta) p_{x,y}(\alpha, \beta) \, d\alpha \, d\beta \\ &= \int_{-\infty}^\infty \int_{-\infty}^\infty a\alpha \, p_{x,y}(\alpha, \beta) \, d\beta \, d\alpha \\ &\qquad + \int_{-\infty}^\infty \int_{-\infty}^\infty b\beta \, p_{x,y}(\alpha, \beta) \, d\alpha \, d\beta. \end{aligned}$$

Integrating out the variable β in the first integral and α in the second, we obtain

$$\begin{aligned} \mathrm{E}[z] &= \int_{-\infty}^\infty a\alpha \, p_x(\alpha) \, d\alpha + \int_{-\infty}^\infty b\beta \, p_y(\beta) \, d\beta \\ &= a\mathrm{E}[x] + b\mathrm{E}[y], \end{aligned}$$

or

$$\bar{z} = a\bar{x} + b\bar{y}.$$

Thus E[ ] can be viewed as a linear operator; that is to say, the expected value of a weighted sum is the weighted sum of the expected values:

$$\mathrm{E}\left[\sum_i a_i x_i\right] = \sum_i a_i \mathrm{E}[x_i]. \tag{2.127}$$

This is true whether or not the $\{x_i\}$ are statistically independent.

Expected value of a product. In general, the expected value of a nonlinear transformation such as $z = xy$ is not the transformation of the expected values; for example, we have

$$\mathrm{E}[z] = \mathrm{E}[xy] = \int_{-\infty}^{\infty}\int_{-\infty}^{\infty} \alpha\beta \, p_{x,y}(\alpha, \beta) \, d\alpha \, d\beta$$

which usually cannot be simplified. If, however, x and y are statistically independent, $p_{x,y}$ factors and

$$\mathrm{E}[xy] = \int_{-\infty}^{\infty}\int_{-\infty}^{\infty} \alpha\beta \, p_x(\alpha) \, p_y(\beta) \, d\alpha \, d\beta.$$

The integrations on α and β may be performed separately to yield

$$\mathrm{E}[xy] = \int_{-\infty}^{\infty} \alpha \, p_x(\alpha) \, d\alpha \int_{-\infty}^{\infty} \beta \, p_y(\beta) \, d\beta = \mathrm{E}[x] \, \mathrm{E}[y],$$

or

$$\overline{xy} = \bar{x}\,\bar{y}; \qquad x \text{ and } y \text{ statistically independent.} \tag{2.128}$$

Thus the statistical independence of random variables guarantees that the mean of the product is the product of the means. It should be emphasized that the converse statement is not necessarily true; $\overline{xy} = \bar{x}\,\bar{y}$ does not usually imply statistical independence of the random variables x and y.

Moments

Of particular importance in the sequel are the expected values of the powers of a random variable. Whenever the value of the integral is finite, we call

$$\mathrm{E}[x^n] \triangleq \int_{-\infty}^{\infty} \alpha^n \, p_x(\alpha) \, d\alpha \tag{2.129a}$$

the nth *moment* of x and

$$\mathrm{E}[(x - \bar{x})^n] \triangleq \int_{-\infty}^{\infty} (\alpha - \bar{x})^n \, p_x(\alpha) \, d\alpha \tag{2.129b}$$

the nth *central moment*. In the trivial case $n = 0$ we have

$$\mathrm{E}[x^0] = \mathrm{E}[1] = 1.$$

The second central moment of x is given the special name *variance* and denoted σ_x^2. From Eq. 2.127

$$\sigma_x^2 \triangleq \mathrm{E}[(x-\bar{x})^2] = \mathrm{E}[x^2] - 2\bar{x}\,\mathrm{E}[x] + \bar{x}^2$$
$$= \overline{x^2} - \bar{x}^2. \tag{2.129c}$$

The square root of the variance, σ_x, is called the *standard deviation.*

If we think of a one-dimensional probability distribution p_x as analogous to a mass distribution along a rod, the moments $\mathrm{E}[x^n]$ also have direct physical analogs. The mean $\bar{x}$ corresponds to the center of gravity; $\overline{x^2}$, to

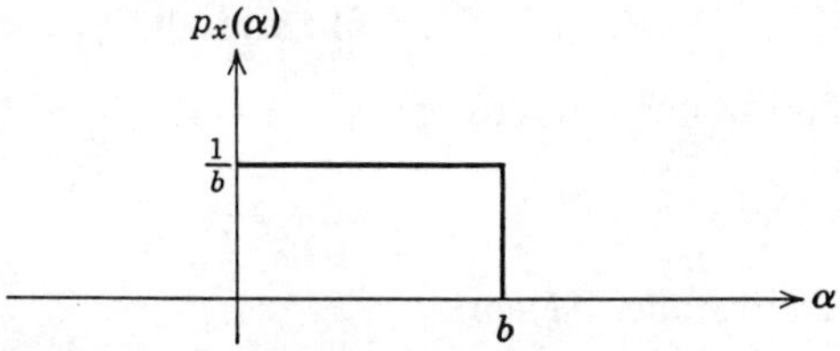

Figure 2.38 The density function of a uniformly distributed random variable.

the moment of inertia around the origin; and σ_x^2, to the central moment of inertia.

As an example, consider the moments of a random variable x that has the uniform density function illustrated in Fig. 2.38. We have

$$\bar{x} = \int_0^b \frac{\alpha}{b}\,d\alpha = \frac{b}{2} \tag{2.130a}$$

$$\overline{x^2} = \int_0^b \frac{\alpha^2}{b}\,d\alpha = \frac{b^2}{3} \tag{2.130b}$$

$$\sigma_x^2 = \overline{x^2} - \bar{x}^2 = \frac{b^2}{12}. \tag{2.130c}$$

To give another example, consider a variable x with the Cauchy density function in Fig. 2.21. Since the integrand is odd, we have

$$\bar{x} = \int_{-\infty}^{\infty} \frac{b\alpha/\pi}{b^2+\alpha^2}\,d\alpha = 0,$$

in which we use the [Cauchy principal value] definition

$$\int_{-\infty}^{\infty} f(x)\,dx \triangleq \lim_{A\to\infty} \int_{-A}^{A} f(x)\,dx. \tag{2.131}$$

The second moment does not exist, however, since the integral

$$\overline{x^2} = \int_{-\infty}^{\infty} \frac{b\alpha^2/\pi}{b^2 + \alpha^2}\, d\alpha$$

is not finite.

It was shown in Eq. 2.127 that the mean of a sum of random variables $\{x_i\}$ is the sum of the means, regardless of whether the variables are or are not statistically independent. Given that the $\{x_i\}$ are *pairwise statistically independent*—but not, in general, otherwise—the same statement holds true also for the variance of a sum; by "pairwise statistically independent" random variables we mean

$$p_{x_i,x_j} = p_{x_i}p_{x_j}; \quad \text{for all } i \text{ and all } j \neq i. \tag{2.132}$$

A general proof is obtained by letting

$$y = \sum_{i=1}^{N} a_i x_i, \tag{2.133a}$$

where the a_i are constants. Then

$$\sigma_y^{\,2} = \mathrm{E}[(y - \bar{y})^2] = \mathrm{E}\left[\left(\sum_i a_i x_i - \sum_i a_i \bar{x}_i\right)^2\right] = \mathrm{E}\left[\left(\sum_i a_i(x_i - \bar{x}_i)\right)^2\right]$$

$$= \mathrm{E}\left[\sum_i a_i^2(x_i - \bar{x}_i)^2 + \sum_i \sum_{j\neq i} a_i a_j (x_i - \bar{x}_i)(x_j - \bar{x}_j)\right].$$

But Eq. 2.132 states that each term in the double summation above involves two statistically independent random variables, the mean of the product of which is the product of the means (Eq. 2.128). Thus the expected value of the double summation is zero and

$$\sigma_y^{\,2} = \mathrm{E}\left[\sum_i a_i^2(x_i - \bar{x}_i)^2\right] = \sum_i a_i^{\,2}\sigma_{x_i}^{\,2}. \tag{2.133b}$$

In particular,

$$\sigma_y^{\,2} = a^2\sigma_x^{\,2}; \qquad \text{for } y = ax. \tag{2.134}$$

Characteristic functions. In Eq. 2.96 we defined the characteristic function of a random variable x as the Fourier transform of the density function p_x:

$$M_x(\nu) = \int_{-\infty}^{\infty} p_x(\alpha)e^{j\nu\alpha}\, d\alpha. \tag{2.135}$$

Alternatively, we can view $M_x(\nu)$ in the light of Eq. 2.126 as the expected value of the random variable $e^{j\nu x}$. Thus

$$M_x(\nu) = \mathrm{E}[e^{j\nu x}] = \overline{e^{j\nu x}}. \tag{2.136}$$

This interpretation requires that we extend our definition of "random variable" to include mappings from Ω into the complex plane, whereas heretofore we have considered only mappings into the real line. A *complex random variable*, w, is defined as a pair of mappings such as

$$w(\omega) = x(\omega) + jy(\omega). \tag{2.137a}$$

Similarly, the expected value of w is defined in terms of the expected values of the real random variables x and y as

$$\bar{w} = \bar{x} + j\bar{y}. \tag{2.137b}$$

The probability of any event defined in terms of w can be calculated from knowledge of the joint density function $p_{x,y}$.

Characteristic functions play a role in probability theory that is equivalent to that played by Fourier transforms in signal analysis. Particularly, many theorems are proved in the transform domain. For example, consider again the problem of finding the density function of the sum of two statistically independent random variables, say $z = x + y$. From Eqs. 2.136 and 2.128 we have directly

$$M_z(\nu) = \overline{e^{j\nu(x+y)}} = \overline{e^{j\nu x}e^{j\nu y}} = \overline{e^{j\nu x}}\ \overline{e^{j\nu y}} = M_x(\nu)\, M_y(\nu),$$

and therefore

$$p_z = p_x * p_y,$$

which is in accord with Eqs. 2.95 and 2.98.

An important attribute of characteristic functions is their relation to moments. Taking the nth derivative with respect to ν of both sides of Eq. 2.135 yields

$$\frac{d^n}{d\nu^n} M_x(\nu) = \int_{-\infty}^{\infty} (j\alpha)^n e^{j\nu\alpha}\, p_x(\alpha)\, d\alpha. \tag{2.138}$$

Evaluating Eq. 2.138 at $\nu = 0$ and denoting the nth derivative by a superscript (n), we have

$$M_x^{(n)}(0) = \int_{-\infty}^{\infty} (j\alpha)^n\, p_x(\alpha)\, d\alpha = (j^n)\mathrm{E}[x^n]. \tag{2.139}$$

Thus,

$$M_x(0) = 1$$

$$-jM_x^{(1)}(0) = \bar{x}$$

$$-M_x^{(2)}(0) = \overline{x^2}$$

$$(-j)^n\, M_x^{(n)}(0) = \overline{x^n}.$$

Characteristic function of Gaussian variable. If x is a Gaussian random variable, its moments are easily obtained from its characteristic function.

First let

$$p_x(\alpha) = \frac{1}{\sqrt{2\pi}} e^{-\alpha^2/2}. \tag{2.140a}$$

Then

$$M_x(\nu) = \int_{-\infty}^{\infty} e^{j\nu\alpha} \left[\frac{1}{\sqrt{2\pi}} e^{-\alpha^2/2} \right] d\alpha = \frac{e^{-\nu^2/2}}{\sqrt{2\pi}} \int_{-\infty}^{\infty} \exp\left[-\frac{1}{2}(\alpha - j\nu)^2 \right] d\alpha.$$

Making the change of variable $s = \alpha - j\nu$ and integrating in the complex plane, we have

$$M_x(\nu) = \frac{e^{-\nu^2/2}}{\sqrt{2\pi}} \int_{-\infty-j\nu}^{\infty-j\nu} \exp\left(-\frac{1}{2} s^2 \right) ds,$$

where the integration is along a line parallel to the real axis. Consider the rectangular contour in Fig. 2.39. Since the function $e^{-s^2/2}$ has no poles, the integral around the entire contour is zero. Also, as l goes to infinity,

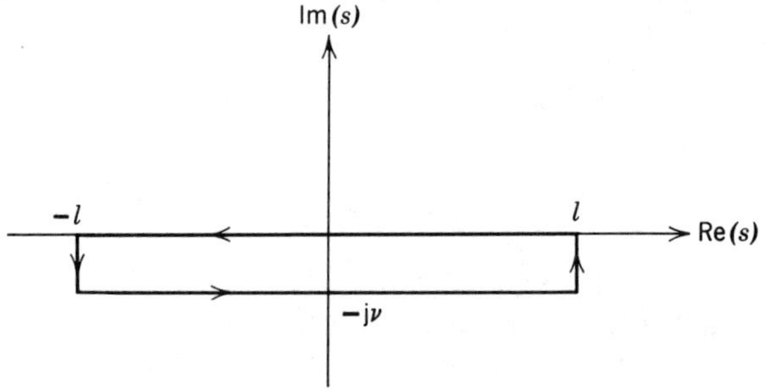

Figure 2.39 The contour of integration for evaluating the Gaussian characteristic function.

the integrand evaluated at $\text{Re}(s) = \pm l$ goes to zero exponentially as $e^{-l^2/2}$. It follows that the contribution to the contour integral from the vertical sides of the rectangle is zero. Thus

$$\int_{-\infty-j\nu}^{\infty-j\nu} e^{-s^2/2}\, ds = \int_{-\infty}^{\infty} e^{-s^2/2}\, ds = \sqrt{2\pi}$$

and

$$M_x(\nu) = e^{-\nu^2/2}. \tag{2.140b}$$

Next consider the random variable y obtained from the Gaussian random variable x by the transformation $y = a + bx$. From Eq. 2.77,

$$p_y(\alpha) = \frac{1}{|b|}\, p_x\!\left(\frac{\alpha - a}{b}\right) = \frac{1}{\sqrt{2\pi b^2}}\, e^{-(\alpha-a)^2/2b^2}.$$

The characteristic function of y follows from Eq. 2.140b:

$$M_y(\nu) = \overline{e^{j\nu(a+bx)}} = e^{j\nu a}\, \overline{e^{j(\nu b)x}} = e^{j\nu a} M_x(b\nu)$$
$$= e^{j\nu a} \exp\left(-\tfrac{1}{2}\nu^2 b^2\right).$$

The moments of y are then given by Eq. 2.139. Specifically, we identify the mean and variance:

$$\bar{y} = -j(ja - \nu b^2) \exp(j\nu a - \tfrac{1}{2}\nu^2 b^2)|_{\nu=0} = a,$$
$$\overline{y^2} = -[-b^2 + (ja - \nu b^2)^2] \exp(j\nu a - \tfrac{1}{2}\nu^2 b^2)|_{\nu=0} = a^2 + b^2,$$
$$\sigma_y^{\,2} = \overline{y^2} - \bar{y}^2 = b^2.$$

In order to place these results in evidence, the density function of y is often written in the standard form

$$p_y(\alpha) = \frac{1}{\sqrt{2\pi}\sigma_y} e^{-(\alpha-\bar{y})^2/2\sigma_y^{\,2}}. \tag{2.141}$$

The function of Eq. 2.141 is called *the general one-dimensional Gaussian density function.*

Now consider the sum

$$z = \sum_{i=1}^{N} y_i,$$

where the y_i are statistically independent Gaussian random variables with

$$E[y_i] = \bar{y}_i,$$
$$E[(y_i - \bar{y}_i)^2] = \sigma_i^2,$$

hence

$$M_{y_i}(\nu) = \exp(-\tfrac{1}{2}\nu^2\sigma_i^{\,2} + j\nu\bar{y}_i).$$

By Eq. 2.98

$$M_z(\nu) = \prod_{i=1}^{N} M_{y_i}(\nu)$$
$$= \exp(-\tfrac{1}{2}\nu^2\sigma^2 + j\nu m), \tag{2.142a}$$

in which

$$\sigma^2 = \sum_{i=1}^{N} \sigma_i^2, \tag{2.142b}$$

$$m = \sum_{i=1}^{N} \bar{y}_i. \tag{2.142c}$$

Noting that $M_z(\nu)$ is the characteristic function of a Gaussian random variable with mean m and variance σ^2, we conclude that the sum of statistically independent Gaussian random variables is also Gaussian.

We may determine the higher moments of a Gaussian random variable by means of a power series expansion of its characteristic function. Consider the random variable y with characteristic function

$$M_y(\nu) = \exp\left(-\tfrac{1}{2}\nu^2\sigma_y^{\,2}\right).$$

With the help of the expansion

$$e^{\alpha} = 1 + \alpha + \frac{1}{2!}\alpha^2 + \cdots + \frac{1}{n!}\alpha^n + \cdots, \tag{2.143}$$

we can write

$$M_y(\nu) = 1 - \tfrac{1}{2}\nu^2\sigma_y^{\,2} + \tfrac{1}{8}\nu^4\sigma_y^{\,4} + \cdots + \frac{(-1)^l}{2^l l!}\nu^{2l}\sigma_y^{\,2l} + \cdots. \tag{2.144a}$$

Moreover,

$$e^{j\nu y} = 1 + j\nu y + \frac{(j\nu)^2 y^2}{2!} + \cdots + \frac{(j\nu)^l y^l}{l!} + \cdots$$

so that,† whenever all moments of y are finite,

$$M_y(\nu) = \overline{e^{j\nu y}} = 1 + j\bar{y}\nu + \frac{(j^2)\overline{y^2}}{2!}\nu^2 + \cdots + \frac{(j^n)\overline{y^n}}{n!}\nu^n + \cdots. \tag{2.144b}$$

Equating coefficients of like powers of ν in Eqs. 2.144a and b, we have (for a zero-mean Gaussian random variable)

$$\overline{y^n} = \begin{cases} 0; & n \text{ odd} \\ \dfrac{n!}{2^{n/2}(n/2)!}\sigma_y^{\,n}; & n \text{ even}, \end{cases} \tag{2.145a}$$

or, more simply,

$$\overline{y^n} = \begin{cases} 0; & n \text{ odd} \\ (n-1)(n-3)(n-5)\cdots(1)\sigma_y^{\,n}; & n \text{ even}. \end{cases} \tag{2.145b}$$

In particular,

$$\overline{y^4} = 3\sigma_y^{\,4}$$

$$\overline{y^6} = 15\sigma_y^{\,6}.$$

2.5 LIMIT THEOREMS

We shall now study several of the limit theorems that form the core of probability theory.

The variance σ_x^2 of a random variable x in some sense is a measure of the variable's "randomness." For instance, Eq. 2.130c states that the

† To obtain Eq. 2.144b rigorously would require proof that the linearity property of the expectation operator E[ ] extends to infinite sums.

variance of a uniformly distributed random variable is $b^2/12$, where b is the width of the density function. Specifying the variance essentially constrains the effective width of the density function. Figure 2.40 illustrates this effect for the Gaussian density function.

A precise statement of the constraint is due to Chebyshev. Let y be a

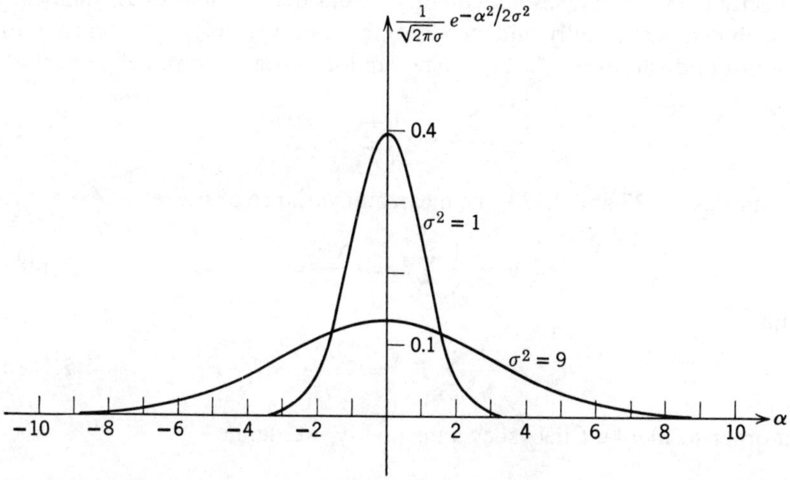

Figure 2.40 The Gaussian probability density function for two values of variance.

zero-mean random variable with finite variance σ_y^2. *Chebyshev's inequality* states that for any positive number ϵ

$$P[|y| \geqslant \epsilon] \leqslant \frac{\sigma_y^2}{\epsilon^2}; \qquad \bar{y} = 0. \tag{2.146}$$

Equation 2.146 can be proved as follows. By definition,

$$\overline{y^2} = \int_{-\infty}^{\infty} \alpha^2\, p_y(\alpha)\, d\alpha.$$

Since the integrand is positive,

$$\overline{y^2} \geqslant \int_{|\alpha| \geqslant \epsilon} \alpha^2\, p_y(\alpha)\, d\alpha.$$

This bound can be weakened further by replacing α^2 with its smallest value, ϵ^2, which yields

$$\overline{y^2} \geqslant \epsilon^2 \int_{|\alpha| \geqslant \epsilon} p_y(\alpha)\, d\alpha$$
$$= \epsilon^2\, P[|y| \geqslant \epsilon].$$

Chebyshev's inequality follows from dividing by ϵ^2 and recalling that $\overline{y^2} = \sigma_y^2$ for a zero-mean variable.

The Weak Law of Large Numbers

The simplest of the limit theorems that we shall consider follows directly from Chebyshev's inequality. Consider the sum of N identically distributed statistically independent random variables $\{x_i\}$, each with mean $\bar{x}$ and variance σ_x^2. Let a new random variable m be defined as

$$m = \frac{1}{N}\sum_{i=1}^{N} x_i. \tag{2.147}$$

From Eqs. 2.127 and 2.133, the mean and variance of m are

$$\bar{m} = \frac{1}{N}\sum_{i=1}^{N} \bar{x}_i = \frac{N\bar{x}}{N} = \bar{x} \tag{2.148a}$$

and

$$\sigma_m^2 = \frac{1}{N^2}\sum_{i=1}^{N} \sigma_{x_i}^2 = \frac{N\sigma_x^2}{N^2} = \frac{\sigma_x^2}{N}. \tag{2.148b}$$

In order to invoke Chebyshev's inequality, we define

$$y \triangleq m - \bar{x},$$

so that

$$\bar{y} = \bar{m} - \bar{x} = 0$$

and

$$\sigma_y^2 = \overline{(m - \bar{x})^2} = \sigma_m^2 = \frac{\sigma_x^2}{N}.$$

Therefore

$$\mathrm{P}[|y| \geqslant \epsilon] \leqslant \frac{\sigma_y^2}{\epsilon^2}$$

becomes the desired result

$$\mathrm{P}[|m - \bar{x}| \geqslant \epsilon] \leqslant \frac{\sigma_x^2}{N\epsilon^2}. \tag{2.149}$$

Equation 2.149 is a statement of the *weak law of large numbers.*

The random variable m is called the *sample mean.* Equation 2.149 states that the probability that the sample mean will differ from the true mean by more than ϵ approaches zero as N becomes large.

The weak law of large numbers provides the mathematical justification for our earlier interpretation of $\mathrm{E}[x]$, or $\bar{x}$, as the number at which the empirical average $\langle x \rangle_N$ of the results of N independent experimental trials tends to stabilize as N becomes large. We need only identify the independent random variable x_i with the result of the ith experimental trial, $i = 1, \ldots, N$, and the sample mean m with the empirical average $\langle x \rangle_N$. When N is large, the weak law statement that with high probability m is close to the number $\bar{x}$ is interpreted in the real world as the statement that—barring an atypical sequence of observations—the value of $\langle x \rangle_N$ will be close to the number $\bar{x}$. The possibility of observing an atypical sequence of trials (one corresponding in the mathematical model to $| m - \bar{x} | \geqslant \epsilon$) is not ruled out; but, if $\sigma_x^2/N\epsilon^2$ is small, such sequences occur rarely.

An interesting special case of Eq. 2.149 is encountered when each random variable x_i is defined in terms of an event A_i of probability p by

$$x_i(\omega) = \begin{cases} 1; & \text{for } \{\omega : \omega \text{ in } A_i\} \\ 0; & \text{for } \{\omega : \omega \text{ in } A_i^{C}\}. \end{cases} \tag{2.150a}$$

Then

$$P[x_i = 1] = P[A_i] \triangleq p, \qquad P[x_i = 0] = P[A_i^{C}] = 1 - p, \tag{2.150b}$$

and, for $i = 1, 2, \ldots, N$, we have

$$\overline{x_i} = p \triangleq \bar{x},$$
$$\overline{x_i^2} = p,$$
$$\sigma_x^2 = \overline{x_i^2} - \overline{x_i}^2 = p(1 - p).$$

Substituting these values in Eq. 2.149 gives

$$P[|m - p| \geqslant \epsilon] \leqslant \frac{p(1 - p)}{N\epsilon^2}. \tag{2.151}$$

Let us now identify the event A_i with the result that A is observed on the ith trial of a simple experiment. The random variable m then corresponds to the relative frequency $f_N(A)$ in a sequence of N independent trials, and Eq. 2.151 may be interpreted to mean that P[A] is the number on which we expect $f_N(A)$ to converge when N is large. Equation 2.151 is the result referred to (Eq. 2.19a) in the discussion of the relation of the mathematical model to the real world.

Chernoff Bound

Greater insight into the weak law can be gained from a different, more graphical derivation. Let $\{y_i\}$, $i = 1, 2, \ldots, N$, be a set of statistically independent zero-mean random variables, each of which has the same

Sections marked by this symbol may be omitted on a first reading.

density function, say p_y, hence the same variance, say σ_y^2, which we assume to be finite. The weak law then states

$$P\left[\left|\frac{1}{N}\sum_{i=1}^{N} y_i\right| \geqslant \epsilon\right] \leqslant \frac{\sigma_y^2}{N\epsilon^2}. \tag{2.152}$$

We begin the new derivation of Eq. 2.152 by defining a random variable

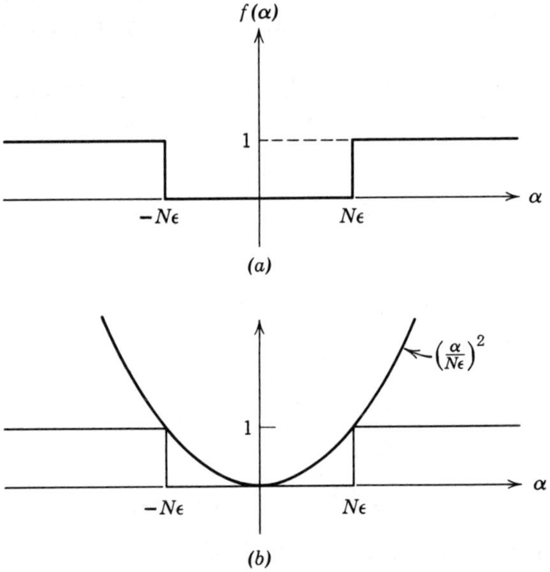

Figure 2.41 Geometric constructions for alternate proof of the weak law of large numbers.

z through the transformation

$$z \triangleq f\left(\sum_{i=1}^{N} y_i\right), \tag{2.153a}$$

where $f(\ )$ is the binary-valued function shown in Fig. 2.41a:

$$f(\alpha) = \begin{cases} 0; & \text{for } |\alpha| < N\epsilon \\ 1; & \text{for } |\alpha| \geqslant N\epsilon. \end{cases} \tag{2.153b}$$

In terms of z we have

$$P\left[\left|\frac{1}{N}\sum_{i=1}^{N} y_i\right| \geqslant \epsilon\right] = P[z = 1].$$

Since z can take on only the two values 0 and 1, we also have

$$\bar{z} = 0 \cdot P[z = 0] + 1 \cdot P[z = 1] = P\left[\left|\frac{1}{N}\sum_{i=1}^{N} y_i\right| \geqslant \epsilon\right]. \tag{2.154a}$$

The expected value of z equals the desired probability. By the theorem on expectation,

$$\bar{z} = \mathrm{E}\left[f\left(\sum_{i=1}^{N} y_i\right)\right]. \tag{2.154b}$$

In general, there is no simple way to evaluate the right-hand side of Eq. 2.154b for arbitrary p_y. The weak law *bound*, however, can be obtained by noting in Fig. 2.41*b* that

$$f(\alpha) \leqslant \left(\frac{\alpha}{N\epsilon}\right)^2; \qquad \text{for all } \alpha. \tag{2.155}$$

Thus

$$\bar{z} = \mathrm{E}\left[f\left(\sum_{i=1}^{N} y_i\right)\right] \leqslant \left(\frac{1}{N\epsilon}\right)^2 \mathrm{E}\left[\left(\sum_{i=1}^{N} y_i\right)^2\right]. \tag{2.156}$$

Since the y_i are statistically independent and each has zero mean and variance σ_y^2, by Eq. 2.133

$$\mathrm{E}\left[\left(\sum_{i=1}^{N} y_i\right)^2\right] = \sum_{i=1}^{N} \sigma_{y_i}^2 = N\sigma_y^2. \tag{2.157}$$

Substituting Eqs. 2.157 and 2.156 in Eq. 2.154a yields Eq. 2.152.

It is obvious from this derivation of Eq. 2.152 that other bounds than the weak law can be obtained by using functions other than $(\alpha/N\epsilon)^2$ to bound $f(\alpha)$ in Eq. 2.155. Indeed, for any function $g(\alpha)$ such that

$$f(\alpha) \leqslant g(\alpha); \qquad \text{all } \alpha,$$

we have

$$\mathrm{P}\left[\left|\frac{1}{N}\sum_{i=1}^{N} y_i\right| \geqslant \epsilon\right] \leqslant \mathrm{E}\left[g\left(\sum_{i=1}^{N} y_i\right)\right]$$

Similarly, if we are interested only in a bound on the positive tail of the random variable $(1/N)\sum_{i=1}^{N} y_i$, we may bound the one-sided step function shown in Fig. 2.42*a* by any function $h(\alpha)$ and obtain

$$\bar{z} = \mathrm{P}\left[\frac{1}{N}\sum_{i=1}^{N} y_i \geqslant \epsilon\right] \leqslant \mathrm{E}\left[h\left(\sum_{i=1}^{N} y_i\right)\right].$$

An especially powerful bound is obtained in this one-sided case if, as shown in Fig. 2.42*b*, we take

$$h(\alpha) = e^{\lambda(\alpha - N\epsilon)}; \qquad \lambda \geqslant 0,\ \epsilon \geqslant 0. \tag{2.158}$$

We then have

$$\bar{z} \leqslant \mathrm{E}\left[h\left(\sum_{i=1}^{N} y_i\right)\right] = \mathrm{E}\left[\exp\left(\lambda\sum_{i=1}^{N} y_i - \lambda N\epsilon\right)\right] = e^{-\lambda N\epsilon}\,\mathrm{E}\left[\prod_{i=1}^{N} e^{\lambda y_i}\right]. \tag{2.159a}$$

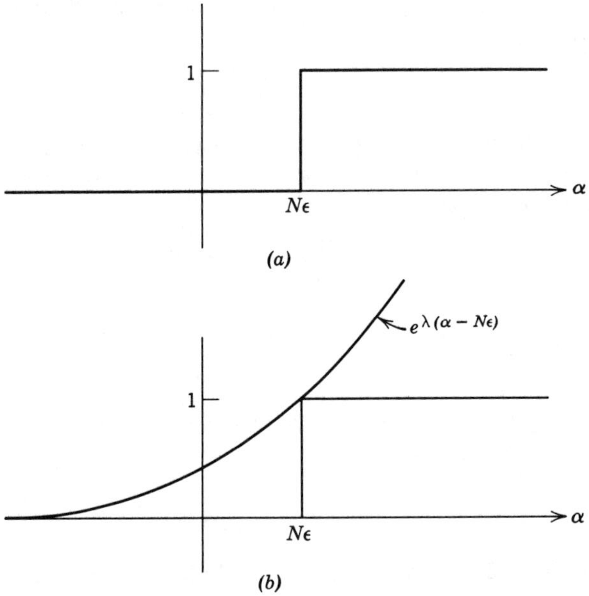

Figure 2.42 Geometric construction for proof of the Chernoff bound.

Since the random variables $\{y_i\}$ are statistically independent, so are the random variables $\{e^{\lambda y_i}\}$. Thus

$$\mathrm{E}\left[\prod_{i=1}^{N} e^{\lambda y_i}\right] = \prod_{i=1}^{N} \mathrm{E}[e^{\lambda y_i}] = [\overline{e^{\lambda y}}]^N . \tag{2.159b}$$

In the last of these equations y denotes any one of the identically distributed random variables $\{y_i\}$. Substituting Eq. 2.159b in Eq. 2.159a yields

$$\bar{z} \leqslant [\overline{e^{\lambda(y-\epsilon)}}]^N . \tag{2.159c}$$

Although the bound of Eq. 2.159c is valid for any $\lambda \geqslant 0$, we should choose λ in such a way that the right-hand side is minimum. We can find this optimum choice, λ_0, by differentiating $\overline{e^{\lambda(y-\epsilon)}}$ with respect to λ and equating the derivative to zero:

$$0 = \frac{d}{d\lambda} \mathrm{E}[e^{\lambda(y-\epsilon)}]_{\lambda=\lambda_0} = \mathrm{E}\left[\frac{d}{d\lambda} e^{\lambda(y-\epsilon)}\right]_{\lambda=\lambda_0}$$

$$= \mathrm{E}[(y-\epsilon)e^{\lambda_0(y-\epsilon)}] = e^{-\lambda_0\epsilon}\mathrm{E}[(y-\epsilon)e^{\lambda_0 y}].$$

Canceling $e^{-\lambda_0 \epsilon}$ and rearranging gives λ_0 implicitly, that is, as the solution to the equation

$$\frac{\mathrm{E}[y e^{\lambda_0 y}]}{\mathrm{E}[e^{\lambda_0 y}]} = \epsilon. \tag{2.160a}$$

The bound of Eq. 2.159c then becomes

$$\bar{z} = \mathrm{P}\left[\frac{1}{N}\sum_{i=1}^{N} y_i \geqslant \epsilon\right] \leqslant [\overline{e^{\lambda_0(y-\epsilon)}}]^N; \qquad \epsilon \geqslant 0. \tag{2.160b}$$

It can be shown[33] that λ_0, as given by Eq. 2.160a, is always greater than or equal to zero for $\epsilon \geqslant 0$ and that λ_0 provides the minimum $\bar{z}$ (rather than the maximum).

The bound of Eqs. 2.160 is called the *Chernoff bound.*[18] It can be used whenever the numerator and denominator of Eq. 2.160a are finite, which is the case for every discrete random variable that takes on a finite number of values and for many continuous random variables. Though less easy to evaluate than the weak law bound, the Chernoff bound is much more powerful: if we define

$$X \triangleq -\ln \overline{e^{\lambda_0(y-\epsilon)}}, \tag{2.161a}$$

then Eq. 2.160b becomes

$$\mathrm{P}\left[\frac{1}{N}\sum_{i=1}^{N} y_i \geqslant \epsilon\right] \leqslant e^{-NX}; \qquad \epsilon \geqslant 0. \tag{2.161b}$$

Thus the Chernoff bound decreases *exponentially* with N, whereas the weak law bound decreases only as $1/N$. Furthermore, it can be shown[34,73] that the exponent X is as large as possible; that is to say, *no bound* of the form

$$\mathrm{P}\left[\frac{1}{N}\sum_{i=1}^{N} y_i \geqslant \epsilon\right] \leqslant e^{-NX'}; \qquad \epsilon \geqslant 0,$$

with X' independent of N, is valid for all N for any $X' > X$. We say that the Chernoff bound is *exponentially tight.*

We extend the Chernoff bound to a set $\{x_i\}$ of identically distributed, independent random variables with nonzero means, $\{\bar{x}_i = \bar{x}\}$, by writing

$$y_i \triangleq x_i - \bar{x}; \qquad i = 1, \ldots, N.$$

Then Eq. 2.160b becomes

$$\mathrm{P}\left[\frac{1}{N}\sum_{i=1}^{N} x_i \geqslant \bar{x} + \epsilon\right] \leqslant [\overline{e^{\lambda_0 x} e^{-\lambda_0(\bar{x}+\epsilon)}}]^N; \qquad \epsilon > 0, \tag{2.162a}$$

in which x denotes any one of the identically distributed variables $\{x_i\}$.

From Eq. 2.160a λ_0 is given implicitly by

$$\epsilon = \frac{\mathrm{E}[(x - \bar{x})e^{\lambda_0(x-\bar{x})}]}{\mathrm{E}[e^{\lambda_0(x-\bar{x})}]} = \frac{\mathrm{E}[xe^{\lambda_0 x}]}{\mathrm{E}[e^{\lambda_0 x}]} - \bar{x}. \tag{2.162b}$$

An identical derivation can be performed when ϵ is taken as a negative constant. The result is

$$\mathrm{P}\left[\frac{1}{N}\sum_{i=1}^{N} x_i \leqslant \bar{x} + \epsilon\right] \leqslant [\overline{e^{\lambda_0 x}} e^{-\lambda_0(\bar{x}+\epsilon)}]^N; \qquad \epsilon < 0, \tag{2.162c}$$

in which λ_0, now negative, is again specified implicitly by Eq. 2.162b.

We can summarize these bounds concisely by defining

$$d \triangleq \bar{x} + \epsilon.$$

In terms of d,

$$[\overline{e^{\lambda_0(x-d)}}]^N \geqslant \begin{cases} \mathrm{P}\left[\frac{1}{N}\sum_{i=1}^{N} x_i \geqslant d\right]; & d > \bar{x} \\ \mathrm{P}\left[\frac{1}{N}\sum_{i=1}^{N} x_i \leqslant d\right]; & d < \bar{x} \end{cases} \tag{2.163a}$$

with λ_0 defined implicitly by

$$\frac{\mathrm{E}[xe^{\lambda_0 x}]}{\mathrm{E}[e^{\lambda_0 x}]} = d. \tag{2.163b}$$

Example. As an example of the Chernoff bound, take

$$x_i = \begin{cases} 1, & \text{with probability } p \\ 0, & \text{with probability } 1 - p \end{cases} \qquad i = 1, 2, \ldots, N. \tag{2.164}$$

We then have

$$\mathrm{E}[e^{\lambda_0 x}] = (1 - p) + pe^{\lambda_0},$$

$$\mathrm{E}[xe^{\lambda_0 x}] = pe^{\lambda_0}.$$

We evaluate λ_0 from Eq. 2.163b: for $0 \leqslant d \leqslant 1$,

$$d = \frac{pe^{\lambda_0}}{(1 - p) + pe^{\lambda_0}}$$

or

$$\frac{1}{d} = \frac{1 - p}{p} e^{-\lambda_0} + 1.$$

Thus

$$e^{-\lambda_0} = \frac{p}{1 - p}\left(\frac{1}{d} - 1\right) = \frac{p(1 - d)}{d(1 - p)}.$$

Finally,

$$\lambda_0 = \ln \frac{d(1-p)}{p(1-d)},$$

which is positive if $d > p$ and negative if $d < p$, as required.

The bracketed term on the left-hand side of Eq. 2.163a then becomes

$$\begin{aligned}
\overline{e^{\lambda_0(x-d)}} &= \mathrm{E}[e^{\lambda_0 x}]e^{-\lambda_0 d} \\
&= [(1-p) + pe^{\lambda_0}](e^{-\lambda_0})^d \\
&= \left[(1-p) + p\,\frac{d(1-p)}{p(1-d)}\right]\left[\frac{p(1-d)}{d(1-p)}\right]^d \\
&= \left(\frac{1-p}{1-d}\right)\left[\frac{p(1-d)}{d(1-p)}\right]^d \\
&= \left(\frac{p}{d}\right)^d\left(\frac{1-p}{1-d}\right)^{1-d} \\
&\triangleq e^{-X}.
\end{aligned}$$

Thus

$$X = -\ln\left[\left(\frac{p}{d}\right)^d\left(\frac{1-p}{1-d}\right)^{1-d}\right], \tag{2.165a}$$

and

$$\left[\left(\frac{p}{d}\right)^d\left(\frac{1-p}{1-d}\right)^{1-d}\right]^N \triangleq e^{-NX} \geqslant \begin{cases} \mathrm{P}\left[\dfrac{1}{N}\sum_{i=1}^{N} x_i \geqslant d\right]; & 1 \geqslant d > p \\ \mathrm{P}\left[\dfrac{1}{N}\sum_{i=1}^{N} x_i \leqslant d\right]; & 0 \leqslant d < p \end{cases} \tag{2.165b}$$

It is helpful to interpret the bound of Eq. 2.165b graphically. Consider

$$\begin{aligned}
X &= -\ln\left[\left(\frac{p}{d}\right)^d\left(\frac{1-p}{1-d}\right)^{1-d}\right] \\
&= -d\ln p - (1-d)\ln(1-p) + d\ln d + (1-d)\ln(1-d) \\
&= T_p(d) - H(d),
\end{aligned} \tag{2.166a}$$

where

$$T_p(\alpha) \triangleq -\alpha\ln p - (1-\alpha)\ln(1-p), \tag{2.166b}$$

$$H(\alpha) \triangleq -\alpha\ln\alpha - (1-\alpha)\ln(1-\alpha). \tag{2.166c}$$

The function $H(\ )$ is called the "binary entropy function." It is tabulated[27] and plotted in Fig. 2.43*a*.

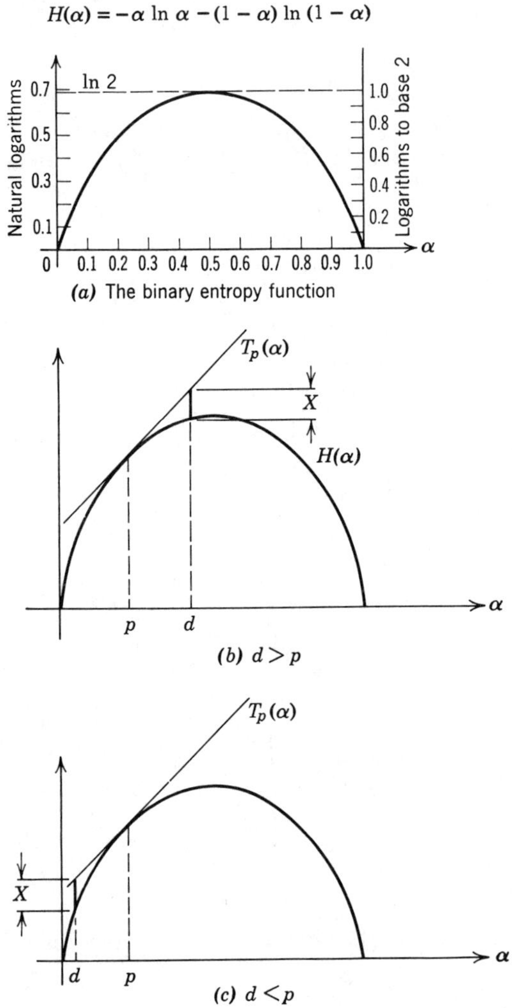

Figure 2.43 The geometric determination of the Chernoff exponent, X, for binomial random variables. $T_p(\alpha)$ is the line tangent to $H(\alpha)$ at the point $\alpha = p$. X is the difference between $T_p(\alpha)$ and $H(\alpha)$ at the point $\alpha = d$.

It can be verified that $T_p(\quad)$ is a linear function of its argument and that $T_p(\alpha)$ and $H(\alpha)$ are equal and have the same slope at $\alpha = p$. Thus X is given by the geometrical constructions shown in Figs. 2.43*b*, *c*. Note that the exponent X increases as $|d - p|$ increases.

An application of the Chernoff bound. An interesting application of the Chernoff bound in the binomial case is found in the estimation of the probability of error that results when the discrete communication channel shown in Fig. 2.44 is used N times in succession, N odd, to communicate one of two input messages. Thus, if $m = m_0$, we transmit a sequence of N zeros over the channel; if $m = m_1$, we transmit a sequence of N ones. The receiver observes the sequence of N received digits and sets $\hat{m} = m_0$ if the majority are zeros and $\hat{m} = m_1$ if the majority are ones. An error occurs if and only if more than half the digits are received in error.

Define a set of random variables $\{x_i\}$ as

$$x_i = \begin{cases} 1, & \text{if the } i\text{th digit is } \textit{not} \text{ received correctly,} \\ 0, & \text{if the } i\text{th digit is received correctly.} \end{cases}$$

If the channel transition probabilities are p and $1-p$ and if the

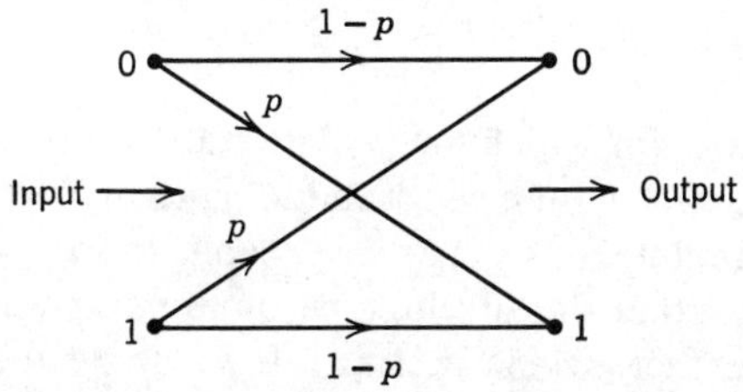

Figure 2.44 A simple discrete communication channel, called the binary symmetric channel. If the channel input is 0, the channel output is 0 with probability $(1 - p)$ and is 1 with probability p. The converse statement applies when the channel input is 1.

occurrence or nonoccurrence of a channel error is statistically independent on each use of the channel, the variables $\{x_i\}$ are identical to those in Eq. 2.164. Moreover, the probability of error for the receiver is

$$\begin{aligned} P[\mathcal{E}] = P[\hat{m} \neq m] &= P\left[\sum_{i=1}^{N} x_i > \frac{N}{2}\right] \\ &= P\left[\frac{1}{N}\sum_{i=1}^{N} x_i > \frac{1}{2}\right]. \end{aligned}$$

Thus we may immediately invoke Eq. 2.165b, with $d = 1 - d = \frac{1}{2}$. If we assume that $p = 0.1$ and $N = 13$, the Chernoff bound yields

$$\begin{aligned} P[\mathcal{E}] &\leqslant \left[\left(\frac{p}{d}\right)^{d}\left(\frac{1-p}{1-d}\right)^{1-d}\right]^{N} \\ &= \left[\left(\frac{0.1}{0.5}\right)^{0.5}\left(\frac{0.9}{0.5}\right)^{0.5}\right]^{13} \\ &= \left(\frac{3}{5}\right)^{13} \approx 1.3 \times 10^{-3}. \end{aligned}$$

On the other hand, substituting $\epsilon = (d - p) = 0.4$ in the weak law bound yields

$$P[\mathcal{E}] \leqslant \frac{p(1-p)}{N\epsilon^2} = \frac{0.1(0.9)}{13(0.4)^2} \approx 0.043.$$

The comparison between the strength of the two bounds is more dramatic if we triple N to 39. The Chernoff bound is then cubed to yield 2.2×10^{-9}, whereas the weak law bound is divided by three to yield 0.014.

Central Limit Theorem

We noted in connection with Fig. 2.7 that the binomial density function (that is, the density function of the sample mean

$$m \triangleq \frac{1}{M} \sum_{k=1}^{M} x_k \tag{2.167}$$

in the particular case for which the $\{x_i\}$ are statistically independent *binary* random variables, each with mean $\bar{x}$ and variance σ_x^2) exhibits an envelope that becomes simultaneously narrower and more bell-shaped as M increases. The fact that the envelope becomes narrower is attributable to the normalization factor $1/M$ in Eq. 2.167: as M increases, the mean $\bar{m} = \bar{x}$ remains constant, whereas the variance $\sigma_m^2 = \sigma_x^2/M$ decreases. We are interested here in investigating the tendency of the envelope to become bell-shaped. Consequently, instead of m, we consider the related random variable z defined by

$$z \triangleq \frac{1}{\sqrt{N}} \sum_{i=1}^{N} (x_i - \bar{x}). \tag{2.168}$$

With this normalization $\bar{z} = 0$ and $\sigma_z^2 = \sigma_x^2$, so that both the mean and the variance of z remain constant as N increases. The behavior of the envelope of p_z as N increases is evidenced in Fig. 2.45.

The bell-shaped tendency illustrated in Fig. 2.45 for the binomial distribution is an example of a much more general group of theorems, called collectively the *central limit theorem*, one statement† of which reads as follows:

Let $\{y_i\}$ denote a set of statistically independent, zero-mean random variables, each with the same density function $p_{y_i} = p_y$ and finite variance σ_y^2. Define

$$z \triangleq \frac{1}{\sqrt{N}} \sum_{i=1}^{N} y_i. \tag{2.169a}$$

† The particular limit theorem stated here is called the Lindeberg-Lévy theorem. This and other related theorems are discussed in References 30 and 35.

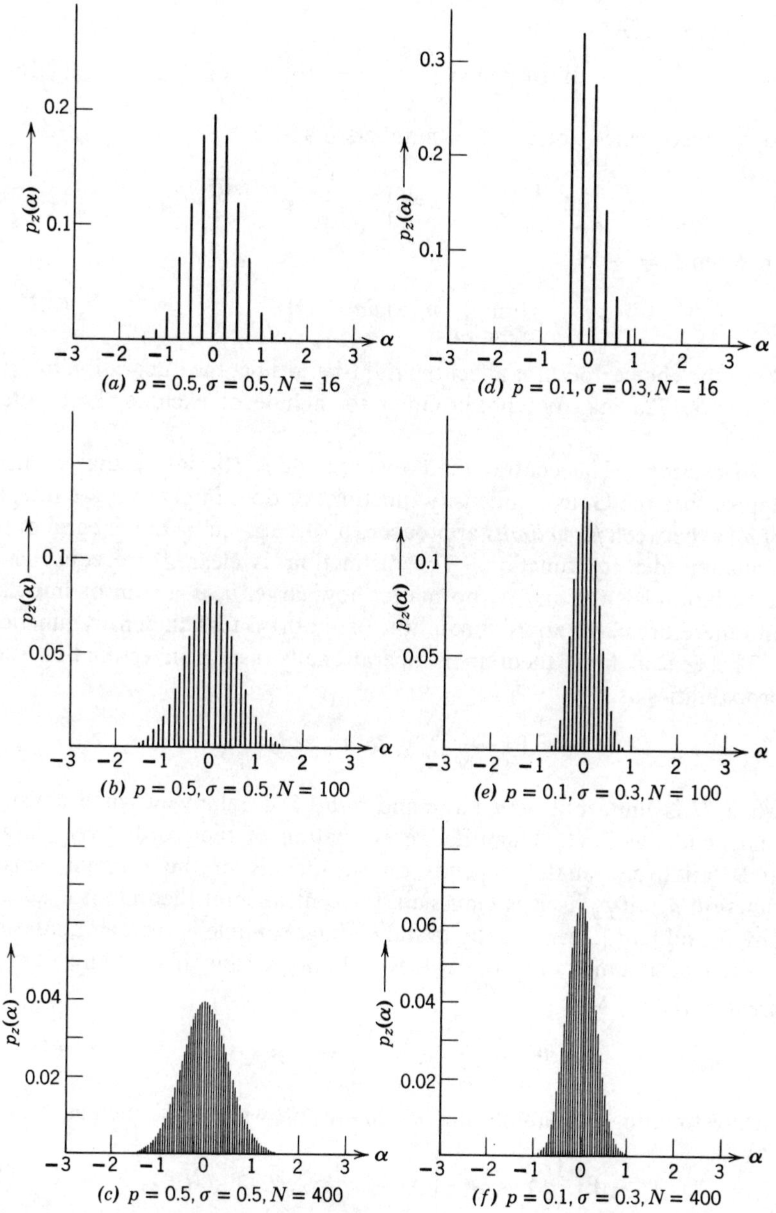

Figure 2.45 The N-term binomial density function normalized to zero-mean and constant variance.

Then, for any α,

$$\lim_{N\to\infty} F_z(\alpha) = \int_{-\infty}^{\alpha} \frac{1}{\sqrt{2\pi}\sigma_y} e^{-\beta^2/2\sigma_y^2}\, d\beta. \tag{2.169b}$$

As a consequence, for any two numbers a and b

$$\lim_{N\to\infty} \int_a^b p_z(\alpha)\, d\alpha = \int_a^b \frac{1}{\sqrt{2\pi}\sigma_y} e^{-\beta^2/2\sigma_y^2}\, d\beta \tag{2.170a}$$

or, when $b = +\infty$,

$$\lim_{N\to\infty} \int_a^\infty p_z(\alpha)\, d\alpha = Q\left(\frac{a}{\sigma_y}\right). \tag{2.170b}$$

Since the choice does not affect the right-hand side, the integration interval of Eq. 2.170a may be chosen either to include or exclude the points a and b.

Discussion. The central limit theorem does *not* imply that p_z itself approaches the Gaussian density function; it does imply that the integral of $p_z(\alpha)$ between *fixed limits* approaches a value given by the integral of the Gaussian density function. The distinction is clear if we consider p_y to be binomial; for any N, no matter how large, p_z is a sum of impulses and therefore never approximates the (smooth) Gaussian density function.

The central limit theorem is operationally useful in estimating such probabilities as

$$\mathrm{P}\left[\frac{1}{\sqrt{N}} \sum_{i=1}^{N} y_i \geqslant a\right] \approx Q\left(\frac{a}{\sigma_y}\right)$$

when N is finite but very large and $|a/\sigma_y|$ is a relatively small constant (independent of N). Quantitative evaluation of the words "very large" and "relatively small" depends on the details of the original density function p_y: if p_y itself is Gaussian, the central limit theorem is exact for any N and $|a/\sigma_y|$. An equally trivial counterexample is the binomial case: if each y_i assumes only the values -1 and 1, and if a is any number greater than $\sqrt{N}$,

$$\mathrm{P}\left[\frac{1}{\sqrt{N}} \sum_{i=1}^{N} y_i \geqslant a\right] = 0 \neq Q\left(\frac{a}{\sigma_y}\right).$$

In estimating probabilities in which a/σ_y grows with N, such as

$$\mathrm{P}\left[\frac{1}{N} \sum_{i=1}^{N} y_i \geqslant \epsilon\right] = \mathrm{P}\left[\frac{1}{\sqrt{N}} \sum_{i=1}^{N} y_i \geqslant \sqrt{N}\,\epsilon\right], \tag{2.171a}$$

the general usefulness of the approximation

$$\mathrm{P}\left[\frac{1}{N} \sum_{i=1}^{N} y_i \geqslant \epsilon\right] \approx Q\left(\frac{\sqrt{N}\,\epsilon}{\sigma_y}\right) \tag{2.171b}$$

is dubious, regardless of how large we take N. Consider, for example, a set of N binary random variables $\{x_i\}$ in which, for each i, x_i assumes the values 0 and 1 with equal probability. With $y_i \triangleq x_i - \frac{1}{2}$, $\sigma_y^2 = \frac{1}{4}$, and $\epsilon = \frac{1}{2}$, we obtain from Eq. 2.171b

$$\mathrm{P}\left[\frac{1}{N}\sum_{i=1}^{N} x_i \geqslant \frac{1}{2} + \epsilon\right] \approx Q\left(\frac{\sqrt{N}\,\epsilon}{\sqrt{\frac{1}{4}}}\right) = Q(\sqrt{N}). \tag{2.172a}$$

We have already seen (cf., Eq. 2.121) that the Q function behaves exponentially as

$$Q(\alpha) \sim e^{-\alpha^2/2}; \qquad \alpha > 0.$$

Thus Eq. 2.172 implies

$$\mathrm{P}\left[\frac{1}{N}\sum_{i=1}^{N} x_i \geqslant 1\right] \sim e^{-0.5N}, \tag{2.172b}$$

whereas the exact expression is

$$\mathrm{P}\left[\frac{1}{N}\sum_{i=1}^{N} x_i \geqslant 1\right] = \mathrm{P}\left[\frac{1}{N}\sum_{i=1}^{N} x_i = 1\right] = 2^{-N} \approx e^{-0.69N}. \tag{2.173}$$

The operational significance of the difference between Eqs. 2.172b and 2.173 may be extremely significant; indeed the fractional error

$$\frac{e^{-0.5N}}{e^{-0.69N}} = e^{+0.19N}$$

grows with N and becomes enormous when N is large. On the other hand, it is readily verified that the Chernoff bound agrees with Eq. 2.173, which is in accord with our earlier statement that the Chernoff bound is exponentially tight. Thus the Chernoff bound should be used in lieu of the central limit calculation in cases such as this, in which the limit of integration in Eq. 2.170b increases with N.

Argument. An appreciation of the validity of the central limit theorem can be gained from the following arguments.

Let $M_y(\nu)$ denote the characteristic function of any one of the N identically distributed zero-mean random variables $\{y_i\}$, and let $M_z(\nu)$ denote the characteristic function of their normalized sum z. Then $M_z(\nu)$ and $M_y(\nu)$ are related by

$$\begin{aligned} M_z(\nu) \triangleq \mathrm{E}[e^{j\nu z}] &= \mathrm{E}\left[\exp\left(j\nu\frac{1}{\sqrt{N}}\sum_{i=1}^{N} y_i\right)\right] = \mathrm{E}\left[\prod_{i=1}^{N}\exp\left(j\frac{\nu}{\sqrt{N}}\,y_i\right)\right] \\ &= \prod_{i=1}^{N}\mathrm{E}\left[\exp\left(j\frac{\nu}{\sqrt{N}}\,y_i\right)\right] = \left[M_y\left(\frac{\nu}{\sqrt{N}}\right)\right]^N, \end{aligned} \tag{2.174}$$

in which we have used the fact that the mean of a product of statistically independent random variables is the product of their means.

Now let us assume that p_y is such that every moment $\{\overline{y^n}\}$, $n = 1, 2, \ldots$, is finite. Then, in accordance with Eq. 2.144b, $M_y(\nu)$ may be expressed in the power-series expansion

$$M_y(\nu) = 1 + (j\nu)\bar{y} + \frac{(j\nu)^2}{2!}\overline{y^2} + \frac{(j\nu)^3}{3!}\overline{y^3} + \cdots. \tag{2.175a}$$

Since $\bar{y} = 0$ and $\overline{y^2} = \sigma_y^{\,2}$, we have

$$M_y(\nu) = 1 - \nu^2\frac{\sigma_y^{\,2}}{2} + \nu^3 f(\nu), \tag{2.175b}$$

where $f(\nu)$ is a continuous function that approaches the constant $(-j\overline{y^3}/6)$ as ν approaches zero.

From Eqs. 2.174 and 2.175b, we have

$$\ln M_z(\nu) = N \ln M_y\left(\frac{\nu}{\sqrt{N}}\right) = N \ln \left[1 - \frac{\nu^2}{N}\frac{\sigma_y^{\,2}}{2} + \left(\frac{\nu}{\sqrt{N}}\right)^3 f\left(\frac{\nu}{\sqrt{N}}\right)\right]. \tag{2.176}$$

The logarithm may be expanded in the power series

$$\ln(1 + w) = w - \frac{w^2}{2} + \frac{w^3}{3} - \cdots, \tag{2.177}$$

which converges for any complex variable w for which $|w| < 1$. Since we are interested in the limit as $N \to \infty$, we may take N sufficiently large that, *for any fixed* ν,

$$\left| -\frac{\nu^2}{N}\frac{\sigma_y^{\,2}}{2} + \left(\frac{\nu}{\sqrt{N}}\right)^3 f\left(\frac{\nu}{\sqrt{N}}\right)\right| < 1.$$

Applying Eq. 2.177 to Eq. 2.176, we have

$$\ln\left[1 - \frac{\nu^2}{N}\frac{\sigma_y^{\,2}}{2} + \left(\frac{\nu}{\sqrt{N}}\right)^3 f\left(\frac{\nu}{\sqrt{N}}\right)\right]$$
$$= \left[-\frac{\nu^2}{N}\frac{\sigma_y^{\,2}}{2} + \left(\frac{\nu}{\sqrt{N}}\right)^3 f\left(\frac{\nu}{\sqrt{N}}\right) + \begin{pmatrix}\text{terms involving the factors}\\ N^{-2}, N^{-5/2}, N^{-3}, \ldots\end{pmatrix}\right].$$

Thus, for any finite value of ν,

$$\lim_{N\to\infty} \ln M_z(\nu) = \lim_{N\to\infty} N\left[-\frac{\nu^2}{N}\frac{\sigma_y^{\,2}}{2} + \left(\frac{\nu}{\sqrt{N}}\right)^3 f\left(\frac{\nu}{\sqrt{N}}\right) + \cdots\right]$$
$$= \frac{-\nu^2\sigma_y^{\,2}}{2}.$$

Since the exponential function is continuous, it follows that

$$\lim_{N\to\infty} M_z(\nu) = e^{-\nu^2\sigma_y{}^2/2}. \tag{2.178}$$

We recognize that the limiting form of $M_z(\nu)$ is the characteristic function of a zero-mean Gaussian random variable with variance $\sigma_y{}^2$.

We must now resist the temptation to claim that the density function

$$\lim_{N\to\infty} p_z(\alpha) = \lim_{N\to\infty} \int_{-\infty}^{\infty} M_z(\nu)e^{-j\nu\alpha}\, d\nu \tag{2.179}$$

is Gaussian. As we have already seen in connection with the binomial distribution, such a claim is false! The operations of limit taking and integration in Eq. 2.179 cannot, in general, be interchanged.

Although the density function of z does tend to Gaussian if p_y is sufficiently smooth, the general central limit theorem statement that the distribution function converges to Gaussian form hinges on the additional "smoothing" that is introduced by integrating the density function p_z to get the distribution function F_z.

APPENDIX 2A REVERSIBLE TRANSFORMATION OF RANDOM VECTORS

The change-of-variables transformation considered in Eq. 2.78 is a special case of a reversible transformation of vectors. A transformation $\mathbf{x} \to \mathbf{y}$, with both $\mathbf{x}$ and $\mathbf{y}$ k-dimensional vectors, is called *reversible* if it is one-to-one, that is, if the inverse transformation $\mathbf{y} \to \mathbf{x}$ also exists for all $\mathbf{x}$ and $\mathbf{y}$ of interest. For example, let

$$\mathbf{y} \triangleq \big(f_1(\mathbf{x}), f_2(\mathbf{x}), \ldots, f_k(\mathbf{x})\big), \tag{2A.1a}$$

where each of the $\{f_i\}$ is a function of k variables; that is, each f_i assigns a (different) number, say $y_i(\omega)$, to a vector $\mathbf{x}(\omega)$. The transformation is reversible if there exists another set of functions $\{g_i\}$ such that

$$\mathbf{x} = \big(g_1(\mathbf{y}), g_2(\mathbf{y}), \ldots, g_k(\mathbf{y})\big). \tag{2A.1b}$$

It is convenient to express Eqs. 2A.1 in the more concise form

$$\mathbf{y} = \mathbf{f}(\mathbf{x}) \tag{2A.2a}$$

$$\mathbf{x} = \mathbf{g}(\mathbf{y}) = \mathbf{g}(\mathbf{f}(\mathbf{x})). \tag{2A.2b}$$

We now relate $p_{\mathbf{y}}$ to $p_{\mathbf{x}}$ for a reversible transformation in which the partial derivatives $\partial f_i/\partial x_j$ and $\partial g_i/\partial y_j$ exist for all i and j, $1 \leqslant i, j \leqslant k$. First we determine the probability distribution function $F_{\mathbf{y}}$ and then we differentiate $F_{\mathbf{y}}$ to obtain $p_{\mathbf{y}}$. By definition,

$$F_{\mathbf{y}}(\boldsymbol{\beta}) = \int_I p_{\mathbf{x}}(\boldsymbol{\alpha})\, d\boldsymbol{\alpha}, \tag{2A.3a}$$

where I is the region

$$I = \{\boldsymbol{\alpha}: f_1(\boldsymbol{\alpha}) \leqslant \beta_1, f_2(\boldsymbol{\alpha}) \leqslant \beta_2, \ldots, f_k(\boldsymbol{\alpha}) \leqslant \beta_k\}. \tag{2A.3b}$$

Taking the derivative $\partial^k/(\partial\beta_1\, \partial\beta_2 \cdots \partial\beta_k)$ of the right-hand side of Eq. 2A.3a to obtain $p_{\mathbf{y}}(\boldsymbol{\beta})$ is complicated by the fact that I is not simply expressed in terms of the variables of integration. This difficulty can be avoided by making the change of variables

$$\boldsymbol{\gamma} = \mathbf{f}(\boldsymbol{\alpha}). \tag{2A.4a}$$

Then it follows from the existence of the inverse transform $\mathbf{g}$ that

$$\boldsymbol{\alpha} = \mathbf{g}(\boldsymbol{\gamma}). \tag{2A.4b}$$

The region of integration I can be expressed simply in terms of $\boldsymbol{\gamma}$ as

$$I = \{\boldsymbol{\gamma}: \boldsymbol{\gamma} \leqslant \boldsymbol{\beta}\}. \tag{2A.4c}$$

Since $\mathbf{g}(\boldsymbol{\gamma})$ may be substituted for $\boldsymbol{\alpha}$ in the integrand of Eq. 2A.3a, the only problem in performing the change of variables of Eq. 2A.4a is to relate the differential volume elements $d\boldsymbol{\alpha}$ and $d\boldsymbol{\gamma}$. The relationship is

$$d\boldsymbol{\alpha} = |J_g(\boldsymbol{\gamma})|\, d\boldsymbol{\gamma}, \tag{2A.5a}$$

where $|J_g(\boldsymbol{\gamma})|$ is the absolute value of the Jacobian $J_g(\boldsymbol{\gamma})$ associated with the transformation $\mathbf{g}$. The Jacobian, by definition, is the determinant

$$J_g(\boldsymbol{\gamma}) = \begin{vmatrix} J_{11} & J_{12} & \cdots & J_{1k} \\ J_{21} & J_{22} & \cdots & J_{2k} \\ \cdot & & & \\ \cdot & & & \\ \cdot & & & \\ J_{k1} & J_{k2} & \cdots & J_{kk} \end{vmatrix}, \tag{2A.5b}$$

with elements

$$J_{ij} = \frac{\partial g_i(\boldsymbol{\gamma})}{\partial \gamma_j}; \qquad i = 1, 2, \ldots, k; \qquad j = 1, 2, \ldots, k. \tag{2A.5c}$$

With the change of variables of Eq. 2A.4a, Eq. 2A.3a becomes

$$\begin{aligned} F_{\mathbf{y}}(\boldsymbol{\beta}) &= \int_{\boldsymbol{\gamma} \leqslant \boldsymbol{\beta}} p_{\mathbf{x}}[\mathbf{g}(\boldsymbol{\gamma})]\, |J_g(\boldsymbol{\gamma})|\, d\boldsymbol{\gamma} \\ &= \int_{-\infty}^{\beta_1} \int_{-\infty}^{\beta_2} \cdots \int_{-\infty}^{\beta_k} p_{\mathbf{x}}[\mathbf{g}(\boldsymbol{\gamma})]\, |J_g(\boldsymbol{\gamma})|\, d\boldsymbol{\gamma}. \end{aligned} \tag{2A.6}$$

Taking the partial derivative is now trivial, and we obtain the desired relation between $p_{\mathbf{y}}$ and $p_{\mathbf{x}}$ when random vectors **y** and **x** are related by the 1:1 transformations $\mathbf{y} = \mathbf{f}(\mathbf{x})$; $\mathbf{x} = \mathbf{g}(\mathbf{y})$:

$$p_{\mathbf{y}}(\boldsymbol{\beta}) = p_{\mathbf{x}}[\mathbf{g}(\boldsymbol{\beta})]\,|J_g(\boldsymbol{\beta})|. \tag{2A.7}$$

Further insight into the relation between $p_{\mathbf{x}}$ and $p_{\mathbf{y}}$ may be gained by recalling the fundamental interpretation of the probability density function: $p_{\mathbf{x}}$ is the function which, when evaluated at a point **a** and multiplied by the volume ΔV_x of a small region ΔI_x including the point **a**, yields the probability that **x** will lie in the region. But, if **x** lies in the region ΔI_x, then $\mathbf{y} = \mathbf{f}(\mathbf{x})$ must lie in a corresponding region ΔI_y, of volume ΔV_y, which contains the point $\mathbf{b} = \mathbf{f}(\mathbf{a})$. Thus

$$p_{\mathbf{y}}(\mathbf{b})\,\Delta V_y = p_{\mathbf{x}}(\mathbf{a})\,\Delta V_x. \tag{2A.8a}$$

Since $\mathbf{a} = \mathbf{g}(\mathbf{b})$, we have

$$p_{\mathbf{y}}(\mathbf{b})\,\Delta V_y = p_{\mathbf{x}}[\mathbf{g}(\mathbf{b})]\,\Delta V_x. \tag{2A.8b}$$

Of course, ΔV_x is not in general equal to ΔV_y; indeed, from Eq. 2A.5a,

$$\frac{\Delta V_x}{\Delta V_y} \approx |J_g(\mathbf{b})|. \tag{2A.8c}$$

Substituting Eq. 2A.8c in Eq. 2A.8b yields

$$p_{\mathbf{y}}(\mathbf{b}) \approx p_{\mathbf{x}}[\mathbf{g}(\mathbf{b})]\,|J_g(\mathbf{b})|, \tag{2A.8d}$$

which is consistent with Eq. 2A.7.

As an example of the use of Eq. 2A.7, consider the polar transformation $\mathbf{x} \to \mathbf{y}$ given by

$$\begin{aligned} y_1 &= f_1(\mathbf{x}) = \sqrt{x_1^2 + x_2^2}, \\ y_2 &= f_2(\mathbf{x}) = \tan^{-1}\frac{x_2}{x_1}. \end{aligned} \tag{2A.9a}$$

As shown in Fig. 2A.1, the inverse transformation is

$$\left.\begin{aligned} x_1 &= g_1(\mathbf{y}) = y_1 \cos y_2 \\ x_2 &= g_2(\mathbf{y}) = y_1 \sin y_2 \end{aligned}\right\}; \qquad y_1 \geqslant 0, \qquad 0 \leqslant y_2 < 2\pi. \tag{2A.9b}$$

Thus

$$\begin{aligned} J_g(\boldsymbol{\beta}) &= \begin{vmatrix} \dfrac{\partial g_1(\boldsymbol{\beta})}{\partial \beta_1} & \dfrac{\partial g_1(\boldsymbol{\beta})}{\partial \beta_2} \\ \dfrac{\partial g_2(\boldsymbol{\beta})}{\partial \beta_1} & \dfrac{\partial g_2(\boldsymbol{\beta})}{\partial \beta_2} \end{vmatrix} = \begin{vmatrix} \cos \beta_2 & -\beta_1 \sin \beta_2 \\ \sin \beta_2 & \beta_1 \cos \beta_2 \end{vmatrix} \\ &= \beta_1 \cos^2 \beta_2 + \beta_1 \sin^2 \beta_2 = \beta_1. \end{aligned} \tag{2A.9c}$$

Introducing the more natural notation $\boldsymbol{\beta} = (r, \theta)$, so that

$$\begin{aligned} J_g(\boldsymbol{\beta}) &= r, \\ g_1(\boldsymbol{\beta}) &= r \cos \theta, \\ g_2(\boldsymbol{\beta}) &= r \sin \theta, \end{aligned} \tag{2A.10a}$$

we have

$$p_{\mathbf{y}}(\boldsymbol{\beta}) = p_{\mathbf{x}}[\mathbf{g}(\boldsymbol{\beta})]\, J_g(\boldsymbol{\beta}),$$

or

$$p_{\mathbf{y}}(r, \theta) = p_{\mathbf{x}}(r \cos \theta, r \sin \theta)\, r; \qquad r \geqslant 0, \qquad 0 \leqslant \theta < 2\pi. \tag{2A.10b}$$

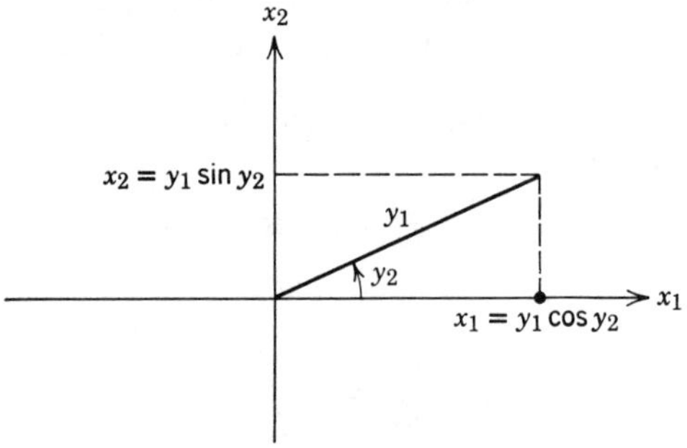

Figure 2A.1 The polar transformation.

For instance, if $p_{\mathbf{x}}$ is the two-dimensional Gaussian density function

$$p_{\mathbf{x}}(\alpha_1, \alpha_2) = \frac{1}{2\pi\sqrt{1 - \rho^2}} \exp\left(-\frac{\alpha_1^2 - 2\rho\alpha_1\alpha_2 + \alpha_2^2}{2(1 - \rho)^2}\right), \tag{2A.11a}$$

then, from Eq. 2A.10b,

$$p_{\mathbf{y}}(r, \theta) = \frac{r}{2\pi\sqrt{1 - \rho^2}} \exp\left[-\frac{r^2(1 - 2\rho \sin \theta \cos \theta)}{2(1 - \rho^2)}\right]; \qquad r \geqslant 0, 0 \leqslant \theta < 2\pi. \tag{2A.11b}$$

PROBLEMS

2.1 Let A, B, C be three events, not necessarily disjoint, defined on a sample space Ω. Prove the three inequalities stated below, and for each discuss the conditions under which the equality sign holds for every legitimate probability assignment.

$$\begin{aligned} \mathrm{P}[A \cup B \cup C] &\leqslant \mathrm{P}[A] + \mathrm{P}[B] + \mathrm{P}[C], \\ \mathrm{P}[A \cup B \cup C] &\geqslant \mathrm{P}[A], \\ \mathrm{P}[ABC] &\leqslant \mathrm{P}[A]. \end{aligned}$$

2.2 Let Ω be the integers 1, 2, . . . , 10 and let each integer be assigned probability $\frac{1}{10}$. Define the events A, B, C by

$$A = \{1, 2, 3, 4, 5\},$$
$$B = \{4, 5, 6, 7, 8\},$$
$$C = \{3, 5, 7, 9, 10\}.$$

a. Calculate the following probabilities:

$$\text{P}[A \cup B^{\text{C}}], \quad \text{P}[A \cap C], \quad \text{P}[(A \cup B)^{\text{C}} \cap C],$$
$$\text{P}[(AB) \cup C], \quad \text{P}[(AB)^{\text{C}} \cup (AC)].$$

b. What is the total number of distinct events implied by the events Ω, A, B, C?

2.3 Consider the probability system of Problem 2.2. Are the following equations true?

$$\text{P}[A \mid BC] = \text{P}[A],$$
$$\text{P}[B \mid AC] = \text{P}[B],$$
$$\text{P}[C \mid AB] = \text{P}[C].$$

Are the three events A, B, and C jointly statistically independent? Are they pairwise statistically independent?

2.4 Consider the following experiment involving four urns. A ball is chosen from urn A, which contains six balls labeled B, three balls labeled C, and three balls labeled D. The letter drawn specifies the urn from which a second drawing is made. Urn B contains five red and five white balls. Urn C contains four red and six white balls. Urn D contains two red and eight white balls.

a. Construct a sample space and probability assignment that describes the experiment.

b. Given that the second ball drawn is red, what is the conditional probability that the first drawing yielded B?

c. Are the two events "first ball labeled C" and "second ball red" independent?

d. Are all results of the first drawing statistically independent of the result of the second drawing?

2.5 Let A and B be two statistically independent events of nonzero probability. Prove or disprove the equation

$$\text{P}[A \cup B] = \text{P}[A] + \text{P}[B].$$

2.6 Consider any event A with nonzero probability and a set of disjoint events $B_1, B_2, \ldots, B_n$ such that

$$\bigcup_{i=1}^{n} B_i = \Omega.$$

Show that

$$\text{P}[B_k \mid A] = \frac{\text{P}[A \mid B_k]\,\text{P}[B_k]}{\sum_{i=1}^{n} \text{P}[A \mid B_i]\,\text{P}[B_i]}.$$

This result is known as Bayes rule (for events).

2.7 An experiment consists of throwing a fair die until two successive results are the same. Construct a mathematical model that describes the experiment and determine the probability of stopping with the nth toss, $n = 0, 1, 2, \ldots$. Verify that these probabilities sum to one.

2.8 A communication network with four terminals I, II, III, IV is connected with four links a, b, c, d, as shown in the figure. Not all links, however, are necessarily available. Let p denote the probability that any particular link is available and assume that the availability of each link is statistically independent of the state of all other links. Two stations can communicate if and only if they are connected by at least one chain of available links.

a. Construct an appropriate probability model with 16 sample points, one for each state of the system.

b. Let $A \triangleq \{\omega\text{: I and IV can communicate}\}$. Calculate $\mathrm{P}[A]$.

c. Let $B \triangleq \{\omega\text{: II and III can communicate}\}$. Calculate $\mathrm{P}[B]$.

d. Calculate $\mathrm{P}[AB]$. How many sample points does this event contain? Are the events A and B statistically independent?

e. Show that $\mathrm{P}[A] = p\,\mathrm{P}[A \mid c \text{ available}] + (1 - p)\,\mathrm{P}[A \mid c \text{ not available}]$. Using this formula, re-evaluate $\mathrm{P}[A]$ by inspection.

f. Prove that $\mathrm{P}[A]$ would be increased if link c were connected between I and III rather than between II and III.

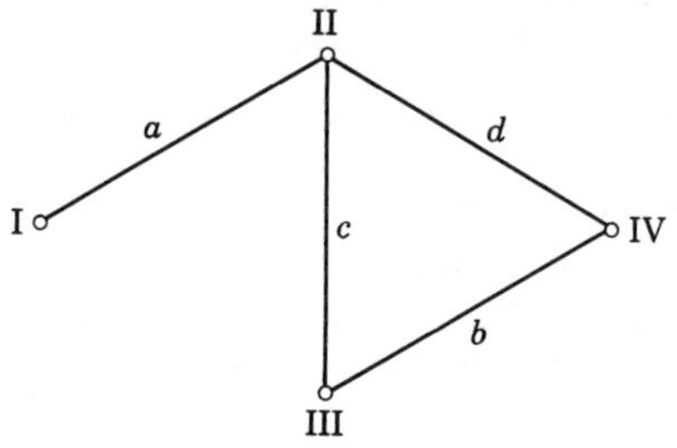

Figure P2.8

2.9 Consider three events A_1, B_1, and C_1, with complements A_2, B_2, and C_2, respectively. Prove that A_1, B_1, and C_1 are statistically independent if and only if the eight equations

$$\mathrm{P}[A_i B_j C_k] = \mathrm{P}[A_i]\,\mathrm{P}[B_j]\,\mathrm{P}[C_k]; \qquad i, j, k = 1, 2$$

are true. Does any subset of these equations imply the others? If so, determine a minimal subset with this property.

2.10 Consider the communication system described here. The transmitter throws one of two fair dice, die I if the message is A and die II if the message is B. Die I has five faces labeled A and one face labeled B, whereas die II has five faces labeled B and one face labeled A. The receiver decides the message is that shown by the thrown die. Assume the two messages are equally likely.

a. Construct a suitable probability system and determine the probability of error (i.e., the probability that the receiver's decision is incorrect).

b. Now assume that the transmitter throws three type I dice if the message is A and three type II dice if the message is B. The receiver decides the message by majority rule. Repeat part a.

c. What is the general expression for the probability of error when the transmitter throws N (N odd) type I or type II dice and the receiver decides by majority rule?

d. The transmitter now throws four type I or type II dice. The receiver again decides by majority rule but asks the transmitter to throw the same four dice again in case of a tie. This continues until a decision is reached. What is the probability of error? What is the probability that the decision will be reached with the Nth repetition?

2.11 A noisy discrete communication channel is available. Once each second one letter from the three-letter alphabet $\{a, b, c\}$ can be transmitted and one letter from the three-letter alphabet $\{1, 2, 3\}$, received. The conditional probabilities of the various received letters, given the various transmitted letters, are specified by the accompanying diagram.

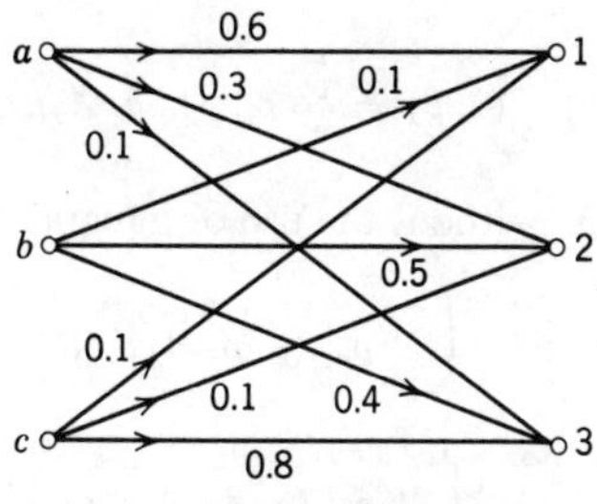

Figure P2.11

A source is available that uses a, b, and c with the following probabilities:

$$P[a] = 0.3,$$
$$P[b] = 0.5,$$
$$P[c] = 0.2.$$

What is the best receiver decision rule (assignment of 1, 2, 3 to a, b, c) and what is the resulting probability of error? What is the minimum probability of error that could be achieved without use of the channel?

2.12 Consider the noisy discrete communication channel illustrated by the accompanying diagram.

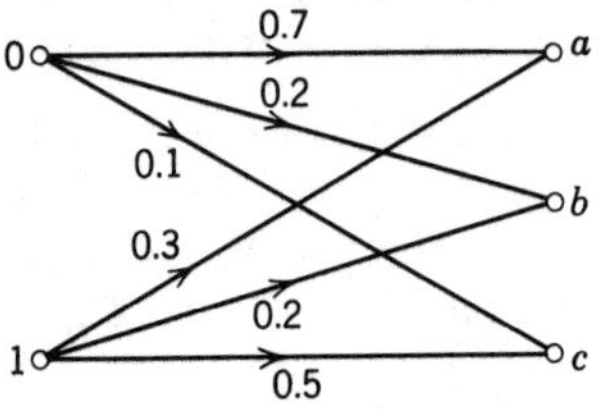

Figure P2.12

a. If P[0] = 0.7 and P[1] = 0.3, determine the optimum decision rule (assignment of a, b, c to 0, 1) and the resulting probability of error.

b. There are eight decision rules. Plot the probability of error for each decision rule versus P[0] on one graph.

c. Each decision rule has a maximum probability of error, which occurs for some least favorable a priori probability P[0]. The decision rule which has the smallest maximum probability of error is called the *minimax decision rule.* Which of the eight rules is minimax?

2.13 Let A_i, $i = 1, 2, \ldots, K$, be a set of *disjoint* events such that

$$\bigcup_{i=1}^{K} A_i = \Omega.$$

a. Prove that, for all α, β,

$$p_{x,y}(\alpha, \beta) = \sum_{i=1}^{K} p_{x,y}(\alpha, \beta, A_i).$$

b. Express the following without the use of integrals:

$$\int_{-\infty}^{\infty}\int_{-\infty}^{\infty} p_{x,y}(\alpha, \beta, A)\, d\alpha\, d\beta$$

$$\int_{-\infty}^{\infty}\int_{-\infty}^{\infty} p_{x,y}(\alpha, \beta \mid A)\, d\alpha\, d\beta$$

$$\int_{-\infty}^{\infty} p_x(\alpha \mid y = \beta, A)\, p_y(\beta \mid A)\, d\beta,$$

where A is any one of the $\{A_i\}$.

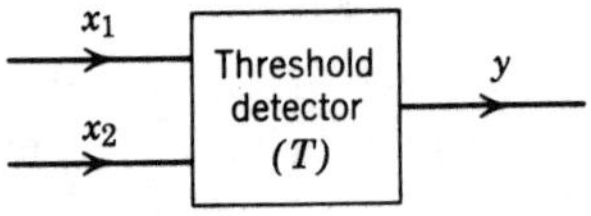

Figure P2.14

2.14 Two statistically dependent random variables x_1 and x_2 are applied at the inputs to a threshold detector, the output from which is equal to the number of inputs that exceed the threshold, say T. Thus $y = 0, 1,$ or 2. Determine the density function p_y in terms of p_{x_1,x_2} and T. (See Fig. P2.14.)

2.15 Consider the random variable z obtained from a random variable θ by the transformation

$$z = \sin \theta.$$

a. Determine p_z when

$$p_\theta(\alpha) = \begin{cases} \dfrac{1}{\pi}; & -\dfrac{\pi}{2} < \alpha \leqslant \dfrac{\pi}{2}, \\ 0; & \text{elsewhere.} \end{cases}$$

b. Determine p_z when ϕ is a constant, N is an integer, and

$$p_\theta(\alpha) = \begin{cases} \dfrac{1}{N2\pi}; & -N\pi + \phi < \alpha \leqslant N\pi + \phi, \\ 0; & \text{elsewhere.} \end{cases}$$

2.16 A random variable x with nonimpulsive density function p_x is transformed into a new random variable y by the transformation

$$y = f(x),$$

where

$$f(\alpha) = F_x(\alpha).$$

Here, as usual, F_x denotes the distribution function of x. Show that

$$p_y(\alpha) = \begin{cases} 1; & 0 \leqslant \alpha \leqslant 1, \\ 0; & \text{elsewhere.} \end{cases}$$

2.17 Let x be a random variable with the density function

$$p_x(\alpha) = \tfrac{1}{2}\, e^{-|\alpha|}.$$

Determine the density function p_y of the random variable

$$y = e^x.$$

2.18 A random variable x with probability density function as shown is applied at the input of each of the five nonlinear devices illustrated on p. 120. Calculate and plot the resulting probability density p_{y_i} for $i = 1, 2, 3, 4, 5$.

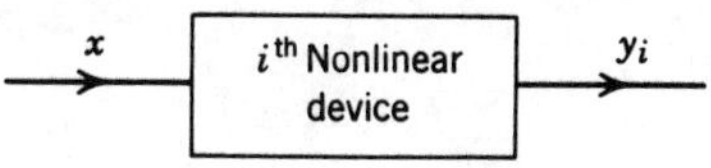

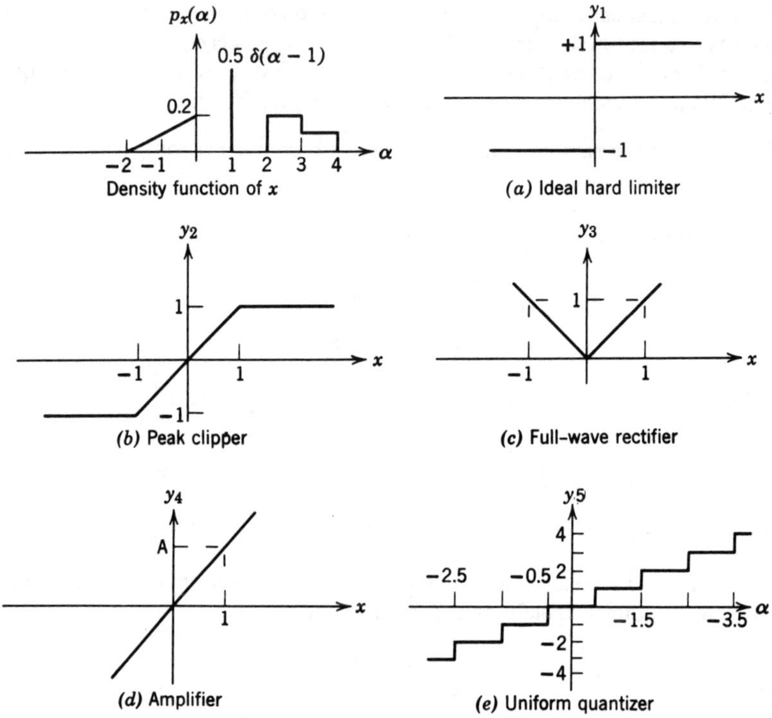

Figure P2.18

2.19 Let x and y be statistically independent random variables with the probability density functions

$$p_x(\alpha) = \begin{cases} \dfrac{1}{\pi\sqrt{1-\alpha^2}}; & -1 \leqslant \alpha \leqslant 1, \\ 0; & \text{elsewhere.} \end{cases}$$

$$p_y(\beta) = \begin{cases} \beta e^{-\beta^2/2}; & \beta \geqslant 0, \\ 0; & \text{elsewhere.} \end{cases}$$

Show that the product $z = xy$ has a Gaussian density function.

2.20 A noise process is studied and the probability that k "zero-crossings" occur in a time interval $[0, \alpha]$ is denoted $P(k, \alpha)$. For example, exactly three "zero-crossings" occur in the time interval $[0, 3]$ for the noise waveform pictured. For all values of α

$$\sum_{k=0}^{\infty} P(k, \alpha) = 1.$$

Let the random variable τ denote the time at which the first zero crossing occurs in the interval $[0, \infty]$. Express p_τ in terms of $P(k, \alpha)$. *Hint.* First calculate $F_\tau(\alpha)$, the probability distribution function of τ evaluated at α.

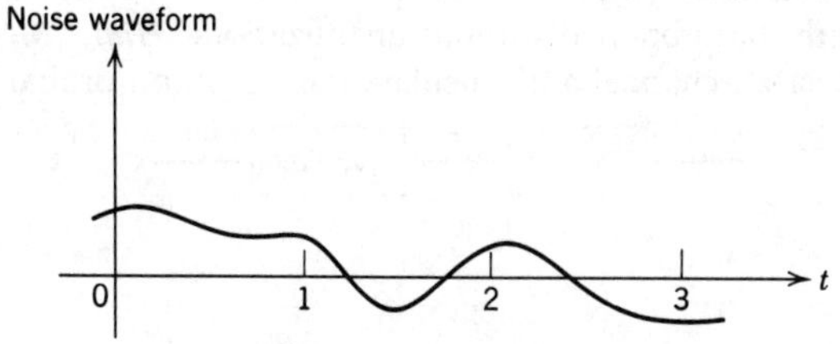

Figure P2.20

2.21 A random variable y with density function

$$p_y(\alpha) = \begin{cases} b\alpha^{-(1+b)}; & \alpha \geqslant 1, \\ 0; & \alpha < 1, \end{cases}$$

is obtained by means of a transformation $y = f(x)$ from the random variable x with density function

$$p_x(\alpha) = \begin{cases} e^{-\alpha}; & \alpha \geqslant 0, \\ 0\ ; & \alpha < 0. \end{cases}$$

Determine a reversible transformation f compatible with the specified density functions.

2.22 Let x and y be statistically independent random variables. New random variables u and v are defined by

$$u = ax + b,$$

$$v = cy + d,$$

where a, b, c, and d are constants. Show that the random variables u and v are also statistically independent.

2.23 A communication system is used to transmit one of two equally likely messages, m_0 and m_1. The channel output is a continuous random variable r, the conditional density functions of which are shown in Fig. P2.23. Determine the optimum receiver decision rule and compute the resulting probability of error.

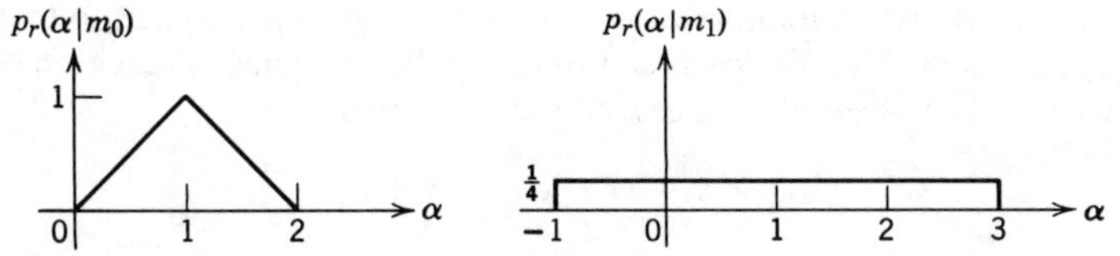

Figure P2.23

2.24 The communication system of Problem 2.23 is now modified by the insertion of a quantizer at the channel output as illustrated in Fig. P2.24. Determine the optimum decision rule for estimating the transmitted message on the basis of the quantizer output r'. Compute the resulting probability of error and compare with that obtained without quantization. *Hint.* Make a discrete model for the over-all channel and calculate the transition probabilities.

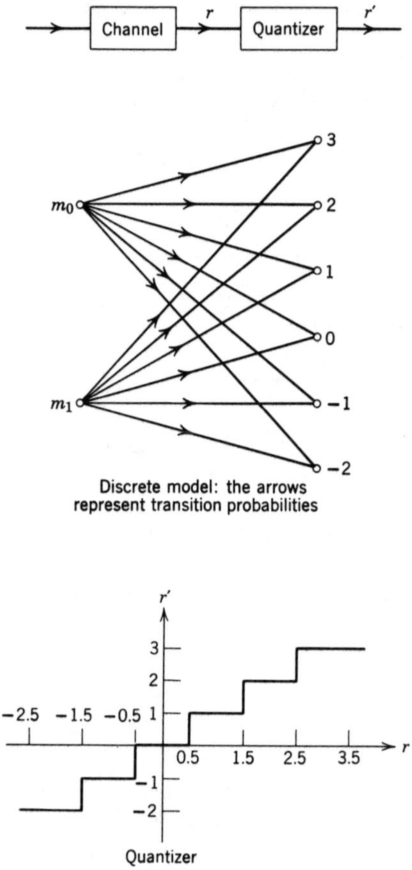

Figure P2.24

2.25 A "diversity" communication system employs two channels to transmit a voltage s to a decision device as shown in Fig. P2.25. Thus the decision device has available two received voltages, r_1 and r_2, in which

$$r_1 = s + n_1, \qquad r_2 = s + n_2.$$

Assume that n_1 and n_2 are zero-mean Gaussian random variables with variances σ_1^2 and σ_2^2 and that s, n_1, and n_2 are jointly statistically independent. The

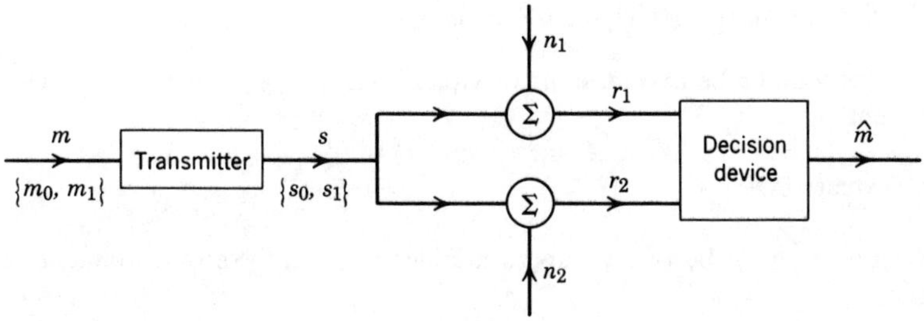

Figure P2.25

system is used to communicate one of two messages m_0 and m_1 with a priori probabilities $P[m_0]$ and $P[m_1]$. For message m_l the signal is

$$s = (-1)^l \sqrt{E}; \qquad l = 0, 1.$$

The optimum decision rule seeks to determine that l for which the a posteriori (conditional) probability of m_l, given r_1 and r_2, is maximum.

a. Determine the structure of the optimum decision device and calculate the resulting probability of error.

b. Compare this result for $\sigma_1 = \sigma_2$ and $P[m_0] = P[m_1]$ with the performance obtained with an optimum decision based only on r_1.

2.26 Derive the inequality

$$Q(\alpha) \triangleq \int_\alpha^\infty \frac{1}{\sqrt{2\pi}} e^{-\beta^2/2}\, d\beta \leqslant \frac{1}{2} e^{-\alpha^2/2}; \qquad \alpha \geqslant 0.$$

For what value of α does the equality hold? For what values of α is this bound tighter than the inequality

$$Q(\alpha) \leqslant \frac{1}{\sqrt{2\pi}\alpha} e^{-\alpha^2/2}\ ?$$

For what values of α are the two bounds both within 10% of the true value of $Q(\alpha)$? *Hint*. Identify $[Q(\alpha)]^2$ as the probability that a pair x, y of independent zero-mean, unit-variance Gaussian random variables lies within the shaded region of (*a*) in Fig. P2.26. Observe that this probability is exceeded by the

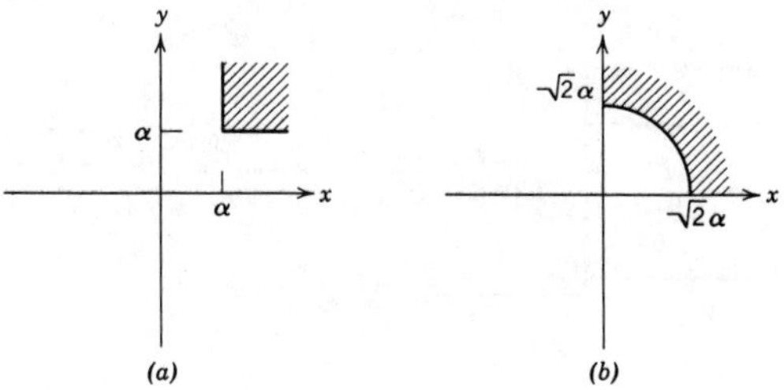

Figure P2.26

probability that x, y lies within the shaded region of (*b*). Evaluate this last probability by means of a change of variables.

2.27 Let y and z be two random variables such that $E[(y - z)^2] = 0$. Define the event

$$A = \{\omega:\ y(\omega) \neq z(\omega)\}$$

and evaluate $P[A]$.

2.28 Let x and y be two random variables with finite second moments and define

$$z = x + y.$$

Prove that

$$\sigma_x^2 + \sigma_y^2 - 2\sigma_x\sigma_y \leqslant \sigma_z^2 \leqslant \sigma_x^2 + \sigma_y^2 + 2\sigma_x\sigma_y,$$

hence

$$\sigma_z^2 \leqslant 2(\sigma_x^2 + \sigma_y^2).$$

2.29 Let x be any random variable for which the two conditions

$$p_x(\alpha) = 0; \qquad \alpha < 0$$

$$\bar{x} \triangleq \int_{-\infty}^{\infty} \alpha\, p_x(\alpha)\, d\alpha < \infty$$

are met. Prove that for all $k > 0$

$$P[x \geqslant k\bar{x}] \leqslant \frac{1}{k}.$$

Is there an acceptable density function p_x for which the equality holds true?

2.30 Let $x_1, x_2, \ldots, x_n$ be a set of N identically distributed statistically independent random variables, each with density function p_x and distribution function F_x. As shown in Fig. P2.30, these variables are applied as the inputs to a box that selects as its output, y_N, the *largest* of the $\{x_i\}$. Clearly, y_N is a random variable.

a. Express p_{y_N} in terms of N, p_x, and F_x.

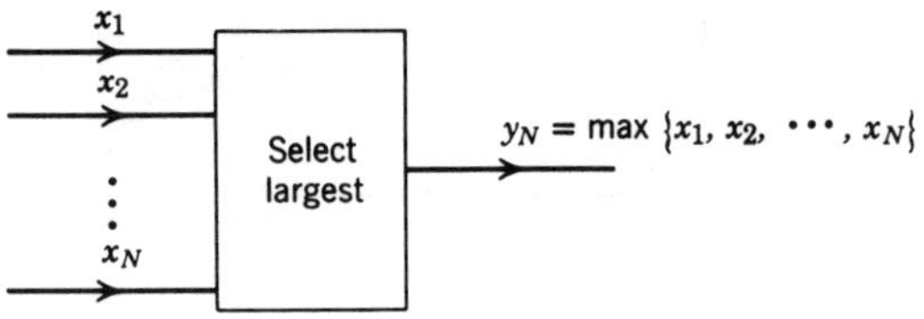

Figure P2.30

b. Assume that the x_i are exponentially distributed random variables:

$$p_x(\alpha) = \begin{cases} e^{-\alpha}; & \alpha \geqslant 0, \\ 0; & \alpha < 0. \end{cases}$$

Calculate the expectation $\bar{y}_N$ for $N = 1, 2$.

Discussion. It can be shown that the general expression for $\bar{y}_N$ in part *b* is

$$\bar{y}_N = \sum_{j=1}^{N} \frac{1}{j}.$$

In certain communication situations involving diversity transmission over independent Rayleigh-fading paths (see Chapter 7) x_i would represent the energy received over the ith path. (Show that the square of a Rayleigh random variable is exponentially distributed.) A "selection diversity" receiver selects the path with the largest energy. We observe that the mean energy of this path, $\bar{y}_N$, increases to infinity as $N \to \infty$. The incremental advantage of adding another diversity channel, however, decreases rapidly as N becomes large.

2.31 Let x be a random variable with mean $\bar{x}$, variance σ_x^2, and characteristic function $M_x(\nu)$. Define

$$y \triangleq ax + b; \qquad a \text{ and } b \text{ constants.}$$

Determine $\bar{y}$, σ_y^2, and $M_y(\nu)$ in terms of $\bar{x}$, σ_x^2, $M_x(\nu)$, a, and b.

2.32 Let x and y be statistically independent random variables with the probability density functions $p_x(\alpha) = p_y(\alpha) = \frac{1}{2}e^{-|\alpha|}$.

a. Calculate the nth moment, $E[x^n]$, of x.
b. Calculate the nth absolute moment, $E[|x|^n]$, of x.
c. Determine the characteristic function of x.
d. Determine and plot the probability density of the sum $z = x + y$.
e. Calculate the probability that x is greater than y.

2.33 A random variable x has characteristic function

$$M_x(\nu) = k\left(\frac{\sin \nu}{\nu}\right)^6.$$

a. Evaluate the constant k.
b. Calculate $\bar{x}$.
c. If $y = x + m$, where m is a constant, calculate $M_y(\nu)$.

2.34 A random variable x which takes on only integer values is said to be "Poisson distributed" if

$$p_x(\alpha) = \sum_{m=0}^{\infty} \delta(\alpha - m)\frac{\lambda^m e^{-\lambda}}{m!}.$$

Plot p_x for $\lambda = 2$, $m \leqslant 5$.

a. Find $\bar{x}$, σ_x^2, and $M_x(\nu)$.
b. Let x and y be statistically independent Poisson variables with constants λ_x and λ_y. Define $z = x + y$. Express p_z, $\bar{z}$, and σ_z^2 in terms of λ_x and λ_y.

2.35 The random variables x_1 and x_2 have the joint density function

$$p_{x_1,x_2}(\alpha_1, \alpha_2) = \frac{1}{\pi^2} \frac{b_1 b_2}{(b_1^2 + \alpha_1^2)(b_2^2 + \alpha_2^2)}; \qquad b_1, b_2 > 0.$$

a. Show that x_1 and x_2 are statistically independent random variables with Cauchy density functions (see Eq. 2.48a).

b. Prove that $M_{x_1}(\nu) = e^{-b_1|\nu|}$.

c. Define $y = x_1 + x_2$. Determine p_y.

d. Let $\{z_i\}$ be a set of N statistically independent Cauchy random variables with $b_i = b$, $i = 1, 2, \ldots, N$. Define

$$z = \frac{1}{N} \sum_{i=1}^{N} z_i.$$

Determine p_z. Is z—which is called the sample mean—a good estimate of the true mean

$$m \triangleq \bar{z}_i.$$

2.36 Let $\{x_i\}$ be a set of N statistically independent random variables and define

$$y = \sum_{i=1}^{N} x_i.$$

a. Which of the following statements are always true? Prove or give a counter example.

(i) $$\bar{y} = \sum_{i=1}^{N} \bar{x}_i.$$

(ii) $$\overline{y_2} = \sum_{i=1}^{N} \overline{x_i^2}.$$

(iii) $$\overline{y^3} = \sum_{i=1}^{N} \overline{x_i^3}.$$

(iv) $$M_y(\nu) = \sum_{i=1}^{N} M_{x_i}(\nu).$$

(v) $$\sigma_y^2 = \sum_{i=1}^{N} \sigma_{x_i}^2.$$

(vi) $$[\overline{y^3} - 3\overline{y^2}\bar{y} + 2\bar{y}^3] = \sum_{i=1}^{N} [\overline{x_i^3} - 3\,\overline{x_i^2}\,\overline{x_i} + 2\bar{x}_i^3].$$

The combination in brackets in (vi) is called the third *semi-invariant moment*. In part b we consider the general form of semi-invariant moments.

b. Define $\mu_y(\nu) \triangleq \ln M_y(\nu)$ and $\mu_i(\nu) \triangleq \ln M_{x_i}(\nu)$.

(i) Show that $$\mu_y(\nu) = \sum_{i=1}^{N} \mu_i(\nu).$$

Assuming that all moments exist, we may expand $\mu_y(\nu)$ and $\mu_i(\nu)$ in a Taylor series:

$$\mu_y(\nu) = \sum_{j=0}^{\infty} a_j \frac{\nu^j}{j!}$$

$$\mu_i(\nu) = \sum_{j=0}^{\infty} a_{ij} \frac{\nu^j}{j!}.$$

Equating coefficients of equal powers of ν, we obtain

$$a_j = \sum_{i=1}^{N} a_{ij}.$$

Thus the jth coefficient in the expansion for a sum of N independent random variables is the sum of the jth coefficients of the constituents. The jth coefficient is called the jth semi-invariant moment and μ_y is called the semi-invariant moment generating function.

(ii) Evaluate a_0, a_1, a_2, and a_3 in terms of the moments of y.

2.37 a. Prove that

$$\mathrm{P}[|x - \bar{x}| \geqslant \epsilon] \leqslant \frac{\overline{(x - \bar{x})^4}}{\epsilon^4}$$

for any random variable x with $\overline{x^4} < \infty$.

b. Assume that x is a Gaussian random variable and let $\epsilon = k\sigma$. Determine the range of k for which the bound of part a is tighter than the Chebyshev bound.

c. Why is the bound of part a not so useful as the Chebyshev bound in proving the weak law of large numbers? *Hint.* Show that, in general,

$$\overline{(x - \bar{x})^4} \neq \sum_{i=1}^{N} \overline{(y_i - \bar{y})^4},$$

where $x \triangleq \sum_{i=1}^{N} y_i$ and the $\{y_i\}$ are statistically independent identically distributed random variables.

2.38 We wish to simulate a communication system on a digital computer and estimate the error probability by measuring the relative frequency of error. Approximate by means of

a. the Chebyshev inequality,
b. the central limit theorem,
c. the Chernoff bound,

how many independent uses of the channel we must simulate in order to be 99.9% certain that the observed relative frequency lies within 5% of the true $\mathrm{P}[\mathcal{E}]$, which we may assume is less than 0.01.

2.39 One of the two equally likely messages is transmitted over a noisy channel by means of the following strategy. If m_0 is the message, the transmitter sends a sequence of N voltage pulses over the channel, each with amplitude $\sqrt{E}$. If

m_1 is the message, N voltage pulses with amplitude $-\sqrt{E}$ are sent. The effect of the channel is to add a (different) statistically independent Gaussian random variable to each amplitude. Thus the channel output is a sequence of N amplitudes

$$r_i = s + n_i; \qquad i = 1, 2, \ldots, N,$$

where $s = +\sqrt{E}$ if the message is m_0 and $s = -\sqrt{E}$ otherwise. Assume for all i that

$$\bar{n}_i = 0; \qquad \overline{n_i^2} = \sigma^2.$$

a. The receiver calculates

$$y = \sum_{i=1}^{N} r_i$$

and sets $\hat{m} = m_0$ if and only if $y > 0$. [We shall see in Chapter 4 that such a receiver is optimum.] Determine the resulting $P[\mathcal{E}]$ and show that

$$P[\mathcal{E}] < e^{-NE/2\sigma^2}.$$

b. A suboptimum receiver makes an independent binary decision about m on the basis of each r_i in turn. Let p denote the minimum attainable probability that any such decision is wrong. Obtain an expression for p. The receiver then forms the sum

$$x = \sum_{i=1}^{N} x_i,$$

where $x_i \triangleq -1$ if the ith decision favors m_1 and $x_i \triangleq +1$ if the ith decision favors m_0. Thus $P[x_i = 1 \mid m_1] = p$ for all i independently. The receiver sets $\hat{m} = m_0$ if $x > 0$ and $\hat{m} = m_1$ if $x \leqslant 0$. Use Chernoff bounding techniques to show that

$$P[\mathcal{E}] < e^{-N[-\ln\sqrt{4p(1-p)}]}.$$

Show that

$$p \gtrsim \tfrac{1}{2} - \sqrt{E/2\pi\sigma^2}$$

when E/σ^2 is very small, so that the probability of error bound in part b then becomes

$$P[\mathcal{E}] < e^{-(NE/2\sigma^2)(2/\pi)}.$$

Comparing this bound with that of part a, we see that the effect of making individual decisions is to multiply E by the factor $2/\pi$ (≈ -2 db).

3

Random Waveforms

We have considered so far how to make the optimum decision about which message is transmitted when a receiver's front end and detector are fixed. With reference to Fig. 3.1, this problem involves limiting our observation of what is received to a quantized voltage sample at point a, or to an unquantized voltage sample at point a'. The decision rules

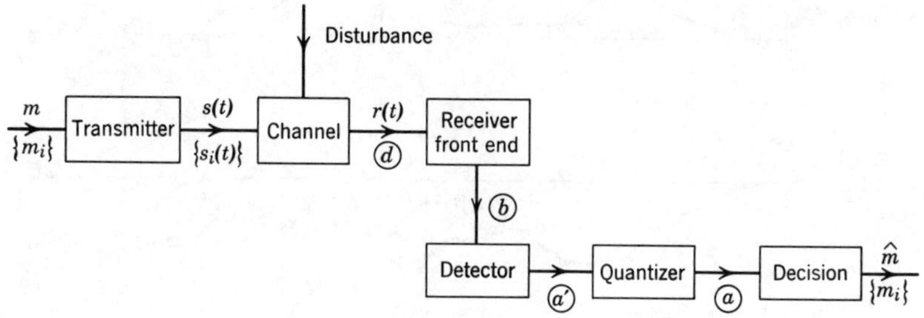

Figure 3.1 A communication system model with a finite number of input messages $\{m_i\}$, $i = 0, 1, \ldots, M - 1$.

established in Chapter 2 are therefore optimum only in the limited sense that they produce the smallest possible probability of error, given that we *cannot redesign* the way in which the receiver obtains the voltage at point a' from the random received waveform $r(t)$. To design a receiver that is optimum in an over-all sense, we must focus back on points b and d and investigate the problem of dealing directly with *random time functions,* instead of just with random voltages.

In this chapter we consider those mathematical aspects of random waveforms that are essential to our study of this problem. As in Chapter 2, the primary objective is to develop the engineering import.

3.1 RANDOM PROCESSES

The appropriate mathematical model for dealing with unpredictable voltages involves the concept of a *random variable*, x, defined as the assignment of a real number $x(\omega)$ to each point ω of a sample space in such a way that a probability distribution function F_x exists. Unpredictable waveforms are dealt with in a similar way: instead of only a single number, however, we now assign to each point ω in Ω a real *time function*, say $x(\omega, t)$. The situation is illustrated in Fig. 3.2, which shows

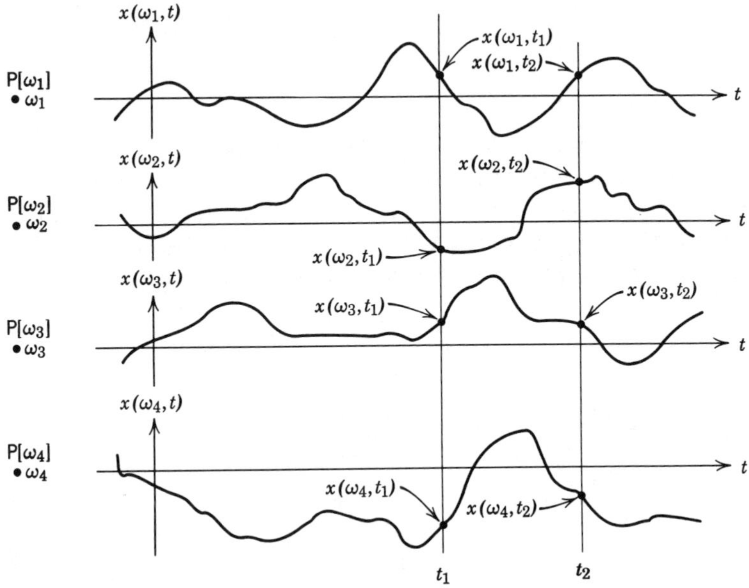

Figure 3.2 A simple random process.

a finite sample space Ω with four points, and four waveforms, labeled

$$x(\omega_i, t); \qquad i = 1, 2, 3, 4.$$

Now let us think of observing this set of waveforms at some time instant, $t = t_1$, as shown in the figure. Since each point ω_i of Ω has associated with it both a number $x(\omega_i, t_1)$ and a probability, the collection of numbers $\{x(\omega_i, t_1)\}$, $i = 1, 2, 3, 4$, forms a random variable. Observing the waveforms at a second time instant, say t_2, yields a different collection of numbers, hence a different random variable. Indeed, this set of four waveforms defines a (different) random variable for each choice of observation instant.

In general, we are interested in the case in which Ω contains an infinite number of points ω, and the set of waveforms $\{x(\omega, t)\}$ is correspondingly rich. For example, $\{x(\omega, t)\}$ might include *every* real waveform defined on $[-\infty < t < \infty]$. Just as with finite Ω, we presume that the collection of waveforms, together with the probability assignment, defines a random variable for each choice of observation instant.

The probability system composed of sample space, set of waveforms, and probability measure is called a *random process* and is denoted by a symbol such as $x(t)$. The individual waveforms of a random process $x(t)$ are called *sample functions*, and the particular sample function associated with the point ω is denoted $x(\omega, t)$. Naming a random process $x(t)$ and denoting the sample function associated with the point ω as $x(\omega, t)$ corresponds to our previous practice of naming a random variable x and denoting the sample value associated with the point ω as $x(\omega)$. We shall find it convenient to use the notation $x(t)$ in two different senses: first (as above) to denote the random process and second to denote the random variable obtained by observing the random process at time t. Whenever the sense is not clear from the context, we write $x(t_i)$ or x_i to denote the random variable observed at time t_i.

Interpretation of the Random-Process Model

Let us consider how the random-process model enters into the problem of designing a receiver such as that diagrammed in Fig. 3.1. First, which of the set of possible transmitter waveforms $\{s_i(t)\}$ is actually transmitted depends on the random input message m. We note immediately that the signal $s(t)$ is a random process with a finite number of sample functions; the probability that $s(t)$ equals $s_i(t)$ is $P[m_i]$.

Next, consider the channel. Let us assume that nature, in some way that we can describe only probabilistically, selects one member of a set containing all possible disturbing waveforms and adds it to $s(t)$. The appropriate mathematical model then involves a sample space Ω on which three random processes and the random input message are defined simultaneously: associated with any particular sample point ω is a message, say m_i, the transmitter signal $s(\omega, t) = s_i(t)$, one of the possible noise waveforms, say $n(\omega, t)$, and the received waveform

$$r(\omega, t) = s(\omega, t) + n(\omega, t). \tag{3.1a}$$

Since Eq. 3.1a holds for every point ω, we write

$$r(t) = s(t) + n(t), \tag{3.1b}$$

where $r(t)$, $s(t)$, and $n(t)$ are random processes. Over Ω the entire set $\{r(\omega, t)\}$ exhausts all possible pairs of noise and signal waveforms.

The problem confronting us when designing the receiver illustrated in Fig. 3.1 may now be stated. We look on the random process $r(t)$ as a black box (encompassing the message source, transmitter, and channel) at whose output terminals *one* of the time functions $r(\omega, t)$ appears. In effect, some hidden mechanism within the box selects a point ω at random and emits the corresponding sample function. The receiver must operate on this sample function—whichever one it may be—in some fixed way to produce an estimate of the message. The crux of the problem is that we must specify the receiver operations in advance, whereas we cannot know in advance which sample function will appear.

Given a fixed receiver design, it is clear that some of the $r(\omega, t)$ will lead to a correct estimate of the message and some will not. Let us denote the set of sample points ω that leads to an incorrect estimate by the symbol $\mathcal{E}$:

$$\mathcal{E} \triangleq \{\omega : r(\omega, t) \Rightarrow \text{error}\}.$$

Our objective is to design the receiver in such a way that the probability of this event, that is, the probability of error $P[\mathcal{E}]$, will be minimum. The subject of Chapter 4 is how to design such a receiver in certain important cases. First, however, we must develop appropriate mathematical techniques for doing so. Accordingly, we now return to the discussion of random processes.

Random Vectors Obtained from Random Processes

By definition, a random process implies the existence of an infinite number of random variables, one for each t in the range $-\infty < t < \infty$. Thus we may speak of the probability density function $p_{x(t_1)}$ of the random variable $x(t_1)$ obtained by observing the random process $x(t)$ at time t_1. More generally, for k time instants $t_1, t_2, \ldots, t_k$ we define the k random variables $x(t_1), x(t_2), \ldots, x(t_k)$ and denote their joint density function by $p_{\mathbf{x}(\mathbf{t})}$, in which we introduce the notation

$$\mathbf{x}(\mathbf{t}) \triangleq (x(t_1), x(t_2), \ldots, x(t_k)). \tag{3.2a}$$

The components of the random vector $\mathbf{x}(\mathbf{t})$ associated with any particular sample point ω are the values of the sample function $x(\omega, t)$ observed at times $t_1, t_2, \ldots, t_k$:

$$\mathbf{x}(\omega, \mathbf{t}) \triangleq (x(\omega, t_1), x(\omega, t_2), \ldots, x(\omega, t_k)). \tag{3.2b}$$

Note that the density function $p_{\mathbf{x}(\mathbf{t})}$ depends on the random process $x(t)$ and the specific time instants $\{t_j\}$.

As an application consider the probability of obtaining a waveform that passes through a set of k "windows", as in Fig. 3.3; that is, the probability of the event

$$A = \{\omega : a_i < x(\omega, t_i) \leqslant b_i;\ i = 1, \ldots, k\}. \tag{3.3a}$$

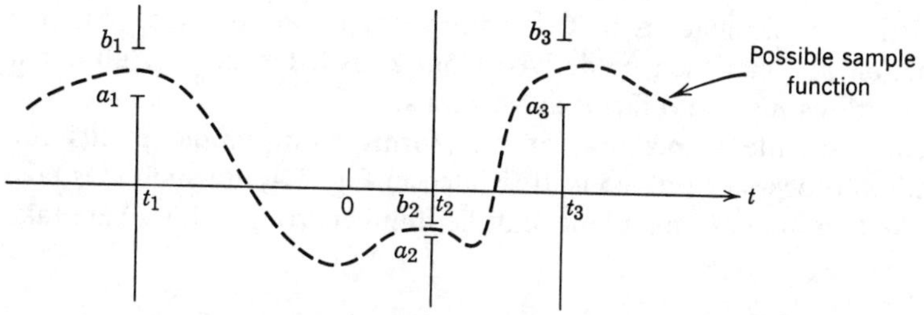

Figure 3.3 The probability of the event $\{\omega: a_1 < x(\omega, t_1) \leqslant b_1, a_2 < x(\omega, t_2) \leqslant b_2, a_3 < x(\omega, t_3) \leqslant b_3\}$ is the probability of the set of sample functions which pass through the windows.

This probability is

$$P[A] = \int_{a_1}^{b_1} \int_{a_2}^{b_2} \cdots \int_{a_k}^{b_k} p_{\mathbf{x}(\mathbf{t})}(\boldsymbol{\alpha})\, d\boldsymbol{\alpha}. \tag{3.3b}$$

In a similar way, we can calculate the probability of any event defined in terms of a finite number of time instants.†

Specification of Random Processes

We say that a random process $x(t)$ is *specified* if and only if a rule is given or implied for determining the joint probability density function $p_{\mathbf{x}(\mathbf{t})}$ for *any finite* set of observation instants $(t_1, t_2, \ldots, t_k)$.

In application, we encounter three methods of specification. The first and simplest is to state the rule directly. For this to be practical the joint density function must depend in a known, elementary way on the time instants. An important example of this method is the Gaussian process, on which we shall concentrate after discussing filtered impulse noise.

For the second method a time function involving one or more parameters is given; for example,

$$g(t) = r \sin(2\pi t + \theta). \tag{3.4}$$

The parameters r and θ are then taken to be random variables, with a specified joint density function $p_{r,\theta}$. The sample functions of the random process $x(t)$ are then

$$x(\omega, t) = r(\omega) \sin[2\pi t + \theta(\omega)]; \qquad \text{all } \omega \text{ in } \Omega, \tag{3.5}$$

† It is not possible in general to calculate directly the probability of events defined in terms of an infinite number of time instants, such as the event B defined by

$$B = \{\omega: x(\omega, t) \leqslant 0 \text{ for all } t \text{ in the interval } [0, 1]\}.$$

Probabilities of this sort can be calculated only indirectly in the limit as k becomes infinite of expressions similar to Eq. 3.3b.

and the sample space is that on which r and θ are defined. Any density function $p_{\mathbf{x(t)}}$ can then be derived from knowledge of $p_{r,\theta}$, although the calculations may be difficult and tedious.

One possible association of waveforms with sample points for the random process of Eq. 3.5 is illustrated in Fig. 3.4, in which Ω is taken to be the two-dimensional plane and the numbers $r(\omega)$ and $\theta(\omega)$ are taken to

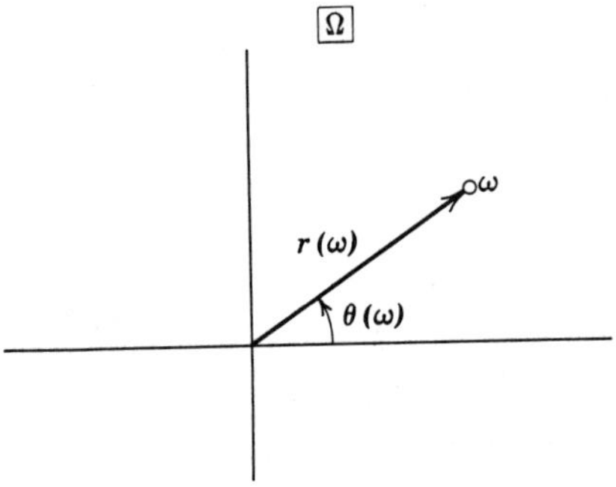

Figure 3.4 Random variables r and θ defined as the polar coordinates of each sample point ω when Ω is a plane.

be the location of the point ω in polar coordinates. A possible joint probability density function is

$$p_{r,\theta}(\alpha, \beta) = \begin{cases} \dfrac{\alpha}{2\pi} e^{-\alpha^2/2}; & 0 \leqslant \alpha < \infty, 0 \leqslant \beta < 2\pi, \\ 0; & \text{otherwise.} \end{cases} \tag{3.6}$$

The third method of specifying a random process is to generate its ensemble by applying a stated operation to the sample functions of a known process. A trivial example is the definition of a new process, say $y(t)$, as the time translate of a given process, say $x(t)$:

$$y(\omega, t) = x(\omega, t + T); \qquad \text{all } \omega \text{ in } \Omega. \tag{3.7}$$

In this case any density function for the new process may be written immediately in terms of the corresponding (known) density function of the original; the random vector

$$\mathbf{y(t)} = (y(t_1), y(t_2), \ldots, y(t_k)) \tag{3.8a}$$

is equal for every sample point to the random vector $\mathbf{x(t + T)}$, where

$$\mathbf{x(t + T)} \triangleq (x(t_1 + T), x(t_2 + T), \ldots, x(t_k + T)). \tag{3.8b}$$

Thus

$$\mathbf{y(t)} = \mathbf{x(t + T)} \tag{3.8c}$$

and

$$p_{y(t)} = p_{x(t+T)}. \tag{3.9}$$

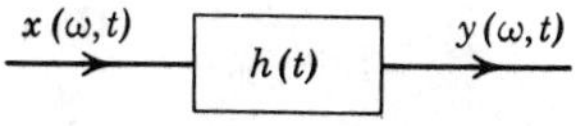

Figure 3.5 The random process $x(t)$ is transformed into $y(t)$ by passing each sample function $x(\omega, t)$ through the linear filter.

A more interesting example of the third method, and one that we shall often encounter, is linear filtering. A new random process $y(t)$ can be obtained by passing the sample functions of a given process, $x(t)$, through a linear filter with impulse response $h(t)$, as shown in Fig. 3.5. The sample functions of the two processes are then related by the convolution integral

$$y(\omega, t) = \int_{-\infty}^{\infty} h(t - \alpha)\, x(\omega, \alpha)\, d\alpha; \text{ all } \omega \text{ in } \Omega. \tag{3.10a}$$

More concisely, we write

$$y(t) = \int_{-\infty}^{\infty} h(t - \alpha)\, x(\alpha)\, d\alpha. \tag{3.10b}$$

In general, it is difficult to determine a density function for the process $y(t)$ from knowledge of the density functions of the process $x(t)$, although when $x(t)$ is a Gaussian process we shall see that doing so is simple.

Stationary Random Processes

In dealing with random waveforms in the real world, we often notice that statistical properties of interest are relatively independent of the time at which observation of the waveform is begun. For example, the empirical average of N consecutive samples taken at 1-sec intervals may be insensitive to the precise time at which the first sample is taken.

A *stationary random process* is defined as one for which all density functions are independent of absolute time reference (time origin). Thus a process $x(t)$ is stationary if, for *every* finite set of time instants $\{t_i\}$, $i = 1, 2, \ldots, k$, and for *every* constant, T,

$$p_{x(t+T)} = p_{x(t)}. \tag{3.11}$$

The notation is that defined in Eq. 3.8.

One implication of stationariness is that the *probability* of the set of sample functions which passes through the windows of Fig. 3.6 is equal to the *probability* of the set of sample functions which passes through the corresponding time-translated windows. It is *not* necessarily true that the two sets consist of the same sample functions.

A second implication of stationariness is that ensemble averages can be associated with the entire process rather than only with the process evaluated at some particular instant of time. For example, a stationary

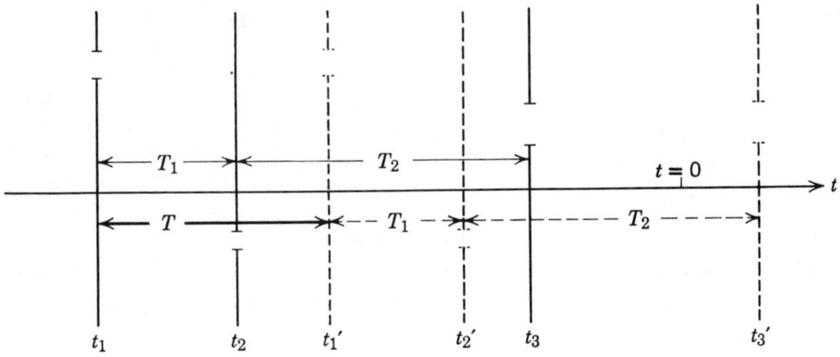

Figure 3.6 Three windows and their time-translates ($t_i' = t_i + T$; $i = 1, 2, 3$).

process $x(t)$ can be said to have a mean value $\bar{x}$ or a second moment $\overline{x^2}$ without specifying the instant of observation t:

$$\mathrm{E}[x(t)] = \bar{x}; \qquad \text{all } t \tag{3.12a}$$

$$\mathrm{E}[x^2(t)] = \overline{x^2}; \qquad \text{all } t. \tag{3.12b}$$

That this is so follows directly from Eq. 3.11. For any two observation instants, t_1 and t_2, we have

$$p_{x(t_1)} = p_{x(t_2)}$$

and thus for any n

$$\mathrm{E}[x^n(t_1)] \triangleq \int_{-\infty}^{\infty} \alpha^n \, p_{x(t_1)}(\alpha) \, d\alpha = \int_{-\infty}^{\infty} \alpha^n \, p_{x(t_2)}(\alpha) \, d\alpha$$

$$\triangleq \mathrm{E}[x^n(t_2)]. \tag{3.12c}$$

More generally, it follows from the theorem of expectation (Eq. 2.126) that the average of any time-invariant function g defined on k samples from a stationary process $x(t)$ is independent of time origin:

$$\overline{g(\mathbf{x(t)})} = \int g(\boldsymbol{\alpha}) \, p_{\mathbf{x(t)}}(\boldsymbol{\alpha}) \, d\boldsymbol{\alpha} = \int g(\boldsymbol{\alpha}) \, p_{\mathbf{x(t+T)}}(\boldsymbol{\alpha}) \, d\boldsymbol{\alpha}$$

$$= \overline{g(\mathbf{x(t+T)})}. \tag{3.12d}$$

A simple example of a stationary random process is the ensemble of waveforms $\{f(t + \tau)\}$ generated from the periodic ramp $f(t)$ shown in Fig. 3.7 by taking τ to be a random variable with the uniform density function

$$p_\tau(\beta) = \begin{cases} \dfrac{1}{T}; & 0 \leqslant \beta \leqslant T, \\ 0; & \text{elsewhere,} \end{cases} \tag{3.13}$$

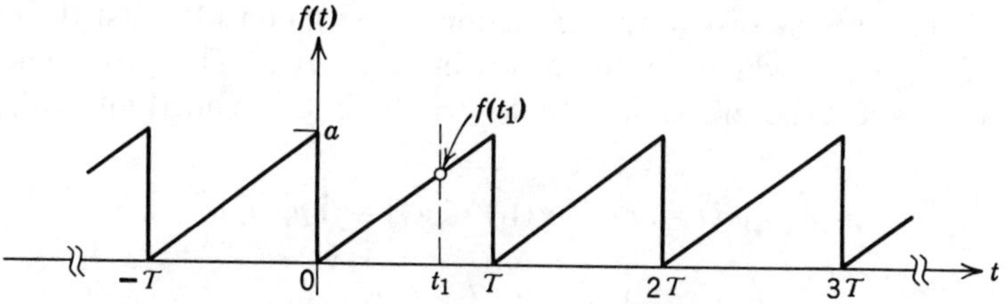

Figure 3.7 A periodic ramp function.

where T is the period of $f(t)$. As a first step in proving that this process, say $x(t)$, is stationary, we demonstrate that the random variables obtained by sampling $x(t)$ at times t_1 and $(t_1 + T)$ have the same density function, independent of T and t_1:

$$p_{x(t_1)} = p_{x(t_1+T)}.$$

The sample function $x(\omega_0, t)$ is illustrated in Fig. 3.8 for a sample point ω_0 such that $\tau(\omega_0) = \tau_0$. Over Ω the random variable τ takes on every value in the interval $[0, T]$; correspondingly, the random variable $x(t_1)$ takes on every value in the interval $[0, a]$. The transformation from τ to $x(t_1)$ is shown in Fig. 3.9.

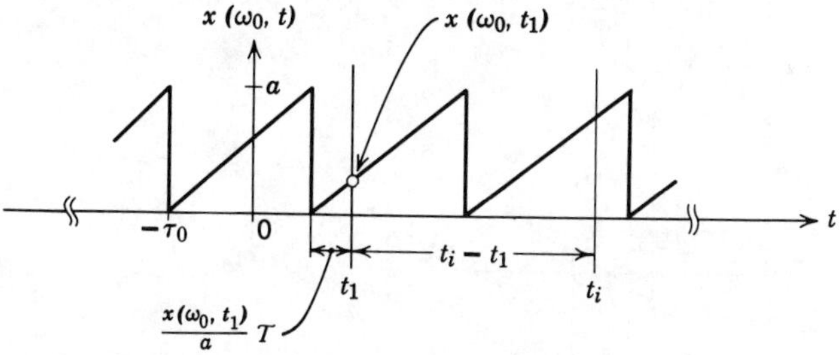

Figure 3.8 When $\tau(\omega_0) = \tau_0$, the sample function $x(\omega_0, t)$ is $f(t + \tau_0)$.

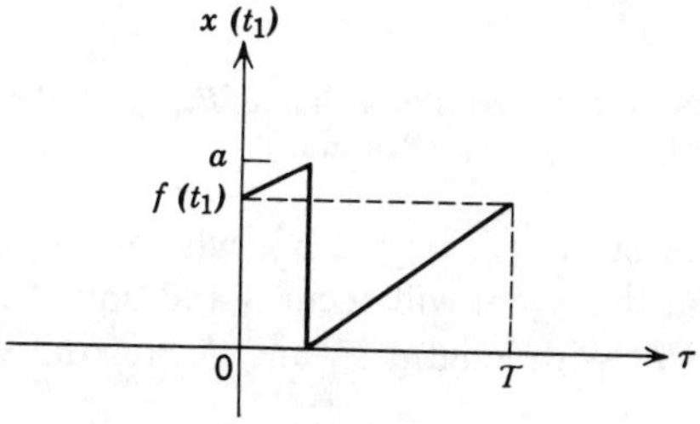

Figure 3.9 The transformation relating the random variables τ and $x(t_1)$ is obtained from Fig. 3.7 by holding t_1 fixed and shifting $f(t)$ to the left by the amount τ.

To determine the distribution function of $x(t_1)$, consider first the event $\{\tau: x(t_1) \leqslant \alpha\}$, in which α is as shown in Fig. 3.10*a*. The probability of this event is just the probability that τ will lie in the shaded interval, I_0.

$$F_{x(t_1)}(\alpha) = \mathrm{P}[\{\tau: x(t_1) \leqslant \alpha\}] = \int_{I_0} p_\tau(\beta)\, d\beta$$
$$= \frac{1}{T}\int_{I_0} d\beta = \frac{T_0}{T} = \frac{\alpha}{a},$$

where T_0 denotes the length of the interval I_0.

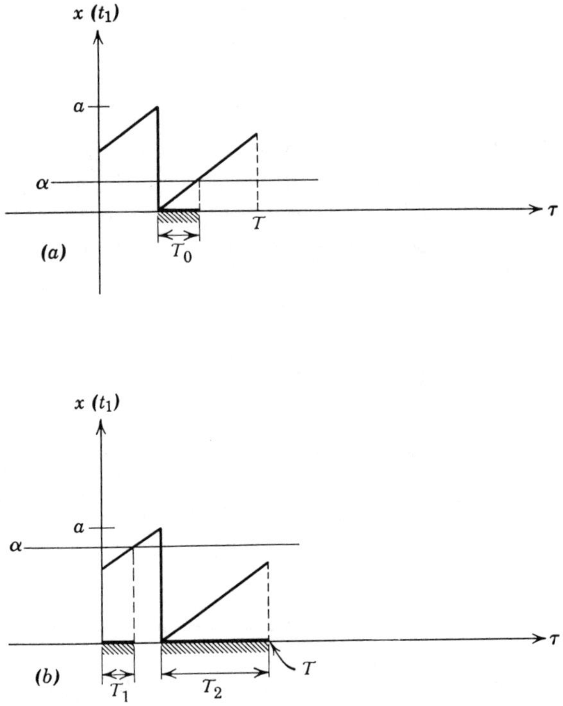

Figure 3.10 The geometrical relations determining $F_{x(t_1)}(\alpha)$; the interval I_0 is shaded in (*a*) and the intervals I_1 and I_2 are shaded in (*b*).

Next consider the event $\{\tau: x(t_1) \leqslant \alpha\}$, where α is as shown in Fig. 3.10*b*. It is clear that this event will occur if and only if τ lies in one of the two intervals I_1 and I_2, with lengths T_1 and T_2, respectively. Thus,

$$F_{x(t_1)}(\alpha) = \frac{T_1 + T_2}{T} = \frac{\alpha}{a}.$$

Since for any α, $0 \leqslant \alpha \leqslant a$, the event $\{\tau: x(t_1) \leqslant \alpha\}$ can occur only as shown either in Fig. 3.10*a* or *b*, we have

$$F_{x(t_1)}(\alpha) = \begin{cases} 0; & \alpha < 0, \\ \dfrac{\alpha}{a}; & 0 \leqslant \alpha \leqslant a, \\ 1; & a < \alpha. \end{cases}$$

Differentiating with respect to α yields

$$p_{x(t_1)}(\alpha) = \begin{cases} \dfrac{1}{a}; & 0 \leqslant \alpha \leqslant a, \\ 0; & \text{elsewhere.} \end{cases} \tag{3.14}$$

Finally, we observe that the derivation of Eq. 3.14 is independent of the observation instant t_1 and therefore must yield the same result when carried through for $x(t_1 + T)$. Thus

$$p_{x(t_1+T)} = p_{x(t_1)} \qquad \text{all } T \text{ and } t_1.$$

We complete the proof that $x(t)$ is stationary by considering the density functions $p_{\mathbf{x(t)}}$ and $p_{\mathbf{x(t+T)}}$ of the random vectors

$$\mathbf{x(t)} = \big(x(t_1), x(t_2), \ldots, x(t_k)\big),$$

$$\mathbf{x(t + T)} = \big(x(t_1 + T), x(t_2 + T), \ldots, x(t_k + T)\big).$$

It is clear from Fig. 3.8 that the knowledge that $x(t_1) = \alpha_1$ uniquely specifies the value of the random variable τ, hence uniquely specifies the sample function of the process $x(t) = f(t + \tau)$ being observed. Given that $x(t_1) = \alpha_1$, the value a_i that will be observed at time t_i is therefore *not* random but depends only on α_1 and the time difference $(t_i - t_1)$: from Fig. 3.8,

$$a_i = f\left(t_i - t_1 + \frac{\alpha_1 T}{a}\right). \tag{3.15a}$$

Hence the conditional density function

$$p_{x(t_i)}(\alpha_i \mid x(t_1) = \alpha_1) = \delta(\alpha_i - a_i)$$

is *independent of the time origin*. Similarly, for any T and t_i,

$$p_{x(t_i+T)}(\alpha_i \,\big|\, x(t_1 + T) = \alpha_1) = \delta(\alpha_i - a_i); \qquad i = 2, 3, \ldots, k,$$

where a_i is the value specified by Eq. 3.15a. It follows immediately that for any $\mathbf{t} = \big(t_1, t_2, \ldots, t_k\big)$

$$p_{\mathbf{x(t)}}(\boldsymbol{\alpha}) = p_{x(t_1)}(\alpha_1) \prod_{i=2}^{k} \delta(\alpha_i - a_i) = p_{\mathbf{x(t+T)}}(\boldsymbol{\alpha}). \tag{3.15b}$$

Thus $x(t)$ is stationary.

The method of analysis used in the foregoing derivation is not restricted to the simple ramp $f(t)$ but can be applied to *any* periodic function $g(t)$. Define the random process $y(t)$ as the ensemble of waveforms $\{g(t + \tau)\}$, where τ is again uniformly distributed over the period T of $g(t)$:

$$y(t) \triangleq g(t + \tau) \tag{3.16a}$$

$$p_\tau(\beta) = \begin{cases} \dfrac{1}{T}; & 0 \leqslant \beta \leqslant T, \\ 0; & \text{elsewhere.} \end{cases} \tag{3.16b}$$

We now use an equivalent but less detailed argument to show that $y(t)$ is stationary.

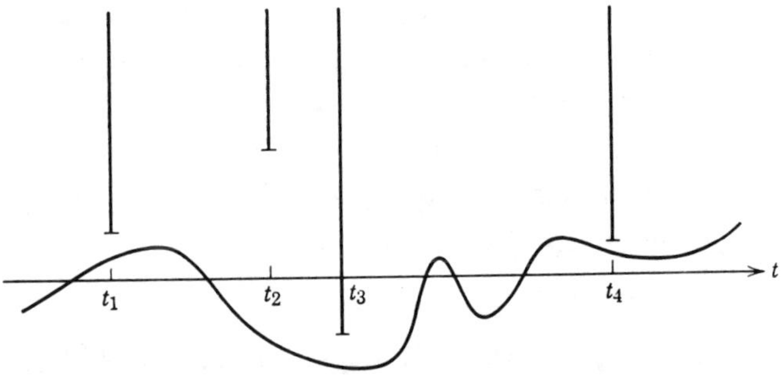

Figure 3.11 A set of barriers and a waveform that passes under them.

For the proof we introduce the translated process

$$z(t) \triangleq y(t + T) = g(t + T + \tau) \tag{3.17a}$$

and the random vectors

$$\begin{aligned} \mathbf{z(t)} &= (z(t_1), z(t_2), \ldots, z(t_k)) \\ &= (y(t_1 + T), y(t_2 + T), \ldots, y(t_k + T)) \\ &= \mathbf{y(t + T)}. \end{aligned} \tag{3.17b}$$

By definition, the process $y(t)$ is stationary if $F_{\mathbf{y(t)}} = F_{\mathbf{z(t)}}$ for all T and all sets of observation instants $\{t_i\}$. These distribution functions are equal whenever

$$\mathrm{P}[\{\tau: \mathbf{y(t)} \leqslant \boldsymbol{\alpha}\}] = \mathrm{P}[\{\tau: \mathbf{z(t)} \leqslant \boldsymbol{\alpha}\}]; \quad \text{all } \boldsymbol{\alpha}; \tag{3.18}$$

that is, whenever the probability of the set of sample functions of $y(t)$ passing under arbitrary barriers such as those of Fig. 3.11 equals the probability of the set of sample functions of $z(t)$ passing under these barriers. The following arguments show that Eq. 3.18 is valid.

We note first that if τ_1' is determined from τ_1 and T by the construction shown in Fig. 3.12, the periodicity of $g(t)$ implies that $g(t + \tau_1)$ and $g(t + T + \tau_1')$ are the *same waveform* for any τ_1 in the interval $[0, T]$. There is a one-to-one correspondence between the sample functions of $y(t)$ and $z(t)$.

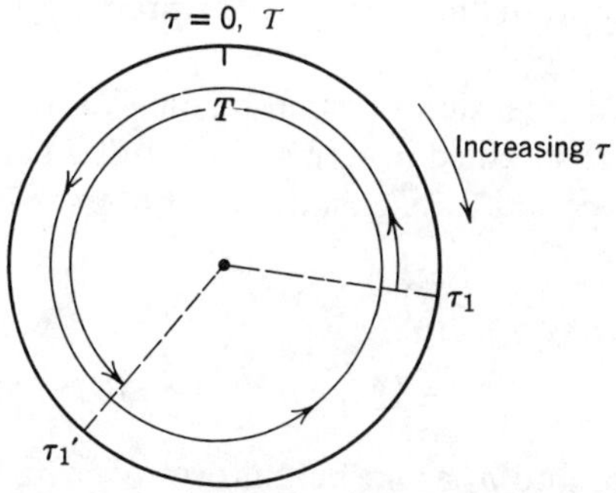

Figure 3.12 The values τ in the interval $[0, T]$ are mapped onto a circle of circumference T. The point τ_1' is that point in the interval $[0, T]$ obtained by starting at τ_1 and moving a distance T counterclockwise around the perimeter.

Next, it is convenient to indicate by heavy arcs the intervals of τ corresponding to those sample functions $\{g(t + \tau)\}$ of $y(t)$ that pass under the barriers of Fig. 3.11. A typical situation might be the one shown in Fig. 3.13*a*. Arcs may also be used, as illustrated in Fig. 3.13*b*, to indicate the intervals of τ corresponding to sample functions $\{g(t + T + \tau)\}$ of $z(t)$ that pass under these barriers. In accordance with the construction of Fig. 3.12, we note that Fig. 3.13*b* is always obtainable from Fig. 3.13*a* by rotating the arcs.

From Eq. 3.16b, the probability that τ lies in any collection of arcs is equal to the total length of the collection. Since rotation does not affect

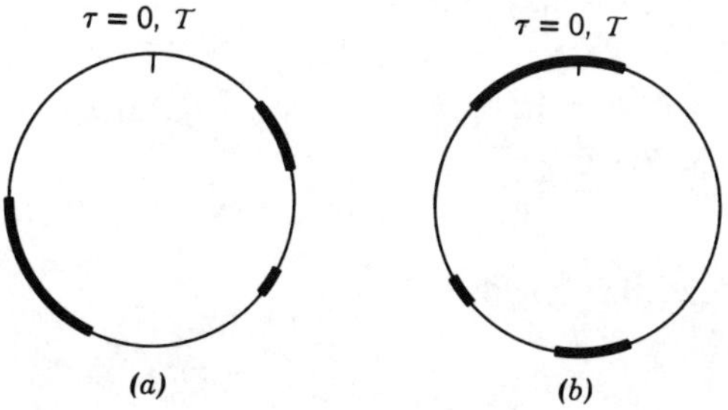

Figure 3.13 The arcs denote the values of τ for which (*a*) sample functions of $y(t)$ and (*b*) sample functions of $z(t)$ pass under the barriers of Fig. 3.11.

arc length, Eq. 3.18 is valid, and

$$F_{y(t)} = F_{z(t)} = F_{y(t+T)}$$

or

$$p_{y(t)} = p_{y(t+T)}. \tag{3.19}$$

This concludes the proof that the random process $y(t)$ is stationary for any periodic function $g(t)$.

A straightforward extension of the foregoing result involves a periodic time function $g(\mathbf{w}, t)$ specified in terms of a set of J parameters $\{w_j\}$, none of which affect the period T. Consider the process

$$x(t) \triangleq g(\mathbf{w}, t + \tau), \tag{3.20a}$$

in which we let

$$\mathbf{w} \triangleq (w_1, w_2, \ldots, w_J) \tag{3.20b}$$

be a random vector and p_τ again be uniform over $[0, T]$. If the random variables $\{w_j\}$ are independent of τ, that is, if

$$p_{\mathbf{w},\tau} = p_{\mathbf{w}} p_\tau, \tag{3.20c}$$

we have

$$p_{x(t)}(\boldsymbol{\alpha}) = \int_{-\infty}^{\infty} p_{x(t)}(\boldsymbol{\alpha} \mid \mathbf{w} = \boldsymbol{\gamma})\, p_{\mathbf{w}}(\boldsymbol{\gamma})\, d\boldsymbol{\gamma}. \tag{3.21}$$

Since, by Eq. 3.19, $p_{x(t)}(\ \mid \mathbf{w} = \boldsymbol{\gamma})$ is independent of the time origin, so also is $p_{x(t)}$. By taking both the period T and the number of components in $\mathbf{w}$ to be very large, we can generate a rich variety of stationary processes.

As an example, we apply this result to the process obtained from the periodic function $\sin 2\pi t$ by letting the amplitude and phase be random variables:

$$x(t) = r \sin (2\pi t + \theta). \tag{3.22a}$$

Here, as in Eq. 3.6, we may choose

$$p_{r,\theta}(\alpha_1, \alpha_2) = \begin{cases} \dfrac{\alpha_1}{2\pi} e^{-\alpha_1^2/2}; & 0 \leqslant \alpha_1, \quad 0 \leqslant \alpha_2 < 2\pi, \\ 0; & \text{elsewhere.} \end{cases} \tag{3.22b}$$

Defining $\tau \triangleq \theta/2\pi$ then yields

$$x(t) = r \sin 2\pi(t + \tau). \tag{3.23}$$

We observe from Eq. 3.22b that r and θ are statistically independent, which implies the independence of r and τ. Moreover, since θ is uniformly distributed over $[0, 2\pi]$, τ is uniformly distributed over $[0, 1]$. Finally, since for any r the function

$$g(r, t) \triangleq r \sin 2\pi t$$

is periodic with period $T = 1$, the preceding discussion implies that the random process $x(t)$ is stationary. In particular,

$$p_{x(t_1)} = p_{x(0)}; \qquad \text{for any } t_1.$$

It is readily verified that

$$p_{x(t_i)}(\alpha) = p_{x(0)}(\alpha) = \frac{1}{\sqrt{2\pi}} e^{-\alpha^2/2}.$$

Example of a nonstationary process. The requirements that a random process must meet in order to be stationary are stringent. A simple example of a nonstationary random process $x(t)$ is the ensemble defined by

$$x(\omega, t) = \sin 2\pi f(\omega)t; \qquad \text{all } \omega \text{ in } \Omega, \tag{3.24a}$$

in which the frequency f is a random variable with the density function

$$p_f(\alpha) = \begin{cases} \dfrac{1}{W}; & 0 \leqslant \alpha \leqslant W, \\ 0; & \text{otherwise.} \end{cases} \tag{3.24b}$$

Three particular members of this ensemble, for which $f = W/4$, $W/2$, and W, are plotted in Fig. 3.14.

To show that $x(t)$ is nonstationary, we need only observe that *every* waveform in the ensemble is

$$\text{zero at } t = 0,$$

$$\text{positive for } 0 < t < \frac{1}{2W},$$

$$\text{negative for } -\frac{1}{2W} < t < 0.$$

Thus the density function of the random variable $x(t_1)$ obtained by sampling $x(t)$ at $t_1 = 1/4W$ is identically zero for negative arguments, whereas the density function of the random variable $x(t_2)$ obtained by sampling $x(t)$ at $t_2 = -1/4W$ is nonzero only for negative arguments. Clearly, $p_{x(t_1)} \neq p_{x(t_2)}$, and Eq. 3.11 is invalid.

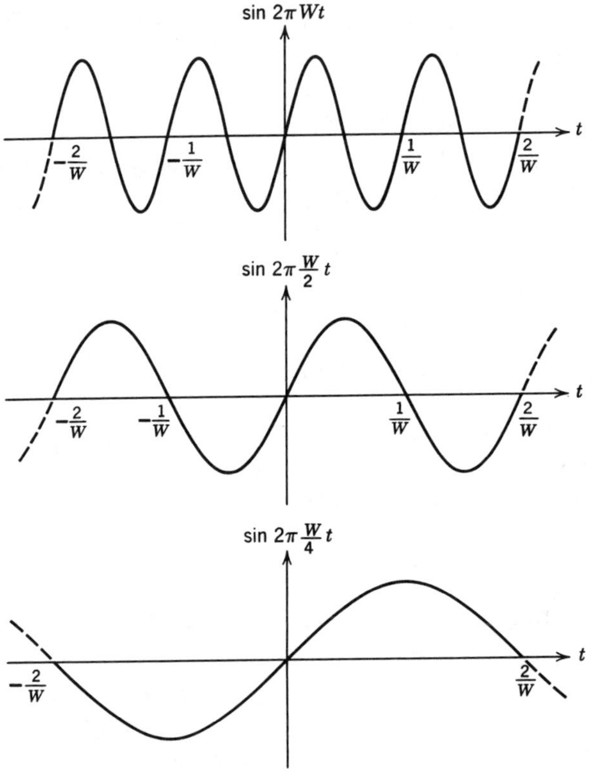

Figure 3.14 Sample functions of a nonstationary random process.

3.2 FILTERED IMPULSE NOISE

The random processes that we have considered so far are helpful in consolidating concepts but are not pertinent examples of the noise disturbances encountered in electrical communication. Filtered impulse noise, however, is ubiquitous; no electrical circuit is ever without it. We now consider one source of filtered impulse noise to provide physical motivation for a subsequent study of Gaussian processes.

Figure 3.15 is a simplified diagram of a triode amplifier. Electrons are emitted thermionically from the heated cathode and migrate to the plate under the influence of the electric field induced by the plate and grid voltages. These electrons then flow through the plate circuit filter $h(t)$ and return to the cathode.

The typical transit time of an electron from cathode to plate is roughly 10^{-9} sec. From Fourier analysis a plate circuit filter with bandwidth W

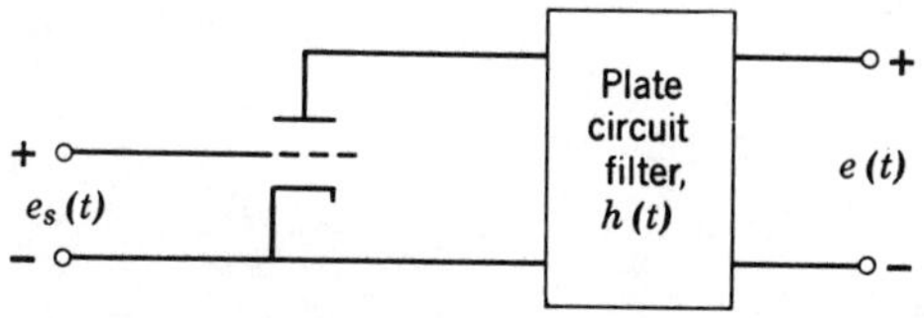

Figure 3.15 A simplified diagram of a triode amplifier stage. The voltage response $e(t)$ to a unit impulse of current is $h(t)$.

has an impulse response with substantial duration, say Δ, of at least $1/W$ sec. It follows that even for a bandwidth of 100 Mc, Δ is greater than 10^{-8} sec and exceeds the transit time by an order of magnitude.

Under these circumstances it is appropriate to conclude that each electron striking the plate delivers a current impulse of magnitude q to the filter $h(t)$, where

$$q = 1.6 \times 10^{-19} \text{ coulomb}$$

is the charge of an electron. Since the plate circuit is linear, the output voltage $e(t)$ is the superposition of the response to each electron individually. As shown in Fig. 3.16*a*, *b*, *c*, we have

$$i(t) = \sum_{\text{all } i} q\, \delta(t - \tau_i) \tag{3.25a}$$

and

$$e(t) = \int_{-\infty}^{\infty} i(\alpha)\, h(t - \alpha)\, d\alpha \tag{3.25b}$$

$$= \sum_{\text{all } i} q\, h(t - \tau_i), \tag{3.25c}$$

where τ_i is the time of occurrence of the ith current impulse.

It is clear from Fig. 3.16 that the output voltage $e(t)$ depends on the precise time structure of the electron arrivals. For instance, if the impulses comprising $i(t)$ occurred periodically, $e(t)$ would be completely predictable from knowledge of the period and phase. On the other hand, because of the thermionic origin of the electrons, we cannot predict precisely the instants $\{\tau_i\}$—hence the output $e(t)$—for any given vacuum tube. We say that $e(t)$ is "noisy."

In a mathematical model of our amplifier we treat the $\{\tau_i\}$ as random variables and $e(t)$ as a random process. Equation 3.25c provides another example of defining a random process by assigning certain parameters of a time function as random variables.

Statistical Characterization

The remaining problem is to determine the density functions associated with the process $e(t)$. For an exact analysis we would first specify the joint density function of the random variables $\{\tau_i\}$, which is a formidable task.

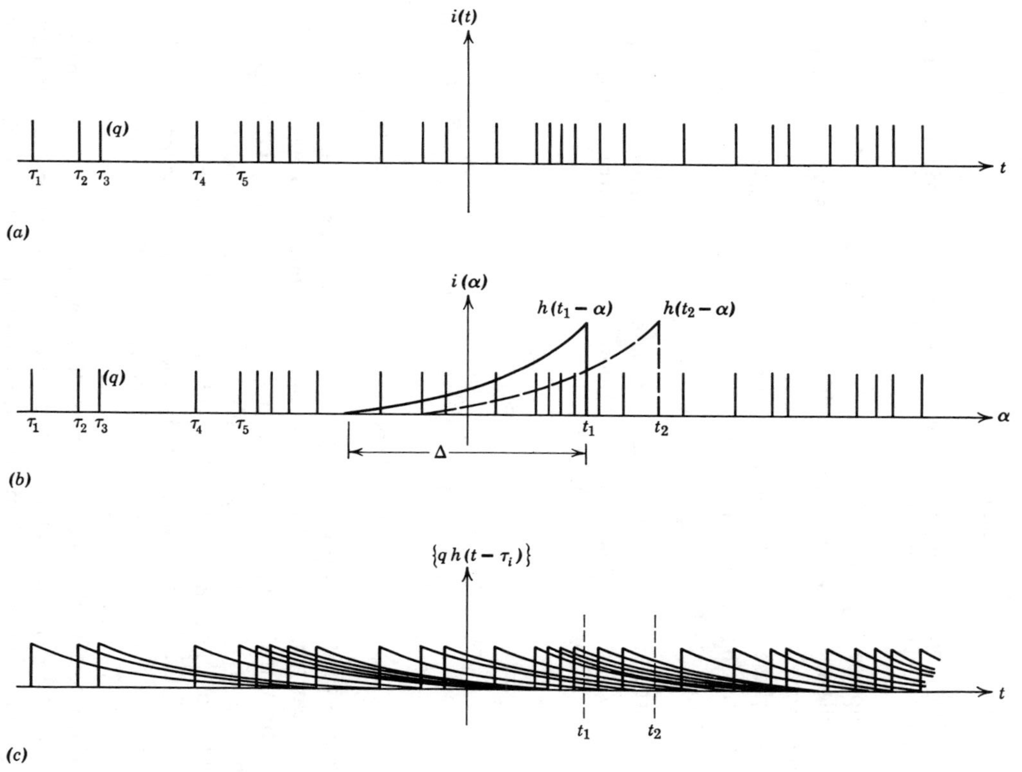

Figure 3.16 The superposition of current impulses in the plate circuit filter. The value of $e(t)$ at any time, say t_1 or t_2, is obtained by adding together the plate response (shown in c) to each individual electron.

In space-charge-limited operation, for instance, the $\{\tau_i\}$ are not statistically independent; a period of greater-than-average emission from the cathode increases the space-charge density, which inhibits the electron flow immediately thereafter.

Fortunately, the fact that the number of electrons contributing to the output voltage at any particular instant is enormous permits an approximate analysis of great usefulness. If the current is 1 ma, an average of $N = 6.25 \times 10^{15}$ electrons strike the plate per second. For $W = 100$ Mc, the effective number of random variables, $h(t - \tau_i)$, contributing to $e(t)$ in Eq. 3.25 is $N \times \Delta \approx 6.25 \times 10^7$.

This situation is a classic example of one to which central limit theorem arguments may be applied. In essence, the statistical dependencies that exist among the $\{\tau_i\}$ are insufficiently pronounced to suppress an overwhelming Gaussian tendency. That this is so has been shown in careful and detailed analyses(79,82) based on reasonable models for the electron stream. The results can be summarized as follows:

1. The random variable $e(t_j)$ obtained by sampling the random process $e(t)$ at the output of an amplifier such as that in Fig. 3.15 at any time t_j has a density function that is approximately Gaussian whenever the electron flow is large.

2. When the amplifier input signal $e_s(t)$ is weak and affects the electron stream only incrementally (as in the input stages of a communication receiver), the output random process may be written

$$e(t) = e_s{}^*(t) + n(t), \tag{3.26}$$

where $e_s{}^*(t)$ is the (nonrandom) output voltage predicted by noiseless circuit theory and $n(t)$ is a random process that is independent of $e_s{}^*(t)$.

3. In measurements made under stable operating conditions the noise process $n(t)$ may be considered stationary with zero mean. Thus the random variables $e(t_j)$ and $n(t_j)$ have mean values

$$\begin{aligned} \overline{e(t_j)} &= e_s{}^*(t_j) \\ \overline{n(t_j)} &= 0. \end{aligned} \tag{3.27}$$

These analytical results are in accord with our intuition. Even more to the point, these results are consistent with empirical evidence: assuming these properties in a mathematical model of vacuum-tube noise leads to calculations of system performance that agree with experimental results under normal operating conditions.

Noise attributable to the random arrival of discrete charge increments is also called *shot noise*.

Statistical Dependency

The preceding discussion makes it reasonable to ascribe a Gaussian probability density function to any time-sample of a filtered impulse noise process such as $n(t)$ in Eq. 3.26:

$$p_{n(t_1)}(\alpha) = \frac{1}{\sqrt{2\pi}\,\sigma} e^{-\alpha^2/2\sigma^2}, \tag{3.28}$$

where $\sigma^2 = \overline{n^2(t_1)}$. The fact that the right-hand side of Eq. 3.28 is independent of t_1 reflects the assumption that $n(t)$ is stationary. It follows that for any other observation time t_2

$$p_{n(t_2)} = p_{n(t_1)}. \tag{3.29}$$

The problem of determining expressions for joint density functions such as $p_{n(t_1),n(t_2)}$, however, must still be considered.

If two random variables are statistically independent, their joint density function is simply the product of their individual densities. On the other hand, an assumption that $n(t_1)$ and $n(t_2)$ are statistically independent is inconsistent with the shot-noise model for many choices of t_1 and t_2.

Let us assume that t_1 and t_2 are separated by an interval shorter than the substantial duration Δ of $h(t)$. Since, from Eq. 3.25b, $e(t)$ results from sliding $h(t - \alpha)$ past $i(\alpha)$ and integrating, many of the impulses that contribute to $e(t_1)$ also contribute to $e(t_2)$, and these two voltages are *physically dependent*. We note in Fig. 3.16 that if $i(\alpha)$ is such that $h(t_1 - \alpha)$ spans a larger than average number of impulses, *both* $e(t_1)$ and $e(t_2)$ will tend to be larger than average whenever $|t_1 - t_2| < \Delta$.

This physical dependence between $e(t_1)$ and $e(t_2)$ must be reflected in a valid mathematical model. In particular, when t_1 and t_2 are close together, knowledge that $n(t_1)$ is larger than average must increase the conditional probability that $n(t_2)$ is larger than average. This implies that for a valid model

$$p_{n_1,n_2} \neq p_{n_1}p_{n_2}; \qquad \text{for } |t_2 - t_1| < \Delta, \tag{3.30a}$$

in which for notational simplicity we define

$$n_1 \triangleq n(t_1), \qquad n_2 \triangleq n(t_2). \tag{3.30b}$$

The problem of ascribing an appropriate functional form to the joint density function p_{n_1,n_2} cannot be resolved without additional analysis.

In Section 3.3 we consider central limit theorem arguments which support the fact that the appropriate choice for p_{n_1,n_2} is the joint Gaussian density function encountered in Chapter 2. For the moment, however, it is instructive to study this density function in more detail and to verify the fact that its properties are consistent with the filtered impulse-noise model. The joint Gaussian density of Eq. 2.58, generalized to allow an arbitrary variance σ^2, is

$$p_{n_1,n_2}(\alpha, \beta) = \frac{1}{2\pi\sigma^2\sqrt{1-\rho^2}} \exp\left[-\frac{\alpha^2 - 2\rho\alpha\beta + \beta^2}{2\sigma^2(1-\rho^2)}\right]; \qquad -1 < \rho < 1. \tag{3.31}$$

We first observe (as in Eq. 2.64) that the individual densities p_{n_1} and p_{n_2} are zero-mean Gaussian: it can be verified readily by integration that

$$p_{n_1}(\alpha) = p_{n_2}(\alpha) = \frac{1}{\sqrt{2\pi}\,\sigma} e^{-\alpha^2/2\sigma^2}. \tag{3.32}$$

This is consistent with Eqs. 3.28 and 3.29.

Second, we observe (as in Eq. 2.85) that the conditional density of n_2, given that n_1 has value α, is

$$\begin{aligned} p_{n_2}(\beta \mid n_1 = \alpha) &\triangleq \frac{p_{n_1,n_2}(\alpha, \beta)}{p_{n_1}(\alpha)} \\ &= \frac{1}{\sqrt{2\pi\sigma^2(1-\rho^2)}} \exp\left[-\frac{(\beta - \rho\alpha)^2}{2\sigma^2(1-\rho^2)}\right]; \qquad |\rho| < 1. \end{aligned} \tag{3.33}$$

The conditional density function is also Gaussian, but the conditional mean of n_2, given $n_1 = \alpha$, is $\rho\alpha$ rather than zero. The conditional variance is $\sigma^2(1 - \rho^2)$. The terms "conditional mean" and "conditional variance" refer to the mean and variance of the conditional density function.

The parameter ρ plays a central role in determining the structure of p_{n_1,n_2}. For example, we recall from Fig. 2.32 that, as $\rho \to 1, p_{n_2}(\beta \mid n_1 = \alpha)$ approaches an impulse function centered on α, the conditional variance becomes smaller and smaller, and there is less and less uncertainty about the value of n_2, once n_1 is known. In the measurement of filtered impulse noise, values of ρ close to 1 pertain to observation times t_1 and t_2 that are close together; the value $\rho = 1$ pertains to the degenerate case in which t_2 equals t_1 and the two measured filter outputs are one and the same.

In contrast, when $\rho = 0$, the random variables n_1 and n_2 are statistically independent, and

$$p_{n_2}(\beta \mid n_1 = \alpha) = p_{n_2}(\beta). \tag{3.34}$$

Knowledge of the value of n_1 tells us nothing about n_2. The corresponding situation occurs in measuring filtered impulse noise when $|t_2 - t_1|$ is much greater than the effective duration of the filter's impulse response, since then there is no significant overlap of the impulse patterns determining the value of the measurements at times t_1 and t_2. Values of ρ intermediate between 0 and 1 correspond to values of $|t_2 - t_1|$ that are comparable to the effective duration of the filter's impulse response.

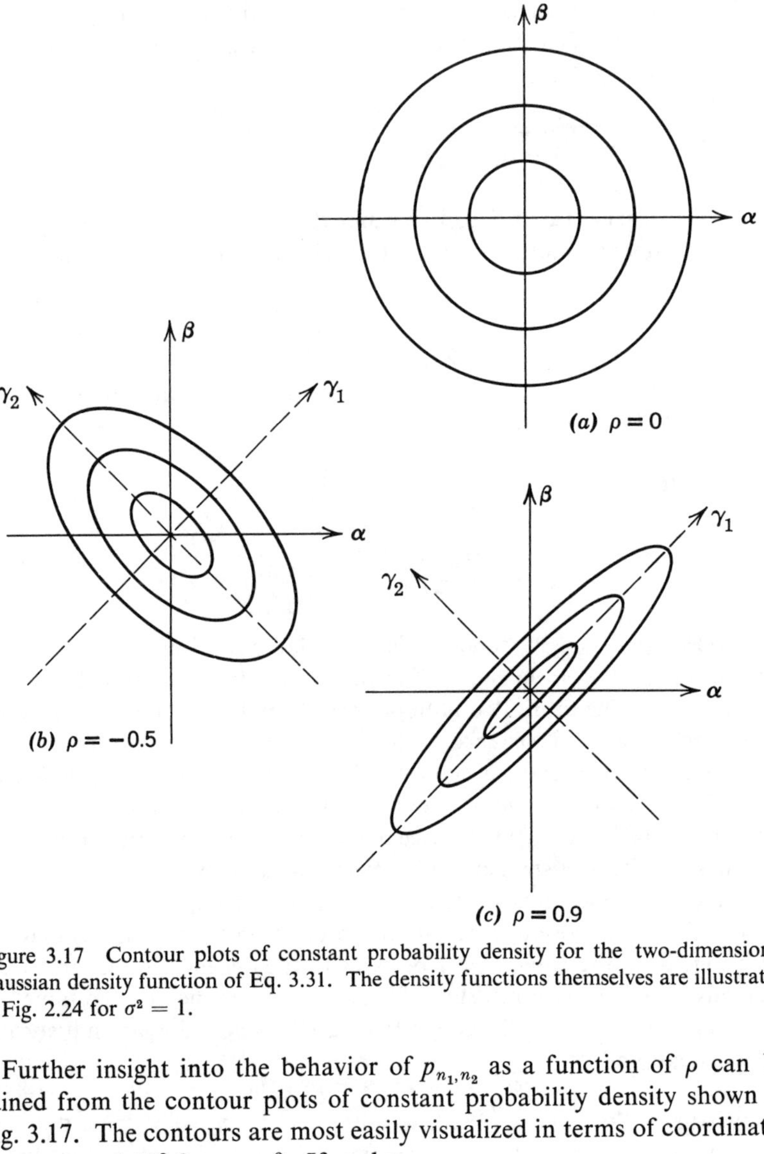

Figure 3.17 Contour plots of constant probability density for the two-dimensional Gaussian density function of Eq. 3.31. The density functions themselves are illustrated in Fig. 2.24 for $\sigma^2 = 1$.

Further insight into the behavior of p_{n_1,n_2} as a function of ρ can be gained from the contour plots of constant probability density shown in Fig. 3.17. The contours are most easily visualized in terms of coordinates γ_1, γ_2 rotated 45° from α, β. If we let

$$\alpha = \gamma_1 \cos \frac{\pi}{4} - \gamma_2 \sin \frac{\pi}{4}, \tag{3.35a}$$

$$\beta = \gamma_1 \sin \frac{\pi}{4} + \gamma_2 \cos \frac{\pi}{4}, \tag{3.35b}$$

the exponent of p_{n_1,n_2} simplifies to

$$\alpha^2 - 2\rho\alpha\beta + \beta^2 = \gamma_1^2(1 - \rho) + \gamma_2^2(1 + \rho). \tag{3.36}$$

Thus for all $|\rho| < 1$ the contours of equal density are ellipses erected on the γ_1, γ_2 axes. When $\rho = 0$, the ellipses degenerate into circles, whereas when $\rho \to +1$ or -1 the ellipses degenerate into the γ_1 and γ_2 axes, respectively.

Joint Gaussian Density Function

Covariance. For any two random variables, say z_i and z_j, the central moment

$$\lambda_{ij} \triangleq \mathrm{E}[(z_i - \bar{z}_i)(z_j - \bar{z}_j)] \tag{3.37}$$

is called the *covariance* when $i \neq j$. (The central moment λ_{ii} is the variance, σ_i^2, of z_i.) Since expectation is linear, we also have

$$\begin{aligned}\lambda_{ij} &= \overline{z_i z_j} - 2\bar{z}_i\bar{z}_j + \bar{z}_i\bar{z}_j \\ &= \overline{z_i z_j} - \bar{z}_i\bar{z}_j.\end{aligned} \tag{3.38}$$

The *covariance coefficient*, ρ_{ij}, of two random variables is defined as

$$\rho_{ij} \triangleq \frac{\lambda_{ij}}{\sigma_i\sigma_j}. \tag{3.39}$$

For the zero-mean Gaussian variables n_1 and n_2 the covariance is $\overline{n_1 n_2}$. Recalling that the conditional mean of n_2, given $n_1 = \alpha$, is $\rho\alpha$, we have

$$\begin{aligned}\overline{n_1 n_2} &= \int_{-\infty}^{\infty}\int_{-\infty}^{\infty} \alpha\beta\, p_{n_1,n_2}(\alpha, \beta)\, d\beta\, d\alpha \\ &= \int_{-\infty}^{\infty} \alpha\, p_{n_1}(\alpha)\, d\alpha \int_{-\infty}^{\infty} \beta\, p_{n_2}(\beta \mid n_1 = \alpha)\, d\beta \\ &= \rho\int_{-\infty}^{\infty} \alpha^2\, p_{n_1}(\alpha)\, d\alpha = \rho\sigma^2.\end{aligned} \tag{3.40}$$

The parameter ρ is therefore identified as the covariance coefficient of the equal-variance random variables n_1 and n_2:

$$\rho = \frac{\overline{n_1 n_2}}{\sigma^2} \triangleq \rho_{12}. \tag{3.41}$$

It is always true that the covariance coefficient of two random variables is restricted to the interval $[-1, 1]$: since the expected value of the square of any random variable is non-negative, we have

$$0 \leqslant \mathrm{E}\left[\left(\frac{z_i - \bar{z}_i}{\sigma_i} \pm \frac{z_j - \bar{z}_j}{\sigma_j}\right)^2\right] = \frac{\sigma_i^{\,2}}{\sigma_i^{\,2}} \pm 2\,\frac{\lambda_{ij}}{\sigma_i\sigma_j} + \frac{\sigma_j^{\,2}}{\sigma_j^{\,2}}, \tag{3.42a}$$

which implies

$$-1 \leqslant \rho_{ij} \leqslant 1. \tag{3.42b}$$

Whenever $|\rho_{ij}| = 1$, the expectation in Eq. 3.42a equals zero. But the second moment of a random variable can vanish only if the random variable is zero for all sample points, except possibly a set of zero probability. Thus

$$\rho_{ij} = \pm 1 \Leftrightarrow \frac{z_i - \bar{z}_i}{\sigma_i} = \pm\,\frac{z_j - \bar{z}_j}{\sigma_j}, \tag{3.43}$$

where the random variables are equal in the sense of Eq. 2.68.

Equation 3.43 is consistent with Figs. 2.32 and 3.17. When $\rho = \pm 1$, then $n_1 = \pm n_2$ and the joint density function p_{n_1,n_2} is impulsive. In such a case we say that the joint Gaussian density function p_{n_1,n_2} is *singular*.

Unequal variances. Equation 3.31 represents the joint density function of two zero-mean Gaussian random variables with equal variances. The unequal-variance case is obtainable from Eq. 3.31 by the elementary transformation

$$x_1 = n_1$$

$$x_2 = bn_2; \qquad b > 0. \tag{3.44a}$$

Then x_1 and x_2 individually are zero-mean Gaussian variables with central moments

$$\lambda_{11} = \sigma_{x_1}^{\;2} = \sigma^2,$$

$$\lambda_{22} = \sigma_{x_2}^{\;2} = b^2\sigma^2,$$

$$\lambda_{12} = \lambda_{21} = \overline{x_1x_2} = \overline{n_1(bn_2)} = b\rho\sigma^2. \tag{3.44b}$$

The covariance coefficient remains unchanged:

$$\rho_{12} \triangleq \frac{\lambda_{12}}{\sigma_{x_1}\sigma_{x_2}} = \rho. \tag{3.44c}$$

In terms of these quantities, the zero-mean unequal-variance Gaussian density can be written by inspection: from Eq. 3.31 and the relation (cf. Eq. 2.88)

$$p_{x_1,x_2}(\alpha, \beta) = \frac{1}{|b|}\, p_{n_1,n_2}\!\left(\alpha, \frac{\beta}{b}\right)$$

we have, with the shortened notation $\sigma_1^2 \triangleq \sigma_{x_1}^2$ and $\sigma_2^2 \triangleq \sigma_{x_2}^2$,

$$p_{x_1,x_2}(\alpha, \beta) = \frac{1}{2\pi\sigma(b\sigma)\sqrt{1-\rho^2}} \exp\left\{-\frac{1}{2(1-\rho^2)}\left[\frac{\alpha^2}{\sigma^2} - \frac{2\rho}{\sigma(b\sigma)}\alpha\beta + \frac{\beta^2}{b^2\sigma^2}\right]\right\}$$

$$= \frac{1}{2\pi\sigma_1\sigma_2\sqrt{1-\rho_{12}^2}} \exp\left\{-\frac{1}{2(1-\rho_{12}^2)}\left[\frac{\alpha^2}{\sigma_1^2} - \frac{2\rho_{12}}{\sigma_1\sigma_2}\alpha\beta + \frac{\beta^2}{\sigma_2^2}\right]\right\}. \tag{3.45}$$

Nonzero means. The general two-dimensional Gaussian density function is obtained from Eq. 3.45 by making the further transformation

$$z_1 = x_1 + \overline{z_1}, \qquad z_2 = x_2 + \overline{z_2}, \tag{3.46}$$

which implies

$$p_{z_1,z_2}(\alpha, \beta) = p_{x_1,x_2}(\alpha - \overline{z_1}, \beta - \overline{z_2}) = \frac{1}{2\pi\sigma_1\sigma_2\sqrt{1-\rho_{12}^2}}$$

$$\times \exp\left\{-\frac{1}{2(1-\rho_{12}^2)}\left[\frac{(\alpha-\overline{z_1})^2}{\sigma_1^2} - \frac{2\rho_{12}}{\sigma_1\sigma_2}(\alpha-\overline{z_1})(\beta-\overline{z_2}) + \frac{(\beta-\overline{z_2})^2}{\sigma_2^2}\right]\right\} \tag{3.47}$$

In writing Eq. 3.47, we have recognized that transformations involving only the addition of constants, as in Eq. 3.46, do not alter central moments, so that

$$\sigma_1^2 \triangleq \mathrm{E}[(z_1 - \overline{z_1})^2] = \overline{x_1^2},$$
$$\sigma_2^2 \triangleq \mathrm{E}[(z_2 - \overline{z_2})^2] = \overline{x_2^2}, \tag{3.48}$$
$$\rho_{12} \triangleq \frac{\mathrm{E}[(z_1 - \overline{z_1})(z_2 - \overline{z_2})]}{\sigma_1\sigma_2} = \frac{\overline{x_1x_2}}{\sigma_1\sigma_2}.$$

Random variables z_1 and z_2 are called *jointly Gaussian* if and only if their density function p_{z_1,z_2} has the form specified by Eqs. 3.47 and 3.48. We observe that the general joint Gaussian density function depends *only* on the means, variances, and covariance (or covariance coefficient). We also observe once again that two jointly Gaussian random variables are statistically independent if and only if their covariance is zero.

General linear transformations. One of the most important properties of the joint Gaussian density function is that *random variables defined as linear transformations of Gaussian variables are also Gaussian.* In this section we show that this is true for any reversible linear transformation applied to the pair of zero-mean Gaussian variables x_1 and x_2 of Eq. 3.45.

The generalization to k Gaussian variables, $k > 2$, is deferred until the next section.

First consider the transformation $(x_1, x_2) \to (x_1, x_3)$ given by

$$x_3 \triangleq ax_1 + bx_2; \qquad b \neq 0. \tag{3.49}$$

The condition $b \neq 0$ guarantees that the transformation is reversible. If $b = 0$, both x_1 and x_3 depend only on the single random variable x_1, and p_{x_1,x_3} is singular (that is, it involves impulses). From Eq. 2.76 the conditional density of x_3, given $x_1 = \alpha$, is

$$p_{x_3}(\beta \mid x_1 = \alpha) = \frac{1}{|b|}\, p_{x_2}\!\left(\frac{\beta - a\alpha}{b} \,\middle|\, x_1 = \alpha\right).$$

Multiplying by $p_{x_1}(\alpha)$ yields

$$p_{x_1,x_3}(\alpha, \beta) = \frac{1}{|b|}\, p_{x_1,x_2}\!\left(\alpha, \frac{\beta - a\alpha}{b}\right). \tag{3.50}$$

Substituting Eq. 3.45 in Eq. 3.50 and simplifying, we have, after considerable (and unrewarding) algebra,

$$p_{x_1,x_3}(\alpha, \beta) = \frac{1}{2\pi\sigma_1\sigma_3\sqrt{1 - \rho_{13}^{\,2}}} \times \exp\left\{-\frac{1}{2(1 - \rho_{13}^{\,2})}\left[\frac{\alpha^2}{\sigma_1^{\,2}} - \frac{2\rho_{13}}{\sigma_1\sigma_3}\alpha\beta + \frac{\beta^2}{\sigma_3^{\,2}}\right]\right\}, \tag{3.51}$$

where

$$\sigma_3^{\,2} \triangleq \overline{x_3^{\,2}} = a^2\overline{x_1^{\,2}} + 2ab\overline{x_1x_2} + b^2\overline{x_2^{\,2}}, \tag{3.52a}$$

$$\rho_{13} \triangleq \frac{\overline{x_1x_3}}{\sigma_1\sigma_3} = \frac{a\overline{x_1^{\,2}} + b\overline{x_1x_2}}{\sigma_1\sigma_3}. \tag{3.52b}$$

We note that Eq. 3.51 once more has the Gaussian form.

Next consider the reversible transformation from the pair (x_1, x_2) to the pair (x_3, x_4) given by

$$\begin{aligned} x_3 &= ax_1 + bx_2; \qquad b \neq 0, \\ x_4 &= cx_1 + dx_2; \qquad bc - ad \neq 0. \end{aligned} \tag{3.53}$$

By writing

$$x_4 = \left(c - \frac{da}{b}\right)x_1 + \frac{d}{b}\,x_3,$$

we observe that the transformation of Eq. 3.53 can be considered as the cascade $(x_1, x_2) \to (x_1, x_3) \to (x_3, x_4)$. Since each individual step results in the general Gaussian form, the cascaded transformation does also, and the proof is complete.

A simple example of a linear transformation is $(n_1, n_2) \to (x_1, x_2)$, in which

$$x_1 \triangleq n_1 \cos\frac{\pi}{4} + n_2 \sin\frac{\pi}{4},$$
$$x_2 \triangleq -n_1 \sin\frac{\pi}{4} + n_2 \cos\frac{\pi}{4}, \tag{3.54}$$

and p_{n_1,n_2} is the zero-mean equal-variance joint Gaussian density function given by Eq. 3.31. Since

$$\sigma_1^2 \triangleq \overline{x_1^2} = \tfrac{1}{2}\overline{n_1^2} + 2(\tfrac{1}{2})\overline{n_1 n_2} + \tfrac{1}{2}\overline{n_2^2} = \sigma^2(1+\rho),$$
$$\sigma_2^2 \triangleq \overline{x_2^2} = \tfrac{1}{2}\overline{n_1^2} - 2(\tfrac{1}{2})\overline{n_1 n_2} + \tfrac{1}{2}\overline{n_2^2} = \sigma^2(1-\rho), \tag{3.55}$$
$$\lambda_{12} \triangleq \overline{x_1 x_2} = -\tfrac{1}{2}\overline{n_1^2} + \tfrac{1}{2}\overline{n_1 n_2} - \tfrac{1}{2}\overline{n_1 n_2} + \tfrac{1}{2}\overline{n_2^2} = 0,$$

from Eq. 3.45 we have

$$p_{x_1,x_2}(\gamma_1, \gamma_2) = \frac{1}{2\pi\sigma^2\sqrt{1-\rho^2}} \exp\left[-\frac{\gamma_1^2}{2\sigma^2(1+\rho)} - \frac{\gamma_2^2}{2\sigma^2(1-\rho)}\right]$$
$$= p_{x_1}(\gamma_1)\, p_{x_2}(\gamma_2). \tag{3.56}$$

We observe that the random variables x_1 and x_2, obtained from the *statistically dependent* variables n_1 and n_2 by the "rotation of coordinates" transformation of Eq. 3.54, are *statistically independent.* By choosing the angle of rotation to be $\frac{1}{2}\tan^{-1}[2\rho_{12}\sigma_1\sigma_2/(\sigma_1^2 - \sigma_2^2)]$ rather than $\pi/4$, the general two-dimensional Gaussian density of Eq. 3.47 can also be transformed into statistically independent form.

Summary. The preceding discussion has established four extremely important properties of two random variables that are *jointly Gaussian,* that is, variables with the joint density function given by Eq. 3.47.

1. The joint Gaussian density function p_{z_1,z_2} depends *only* on the means $\overline{z_1}$ and $\overline{z_2}$, the variances $\sigma_{z_1}^2$ and $\sigma_{z_2}^2$, and the covariance

$$\lambda_{12} = \mathrm{E}[(z_1 - \overline{z_1})(z_2 - \overline{z_2})].$$

2. If z_1 and z_2 are jointly Gaussian, they are individually Gaussian.
3. Two variables that are jointly Gaussian are statistically independent if and only if their covariance is zero.
4. Linear transformations on variables that are jointly Gaussian yield new variables that are also jointly Gaussian.

These four properties are *not* true in general for two random variables that are *not* jointly Gaussian.

In Section 3.3 we derive from multidimensional central limit theorem arguments a density function for k random variables that is called *k-dimensional Gaussian.* Random vectors with this density function are *jointly Gaussian.* We shall see that the four properties summarized for the case $k = 2$ extend without change to the case of arbitrary k:

1. The density function $p_{\mathbf{z}}$ of a jointly Gaussian random vector $\mathbf{z} = (z_1, z_2, \ldots, z_k)$ depends only on the means $\{\bar{z}_i\}$ and the set of central moments $\{\lambda_{ij}\}$:

$$\lambda_{ij} = \lambda_{ji} \triangleq \mathrm{E}[(z_i - \bar{z}_i)(z_j - \bar{z}_j)]; \qquad i = 1, 2, \ldots, k, \quad j = 1, 2, \ldots, k.$$

2. Any subset of jointly Gaussian random variables is jointly Gaussian.
3. A set of k Gaussian random variables is statistically independent if and only if the covariances $\lambda_{ij} = 0$ for all i and $j \neq i$. In this case,

$$p_{\mathbf{z}}(\boldsymbol{\alpha}) = \prod_{i=1}^{k} p_{z_i}(\alpha_i) = \frac{1}{(2\pi)^{k/2}\sigma_1\sigma_2 \cdots \sigma_k} \exp\left(-\frac{1}{2}\sum_{i=1}^{k}\frac{\alpha_i^2}{\sigma_i^2}\right), \tag{3.57}$$

in which we have written σ_i^2 in lieu of λ_{ii} and assumed all $\bar{z}_i = 0$.
4. Any linear transformation of a set of k jointly Gaussian random variables yields new variables that are also jointly Gaussian. In particular, a weighted sum of Gaussian variables is Gaussian.

Even for $k = 2$ we have seen that the algebra is tedious and that the general expression for $p_{\mathbf{z}}$ is sufficiently cumbrous that notation is a problem. For $k > 2$ the simplification that results from the use of matrix notation is essential. This notation is reviewed in Appendix 3A and is applied in Section 3.3 to verify the foregoing properties of joint Gaussian variables. Since only the properties themselves, and not their proofs, are used in the sequel, Section 3.3 may be omitted on a first reading.

3.3 THE MULTIVARIATE CENTRAL LIMIT THEOREM

Insight into the appropriate mathematical model for filtered impulse noise is gained from consideration of the multivariate central limit theorem, which reduces for a single random variable to the central limit theorem of Chapter 2. The theorem is proved by means of the *joint characteristic function*, denoted $M_{\mathbf{x}}(\mathbf{v})$, of a set of k random variables

$$\mathbf{x} = (x_1, x_2, \ldots, x_k). \tag{3.58}$$

Joint Characteristic Functions

We define $M_{\mathbf{x}}(\boldsymbol{\nu})$ to be that function obtained from the joint density function $p_{\mathbf{x}}$ by performing a Fourier transformation on each argument:

$$M_{\mathbf{x}}(\nu_1, \nu_2, \ldots, \nu_k)$$

$$\triangleq \int_{-\infty}^{\infty} \int_{-\infty}^{\infty} \cdots \int_{-\infty}^{\infty} p_{\mathbf{x}}(\alpha_1, \alpha_2, \ldots, \alpha_k) e^{\mathrm{j}\nu_1\alpha_1} e^{\mathrm{j}\nu_2\alpha_2} \cdots e^{\mathrm{j}\nu_k\alpha_k}\, d\alpha_1\, d\alpha_2 \cdots d\alpha_k.$$

Using matrix notation and the theorem of expectation, we can write this more concisely as

$$M_{\mathbf{x}}(\boldsymbol{\nu}) \triangleq \int_{-\infty}^{\infty} p_{\mathbf{x}}(\boldsymbol{\alpha}) e^{\mathrm{j}\boldsymbol{\nu}\boldsymbol{\alpha}^{\mathsf{T}}}\, d\boldsymbol{\alpha}$$

$$= \overline{e^{\mathrm{j}\boldsymbol{\nu}\boldsymbol{\alpha}^{\mathsf{T}}}} = \mathrm{E}\left[\exp\left(\mathrm{j}\sum_{i=1}^{k} \nu_i x_i\right)\right] = \mathrm{E}\left[\prod_{i=1}^{k} e^{\mathrm{j}\nu_i x_i}\right]. \tag{3.59}$$

If the $\{x_i\}$ are statistically independent,

$$M_{\mathbf{x}}(\boldsymbol{\nu}) = \prod_{i=1}^{N} \mathrm{E}[e^{\mathrm{j}\nu_i x_i}] = \prod_{i=1}^{N} M_{x_i}(\nu_i). \tag{3.60}$$

Note that $M_{\mathbf{x}}(\boldsymbol{\nu})$ is a function of k arguments: $\boldsymbol{\nu} = (\nu_1, \nu_2, \ldots, \nu_k)$. Equation 3.60 should be contrasted with Eq. 2.98, the characteristic function of a sum of independent random variables, which is a function of only *one* variable ν.

Just as in the one-dimensional case, the joint density function $p_{\mathbf{x}}$ can be regained from $M_{\mathbf{x}}$ by the inverse Fourier transform; in matrix notation this is written

$$p_{\mathbf{x}}(\boldsymbol{\alpha}) = \frac{1}{(2\pi)^k} \int_{-\infty}^{\infty} M_{\mathbf{x}}(\boldsymbol{\nu}) e^{-\mathrm{j}\boldsymbol{\nu}\boldsymbol{\alpha}^{\mathsf{T}}}\, d\boldsymbol{\nu}. \tag{3.61}$$

The only essential difference between single and multidimensional Fourier transformations is the amount of labor required to evaluate the integrals.

Moments. In addition to their role in establishing limit theorems, joint characteristic functions are useful in calculating moments. This property has already been exploited in connection with one-dimensional characteristic functions. The general k-dimensional case is a straightforward extension. We first note from the definition of Eq. 3.59 that if we define the complex random variable w as

$$w \triangleq \mathrm{j}\boldsymbol{\nu}\mathbf{x}^{\mathsf{T}} = \mathrm{j}(\nu_1 x_1 + \nu_2 x_2 + \cdots + \nu_k x_k), \tag{3.62a}$$

then

$$M_{\mathbf{x}}(\boldsymbol{\nu}) = \overline{e^{w}}. \tag{3.62b}$$

If the moments exist,† we can expand $\overline{e^w}$ in a power series to obtain

$$\overline{e^w} = \mathrm{E}\left[1 + w + \frac{w^2}{2!} + \frac{w^3}{3!} + \cdots\right]$$

$$= 1 + \bar{w} + \frac{\overline{w^2}}{2!} + \frac{\overline{w^3}}{3!} + \cdots. \tag{3.62c}$$

Let us examine the second term in the expansion. From Eq. 3.62a

$$\bar{w} = \mathrm{j}(\nu_1\bar{x}_1 + \nu_2\bar{x}_2 + \cdots + \nu_k\bar{x}_k), \tag{3.62d}$$

which involves only the means of the $\{x_i\}$. In the derivation of the multivariate central limit, we shall be concerned with zero-mean random variables. Therefore, we now particularize to the case in which the means $\{\bar{x}_i\}$ are all zero. Letting $\mathbf{0}$ denote the vector each component of which is zero, we have

$$\mathrm{E}[\mathbf{x}] \triangleq \boldsymbol{(}\bar{x}_1, \bar{x}_2, \ldots, \bar{x}_k\boldsymbol{)} = \boldsymbol{(}0, 0, \ldots, 0\boldsymbol{)} \triangleq \mathbf{0}.$$

The second term in Eq. 3.62c is then $\bar{w} = 0$.

Let us next examine the third term, $\overline{w^2}/2$. Since

$$w^2 = \mathrm{j}^2\left(\sum_{i=1}^{k} \nu_i x_i\right)^2 = -\sum_{i=1}^{k}\sum_{j=1}^{k} \nu_i x_i x_j \nu_j,$$

taking the expectation yields

$$\overline{w^2} = -\sum_{i=1}^{k}\sum_{j=1}^{k} \nu_i \overline{x_i x_j} \nu_j.$$

For zero-mean random variables x_i and x_j the covariance λ_{ij} is

$$\lambda_{ij} = \overline{x_i x_j}; \qquad \overline{x_i} = \overline{x_j} = 0.$$

Thus

$$\overline{w^2} = -\sum_{i=1}^{k}\sum_{j=1}^{k} \nu_i \lambda_{ij} \nu_j, \tag{3.62e}$$

and $\overline{x_i x_j}$ may be evaluated by determining the coefficient multiplying $\nu_i\nu_j$ in the power series expansion of $M_{\mathbf{x}}(\boldsymbol{\nu})$.

Similarly, examination of $\overline{w^3}$ and higher order terms shows that the coefficient of any term such as $(\nu_i\nu_j \cdots \nu_l)$ in the power-series expansion of

† Since $|M_{\mathbf{x}}(\boldsymbol{\nu})| = \left|\int_{-\infty}^{\infty} e^{\mathrm{j}\boldsymbol{\nu}\boldsymbol{\alpha}^{\mathrm{T}}} p_{\mathbf{x}}(\boldsymbol{\alpha})\, d\boldsymbol{\alpha}\right| \leqslant \int_{-\infty}^{\infty} |e^{\mathrm{j}\boldsymbol{\nu}\boldsymbol{\alpha}^{\mathrm{T}}}|\, p_{\mathbf{x}}(\boldsymbol{\alpha})\, d\boldsymbol{\alpha} = 1$, the characteristic function is finite for all $\boldsymbol{\nu}$. If only the first J moments of w exist, it follows that $\overline{e^w}$ may be expanded in terms of $\overline{w^j}$, $1 \leqslant j \leqslant J$, plus a remainder term that vanishes as $\boldsymbol{\nu} \to \mathbf{0}$.

$M_{\mathbf{x}}(\boldsymbol{\nu})$ is proportional to the corresponding mixed moment $(\overline{x_i x_j \cdots x_l})$. Thus all moments that exist may be evaluated by expanding $M_{\mathbf{x}}(\boldsymbol{\nu})$ in a power series.

The covariance matrix. The form of the expression for $\overline{w^2}$ in Eq. 3.62e can be simplified by using matrix notation. Recognizing that the double summation is a quadratic form (cf. Eq. 3A.19), we can write

$$\overline{w^2} = -\boldsymbol{\nu}\Lambda_x\boldsymbol{\nu}^{\mathsf{T}}, \tag{3.63}$$

for which we define the matrix

$$\Lambda_x \triangleq \begin{pmatrix} \lambda_{11} & \lambda_{12} & \cdots & \lambda_{1k} \\ \lambda_{21} & \lambda_{22} & \cdots & \lambda_{2k} \\ \cdot & & & \\ \cdot & & & \\ \cdot & & & \\ \lambda_{k1} & \lambda_{k2} & \cdots & \lambda_{kk} \end{pmatrix}. \tag{3.64}$$

Λ_x is called the *covariance matrix* of $\mathbf{x}$. Since $\lambda_{ij} = \lambda_{ji}$ for all i and j, a covariance matrix is symmetric about its principal diagonal.

The covariance matrix plays a central role in the multidimensional central limit theorem. Observing that†

$$\mathbf{x}^{\mathsf{T}}\,\mathbf{x} = \begin{pmatrix} x_1 \\ x_2 \\ \cdot \\ \cdot \\ \cdot \\ x_k \end{pmatrix} (x_1, x_2, \ldots, x_k) = \begin{pmatrix} x_1^2 & x_1x_2 & \cdots & x_1x_k \\ x_2x_1 & x_2^2 & \cdots & x_2x_k \\ \cdot & & & \\ \cdot & & & \\ \cdot & & & \\ x_kx_1 & x_kx_2 & \cdots & x_k^2 \end{pmatrix}, \tag{3.65}$$

we can write Λ_x in the compact form

$$\Lambda_x = \mathrm{E}[\mathbf{x}^{\mathsf{T}}\,\mathbf{x}] = \overline{\mathbf{x}^{\mathsf{T}}\,\mathbf{x}}, \tag{3.66}$$

where the expectation E[**A**] of a matrix **A** with elements $\{a_{ij}\}$ is defined as the matrix whose elements are $\{\bar{a}_{ij}\}$. With this notation and the fact that

$$\boldsymbol{\nu}\mathbf{x}^{\mathsf{T}} = \sum_{i=1}^{k} \nu_i x_i = \mathbf{x}\boldsymbol{\nu}^{\mathsf{T}}, \tag{3.67a}$$

† Since $\mathbf{x}\mathbf{x}^{\mathsf{T}} = \mathbf{x}\cdot\mathbf{x} = \sum_{i=1}^{k} x_i^2$, Eq. 3.65 is a good example that matrix multiplication is *not* commutative.

we observe that Eq. 3.63 may also be derived directly by the sequence of equalities

$$\overline{w^2} \triangleq \mathrm{E}[(j\boldsymbol{\nu}\mathbf{x}^{\mathsf{T}})^2] = -\mathrm{E}[(\boldsymbol{\nu}\mathbf{x}^{\mathsf{T}})(\mathbf{x}\boldsymbol{\nu}^{\mathsf{T}})]$$

$$= -\boldsymbol{\nu}\overline{\mathbf{x}^{\mathsf{T}}\,\mathbf{x}}\boldsymbol{\nu}^{\mathsf{T}} = -\boldsymbol{\nu}\Lambda_x\boldsymbol{\nu}^{\mathsf{T}}. \tag{3.67b}$$

Central Limit Argument

The development of the multivariate central limit theorem which follows exactly mirrors the development of the corresponding one-dimensional theorem in Chapter 2. The only distinction is that the use of matrix notation now permits us to treat a sum of random vectors rather than just a sum of random variables.

Let us consider the vector $\mathbf{z} = (z_1, z_2, \ldots, z_k)$ defined as

$$\mathbf{z} = \frac{1}{\sqrt{N}}\sum_{i=1}^{N}\mathbf{x}_i. \tag{3.68}$$

We assume that each $\mathbf{x}_i$ is a k-component vector that is *statistically independent* of all others:

$$p_{\mathbf{x}_1,\mathbf{x}_2,\ldots,\mathbf{x}_N} = \prod_{i=1}^{N} p_{\mathbf{x}_i}. \tag{3.69a}$$

Also, we assume that each $\mathbf{x}_i$ has the same density function, say $p_{\mathbf{x}}$, with zero mean, covariance matrix Λ_x, and characteristic function $M_{\mathbf{x}}$:

$$\left.\begin{aligned} p_{\mathbf{x}_i} &= p_{\mathbf{x}} \\ \mathrm{E}[\mathbf{x}_i] &= \mathbf{0} \\ \mathrm{E}[\mathbf{x}_i^{\mathsf{T}}\,\mathbf{x}_i] &= \Lambda_x \\ M_{\mathbf{x}_i} &= M_{\mathbf{x}} \end{aligned}\right\}; \qquad i = 1, 2, \ldots, N. \tag{3.69b}$$

Thus we have

$$\mathrm{E}[\mathbf{z}] = \mathbf{0}. \tag{3.70a}$$

The normalization of $\mathbf{z}$ by the factor $1/\sqrt{N}$ in Eq. 3.68 is such that

$$\Lambda_z = \mathrm{E}[\mathbf{z}^{\mathsf{T}}\,\mathbf{z}] = \frac{1}{N}\mathrm{E}\left[\left(\sum_{i=1}^{N}\mathbf{x}_i^{\mathsf{T}}\right)\left(\sum_{j=1}^{N}\mathbf{x}_j\right)\right]$$

$$= \frac{1}{N}\mathrm{E}\left[\sum_{i=1}^{N}\mathbf{x}_i^{\mathsf{T}}\,\mathbf{x}_i + \sum_{i=1}^{N}\sum_{\substack{j=1\\(j\neq i)}}^{N}\mathbf{x}_i^{\mathsf{T}}\,\mathbf{x}_j\right]$$

$$= \frac{1}{N}\sum_{i=1}^{N}\mathrm{E}[\mathbf{x}_i^{\mathsf{T}}\,\mathbf{x}_i] = \Lambda_x. \tag{3.70b}$$

Here we have used the fact that $\mathbf{x}_i$ and $\mathbf{x}_j$ are statistically independent to evaluate

$$\mathrm{E}[\mathbf{x}_i^{\mathsf{T}}\,\mathbf{x}_j] = \mathrm{E}[\mathbf{x}_i^{\mathsf{T}}]\,\mathrm{E}[\mathbf{x}_j] = (0); \qquad j \neq i,$$

in which (0) denotes the matrix each element of which is zero.

We now take up the limiting form of the characteristic function of $\mathbf{z}$:

$$\begin{aligned} M_{\mathbf{z}}(\boldsymbol{\nu}) &\triangleq \mathrm{E}[e^{\mathrm{j}\boldsymbol{\nu}\mathbf{z}^{\mathsf{T}}}] \\ &= \mathrm{E}\left[\exp\left(\mathrm{j}\boldsymbol{\nu}\frac{1}{\sqrt{N}}\sum_{i=1}^{N}\mathbf{x}_i^{\mathsf{T}}\right)\right] \\ &= \mathrm{E}\left[\prod_{i=1}^{N}\exp\left(\mathrm{j}\frac{\boldsymbol{\nu}}{\sqrt{N}}\mathbf{x}_i^{\mathsf{T}}\right)\right]. \end{aligned}$$

Since the random vectors $\{\mathbf{x}_i\}$ are statistically independent, so are the random variables $\{\exp(\mathrm{j}\,\boldsymbol{\nu}\,\mathbf{x}_i^{\mathsf{T}}/\sqrt{N})\}$, and the mean of their product is therefore the product of their means:

$$\begin{aligned} M_{\mathbf{z}}(\boldsymbol{\nu}) &= \prod_{i=1}^{N}\mathrm{E}\left[\exp\left(\mathrm{j}\frac{\boldsymbol{\nu}}{\sqrt{N}}\mathbf{x}_i^{\mathsf{T}}\right)\right] \\ &= \prod_{i=1}^{N} M_{\mathbf{x}_i}\!\left(\frac{\boldsymbol{\nu}}{\sqrt{N}}\right) = \left[M_{\mathbf{x}}\!\left(\frac{\boldsymbol{\nu}}{\sqrt{N}}\right)\right]^{N}. \end{aligned}$$

Taking logarithms on both sides, we have

$$\ln M_{\mathbf{z}}(\boldsymbol{\nu}) = N \ln M_{\mathbf{x}}\!\left(\frac{\boldsymbol{\nu}}{\sqrt{N}}\right). \tag{3.71}$$

The limiting behavior of the right-hand side of Eq. 3.71 can be determined by expanding first $M_{\mathbf{x}}(\boldsymbol{\nu}/\sqrt{N})$, and then $\ln M_{\mathbf{x}}(\boldsymbol{\nu}/\sqrt{N})$, in a power series. We assume for simplicity that all moments $\overline{w^j}$, $j = 1, 2, \ldots$, are finite. The proof may be extended to the case in which only $\overline{w^2}$ is finite by expanding in a power series with remainder. If $\overline{w^2}$ is not finite, the central limit theorem is not valid. From Eqs. 3.62 and 3.70

$$M_{\mathbf{x}}(\boldsymbol{\nu}) = 1 + \bar{w} + \frac{\overline{w^2}}{2!} + \frac{\overline{w^3}}{3!} + \cdots,$$

where

$$\begin{aligned} w &\triangleq \mathrm{j}\boldsymbol{\nu}\mathbf{x}^{\mathsf{T}} = \mathrm{j}\sum_{i=1}^{N}\nu_i x_i, \\ \bar{w} &= 0, \\ \overline{w^2} &= -\boldsymbol{\nu}\Lambda_x\boldsymbol{\nu}^{\mathsf{T}} = -\boldsymbol{\nu}\Lambda_z\boldsymbol{\nu}^{\mathsf{T}}. \end{aligned}$$

Thus

$$M_{\mathbf{x}}\left(\frac{\boldsymbol{\nu}}{\sqrt{N}}\right) = 1 - \frac{1}{2N}\boldsymbol{\nu}\Lambda_z\boldsymbol{\nu}^{\mathsf{T}} + \frac{1}{N^{3/2}} f_{\boldsymbol{\nu}}\left(\frac{1}{\sqrt{N}}\right), \tag{3.72a}$$

where

$$f_{\boldsymbol{\nu}}\left(\frac{1}{\sqrt{N}}\right) \triangleq \left[\frac{\overline{w^3}}{3!} + \frac{\overline{w^4}}{4!\sqrt{N}} + \cdots\right] \tag{3.72b}$$

is a continuous function of $\sqrt{N}$ that for any fixed $\boldsymbol{\nu}$ approaches the constant $\overline{w^3}/6$ as N becomes large. By taking N large enough, we can make

$$\left|\frac{\overline{w^2}}{2N} + \frac{1}{N^{3/2}} f_{\boldsymbol{\nu}}\left(\frac{1}{\sqrt{N}}\right)\right|$$

as small as we wish. It follows that for sufficiently large N we may invoke the expansion

$$\ln(1 + u) = u - \frac{u^2}{2} + \frac{u^3}{3} - \cdots; \qquad |u| < 1$$

and write

$$\ln M_{\mathbf{x}}\left(\frac{\boldsymbol{\nu}}{\sqrt{N}}\right) = -\frac{1}{2N}\boldsymbol{\nu}\Lambda_z\boldsymbol{\nu}^{\mathsf{T}} + \frac{1}{N^{3/2}} f_{\boldsymbol{\nu}}\left(\frac{1}{\sqrt{N}}\right) + \text{(other terms)}.$$

Since the "other terms" involve powers of N more negative than $N^{-3/2}$, we have, for any fixed $\boldsymbol{\nu}$,

$$\begin{aligned}
\lim_{N\to\infty} \ln M_{\mathbf{z}}(\boldsymbol{\nu}) &= \lim_{N\to\infty} N \ln M_{\mathbf{x}}\left(\frac{\boldsymbol{\nu}}{\sqrt{N}}\right) \\
&= \lim_{N\to\infty} N\left[-\frac{1}{2N}\boldsymbol{\nu}\Lambda_z\boldsymbol{\nu}^{\mathsf{T}} + \frac{1}{N^{3/2}} f_{\boldsymbol{\nu}}\left(\frac{1}{\sqrt{N}}\right) + \text{(other terms)}\right] \\
&= -\frac{1}{2}\boldsymbol{\nu}\Lambda_z\boldsymbol{\nu}^{\mathsf{T}}.
\end{aligned}$$

From the continuity of the exponential function

$$\lim_{N\to\infty} M_{\mathbf{z}}(\boldsymbol{\nu}) = \exp\left(-\tfrac{1}{2}\boldsymbol{\nu}\Lambda_z\boldsymbol{\nu}^{\mathsf{T}}\right). \tag{3.73a}$$

Equation 3.73a is our desired result. For any $p_{\mathbf{x}}$ the characteristic function $M_{\mathbf{z}}(\boldsymbol{\nu})$ of a normalized sum $\mathbf{z} = (1/\sqrt{N})\sum_{i=1}^{N}\mathbf{x}_i$ of identically distributed zero-mean random vectors $\{\mathbf{x}_i\}$ approaches $\exp\left[-\tfrac{1}{2}\boldsymbol{\nu}\Lambda_z\boldsymbol{\nu}^{\mathsf{T}}\right]$. This limiting function involves only the covariance matrix $\Lambda_z = \Lambda_x$. Note that when $k = 1$ Eq. 3.73a reduces to

$$\lim_{N\to\infty} M_z(\nu) = \exp\left(-\tfrac{1}{2}\nu\lambda_{11}\nu\right) = \exp\left(-\tfrac{1}{2}\nu^2\sigma^2\right) \tag{3.73b}$$

and is in accord with the one-dimensional central limit result of Eq. 2.178.

Gaussian Random Variables

In Chapter 2 we called a single random variable "Gaussian" if its characteristic function had the form of the right-hand side of Eq. 3.73b. We now generalize the definition to k variables by saying that any zero-mean random vector $\mathbf{y}$ is *Gaussian if and only if*

$$M_{\mathbf{y}}(\boldsymbol{\nu}) = \exp\left(-\tfrac{1}{2}\boldsymbol{\nu}\Lambda_y\boldsymbol{\nu}^{\mathsf{T}}\right). \tag{3.74}$$

Alternatively, we say that the components $\{y_i\}$ of $\mathbf{y}$ are "jointly Gaussian." Equation 3.73a states that $M_{\mathbf{z}}(\boldsymbol{\nu})$ approaches the Gaussian form as $N \to \infty$.

The density function of a zero-mean Gaussian vector $\mathbf{y}$ is determined by taking the inverse Fourier transform of $M_{\mathbf{y}}$. However, just as in the one-dimensional case, we must refrain from claiming that the density function $p_{\mathbf{z}}$ of a normalized sum $\mathbf{z}$ necessarily converges to Gaussian form as N gets large. Whenever $p_{\mathbf{x}}$ does not contain impulses, the convergence occurs. However, if $p_{\mathbf{x}}$ contains impulses, so does $p_{\mathbf{z}}$. As in Chapter 2, it is only the distribution function $F_{\mathbf{z}}$ that always becomes Gaussian (provided Λ_x exists).

The definition of "jointly Gaussian" is extended to vectors with nonzero means in an obvious way. If $\mathbf{x}$ is a k-dimensional vector with mean

$$\mathrm{E}[\mathbf{x}] \triangleq \mathbf{m}_x \triangleq (\overline{x_1}, \overline{x_2}, \ldots, \overline{x_k}), \tag{3.75a}$$

then $\mathbf{x}$ is called Gaussian if and only if the zero-mean vector

$$\mathbf{y} = \mathbf{x} - \mathbf{m}_x \tag{3.75b}$$

is Gaussian; that is, if and only if

$$M_{\mathbf{y}}(\boldsymbol{\nu}) = \exp\left(-\tfrac{1}{2}\boldsymbol{\nu}\Lambda_y\boldsymbol{\nu}^{\mathsf{T}}\right). \tag{3.75c}$$

We therefore have

$$\begin{aligned} M_{\mathbf{x}}(\boldsymbol{\nu}) &\triangleq \overline{e^{j\boldsymbol{\nu}\mathbf{x}^{\mathsf{T}}}} = \overline{e^{j\boldsymbol{\nu}(\mathbf{y}^{\mathsf{T}}+\mathbf{m}_x{}^{\mathsf{T}})}} \\ &= \overline{e^{j\boldsymbol{\nu}\mathbf{y}^{\mathsf{T}}}}\, e^{j\boldsymbol{\nu}\mathbf{m}_x{}^{\mathsf{T}}} = M_{\mathbf{y}}(\boldsymbol{\nu})e^{j\boldsymbol{\nu}\mathbf{m}_x{}^{\mathsf{T}}} \\ &= \exp\left(-\tfrac{1}{2}\boldsymbol{\nu}\Lambda_y\boldsymbol{\nu}^{\mathsf{T}} + j\boldsymbol{\nu}\mathbf{m}_x{}^{\mathsf{T}}\right). \end{aligned}$$

Since, in accordance with the definition of Eq. 3.37, the covariance λ_{ij} of x_i and x_j is

$$\lambda_{ij} \triangleq \mathrm{E}[(x_i - \overline{x}_i)(x_j - \overline{x}_j)] = \mathrm{E}[y_iy_j],$$

the covariance matrices of $\mathbf{x}$ and $\mathbf{y}$ are the same:

$$\Lambda_x = \Lambda_y.$$

(We again note that central moments are invariant to transformations involving only the addition of constants.) We conclude that the general form of the *Gaussian characteristic function* is

$$M_{\mathbf{x}}(\boldsymbol{\nu}) = \exp\left(-\tfrac{1}{2}\boldsymbol{\nu}\Lambda_x\boldsymbol{\nu}^{\mathsf{T}} + \mathrm{j}\boldsymbol{\nu}\mathbf{m}_x^{\mathsf{T}}\right), \tag{3.76a}$$

where

$$\mathbf{m}_x \triangleq (\bar{x}_1, \bar{x}_2, \ldots, \bar{x}_k), \tag{3.76b}$$

$$\Lambda_x \triangleq \mathrm{E}[(\mathbf{x} - \mathbf{m}_x)^{\mathsf{T}} (\mathbf{x} - \mathbf{m}_x)]. \tag{3.76c}$$

Filtered Impulse Noise Process

The appropriateness of assuming that samples $\mathbf{n(t)} = (n(t_1), n(t_2), \ldots, n(t_k))$ observed from a filtered impulse noise source at any set of times $\{t_j\}$ are modeled mathematically by a joint Gaussian density function hinges on the multivariate central limit theorem. Let $\mathbf{h}_i$ be the random vector obtained by sampling the plate response to the ith current impulse in Fig. 3.16 at times $t_1, t_2, \ldots, t_k$:

$$\mathbf{h}_i \triangleq (h(t_1 - \tau_i), h(t_2 - \tau_i), \ldots, h(t_k - \tau_i)). \tag{3.77a}$$

As in Eq. 3.25, $h(t)$ is the (known) filter impulse response, and the random variable τ_i is the arrival time of the ith impulse. Whenever the impulse arrival times $\{\tau_i\}$ are substantially independent and the average number of impulses arriving during the effective duration of the filter's impulse response is extremely large, the central limit theorem implies that the density function of

$$\mathbf{n(t)} = \sum_i \mathbf{h}_i \tag{3.77b}$$

is closely approximated by the joint Gaussian density function.

Properties of Gaussian Random Variables

Before considering the form of the multivariate Gaussian density function, it is instructive to observe certain properties implied by the definition of the Gaussian characteristic function. We now show that any set of k *jointly Gaussian* random variables, say $\mathbf{x} = (x_1, x_2, \ldots, x_k)$, exhibits the four properties claimed on p. 156.

Property 1. The joint density function of the $\{x_i\}$, $p_{\mathbf{x}}$, depends only on the means $\mathbf{m}_x$ and the central moments λ_{ij}, $i = 1, 2, \ldots, k; j = 1, 2, \ldots, k$.

Proof follows from the fact that the Gaussian characteristic function $M_{\mathbf{x}}$ depends only on $\mathbf{m}_x$ and the covariance matrix Λ_x, with elements $\{\lambda_{ij}\}$. Thus $p_{\mathbf{x}}$, the Fourier transform of $M_{\mathbf{x}}$, also depends only on these quantities.

Property 2. Any subset of the $\{x_i\}$, say $\mathbf{x}_0 \triangleq (x_1, x_2, \ldots, x_l)$, where $1 \leqslant l < k$, is also jointly Gaussian.

Proof follows from noting that, if $\boldsymbol{\nu}_0 \triangleq (\nu_1, \nu_2, \ldots, \nu_l)$,

$$M_{\mathbf{x}_0}(\boldsymbol{\nu}_0) \triangleq \mathrm{E}[e^{\mathrm{j}(\nu_1 x_1 + \nu_2 x_2 + \cdots + \nu_l x_l)}]$$

$$= \mathrm{E}[e^{\mathrm{j}(\nu_1 x_1 + \nu_2 x_2 + \cdots + \nu_l x_l + 0 \cdot x_{l+1} + \cdots + 0 \cdot x_k)}]$$

$$= M_{\mathbf{x}}(\nu_1, \nu_2, \ldots, \nu_l, 0, 0, \ldots, 0). \tag{3.78a}$$

From Eq. 3.76

$$M_{\mathbf{x}}(\boldsymbol{\nu}) = \exp\left(-\frac{1}{2}\sum_{i=1}^{k}\sum_{j=1}^{k}\nu_i\lambda_{ij}\nu_j + \mathrm{j}\sum_{i=1}^{k}\nu_i\overline{x_i}\right). \tag{3.78b}$$

Substituting Eq. 3.78b in Eq. 3.78a and discarding terms that are equal to zero, we again have the Gaussian form

$$M_{\mathbf{x}_0}(\boldsymbol{\nu}_0) = \exp\left(-\frac{1}{2}\sum_{i=1}^{l}\sum_{j=1}^{l}\nu_i\lambda_{ij}\nu_j + \mathrm{j}\sum_{i=1}^{l}\nu_i\overline{x}_i\right). \tag{3.78c}$$

As a special case, we note that each component x_i of a Gaussian vector $\mathbf{x}$ is individually Gaussian, with variance $\sigma_i^2 = \lambda_{ii}$ and mean $\overline{x}_i$:

$$M_{x_i}(\nu_i) = M_{\mathbf{x}}(0, 0, \ldots, \nu_i, \ldots, 0) = \exp(-\tfrac{1}{2}\nu_i^2\sigma_i^2 + \mathrm{j}\nu_i\overline{x_i}). \tag{3.78d}$$

Property 3. The $\{x_i\}$ are statistically independent if their covariance matrix is *diagonal*; that is, if all covariances $\{\lambda_{ij}\}$ are zero for $j \neq i$:

$$\lambda_{ij} = \sigma_i^2\,\delta_{ij}, \tag{3.79a}$$

in which we use the Kronecker delta, defined by

$$\delta_{ij} \triangleq \begin{cases} 1; & \text{for } j = i, \\ 0; & \text{for } j \neq i. \end{cases} \tag{3.79b}$$

Proof follows from substituting the diagonal covariance matrix

$$\Lambda_x = \begin{pmatrix} \sigma_1^2 & & & & \\ & \sigma_2^2 & & 0 & \\ & & \cdot & & \\ & & & \cdot & \\ & 0 & & & \cdot & \\ & & & & & \sigma_k^2 \end{pmatrix} \tag{3.80a}$$

in the expression for the characteristic function:

$$M_{\mathbf{x}}(\boldsymbol{\nu}) = \exp\left(-\tfrac{1}{2}\boldsymbol{\nu}\Lambda_x\boldsymbol{\nu}^{\mathsf{T}} + \mathrm{j}\boldsymbol{\nu}\mathbf{m}_x^{\mathsf{T}}\right)$$

$$= \exp\left(-\frac{1}{2}\sum_{i=1}^{k}\nu_i^2\sigma_i^2 + \mathrm{j}\sum_{i=1}^{k}\nu_i\bar{x}_i\right)$$

$$= \prod_{i=1}^{k}\exp\left(-\tfrac{1}{2}\nu_i^2\sigma_i^2 + \mathrm{j}\nu_i\bar{x}_i\right) = \prod_{i=1}^{k}M_{x_i}(\nu_i). \tag{3.80b}$$

Taking the inverse Fourier transform in accordance with Eq. 3.61, we obtain

$$p_{\mathbf{x}}(\boldsymbol{\alpha}) = \frac{1}{(2\pi)^k}\int_{-\infty}^{\infty} M_{\mathbf{x}}(\boldsymbol{\nu})e^{-\mathrm{j}\boldsymbol{\nu}\boldsymbol{\alpha}^{\mathsf{T}}}\,d\boldsymbol{\nu}$$

$$= \prod_{i=1}^{k}\frac{1}{2\pi}\int_{-\infty}^{\infty} M_{x_i}(\nu_i)e^{-\mathrm{j}\nu_i\alpha_i}\,d\nu_i$$

$$= \prod_{i=1}^{k} p_{x_i}(\alpha_i), \tag{3.80c}$$

which completes the proof. Equation 3.80c states that *any* set of (not necessarily Gaussian) random variables is *statistically independent whenever their joint characteristic function factors.* For *Gaussian* variables the factorability of the characteristic function is guaranteed by the condition that the covariance matrix be diagonal.

Property 4. Let $y = (y_1, y_2, \ldots, y_k)$ be a set of random variables obtained from $\mathbf{x}$ by means of the transformation

$$\mathbf{y}^{\mathsf{T}} = \mathbf{A}\mathbf{x}^{\mathsf{T}} + \mathbf{a}^{\mathsf{T}}, \tag{3.81}$$

where $\mathbf{A}$ is any $k \times k$ matrix. Then $\mathbf{y}$ is also jointly Gaussian.

Proof follows from showing that the joint characteristic function of $\mathbf{y}$ has the Gaussian form of Eq. 3.76. By definition,

$$M_{\mathbf{y}}(\boldsymbol{\nu}) \triangleq \overline{e^{\mathrm{j}\boldsymbol{\nu}\mathbf{y}^{\mathsf{T}}}} = \overline{e^{\mathrm{j}\boldsymbol{\nu}(\mathbf{A}\mathbf{x}^{\mathsf{T}}+\mathbf{a}^{\mathsf{T}})}}$$

$$= \overline{e^{\mathrm{j}(\boldsymbol{\nu}\mathbf{A})\mathbf{x}^{\mathsf{T}}}}\,e^{\mathrm{j}\boldsymbol{\nu}\mathbf{a}^{\mathsf{T}}}$$

$$= M_{\mathbf{x}}(\boldsymbol{\nu}\mathbf{A})e^{\mathrm{j}\boldsymbol{\nu}\mathbf{a}^{\mathsf{T}}}.$$

Since $M_{\mathbf{x}}(\boldsymbol{\nu})$ is Gaussian,

$$M_{\mathbf{y}}(\boldsymbol{\nu}) = \{\exp[-\tfrac{1}{2}(\boldsymbol{\nu}\mathbf{A})\Lambda_x(\boldsymbol{\nu}\mathbf{A})^{\mathsf{T}} + \mathrm{j}(\boldsymbol{\nu}\mathbf{A})\mathbf{m}_x^{\mathsf{T}}]\}\,e^{\mathrm{j}\boldsymbol{\nu}\mathbf{a}^{\mathsf{T}}}$$

$$= \exp[-\tfrac{1}{2}\boldsymbol{\nu}(\mathbf{A}\Lambda_x\mathbf{A}^{\mathsf{T}})\boldsymbol{\nu}^{\mathsf{T}} + \mathrm{j}\boldsymbol{\nu}(\mathbf{A}\mathbf{m}_x^{\mathsf{T}} + \mathbf{a}^{\mathsf{T}})]. \tag{3.82}$$

We now identify $(\mathbf{A}\mathbf{m}_x^{\mathsf{T}} + \mathbf{a}^{\mathsf{T}})$ and $(\mathbf{A}\Lambda_x\mathbf{A}^{\mathsf{T}})$ as $\mathbf{m}_y^{\mathsf{T}}$ and Λ_y, respectively. First, from Eq. 3.81,

$$\mathbf{m}_y^{\mathsf{T}} \triangleq \bar{\mathbf{y}}^{\mathsf{T}} = \mathrm{E}[\mathbf{A}\mathbf{x}^{\mathsf{T}} + \mathbf{a}^{\mathsf{T}}]$$

$$= \mathbf{A}\mathbf{m}_x^{\mathsf{T}} + \mathbf{a}^{\mathsf{T}}. \tag{3.83a}$$

Second, from Eq. 3.76,

$$\Lambda_y \triangleq \mathrm{E}[(\mathbf{y}^{\mathsf{T}} - \mathbf{m}_y^{\mathsf{T}})(\mathbf{y} - \mathbf{m}_y)].$$

But

$$\mathbf{y}^{\mathsf{T}} - \mathbf{m}_y^{\mathsf{T}} = (\mathbf{A}\mathbf{x}^{\mathsf{T}} + \mathbf{a}^{\mathsf{T}}) - (\mathbf{A}\mathbf{m}_x^{\mathsf{T}} + \mathbf{a}^{\mathsf{T}}) = \mathbf{A}(\mathbf{x}^{\mathsf{T}} - \mathbf{m}_x^{\mathsf{T}}),$$

and transposing yields

$$\mathbf{y} - \mathbf{m}_y = (\mathbf{x} - \mathbf{m}_x)\mathbf{A}^{\mathsf{T}}.$$

Thus

$$\Lambda_y = \mathrm{E}[\mathbf{A}(\mathbf{x}^{\mathsf{T}} - \mathbf{m}_x^{\mathsf{T}})(\mathbf{x} - \mathbf{m}_x)\mathbf{A}^{\mathsf{T}}]$$

$$= \mathbf{A}\Lambda_x\mathbf{A}^{\mathsf{T}}. \tag{3.83b}$$

Substituting Eqs. 3.83a and b in Eq. 3.82, we have

$$M_{\mathbf{y}}(\boldsymbol{\nu}) = \exp\left(-\tfrac{1}{2}\boldsymbol{\nu}\Lambda_y\boldsymbol{\nu}^{\mathsf{T}} + \mathrm{j}\boldsymbol{\nu}\mathbf{m}_y^{\mathsf{T}}\right).$$

We conclude that **y**, the result of a matrix transformation on the Gaussian vector **x**, is also Gaussian.

A special case of Eq. 3.81 is the particular $(k \times k)$ transformation

$$\mathbf{A} = \begin{pmatrix} a_{11} & a_{12} & a_{13} & \cdots & a_{1k} \\ 0 & 1 & 0 & \cdots & 0 \\ 0 & 0 & 1 & \cdots & 0 \\ \cdot & & & \cdot & \\ \cdot & & & & \cdot \\ \cdot & & & & \cdot \\ 0 & 0 & 0 & \cdots & 1 \end{pmatrix}, \quad \mathbf{a} = \mathbf{0}. \tag{3.84a}$$

Then

$$y_1 = \sum_{i=1}^{k} a_{ij}x_j \tag{3.84b}$$

$$y_j = x_j; \qquad j \neq 1. \tag{3.84c}$$

It follows that y_1, hence any arbitrary weighted sum of the jointly Gaussian random variables $\{x_i\}$, is Gaussian whether or not the $\{x_i\}$

are statistically independent. (Note that we had previously established in Eq. 2.142 the restricted result that a sum of *independent* Gaussian variables is Gaussian.)

In matrix algebra[43] it is shown that for any nonsingular† covariance matrix Λ_y a reversible transformation $\mathbf{B}\mathbf{y}^{\mathsf{T}} = \mathbf{x}^{\mathsf{T}}$ exists such that

$$\Lambda_x \triangleq \mathbf{B}\Lambda_y\mathbf{B}^{\mathsf{T}} \tag{3.85}$$

is diagonal. Thus an arbitrary nonsingular set of Gaussian random variables $\{y_i\}$ can always be transformed into a set of statistically independent Gaussian random variables $\{x_i\}$. Conversely, the transformation $\mathbf{A} = \mathbf{B}^{-1}$ applied to the $\{x_i\}$ regains the statistically dependent variables $\{y_i\}$. A diagonalizing transformation $\mathbf{B}$ also exists when Λ_y is singular, but in this case $\mathbf{B}$ is irreversible.

The Multivariate Gaussian Density Function

The form of the joint Gaussian density function is easily obtained by first considering a set, say $\mathbf{x} = (x_1, x_2, \ldots, x_k)$, of statistically independent zero-mean Gaussian random variables:

$$p_{\mathbf{x}}(\boldsymbol{\alpha}) = \prod_{i=1}^{k} p_{x_i}(\alpha_i) = \prod_{i=1}^{k} \frac{1}{\sqrt{2\pi}\sigma_i} e^{-\alpha_i^2/2\sigma_i^2}; \qquad \sigma_i^2 = \overline{x_i^2}. \tag{3.86a}$$

In matrix notation

$$p_{\mathbf{x}}(\boldsymbol{\alpha}) = \frac{1}{(2\pi)^{k/2}|\Lambda_x|^{1/2}} \exp\left(-\tfrac{1}{2}\boldsymbol{\alpha}\Lambda_x^{-1}\boldsymbol{\alpha}^{\mathsf{T}}\right), \tag{3.86b}$$

where Λ_x is the diagonal matrix

$$\Lambda_x = \begin{pmatrix} \sigma_1^2 & & & 0 \\ & \sigma_2^2 & & \\ & & \ddots & \\ 0 & & & \sigma_k^2 \end{pmatrix} \tag{3.86c}$$

† As in Appendix 2A, we say that Λ_y, or $\mathbf{y}$, is *singular* whenever the determinant $|\Lambda_y| = 0$, which implies that the inverse matrix Λ_y^{-1} does not exist. In this case some of the component random variables comprising $\mathbf{y}$ are equal to linear combinations of the others, so that $p_{\mathbf{y}}$ contains impulses. A singular random vector $\mathbf{y}$ results when a nonsingular random vector $\mathbf{z}$ is transformed by an *irreversible* matrix $\mathbf{C}$; that is, when $\mathbf{y}^{\mathsf{T}} = \mathbf{C}\mathbf{z}^{\mathsf{T}}$ and $|\mathbf{C}| = 0$, so that $\mathbf{z}$ cannot be regained from knowledge of $\mathbf{y}$.

with inverse

$$\Lambda_x^{-1} = \begin{pmatrix} \frac{1}{\sigma_1^2} & & & 0 \\ & \frac{1}{\sigma_2^2} & & \\ & & \ddots & \\ 0 & & & \frac{1}{\sigma_k^2} \end{pmatrix} \tag{3.86d}$$

and determinant

$$|\Lambda_x| = \sigma_1^2\sigma_2^2 \cdots \sigma_k^2. \tag{3.86e}$$

Next, let us consider the (Gaussian) random vector obtained from $\mathbf{x}$ by the reversible matrix transformation

$$\mathbf{y} = \mathbf{x}\mathbf{A}^{\mathsf{T}} + \mathbf{m}_y = \mathbf{f}(\mathbf{x}). \tag{3.87a}$$

Here, the notation $\mathbf{f}(\ )$ is that of Appendix 2A. The inverse transformation is defined as

$$\mathbf{x} \triangleq \mathbf{g}(\mathbf{y}) = (\mathbf{y} - \mathbf{m}_y)\mathbf{B}^{\mathsf{T}}, \tag{3.87b}$$

where $\mathbf{B}$ is the matrix inverse to $\mathbf{A}$:

$$\mathbf{B} = \mathbf{A}^{-1}. \tag{3.87c}$$

It follows from Eq. 2A.7 that

$$p_{\mathbf{y}}(\boldsymbol{\beta}) = p_{\mathbf{x}}(\mathbf{g}(\boldsymbol{\beta}))\,|J_g(\boldsymbol{\beta})|\,, \tag{3.88}$$

where $|J_g(\boldsymbol{\beta})|$ is the absolute value of the Jacobian of the transformation $\mathbf{g}(\ )$.

By definition, the (i, j)th element of $J_g(\boldsymbol{\beta})$ is

$$J_{ij} = \frac{\partial g_i(\boldsymbol{\beta})}{\partial \beta_j}. \tag{3.89a}$$

From Eq. 3.87b

$$\begin{aligned} \mathbf{g}(\boldsymbol{\beta}) &= (\boldsymbol{\beta} - \mathbf{m}_y)\mathbf{B}^{\mathsf{T}} \\ &\triangleq (g_1(\boldsymbol{\beta}), g_2(\boldsymbol{\beta}), \ldots, g_k(\boldsymbol{\beta})). \end{aligned}$$

Denoting the (i, j) element of $\mathbf{B}$ by b_{ij}, we have

$$g_i(\boldsymbol{\beta}) = \sum_{j=1}^{k} b_{ij}(\beta_j - \bar{y}_j) \tag{3.89b}$$

and

$$\frac{\partial g_i(\boldsymbol{\beta})}{\partial \beta_j} = b_{ij}. \tag{3.89c}$$

We conclude that the Jacobean is just the determinant of the matrix **B**,

$$J_g(\boldsymbol{\beta}) = |\mathbf{B}|, \tag{3.89d}$$

and is independent of $\boldsymbol{\beta}$.

Substitution of Eqs. 3.86b and 3.89d in Eq. 3.88 then yields

$$p_\mathbf{y}(\boldsymbol{\beta}) = \frac{1}{(2\pi)^{k/2}}\left(\frac{|\mathbf{B}|^2}{|\Lambda_x|}\right)^{1/2} \exp\left[-\tfrac{1}{2}(\boldsymbol{\beta} - \mathbf{m}_y)\mathbf{B}^\mathsf{T}\Lambda_x^{-1}\mathbf{B}(\boldsymbol{\beta}^\mathsf{T} - \mathbf{m}_y^\mathsf{T})\right].$$

The last step in determining the general form of the multivariate Gaussian density function is identification of terms. Since $\mathbf{B} = \mathbf{A}^{-1}$ and

$$\Lambda_y \triangleq \mathrm{E}[(\mathbf{y}^\mathsf{T} - \mathbf{m}_y^\mathsf{T})(\mathbf{y} - \mathbf{m}_y)] = \mathrm{E}[\mathbf{A}\mathbf{x}^\mathsf{T}\,\mathbf{x}\mathbf{A}^\mathsf{T}] = \mathbf{A}\Lambda_x\mathbf{A}^\mathsf{T},$$

invoking Eqs. 3A.28 and 3A.30 we have

$$\mathbf{B}^\mathsf{T}\Lambda_x^{-1}\mathbf{B} = (\mathbf{A}^{-1})^\mathsf{T}\Lambda_x^{-1}\mathbf{A}^{-1} = (\mathbf{A}\Lambda_x\mathbf{A}^\mathsf{T})^{-1} = \Lambda_y^{-1}.$$

Using the well-known results for determinants[43] that

$$|\mathbf{A}^\mathsf{T}| = |\mathbf{A}|$$

and that for any two $(k \times k)$ matrices

$$|\mathbf{CD}| = |\mathbf{C}|\,|\mathbf{D}|,$$

which implies

$$|\mathbf{I}| = |\mathbf{A}^{-1}\mathbf{A}| = |\mathbf{A}^{-1}|\,|\mathbf{A}| = 1$$

or

$$|\mathbf{B}| = \frac{1}{|\mathbf{A}|},$$

we have

$$\frac{|\mathbf{B}|^2}{|\Lambda_x|} = \frac{1}{|\mathbf{A}|\,|\Lambda_x|\,|\mathbf{A}^\mathsf{T}|} = \frac{1}{|\mathbf{A}\Lambda_x\mathbf{A}^\mathsf{T}|} = \frac{1}{|\Lambda_y|}.$$

Accordingly, $p_\mathbf{y}$ may be written concisely as

$$p_\mathbf{y}(\boldsymbol{\beta}) = \frac{1}{(2\pi)^{k/2}\,|\Lambda_y|^{1/2}} \exp\left[-\tfrac{1}{2}(\boldsymbol{\beta} - \mathbf{m}_y)\Lambda_y^{-1}(\boldsymbol{\beta} - \mathbf{m}_y)^\mathsf{T}\right]. \tag{3.90}$$

Equation 3.90 is the general form of the nonsingular Gaussian density function. We observe that it depends only on the mean vector $\mathbf{m}_y$ and the covariance matrix Λ_y. That Eq. 3.90 represents the most general form of the nonsingular Gaussian density function follows from the fact that *any* such set of Gaussian variables may be obtained by matrix transformation from a statistically independent set. As a final point, we note that, since $p_{\mathbf{y}}$ and $M_{\mathbf{y}}$ are Fourier transforms of each other, the righthand side of Eq. 3.90 is the inverse transform of

$$M_{\mathbf{y}}(\boldsymbol{\nu}) = \exp\left(-\tfrac{1}{2}\boldsymbol{\nu}\Lambda_y\boldsymbol{\nu}^{\mathrm{T}} + j\boldsymbol{\nu}\mathbf{m}_y^{\mathrm{T}}\right). \tag{3.91}$$

As an example of Eq. 3.90, consider the two-dimensional case with covariance matrix

$$\Lambda_y = \begin{pmatrix} \sigma^2 & \rho\sigma^2 \\ \rho\sigma^2 & \sigma^2 \end{pmatrix}; \qquad |\rho| < 1.$$

Then

$$|\Lambda_y| = \sigma^4(1 - \rho^2)$$

and

$$\Lambda_y^{-1} = \frac{1}{|\Lambda_y|}\begin{pmatrix} \sigma^2 & -\rho\sigma^2 \\ -\rho\sigma^2 & \sigma^2 \end{pmatrix} = \frac{1}{\sigma^2(1-\rho^2)}\begin{pmatrix} 1 & -\rho \\ -\rho & 1 \end{pmatrix}.$$

If $\mathbf{m}_y = (0, 0)$, we have

$$p_{y_1,y_2}(\beta_1, \beta_2) = \frac{1}{2\pi\sigma^2\sqrt{1-\rho^2}} \exp\left[\frac{-1}{2\sigma^2(1-\rho^2)}(\beta_1, \beta_2)\begin{pmatrix} 1 & -\rho \\ -\rho & 1 \end{pmatrix}\begin{pmatrix} \beta_1 \\ \beta_2 \end{pmatrix}\right]$$

$$= \frac{1}{2\pi\sigma^2\sqrt{1-\rho^2}} \exp\left[-\frac{\beta_1^2 - 2\rho\beta_1\beta_2 + \beta_2^2}{2\sigma^2(1-\rho^2)}\right].$$

This density function has already been studied in detail in Section 3.2.

3.4 THE GAUSSIAN PROCESS

Consider a random process $x(t)$, and let $\mathbf{x(t)} = (x(t_1), x(t_2), \ldots, x(t_k))$ denote the random variables obtained by sampling $x(t)$ at the set of k time instants $\{t_i\}$. If the variables $\mathbf{x(t)}$ are jointly Gaussian for *every* finite set of observation instants $\{t_i\}$, then $x(t)$ is called a *Gaussian process.*

The conditions that a process must meet in order to be Gaussian are stringent. The one-dimensional central limit theorem of Chapter 2 has been used, however, to argue that the output of a filtered impulse noise source, observed at any single time t_1, can be adequately modeled mathematically by a Gaussian random variable. More generally, the multivariate central limit theorem justifies the assumption that k output samples observed at any set of times $\{t_i\}$ can be adequately modeled by k random variables that are jointly Gaussian. The important condition for the validity of such a mathematical model is that the values of the observed samples depend on the sum of a large number of relatively independent perturbations. Since there are many circumstances, such as thermal noise in resistors, diffusion noise in transistors, spontaneous emission noise in masers and intergalactic noise in radio astronomy, in which this condition is met, Gaussian processes are of the utmost practical (as well as mathematical) importance.

Specification of Gaussian Processes

We have seen that an arbitrary random process is considered specified if and only if a rule is implied for determining the joint density function of samples taken at *any* finite set of time instants $\{t_i\}$, $i = 1, 2, \ldots, k$. One of the important properties of a set of jointly Gaussian variables, say $\mathbf{x} = (x_1, x_2, \ldots, x_k)$, is that $p_{\mathbf{x}}$ depends only on the mean values

$$\mathrm{E}[\mathbf{x}] \triangleq \mathbf{m}_x = (\overline{x_1}, \overline{x_2}, \ldots, \overline{x_k}) \tag{3.92a}$$

and the set of covariances† $\{\lambda_{ij}\}$, $i = 1, 2, \ldots, k$; $j = 1, 2, \ldots, k$, in which

$$\begin{aligned} \lambda_{ij} &\triangleq \mathrm{E}[(x_i - \overline{x_i})(x_j - \overline{x_j})] \\ &= \overline{x_i x_j} - \overline{x_i}\,\overline{x_j}. \end{aligned} \tag{3.92b}$$

Letting x_i denote the random variable $x(t_i)$, $i = 1, 2, \ldots, k$, we see that a Gaussian process $x(t)$ is completely specified by knowledge of how the means and covariances depend on the sampling instants $\{t_i\}$.

The mean function. To be able to specify $\mathbf{m}_x$ for any set of instants $\{t_i\}$, it is necessary and sufficient that we know a function $m_x(t)$, called the *mean function* of $x(t)$, defined by

$$m_x(t) \triangleq \mathrm{E}[x(t)]. \tag{3.93}$$

For example, since x_i and x_j denote the random variables obtained by sampling the process at times t_i and t_j, respectively,

$$\overline{x_i} = m_x(t_i) \tag{3.94a}$$

$$\overline{x_j} = m_x(t_j). \tag{3.94b}$$

The covariance function. Similarly, in order to be able to specify the set of covariances $\{\lambda_{ij}\}$ for *any* set of instants $\{t_i\}$, it is necessary and sufficient that we know a function $\mathscr{L}_x(t, s)$, called the *covariance function* of $x(t)$, defined by

$$\mathscr{L}_x(t, s) \triangleq \mathrm{E}[(x(t) - m_x(t))(x(s) - m_x(s))]. \tag{3.95a}$$

† We refer generically to the λ_{ij} as "covariances," even though terms for which $j = i$ are variances.

Then for samples x_i and x_j taken at t_i and t_j, respectively, we have

$$\lambda_{ij} = \mathscr{L}_x(t_i, t_j). \tag{3.95b}$$

In interpreting $\mathscr{L}_x(t, s)$, we think of observing each sample function $x(\omega, t)$ of the process first at some particular time t and again at some time s, as shown in Fig. 3.18. The product of these two samples (with means subtracted) is $[x(\omega, t) - m_x(t)][x(\omega, s) - m_x(s)]$. The covariance function $\mathscr{L}_x(t, s)$ describes how the expected value of this product, over the ensemble of points ω in Ω, varies as a function of the sampling instants t and s.

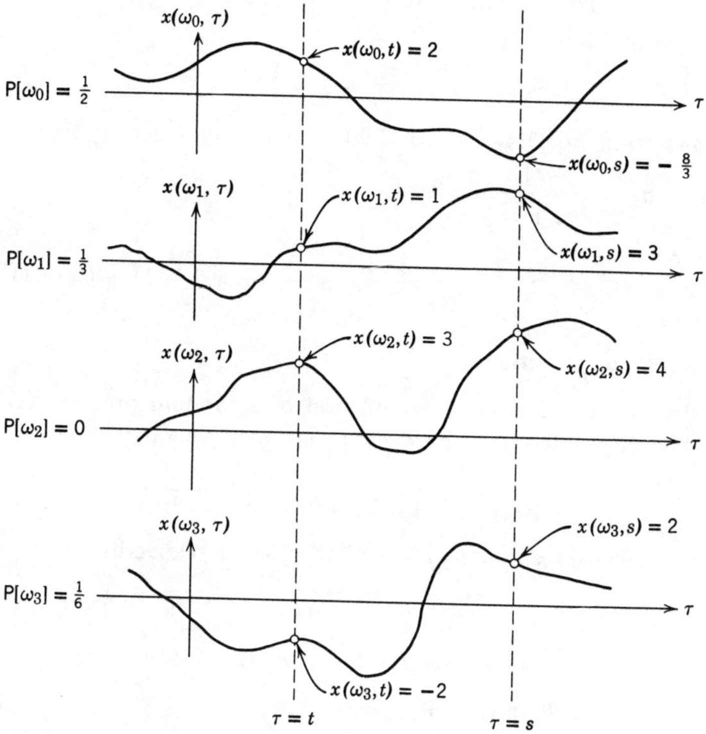

Figure 3.18 Interpretation of the covariance function. For this particular choice of t and s we see that $m_x(t) = 1$, $m_x(s) = 0$. Let z be a random variable defined by $z(\omega) \triangleq [x(\omega, t) - 1][x(\omega, s)]$. Then

$$z(\omega_0) = (2 - 1)(-8/3) = -8/3$$
$$z(\omega_1) = (1 - 1)(3) = 0$$
$$z(\omega_2) = (3 - 1)(4) = 8$$
$$z(\omega_3) = (-2 - 1)(2) = -6$$

and $\mathscr{L}_x(t, s) = E[z] = -7/3$.

Example. Suppose it is known that a random process $x(t)$ is Gaussian and

$$m_x(t) = \sin \pi t, \tag{3.96a}$$

$$\mathscr{L}_x(t, s) = e^{-|t-s|}. \tag{3.96b}$$

The set of covariances of two samples x_1 and x_2 taken at times $t_1 = 1$ and $t_2 = \frac{3}{2}$ is

$$\sigma_1^{\,2} \triangleq \lambda_{11} = e^{-|t_1-t_1|} = 1,$$

$$\sigma_2^{\,2} \triangleq \lambda_{22} = e^{-|t_2-t_2|} = 1,$$

$$\rho_{12}\sigma_1\sigma_2 \triangleq \lambda_{12} = \lambda_{21} = e^{-|t_1-t_2|} = e^{-\frac{1}{2}}.$$

The vector of the means is

$$\mathbf{m} = (m_x(t_1), m_x(t_2)) = (0, -1).$$

It follows from Eq. 3.47 (or Eq. 3.90) that the joint density function is

$$p_{x_1,x_2}(\alpha, \beta) = \frac{1}{2\pi\sqrt{1 - e^{-1}}} \times \exp\left\{-\frac{1}{2(1 - e^{-1})}\left[\alpha^2 - \frac{2}{\sqrt{e}}\alpha(\beta + 1) + (\beta + 1)^2\right]\right\}.$$

The Correlation Function

In addition to the covariance function of a random process $x(t)$, we frequently encounter the *correlation function*, denoted $\mathcal{R}_x(t, s)$, and defined as

$$\mathcal{R}_x(t, s) \triangleq \mathrm{E}[x(t)\, x(s)] = \overline{x(t)\, x(s)}. \tag{3.97}$$

From Eq. 3.95 we see that $\mathcal{R}_x(t, s)$ and $\mathscr{L}_x(t, s)$ are related by

$$\begin{aligned} \mathscr{L}_x(t, s) &= \overline{[x(t) - m_x(t)][x(s) - m_x(s)]} \\ &= \overline{x(t)\, x(s)} - m_x(t)\, \overline{x(s)} - m_x(s)\, \overline{x(t)} + m_x(t)\, m_x(s) \\ &= \mathcal{R}_x(t, s) - m_x(t)\, m_x(s). \end{aligned} \tag{3.98}$$

It follows that a Gaussian process is completely specified by knowledge of $m_x(t)$ and either $\mathscr{L}_x(t, s)$ or $\mathcal{R}_x(t, s)$.

Finally, it should be noted that all three of these functions—say $m_y(t)$, $\mathscr{L}_y(t, s)$, and $\mathcal{R}_y(t, s)$—may also be defined for any process $y(t)$ that is *not* Gaussian. In the non-Gaussian case, however, knowledge of these functions alone does *not* imply that the process is completely specified. For example, consider the two random processes $y(t)$ and $z(t)$ shown in

Fig. 3.19; in both cases every sample function is a constant, and it is clear that

$$m_y(t) = m_z(t) = 0$$

$$\mathcal{R}_y(t, s) = \mathcal{R}_z(t, s) = 1.$$

But, for any observation instant $t = t_1$,

$$p_{y(t_1)}(\alpha) = \tfrac{1}{4}[\delta(\alpha - \sqrt{2}) + 2\delta(\alpha) + \delta(\alpha + \sqrt{2})],$$

whereas

$$p_{z(t_1)}(\alpha) = \tfrac{1}{2}[\delta(\alpha - 1) + \delta(\alpha + 1)].$$

Stationary Gaussian Processes

To be stationary an arbitrary random process must be such that all joint density functions are invariant to any translation in time origin. For a Gaussian process $x(t)$, the joint density function $p_{\mathbf{x}}$ of k samples $\{x_i\}$ observed at times $\{t_i\}$, $i = 1, 2, \ldots, k$, depends only on the set of means $\{\bar{x}_i\}$ and covariances $\{\lambda_{ij}\}$. Thus $p_{\mathbf{x}}$ is unaffected by a translation T in time origin if and only if

$$m_x(t_i) \triangleq \mathrm{E}[x(t_i)] = \mathrm{E}[x(t_i + T)] \triangleq m_x(t_i + T) = \bar{x} = \text{a constant} \tag{3.99a}$$

and also

$$\begin{aligned}\lambda_{ij} &= \mathscr{L}_x(t_i, t_j) = \mathrm{E}[x(t_i)\, x(t_j)] - \bar{x}^2 \\ &= \mathrm{E}[x(t_i + T)\, x(t_j + T)] - \bar{x}^2 = \mathscr{L}_x(t_i + T, t_j + T)\end{aligned} \tag{3.99b}$$

for all t_i, t_j, and all T. In particular, if we choose $T = -t_j$ in Eq. 3.99b, we have

$$\lambda_{ij} = \mathrm{E}[x(t_i - t_j)\, x(0)] - \bar{x}^2$$

for all t_i, t_j, which implies that

$$\mathscr{L}_x(t, s) = \mathscr{L}_x(t - s, 0) \tag{3.99c}$$

for all t and s. The covariance function must depend only on the interval $(t - s)$ between observations and not directly on these observation instants themselves. A Gaussian process is stationary whenever Eqs. 3.99a and c are satisfied. In order to simplify notation, it is conventional to drop the second argument in Eq. 3.99c and write $\mathscr{L}_x(t - s)$ instead of $\mathscr{L}_x(t - s, 0)$. The conditions that a Gaussian process must meet in order to be stationary are then

$$m_x(t) = \bar{x} = \text{a constant} \tag{3.100a}$$

$$\mathscr{L}_x(t, s) = \mathscr{L}_x(t - s). \tag{3.100b}$$

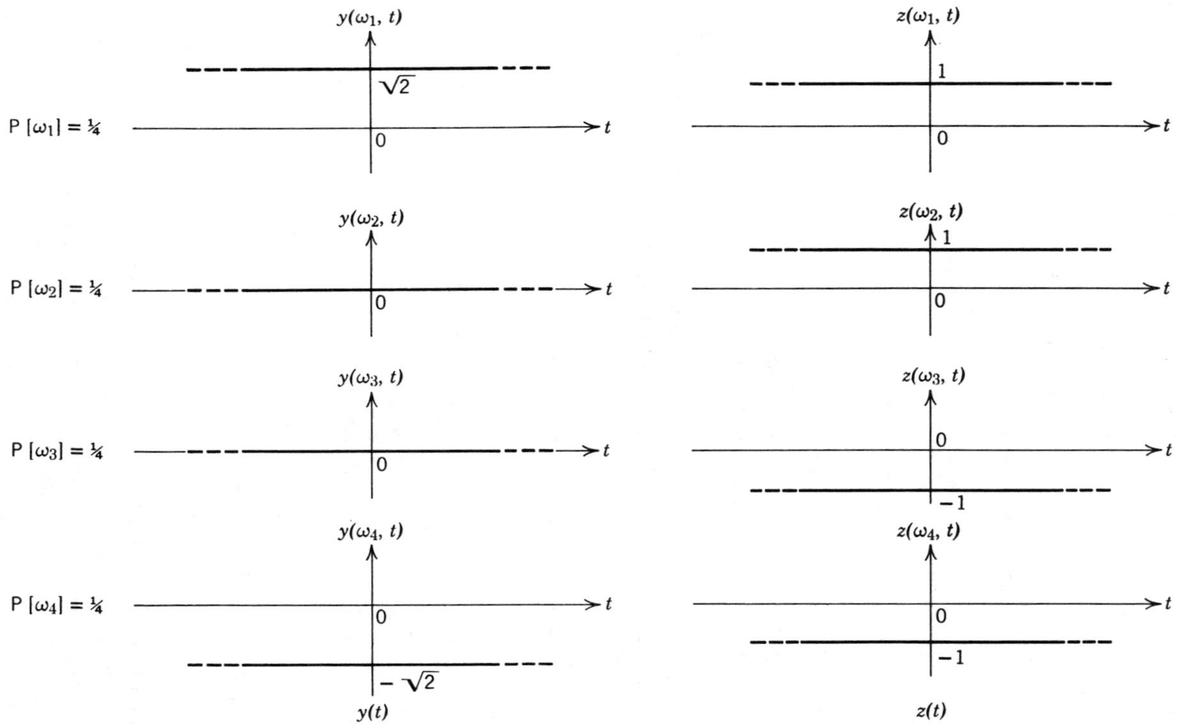

Figure 3.19 Two different random processes with the same mean and covariance functions.

An example of a covariance function meeting this condition is Eq. 3.96b. Given that Eq. 3.100a is satisfied, a requirement equivalent to Eq. 3.100b (with the same notational convention) is

$$\mathcal{R}_x(t, s) = \mathcal{R}_x(t - s). \tag{3.100c}$$

Notice that these conditions are *not* sufficient to guarantee stationariness for random processes that are not Gaussian. The following random process is a counterexample. Let Ω contain five sample points, and let each point be assigned probability $\frac{1}{5}$. Let $z(t)$ be the process whose sample functions $z(\omega, t)$ are

$$\begin{aligned} z(\omega_1, t) &= -\sqrt{2} \cos t, \\ z(\omega_2, t) &= -\sqrt{2} \sin t, \\ z(\omega_3, t) &= \sqrt{2} (\cos t + \sin t), \\ z(\omega_4, t) &= (\cos t - \sin t), \\ z(\omega_5, t) &= (\sin t - \cos t). \end{aligned} \tag{3.101}$$

It can be verified by direct calculation that

$$\overline{z(t)} = \frac{1}{5} \sum_{i=1}^{5} z(\omega_i, t) = 0; \qquad \text{for all } t$$

$$\overline{z(t)\, z(s)} = \frac{1}{5} \sum_{i=1}^{5} z(\omega_i, t)\, z(\omega_i, s) = \frac{6}{5} \cos (t - s).$$

Thus the conditions of Eq. 3.100 are met.

On the other hand, it is easy to show that $z(t)$ is not stationary. For instance, consider the two random variables z_1 and z_2 obtained by observing $z(t)$ at times $t_1 = 0$ and $t_2 = \pi/4$. We have directly from Eq. 3.101

$$p_{z_1}(\alpha) = \tfrac{1}{5}[\delta(\alpha + \sqrt{2}) + \delta(\alpha) + \delta(\alpha - \sqrt{2}) + \delta(\alpha - 1) + \delta(\alpha + 1)]$$

$$p_{z_2}(\alpha) = \tfrac{1}{5}[2\delta(\alpha + 1) + \delta(\alpha - 2) + 2\delta(\alpha)].$$

Thus $p_{z_1} \neq p_{z_2}$.

Gaussian Processes through Linear Filters

We have argued in Sections 3.2 and 3.3 that filtered impulse noise becomes Gaussian when the number of impulses per second becomes large. More precisely, we require that the average number of impulses occurring during the effective duration of the filter's impulse response be large (as indicated in Fig. 3.16) and that the arrival times of the impulses be substantially independent of one another. In general, it follows from the

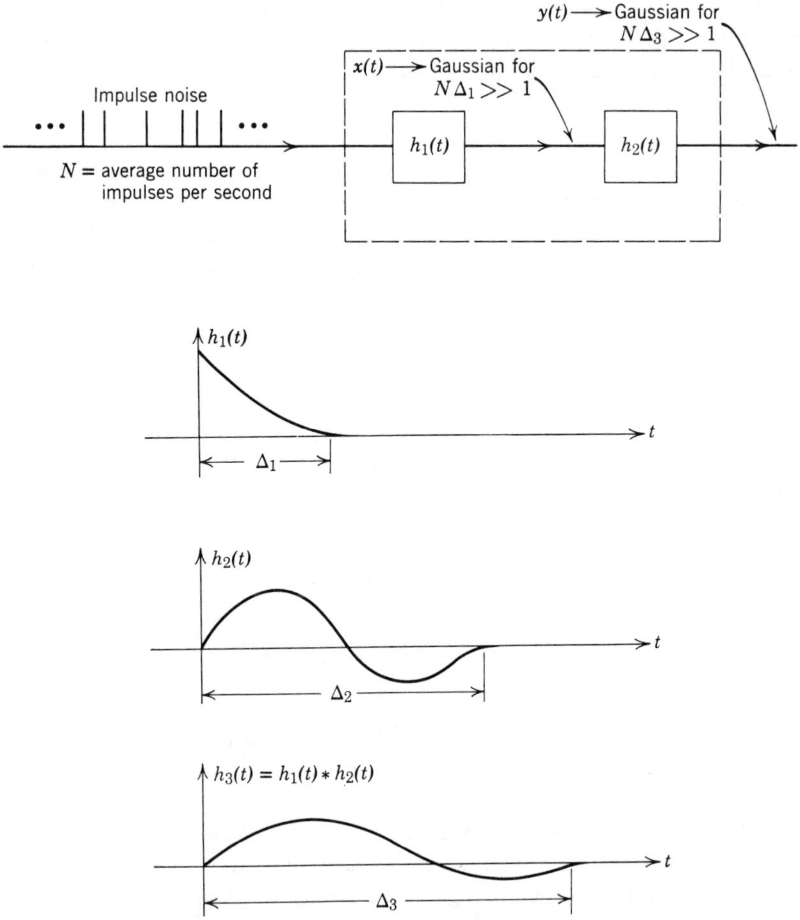

Figure 3.20 Two smoothing filters in cascade. The dashed box may be considered either as a single filter with impulse response $h_3(t)$ and effective duration Δ_3 or as two filters in cascade. [The effective duration Δ of any filter response $h(t)$ containing impulses is zero; the output of such a filter is also impulsive and obviously does *not* become Gaussian as $N \to \infty$.]

same argument that the output of a second filter connected in cascade behind the first, as shown in Fig. 3.20, also becomes Gaussian. All that is required is that the effective duration of the over-all impulse response of the pair of filters in cascade should again be sufficiently long.

The preceding arguments suggest that *the output of any linear filter is a Gaussian process whenever its input is a Gaussian process.* Although formal proof of this fact is mathematically involved, the observation that the input and output processes $x(t)$ and $y(t)$ in Fig. 3.20 are related by

$$y(t) = \int_{-\infty}^{\infty} x(\alpha)\, h_2(t - \alpha)\, d\alpha \tag{3.102}$$

provides further substantiation. Approximating this integral by a sum,

$$y(t) \approx \sum_i x(\alpha_i)\, h(t - \alpha_i)\, \Delta\alpha_i,$$

we note that the conclusion that $y(t)$ is Gaussian is consistent with the property that a weighted sum of Gaussian random variables is Gaussian.

As mentioned in connection with Eq. 3.10, Eq. 3.102 is an example of specifying a new random process by means of applying a stated operation [convolution with $h_2(t)$] to the sample functions of a given process. The relative mathematical ease with which Gaussian noise can be handled in communication problems stems from the fact that a Gaussian input to a linear filter yields a Gaussian output. This, of course, is not true for non-Gaussian inputs.

3.5 CORRELATION FUNCTIONS AND POWER SPECTRA

We have seen that the random process at the output of a linear filter is Gaussian whenever the input is Gaussian. Since any Gaussian process is specified by its mean and correlation functions, the effect of the linear filter on a Gaussian input is described completely by the effect of the linear filter on the mean and correlation functions. We now consider how to calculate these functions; the results are valid whether or not the input process is Gaussian.

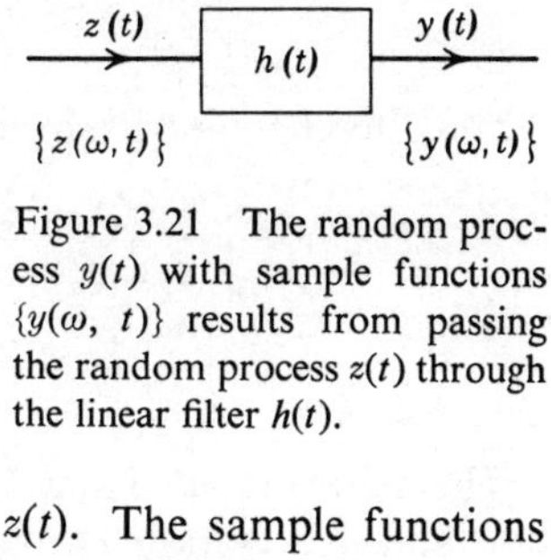

Figure 3.21 The random process $y(t)$ with sample functions $\{y(\omega, t)\}$ results from passing the random process $z(t)$ through the linear filter $h(t)$.

The Expectation of an Integral

In Fig. 3.21 we show a linear filter $h(t)$ whose input is an arbitrary random process $z(t)$. The sample functions of the random process $y(t)$ at the filter output are related to the sample functions of $z(t)$ by the convolution integral

$$y(\omega, t) = \int_{-\infty}^{\infty} z(\omega, \alpha)\, h(t - \alpha)\, d\alpha; \quad \text{all } \omega \text{ in } \Omega. \tag{3.103}$$

From Eq. 3.93 the mean function of $y(t)$ is

$$m_y(t) = \mathrm{E}[y(t)] = \mathrm{E}\left[\int_{-\infty}^{\infty} z(\alpha)\, h(t - \alpha)\, d\alpha\right]. \tag{3.104}$$

Simplification of Eq. 3.104 is straightforward when the number of points in the sample space Ω is finite. Let us assume that there are k points $\{\omega_i\}$, $i = 1, 2, \ldots, k$, to each of which is assigned probability P_i. Then

$$m_y(t) = \sum_{i=1}^{k} P_i\, y(\omega_i, t) = \sum_{i=1}^{k} P_i \int_{-\infty}^{\infty} z(\omega_i, \alpha)\, h(t - \alpha)\, d\alpha. \tag{3.105a}$$

By interchanging the order of summation and integration in Eq. 3.105a, we obtain

$$\begin{aligned} m_y(t) &= \int_{-\infty}^{\infty} \sum_{i=1}^{k} P_i\, z(\omega_i, \alpha)\, h(t - \alpha)\, d\alpha \\ &= \int_{-\infty}^{\infty} \overline{z(\alpha)}\, h(t - \alpha)\, d\alpha. \end{aligned} \tag{3.105b}$$

Under these conditions the autocorrelation function of $y(t)$ may be obtained by a similar procedure:

$$\begin{aligned} \mathcal{R}_y(t, s) &\triangleq \overline{y(t)\, y(s)} \\ &= \mathrm{E}\left[\int_{-\infty}^{\infty} z(\alpha)\, h(t - \alpha)\, d\alpha \int_{-\infty}^{\infty} z(\beta)\, h(s - \beta)\, d\beta\right] \\ &= \sum_{i=1}^{k} P_i \int_{-\infty}^{\infty} z(\omega_i, \alpha)\, h(t - \alpha)\, d\alpha \int_{-\infty}^{\infty} z(\omega_i, \beta)\, h(s - \beta)\, d\beta \\ &= \sum_{i=1}^{k} P_i \int_{-\infty}^{\infty}\int_{-\infty}^{\infty} z(\omega_i, \alpha)\, z(\omega_i, \beta)\, h(t - \alpha)\, h(s - \beta)\, d\alpha\, d\beta. \end{aligned} \tag{3.106a}$$

Again interchanging the order of finite summation and integration, we have

$$\begin{aligned} \mathcal{R}_y(t, s) &= \int_{-\infty}^{\infty}\int_{-\infty}^{\infty} \left[\sum_{i=1}^{k} P_i\, z(\omega_i, \alpha)\, z(\omega_i, \beta)\right] h(t - \alpha)\, h(s - \beta)\, d\alpha\, d\beta \\ &= \int_{-\infty}^{\infty}\int_{-\infty}^{\infty} \overline{z(\alpha)\, z(\beta)}\, h(t - \alpha)\, h(s - \beta)\, d\alpha\, d\beta. \end{aligned} \tag{3.106b}$$

The mathematical issues involved in interchanging the order of integration and expectation become sensitive when the sample space becomes infinite. Both the interchange and the resulting input-output relations

$$m_y(t) = \int_{-\infty}^{\infty} m_z(\alpha)\, h(t - \alpha)\, d\alpha, \tag{3.107}$$

$$\mathcal{R}_y(t, s) = \int_{-\infty}^{\infty}\int_{-\infty}^{\infty} \mathcal{R}_z(\alpha, \beta)\, h(t - \alpha)\, h(s - \beta)\, d\alpha\, d\beta, \tag{3.108}$$

remain valid, however, whenever the double integral of Eq. 3.108 is finite for all t and s.[23,63]

For neither of these equations do we require that $z(t)$ be Gaussian. When $z(t)$—hence $y(t)$—is Gaussian, however, evaluation of these two integrals completely specifies the process $y(t)$.

Power Spectrum

Important additional insight into the effect of filtering a random process $z(t)$, which again need not necessarily be Gaussian, can be gained from Eq. 3.108 in the special case in which $\mathcal{R}_z(t, s)$ depends *only* on the interval $(t - s)$ between the sampling instants t and s. In particular, if this condition is satisfied, we shall find it possible to investigate the distribution of mean power in $z(t)$ as a function of frequency. Accordingly, in the rest of this section we shall assume that

$$\mathcal{R}_z(t, s) = \mathcal{R}_z(\tau), \tag{3.109}$$

where

$$\tau \triangleq t - s$$

and the notation is that of Eq. 3.100.

Equation 3.109, when substituted in Eq. 3.108, implies that

$$\mathcal{R}_y(t, s) = \int_{-\infty}^{\infty}\int_{-\infty}^{\infty} \mathcal{R}_z(\alpha - \beta)\, h(t - \alpha)\, h(s - \beta)\, d\alpha\, d\beta.$$

Making the change of variables $\nu = t - \alpha$, $\mu = s - \beta$, we obtain

$$\mathcal{R}_y(t, s) = \int_{-\infty}^{\infty}\int_{-\infty}^{\infty} \mathcal{R}_z(t - s + \mu - \nu)\, h(\mu)\, h(\nu)\, d\mu\, d\nu. \tag{3.110a}$$

Since the right-hand side of this equation depends only on $(t - s)$, we see that whenever $\mathcal{R}_z(t, s)$ is a function only of $\tau = t - s$, so also is $\mathcal{R}_y(t, s)$:

$$\mathcal{R}_z(t, s) = \mathcal{R}_z(\tau) \Rightarrow \mathcal{R}_y(t, s) = \mathcal{R}_y(\tau). \tag{3.110b}$$

Equation 3.110a can be simplified if we introduce the Fourier transforms of $\mathcal{R}_y(\tau)$ and $\mathcal{R}_z(\tau)$, say $\mathcal{S}_y(f)$ and $\mathcal{S}_z(f)$:

$$\mathcal{S}_y(f) \triangleq \int_{-\infty}^{\infty} \mathcal{R}_y(\tau)e^{-j2\pi f\tau}\, d\tau, \tag{3.111a}$$

$$\mathcal{S}_z(f) \triangleq \int_{-\infty}^{\infty} \mathcal{R}_z(\tau)e^{-j2\pi f\tau}\, d\tau. \tag{3.111b}$$

It follows by inverse transformation that

$$\mathcal{R}_y(\tau) = \int_{-\infty}^{\infty} \mathcal{S}_y(f)e^{+j2\pi f\tau}\, df \tag{3.112a}$$

and

$$\mathcal{R}_z(\tau) = \int_{-\infty}^{\infty} \mathcal{S}_z(f)e^{+j2\pi f\tau}\, df. \tag{3.112b}$$

When τ is substituted for $t - s$ and Eq. 3.112b is used to express $\mathcal{R}_z(\tau + \mu - \nu)$ in terms of $\mathcal{S}_z(f)$, Eq. 3.110a becomes

$$\mathcal{R}_y(\tau) = \int_{-\infty}^{\infty} \int_{-\infty}^{\infty} \int_{-\infty}^{\infty} \mathcal{S}_z(f) e^{+j2\pi f(\tau+\mu-\nu)} h(\mu)\, h(\nu)\, df\, d\mu\, d\nu$$

$$= \int_{-\infty}^{\infty} \mathcal{S}_z(f) e^{j2\pi f\tau}\, df \int_{-\infty}^{\infty} h(\mu) e^{j2\pi f\mu}\, d\mu \int_{-\infty}^{\infty} h(\nu) e^{-j2\pi f\nu}\, d\nu.$$

The integral on ν is recognized as the filter's transfer function $H(f)$, and the integral on μ is recognized as $H^*(f)$. Thus

$$\mathcal{R}_y(\tau) = \int_{-\infty}^{\infty} \mathcal{S}_z(f)\, |H(f)|^2\, e^{j2\pi f\tau}\, df, \tag{3.113}$$

and, comparing Eq. 3.113 with Eq. 3.112a, we have

$$\mathcal{S}_y(f) = \mathcal{S}_z(f)\, |H(f)|^2. \tag{3.114}$$

We may interpret Eq. 3.114 as follows. First, we note that the mean square value of the filter output process $y(t)$ is independent of time whenever Eq. 3.109 is satisfied:

$$\overline{y^2(t)} = \mathcal{R}_y(t, t) = \mathcal{R}_y(t - t) = \mathcal{R}_y(0). \tag{3.115}$$

Next, we consider $y(t)$ as an ensemble of voltage or current waveforms applied across a 1-Ω resistor, so that $y^2(\omega, t)$ is the instantaneous power dissipated in the resistor at time t by the waveform associated with sample point ω. We therefore interpret $\mathcal{R}_y(0)$ as the expected value of the power dissipated in the resistor at any instant.

From Eqs. 3.112a and 3.114 we have

$$\mathcal{R}_y(0) = \int_{-\infty}^{\infty} \mathcal{S}_y(f)\, df = \int_{-\infty}^{\infty} \mathcal{S}_z(f)\, |H(f)|^2\, df. \tag{3.116}$$

If we now let $H(f)$ be the particular filter, shown in Fig. 3.22, for which

$$H(f) = \begin{cases} 1; & \text{for } f_1 \leqslant |f| \leqslant f_2, \\ 0; & \text{elsewhere,} \end{cases} \tag{3.117a}$$

we obtain

$$\mathcal{R}_y(0) = \int_{-f_2}^{-f_1} \mathcal{S}_z(f)\, df + \int_{f_1}^{f_2} \mathcal{S}_z(f)\, df. \tag{3.117b}$$

We shall soon see that $\mathcal{S}_z(f)$ is always an even function of frequency. Since Eq. 3.117 implies that the mean power delivered by $z(t)$ in any narrow frequency band of width Δf centered on f' is approximately $2\mathcal{S}_z(f')\, \Delta f$, as shown in Fig. 3.23, $\mathcal{S}_z(f)$ describes the distribution of

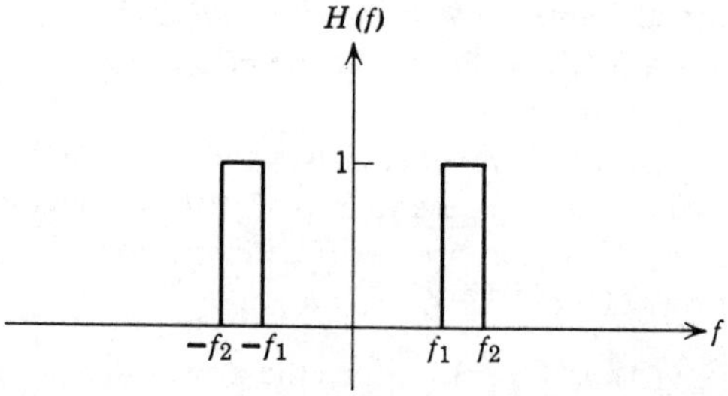

Figure 3.22 Ideal bandpass filter. Although not physically realizable (the impulse response is not identically zero for $t < 0$), ideal rectangular filters are useful for purposes of analysis.

mean power with frequency in the process $z(t)$. For this reason $\mathcal{S}_z(f)$ is called the *power density function of* $z(t)$.

Wide sense stationariness. It is essential in the derivation of Eq. 3.117b that $\mathcal{R}_z(t, s) = \mathcal{R}_z(t - s)$; if this condition is not met, the Fourier transformation of Eq. 3.111 cannot be made and the power density function $\mathcal{S}_z(f)$ is not defined.

Since knowledge of $\mathcal{S}_y(f)$ at the output of a linear filter implies knowledge of $\mathcal{R}_y(\tau)$, Eq. 3.114 (together with the relation between the mean functions given by Eq. 3.107) *completely describes* the effect of a linear filter on a *Gaussian* input process. When $z(t)$ is *not* Gaussian, this is not the case, although Eqs. 3.115 and 3.116 still permit us to calculate the total mean square instantaneous power out of the filter. The ability to do this and to talk about the power density of a random process is sufficiently important in its own right that processes $z(t)$ which meet the conditions

$$m_z(t) = \text{constant} \tag{3.118a}$$

$$\mathcal{R}_z(t, s) = \mathcal{R}_z(t - s) \tag{3.118b}$$

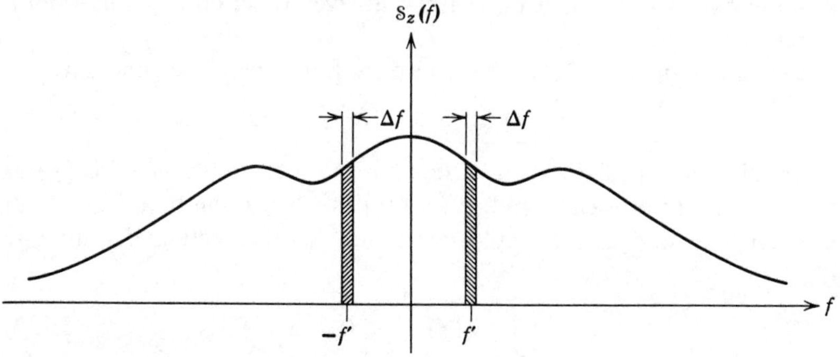

Figure 3.23 The mean power delivered by $z(t)$ in a frequency band of width Δf centered on f' is equal to the shaded area.

are given the special name *wide-sense stationary*.† Stationariness, as we defined it in Section 3.1, is often called *strict-sense stationariness* in order to avoid possible confusion.

Any strict-sense stationary process is wide-sense stationary, but the converse is not true. The process of Eqs. 3.101 is a counterexample. *A wide-sense stationary Gaussian process is also strict-sense stationary*, since all of the conditions of Eqs. 3.100 are met.

Properties of $\mathcal{S}_z(f)$ and $\mathcal{R}_z(\tau)$. Since the power density function $\mathcal{S}_z(f)$ of a wide-sense stationary random process $z(t)$ is the Fourier transform of the correlation function $\mathcal{R}_z(\tau)$, the properties of the two functions are intimately related. First, we note that $\mathcal{R}_z(\tau)$ is a *real, even* function of τ:

$$\mathcal{R}_z(-\tau) = \mathcal{R}_z(\tau). \tag{3.119}$$

This follows from the definition of Eq. 3.97; $z(t)$ is real, and

$$\begin{aligned}\mathcal{R}_z(\tau) &= \mathcal{R}_z(t - s) \triangleq \overline{z(t)\, z(s)} \\ &= \overline{z(s)\, z(t)} \triangleq \mathcal{R}_z(s - t) = \mathcal{R}_z(-\tau).\end{aligned}$$

Equation 3.119 implies that $\mathcal{S}_z(f)$ is a *real, even* function of f. We prove this by observing that, since $\mathcal{R}_z(\tau)$ is even and $\sin 2\pi f\tau$ is odd,

$$\int_{-\infty}^{\infty} \mathcal{R}_z(\tau) \sin 2\pi f\tau \, d\tau = 0.$$

But

$$\int_{-\infty}^{\infty} \mathcal{R}_z(\tau) e^{-j2\pi f\tau} \, d\tau = \int_{-\infty}^{\infty} \mathcal{R}_z(\tau)(\cos 2\pi f\tau - j \sin 2\pi f\tau) \, d\tau,$$

hence

$$\mathcal{S}_z(f) = \int_{-\infty}^{\infty} \mathcal{R}_z(\tau) \cos 2\pi f\tau \, d\tau. \tag{3.120}$$

Since the right-hand side of Eq. 3.120 is an even function of f, the proof is complete.

Next, we claim that $\mathcal{S}_z(f)$ must also be a non-negative function:

$$\mathcal{S}_z(f) \geqslant 0; \qquad \text{for all } f. \tag{3.121}$$

This is clearly a necessary condition for the interpretation of $\mathcal{S}_z(f)$ as power density to be meaningful. Proof follows by noting that if Eq. 3.121 were not true an f_1 and f_2 could be chosen for the rectangular filter in Fig. 3.24 such that

$$\int_{f_1}^{f_2} \mathcal{S}_z(f) \, df < 0. \tag{3.122}$$

† In many texts, processes satisfying only Eq. 3.118b are called wide-sense stationary.

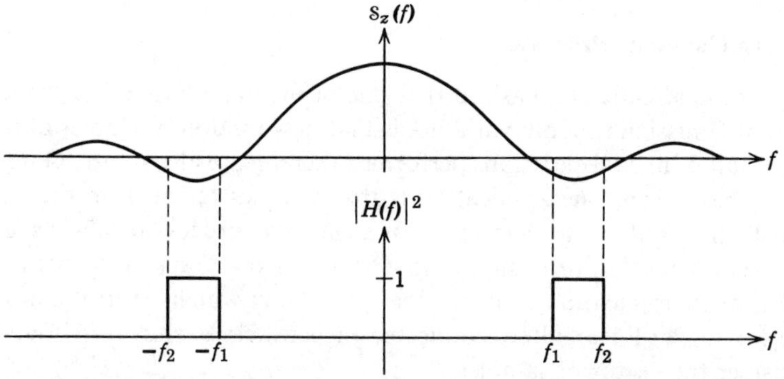

Figure 3.24 Proof (by contradiction) that a power density function cannot be negative.

But, from Eq. 3.117 and the evenness of $\mathcal{S}_z(f)$, this integral is one half the expected value of the square of the filter output $y(t)$ and thus Eq. 3.122 would be in contradiction to the fact that $\overline{y^2(t)}$ must be non-negative.

The fact that $\mathcal{S}_z(f)$ is non-negative does not imply that $\mathcal{R}_z(\tau)$ is also non-negative. It does imply that the correlation function of any wide-sense stationary process $z(t)$ satisfies the inequality

$$|\mathcal{R}_z(\tau)| \leqslant \mathcal{R}_z(0); \qquad \text{for all } \tau, \tag{3.123}$$

since

$$|\mathcal{R}_z(\tau)| = \left| \int_{-\infty}^{\infty} \mathcal{S}_z(f) e^{j2\pi f\tau}\, df \right|$$

$$\leqslant \int_{-\infty}^{\infty} |\mathcal{S}_z(f)|\, |e^{j2\pi f\tau}|\, df$$

$$= \int_{-\infty}^{\infty} \mathcal{S}_z(f)\, df = \mathcal{R}_z(0).$$

Equation 3.123 permits interpretation of the conditions under which the filter input-output relations of Eqs. 3.107 and 3.108 are valid. For wide-sense stationary processes,

$$|\mathcal{R}_y(t, s)| = |\mathcal{R}_y(t - s)| \leqslant \mathcal{R}_y(0) = \overline{y^2(t)},$$

so that requiring the double integral of Eq. 3.108 to be finite is equivalent to requiring that the mean power of the output process be finite for all t. It can be shown that this requirement suffices even when $y(t)$ is not stationary.

Jointly Gaussian Processes

We have already emphasized that one of the most important properties of joint Gaussian random variables is that new random variables obtained as a result of linear operations performed thereon are also jointly Gaussian. As we have seen, one application is that samples taken from the output $y(t)$ of a linear filter whose input $x(t)$ is a Gaussian process are always jointly Gaussian, which in turn implies that $y(t)$ is also a Gaussian process.

A second application concerns the situation in which $x(t)$ is the input to two (or more) linear filters connected in parallel, as shown in Fig. 3.25. Consider the vector of samples

$$\mathbf{w} = \big(y(t_1), y(t_2), \ldots, y(t_k), z(s_1), z(s_2), \ldots, z(s_l)\big) \tag{3.124}$$

obtained by observing the output $y(t)$ of the first filter at times $\{t_i\}$ and

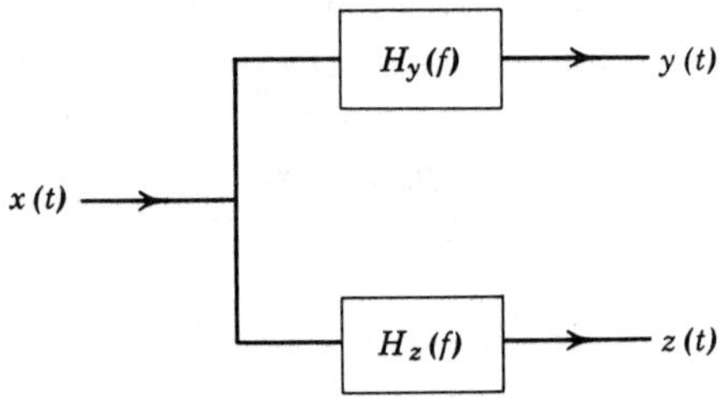

Figure 3.25 If $x(t)$ is a Gaussian process, then the processes $y(t)$ and $z(t)$ are jointly Gaussian.

the output $z(t)$ of the second filter at times $\{s_j\}$. Since $\mathbf{w}$ results from linear operations on $x(t)$, $\mathbf{w}$ is Gaussian for any $\{t_i\}$ and any $\{s_j\}$. The statement remains true if $\mathbf{w}$ results from sampling N rather than just two filters connected in parallel. We call N processes *jointly Gaussian* if every vector such as $\mathbf{w}$ formed from these processes is jointly Gaussian.

Two jointly Gaussian processes $y(t)$ and $z(t)$ are individually specified whenever their mean and correlation functions are known. In order to specify the joint density function of vectors such as $\mathbf{w}$, however, we must know the covariances associated with *every pair* of components. Thus, if $y(t)$ and $z(t)$ are to be *jointly specified*, we must also know the covariance

$$\mathrm{E}[y(t_i)\, z(s_j)] - m_y(t_i)\, m_z(s_j) \tag{3.125}$$

for any pair of observation instants (t_i, s_j). The additional knowledge that we need is embodied in the function

$$\mathcal{R}_{yz}(t, s) \triangleq \mathrm{E}[y(t)\, z(s)]; \qquad \text{all } t \text{ and } s, \tag{3.126}$$

which is called the *crosscorrelation function* of the processes $y(t)$ and $z(t)$.

For the case illustrated by Fig. 3.25, the crosscorrelation function is readily obtained from $x(t)$ and the two filter impulse responses $h_y(t)$ and $h_z(t)$.

$$\mathcal{R}_{yz}(t, s) = \overline{y(t)\, z(s)} = \mathrm{E}\left[\int_{-\infty}^{\infty} x(t-\alpha)\, h_y(\alpha)\, d\alpha \int_{-\infty}^{\infty} x(s-\beta)\, h_z(\beta)\, d\beta\right]$$

$$= \int_{-\infty}^{\infty}\int_{-\infty}^{\infty} \overline{x(t-\alpha)\, x(s-\beta)}\, h_y(\alpha)\, h_z(\beta)\, d\alpha\, d\beta$$

$$= \int_{-\infty}^{\infty}\int_{-\infty}^{\infty} \mathcal{R}_x(t-\alpha, s-\beta)\, h_y(\alpha)\, h_z(\beta)\, d\alpha\, d\beta. \tag{3.127a}$$

If $x(t)$ is stationary, this simplifies to

$$\mathcal{R}_{yz}(t, s) = \int_{-\infty}^{\infty}\int_{-\infty}^{\infty} \mathcal{R}_x(t-s+\beta-\alpha)\, h_y(\alpha)\, h_z(\beta)\, d\alpha\, d\beta$$

$$= \int_{-\infty}^{\infty}\int_{-\infty}^{\infty}\int_{-\infty}^{\infty} \mathcal{S}_x(f) e^{\mathrm{i}2\pi f(t-s+\beta-\alpha)} h_y(\alpha)\, h_z(\beta)\, d\alpha\, d\beta\, df$$

$$= \int_{-\infty}^{\infty} \mathcal{S}_x(f) e^{\mathrm{i}2\pi f(t-s)} \int_{-\infty}^{\infty} h_y(\alpha) e^{-\mathrm{i}2\pi f\alpha}\, d\alpha \int_{-\infty}^{\infty} h_z(\beta) e^{+\mathrm{i}2\pi f\beta}\, d\beta. \tag{3.127b}$$

Recognizing the integrals on α and β as $H_y(f)$ and $H_z^*(f)$, respectively, we have

$$\mathcal{R}_{yz}(t-s) = \int_{-\infty}^{\infty} \mathcal{S}_x(f)\, H_y(f)\, H_z^*(f) e^{\mathrm{i}2\pi f(t-s)}\, df. \tag{3.128}$$

Equation 3.128 is our desired result. Since $\mathcal{R}_{yz}(t, s)$, as well as $\mathcal{R}_y(t, s)$ and $\mathcal{R}_z(t, s)$, depends *only* on $(t - s)$ when $x(t)$ is stationary, we observe that the density function of any vector such as **w** is independent of time origin whenever the input $x(t)$ is a stationary Gaussian process. In this case $y(t)$ and $z(t)$ are called "jointly stationary."†

An important particular case occurs when $H_y(f)$ and $H_z(f)$ are non-overlapping, as shown in Fig. 3.26. Equation 3.128 then states that

$$\mathcal{R}_{yz}(t-s) = 0; \qquad \text{for all } t \text{ and } s. \tag{3.129}$$

In addition, $x(t)$ stationary implies $m_x(t)$ a constant, so that $m_y(t)\, m_z(t) = 0$. (At least one of the filters must have zero response to a constant (dc) input if they are nonoverlapping.) Thus any covariance involving both

† If $x(t)$ is stationary only in the wide sense, $y(t)$ and $z(t)$ are called "jointly wide-sense stationary."

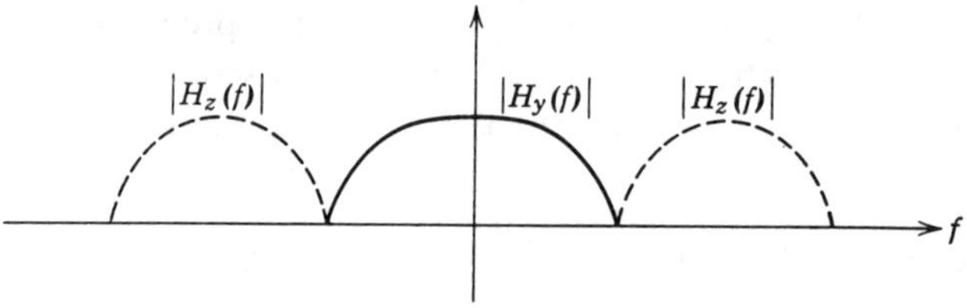

Figure 3.26 The filters $H_y(f)$ and $H_z(f)$ are disjoint in frequency.

$y(t)$ and $z(t)$, as in Eq. 3.125, must be zero. For $x(t)$ Gaussian as well as stationary it follows that

$$p_{\mathbf{w}} = p_{\mathbf{y(t),z(s)}} = p_{\mathbf{y(t)}}p_{\mathbf{z(s)}} \tag{3.130}$$

for *any* vectors

$$\mathbf{y(t)} = \big(y(t_1), y(t_2), \ldots, y(t_k)\big)$$

$$\mathbf{z(s)} = \big(z(s_1), z(s_2), \ldots, z(s_l)\big).$$

When Eq. 3.130 is satisfied for all $\{t_i\}$ and $\{s_j\}$, we say that the *processes $y(t)$ and $z(t)$ are statistically independent.*

White Gaussian Noise

When dealing with a Gaussian process, say $x(t)$, it is frequently convenient to decompose the process into the sum of its mean function and a zero-mean noise term, say $n(t)$. Thus we let

$$x(t) = m_x(t) + n(t), \tag{3.131a}$$

where $n(t)$ is a Gaussian process with zero mean:

$$\overline{n(t)} = \overline{x(t)} - m_x(t) = 0; \qquad \text{for all } t. \tag{3.131b}$$

In most applications of interest, such as the shot noise of Eq. 3.26, the mean function $m_x(t)$ represents a known (nonrandom) signal term, and the Gaussian noise process $n(t)$ is (strict-sense) stationary. Since $\overline{n(t)} = 0$, the covariance function $\mathscr{L}_n(t, s)$ is then (from Eq. 3.98) equal to the correlation function:

$$\mathscr{L}_n(t, s) = \mathcal{R}_n(t, s) = \mathcal{R}_n(\tau); \quad \tau = t - s. \tag{3.131c}$$

Thus the Fourier transform of $\mathcal{R}_n(\tau)$, that is, the power density function $\mathcal{S}_n(f)$, completely specifies the zero mean process $n(t)$.

In many communication applications we are confronted with physical noise sources in which the Gaussian noise added onto the desired signal has a power spectrum that is essentially flat up to frequencies much higher than those that are significant in the signal itself. In such cases

Eqs. 3.115 and 3.116 imply that the mean square value of the noise interference can be reduced (without adversely affecting the desired signal) by passing the sum of signal and noise through a filter $H(f)$ that passes the signal without important change but eliminates much of the noise, as shown in Fig. 3.27. Insofar as the power spectrum of the noise at the filter output is concerned, it makes little difference precisely how the input-noise power spectrum approaches zero outside the passband of $H(f)$. Accordingly, one frequently assumes that this input spectrum is flat for *all* frequencies and introduces the concept of white Gaussian noise,

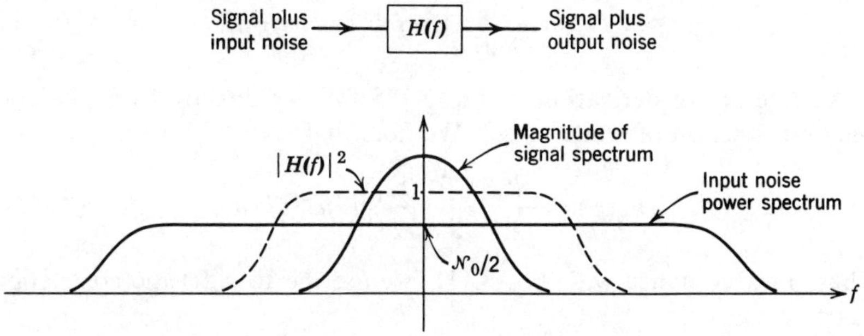

Figure 3.27 Wideband Gaussian noise at the input to a narrow band filter. The filter output is substantially the same as it would be if the input noise were white and Gaussian.

denoted $n_w(t)$ and defined as a stationary, zero-mean Gaussian process with power spectrum†

$$\mathcal{S}_w(f) \triangleq \frac{\mathcal{N}_0}{2}; \qquad -\infty < f < \infty. \tag{3.132}$$

Actually, white noise (whether Gaussian or not) must be fictitious because its total mean power would be

$$\overline{n_w^2(t)} = \int_{-\infty}^{\infty} \mathcal{S}_w(f)\, df = \infty, \tag{3.133a}$$

which is not meaningful. The utility of the concept of white noise derives from the fact that such a noise, when passed through a linear filter for which

$$\int_{-\infty}^{\infty} |H(f)|^2\, df < \infty, \tag{3.133b}$$

produces at the filter output a stationary, zero-mean noise $n(t)$ that *is*

† The dimensions of $\mathcal{N}_0$ are watts per cycle per second, or joules. We shall always define power spectra on a bilateral frequency basis, $-\infty < f < \infty$.

meaningful. From Eqs. 3.114 and 3.132 we have

$$\mathcal{S}_n(f) = \frac{\mathcal{N}_0}{2} |H(f)|^2, \tag{3.134a}$$

and thus

$$\overline{n^2(t)} = \frac{\mathcal{N}_0}{2} \int_{-\infty}^{\infty} |H(f)|^2 \, df, \tag{3.134b}$$

which, by Eq. 3.133b, is finite. The correlation function at the output, from Eqs. 3.120 and 3.134a, is

$$\mathcal{R}_n(\tau) = \frac{\mathcal{N}_0}{2} \int_{-\infty}^{\infty} |H(f)|^2 \cos 2\pi f \tau \, df. \tag{3.135}$$

An alternative derivation of Eq. 3.135 follows directly from the correlation function of white noise. We note that

$$\mathcal{S}_w(f) = \frac{\mathcal{N}_0}{2} = \int_{-\infty}^{\infty} \frac{\mathcal{N}_0}{2} \delta(\tau) e^{-i2\pi f \tau} \, d\tau. \tag{3.136a}$$

Thus, in accordance with Eq. 3.111, we ascribe to $n_w(t)$ the correlation function

$$\mathcal{R}_w(\tau) = \frac{\mathcal{N}_0}{2} \delta(\tau), \tag{3.136b}$$

which is again a nonphysical but useful result. Equation 3.136b implies that any two samples of white Gaussian noise, no matter how closely together in time they are taken, are statistically independent. In a sense, white Gaussian noise represents the ultimate in "randomness." Substituting Eq. 3.136b in Eq. 3.110a, with $t - s = \tau$, we have

$$\mathcal{R}_n(\tau) = \frac{\mathcal{N}_0}{2} \int_{-\infty}^{\infty} \int_{-\infty}^{\infty} \delta(\tau + \mu - \nu) \, h(\mu) \, h(\nu) \, d\mu \, d\nu$$

$$= \frac{\mathcal{N}_0}{2} \int_{-\infty}^{\infty} h(\nu - \tau) \, h(\nu) \, d\nu. \tag{3.137}$$

Expressing $h(\nu)$ as the inverse Fourier transform of $H(f)$ and interchanging the order of integration again leads to Eq. 3.135. The integral in Eq. 3.137 is frequently referred to as the "correlation function" of the (deterministic) function $h(t)$.

As an example of the application of these results, consider the ideal lowpass filter shown in Fig. 3.28, whose transfer function is given by

$$W(f) \triangleq \begin{cases} 1; & |f| < W, \\ 0; & \text{elsewhere}. \end{cases} \tag{3.138}$$

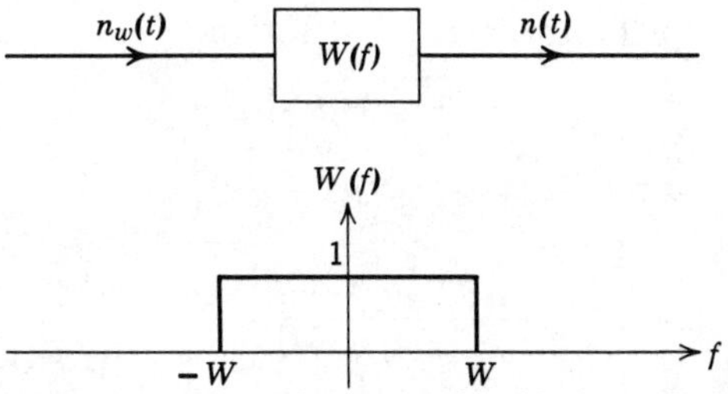

Figure 3.28 White noise into an ideal lowpass filter.

When the input to this filter is white Gaussian noise, $n_w(t)$, the mean function $m_n(t)$ of the output $n(t)$ is

$$m_n(t) = \int_{-\infty}^{\infty} \overline{n_w(\alpha)}\, h(t - \alpha)\, d\alpha.$$

But, from the definition of $n_w(t)$,

$$\overline{n_w(\alpha)} = 0; \qquad \text{for all } \alpha,$$

so that

$$m_n(t) = 0; \qquad \text{for all } t. \tag{3.139}$$

The correlation and covariance functions at the output, from Eqs. 3.131c and 3.135, are

$$\mathscr{L}_n(\tau) = \mathcal{R}_n(\tau) = \int_{-\infty}^{\infty} \mathcal{S}_w(f)\, |W(f)|^2 \cos 2\pi f\tau\, df$$

$$= \frac{\mathcal{N}_0}{2} \int_{-W}^{W} \cos 2\pi f\tau\, df$$

$$= \frac{\mathcal{N}_0}{2} \frac{\sin 2\pi f\tau}{2\pi\tau}\bigg|_{-W}^{W} = W\mathcal{N}_0 \frac{\sin 2\pi W\tau}{2\pi W\tau}. \tag{3.140}$$

Hence

$$\mathscr{L}_n(0) = \mathcal{R}_n(0) = \overline{n^2(t)} = W\mathcal{N}_0; \qquad \text{for all } t.$$

Now consider k samples $\{n_i\}$ taken from the output process $n(t)$ at the time instants $\{t_i\}$ given by

$$t_i = \frac{i}{2W} + T; \qquad i = 1, 2, \ldots, k, \tag{3.141a}$$

where T is any constant. It is interesting to note that the $\{n_i\}$ are *statistically independent* with zero mean and variance $W\mathcal{N}_0$:

$$\overline{n_i} = \overline{n(t_i)} = m_n(t_i) = 0, \tag{3.141b}$$

$$\lambda_{ij} = \overline{n_i n_j} = \mathcal{L}_n(t_i - t_j) = \mathcal{L}_n\left(\frac{i-j}{2W}\right)$$

$$= W\mathcal{N}_0 \frac{\sin \pi(i-j)}{\pi(i-j)} = \begin{cases} W\mathcal{N}_0; & \text{for } i = j, \\ 0; & \text{otherwise.} \end{cases} \tag{3.141c}$$

Thus the density function of the k Gaussian random variables $\{n_i\}$ is

$$p_{\mathbf{n}}(\boldsymbol{\alpha}) = \frac{1}{(2\pi W\mathcal{N}_0)^{k/2}} \exp\left(-\frac{1}{2W\mathcal{N}_0}\sum_{i=1}^{k} \alpha_i^{\,2}\right).$$

APPENDIX 3A MATRIX NOTATION

Matrix notation simplifies dealing with linear transformations. Consider, for example, the set of linear equations

$$\begin{aligned} y_1 &= a_{11}x_1 + a_{12}x_2 + \cdots + a_{1k}x_k + m_1 \\ y_2 &= a_{21}x_1 + a_{22}x_2 + \cdots + a_{2k}x_k + m_2 \\ &\cdot \\ &\cdot \\ &\cdot \\ y_k &= a_{k1}x_1 + a_{k2}x_2 + \cdots + a_{kk}x_k + m_k. \end{aligned} \tag{3A.1}$$

We may say that the variables $\{x_i\}$, $i = 1, 2, \ldots, k$, are *linearly transformed* into the new variables $\{y_j\}$, $j = 1, 2, \ldots, k$. In matrix notation these equations would be written more concisely as

$$\mathbf{y}^{\mathsf{T}} = \mathbf{A}\mathbf{x}^{\mathsf{T}} + \mathbf{m}^{\mathsf{T}}. \tag{3A.2}$$

Definitions

In order to give explicit meaning to Eq. 3A.2, several definitions are necessary.

1. An $(n \times k)$ matrix $\mathbf{B}$ is defined as an n-row, k-column array of numbers such as

$$\mathbf{B} = \begin{pmatrix} b_{11} & b_{12} & \cdots & b_{1k} \\ b_{21} & b_{22} & \cdots & b_{2k} \\ \cdot & & & \\ \cdot & & & \\ \cdot & & & \\ b_{n1} & b_{n2} & \cdots & b_{nk} \end{pmatrix}. \tag{3A.3}$$

2. The (i, j)th *element*, b_{ij}, of a matrix $\mathbf{B}$ is the number that is located at the intersection of the ith row and the jth column.

3. The *transpose* of an $(n \times k)$ matrix $\mathbf{B}$ is the $(k \times n)$ matrix, denoted $\mathbf{B}^{\mathsf{T}}$, obtained by interchanging the rows and columns of $\mathbf{B}$. An equivalent statement is that the (i, j)th element of $\mathbf{B}^{\mathsf{T}}$ is the (j, i)th element of $\mathbf{B}$. The transpose of matrix $\mathbf{B}$ in Eq. 3A.3 is

$$\mathbf{B}^{\mathsf{T}} = \begin{pmatrix} b_{11} & b_{21} & \cdots & b_{n1} \\ b_{12} & b_{22} & \cdots & b_{n2} \\ \cdot & & & \\ \cdot & & & \\ \cdot & & & \\ b_{1k} & b_{2k} & \cdots & b_{nk} \end{pmatrix}. \tag{3A.4}$$

4. We call a $1 \times k$ (single-row) matrix a *vector*. For example,

$$\mathbf{z} = (z_1, z_2, \ldots, z_k). \tag{3A.5a}$$

The transpose of a row matrix $\mathbf{z}$, denoted $\mathbf{z}^{\mathsf{T}}$, is a $k \times 1$ (single-column) matrix,

$$\mathbf{z}^{\mathsf{T}} = \begin{pmatrix} z_1 \\ z_2 \\ \cdot \\ \cdot \\ \cdot \\ z_k \end{pmatrix}. \tag{3A.5b}$$

5. Two matrices are said to be *equal* if and only if every pair of corresponding elements is equal. Thus the equation $\mathbf{A} = \mathbf{B}$ implies

$$a_{ij} = b_{ij}; \qquad \text{for all } i \text{ and } j. \tag{3A.6}$$

6. The *sum* $[\mathbf{A} + \mathbf{B}]$ of two $(n \times k)$ matrices $\mathbf{A}$ and $\mathbf{B}$ is the new $(n \times k)$ matrix $\mathbf{C}$ whose elements are given by

$$c_{ij} = a_{ij} + b_{ij}; \qquad \text{for all } i \text{ and } j. \tag{3A.7a}$$

Thus

$$\mathbf{C} = \mathbf{A} + \mathbf{B} \tag{3A.7b}$$

if and only if Eq. 3A.7a is satisfied. Matrix addition, like arithmetic addition, is associative and commutative. The sum of two matrices that do not have the same dimensions $(n \times k)$ is not defined.

7. The *scalar product* of an $(n \times k)$ matrix $\mathbf{A}$ by a constant c is the new $(n \times k)$ matrix $\mathbf{B}$ whose elements are given by

$$b_{ij} = ca_{ij}; \qquad \text{for all } i \text{ and } j. \tag{3A.8a}$$

Thus

$$\mathbf{B} = c\mathbf{A} \tag{3A.8b}$$

if and only if Eq. 3A.8a is satisfied. Scalar multiplication is associative and commutative.

8. The *matrix product* $\mathbf{AB}$ of an $(n \times k)$ matrix $\mathbf{A}$ by a $(k \times m)$ matrix $\mathbf{B}$ is the new $(n \times m)$ matrix $\mathbf{C}$ whose elements are given by

$$c_{ij} = \sum_{l=1}^{k} a_{il} b_{lj}; \qquad \text{for all } i \text{ and } j. \tag{3A.9a}$$

Thus

$$\mathbf{C} = \mathbf{AB} \tag{3A.9b}$$

if and only if Eq. 3A.9a is satisfied. If the number of *columns* in the first matrix, $\mathbf{A}$, is not equal to the number of *rows* in the second matrix, $\mathbf{B}$, the two matrices are said to be *nonconformable* and the product $\mathbf{AB}$ is not defined. Thus the matrix product of two vectors is *not defined*; but the matrix product of a k-component vector $\mathbf{x}$ and a k-component transposed vector $\mathbf{y}^{\mathsf{T}}$ is identical to the vector dot product of $\mathbf{x}$ and $\mathbf{y}$:

$$\mathbf{x}\mathbf{y}^{\mathsf{T}} = \sum_{l=1}^{k} x_l y_l = \mathbf{x} \cdot \mathbf{y}. \tag{3A.10}$$

Equation 3A.10 is an important relation which we shall use frequently. It is immediately helpful in visualizing the meaning of Eq. 3A.9a. As shown in Fig. 3A.1, we can think of c_{ij} as the dot product of the vector $\mathbf{a}_{i\cdot}$ that corresponds to the ith row of $\mathbf{A}$ and the vector $\mathbf{b}_{\cdot j}$ whose transpose corresponds to the jth column of $\mathbf{B}$. Thus

$$c_{ij} = \mathbf{a}_{i\cdot} \cdot \mathbf{b}_{\cdot j}. \tag{3A.11}$$

The notation $\mathbf{a}_{i\cdot}$ and $\mathbf{b}_{\cdot j}$ is mnemonic in that the dots indicate indices ranging over the dimension of the vector; for a k-column matrix $\mathbf{A}$ and an n-row matrix $\mathbf{B}$, $\mathbf{a}_{i\cdot} = (a_{i1}, a_{i2}, \ldots, a_{ik})$ and $\mathbf{b}_{\cdot j} = (b_{1j}, b_{2j}, \ldots, b_{nj})$. Equation 3A.11 may be visualized in terms of picking up the jth column of $\mathbf{B}$, laying it horizontally over the ith row of $\mathbf{A}$, multiplying the superimposed numbers by pairs, and summing the products. As an example,

$$\begin{pmatrix} 3 & 1 & 2 \\ 2 & 0 & 6 \end{pmatrix} \cdot \begin{pmatrix} 0 & 3 & 6 & 1 \\ 7 & 1 & 2 & 3 \\ 4 & 5 & 3 & 4 \end{pmatrix} = \begin{pmatrix} 15 & 20 & 26 & 14 \\ 24 & 36 & 30 & 26 \end{pmatrix},$$

$$\mathbf{C} = \begin{pmatrix} a_{11} & a_{12} & \cdots & a_{1k} \\ a_{21} & a_{22} & \cdots & a_{2k} \\ \vdots & & & \\ \boxed{a_{i1} \quad a_{i2} \quad \cdots \quad a_{ik}} \\ \vdots & & & \\ a_{n1} & a_{n2} & \cdots & a_{nk} \end{pmatrix} \begin{pmatrix} b_{11} & b_{12} & \cdots & \boxed{b_{1j}} & \cdots & b_{1m} \\ b_{21} & b_{22} & \cdots & b_{2j} & \cdots & b_{2m} \\ \vdots & & & & & \\ b_{k1} & b_{k2} & \cdots & b_{kj} & \cdots & b_{km} \end{pmatrix}$$

$\mathbf{a}_{i\cdot}$

$(\mathbf{b}_{\cdot j})^{\mathsf{T}}$

$\mathbf{b}_{\cdot j} \rightarrow \boxed{b_{1j} \quad b_{2j} \quad \cdots \quad b_{kj}}$

$\mathbf{a}_{i\cdot} \rightarrow \boxed{a_{i1} \quad a_{i2} \quad \cdots \quad a_{ik}}$

$\begin{matrix} b_{1j} \\ b_{2j} \\ \vdots \\ b_{kj} \end{matrix}$

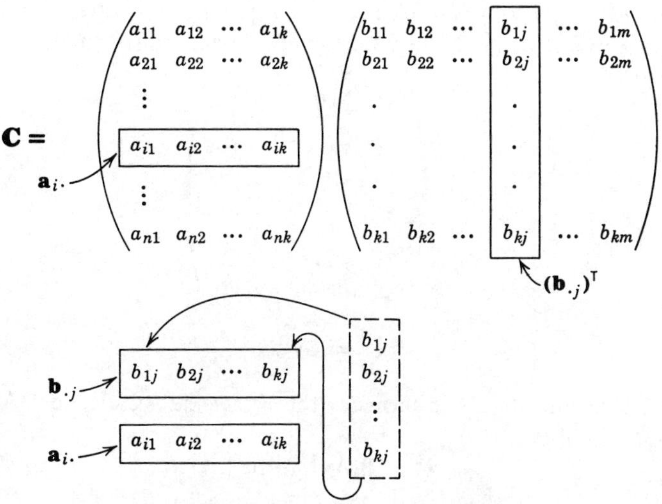

$$c_{ij} = \mathbf{a}_{i\cdot} \cdot \mathbf{b}_{\cdot j} = (a_{i1}b_{1j} + a_{i2}b_{2j} + \cdots + a_{ik}b_{kj})$$

Figure 3.A.1   Matrix multiplication. The matrix $\mathbf{C} = \mathbf{AB}$ is an $n \times m$ matrix with elements $\{c_{ij}\}$ that may be obtained as shown.

which may be readily verified by inspection; for instance, the $(2, 3)$ element in the product is computed

$$\left.\begin{matrix} \mathbf{a}_{2\cdot} = (2 \quad 0 \quad 6) \\ \mathbf{b}_{\cdot 3} = (6 \quad 2 \quad 3) \end{matrix}\right\} c_{23} = 12 + 0 + 18 = 30.$$

The foregoing definitions are sufficient to explain the meaning of Eq. 3A.2. We take the matrix $\mathbf{A}$ to be the square $(k \times k)$ matrix whose elements are the coefficients $\{a_{ij}\}$ in Eq. 3A.1 and let

$$\mathbf{y}^{\mathsf{T}} = \begin{pmatrix} y_1 \\ y_2 \\ \cdot \\ \cdot \\ \cdot \\ y_k \end{pmatrix}, \quad \mathbf{x}^{\mathsf{T}} = \begin{pmatrix} x_1 \\ x_2 \\ \cdot \\ \cdot \\ \cdot \\ x_k \end{pmatrix}, \quad \mathbf{m}^{\mathsf{T}} = \begin{pmatrix} m_1 \\ m_2 \\ \cdot \\ \cdot \\ \cdot \\ m_k \end{pmatrix}. \tag{3A.12}$$

The product $\mathbf{Ax}^{\mathsf{T}}$ is therefore a $(k \times 1)$, column matrix, and equating corresponding elements on the right- and left-hand sides of Eq. 3A.2 reproduces the set of equations in Eq. 3A.1.

Matrix notation is especially helpful when one is confronted with a sequence of linear transformations. For example, if the k variables

$\mathbf{y} = (y_1, y_2, \ldots, y_k)$ in Eq. 3A.1 are subsequently transformed into l new variables $\mathbf{z} = (z_1, z_2, \ldots, z_l)$ by means of a linear transformation

$$\mathbf{B} = \begin{pmatrix} b_{11} & b_{12} & \cdots & b_{1k} \\ b_{21} & b_{22} & \cdots & b_{2k} \\ \cdot & & & \\ \cdot & & & \\ \cdot & & & \\ b_{l1} & b_{l2} & \cdots & b_{lk} \end{pmatrix}, \tag{3A.13a}$$

then

$$\mathbf{z}^{\mathsf{T}} = \mathbf{B}\mathbf{y}^{\mathsf{T}}. \tag{3A.13b}$$

If we wish to find the z's in terms of the x's, we substitute Eq. 3A.13b in Eq. 3A.2 and obtain

$$\mathbf{z}^{\mathsf{T}} = \mathbf{B}[\mathbf{A}\mathbf{x}^{\mathsf{T}} + \mathbf{m}^{\mathsf{T}}]. \tag{3A.13c}$$

Properties of Matrix Multiplication

The definition of matrix multiplication (Eq. 3A.9) implies certain properties that are important.

1. Matrix multiplication and addition are *distributive*; that is,

$$\mathbf{A}(\mathbf{B} + \mathbf{C}) = \mathbf{AB} + \mathbf{AC}. \tag{3A.14}$$

This can be verified directly from the definition.

2. Matrix multiplication is *associative*; that is,

$$(\mathbf{AB})\mathbf{C} = \mathbf{A}(\mathbf{BC}). \tag{3A.15}$$

This can be verified, with some labor, by showing that the (i, j)th element, say d_{ij}, of the triple product is given by

$$d_{ij} = \sum_l \sum_m a_{il} b_{lm} c_{mj}, \tag{3A.16}$$

regardless of which multiplication is carried out first.†

3. Matrix multiplication is *not* generally *commutative*; that is,

$$\mathbf{AB} \neq \mathbf{BA}. \tag{3A.17}$$

Indeed, two matrices conformable in one order need not be conformable

† Use of these first two properties permits us to simplify Eq. 3A.13c still further: we may write $\mathbf{z}^{\mathsf{T}} = \mathbf{C}\mathbf{x}^{\mathsf{T}} + \mathbf{n}^{\mathsf{T}}$, where $\mathbf{C} = \mathbf{AB}$ and $\mathbf{n}^{\mathsf{T}} = \mathbf{B}\mathbf{m}^{\mathsf{T}}$. Thus a sequence of linear transformations is a linear transformation.

in the other. Even in the case of two ($k \times k$) matrices, however, multiplication is not usually commutative. For example,

$$\begin{pmatrix} 1 & 0 \\ 1 & 0 \end{pmatrix}\begin{pmatrix} 1 & 1 \\ 0 & 0 \end{pmatrix} = \begin{pmatrix} 1 & 1 \\ 1 & 1 \end{pmatrix} \neq \begin{pmatrix} 1 & 1 \\ 0 & 0 \end{pmatrix}\begin{pmatrix} 1 & 0 \\ 1 & 0 \end{pmatrix} = \begin{pmatrix} 2 & 0 \\ 0 & 0 \end{pmatrix}.$$

4. The transpose of a matrix product is the commuted product of the transposes; that is

$$(\mathbf{AB})^{\mathsf{T}} = \mathbf{B}^{\mathsf{T}}\mathbf{A}^{\mathsf{T}}. \tag{3A.18}$$

This property is easily proved. First consider the left-hand side of Eq. 3A.18. The (i, j)th element of $(\mathbf{AB})^{\mathsf{T}}$ is the (j, i)th element of $\mathbf{AB}$, which by Eq. 3A.11 is $\mathbf{a}_{j\cdot} \cdot \mathbf{b}_{\cdot i}$. Next consider the right-hand side: the ith row of $\mathbf{B}^{\mathsf{T}}$ is the ith column of $\mathbf{B}$, and the jth column of $\mathbf{A}^{\mathsf{T}}$ is the jth row of $\mathbf{A}$. Hence the (i, j)th element of $\mathbf{B}^{\mathsf{T}}\mathbf{A}^{\mathsf{T}}$ is also $\mathbf{a}_{j\cdot} \cdot \mathbf{b}_{\cdot i}$. As an example,

$$\left[\begin{pmatrix} 1 & 2 \\ 3 & 4 \end{pmatrix}\begin{pmatrix} 5 & 6 \\ 7 & 8 \end{pmatrix}\right]^{\mathsf{T}} = \begin{pmatrix} 19 & 22 \\ 43 & 50 \end{pmatrix}^{\mathsf{T}}$$

$$= \begin{pmatrix} 19 & 43 \\ 22 & 50 \end{pmatrix} = \begin{pmatrix} 5 & 7 \\ 6 & 8 \end{pmatrix}\begin{pmatrix} 1 & 3 \\ 2 & 4 \end{pmatrix}.$$

5. A number b equal to a double sum of the form

$$\begin{aligned} b = \sum_{i=1}^{k}\sum_{j=1}^{k} x_i a_{ij} y_j &= x_1 a_{11} y_1 + x_1 a_{12} y_2 + \cdots + x_1 a_{1k} y_k \\ &+ x_2 a_{21} y_1 + x_2 a_{22} y_2 + \cdots + x_2 a_{2k} y_k \\ &\cdot \\ &\cdot \\ &\cdot \\ &+ x_k a_{k1} y_1 + x_k a_{k2} y_2 + \cdots + x_k a_{kk} y_k \end{aligned} \tag{3A.19a}$$

can be written succinctly

$$b = \mathbf{x}\mathbf{A}\mathbf{y}^{\mathsf{T}} = \sum_{i=1}^{k}\sum_{j=1}^{k} x_i a_{ij} y_j, \tag{3A.19b}$$

where $\mathbf{x} = (x_1, x_2, \ldots, x_k)$, $\mathbf{y} = (y_1, y_2, \ldots, y_k)$, and $\mathbf{A}$ is the ($k \times k$) matrix with elements $\{a_{ij}\}$. This type of sum is called a *bilinear form.* When $\mathbf{y} = \mathbf{x}$, it is called a *quadratic form.* Expressions of this kind are useful in Section 3.3.

Inverse Matrices

The last matrix concept we shall consider is that of an *inverse.* The inverse of a square ($k \times k$) matrix $\mathbf{A}$ is written $\mathbf{A}^{-1}$ and is also a ($k \times k$)

matrix. If the set of k equations

$$\mathbf{y}^{\mathsf{T}} = \mathbf{A}\mathbf{x}^{\mathsf{T}} \tag{3A.20a}$$

can be solved uniquely for the k x's in terms of the k y's, $\mathbf{A}^{-1}$ is the matrix of coefficients in the resulting equations. Thus, if Eq. 3A.20a implies that

$$\mathbf{x}^{\mathsf{T}} = \mathbf{B}\mathbf{y}^{\mathsf{T}}, \tag{3A.20b}$$

then

$$\mathbf{B} = \mathbf{A}^{-1}. \tag{3A.20c}$$

Combining Eqs. 3A.20c with Eqs. 3A.20a and 3A.20b, we have both

$$\mathbf{y}^{\mathsf{T}} = \mathbf{A}(\mathbf{B}\mathbf{y}^{\mathsf{T}}) = (\mathbf{A}\mathbf{A}^{-1})\mathbf{y}^{\mathsf{T}} \tag{3A.21a}$$

and

$$\mathbf{x}^{\mathsf{T}} = \mathbf{B}(\mathbf{A}\mathbf{x}^{\mathsf{T}}) = (\mathbf{A}^{-1}\mathbf{A})\mathbf{x}^{\mathsf{T}}. \tag{3A.21b}$$

It follows that

$$\mathbf{A}\mathbf{A}^{-1} = \mathbf{A}^{-1}\mathbf{A} = \mathbf{I}, \tag{3A.22}$$

where $\mathbf{I}$ is the *diagonal* matrix

$$\mathbf{I} \triangleq \begin{pmatrix} 1 & & & & \\ & 1 & & 0 & \\ & & 1 & & \\ & 0 & & \ddots & \\ & & & & 1 \end{pmatrix} \tag{3A.23}$$

in which all off-diagonal elements are zero (symbolized by the large 0's), and all *principal diagonal* elements (of the form c_{ii}) are unity.

The matrix $\mathbf{I}$ is called the *identity matrix* and has the property that it transforms any matrix into itself:

$$\mathbf{C}\mathbf{I} = \mathbf{I}\mathbf{C} = \mathbf{C}. \tag{3A.24}$$

Equation 3A.22 is taken to be the definition of *inverse*: the matrix $\mathbf{A}^{-1}$ inverse to $\mathbf{A}$ is that matrix which, when premultiplied or postmultiplied by $\mathbf{A}$, yields the identity matrix. It is clear from the definition that

$$(\mathbf{A}^{-1})^{-1} = \mathbf{A}. \tag{3A.25}$$

When matrix $\mathbf{A}$ does not correspond to a reversible transformation (that is, if the x's in Eq. 3A.20a cannot be uniquely determined from knowledge of the y's and vice versa), the matrix inverse to $\mathbf{A}$ is *not defined* and $\mathbf{A}$ is called *singular*. This must always be the case when $\mathbf{A}$ is not square. When $\mathbf{A}$ is square, it is singular whenever the simultaneous equations of Eq. 3A.20a are linearly dependent, which implies that the determinant of **A**, denoted $|\mathbf{A}|$, is zero:

$$|\mathbf{A}| = 0 \Leftrightarrow \mathbf{A} \text{ is singular.} \tag{3A.26}$$

Otherwise, **A** is nonsingular and $\mathbf{A}^{-1}$ exists.

The elements comprising $\mathbf{A}^{-1}$ are given directly by solving Eq. 3A.20a to obtain Eq. 3A.20b. If $\mathbf{B} = \mathbf{A}^{-1}$, then we know from the elementary theory of determinants[37] that

$$b_{ij} = (-1)^{i+j} \frac{|\mathbf{A}_{ji}|}{|\mathbf{A}|}, \tag{3A.27}$$

where $\mathbf{A}_{ji}$ is the matrix obtained from **A** by deleting the jth row and ith column, and $|\mathbf{A}_{ji}|$ is its determinant. Note that the order of the indices i and j is different on the two sides of Eq. 3A.27.

As an example, the inverse of the matrix

$$\mathbf{A} = \begin{pmatrix} 1 & 1 & 0 \\ 2 & 1 & 3 \\ 1 & 4 & 1 \end{pmatrix}, \qquad |\mathbf{A}| = -10,$$

is

$$\mathbf{A}^{-1} = \frac{1}{10} \begin{pmatrix} 11 & 1 & -3 \\ -1 & -1 & 3 \\ -7 & 3 & 1 \end{pmatrix}.$$

It can be readily verified that Eq. 3A.22 is satisfied.

The last result we shall need is

$$(\mathbf{AB})^{-1} = \mathbf{B}^{-1}\mathbf{A}^{-1}. \tag{3A.28}$$

This follows directly from the equation

$$(\mathbf{B}^{-1}\mathbf{A}^{-1})(\mathbf{AB}) = \mathbf{B}^{-1}(\mathbf{A}^{-1}\mathbf{A})\mathbf{B} = \mathbf{B}^{-1}\mathbf{B} = \mathbf{I}. \tag{3A.29}$$

Finally, taking $\mathbf{B} = \mathbf{A}^{-1}$ in Eq. 3A.18 yields

$$(\mathbf{A}^{-1})^{\mathsf{T}} = (\mathbf{A}^{\mathsf{T}})^{-1}. \tag{3A.30}$$

PROBLEMS

3.1 An elementary random process comprises four sample functions, to each of which is assigned equal probability.

$$x(\omega_1, t) = 1 \qquad x(\omega_3, t) = \sin \pi t,$$
$$x(\omega_2, t) = -2 \qquad x(\omega_4, t) = \cos \pi t.$$

a. Is the process stationary?

b. Calculate $\overline{x(t)}$ and $\overline{x(t_1)\,x(t_2)}$.

c. What is the probability of the set of sample functions passing through the windows of Fig. P3.1*a*?—Fig. P3.1*b*?

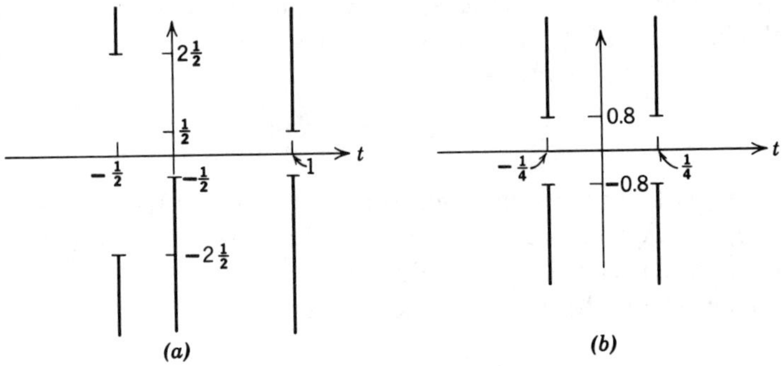

Figure P3.1

3.2 Let $\mathbf{x} = (x_1, x_2)$, where x_1 and x_2 are zero-mean Gaussian random variables. Assume for (a) and (b) that $\overline{x_1^2} = \overline{x_2^2} = 1$ and that x_1 and x_2 are statistically independent.

a. Evaluate $\overline{|\mathbf{x}|^2}$, $\overline{|\mathbf{x}|}^2$.

b. For each of the four accompanying figures, express the probability that $\mathbf{x}$ lies in the shaded region in terms of the function $Q(\alpha)$, where

$$Q(\alpha) \triangleq \int_\alpha^\infty \frac{1}{\sqrt{2\pi}}\, e^{-\beta^2/2}\, d\beta.$$

c. Repeat (b) for Fig. P3.2*a* and *b*, with $\overline{x_1^2} = 1$, $\overline{x_2^2} = 2$, $\overline{x_1x_2} = -\frac{1}{2}$.

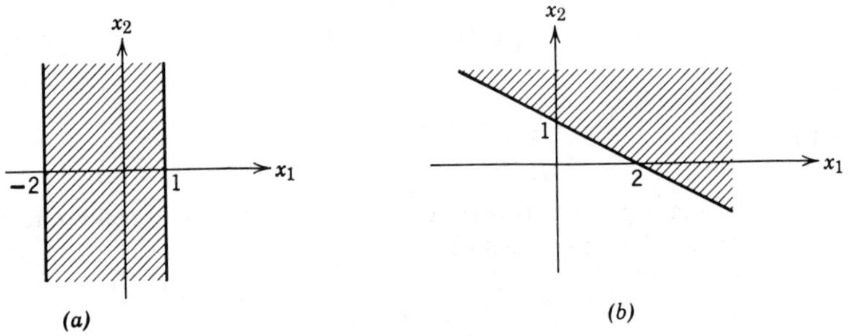

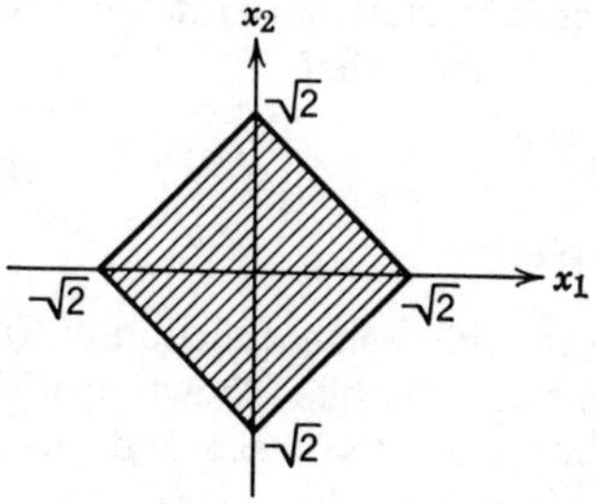

(c)

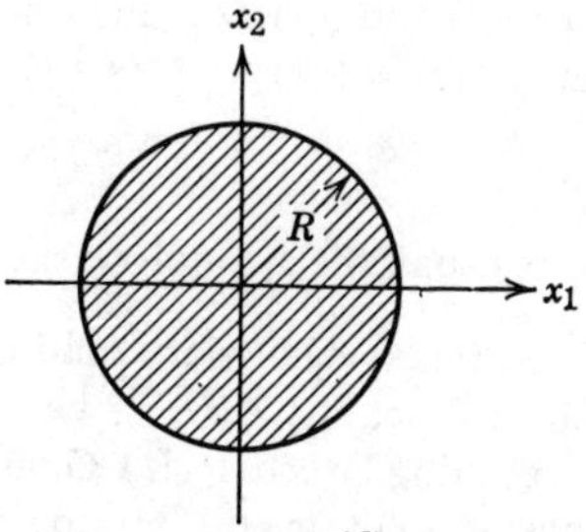

(d)

Figure P3.2

3.3 Let $\mathbf{x} = (x_1, x_2, x_3)$ be a zero-mean Gaussian vector with covariance matrix

$$\Lambda_x = \begin{pmatrix} 3 & 3 & 0 \\ 3 & 5 & 0 \\ 0 & 0 & 6 \end{pmatrix}.$$

(This is a concise way of writing $\overline{x_1^2} = \overline{x_1x_2} = 3$; $\overline{x_2^2} = 5$; $\overline{x_3^2} = 6$; $\overline{x_1x_3} = \overline{x_2x_3} = 0$.)

a. Give an expression for $p_{\mathbf{x}}$. [Observe that x_3 is statistically independent of the pair (x_1, x_2).]

b. If $y = x_1 + 2x_2 - x_3$, determine p_y.

c. If $\mathbf{z} = (z_1, z_2, z_3)$, determine $p_{\mathbf{z}}$, where

$$z_1 = 5x_1 - 3x_2 - x_3,$$
$$z_2 = -x_1 + 3x_2 - x_3,$$
$$z_3 = x_1 + x_3.$$

d. Determine $p_{x_1}(\alpha \mid x_2 = \beta)$.

3.4 A channel is disturbed by two zero-mean jointly Gaussian noise processes, $n_1(t)$ and $n_2(t)$. It is known that

$$\mathcal{R}_i(\tau) \triangleq \overline{n_i(t)\, n_i(t - \tau)} = \frac{\sin \pi\tau}{\pi\tau}; \qquad i = 1, 2,$$

$$\mathcal{R}_{12}(\tau) \triangleq \overline{n_1(t)\, n_2(t - \tau)} = \frac{\sin \pi\tau}{2\pi\tau}.$$

Write the joint density function of the three random variables x_1, x_2, and x_3, where

$$x_1 \triangleq n_1(t)\big|_{t=0},$$
$$x_2 \triangleq n_1(t)\big|_{t=1},$$
$$x_3 \triangleq n_2(t)\big|_{t=0}.$$

3.5 Let $x(t)$ and $y(t)$ be statistically independent, stationary random processes and define $z(t) = x(t)\,y(t)$. Is $z(t)$ stationary? Show that

$$\mathcal{S}_z(f) = \mathcal{S}_x(f) * \mathcal{S}_y(f),$$

where, as usual, the symbol $*$ denotes convolution.

3.6 Let $x(t)$, a Gaussian random process with mean function $m_x(t)$ and covariance function $\mathscr{L}_x(t, s)$, be passed through the filter shown in Fig. P3.6. Is the resulting process $y(t)$ Gaussian? What are the mean and covariance functions of $y(t)$? Is $y(t)$ stationary if $x(t)$ is stationary?

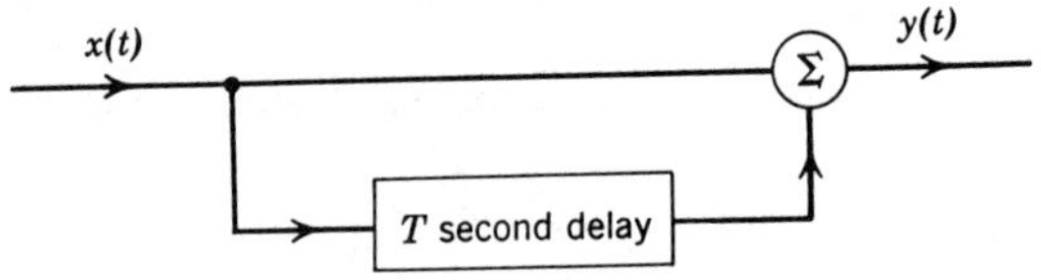

Figure P3.6

3.7 A stationary zero-mean random process is the input to three linear filters, as shown in Fig. P3.7. The power density spectrum of $x(t)$ is $\mathcal{S}_x(f) = \mathcal{N}_0/2$. The filter impulse responses are

$$h_1(t) = \begin{cases} 1; & 0 \leqslant t < 1, \\ 0; & \text{elsewhere.} \end{cases}$$

$$h_2(t) = \begin{cases} 2e^{-t}; & 0 \leqslant t, \\ 0; & \text{elsewhere.} \end{cases}$$

$$h_3(t) = \begin{cases} \sqrt{2}\,\sin 2\pi t; & 0 \leqslant t < 2, \\ 0; & \text{elsewhere.} \end{cases}$$

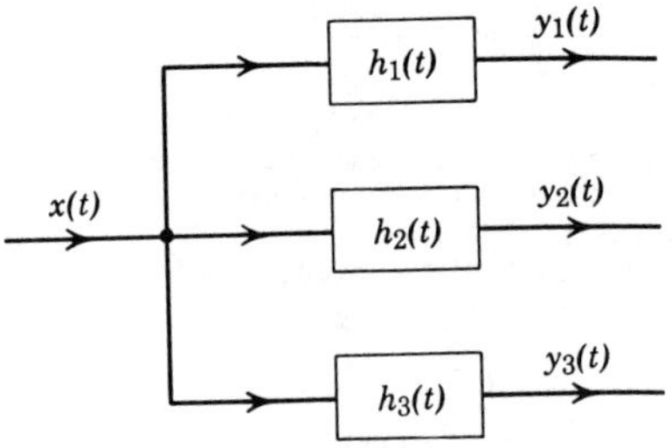

Figure P3.7

a. Determine $\overline{y_i(t)}$ and $\overline{y_i^2(t)}$ for $i = 1, 2, 3$.
b. Is there any pair of output processes for which $\overline{y_i(t)\, y_j(t)} = 0$ for all t?
c. Is there any pair of output processes for which $\overline{y_i(t)\, y_j(s)} = 0$ for all t, s?

3.8 A stationary Gaussian random process $x(t)$ with mean $m_x(t) = m_x$ and covariance function $\mathscr{L}_x(\tau)$ is passed through two linear filters with impulse responses $h(t)$ and $g(t)$, yielding processes $y(t)$ and $z(t)$ as shown in Fig. P3.8.

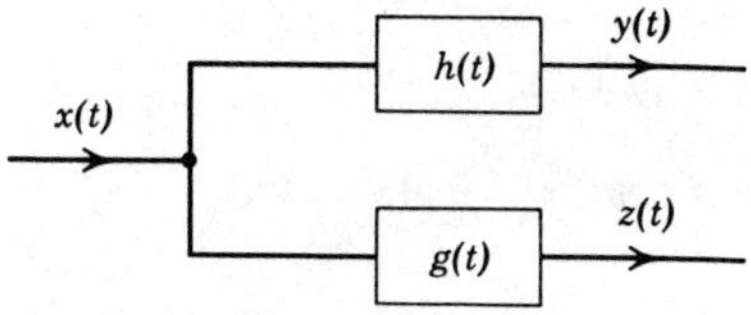

Figure P3.8

a. What is the joint density function of the random variables $y_1 \triangleq y(t_1)$ and $z_2 \triangleq z(t_2)$?
b. Evaluate $\overline{y(t)\, x(t - \tau)}$. To what does this expression reduce when $x(t)$ is white noise?
c. What conditions on $h(t)$ and $g(t)$ are necessary and sufficient to ensure that $y(t)$ and $z(t)$ are statistically independent?
d. If $m_x = 0$ and $\mathscr{L}_x(\tau) = (\sin \pi\tau)^2/(\pi\tau)^2$, find the instantaneous power of $y(t)$ when $h(t)$ is an ideal filter with transfer function

$$H(f) = \begin{cases} 1; & \frac{1}{2} < |f| < 1, \\ 0; & \text{elsewhere.} \end{cases}$$

3.9 A zero-mean stationary Gaussian process with spectral density $S_x(f)$ is the input to a linear filter whose impulse response is shown in Fig. P3.9. A sample, y, is taken of the output process at time T. The random variable y is often referred to as the T-second time average of the process $x(t)$.

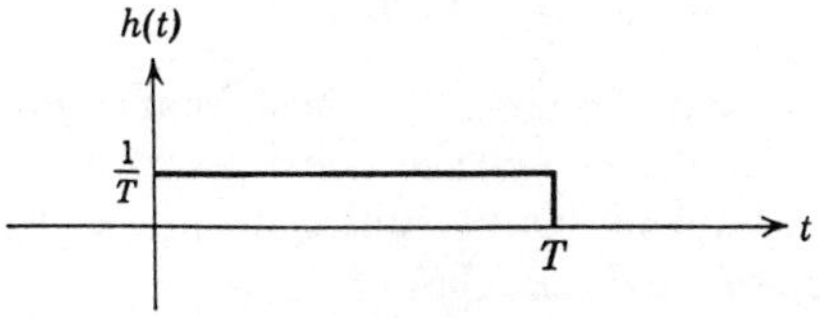

Figure P3.9

a. Calculate $\bar{y}$.
b. Calculate σ_y^2 in terms of $S_x(f)$ and T.

c. Upper bound σ_y^2 under the conditions $\mathcal{S}_x(f) \leqslant S$ for all f.

d. Derive a tight upper bound on $\mathrm{P}[\,|y - \bar{y}| \geqslant \epsilon]$ and contrast with the weak law of large numbers.

3.10 It is desired to generate a stationary random process with the correlation function

$$\mathcal{R}_x(\tau) = e^{-|\tau|}, \tag{1}$$

hence the power spectrum

$$\mathcal{S}_x(f) = \frac{2}{1 + (2\pi f)^2}. \tag{2}$$

We propose doing this in two ways:

I. By setting $x(t) = A \cos(2\pi f t + \theta)$, in which A, f, and θ are *statistically independent* random variables.

II. By taking

$$x(t) = \int_0^\infty h(\alpha)\, n(t - \alpha)\, d\alpha,$$

in which $n(t)$ is white noise and $h(t)$ is some appropriate impulse response.

a. Specify density functions for p_A, p_f, and p_θ that yield the desired power density spectrum of Eq. 2. Do you need to specify the density functions for A, f, and θ completely or is specifying less statistical information about them sufficient?

b. Pick $h(t)$ to yield the spectrum of Eq. 2 via method II.

c. Sketch a typical sample function generated by method I; by method II. Do you expect them to look similar? Explain.

3.11 Let x and y be statistically independent Gaussian random variables, each with zero mean and unit variance. Define the (Gaussian) process

$$z(t) = x \cos 2\pi t + y \sin 2\pi t.$$

a. Determine the covariance function of $z(t)$ and express p_{z_1,z_2} in terms of it, where $z_i \triangleq z(t_i)$ for $i = 1, 2$. Is the process $z(t)$ stationary?

b. Define $r \triangleq \sqrt{x^2 + y^2}$, $\theta \triangleq \tan^{-1} x/y$, and determine $p_{r,\theta}$. Note that

$$z(t) = r \sin(2\pi t + \theta).$$

c. Consider three random variables obtained from $z(t)$ by sampling at times $t = 0, \frac{1}{4}, \frac{1}{2}$. Determine the covariance matrix of these variables. Does the inverse matrix exist? Explain. Use impulse functions to write the joint probability density function of these variables.

3.12 Determine the correlation function $\mathcal{R}_x(t, s)$ of the random process

$$x(t) = \sum_{i=-\infty}^{\infty} w_i\, u(t - iT - \tau),$$

where the $\{w_i\}$ and τ are statistically independent random variables with

$$p_{w_i}(\alpha) = \tfrac{1}{2}[\delta(\alpha + 1) + \delta(\alpha - 1)]; \quad \text{all } i,$$

$$p_\tau(\alpha) = \begin{cases} \dfrac{1}{T}, & 0 \leqslant \alpha < T, \\ 0, & \text{elsewhere.} \end{cases}$$

The waveform $u(t)$ is shown in Fig. P3.12*a* and a typical sample function appears in Fig. P3.12*b*.

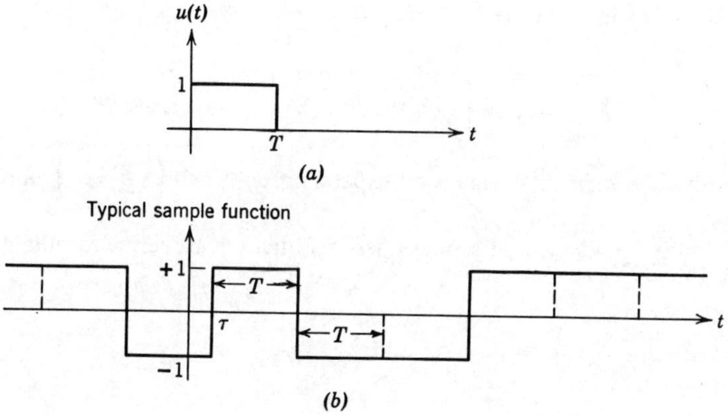

Figure P3.12

3.13 The general expression for the mixed moments of N zero-mean jointly Gaussian random variables $x_1, x_2, \ldots, x_N$ is

$$\overline{x_{i_1}x_{i_2}\cdots x_{i_L}} = \begin{cases} 0; & L \text{ odd}, \\ \displaystyle\sum_{\substack{\text{all distinct} \\ \text{pairs of} \\ \text{subscripts}}} [\lambda_{j_1j_2}\lambda_{j_3j_4}\cdots\lambda_{j_{L-1}j_L}]; & L \text{ even}, \end{cases}$$

where, as usual for zero-mean variables, $\lambda_{lk} \triangleq \overline{x_l x_k}$. For example

$$\overline{x_1x_2x_3x_4} = \lambda_{12}\lambda_{34} + \lambda_{13}\lambda_{24} + \lambda_{14}\lambda_{23},$$

$$\overline{x_1x_2x_3} = 0.$$

If some of the variables appear in the moment with a power of 2 or higher, the formula is to be applied by treating each repeated subscript as if it were distinct;

thus

$$\overline{x_1{}^2x_2x_3} = \lambda_{11}\lambda_{23} + \lambda_{12}\lambda_{13} + \lambda_{13}\lambda_{12} = \lambda_{11}\lambda_{23} + 2\lambda_{12}\lambda_{13};$$
$$\overline{x_1{}^4} = 3\lambda_{11}{}^2 = 3\sigma_1{}^4.$$

a. Evaluate $\overline{x_1{}^2x_2{}^2}$ and $\overline{x_1{}^3x_2}$ directly and by use of the formula.

b. Apply the formula to $\overline{x_1x_2x_3x_4x_5x_6}$.

c. Verify that the number of terms entering into the formula for $\overline{x_1x_2\cdots x_L}$, L even, is

$$(L-1)(L-3)\cdots(3)(1) = \frac{L!}{2^{L/2}(L/2)!}.$$

d. Using (c), evaluate $\overline{x_1{}^L}$ and $\overline{x_1{}^4x_2{}^4}$.

e. Note that

$$\overline{\left(\sum_{i=1}^{N} \nu_i x_i\right)^L} = \left[\sum_{i=1}^{N}\sum_{k=1}^{N} \nu_i(\overline{x_i x_k})\nu_k\right]^{L/2}; \qquad L \text{ even}$$

and prove the moment formula by expanding both $\overline{\exp\left(j\sum_{i=1}^{N}\nu_i x_i\right)}$ and $\exp\left(-\frac{1}{2}\sum_{i=1}^{N}\sum_{k=1}^{N}\nu_i\lambda_{ik}\nu_k\right)$ in a power series. First equate terms to obtain

$$\overline{\left(\sum_{i=1}^{N} \nu_i x_i\right)^L} = 0; \qquad L \text{ odd}$$

$$\overline{\left(\sum_{i=1}^{N} \nu_i x_i\right)^L} = \frac{L!}{2^{L/2}(L/2)!}\left(\sum_{i=1}^{N}\sum_{k=1}^{N}\nu_i\lambda_{ik}\nu_k\right)^{L/2}; \qquad L \text{ even.}$$

Next equate coefficients of terms such as $\nu_1\nu_2\cdots\nu_L$ on both sides of this expression.

3.14 In the circuit shown in Fig. P3.14, $x(t)$ is a Gaussian random process with zero-mean and correlation function

$$\mathcal{R}_x(t, s) = \frac{2\sin\pi(t-s)}{\pi(t-s)}.$$

Find expressions [in terms of $h(t)$ or $H(f)$] for $m_y(t)$ and $\mathscr{L}_y(t, s)$. Is $y(t)$ wide-sense stationary? *Hint.* Use the results of Problem 3.13 and the convolution $\leftrightarrow$ multiplication theorem of Fourier analysis.

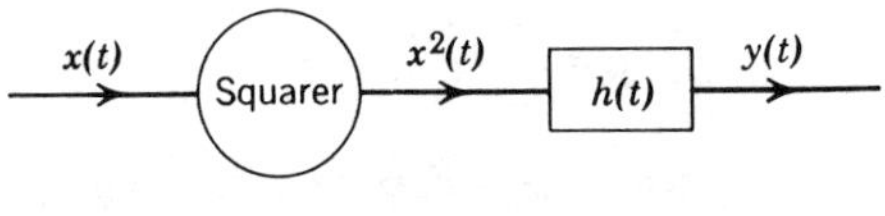

Figure P3.14

3.15 The process

$$x(t) \triangleq \sum_{i=-\infty}^{\infty} A\,\delta(t - \tau_i)$$

is called a "Poisson impulse train" when the $\{\tau_i\}$ are random variables so distributed that the probability $P(n, T)$ of exactly n impulses occurring in any interval I of duration T is

$$P(n, T) = e^{-mT}\frac{(mT)^n}{n!}; \qquad n = 0, 1, 2, \ldots,$$

independent of the number of impulses arriving during all time intervals disjoint from I. We assume without loss of generality that $\tau_i < \tau_{i+1}$, all i, as indicated in Fig. P3.15. The parameter m is a positive constant.

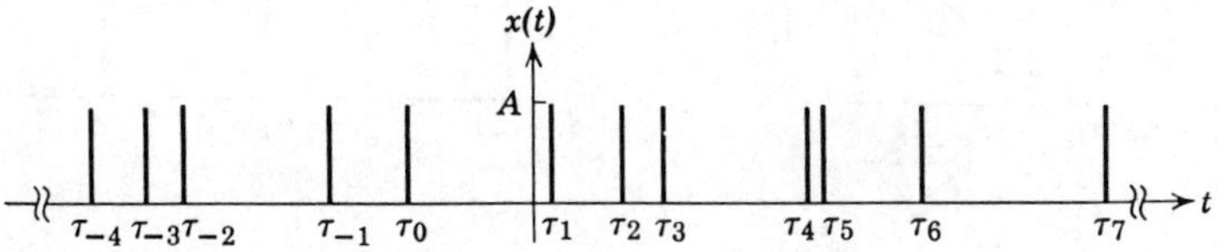

Figure P3.15

a. Verify that

$$\sum_{n=0}^{\infty} P(n, T) = 1.$$

b. Let I consist of two subintervals with durations T_1 and T_2, and let n_1 and n_2 denote the number of impulses occurring in these subintervals. Use characteristic functions to verify that

$$P[n_1 + n_2 = n] = P(n, T_1 + T_2).$$

c. Let the random variable N denote the number of impulses occurring in any interval of T seconds duration. Evaluate $\bar{N}$ and σ_N^2.

d. Define the random variable

$$l_i \triangleq \tau_{i+1} - \tau_i.$$

Thus l_i is the length of time between the occurrence of the ith and $(i + 1)$st impulse. Determine $\overline{l_i}$, $\overline{l_i^2}$, and the probability density function p_{l_i}. *Hint.* First determine $P[l_i \leqslant \alpha]$.

e. Repeat (d) for the random variable

$$l_k \triangleq \tau_{i+k} - \tau_i,$$

in which k is an arbitrary positive integer.

3.16 The Poisson impulse train $x(t)$ of Problem 3.15 is applied as input to a linear filter, as shown in Fig. P3.16a. When $h(t)$ is chosen as shown in Fig. P3.16b, the output process is

$$y(t) = A \sum_{i=-\infty}^{\infty} h(t - \tau_i) = \frac{A}{\Delta} N_\Delta,$$

in which N_Δ is the number of impulses occurring in the interval $[t - \Delta, t]$.

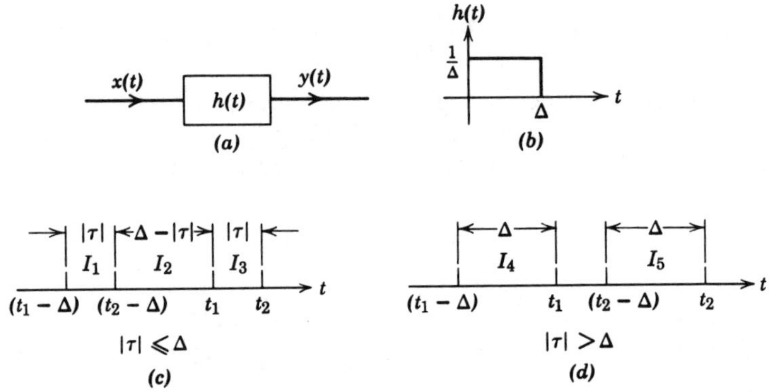

Figure P3.16

a. Show that for this $h(t)$

$$\overline{y(t_1)\,y(t_2)} = \mathcal{R}_y(\tau) = \begin{cases} \dfrac{A^2}{\Delta^2}\,\overline{(N_1 + N_2)(N_2 + N_3)}; & |\tau| \leqslant \Delta, \\ \dfrac{A^2}{\Delta^2}\,\overline{N_4 N_5}; & |\tau| > \Delta, \end{cases}$$

in which $\tau \triangleq t_2 - t_1$ and N_i $(i = 1, 2, 3, 4, 5)$ is the number of impulses occurring in the corresponding interval I_i shown in Fig. P3.15c and d.

b. Use the results of Problem 3.15c to reduce the expression for $\mathcal{R}_y(\tau)$ to the form

$$\mathcal{R}_y(\tau) = \begin{cases} A^2\left[m^2 + \dfrac{m}{\Delta}\left(1 - \dfrac{|\tau|}{\Delta}\right)\right]; & |\tau| \leqslant \Delta, \\ m^2 A^2; & |\tau| > \Delta. \end{cases}$$

c. Observe that the process $y(t)$ tends to the process $x(t)$ as $\Delta \to 0$ and verify that

$$\mathcal{S}_x(f) = mA^2 + m^2A^2\,\delta(f).$$

Prove as a consequence that, for a *general* filter $h(t)$,

$$\mathcal{S}_y(f) = mA^2\,|H(f)|^2 + [mA\,H(0)]^2\,\delta(f).$$

This result, known as Campbell's theorem,is exploited in (d) and (e).

d. The process $x(t)$, with A specialized to the electron charge q, is a good model for the emission of electrons from the cathode of a vacuum diode as long as the electrons do not interact with each other, which is a reasonable approximation with temperature-limited operation. Let $qh(t)$, with $\int_0^\infty h(t)\,dt = H(0) = 1$, denote the plate current increment due to a single electron emitted at $t = 0$. Then $y(t)$ is the total diode current.

Let I_{dc} denote the dc current and show that

$$y(t) = I_{\text{dc}} + n(t),$$

where $n(t)$ is a zero-mean noise process with power spectrum

$$\mathcal{S}_n(f) = q\,|I_{\text{dc}}|$$

over the range of f for which $H(f)$, the Fourier transform of $h(t)$, is approximately constant. Argue that an implication is that the noise in a vacuum tube amplifier is *not* strictly signal independent except in the limit of arbitrarily small signal dynamic range.

e. Both forward and reverse currents tend to flow simultaneously across the diffusion layer of a solid-state diode (or transistor) when bias is applied. In normal operation the forward current is composed chiefly of one type of carrier (say holes) and the reverse current of the other (say electrons). The Poisson impulse train $x(t)$ provides a good model for both the forward and reverse diffusion *individually*, with A specialized to $+q$ and $-q$, respectively. The resulting terminal current may be written

$$y(t) = I_f - I_r + n(t),$$

in which I_f and I_r denote the dc value of forward and reverse current and $n(t)$ is again a zero-mean noise process. Assume that the forward and reverse diffusion processes are statistically independent and show that

$$\mathcal{S}_n(f) = q(|I_f| + |I_r|)$$

over the range of f for which the Fourier transform $q\,H(f)$ of the diode's response to the diffusion of a single charge-carrier at $t = 0$ is approximately constant.

3.17 Determine the expression for Campbell's theorem (cf. Problem 3.16) for the case, illustrated in Fig. P3.17, in which the filter input

$$x(t) = \sum_i A_i\,\delta(t - \tau_i)$$

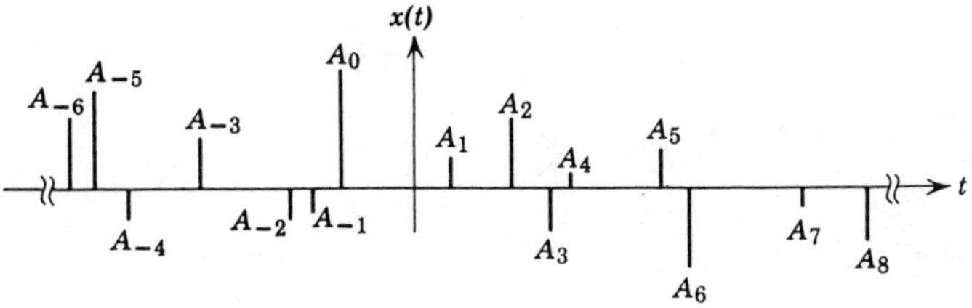

Figure P3.17

is a Poisson impulse train with random amplitudes $\{A_i\}$. Assume the $\{A_i\}$ are identically distributed random variables, with mean $\bar{A}$ and second moment $\overline{A^2}$, which are statistically independent of each other and of the $\{\tau_i\}$. *Hint.* Show that

$$\overline{y(t_1)\,y(t_2)} = \overline{A^2}\,\mathrm{E}\left[\sum_i h(t_1 - \tau_i)\,h(t_2 - \tau_i)\right] + \bar{A}^2\,\mathrm{E}\left[\sum_i \sum_{j \neq i} h(t_1 - \tau_i)\,h(t_2 - \tau_j)\right].$$

3.18 Property 4 on p. 156 states that every weighted linear sum of jointly Gaussian random variables is a Gaussian random variable.

a. Prove the converse statement that if

$$y = \sum_{i=1}^{k} a_i x_i,$$

is a Gaussian random variable for every (nonzero) constant vector $\mathbf{a} = (a_1, a_2, \ldots, a_k)$, the $\{x_i\}$ are jointly Gaussian. *Hint.* Calculate the joint characteristic function of the $\{x_i\}$ by noting that

$$M_{\mathbf{x}}(\mathbf{v}) = M_y(1)\,|_{\mathbf{a}=\mathbf{v}} = e^{-\frac{1}{2}\sigma_y^2} e^{j\bar{y}}$$

and compare with Eq. 3.76 after evaluating σ_y^2 and $\bar{y}$.

b. The converse statement may be taken as an alternate definition of jointly Gaussian random variables. Prove properties 2 and 4 (p. 156) directly from this definition without recourse to the multivariate characteristic function. Observe that with this alternate definition the multivariate central limit theorem can be reduced to a single-variable theorem.

4

Optimum Receiver Principles

The concepts and methods of random processes studied in Chapter 3, together with the a posteriori probability viewpoint of communication discussed in Chapter 2, provide the background necessary to treat the problem of optimum communication receiver design. In this chapter we apply this background to the particular communication system diagrammed in Fig. 4.1. Here one of a discrete set of specified waveforms

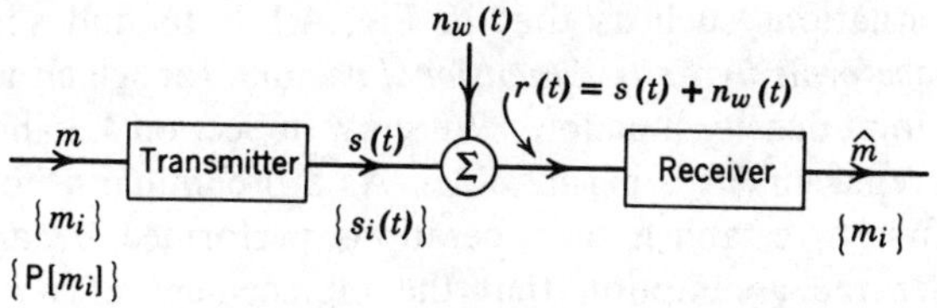

Figure 4.1 Communication over an additive white Gaussian noise channel.

$\{s_i(t)\}$, $i = 0, 1, \ldots, M-1$, is transmitted over a channel disturbed by the addition of white Gaussian noise, so that the received signal process is

$$r(t) = s(t) + n_w(t). \tag{4.1}$$

Which waveform is actually transmitted depends on the random message input, m; when $m = m_i$, the transmitted signal is $s_i(t)$. Thus the correspondence

$$m = m_i \Leftrightarrow s(t) = s_i(t) \tag{4.2}$$

defines the transmitter. The a priori probabilities $\{P[m_i]\}$ specify the input source.

The first part of this chapter is devoted to investigating how the received signal $r(t)$ should be processed in order to produce an estimate, $\hat{m}$, of the transmitter input m that is optimum in the sense that the probability of error

$$P[\mathcal{E}] \triangleq P[\hat{m} \neq m] \tag{4.3}$$

is minimum. The investigation results in the determination of the optimum receiver structure; that is, in the specification of what operations to perform on $r(t)$.

In formulating the optimum receiver design problem, we assume that the a priori probabilities $\{P[m_i]\}$ and signals $\{s_i(t)\}$ are known. The chapter concludes with a discussion of how the minimum achievable probability of error depends on the choice of these a priori data. In particular, certain signal sets of practical importance are evaluated and compared.

In Chapter 7 we extend the results of this chapter to the design and evaluation of optimum receivers for certain channels that disturb the transmitted signal in ways more complicated than by the simple addition of white Gaussian noise.

4.1 BASIC APPROACH TO OPTIMUM RECEIVER DESIGN

In Chapter 3 we have seen that the transmitted signal $s(t)$, the disturbing noise $n_w(t)$, and the received signal $r(t)$ in Fig. 4.1 are random processes. In addition, we have seen that a random process is specified in terms of the joint density functions that it implies. The key to analyzing communication situations such as that in Fig. 4.1 is to find some way to *replace all waveforms by finite dimensional vectors*, for which we can then calculate the joint density function. We show in Section 4.3 and Appendix 4A that this replacement is permissible. As a preliminary, however, it is convenient first to establish the operations performed by an optimum receiver under the assumption that the replacement of waveforms by vectors has already been accomplished.

4.2 VECTOR CHANNELS

The N-dimensional vector communication system diagrammed in Fig. 4.2 is a straightforward extension of the single random variable system discussed in Chapter 2 in connection with Fig. 2.34. The transmitter is defined by a set of M signal vectors, $\{\mathbf{s}_i\}$. When $m = m_i$, the vector $\mathbf{s}_i$ is transmitted,

$$\mathbf{s}_i = (s_{i1}, s_{i2}, \ldots, s_{iN}); \qquad i = 0, 1, \ldots, M-1. \tag{4.4a}$$

The vector channel disturbs the transmission and emits a random vector

$$\mathbf{r} = (r_1, r_2, \ldots, r_N). \tag{4.4b}$$

We consider a vector channel to be defined mathematically if and only if the entire set of M conditional density functions $\{p_{\mathbf{r}}(\ \mid \mathbf{s} = \mathbf{s}_i)\}$ is known. For brevity, we follow the usage of Eq. 2.104c and denote this set by $p_{\mathbf{r}|\mathbf{s}}$.

For our vector communication system the optimum receiver is specified as follows: given that any particular vector, say $\mathbf{r} = \boldsymbol{\rho}$, is received, where

$$\boldsymbol{\rho} \triangleq (\rho_1, \rho_2, \ldots, \rho_N), \tag{4.5}$$

the optimum receiver must determine from its knowledge of $p_{\mathbf{r}|\mathbf{s}}$, $\{\mathbf{s}_i\}$, and $\{P[m_i]\}$ which one of the possible transmitter inputs $\{m_i\}$ has maximum a posteriori probability. More precisely, the optimum receiver sets $\hat{m} = m_k$ whenever

$$P[m_k \mid \mathbf{r} = \boldsymbol{\rho}] > P[m_i \mid \mathbf{r} = \boldsymbol{\rho}]; \quad \text{for } i = 0, 1, \ldots, M-1, i \neq k. \tag{4.6}$$

Proof that such a *maximum a posteriori probability* receiver is in fact optimum follows from noting that when the receiver sets $\hat{m} = m_k$, the conditional probability of a correct decision, given that $\mathbf{r} = \boldsymbol{\rho}$, is

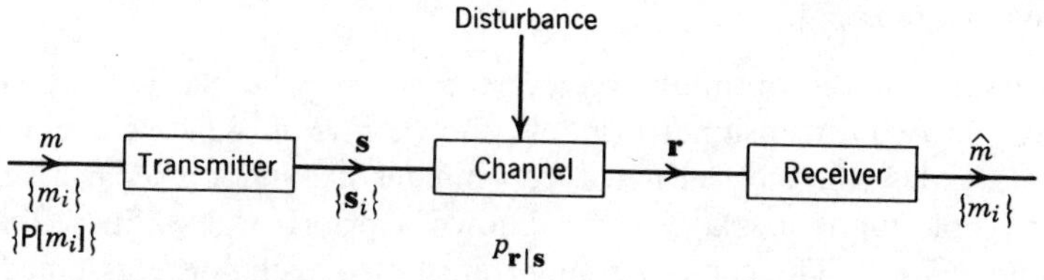

Figure 4.2 A vector communication system.

$$P[\mathcal{C} \mid \mathbf{r} = \boldsymbol{\rho}] = P[m_k \mid \mathbf{r} = \boldsymbol{\rho}]. \tag{4.7a}$$

The unconditional probability of correct decision can be written

$$P[\mathcal{C}] = \int_{-\infty}^{\infty} P[\mathcal{C} \mid \mathbf{r} = \boldsymbol{\rho}] \, p_{\mathbf{r}}(\boldsymbol{\rho}) \, d\boldsymbol{\rho}. \tag{4.7b}$$

Since

$$p_{\mathbf{r}}(\boldsymbol{\rho}) \geqslant 0,$$

it is clear that $P[\mathcal{C}]$ is maximized by maximizing $P[\mathcal{C} \mid \mathbf{r} = \boldsymbol{\rho}]$ for each received vector $\boldsymbol{\rho}$. If two or more m_i yield the same a posteriori probability, the receiver may select $\hat{m}$ from among them in any arbitrary way—for instance, by choosing the one with the smallest index—without affecting the probability of error.

Determination of the a posteriori probabilities $\{P[m_i \mid \mathbf{r} = \boldsymbol{\rho}]\}$ follows from the mixed form of Bayes rule, Eq. 2.103a:

$$P[m_i \mid \mathbf{r} = \boldsymbol{\rho}] = \frac{P[m_i] p_{\mathbf{r}}(\boldsymbol{\rho} \mid m_i)}{p_{\mathbf{r}}(\boldsymbol{\rho})}. \tag{4.8a}$$

Since the event $m = m_i$ implies the event $\mathbf{s} = \mathbf{s}_i$, and conversely, we have

$$p_{\mathbf{r}}(\boldsymbol{\rho} \mid m_i) = p_{\mathbf{r}}(\boldsymbol{\rho} \mid \mathbf{s} = \mathbf{s}_i). \tag{4.8b}$$

Finally, since $p_{\mathbf{r}}(\boldsymbol{\rho})$ is independent of the index i, we conclude from Eqs. 4.6 and 4.8 that the optimum receiver, on observing $\mathbf{r} = \boldsymbol{\rho}$, sets $\hat{m} = m_k$ whenever the *decision function*

$$P[m_i]\, p_{\mathbf{r}}(\boldsymbol{\rho} \mid \mathbf{s} = \mathbf{s}_i); \qquad i = 0, 1, \ldots, M-1, \tag{4.9}$$

is maximum for $i = k$.

A receiver that determines $\hat{m}$ by maximizing only the factor $p_{\mathbf{r}}(\boldsymbol{\rho} \mid \mathbf{s} = \mathbf{s}_i)$ without regard to the factor $P[m_i]$ is called a *maximum-likelihood* receiver. Such a receiver is often used when the a priori probabilities $\{P[m_i]\}$ are not known. A maximum-likelihood receiver yields the minimum probability of error when the transmitter inputs are all equally likely.

Decision Regions

The nature of the optimum vector receiver may be clarified by considering the two-dimensional example shown in Fig. 4.3*a*, wherein the vectors are described in terms of coordinates φ_1 and φ_2. We assume three possible input messages, with known a priori probabilities $P[m_0]$, $P[m_1]$, and $P[m_2]$. The corresponding transmitted vectors are assumed to be

$$\begin{aligned} \mathbf{s}_0 &= (1, 2), \\ \mathbf{s}_1 &= (2, 1), \\ \mathbf{s}_2 &= (1, -2). \end{aligned} \tag{4.10}$$

If we now receive some point $\mathbf{r} = \boldsymbol{\rho}$, as shown, the receiver can calculate $P[m_i]\, p_{\mathbf{r}}(\boldsymbol{\rho} \mid \mathbf{s} = \mathbf{s}_i)$ from knowledge of the functions $p_{\mathbf{r}|\mathbf{s}}$ which define the channel and thereby determine $\hat{m}$ in accordance with the preceding discussion.

We note that this calculation can be carried out for every point $\boldsymbol{\rho}$ in the (φ_1, φ_2) plane and that each such point is thereby assigned to one and only one of the possible inputs $\{m_i\}$. Thus the decision rule of Eq. 4.9 implies a partitioning of the entire plane into disjoint regions, say $\{I_i\}$, $i = 0, 1, 2$, similar in general to those shown in Fig. 4.3*b*. Each region comprises all points such that whenever the received vector $\mathbf{r}$ is in I_k the optimum receiver sets $\hat{m}$ equal to m_k. The correspondence

$$\mathbf{r} \text{ in } I_k \Leftrightarrow \hat{m} = m_k \tag{4.11}$$

defines the optimum receiver.

The regions $\{I_i\}$ are called optimum *decision regions* and are a natural extension of the *decision intervals* considered in Fig. 2.35. We note for future reference that the optimum receiver makes an error when $m = m_k$ if and only if $\mathbf{r}$ falls outside I_k.

It is clear that the concept of decision regions, which for simplicity we have illustrated for a two-dimensional plane, extends directly to the case

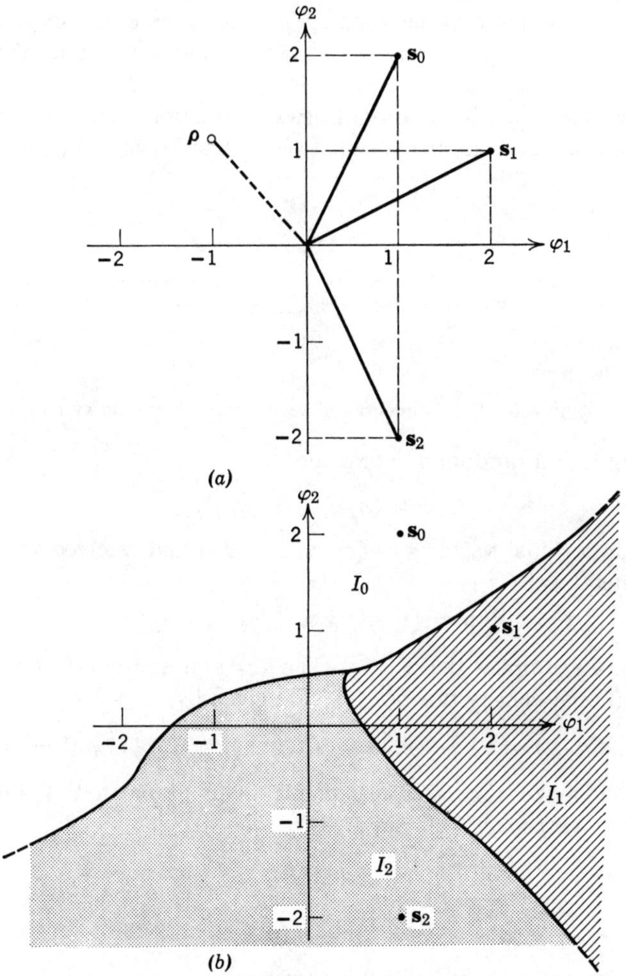

Figure 4.3 A three-signal vector communication problem: (*a*) three two-dimensional signal vectors and a possible received signal $\boldsymbol{\rho}$; (*b*) decision regions.

of an arbitrary number of possible inputs $\{m_i\}$ and to corresponding signals $\{\mathbf{s}_i\}$ that are defined on an arbitrary number of dimensions. The decision function of Eq. 4.9 then implies a partitioning of an N-dimensional received signal space into M disjoint N-dimensional decision regions $\{I_i\}$.

Additive Gaussian Noise

The actual boundaries of the decision regions in any particular case depend by Eq. 4.9 on the a priori probabilities $\{P[m_i]\}$, the signals $\{\mathbf{s}_i\}$, and the definition of the channel $p_{\mathbf{r}|\mathbf{s}}$. In some instances the calculation of these boundaries may be simple; in most it is exceedingly difficult. Fortunately, many situations of practical interest fall into the simple category.

To illustrate a relatively straightforward situation, consider the case in which the channel disturbs the signal vector (as shown in Fig. 4.4) simply

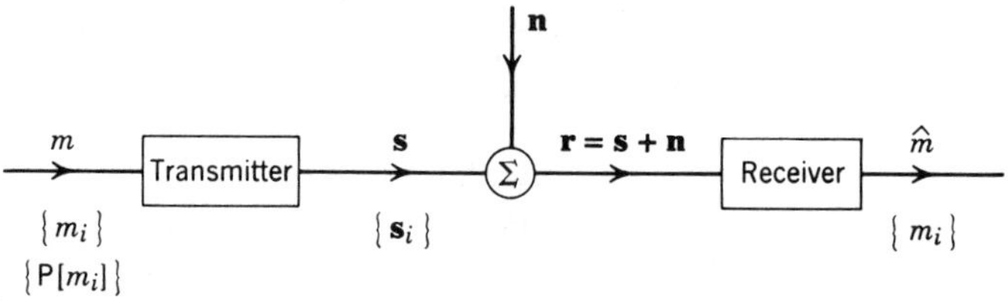

Figure 4.4 An N-dimensional vector communication system.

by adding to it a random noise vector

$$\mathbf{n} = (n_1, n_2, \ldots, n_N). \tag{4.12}$$

The random signal vector $\mathbf{s} = (s_1, s_2, \ldots, s_N)$ and received vector $\mathbf{r}$ are then related by

$$\mathbf{r} = \mathbf{s} + \mathbf{n} = (s_1 + n_1, s_2 + n_2, \ldots, s_N + n_N). \tag{4.13}$$

Since Eq. 4.13 implies that $\mathbf{r} = \boldsymbol{\rho}$ when $\mathbf{s} = \mathbf{s}_i$ if and only if $\mathbf{n} = \boldsymbol{\rho} - \mathbf{s}_i$, the conditional density functions $p_{\mathbf{r}|\mathbf{s}}$ are given by

$$p_{\mathbf{r}}(\boldsymbol{\rho} \mid \mathbf{s} = \mathbf{s}_i) = p_{\mathbf{n}}(\boldsymbol{\rho} - \mathbf{s}_i \mid \mathbf{s} = \mathbf{s}_i); \qquad i = 0, 1, \ldots, M - 1. \tag{4.14}$$

We now make the often-reasonable assumption that $\mathbf{n}$ and $\mathbf{s}$ are *statistically independent* (cf. Eq. 2.104):

$$p_{\mathbf{n}|\mathbf{s}} = p_{\mathbf{n}}. \tag{4.15a}$$

Hence

$$p_{\mathbf{n}}(\boldsymbol{\rho} - \mathbf{s}_i \mid \mathbf{s} = \mathbf{s}_i) = p_{\mathbf{n}}(\boldsymbol{\rho} - \mathbf{s}_i); \qquad \text{all } i. \tag{4.15b}$$

The decision function of Eq. 4.9 is therefore

$$P[m_i]\, p_{\mathbf{n}}(\boldsymbol{\rho} - \mathbf{s}_i). \tag{4.16}$$

In order to simplify the decision function still more, we must specify the noise density function $p_{\mathbf{n}}$. An especially simple and important case is that in which the N components of $\mathbf{n}$ are statistically independent, zero-mean, Gaussian random variables, each with variance σ^2. From

Eq. 3.57 we then have

$$p_{\mathrm{n}}(\boldsymbol{\alpha}) = \frac{1}{(2\pi\sigma^2)^{N/2}} \exp\left(-\frac{1}{2\sigma^2}\sum_{j=1}^{N}\alpha_j^{\,2}\right). \tag{4.17a}$$

The notation can be contracted by observing that the squared-length of any vector $\boldsymbol{\alpha}$ is defined to be the dot product of $\boldsymbol{\alpha}$ with itself. In the familiar case of $N = 2$ or 3 we have

$$|\boldsymbol{\alpha}|^2 = \boldsymbol{\alpha} \cdot \boldsymbol{\alpha} = \sum_{j=1}^{N}\alpha_j^{\,2}, \tag{4.17b}$$

where the $\{\alpha_j\}$ are the Cartesian coordinates of $\boldsymbol{\alpha}$. For larger N length is defined in the same way and Eq. 4.17b remains valid. Thus Eq. 4.17a can be written

$$p_{\mathrm{n}}(\boldsymbol{\alpha}) = \frac{1}{(2\pi\sigma^2)^{N/2}} e^{-|\boldsymbol{\alpha}|^2/2\sigma^2}. \tag{4.17c}$$

Substituting Eq. 4.17c in Eq. 4.16, we see that for this p_{n} the optimum receiver sets $\hat{m} = m_k$ whenever

$$\mathrm{P}[m_i]\, e^{-|\boldsymbol{\rho}-\mathbf{s}_i|^2/2\sigma^2} \tag{4.18}$$

is maximum for $i = k$. [The factor $(2\pi\sigma^2)^{-N/2}$ is independent of i and its discard entails no loss of optimality.] Finally, we note that maximizing the expression of Eq. 4.18 is equivalent to finding that value of i which *minimizes*

$$|\boldsymbol{\rho} - \mathbf{s}_i|^2 - 2\sigma^2 \ln \mathrm{P}[m_i]. \tag{4.19}$$

The decision function of Eq. 4.19 is easily visualized geometrically. We recognize that the term $|\boldsymbol{\rho} - \mathbf{s}_i|^2$ is the square of the Euclidean distance between the points $\boldsymbol{\rho}$ and $\mathbf{s}_i$:

$$|\boldsymbol{\rho} - \mathbf{s}_i|^2 = \sum_{j=1}^{N}(\rho_j - s_{ij})^2.$$

Whenever all m_i have equal a priori probability, the optimum decision rule is to assign a received point $\boldsymbol{\rho}$ to m_k if and only if $\boldsymbol{\rho}$ is *closer* to the point $\mathbf{s}_k$ than to any other possible signal. For example, consider the two-dimensional signal set of Eq. 4.10. If all three messages are equally probable, the decision regions are those shown in Fig. 4.5*a*; when the three messages have unequal a priori probabilities, the decision regions are modified in accordance with Eq. 4.19, as indicated in Fig. 4.5*b*.

Once the decision regions $\{I_i\}$ have been determined, an expression for the conditional probability of correct decision follows immediately:

$$\mathrm{P}[\mathcal{C} \mid m_i] = \mathrm{P}[\mathbf{r} \text{ in } I_i \mid m_i] = \int_{I_i} p_{\mathbf{r}}(\boldsymbol{\rho} \mid \mathbf{s} = \mathbf{s}_i)\, d\boldsymbol{\rho}. \tag{4.20a}$$

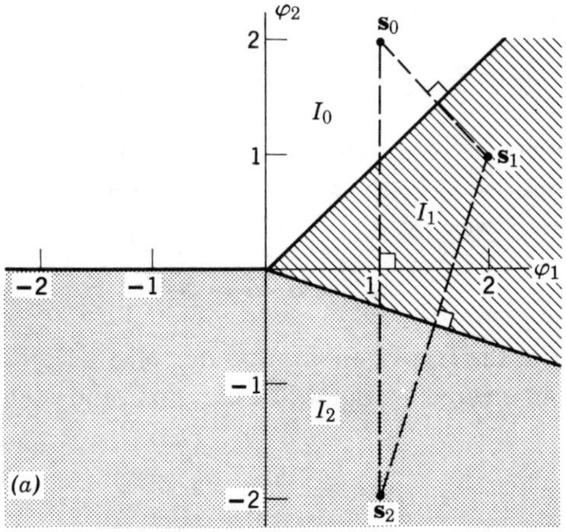

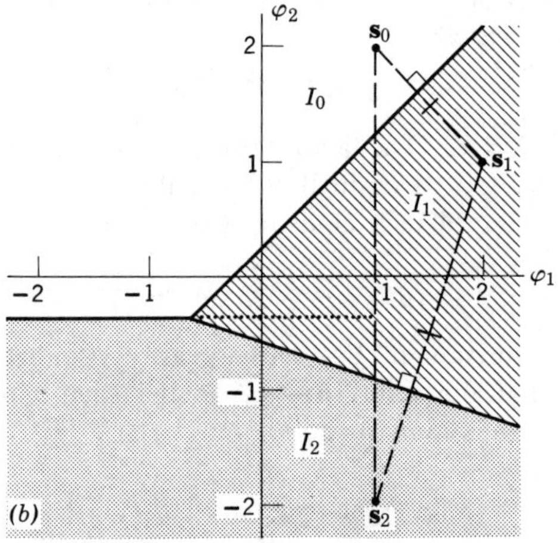

Figure 4.5 Optimum decision regions for additive Gaussian noise: (*a*) the boundaries of the $\{I_i\}$ are the perpendicular bisectors of the sides of the signal triangle whenever $P[m_0] = P[m_1] = P[m_2]$; (*b*) the boundaries of the $\{I_i\}$ are displaced when $P[m_1] > P[m_0] > P[m_2]$.

For additive equal-variance Gaussian noise this becomes

$$P[\mathcal{C} \mid m_i] = \int_{I_i} p_{\mathbf{n}}(\boldsymbol{\rho} - \mathbf{s}_i)\, d\boldsymbol{\rho}$$

$$= \frac{1}{(2\pi\sigma^2)^{N/2}} \int_{I_i} e^{-|\boldsymbol{\rho} - \mathbf{s}_i|^2/2\sigma^2}\, d\boldsymbol{\rho}. \tag{4.20b}$$

The over-all probability of error is

$$P[\mathcal{E}] \triangleq 1 - P[\mathcal{C}] = 1 - \sum_{i=0}^{M-1} P[m_i]\, P[\mathcal{C} \mid m_i]. \tag{4.20c}$$

In Section 4.4 these expressions are evaluated for certain (important) situations in which the decision regions are such that the integrals can be easily calculated or approximated.

Multivector Channels

In the "diversity" communication system shown in Fig. 4.6, in which the transmitted vector $\mathbf{s}$ is applied at the input of two different channels and the receiver observes the output of both, it is natural to describe the

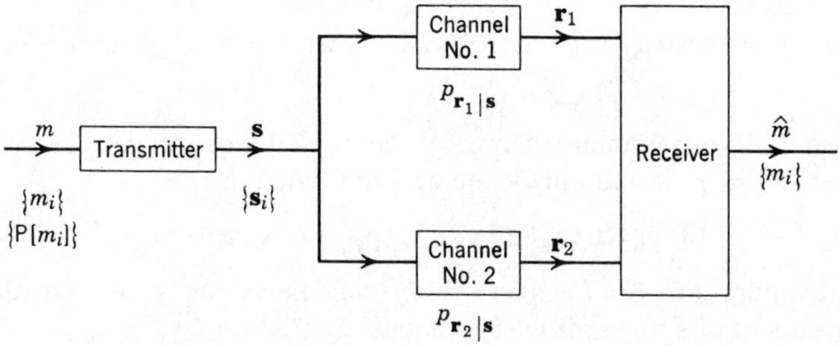

Figure 4.6 A "diversity" vector communication system. [In many situations the vectors $\mathbf{s}$, $\mathbf{r}_1$, and $\mathbf{r}_2$ all have the same number of components, but this need not be so.]

total receiver input $\mathbf{r}$ in terms of vectors $\mathbf{r}_1$ and $\mathbf{r}_2$ that are associated with each channel individually. Thus we write

$$\mathbf{r} = (\mathbf{r}_1, \mathbf{r}_2) \triangleq (r_{11}, r_{12}, \ldots, r_{1k}, r_{21}, r_{22}, \ldots, r_{2l}), \tag{4.21a}$$

where

$$\mathbf{r}_1 = (r_{11}, r_{12}, \ldots, r_{1k}), \tag{4.21b}$$

$$\mathbf{r}_2 = (r_{21}, r_{22}, \ldots, r_{2l}). \tag{4.21c}$$

Given that vectors $\mathbf{r}_1 = \boldsymbol{\rho}_1$ and $\mathbf{r}_2 = \boldsymbol{\rho}_2$ are received, the a posteriori probability of the ith message is

$$P[m_i \mid \mathbf{r} = \boldsymbol{\rho}] = P[m_i \mid \mathbf{r}_1 = \boldsymbol{\rho}_1, \mathbf{r}_2 = \boldsymbol{\rho}_2], \tag{4.22a}$$

where $\boldsymbol{\rho} \triangleq (\boldsymbol{\rho}_1, \boldsymbol{\rho}_2)$. With this notation, the optimum decision rule of Eq. 4.9 is written: set $\hat{m} = m_k$ if and only if

$$P[m_i]\, p_{\mathbf{r}}(\boldsymbol{\rho} \mid \mathbf{s} = \mathbf{s}_i) = P[m_i]\, p_{\mathbf{r}_1,\mathbf{r}_2}(\boldsymbol{\rho}_1, \boldsymbol{\rho}_2 \mid \mathbf{s} = \mathbf{s}_i) \tag{4.22b}$$

is maximum for $i = k$.

The theorem of irrelevance. In many cases of practical importance a channel presents some data at its output which an optimum receiver can ignore. For instance, consider the arbitrary vector channel in Fig. 4.7, in which two inputs $\mathbf{r}_1$ and $\mathbf{r}_2$ are available to the receiver. Let us determine the conditions under which the receiver may disregard $\mathbf{r}_2$ without affecting the probability of error.

The optimum decision rule is again given by Eq. 4.22b. If we factor the right-hand side of this equation in accordance with Bayes rule (Eq. 2.103),

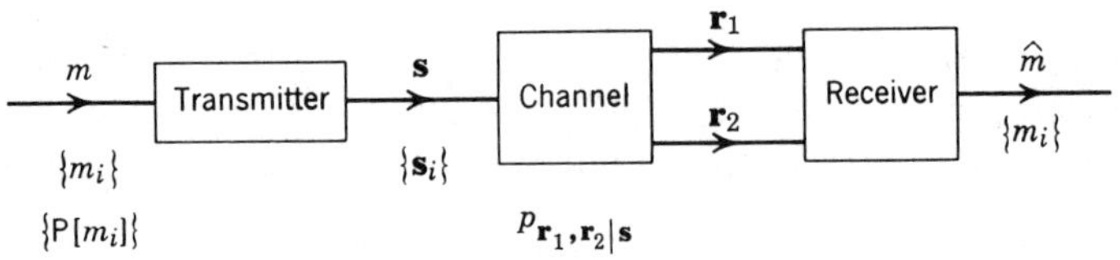

Figure 4.7 An arbitrary vector communication system described in terms of two output vectors.

we see that an optimum receiver sets $\hat{m} = m_k$ following the observation $\mathbf{r}_1 = \boldsymbol{\rho}_1$, $\mathbf{r}_2 = \boldsymbol{\rho}_2$ if and only if the decision function

$$P[m_i]\, p_{\mathbf{r}_1}(\boldsymbol{\rho}_1 \mid \mathbf{s} = \mathbf{s}_i)\, p_{\mathbf{r}_2}(\boldsymbol{\rho}_2 \mid \mathbf{s} = \mathbf{s}_i, \mathbf{r}_1 = \boldsymbol{\rho}_1) \tag{4.23}$$

is maximum for $i = k$. If $\mathbf{r}_2$ *when conditioned on* $\mathbf{r}_1$ is statistically independent of $\mathbf{s}$, then for every value of $\boldsymbol{\rho}_2$

$$\begin{aligned} p_{\mathbf{r}_2}(\boldsymbol{\rho}_2 \mid \mathbf{s} = \mathbf{s}_i, \mathbf{r}_1 = \boldsymbol{\rho}_1) &= p_{\mathbf{r}_2}(\boldsymbol{\rho}_2 \mid \mathbf{r}_1 = \boldsymbol{\rho}_1) \\ &= \text{a number independent of } i. \end{aligned} \tag{4.24}$$

When this is so, the knowledge that $\mathbf{r}_2 = \boldsymbol{\rho}_2$ can never enter into the determination of which value of i maximizes the expression of Eq. 4.23; an optimum receiver may therefore totally ignore $\mathbf{r}_2$. Thus we have the important *theorem of irrelevance: an optimum receiver may disregard a vector* $\mathbf{r}_2$ *if and only if*

$$p_{\mathbf{r}_2|\mathbf{r}_1,\mathbf{s}} = p_{\mathbf{r}_2|\mathbf{r}_1}. \tag{4.25a}$$

Equation 4.25a is a necessary and sufficient condition for ignoring $\mathbf{r}_2$. A sufficient condition is that

$$p_{\mathbf{r}_2|\mathbf{r}_1,\mathbf{s}} = p_{\mathbf{r}_2}. \tag{4.25b}$$

The meaning and utility of this theorem may be demonstrated by considering three examples, each of which involves two additive noise vectors $\mathbf{n}_1$ and $\mathbf{n}_2$ that are statistically independent of one another and of $\mathbf{s}$. The first example, shown in Fig. 4.8, illustrates a situation in which Eq. 4.25b is valid: the received vector $\mathbf{r}_2$ is just the noise $\mathbf{n}_2$, which is statistically independent of both $\mathbf{n}_1$ and $\mathbf{s}$, hence of $\mathbf{s}$ and $\mathbf{r}_1 = \mathbf{n}_1 + \mathbf{s}$.

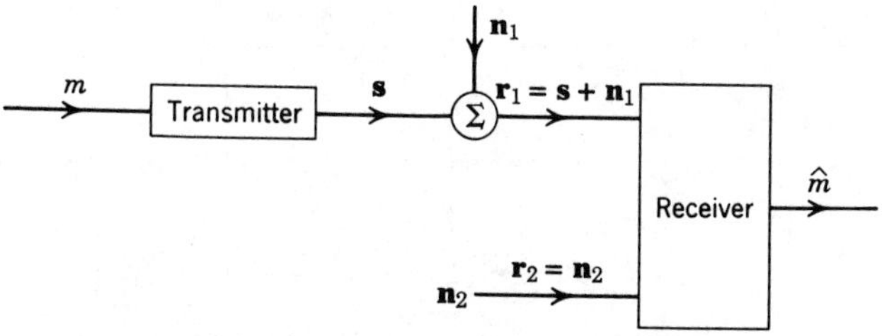

Figure 4.8 The vector $\mathbf{r}_2$ is irrelevant because $p_{\mathbf{r}_2|\mathbf{r}_1,\mathbf{s}} = p_{\mathbf{r}_2}$.

Accordingly,

$$p_{\mathbf{r}_2|\mathbf{r}_1,\mathbf{s}} = p_{\mathbf{r}_2} \tag{4.26}$$

and $\mathbf{r}_2$ is irrelevant, which is obviously sensible.

The second example, shown in Fig. 4.9, illustrates a situation in which Eq. 4.25a is valid but Eq. 4.25b is not. We have two vector channels in cascade and a receiver that has access to the intermediate output $\mathbf{r}_1$ as well as to the final output $\mathbf{r}_2$. Since $\mathbf{r}_2$ is a corrupted version of $\mathbf{r}_1$, hence

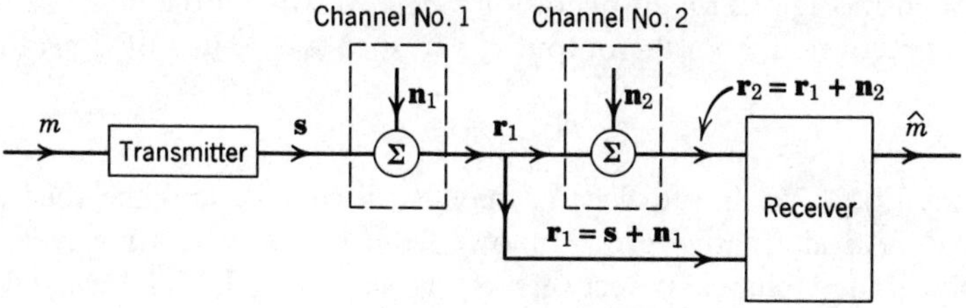

Figure 4.9 The vector $\mathbf{r}_2$ is irrelevant because $p_{\mathbf{r}_2|\mathbf{r}_1,\mathbf{s}} = p_{\mathbf{r}_2|\mathbf{r}_1}$.

depends on m only through $\mathbf{r}_1$, we feel intuitively that $\mathbf{r}_2$ can tell us nothing about $\mathbf{s}$ that is not already conveyed by $\mathbf{r}_1$. We prove this formally by noting that, since $\mathbf{r}_2 = \mathbf{r}_1 + \mathbf{n}_2$, when $\mathbf{r}_1$ is known $\mathbf{r}_2$ depends only on the noise $\mathbf{n}_2$, which is independent of $\mathbf{s}$. Thus for all $\boldsymbol{\rho}_2$ and i

$$p_{\mathbf{r}_2}(\boldsymbol{\rho}_2 \mid \mathbf{r}_1 = \boldsymbol{\rho}_1, \mathbf{s} = \mathbf{s}_i) = p_{\mathbf{n}_2}(\boldsymbol{\rho}_2 - \boldsymbol{\rho}_1) = p_{\mathbf{r}_2}(\boldsymbol{\rho}_2 \mid \mathbf{r}_1 = \boldsymbol{\rho}_1).$$

The condition of Eq. 4.25a is satisfied, and the theorem of irrelevance states that $\mathbf{r}_2$ is of no value to an optimum receiver.

The third example, shown in Fig. 4.10, illustrates a situation in which $\mathbf{r}_2$ *cannot* be discarded by an optimum receiver. We have

$$\begin{aligned} p_{\mathbf{r}_2}(\boldsymbol{\rho}_2 \mid \mathbf{r}_1 = \boldsymbol{\rho}_1, \mathbf{s} = \mathbf{s}_i) &= p_{\mathbf{r}_2}(\boldsymbol{\rho}_2 \mid \mathbf{n}_1 = \boldsymbol{\rho}_1 - \mathbf{s}_i, \mathbf{s} = \mathbf{s}_i) \\ &= p_{\mathbf{n}_2}(\boldsymbol{\rho}_2 - \boldsymbol{\rho}_1 + \mathbf{s}_i \mid \mathbf{n}_1 = \boldsymbol{\rho}_1 - \mathbf{s}_i, \mathbf{s} = \mathbf{s}_i) \\ &= p_{\mathbf{n}_2}(\boldsymbol{\rho}_2 - \boldsymbol{\rho}_1 + \mathbf{s}_i), \end{aligned}$$

which does depend explicitly on i. Thus Eq. 4.25 is not satisfied and $\mathbf{r}_2$ is not irrelevant, even though $\mathbf{r}_2$ and $\mathbf{s}$ are pairwise independent. This is

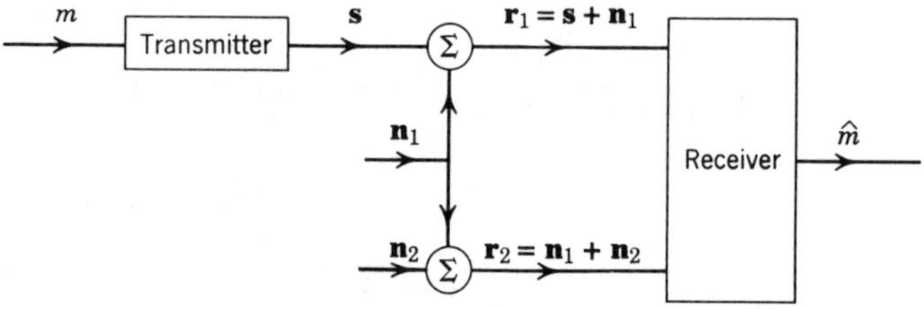

Figure 4.10 The vector $\mathbf{r}_2$ is not irrelevant.

clearly sensible, since (as an extreme case) knowledge of $\mathbf{r}_2$ provides a good estimate of $\mathbf{n}_1$, hence of $\mathbf{s}$, when $p_{\mathbf{n}_2}$ is such that with high probability $\mathbf{n}_2$ is very small compared to $\mathbf{n}_1$.

The theorem of reversibility. An important corollary of the theorem of irrelevance is the *theorem of reversibility*, which states that *the minimum attainable probability of error is not affected by the introduction of a reversible operation at the output of a channel*, as in Fig. 4.11*a*. As indicated in Fig. 4.11*b*, an operation $\mathbf{G}$ is reversible if the input $\mathbf{r}_2$ can be exactly recovered from the output $\mathbf{r}_1$. In such a case it is obvious that

$$p_{\mathbf{r}_2|\mathbf{r}_1,\mathbf{s}} = p_{\mathbf{r}_2|\mathbf{r}_1},$$

so that Eq. 4.25a is satisfied, $\mathbf{r}_2$ may be discarded, and the theorem is proved. An alternative proof follows from noting that a receiver for $\mathbf{r}_1$ can be built which first recovers $\mathbf{r}_2$, as shown in Fig. 4.11*c*, and then operates on $\mathbf{r}_2$ to determine $\hat{m}$.

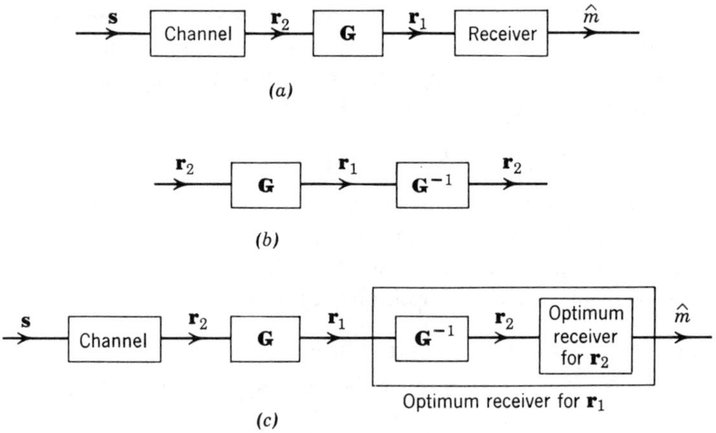

Figure 4.11 Insertion of a reversible operation, $\mathbf{G}$, between channel and receiver. The operation inverse to $\mathbf{G}$ is denoted $\mathbf{G}^{-1}$. For example, $\mathbf{G}$ might be the addition, and $\mathbf{G}^{-1}$ the subtraction, of a fixed vector $\mathbf{a}$.

4.3 WAVEFORM CHANNELS

The foregoing discussion of irrelevance provides the analytic tool that is required in order to replace the waveform communication problem of Fig. 4.1 by an equivalent vector communication problem. We therefore return to consideration of this figure, in which the received waveform $r(t)$ is given by

$$r(t) = s(t) + n_w(t) \tag{4.27}$$

and $n_w(t)$ is a zero-mean white Gaussian noise process with power density

$$\mathcal{S}_w(f) = \frac{\mathcal{N}_0}{2}; \qquad -\infty < f < \infty. \tag{4.28}$$

We first represent the signal process $s(t)$ in an equivalent vector form and then show that the relevant noise process may also be represented by a random vector.

Waveform Synthesis

A convenient way to synthesize the signal set $\{s_i(t)\}$ at the transmitter of Fig. 4.1 is shown in Fig. 4.12. A set of N filters is used, with the impulse response of the jth filter denoted by $\varphi_j(t)$. When the transmitter input is m_i, the first filter is excited by an impulse of value s_{i1}, the second filter by an impulse of value s_{i2}, and so on, with the Nth filter excited by an impulse of value s_{iN}. The filter outputs are summed to yield $s_i(t)$. Thus the transmitted waveform is one of the M signals

$$s_i(t) = \sum_{j=1}^{N} s_{ij}\, \varphi_j(t); \qquad i = 0, 1, \ldots, M-1. \tag{4.29}$$

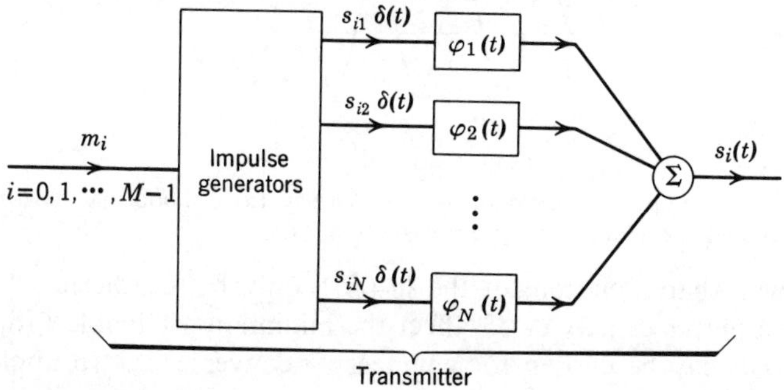

Figure 4.12 Signal synthesis. The output $s_i(t)$ depends on i through the choice of the impulse weighting coefficients $\{s_{ij}\}$.

For ease of analysis we assume that the N "building-block" waveforms $\{\varphi_j(t)\}$ are *orthonormal*, by which we mean

$$\int_{-\infty}^{\infty} \varphi_j(t)\, \varphi_l(t)\, dt = \begin{cases} 1; & j = l \\ 0; & j \neq l \end{cases} \tag{4.30}$$

for all j and l, $1 \leqslant j, l \leqslant N$.

We shall soon see that the error performance which can be achieved with signal sets generated in this way is completely independent of the

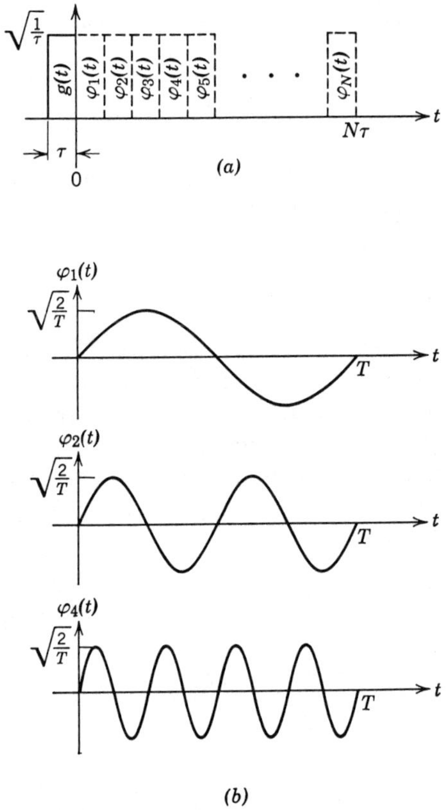

Figure 4.13 Examples of orthonormal waveforms: (*a*) orthonormal time-translated pulses; (*b*) orthonormal frequency-translated pulses.

actual waveshapes chosen for the $\{\varphi_j(t)\}$; only the coefficients $\{s_{ij}\}$ and the noise power density $\mathcal{N}_0/2$ affect the minimum attainable P[$\mathcal{E}$]. Thus the $\{\varphi_j(t)\}$ may be chosen for engineering convenience. In application, one frequently encounters the set of time-translated pulses

$$\varphi_j(t) = g(t - j\tau); \qquad j = 1, 2, \ldots, N \tag{4.31a}$$

shown in Fig. 4.13*a*, where $g(t)$ is the unit energy pulse

$$g(t) = \begin{cases} \sqrt{\dfrac{1}{\tau}}; & -\tau \leqslant t < 0, \\ 0; & \text{elsewhere.} \end{cases} \tag{4.31b}$$

A second common example is the set of frequency-translated pulses

$$\varphi_j(t) = \begin{cases} \sqrt{\dfrac{2}{T}} \sin 2\pi \dfrac{j}{T} t; & 0 \leqslant t < T, \\ 0; & \text{elsewhere,} \end{cases} \quad j = 1, 2, \ldots, N \tag{4.32}$$

shown in Fig. 4.13*b*. It may be readily verified that both sets of waveforms satisfy the orthonormality condition of Eq. 4.30. [The prefix "ortho" comes from "orthogonal," meaning that the integral of $\varphi_j(t)\, \varphi_l(t)$ is zero whenever $j \neq l$; the suffix "normal" means that the integral is unity whenever $j = l$.]

It may seem restrictive at first to consider only waveforms $\{s_i(t)\}$ that are constructed in accordance with Eq. 4.29. This is not so: *any set of M finite-energy waveforms can be synthesized in this way.* This and the fact that the *number of filters required to do so never exceeds M*, is proved in Appendix 4A. It follows that there is no loss of generality entailed in considering only transmitters that operate as shown in Fig. 4.12.

Geometric Interpretation of Signals

Once a convenient set of orthonormal functions $\{\varphi_j(t)\}$ has been adopted, each of the transmitter waveforms $\{s_i(t)\}$ is completely determined by the vector of its coefficients:

$$\mathbf{s}_i = (s_{i1}, s_{i2}, \ldots, s_{iN}); \qquad i = 0, 1, \ldots, M - 1. \tag{4.33}$$

As usual, we visualize the M vectors $\{\mathbf{s}_i\}$ as defining M points in an N-dimensional geometric space, called the *signal space*, with N mutually perpendicular axes labeled $\varphi_1, \varphi_2, \ldots, \varphi_N$. If we let $\boldsymbol{\varphi}_j$ denote the unit vector along the jth-axis, $j = 1, 2, \ldots, N$, each N-tuple in Eq. 4.33 denotes the vector

$$\mathbf{s}_i = s_{i1}\boldsymbol{\varphi}_1 + s_{i2}\boldsymbol{\varphi}_2 + \cdots + s_{iN}\boldsymbol{\varphi}_N. \tag{4.34}$$

The idea of visualizing transmitter signals geometrically is of fundamental importance. For example, Fig. 4.3 (which we have already considered) represents a two-dimensional space with three signals: $N = 2$,

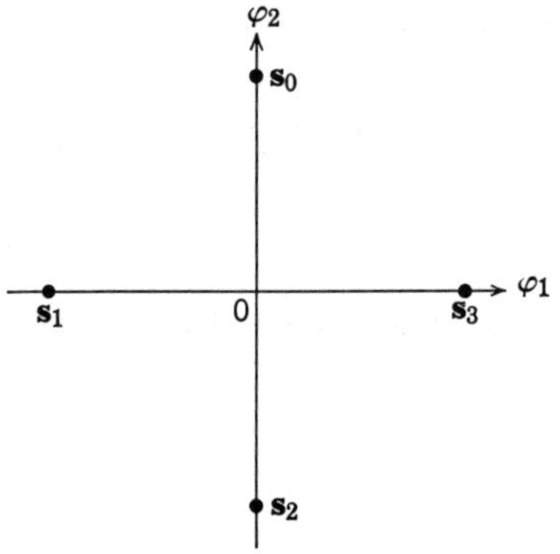

Figure 4.14 Four signals in a two-dimensional signal space. Each vector $\mathbf{s}_i$ is located a distance $\sqrt{E_s}$ from the origin.

$M = 3$. As another example, consider the set of two orthonormal functions

$$\varphi_1(t) = \begin{cases} \sqrt{\dfrac{2}{T}} \sin 2\pi f_0 t; & 0 \leqslant t < T \\ 0; & \text{elsewhere} \end{cases} \tag{4.35a}$$

$$\varphi_2(t) = \begin{cases} \sqrt{\dfrac{2}{T}} \cos 2\pi f_0 t; & 0 \leqslant t < T \\ 0; & \text{elsewhere,} \end{cases} \tag{4.35b}$$

where f_0 is an integral multiple of $1/T$. If we choose

$$\begin{aligned} \mathbf{s}_0 &= (0, \sqrt{E_s}) \\ \mathbf{s}_1 &= (-\sqrt{E_s}, 0) \\ \mathbf{s}_2 &= (0, -\sqrt{E_s}) \\ \mathbf{s}_3 &= (\sqrt{E_s}, 0), \end{aligned} \tag{4.36}$$

the vector diagram of Fig. 4.14 represents the set of four phase-modulated transmitter waveforms

$$s_i(t) = \begin{cases} \sqrt{\dfrac{2E_s}{T}} \cos 2\pi\left(f_0 t + \dfrac{i}{4}\right); & 0 \leqslant t < T \\ 0; & \text{elsewhere} \end{cases} \qquad i = 0, 1, 2, 3, \tag{4.37a}$$

where

$$E_s = \int_{-\infty}^{\infty} s_i^2(t)\, dt; \qquad i = 0, 1, 2, 3 \tag{4.37b}$$

is the energy dissipated if $s_i(t)$ is a voltage across a 1-ohm load. Similarly, if $\varphi_1(t)$ and $\varphi_2(t)$ are two nonoverlapping unit pulses, the vectors of Eq. 4.36 and the diagram of Fig. 4.14 represent the four entirely different waveforms shown in Fig. 4.15. The actual waveforms $\{s_i(t)\}$ depend on

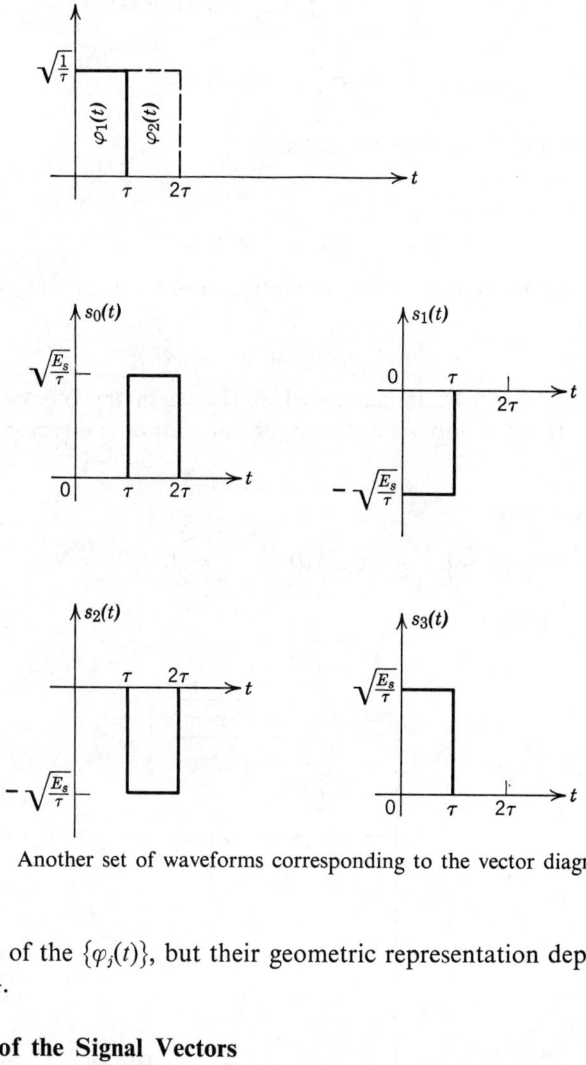

Figure 4.15 Another set of waveforms corresponding to the vector diagram of Fig. 4.14.

the choice of the $\{\varphi_j(t)\}$, but their geometric representation depends only on the $\{\mathbf{s}_i\}$.

Recovery of the Signal Vectors

So far we have considered the synthesis of the signal waveforms $\{s_i(t)\}$ from corresponding signal vectors $\{\mathbf{s}_i\}$. It is also straightforward to recover the vectors from the waveforms. We observe that by virtue of the orthonormality of the $\{\varphi_j(t)\}$

$$\begin{aligned}\int_{-\infty}^{\infty} s_i(t)\,\varphi_l(t)\,dt &= \int_{-\infty}^{\infty}\left[\sum_{j=1}^{N} s_{ij}\,\varphi_j(t)\right]\varphi_l(t)\,dt \\ &= \sum_{j=1}^{N} s_{ij}\int_{-\infty}^{\infty} \varphi_j(t)\,\varphi_l(t)\,dt \\ &= \sum_{j=1}^{N} s_{ij}\,\delta_{jl} = s_{il},\end{aligned} \tag{4.38}$$

in which we use the Kronecker delta

$$\delta_{jl} \triangleq \begin{cases} 1; & l = j \\ 0; & l \neq j. \end{cases} \tag{4.39}$$

Carrying out the multiplication and integration for each $\varphi_l(t)$, $1 \leqslant l \leqslant N$, we obtain

$$\mathbf{s}_i = (s_{i1}, s_{i2}, \ldots, s_{iN}).$$

The procedure can be implemented as shown in the block diagram of Fig. 4.16. If $s(t)$ is applied at the input, the output is a vector

$$\mathbf{s} \triangleq (s_1, s_2, \ldots, s_N) \tag{4.40a}$$

with components

$$s_j \triangleq \int_{-\infty}^{\infty} s(t)\,\varphi_j(t)\,dt; \qquad j = 1, 2, \ldots, N. \tag{4.40b}$$

If $s(t) = s_i(t)$, then $\mathbf{s} = \mathbf{s}_i$.

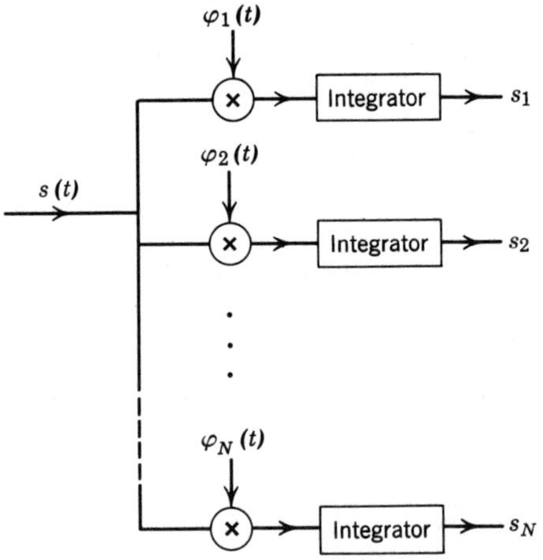

Figure 4.16 Extraction of $\mathbf{s} = (s_1, s_2, \ldots, s_N)$ from $s(t)$. Each of the integrations extends over the duration of the $\varphi_j(t)$ with which it is associated.

Irrelevant Data

Now suppose that the input to the bank of N multipliers and integrators in Fig. 4.16 is not $s(t)$, but rather the received random process $r(t)$ of Fig. 4.1. In this case the integrator outputs, say

$$r_j \triangleq \int_{-\infty}^{\infty} r(t)\, \varphi_j(t)\, dt; \qquad j = 1, 2, \ldots, N, \tag{4.41a}$$

are random variables† which together constitute a random vector

$$\mathbf{r}_1 \triangleq (r_1, r_2, \ldots, r_N). \tag{4.41b}$$

Since $r(t) = s(t) + n_w(t)$, we have

$$\mathbf{r}_1 = \mathbf{s} + \mathbf{n}, \tag{4.42}$$

where

$$\mathbf{n} = (n_1, n_2, \ldots, n_N) \tag{4.43a}$$

is the random vector with components

$$n_j \triangleq \int_{-\infty}^{\infty} n_w(t)\, \varphi_j(t)\, dt; \qquad j = 1, 2, \ldots, N. \tag{4.43b}$$

We assume that $n_w(t)$, hence $\mathbf{n}$, is statistically independent of $\mathbf{s}$.

Were it not for the noise vector $\mathbf{n}$, we have seen that $\mathbf{r}_1$ would coincide with whichever one of the $\{\mathbf{s}_i\}$ was actually transmitted. When the presence of $\mathbf{n}$ cannot be neglected, this, of course, is no longer true. What is true, however, is that the vector $\mathbf{r}_1$ in and by itself does contain *all data from $r(t)$ that is relevant to the optimum determination of the transmitted message.* The objective of this section is to prove this important fact.

The first step in the proof is to note that the waveform equation corresponding to the vector equality of Eq. 4.42 is

$$r_1(t) \triangleq \sum_{j=1}^{N} r_j\, \varphi_j(t) = s(t) + n(t), \tag{4.44a}$$

in which

$$s(t) = \sum_{j=1}^{N} s_j\, \varphi_j(t) \tag{4.44b}$$

$$n(t) \triangleq \sum_{j=1}^{N} n_j\, \varphi_j(t). \tag{4.44c}$$

† The value $r_j(\omega)$ assigned to any point ω of the sample space on which $r(t)$ is defined is $\int_{-\infty}^{\infty} r(\omega, t)\, \varphi_j(t)\, dt$.

The next step in the proof is to note that in terms of these random processes we may write

$$r(t) = r_1(t) + r_2(t), \tag{4.45a}$$

where

$$\begin{aligned} r_2(t) &\triangleq r(t) - r_1(t) \\ &= [s(t) + n_w(t)] - [s(t) + n(t)] \\ &= n_w(t) - n(t) \end{aligned} \tag{4.45b}$$

is a random process that is independent of the signal transmitted. The fact that $r_2(t)$ is not in general identically zero implies that the noise process $n_w(t)$ cannot be represented with complete fidelity by the finite orthonormal set $\{\varphi_j(t)\}$.

We have succeeded in Eq. 4.45a in decomposing the received waveform $r(t)$ into two waveforms, $r_1(t)$ and $r_2(t)$, the first entirely specified by the vector $\mathbf{r}_1$ and the second independent of the transmitted signal. We now show that the optimum receiver may disregard $r_2(t)$ and therefore base its decision solely upon the vector $\mathbf{r}_1 = \mathbf{s} + \mathbf{n}$.

Observe that any finite set of time samples taken from $r_2(t)$, say

$$\mathbf{r}_2 = \big(r_2(t_1), r_2(t_2), \ldots, r_2(t_q)\big), \tag{4.46}$$

depends only on $n_w(t)$. Since this is true also of $\mathbf{n}$, the vectors $\mathbf{r}_2$ and $\mathbf{n}$ are jointly independent of $\mathbf{s}$. As a preliminary to invoking the theorem of irrelevance (Eq. 4.25b and Fig. 4.8), we observe in consequence that

$$\begin{aligned} p_{\mathbf{r}_2|\mathbf{r}_1,\mathbf{s}} = p_{\mathbf{r}_2|\mathbf{n},\mathbf{s}} &= \frac{p_{\mathbf{r}_2,\mathbf{n},\mathbf{s}}}{p_{\mathbf{n},\mathbf{s}}} \\ &= \frac{p_{\mathbf{r}_2,\mathbf{n}}\, p_{\mathbf{s}}}{p_{\mathbf{n}}\, p_{\mathbf{s}}} = p_{\mathbf{r}_2|\mathbf{n}}. \end{aligned}$$

Thus $\mathbf{r}_2$ may be discarded by the optimum receiver provided that it is also independent of $\mathbf{n}$. Since a random process is completely described by the statistical behavior of finite sets of time samples, it follows that the entire process $r_2(t)$ may be discarded whenever the statistical independence of $\mathbf{r}_2$ and $\mathbf{n}$ holds true for every possible finite set of sampling instants $\{t_l\}$, $l = 1, 2, \ldots, q$. In other words, the random process $r_2(t)$ may be ignored if it is statistically independent of the process $n(t)$.

The required proof of statistical independence rests on the fact that both $n(t)$ and $r_2(t)$ result from linear operations—integration, addition, and subtraction—on the Gaussian process $n_w(t)$. Thus $n(t)$ and $r_2(t)$ are jointly Gaussian processes, so that by analogy with Eq. 3.130 any two random vectors obtained from $n(t)$ and $r_2(t)$, respectively, are statistically independent if the covariance

$$\mathrm{E}[n(s)\, r_2(t)] - \mathrm{E}[n(s)]\, \mathrm{E}[r_2(t)]$$

vanishes for all observation instants t and s. In particular, since $n_w(t)$, hence $n(s)$ and $r_2(t)$ as well, are zero mean, it suffices to show that

$$\mathrm{E}[n(s)\, r_2(t)] = 0; \qquad \text{for all } t \text{ and } s. \tag{4.47a}$$

From Eq. 4.44c we have

$$\mathrm{E}[n(s)\, r_2(t)] = \mathrm{E}\left[r_2(t) \sum_{j=1}^{N} n_j\, \varphi_j(s) \right]$$

$$= \sum_{j=1}^{N} \varphi_j(s)\, \mathrm{E}[n_j\, r_2(t)], \tag{4.47b}$$

so that we need prove only that

$$\overline{n_j r_2(t)} = 0; \qquad \text{for all } j \text{ and } t. \tag{4.47c}$$

In order to verify Eq. 4.47c, we note from the definitions of Eqs. 4.43 and 4.45 that

$$\overline{n_j r_2(t)} = \overline{n_j[n_w(t) - n(t)]} = \overline{n_j n_w(t)} - \overline{n_j n(t)}$$

$$= \int_{-\infty}^{\infty} \overline{n_w(t)\, n_w(\alpha)}\, \varphi_j(\alpha)\, d\alpha - \sum_{l=1}^{N} \overline{n_j n_l}\, \varphi_l(t). \tag{4.48a}$$

The integral can be evaluated with the help of Eq. 3.136b:

$$\int_{-\infty}^{\infty} \overline{n_w(t)\, n_w(\alpha)}\, \varphi_j(\alpha)\, d\alpha = \int_{-\infty}^{\infty} \mathcal{R}_w(t - \alpha)\, \varphi_j(\alpha)\, d\alpha$$

$$= \frac{\mathcal{N}_0}{2} \int_{-\infty}^{\infty} \delta(t - \alpha)\, \varphi_j(\alpha)\, d\alpha = \frac{\mathcal{N}_0}{2}\, \varphi_j(t). \tag{4.48b}$$

Evaluation of the sum follows from the fact that

$$\overline{n_l n_j} = \int_{-\infty}^{\infty} \int_{-\infty}^{\infty} \overline{n_w(\alpha)\, n_w(\beta)}\, \varphi_l(\alpha)\, \varphi_j(\beta)\, d\alpha\, d\beta$$

$$= \frac{\mathcal{N}_0}{2} \int_{-\infty}^{\infty} \int_{-\infty}^{\infty} \delta(\alpha - \beta)\, \varphi_l(\alpha)\, \varphi_j(\beta)\, d\alpha\, d\beta$$

$$= \frac{\mathcal{N}_0}{2} \int_{-\infty}^{\infty} \varphi_l(\beta)\, \varphi_j(\beta)\, d\beta = \frac{\mathcal{N}_0}{2}\, \delta_{lj}. \tag{4.48c}$$

Thus

$$\sum_{l=1}^{N} \overline{n_l n_j}\, \varphi_l(t) = \frac{\mathcal{N}_0}{2}\, \varphi_j(t). \tag{4.48d}$$

Substituting Eqs. 4.48b and 4.48d into Eq. 4.48a, we have

$$\overline{n_j r_2(t)} = \frac{\mathcal{N}_0}{2}\,\varphi_j(t) - \frac{\mathcal{N}_0}{2}\,\varphi_j(t) = 0; \qquad \text{for all } j \text{ and } t, \tag{4.48e}$$

which was to be shown.

This completes the proof that the process $r_2(t)$ is statistically independent of $n(t)$. We conclude that the vector $\mathbf{r}_1$ defined by Eqs. 4.41 does in fact contain all data relevant to the optimum determination of $\hat{m}$ for the communication system of Fig. 4.1.

Joint Density Function of the Relevant Noise

In addition to the result that $r_2(t)$ is irrelevant, the foregoing analysis yields valuable information about $\mathbf{r}_1$. First, Eq. 4.42 establishes that the relevant effect of the additive white Gaussian noise $n_w(t)$ is to disturb the transmitted vector $\mathbf{s}$ by the addition of a random noise vector $\mathbf{n}$:

$$\mathbf{r}_1 = \mathbf{s} + \mathbf{n}. \tag{4.49a}$$

Second, the discussion leading to Eq. 4.47 implies that $\mathbf{n}$ is a set of N jointly Gaussian random variables, $\{n_j\}$, each of which has zero mean:

$$\overline{n_j} = 0; \qquad j = 1, 2, \ldots, N. \tag{4.49b}$$

Third, Eq. 4.48c establishes that the $\{n_j\}$ have zero covariance and equal variance:

$$\overline{n_l n_j} = \begin{cases} \dfrac{\mathcal{N}_0}{2}; & l = j \\ 0; & l \neq j. \end{cases} \tag{4.49c}$$

Thus the joint density function $p_{\mathbf{n}}$, in the notation of Eq. 4.17, is

$$p_{\mathbf{n}}(\boldsymbol{\alpha}) = \frac{1}{(\pi\mathcal{N}_0)^{N/2}}\, e^{-|\boldsymbol{\alpha}|^2/\mathcal{N}_0}, \tag{4.49d}$$

which implies that the $\{n_j\}$ are statistically independent. In particular, we note that $p_{\mathbf{n}}$ is *spherically symmetric*, that is, that $p_{\mathbf{n}}(\boldsymbol{\alpha})$ depends on the magnitude but not on the direction of the argument vector $\boldsymbol{\alpha}$.

Invariance of the Vector Channel to Choice of Orthonormal Base

Since a receiver need never consider the process $r_2(t)$ of Eq. 4.45, we shall henceforth disregard it and designate the relevant received vector simply by $\mathbf{r}$ rather than by $\mathbf{r}_1$.

Once provision is made for calculating the vector $\mathbf{r}$, the remaining receiver design problem is precisely the same as the vector receiver problem which we have already considered in connection with Fig. 4.2 and Eqs. 4.13 and 4.17, with the variance σ^2 set equal to $\mathcal{N}_0/2$. The relationship between the vector and waveform channels is illustrated in Fig. 4.17, in which we break both the transmitter and receiver into two parts. The "vector transmitter" accepts the input message m and generates the vector $\mathbf{s}_i$ whenever $m = m_i$; the "modulator" then constructs $s_i(t)$ from $\mathbf{s}_i$ and the waveforms $\{\varphi_j(t)\}$, which we call the *orthonormal base*. At the receiver the "detector" operates on the received waveform $r(t)$ and

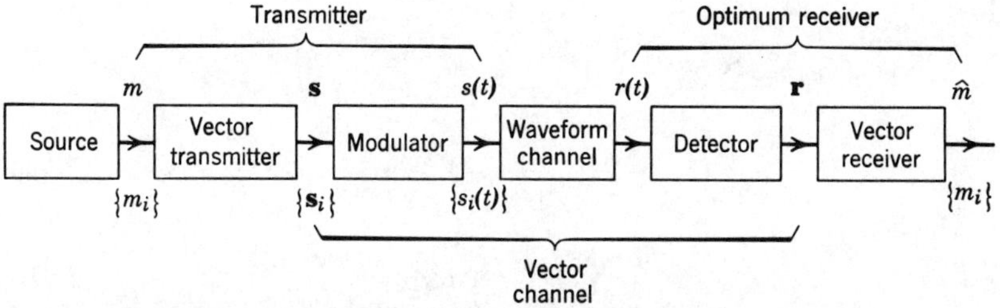

Figure 4.17 Reduction of waveform channel to vector channel. The modulator converts $\mathbf{s}$ to $s(t)$ by the mechanism of Fig. 4.12. The detector extracts the relevant received vector $\mathbf{r}$ from $r(t)$ by the mechanism of Fig. 4.16.

produces the relevant vector $\mathbf{r}$; the "vector receiver" then determines which message is most probable from observation of $\mathbf{r}$ and knowledge of the $\{\mathbf{s}_i\}$ and $\{P[m_i]\}$.

We have already noted that a particular geometric configuration of the signal vectors $\{\mathbf{s}_i\}$ may be converted to many different sets of waveforms $\{s_i(t)\}$ by appropriate choice of the orthonormal base. In addition, we now note that the derivation of $p_{\mathbf{n}}$ relies only on the fact that the $\{\varphi_j(t)\}$ are orthonormal and depends in no way on the specific waveshapes of these functions. Thus, as claimed earlier, whenever their vector representations $\{\mathbf{s}_i\}$ are the same, systems with different sets of transmitter signals $\{s_i(t)\}$, $i = 0, 1, \ldots, M - 1$, reduce to the same vector channel and yield the same minimum probability of error, $P[\mathcal{E}]$. The expression for $P[\mathcal{E}]$ is given in Eq. 4.20, with σ^2 specialized to $\mathcal{N}_0/2$ in accordance with Eq. 4.49c.

4.4 RECEIVER IMPLEMENTATION

We have seen so far that the optimum receiver in Fig. 4.17 performs two functions: first, the receiver calculates the relevant data vector

$$\mathbf{r} = (r_1, r_2, \ldots, r_N), \tag{4.50a}$$

where

$$r_j = \int_{-\infty}^{\infty} r(t)\, \varphi_j(t)\, dt; \qquad j = 1, 2, \ldots, N. \tag{4.50b}$$

Then, in accordance with Eq. 4.19 (with $\sigma^2 = \mathcal{N}_0/2$), the receiver sets $\hat{m} = m_k$ if the decision function

$$|\mathbf{r} - \mathbf{s}_i|^2 - \mathcal{N}_0 \ln \mathrm{P}[m_i] \tag{4.51}$$

is *minimum* for $i = k$. In practice, squarers are avoided by recognizing that

$$|\mathbf{r} - \mathbf{s}_i|^2 = \sum_{j=1}^{N} (r_j - s_{ij})^2$$

$$= \sum_{j=1}^{N} (r_j^2 - 2r_j s_{ij} + s_{ij}^2) = |\mathbf{r}|^2 - 2\mathbf{r} \cdot \mathbf{s}_i + |\mathbf{s}_i|^2, \tag{4.52a}$$

in which

$$\mathbf{r} \cdot \mathbf{s}_i \triangleq \sum_{j=1}^{N} r_j s_{ij} \tag{4.52b}$$

is the dot product of the vectors $\mathbf{r}$ and $\mathbf{s}_i$. Since $|\mathbf{r}|^2$ is independent of i, a decision rule equivalent to Eq. 4.52 is to *maximize* the expression

$$(\mathbf{r} \cdot \mathbf{s}_i) + c_i, \tag{4.53a}$$

where

$$c_i \triangleq \tfrac{1}{2}(\mathcal{N}_0 \ln \mathrm{P}[m_i] - |\mathbf{s}_i|^2), \qquad i = 0, 1, \ldots, M - 1. \tag{4.53b}$$

Correlation Receiver

When the relevant received vector $\mathbf{r}$ is obtained from the received waveform by the bank of N multipliers and integrators shown in Fig. 4.16, the receiver is called a correlation receiver. When M is not large, the numbers

$$\mathbf{r} \cdot \mathbf{s}_i = \sum_{j=1}^{N} r_j s_{ij}; \qquad i = 0, 1, \ldots, M - 1$$

can be obtained from $\mathbf{r}$ and knowledge of the $\{\mathbf{s}_i\}$ by attaching a set of M resistor weighting networks (with weights proportional to the $\{s_{ij}\}$) to the integrator outputs or by other analog computer techniques. When M is very large, digital computation of the $\{\mathbf{r} \cdot \mathbf{s}_i\}$ becomes preferable. A block diagram of an optimum correlation receiver is shown in Fig. 4.18.

Matched Filter Receiver

If each member of the orthonormal base $\{\varphi_j(t)\}$ is identically zero outside some finite time interval, say $0 \leqslant t \leqslant T$, the use of the multipliers

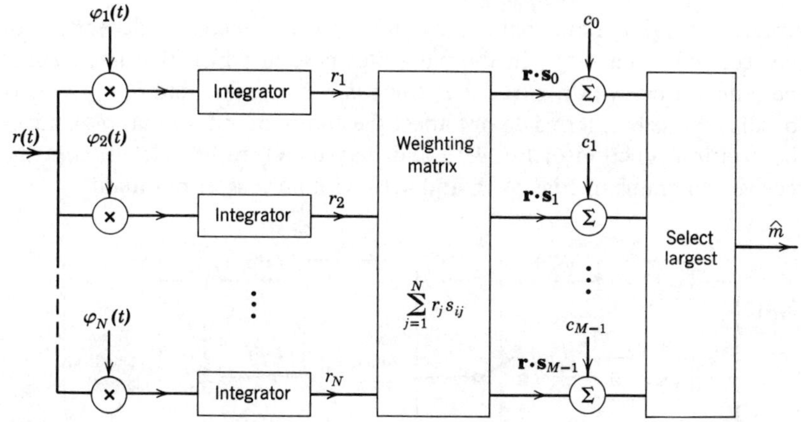

Figure 4.18 Diagram of the correlation receiver. The bias terms $\{c_i\}$ are given by Eq. 4.53b.

shown in Fig. 4.18 can be avoided. This is desirable, since accurate analog multipliers are hard to build. Consider, for instance, the output $u_j(t)$ of a linear filter with impulse response $h_j(t)$. When $r(t)$ is the filter input, we have

$$u_j(t) = \int_{-\infty}^{\infty} r(\alpha)\, h_j(t - \alpha)\, d\alpha. \tag{4.54a}$$

If we now set

$$h_j(t) = \varphi_j(T - t), \tag{4.54b}$$

the output is

$$u_j(t) = \int_{-\infty}^{\infty} r(\alpha)\, \varphi_j(T - t + \alpha)\, d\alpha. \tag{4.54c}$$

Finally, the output sampled at time $t = T$ is

$$u_j(T) = \int_{-\infty}^{\infty} r(\alpha)\, \varphi_j(\alpha)\, d\alpha \triangleq r_j, \tag{4.54d}$$

where the second equality follows from Eq. 4.50b. Thus the optimum decision rule of Eq. 4.53 can also be implemented by the receiver shown in Fig. 4.19.

A filter whose impulse response is a delayed, time-reversed version of a signal $\varphi_j(t)$ is called *matched* to $\varphi_j(t)$ and the optimum receiver realization of Fig. 4.19 is a *matched filter* receiver. The requirement that $\varphi_j(t)$ vanish for $t > T$ is necessary in order that the matched filter may be physically realizable, that is, in order that $h_j(t) \equiv 0$ for $t < 0$.

For both the correlation and matched filter optimum receiver realizations we note that the "bias" terms

$$c_i = \tfrac{1}{2}(\mathcal{N}_0 \ln \mathrm{P}[m_i] - |\mathbf{s}_i|^2)$$

represent a priori data that are available to the receiver independent of the received signal $r(t)$. In the particular case in which the bias term is the same for every i (in particular, when $|\mathbf{s}_i|^2$ is constant and $P[m_i] = 1/M$ for all i), these bias terms do not affect the choice of index i that maximizes the decision function of Eq. 4.53 and may therefore be deleted from the receiver diagrams in Figs. 4.18 and 4.19 without loss of optimality.

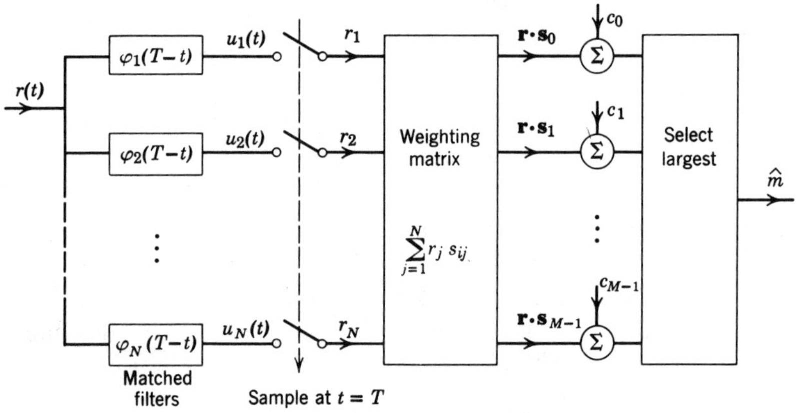

Figure 4.19 Diagram of the matched-filter receiver.

A simple example of a matched filter occurs when the signal to be matched is

$$\varphi_j(t) = \begin{cases} -\sqrt{\dfrac{2}{T}} \cos 2\pi f_j t; & 0 \leqslant t \leqslant T \\ 0; & \text{elsewhere,} \end{cases} \tag{4.55a}$$

where f_j is an integral multiple of $1/2T$. Then

$$h_j(t) = \varphi_j(T - t)$$

$$= \begin{cases} +\sqrt{\dfrac{2}{T}} \cos 2\pi f_j t; & 0 \leqslant t \leqslant T \\ 0; & \text{elsewhere,} \end{cases} \tag{4.55b}$$

as shown in Fig. 4.20*a*.

The voltage response of the infinite-Q parallel tuned circuit shown in Fig. 4.20*b* to a unit impulse of current is

$$h(t) = \frac{1}{C} \cos \frac{t}{\sqrt{LC}}; \qquad 0 \leqslant t < \infty,$$

where we have assumed that the initial energy storage in L and C at time $t = 0$ is zero. It is clear that when $1/\sqrt{LC} = 2\pi f_j$ and $1/C = \sqrt{2/T}$ the impulse response $h(t)$ coincides with $h_j(t)$ over the interval $0 \leqslant t \leqslant T$, although it does not do so for $t > T$. Thus the matched filtering operation for $\varphi_j(t)$ can be instrumented as shown in Fig. 4.20*c*. The parallel switch closing briefly at time $t = 0$ dumps any residual energy in the filter, ensuring that signal energy received earlier than $t = 0$ does not contribute to the output at time $t = T$. The series switch closing briefly at $t = T$ samples the filter output at the proper time. The entire cycle can be repeated during the interval $T \leqslant t \leqslant 2T$, although care must be taken to

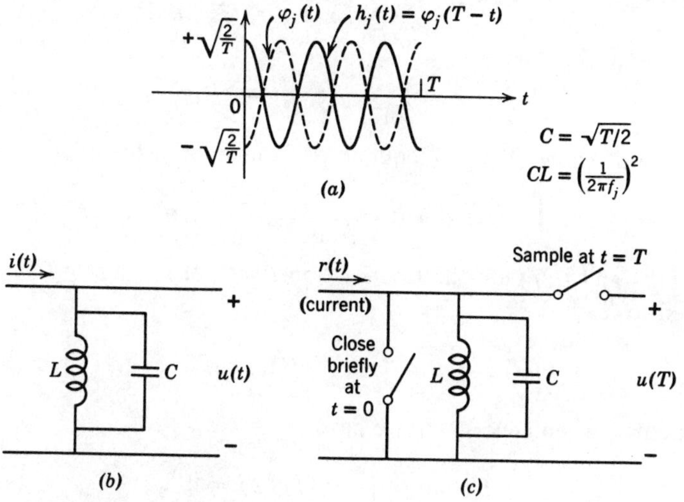

Figure 4.20 Integrate-and-dump filter. In application the resonant circuit may be lossy, so long as its time constant is much greater than T.

be sure that the desired output is always sampled just before the filter is dumped. A matched filter of this sort is called an *integrate-and-dump*[87] circuit. Such a filter is not time invariant, but it does give the desired impulse response as long as the timing of the switches is properly synchronized with respect to $\varphi_j(t)$.

Parseval relationships. The vector decision function of Eq. 4.53 can be interpreted directly in terms of time functions by means of the following Parseval relationship. Consider an orthonormal set $\{\varphi_j(t)\}$, $j = 1, 2, \ldots, N$, and any two waveforms defined by

$$f(t) \triangleq \sum_{j=1}^{N} f_j \, \varphi_j(t) \tag{4.56a}$$

$$g(t) \triangleq \sum_{j=1}^{N} g_j \, \varphi_j(t), \tag{4.56b}$$

with corresponding vector representations

$$\mathbf{f} = (f_1, f_2, \ldots, f_N) \tag{4.57a}$$

$$\mathbf{g} = (g_1, g_2, \ldots, g_N). \tag{4.57b}$$

Then

$$\begin{aligned}\int_{-\infty}^{\infty} f(t)\, g(t)\, dt &= \int_{-\infty}^{\infty} \sum_{j=1}^{N} \sum_{l=1}^{N} f_j g_l\, \varphi_j(t)\, \varphi_l(t)\, dt \\ &= \sum_{j=1}^{N} \sum_{l=1}^{N} f_j g_l \int_{-\infty}^{\infty} \varphi_j(t)\, \varphi_l(t)\, dt \\ &= \sum_{j=1}^{N} \sum_{l=1}^{N} f_j g_l\, \delta_{jl} = \sum_{j=1}^{N} f_j g_j = \mathbf{f} \cdot \mathbf{g}.\end{aligned}$$

Thus the well-known Parseval equation[62] from Fourier theory,

$$\int_{-\infty}^{\infty} f(t)\, g(t)\, dt = \int_{-\infty}^{\infty} F(f)\, G^*(f)\, df,$$

where $F(f)$ and $G(f)$ are the Fourier transforms of $f(t)$ and $g(t)$, can be extended to read

$$\int_{-\infty}^{\infty} f(t)\, g(t)\, dt = \int_{-\infty}^{\infty} F(f)\, G^*(f)\, df = \mathbf{f} \cdot \mathbf{g}. \tag{4.58a}$$

In particular, when $g(t) = f(t)$, we have

$$\int_{-\infty}^{\infty} f^2(t)\, dt = \int_{-\infty}^{\infty} |F(f)|^2\, df = |\mathbf{f}|^2. \tag{4.58b}$$

Equation 4.58a states that the "correlation" of $f(t)$ and $g(t)$, defined as the integral of their product, equals the dot product of the corresponding vectors. Equation 4.58b states that the "energy" of $f(t)$, normalized to a one-ohm load, equals the square of the length of the corresponding vector $\mathbf{f}$.

Equation 4.58b provides an immediate interpretation of the bias term c_i in the additive white Gaussian noise decision rule of Eq. 4.53. We have

$$c_i = \tfrac{1}{2}(\mathcal{N}_0 \ln \mathrm{P}[m_i] - E_i), \tag{4.59a}$$

where

$$E_i \triangleq \int_{-\infty}^{\infty} s_i^2(t)\, dt = \text{energy of the } i\text{th signal}. \tag{4.59b}$$

Moreover, from Eqs. 4.29 and 4.50 we also have

$$\begin{aligned}\int_{-\infty}^{\infty} r(t)\, s_i(t)\, dt &= \int_{-\infty}^{\infty} r(t) \left[\sum_{j=1}^{N} s_{ij}\, \varphi_j(t)\right] dt \\ &= \sum_{j=1}^{N} s_{ij} \int_{-\infty}^{\infty} r(t)\, \varphi_j(t)\, dt = \sum_{j=1}^{N} s_{ij} r_j = \mathbf{r} \cdot \mathbf{s}_i.\end{aligned}$$

Thus, in terms of the complete received waveform $r(t)$, the optimum decision function of Eq. 4.53a is

$$\int_{-\infty}^{\infty} r(t)\, s_i(t)\, dt + c_i. \tag{4.60}$$

In view of Eq. 4.60, the matched filter (or the correlation) receiver can be instrumented directly in terms of the $\{s_i(t)\}$, $i = 0, 1, \ldots, M - 1$, as indicated in Fig. 4.21. At first glance this might appear to eliminate the need for the weighting and summing operations in Figs. 4.18 and 4.19.

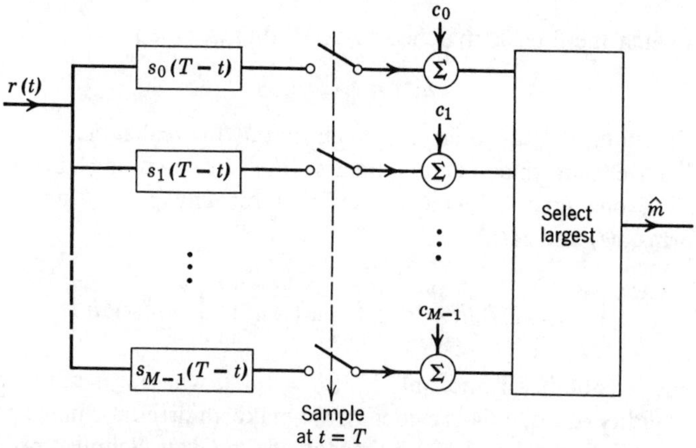

Figure 4.21 An optimum receiver with M filters matched directly to the signals $\{s_i(t)\}$, which are assumed to have duration T.

Actually, of course, these operations are still being performed but now occur within the M matched filters (or correlators). We have already remarked (and prove in Appendix 4A) that the number, N, of orthonormal functions required to express any set of M signals $\{s_i(t)\}$ in the form of Eq. 4.29 is always less than or equal to M. When $M \gg N$, a situation often encountered in practice, it is usually much less expensive to use N filters (or correlators) matched to the $\{\varphi_j(t)\}$, plus an analog or digital computer, than it is to use M filters (or correlators) matched directly to the $\{s_i(t)\}$.

Signal-to-noise ratio. We may gain insight into the optimality of the matched filtering operation by a signal-to-noise ratio analysis. Consider the situation illustrated in Fig. 4.22, in which $h(t)$ is an arbitrary linear filter, T is an arbitrary observation instant, and $\varphi(t)$ is any known signal. [In particular, we may choose $\varphi(t)$ to be one of the orthonormal base functions.] The sampled output r may be written

$$r = \bar{r} + n, \tag{4.61}$$

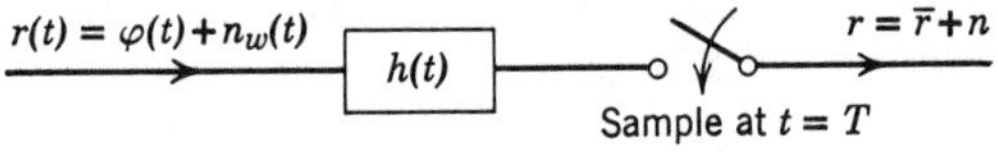

Figure 4.22 An arbitrary filter, the output of which is sampled at $t = T$.

where $\bar{r}$, the mean of r, depends on $\varphi(t)$ and the noise term n depends on $n_w(t)$. We now show that the maximum attainable signal-to-noise power ratio, defined as

$$\mathcal{S}/\mathcal{N} \triangleq \bar{r}^2/\overline{n^2}, \tag{4.62}$$

occurs when the filter is matched to $\varphi(t)$; that is, when

$$h(t) = \varphi(T - t). \tag{4.63}$$

In application, T is taken large enough that $h(t)$ is realizable.

We prove that this $h(t)$ maximizes $\mathcal{S}/\mathcal{N}$ by invoking the Schwarz inequality, one form of which states that for any pair of finite-energy waveforms $a(t)$ and $b(t)$,

$$\left[\int_{-\infty}^{\infty} a(t)\, b(t)\, dt\right]^2 \leqslant \left[\int_{-\infty}^{\infty} a^2(t)\, dt\right]\left[\int_{-\infty}^{\infty} b^2(t)\, dt\right]. \tag{4.64}$$

The equality obtains if and only if $b(t) = ca(t)$, where c is any constant.

The validity of Eq. 4.64 is evident if we make an orthonormal expansion of the waveforms $a(t)$ and $b(t)$ by means of the Gram-Schmidt procedure discussed in Appendix 4A. We then have

$$a(t) = a_1\, \psi_1(t) + a_2\, \psi_2(t)$$

$$b(t) = b_1\, \psi_1(t) + b_2\, \psi_2(t),$$

where

$$\int_{-\infty}^{\infty} \psi_i(t)\, \psi_j(t)\, dt = \delta_{ij}; \qquad i, j = 1, 2.$$

Figure 4.23 illustrates that the angle between the two vectors

$$\begin{aligned} \mathbf{a} &\triangleq (a_1, a_2) \\ \mathbf{b} &\triangleq (b_1, b_2) \end{aligned} \tag{4.65a}$$

is given by

$$\cos\theta = \frac{\mathbf{a}\cdot\mathbf{b}}{|\mathbf{a}|\,|\mathbf{b}|} = \frac{\displaystyle\int_{-\infty}^{\infty} a(t)\, b(t)\, dt}{\left[\displaystyle\int_{-\infty}^{\infty} a^2(t)\, dt \int_{-\infty}^{\infty} b^2(t)\, dt\right]^{1/2}}. \tag{4.65b}$$

The second equality above rests on the Parseval relations of Eq. 4.58.

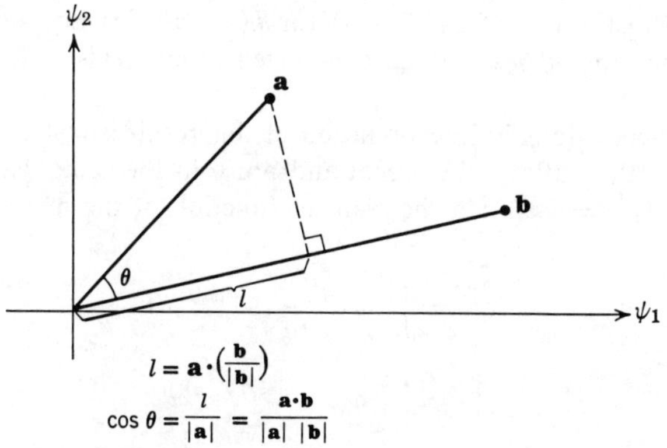

Figure 4.23 The angle between two vectors.

The Schwarz inequality (Eq. 4.64) results from recognizing that $|\cos\theta| \leqslant 1$. Furthermore, $|\cos\theta| = 1$ if and only if $\mathbf{b} = c\mathbf{a}$, that is, if and only if $a(t) = c\,b(t)$.

We now apply the Schwarz inequality to the maximization of $\mathcal{S}/\mathcal{N}$. For the random variable r of Fig. 4.22,

$$\bar{r} = \int_{-\infty}^{\infty} \varphi(T-\alpha)\, h(\alpha)\, d\alpha$$

and

$$\overline{n^2} = \mathrm{E}\left[\int_{-\infty}^{\infty}\int_{-\infty}^{\infty} n_w(T-\alpha)\, n_w(T-\beta)\, h(\alpha)\, h(\beta)\, d\alpha\, d\beta\right]$$

$$= \frac{\mathcal{N}_0}{2}\int_{-\infty}^{\infty}\int_{-\infty}^{\infty} \delta(\beta-\alpha)\, h(\alpha)\, h(\beta)\, d\alpha\, d\beta$$

$$= \frac{\mathcal{N}_0}{2}\int_{-\infty}^{\infty} h^2(\alpha)\, d\alpha.$$

From Schwarz's inequality, for any $h(t)$ we have

$$\frac{\mathcal{S}}{\mathcal{N}} \triangleq \frac{\bar{r}^2}{\overline{n^2}} = \frac{\left[\int_{-\infty}^{\infty} \varphi(T-\alpha)\, h(\alpha)\, d\alpha\right]^2}{(\mathcal{N}_0/2)\int_{-\infty}^{\infty} h^2(\alpha)\, d\alpha}$$

$$\leqslant \frac{\int_{-\infty}^{\infty} \varphi^2(T-\alpha)\, d\alpha \int_{-\infty}^{\infty} h^2(\alpha)\, d\alpha}{(\mathcal{N}_0/2)\int_{-\infty}^{\infty} h^2(\alpha)\, d\alpha} = \frac{\int_{-\infty}^{\infty} \varphi^2(\alpha)\, d\alpha}{\mathcal{N}_0/2}. \tag{4.66}$$

Since the substitution of $c\varphi(T - \alpha)$ for $h(\alpha)$ satisfies Eq. 4.66 with the equality, the ratio $\mathcal{S}/\mathcal{N}$ is indeed maximized when $h(t)$ is matched to $\varphi(t)$, as claimed.

The frequency-domain interpretation of this result is instructive. Since amplitude scaling affects the signal and noise in the same way, we need consider only $c = 1$. Then the transfer function of the matched filter is given by

$$H(f) = \int_{-\infty}^{\infty} \varphi(T - t)e^{-j2\pi ft}\, dt$$

$$= \int_{-\infty}^{\infty} \varphi(\alpha)e^{-j2\pi f(T-\alpha)}\, d\alpha$$

$$= e^{-j2\pi fT}\, \Phi^*(f), \tag{4.67a}$$

where the signal spectrum is

$$\Phi(f) = |\Phi(f)|\, e^{j\theta(f)} \triangleq \int_{-\infty}^{\infty} \varphi(t)e^{-j2\pi ft}\, dt. \tag{4.67b}$$

Thus

$$H(f) = |\Phi(f)|\, e^{-j[\theta(f)+2\pi fT]}. \tag{4.67c}$$

In accordance with the inverse Fourier transform,

$$\varphi(t) = \int_{-\infty}^{\infty} \Phi(f)e^{j2\pi ft}\, df, \tag{4.68}$$

we may interpret the filter input $\varphi(t)$ to be a composite of many small (complex) sinusoids: the sinusoid at frequency f_1 has amplitude $|\Phi(f_1)|\, df$ and phase $\theta(f_1)$. In passing through the filter this component is multiplied by $H(f_1)$, which changes its magnitude to $|\Phi(f_1)|^2$ and its phase to

$$\theta(f_1) - [\theta(f_1) + 2\pi f_1 T] = -2\pi f_1 T.$$

Thus the filter-output sinusoid at frequency f_1 is

$$|\Phi(f_1)|^2\, df\, e^{j2\pi f_1(t-T)},$$

which has a maximum at $t = T$. Since this is true for every f_1, all of the frequency components of $\varphi(t)$ are brought into phase coincidence and reinforce each other at $t = T$; as shown in Fig. 4.24, an output signal peak is produced at this instant.

Appreciation of the effect of the spectral-amplitude shaping caused by $|H(f)|$ can be gained by contrasting the matched filter with an *inverse filter*, which has the transfer function

$$\frac{e^{-j2\pi fT}}{\Phi(f)} = \frac{1}{|\Phi(f)|}\, e^{-j[\theta(f)+2\pi fT]}. \tag{4.69}$$

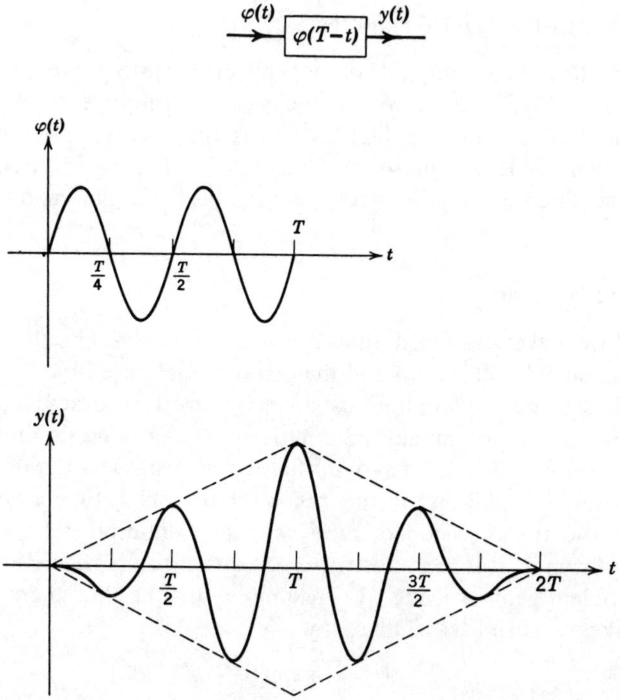

Figure 4.24 An example illustrating that the output of the matched filter is maximum at the instant $t = T$.

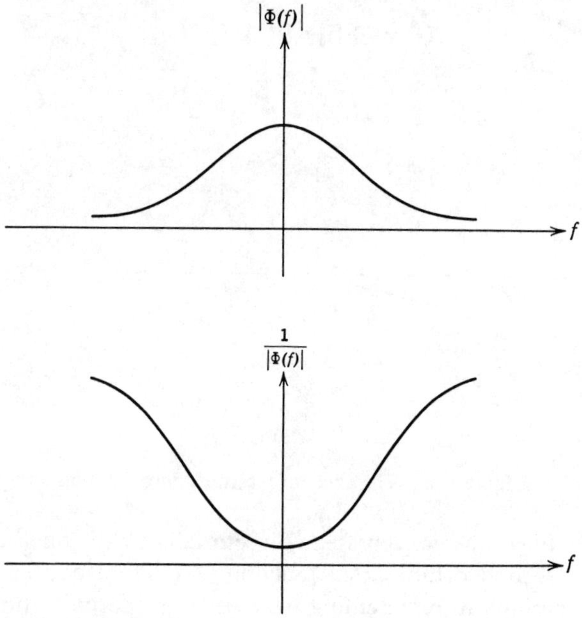

Figure 4.25 The inverse filter has high gain at frequencies for which $|\Phi(f)|$ is small, whereas the matched filter gain is proportional to $|\Phi(f)|$.

The inverse filter also brings all components of $\varphi(t)$ into phase coincidence. As shown in Fig. 4.25, however, the weaker components of $\varphi(t)$ are accentuated by the inverse filter, whereas they are suppressed by the matched filter. Since the noise spectrum $\mathcal{S}_w(f)$ is flat over all frequencies, the inverse filter exalts the out-of-band noise and the matched filter subdues it.

Component Accuracy

So far we have presumed that the receiver knows exactly both the transmitter signal vectors $\{\mathbf{s}_i\}$ and the orthonormal base functions $\{\varphi_j(t)\}$. In practice, of course, limitations on component accuracy render this knowledge only approximate. Alternatively, in the interests of economy we might wish to settle for a system that is somewhat less than optimum.

In general, calculation of the precise trade-off between error performance and the precision of receiver instrumentation is both tedious and unrewarding. It is more instructive to visualize the nature and extent of the problem geometrically. For example, assume that there are two equally likely transmitter signals, say

$$s(t) = \pm s_1\varphi_1(t). \tag{4.70a}$$

The corresponding vector representation is illustrated by the black dots in Fig. 4.26. The receiver's approximations to these signals might be

$$\tilde{s}(t) = \pm[\tilde{s}_1\varphi_1(t) + \tilde{s}_2\varphi_2(t)]. \tag{4.70b}$$

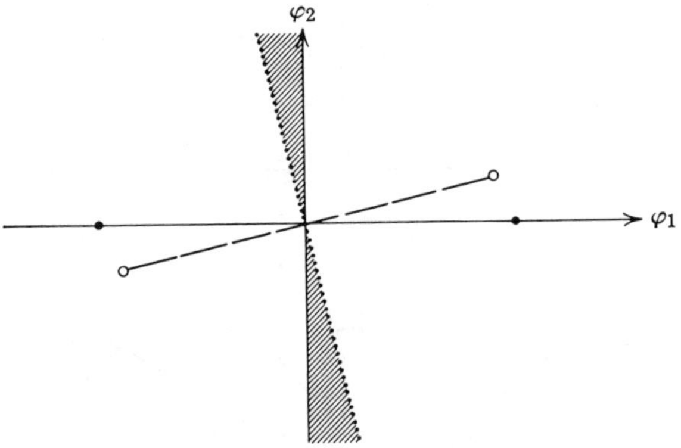

Figure 4.26 The effect of receiver approximation.

These approximations are represented vectorially by the open dots in the figure. The second orthonormal function $\varphi_2(t)$ is introduced to permit complete generality in representing the receiver's approximation of $\varphi_1(t)$.

A receiver matched to these approximate signals would employ the decision boundary indicated by the dotted line in Fig. 4.26, whereas an optimum receiver would use the φ_2-axis as the decision boundary. It is clear that the degradation in error performance is small as long as the receiver's approximations of the $\{s_i(t)\}$ are sufficiently accurate that the probability of the received vector **r** falling into the shaded area is small compared with the optimum $P[\mathcal{E}]$. This condition is met in general whenever

$$|\tilde{\mathbf{s}}_i - \mathbf{s}_i|^2 = \int_{-\infty}^{\infty} [\tilde{s}_i(t) - s_i(t)]^2 \, dt$$

is small compared with the square of each intersignal distance, $|\mathbf{s}_i - \mathbf{s}_k|^2$, for all i and $k \neq i$.

4.5 PROBABILITY OF ERROR

We have seen in Section 4.3 that the problem of communicating one of a set of M specified signals $\{s_i(t)\}$ over a channel disturbed only by additive white Gaussian noise always reduces to a corresponding vector communication problem. In particular, we recall that the transmitter signals are represented by M points $\{\mathbf{s}_i\}$ in an N-dimensional space and that the relevant noise disturbance is represented by an N-dimensional random vector, **n**, with the spherically symmetric density function

$$p_{\mathbf{n}}(\boldsymbol{\alpha}) = \frac{1}{(\pi \mathcal{N}_0)^{N/2}} e^{-|\boldsymbol{\alpha}|^2/\mathcal{N}_0}. \tag{4.71a}$$

In accordance with the discussion leading to Eq. 4.19, the optimum receiver divides the signal space into a set of M disjoint decision regions $\{I_i\}$; any point $\boldsymbol{\rho}$ is assigned to I_k if and only if

$$|\boldsymbol{\rho} - \mathbf{s}_k|^2 - \mathcal{N}_0 \ln P[m_k] < |\boldsymbol{\rho} - \mathbf{s}_i|^2 - \mathcal{N}_0 \ln P[m_i]; \qquad \text{for all } i \neq k. \tag{4.71b}$$

The receiver output $\hat{m}$ is then set equal to m_k whenever the received vector

$$\mathbf{r} = \mathbf{s} + \mathbf{n} \tag{4.71c}$$

lies in I_k. Since the vector communication problem is invariant to the specific orthonormal base $\{\varphi_j(t)\}, j = 1, 2, \ldots, N$, that relates the $\{\mathbf{s}_i\}$ and the $\{s_i(t)\}$, the probability of error is independent of the waveshapes ascribed to the $\{\varphi_j(t)\}$.

In this section we evaluate the minimum attainable error probability (Eqs. 4.20, with $\sigma^2 = \mathcal{N}_0/2$) for certain important vector signal configurations. Except for $M = 2$, we assume that all M a priori probabilities

$\{P[m_i]\}$ are equal. The assumption is justified from an operational point of view in the discussion of "completely symmetric signals" at the end of this chapter.

Equivalent Signal Sets

In addition to signal sets that are equivalent by virtue of the fact that their geometrical configurations are identical, different geometrical configurations may also be equivalent insofar as error probability is concerned. Insight into this fact is gained by considering the geometry of the decision regions.

Rotation and translation of coordinates. In Fig. 4.27*a* we show a signal $\mathbf{s}_i$ and its decision region I_i. Whenever $\mathbf{s}_i$ is transmitted, a correct

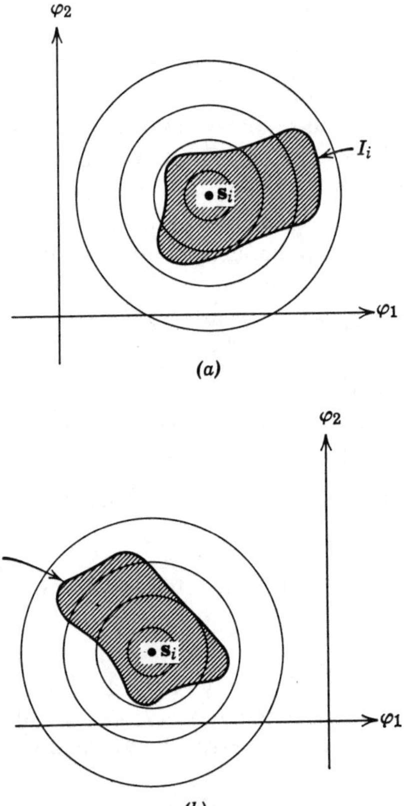

Figure 4.27 Equivalent decision regions. The concentric circles represent loci of constant $p_{\mathbf{n}}$.

decision results if $\mathbf{n} + \mathbf{s}_i$ falls within I_i. The probability of this event is unaffected if $\mathbf{s}_i$ and I_i are translated together through signal space. This follows, in accordance with Eqs. 4.71, from the fact that the noise $\mathbf{n}$ is additive and its density function $p_{\mathbf{n}}$ is independent of the signal. Moreover, since $p_{\mathbf{n}}$ is spherically symmetric, as indicated by the contours of constant probability density in the illustration, the probability that $\mathbf{n} + \mathbf{s}_i$ will fall in I_i is also unaffected by a rotation of I_i about $\mathbf{s}_i$. Thus $\mathbf{s}_i$ and I_i may be simultaneously translated and rotated, as in Fig. 4.27*b*, without affecting the conditional probability of a correct decision, $P[\mathcal{C} \mid m_i]$.

Minimum-energy signals. Although the probability of a correct decision is invariant to translation, such a transformation does affect the energy required to transmit each signal: in general, $\mathbf{s}_i' = \mathbf{s}_i - \mathbf{a}$ implies

$$E_i \triangleq \int_{-\infty}^{\infty} s_i^2(t)\, dt = |\mathbf{s}_i|^2 \neq |\mathbf{s}_i - \mathbf{a}|^2 = |\mathbf{s}_i'|^2 \triangleq E_i' . \tag{4.72}$$

When there is a constraint, say E_s, on the peak energy permitted for any signal, the vectors $\{\mathbf{s}_i\}$ are constrained to lie within a sphere of radius $\sqrt{E_s}$, as indicated in Fig. 4.28. A somewhat weaker constraint is that the mean energy $\overline{E_m}$, defined as

$$\overline{E_m} \triangleq \sum_{i=0}^{M-1} P[m_i]\, E_i = \sum_{i=0}^{M-1} P[m_i]\, |\mathbf{s}_i|^2, \tag{4.73}$$

be less than some fixed value. For a given configuration of signal points the mean energy can be minimized, without affecting the probability of

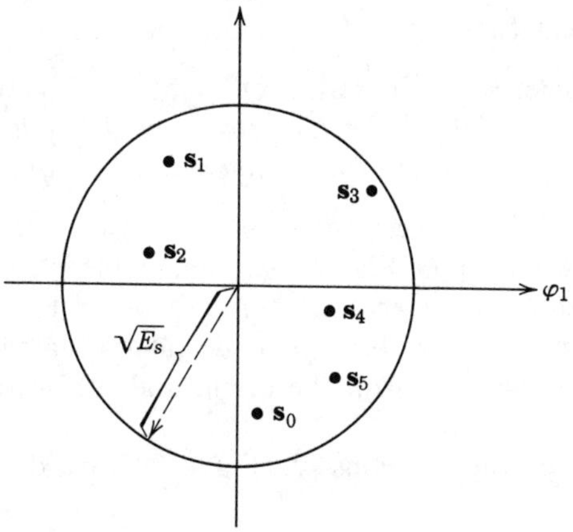

Figure 4.28 Peak energy constraint.

error, by subtracting from each signal $\mathbf{s}_i$ a constant vector $\mathbf{a}$ so chosen that

$$\sum_{i=0}^{M-1} \mathrm{P}[m_i]\,|\mathbf{s}_i - \mathbf{a}|^2$$

is minimum.

How to choose $\mathbf{a}$ is obvious once we have recognized that the expression for $\overline{E_m}$ is precisely the expression for the moment of inertia around the origin of a system of M point masses, where the mass of the ith point is $\mathrm{P}[m_i]$ and its position is $\mathbf{s}_i$. Since the moment of inertia is minimum when taken around the centroid (center of gravity) of a system, it follows that $\mathbf{a}$ should be chosen in such a way that the resulting centroid coincides with the origin. Given a set of probabilities $\{\mathrm{P}[m_i]\}$ and a set of signals $\{\mathbf{s}_i\}$, the appropriate choice of $\mathbf{a}$ is therefore

$$\mathbf{a} = \sum_{i=0}^{M-1} \mathrm{P}[m_i]\,\mathbf{s}_i \triangleq \mathrm{E}[\mathbf{s}]. \tag{4.74a}$$

As proof, we note that for any other translation, say $\mathbf{b}$, we have

$$\begin{aligned} \mathrm{E}[|\mathbf{s} - \mathbf{b}|^2] &= \mathrm{E}[|(\mathbf{s} - \mathbf{a}) + (\mathbf{a} - \mathbf{b})|^2] \\ &= \mathrm{E}[|\mathbf{s} - \mathbf{a}|^2] + 2(\mathbf{a} - \mathbf{b}) \cdot (\mathrm{E}[\mathbf{s}] - \mathbf{a}) + |\mathbf{a} - \mathbf{b}|^2 \qquad (4.74b) \\ &= \mathrm{E}[|\mathbf{s} - \mathbf{a}|^2] + |\mathbf{a} - \mathbf{b}|^2, \end{aligned}$$

where the last equality follows from Eq. 4.74a. The mean energy is increased when $\mathbf{b} \neq \mathbf{a}$. If the mean energy still exceeds the allowable maximum after the translation $\mathbf{a}$ is made, further reduction is possible only by transformations such as radial scaling that do affect the probability of error.

Rectangular Signal Sets

When the geometric configuration of M equally likely signal vectors is rectangular, the calculation of the error probability is especially easy. The simplest situation is that in which there are only two signals.

Binary signals. The general case of two signal vectors, each with probability $\frac{1}{2}$, is shown in Fig. 4.29*a*. From the standpoint of error probability, an equivalent signal set is that shown in Fig. 4.29*b*, in which the signal configuration has been rotated and translated in such a way that the centroid coincides with the origin and the vector $(\mathbf{s}_0 - \mathbf{s}_1)$ lies along the φ_1 axis.

The optimum decision regions for Fig. 4.29*b* are determined by the expression

$$\min_i \; \{|\boldsymbol{\rho} - \mathbf{s}_i|^2 - \mathcal{N}_0 \ln \mathrm{P}[m_i]\}. \tag{4.75}$$

For equal a priori probabilities, this decision rule is just

$$\min_i |\boldsymbol{\rho} - \mathbf{s}_i|^2.$$

It is clear from Fig. 4.29*b* that the locus of all points $\boldsymbol{\rho}$ equally distant from $\mathbf{s}_0$ and $\mathbf{s}_1$ is the φ_2 axis. Thus an error occurs when $\mathbf{s}_1$ is transmitted

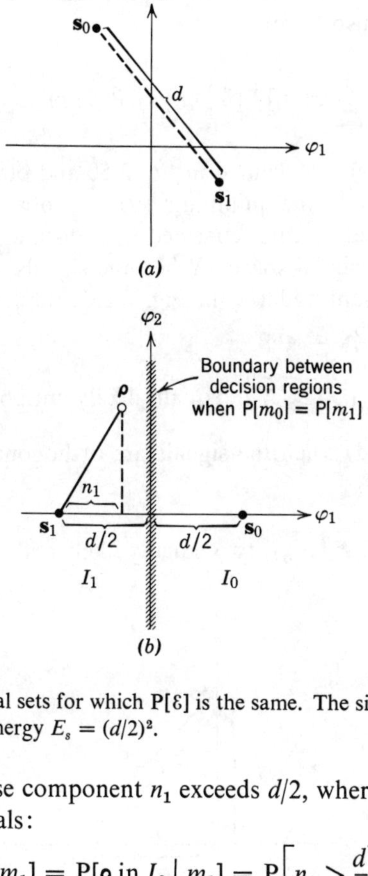

Figure 4.29 Binary signal sets for which P[ℰ] is the same. The signals in (*b*) are called "antipodal"; each has energy $E_s = (d/2)^2$.

if and only if the noise component n_1 exceeds $d/2$, where d is the distance between the two signals:

$$P[\mathcal{E} \mid m_1] = P[\boldsymbol{\rho} \text{ in } I_0 \mid m_1] = P\left[n_1 > \frac{d}{2}\right],$$

where

$$d^2 \triangleq |\mathbf{s}_0 - \mathbf{s}_1|^2 = \int_{-\infty}^{\infty} [s_0(t) - s_1(t)]^2 \, dt. \tag{4.76a}$$

But n_1 is zero-mean Gaussian with variance $\mathcal{N}_0/2$, so that

$$P[\mathcal{E} \mid m_1] = \int_{d/2}^{\infty} \frac{1}{\sqrt{\pi \mathcal{N}_0}} e^{-\alpha^2/\mathcal{N}_0} \, d\alpha.$$

Setting $\gamma = \alpha\sqrt{2/\mathcal{N}_0}$, we have

$$P[\mathcal{E} \mid m_1] = \int_{\frac{d/2}{\sqrt{\mathcal{N}_0/2}}}^{\infty} \frac{1}{\sqrt{2\pi}} e^{-\gamma^2/2}\, d\gamma \triangleq Q\left(\frac{d}{\sqrt{2\mathcal{N}_0}}\right).$$

Since, by symmetry, the conditional probability of error is the same for either signal, we also have

$$P[\mathcal{E}] = \sum_{i=0}^{1} P[m_i]\, P[\mathcal{E} \mid m_i] = P[\mathcal{E} \mid m_1] = Q\left(\frac{d}{\sqrt{2\mathcal{N}_0}}\right). \tag{4.76b}$$

The function $Q(\ )$ was defined in Eq. 2.50 and plotted in Fig. 2.36.

Equation 4.76b is the minimum error probability for any pair of equally likely signal vectors separated by a distance d, regardless of their actual location in signal space. When the signals have minimum energy and are therefore antipodal as in Fig. 4.29*b*, the length of each vector is $\sqrt{E_s}$, so that $d = 2\sqrt{E_s}$ and

$$P[\mathcal{E}] = Q(\sqrt{2E_s/\mathcal{N}_0});\ \text{equally likely antipodal signals.} \tag{4.77}$$

On the other hand, when the signals are orthogonal, as in Fig. 4.30, we have $d = \sqrt{2E_s}$ and

$$P[\mathcal{E}] = Q(\sqrt{E_s/\mathcal{N}_0});\ \text{two equally likely orthogonal signals.} \tag{4.78}$$

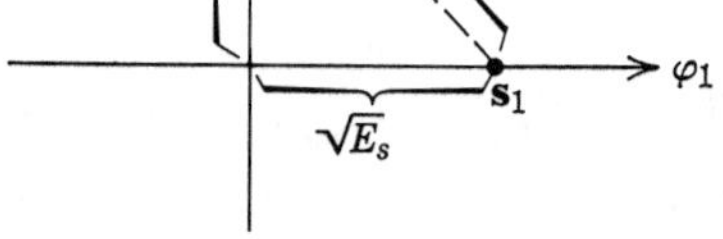

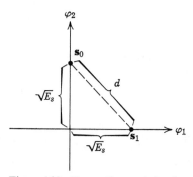

Figure 4.30 Two orthogonal signals.

It is common engineering practice to express energy ratios in units of decibels (db), where

$$\left.\frac{E_s}{\mathcal{N}_0}\right|_{\text{db}} \triangleq 10 \log_{10} \frac{E_s}{\mathcal{N}_0}.$$

For example

$\dfrac{E_s}{\mathcal{N}_0}$	$\left.\dfrac{E_s}{\mathcal{N}_0}\right\vert_{\text{db}}$
0.1	−10 db
1.0	0 db
2.0	3 db
3.0	4.8 db
10.0	10 db
100.0	20 db

The probabilities of error for antipodal and orthogonal signaling are plotted in Fig. 4.31 with $E_s/\mathcal{N}_0$ in units of db. The figure illustrates that antipodal signaling is 3 db more efficient than orthogonal signaling in communicating one of two equally likely messages.

With binary signals, it is also easy to determine P[$\mathcal{E}$] when the a priori probabilities are not equal. As shown in Fig. 4.32, the decision boundary is shifted from $\mathbf{s}_1$ toward $\mathbf{s}_0$ by an amount

$$\Delta = \frac{\mathcal{N}_0/2}{d} \ln \frac{\mathrm{P}[m_1]}{\mathrm{P}[m_0]}. \tag{4.79a}$$

Equation 4.79a is derived from the decision rule of Eq. 4.75 by solving the equation

$$|\boldsymbol{\rho} - \mathbf{s}_1|^2 - \mathcal{N}_0 \ln \mathrm{P}[m_1] = |\boldsymbol{\rho} - \mathbf{s}_0|^2 - \mathcal{N}_0 \ln \mathrm{P}[m_0]$$

for $\boldsymbol{\rho} = (\rho_1, \rho_2)$. For any value of ρ_2 we then have

$$\left(\rho_1 + \frac{d}{2}\right)^2 - \mathcal{N}_0 \ln \mathrm{P}[m_1] = \left(\rho_1 - \frac{d}{2}\right)^2 - \mathcal{N}_0 \ln \mathrm{P}[m_0]. .$$

Since Δ is the value of ρ_1 satisfying this equation,

$$2\Delta d = \mathcal{N}_0 \ln \frac{\mathrm{P}[m_1]}{\mathrm{P}[m_0]}.$$

The resulting error probability is

$$\mathrm{P}[\mathcal{E}] = \mathrm{P}[m_0]\, Q\left(\frac{d - 2\Delta}{\sqrt{2\mathcal{N}_0}}\right) + \mathrm{P}[m_1]\, Q\left(\frac{d + 2\Delta}{\sqrt{2\mathcal{N}_0}}\right). \tag{4.79b}$$

Rectangular decision regions. The ease of calculating the error probability for binary signals is directly attributable to the fact that an error occurs if and only if *one* random variable exceeds a given magnitude. A situation that is only slightly more complicated exists whenever the decision region boundaries are rectangular. Consider, for example, the

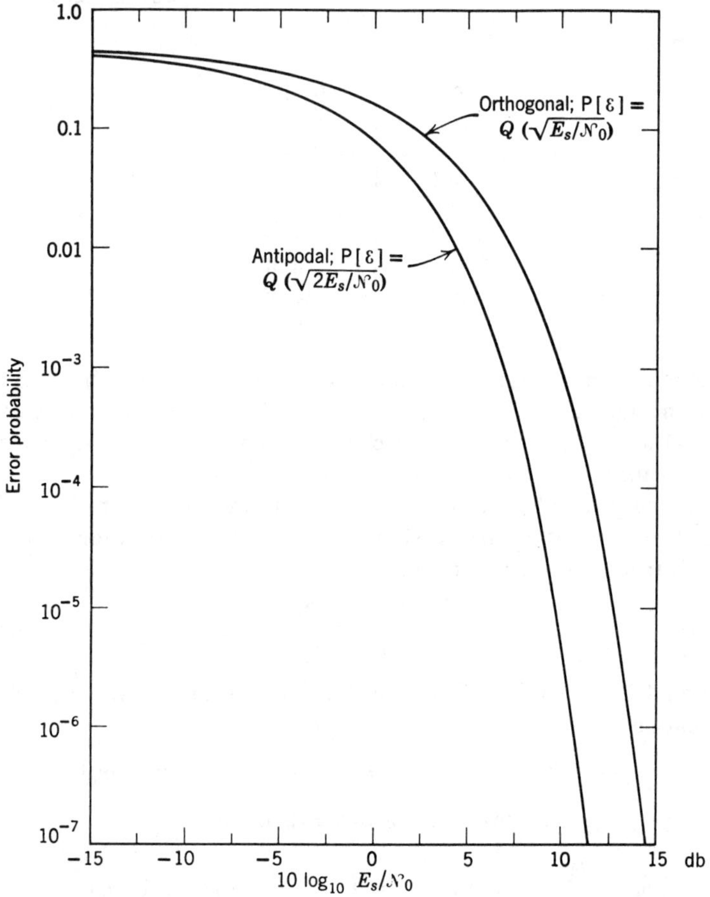

Figure 4.31 Probability of error for binary antipodal and binary orthogonal signaling with equally likely messages.

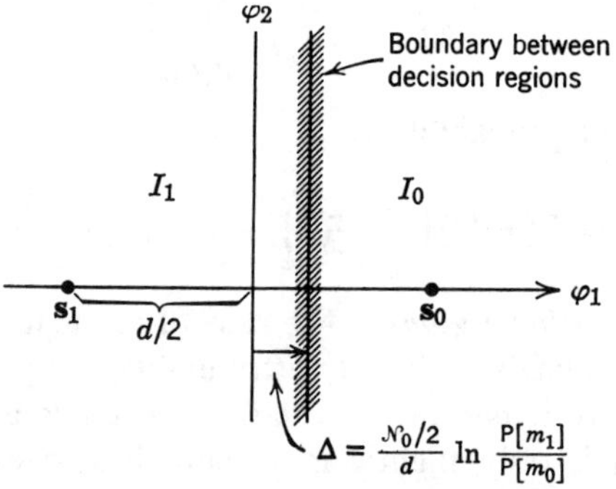

Figure 4.32 Decision regions for antipodal signals with distance d and unequal a priori probabilities.

signal $\mathbf{s}_i$ and decision region I_i shown in Fig. 4.33*a*. After translating $\mathbf{s}_i$ to the origin and rotating the configuration as shown in Fig. 4.33*b*, we see immediately that $\mathbf{s}_i + \mathbf{n}$ falls within I_i whenever, simultaneously,

$$(a_1 < n_1 < b_1) \quad \text{and} \quad (a_2 < n_2 < b_2). \tag{4.80a}$$

But n_1 and n_2 are statistically independent (cf. Eq. 4.49), and the density

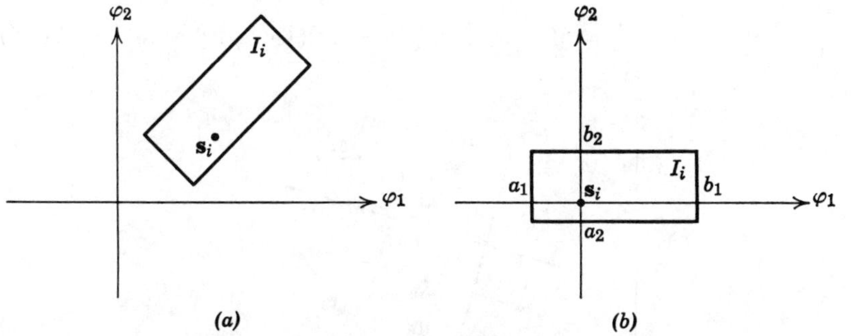

Figure 4.33 A single rectangular decision region.

function, say p_n, of each is the same:

$$p_{n_j}(\alpha) = p_n(\alpha) = \frac{1}{\sqrt{\pi \mathcal{N}_0}} e^{-\alpha^2/\mathcal{N}_0}; \qquad j = 1, 2. \tag{4.80b}$$

Thus

$$\begin{aligned} P[\mathcal{C} \mid m_i] &= P[a_1 < n_1 < b_1, a_2 < n_2 < b_2] \\ &= P[a_1 < n_1 < b_1]\, P[a_2 < n_2 < b_2] \\ &= \int_{a_1}^{b_1} p_n(\alpha)\, d\alpha \int_{a_2}^{b_2} p_n(\alpha)\, d\alpha. \end{aligned} \tag{4.80c}$$

The optimum decision boundaries are always rectangular when the signal vector configuration is rectangular and all signals are equally likely. A simple example is the rectangular configuration of six equally likely signals shown in Fig. 4.34. We have

$$P[\mathcal{C} \mid m_0] = \int_{-\infty}^{d/2} p_n(\alpha)\, d\alpha \int_{-\infty}^{d/2} p_n(\alpha)\, d\alpha = (1 - p)^2, \tag{4.81a}$$

where $p = Q(d/\sqrt{2\mathcal{N}_0})$ is the probability of error for two signals separated by a distance d. From symmetry,

$$P[\mathcal{C} \mid m_0] = P[\mathcal{C} \mid m_1] = P[\mathcal{C} \mid m_2] = P[\mathcal{C} \mid m_3]. \tag{4.81b}$$

Similarly,

$$P[\mathcal{C} \mid m_4] = P[\mathcal{C} \mid m_5] = \int_{-d/2}^{d/2} p_n(\alpha)\, d\alpha \int_{-d/2}^{\infty} p_n(\alpha)\, d\alpha$$

$$= (1 - 2p)(1 - p). \tag{4.81c}$$

Thus

$$P[\mathcal{C}] = \sum_{i=0}^{5} P[\mathcal{C} \mid m_i]\, P[m_i]$$

$$= \tfrac{4}{6}(1 - p)^2 + \tfrac{2}{6}(1 - 2p)(1 - p). \tag{4.81d}$$

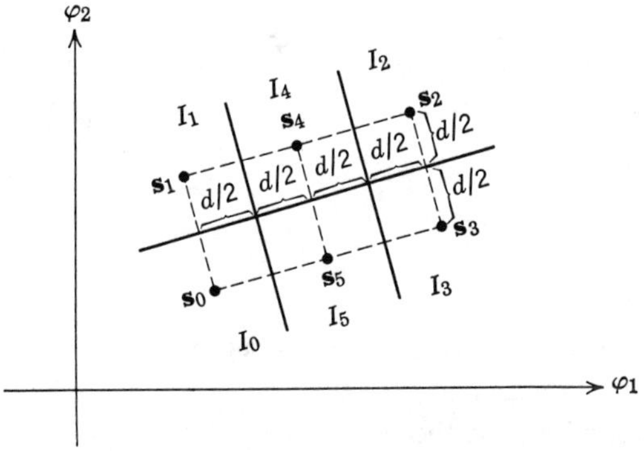

Figure 4.34 Rectangular decision regions.

Vertices of a hypercube. A special case of rectangular decision regions occurs when $M = 2^N$ equally likely messages are located on the vertices of an N-dimensional hypercube centered on the origin. This configuration is shown geometrically in Fig. 4.35 for $N = 2$ and 3. Analytically, we have

$$\mathbf{s}_i = (s_{i1}, s_{i2}, \ldots, s_{iN}); \quad i = 0, 1, \ldots, 2^N - 1, \tag{4.82a}$$

where

$$s_{ij} = \begin{cases} +\,d/2 \\ \text{or} & \text{for all } i, j. \\ -d/2 \end{cases} \tag{4.82b}$$

To evaluate the error probability, assume that the signal

$$\mathbf{s}_0 \triangleq \left(-\frac{d}{2}, -\frac{d}{2}, \ldots, -\frac{d}{2}\right) \tag{4.83}$$

is transmitted. We first claim that no error is made if

$$n_j < \frac{d}{2}; \qquad \text{for all } j = 1, 2, \ldots, N. \tag{4.84a}$$

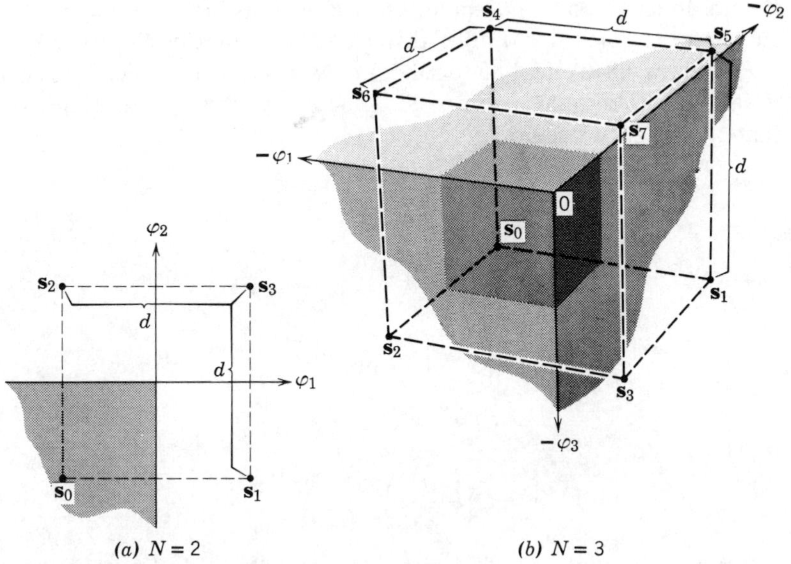

Figure 4.35 Signals on the vertices of two- and three-dimensional cubes: (*a*) $N = 2$; (*b*) $N = 3$. The decision regions I_0 are shaded.

The proof is immediate. When $\mathbf{r} = \boldsymbol{\rho}$ is received the jth component of $\boldsymbol{\rho} - \mathbf{s}_i$ is

$$(\rho_j - s_{ij}) = \begin{cases} n_j; & \text{if } s_{ij} = -\dfrac{d}{2} \\ n_j - d\,; & \text{if } s_{ij} = +\dfrac{d}{2}. \end{cases} \tag{4.84b}$$

Since Eq. 4.84a implies

$$d - n_j > n_j; \quad \text{all } j, \tag{4.84c}$$

it follows that

$$|\boldsymbol{\rho} - \mathbf{s}_i|^2 = \sum_{j=1}^{N} (\rho_j - s_{ij})^2 > \sum_{j=1}^{N} n_j^{\,2} = |\boldsymbol{\rho} - \mathbf{s}_0|^2 \tag{4.84d}$$

for all $\mathbf{s}_i \neq \mathbf{s}_0$ whenever Eq. 4.84a is satisfied.

We next claim that an error is made if, for at least one j,

$$n_j > \frac{d}{2}. \tag{4.85}$$

This follows from the fact that $\boldsymbol{\rho}$ is closer to $\mathbf{s}_j$ than to $\mathbf{s}_0$ whenever Eq. 4.85 is satisfied, where $\mathbf{s}_j$ denotes that signal with components $+d/2$ in the jth direction and $-d/2$ in all other directions. (Of course, $\boldsymbol{\rho}$ may be still closer to some signal other than $\mathbf{s}_j$, but it cannot be closest to $\mathbf{s}_0$.)

Equations 4.84d and 4.85 together imply that a correct decision is made if and only if Eq. 4.84a is satisfied. The probability of this event, given that $m = m_0$, is therefore

$$\begin{aligned} P[\mathcal{C} \mid m_0] &= P\left[\text{all } n_j < \frac{d}{2};\quad j = 1, 2, \ldots, N\right] \\ &= \prod_{j=1}^{N} P\left[n_j < \frac{d}{2}\right] \\ &= \left(1 - \int_{d/2}^{\infty} p_n(\alpha)\, d\alpha\right)^N \\ &= (1 - p)^N, \end{aligned}$$

in which,

$$p = Q\left(\frac{d}{\sqrt{2\mathcal{N}_0}}\right) \tag{4.86}$$

is again the probability of error for two equally likely signals separated by distance d. Finally, from symmetry

$$P[\mathcal{C} \mid m_i] = P[\mathcal{C} \mid m_0]; \qquad \text{for all } i, \tag{4.87a}$$

hence

$$P[\mathcal{C}] = (1 - p)^N. \tag{4.87b}$$

In order to express this result in terms of signal energy, we again recognize that the distance squared from the origin to each signal $\mathbf{s}_i$ is the same. The transmitted energy is therefore independent of i, hence may be designated E_s. From Eqs. 4.58b and 4.82b we have

$$|\mathbf{s}_i|^2 = \sum_{j=1}^{N} s_{ij}^{\;2} = N\frac{d^2}{4} = E_s, \tag{4.88a}$$

$$d = 2\sqrt{\frac{E_s}{N}}, \tag{4.88b}$$

and

$$p = Q\left(\sqrt{\frac{2E_s}{N\mathcal{N}_0}}\right). \tag{4.89}$$

The simple form of the result $P[\mathcal{C}] = (1 - p)^N$ suggests that a more immediate derivation may exist. Indeed one does. Note that the jth coordinate of the random signal $\mathbf{s}$ is a priori equally likely to be $+d/2$

or $-d/2$, independent of all other coordinates. Moreover, the noise n_j disturbing the jth coordinate is independent of the noise in all other coordinates. Hence, by the theorem on irrelevance, a decision may be made on the jth coordinate without examining any other coordinate. This single-coordinate decision corresponds to the problem of binary signals separated by distance d, for which the probability of correct decision is $1 - p$. Since in the original hypercube problem a correct decision is made if and only if a correct decision is made on every coordinate, and since these decisions are independent, it follows immediately that

$$P[\mathcal{C}] = (1 - p)^N. \tag{4.90}$$

Orthogonal and Related Signal Sets

Another class of equally likely signals for which the minimum attainable error probability is quite easy to calculate is the set of M equal-energy orthogonal vectors. Closely related to them are the simplex and bi-orthogonal signal sets. In treating these sets it is convenient to index the orthonormal axes $\{\varphi_j\}$ from $j = 0$ to $N - 1$ rather than from $j = 1$ to N, where N is the dimensionality of the signal space.

Orthogonal signals. When M equally likely and equal-energy signals are mutually orthogonal, so that $N = M$ and

$$\int_{-\infty}^{\infty} s_i(t)\, s_k(t)\, dt = \mathbf{s}_i \cdot \mathbf{s}_k = E_s\, \delta_{ik}; \qquad i, k = 0, 1, \ldots, M - 1, \tag{4.91}$$

the optimum decision region boundaries are no longer rectangular and are difficult to visualize. It is easier to proceed analytically. Letting $\boldsymbol{\varphi}_j$ denote the unit vector along the jth coordinate axis and

$$\mathbf{s}_j = \sqrt{E_s}\, \boldsymbol{\varphi}_j; \qquad j = 0, 1, \ldots, M - 1, \tag{4.92a}$$

we note that the squared distance from $\mathbf{s}_j$ to the received vector $\mathbf{r}$ is

$$\begin{aligned} |\mathbf{r} - \mathbf{s}_j|^2 &= |\mathbf{r}|^2 + |\mathbf{s}_j|^2 - 2\mathbf{r} \cdot (\sqrt{E_s}\, \boldsymbol{\varphi}_j) \\ &= |\mathbf{r}|^2 + E_s - 2r_j\sqrt{E_s}, \end{aligned} \tag{4.92b}$$

where r_j is the jth component of $\mathbf{r}$.

When $\mathbf{s}_k$ is transmitted, it follows that

$$|\mathbf{r} - \mathbf{s}_k|^2 < |\mathbf{r} - \mathbf{s}_i|^2; \qquad \text{all } i \neq k \tag{4.93a}$$

if and only if

$$-2r_k\sqrt{E_s} < -2r_i\sqrt{E_s},$$

i.e.

$$r_i < r_k; \qquad \text{all } i \neq k. \tag{4.93b}$$

As shown in Fig. 4.36, when $\mathbf{s}_0$ is transmitted we have

$$r_0 = n_0 + \sqrt{E_s} \tag{4.94a}$$

$$r_i = n_i; \qquad i > 0. \tag{4.94b}$$

Thus

$$\begin{aligned} P[\mathcal{C} \mid m_0, r_0 = \alpha] &= P[n_1 < \alpha, n_2 < \alpha, \ldots, n_{M-1} < \alpha] \\ &= (P[n_1 < \alpha])^{M-1}, \end{aligned} \tag{4.95a}$$

in which the last equality stems from the fact that all n_i are statistically

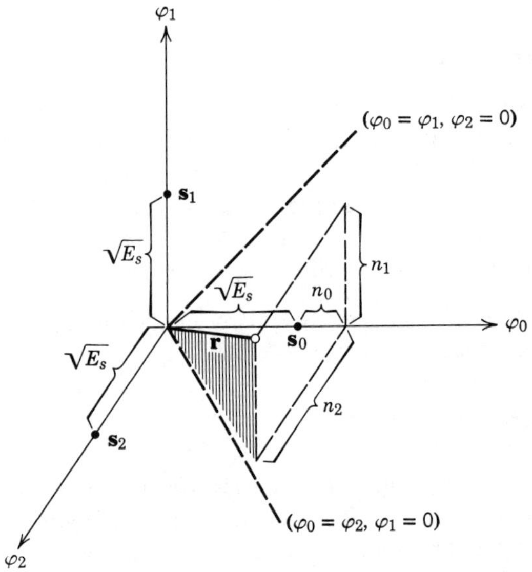

Figure 4.36 Three orthogonal signals. When $\mathbf{s}_0$ is transmitted, a correct decision is made if and only if n_1 and n_2 are both less than $\alpha = \sqrt{E_s} + n_0$. The heavy dashed lines are the intersections of the decision boundaries with the planes $\varphi_2 = 0$ and $\varphi_1 = 0$.

independent and identically distributed. Multiplying by

$$p_{r_0}(\alpha) = p_n(\alpha - \sqrt{E_s}) \tag{4.95b}$$

and integrating yields, for M equally likely equal-energy signals,

$$P[\mathcal{C} \mid m_0] = \int_{-\infty}^{\infty} p_n(\alpha - \sqrt{E_s})\, d\alpha \left[\int_{-\infty}^{\alpha} p_n(\beta)\, d\beta\right]^{M-1}, \tag{4.96a}$$

with

$$p_n(\alpha) \triangleq \frac{1}{\sqrt{\pi \mathcal{N}_0}}\, e^{-\alpha^2/\mathcal{N}_0} \tag{4.96b}$$

From symmetry,

$$P[\mathcal{C} \mid m_i] = P[\mathcal{C} \mid m_0] = P[\mathcal{C}], \tag{4.96c}$$

so that Eq. 4.96a is also the expression for the unconditional probability of a correct decision.

The integral in Eq. 4.96a cannot be simplified further but has been tabulated[36] as a function of M and $E_s/\mathcal{N}_0$; a plot of $P[\mathcal{E}] = 1 - P[\mathcal{C}]$ is provided in Fig. 4.37.

Simplex signals. A useful application of the energy minimization ideas discussed earlier is to M equally likely orthogonal signals. From Eqs.

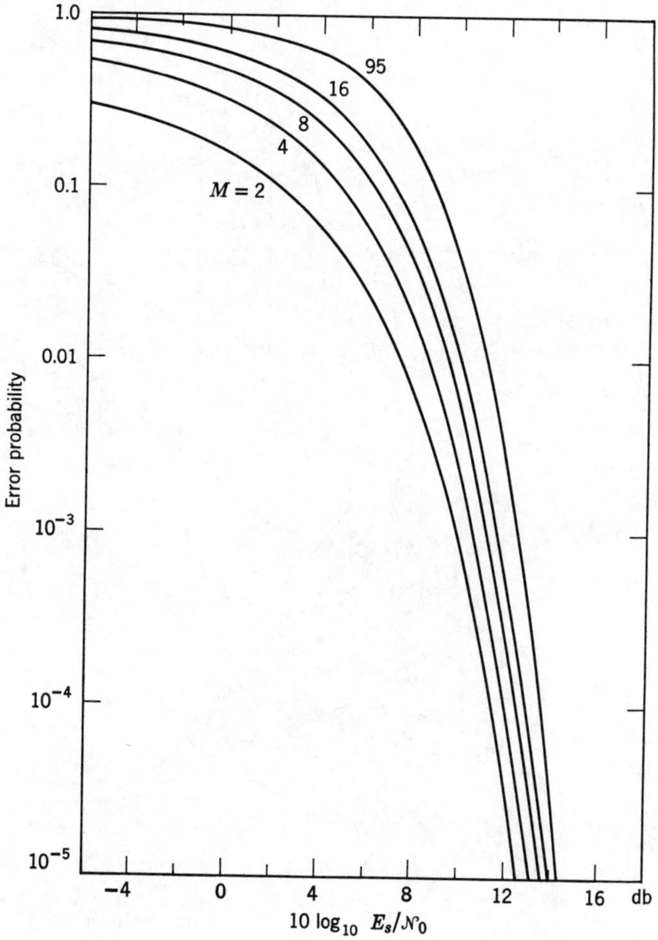

Figure 4.37 Error probability for M orthogonal signals.

4.74a and 4.92a the minimizing translation is

$$\mathbf{a} = \mathrm{E}[\mathbf{s}] = \frac{1}{M}\sum_{i=0}^{M-1}\mathbf{s}_i = \frac{\sqrt{E_s}}{M}\sum_{i=0}^{M-1}\boldsymbol{\varphi}_i. \tag{4.97a}$$

The resulting signal set

$$\{\mathbf{s}_i'\} = \{\mathbf{s}_i - \mathbf{a}\}; \qquad i = 0, 1, \ldots, M-1 \tag{4.97b}$$

is called a *simplex* and is the optimum[52] (minimum P[ℰ] set of M signals for use in white Gaussian noise when energy is constrained and $\mathrm{P}[m_i] = 1/M$ for all i. The simplex signals for $M = 2$, 3, and 4 are shown in Fig. 4.38. Since

$$\sum_{i=0}^{M-1}\mathbf{s}_i' = \sum_{i=0}^{M-1}\mathbf{s}_i - M\mathbf{a} = \mathbf{0}, \tag{4.98}$$

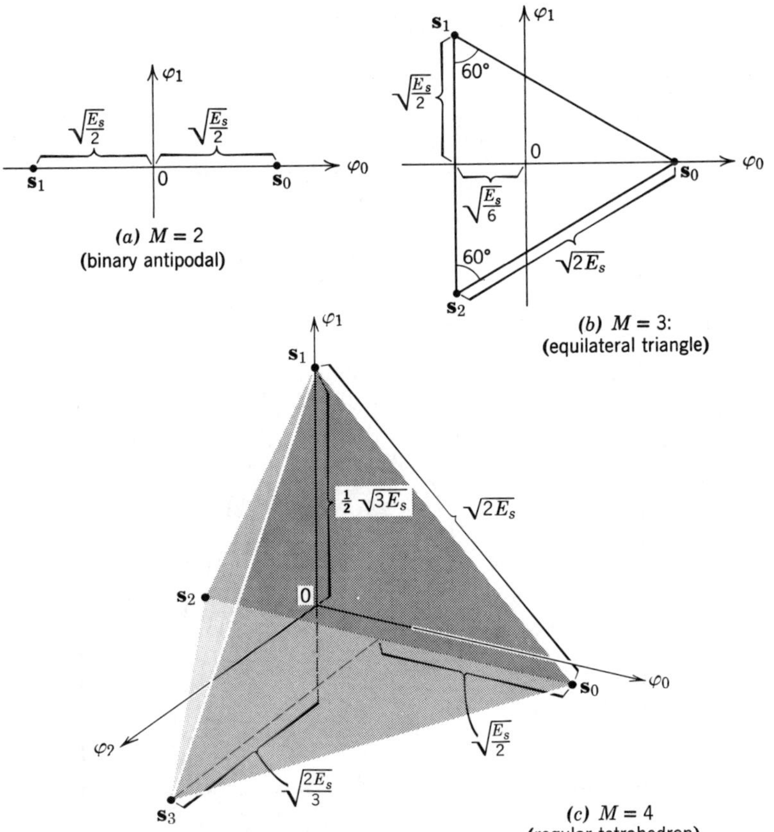

Figure 4.38 Simplex signals. All $\mathbf{s}_i$ are at distance $\sqrt{E_s(1 - 1/M)}$ from the origin.

any one of the $\{\mathbf{s}_i'\}$ can be expressed as a linear combination of the others. The M simplex signals therefore span a space of $N = M - 1$ dimensions. By virtue of the orthonormality of the $\{\boldsymbol{\varphi}_j\}$, for all i, k

$$\begin{aligned}\mathbf{s}_i' \cdot \mathbf{s}_k' &= (\mathbf{s}_i - \mathbf{a}) \cdot (\mathbf{s}_k - \mathbf{a}) \\ &= (\mathbf{s}_i \cdot \mathbf{s}_k) - \mathbf{a} \cdot (\mathbf{s}_k + \mathbf{s}_i) + |\mathbf{a}|^2 \\ &= E_s\,\delta_{ik} - 2\frac{E_s}{M} + \frac{E_s}{M} \\ &= \begin{cases} E_s\left(1 - \dfrac{1}{M}\right); & \text{for } i = k \\ -\dfrac{E_s}{M}; & \text{otherwise.} \end{cases}\end{aligned} \tag{4.99}$$

We see that each signal in a simplex has the same energy, which is reduced by the factor $(1 - 1/M)$ from that required for the orthogonal signals, with *no change in error probability*. (Translations do not effect $P[\mathcal{E}]$.) When $M = 2$, the saving is 3 db; for large M the saving is negligible.

Equation 4.99 may be used as the definition of a simplex. We note that a set of M vectors $\{\mathbf{s}_i'\}$ satisfying Eq. 4.99 may be transformed to a set of orthogonal vectors by adding a vector $\sqrt{E_s/M}\,\boldsymbol{\psi}$ to each $\mathbf{s}_i'$, where $\boldsymbol{\psi}$ is any unit vector orthogonal to all of the $\{\mathbf{s}_i'\}$.

Biorthogonal signals. The final specific signal configuration considered here is the biorthogonal set, illustrated for $N = 2$ and 3 in Fig. 4.39. This signal set can be obtained from an original orthogonal set of N signals by augmenting it with the negative of each signal. Obviously, for the biorthogonal set

$$M = 2N. \tag{4.100}$$

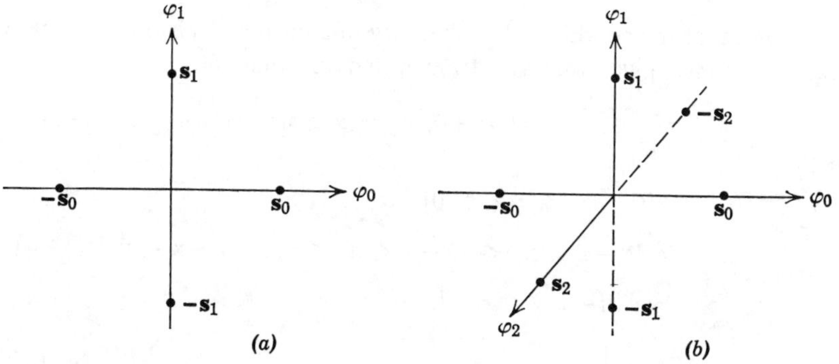

Figure 4.39 Biorthogonal signals, all at distance $\sqrt{E_s}$ from origin.

We denote the additional signals by $-\mathbf{s}_j$, $j = 0, 1, \ldots, N-1$, and assume each signal has energy E_s.

It is clear from Fig. 4.40 that the received message point is closer to $\mathbf{s}_0$ than to $-\mathbf{s}_0$ if and only if

$$r_0 > 0. \tag{4.101a}$$

Also, $\mathbf{r}$ is closer to $\mathbf{s}_0$ than to $\mathbf{s}_i$ if and only if

$$r_0 > r_i; \qquad i > 0, \tag{4.101b}$$

and $\mathbf{r}$ is closer to $\mathbf{s}_0$ than to $-\mathbf{s}_i$ if and only if

$$r_0 > -r_i; \qquad i > 0. \tag{4.101c}$$

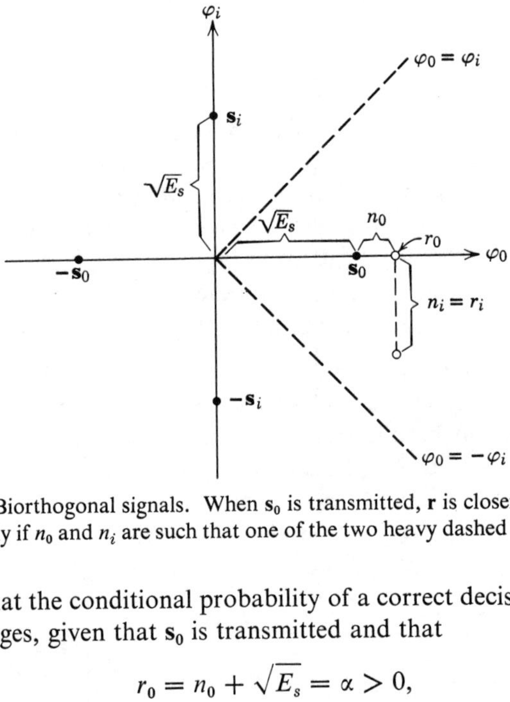

Figure 4.40 Biorthogonal signals. When $\mathbf{s}_0$ is transmitted, $\mathbf{r}$ is closer to $\pm\mathbf{s}_i$ than it is to $\mathbf{s}_0$ if and only if n_0 and n_i are such that one of the two heavy dashed lines is crossed.

It follows that the conditional probability of a correct decision for equally likely messages, given that $\mathbf{s}_0$ is transmitted and that

$$r_0 = n_0 + \sqrt{E_s} = \alpha > 0, \tag{4.102a}$$

is just

$$\begin{aligned} &P[\mathcal{C} \mid m_0, r_0 = \alpha > 0] \\ &= P[-\alpha < n_1 < \alpha, -\alpha < n_2 < \alpha, \ldots, -\alpha < n_{N-1} < \alpha] \\ &= \{P[-\alpha < n < \alpha]\}^{N-1} \\ &= \left[\int_{-\alpha}^{\alpha} p_n(\beta)\, d\beta\right]^{N-1}. \end{aligned} \tag{4.102b}$$

The notation is that of Eq. 4.96b. Multiplying by $p_{r_0}(\alpha) = p_n(\alpha - \sqrt{E_s})$ and integrating over α from 0 to ∞ (because of the condition of Eq. 4.102a), we obtain

$$P[\mathcal{C} \mid m_0] = \int_0^\infty p_n(\alpha - \sqrt{E_s})\, d\alpha \left[\int_{-\alpha}^{\alpha} p_n(\beta)\, d\beta\right]^{N-1}. \qquad (4.103)$$

Once again, by virtue of symmetry and the equal a priori probability of the $\{m_i\}$, Eq. 4.103 is also the expression for $P[\mathcal{C}]$. Noting that $N - 1 = (M/2) - 1$, we have†

$$P[\mathcal{C}] = \int_0^\infty p_n(\alpha - \sqrt{E_s})\, d\alpha \left[1 - 2\int_{\alpha}^{\infty} p_n(\beta)\, d\beta\right]^{\frac{M}{2} - 1}. \qquad (4.104)$$

The difference in error performance for M biorthogonal and M orthogonal signals is negligible when M and E_s/N_0 are large, but the number of dimensions required is reduced by one half in the biorthogonal case.

Completely Symmetric Signal Sets and A Priori Knowledge

In almost all of the specific cases we have considered—in particular, the binary, orthogonal, simplex, biorthogonal, and vertices-of-a-hypercube signal sets—the error probability calculation is greatly simplified by the "complete symmetry" of the geometrical configuration of the $\{\mathbf{s}_i\}$. By *complete symmetry* we mean that any relabeling of the signal points can be undone by a rotation of coordinates, translation, and/or inversion of axes. As a counterexample, the signals of Fig. 4.34 are *not* completely symmetric.

Given complete symmetry, the condition

$$P[m_i] = \frac{1}{M}; \qquad \text{for all } i \qquad (4.105)$$

leads to congruent decision regions $\{I_i\}$ and thus to a conditional probability of correct decision that is independent of the particular signal transmitted:

$$P[\mathcal{C} \mid m_i] = \text{a constant}; \qquad \text{for all } i. \qquad (4.106a)$$

If such a congruent-decision-region receiver is used with message probabilities $\{P[m_i]\}$ that are not all the same, the resulting probability of correct decision is

$$P[\mathcal{C}] = \sum_{i=0}^{M-1} P[m_i]\, P[\mathcal{C} \mid m_i] = P[\mathcal{C} \mid m_0], \qquad (4.106b)$$

which is unchanged from the equally likely message case. Thus the error performance of a congruent-decision-region receiver is invariant to the

† The integral of Eq. 4.104 is tabulated and plotted in reference 36.

actual source statistics $\{P[m_i]\}$. (Of course, if the source statistics are known in advance, the probability of correct decision can be increased by the use of a noncongruent-decision-region receiver designed in accordance with Eq. 4.71b.)

Invariance to message probabilities can be exploited by a communication system designer, who seldom knows in advance the exact input statistics of the source. If the transmitter is designed with completely symmetric signals and an optimum receiver is designed on the assumption that all messages are equally likely, Eqs. 4.106 will be satisfied and the error probability of the system can be specified independent of the message source to which it is connected. A receiver designed to be optimum under the assumption of equally likely messages is called a *maximum likelihood receiver*. (See also the discussion following Eq. 4.9.)

Minimax receivers. The foregoing discussion provides a powerful argument in support of a design assumption that all a priori message probabilities are equal. Even more cogently, with completely symmetric signals this assumption leads to a receiver design that is *minimax*, a term we now define.

For a fixed transmitter and channel, the probability of error depends only on the receiver and the message probabilities. For a given receiver (with transmitter and channel fixed) the probability of error depends only on the message source statistics and reaches a maximum value for some choice of these statistics. This maximum value of the $P[\mathcal{E}]$ is a useful criterion of goodness for the receiver in the absence of a priori knowledge of the $\{P[m_i]\}$: it represents a guaranteed minimum performance level beneath which the system will never operate, regardless of the statistics of the message source to which it may be connected. With this criterion, the receiver with the *smallest maximum* $P[\mathcal{E}]$ is most desirable. It is called the *minimax receiver*.

The argument that the maximum likelihood receiver is minimax when the $\{\mathbf{s}_i\}$ are completely symmetric is very simple. First, this receiver yields a probability of error that is independent of the actual $\{P[m_i]\}$ with which it may be used. Second, by the definition of optimum, any other receiver yields a greater probability of error when used with equally likely signals, hence must have a larger maximum. This concludes the proof.

Union Bound on the Probability of Error

An approximation to the $P[\mathcal{E} \mid m_i]$ for any set of M equally likely signals $\{\mathbf{s}_i\}$ in white Gaussian noise is obtained by noting that an error occurs when $\mathbf{s}_i$ is transmitted if and only if the received vector $\mathbf{r}$ is closer to at least one signal $\mathbf{s}_k$, $k \neq i$, than it is to $\mathbf{s}_i$. If $\mathcal{E}_{ik}$ is used to denote the event that $\mathbf{r}$ is closer to $\mathbf{s}_k$ than to $\mathbf{s}_i$ when $\mathbf{s}_i$ is transmitted, we have

$$P[\mathcal{E} \mid m_i] = P[\mathcal{E}_{i0} \cup \mathcal{E}_{i1} \cup \cdots \cup \mathcal{E}_{i,i-1} \cup \mathcal{E}_{i,i+1} \cup \cdots \cup \mathcal{E}_{i,M-1}]. \quad (4.107)$$

From Eq. 2.10 the probability of a finite union of events is bounded above by the sum of the probabilities of the constituent events, a result made geometrically evident in Fig. 4.41. Thus

$$P[\mathcal{E} \mid m_i] \leqslant \sum_{\substack{k=0 \\ (k \neq i)}}^{M-1} P[\mathcal{E}_{ik}]. \quad (4.108)$$

Note that $P[\mathcal{E}_{ik}]$ is not in general equal to $P[\hat{m} = m_k \mid m_i]$, because the latter is the probability that $\mathbf{r} = \mathbf{s}_i + \mathbf{n}$ is closer to $\mathbf{s}_k$ than to *every* other

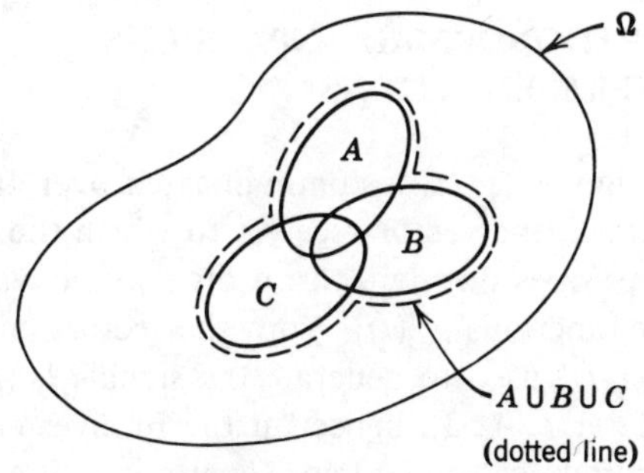

Figure 4.41 Venn diagram. It is apparent that $P[A \cup B \cup C] \leqslant P[A] + P[B] + P[C]$.

signal vector. To emphasize that $P[\mathcal{E}_{ik}]$ depends only on two vectors, $\mathbf{s}_i$ and $\mathbf{s}_k$, hereafter we write $P_2[\mathbf{s}_i, \mathbf{s}_k]$ in place of $P[\mathcal{E}_{ik}]$. Equation 4.108 then becomes

$$P[\mathcal{E} \mid m_i] \leqslant \sum_{\substack{k=0 \\ (k \neq i)}}^{M-1} P_2[\mathbf{s}_i, \mathbf{s}_k]. \quad (4.109)$$

We next observe that $P_2[\mathbf{s}_i, \mathbf{s}_k]$ is just the probability of error for a system that uses the vectors $\mathbf{s}_i$ and $\mathbf{s}_k$ as signals to communicate one of two equally likely messages. The bound of Eq. 4.109, and this interpretation of $P_2[\mathbf{s}_i, \mathbf{s}_k]$, holds for channels more general than that of additive Gaussian noise. For the Gaussian channel, however, the expression for $P_2[\mathbf{s}_i, \mathbf{s}_k]$ is particularly simple; from Eq. 4.76b, we have

$$P_2[\mathbf{s}_i, \mathbf{s}_k] = Q\left(\frac{|\mathbf{s}_i - \mathbf{s}_k|}{\sqrt{2\mathcal{N}_0}}\right). \quad (4.110)$$

The union bound of Eq. 4.109 is especially useful when the signal set $\{\mathbf{s}_i\}$ is completely symmetric, for in this case the unconditioned error probability $P[\mathcal{E}]$ equals $P[\mathcal{E} \mid m_i]$ and most of the terms $\{P_2[\mathbf{s}_i, \mathbf{s}_k]\}$ are identical. The following examples illustrate the application of the bound.

Orthogonal Signals:

$$P[\mathcal{E}] = P[\mathcal{E} \mid m_i] \leqslant (M - 1)Q(\sqrt{E_s/\mathcal{N}_0}). \tag{4.111}$$

Biorthogonal Signals:

$$P[\mathcal{E}] = P[\mathcal{E} \mid m_i] \leqslant (M - 2)Q(\sqrt{E_s/\mathcal{N}_0}) + Q(\sqrt{2E_s/\mathcal{N}_0}). \tag{4.112}$$

In many instances the union bound is a useful approximation to the actual $P[\mathcal{E}]$. It becomes increasingly tight for fixed M as $E_s/\mathcal{N}_0$ is increased.

APPENDIX 4A ORTHONORMAL EXPANSIONS AND VECTOR REPRESENTATIONS

When one of M signals $\{s_i(t)\}$ is communicated over an additive white Gaussian noise channel, the vector receiver to which the optimum waveform receiver reduces does not depend on the specific waveshapes of the N orthonormal base functions $\{\varphi_j(t)\}$. Only the vectors $\{\mathbf{s}_i\}$ are important; the particular set $\{\varphi_j(t)\}$ used to generate the signals $\{s_i(t)\}$ has no effect on the decision rule (Eq. 4.53), hence on the receiver error probability. In the design of communication systems for use in white Gaussian noise, the problem is to choose a good set of vectors $\{\mathbf{s}_i\}$ and a convenient set of functions $\{\varphi_j(t)\}$ that will propagate satisfactorily over the channel.

To prove that the transmitter structure of Fig. 4.12 and the correlation and matched filter receivers of Figs. 4.18 and 4.19 are completely general, we must show that *any* set of M finite-energy waveforms can always be expressed as

$$s_i(t) = \sum_{j=1}^{N} s_{ij}\, \varphi_j(t); \qquad i = 0, 1, \ldots, M - 1, \tag{4A.1a}$$

in which the waveforms $\{\varphi_j(t)\}$ are an appropriately chosen set of orthonormal functions:

$$\int_{-\infty}^{\infty} \varphi_l(t)\, \varphi_j(t)\, dt = \delta_{lj}; \qquad 1 \leqslant l, j \leqslant N. \tag{4A.1b}$$

In this appendix we prove the generality of Eq. 4A.1 and discuss some of its implications.

The Gram-Schmidt orthogonalization procedure. One convenient way in which an appropriate orthonormal set $\{\varphi_j(t)\}$ can be obtained from any given signal set $\{s_i(t)\}$ is by the Gram-Schmidt[43] orthogonalization procedure described in the following sequence of steps.

1. First consider $s_0(t)$. If $s_0(t) \equiv 0$ (has zero energy), renumber the signals. For $s_0(t) \not\equiv 0$, set

$$\varphi_1(t) = \frac{s_0(t)}{\sqrt{E_0}}, \tag{4A.2a}$$

where

$$E_0 \triangleq \int_{-\infty}^{\infty} s_0^2(t)\, dt. \tag{4A.2b}$$

Then $\varphi_1(t)$ is a waveform with unit energy. Since $s_0(t) = \sqrt{E_0}\,\varphi_1(t)$, the coefficient $s_{01} = \sqrt{E_0}$. The associated vector $\mathbf{s}_0$ is shown in Fig. 4A.1*a*.

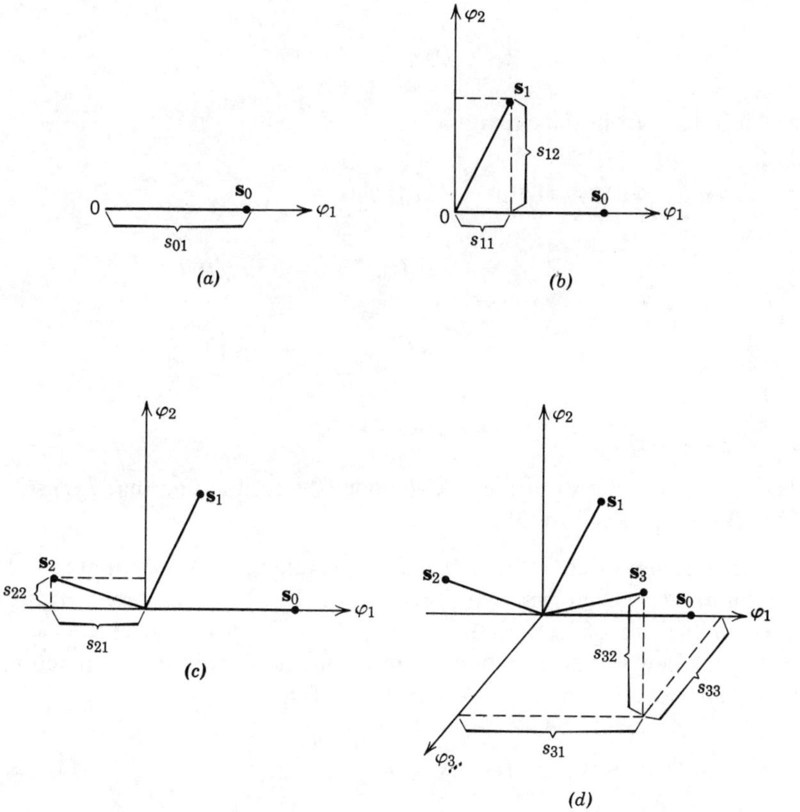

Figure 4A.1 Vectors obtained by the Gram-Schmidt procedure: $M = 4$, $N = 3$. Here $\mathbf{s}_2$ can be expressed as a linear combination of φ_1 and φ_2, so that $\theta_2(t) \equiv 0$.

2. Second, define the auxiliary function $\theta_1(t)$ as

$$\theta_1(t) = s_1(t) - s_{11}\,\varphi_1(t), \tag{4A.3a}$$

where

$$s_{11} \triangleq \int_{-\infty}^{\infty} s_1(t)\,\varphi_1(t)\,dt. \tag{4A.3b}$$

If $\theta_1(t) \not\equiv 0$, set

$$\varphi_2(t) = \frac{\theta_1(t)}{\sqrt{E_{\theta_1}}}, \tag{4A.3c}$$

where

$$E_{\theta_1} \triangleq \int_{-\infty}^{\infty} \theta_1^{\,2}(t)\,dt. \tag{4A.3d}$$

Then $\varphi_2(t)$ also has unit energy, and $s_{12} = \sqrt{E_{\theta_1}}$. Furthermore,

$$\int_{-\infty}^{\infty} \varphi_2(t)\,\varphi_1(t)\,dt = 0, \tag{4A.3e}$$

which follows from the equations

$$\begin{aligned}\sqrt{E_{\theta_1}}\int_{-\infty}^{\infty}\varphi_2(t)\,\varphi_1(t)\,dt &= \int_{-\infty}^{\infty}\theta_1(t)\,\varphi_1(t)\,dt \\ &= \int_{-\infty}^{\infty}[s_1(t) - s_{11}\,\varphi_1(t)]\varphi_1(t)\,dt \\ &= \int_{-\infty}^{\infty}s_1(t)\,\varphi_1(t)\,dt - s_{11}\int_{-\infty}^{\infty}\varphi_1^{\,2}(t)\,dt \\ &= s_{11} - s_{11} = 0.\end{aligned}$$

The vector $\mathbf{s}_1$ is shown in Fig. 4A.1*b* under the assumption that $\theta_1(t) \not\equiv 0$. If $\theta_1(t) \equiv 0$, proceed to (3).

3. The general step in the procedure is as follows. Assume that $(l - 1)$ orthonormal waveforms $\varphi_1(t), \varphi_2(t), \ldots, \varphi_{l-1}(t)$ have been defined through the use of $s_0(t), s_1(t), \ldots, s_{k-1}(t)$. It is clear that $(l - 1) \leqslant k$, since each new signal introduces at most one new orthonormal function. Now consider $s_k(t)$ and define the auxiliary function

$$\theta_k(t) = s_k(t) - \sum_{j=1}^{l-1} s_{kj}\,\varphi_j(t), \tag{4A.4a}$$

where

$$s_{kj} \triangleq \int_{-\infty}^{\infty} s_k(t)\,\varphi_j(t)\,dt; \qquad j = 1, 2, \ldots, l-1. \tag{4A.4b}$$

If $\theta_k(t) \not\equiv 0$, set

$$\varphi_l(t) = \frac{\theta_k(t)}{\sqrt{E_{\theta_k}}}, \tag{4A.4c}$$

where

$$E_{\theta_k} \triangleq \int_{-\infty}^{\infty} \theta_k^2(t)\, dt. \tag{4A.4d}$$

Clearly, $\varphi_l(t)$ has unit energy, and $s_{kl} = \sqrt{E_{\theta_k}}$. Also,

$$\int_{-\infty}^{\infty} \varphi_l(t)\, \varphi_m(t)\, dt = 0; \qquad \text{for } 1 \leqslant m \leqslant l - 1, \tag{4A.4e}$$

which follows from the equations

$$\begin{aligned}
\sqrt{E_{\theta_k}} \int_{-\infty}^{\infty} \varphi_k(t)\, \varphi_m(t)\, dt &= \int_{-\infty}^{\infty} \theta_k(t)\, \varphi_m(t)\, dt \\
&= \int_{-\infty}^{\infty} \left[s_k(t) - \sum_{j=1}^{l-1} s_{kj}\, \varphi_j(t) \right] \varphi_m(t)\, dt \\
&= \int_{-\infty}^{\infty} s_k(t)\, \varphi_m(t)\, dt - \sum_{j=1}^{l-1} s_{kj} \int_{-\infty}^{\infty} \varphi_j(t)\, \varphi_m(t)\, dt \\
&= s_{km} - \sum_{j=1}^{l-1} s_{kj}\, \delta_{jm} \\
&= s_{km} - s_{km} = 0; \qquad 1 \leqslant m \leqslant l - 1.
\end{aligned}$$

The foregoing procedure can be continued until all M signals $\{s_i(t)\}$ have been exhausted, as shown in Figs. 4A.1*c*, *d*. There will then have been established $N \leqslant M$ orthonormal waveforms $\{\varphi_j(t)\}$ with the equality holding if and only if all M signals are *linearly independent*—that is, if and only if no one signal can be expressed as a linear combination of the others. The integer N is called the *dimensionality* of the signal space defined by the $\{s_i(t)\}$. By the nature of the construction, it is clear that each $s_i(t)$, $i = 0, 1, \ldots, M - 1$, can indeed be expressed as a linear combination of the $\{\varphi_j(t)\}$ and thus that Eq. 4A.1 is satisfied.

A simple example of the Gram-Schmidt procedure is provided by the four waveforms shown in Fig. 4A.2. Starting with $s_0(t)$, we have

$$E_0 = 4 + 4 + 4 = 12,$$

and

$$\varphi_1(t) = \frac{s_0(t)}{\sqrt{E_0}} = \frac{s_0(t)}{\sqrt{12}}, \qquad s_{01} = \sqrt{12}.$$

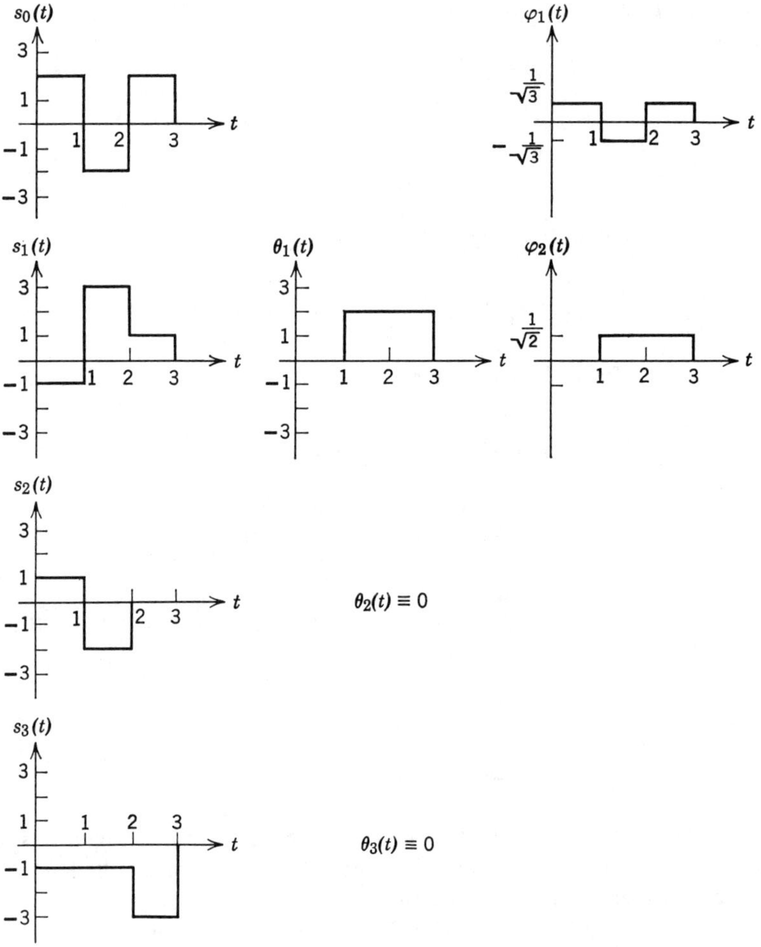

Figure 4A.2 An illustration of the Gram-Schmidt procedure.

Next, introducing $s_1(t)$, we have

$$s_{11} = \int_{-\infty}^{\infty} s_1(t)\, \varphi_1(t)\, dt = \sqrt{\tfrac{1}{3}}(-1 - 3 + 1) = -\sqrt{3}$$

$$\theta_1(t) = s_1(t) + \sqrt{3}\, \varphi_1(t)$$

$$E_{\theta_1} = 8, \qquad s_{12} = \sqrt{8}$$

$$\varphi_2(t) = \frac{1}{\sqrt{8}}\, \theta_1(t).$$

Introducing $s_2(t)$, we obtain

$$s_{21} = \int_{-\infty}^{\infty} s_2(t)\, \varphi_1(t)\, dt = \sqrt{3},$$

$$s_{22} = \int_{-\infty}^{\infty} s_2(t)\, \varphi_2(t)\, dt = -\sqrt{2},$$

$$\theta_2(t) = s_2(t) - \sqrt{3}\, \varphi_1(t) + \sqrt{2}\, \varphi_2(t) \equiv 0.$$

Finally, introducing $s_3(t)$, we have

$$s_{31} = \int_{-\infty}^{\infty} s_3(t)\, \varphi_1(t)\, dt = -\sqrt{3},$$

$$s_{32} = \int_{-\infty}^{\infty} s_3(t)\, \varphi_2(t)\, dt = -2\sqrt{2},$$

$$\theta_3(t) = s_3(t) + \sqrt{3}\, \varphi_1(t) + 2\sqrt{2}\, \varphi_2(t) \equiv 0.$$

Thus the four signals $\{s_i(t)\}$ span a space of two dimensions, and the vector representations are

$$\begin{aligned} s_0(t) &= \sqrt{12}\, \varphi_1(t) & \mathbf{s}_0 &= (\sqrt{12}, 0), \\ s_1(t) &= -\sqrt{3}\, \varphi_1(t) + \sqrt{8}\, \varphi_2(t) & \mathbf{s}_1 &= (-\sqrt{3}, \sqrt{8}), \\ s_2(t) &= +\sqrt{3}\, \varphi_1(t) - \sqrt{2}\, \varphi_2(t) & \mathbf{s}_2 &= (\sqrt{3}, -\sqrt{2}), \\ s_3(t) &= -\sqrt{3}\, \varphi_1(t) - \sqrt{8}\, \varphi_2(t) & \mathbf{s}_3 &= (-\sqrt{3}, -\sqrt{8}), \end{aligned} \tag{4A.5}$$

as shown in Fig. 4A.3.

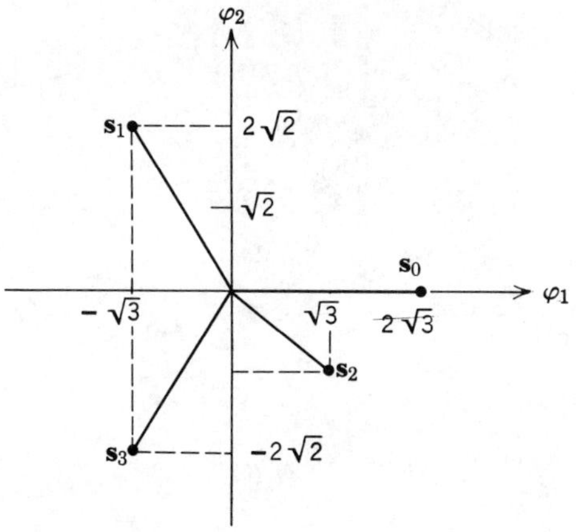

Figure 4A.3 A vector representation of the $\{s_i(t)\}$ of Fig. 4A.2.

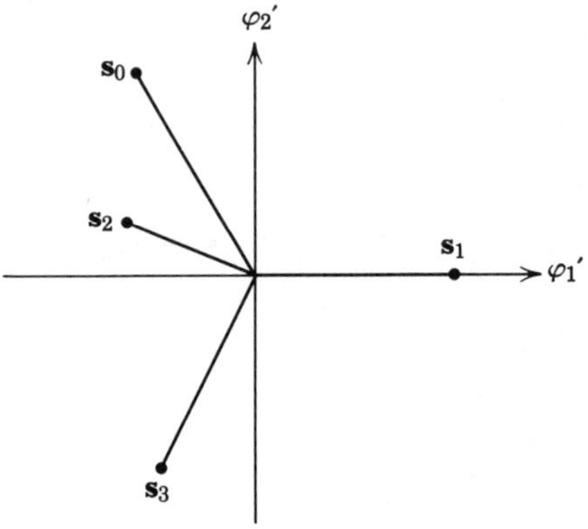

Figure 4A.4 An alternative vector diagram for the $\{s_i(t)\}$ of Fig. 4A.2.

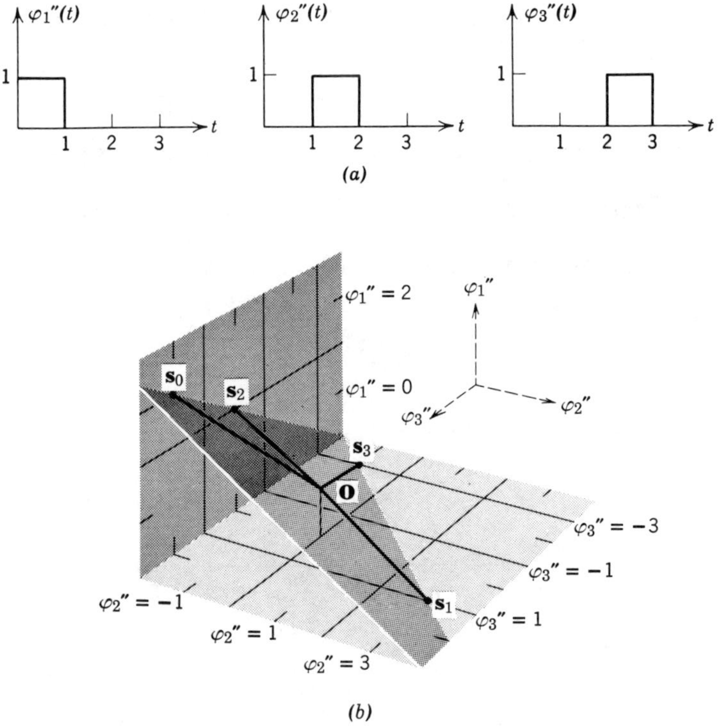

Figure 4A.5 A third vector representation of the signals of Fig. 4A.2

We have shown that it is always possible to represent a finite set of signals $\{s_i(t)\}$ by means of at least one finite weighted sum of orthonormal functions $\{\varphi_j(t)\}$ and therefore that the derivation of the optimum receivers of Figs. 4.18 and 4.19 is always valid.

Note that any given set $\{s_i(t)\}$ can be expanded in many different orthonormal sets, all of which ultimately yield the same receiver, hence the same decisions and the same probability of error. For example, if the Gram-Schmidt procedure for the signals of Fig. 4A.2 were carried out by considering signals in the order $s_1(t)$, $s_2(t)$, $s_3(t)$, $s_0(t)$, a different pair of orthonormal functions $\varphi_1'(t)$, $\varphi_2'(t)$, and a different set of coefficients $\{s_{ij}'\}$ would have been obtained. In particular, $\mathbf{s}_1$ would lie on the φ_1'-axis and $\mathbf{s}_2$ would have a positive projection on the φ_2'-axis, as shown in Fig. 4A.4. Alternatively, a set $\{\varphi_j''(t)\}$ might be obtained without use of the Gram-Schmidt procedure, although the resulting number of functions might be larger than the dimensionality, N. Such a set is shown in Fig. 4A.5*a* and the corresponding vectors in Fig. 4A.5*b*. Note that the four signal points remain coplanar and have the same relative positions. The important fact is that the signal points $\{\mathbf{s}_i\}$ always retain the same geometrical configuration, regardless of the particular set of coordinates in terms of which they are described.

PROBLEMS

4.1 The random variable n in Fig. P4.1*a* is Gaussian, with zero mean. If one of two equally likely messages is transmitted, using the signals of Fig. P4.1*b*, an optimum receiver yields $P[\mathcal{E}] = 0.01$.

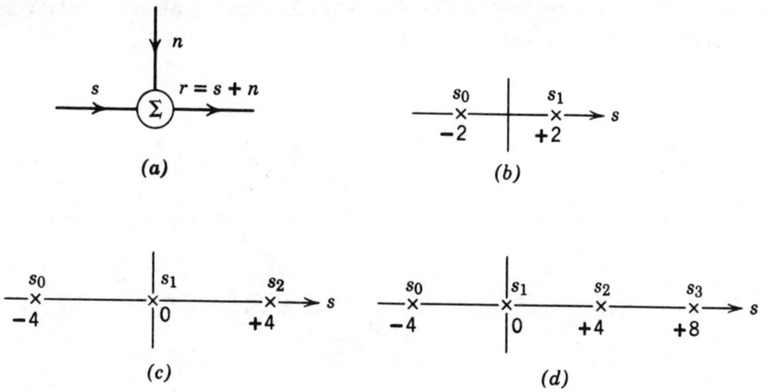

Figure P4.1

a. What is the minimum attainable probability of error, $P[\mathcal{E}]_{min}$, when the channel of Fig. P4.1*a* is used with three equally likely messages and the signals of (*c*)? With four equally likely messages and the signals of (*d*)?

b. How do the answers to part (a) change if it is known that $\bar{n} = 1$ rather than 0?

4.2 One of four equally likely messages is to be communicated over a vector channel which adds a (different) statistically independent zero-mean Gaussian random variable with variance $\mathcal{N}_0/2$ to each transmitted vector component. Assume that the transmitter uses the signal vectors shown in Fig. P4.2 and express the $P[\mathcal{E}]$ produced by an optimum receiver in terms of the function $Q(\alpha)$.

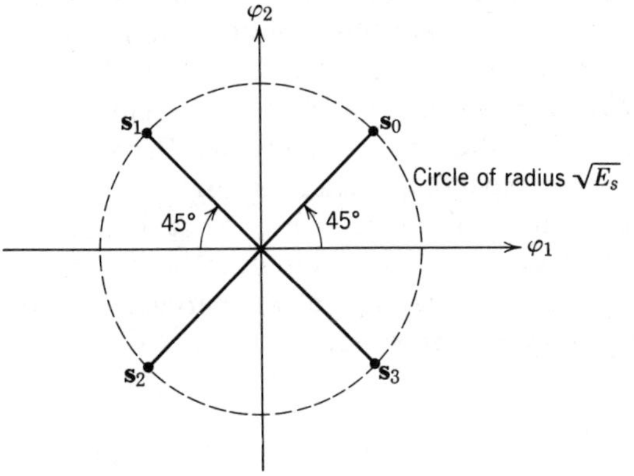

Figure P4.2

4.3 It is known that $P[\mathcal{E}]_{min} = q$ when the two signal vectors $\mathbf{s}_0$ and $\mathbf{s}_1$ shown in Fig. P4.3*a* are transmitted with equal probability over a channel disturbed by additive white Gaussian noise. Compute $P[\mathcal{E}]_{min}$ in terms of q, θ, and l when the nine vectors indicated by ×'s in Fig. P4.3*b* are used as signals with equal probability over the same channel.

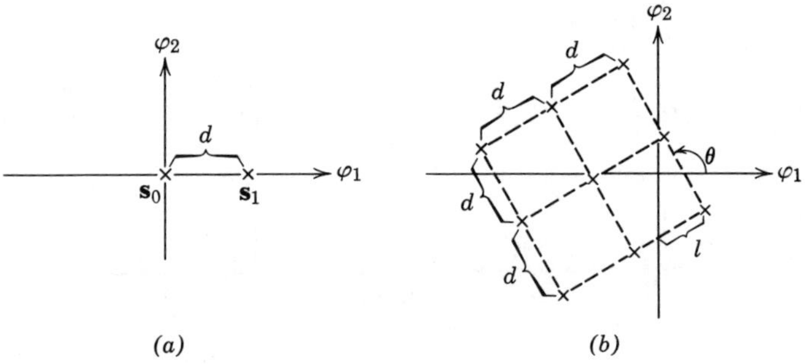

Figure P4.3

4.4 One of 16 equally likely messages is to be communicated over an additive Gaussian noise channel with $\mathcal{S}_n(f) = \mathcal{N}_0/2$. The transmitter utilizes a signal set $\{s_i(t)\}$ whose vector representation is indicated by $\times$'s in Fig. P4.4.

a. Draw the optimum decision regions.

b. Determine $P[\mathcal{E}]_{\min}$ in terms of $Q(\alpha)$.

c. Find a set of 16 two-dimensional signal vectors (not necessarily optimum) such that the transmitted energy is never greater than E_s but for which the attainable $P[\mathcal{E}]$ is less than the answer to part (b).

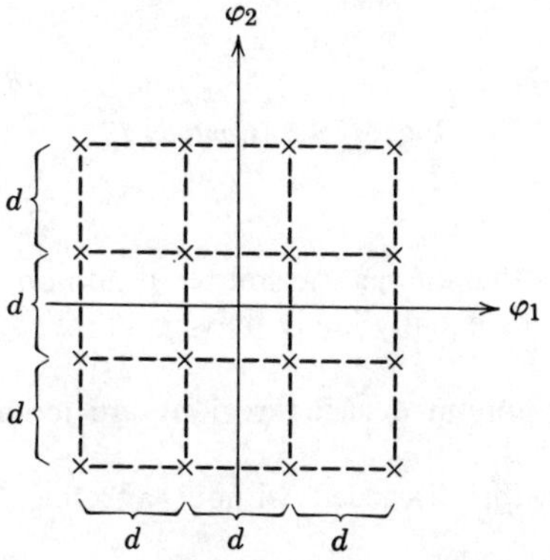

Figure P4.4

4.5 One of the two signals $s_0 = -1$, $s_1 = +1$ is transmitted over the channel shown in Fig. P4.5*a*. The two noise random variables n_1 and n_2 are statistically independent of the transmitted signal and of each other. Their density functions are

$$p_{n_1}(\alpha) = p_{n_2}(\alpha) = \tfrac{1}{2}\, e^{-|\alpha|}.$$

a. Prove that the optimum decision regions for equally likely messages are as shown in Fig. P4.5*b*. *Hint.* Use geometric reasoning and the fact that $|\rho_1 - 1| + |\rho_2 - 1| = a + b$, as shown on the next page in Fig. P4.5*d*.

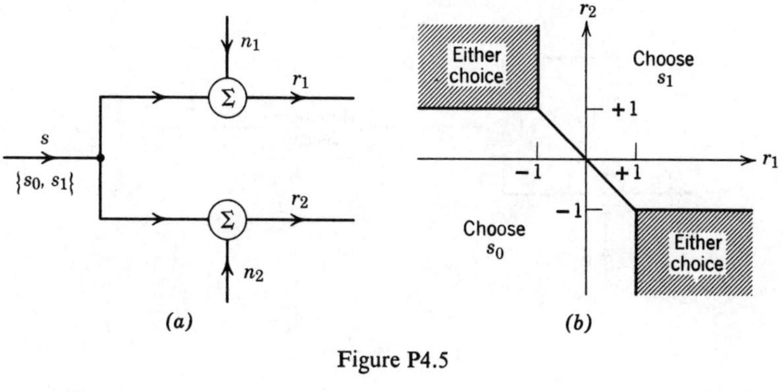

Figure P4.5

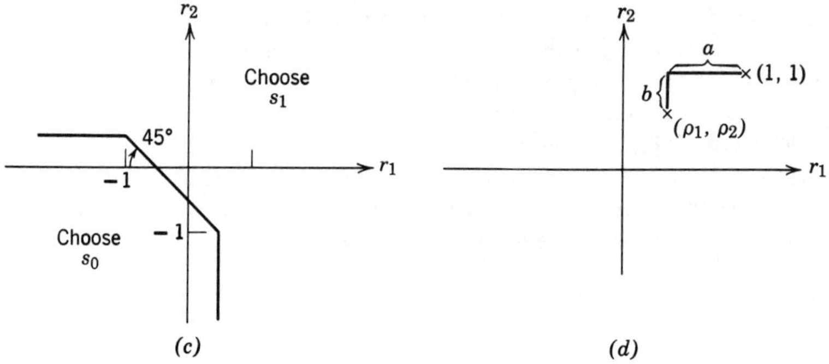

Figure P4.5 (*Continued*)

b. A receiver decides that s_1 was transmitted if and only if $(r_1 + r_2) > 0$. Is this receiver optimum for equally likely messages? What is its probability of error?

c. Prove that the optimum decision regions are modified as indicated in Fig. P4.5*c* when $P[s_1] > \frac{1}{2}$.

d. The channel may be discarded without affecting $P[\mathcal{E}]_{\min}$ if $P[s_1] \geqslant q$. Evaluate q.

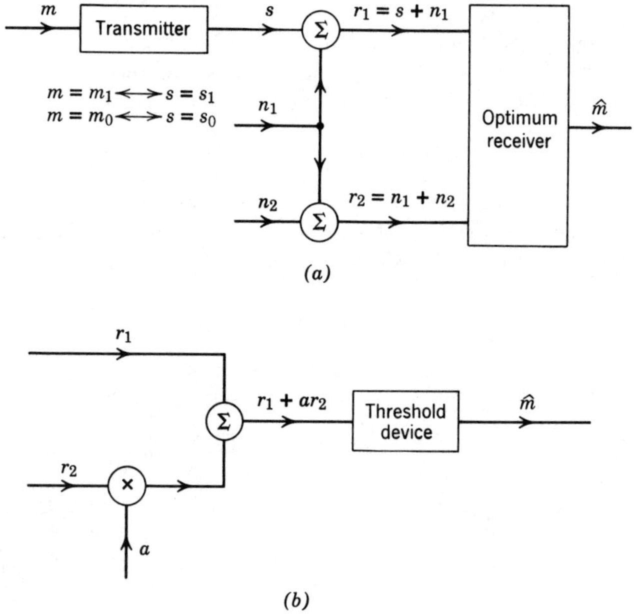

Figure P4.6

4.6 In the communication system diagrammed in Fig. P4.6*a*, the transmitted signal s and the noises n_1 and n_2 are all random voltages and all statistically independent. Assume that

$$P[m_0] = P[m_1] = \tfrac{1}{2},$$

$$s_1 = -s_0 = \sqrt{E_s},$$

$$p_{n_1}(\alpha) = p_{n_2}(\alpha) = \frac{1}{\sqrt{2\pi}\,\sigma} e^{-\alpha^2/2\sigma^2}.$$

a. Show that the optimum receiver can be realized as diagrammed in Fig. P4.6*b*, where a is an appropriately chosen constant.

b. What is the optimum value of a?

c. What is the optimum threshold setting?

d. Express the resulting P[ℰ] in terms of $Q(\alpha)$.

e. By what factor would E_s have to be increased to yield this same probability of error if the receiver were restricted to observing *only* r_1.

4.7 The voltage waveforms $x(t)$ and $y(t)$, plotted below, have the properties that when applied across a 1-ohm resistor

$$\int_0^T x^2(t)\,dt = \int_0^T y^2(t)\,dt = 16 \text{ joules.}$$

$$\int_0^T x(t)\,y(t)\,dt = 0.$$

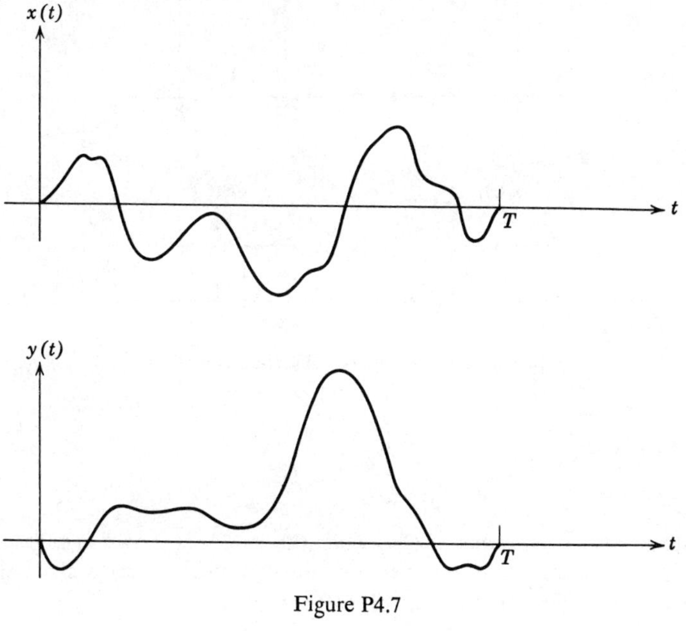

Figure P4.7

These signals can be used to communicate one of two equally likely messages over a channel perturbed by additive white Gaussian noise with power density of 4 watts/cycle/sec (on a bilateral frequency scale).

a. Calculate the minimum attainable probability of error when the two signals used are $x(t)$ and $-x(t)$.

b. Calculate the minimum attainable probability of error when the two signals used are $x(t)$ and $y(t)$.

4.8 a. Calculate $P[\mathcal{E}]_{\min}$ when the signal sets specified by Figs. P4.8*a*, *b*, and *c* are used to communicate one of two equally likely messages over a channel disturbed by additive Gaussian noise with $\mathcal{S}_n(f) = 0.15$.

b. Repeat part (a) for a priori message probabilities $(\frac{1}{4}, \frac{3}{4})$.

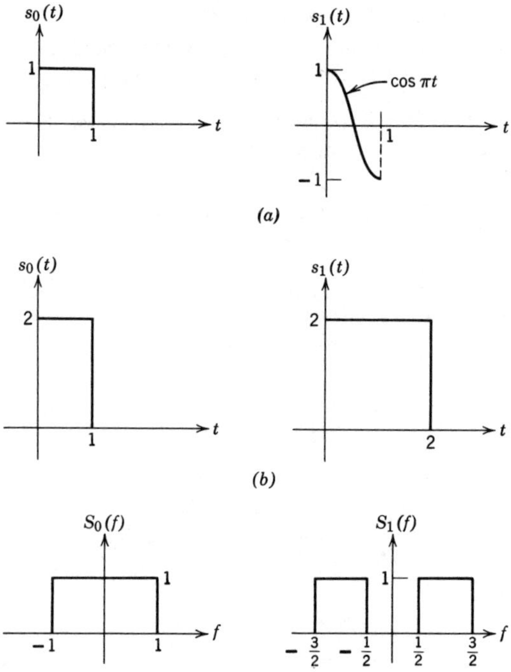

[$S_i(f)$, the Fourier transform of $s_i(t)$, is pure real.]

(*c*)

Figure P4.8

4.9 Express $P[\mathcal{E}]_{\min}$ in terms of $Q(\alpha)$ when the signal set shown in Fig. P4.9 is used to communicate one of eight equally likely messages over a channel disturbed by additive Gaussian noise with $\mathcal{S}_n(f) = \mathcal{N}_0/2$.

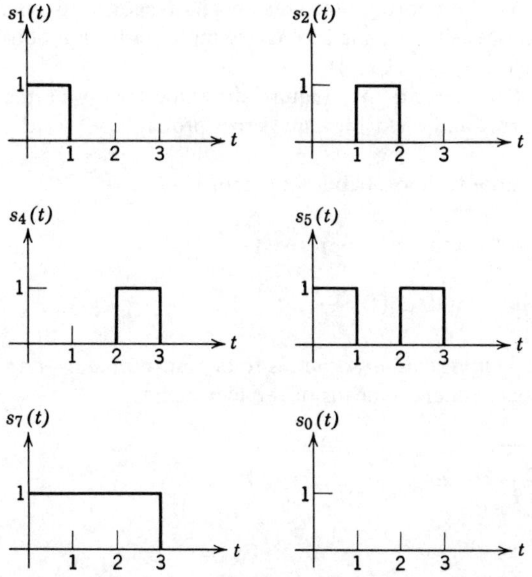

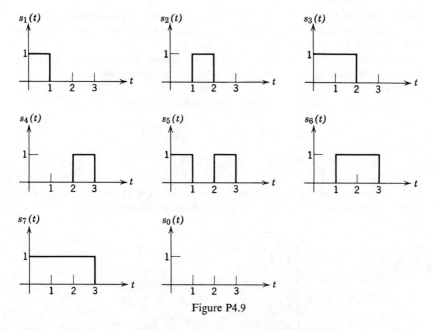

Figure P4.9

4.10 One of two equally likely messages is to be transmitted over an additive white Gaussian noise channel with $\mathcal{S}_n(f) = 0.05$ by means of binary pulse position modulation. Specifically,

$$s_0(t) = p(t),$$

$$s_1(t) = p(t - 2),$$

in which the pulse $p(t)$ is shown in Fig. P4.10.

a. What mathematical operations are performed by the optimum receiver?

b. What is the resulting probability of error?

c. Indicate two methods of implementing the receiver, each of which uses a single linear filter followed by a sampler and comparison device. Method I requires that two samples from the filter output be fed into the comparison device. Method II requires that just one sample be used. For each method

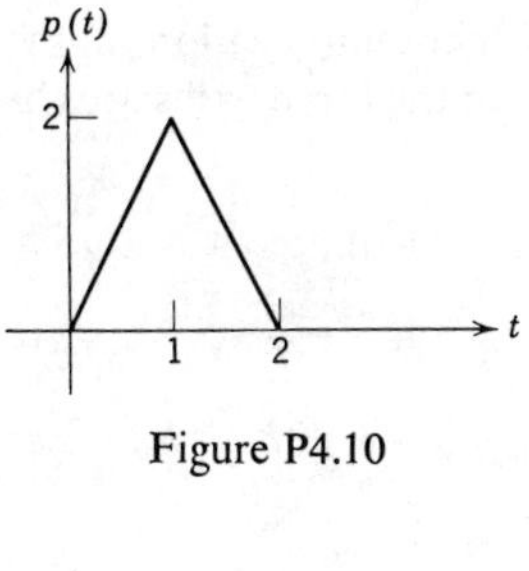

Figure P4.10

sketch the impulse response of the appropriate filter and its response to $p(t)$. Which of these methods is most easily extended to M-ary pulse position modulation, where $s_i(t) = p(t - 2i)$, $i = 0, 1, \ldots, M - 1$?

d. Suggest another pair of waveforms that require the same energy as the binary pulse-position waveforms and yield the same error probability; yield a lower error probability.

e. Calculate the minimum attainable probability of error if

$$s_0(t) = p(t) \quad \text{and} \quad s_1(t) = p(t - 1).$$

Repeat for

$$s_0(t) = p(t) \quad \text{and} \quad s_1(t) = -p(t - 1).$$

4.11 One of two equally likely messages, m_0 or m_1, is to be transmitted over an additive white Gaussian noise channel by means of the two signals

$$s_0(t) = \begin{cases} \sqrt{\dfrac{2E_s}{T}} \cos 2\pi f_1 t; & 0 \leqslant t \leqslant T \\ 0; & \text{elsewhere,} \end{cases}$$

$$s_1(t) = \begin{cases} \sqrt{\dfrac{2E_s}{T}} \cos 2\pi (f_1 + \Delta) t; & 0 \leqslant t \leqslant T \\ 0; & \text{elsewhere,} \end{cases}$$

where $T = 2$ msec, $f_1 = 1$ Mc, and $\Delta = 250$ cps. The noise has power density spectrum $\mathcal{N}_0/2$. If $E_s/\mathcal{N}_0 = 6$, calculate the probability of error to two significant digits. Repeat for $\Delta = 500$ cps.

4.12 M signals $s_0(t), s_1(t), \ldots, s_{M-1}(t)$ exist for $0 \leqslant t \leqslant T$, but each is identical to all others in the subinterval $[t_1, t_2]$, where $0 < t_1 < t_2 < T$.

a. Show that the optimum receiver may ignore this subinterval. Equivalently, show that if $\mathbf{s}_0, \mathbf{s}_1, \ldots, \mathbf{s}_{M-1}$ all have the same projection in one dimension, then this dimension may be ignored. Assume an additive white Gaussian noise channel.

b. Does this result necessarily hold true if the noise is Gaussian but not white? Explain.

4.13 Consider the multipath communication model shown in Fig. P4.13*a*, for which $P[m_0] = \frac{1}{2}$. Assume that the three paths are characterized by the following parameters:

Constant attenuation	$\alpha_1 = 0.2$	$\alpha_2 = 0.4$	$\alpha_3 = 0.6$.
Constant delay	$\tau_1 = 1$ msec	$\tau_2 = 1.5$ msec	$\tau_3 = 2$ msec.
White noise power density	$S_{n_1}(f) = 0.002$	$S_{n_2}(f) = 0.006$	$S_{n_3}(f) = 0.004$.

The three noise processes are Gaussian and statistically independent of each other and the signal transmitted. The transmitter is defined by the mapping

$$m = m_0 \Leftrightarrow s(t) = s_0(t) = \begin{cases} 5\cos 2\pi 10^3 t; & 0 \leqslant t \leqslant 3 \times 10^{-3} \\ 0; & \text{elsewhere.} \end{cases}$$

$$m = m_1 \Leftrightarrow s(t) = -s_0(t).$$

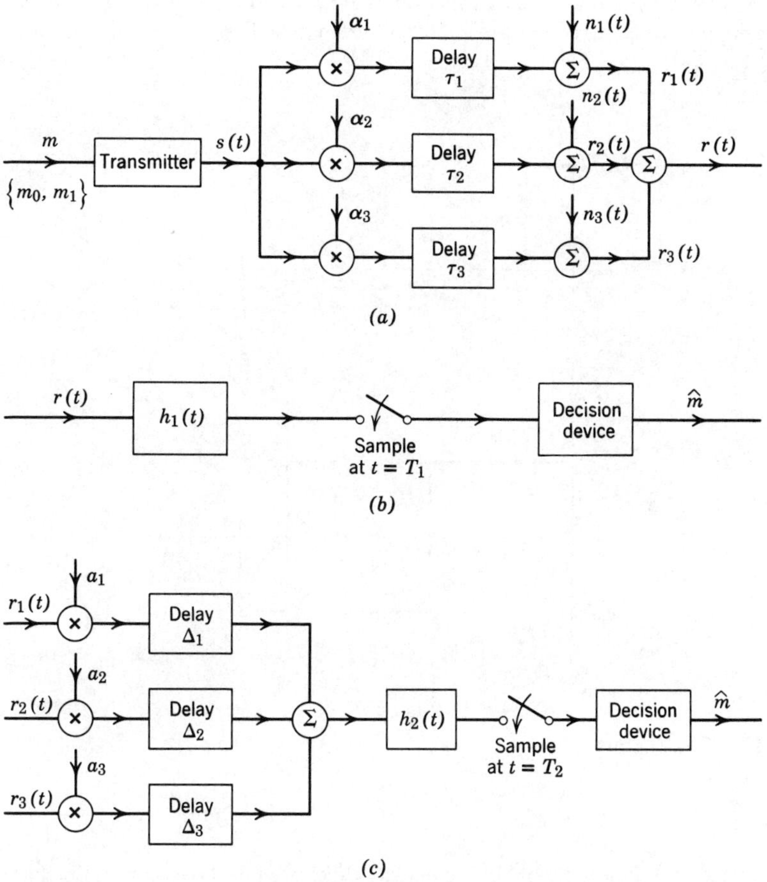

Figure P4.13

a. Show that the optimum receiver can be realized in the form illustrated in Fig. P4.13*b*. Determine $h_1(t)$, T_1, and the specification of the decision device. Suggest a reasonable implementation for $h_1(t)$. Calculate P[$\mathcal{E}$] to two significant digits.

b. Now assume that the receiver has access to the three multipath outputs individually. Demonstrate that in this case (called *diversity* reception) the optimum receiver can be realized in the form shown in Fig. P4.13*c*, in which the Δ's are constant delays and the a's are constant multipliers. Determine the Δ's, the a's, $h_2(t)$, T_2, and the specification of the decision device. Calculate the probability of error to two significant digits.

4.14 Specify a matched filter for each of the signals shown in Fig. P4.14 and sketch each filter output as a function of time when the signal matched to it is the input. Sketch the output of the filter matched to $s_2(t)$ when the input is $s_1(t)$.

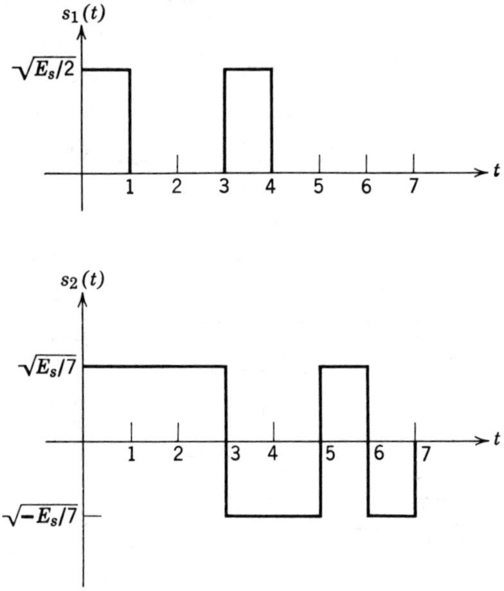

Figure P4.14

4.15 Two signals,

$$s_0(t) = -s_1(t) = \begin{cases} e^{-t}; & t \geqslant 0, \\ 0; & \text{elsewhere,} \end{cases}$$

are used with equal probability over an additive white Gaussian noise channel. The receiver bases its decision solely on observation of the received process

$$r(t) = s(t) + n_w(t)$$

over the restricted interval $0 \leqslant t \leqslant 2$. Express the minimum attainable $P[\mathcal{E}]$ in terms of $Q(\alpha)$. Contrast numerically with the performance of an optimum receiver that observes all of $r(t)$, $-\infty < t < \infty$.

4.16 A transmitter uses the signals $\{s_i(t)\}$ to communicate one of $M > 2$ equally likely messages over an additive white Gaussian noise channel with power density $\mathcal{N}_0/2$, where for $i = 0, 1, \ldots, M-1$

$$s_i(t) = \begin{cases} \sqrt{\dfrac{2E_s}{T}} \cos\left(2\pi \dfrac{k}{T} t + \dfrac{2\pi i}{M}\right); & 0 \leqslant t < T, \quad k \text{ an integer} \\ 0; & \text{elsewhere.} \end{cases}$$

a. Sketch the signal vectors and optimum decision regions for $M = 5$.

b. Use geometric arguments to show that the minimum attainable $P[\mathcal{E}]$ is bounded by

$$p \leqslant P[\mathcal{E}] \leqslant 2p,$$

where

$$p = Q\left(\sqrt{\frac{2E_s}{\mathcal{N}_0}} \sin \frac{\pi}{M}\right).$$

[This very neat result is due to E. Arthurs and H. Dym.[4]]

4.17 Assume that a set $\{\boldsymbol{\theta}_i\}$ of M vectors satisfies the equations

$$\boldsymbol{\theta}_i \cdot \boldsymbol{\theta}_j = \begin{cases} 1; & i = j, \\ \rho; & i \neq j. \end{cases}$$

a. Prove that $1 \geqslant \rho \geqslant -1/(M-1)$, where the right-hand equality is satisfied by the unit-energy simplex. *Hint.* Consider

$$\left|\sum_{i=0}^{M-1} \boldsymbol{\theta}_i\right|^2.$$

b. Prove for any allowable ρ that the signal set $\{\mathbf{s}_i\}$, with $\mathbf{s}_i \triangleq \sqrt{E_\rho}\, \boldsymbol{\theta}_i$ for all i, has the same error probability as the simplex signal set with energy

$$E_s = E_\rho\left(1 - \frac{1}{M}\right)(1 - \rho),$$

hence the same error probability as the orthogonal signal set with energy

$$E_0 = E_\rho(1 - \rho).$$

Hint. Consider the set $\{(\mathbf{s}_i - \mathbf{a})\}$, with $\mathbf{a} = \dfrac{1}{M} \sum_{i=0}^{M-1} \mathbf{s}_i$.

4.18 Either of the two signal waveform sets illustrated in the Fig. P4.18 may be used to communicate one of four equally likely messages over an additive white Gaussian noise channel.

a. Show that both sets use the same energy.

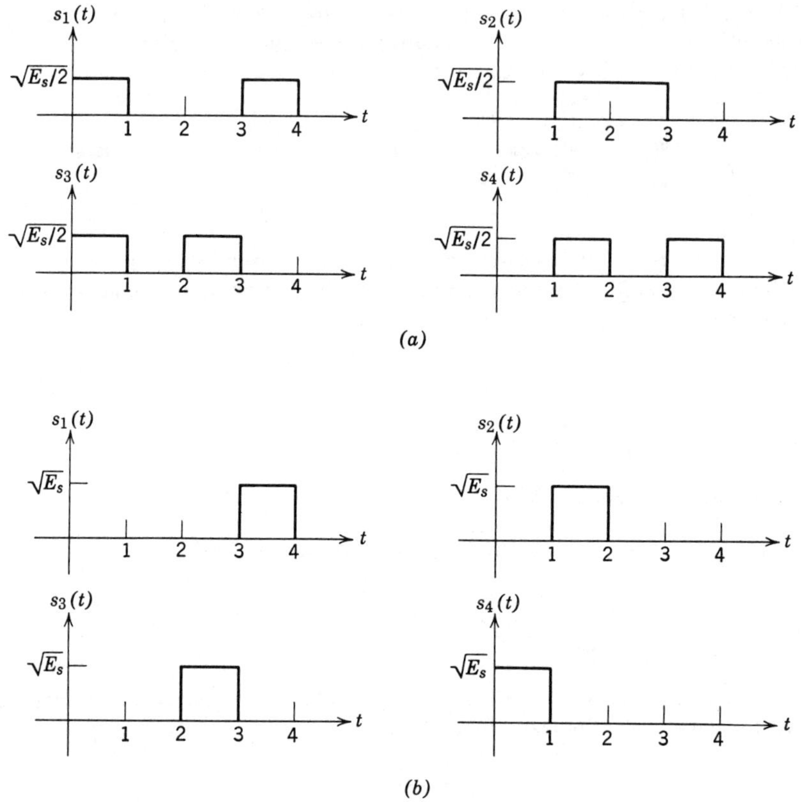

Figure P4.18

b. Exploit the union bound to show that the set of Fig. P4.18*b* uses energy almost 3 db more effectively than the set of Fig. 4.18*a* when a small P[ℰ] is required.

5

Efficient Signaling for Message Sequences

Preceding chapters have dealt with the problem of communicating a single input message chosen at random from some finite set of possible inputs. In practice, however, we are not often interested in communication systems that transmit only a single message and then cease operation forever, but rather in systems that communicate a sequence of messages, one after another, for many years.

Of course, we might choose to consider the transmission of a sequence of K inputs, each chosen from a set of M possible messages, as the transmission of a single input chosen from a set of M^K possibilities. This is the single-transmission, or "one-shot," approach. Alternatively, we can reformulate the single-transmission theory considered thus far in such a way that the sequential nature of the communication problem will be explicitly reflected in our analysis. In doing so we shall gain rich dividends, the concepts of channel capacity and communication efficiency. We shall also gain insight into the interrelationships between time, bandwidth, probability of error, and signal-to-noise ratio. In this chapter we consider these issues from a theoretical point of view. In the next we discuss certain aspects of the problem of system implementation.

5.1 SEQUENTIAL SOURCES

Given a message source that produces a sequence of discrete symbols, we are interested in characterizing how much transmission capability is required to communicate the source output to a distant terminal. In the simplest case we might have a source that produces statistically independent binary digits, each of which is equally likely to be 0 or 1, at a uniform rate of R digits/sec. During any time interval T that is an integral multiple of $1/R$, this source generates a sequence of RT binary digits, and each of the 2^{RT} possible sequences is equally likely to occur. For example, if $R = \frac{3}{2}$ and $T = 2$, one of the eight sequences

$$\begin{matrix} 000 & 010 & 100 & 110 \\ 001 & 011 & 101 & 111 \end{matrix}$$

is produced, and each has a priori probability $\frac{1}{8}$. Thus the transmitter must be able to communicate one of

$$M = 2^{RT} \tag{5.1}$$

equally likely messages during each successive T-sec interval.

Source Rate

For the situation just considered, we call R the *source rate*, measured in units of *b*inary dig*its* (abbreviated *bits*) per second. Similarly, for other sources, not necessarily binary, that produce one of a set of M equally likely messages in any time interval T we define the source rate in such a way that Eq. 5.1 remains valid:

$$R \triangleq \frac{1}{T} \log_2 M \quad \text{bits/sec.} \tag{5.2}$$

As an example of the application of this definition, consider a source that generates one symbol selected from an L-symbol alphabet each $1/R'$ sec. If the symbols are equally probable and successive selections are statistically independent, in time T the source effectively specifies one of

$$M = L^{R'T} \tag{5.3a}$$

equally likely messages. The source rate is therefore

$$R = \frac{1}{T} \log_2 M = R' \log_2 L \quad \text{bits/sec.} \tag{5.3b}$$

To see that the rate of a source is a meaningful measure of the transmission capability required to communicate the source output, we need only recognize that a set of M messages can be converted into a set of binary sequences simply by numbering the original messages and writing these numbers in binary form. For example, we might have

Message	Message No.	Sequence	Message	Message No.	Sequence
a	0	000	e	4	100
b	1	001	f	5	101
c	2	010	g	6	110
d	3	011	h	7	111

The identity of any input message can be specified by communicating the associated binary sequence. When M is a power of 2 and each message is equally likely, successive binary digits obtained in this way are statistically independent and equally likely to be 0 or 1. In this text we restrict our attention to the problem of communicating such a binary sequence. It can be shown[27] that the restriction entails no significant loss of generality.

The deep significance of source rate (which is frequently called "information rate") is clarified by the following considerations. Assume that we have two independent sources, the first of which produces one of M_1 and the second of which produces one of M_2 equally likely messages during each interval of T sec. If each source is connected to a separate transmitter, the required transmission capabilities are, respectively,

$$R_1 = \frac{1}{T} \log M_1 \quad \text{bits/sec.} \tag{5.4a}$$

and

$$R_2 = \frac{1}{T} \log M_2 \quad \text{bits/sec.} \tag{5.4b}$$

On the other hand, if both sources are connected simultaneously to a single transmitter, it must be able to specify one of $M = M_1 M_2$ messages in time T, hence must accommodate a rate of

$$\begin{aligned} R &= \frac{1}{T} \log M = \frac{1}{T} \log M_1 M_2 \\ &= \frac{1}{T} \log M_1 + \frac{1}{T} \log M_2 = R_1 + R_2 \quad \text{bits/sec.} \end{aligned} \tag{5.4c}$$

The important point is that, by virtue of the logarithm in the definition of rate, the rate of the two sources combined is the sum of their individual rates.

The utility of a communication system is measured by the (maximum) source rate that it will accommodate: other things being equal, one system with rate R can handle as much traffic as two systems with rate $R/2$. In contrast, note that a system capable of transmitting one of M equally likely messages per unit time is not equivalent to two such systems, each of capability $M/2$.

Transmitter Power

In Chapter 4, which dealt with the transmission of a single message, we considered the selection of signals subject to a constraint on the transmitted energy, E_s. We are now concerned with the transmission of a (possibly unending) sequence of messages, so that an energy constraint is no longer meaningful. But it is both meaningful and instructive to impose a bound on the average transmitted power, denoted P_s. For a signal $s(t)$ of duration T the *average power* is defined by

$$P_s \triangleq \frac{1}{T}\int_0^T s^2(t)\,dt = \frac{1}{T}\int_{-\infty}^{\infty} s^2(t)\,dt = \frac{E_s}{T}. \tag{5.5}$$

Thus, a constraint on P_s implies that the available transmitter energy increases linearly with time.

If a source has rate R, it can be thought of as producing one binary digit each $1/R$ sec. Subject to an average power constraint P_s, the average energy available per bit, say E_b, is therefore

$$E_b = \frac{P_s}{R} \text{ joules/bit.} \tag{5.6}$$

The average energy per bit required by different communication systems to obtain a given standard of error performance is a measure of their relative efficiencies.

5.2 BIT-BY-BIT AND BLOCK-ORTHOGONAL SIGNALING

To see that different communication systems may yield drastically different performances for the same value of E_b, let us contrast the results achieved when a sequence of

$$K = RT \tag{5.7}$$

equally likely binary digits is communicated by two specific signaling schemes. The first (a rather obvious choice) transmits a signal consisting of a sequence of K nonoverlapping pulse translates, each of which has the same waveshape but is positive when the corresponding bit in the input sequence is 1 and negative when it is 0, as shown in Fig. 5.1. The energy of each elementary pulse is E_b, and the total energy expended is KE_b. The second signaling scheme uses a signal set of 2^K orthogonal pulses, each having energy $E_s = KE_b$. The choice of transmitted signal is made by observing the entire input sequence at once and transmitting the ith pulse when the binary number specified by this sequence is i.

In many applications the entire K bit sequence must be transmitted correctly. A naval fire-control system, in which a 1 for the jth digit could designate that the target is above the surface and a 0 that it is below, is an example. In such cases the sequence is considered to be communicated correctly if and only if every one of its K bits is reproduced without error at

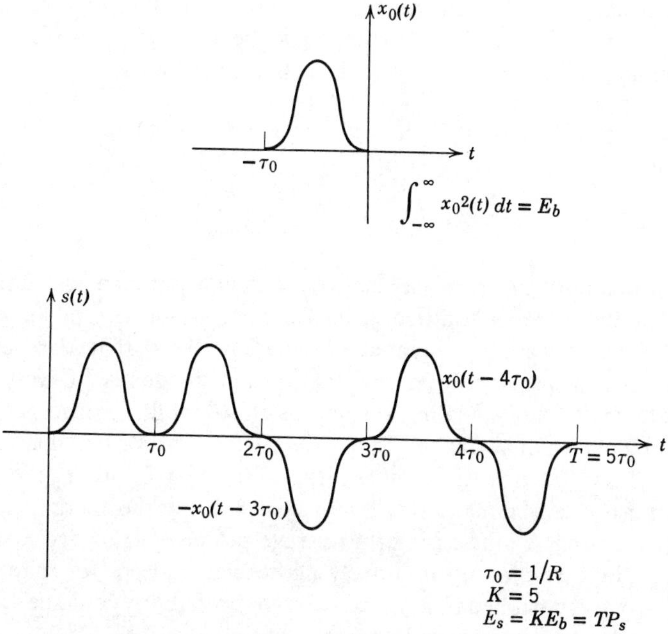

Figure 5.1 Bit-by-bit waveform for message sequence 11010.

the receiver output. We therefore compare our two signaling systems by calculating the probability, which we again denote by P[$\mathcal{E}$], that one or more bits will be received incorrectly when the transmission is disturbed by additive white Gaussian noise.

Bit-by-Bit Signaling

For the first system under consideration the transmitted signal is given by

$$s(t) = \sum_{j=1}^{K} s_j\, x_0(t - j\tau_0), \tag{5.8a}$$

where

$$s_j = \begin{cases} +1 & \text{if the } j\text{th bit is } 1 \\ -1 & \text{if the } j\text{th bit is } 0 \end{cases} \tag{5.8b}$$

and $x_0(t)$ is a pulse with energy E_b and duration $\tau_0 = 1/R$. By letting

$$\varphi_j(t) \triangleq \frac{x_0(t - j\tau_0)}{\sqrt{E_b}}; \qquad j = 1, 2, \ldots, K, \tag{5.9}$$

we associate the $M = 2^K$ possible signals with the 2^K vertices of a K-dimensional hypercube. In Chapter 4 we noted (Eq. 4.87) that the probability of at least one error with such a signal set is

$$\mathrm{P}[\mathcal{E}] = 1 - (1 - p)^K = 1 - (1 - p)^{RT}, \tag{5.10a}$$

in which

$$p \triangleq Q\left(\sqrt{\frac{2E_b}{\mathcal{N}_0}}\right) = Q\left(\sqrt{\frac{2P_s}{R\mathcal{N}_0}}\right) \tag{5.10b}$$

is the probability of error for a binary decision between two antipodal signals of energy E_b in additive white Gaussian noise with power density $\mathcal{N}_0/2$. Since it was also pointed out in Chapter 4 that the optimum receiver in this case can decide on each bit independently of every other, we characterize this signaling scheme as "bit-by-bit" transmission.

For any choice of R and P_s Eqs. 5.10 state that the probability of error tends to 1 as T, hence K, becomes large. For fixed T and $\mathcal{N}_0$ the probability of error can be made small *only* by increasing the energy expended per bit, E_b, either by increasing the average power P_s or by decreasing the rate R. These results are intuitively agreeable; indeed, for many years communicators assumed that decreased error probability could be achieved only by increasing power or decreasing rate.

Block-Orthogonal Signaling

To see that this assumption is false, we need only consider the second of our examples, in which one out of 2^K orthogonal pulses is transmitted every T sec. For the particular example of the discrete pulse-position-modulated (abbreviated PPM) orthogonal signal set illustrated in Fig. 5.2, the transmitted signal can be written

$$s_i(t) = \sqrt{E_s}\,\varphi(t - i\tau_1); \qquad i = 0, 1, \ldots, 2^K - 1, \tag{5.11a}$$

where i is the binary number specified by the K-bit input sequence and $\varphi(t)$ is a unit-energy pulse of duration

$$\tau_1 = \frac{T}{2^K}. \tag{5.11b}$$

We have seen in Chapter 4 (Eq. 4.111) that for any set of M equally likely equal-energy orthogonal signals the probability of error is bounded by

$$\mathrm{P}[\mathcal{E}] \leqslant (M - 1)\, Q\left(\sqrt{\frac{E_s}{\mathcal{N}_0}}\right) < Me^{-E_s/2\mathcal{N}_0}, \tag{5.12}$$

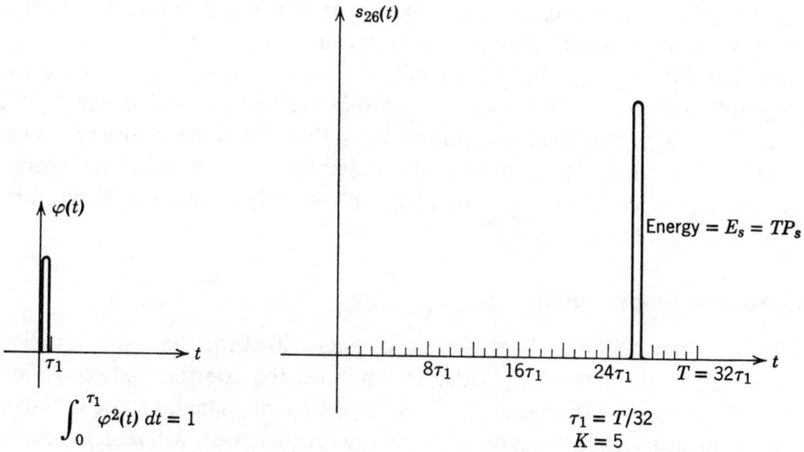

Figure 5.2 Block orthogonal waveform for messsage sequence 11010.

with the second inequality following from Eq. 2.122. A bound that is sometimes tighter is derived in Section 5.6, but Eq. 5.12 suffices to provide insight into the behavior of P[ℰ].

By substituting

$$M = 2^K = 2^{RT} \tag{5.13a}$$

and

$$E_s = KE_b = TP_s, \tag{5.13b}$$

Eq. 5.12 can be rewritten in the form

$$P[\mathcal{E}] < 2^{RT}e^{-TP_s/2\mathcal{N}_0} = \exp\left[-T\left(\frac{P_s}{2\mathcal{N}_0} - R\ln 2\right)\right]. \tag{5.14a}$$

We see that the probability of error *approaches zero exponentially with increasing T, as long as the rate R satisfies the bound*

$$R < \frac{P_s}{2\mathcal{N}_0}\frac{1}{\ln 2} \approx 0.72\frac{P_s}{\mathcal{N}_0}. \tag{5.14b}$$

Expressions equivalent to Eqs. 5.14 are

$$P[\mathcal{E}] < 2^K e^{-K(E_b/2\mathcal{N}_0)} = \exp\left[-K\left(\frac{E_b}{2\mathcal{N}_0} - \ln 2\right)\right] \tag{5.15a}$$

and

$$\frac{E_b}{\mathcal{N}_0} > 2\ln 2 \approx 1.39. \tag{5.15b}$$

The contrast between the results obtained with bit-by-bit transmission (Eqs. 5.10) and those obtained when orthogonal signals are used to transmit a whole block of K input bits simultaneously ("block-orthogonal signaling") is dramatic. In the first case increasing K forces the probability of error toward unity regardless of how large we make the energy ratio per bit, $E_b/\mathcal{N}_0$. In the second, by increasing K we can force the probability of error to be as close to zero as we wish, provided that $E_b/\mathcal{N}_0$ exceeds 1.39. An alternative statement is that the signal-to-noise power ratio $P_s/\mathcal{N}_0$ implies a bound on the maximum rate of communication; at rates below this maximum the P[$\mathcal{E}$] can be made as small as we wish by choosing T sufficiently large.

Geometric Interpretation

The geometry of the signal-vector constellations for the two signaling schemes just considered provides insight into the contrast between their performances. As shown in Fig. 5.3 for bit-by-bit signaling, the distance between nearest neighbors remains fixed as K increases, whereas the number of nearest neighbors and the number of dimensions occupied by the signal set increase linearly with K. The probability that at least one of the

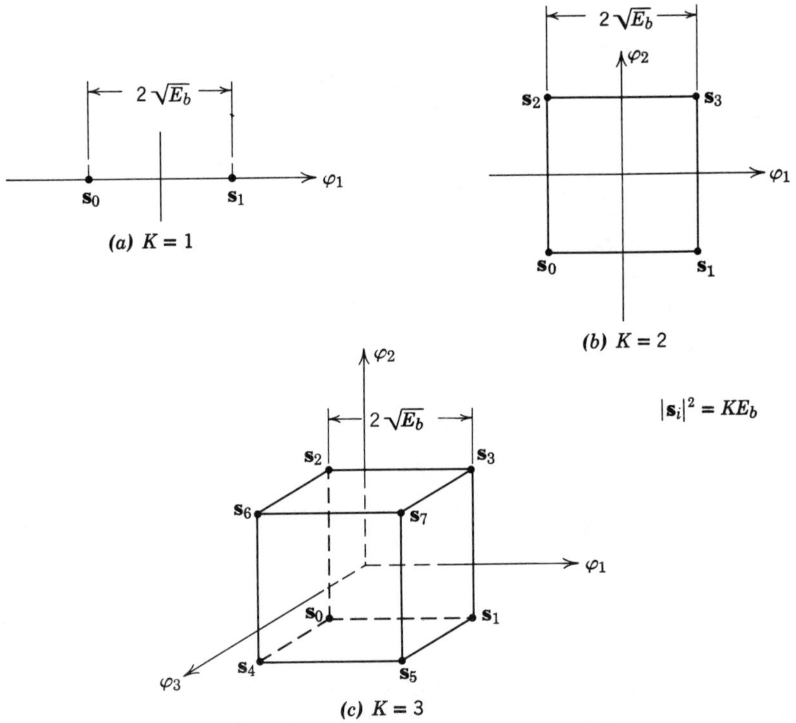

Figure 5.3 Bit-by-bit signal geometry.

K relevant noise components will carry the received signal vector closer to a neighbor than to the transmitted vector becomes large as K increases; there are K chances for this to happen.

On the other hand, in the block-orthogonal case the distance between nearest neighbors grows linearly with $\sqrt{K}$, as indicated by Fig. 5.4. When K increases from $j-1$ to j, this growth in distance is achieved by introducing a new dimension for each of the 2^{j-1} additional signals and rescaling in amplitude. Even though the number of nearest-neighbors grows as 2^K (all signals are nearest neighbors), the growth in the distance

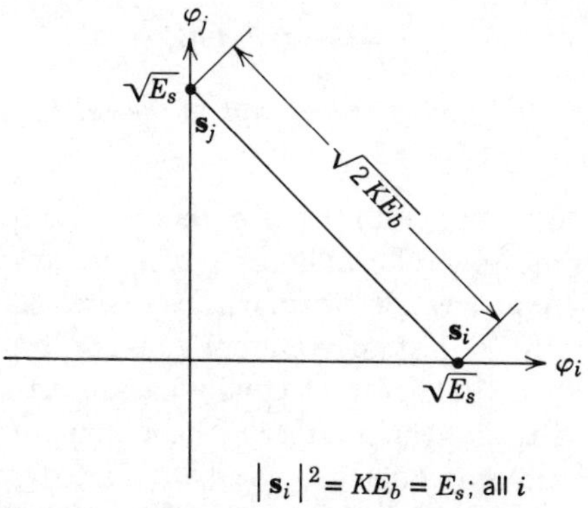

Figure 5.4 Block-orthogonal signal geometry. The geometry obtains for each pair of signals $(\mathbf{s}_i, \mathbf{s}_j)$; $0 \leqslant i, j \leqslant 2^K - 1$, $j \neq i$.

between signals dominates the probability-of-error behavior for large values of $E_b/\mathcal{N}_0$. Conversely, for small $E_b/\mathcal{N}_0$ we shall see that the growth in number of neighbors dominates and that $P[\mathcal{E}] \to 1$ as K becomes large.

5.3 TIME, BANDWIDTH, AND DIMENSIONALITY

It might seem that the block-orthogonal PPM signaling scheme provides a solution to the general problem of accurate, efficient communication over a Gaussian channel. Unfortunately, such is not the case: for R close to $0.72P_s/\mathcal{N}_0$, a very large value of T is required to obtain a large negative exponent in the bound of Eq. 5.14a; however, very large T in turn implies that the number 2^{RT} of orthogonal waveforms required in the signal set is enormous. We shall see that a channel with a given finite bandwidth cannot accommodate 2^{RT} orthogonal waveforms as T increases while R is fixed. All physical channels are characterized by a finite-bandwidth constraint, hence no block-orthogonal signaling scheme can be built for fixed rate and arbitrarily large T.

Signal Dimensionality as a Function of T

A measure of the constraint imposed by finite bandwidth on the dimensionality of a signal set can be gained from theorems due to Shannon and to Landau and Pollak, which we state without proof.†

Dimensionality theorem.

Let $\{\varphi_j(t)\}$ denote any set of orthogonal waveforms of duration T and "bandwidth" W. More precisely, require that each $\varphi_j(t)$

(1) *be identically zero outside a time interval of duration T and*

(2) *have no more than $\frac{1}{12}$ of its energy outside the frequency interval*

$$-W < f < W.$$

Then the number of different waveforms in the set $\{\varphi_j(t)\}$ is overbounded (conservatively) by $2.4TW$ when TW is large.

The definition of bandwidth in this theorem may seem somewhat arbitrary, but any meaningful evaluation of the bandwidth occupied by a time-limited, low-frequency waveform can be expressed as some constant times that bandwidth, W, just large enough to incorporate $\frac{11}{12}$ of the waveform's energy.‡ Thus the theorem actually has unrestricted applicability. The important fact is that the number of orthogonal waveforms (dimensions) that can be accommodated by a "bandlimited" channel can grow *no faster than linearly with time*, T, regardless of how "bandwidth" is defined.

The converse statement, that the number of dimensions (say N) available with a bandlimited channel *can* grow linearly with T, is easy to demonstrate. We wish to show that

$$N = DT, \tag{5.16}$$

where D, the *number of dimensions available per second*, varies linearly with W but is relatively insensitive to T. As a first example consider a pulse $x(t)$ that is identically zero outside a time interval of duration τ and occupies some (suitably defined) bandwidth W. Then T/τ such pulses can be placed without overlap into a time interval of duration T. Since non-overlapping pulses are orthogonal, this scheme provides a means of obtaining $D = 1/\tau$ dimensions per second.

Insight into the relationship between D and W is gained by considering the inverse scaling that exists between the time and frequency domains;

† See Appendix 5A. Dollard[23] has obtained the tighter result that if each $\varphi_j(t)$ has no more than η_W^2 of its energy outside of $(-W, W)$, then the number of different waveforms is overbounded by $2TW/(1 - \eta_W^2)$ for all values of TW.
‡ Appendix 5B.

if the Fourier transform of $x(t)$ is $X(f)$, the Fourier transform of $x(\alpha t)$ is

$$\int_{-\infty}^{\infty} x(\alpha t)e^{-j2\pi ft}\,dt = \frac{1}{\alpha}\int_{-\infty}^{\infty} x(\xi)e^{-j2\pi(f/\alpha)\xi}\,d\xi$$

$$= \frac{1}{\alpha}X\left(\frac{f}{\alpha}\right). \tag{5.17}$$

Thus, if a pulse $x(t)$ of duration τ occupies a bandwidth W, the pulse $x(\alpha t)$ has duration τ/α and occupies a bandwidth αW. It follows that $D = \alpha/\tau$ of the pulses $x(\alpha t)$ can be placed without overlap in a one second interval, which verifies the fact that D is proportional to bandwidth.

As a second example of the converse statement, consider T-second pulses of sine and cosine waves separated in frequency by $1/T$ cps, such as

$$\left.\begin{aligned} s_0(t) &= 1 \\ s_1(t) &= \sqrt{2}\sin 2\pi\frac{t}{T} \\ s_2(t) &= \sqrt{2}\cos 2\pi\frac{t}{T} \\ s_3(t) &= \sqrt{2}\sin 4\pi\frac{t}{T} \\ s_4(t) &= \sqrt{2}\cos 4\pi\frac{t}{T} \end{aligned}\right\} -\frac{T}{2} \leqslant t \leqslant \frac{T}{2}.$$

Each waveform is zero for $|t| > T/2$. Clearly, all such waveforms are mutually orthogonal. The corresponding signal spectra are related to the spectrum, $S_0(f)$, of $s_0(t)$ as indicated by Fig. 5.5. It can be verified through integration by parts and use of the tabulated sine-integral function[46] that

$$\int_{-1/T}^{1/T} |S_0(f)|^2\,df > 0.9\int_{-\infty}^{\infty} |S_0(f)|^2\,df. \tag{5.18}$$

It follows from Eq. 5.18 and Fig. 5.5 that, when TW is an integer, a total of $1 + 2[W/(1/T)] = 1 + 2TW$ such signals can be accommodated in a bilateral frequency interval of bandwidth $(W + 1/T)$ with at least 90 per cent of the energy of every signal contained within this bandwidth.

A difficulty in transmitting sequences of orthogonal pulses is that most physical channels introduce distortion; pulses that do not overlap when transmitted tend to be smeared together when they are received, as indicated in Fig. 5.6. The result, called *intersymbol interference*, is that strict orthogonality is lost and the value of D attainable in practice reduced. A brute-force remedy is to provide sufficient dead time between pulses that the interference is reduced to manageable proportions; elegant

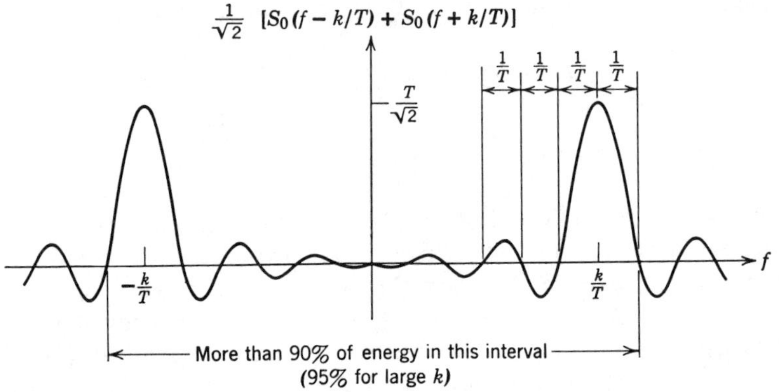

Figure 5.5 Spectrum of T-sec cosine pulse at frequency k/T. The spectrum when $k = 0$ is $S_0(f) = T(\sin \pi fT)/\pi fT$.

approaches require careful waveshaping of the transmitted pulses and/or elaborate filters. In practice, the maximum number of essentially orthogonal waveforms that can be transmitted in time T through a channel with nominal bandwidth W is between TW and $\frac{3}{2}$ TW; the choice of definition for W and the cost of implementation are the determining factors.

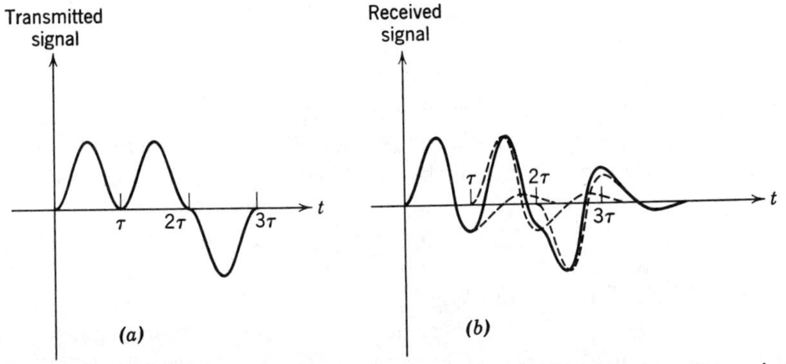

Figure 5.6 Intersymbol interference. The solid curve in (*b*) is the composite received signal, obtained by summing the responses (dashed curves) due to each of the three transmitted pulses shown in (*a*).

Bandwidth Requirements with Block-Orthogonal Signaling

It is now easy to show that bandlimited transmission channels preclude the unrestricted use of block-orthogonal signaling. As we have seen, when a transmitter is connected to a source that provides input bits at a rate R per second, the number of bits that must be transmitted in time T is RT and the number of different signals required is $M = 2^{RT}$. If we insist that these signals be orthogonal, the dimensionality theorem states that the number of orthogonal signals, M, and the bandwidth, W, satisfy

$$M = 2^{RT} \leqslant 2.4TW, \tag{5.19a}$$

or

$$W \geqslant \frac{2^{RT}}{2.4T}. \tag{5.19b}$$

As T becomes large, W grows almost exponentially and therefore exceeds the bandwidth of any physical channel.

The import of an exponential growth in bandwidth is made tangible by the following example. Consider a system operating at the modest rate of 100 bits/sec and assume that R and $P_s/\mathcal{N}_0$ in Eq. 5.14a are such that $T = 1$ sec is necessary to achieve the desired probability of error. Then

$$W \geqslant \frac{2^{100}}{2.4} \approx 10^{30} \text{ cps},$$

which is clearly outlandish. Viewed in the time domain, Eq. 5.19a states that if we wished to realize this system by using a block-orthogonal PPM scheme the number of nonoverlapping pulses per second would have to be 2^{100}, which implies a pulse duration of 10^{-21} nanosecond!

5.4 EFFICIENT SIGNAL SELECTION

In Section 5.2 we observed that block-orthogonal signaling over an additive white Gaussian noise channel would yield a probability of error that approaches zero exponentially with increasing block duration T for rates R less than 0.72 $P_s/\mathcal{N}_0$. The drawback was that the bandwidth requirement becomes exponentially large (substantially infinite) for large T. We now show that it is possible to achieve a probability-of-error behavior analogous to that of orthogonal signaling while simultaneously meeting the bandlimited channel constraint that the dimensionality of the signal space grow only linearly with T.

A direct demonstration of this fact is not possible for two reasons. First, unless some regular structure is imposed (as in the two examples in Section 5.2), the mere task of specifying a set of $M = 2^{RT}$ different signals is enormous when T is large. Second, even if the problem of signal specification were manageable, in general we would be unable to analyze the P[ℰ] that results from use of the specified signal set. Strangely enough, it is much easier to demonstrate that as T becomes large a great many signal sets with linearly increasing dimensionality yield an exponentially decreasing probability of error (for rates that are not too high) than it is to exhibit a single specific set of signals behaving in this way.

Signaling with Sequences of Binary Waveforms

As a first example, let us consider a case in which the available number of dimensions per second, D, exceeds the rate R:

$$D > R. \tag{5.20a}$$

For simplicity, we again (as in Section 5.2) restrict the signals to lie on the vertices of a hypercube. Since the number of vertices on a hypercube of DT dimensions is 2^{DT} and the number of signals required is $M = 2^{RT}$, not all of the vertices need be used. In fact, the fraction of vertices that we must use,

$$\frac{2^{RT}}{2^{DT}} = 2^{-(D-R)T}, \tag{5.20b}$$

approaches zero as T increases. Thus there is a possibility that we can avoid the convergence of the probability of error to unity with increasing T which we observed in Section 5.2 as a consequence of the nearest-neighbor structure when $D = R$.

Restricting the signals $\{s_i(t)\}$ to the vertices of a hypercube implies that each signal has the form

$$s_i(t) = \sum_{j=1}^{N} s_{ij}\varphi_j(t); \qquad \text{for } i = 0, 1, \ldots, M-1, \tag{5.21a}$$

where

$$s_{ij} = \pm\sqrt{E_N}; \qquad \text{all } i \text{ and } j, \tag{5.21b}$$

$$N \triangleq DT, \text{ the number of dimensions in time } T, \tag{5.21c}$$

and E_N is defined as the *available signal energy per dimension.* As in Chapter 4, $\{\varphi_j(t)\}$ can be any set of orthonormal waveforms:

$$\int_{-\infty}^{\infty} \varphi_j(t)\,\varphi_l(t)\,dt = \delta_{jl}; \qquad \text{all } l \text{ and } j.$$

For example, the $\{\varphi_j(t)\}$ might be successively delayed, nonoverlapping replicas of some finite-duration, unit-energy pulse, as shown in Fig. 5.7.

The constraint on the average transmitted power, P_s, requires

$$E_s = P_s T = \sum_{j=1}^{N} s_{ij}^{\,2} = NE_{\mathrm{N}}, \tag{5.22a}$$

or

$$E_{\mathrm{N}} = \frac{E_s}{N} = \frac{P_s}{D} \text{ joules/dimension.} \tag{5.22b}$$

For the $\{\varphi_j(t)\}$ of Fig. 5.7 the signals $\{s_i(t)\}$ are sequences of positive and negative nonoverlapping pulses, each pulse containing energy E_{N}.

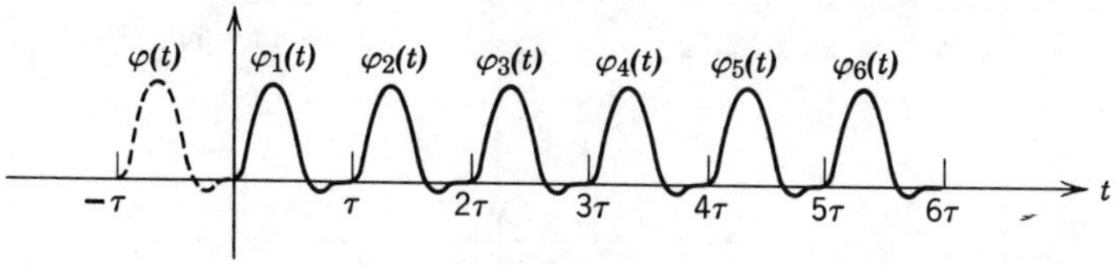

$$\int_{-\infty}^{\infty} \varphi_j^{\,2}(t)\, dt = 1$$

$$\varphi_j(t) = \varphi(t - j\tau)$$

Figure 5.7 Orthonormal (pulse position) waveforms.

The average probability of error. The problem of signal selection for this particular example reduces to the assignment of the vectors of coefficients $\{s_{ij}\}$ in Eq. 5.21a:

$$\mathbf{s}_i \triangleq (s_{i1}, s_{i2}, \ldots, s_{iN}); \qquad i = 0, 1, \ldots, M-1. \tag{5.23}$$

As we have mentioned, a good specific assignment is hard to find and hard to analyze. These complications can be circumvented by bounding the attainable probability of error by an ingenious indirect argument due to Shannon.[75] *The key to the derivation is to consider not just one communication system, but rather a whole collection of communication systems, each consisting of a transmitter, channel, and optimum receiver.* As shown in Fig. 5.8, the systems are identical, except that each employs a *different* set of signals $\{\mathbf{s}_i\}$.

There are $2^N = 2^{DT}$ different vertices available on our N-dimensional signal space hypercube and $M = 2^{RT}$ signals $\{\mathbf{s}_i\}$ to be assigned thereon; it follows that there are $(2^N)^M = 2^{NM}$ distinct ways to assign the M signals. We assume that each of these 2^{NM} signal sets is used by one (and only one) of the communication systems in our collection, and that each system uses a receiver that is optimum for its signal set. Following common usage, we refer to the signal sets as *codes*, and to the signal vectors as *codewords*.

It is clear that each system in our collection has a definite probability of error, say P_l for the lth system, $l = 1, 2, \ldots, 2^{NM}$. Some of the systems—for example, those with codes in which all M of the vectors $\{\mathbf{s}_i\}$ are assigned to the same vertex—have a very large probability of error. On the other hand, most of the systems have a probability of error that is

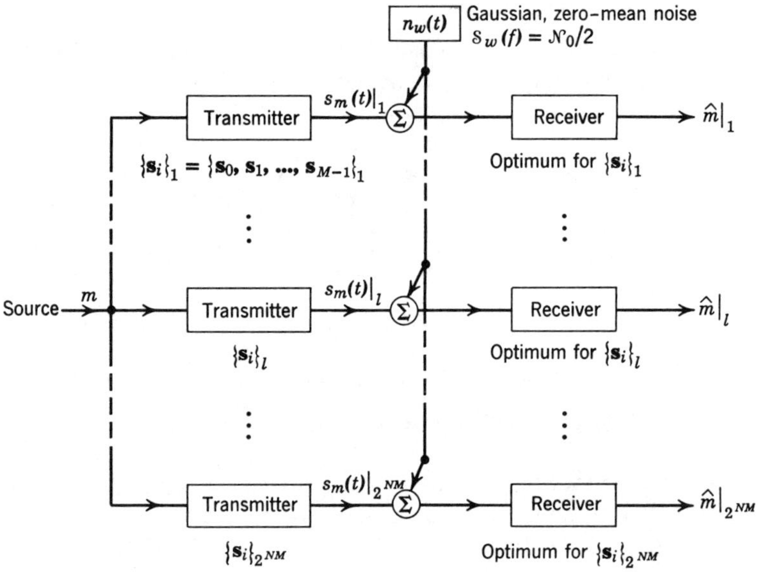

Figure 5.8 Collection of communication systems, each using a different set of M signals $\{\mathbf{s}_i\}_l$, $l = 1, 2, \ldots, 2^{NM}$.

quite small, a fact that we shall prove by calculating a bound on the arithmetic average, denoted $\overline{P[\mathcal{E}]}$, over the entire collection:

$$\overline{P[\mathcal{E}]} \triangleq \frac{1}{2^{NM}} \sum_{l=1}^{2^{NM}} P_l. \tag{5.24}$$

Clearly, not all of the P_l can be greater than $\overline{P[\mathcal{E}]}$.

It may be surprising that one can bound the average probability of error for a collection of communication systems when one cannot calculate the probability of error of an individual system. Such was Shannon's insight.

To calculate a bound on $\overline{P[\mathcal{E}]}$, we first interpret Eq. 5.24 as a statistical rather than an arithmetic average. Although this interpretation is not essential, it simplifies the derivation by permitting us to use the notation and results of the preceding three chapters. Consider a probability system in which each point ω of the sample space has associated with it one of the systems of Fig. 5.8 as well as a message, a noise waveform, and the resulting received waveform. The probability assigned to the system utilizing code $\{\mathbf{s}_i\}$ is

$$P[\{\mathbf{s}_i\}] = 2^{-NM}, \tag{5.25a}$$

and is statistically independent of the message and the noise process. If the code for the lth system is $\{\mathbf{s}_i\}_l$, we have

$$P[\,\mathcal{E} \mid \{\mathbf{s}_i\}_l] = P_l. \tag{5.25b}$$

By using Eqs. 5.25, Eq. 5.24 may be rewritten

$$\overline{P[\mathcal{E}]} = E[P_l] = \sum_{\text{all codes}} P[\mathcal{E} \mid \{\mathbf{s}_i\}]\, P[\{\mathbf{s}_i\}]. \tag{5.26}$$

We now bound $\overline{P[\mathcal{E}]}$. When message m_k is transmitted, the conditional probability of error, $\overline{P[\mathcal{E} \mid m_k]}$, averaged over the collection of codes is

$$\overline{P[\mathcal{E} \mid m_k]} = \sum_{\text{all codes}} P[\{\mathbf{s}_i\}]\, P[\mathcal{E} \mid m_k, \{\mathbf{s}_i\}], \tag{5.27}$$

in which $P[\mathcal{E} \mid m_k, \{\mathbf{s}_i\}]$ is the conditional probability of error, given $m = m_k$, for a specific code $\{\mathbf{s}_i\}$. Application of the union bound of Eq. 4.109 to each specific code yields

$$P[\mathcal{E} \mid m_k, \{\mathbf{s}_i\}] \leqslant \sum_{\substack{i=0 \\ (i \neq k)}}^{M-1} P_2[\mathbf{s}_i, \mathbf{s}_k], \tag{5.28}$$

where $P_2[\mathbf{s}_i, \mathbf{s}_k]$ is the probability of error when the two signal vectors $\mathbf{s}_i$ and $\mathbf{s}_k$ are used to communicate one of two equally likely messages.

If it were easy to evaluate the right-hand side of Eq. 5.28, there would be no need to consider the collection (ensemble) of possible communication systems. This evaluation, however, requires both explicit knowledge of the signal set $\{\mathbf{s}_i\}$ and unlimited patience. The crucial advantage to be gained by considering the ensemble of systems is that both difficulties are avoided by an interchange in order of summations. Substituting Eq. 5.28 in Eq. 5.27, we have

$$\overline{P[\mathcal{E} \mid m_k]} \leqslant \sum_{\text{all codes}} P[\{\mathbf{s}_i\}] \sum_{\substack{i=0 \\ (i \neq k)}}^{M-1} P_2[\mathbf{s}_i, \mathbf{s}_k].$$

Interchanging the order of summations yields

$$\begin{aligned}\overline{P[\mathcal{E} \mid m_k]} &\leqslant \sum_{\substack{i=0 \\ (i \neq k)}}^{M-1} \left\{ \sum_{\text{all codes}} P[\{\mathbf{s}_i\}]\, P_2[\mathbf{s}_i, \mathbf{s}_k] \right\} \\ &= \sum_{\substack{i=0 \\ (i \neq k)}}^{M-1} \overline{P_2[\mathbf{s}_i, \mathbf{s}_k]},\end{aligned} \tag{5.29}$$

in which the bar denotes expectation over the ensemble of communication systems. Thus interchanging the order of summations makes averaging over the code ensemble the next step in the bounding of $\overline{\mathrm{P}[\mathcal{E}]}$.

For the additive white Gaussian noise channel, $\mathrm{P}_2[\mathbf{s}_i, \mathbf{s}_k]$ depends only on the Euclidean distance between $\mathbf{s}_i$ and $\mathbf{s}_k$. In accordance with Eq. 4.110,

$$\mathrm{P}_2[\mathbf{s}_i, \mathbf{s}_k] = Q\left(\frac{|\mathbf{s}_i - \mathbf{s}_k|}{\sqrt{2\mathcal{N}_0}}\right). \tag{5.30}$$

If $\mathbf{s}_i$ and $\mathbf{s}_k$ differ in h coordinates, the square of the distance between them is

$$|\mathbf{s}_i - \mathbf{s}_k|^2 = \sum_{j=1}^{N} (s_{ij} - s_{kj})^2 = h\,(2\sqrt{E_{\mathrm{N}}})^2 = 4hE_{\mathrm{N}}. \tag{5.31}$$

Over the ensemble of codes, the probability assignment of Eq. 5.25a implies that $\mathbf{s}_i$ is equally likely to be any of the 2^N vertices of the signal-space hypercube, independently of $\mathbf{s}_k$. Thus the probability that s_{ij} equals s_{kj} is $\frac{1}{2}$, independently for all $j = 1, 2, \ldots, N$. As a consequence, the probability that $\mathbf{s}_i$ and $\mathbf{s}_k$ will differ in h coordinates is just the probability of getting h Heads in N tosses of an unbiased coin:

$$\mathrm{P}[h] = \binom{N}{h}\left(\frac{1}{2}\right)^N. \tag{5.32a}$$

The expected value of $\mathrm{P}_2[\mathbf{s}_i, \mathbf{s}_k]$ over the ensemble of codes is therefore

$$\begin{aligned}\overline{\mathrm{P}_2[\mathbf{s}_i, \mathbf{s}_k]} &= \mathrm{E}\left[Q\left(\frac{|\mathbf{s}_i - \mathbf{s}_k|}{\sqrt{2\mathcal{N}_0}}\right)\right] \\ &= \sum_{h=0}^{N} \mathrm{P}[h]\, Q\left(\frac{\sqrt{4hE_{\mathrm{N}}}}{\sqrt{2\mathcal{N}_0}}\right) = \sum_{h=0}^{N} 2^{-N}\binom{N}{h} Q\left(\sqrt{\frac{2hE_{\mathrm{N}}}{\mathcal{N}_0}}\right).\end{aligned} \tag{5.32b}$$

Since the right-hand side of Eq. 5.32b is independent of the indices i and k, it is convenient to introduce the simpler notation

$$\overline{\mathrm{P}_2[\mathcal{E}]} \triangleq \overline{\mathrm{P}_2[\mathbf{s}_i, \mathbf{s}_k]}. \tag{5.33}$$

With this notation we observe that

$$\overline{\mathrm{P}[\mathcal{E} \mid m_k]} \leqslant \sum_{\substack{i=0 \\ (i \neq k)}}^{M-1} \overline{\mathrm{P}_2[\mathbf{s}_i, \mathbf{s}_k]} = (M-1)\overline{\mathrm{P}_2[\mathcal{E}]} < M\,\overline{\mathrm{P}_2[\mathcal{E}]}$$

and

$$\begin{aligned}\overline{\mathrm{P}[\mathcal{E}]} &= \sum_{k=0}^{M-1} \overline{\mathrm{P}[\mathcal{E} \mid m_k]}\, \mathrm{P}[m_k] \\ &< M\,\overline{\mathrm{P}_2[\mathcal{E}]} \sum_{k=0}^{M-1} \mathrm{P}[m_k] = M\,\overline{\mathrm{P}_2[\mathcal{E}]}.\end{aligned} \tag{5.34}$$

Bounding $\overline{\mathrm{P}[\mathcal{E}]}$ now reduces to bounding $\overline{\mathrm{P}_2[\mathcal{E}]}$.

Recalling from Eq. 2.122 that

$$Q(\alpha) < e^{-\alpha^2/2},$$

we substitute in Eq. 5.32b and obtain

$$\overline{P_2[\mathcal{E}]} < \sum_{h=0}^{N} 2^{-N}\binom{N}{h} e^{-hE_N/\mathcal{N}_0} = 2^{-N}\sum_{h=0}^{N}\binom{N}{h}\,[e^{-E_N/\mathcal{N}_0}]^h.$$

But

$$[1 + a]^N = \sum_{h=0}^{N}\binom{N}{h}a^h,$$

which implies

$$\overline{P_2[\mathcal{E}]} < 2^{-N}[1 + e^{-E_N/\mathcal{N}_0}]^N. \tag{5.35}$$

This may be written more concisely as

$$\overline{P_2[\mathcal{E}]} < 2^{-NR_0}, \tag{5.36a}$$

in which we introduce the *exponential bound parameter* R_0, identified from Eq. 5.35 as

$$\begin{aligned} R_0 &= \log_2\left(\frac{2}{1 + e^{-E_N/\mathcal{N}_0}}\right) \\ &= 1 - \log_2(1 + e^{-E_N/\mathcal{N}_0}); \quad \text{antipodal signaling.} \end{aligned} \tag{5.36b}$$

Finally, the combination of Eqs. 5.34 and 5.36 yields the end result of our analysis, the bound

$$\begin{aligned} \overline{P[\mathcal{E}]} &< M\,\overline{P_2[\mathcal{E}]} \\ &< M\,2^{-NR_0}. \end{aligned} \tag{5.37}$$

Defining R_N as the transmitter rate in bits per dimension,

$$R_N \triangleq \frac{R}{D} = \frac{\text{bits/second}}{\text{dimensions/second}}, \tag{5.38a}$$

so that

$$M = 2^{TR} = 2^{NR_N}, \tag{5.38b}$$

we can rewrite the bound in the convenient form

$$\overline{P[\mathcal{E}]} < 2^{-N[R_0 - R_N]}. \tag{5.38c}$$

Equations 5.38 state that *as long as R_N is less than the exponential bound parameter R_0, the average probability of error—hence the probability of error for at least one code in the collection—can be made arbitrarily small by taking N sufficiently large.* The number of dimensions N is frequently called the code *block length.*

The parameter R_0 is plotted in Fig. 5.9 as a function of the signal-energy-to-noise ratio per dimension, $E_N/\mathcal{N}_0$. Since the maximum value of R_0 is unity (corresponding to $E_N \to \infty$ in Eq. 5.36), the exponent $[R_0 - R_N]$ in Eq. 5.38 can never be positive for a rate R_N greater than or equal to 1 bit/dimension. This is consistent with the result given in Section 5.2 for bit-by-bit signaling: when $R_N = 1$, we have $R = D$, which implies that the required number of signals equals the number of available hypercube vertices. Using antipodal signaling (binary codes) restricts the system

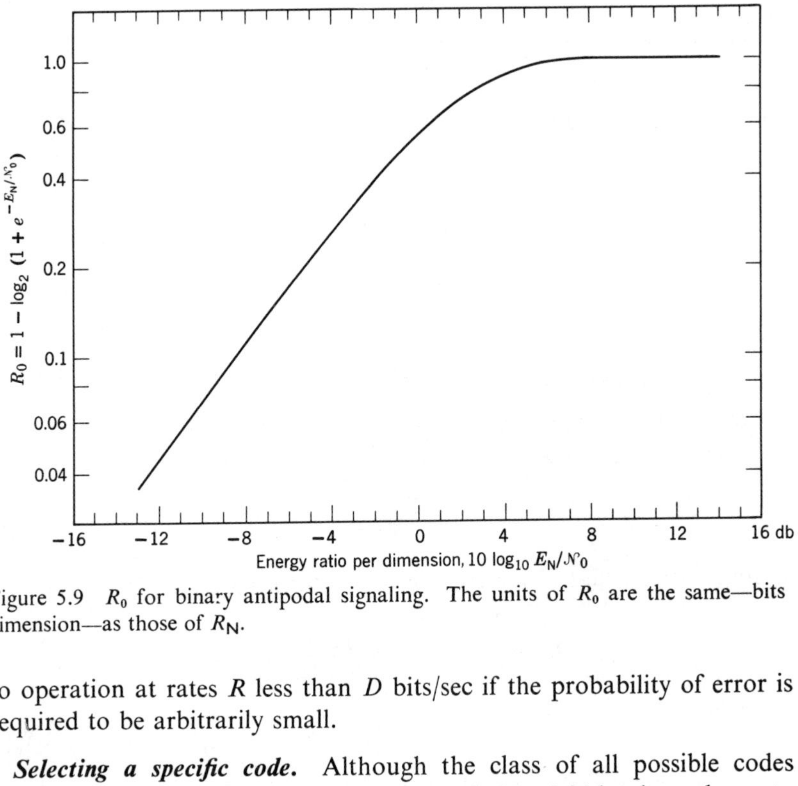

Figure 5.9 R_0 for binary antipodal signaling. The units of R_0 are the same—bits dimension—as those of R_N.

to operation at rates R less than D bits/sec if the probability of error is required to be arbitrarily small.

Selecting a specific code. Although the class of all possible codes (signaling sets) constructed in accordance with Eqs. 5.21 has been shown to yield an average probability of error that decays exponentially with increasing N when the bit rate per dimension is not too great, we have not yet considered the problem of selecting a *single, specific code.* It is evident that this problem is not a sensitive one insofar as error probability is concerned. The quantity $\overline{P[\mathcal{E}]}$ is the average value of the positive quantities $\{P_l\}$, where P_l is the probability of error for the lth code in the class. Since only a fraction $1/\lambda$ of a set of positive numbers can be larger than λ times their average, at least 90 per cent of all codes in the collection must have a $P[\mathcal{E}]$ no larger than $10\ \overline{P[\mathcal{E}]}$, and 99 per cent of all codes must have a $P[\mathcal{E}]$ no larger than $100\ \overline{P[\mathcal{E}]}$.

For rates such that $\overline{P[\mathcal{E}]}$ decays exponentially with N, it is possible when designing a system to choose N large enough so that 10, 100, or even $1000\ \overline{P[\mathcal{E}]}$ will be as small as we like. For example, if $N = N_1$ is sufficient to guarantee $\overline{P[\mathcal{E}]} < 10^{-8}$, clearly $N = \frac{5}{4}N_1$ is sufficient to guarantee $100\ \overline{P[\mathcal{E}]} < 10^{-8}$. Measured in terms of the required fractional increase in code length N, only a small price need be paid to gain reasonable assurance that a code picked at random is good. Of course, once a good code has been chosen, it can be used for many transmissions and in many systems.

Discussion. An intuitive understanding of why a $\overline{P[\mathcal{E}]}$ that decays exponentially with N results for $R_N < R_0$ can be gained from the following considerations. We recall that R_0 specifies the exponential bound on $\overline{P_2[\mathcal{E}]}$, the mean probability of error (over the ensemble of codes) when one of two signals is equally likely to be transmitted over a channel disturbed by additive white Gaussian noise:

$$\overline{P_2[\mathcal{E}]} = \overline{Q\left(\frac{|\mathbf{s}_1 - \mathbf{s}_2|}{\sqrt{2\mathcal{N}_0}}\right)} < 2^{-NR_0}.$$

On the average, two signals chosen independently at random from 2^N hypercube vertices differ from one another in approximately $N/2$ coordinates. Thus the root mean square distance between two such signals increases linearly with $\sqrt{N}$. Since Gaussian noise produces a probability of error that decays exponentially with the square of the Euclidean distance between two signals, it is reasonable that $\overline{P_2[\mathcal{E}]}$ should decay exponentially with N.

Two phenomena enter into the occurrence of an error when $M = 2$ and the signals are chosen at random. The first is that the noise may be unusually large and cause an error even though the Euclidean distance between the two signals is typical, as shown in Fig. 5.10*a*. The second is that the noise may be typical but the two signals may be poor in the sense that the distance between them is unusually small (see Fig. 5.10*b*). The value of R_0 in Eq. 5.36 represents the combined influences of these two phenomena. When $E_N/\mathcal{N}_0$ is large, R_0 approaches unity, and the $\overline{P_2[\mathcal{E}]}$ approaches 2^{-N}. But 2^{-N} is just the probability of assigning the two signals to the same hypercube vertex; we recognize that it is the second phenomenon that dominates R_0 when $E_N/\mathcal{N}_0$ is large. On the other hand, when $E_N/\mathcal{N}_0$ is small, errors are likely to occur even when the two signals

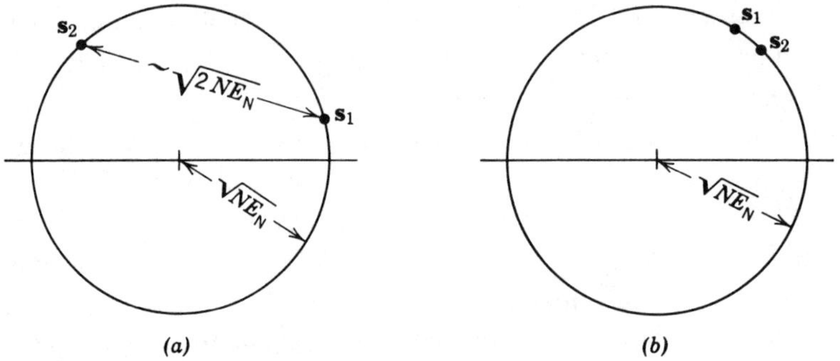

Figure 5.10 Two possible signal pairs: (*a*) typical spacing; (*b*) small spacing.

are typical in the sense that they differ in approximately $N/2$ components. Under these circumstances R_0 is dominated by the first phenomenon.

This heuristic discussion is extended to the case of M randomly selected signals by recognizing that there are three distinct and statistically independent selections entering into the occurence of error:

1. The data source selects the transmitter input m.
2. Nature selects the relevant noise $\mathbf{n}$.
3. The communication system engineer selects the signals $\{\mathbf{s}_i\}$.

$\overline{P[\mathcal{E}]}$ denotes the probability of the event error in the product ensemble describing the three selections. It is convenient to visualize these selections as taking place in the order listed and to assume m is m_k. We may also visualize that the system engineer first selects the transmitted signal $\mathbf{s}_k$ and then the remaining $M - 1$ signals. An error occurs if and only if one or more of the $M - 1$ remaining signals (which over the ensemble are selected without reference to $\mathbf{s}_k$, $\mathbf{n}$, or each other) lie closer to $\mathbf{r} = \mathbf{s}_k + \mathbf{n}$

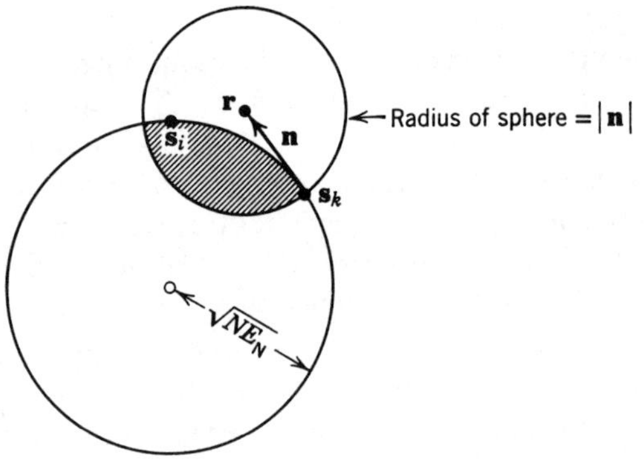

Figure 5.11 An error occurs if any signal $\mathbf{s}_i$ falls into the shaded region, since then $|\mathbf{r} - \mathbf{s}_i| < |\mathbf{r} - \mathbf{s}_k| = |\mathbf{n}|$.

than the distance $|\mathbf{n}|$ from $\mathbf{s}_k$ to $\mathbf{r}_b$ as indicated in Fig. 5.11. For each of the remaining signals the probability of falling into this forbidden region is, by definition, $\overline{P_2[\mathcal{E}]}$. Since there are $(M - 1)$ chances for some signal to fall into the forbidden region, we immediately have the union bound

$$\overline{P[\mathcal{E}]} \leqslant (M - 1)\,\overline{P_2[\mathcal{E}]}.$$

The average probability of error approaches zero with increasing N as long as the number of messages $M = 2^{NR_N}$ grows with N less rapidly than $\overline{P_2[\mathcal{E}]}$ decays.

Comparison with block-orthogonal signaling. It is interesting to compare the bound of Eq. 5.38 with the behavior exhibited in Eqs. 5.15 for block-orthogonal signaling, namely,

$$P[\mathcal{E}] < 2^{-K[(E_b/\mathcal{N}_0)(1/2 \ln 2)-1]}, \tag{5.39a}$$

where K as usual denotes the number of transmitter input bits during an interval T. Thus the energy per bit utilized with orthogonal signaling must satisfy the bound

$$\frac{E_b}{\mathcal{N}_0} > 2 \ln 2; \qquad \text{for orthogonal signals} \tag{5.39b}$$

in order that the bound on probability of error tend to zero with increasing block size, K.

The corresponding limitation on $E_b/\mathcal{N}_0$ with binary coding is obtained by rewriting Eq. 5.38c in the same form as Eq. 5.39a. Since

$$K = RT = NR_N,$$

we have

$$\overline{P[\mathcal{E}]} < 2^{-N[R_0 - R_N]} = 2^{-K[(R_0/R_N)-1]}. \tag{5.40a}$$

Moreover,

$$E_N = \text{energy per dimension} = \left(\frac{\text{energy}}{\text{bit}}\right)\left(\frac{\text{bits}}{\text{dimension}}\right) = E_b R_N, \tag{5.40b}$$

so that (from Eq. 5.36)

$$\frac{R_0}{R_N} = E_b\frac{R_0}{E_N} = \frac{E_b}{\mathcal{N}_0}\cdot\frac{R_0}{E_N/\mathcal{N}_0} = \frac{E_b}{\mathcal{N}_0}\cdot\frac{1 - \log_2(1 + e^{-E_N/\mathcal{N}_0})}{E_N/\mathcal{N}_0}. \tag{5.40c}$$

Thus

$$\overline{P[\mathcal{E}]} < 2^{-K[(E_b/\mathcal{N}_0)(1/\alpha)-1]}, \tag{5.41a}$$

where

$$\alpha \triangleq \frac{E_N/\mathcal{N}_0}{1 - \log_2(1 + e^{-E_N/\mathcal{N}_0})}. \tag{5.41b}$$

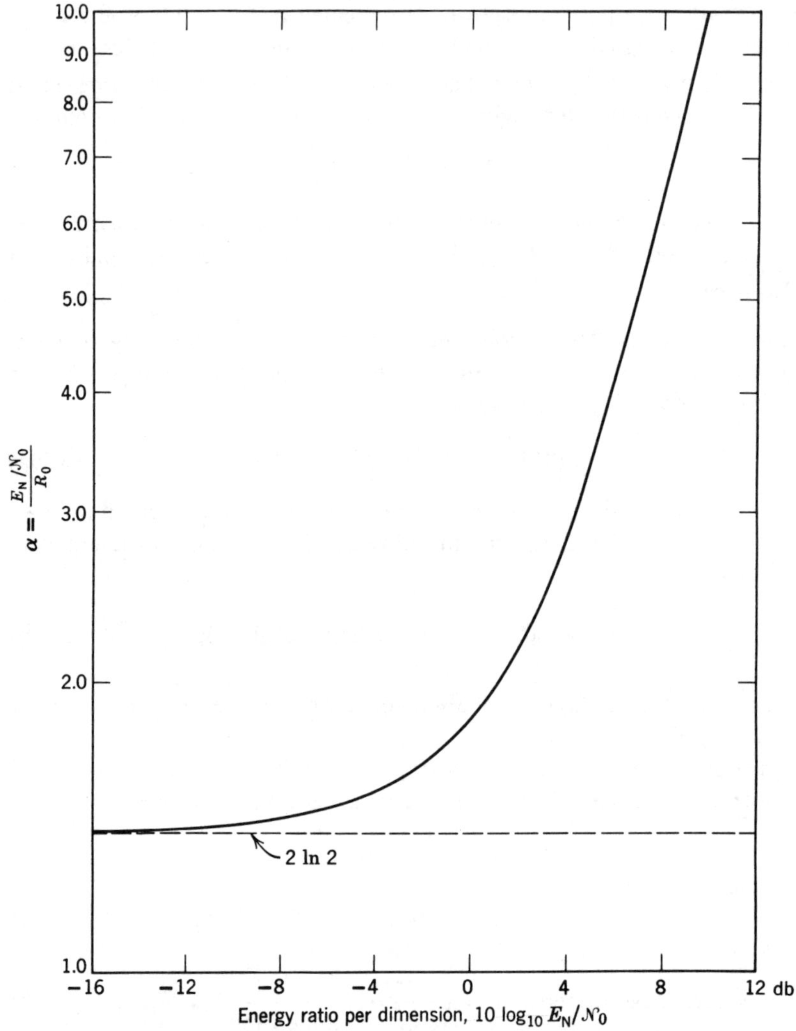

Figure 5.12 Lower bound to the allowable ratio $E_b/\mathcal{N}_0$ for binary-coded systems.

For the bound on $\overline{P[\mathcal{E}]}$ to go to zero with increasing K, we require

$$\frac{E_b}{\mathcal{N}_0} > \alpha; \qquad \text{for binary-coded signals.} \tag{5.41c}$$

The parameter α is plotted in Fig. 5.12 as a function of $E_N/\mathcal{N}_0$. Its minimum value—attained as $E_N/\mathcal{N}_0 \to 0$—is 2 ln 2, and α exceeds this minimum only slightly for $E_N/\mathcal{N}_0 < -10$ db. Thus the exponential decay of the average probability of error bound over all codes of the class considered here is *substantially equivalent to that obtained with block-orthogonal signaling, provided that D can be made large enough so that* $E_N/\mathcal{N}_0$ *is small.* This corroborates our earlier observation that under this condition it is the noise that dominates R_0.

In Chapter 4, we claimed that simplex signals are optimum for communication over an additive white Gaussian noise channel and that orthogonal signals are substantially equivalent to simplex signals when the number of signals, M, is large. Since the exponential decay of $\overline{P[\mathcal{E}]}$ becomes substantially equivalent to that obtained with block-orthogonal signals, we conclude that the class of hypercube-vertex (binary-coded) signals may be considered to be "exponentially optimum" provided that the noise, the available number of dimensions per second D, and the received signal power P_s are so related that

$$E_N = \frac{\text{energy/sec}}{\text{dimensions/sec}} = \frac{P_s}{D} < \frac{\mathcal{N}_0}{10} \tag{5.42a}$$

or

$$D > 10 \frac{P_s}{\mathcal{N}_0}. \tag{5.42b}$$

Signaling with Multilevel Sequences

We have just inferred that the signal class consisting of binary-waveform sequences is exponentially optimum whenever the ratio $P_s/\mathcal{N}_0$ is much smaller than the number of dimensions available per second, D. We have also observed in Fig. 5.9 that for this signal class R_0 saturates at one bit per dimension when $E_N/\mathcal{N}_0 \gg 1$. Since we certainly expect that large enough $E_N/\mathcal{N}_0$ should permit reliable communication at rates above one bit per dimension, we anticipate that the class of binary-waveform sequences will *not* be exponentially optimum when $E_N/\mathcal{N}_0$ is large.

As noted in connection with Eq. 5.20, the saturation of R_0 in Fig. 5.9 is attributable to the fact that the total number of distinct binary-waveform sequences occupying DT dimensions is 2^{DT}, so that R cannot exceed D bits/sec. The only way to avoid this saturation effect is to augment the class of allowable signals. Since in many situations $P_s/\mathcal{N}_0$ is large but the bandwidth is limited—for example, in digital communication over toll-grade telephone lines†—it is important to consider signal sets $\{\mathbf{s}_i\}$ that are not constrained to lie on the vertices of a hypercube.

† Although the noise on telephone circuits is not simply Gaussian, experiments[54] have demonstrated that a sizable improvement in rate can be achieved by the use of nonbinary waveforms of the kind to be discussed here.

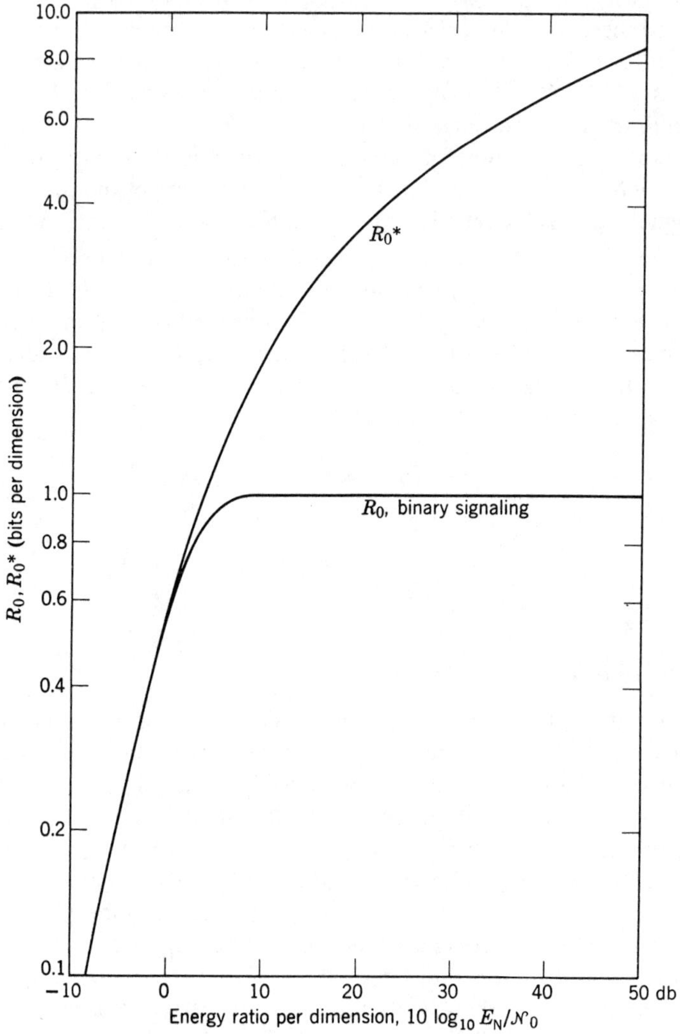

Figure 5.13 Comparison of R_0^* and R_0 for binary signaling.

Shannon,[74] in a derivation beyond the scope of this book, considers additive white Gaussian noise and N-dimensional signal sets $\{\mathbf{s}_i\}$ that are constrained only in energy:†

$$|\mathbf{s}_i|^2 \leqslant NE_N = N\frac{P_s}{D}; \qquad i = 0, 1, \ldots, M-1. \qquad (5.43)$$

† See also Gallager.[32]

He then shows that *sets of* $M = 2^{NR_N}$ *signals exist for which the error probability is bounded by*

$$P[\mathcal{E}] < 2^{-N[R_0^* - R_N]}; \qquad 0 < R_N < R_0^*, \tag{5.44a}$$

with

$$R_0^* \triangleq \frac{\log_2 e}{2}\left[1 + \frac{E_N}{\mathcal{N}_0} - \sqrt{1 + \left(\frac{E_N}{\mathcal{N}_0}\right)^2}\,\right] + \frac{1}{2}\log_2\left[\frac{1}{2}\left(1 + \sqrt{1 + \left(\frac{E_N}{\mathcal{N}_0}\right)^2}\,\right)\right]. \tag{5.44b}$$

In addition, he proves that *no* set of $M = 2^{NR_N}$ signals satisfying Eq. 5.43 exists such that the bound of Eq. 5.44a is valid for *arbitrary* N and R_N when R_0^* is replaced by a larger number. (We shall see in Section 5.6, however, that more elaborate bounding techniques do yield tighter results for particular values of R_N.)

In Fig. 5.13 R_0^* is plotted as a function of $E_N/\mathcal{N}_0$, together with the R_0 achieved by the ensemble of binary-waveform sequences. Our intuitive feeling that rates greater than D bits/sec must be attainable for large values of $P_s/\mathcal{N}_0$ is justified. For $E_N/\mathcal{N}_0 < 0$ db, R_0 nearly coincides with R_0^*, but for $E_N/\mathcal{N}_0 > 0$ db the binary-waveform sequences are less desirable. For $E_N/\mathcal{N}_0 > 10$ db they are exceedingly inefficient.

We now consider certain signal classes that yield a bound parameter R_0 that is substantially as large as R_0^*, even for large values of $E_N/\mathcal{N}_0$. The adverse effect of saturation is circumvented by not restricting the signal vectors $\{\mathbf{s}_i\}$ to the vertices of a hypercube. An especially convenient augmented class of allowable signals, in terms of analysis and implementation,† is one in which the components $\{s_{ij}\}$ of the signal vectors are still restricted to a finite number of different values, but in which this number, say A, is now an integer greater than 2. The total number of allowable signals of the form

$$\mathbf{s}_i = (s_{i1}, s_{i2}, \ldots, s_{iN}), \tag{5.45a}$$

$$s_i(t) = \sum_{j=1}^{N} s_{ij}\varphi_j(t) \tag{5.45b}$$

is therefore

$$A^N = 2^{N \log_2 A}. \tag{5.45c}$$

For this class of signal, saturation does not occur until

$$M = 2^{NR_N} = A^N \tag{5.45d}$$

or

$$R_N = \log_2 A. \tag{5.45e}$$

† Questions of implementation are considered in Chapter 6.

For example, if $A = 4$, the saturation value of R_N is 2 bits/dimension rather than 1. Thus we may hope to obtain a bound of the form

$$P[\mathcal{E}] < 2^{-N[R_0 - R_N]}$$

in which R_0 is greater than 1.

To complete the specification of the enlarged signal class, we must state the A values permitted to the $\{s_{ij}\}$. We consider only the case in which each s_{ij} can be assigned any one of A amplitudes equally spaced over the interval $[-\sqrt{E_N}, \sqrt{E_N}]$, as shown in Fig. 5.14 for $A = 8$. Such

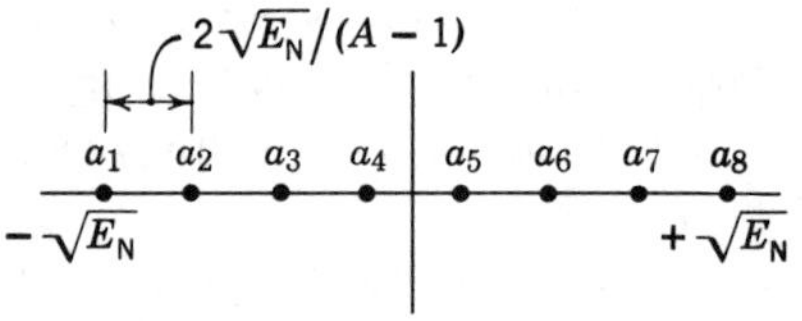

Figure 5.14 Possible set of values permitted the $\{s_{ij}\}$; $A = 8$.

an assignment guarantees that $|\mathbf{s}_i|^2 \leqslant NE_N$ for all i. For example, the 16 allowable signals when $A = 4$ and $N = 2$ are illustrated in Fig. 5.15. The set of values permitted the $\{s_{ij}\}$ is called the *signal alphabet* and denoted $\{a_l\}$, $l = 1, 2, \ldots, A$. The members of the alphabet are called *letters*, and the set of all A^N allowable signal vectors is called the *code base.*

To determine R_0 as a function of A and $E_N/\mathcal{N}_0$, we again bound the mean probability of error, $\overline{P[\mathcal{E}]}$, over an appropriate ensemble of communication systems. Since each message may be assigned any one of the A^N vectors in the code base, the total number of distinct codes—assignments of M messages to code-base vectors—is $(A^N)^M = A^{NM}$. As when $A = 2$, codes in which several messages are assigned to the same vector are included in the count. For bounding $\overline{P[\mathcal{E}]}$, we consider an ensemble containing A^{NM} communication systems, each of which uses a different code $\{\mathbf{s}_i\}$ together with a receiver that is optimum for that code.

We recall that $\overline{P[\mathcal{E}]}$ is the ensemble average of the probability of error of each system in the ensemble. In evaluating $\overline{P[\mathcal{E}]}$ for $A = 2$, we assigned each of the 2^{NM} systems equal probability, which implied

$$\overline{P[\mathcal{E}]} = \frac{1}{2^{NM}} \sum_{\text{all codes}} P[\mathcal{E} \mid \{\mathbf{s}_i\}].$$

When $A > 2$, the ensemble average probability of error, $\overline{P[\mathcal{E}]}$, is reduced, hence the value of R_0 increased, by assigning nonequal probabilities to the A^{NM} systems in the ensemble. The reason is that the signal alphabet $\{a_l\}$ is asymmetric, as seen in Fig. 5.14: although each letter is equally distant from its nearest neighbor, the letters $+\sqrt{E_N}$ and $-\sqrt{E_N}$ have neighbors only on one side. These end letters are, in a sense, more distinguishable, and we anticipate that the probability of error will be smaller for systems with codes $\{\mathbf{s}_i\}$ in which letters near the ends are used more frequently than the interior letters.

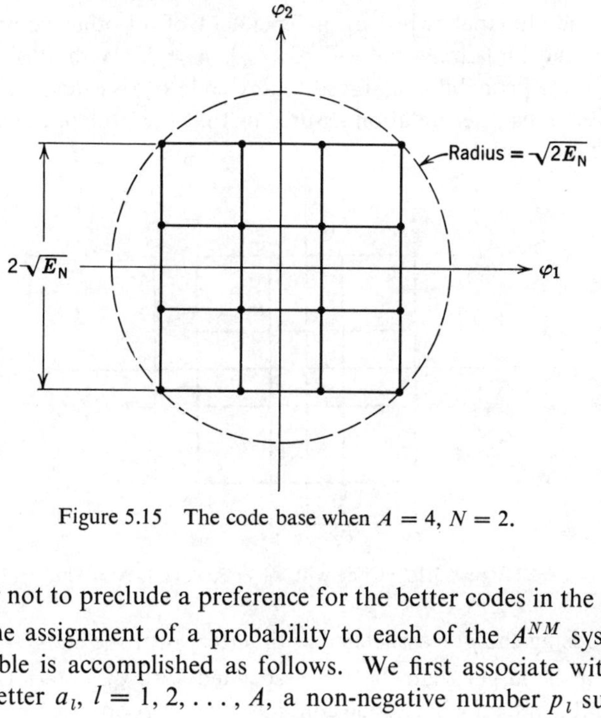

Figure 5.15 The code base when $A = 4$, $N = 2$.

In order not to preclude a preference for the better codes in the analysis of $\overline{P[\mathcal{E}]}$, the assignment of a probability to each of the A^{NM} systems in the ensemble is accomplished as follows. We first associate with every alphabet letter a_l, $l = 1, 2, \ldots, A$, a non-negative number p_l such that

$$p_1 + p_2 + \cdots + p_A = 1. \tag{5.46a}$$

Next, for each system we observe its entire code $\{\mathbf{s}_i\}$ and count the total number of times, say N_l, $l = 1, 2, \ldots, A$, that letter a_l appears therein. To this system we assign the probability

$$P[\{\mathbf{s}_i\}] = p_1^{N_1} p_2^{N_2} \cdots p_A^{N_A}. \tag{5.46b}$$

Since each code comprises M codewords with N symbols apiece, it is clear that for every system $N_1 + N_2 + \cdots + N_A = NM$. For example, a code $\{\mathbf{s}_i\}$ containing $M = 5$ members is shown in Fig. 5.16, with $N = 2$ and $A = 4$. For this code

$$N_1 = 4, \qquad N_2 = 2, \qquad N_3 = 2, \qquad N_4 = 2.$$

If we choose $p_1 = p_4 = \frac{4}{10}$ and $p_2 = p_3 = \frac{1}{10}$, then

$$\mathrm{P}[\{\mathbf{s}_i\}] = p_1^4 p_2^2 p_3^2 p_4^2 = 4.096 \times 10^{-7}.$$

Another way of expressing this probability assignment is to state that, over the ensemble, the probability that component s_{ij} will be the lth letter of the alphabet is just p_l, independent of all other components in $\mathbf{s}_i$ and in the remaining code words $\{\mathbf{s}_k\}$, $k \neq i$. With this alternative definition, the probability assigned to any code $\{\mathbf{s}_i\}$ is exactly that given in Eq. 5.46b. This interpretation assures us that the probability assignment of Eqs. 5.46 is valid.

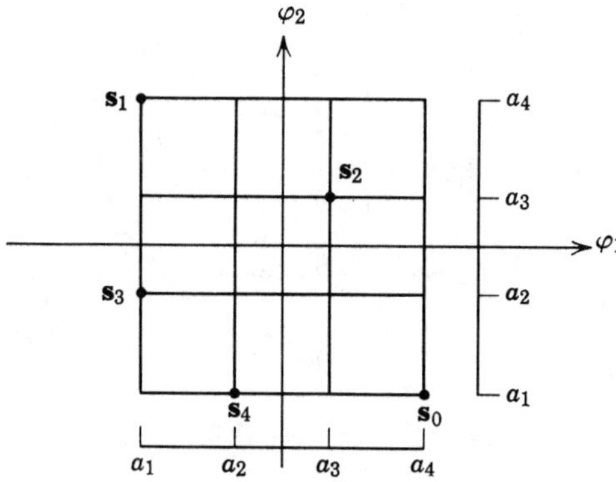

Figure 5.16 Code with $M = 5$, $A = 4$, $N = 2$.

By choosing the p_l's associated with letters near the ends, $+\sqrt{E_\mathrm{N}}$ and $-\sqrt{E_\mathrm{N}}$, to be larger than the p_l's associated with the interior letters we can permit a system whose code contains a larger proportion of end letters to contribute more strongly to the average probability of error than a system whose code contains a smaller proportion. If we choose to let each p_l equal $1/A$, every possible code is equally likely, and all systems will contribute equally to $\overline{\mathrm{P}[\mathcal{E}]}$. We first calculate R_0 for arbitrary $\{p_l\}$; then we specialize the $\{p_l\}$ to values that maximize R_0.†

The procedure for obtaining an exponential bound on $\overline{\mathrm{P}[\mathcal{E}]}$ for the ensemble specified by Eqs. 5.46 is parallel to that followed in the case of

† If, in selecting a specific code, letters are chosen for codewords independently but with the optimum $\{p_l\}$, the probability is high that a code with performance comparable to that afforded by the maximum R_0 will be obtained.

binary antipodal letters. We again have

$$\overline{P[\mathcal{E} \mid m_k]} = \sum_{\text{all codes}} P[\mathcal{E} \mid m_k, \{\mathbf{s}_i\}]\, P[\{\mathbf{s}_i\}],$$

$$P[\mathcal{E} \mid m_k, \{\mathbf{s}_i\}] \leqslant \sum_{\substack{i=0 \\ (i \neq k)}}^{M-1} P_2[\mathbf{s}_i, \mathbf{s}_k],$$

$$\begin{aligned} \overline{P[\mathcal{E} \mid m_k]} &\leqslant \sum_{\text{all codes}} P[\{\mathbf{s}_i\}] \sum_{\substack{i=0 \\ (i \neq k)}}^{M-1} P_2[\mathbf{s}_i, \mathbf{s}_k] \\ &= \sum_{\substack{i=0 \\ (i \neq k)}}^{M-1} \overline{P_2[\mathbf{s}_i, \mathbf{s}_k]}. \end{aligned} \tag{5.47}$$

Provided that we can obtain a bound of the form

$$\overline{P_2[\mathbf{s}_i, \mathbf{s}_k]} = \overline{P_2[\mathcal{E}]} < 2^{-NR_0} \tag{5.48}$$

for any k and all $i \neq k$, it will follow as before that

$$\overline{P[\mathcal{E} \mid m_k]} \leqslant \sum_{\substack{i=0 \\ i \neq k}}^{M-1} \overline{P_2[\mathcal{E}]} < M 2^{-NR_0},$$

and therefore

$$\overline{P[\mathcal{E}]} < 2^{-N[R_0 - R_N]}, \tag{5.49}$$

which is the result that we desire.

It remains to prove the validity of Eq. 5.48 and to evaluate R_0. Since the noise is additive white Gaussian, we again have

$$\begin{aligned} P_2[\mathbf{s}_i, \mathbf{s}_k] &= Q\left(\frac{|\mathbf{s}_i - \mathbf{s}_k|}{\sqrt{2\mathcal{N}_0}}\right) \\ &< \exp\left[-\frac{1}{4\mathcal{N}_0} \sum_{j=1}^{N} (s_{ij} - s_{kj})^2\right] \\ &= \prod_{j=1}^{N} \exp\left[-\frac{1}{4\mathcal{N}_0} (s_{ij} - s_{kj})^2\right], \end{aligned}$$

where $\{s_{ij}\}$ and $\{s_{kj}\}$ are the components of $\mathbf{s}_i$ and $\mathbf{s}_k$, respectively. Averaging over the ensemble of codes yields

$$\overline{P_2[\mathbf{s}_i, \mathbf{s}_k]} < E\left[\prod_{j=1}^{N} \exp\left\{-\frac{1}{4\mathcal{N}_0} (s_{ij} - s_{kj})^2\right\}\right]. \tag{5.50}$$

Evaluation of the right-hand side of Eq. 5.50 is facilitated if we denote the distance between the lth letter and the hth letter of the transmitter alphabet $\{a_l\}$ by the symbol d_{lh}:

$$d_{lh} \triangleq |a_l - a_h|; \qquad l, h = 1, 2, \ldots, A. \tag{5.51a}$$

For example, with the letters of Fig. 5.14

$$d_{lh} = \frac{2\sqrt{E_{\rm N}}}{A-1}\,|l-h|. \tag{5.51b}$$

If $s_{ij} = a_l$ and $s_{kj} = a_h$, we then have

$$(s_{ij} - s_{kj})^2 = d_{lh}^{\ 2}. \tag{5.51c}$$

We next recall that over the ensemble of codes the probability of the joint event $(s_{ij} = a_l, s_{kj} = a_h)$ is $p_l p_h$, independently of the coordinate j we are considering and independently of all other letter assignments. Thus

$$\mathrm{P}[(s_{ij} - s_{kj})^2 = d_{lh}^{\ 2}] = p_l p_h, \tag{5.52}$$

independently for all j, i, and k.

The desirability of assigning probabilities to the different members of our ensemble of communication systems in accordance with Eqs. 5.46 now becomes evident. The statistical independence of the $\{(s_{ij} - s_{kj})^2\}$ permits us to simplify Eq. 5.50 by using the fact that the expected value of a product of statistically independent random variables is the product of their expected values. Since the random variables $\{(s_{ij} - s_{kj})^2\}$, hence the random variables

$$\exp\left[-\frac{1}{4\mathcal{N}_0}(s_{ij} - s_{kj})^2\right], \qquad j = 1, 2, \ldots, N,$$

are statistically independent, Eq. 5.50 yields

$$\overline{\mathrm{P}_2[\mathbf{s}_i, \mathbf{s}_k]} < \prod_{j=1}^{N} \mathrm{E}\left[\exp\left\{-\frac{1}{4\mathcal{N}_0}(s_{ij} - s_{kj})^2\right\}\right].$$

The rest is definition. From Eq. 5.52

$$\mathrm{E}\left[\exp\left\{-\frac{1}{4\mathcal{N}_0}(s_{ij} - s_{kj})^2\right\}\right] = \sum_{l=1}^{A}\sum_{h=1}^{A} \mathrm{P}[(s_{ij} - s_{kj})^2 = d_{lh}^{\ 2}]\, e^{-d_{lh}^{\ 2}/4\mathcal{N}_0}$$

$$= \sum_{l=1}^{A}\sum_{h=1}^{A} p_l p_h e^{-d_{lh}^{\ 2}/4\mathcal{N}_0}.$$

Defining

$$b_{lh} \triangleq e^{-d_{lh}^{\ 2}/4\mathcal{N}_0} \tag{5.53a}$$

and

$$R_0 \triangleq -\log_2\left(\sum_{l=1}^{A}\sum_{h=1}^{A} p_l b_{lh} p_h\right), \tag{5.53b}$$

we have

$$\overline{\mathrm{P}_2[\mathbf{s}_i, \mathbf{s}_k]} < \prod_{j=1}^{N} 2^{-R_0} = 2^{-NR_0}. \tag{5.54}$$

Since the bound of Eq. 5.54 is valid for all i and k, we can again denote $\overline{P_2[\mathbf{s}_i, \mathbf{s}_k]}$ by $\overline{P_2[\mathcal{E}]}$. Thus Eq. 5.48, and therefore the bound

$$\overline{P[\mathcal{E}]} < 2^{-N[R_0 - R_N]}, \tag{5.55}$$

is verified, with R_0 given by Eqs. 5.53. The average probability of error for an ensemble of communication systems using codes with letters selected from an A-letter alphabet decreases exponentially to zero with increasing codeword length, N, as long as $R_N < R_0$. Only the value of R_0 has changed from when $A = 2$; the form of the bound is the same.

The bound of Eq. 5.55 has been derived for any set of A amplitudes $\{a_l\}$ and any set of letter probabilities $\{p_l\}$. In the special case when we choose all $p_l = 1/A$, the expression for R_0 reduces to

$$R_0 = -\log_2 \frac{1}{A^2} \sum_{l=1}^{A} \sum_{h=1}^{A} e^{-d_{lh}^2/4\mathcal{N}_0}. \tag{5.56}$$

For $A = 2$ and $a_1 = +\sqrt{E_N}$, $a_2 = -\sqrt{E_N}$, we have $d_{11} = d_{22} = 0$, $d_{12} = d_{21} = 2\sqrt{E_N}$, and

$$\begin{aligned} R_0 &= -\log_2 \tfrac{1}{4}[e^{-E_N/\mathcal{N}_0} + e^0 + e^0 + e^{-E_N/\mathcal{N}_0}] \\ &= \log_2 \frac{2}{1 + e^{-E_N/\mathcal{N}_0}}, \end{aligned}$$

which agrees with the previous result of Eq. 5.36. More generally, given any choice of amplitudes $\{a_l\}$, Eq. 5.56 can be evaluated on a digital computer. This has been done for the alphabets chosen as in Fig. 5.14 with $A = 2$, 3, 4, 8, 16, 32, and 64. Curves of R_0 as a function of $E_N/\mathcal{N}_0$ are shown in Fig. 5.17. We see that the upper envelope of the curves has small dips at the crossover points.

In Appendix 5C we consider the problem of choosing an optimum probability assignment for the $\{p_l\}$, given any particular signaling alphabet $\{a_l\}$. The curves of R_0 that result when the optimum $\{p_l\}$ are used with the equally spaced letters of Fig. 5.14 are shown in Fig. 5.18, together with R_0^*. We see that the dips disappear and the upper envelope is smooth. The upper envelope of the nonoptimized curves of Fig. 5.17 is also included in Fig. 5.18, as dotted lines. The advantage of using optimum $\{p_l\}$, compared with equally likely $\{p_l\}$, is small as long as the value A is properly chosen.

It is clear from Fig. 5.18 that a relatively simple ensemble of codes with A equally spaced letters having equal probabilities can always be chosen so that R_0 is close to R_0^*; for no value of $E_N/\mathcal{N}_0$ does the R_0^* curve exceed the nonoptimum envelope by more than 35 per cent.

The reason for the discrepancy between R_0^* and the R_0 for multi-amplitude-waveform sequences is easily discerned. First, the condition

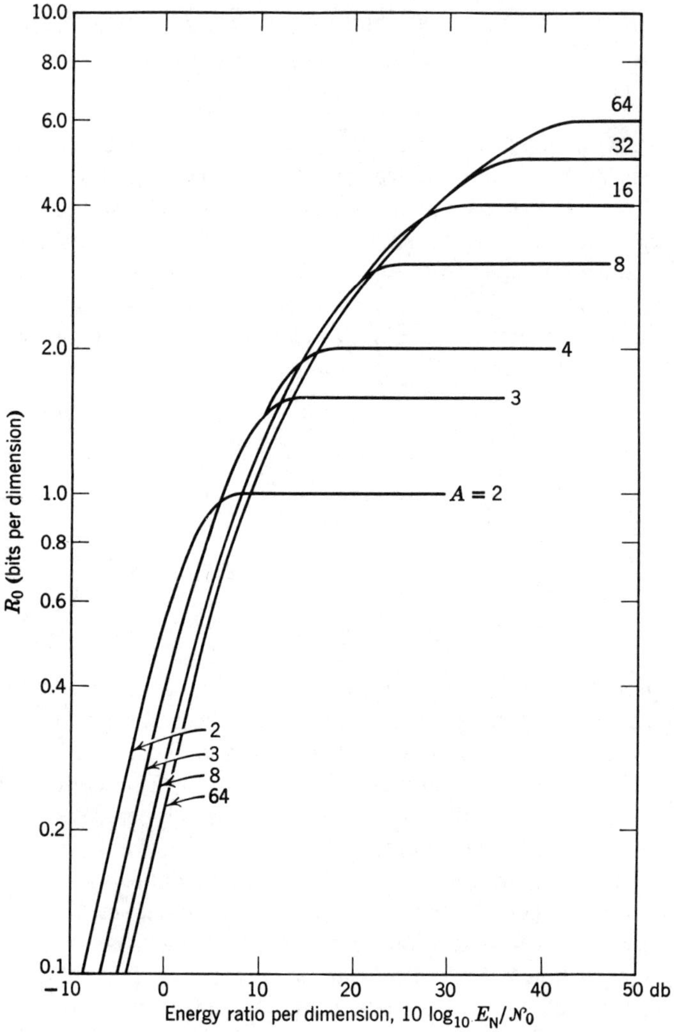

Figure 5.17 R_0 for equispaced A-level amplitude modulation and $p_l = 1/A$; $l = 1, 2, \ldots, A$.

imposed by Shannon in the derivation of R_0^* was that (cf. Eq. 5.43) the *total length* of each signal vector $\mathbf{s}_i$ must be no greater than $\sqrt{NE_N}$. On the other hand, in the derivation of R_0 we required that no vector *component* s_{ij} could be greater than $\sqrt{E_N}$, which is sufficient but not necessary to satisfy Eq. 5.43. The first restriction is a constraint on the total energy of each signal, whereas the second is more akin to a peak-power constraint. If we consider the case in which the $\{a_l\}$ are equally spaced over

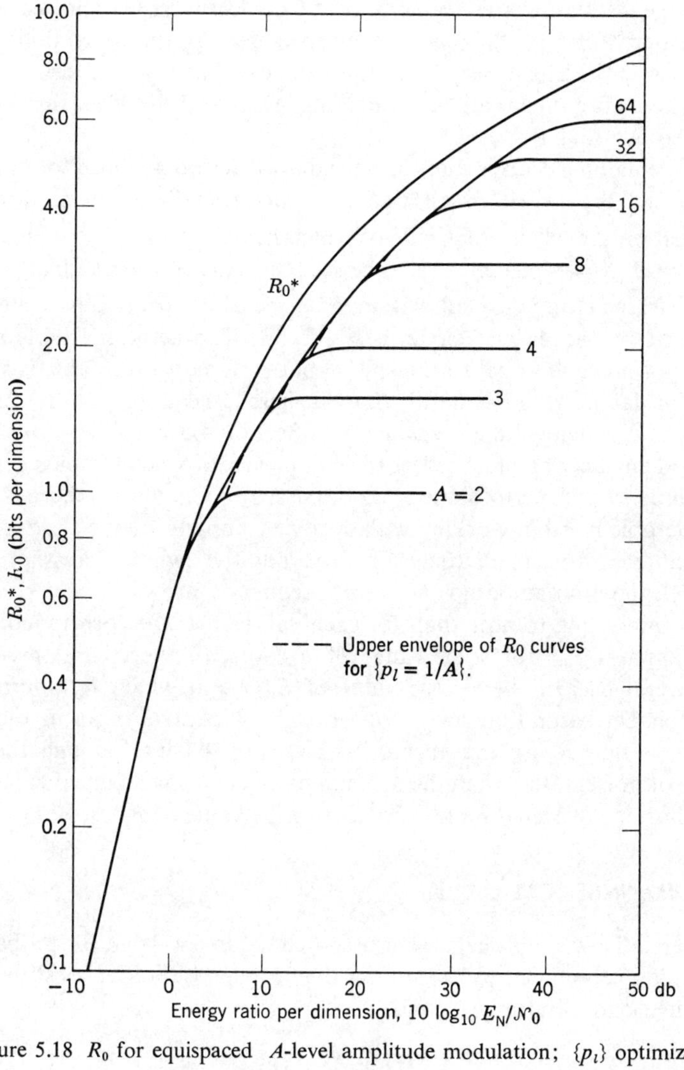

Figure 5.18 R_0 for equispaced A-level amplitude modulation; $\{p_l\}$ optimized.

$[-\sqrt{E_N}, +\sqrt{E_N}]$, each $p_l = 1/A$, and A is large, the expected value of the squared length of any $\mathbf{s}_i$ is

$$\mathrm{E}[|\mathbf{s}_i|^2] = \mathrm{E}\left[\sum_{j=1}^{N} s_{ij}^2\right] = \sum_{j=1}^{N} \mathrm{E}[s_{ij}^2] = N\,\mathrm{E}[s_{ij}^2]$$

$$= \frac{N}{A}\sum_{l=1}^{A} a_l^2 \approx \frac{NE_N}{3}. \tag{5.57}$$

For large A there is a factor of 3, or 4.8 db, between the allowed energy in the derivation of R_0^* and the mean energy in the derivation of R_0. When $A = 3$, $\mathrm{E}[|\mathbf{s}_i|^2] = \frac{2}{3}NE_{\mathrm{N}}$ and the discrepancy is 2 db. Energy differences account for all but something less than 1 db of the discrepancy between R_0^* and R_0.†

The remaining 1 db is due to the signal structure assumed for our code ensemble. We restricted all signal vectors to fall within a *hypercube* centered on the origin, each side of which has length $2\sqrt{E_{\mathrm{N}}}$, as illustrated for $N = 2$, $A = 4$ in Fig. 5.15. The set of signals considered by Shannon is constrained only to fall within a *hypersphere* of radius $\sqrt{NE_{\mathrm{N}}}$, as indicated by the dashed circle in Fig. 5.15. The additional volume for locating signals, internal to the sphere but external to the cube, is significant for large N. (The term "hypersphere" means an N-dimensional sphere and is defined mathematically in Section 5.5.)

Good engineering must reflect the complexity of system implementation as well as system performance; as discussed in Chapter 6, there is often considerable merit in working with a slightly nonoptimum class of signals to facilitate implementation. For the additive white Gaussian noise channel, the multiamplitude waveform sequences are such a class.

It is interesting to note that, for each value of A, the corresponding R_0 approximates R_0^* for some range of $E_{\mathrm{N}}/\mathcal{N}_0$. In every case this range lies several decibels below the value of $E_{\mathrm{N}}/\mathcal{N}_0$ at which R_0 approaches the alphabet saturation level, $\log_2 A$. The explanation, as in the case $A = 2$, is that R_0 is "optimized" by choosing A large enough that the effects of noise, rather than the probability of choosing a bad code because of a shortage of signal points, dominates the value of R_0.

5.5 CHANNEL CAPACITY

The relatively simple argument used in Section 5.4—that the probability of a union is bounded by the sum of the probabilities of its constituents—is sufficient to obtain the bound

$$\overline{\mathrm{P}[\mathcal{E}]} < M\,\overline{\mathrm{P}_2[\mathcal{E}]}, \tag{5.58a}$$

and thence the result

$$\overline{\mathrm{P}[\mathcal{E}]} < 2^{-N[R_0 - R_{\mathrm{N}}]}. \tag{5.58b}$$

Equation 5.58b guarantees that signal sets exist which afford communication through white Gaussian noise at any rate $R_{\mathrm{N}} < R_0$ with arbitrarily

† This same consideration accounts for the discrepancy in Fig. 5.17 between the curves of R_0 for large A and for $A = 2$ when the $\{p_l\}$ are equal to $1/A$ and $E_{\mathrm{N}}/\mathcal{N}_0$ is small.

low error probability. The value of N obtained by setting the right-hand side equal to the desired error probability is an upper bound on the number of dimensions necessary to achieve such performance.

On the other hand, Eqs. 5.58 do not imply that an arbitrarily low probability of error cannot be obtained for rates R_N greater than R_0. Indeed, we have already seen that $R_0^* > R_0$. The central question concerning the ultimate limitations imposed by noise remains.

Capacity Theorem

A complete answer to this question is provided by specialization of a theorem, due to Shannon,[72,75] called the *capacity theorem*. Roughly speaking, this remarkable theorem states that there is a maximum, called *channel capacity*, to the rate at which any communication system can operate satisfactorily when constrained in power; operation at a rate greater than capacity condemns the system to a high probability of error, regardless of the choice of signal set or receiver. The theorem is extremely general and is not restricted to Gaussian channels. For such channels, however, it is clear that the capacity is at least as great as R_0, since we have already proved the existence of systems that yield arbitrarily small error probabilities for any rate less than R_0.

Recalling that the number, D, of dimensions that can be accommodated per second by a bandlimited channel is not sharply specified, we state the capacity theorem in terms of the parameters E_N and R_N, where $R_N = R/D$ again denotes the transmitter input rate in bits per dimension. The energy of each signal is constrained to be no greater than NE_N, where N is the dimensionality of the signal space.

In the particular case of transmission over an additive white Gaussian noise channel the capacity theorem may be stated as follows:

Theorem. There exists a constant, C_N, given by

$$C_N = \tfrac{1}{2} \log_2 \left(1 + 2\frac{E_N}{\mathcal{N}_0}\right) \tag{5.59}$$

and called the *Gaussian channel capacity*, with the following properties:

Negative Statement. If $R_N > C_N$ and the number of equally likely messages, $M = 2^{NR_N}$, is large, the probability of error is close to 1 for every possible set of M transmitter signals.

Positive Statement. If $R_N < C_N$ and M is sufficiently large, there exist sets of M transmitter signals such that the probability of error achieved with optimum receivers is arbitrarily small.

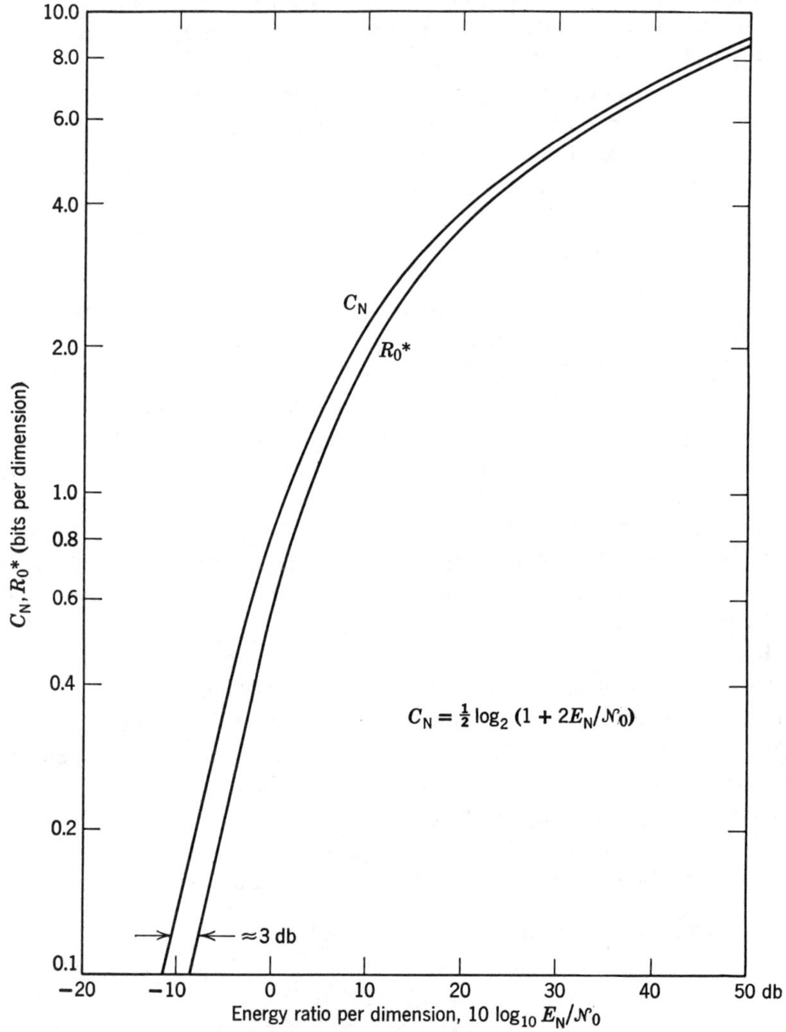

Figure 5.19 Comparison of capacity and R_0^*.

A plot of C_N as a function of $E_N/\mathcal{N}_0$ is given in Fig. 5.19, together with R_0^*. We see that

$$\tfrac{1}{2}C_N \leqslant R_0^* \leqslant C_N. \tag{5.60}$$

Thus the apparent limitation $R_N < R_0$ on rate evidenced by Eq. 5.58 is attributable to the manner of bounding and is not an inescapable attribute of $E_N/\mathcal{N}_0$. The bound $R_N < C_N$ is inescapable.

The bound $R_N < C_N$ (bits/dimension) implies that

$$R < DC_N \text{ (bits/sec).} \tag{5.61a}$$

The number of dimensions per second that can be accommodated by a bandlimited channel is bounded† (cf. Appendix 5A, Eq. 5A.6) by

$$D \leqslant 2W. \tag{5.61b}$$

If we achieve the upper bound $D = 2W$, then $E_N = P_s/D = P_s/2W$, and we have the well-known result

$$R < 2WC_N = W \log_2 \left(1 + \frac{P_s}{W\mathcal{N}_0}\right) \triangleq C, \tag{5.61c}$$

where C is the capacity in bits per second and P_s, defined by Eq. 5.5, is the maximum average power allotted to any transmitted signal.

Proof of the Capacity Theorem

This proof of Shannon's[72] capacity theorem for the Gaussian channel is essentially geometric. The proof is long but straightforward.

Sphere hardening. Let us begin by considering a signal space of N dimensions and a set of $M = 2^{NR_N}$ signals, each with energy less than or equal to NE_N:

$$|\mathbf{s}_i|^2 \leqslant NE_N; \qquad \text{all } i. \tag{5.62}$$

When Eq. 5.62 is met, we say that the signals lie within an *N-dimensional sphere*‡ of radius $\sqrt{NE_N}$.

For this proof, we introduce vectors so normalized that the size of the constraining sphere is independent of N:

$$\underline{\mathbf{s}}_i \triangleq \mathbf{s}_i/\sqrt{N}; \qquad i = 0, 1, \ldots, M-1, \tag{5.63a}$$

$$\underline{\mathbf{n}} \triangleq \mathbf{n}/\sqrt{N}, \tag{5.63b}$$

$$\underline{\mathbf{r}} \triangleq \mathbf{r}/\sqrt{N} = \underline{\mathbf{s}}_i + \underline{\mathbf{n}}; \qquad m = m_i, \tag{5.63c}$$

† The discrepancy between the bound of Eq. 5.61b and the dimensionality theorem of Sect. 5.3, $D < 2.4W$, arises out of a distinction in the conditions of validity of the two bounds. The distinction is discussed in App. 5A.

‡ An N-dimensional sphere, say I_s, of radius ρ and centered on the origin, is defined as the set of points $\mathbf{x} = (x_1, x_2, \ldots, x_N)$ such that $x_1^2 + x_2^2 + \cdots + x_N^2 \leqslant \rho^2$. Thus $I_s \triangleq \{\mathbf{x} : |\mathbf{x}|^2 \leqslant \rho^2\}$. The intersection of an N-dimensional sphere of radius ρ with any two-dimensional plane passing through its center is a circle of radius ρ. Similarly, the projection of the N-dimensional sphere into any set of three dimensions—achieved by setting all x_i equal to zero except for the three x_i pertaining to the three dimensions of interest—is a three-dimensional sphere of radius ρ. For instance,

$$I_s|_{\text{projected in first three dimensions}} = \{\mathbf{x} : x_1^2 + x_2^2 + x_3^2 \leqslant \rho^2\}.$$

where $\mathbf{s}_i$, $\mathbf{n}$, and $\mathbf{r}$ are defined as usual in terms of orthonormal functions. We then have

$$|\underline{\mathbf{s}}_i|^2 = \frac{|\mathbf{s}_i|^2}{N} \leqslant E_{\mathrm{N}} \text{ (joules/dimension)}, \tag{5.64}$$

so that all normalized signals lie within a "signal sphere", say I_s, of radius $\sqrt{E_{\mathrm{N}}}$, where E_{N} is the average energy available per dimension.

It is interesting to examine the mean-squared length of the N-dimensional noise vector $\underline{\mathbf{n}}$ under this normalization:

$$|\underline{\mathbf{n}}|^2 = \frac{1}{N}|\mathbf{n}|^2 = \frac{1}{N}\sum_{j=1}^{N} n_j^{\,2}, \tag{5.65a}$$

where $\{n_j\}$ is a set of N zero-mean, statistically independent random variables, each with variance $\mathcal{N}_0/2$. Hence

$$\mathrm{E}[|\underline{\mathbf{n}}|^2] = \frac{1}{N}\overline{\sum_{j=1}^{N} n_j^{\,2}} = \frac{1}{N}\sum_{j=1}^{N}\overline{n_j^{\,2}} = \frac{1}{N}\sum_{j=1}^{N}\frac{\mathcal{N}_0}{2} = \frac{\mathcal{N}_0}{2}. \tag{5.65b}$$

We see that the average squared length of the normalized noise vector is $\mathcal{N}_0/2$, independently of the number of dimensions N.

Although the average squared length of the noise vector is independent of N, it is crucial to our proof that the *variance of the squared length is not.* Since the variance of a sum of independent random variables equals the sum of the variances, the variance of $|\underline{\mathbf{n}}|^2$, say $\sigma^2(|\underline{\mathbf{n}}|^2)$, is

$$\begin{aligned}\sigma^2(|\underline{\mathbf{n}}|^2) &= \frac{1}{N^2}\sigma^2\left(\sum_{j=1}^{N} n_j^{\,2}\right) = \frac{1}{N^2}\sum_{j=1}^{N}\sigma^2(n_j^{\,2}) \\ &= \frac{1}{N^2}\sum_{j=1}^{N}\left[\overline{n_j^{\,4}} - (\overline{n_j^{\,2}})^2\right].\end{aligned} \tag{5.65c}$$

Equation 5.65c may be evaluated by invoking Eq. 2.145, which states that for zero-mean Gaussian random variables $\{n_j\}$

$$\overline{n_j^{\,4}} = 3(\overline{n_j^{\,2}})^2; \qquad j = 1, \dots, N.$$

Thus

$$\sigma^2(|\underline{\mathbf{n}}|^2) = \frac{1}{N^2}\sum_{j=1}^{N} 2(\overline{n_j^{\,2}})^2 = \frac{2}{N}\left(\frac{\mathcal{N}_0}{2}\right)^2. \tag{5.65d}$$

We see that the variance of $|\underline{\mathbf{n}}|^2$ tends to zero with increasing N. It follows from Chebyshev's inequality that

$$\mathrm{P}\left[\left|\,|\underline{\mathbf{n}}|^2 - \frac{\mathcal{N}_0}{2}\right| \geqslant \Delta\right] \leqslant \frac{2}{N}\frac{(\mathcal{N}_0/2)^2}{\Delta^2} \tag{5.66}$$

for any positive Δ, no matter how small.

Equation 5.66 states that for large enough N the probability that the squared length of the normalized noise vector $\underline{\mathbf{n}}$ differs from its average value of $\mathcal{N}_0/2$ by more than Δ is arbitrarily close to 0. Since the noise vector is equally likely to point in any direction, we may picture the noise vector when N is very large as falling close to the surface of a sphere of radius $\sqrt{\mathcal{N}_0/2}$ without directional preference, as shown in Fig. 5.20. This phenomenon is referred to as *sphere hardening*.

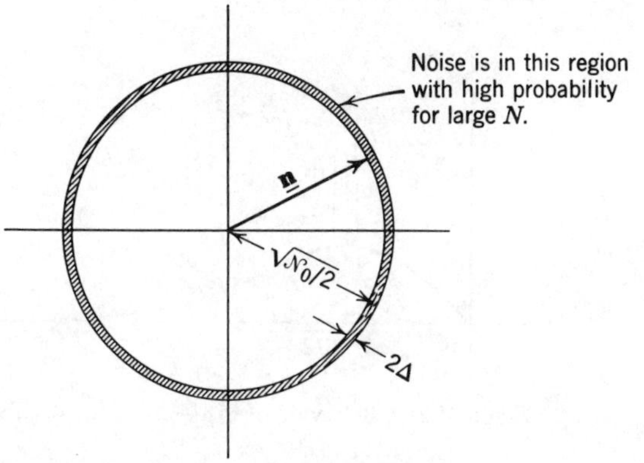
Noise is in this region with high probability for large N.
n
√N0/2
2Δ

Figure 5.20 Sphere hardening.

Insight into the phenomenon of sphere hardening may be obtained by calculating the probability that $\underline{\mathbf{n}}$ falls into the shell between concentric spheres of radius $\rho - \Delta$ and ρ, with $\Delta/\rho \ll 1$. Since the components of $\underline{\mathbf{n}}$ are zero-mean Gaussian random variables of variance $\mathcal{N}_0/2N$, the density function of the normalized noise vector is

$$p_{\underline{\mathbf{n}}}(\boldsymbol{\alpha}) = \frac{1}{[\pi(\mathcal{N}_0/N)]^{N/2}} \exp\left(-\frac{N}{\mathcal{N}_0}|\boldsymbol{\alpha}|^2\right). \tag{5.67a}$$

When Δ/ρ is small,

$$p_{\underline{\mathbf{n}}}(\boldsymbol{\alpha}) \approx \left(\frac{N}{\pi\mathcal{N}_0}\right)^{N/2} \exp\left(-\frac{N}{\mathcal{N}_0}\rho^2\right); \qquad \text{for } \rho - \Delta < |\boldsymbol{\alpha}| \leqslant \rho. \tag{5.67b}$$

Thus

$$\mathrm{P}\left[\rho\left(1 - \frac{\Delta}{\rho}\right) < |\underline{\mathbf{n}}| \leqslant \rho\right] \approx \left(\frac{N}{\pi\mathcal{N}_0}\right)^{N/2} \exp\left(-\frac{N}{\mathcal{N}_0}\rho^2\right) [\text{volume of shell}].$$

In Appendix 5D we show (Eq. 5D.8) that the volume of the shell is proportional to $\rho^N(\Delta/\rho)$. Thus the probability that $\underline{\mathbf{n}}$ lies within the shell is proportional to the product of two factors, one of which $(e^{-(N/\mathcal{N}_0)\rho^2})$ *decreases* and the other of which (ρ^N) *increases* sharply with increasing ρ.

For Δ/ρ = a constant $\ll 1$ we have

$$\mathrm{P}\left[\rho\left(1-\frac{\Delta}{\rho}\right) < |\underline{\mathbf{n}}| \leqslant \rho\right] \sim \left[\rho \exp\left(-\frac{\rho^2}{\mathcal{N}_0}\right)\right]^N. \tag{5.67c}$$

The right-hand side of Eq. 5.67c has a single maximum at $\rho^2 = \mathcal{N}_0/2$, as shown in Fig. 5.21. As N becomes large, the consequence is that only values of $|\underline{\mathbf{n}}|^2$ in the vicinity of this maximum, $\mathcal{N}_0/2$, have significant probability. Figure 5.21 provides a graphic demonstration of the "sphere-hardening" phenomenon.

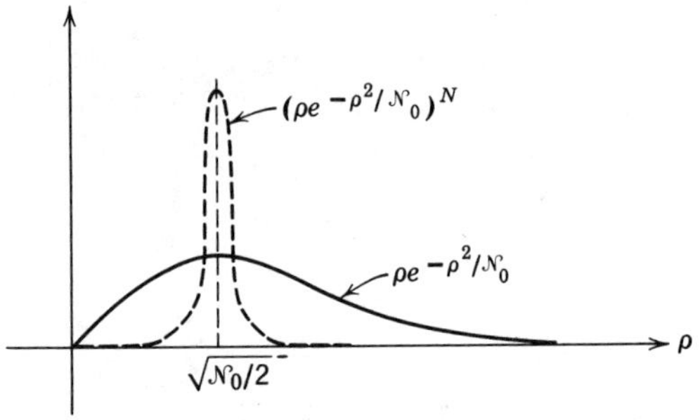

Figure 5.21 Behavior of $\mathrm{P}[\rho - \Delta < |\mathbf{n}| \leqslant \rho]$ with ρ.

Proof of the negative statement. The negative part of the capacity theorem states that the probability of error tends to one with increasing N if the rate exceeds capacity. The statement is readily proved by means of sphere-hardening arguments. We first recall that the receiver for any set of transmitter signals $\{\mathbf{s}_i\}$ is defined by a set of decision regions. If the decision region associated with the normalized signal $\underline{\mathbf{s}}_i$ is significantly smaller than a sphere of radius $\sqrt{\mathcal{N}_0/2}$ centered on $\underline{\mathbf{s}}_i$, the probability that ($\underline{\mathbf{r}} = \underline{\mathbf{s}}_i + \underline{\mathbf{n}}$) will fall into this decision region must, by sphere-hardening arguments, tend to zero as N increases. Hence decision regions must be comparable to or larger than spheres of radius $\sqrt{\mathcal{N}_0/2}$. The negative statement rests on the observation that *if the number of signals is too large* the typical decision region will be forced by volume (power) constraints to have an effective size smaller than that of a sphere of radius $\sqrt{\mathcal{N}_0/2}$.

To make the proof precise, we first show that sphere-hardening is also exhibited by the received signal; that is, with high probability $\underline{\mathbf{r}}$ will fall within a sphere of radius $\sqrt{E_{\mathrm{N}} + \mathcal{N}_0/2 + \Delta}$. Proceeding as with $|\underline{\mathbf{n}}|^2$, we have, when $\underline{\mathbf{s}}_k$ is transmitted,

$$|\underline{\mathbf{r}}|^2 = |\underline{\mathbf{s}}_k + \underline{\mathbf{n}}|^2 = |\underline{\mathbf{s}}_k|^2 + 2\underline{\mathbf{s}}_k \cdot \underline{\mathbf{n}} + |\underline{\mathbf{n}}|^2$$

$$= |\underline{\mathbf{s}}_k|^2 + \frac{2}{N}\sum_{j=1}^{N} s_{kj} n_j + |\underline{\mathbf{n}}|^2, \tag{5.68a}$$

where $\underline{\mathbf{s}}_k = \frac{1}{\sqrt{N}}(s_{k1}, s_{k2}, \ldots, s_{kN})$. Since each noise variable n_j has zero mean,

$$\begin{aligned}
\mathrm{E}[|\underline{\mathbf{r}}|^2] &= |\underline{\mathbf{s}}_k|^2 + \frac{\mathcal{N}_0}{2} + \frac{2}{N}\sum_{j=1}^{N} s_{kj}\, \mathrm{E}[n_j] \\
&= |\underline{\mathbf{s}}_k|^2 + \frac{\mathcal{N}_0}{2} \\
&\leqslant E_{\mathsf{N}} + \frac{\mathcal{N}_0}{2}. \qquad (5.68\text{b})
\end{aligned}$$

Next, denoting the variance of the squared length of $\underline{\mathbf{r}}$ by $\sigma^2(|\underline{\mathbf{r}}|^2)$ and noting that the variance of a sum of two random variables is never greater than twice the sum of the variances—a consequence of the inequality $(a + b)^2 \leqslant 2(a^2 + b^2)$—when $\underline{\mathbf{s}}_k$ is transmitted we have

$$\begin{aligned}
\sigma^2(|\underline{\mathbf{r}}|^2) &\leqslant 2[\sigma^2(2\underline{\mathbf{s}}_k \cdot \underline{\mathbf{n}}) + \sigma^2(|\underline{\mathbf{n}}|^2)] \\
&= 2\left[\frac{4}{N^2}\sum_{j=1}^{N}\sigma^2(s_{kj}n_j) + \frac{2}{N}\left(\frac{\mathcal{N}_0}{2}\right)^2\right] \\
&= 2\left[\frac{4}{N^2}\sum_{j=1}^{N}s_{kj}{}^2\sigma^2(n_j) + \frac{2}{N}\left(\frac{\mathcal{N}_0}{2}\right)^2\right] \\
&= 2\left[\frac{4}{N^2}\frac{\mathcal{N}_0}{2}\sum_{j=1}^{N}s_{kj}{}^2 + \frac{2}{N}\left(\frac{\mathcal{N}_0}{2}\right)^2\right] \\
&\leqslant \frac{2}{N}\left[2\mathcal{N}_0 E_{\mathsf{N}} + 2\left(\frac{\mathcal{N}_0}{2}\right)^2\right]. \qquad (5.68\text{c})
\end{aligned}$$

The variance of the squared length of the received signal also vanishes with increasing N. Hence the received signal tends to be close to the surface of a sphere of radius $\sqrt{|\underline{\mathbf{s}}_k|^2 + \mathcal{N}_0/2}$. In particular,

$$\mathrm{P}\left[|\underline{\mathbf{r}}|^2 \geqslant E_{\mathsf{N}} + \frac{\mathcal{N}_0}{2} + \Delta\right] \leqslant \frac{\sigma^2(|\underline{\mathbf{r}}|^2)}{\Delta^2} \sim \frac{1}{N\Delta^2} \qquad (5.69)$$

and tends to zero as N gets large. This tendency of the received vector to fall within a sphere of fixed diameter sharply limits the effective volume of the decision regions.

We are now ready to prove the negative capacity theorem. We show that for any small positive quantity ϵ the probability of correct decision in the transmission of one of $M = 2^{NR_{\mathsf{N}}}$ equally likely messages is less than ϵ for sufficiently large N whenever $R_{\mathsf{N}} > C_{\mathsf{N}} = \frac{1}{2}\log(1 + 2E_{\mathsf{N}}/\mathcal{N}_0)$, regardless of the choice of signal set and receiver.

According to the sphere-hardening argument, for large N the received vector $\underline{\mathbf{r}}$ is effectively constrained to lie within a sphere, say I_r, of radius $\sqrt{E_N + \mathcal{N}_0/2 + \Delta}$. Writing the probability of correct decision as the sum of two terms,

$$P[\mathcal{C}] = P[\mathcal{C}, \underline{\mathbf{r}} \text{ in } I_r] + P[\mathcal{C}, \underline{\mathbf{r}} \text{ outside } I_r], \tag{5.70a}$$

we observe that the second term satisfies, for any $\epsilon > 0$, the inequalities

$$P[\mathcal{C}, \underline{\mathbf{r}} \text{ outside } I_r] \leqslant P[\underline{\mathbf{r}} \text{ outside } I_r] < \frac{\epsilon}{2}. \tag{5.70b}$$

The last inequality follows, for large enough N, from Eq. 5.69.

It remains to be shown that the first term in Eq. 5.70a is also less than $\epsilon/2$ for sufficiently large N whenever $R_N > C_N$.

Let I_i, $i = 0, 1, \ldots, M - 1$, denote that part of the decision region for the ith signal lying entirely within I_r, as shown in Fig. 5.22; let V_i

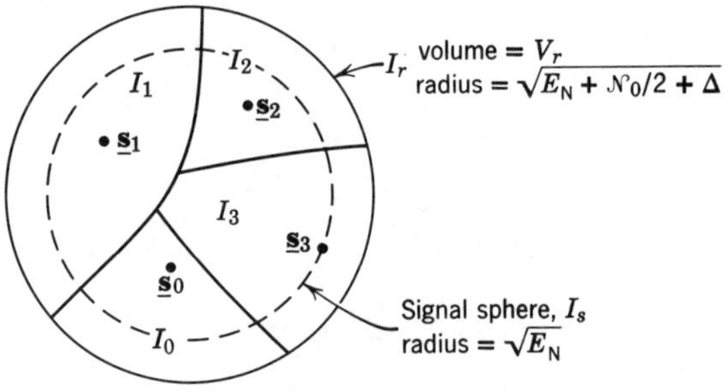

Figure 5.22 Decision regions within I_r.

denote the volume of I_i and let V_r denote the volume of I_r. Because the decision regions are disjoint,

$$V_r = V_0 + V_1 + \cdots + V_{M-1} \tag{5.71}$$

and

$$\begin{aligned} P[\mathcal{C}, \underline{\mathbf{r}} \text{ in } I_r] &= \sum_{i=0}^{M-1} P[\underline{\mathbf{r}} \text{ in } I_i \mid m_i]\, P[m_i] \\ &= \frac{1}{M} \sum_{i=0}^{M-1} P[\underline{\mathbf{r}} \text{ in } I_i \mid m_i]. \end{aligned} \tag{5.72}$$

We now observe that, for each i,

$$P[\underline{\mathbf{r}} \text{ in } I_i \mid m_i] \leqslant P[|\underline{\mathbf{n}}| \leqslant \rho_i], \tag{5.73}$$

where ρ_i is defined to be the radius of an N-dimensional *sphere* of volume V_i (this sphere and I_i both have the same volume). Equation 5.73 states that *no decision region of given volume is better than a spherical decision region of the same volume centered on the signal.* Proof of the optimality of spheres follows immediately from the observation that $p_{\underline{n}}$ is a spherically symmetric density function decreasing monotonically with increasing $|\underline{n}|$. As a consequence, any volume element lying farther from $\underline{s}_i$ than the radius ρ_i has less probability of containing $\underline{r} = \underline{s}_i + \underline{n}$ than it would if it were located within a distance ρ_i from the signal. On the other hand, all volume elements in the sphere do lie within distance ρ_i from $\underline{s}_i$.

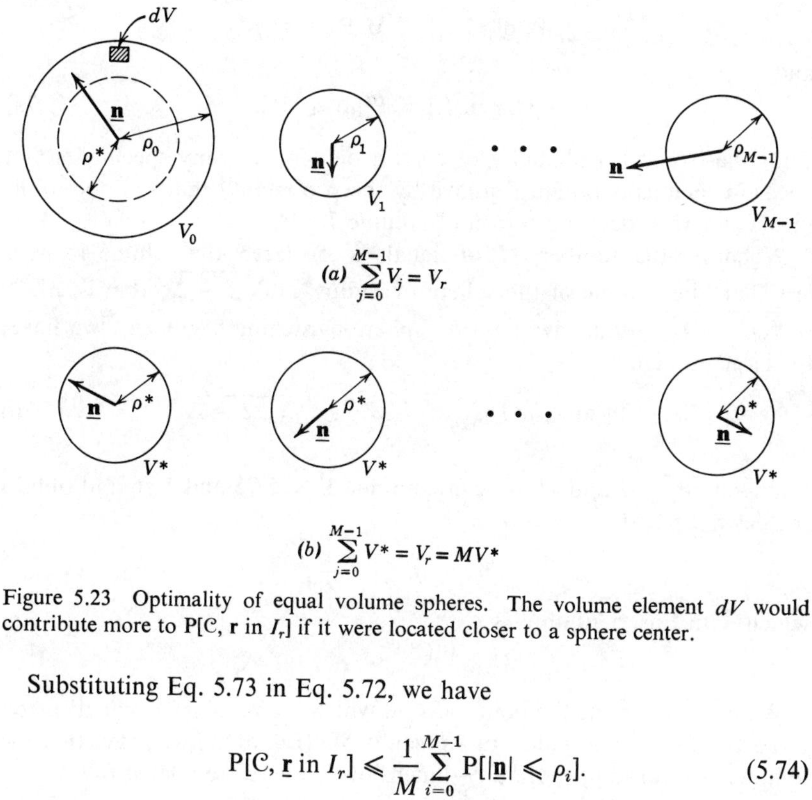

Figure 5.23 Optimality of equal volume spheres. The volume element dV would contribute more to P[C, **r** in I_r] if it were located closer to a sphere center.

Substituting Eq. 5.73 in Eq. 5.72, we have

$$P[\mathcal{C}, \underline{r} \text{ in } I_r] \leqslant \frac{1}{M} \sum_{i=0}^{M-1} P[|\underline{n}| \leqslant \rho_i]. \tag{5.74}$$

Each term on the right-hand side of this inequality is the probability that $\underline{n}$ will lie on or within a sphere of volume V_i. The right-hand side is thus the arithmetic mean of the probabilities of noise falling in spheres of radii $\rho_0, \rho_1, \ldots, \rho_{M-1}$, as indicated in Fig. 5.23*a*.

If the original decision regions $\{I_i\}$ all contained the same volume, we would have (from Eq. 5.71)

$$V_i = \frac{V_r}{M},$$

and each of the ρ_i would equal the radius, say ρ^*, of the sphere of volume V_r/M. In this case every volume element dV in the set of M spheres would lie at a distance no greater than ρ^* from the center of one of the spheres, as shown in Fig. 5.23*b*. On the other hand, when the V_i—hence the ρ_i—are *not* all equal, some volume elements are more distant than ρ^* from a center and therefore contribute less probability to the sum in Eq. 5.74. It follows that

$$\sum_{i=0}^{M-1} \mathrm{P}[|\underline{\mathbf{n}}| \leqslant \rho_i] \leqslant M\, \mathrm{P}[|\underline{\mathbf{n}}| \leqslant \rho^*]$$

and

$$\mathrm{P}[\mathcal{C}, \underline{\mathbf{r}} \text{ in } I_r] \leqslant \mathrm{P}[|\underline{\mathbf{n}}| \leqslant \rho^*]. \tag{5.75}$$

Thus the over-all probability of correct decision for any specified set of decision regions is bounded above by the probability that the noise falls into a spherical decision region of volume V_r/M.

Whenever the number, M, of signals is too large, the volume V_r/M is less than the volume of the sphere of radius $\sqrt{\mathcal{N}_0/2 - \Delta}$; that is, $\rho^* < \sqrt{\mathcal{N}_0/2 - \Delta}$. Again invoking the sphere-hardening argument, we have, for large enough N,

$$\mathrm{P}[|\underline{\mathbf{n}}| \leqslant \rho^*] < \frac{\epsilon}{2}, \quad \text{if } \rho^* < \sqrt{\mathcal{N}_0/2 - \Delta}. \tag{5.76}$$

For such large M and N, we can combine Eqs. 5.75 and 5.76 and obtain the desired result

$$\mathrm{P}[\mathcal{C}, \underline{\mathbf{r}} \text{ in } I_r] < \frac{\epsilon}{2},$$

which with Eqs. 5.70 implies

$$\mathrm{P}[\mathcal{C}] < \epsilon.$$

We now determine the point beyond which the number of signals is too large and Eq. 5.76 is valid. In Appendix 5D (Eq. 5D.5) we prove that the volume V and radius ρ of an N-dimensional sphere are related by

$$V = B_N\, \rho^N, \tag{5.77a}$$

where B_N is a positive constant that depends only on N. Thus the statement that $\rho^* < \sqrt{\mathcal{N}_0/2 - \Delta}$ or the equivalent statement that V_r/M is less than the volume of a sphere of radius $\sqrt{\mathcal{N}_0/2 - \Delta}$ may be written

$$\frac{V_r}{M} < B_N\left(\frac{\mathcal{N}_0}{2} - \Delta\right)^{N/2}. \tag{5.77b}$$

Since V_r is the volume of a sphere of radius $\sqrt{E_{\mathrm{N}} + \mathcal{N}_0/2 + \Delta}$, Eq. 5.77b becomes

$$\frac{B_N(E_{\mathrm{N}} + \mathcal{N}_0/2 + \Delta)^{N/2}}{M} < B_N\left(\frac{\mathcal{N}_0}{2} - \Delta\right)^{N/2},$$

or

$$M > \left(\frac{E_{\mathrm{N}} + \mathcal{N}_0/2 + \Delta}{\mathcal{N}_0/2 - \Delta}\right)^{N/2}. \tag{5.77c}$$

Finally, since $M = 2^{NR_{\mathrm{N}}}$, Eq. 5.77c may be written

$$2^{NR_{\mathrm{N}}} > \left(\frac{E_{\mathrm{N}} + \mathcal{N}_0/2 + \Delta}{\mathcal{N}_0/2 - \Delta}\right)^{N/2}$$

or

$$R_{\mathrm{N}} > \frac{1}{2}\log_2 \frac{E_{\mathrm{N}} + \mathcal{N}_0/2 + \Delta}{\mathcal{N}_0/2 - \Delta}. \tag{5.77d}$$

Clearly, if

$$R_{\mathrm{N}} > C_{\mathrm{N}} \triangleq \frac{1}{2}\log_2\left(1 + 2\frac{E_{\mathrm{N}}}{\mathcal{N}_0}\right) = \frac{1}{2}\log_2 \frac{E_{\mathrm{N}} + \mathcal{N}_0/2}{\mathcal{N}_0/2}, \tag{5.78a}$$

we can take Δ sufficiently small that the inequality of Eq. 5.77d, hence of Eq. 5.76, is satisfied. Consequently, the condition $R_{\mathrm{N}} > C_{\mathrm{N}}$ implies that

$$\mathrm{P}[\mathcal{C}] < \epsilon, \tag{5.78b}$$

or

$$\mathrm{P}[\mathcal{E}] > 1 - \epsilon. \tag{5.78c}$$

Equation 5.78a provides an upper bound on the number of message bits per dimension which, if exceeded, causes $\mathrm{P}[\mathcal{E}]$ to be close to 1 for large N. We summarize the steps in the foregoing proof by a sequence of equations:

$$\begin{aligned}
\mathrm{P}[\mathcal{C}] &= \mathrm{P}[\mathcal{C}, \underline{\mathbf{r}} \text{ in } I_r] + \mathrm{P}[\mathcal{C}, \underline{\mathbf{r}} \text{ outside of } I_r] \\
&< \frac{1}{M}\sum_{i=0}^{M-1} \mathrm{P}[\underline{\mathbf{r}} \text{ in } I_i \mid m_i] + \frac{\epsilon}{2} \\
&< \frac{1}{M}\sum_{i=0}^{M-1} \mathrm{P}[|\underline{\mathbf{n}}| < \rho_i] + \frac{\epsilon}{2} \\
&< \mathrm{P}[|\underline{\mathbf{n}}| < \rho^*] + \frac{\epsilon}{2} \\
&< \epsilon.
\end{aligned}$$

This sequence is valid if

$$\begin{aligned}\sqrt{\mathcal{N}_0/2 - \Delta} &> \rho^* \\ &= \left(\frac{1}{B_N}\frac{V_r}{M}\right)^{1/N} \\ &= \frac{\sqrt{E_{\mathrm{N}} + \mathcal{N}_0/2 + \Delta}}{M^{1/N}},\end{aligned}$$

which implies

$$M > \left(1 + 2\frac{E_{\mathrm{N}}}{\mathcal{N}_0}\right)^{N/2}$$

or

$$R_{\mathrm{N}} > \frac{1}{2}\log_2\left(1 + \frac{2E_{\mathrm{N}}}{\mathcal{N}_0}\right).$$

The derivation of Eqs. 5.78 is completely independent of the particular set of transmitter vectors $\{\mathbf{s}_i\}$; the result is valid for *any* set that meets the signal energy constraint of Eq. 5.62. Thus the negative statement of the channel capacity theorem is proved. Since transmission with a set of $2^{NR_{\mathrm{N}}}$ vectors having N components includes the possibility of k transmissions, each with a set of $2^{NR_{\mathrm{N}}/k}$ vectors having N/k components, the theorem holds true for any transmission strategy. We see that the probability of communicating a block of $RT = NR_{\mathrm{N}}$ bits without any error whatsoever must approach zero as T grows large if R_{N} exceeds C_{N}.

This proof is described as "sphere packing." It is a negative proof, in that no claim is made about the existence of signals $\{\mathbf{s}_i\}$ such that the decision regions $\{I_i\}$ actually are spheres of equal radius. Clearly, geometry does not permit. The essence of the argument is simply that the "packed spheres" idealization implies a bound on performance that no realizable set of signals can surpass.

Proof of the positive statement. We now prove the positive channel capacity statement that if $R_{\mathrm{N}} < C_{\mathrm{N}}$ then for any positive number ϵ (no matter how small) there exists a large enough value of N and a set of $M = 2^{NR_{\mathrm{N}}}$ signals $\{\mathbf{s}_i\}$ such that the attainable probability of error is less than ϵ. The proof is complicated by two facts: first, in general it is not possible to exhibit explicitly such a set of signals $\{\mathbf{s}_i\}$, and, second, even if such a set could be exhibited, the calculation of its probability of error would be enormously difficult. These complications, which we encountered before in connection with R_0, may again be circumvented by considering not just one communication system but rather a whole ensemble of systems, each consisting of a transmitter, channel, and optimum receiver. As before, we construct our ensemble in such a way that the mean probability of error, $\overline{P[\mathcal{E}]}$, may be easily calculated. We prove the theorem by showing that $\overline{P[\mathcal{E}]} < \epsilon$ for sufficiently large N; the ensemble must then contain individual systems for which the probability of error is also less than ϵ.

Specification of Codes for the Ensemble of Systems. The capacity theorem for the Gaussian channel concerns normalized N-dimensional signals $\{\underline{\mathbf{s}}_i\}$ each of which satisfies the average power constraint

$$|\underline{\mathbf{s}}_i| \leqslant \sqrt{E_N}; \qquad i = 0, 1, \ldots, M-1, \tag{5.79a}$$

where, as before,

$$\underline{\mathbf{s}}_i \triangleq \mathbf{s}_i/\sqrt{N}. \tag{5.79b}$$

Since any vector $\underline{\mathbf{s}}_i$ may lie anywhere in the N-dimensional signal sphere I_s implied by Eq. 5.79a, the codes of an ensemble of systems can be specified by stating an appropriate density function over I_s, say

$$p_{\{\underline{\mathbf{s}}_i\}} \triangleq p_{\underline{\mathbf{s}}_0, \underline{\mathbf{s}}_1, \ldots, \underline{\mathbf{s}}_{M-1}}. \tag{5.80}$$

In terms of the density function, the ensemble average probability of error is

$$\overline{P[\mathcal{E}]} = \int P[\mathcal{E} \mid \{\underline{\mathbf{s}}_i\} = \boldsymbol{\gamma}]\, p_{\{\underline{\mathbf{s}}_i\}}(\boldsymbol{\gamma})\, d\boldsymbol{\gamma}. \tag{5.81}$$

Since there are M vectors $\underline{\mathbf{s}}_i$, and each comprises N components, $\boldsymbol{\gamma}$ is an NM dimensional vector. The multiple integral of Eq. 5.81 is over all NM arguments.

A simple and convenient choice for $p_{\{\underline{\mathbf{s}}_i\}}$ which facilitates calculation of $\overline{P[\mathcal{E}]}$ and also satisfies the constraint of Eq. 5.79a is

$$p_{\underline{\mathbf{s}}_i}(\boldsymbol{\alpha}) = \begin{cases} \dfrac{1}{V_s} & \text{for } |\boldsymbol{\alpha}|^2 \leqslant E_N \\ 0 & \text{for } |\boldsymbol{\alpha}|^2 > E_N \end{cases}; \qquad \text{all } i, \tag{5.82a}$$

and

$$p_{\{\underline{\mathbf{s}}_i\}} = \prod_{i=0}^{M-1} p_{\underline{\mathbf{s}}_i}, \tag{5.82b}$$

where V_s denotes the volume of I_s. Equations 5.82 state that over the ensemble of systems the signal vectors are statistically independent and the probability that any signal vector will fall outside of the signal sphere I_s is zero. Furthermore, if I is a region of volume V entirely contained within the signal sphere,

$$P[\underline{\mathbf{s}}_i \text{ in } I] = \int_I p_{\underline{\mathbf{s}}_i}(\boldsymbol{\alpha})\, d\boldsymbol{\alpha} = \frac{1}{V_s} \int_I d\boldsymbol{\alpha} = \frac{V}{V_s}. \tag{5.82c}$$

Thus, if we select one system at random from the ensemble for examination, the probability that the signal, $\underline{\mathbf{s}}_i$, assigned to the ith message is located in a region I of the signal sphere is directly proportional to the volume of the region I.

Although $\underline{\mathbf{s}}_i$ is equally likely to lie in any volume element within the signal sphere, it is *not* true that $\underline{\mathbf{s}}_i$ is equally likely to lie at any radius ρ, $0 \leqslant \rho \leqslant \sqrt{E_N}$. Indeed, for any $\Delta > 0$,

$$\begin{aligned} \mathrm{P}[|\underline{\mathbf{s}}_i| \leqslant \sqrt{E_N - \Delta}] &= \mathrm{P}[\underline{\mathbf{s}}_i \text{ in sphere of radius } \sqrt{E_N - \Delta}] \\ &= \frac{\text{volume of sphere of radius } \sqrt{E_N - \Delta}}{V_s} \\ &= \frac{B_N(E_N - \Delta)^{N/2}}{B_N {E_N}^{N/2}} = \left(1 - \frac{\Delta}{E_N}\right)^{N/2}, \end{aligned} \tag{5.83}$$

which is very close to zero for large N. Equation 5.83 is a concomitant of the fact that almost all of the volume in a high-dimensional sphere is located near the surface. The probability assignment of Eq. 5.82 therefore implies that nearly all of the signals $\{\underline{\mathbf{s}}_i\}$ have energy close to E_N.

Calculation of $\overline{\mathrm{P}[\mathcal{E}]}$. We now show that over this ensemble of communication systems $\overline{\mathrm{P}[\mathcal{E}]} < \epsilon$ if N is sufficiently large. Note that $\overline{\mathrm{P}[\mathcal{E}]}$ depends on three statistically independent sets of random variables:

1. The choice of message, m, with $\mathrm{P}[m_i] = 1/M$.
2. The noise $\underline{\mathbf{n}}$, with $p_{\underline{\mathbf{n}}}$ given by Eq. 5.67a.
3. The choice of code $\{\underline{\mathbf{s}}_i\}$, with $p_{\{\underline{\mathbf{s}}_i\}}$ given by Eq. 5.82.

Thus we may calculate $\overline{\mathrm{P}[\mathcal{E}]}$ from the conditional probability of error

$$\mathrm{P}[\mathcal{E} \mid m_k, \underline{\mathbf{n}}, \{\underline{\mathbf{s}}_i\}] = \begin{cases} 0 & \text{if } m_k, \underline{\mathbf{n}} \text{ and } \{\underline{\mathbf{s}}_i\} \text{ are such that} \\ & |\underline{\mathbf{s}}_k - (\underline{\mathbf{s}}_k + \underline{\mathbf{n}})| < |\underline{\mathbf{s}}_i - (\underline{\mathbf{s}}_k + \underline{\mathbf{n}})| \text{ for} \\ & \text{all } i \neq k, \text{ so that no error is made,} \\ 1 & \text{otherwise} \end{cases} \tag{5.84a}$$

by first multiplying by

$$\mathrm{P}[m_k] p_{\underline{\mathbf{n}}} p_{\underline{\mathbf{s}}_0} p_{\underline{\mathbf{s}}_1} \cdots p_{\underline{\mathbf{s}}_{M-1}}, \tag{5.84b}$$

then integrating out the continuous variables $\{\underline{\mathbf{s}}_i\}$ and $\mathbf{n}$, and finally summing over the index k.

Clearly, the order in which the conditioning random variables are integrated out does not affect the value of $\overline{\mathrm{P}[\mathcal{E}]}$. But eliminating $\underline{\mathbf{n}}$ and k first amounts (for each code $\{\underline{\mathbf{s}}_i\}$ in the ensemble) to evaluating $\mathrm{P}[\mathcal{E} \mid \{\underline{\mathbf{s}}_i\}]$.

This problem—finding the P[$\mathcal{E}$] for a specific code—we have already foresworn as too difficult. Once more, the crucial advantage of the random-coding argument is that it permits us to eliminate the $\{\underline{\mathbf{s}}_i\}$ first (to integrate over the ensemble of systems first) and thereby to simplify the computation. We therefore proceed in the following order:

i. Eliminate (that is, integrate over) $\{\underline{\mathbf{s}}_i\}$ for all $i \neq k$ to obtain $P[\mathcal{E} \mid m_k, \underline{\mathbf{s}}_k, \underline{\mathbf{n}}]$.
ii. Eliminate $\underline{\mathbf{s}}_k$ and $\underline{\mathbf{n}}$ to obtain $\overline{P[\mathcal{E} \mid m_k]}$.
iii. Eliminate m_k to obtain $\overline{P[\mathcal{E}]}$.

It is the fact that step i can be performed by use of a geometric argument that permits a simple proof.

(i) *Elimination of* $\{\underline{\mathbf{s}}_i\}$, $i \neq k$. In calculating $P[\mathcal{E} \mid m_k, \underline{\mathbf{s}}_k, \underline{\mathbf{n}}]$ the transmitted vector and the disturbing noise have, by definition, the fixed known values $\underline{\mathbf{s}}_k$ and $\underline{\mathbf{n}}$. These two vectors together specify a two-dimensional

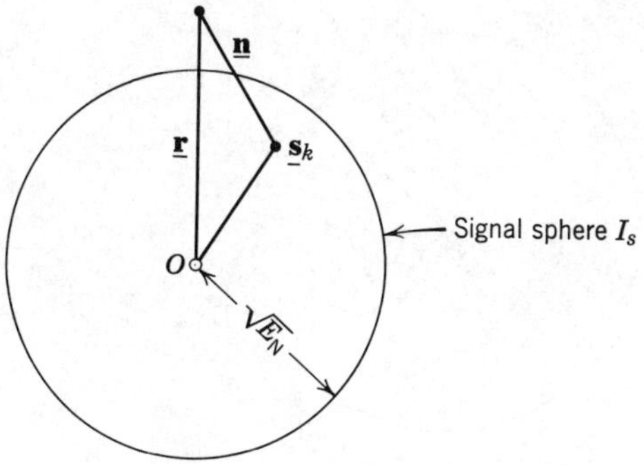

Figure 5.24 Plane containing $\underline{\mathbf{s}}_k$, $\underline{\mathbf{n}}$, $\underline{\mathbf{r}}$, and origin.

plane intersecting the N-dimensional signal sphere I_s in a circle of radius $\sqrt{E_N}$, as shown in Fig. 5.24. All points in the signal space that are closer than $\underline{\mathbf{s}}_k$ to the received vector $\underline{\mathbf{r}} = \underline{\mathbf{s}}_k + \underline{\mathbf{n}}$ are located in a "noise" sphere around $\underline{\mathbf{r}}$ of radius $|\underline{\mathbf{n}}|$. Since we have already stipulated that each receiver in the ensemble of communication systems is optimum, the presence of one or more of the other signals in this noise sphere will cause an error. All signals, however, are confined to I_s. Thus the intersection of I_s and the noise sphere centered on $\underline{\mathbf{r}}$ forms the locus of all allowable transmitter signals that cause an error, given $\underline{\mathbf{s}}_k$ transmitted and $\underline{\mathbf{r}} = \underline{\mathbf{s}}_k + \underline{\mathbf{n}}$ received.

This locus is an N-dimensional solid whose projection onto the plane of $\underline{\mathbf{s}}_k$ and $\underline{\mathbf{n}}$ is the crosshatched region shown in Fig. 5.25*a*. Furthermore, this N-dimensional solid has an identical lens-shaped cross section when projected onto *any* plane containing $\underline{\mathbf{r}}$ and the origin. Consequently, this solid, to which we shall henceforth refer as an N-dimensional lens, is completely contained within an N-dimensional sphere of radius h centered on the point $0'$. This follows from the fact that the cross section of this sphere, when projected on any plane containing $\underline{\mathbf{r}}$, is a circle of radius h centered on $0'$. Thus the volume of the lens, V_{lens}, is bounded by

$$V_{\text{lens}} < B_N h^N, \tag{5.85}$$

a fact to which we shall return later. It is helpful when visualizing the geometrical relationships just described to consider the case in which the spheres are three-dimensional ($N = 3$), illustrated in Fig. 5.25*b*.

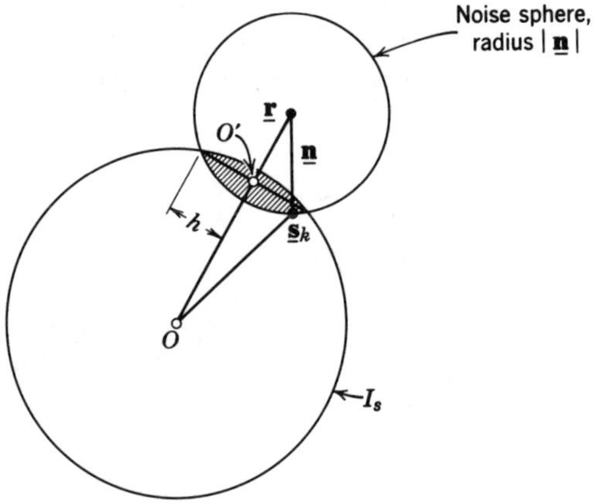

Figure 5.25*a* Projection of locus of signals causing error.

Given $\underline{\mathbf{s}}_k$ and $\underline{\mathbf{n}}$, an error occurs in any system in the ensemble whose code includes at least one other signal vector within the lens. From Eq. 5.82c the probability of the set of systems whose ith signal vector, $\underline{\mathbf{s}}_i$, lies in the lens is

$$\mathrm{P}[\underline{\mathbf{s}}_i \text{ in lens}] = \frac{V_{\text{lens}}}{V_s}; \qquad i \neq k.$$

There are $(M - 1)$ nontransmitted vectors in each code. Since the probability of a union of events is bounded above by the sum of their probabilities, it follows that the probability of the set of systems having one or more nontransmitted signal vectors in the lens is

$$\mathrm{P}[\underline{\mathbf{s}}_0 \text{ or } \cdots \text{ or } \underline{\mathbf{s}}_i \text{ or } \cdots \text{ or } \underline{\mathbf{s}}_{M-1} \text{ in lens}] \leqslant (M-1)\frac{V_{\text{lens}}}{V_s}; \qquad i \neq k.$$

Thus we have

$$P[\mathcal{E} \mid m_k, \underline{\mathbf{s}}_k, \underline{\mathbf{n}}] < M \frac{V_{\text{lens}}}{V_s}. \tag{5.86a}$$

It is clear from Fig. 5.25*a* that the volume V_{lens} depends on $\underline{\mathbf{s}}_k$ and $\underline{\mathbf{n}}$. For certain choices of these vectors $M(V_{\text{lens}}/V_s)$ will exceed unity, in which case tighter results can be obtained by invoking the trivial bound

$$P[\mathcal{E} \mid m_k, \underline{\mathbf{s}}_k, \underline{\mathbf{n}}] \leqslant 1. \tag{5.86b}$$

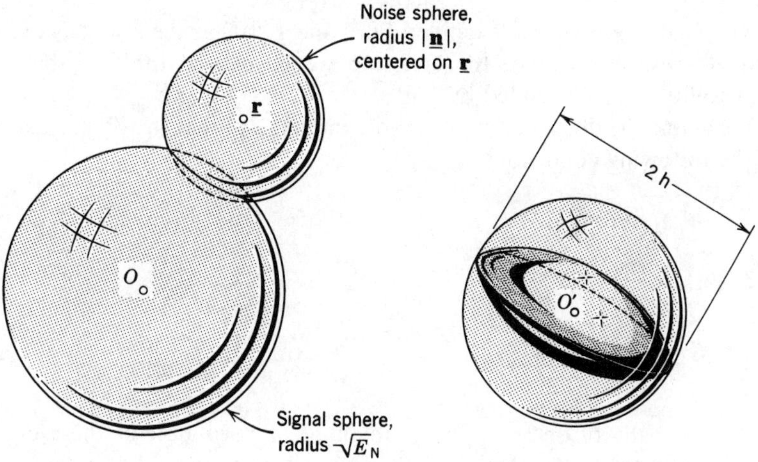

(b)

Figure 5.25*b* The intersection of two spheres is a lens. The enlargement shows the lens enclosed within a third sphere, of radius h, centered on O'.

(ii) *Elimination of* $\underline{\mathbf{s}}_k$ *and* $\underline{\mathbf{n}}$. We are now prepared to undertake the second step of the proof, namely, to eliminate the continuous variables $\underline{\mathbf{s}}_k$ and $\underline{\mathbf{n}}$ from the conditional probability of error bounded in Eqs. 5.86:

$$\overline{P[\mathcal{E} \mid m_k]} = \int P[\mathcal{E} \mid m_k, \underline{\mathbf{s}}_k = \boldsymbol{\alpha}, \underline{\mathbf{n}} = \boldsymbol{\beta}]\, p_{\underline{\mathbf{s}}_k}(\boldsymbol{\alpha})\, p_{\underline{\mathbf{n}}}(\boldsymbol{\beta})\, d\boldsymbol{\alpha}\, d\boldsymbol{\beta},$$

where the integral is taken over all possible values of $\underline{\mathbf{s}}_k$ and $\underline{\mathbf{n}}$. In order to apply the bounds of Eqs. 5.86a and b, we perform the integration in two parts. In the first an integral is taken over a domain $\mathfrak{D}$ of values of $\underline{\mathbf{s}}_k$ and $\underline{\mathbf{n}}$ for which all pairs $(\underline{\mathbf{s}}_k, \underline{\mathbf{n}})$ are such that V_{lens} is less than a (small) constant, say V^*_{lens}. The second integral is over the remaining domain, $\mathfrak{D}^{\mathsf{C}}$, of values of $\underline{\mathbf{s}}_k$ and $\underline{\mathbf{n}}$. The probability of $\mathfrak{D}^C$ is later shown to be sufficiently small that the bound of Eq. 5.86b may be used safely. Thus

$$\overline{P[\mathcal{E} \mid m_k]} < \int_{\mathfrak{D}} \left(M \frac{V^*_{\text{lens}}}{V_s} \right) p_{\underline{\mathbf{s}}_k}(\boldsymbol{\alpha})\, p_{\underline{\mathbf{n}}}(\boldsymbol{\beta})\, d\boldsymbol{\alpha}\, d\boldsymbol{\beta} + \int_{\mathfrak{D}^C} p_{\underline{\mathbf{s}}_k}(\boldsymbol{\alpha})\, p_{\underline{\mathbf{n}}}(\boldsymbol{\beta})\, d\boldsymbol{\alpha}\, d\boldsymbol{\beta}$$

$$= M \frac{V^*_{\text{lens}}}{V_s} P[\mathfrak{D}] + P[\mathfrak{D}^C]$$

$$\leqslant M \frac{V^*_{\text{lens}}}{V_s} + P[\mathfrak{D}^C]. \tag{5.87}$$

In the evaluation we have defined $P[\mathfrak{D}]$ and $P[\mathfrak{D}^C]$ as the integrals over $\mathfrak{D}$ and $\mathfrak{D}^C$ respectively. In the last step we have used the fact that any probability is overbounded by unity.

We define the domain $\mathfrak{D}^C$ to be those pairs $(\underline{\mathbf{s}}_k, \underline{\mathbf{n}})$ that satisfy at least one of the following conditions:

1. $|\underline{\mathbf{s}}_k|^2 < E_N - \Delta$
2. $|\underline{\mathbf{n}}|^2 > \frac{\mathcal{N}_0}{2} + \Delta$
3. $|\underline{\mathbf{r}}|^2 < |\underline{\mathbf{s}}_k|^2 + \frac{\mathcal{N}_0}{2} - \Delta.$

The probability of $\mathfrak{D}^C$ is the probability of the union of these events and is bounded by the sum of their probabilities:

$$P[\mathfrak{D}^C] \leqslant P[|\underline{\mathbf{s}}_k|^2 < E_N - \Delta] + P\left[|\underline{\mathbf{n}}|^2 > \frac{\mathcal{N}_0}{2} + \Delta\right] + P\left[|\underline{\mathbf{r}}|^2 < |\underline{\mathbf{s}}_k|^2 + \frac{\mathcal{N}_0}{2} - \Delta\right].$$

By Eqs. 5.83, 5.66, and 5.68 each of the three terms on the right is less than $\epsilon/6$ for sufficiently large N, so that†

$$P[\mathfrak{D}^C] < \frac{\epsilon}{2}. \tag{5.88}$$

We now show that the first term on the right-hand side of Eq. 5.87 is also overbounded by $\epsilon/2$ for large N. For all pairs $(\underline{\mathbf{s}}_k, \underline{\mathbf{n}})$ in $\mathfrak{D}$ we have,

† To be precise, Eqs. 5.68b and c together with the Chebyshev inequality imply that the conditional probability of the event $|\mathbf{r}|^2 < |\boldsymbol{\alpha}|^2 + \mathcal{N}_0/2 - \Delta$, given $\mathbf{s}_k = \boldsymbol{\alpha}$, approaches zero as N becomes large. But for any event A such that $P[A \mid \mathbf{s}_k = \boldsymbol{\alpha}] < \epsilon/6$ for all allowable $\boldsymbol{\alpha}$ we also have $P[A] < \epsilon/6$.

from the defining conditions,

$$|\underline{\mathbf{n}}| \leqslant \sqrt{\mathcal{N}_0/2 + \Delta}$$

and (5.89)

$$|\underline{\mathbf{r}}| \geqslant \sqrt{E_N + \mathcal{N}_0/2 - 2\Delta}.$$

From Fig. 5.25*a* it is clear that the size of the lens increases with decreasing $|\underline{\mathbf{r}}|$ and with increasing $|\underline{\mathbf{n}}|$. Hence the largest lens for pairs $(\underline{\mathbf{s}}_k, \underline{\mathbf{n}})$ in $\mathfrak{D}$ is achieved when the conditions of Eqs. 5.89 are satisfied with the equality, as shown in Fig. 5.26; from Eq. 5.85 we have

$$V^*_{\text{lens}} < B_N(h^*)^N, \tag{5.90a}$$

where h^* is defined in the figure.

To show that V^*_{lens} is small enough so that MV^*_{lens}/V_s is less than $\epsilon/2$, we require a bound on h^*. It is clear from Fig. 5.26 that h^* is a continuous

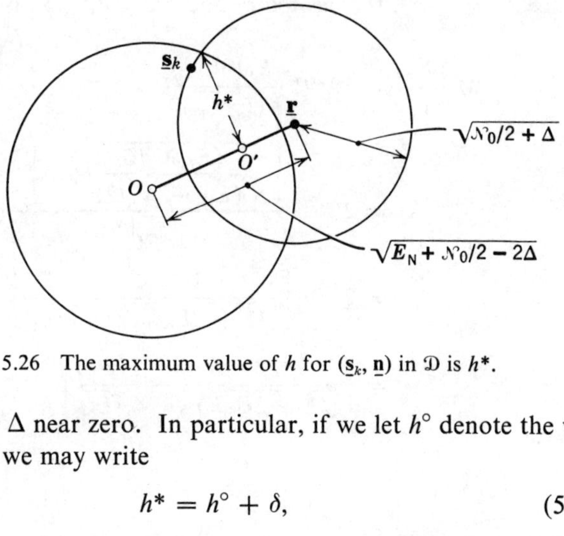

Figure 5.26 The maximum value of h for $(\underline{\mathbf{s}}_k, \underline{\mathbf{n}})$ in $\mathfrak{D}$ is h^*.

function of Δ for Δ near zero. In particular, if we let h° denote the value of h^* for $\Delta = 0$, we may write

$$h^* = h^\circ + \delta, \tag{5.90b}$$

where δ is positive and may be made arbitrarily small by taking Δ small. It is an easy matter to compute h°, since $\underline{\mathbf{s}}_k$, $\underline{\mathbf{n}}$, and $\underline{\mathbf{r}}$ form a right triangle when $\Delta = 0$, as shown in Fig. 5.27. Calculating the area of this triangle first with $\underline{\mathbf{r}}$ as the base and then with $\underline{\mathbf{s}}_k$ as the base, we have

$$h^\circ \sqrt{E_N + \frac{\mathcal{N}_0}{2}} = \sqrt{E_N}\sqrt{\frac{\mathcal{N}_0}{2}},$$

hence

$$h^\circ = \sqrt{\frac{E_N\mathcal{N}_0/2}{E_N + \mathcal{N}_0/2}}. \tag{5.90c}$$

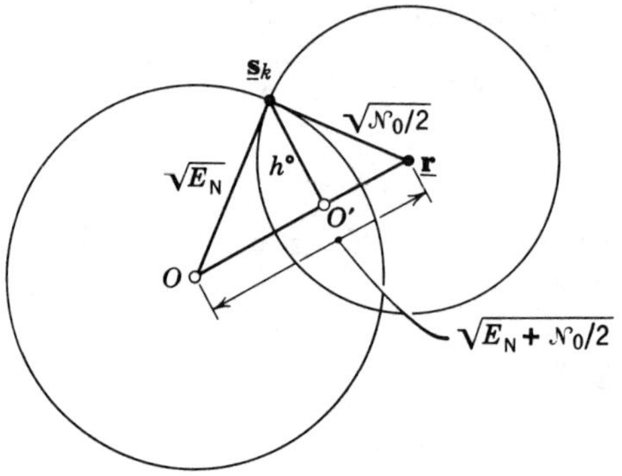

Figure 5.27 Geometry when $\Delta = 0$.

Since V_s is the volume of the signal sphere I_s, which has radius $\sqrt{E_N}$, and,since $M = 2^{NR_N}$, the desired bound on MV^*_{lens}/V_s is

$$
\begin{aligned}
M\frac{V^*_{\text{lens}}}{V_s} &< 2^{NR_N}\frac{B_N(h^*)^N}{B_N(\sqrt{E_N})^N} \\
&= 2^{NR_N}\frac{\left[\sqrt{\dfrac{(E_N\mathcal{N}_0/2)}{(E_N+\mathcal{N}_0/2)}}+\delta\right]^N}{[\sqrt{E_N}]^N} \\
&= 2^{NR_N}\left[\frac{1}{\sqrt{1+2E_N/\mathcal{N}_0}}+\frac{\delta}{\sqrt{E_N}}\right]^N \\
&= \left[\frac{2^{R_N}}{\sqrt{1+2E_N/\mathcal{N}_0}}+\frac{2^{R_N}\,\delta}{\sqrt{E_N}}\right]^N.
\end{aligned}
\tag{5.91}
$$

Whenever

$$\frac{2^{R_N}}{\sqrt{1+2E_N/\mathcal{N}_0}} < 1, \tag{5.92}$$

Δ, hence δ, can be taken small enough so that the term within square brackets in Eq. 5.91 is less than 1. Equation 5.92 is equivalent to the statement that $R_N < C_N \triangleq \frac{1}{2}\log_2(1 + 2E_N/\mathcal{N}_0)$. Thus for sufficiently large N

$$M\frac{V^*_{\text{lens}}}{V_s} < \frac{\epsilon}{2}, \quad \text{if} \quad R_N < C_N$$

and

$$\overline{P[\mathcal{E} \mid m_k]} < M\frac{V^*_{\text{lens}}}{V_s} + P[\mathcal{D}^C] < \epsilon.$$

(iii) *Elimination of* m_k. The final step in the proof of the positive channel capacity statement is to sum over the index k.

$$\overline{P[\mathcal{E}]} = \sum_{k=0}^{M-1} \overline{P[\mathcal{E} \mid m_k]}\, P[m_k]$$
$$< \sum_{k=0}^{M-1} \epsilon\, P[m_k] = \epsilon. \tag{5.93}$$

This completes the proof.

Discussion

The concept of channel capacity is the fundament of modern communication theory. Before Shannon's work communication engineers believed that noise in the channel set an inescapable limit on the *accuracy* of communication of a fixed-rate source. The capacity theorem states that noise (together with the available number of dimensions per second and the available signal power) sets an inescapable limit only on the *rate* at which accurate communication can be achieved, but *not* on the accuracy.

This theorem, proved here for an additive white Gaussian noise channel, is actually of vast applicability. It holds true for very general mathematical channel models. More important, every physical communication channel also exhibits phenomena that are consistent with the concept of an input bit rate that cannot be exceeded if communication accuracy is to be preserved. In addition, this rate is usually significantly greater than that at which reliable system operation can be achieved by conventional means such as bit-by-bit signaling.

To a considerable extent, research in communication theory is concerned with finding practical means of simultaneously attaining the higher accuracy and higher data rates predicted by channel capacity. Some of the problems inherent in trying to do so are considered in Chapter 6.

5.6 RELIABILITY FUNCTIONS

In Section 5.4 the ensemble average probability of error for communication over an additive white Gaussian noise channel was shown to satisfy the bound

$$\overline{P[\mathcal{E}]} < 2^{-N[R_0 - R_N]}, \tag{5.94}$$

where N is the code block length, and R_N is the rate in bits per dimension. Equation 5.94 was arrived at by means of the simple argument that the probability of a union is no greater than the sum of the probabilities of its constituents.

The bound of Eq. 5.94 indicates that arbitrarily small error probabilities can certainly be achieved if $R_N < R_0$. More elaborate bounding techniques were used in Section 5.5 to prove the channel capacity statement that arbitrarily small error probabilities can be achieved if and only if $R_N < C_N$. The channel capacity statement is stronger, in the sense that $C_N \geqslant R_0$. In another sense, however, Eq. 5.94 is stronger, in that knowledge of R_0 enables the bounding of the error probability as a function of N and R_N, whereas knowledge of C_N alone does not.

More complete knowledge of the achievable error performance than that provided by either C_N or R_0 is embodied in a function called the channel *reliability function.* We now derive the reliability function for the infinite-bandwidth white Gaussian noise channel. The procedure is to obtain a bound on the attainable probability of error for block orthogonal signals which is tighter than that afforded by the union argument alone.

Block-Orthogonal Signaling

When one of a set of $M = 2^{RT}$ equally likely orthogonal signals of energy $E_s = P_s T$ is transmitted in white Gaussian noise of power density $\mathcal{N}_0/2$, the union bound of Eq. 5.14a may be rewritten as

$$\mathrm{P}[\mathcal{E}] < 2^{-T(\frac{1}{2}C_\infty - R)}, \tag{5.95a}$$

in which we have introduced the definition

$$C_\infty \triangleq \frac{P_s}{\mathcal{N}_0}\log_2 e = \lim_{D\to\infty} DC_N = \lim_{D\to\infty}\frac{D}{2}\log_2\left(1 + \frac{2P_s}{\mathcal{N}_0 D}\right). \tag{5.95b}$$

C_∞ is the limiting value of the white Gaussian noise channel capacity (in bits per second) of Eq. 5.59 as the available dimensions per second, D, hence the channel bandwidth, tends to infinity while P_s and $\mathcal{N}_0$ remain fixed.

From Eq. 4.96, the exact expression for the probability bounded in Eqs. 5.95 is $\mathrm{P}[\mathcal{E}] = 1 - \mathrm{P}[\mathcal{C}]$, in which

$$\mathrm{P}[\mathcal{C}] = \int_{-\infty}^{\infty} p_n(\mu - \sqrt{E_s})\,d\mu\left[\int_{-\infty}^{\mu} p_n(\nu)\,d\nu\right]^{M-1}, \tag{5.96a}$$

$$p_n(\nu) = \frac{1}{\sqrt{\pi\mathcal{N}_0}}\,e^{-\nu^2/\mathcal{N}_0}. \tag{5.96b}$$

We now overbound $1 - \mathrm{P}[\mathcal{C}]$ by arguments similar to, but more sensitive than, the union bound. As a preliminary step we normalize Eq. 5.96 by making the change of variables $\alpha = \mu/\sqrt{\mathcal{N}_0/2}$, $\beta = \nu/\sqrt{\mathcal{N}_0/2}$, so that

$$\mathrm{P}[\mathcal{C}] = \int_{-\infty}^{\infty} p(\alpha - b)\, d\alpha \left[\int_{-\infty}^{\alpha} p(\beta)\, d\beta\right]^{M-1}, \tag{5.97a}$$

in which

$$p(\gamma) = \frac{1}{\sqrt{2\pi}}\, e^{-\gamma^2/2} \tag{5.97b}$$

and

$$b \triangleq \sqrt{2E_s/\mathcal{N}_0}. \tag{5.97c}$$

Thus the probability of error, expressed in terms of the $Q(\ )$ function of Eq. 2.50, is

$$\mathrm{P}[\mathcal{E}] = 1 - \mathrm{P}[\mathcal{C}] = \int_{-\infty}^{\infty} p(\alpha - b)\, d\alpha\{1 - [1 - Q(\alpha)]^{M-1}\}. \tag{5.97d}$$

The term in braces is the probability that at least one of $M - 1$ (independent) noise components exceeds α; by the union argument it is bounded above by the sum of the probabilities that individual components exceed α:

$$\{1 - [1 - Q(\alpha)]^{M-1}\} \leqslant (M - 1)\, Q(\alpha) < M\, Q(\alpha). \tag{5.98a}$$

Since it is a probability, it is also overbounded by one:

$$\{1 - [1 - Q(\alpha)]^{M-1}\} \leqslant 1. \tag{5.98b}$$

The unity bound is tighter when α is small and $Q(\alpha)$ large; the bound $MQ(\alpha)$ is tighter when α is large. It is therefore convenient to split the range of integration on α into two parts, thereby obtaining

$$\mathrm{P}[\mathcal{E}] < \int_{-\infty}^{a} p(\alpha - b)\, d\alpha + M \int_{a}^{\infty} p(\alpha - b) e^{-\alpha^2/2}\, d\alpha; \qquad 0 \leqslant a.$$

Here we have also invoked Eq. 2.122 and the condition $a \geqslant 0$ to overbound $Q(\alpha)$ by $e^{-\alpha^2/2}$. Denoting the first integral by P_1 and the second by P_2, we have

$$\mathrm{P}[\mathcal{E}] < P_1 + MP_2. \tag{5.99}$$

The bound is minimized by choosing a as the solution to

$$0 = \frac{d}{da}[P_1 + MP_2] = p(a - b) - Mp(a - b)e^{-a^2/2},$$

whence

$$e^{a^2/2} = M. \tag{5.100}$$

The next step is to bound P_1 and P_2. We have

$$P_1 = \int_{-\infty}^{a} \frac{1}{\sqrt{2\pi}} e^{-(\alpha-b)^2/2}\, d\alpha = \int_{-\infty}^{a-b} \frac{1}{\sqrt{2\pi}} e^{-\gamma^2/2}\, d\gamma = Q(b-a).$$

Thus

$$P_1 \leqslant e^{-(a-b)^2/2}; \qquad a \leqslant b. \tag{5.101}$$

Also,

$$\begin{aligned} P_2 &= \int_{a}^{\infty} \frac{1}{\sqrt{2\pi}} e^{-\frac{1}{2}[(\alpha-b)^2+\alpha^2]}\, d\alpha \\ &= e^{-b^2/4} \int_{a}^{\infty} \frac{1}{\sqrt{2\pi}} e^{-(\alpha-b/2)^2}\, d\alpha \\ &= e^{-b^2/4} \frac{1}{\sqrt{2}} \int_{\sqrt{2}(a-b/2)}^{\infty} \frac{1}{\sqrt{2\pi}} e^{-\gamma^2/2}\, d\gamma \\ &= \frac{1}{\sqrt{2}} e^{-b^2/4}\, Q\left(\sqrt{2}\left[a - \frac{b}{2}\right]\right). \end{aligned}$$

Thus

$$P_2 < \begin{cases} e^{-b^2/4}; & a \leqslant \dfrac{b}{2}, \\ e^{-(b^2/4)-(a-b/2)^2}; & a \geqslant \dfrac{b}{2}. \end{cases} \tag{5.102}$$

(In Eq. 5.102 it is important to note the values of a for which the inequalities are valid.) Substituting Eqs. 5.102 and 5.101 in Eq. 5.99 and replacing M with $e^{a^2/2}$ in accordance with Eq. 5.100 yields

$$\mathrm{P}[\mathcal{E}] < \begin{cases} e^{-(a-b)^2/2} + e^{a^2/2} e^{-b^2/4}; & 0 \leqslant a \leqslant \dfrac{b}{2}, \\ e^{-(a-b)^2/2} + e^{a^2/2} e^{-(b^2/4)-(a-b/2)^2}; & \dfrac{b}{2} \leqslant a \leqslant b. \end{cases} \tag{5.103}$$

The final step in bounding $\mathrm{P}[\mathcal{E}]$ is to simplify Eq. 5.103. Since

$$\frac{(a-b)^2}{2} - \left(\frac{b^2}{4} - \frac{a^2}{2}\right) = \left(a - \frac{b}{2}\right)^2 \geqslant 0,$$

the second term in the bound on $\mathrm{P}[\mathcal{E}]$ for $0 \leqslant a \leqslant b/2$ is larger than the first. For $b/2 \leqslant a \leqslant b$, the exponents of the two terms are the same. Thus

$$\mathrm{P}[\mathcal{E}] < \begin{cases} 2e^{-(b^2/4)+(a^2/2)}; & 0 \leqslant a \leqslant \dfrac{b}{2}, \\ 2e^{-(a-b)^2/2}; & \dfrac{b}{2} \leqslant a \leqslant b. \end{cases} \tag{5.104}$$

Equation 5.104 can be written in terms of the original parameters of the communication problem by substituting

$$a = \sqrt{2 \ln M} = \sqrt{RT(2 \ln 2)},$$
$$b = \sqrt{2E_s/\mathcal{N}_0} = \sqrt{2(TP_s/\mathcal{N}_0)} = \sqrt{TC_\infty(2 \ln 2)}. \qquad (5.105)$$

We then have

$$\mathrm{P}[\mathcal{E}] < 2 \cdot 2^{-TE^*(R)}, \qquad (5.106a)$$

in which

$$E^*(R) = \begin{cases} \frac{1}{2}C_\infty - R; & 0 \leqslant R \leqslant \frac{1}{4}C_\infty, \\ (\sqrt{C_\infty} - \sqrt{R})^2; & \frac{1}{4}C_\infty \leqslant R \leqslant C_\infty. \end{cases} \qquad (5.106b)$$

Equation 5.106 is the desired result: the exponential factor $E^*(R)$ is the channel *reliability function.* A normalized plot of $E^*(R)$ is shown in

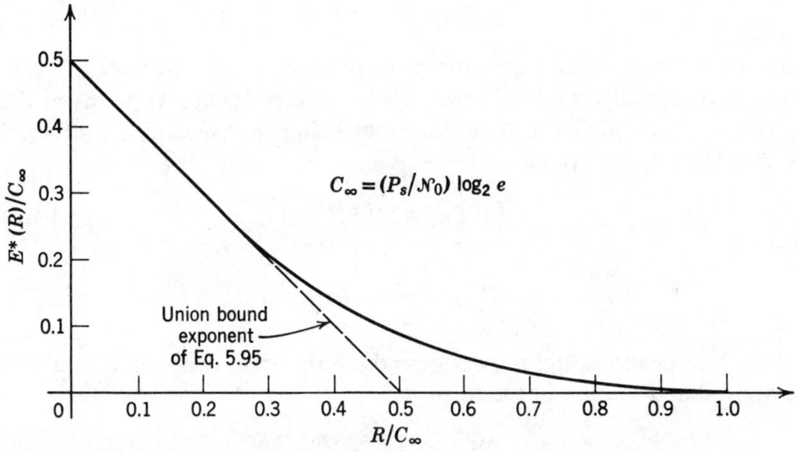

Figure 5.28 Channel reliability function for orthogonal signaling.

Fig. 5.28. We note that $E^*(R)$ coincides with the exponent of the union bound for $R < C_\infty/4$, but yields a tighter result for $C_\infty/4 < R < C_\infty$. The fact that $E^*(R) = 0$ for $R = C_\infty$ reflects the channel capacity constraint.

It is possible to show[32,93] that the foregoing bound is *exponentially tight*; this means that for no rate R can a number greater than $E^*(R)$ be substituted in Eq. 5.106a without invalidating the inequality for large values of T. The equivalent mathematical statement is

$$\mathrm{P}[\mathcal{E}] \geqslant Be^{-TE^*(R)}, \qquad (5.106c)$$

in which the coefficient B decreases only slowly (nonexponentially) as a function of T. Although stated for orthogonal signals, Eq. 5.106c pertains also to any other signal set. This follows from the fact that orthogonal signals provide substantially the same error performance as optimum (simplex) signals when M is large. Thus the reliability function of Eq. 5.106b is *both an upper and a lower bound on the exponential behavior of the error probability attainable with the infinite bandwidth additive white Gaussian noise channel.*

Other Channels

Bounds analogous to Eqs. 5.106a and c can be derived for an extremely broad class of realistic communication channel models.[6,27,32] In particular, random coding arguments somewhat more elaborate than those we have encountered here can be used to evaluate a reliability function and write a tight upper bound in the form

$$\overline{\mathrm{P}[\mathcal{E}]} \leqslant A2^{-TE'(R)}. \tag{5.107a}$$

The bound is on the mean error probability over an ensemble of communication systems, each of which uses a different code. In terms of the dimensions per codeword, N, and the dimensions per second, D, afforded by the channel, the bound is

$$\overline{\mathrm{P}[\mathcal{E}]} \leqslant A2^{-NE(R_N)}, \tag{5.107b}$$

where

$$E(R_N) = \frac{1}{D} E'(DR_N). \tag{5.107c}$$

For these channels tight lower bounds to the error probability can also be derived and written in the form

$$\mathrm{P}[\mathcal{E}] \geqslant \tilde{A}2^{-N\tilde{E}(R_N)}. \tag{5.108}$$

Combining Eqs. 5.107b and 5.108, we have

$$\tilde{A}2^{-N\tilde{E}(R_N)} \leqslant \mathrm{P}[\mathcal{E}] \leqslant A2^{-NE(R_N)}. \tag{5.109}$$

Since the the coefficients $\tilde{A}$ and A both can be shown to vary only slowly with N, the reliability functions $\tilde{E}(R_N)$ and $E(R_N)$, evaluated for a particular channel, represent upper and lower bounds on the exponential behavior of the probability of error attainable when communicating over that channel. In writing Eq. 5.109, we have used the fact that not all of the systems in an ensemble can yield a $\mathrm{P}[\mathcal{E}] > \overline{\mathrm{P}[\mathcal{E}]}$, so that at least one code exists for which the upper bound of Eq. 5.109 is valid.

The generic form of the functions $\tilde{E}(R_N)$ and $E(R_N)$ is illustrated in Fig. 5.29. Of course, for different channels the values of the parameters

C_N, R_0, R_c, R_e, and $E(0)$ are different; the *shape* of the curves shown, however, is extremely general.† In particular, the equality

$$\tilde{E}(R_N) = E(R_N); \qquad R_c \leqslant R_N \leqslant C_N, \tag{5.110}$$

where R_c is called the *critical rate*, is always true. Thus the exponential behavior of the attainable P[ℰ] is precisely determined for rates near channel capacity.

Equation 5.110 is a remarkable result: $E(R_N)$ relates to the average error behavior over an ensemble of all N-symbol codes of rate R_N,

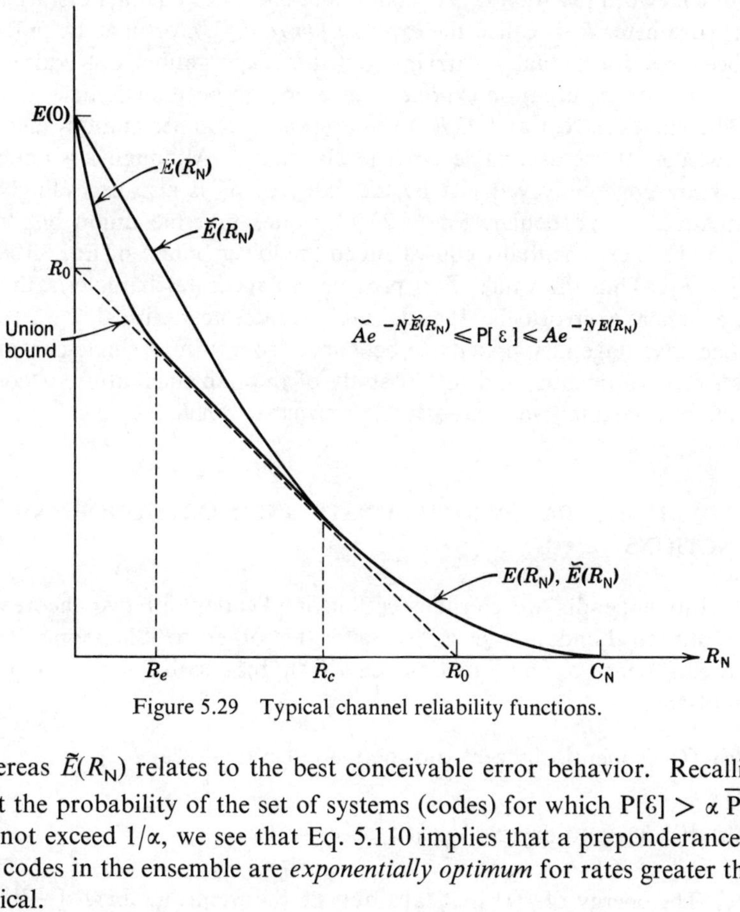

Figure 5.29 Typical channel reliability functions.

whereas $\tilde{E}(R_N)$ relates to the best conceivable error behavior. Recalling that the probability of the set of systems (codes) for which $P[\mathcal{E}] > \alpha\, \overline{P[\mathcal{E}]}$ cannot exceed $1/\alpha$, we see that Eq. 5.110 implies that a preponderance of the codes in the ensemble are *exponentially optimum* for rates greater than critical.

† In certain instances the curves may exhibit degeneracies. As an example, for the infinite bandwidth white Gaussian noise channel $E(0) = R_0$ and $\tilde{E}(R_N) = E(R_N)$ for all R_N.

The union bound,

$$\overline{P[\mathcal{E}]} < 2^{-N[R_0 - R_N]}, \tag{5.111}$$

is indicated in Fig. 5.29 by the dashed line. The ensemble exponent $E(R_N)$ always coincides with the union exponent for $R_e \leqslant R_N \leqslant R_c$, but in general

$$E(R_N) > R_0 - R_N; \qquad 0 \leqslant R_N \leqslant R_e. \tag{5.112}$$

The improvement at low rates is obtained by expurgating the ensemble to eliminate those systems in which the error probability is dominated by poor codeword selection rather than by the effects of channel disturbance. The parameter R_e is called the *expurgation rate.* Unfortunately, practical procedures for actually carrying out the expurgation procedure and attaining the expurgation exponent have not yet been devised.

The curves $\tilde{E}(R_N)$ and $E(R_N)$ for a specific channel embody detailed knowledge of the attainable error performance. Although less detailed, the knowledge conveyed just by the value of R_0 is also exceedingly informative. In particular, Fig. 5.29 illustrates that the union bound of Eq. 5.111 is exponentially equivalent to the lower bound of Eq. 5.108 for $R_N \approx R_c$. Thus the value of R_0 provides an accurate characterization of the exponential error behavior attainable at rates near critical.

The advantage in simplicity to be gained from using a single-parameter descriptor is obvious, and in our study of the implementation of coding in the next chapter we focus attention primarily on R_0.

APPENDIX 5A BANDWIDTH-CONSTRAINED ORTHONORMAL FUNCTIONS

In this appendix we consider certain implications of two theorems,[53] one due to Landau and Pollak and the other to Shannon. These theorems concern any function, say $f(t)$, that satisfies the following conditions:

(a) $f(t)$ is identically zero outside the interval $[-T/2, T/2]$.

(b) $f(t)$ has unit energy: $\int_{-\infty}^{\infty} |F(f)|^2 \, df = 1.$

(c) The energy of $f(t)$ that falls outside the frequency band $[-W, W]$ is at most $\eta_W{}^2$:

$$\int_{-W}^{W} |F(f)|^2 \, df \geqslant 1 - \eta_W{}^2.$$

The theorems state that there exists a particular set of orthonormal functions† $\{\Psi_i(t)\}$, $i = 0, 1, 2, \ldots$, with the following properties. Each $\Psi_i(t)$ is identically zero for $|t| > T/2$, and for every $f(t)$ satisfying (a), (b), and (c)

$$\int_{-\infty}^{\infty} \left[f(t) - \sum_{i=0}^{L-1} f_i \Psi_i(t) \right]^2 dt < \epsilon^2, \tag{5A.1}$$

where

$$f_i \triangleq \int_{-\infty}^{\infty} f(t)\, \Psi_i(t)\, dt \tag{5A.2}$$

and

(i) Landau and Pollak
$$\begin{cases} L = \text{largest integer} \leqslant 2TW + 1 \\ \epsilon^2 = 12\eta_W{}^2 \end{cases} \tag{5A.3}$$

(ii) Shannon

$$\begin{cases} L = \text{largest integer} \leqslant 2TW + \dfrac{12}{\Delta}\left(1 + \dfrac{1}{\pi^2} \ln 2TW\right) \\ \epsilon^2 = \dfrac{12\eta_W{}^2}{(12 - \Delta)} \end{cases} \quad \text{for all } \Delta, \quad 0 < \Delta < 12. \tag{5A.4}$$

5A.1 Constrained Linear Combinations

Suppose that $\{\varphi_j(t)\}$ is a set of N orthonormal functions such that *every* unit-energy linear combination of them, for example,

$$g(t) = \sum_{j=1}^{N} g_j \varphi_j(t); \qquad \sum_{j=1}^{N} g_j{}^2 = 1, \tag{5A.5}$$

satisfies conditions (a), (b), and (c) with $\eta_W{}^2 = \frac{1}{12}$. (In particular, each of the $\varphi_j(t)$ satisfies the conditions.) Then the theorem of Landau and Pollak may be used to show that the number of functions, N, in the set $\{\varphi_j(t)\}$ is constrained by

$$N \leqslant L \leqslant 2TW + 1,$$

hence

$$\lim_{T \to \infty} \frac{N}{T} \leqslant 2W \text{ dimensions/sec.} \tag{5A.6}$$

† The orthonormal functions $\{\Psi_i(t)\}$ are related to the prolate spheroidal wave functions with parameters T and W, say $\{\psi_i(t)\}$, by

$$\Psi_i(t) = \begin{cases} \dfrac{1}{\lambda_i} \psi_i(t); & |t| \leqslant \dfrac{T}{2} \\ 0; & \text{otherwise.} \end{cases}$$

The $\{\lambda_i\}$ are normalization constants.

Proof is by contradiction. Suppose that $\eta_W{}^2 = \frac{1}{12}$ and $N > L$. Then a linear combination of the $\{\varphi_j(t)\}$ exists[10] which is orthogonal to each of L functions $\{\Psi_i(t)\}$. Let $g(t)$ be this linear combination, normalized to unit energy. Then

$$g_i = \int_{-\infty}^{\infty} g(t)\,\Psi_i(t)\,dt = 0; \qquad i = 0, 1, \ldots, L-1, \tag{5A.7}$$

and

$$\int_{-\infty}^{\infty}\left[g(t) - \sum_{i=0}^{L-1} g_i\,\Psi_i(t)\right]^2 dt = \int_{-\infty}^{\infty} g^2(t)\,dt = 1. \tag{5A.8}$$

On the other hand, for $\eta_W{}^2 = 12$ the Landau and Pollak result requires

$$\int_{-\infty}^{\infty}\left[g(t) - \sum_{i=0}^{L-1} g_i\,\Psi_i(t)\right]^2 dt < 12\eta_W{}^2 = 1, \tag{5A.9}$$

which contradicts Eq. 5A.8, hence contradicts the hypothesis $N > L$.

5.A2 Constrained Orthonormal Functions

We now use the theorem of Shannon to bound the number of T-sec duration orthonormal functions $\{\varphi_j(t)\}$ that satisfy conditions somewhat weaker than those of Section 5A.1; instead of requiring that *every* linear combination of the $\{\varphi_j(t)\}$ meet the bandwidth constraint of condition (c), we now require only that each $\varphi_j(t)$ meet this condition individually. Thus each $\varphi_j(t)$, $j = 1, 2, \ldots, N$, is required to have at most a fraction $\eta_W{}^2$ of its energy outside the band $[-W, W]$, although it is possible that some linear combination of the $\{\varphi_j(t)\}$ have more. In this case we shall obtain the (weaker) bound

$$\frac{N}{T} < 2W \frac{12 - \Delta}{12(1 - \eta_W{}^2) - \Delta}\left[1 + \frac{12}{2TW\Delta}\left(1 + \frac{1}{\pi^2}\ln 2TW\right)\right];$$

$$\text{for all } \Delta, \quad 0 < \Delta < 12, \tag{5A.10a}$$

hence

$$\lim_{T\to\infty} \frac{N}{T} \leqslant \frac{2W}{1 - \eta_W{}^2}. \tag{5A.10b}$$

Although both bounds in Eqs. 5A.10 are always greater than $2W$, they exceed $2W$ by very little when $2TW$ is large and $\eta_W{}^2$ is small. For $2TW \geqslant 100$ and $\eta_W{}^2 = \frac{1}{12}$ Eq. 5A.10a states that $N/2TW < 1.2$.

The first step in proving Eq. 5A.10a is to note from Eq. 5A.1 that

$$\int_{-\infty}^{\infty}\left[\varphi_j(t) - \sum_{i=0}^{L-1} a_{ij}\,\Psi_i(t)\right]^2 dt < \epsilon^2; \qquad j = 1, 2, \ldots, N, \tag{5A.11}$$

where

$$a_{ij} = \int_{-\infty}^{\infty} \varphi_j(t)\,\Psi_i(t)\,dt. \tag{5A.12}$$

But the left-hand side of Eq. 5A.11 is

$$\int_{-\infty}^{\infty} \varphi_j^2(t)\,dt - 2\sum_{i=0}^{L-1} a_{ij} \int_{-\infty}^{\infty} \varphi_j(t)\,\Psi_i(t)\,dt + \sum_{i=0}^{L-1} a_{ij}^2 \int_{-\infty}^{\infty} \Psi_i^2(t)\,dt$$
$$= 1 - 2\sum_{i=0}^{L-1} a_{ij}^2 + \sum_{i=0}^{L-1} a_{ij}^2 = 1 - \sum_{i=0}^{L-1} a_{ij}^2. \qquad (5A.13)$$

Substituting Eq. 5A.13 in Eq. 5A.11 and summing over j, we have

$$\sum_{j=1}^{N}\left[1 - \sum_{i=0}^{L-1} a_{ij}^2\right] = N - \sum_{i=0}^{L-1}\left(\sum_{j=1}^{N} a_{ij}^2\right) < N\epsilon^2$$

or

$$\sum_{i=0}^{L-1}\left(\sum_{j=1}^{N} a_{ij}^2\right) > N(1-\epsilon^2). \qquad (5A.14)$$

The next step is to note that the $\{\Psi_i(t)\}$ may be expanded in terms of the $\{\varphi_j(t)\}$ in accordance with the Gram-Schmidt procedure of Appendix 4A:

$$\Psi_i(t) = \sum_{j=1}^{N} a_{ij}\,\varphi_j(t) + \theta_i(t),$$

where $\theta_i(t)$ represents the part of $\Psi_i(t)$ that is orthogonal to all of the $\{\varphi_i(t)\}$. Thus

$$1 = \int_{-\infty}^{\infty} \Psi_i^2(t)\,dt = \sum_{j=1}^{N} a_{ij}^2 + \int_{-\infty}^{\infty} \theta_i^2(t)\,dt$$

and

$$1 \geqslant \sum_{j=1}^{N} a_{ij}^2. \qquad (5A.15)$$

Substitution of Eq. 5A.15 in Eq. 5A.14 yields

$$\sum_{i=0}^{L-1} 1 = L > N(1-\epsilon^2)$$

or

$$N < \frac{L}{1-\epsilon^2}. \qquad (5A.16)$$

Substituting the values of L and ϵ^2 from Eq. 5A.4 yields Eq. 5A.10.

5.A3 Discussion

We conclude that the number of orthonormal functions with energy concentrated in $[-W, W]$ increases linearly with T, at best. The proportionality constant of the bound is linear in W and equals $2W$ when all linear combinations must also have energy concentrated in $[-W, W]$. The proportionality constant of the bound is slightly larger than $2W$ if only the orthonormal functions themselves must satisfy the energy concentration condition.

APPENDIX 5B BANDLIMITED WAVEFORMS

Consider an ideal bandlimited waveform such as

$$g(t) = \int_{-W}^{W} G(f)e^{j2\pi ft}\, df, \tag{5B.1}$$

where

$$G(f) = \int_{-\infty}^{\infty} g(t)e^{-j2\pi ft}\, dt. \tag{5B.2}$$

In this appendix we show that if $g(t)$ is identically zero over any interval $a \leqslant t \leqslant b$ of nonzero length, then $g(t)$ is identically zero for all t.

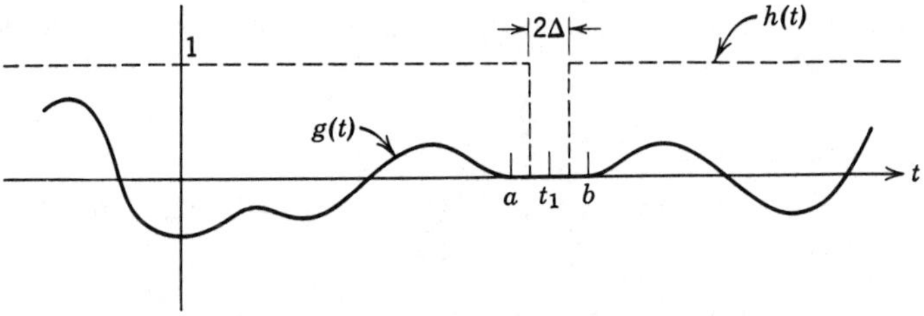

Figure 5B.1 A function $g(t)$ identically zero in $[a, b]$.

Preliminary insight is gained from an apparent inconsistency. Assume

$$g(t) \equiv 0; \qquad a \leqslant t \leqslant b \tag{5B.3}$$

and define

$$h(t) = \begin{cases} 0; & |t - t_1| < \Delta \\ 1; & \text{elsewhere,} \end{cases} \tag{5B.4}$$

where Δ and t_1 are chosen so that $t_1 + \Delta$ and $t_1 - \Delta$ both fall within the interval $[a, b]$. Then, as shown in Fig. 5B.1,

$$g(t) = g(t)\, h(t). \tag{5B.5}$$

Taking the Fourier transform of both sides of Eq. 5B.5 yields

$$G(f) = G(f) * H(f). \tag{5B.6}$$

But

$$|H(f)| = \delta(f) + 2\Delta \left| \frac{\sin 2\pi f\Delta}{2\pi f\Delta} \right|. \tag{5B.7}$$

It is evident in Fig. 5B.2 that convolving a bandlimited spectrum $G(f)$ with $H(f)$ yields a spectrum that is not bandlimited. We infer that Eqs. 5B.1, 5B.3, and 5B.6 cannot all be valid simultaneously unless $G(f) \equiv 0$.

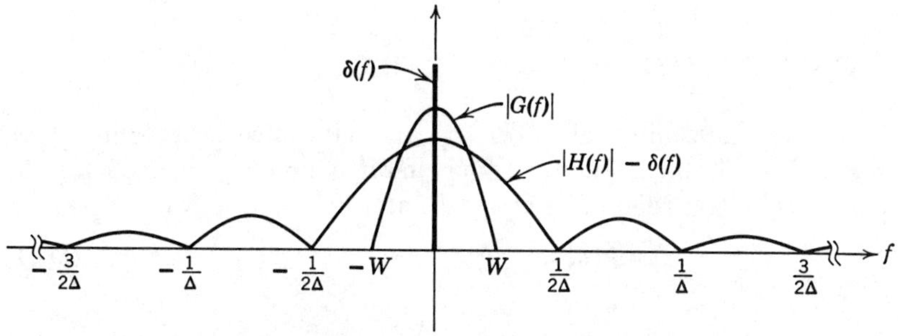

Figure 5B.2 Spectra of $g(t)$ and $h(t)$.

A formal proof that provides additional insight involves the power series expansion of $g(t)$. From Eq. 5B.1, the kth derivative of $g(t)$ is

$$g^{(k)}(t) = \int_{-W}^{W} (j2\pi f)^k G(f) e^{j2\pi f t}\, df. \tag{5B.8}$$

Thus

$$|g^{(k)}(t)| \leqslant (2\pi W)^k \int_{-W}^{W} |G(f)|\, df < (2\pi W)^k \int_{-W}^{W} [1 + |G(f)|^2]\, df$$

or, if E_g is the energy of $g(t)$,

$$|g^{(k)}(t)| < (2\pi W)^k (E_g + 2W). \tag{5B.9}$$

The k-term power-series expansion of $g(t)$ around the point t_1 is

$$g(t) = g(t_1) + g^{(1)}(t_1)(t - t_1) + \frac{g^{(2)}(t_1)}{2!}(t - t_1)^2 + \cdots + \frac{g^{(k-1)}(t_1)}{(k-1)!}(t - t_1)^{k-1} + R_k, \tag{5B.10}$$

in which the remainder term R_k is given by

$$R_k = \frac{(t - t_1)^k}{k!} g^{(k)}(\tau) \tag{5B.11}$$

with τ some number between t and t_1. Thus

$$|R_k| < \frac{|t - t_1|^k}{k!} (2\pi W)^k (E_g + 2W). \tag{5B.12}$$

Precise knowledge of $g(t)$ over any interval of nonzero length permits the calculation of every derivative of $g(t)$ at the midpoint of this interval and thus the construction of the power series. Moreover, the bound of Eq. 5B.12, hence $|R_k|$, goes to zero as $k \to \infty$ for every t, so that the infinite power series is everywhere absolutely convergent and represents the function $g(t)$ completely. It follows that if $g(t) \equiv 0$ over any interval, it is identically zero everywhere.

APPENDIX 5C OPTIMIZATION OF R_0

Given any transmitter alphabet $\{a_l\}$ and associated probabilities $\{p_l\}$, $l = 1, 2, \ldots, A$, the random coding union bound of Eq. 5.55 for the additive white Gaussian noise channel states that

$$\overline{P[\mathcal{E}]} < 2^{-N[R_0 - R_N]}, \tag{5C.1}$$

where

$$R_0 \triangleq -\log_2 \sum_{l=1}^{A} \sum_{h=1}^{A} p_l b_{lh} p_h \tag{5C.2}$$

and

$$b_{lh} \triangleq e^{-d_{lh}^2/2\mathcal{N}_0} = b_{hl}. \tag{5C.3}$$

In Eq. 5C.1, $\overline{P[\mathcal{E}]}$ is the average probability of error for codes of length N over the ensemble of communication systems in which the probability that any signal component s_{ij} is assigned letter a_l is p_l, independent of all other component assignments.

We desire to find the $\{p_l\}$ for which R_0 is maximum, subject to the constraints

$$p_l \geqslant 0; \qquad l = 1, 2, \ldots, A \tag{5C.4a}$$

and

$$\sum_{l=1}^{A} p_l = 1. \tag{5C.4b}$$

The exponent R_0 may be maximized by minimizing the double summation in Eq. 5C.2. Let 2λ be a Lagrange multiplier. Then

$$\frac{\partial}{\partial p_l}\left[\sum_{l=1}^{A}\sum_{h=1}^{A} p_l b_{lh} p_h - 2\lambda \sum_{l=1}^{A} p_l\right] = 2\left[\sum_{h=1}^{A} b_{lh} p_h - \lambda\right]; \qquad l = 1, 2, \ldots, A. \tag{5C.5}$$

Setting each partial derivative equal to zero yields the set of A inhomogeneous linear equations

$$\sum_{h=1}^{A} b_{lh} p_h = \lambda; \qquad l = 1, 2, \ldots, A. \tag{5C.6}$$

The value of λ is determined from the constraint $\sum_{h=1}^{A} p_h = 1$.

Whenever the $\{p_l\}$ that solve Eq. 5C.6 are all non-negative, these $\{p_l\}$ maximize R_0. We then have

$$\sum_{l=1}^{A}\sum_{h=1}^{A} p_l b_{lh} p_h = \lambda \sum_{l=1}^{A} p_l = \lambda \tag{5C.7}$$

and

$$R_{0,\max} = -\log_2 \lambda; \qquad \text{all } p_l \geqslant 0. \tag{5C.8}$$

If the b_{lh} all sum to the same number,

$$\sum_{h=1}^{A} b_{lh} = b; \qquad l = 1, 2, \ldots, A, \tag{5C.9a}$$

the solution to Eq. 5C.6 assigns equal probability to each letter of the alphabet. This is immediately apparent from the fact that Eq. 5C.6 then becomes

$$\sum_{h=1}^{A} b_{lh} p_h = \frac{1}{A} \sum_{h=1}^{A} b_{lh} = \frac{b}{A} = \lambda; \qquad l = 1, 2, \ldots, A. \tag{5C.9b}$$

In this case

$$R_{0,\max} = -\log_2 \frac{b}{A}. \tag{5C.9c}$$

When some of the $\{p_l\}$ that solve Eq. 5C.6 are negative, the Lagrange solution is not a valid probability assignment. The implication is that some of the $\{p_l\}$ should be set to zero, which means that there are too many letters in the transmitter alphabet $\{a_l\}$. The engineering solution is to reduce the number of letters, so that they may be spread farther apart without violating the energy constraint of Fig. 5.14.

APPENDIX 5D THE VOLUME OF AN N-DIMENSIONAL SPHERE

An N-dimensional sphere of radius ρ is defined to be the locus of all points

$$\boldsymbol{\alpha} = (\alpha_1, \alpha_2, \ldots, \alpha_N) \tag{5D.1}$$

such that

$$|\boldsymbol{\alpha}|^2 = \sum_{j=1}^{N} \alpha_j^2 \leqslant \rho^2. \tag{5D.2}$$

Thus the volume of an N-dimensional sphere of radius ρ is

$$\begin{aligned} V(\rho) &\triangleq \int\limits_{|\boldsymbol{\alpha}|^2 \leqslant \rho^2} d\boldsymbol{\alpha} \\ &= \iint\limits_{\alpha_1^2+\alpha_2^2+\cdots+\alpha_N^2 \leqslant \rho^2} \cdots \int d\alpha_1\, d\alpha_2 \cdots d\alpha_N. \end{aligned} \tag{5D.3}$$

Making the changes of variable

$$\beta_j = \frac{\alpha_j}{\rho}; \qquad j = 1, 2, \ldots, N, \tag{5D.4}$$

we have

$$V(\rho) = \rho^N \iint_{\beta_1{}^2+\beta_2{}^2+\cdots+\beta_N{}^2\leqslant 1} \cdots \int d\beta_1\, d\beta_2 \cdots d\beta_N$$
$$= \rho^N V(1) \triangleq B_N \rho^N. \tag{5D.5}$$

We still have to determine the volume, B_N, of an N-dimensional sphere of unit radius. We begin indirectly by considering a set $\mathbf{n} = (n_1, n_2, \ldots, n_N)$ of N zero-mean, unit-variance, statistically independent Gaussian random variables, with probability density function

$$p_{\mathbf{n}}(\boldsymbol{\alpha}) = \frac{1}{(2\pi)^{N/2}}\, e^{-|\boldsymbol{\alpha}|^2/2}. \tag{5D.6}$$

Now consider the probability that $\mathbf{n}$ will lie in the thin spherical shell contained between concentric spheres of radii ρ and $\rho - \Delta$. If Δ is small, $|\mathbf{n}|$ is very nearly constant for all $\mathbf{n}$ in the shell. This probability is therefore very nearly equal to the volume of the shell times the value of $p_{\mathbf{n}}(\boldsymbol{\alpha})$ when $|\boldsymbol{\alpha}| = \rho$:

$$\mathrm{P}[(\rho - \Delta) < |\mathbf{n}| \leqslant \rho] \approx \frac{1}{(2\pi)^{N/2}}\, e^{-\rho^2/2}[V(\rho) - V(\rho - \Delta)]. \tag{5D.7}$$

But

$$\begin{aligned} V(\rho) - V(\rho - \Delta) &= B_N[(\rho)^N - (\rho - \Delta)^N] \\ &= B_N\left[N\rho^{N-1}\Delta - \frac{N(N-1)}{2!}\,\rho^{N-2}\Delta^2 + \cdots\right] \\ &\approx NB_N\rho^{N-1}\Delta; \qquad \frac{\Delta}{\rho} \ll \frac{2}{N-1}. \end{aligned} \tag{5D.8}$$

Therefore

$$\mathrm{P}[(\rho - \Delta) < |\mathbf{n}| \leqslant \rho] \approx \frac{B_N}{(2\pi)^{N/2}}\, e^{-\rho^2/2} N\rho^{N-1}\Delta. \tag{5D.9}$$

We can also write $\mathrm{P}[(\rho - \Delta) < |\mathbf{n}| \leqslant \rho]$ in terms of the density function of the random variable $|\mathbf{n}|$:

$$\mathrm{P}[(\rho - \Delta) < |\mathbf{n}| \leqslant \rho] \approx p_{|\mathbf{n}|}(\rho)\,\Delta.$$

Substituting back in Eq. 5D.9, canceling the Δ's, and noting that in the limit as Δ tends to zero the approximations become exact, we have

$$p_{|\mathbf{n}|}(\rho) = \frac{N\rho^{N-1}B_N}{(2\pi)^{N/2}}\, e^{-\rho^2/2}. \tag{5D.10a}$$

The constant B_N may now be evaluated by use of the fact that the area under any probability density is unity:

$$1 = \int_0^\infty p_{|\mathbf{n}|}(\rho)\, d\rho = \frac{NB_N}{(2\pi)^{(N-1)/2}} \int_0^\infty \frac{\rho^{N-1}}{\sqrt{2\pi}}\, e^{-\rho^2/2}\, d\rho. \tag{5D.10b}$$

There are two cases: when N is odd, $N - 1$ is even; the integral is therefore one half the $(N - 1)$st moment of the unit-variance Gaussian density function. From Eqs. 5D.10b and 2.145,

$$B_N = \frac{2^N(\pi)^{(N-1)/2}[(N-1)/2]!}{N!}; \qquad N \text{ odd}. \tag{5D.11}$$

When N is even, $N - 1$ is odd. Making the change of variable $\beta = \rho^2/2$, we have

$$\int_0^\infty \frac{\rho^{N-1}}{\sqrt{2\pi}} e^{-\rho^2/2}\, d\rho = \frac{2^{(N-2)/2}}{\sqrt{2\pi}} \int_0^\infty \beta^{(N-2)/2} e^{-\beta}\, d\beta. \tag{5D.12}$$

Repeated integration by parts yields

$$\int_0^\infty \beta^{(N-2)/2} e^{-\beta}\, d\beta = \left(\frac{N-2}{2}\right)!. \tag{5D.13}$$

Substitution of Eqs. 5D.13 and 5D.12 in Eq. 5D.10b leads to

$$B_N = \frac{(2\pi)^{N/2}}{N2^{(N-2)/2}\left(\dfrac{N-2}{2}\right)!} = \frac{\pi^{N/2}}{\left(\dfrac{N}{2}\right)!}; \qquad N \text{ even}. \tag{5D.14}$$

As a check, we note that $B_2 = \pi$, $B_3 = \frac{4}{3}\pi$.

It may be verified from Stirling's approximation to the factorial that

$$\frac{B_N}{B_{N-1}} \approx \sqrt{2\pi/N}; \qquad N \text{ large}. \tag{5D.15}$$

Indeed, from Eq. 5D.14, we have immediately

$$\frac{B_N}{B_{N-1}} \cdot \frac{B_{N-1}}{B_{N-2}} = \frac{2\pi}{N}; \qquad \text{all even } N. \tag{5D.16}$$

PROBLEMS

5.1a. A communication system has an input buffer for storing messages before transmission. The buffer contains 10^4 magnetic cores, each of which has two distinct flux states. The message source specifies one of 1024 messages each second. How many seconds of source output can be stored in the buffer?

b. Assume that each (binary) core in (a) costs one dollar, installed. At what price per installed core would a buffer using multistate cores, each with eight distinct flux states, be competitive?

5.2a. Equation 5.15a provides a useful bound on the error probability with orthogonal signaling when $E_b > \mathcal{N}_0 2 \ln 2 \triangleq E_{\min}$. Use the bound to estimate how large the number of messages M must be to guarantee $P[\mathcal{E}] < 10^{-6}$ when

$$10 \log_{10} \frac{E_b}{E_{\min}} = \begin{cases} \text{(i)} & 1 \text{ db} \\ \text{(ii)} & 3 \text{ db} \\ \text{(iii)} & 6 \text{ db}. \end{cases}$$

b. Assume that the communication system is connected to a source that produces one bit every 10 msec. Determine (for i, ii, and iii) how many seconds of source output must be buffered at the transmitter. Also determine the channel bandwidth, W, required when the number of orthogonal signals, D, that can be transmitted per second equals $\frac{3}{2}W$.

5.3 Equation 5.14 bounds the attainable $P[\mathcal{E}]$ for M equally likely orthogonal signals and an additive white Gaussian noise channel in terms of the signaling interval T, the available transmitter power P_s, and the information rate R (in bits per second). Derive similar bounds for (a) M simplex signals, (b) M biorthogonal signals. Discuss the relative advantages of the three signaling systems from an engineering point of view.

5.4 Consider the Gaussian pulse $x(t) = (\sqrt{2\pi}\,\sigma)^{-1} e^{-t^2/2\sigma^2}$ and signals such as

$$s_i(t) = \sum_{j=1}^{N} s_{ij}\, x(t - j\tau); \qquad i = 0, 1, \ldots, M - 1$$

constructed from successive τ-sec translates of $x(t)$. Constrain the interpulse interference by requiring

$$\int_{-\infty}^{\infty} x(t - l\tau)\, x(t - j\tau)\, dt \leqslant 0.05 \int_{-\infty}^{\infty} x^2(t)\, dt; \qquad \text{all } j \text{ and } l \neq j,$$

and constrain the signal bandwidth W by requiring that $x(t)$ have no more than 10% of its energy outside the frequency interval $[-W, W]$. Determine the largest permissible value of the coefficient k in the equation $N = kTW$ when $N \gg 1$.

5.5 Consider a set of A orthonormal waveforms $\{\varphi_k(t)\}$, $k = 1, 2, \ldots, A$, each of which is identically zero outside the time interval $[-\tau, 0]$. These waveforms are used to construct signals $\{s_i(t)\}$ of the form

$$s(t) = \sqrt{P_s\tau}\,[\varphi_{k_1}(t - \tau) + \varphi_{k_2}(t - 2\tau) + \cdots + \varphi_{k_J}(t - J\tau)],$$

in which the $\{k_j\}$ are integers between 1 and A. Thus each signal in the set $\{s_i(t)\}$ is specified by a vector of the form $(k_1, k_2, \ldots, k_J)$.

a. Assume $A = 4$, $J = 5$, and

$$\varphi_k(t) = \begin{cases} \sqrt{2/\tau}\,\sin 2\pi \dfrac{k}{\tau} t; & -\tau \leqslant t < 0, \\ 0; & \text{elsewhere.} \end{cases}$$

Sketch the signal specified by the vector $(2, 1, 4, 2, 3)$.

b. Consider the set of all distinct waveforms in the form of $s(t)$. How many waveforms are there in this set for arbitrary A and J? Are all of these waveforms mutually orthogonal?

c. Consider the ensemble comprising all waveforms of (b), to each of which is assigned equal probability. Pick two waveforms, independently at random, from this ensemble. What is the probability that they differ in h of the J positions?

d. What is the smallest attainable probability of error if these two waveforms (differing in h of J positions) are used as the signals in communicating one of two equally likely messages over an additive Gaussian noise channel with $\mathcal{S}_n(f) = \mathcal{N}_0/2$?

e. What is the average, say $\overline{P_2[\mathcal{E}]}$, of the error probability of (d) over the ensemble of (c)? Show that

$$\overline{P_2[\mathcal{E}]} < 2^{-NR_0},$$

where $N \triangleq AJ$ is the dimensionality of the (code base) ensemble. Derive an expression for the value of R_0. Discuss the relation between this value and that obtained by specializing the expression of Eq. 5.56. *Hint.* Note that the dimensionality of each particular signal in the code base is J, not N.

f. Use the union bound to show that the average probability of error, $\overline{P[\mathcal{E}]}$, for $M = 2^{NR_N}$ equally likely messages satisfies

$$\overline{P[\mathcal{E}]} < 2^{-N[R_0 - R_N]}$$

when the M signals are drawn independently at random from the ensemble of (c).

g. Verify that the energy per bit is given by

$$E_b = \frac{P_s \tau}{A R_N}.$$

What is the minimum value of E_b for which the bound of (f) is useful? Show that the bound of (f) can be rewritten in the form

$$\overline{P[\mathcal{E}]} < \exp\left\{-K\left[\frac{E_b}{2\mathcal{N}_0}\frac{1}{x}\ln\frac{A}{1 + (A-1)e^{-x}} - \ln 2\right]\right\},$$

where $x \triangleq P_s\tau/2\mathcal{N}_0$, and determine the minimum value of E_b in the limit $x \to 0$.

h. Compare the limiting value of E_b in (g) with that obtained in the text for binary antipodal signals. How would the two values compare if the letters $\{\varphi_k(t)\}$ formed a simplex rather than an orthogonal set?

i. Show that the minimum value of E_b does not greatly exceed its limiting value when $A \gg 1$ and the letter duration τ is chosen to satisfy

$$\frac{P_s \tau}{\mathcal{N}_0} = 2 \ln A.$$

j. For large A and τ chosen as in (i) show that the number of dimensions per second, D, required by the signaling system is

$$D = \frac{A}{2 \ln A}\frac{P_s}{\mathcal{N}_0}.$$

If in addition we choose R (in bits per second) so that E_b is twice the limiting value determined in (h), show that

$$D = R\frac{A}{\ln A}\, 2 \ln 2.$$

5.6 A set of A phase-shift waveforms $\{\psi_k(t)\}$, in which $L > 0$ is an integer and

$$\psi_k(t) \triangleq \begin{cases} \sqrt{\frac{2}{\tau}} \sin 2\pi\left[\frac{L}{\tau}t + \frac{k}{A}\right]; & -\tau \leqslant t < 0, \quad k = 1, 2, \ldots, A, \\ 0; & \text{otherwise,} \end{cases}$$

is used to construct coded signals $\{s_i(t)\}$ in the form

$$s(t) = \sqrt{P_s\tau}\sum_{j=1}^{J}\psi_{k_j}(t - j\tau).$$

As in Problem 5.5, any $s_i(t)$ is specified by a vector $(k_1, k_2, \ldots, k_J)$ whose components are integers between 1 and A.

a. Consider a code-base ensemble in which each distinct waveform in the form of $s(t)$ is assigned equal probability. Assuming that there is additive white Gaussian noise and that the signals $\{s_i(t)\}$ are chosen independently at random, show that the value of R_0 in the bound $\overline{P[\mathcal{E}]} < 2^{-N[R_0 - R_N]}$ is

$$R_0 = -\tfrac{1}{2}\log_2 \frac{1}{A}\sum_{k=1}^{A}\exp\left[-\frac{P_s\tau}{\mathcal{N}_0}\sin^2 k\frac{\pi}{A}\right]; \qquad A \geqslant 3.$$

What is the value of R_0 when $A = 2$? (Note that the dimensionality of the code base, N, is different for $A = 2$ and $A \geqslant 3$.)

b. Discuss the relation between the values of R_0 obtained in (a) for $A = 2$ and $A = 4$ and the value of R_0 for binary antipodal signaling.

c. Show that in the limit as $\overline{E_N}/\mathcal{N}_0 \to 0$

$$R_0 \to \frac{\overline{E_N}}{\mathcal{N}_0}\frac{1}{2\ln 2}, \qquad \text{for every } A \geqslant 2,$$

in which $\overline{E_N}$ is the average energy transmitted per dimension. Discuss and interpret this rather surprising result. *Hint.*

$$\sum_{k=1}^{A-1}\sin^2\frac{k\pi}{A} = \frac{A}{2}; \qquad A \geqslant 2.$$

5.7a. Show that Hartley's result, Eq. 1.1, can be written in the form $R_N = \log_2(1 + A/\Delta)$. Compare and contrast the conditions and content of this result and the capacity theorem for additive white Gaussian noise,

$$C_N = \tfrac{1}{2}\log_2(1 + 2\,E_N/\mathcal{N}_0).$$

b. Obtain rough numerical comparisons of the two statements by setting $A = \sqrt{3E_N}$ and choosing Δ so that the error probability per dimension in Hartley's formulation is 10^{-2}; 10^{-4}; 10^{-6}. Discuss.

5.8 Consider communicating over a channel disturbed by additive Gaussian noise with $\mathcal{S}_n(f) = \mathcal{N}_0/2$ by means of signals constructed from D orthonormal waveforms per second. Constrain the average power of each signal to be no greater than P_s.

a. Show that the channel capacity in *bits per second* increases monotonically toward its maximum value, $C_\infty = (P_s/\mathcal{N}_0)\log_2 e$, as D increases, whereas the capacity in *bits per dimension* decreases monotonically with D.

b. Similarly, show for binary antipodal codes that R_0 decreases, but DR_0 increases, monotonically with D. Show that the value of D required in order to achieve the bound

$$\overline{P[\mathcal{E}]} < 2^{-T[\frac{1}{2}C_\infty(1-\alpha)-R]}$$

when $0 < \alpha \ll 1$ is given approximately for antipodal codes by

$$D \approx \frac{P_s}{4\alpha\mathcal{N}_0}.$$

5.9a. Prove by induction that for any set of k events $\{A_i\}$

$$P\left[\bigcup_{i=1}^{k} A_i\right] \geqslant \sum_{i=1}^{k} P[A_i] - \sum_{i=2}^{k}\sum_{j=1}^{i-1} P[A_iA_j].$$

Hint. Apply the bound

$$P\left[\bigcup_{i=1}^{k-1} B_i\right] \leqslant \sum_{i=1}^{k-1} P[B_i]$$

to the events $\{A_iA_k\}$, $i < k$.

b. Now let one of $M = 2^{RT}$ equally likely messages be transmitted over an additive white Gaussian channel by means of M orthogonal signals, each with energy E_s. Use the theorem of (a) to prove that

$$P[\mathcal{E}] \geqslant (M-1)\,Q(\sqrt{E_s/\mathcal{N}_0}) - \binom{M-1}{2}\overline{Q^2(y)},$$

where the overhead bar denotes the mean of $Q^2(y)$ when y is a unit-variance Gaussian random variable with mean $\sqrt{2E_s/\mathcal{N}_0}$.

c. By using the bounds

$$Q(\alpha) > \frac{e^{-\alpha^2/2}}{\sqrt{2\pi}\,\alpha}\left(1 - \frac{1}{\alpha^2}\right); \qquad \alpha > 0,$$

$$Q(\alpha) \leqslant \begin{cases} e^{-\alpha^2/2}; & \alpha \geqslant 0, \\ 1; & \alpha < 0, \end{cases}$$

and the fact (see Appendix 7C for the general result) that

$$\frac{1}{\sqrt{2\pi}\sigma}\int_0^\infty e^{-(y-m)^2/2\sigma^2}\, e^{-y^2}\, dy < \overline{e^{-y^2}} = \frac{e^{-m^2/(1+2\sigma^2)}}{\sqrt{1+2\sigma^2}},$$

prove that

$$P[\mathcal{E}] > B2^{-T[\frac{1}{2}C_\infty - R]}; \qquad R < \frac{C_\infty}{6},$$

in which the coefficient B decays as $1/\sqrt{T}$ when T is large. [As stated in the text, stronger (but more laborious) arguments may be used to obtain a lower bound valid for all $R < C_\infty$.]

5.10 Use Stirling's approximation,

$$N! \approx \sqrt{2\pi N}\left(\frac{N}{e}\right)^N,$$

to prove that $B_N/B_{N-1} \approx \sqrt{2\pi/N}$, N large, where B_N (given in Eqs. 5D.11 and 5D.14) is the volume of an N-dimensional sphere of unit radius.

5.11 In Eq. 5.67c and in Appendix 5D we consider the probability density function of the length of an N-component random vector $\mathbf{n}$, each component of which is a statistically independent, zero mean, unit-variance Gaussian random variable. The probability density function of the squared length of $\mathbf{n}$, say

$$y_N \triangleq |\mathbf{n}|^2 = \sum_{i=1}^{N} n_i^2,$$

is called the "chi-square density function with N degrees of freedom." Let us denote this density function by p_N.

a. Use the result of Appendix 7C to determine the characteristic function of y_N.

b. Express p_N in terms of its characteristic function and by means of a single integration-by-parts show that

$$p_{N+2}(\alpha) = \frac{\alpha}{N}\, p_N(\alpha); \qquad N \geqslant 1.$$

Hence

$$p_N(\alpha) = \begin{cases} \dfrac{\alpha^{(N-1)/2}}{(N-2)!\,!}\, p_1(\alpha); & N \text{ odd,} \\[2ex] \dfrac{\alpha^{(N-2)/2}}{(N-2)!\,!}\, p_2(\alpha); & N \text{ even,} \end{cases}$$

where

$$(N-2)!\,! \triangleq \begin{cases} (N-2)(N-4)\cdots 1; & N \text{ odd} \\ (N-2)(N-4)\cdots 2; & N \text{ even.} \end{cases}$$

c. Complete the derivation of $p_N(\alpha)$ by showing that

$$p_1(\alpha) = \begin{cases} \dfrac{e^{-\alpha/2}}{\sqrt{2\pi\alpha}}; & \alpha \geqslant 0, \\[2ex] 0; & \alpha < 0, \end{cases} \qquad p_2(\alpha) = \begin{cases} \frac{1}{2}e^{-\alpha/2}; & \alpha \geqslant 0, \\ 0; & \alpha < 0. \end{cases}$$

d. Show that the transformation $|\mathbf{n}| = \sqrt{y_N}$ reduces p_N to the density function given in Eq. 5D.10a.

6

Implementation of Coded Systems

The problem of finding appropriate classes of signals for the communication of data over bandlimited channels disturbed by additive white Gaussian noise was discussed in Chapter 5. We concluded that power-constrained communication systems, using signals of T sec duration, exist which simultaneously (1) require signals (codewords) whose dimensionality, N, increases only linearly with T; (2) accommodate a number of messages, M, that increases exponentially with T; (3) afford a probability of error that decreases exponentially with T. More specifically, we considered systems that communicate one of M equally likely messages over an additive white Gaussian noise channel by means of signals,

$$s_i(t) = \sum_{j=1}^{N} s_{ij}\varphi_j(t); \qquad i = 0, 1, \ldots, M - 1, \tag{6.1}$$

in which each coefficient s_{ij} is chosen to be one of A amplitudes equally spaced over the interval $[-\sqrt{E_N}, \sqrt{E_N}]$. For signals of this form the probability of error achievable with optimum a posteriori probability computing receivers satisfies the simple union bound

$$P[\mathcal{E}] < 2^{-N[R_0 - R_N]}, \tag{6.2a}$$

where

$$M = 2^{NR_N} \tag{6.2b}$$

and R_0 (as a function of the energy-to-noise ratio per dimension, $E_N/\mathcal{N}_0$) is given by the curves of Figs. 5.17 and 5.18.

If we know that such communication systems exist in principle, the remaining task is to determine how to build them. This is the subject of this chapter. In particular, given an appropriate set of orthonormal waveforms $\{\varphi_j(t)\}$, we are confronted with the problems of transmitter and receiver implementation. The latter—which is by far the more grievous—can be separated into problems concerning quantization of the received signal, decoding, and two-way systems. We shall consider the different problem areas in the order listed.

In the design of a communication system one is never interested in building an "optimum" system irrespective of cost. The appropriate engineering objective is to build the most economical system that meets a required standard of performance. Given a transmission channel, two factors that relate directly to questions of economy are (1) the data rate R, in bits per second, at which the channel is used, and (2) the complexity of the terminal equipment required to meet the performance standard at rate R.

That these two factors are interrelated is made evident by rewriting Eq. 6.2 in terms of the time parameters T and R. If D is the number of orthogonal functions per second accommodated by the channel and T is the time duration of each signal in seconds, we have

$$N = DT \tag{6.3a}$$

$$M = 2^{RT} \tag{6.3b}$$

and therefore

$$\mathrm{P}[\mathcal{E}] < 2^{-T[DR_0 - R]}. \tag{6.3c}$$

It is clear from Eq. 6.3c that any required standard of performance, measured in terms of the allowable $\mathrm{P}[\mathcal{E}]$, can be attained by choosing T, DR_0, and R appropriately. In its simplest expression the engineering design problem is to determine the three parameters in such a way that the over-all cost of the system is minimum. Each parameter affects the cost qualitatively in the following way when the other parameters are fixed.

1. If we increase T, the cost increases: each signal (codeword) is specified by more vector components and there are many more signals ($M = 2^{RT}$) in the code.
2. If we increase DR_0, the cost increases: the maximum value of D is constrained by the transmission channel bandwidth and the maximum value of R_0 is constrained by the allowable value of $E_N/\mathcal{N}_0$. Forcing D close to its maximum value is costly, as is increasing $E_N/\mathcal{N}_0$.
3. If we decrease R, the cost increases: three complete systems, each with rate R, are required to communicate the same amount of data per second as one system with rate $3R$.

The appropriate choice of T, DR_0, and R in any given communication problem depends on the details of that problem. For instance, whether it is more economical to use three channels at rate R with simple terminal equipment or to use one channel at rate $3R$ with complicated terminal equipment, depends on the relative costs of transmission facility and complex terminal equipment. Such questions cannot be considered quantitatively until "terminal equipment complexity" has been defined in a meaningful way and the growth of complexity (hence cost) determined as a function of T and DR_0.

It is with these objectives in mind that we now address the problems of transmitter and receiver implementation. Initially, the number of degrees of freedom per second, D, is considered fixed. In Section 6.5 we discuss an example in which D is also a design parameter to be specified.

6.1 TRANSMITTER IMPLEMENTATION

The structure of the signals in Eq. 6.1 suggests a transmitter designed in two stages as shown in Fig. 6.1 (and previously, with different nomenclature, in Fig. 4.12). The first stage, called the coder (or encoder)

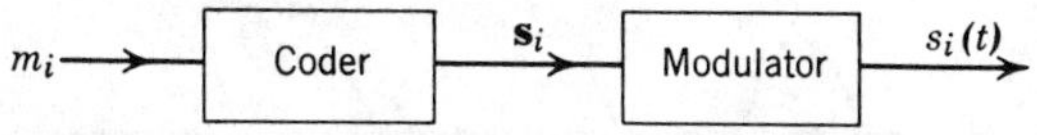

Figure 6.1 Two-stage transmitter: $i = 0, 1, \ldots, M-1$.

observes the message to be communicated, m_i, and generates a corresponding sequence of N output digits, $\mathbf{s}_i$. The second stage, called the modulator or waveform generator, accepts the coder output

$$\mathbf{s}_i = (s_{i1}, s_{i2}, \ldots, s_{iN}) \tag{6.4a}$$

and generates the waveform

$$s_i(t) = \sum_{j=1}^{N} s_{ij}\varphi_j(t). \tag{6.4b}$$

First, let us investigate the complexity of the modulator as a function of T. We are interested in the case in which a new transmitter input message is accepted, and a new waveform generated, every T sec. If the $\{\varphi_j(t)\}$ are chosen to be nonoverlapping time translations of a single waveform with duration T/N, as shown in Fig. 6.2, the same signal

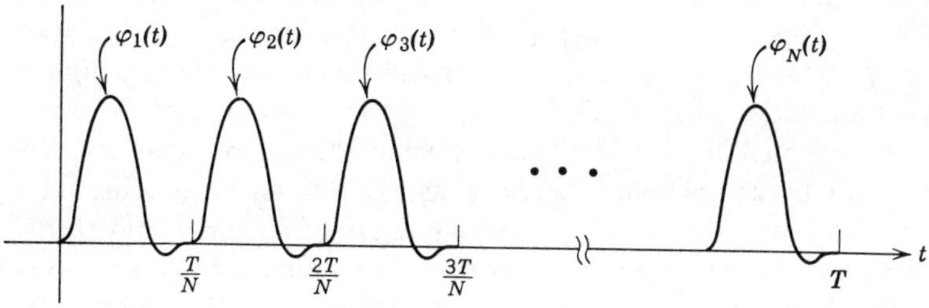

Figure 6.2 Pulse position orthonormal functions.

generator and amplitude modulator can be used over and over again, N times in succession. Alternatively, we can start with a small set of finite-duration orthonormal functions, such as the sinusoids $\varphi_1(t)$, $\varphi_2(t)$, and $\varphi_3(t)$ in Fig. 6.3, and choose the $\{\varphi_j(t)\}$ to be this set and their nonoverlapping time translates. In either case, since T/N is constant, the complexity of the waveform generator part of the transmitter is relatively independent of T.

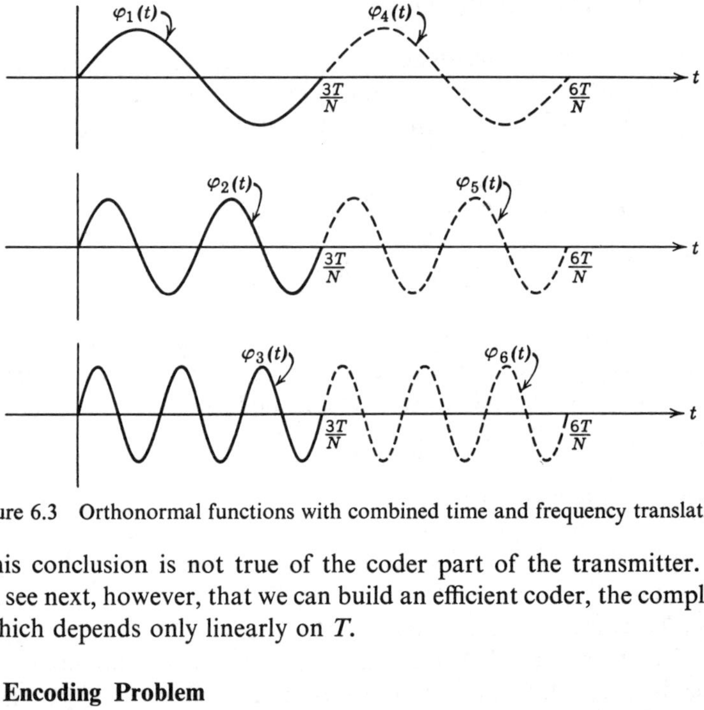

Figure 6.3 Orthonormal functions with combined time and frequency translation.

This conclusion is not true of the coder part of the transmitter. We shall see next, however, that we can build an efficient coder, the complexity of which depends only linearly on T.

The Encoding Problem

The first problem in encoder design is that of input message storage. As in Chapter 5, we assume that the input message m during each T-sec interval is a sequence of $K = NR_N$ binary digits, say $\mathbf{x}$. The sequence $\mathbf{x}$ may be any one of the set $\{\mathbf{x}_i\}$ of all 2^K vectors with components 0 or 1. We may visualize the data source as providing one new binary digit of $\mathbf{x}$ to the transmitter every $T/K = 1/R$ sec. In this case part of the encoder must be devoted to accepting and storing the vector $\mathbf{x}$ as it arrives, component by component. A convenient device for accomplishing this is a shift-register, which accepts binary digits at its input and shifts its contents one stage to the right each time a new digit arrives, as shown in Fig. 6.4. Since K is proportional to N, hence to T, the complexity of such a shift-register depends linearly on T.

In addition to accumulating the input message vector, the coder must implement an appropriate mapping $\mathbf{x}_i \Rightarrow \mathbf{s}_i$, $i = 0, 1, \ldots, M-1$. The problems involved are not trivial. Indeed, the construction of an appropriate coder could easily be an engineering impossibility. To see this, we need consider only the magnitude of the numbers involved; since

$$M = 2^K = 2^{RT} = 2^{NR_N}, \tag{6.5}$$

the required number of vectors in the set $\{\mathbf{s}_i\}$ is enormous when T is large. For example, $N = 200$ and $R_N = \frac{1}{2}$ imply $M = 2^{100} \approx 10^{30}$.

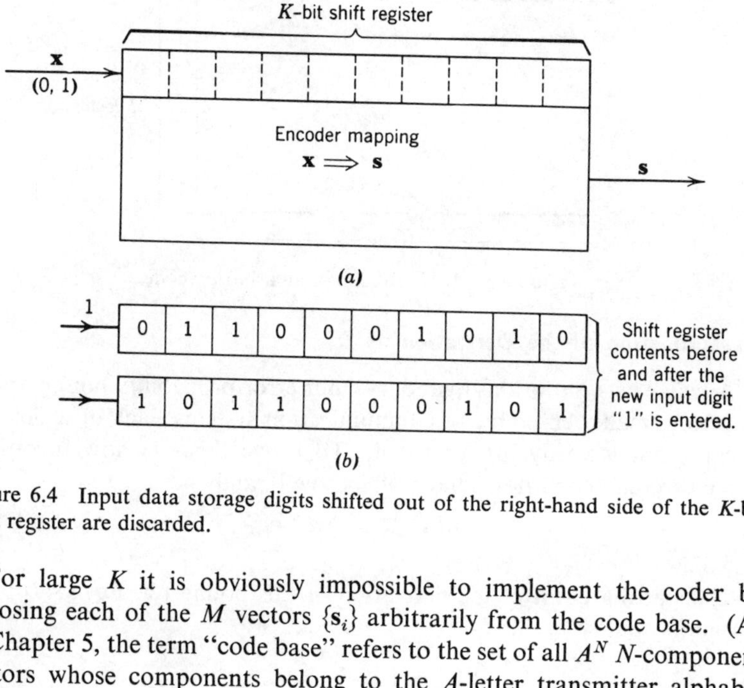

Figure 6.4 Input data storage digits shifted out of the right-hand side of the K-bit shift register are discarded.

For large K it is obviously impossible to implement the coder by choosing each of the M vectors $\{\mathbf{s}_i\}$ arbitrarily from the code base. (As in Chapter 5, the term "code base" refers to the set of all A^N N-component vectors whose components belong to the A-letter transmitter alphabet $\{a_l\}$.) To do so would require provisions for storing each selected vector in an ordered table containing MN entries, as shown in Fig. 6.5, and for reading out the ith table entry, $\mathbf{s}_i$, whenever $\mathbf{x}_i$ is the message input. The complexity of such a table-storage facility is proportional to the table size, MN, which grows with the time interval T as $T2^{RT}$. The size of the memory that would be required is simply too large.

On the other hand, the error probability bound of Eq. 6.2 has thus far been established only by considering the average probability of error over the ensemble of all A^{NM} possible codes. As we have seen (cf. p. 304), most of the codes in this ensemble must be good ones. But we have also seen that some codes—for instance, those in which all $\mathbf{s}_i$ are the same—are bad. It is not inconceivable that all of the easily implementable codes might be bad and that *only* those requiring table-storage implementation are good. The dilemma is obvious: *it is not yet clear that any code that can be instrumented obeys our error probability bound.*

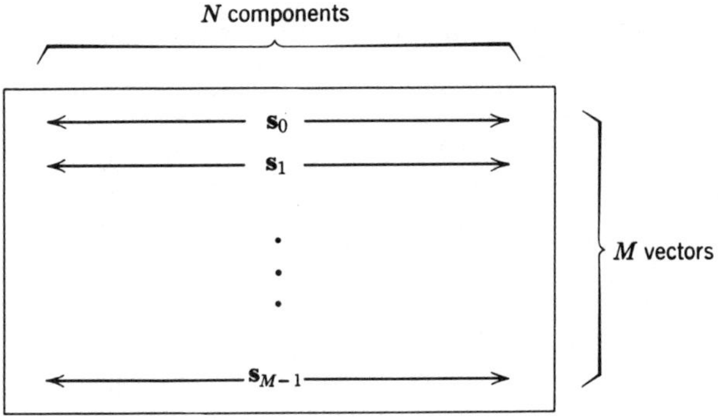

Figure 6.5 Table storage of an arbitrary code.

Recapitulation of the Derivation of R_0

A way exists out of this quandary: our error probability bound applies also to a smaller ensemble of communication systems, each of which uses a code that is easily instrumented. To prove this, we now investigate more carefully conditions under which the bound

$$\overline{P[\mathcal{E}]} < 2^{-N[R_0 - R_N]} \tag{6.6}$$

is valid.

The starting point of the derivation of this bound (cf. Eq. 5.47) is the union inequality

$$P[\mathcal{E} \mid m_k] \leqslant \sum_{\substack{i=0 \\ (i \neq k)}}^{M-1} P_2[\mathbf{s}_i, \mathbf{s}_k], \tag{6.7}$$

in which $P_2[\mathbf{s}_i, \mathbf{s}_k]$ is the probability of error when specific vectors $\mathbf{s}_i$ and $\mathbf{s}_k$ are used to communicate one of two equally likely messages. For an ensemble of communication systems chosen in such a way that the mean of $P_2[\mathbf{s}_i, \mathbf{s}_k]$ is bounded independent of the indices i and k by

$$\overline{P_2[\mathbf{s}_i, \mathbf{s}_k]} = \overline{P_2[\mathcal{E}]} \leqslant 2^{-NR_0}; \qquad \text{for all } i \text{ and } k, \tag{6.8}$$

substitution of Eq. 6.8 in Eq. 6.7 yields

$$\overline{P[\mathcal{E} \mid m_k]} \leqslant (M-1)2^{-NR_0}, \tag{6.9}$$

which in turn implies Eq. 6.6. Thus Eq. 6.8 represents the crucial property that an ensemble must evidence for the derivation of Eq. 6.6 to be valid.

For the ensemble of codes considered in Chapter 5, the validity of Eq. 6.8 was ensured for all i and k by the nature of the probability assignment to the codes of the ensemble; the probability that any vector in the code base was assigned to the signal $\mathbf{s}_k$ did not depend on k nor on which code-base vectors were assigned to the $M - 1$ other signals $\{\mathbf{s}_i\}$, $i \neq k$. As a consequence the expectation

$$\overline{P_2[\mathbf{s}_i, \mathbf{s}_k]} \triangleq \sum_{\substack{\text{all } \boldsymbol{\alpha}, \boldsymbol{\beta} \text{ in} \\ \text{the code} \\ \text{base}}} P_2[\boldsymbol{\alpha}, \boldsymbol{\beta}]\, P[\mathbf{s}_i = \boldsymbol{\alpha}, \mathbf{s}_k = \boldsymbol{\beta}] \tag{6.10}$$

was *independent* of i and k. Moreover, the statistical independence of $\mathbf{s}_i$ and $\mathbf{s}_k$,

$$P[\mathbf{s}_i = \boldsymbol{\alpha}, \mathbf{s}_k = \boldsymbol{\beta}] = P[\mathbf{s}_i = \boldsymbol{\alpha}]\, P[\mathbf{s}_k = \boldsymbol{\beta}];$$

$$\text{for all } (i, k) \text{ and all } (\boldsymbol{\alpha}, \boldsymbol{\beta}) \text{ in the code base,} \tag{6.11a}$$

together with the independence of the components of each $\mathbf{s}_i$,

$$P[\mathbf{s}_i = \boldsymbol{\alpha}] = \prod_{j=1}^{N} P[s_{ij} = \alpha_j]; \qquad \text{all } i \text{ and } \boldsymbol{\alpha}, \tag{6.11b}$$

made it possible to calculate the numerical value of R_0.

Now consider two distinct ensembles of communication systems such that the probability assigned to the event $[\mathbf{s}_i = \boldsymbol{\alpha}, \mathbf{s}_k = \boldsymbol{\beta}]$ in one ensemble is the same as the probability assigned to this event in the other. If this is true for all (i, k) and all $(\boldsymbol{\alpha}, \boldsymbol{\beta})$ in the code base, it is clear that $\overline{P_2[\mathcal{E}]}$ is the same for both ensembles. Thus Eqs. 6.11a and b *incorporate the only properties of an ensemble we need to establish the random coding bound and the value of* R_0.

Equation 6.11a requires only that any two signals $\mathbf{s}_i$ and $\mathbf{s}_k$ be statistically independent; although heretofore we have considered an ensemble in which all M signals $\{\mathbf{s}_i\}$ are statistically independent, it is sufficient that they be *independent by pairs*. The sufficiency of this much weaker condition enables us to validate our random coding bound for an ensemble of communication systems, each of which has an easily implemented coder.

Parity-Check Codes

We now consider an ensemble of codes which simultaneously meets two requirements: (a) over the ensemble, codewords are statistically independent by pairs and (b) each code in the ensemble can be implemented by means of a device whose complexity (appropriately measured) grows linearly with $K = RT$.

The parameter K is called the *constraint span* of the code. We first treat the binary case in which the codewords $\{\mathbf{s}_i\}$ are vectors with components restricted to $\pm\sqrt{E_N}$.

The coding device is diagrammed in Fig. 6.6. Each of the first K blocks in the top rectangle (which we call the x-register) represents a stage in a binary shift register. The encoder input sequence $\mathbf{x}$ is fed into this shift

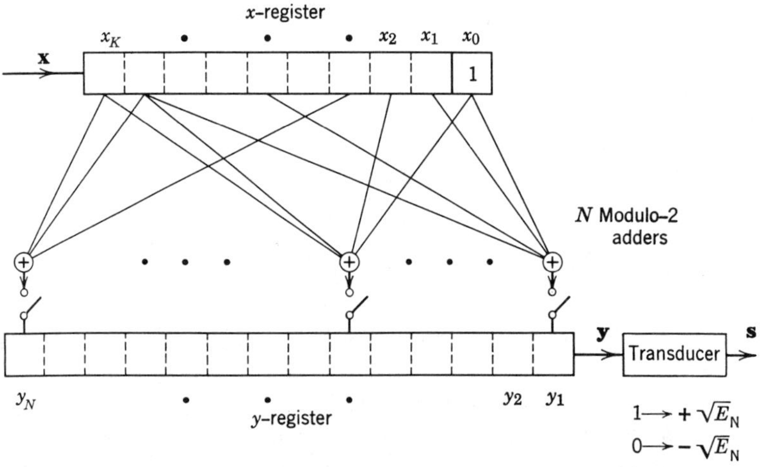

Figure 6.6 Parity check coder. There is one modulo-2 adder associated with each stage y_j of the y-register, $j = 1, 2, \ldots, N$. The switches close at time $t = T$.

register one bit at a time, so that at the end of T sec the K binary digits of $\mathbf{x}$ are stored in the K shift-register stages in the positions indicated in the figure. The $(K + 1)$th square, labeled x_0, represents a storage element that always contains 1.

The N symbols $\oplus$ in Fig. 6.6 represent modulo-2 adders, and the lines from squares to adders represent connections. The output at time T from the jth adder, say y_j, is the modulo-2 sum of the digits $\{x_h\}$ stored in the stages of the x-register to which the jth adder is connected. Since modulo-2 addition is defined by the equations

$$0 \oplus 0 = 1 \oplus 1 = 0$$

$$0 \oplus 1 = 1 \oplus 0 = 1,$$

we see that y_j is 1 if the number of 1's stored in these stages is odd and zero otherwise. The $\{y_j\}$ are called *parity checks* and the device is called a *parity-check coder*.

At time T the $\{y_j\}$ are fed in parallel to the lower rectangle, called the y-register, each square of which again represents a stage of shift-register. During the interval $[T, 2T]$, these N binary digits are shifted out, one at a time. Thus the y-register output is some sequence, say $\mathbf{y}$, of 0's and 1's:

$$\mathbf{y} \triangleq (y_1, y_2, \ldots, y_N); \qquad y_j = 0, 1, \quad \text{all } j. \tag{6.12}$$

We can convert this sequence into a signal vector, $\mathbf{s}$, of the desired binary form by the simple expedient of transforming 1 into $+\sqrt{E_N}$ and 0 into $-\sqrt{E_N}$ in the transducer:

$$\begin{aligned} y_j = 1 &\Rightarrow s_j = +\sqrt{E_N} \\ y_j = 0 &\Rightarrow s_j = -\sqrt{E_N}. \end{aligned} \tag{6.13}$$

Since $N = K/R_N$, the complexity of a parity-check coder, measured in terms of the total number of shift-register stages, is proportional to K.

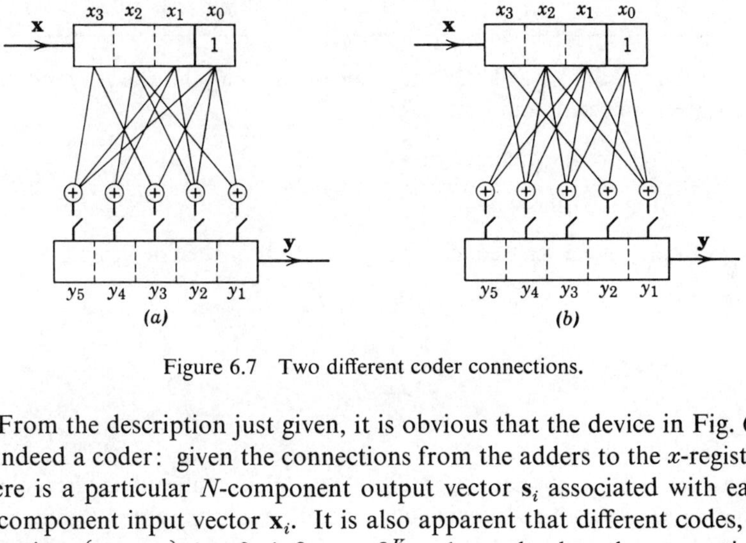

Figure 6.7 Two different coder connections.

From the description just given, it is obvious that the device in Fig. 6.6 is indeed a coder: given the connections from the adders to the x-register, there is a particular N-component output vector $\mathbf{s}_i$ associated with each K-component input vector $\mathbf{x}_i$. It is also apparent that different codes, or mappings $\{\mathbf{x}_i \Rightarrow \mathbf{s}_i\}$, $i = 0, 1, 2, \ldots, 2^K - 1$, result when the connections are made in different ways.

As an example, consider the two coders diagrammed in Fig. 6.7. For both, $K = 3$ and $N = 5$. By convention, we shall always let $\mathbf{x}_i$ denote the input vector corresponding to the number i written in binary form, with the first component taken as the most significant digit. By inspection, the two mapping $\mathbf{x} \Rightarrow \mathbf{y}$ are as given in Table 6.1. The two codes $\{\mathbf{s}_i\}$ are obtained by substituting $+\sqrt{E_N}$ for 1 and $-\sqrt{E_N}$ for 0 in the $\{\mathbf{y}_i\}$. Since the vectors $\{\mathbf{y}_i\}$ for the second device occur in pairs, it is obvious that this is a poor way to connect the coder; but we shall soon see that most connections yield good codes.

Insight into the structure of the $\{\mathbf{y}_i\}$ generated by a parity-check coder is gained by considering the set of *connection coefficients* $\{f_{hj}\}$. Define

Table 6.1 *Codes Obtained from Two Parity-Check Coders*

	x_1	x_2	x_3		First Coder y_1	y_2	y_3	y_4	y_5		Second Coder y_1	y_2	y_3	y_4	y_5
$\mathbf{x}_0$:	0	0	0	$\mathbf{y}_0$:	1	1	1	0	1	$\mathbf{y}_0$:	1	1	1	0	0
$\mathbf{x}_1$:	0	0	1	$\mathbf{y}_1$:	1	1	0	0	0	$\mathbf{y}_1$:	1	0	1	1	0
$\mathbf{x}_2$:	0	1	0	$\mathbf{y}_2$:	0	0	1	1	1	$\mathbf{y}_2$:	0	1	0	1	1
$\mathbf{x}_3$:	0	1	1	$\mathbf{y}_3$:	0	0	0	1	0	$\mathbf{y}_3$:	0	0	0	0	1
$\mathbf{x}_4$:	1	0	0	$\mathbf{y}_4$:	1	0	1	1	0	$\mathbf{y}_4$:	0	1	0	1	1
$\mathbf{x}_5$:	1	0	1	$\mathbf{y}_5$:	1	0	0	1	1	$\mathbf{y}_5$:	0	0	0	0	1
$\mathbf{x}_6$:	1	1	0	$\mathbf{y}_6$:	0	1	1	0	0	$\mathbf{y}_6$:	1	1	1	0	0
$\mathbf{x}_7$:	1	1	1	$\mathbf{y}_7$:	0	1	0	0	1	$\mathbf{y}_7$:	1	0	1	1	0

f_{hj} as 1 if the hth stage of the x-register in Fig. 6.6 and the jth modulo-2 adder are connected, and 0 otherwise:

$$f_{hj} = \begin{cases} 1, & \text{if } x_h \text{ affects } y_j, \\ 0, & \text{otherwise}, \end{cases} \qquad 0 \leqslant h \leqslant K, \qquad 1 \leqslant j \leqslant N. \tag{6.14}$$

For example, in the first coder of Fig. 6.7 each of the coefficients

$$\begin{gathered} f_{01}, f_{02}, f_{03}, f_{05} \\ f_{12}, f_{14}, f_{15} \\ f_{21}, f_{22}, f_{24} \\ f_{33}, f_{35} \end{gathered}$$

is 1, and all other f_{hj} are 0.

The set $\{f_{hj}\}$ completely specifies the coder connections, hence the mapping $\mathbf{x}_i \Rightarrow \mathbf{y}_i$, all i. In particular, we observe from Fig. 6.6 that

$$\begin{aligned} y_1 &= f_{01} \oplus x_1 f_{11} \oplus x_2 f_{21} \oplus \cdots \oplus x_K f_{K1} \\ y_2 &= f_{02} \oplus x_1 f_{12} \oplus x_2 f_{22} \oplus \cdots \oplus x_K f_{K2} \\ &\vdots \\ y_N &= f_{0N} \oplus x_1 f_{1N} \oplus x_2 f_{2N} \oplus \cdots \oplus x_K f_{KN}, \end{aligned} \tag{6.15a}$$

where the $\{x_h\}$ are the components of the input vector

$$\mathbf{x} \triangleq (x_1, x_2, \ldots, x_K). \tag{6.15b}$$

Equations 6.15 can be simplified by the use of vector notation. The modulo-2 sum of two binary vectors, say **a** and **b**, is defined as

$$\mathbf{a} \oplus \mathbf{b} = (a_1 \oplus b_1, a_2 \oplus b_2, \ldots, a_N \oplus b_N). \tag{6.16}$$

For example,

$$(0, 1, 1, 0) \oplus (1, 0, 1, 0) = (1, 1, 0, 0)$$

and, for any binary vector **c**,

$$\mathbf{c} \oplus \mathbf{c} = (0, 0, \ldots, 0) \triangleq \mathbf{0}. \tag{6.17}$$

With this definition, Eq. 6.15a can be written in the more concise form

$$\mathbf{y} = \mathbf{f}_0 \oplus x_1\mathbf{f}_1 \oplus x_2\mathbf{f}_2 \oplus \cdots \oplus x_K\mathbf{f}_K, \tag{6.18a}$$

in which

$$\mathbf{y} \triangleq (y_1, y_2, \ldots, y_N) \tag{6.18b}$$

$$\mathbf{f}_h \triangleq (f_{h1}, f_{h2}, \ldots, f_{hN}); \qquad 0 \leqslant h \leqslant K. \tag{6.18c}$$

Thus the *connection vectors* $\{\mathbf{f}_h\}$ for the first coder in Fig. 6.7 are

$$\mathbf{f}_0 = (1, 1, 1, 0, 1)$$

$$\mathbf{f}_1 = (0, 1, 0, 1, 1)$$

$$\mathbf{f}_2 = (1, 1, 0, 1, 0)$$

$$\mathbf{f}_3 = (0, 0, 1, 0, 1).$$

When **x** is the binary vector each of whose components except x_h is 0, the corresponding output vector is $\mathbf{y} = \mathbf{f}_0 \oplus \mathbf{f}_h$. More generally, **y** is the modulo-2 sum of $\mathbf{f}_0$ and those $\mathbf{f}_h$ corresponding to nonzero components of **x**.

The ensemble of binary codes. We now discuss the set of all binary codes that can be generated by a parity-check coder and show that the average probability of error over this set obeys the random coding bound of Eq. 6.6 without degradation of R_0. For any K and N a particular code is specified by the set of $(K + 1)$ connection vectors $\{\mathbf{f}_h\}$, $h = 0, 1, 2, \ldots, K$. Each of these vectors has N components and each component can be 0 or 1. There are $N(K + 1)$ components f_{hj} to be assigned, hence $2^{N(K+1)}$ ways to connect the coder.

Suppose that each of the $2^{N(K+1)}$ coders appears in an ensemble with equal probability, $2^{-N(K+1)}$. This implies that each of the connection coefficients $\{f_{hj}\}$ is equally likely to be 0 or 1 and that each coefficient is statistically independent of all others. An equivalent statement is that each of the connection vectors $\mathbf{f}_h$ is equally likely to be any one of the 2^N binary vectors of length N and that the $\{\mathbf{f}_h\}$ are statistically independent.

We say that a random binary vector (such as any $\mathbf{f}_h$) is *EL* if its components are statistically independent and equally likely to be 0 or 1. In proving the random coding bound for parity-check coders, the following property of the modulo-2 sum of two random N-component binary vectors, say $\mathbf{a}$ and $\mathbf{b}$, is of central importance:

If $\mathbf{a}$ *is EL and statistically independent of* $\mathbf{b}$, *then* $\mathbf{c} = \mathbf{a} \oplus \mathbf{b}$ *is also EL and independent of* $\mathbf{b}$.

In equation form this statement is

$$\mathrm{P}[\mathbf{c} = \boldsymbol{\alpha}] = \mathrm{P}[\mathbf{c} = \boldsymbol{\alpha} \mid \mathbf{b} = \boldsymbol{\beta}] = 2^{-N}; \qquad \text{for all } \boldsymbol{\alpha}, \boldsymbol{\beta}, \tag{6.19}$$

where $\boldsymbol{\alpha}$ and $\boldsymbol{\beta}$ are N-component binary vectors.

The proof of Eq. 6.19 is straightforward. From Eq. 6.17, if $\mathbf{c} = \mathbf{a} \oplus \mathbf{b}$, then

$$\mathbf{c} \oplus \mathbf{b} = \mathbf{a} \oplus \mathbf{b} \oplus \mathbf{b} = \mathbf{a}. \tag{6.20a}$$

Thus $\mathbf{c} = \boldsymbol{\alpha}$ when $\mathbf{b} = \boldsymbol{\beta}$ if and only if

$$\mathbf{a} = \boldsymbol{\alpha} \oplus \boldsymbol{\beta}. \tag{6.20b}$$

But $\mathbf{a}$ is *EL* and independent of $\mathbf{b}$. Therefore for any $\boldsymbol{\alpha}$ and $\boldsymbol{\beta}$

$$\mathrm{P}[\mathbf{c} = \boldsymbol{\alpha} \mid \mathbf{b} = \boldsymbol{\beta}] = \mathrm{P}[\mathbf{a} = \boldsymbol{\alpha} \oplus \boldsymbol{\beta} \mid \mathbf{b} = \boldsymbol{\beta}] = \mathrm{P}[\mathbf{a} = \boldsymbol{\alpha} \oplus \boldsymbol{\beta}] = 2^{-N}, \tag{6.20c}$$

and

$$\mathrm{P}[\mathbf{c} = \boldsymbol{\alpha}] = \sum_{\text{all } \boldsymbol{\beta}} \mathrm{P}[\mathbf{c} = \boldsymbol{\alpha} \mid \mathbf{b} = \boldsymbol{\beta}]\, \mathrm{P}[\mathbf{b} = \boldsymbol{\beta}] = 2^{-N}. \tag{6.20d}$$

As claimed, $\mathbf{c}$ is *EL* and statistically independent of $\mathbf{b}$.

We now invoke this property to show that if $\mathbf{x}_i$ is the input to a parity-check coder then over the ensemble of encoder connections (1) the coder output vector $\mathbf{y}_i$ is *EL* and (2) the coder output vector $\mathbf{y}_i$ is pairwise statistically independent of the vector $\mathbf{y}_k$ produced by any other input $\mathbf{x}_k$, $k \neq i$. These two results will be used to establish that

$$\overline{\mathrm{P}_2[\mathbf{s}_i, \mathbf{s}_k]} < 2^{-NR_0}, \tag{6.21}$$

where R_0 is the error exponent for binary-waveform sequences given by Eq. 5.36.

Proof that any $\mathbf{y}_i$ is *EL* follows from the fact (Eq. 6.18a) that

$$\mathbf{y}_i = \mathbf{f}_0 \oplus x_{i1}\mathbf{f}_1 \oplus x_{i2}\mathbf{f}_2 \oplus \cdots \oplus x_{iK}\mathbf{f}_K.$$

Letting $\mathbf{a}$ denote the modulo-2 sum of the input-dependent terms, we have

$$\mathbf{y}_i = \mathbf{f}_0 \oplus \mathbf{a}. \tag{6.22a}$$

But, over the ensemble, $\mathbf{f}_0$ is both *EL* and statistically independent of all other $\mathbf{f}_h$, hence of $\mathbf{a}$. Accordingly, for any i, $\mathbf{y}_i$ is *EL*:

$$P[\mathbf{y}_i = \boldsymbol{\alpha}] = 2^{-N}; \qquad \text{for all } \boldsymbol{\alpha}. \tag{6.22b}$$

(Note, however, that if $\mathbf{f}_0$ were *not* included in the ensemble of connection vectors the output $\mathbf{y}_0$ produced by the all-zero input sequence $\mathbf{x}_0$ would also be identically zero, hence not *EL*.)

Proof that the pair of output vectors $\mathbf{y}_i$ and $\mathbf{y}_k$ are statistically independent when $i \neq k$ follows from the observation that $\mathbf{x}_i$ and $\mathbf{x}_k$ differ in at least one component. Let l denote such a component and assume initially that

$$x_{il} = 1, \qquad x_{kl} = 0. \tag{6.23a}$$

We can therefore write

$$\mathbf{y}_i = \mathbf{f}_l \oplus \mathbf{b}, \tag{6.23b}$$

where $\mathbf{f}_l$ enters neither into $\mathbf{b}$ nor $\mathbf{y}_k$, hence is independent of both. Since $\mathbf{f}_l$ is *EL* and statistically independent of the pair $(\mathbf{b}, \mathbf{y}_k)$, so also is $\mathbf{y}_i$. Indeed, for all N-component binary vectors $\boldsymbol{\alpha}, \boldsymbol{\beta}, \boldsymbol{\gamma}$ we have

$$\begin{aligned} P[\mathbf{y}_i = \boldsymbol{\alpha} \mid \mathbf{b} = \boldsymbol{\beta}, \mathbf{y}_k = \boldsymbol{\gamma}] &= P[\mathbf{f}_l = \boldsymbol{\alpha} \oplus \boldsymbol{\beta} \mid \mathbf{b} = \boldsymbol{\beta}, \mathbf{y}_k = \boldsymbol{\gamma}] \\ &= P[\mathbf{f}_l = \boldsymbol{\alpha} \oplus \boldsymbol{\beta}] = 2^{-N}. \end{aligned} \tag{6.23c}$$

Thus

$$\begin{aligned} P[\mathbf{y}_i = \boldsymbol{\alpha} \mid \mathbf{y}_k = \boldsymbol{\gamma}] &= \sum_{\text{all } \boldsymbol{\beta}} P[\mathbf{y}_i = \boldsymbol{\alpha} \mid \mathbf{b} = \boldsymbol{\beta}, \mathbf{y}_k = \boldsymbol{\gamma}]\, P[\mathbf{b} = \boldsymbol{\beta} \mid \mathbf{y}_k = \boldsymbol{\gamma}] \\ &= 2^{-N} \sum_{\text{all } \boldsymbol{\beta}} P[\mathbf{b} = \boldsymbol{\beta} \mid \mathbf{y}_k = \boldsymbol{\gamma}] \\ &= 2^{-N} = P[\mathbf{y}_i = \boldsymbol{\alpha}]. \end{aligned} \tag{6.23d}$$

For this proof, we have assumed that $x_{il} = 1$ and $x_{kl} = 0$. If on the contrary $x_{il} = 0$ and $x_{kl} = 1$, the statistical independence of $\mathbf{y}_i$ and $\mathbf{y}_k$ follows from interchanging the indices i and k in the preceding argument.

With these two results, we now establish that the probability of error bound of Eq. 6.6 applies to the ensemble of binary codes $\{\mathbf{s}_i\}$ defined by the set of all equally likely parity-check encoders. Since each output vector $\mathbf{y}_i$ implies a definite signal vector $\mathbf{s}_i$, the pairwise statistical independence of the $\mathbf{y}_i$ implies pairwise statistical independence of the $\mathbf{s}_i$. Furthermore, since each $\mathbf{y}_i$ is equally likely to be any binary vector with components 0 and 1, each $\mathbf{s}_i$ is equally likely to be any binary vector with components $\pm\sqrt{E_N}$. Thus Eqs. 6.11a and b are both satisfied. We conclude that the probability of error for communication over an additive white Gaussian noise channel, when averaged over the ensemble of all parity-check-coded systems, satisfies

$$\overline{P[\mathcal{E}]} < 2^{-N[R_0 - R_N]} \tag{6.24a}$$

with (from Eq. 5.36)

$$R_0 = 1 - \log_2 (1 + e^{-E_N/\mathcal{N}_0}). \tag{6.24b}$$

We have already noted (Eq. 5.42) that this value of R_0 is exponentially optimum for small values of the energy-to-noise ratio per degree of freedom,† $E_N/\mathcal{N}_0$. Under these conditions the use of a transmitter whose complexity grows only linearly with K, hence with the signal duration T, does not imply a loss in signaling efficiency.

Multiamplitude codes. Parity-check coders also provide an effective escape from the difficulty of storing an exponentially large set of multi-amplitude-component signal vectors $\{\mathbf{s}_i\}$ for use on channels with high

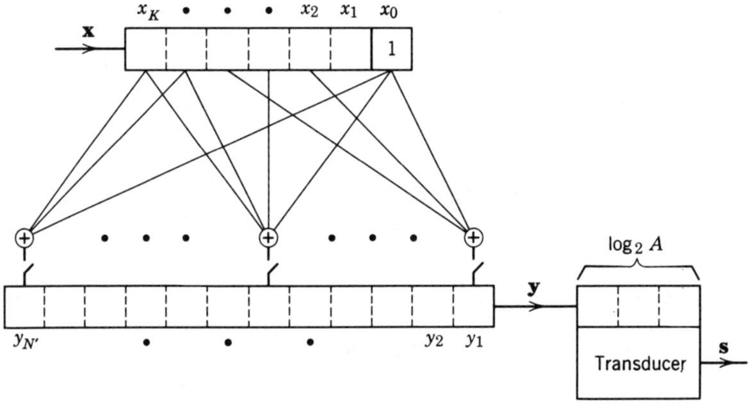

Figure 6.8 A multiamplitude parity-check coder. The transducer produces one component of **s** from each successive block of $\log_2 A$ components of **y**.

energy-to-noise ratio per degree of freedom. An appropriate coder for such a condition is shown in Fig. 6.8. Whenever A, the number of signal amplitudes (alphabet letters) on which we wish to assign the $\{s_{ij}\}$, is a power of 2, we use

$$N' = N \log_2 A$$

stages in the y-register, instead of only N. As usual, N is the number of dimensions occupied by the signal set $\{\mathbf{s}_i\}$.

The amplitudes of the coefficients of the signal vectors are obtained from the output of the y-register by feeding **y**, $\log_2 A$ digits at a time, into the

† The "degrees of freedom" of a signal set $\{s_i(t)\}$ is defined as the number, N, of orthonormal functions $\{\varphi_j(t)\}$ used in its construction, i.e., as the signal set dimensionality.

transducer shown in Fig. 6.8. Clearly, these $\log_2 A$ digits may be used to specify one of A different amplitudes. In a typical case, say $A = 8$, the transducer might be a digital-to-analog convertor specified by the transformations

Input	Output	Input	Output
0 1 1	$+\sqrt{E_N}$	1 0 0	$-\frac{1}{7}\sqrt{E_N}$
0 1 0	$+\frac{5}{7}\sqrt{E_N}$	1 0 1	$-\frac{3}{7}\sqrt{E_N}$
0 0 1	$+\frac{3}{7}\sqrt{E_N}$	1 1 0	$-\frac{5}{7}\sqrt{E_N}$
0 0 0	$+\frac{1}{7}\sqrt{E_N}$	1 1 1	$-\sqrt{E_N}$

We now show that the multiamplitude random coding bound of Eq. 5.55 applies for an ensemble of parity-check coders and a fixed transducer. The $2^{N'(K+1)}$ distinct coder connections are assumed to be equally likely. Since $\mathbf{s}_i$ and $\mathbf{s}_k$ depend only on $\mathbf{y}_i$ and $\mathbf{y}_k$, respectively, and (as in the binary transducer case) $\mathbf{y}_i$ and $\mathbf{y}_k$ are pairwise statistically independent for any i and $k \neq i$, it is clear that $\mathbf{s}_i$ and $\mathbf{s}_k$ are pairwise statistically independent. Furthermore, for all i each component y_{ij}, $j = 1, 2, \ldots, N'$, is statistically independent of all other components in $\mathbf{y}_i$ and equally likely to be 0 or 1. Thus each component of any vector $\mathbf{s}_i$ at the transducer output is statistically independent of all of the other components in $\mathbf{s}_i$ and when A is a power of two is equally likely to be any one of the A possible values. The conditions of Eqs. 6.11a and b for the validity of the random coding bound are therefore met, and we again have

$$\overline{P[\mathcal{E}]} < 2^{-N[R_0 - R_N]}, \tag{6.25a}$$

in which R_0 is given by Eq. 5.56, with A a power of 2 and

$$p_l = \frac{1}{A}; \qquad l = 1, 2, \ldots, A. \tag{6.25b}$$

The simple coding strategy just considered is sufficient to attain near exponential optimality whenever the energy-to-noise ratio per degree of freedom is such that Shannon's upper bound, R_0^*, is closely approximated by the R_0 of Eq. 5.56, as plotted in Fig. 5.17. If this cannot be accomplished satisfactorily with A's that are powers of 2 and equally likely p_l's, matters can be improved by elaborating the procedure at the cost of making

$N'/N > \log_2 A$. For example, if $A = 3$ is satisfactory, we can use $N'/N = 3$ and the transducer mapping

$$\left.\begin{matrix} 0 & 1 & 1 \\ 0 & 1 & 0 \\ 0 & 0 & 1 \end{matrix}\right\} \Rightarrow +\sqrt{E_N}$$

$$\left.\begin{matrix} 0 & 0 & 0 \\ 1 & 0 & 0 \end{matrix}\right\} \Rightarrow 0$$

$$\left.\begin{matrix} 1 & 0 & 1 \\ 1 & 1 & 0 \\ 1 & 1 & 1 \end{matrix}\right\} \Rightarrow -\sqrt{E_N}$$

The signaling amplitudes $+\sqrt{E_N}$, 0, $-\sqrt{E_N}$ are now used with the unequal probabilities $\frac{3}{8}$, $\frac{2}{8}$, $\frac{3}{8}$; however, as we found in Chapter 5, it is desirable to use the amplitude zero with a probability less than 1/3 when $A = 3$. Clearly, any A and any desired probability set $\{p_l\}$ can be approximated by making N'/N sufficiently large and using an appropriate transducer mapping.

Invariance of $P[\mathcal{E} \mid m_k]$. We noted in Section 4.5 that certain completely symmetric signal sets $\{\mathbf{s}_i\}$, such as the set of M orthogonal signals and the set of M simplex signals, exhibit the following important property: with equally likely messages and white Gaussian noise, the optimum—that is, the maximum likelihood—receiver yields a probability of error which is independent of the signal actually transmitted.

$$P[\mathcal{E} \mid m_k] = P[\mathcal{E} \mid m_0]; \qquad \text{for } k = 0, 1, \ldots, M - 1. \tag{6.26}$$

We show in this section that every *binary* parity-check code also exhibits this property.

The first step in proving this invariance is to observe the effect of adding an arbitrary N-component binary vector, say

$$\mathbf{a} = (a_1, a_2, \ldots, a_N),$$

modulo-2 to *each* of the encoder output vectors $\{\mathbf{y}_i\}$: the jth component of every $\mathbf{y}_i$ is complemented when $a_j = 1$ and is left unaltered when $a_j = 0$. By "complement" we mean the transformation

$$0 \to 1, \qquad 1 \to 0.$$

Since with a binary code the transmitted vectors $\{\mathbf{s}_i\}$ are obtained from the $\{\mathbf{y}_i\}$ by

$$y_{ij} = 0 \Rightarrow s_{ij} = -\sqrt{E_N}$$
$$y_{ij} = 1 \Rightarrow s_{ij} = +\sqrt{E_N}$$

and

$$s_i(t) = \sum_{j=1}^{N} s_{ij}\, \varphi_j(t),$$

the effect on the $\{s_i(t)\}$ of adding $\mathbf{a}$ to each $\mathbf{y}_i$ is to transform

$$\varphi_j(t) \rightarrow -\varphi_j(t)$$

for all j such that $a_j = 1$. Such a transformation does not affect the orthonormality of the $\{\varphi_j(t)\}$. Since the minimum probability of error with additive white Gaussian noise is invariant to the particular choice of $\{\varphi_j(t)\}$ (cf. Chapter 4), for any binary parity-check code we have

$$P[\mathcal{E} \mid m_k, \{\mathbf{y}_i\}] = P[\mathcal{E} \mid m_k, \{\mathbf{y}_i \oplus \mathbf{a}\}]; \qquad \text{for all } k \text{ and any } \mathbf{a}. \tag{6.27}$$

An immediate implication of Eq. 6.27 is that the minimum error probability for any binary parity-check coder such as that diagrammed in Fig. 6.6 is independent of the choice of connection vector $\mathbf{f}_0$. In particular, setting $\mathbf{a} = \mathbf{f}_0$ in Eq. 6.27 is equivalent to having chosen $\mathbf{f}_0 = \mathbf{0}$ initially; in the binary case, although including $\mathbf{f}_0$ in the ensemble of codes simplifies the proof that the ensemble obeys the error probability bound, its inclusion has no effect on the actual error behavior of any code in the ensemble. Note, however, that this statement is *not* true in general when the number of amplitudes in the transmitter alphabet A is greater than two; in the multiamplitude case $\mathbf{f}_0$ enters into determination of the magnitude of the signal coefficients $\{s_{ij}\}$ rather than only into the determination of their sign.

We are now in a position to prove that any particular binary parity-check code obeys Eq. 6.26, so that the error probability of the maximum likelihood receiver is independent of which message is transmitted.

Without disturbing the error probabilities, we may take $\mathbf{f}_0 = \mathbf{0}$. The coder output vector $\mathbf{y}$ is then related to the coder input vector $\mathbf{x} = (x_1, x_2, \ldots, x_K)$ by

$$\mathbf{y} = x_1\mathbf{f}_1 \oplus x_2\mathbf{f}_2 \oplus \cdots \oplus x_K\mathbf{f}_K, \tag{6.28}$$

in which the $\{\mathbf{f}_h\}$ are the connection vectors of the particular code under consideration. The key to proving Eq. 6.26 is to note that Eq. 6.28 implies the following property:

If $\mathbf{a}$ *is any member of* $\{\mathbf{y}_i\}$, *the two sets* $\{\mathbf{y}_i \oplus \mathbf{a}\}$, $i = 0, 1, \ldots, M-1$, *and* $\{\mathbf{y}_i\}$ *both comprise the same vectors.*

As an example, if $\mathbf{a} = \mathbf{y}_2$ and the $\{\mathbf{y}_i\}$ are

$$\begin{aligned}\mathbf{y}_0 &= 0\ 0\ 0\ 0\ 0\\ \mathbf{y}_1 &= 0\ 1\ 0\ 1\ 1\\ \mathbf{y}_2 &= 1\ 1\ 0\ 1\ 0\\ \mathbf{y}_3 &= 1\ 0\ 0\ 0\ 1,\end{aligned}$$

then

$$\begin{aligned}\mathbf{y}_0 \oplus \mathbf{a} &= 1\ 1\ 0\ 1\ 0 = \mathbf{y}_2\\ \mathbf{y}_1 \oplus \mathbf{a} &= 1\ 0\ 0\ 0\ 1 = \mathbf{y}_3\\ \mathbf{y}_2 \oplus \mathbf{a} &= 0\ 0\ 0\ 0\ 0 = \mathbf{y}_0\\ \mathbf{y}_3 \oplus \mathbf{a} &= 0\ 1\ 0\ 1\ 1 = \mathbf{y}_1.\end{aligned}$$

The $\{\mathbf{y}_i \oplus \mathbf{a}\}$ differ from the $\{\mathbf{y}_i\}$ by a relabeling of subscripts.

The general proof of this *closure* property depends on the fact that Eq. 6.28 is *linear* in the sense that if the coder input is $\mathbf{x}_i \oplus \mathbf{x}_k$ the output is $\mathbf{y}_i \oplus \mathbf{y}_k$. For fixed k the coder input set $\{\mathbf{x}_i \oplus \mathbf{x}_k\}$, $i = 0, 1, \ldots, M - 1$, contains each of the 2^K binary vectors of length K once and only once. Thus $\{\mathbf{x}_i \oplus \mathbf{x}_k\}$ is a relabeling of $\{\mathbf{x}_i\}$, which implies that when $\mathbf{a} = \mathbf{y}_k$, $\{\mathbf{y}_i \oplus \mathbf{a}\}$ is a relabeling of $\{\mathbf{y}_i\}$. Codes for which this is so are called "group codes."[66,76]

Proof of Eq. 6.26 follows from the closure property. From Eq. 6.27 we know that

$$\mathrm{P}[\mathcal{E} \mid m_k, \{\mathbf{y}_i \oplus \mathbf{a}\}] = \mathrm{P}[\mathcal{E} \mid m_k, \{\mathbf{y}_i\}]. \tag{6.29a}$$

If we choose $\mathbf{a} = \mathbf{y}_k$, then

$$\mathbf{y}_k \oplus \mathbf{a} = \mathbf{0} = \mathbf{y}_0. \tag{6.29b}$$

Thus the transmitted vector with the code $\{\mathbf{y}_i \oplus \mathbf{a}\}$ when $m = m_k$ is the same as the transmitted vector with the code $\{\mathbf{y}_i\}$ when $m = m_0$. Since the remaining signal vectors are also the same, we have

$$\mathrm{P}[\mathcal{E} \mid m_k, \{\mathbf{y}_i \oplus \mathbf{a}\}] = \mathrm{P}[\mathcal{E} \mid m_0, \{\mathbf{y}_i\}]. \tag{6.29c}$$

Equating the right-hand sides of Eqs. 6.29 a and c yields Eq. 6.26, which was to be proved.

An immediate corollary of Eq. 6.26 is that the probability of error resulting when any binary parity-check code is used over an additive white Gaussian noise channel is invariant to the actual a priori probabilities $\{\mathrm{P}[m_i]\}$ whenever the receiver is maximum likelihood, hence optimum for equally likely messages. This corollary provides additional cogent justification for the equally likely a priori probability assumption; in accordance with the discussion of minimax receivers in Section 4.5, any receiver that is optimum for equally likely message inputs and for which $P[\mathcal{E} \mid m_k]$ is independent of k is also *minimax*.

Unfortunately, with multiamplitude codes the invariance of $P[\mathcal{E} \mid m_k]$ to k is lost in the asymmetric transformation $\{\mathbf{y}_i\} \to \{\mathbf{s}_i\}$. In principle significant sensitivity of the error probability with respect to m_k can be remedied in multiamplitude codes by means of an appropriate expurgation procedure. For example, if we denote by P the error probability that would result if a given N-dimension, K-bit—abbreviated (N, K)—code were used with equal a priori probabilities, then

$$P = \sum_k P[m_k]\, P[\mathcal{E} \mid m_k]$$

$$= \frac{1}{M} \sum_{k=0}^{M-1} P[\mathcal{E} \mid m_k]. \tag{6.30a}$$

Clearly, no more than half of the $P[\mathcal{E} \mid m_k]$ can be greater than twice P. If we delete those members of $\{\mathbf{s}_i\}$ for which

$$P[\mathcal{E} \mid m_k] > 2P, \tag{6.30b}$$

we have left a new code consisting of at least 2^{K-1} signals for each of which

$$P[\mathcal{E} \mid m_i] \leqslant 2P. \tag{6.30c}$$

Moreover, the rate of this expurgated code in bits per dimension,

$$R_N = \frac{K-1}{N}, \tag{6.30d}$$

is very nearly equal to the original unexpurgated rate, K/N, when K is large. The difficulty with the expurgation procedure is that one needs to know the $\{P[\mathcal{E} \mid m_i]\}$ in order to apply it: as already pointed out many times, in general we cannot hope to calculate all 2^K of these conditional probabilities when K is large.

Orthogonal and simplex codes. Parity-check coders may also be used to generate orthogonal and simplex signals, with $N = 2^K$ and $2^K - 1$, respectively. It is particularly interesting that with this technique each resulting signal vector, say $\mathbf{s}_i$, is binary; that is,

$$\mathbf{s}_i = (s_{i1}, s_{i2}, \ldots, s_{iN}); \qquad i = 0, 1, \ldots, 2^K - 1,$$

with

$$s_{ij} = +\sqrt{E_N} \quad \text{or} \quad -\sqrt{E_N}; \qquad \text{for all } i, j.$$

To see how to generate such signal sets, consider the case $K = 2$ and $N = 2^K = 4$. We take $\mathbf{f}_0 = \mathbf{0}$ and choose the parity-check coder-connection vectors $\mathbf{f}_1$ and $\mathbf{f}_2$ to be

$$\begin{aligned} \mathbf{f}_1 &= 1 \quad 0 \quad 1 \quad 0 \\ \mathbf{f}_2 &= 1 \quad 1 \quad 0 \quad 0. \end{aligned} \tag{6.31a}$$

Then, in accordance with Eq. 6.28, the $\{\mathbf{y}_i\}$ are

$$\begin{aligned} \mathbf{y}_0 &= 0 \quad 0 \quad 0 \quad 0 \\ \mathbf{y}_1 &= 1 \quad 0 \quad 1 \quad 0 \\ \mathbf{y}_2 &= 1 \quad 1 \quad 0 \quad 0 \\ \mathbf{y}_3 &= 0 \quad 1 \quad 1 \quad 0. \end{aligned} \tag{6.31b}$$

The corresponding binary vectors $\{\mathbf{s}_i\}$ are

$$\begin{aligned} \mathbf{s}_0 &= \sqrt{E_N}\,(-1, \quad -1, \quad -1, \quad -1) \\ \mathbf{s}_1 &= \sqrt{E_N}\,(+1, \quad -1, \quad +1, \quad -1) \\ \mathbf{s}_2 &= \sqrt{E_N}\,(+1, \quad +1, \quad -1, \quad -1) \\ \mathbf{s}_3 &= \sqrt{E_N}\,(-1, \quad +1, \quad +1, \quad -1). \end{aligned}$$

It is apparent that the dot product of any two vectors $\mathbf{s}_i$ and $\mathbf{s}_k$ is

$$\mathbf{s}_i \cdot \mathbf{s}_k = NE_N\,\delta_{ik}. \tag{6.32}$$

Thus these vectors $\{\mathbf{s}_i\}$ form an orthogonal set, and each has length $\sqrt{NE_N}$.

The reason for the orthogonality of the $\{\mathbf{s}_i\}$ becomes clear when we consider the structure of the $\{\mathbf{f}_h\}$. Each $\mathbf{f}_h$ consists of alternate groups of 1's and 0's. In $\mathbf{f}_1$ the groups are of length 2^0; in $\mathbf{f}_2$ the groups are of length 2^1. It is because of this that each vector $\mathbf{y}_k$ differs from every other vector $\mathbf{y}_i$ in exactly $N/2$ coordinates, which fact in turn implies orthogonality between the $\{\mathbf{s}_i\}$.

We now prove for every K and $N = 2^K$ that, if the coder-connection vectors are alternate groups of 1's and 0's, with $\mathbf{f}_h$ having groups of length 2^{h-1}, the resulting coder generates a set of 2^K orthogonal vectors. Let $\{\mathbf{f}_h\}$, $h = 1, 2, \ldots, k$, denote the connection vectors for the case ($N = 2^k$, $K = k$) and let $\{\mathbf{g}_h\}$, $h = 1, 2, \ldots, k + 1$, denote the connection vectors for the case ($N = 2^{k+1}$, $K = k + 1$). The alternate grouping implies

$$\begin{aligned} \mathbf{g}_1 &= (\mathbf{f}_1, \mathbf{f}_1) \\ \mathbf{g}_2 &= (\mathbf{f}_2, \mathbf{f}_2) \\ &\ \ \vdots \\ \mathbf{g}_k &= (\mathbf{f}_k, \mathbf{f}_k), \end{aligned} \tag{6.33a}$$

in which we use the notation

$$(\mathbf{z}_1, \mathbf{z}_2) \triangleq (z_{11}, z_{12}, \ldots, z_{1N}, z_{21}, z_{22}, \ldots, z_{2N}). \tag{6.33b}$$

The $(k + 1)$th connection vector is

$$\mathbf{g}_{k+1} = (\underbrace{1, 1, \ldots, 1}_{2^k \text{ 1's}}, \underbrace{0, 0, \ldots, 0}_{2^k \text{ 0's}}). \tag{6.33c}$$

Proof of orthogonality is by induction. Assume that the set of vectors $\{\mathbf{s}_i\}$ is orthogonal for $K = k$. From Eqs. 6.28 and 6.33 the set of signals for $K = k + 1$, say $\{\mathbf{s}_i'\}$, can be written in terms of the signals $\{\mathbf{s}_i\}$ for $K = k$ as

$$\left.\begin{aligned} \mathbf{s}_{2i}' &= (\mathbf{s}_i, \mathbf{s}_i) \\ \mathbf{s}_{2i+1}' &= (-\mathbf{s}_i, \mathbf{s}_i) \end{aligned}\right\} \quad \text{for } i = 0, 1, 2, \ldots, 2^k - 1. \tag{6.34}$$

Equations 6.34 follow from the fact that since x_{k+1} by convention is the least significant digit, $\mathbf{g}_{k+1}$ enters into the determination of $\mathbf{s}_{2i+1}'$ but not into the determination of $\mathbf{s}_{2i}'$, for all $i \leqslant 2^k - 1$. The effect of including $\mathbf{g}_{k+1}$ is to change the sign of the first 2^k components of the signal vector that would result if $\mathbf{g}_{k+1}$ were not included.

From Eq. 6.33b,

$$(\mathbf{z}_1, \mathbf{z}_2) \cdot (\mathbf{z}_3, \mathbf{z}_4) = (\mathbf{z}_1 \cdot \mathbf{z}_3) + (\mathbf{z}_2 \cdot \mathbf{z}_4).$$

By virtue of the orthogonality (assumed for the induction) between the 2^k-component vectors $\{\mathbf{s}_i\}$, we therefore have

$$(\mathbf{s}_i, \mathbf{s}_i) \cdot (\mathbf{s}_l, \mathbf{s}_l) = 2^k E_{\mathrm{N}}\, \delta_{il} + 2^k E_{\mathrm{N}}\, \delta_{il} = 2^{k+1} E_{\mathrm{N}}\, \delta_{il}, \tag{6.35a}$$

$$(-\mathbf{s}_i, \mathbf{s}_i) \cdot (-\mathbf{s}_l, \mathbf{s}_l) = 2^k E_{\mathrm{N}}\, \delta_{il} + 2^k E_{\mathrm{N}}\, \delta_{il} = 2^{k+1} E_{\mathrm{N}}\, \delta_{il}, \tag{6.35b}$$

$$(\mathbf{s}_i, \mathbf{s}_i) \cdot (-\mathbf{s}_l, \mathbf{s}_l) = -2^k E_{\mathrm{N}}\, \delta_{il} + 2^k E_{\mathrm{N}}\, \delta_{il} = 0. \tag{6.35c}$$

Thus the orthogonality of the signal vectors in the case $K = k$ guarantees the orthogonality in the case $K = k + 1$. Since we have seen that the theorem is true for $K = 2$, the proof is complete. That the theorem is also true for $K = 1$ is obvious by inspection. (It is convenient to begin the induction argument with $K = 2$ because of the insight afforded into the structure of the $\{\mathbf{f}_h\}$.)

The advantage of generating orthogonal waveforms in this way is obvious; from an engineering point of view their generation is relatively simple. Of course, this is also true of short pulses positioned in time so that they do not overlap. With parity-check waveforms, however, the problem of a high peak-power requirement is avoided, as illustrated in Fig. 6.9.

To obtain a set of 2^K simplex waveforms it is only necessary to modify the coder just described by deleting the Nth stage of the y-register, leaving the first $2^K - 1$ stages unchanged. This corresponds to deleting the last component of each of the $\{\mathbf{f}_h\}$. Since our choice of the $\{\mathbf{f}_h\}$ was such that $f_{hN} = 0$ for all h, it follows that $y_{iN} = 0$ for all $\mathbf{y}_i$; thus truncating the code words to length $2^K - 1$ does not affect the error performance of the $\{\mathbf{s}_i\}$. (Recall that in Chapter 4 simplex waveforms were obtained from orthogonal waveforms by a translation that did not affect P[$\mathcal{E}$].)

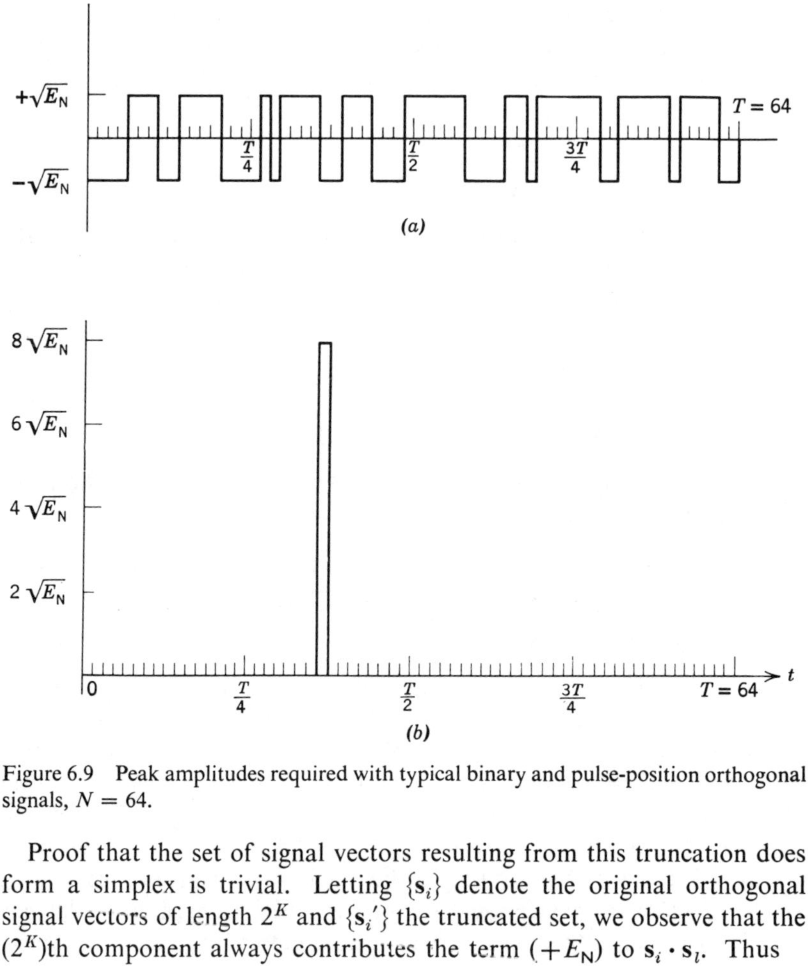

Figure 6.9 Peak amplitudes required with typical binary and pulse-position orthogonal signals, $N = 64$.

Proof that the set of signal vectors resulting from this truncation does form a simplex is trivial. Letting $\{\mathbf{s}_i\}$ denote the original orthogonal signal vectors of length 2^K and $\{\mathbf{s}_i'\}$ the truncated set, we observe that the (2^K)th component always contributes the term $(+E_N)$ to $\mathbf{s}_i \cdot \mathbf{s}_l$. Thus

$$\mathbf{s}_i' \cdot \mathbf{s}_l' = \mathbf{s}_i \cdot \mathbf{s}_l - E_N$$
$$= \begin{cases} (2^K - 1)E_N; & \text{for } i = l \\ -E_N; & \text{for } i \neq l. \end{cases} \tag{6.36}$$

Since Eq. 6.36 reduces to the simplex definition of Eq. 4.99 when 2^K is identified with M and ME_N with E_s, the proof is complete.

The encoder for simplex vectors in the case $K = 3$, $N = 2^K - 1 = 7$, is shown in Fig. 6.10. The connection vectors are

$$\begin{aligned} \mathbf{f}_1 &= 1 \quad 0 \quad 1 \quad 0 \quad 1 \quad 0 \quad 1 \\ \mathbf{f}_2 &= 1 \quad 1 \quad 0 \quad 0 \quad 1 \quad 1 \quad 0 \\ \mathbf{f}_3 &= 1 \quad 1 \quad 1 \quad 1 \quad 0 \quad 0 \quad 0. \end{aligned} \tag{6.37}$$

It is interesting to note that each column on the right-hand side of Eqs. 6.37 represents a different one of the $(2^K - 1)$ distinct non-null parity-check connections. It can be shown that this is true for all K: simplex codes with 2^K words can be generated by performing all distinct

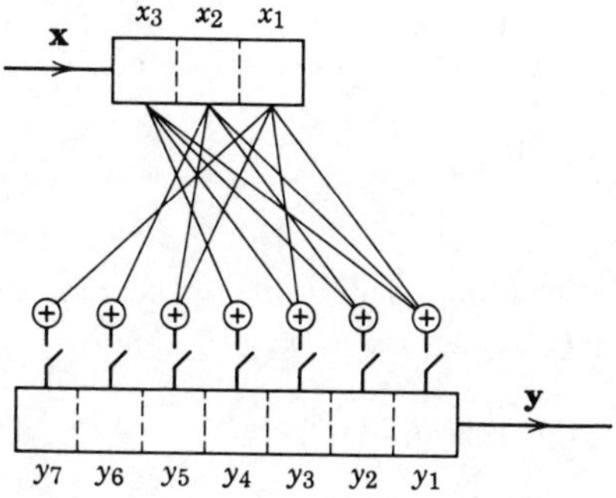

Figure 6.10 Parity-check encoder for simplex ($K = 3$, $N = 2^K - 1 = 7$):
$\mathbf{y} = (x_1 \oplus x_2 \oplus x_3, x_2 \oplus x_3, x_1 \oplus x_3, x_3, x_1 \oplus x_2, x_2, x_1)$.

non-null parity checks on a sequence of K message bits. An especially simple implementation of a simplex coder is a K-bit shift register connected in a maximal-length feedback configuration.[36,66] An example is shown in Fig. 6.11.

Discussion. Much study has been devoted to parity-check coders, particularly for the binary signal case. Catalogs of optimum, that is, minimum P[$\mathcal{E}$], binary codes have been compiled[66] for many cases in which either K or $N - K$ or both are small. The known techniques for finding optimum codes are essentially those of exhaustive enumeration and evaluation and usually cannot be applied when both K and $(N - K)$ are large. No general algorithm is known for constructing explicit codes for which it can be proved that the probability of error is overbounded by Eq. 6.6.

At first glance it is startling that the error probability averaged over all (N, K) binary codes is, in general, smaller than the behavior of the best code for which the error probability can be calculated. In some sense it appears that it is the absence of simple structure that makes a code good. Unfortunately, however, it is not possible to calculate the error probability of specific large codes that are not highly structured.

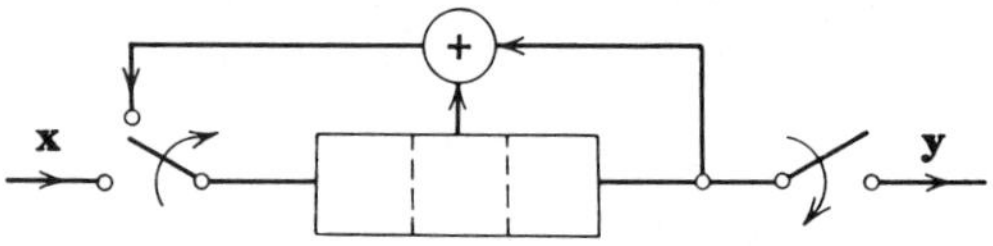

Operate switches after $\mathbf{x}$ is loaded into x-register and step seven times

Shift	Contents of x-register		
0	x_3	x_2	x_1
1	$x_1 \oplus x_2$	x_3	x_2
2	$x_2 \oplus x_3$	$x_1 \oplus x_2$	x_3
3	$x_1 \oplus x_2 \oplus x_3$	$x_2 \oplus x_3$	$x_1 \oplus x_2$
4	$x_1 \oplus x_3$	$x_1 \oplus x_2 \oplus x_3$	$x_2 \oplus x_3$
5	x_1	$x_1 \oplus x_3$	$x_1 \oplus x_2 \oplus x_3$
6	x_2	x_1	$x_1 \oplus x_3$
7	x_3	x_2	x_1

Figure 6.11 Maximal length shift register encoder for simplex ($N = 7$, $K = 3$): $\mathbf{y} = (x_1, x_2, x_3, x_1 \oplus x_2, x_2 \oplus x_3, x_1 \oplus x_2 \oplus x_3, x_1 \oplus x_3)$.

6.2 RECEIVER QUANTIZATION

We have been studying the problem of building a transmitter that is capable of efficiently communicating one of

$$M = 2^{NR_{\mathrm{N}}} = 2^{RT} \tag{6.38a}$$

messages even when NR_{N} is large. For the additive white Gaussian noise channel we have observed that it is not difficult to construct an ensemble in which the transmitters are easily implemented and for which the bound

$$\overline{P[\mathcal{E}]} < 2^{-N[R_0 - R_{\mathrm{N}}]} \tag{6.38b}$$

is satisfied with an R_0 that is nearly optimum.

The problem of implementing an efficient receiver is not so easily resolved. The bound of Eq. 6.38b was derived under the assumption that each member of the ensemble of communication systems has an optimum receiver. Optimum receivers for signals

$$s_i(t) = \sum_{j=1}^{N} s_{ij}\, \varphi_j(t); \qquad i = 0, 1, \ldots, M-1 \tag{6.39}$$

have been studied in Chapter 4. As illustrated in Fig. 6.12, one implementation is a bank of N filters matched to the $\{\varphi_j(t)\}$, followed by circuits that compute the M dot products

$$\mathbf{r} \cdot \mathbf{s}_i = \sum_{j=1}^{N} r_j s_{ij} \tag{6.40a}$$

and determine for which i the decision variable

$$g_i \stackrel{\Delta}{=} \mathbf{r} \cdot \mathbf{s}_i - \tfrac{1}{2} |\mathbf{s}_i|^2; \qquad i = 0, 1, \cdots, M-1 \tag{6.40b}$$

is maximum. (In Eq. 6.40 and throughout this chapter we assume equal a priori message probabilities.)

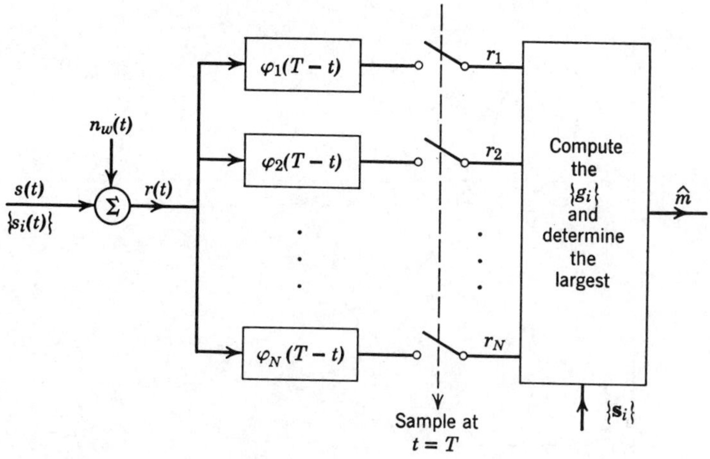

Figure 6.12 An optimum receiver realization: $\mathbf{r} = (r_1, r_2, \ldots, r_N)$.

Clearly, the complexity of implementing the bank of matched filters illustrated in Fig. 6.12 grows no faster than linearly with N. Indeed, as stated in Section 6.1 in connection with modulator design, the complexity is independent of N if the $\{\varphi_j(t)\}$ are chosen to be nonoverlapping time-translates of a single waveform of duration τ. As shown in Fig. 6.13, in this case we can use a single matched filter and sample its output at times $j\tau, j = 1, 2, \ldots, N$.

On the other hand, there remains the problem of calculating the set of decision variables $\{g_i\}$. At first glance it might appear that a high-speed digital computer could resolve this difficulty. But for large T this is not so; from Eqs. 6.40 the number of calculations involved in determining the $\{g_i\}$ is NM. For $R = 1000$ bits/sec and $T = \frac{1}{10}$ sec, we have

$$M = 2^{RT} = 2^{100} > 10^{30},$$

which in a serial computer would allow 10^{-22} nanosecond for computing each sum. One cannot trifle with exponential growth.

An alternative is to calculate the $\{g_i\}$ in time-parallel rather than in time-sequence, perhaps by resistor weighting networks and summing busses. But this would require approximately NM resistors, and exponential growth in number of components is no more attractive than exponential growth in speed of computation. In general, the only recourse is to accept a receiver that is less than optimum.

Once we are reconciled to some loss in performance, the problem is to determine receiving procedures with acceptable degradation. In this framework special-purpose digital computers, called *decoders*, assume a

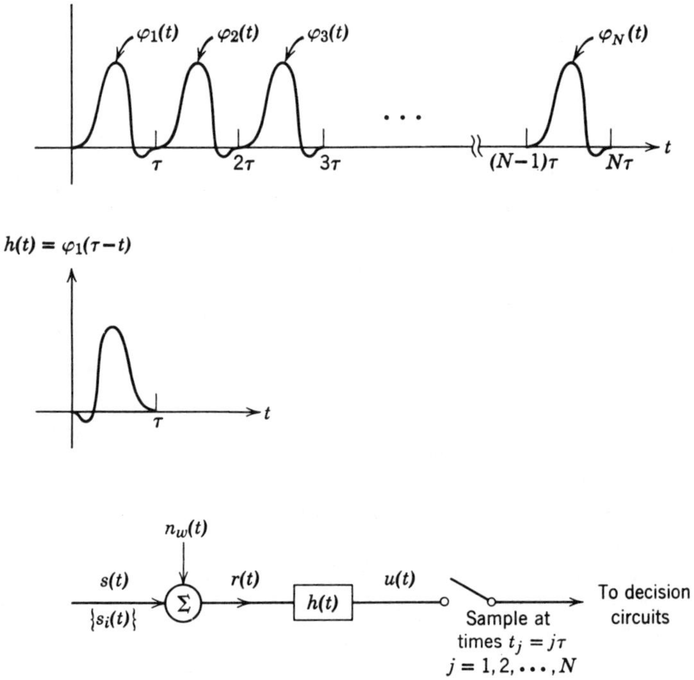

Figure 6.13 Optimum receiver realization for a time-translated orthonormal set $\{\varphi_j(t)\}$:

$$\begin{aligned}
u(t_j) &= \int_{-\infty}^{\infty} r(\alpha)h(t_j - \alpha)\,d\alpha \\
&= \int_{-\infty}^{\infty} r(\alpha)\varphi_1(\tau - t_j + \alpha)\,d\alpha \\
&= \int_{-\infty}^{\infty} r(\alpha)\varphi_1[\alpha - (j-1)\tau]\,d\alpha \\
&= \int_{-\infty}^{\infty} r(\alpha)\varphi_j(\alpha)\,d\alpha = r_j.
\end{aligned}$$

role of central importance, primarily because of the great flexibility with which they process data.

When a decoder is used, the performance degradation arises from two sources. First, the vector **r** at the output of the matched-filter bank has components $\{r_j\}$ that are defined on a continuum, whereas a digital computer operates only with discrete numbers. Thus some form of amplitude quantization is usually introduced ahead of the computer. Second, the number of computations demanded of the computer must be restricted to growing no faster than linearly with the signal duration T. The first source of degradation is considered in the remainder of this section; the second is considered in Section 6.4.

Measure of Degradation

It is evident that transforming the N-component vector **r** into a discrete vector suitable for computer processing is an irreversible operation and in general degrades the attainable error performance. It is intuitively reasonable that this degradation will be small if the quantization is extremely fine. On the other hand, coarse quantization is desirable because it decreases the memory requirements, hence the cost of the decoder: if each component of **r** is quantized into one of Q levels (Q a power of 2), $N \log_2 Q$ bits of memory are required to store the quantized vector in the computer.

The appropriate engineering balance between system cost and performance cannot be adjudged without some quantitative measure of the effect of quantization on the probability of error. An especially useful measure of degradation in a coding situation is provided by the exponent in the random coding bound.

Heretofore the exponential parameter R_0 in the bound $\overline{P[\mathcal{E}]} < 2^{-N(R_0 - R_N)}$ has been determined only for an ensemble of communication systems utilizing parity-check coders, transducers, and *optimum* (unquantized) receivers. We now consider the parameter R_0' in a corresponding bound $\overline{P[\mathcal{E}]} < 2^{-N(R_0' - R_N)}$ for an ensemble of systems with the same transmitters but with receivers having the structure of Fig. 6.14, in which a quantizer Q is inserted between matched filter and decoder. The decoder itself is assumed to be optimum in the sense that it determines, from the quantized vector $\mathbf{r}'$ and knowledge of the signal set $\{\mathbf{s}_i\}$, which message has maximum a posteriori probability $P[m_i \mid \mathbf{r}' = \boldsymbol{\gamma}, \{\mathbf{s}_i\}]$. The difference between R_0 and R_0' provides a meaningful measure of the degradation due to quantization.†

† Methods other than the direct quantization of each component of **r** may also be used to produce a discrete decoder input vector. (See problem 6.10.)

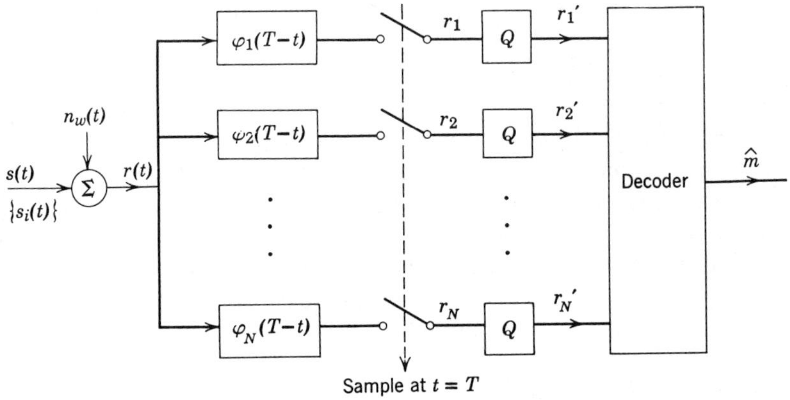

Figure 6.14 Quantized receiver. The decoder input vector is $\mathbf{r}' = (r_1', r_2', \ldots, r_N')$.

The Quantized-Channel Model

With an additive white Gaussian noise channel, each component s_j of the transmitted vector $\mathbf{s}$ is corrupted by the addition of a statistically independent Gaussian noise variable. Thus, if $\{a_l\}$ denotes the transmitter alphabet, when $s_j = a_l$ the jth component of the (unquantized) received vector $\mathbf{r}$ is described by the density function

$$p_{r_j}(\gamma \mid s_j = a_l) = \frac{1}{\sqrt{\pi \mathcal{N}_0}} e^{-(\gamma - a_l)^2/\mathcal{N}_0}. \tag{6.41}$$

As illustrated in Fig. 6.15, the quantizer maps r_j into an output component r_j' that cannot assume an arbitrary value on the real line but is

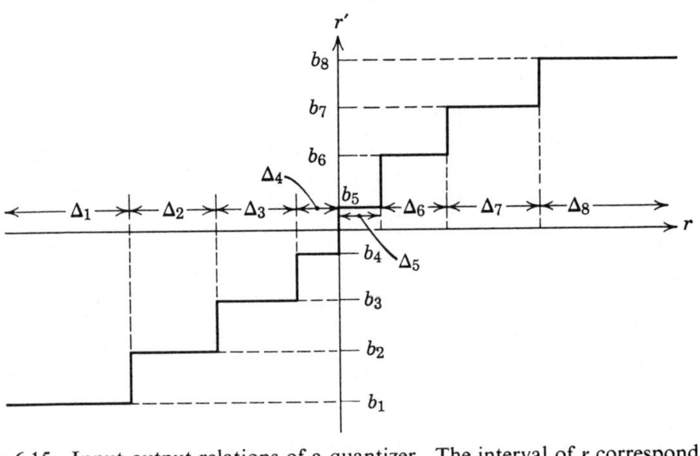

Figure 6.15 Input-output relations of a quantizer. The interval of r corresponding to $r' = b_h$ is Δ_h.

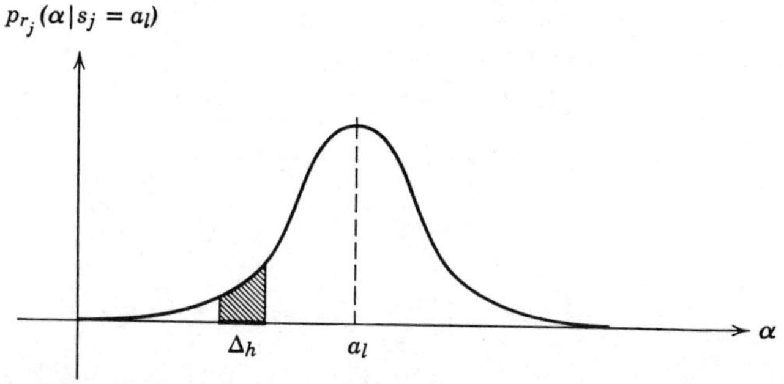

Figure 6.16 The transition probability q_{lh} is the area of the shaded region.

restricted to being some letter of the *quantizer output alphabet*, say $\{b_h\}$, $h = 1, 2, \ldots, Q$. Given that s_j is a_l, we denote the probability that r_j' is b_h by the symbol q_{lh}:

$$q_{lh} \triangleq \mathrm{P}[r_j' = b_h \mid s_j = a_l]. \tag{6.42}$$

As shown in Fig. 6.16, the value of q_{lh} for any particular quantizer is the integral of the Gaussian density function of Eq. 6.41 over the hth quantization interval. The set of probabilities $\{q_{lh}\}$, $l = 1, 2, \ldots, A$, $h = 1, 2, \ldots, Q$, specifies the probabilistic connections between the transmitter alphabet $\{a_l\}$ and the quantizer output alphabet $\{b_h\}$. The $\{q_{lh}\}$, called *transition probabilities*, may be conveniently displayed in a diagram (see Fig. 6.17*a*) when A and Q are small and in a matrix (see Fig. 6.17*b*) when A and Q are large.

The components of the Gaussian noise vector which the channel adds to the signal vector **s** are statistically independent. If we assume that each

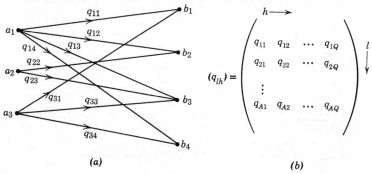

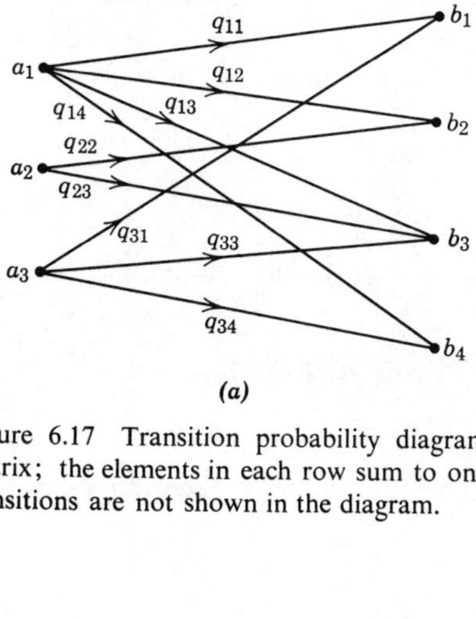

$$(q_{lh}) = \begin{pmatrix} q_{11} & q_{12} & \cdots & q_{1Q} \\ q_{21} & q_{22} & \cdots & q_{2Q} \\ \vdots & & & \\ q_{A1} & q_{A2} & \cdots & q_{AQ} \end{pmatrix}$$

(b)

Figure 6.17 Transition probability diagram and matrix: (*a*) $A = 3$, $Q = 4$; (*b*) matrix; the elements in each row sum to one. In the interest of clarity all possible transitions are not shown in the diagram.

matched filter output r_j, $j = 1, 2, \ldots, N$, is subjected to an identical quantizer, each component s_j is affected independently by the same set of transition probabilities $\{q_{lh}\}$. Thus if

$$\boldsymbol{\alpha} = (\alpha_1, \alpha_2, \ldots, \alpha_N)$$

$$\boldsymbol{\gamma} = (\gamma_1, \gamma_2, \ldots, \gamma_N),$$

then

$$P[\mathbf{r}' = \boldsymbol{\gamma} \mid \mathbf{s} = \boldsymbol{\alpha}] = \prod_{j=1}^{N} P[r_j' = \gamma_j \mid s_j = \alpha_j]. \tag{6.43}$$

Here, each α_j may be any member of the transmitter alphabet $\{a_l\}$ and each γ_j may be any member of the quantizer output alphabet $\{b_h\}$. For example, if

$$\boldsymbol{\alpha} = (a_6, a_2, a_5)$$

$$\boldsymbol{\gamma} = (b_3, b_7, b_1),$$

then, in accordance with Eqs. 6.42 and 6.43,

$$P[\mathbf{r}' = \boldsymbol{\gamma} \mid \mathbf{s} = \boldsymbol{\alpha}] = q_{6,3}\, q_{2,7}\, q_{5,1}.$$

Calculation of R_0'

We are now in a position to calculate a bound on the mean probability of error for an ensemble of quantized receiver communication systems. We assume that the connection vectors for the parity-check encoders are *EL* and statistically independent over the ensemble. Consequently, the signals $\{\mathbf{s}_i\}$ are statistically independent by pairs:

$$P[\mathbf{s}_i = \boldsymbol{\alpha}, \mathbf{s}_k = \boldsymbol{\beta}] = P[\mathbf{s}_i = \boldsymbol{\alpha}]\, P[\mathbf{s}_k = \boldsymbol{\beta}]; \qquad \text{all } i, k \neq i. \tag{6.44a}$$

Furthermore, the components of each signal are statistically independent,

$$P[\mathbf{s}_i = \boldsymbol{\alpha}] = \prod_{j=1}^{N} P[s_{ij} = \alpha_j]; \qquad i = 0, 1, \ldots, M-1, \tag{6.44b}$$

and for each a_l in the transmitter alphabet

$$P[s_{ij} = a_l] = p_l; \qquad \text{all } i, j. \tag{6.44c}$$

The $\{p_l\}$ depend on the choice of N' and of the digital-analog transducer of Fig. 6.8.

Formulation of the bound. The derivation of the bound

$$\overline{P[\mathcal{E}]} < 2^{-N[R_0' - R_N]} \tag{6.45}$$

is formulated in a manner identical to that we have encountered before.

We start with the union bound

$$P[\mathcal{E} \mid m_k] \leqslant \sum_{\substack{i=0 \\ (i \neq k)}}^{M-1} P_2[\mathbf{s}_i, \mathbf{s}_k]. \tag{6.46}$$

By virtue of Eqs. 6.44 the expectation of $P_2[\mathbf{s}_i, \mathbf{s}_k]$ over the ensemble of systems is independent of the subscripts i and k. Hence

$$\overline{P_2[\mathbf{s}_i, \mathbf{s}_k]} = \overline{P_2[\mathcal{E}]}; \qquad \text{all } i, k \neq i \tag{6.47a}$$

and

$$\overline{P[\mathcal{E}]} = \overline{P[\mathcal{E} \mid m_k]} < M\overline{P_2[\mathcal{E}]}. \tag{6.47b}$$

Since $M = 2^{NR_N}$, we need only show that

$$\overline{P_2[\mathcal{E}]} < 2^{-NR_0'} \tag{6.47c}$$

to obtain the desired bound of Eq. 6.45.

Verification of Eq. 6.47c and evaluation of R_0' remain to be done. We recall that $P_2[\mathbf{s}_i, \mathbf{s}_k]$ is the probability of error when $\mathbf{s}_i$ and $\mathbf{s}_k$ are used to communicate one of two equally likely messages. Let $\boldsymbol{\alpha}$ and $\boldsymbol{\beta}$ be two vectors with components in the transmitter alphabet $\{a_l\}$, let $\boldsymbol{\gamma}$ be a vector with components in the receiver alphabet $\{b_h\}$, and assume for the moment that

$$\mathbf{s}_i = \boldsymbol{\alpha}, \qquad \mathbf{s}_k = \boldsymbol{\beta}, \qquad \mathbf{r}' = \boldsymbol{\gamma}. \tag{6.48}$$

The optimum decoder in this two-message case makes an error when m_k is the transmitter input and $\mathbf{r}' = \boldsymbol{\gamma}$ is received if and only if

$$P[\mathbf{r}' = \boldsymbol{\gamma} \mid \mathbf{s}_i = \boldsymbol{\alpha}) \geqslant P[\mathbf{r}' = \boldsymbol{\gamma} \mid \mathbf{s}_k = \boldsymbol{\beta}]. \tag{6.49}$$

Equivalent forms of the error condition are

$$\ln \frac{P[\mathbf{r}' = \boldsymbol{\gamma} \mid \mathbf{s}_i = \boldsymbol{\alpha}]}{P[\mathbf{r}' = \boldsymbol{\gamma} \mid \mathbf{s}_k = \boldsymbol{\beta}]} \geqslant 0,$$

and, in view of Eq. 6.43,

$$\sum_{j=1}^{N} \ln \frac{P[r_j' = \gamma_j \mid s_{ij} = \alpha_j]}{P[r_j' = \gamma_j \mid s_{kj} = \beta_j]} \geqslant 0. \tag{6.50}$$

We simplify notation by defining

$$z_j \triangleq \ln \frac{P[r_j' = \gamma_j \mid s_{ij} = \alpha_j]}{P[r_j' = \gamma_j \mid s_{kj} = \beta_j]}, \qquad \text{for } j = 1, 2, \ldots, N \tag{6.51a}$$

and

$$\mathrm{z} \triangleq \sum_{j=1}^{N} z_j. \tag{6.51b}$$

Given $\mathbf{s}_i = \boldsymbol{\alpha}$, $\mathbf{s}_k = \boldsymbol{\beta}$, and $\mathbf{r}' = \boldsymbol{\gamma}$, an optimum receiver in our two-message case computes the number Z, and sets $\hat{m} = m_k$ if $Z < 0$. Thus, when $m = m_k$, an error is made if and only if

$$Z \geqslant 0. \tag{6.52}$$

Ensemble averaging. Over the ensemble of codes and channel noise, we recognize that s_{ij}, s_{kj}, and r_j' are random variables, with s_{ij} and s_{kj} ranging over the transmitter alphabet $\{a_l\}$ and r_j' ranging over the quantizer alphabet $\{b_h\}$. Hence z_j, which is uniquely determined for stated values of s_{ij}, s_{kj}, and r_j', is also a random variable. In particular, from Eqs. 6.42 and 6.51 we have

$$(s_{ij} = a_u, s_{kj} = a_l, r_j' = b_h) \Rightarrow \left(z_j = \ln \frac{q_{uh}}{q_{lh}}\right); \qquad \begin{matrix} 1 \leqslant u, l \leqslant A \\ 1 \leqslant h \leqslant Q. \end{matrix} \tag{6.53}$$

The probability assignment for z_j follows from the statistical independence of s_{ij} and s_{kj}. We have

$$\begin{aligned} \mathrm{P}[s_{ij} &= a_u, s_{kj} = a_l, r_j' = b_h \mid m_k] \\ &= \mathrm{P}[s_{ij} = a_u]\,\mathrm{P}[s_{kj} = a_l]\,\mathrm{P}[r_j' = b_h \mid m_k, s_{kj} = a_l] \\ &= p_u p_l q_{lh}. \end{aligned} \tag{6.54}$$

Finally, by virtue of Eqs. 6.43 and 6.44b we note that the random variables $\{z_j\}$, $j = 1, 2, \ldots, N$, are statistically independent, hence that Z is a sum of statistically independent, identically distributed random variables.

We shall bound $\overline{\mathrm{P}_2[\mathbf{s}_i, \mathbf{s}_k]}$, using the technique first introduced in the derivation of the Chernoff bound in Chapter 2. If we define the unit step function

$$f(Z) = \begin{cases} 1; & Z \geqslant 0 \\ 0; & Z < 0, \end{cases} \tag{6.55a}$$

then, from Eq. 6.52, we have

$$\overline{\mathrm{P}_2[\mathbf{s}_i, \mathbf{s}_k]} = \overline{\mathrm{P}_2[\mathcal{E}]} = \overline{f(Z)}, \tag{6.55b}$$

where the average is over the joint ensemble of codes and channel disturbances.

Evaluation of the bound. Direct evaluation of $\overline{f(Z)}$ is not, in general, possible. For the special case of no quantization, which was described in Chapter 5, the corresponding bound on $\overline{\mathrm{P}_2[\mathcal{E}]}$ was expressed in terms of the function $Q(\ )$ rather than the unit step function $f(\ )$. The averaging was easily carried out after the substitution of an exponential bound on

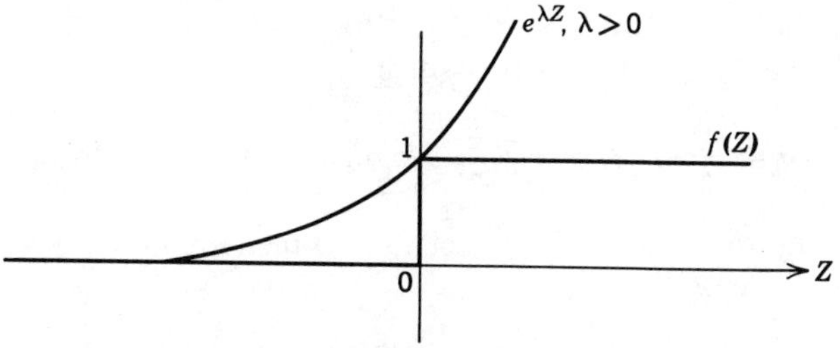

Figure 6.18 Exponential overbound to the unit step.

the $Q(\ \ )$ function. A similar strategy, which we now adopt, is to overbound the unit step $f(Z)$ by the exponential $e^{\lambda Z}$.

As shown in Fig. 6.18,

$$f(Z) \leqslant e^{\lambda Z}, \qquad \text{for any } \lambda \geqslant 0. \tag{6.56}$$

Substitution of Eq. 6.56 in Eq. 6.55b yields

$$\begin{aligned}\overline{P_2[\mathcal{E}]} &= \overline{f(Z)} \leqslant \overline{e^{\lambda Z}} \\ &= E\left[\exp\left(\lambda \sum_{j=1}^{N} z_j\right)\right] = E\left[\prod_{j=1}^{N} e^{\lambda z_j}\right] \\ &= \prod_{j=1}^{N} \overline{e^{\lambda z_j}} = [\overline{e^{\lambda z}}]^N; \qquad \lambda \geqslant 0,\end{aligned} \tag{6.57}$$

in which z denotes any one of the identically distributed, statistically independent random variables $\{z_j\}$. Defining

$$R_0'(\lambda) \triangleq -\log_2 \overline{e^{\lambda z}}, \tag{6.58a}$$

we have

$$\overline{P_2[\mathcal{E}]} \leqslant 2^{-NR_0'(\lambda)}; \qquad \lambda \geqslant 0. \tag{6.58b}$$

In the derivation of Eq. 6.58 we have exploited the fact that the random variables $\{z_j\}$, hence the random variables $\{e^{\lambda z_j}\}$, are statistically independent; this enables us to equate the mean of the product of the $\{e^{\lambda z_j}\}$ and the product of their means. Indeed, the motivation for adopting the exponential bound of Eq. 6.56 is that it permits exploitation of this fact.

The bound of Eq. 6.58b is valid for any $\lambda \geqslant 0$. We now choose the parameter λ in such a way that the bound is as tight as possible. From Eqs. 6.53 and 6.54,

$$\begin{aligned}\overline{e^{\lambda z}} &= \sum_u \sum_l \sum_h p_u p_l q_{lh} \exp\left(\lambda \ln \frac{q_{uh}}{q_{lh}}\right) \\ &= \sum_u \sum_l \sum_h p_u p_l q_{lh}^{1-\lambda} q_{uh}^{\lambda},\end{aligned} \tag{6.59}$$

where the indices u and l run from 1 to A and h runs from 1 to Q. We therefore seek the value of λ for which

$$0 = \frac{d}{d\lambda}(\overline{e^{\lambda z}}) = \sum_u \sum_l \sum_h p_u p_l q_{lh}^{1-\lambda} q_{uh}^{\lambda}(\ln q_{uh} - \ln q_{lh}). \quad (6.60a)$$

Since the right-hand side of Eq. 6.60a is symmetrical in the indices u and l, the solution to Eq. 6.60a is

$$\lambda = \tfrac{1}{2}, \quad (6.60b)$$

which, of course, satisfies the condition $\lambda \geqslant 0$. If we define

$$R_0' \triangleq R_0'(\lambda)_{\max} = R_0'(\tfrac{1}{2}) = -\log_2\left[\sum_u \sum_l \sum_h p_u p_l \sqrt{q_{uh} q_{lh}}\right], \quad (6.61a)$$

Eq. 6.58b becomes

$$\overline{\mathrm{P}_2[\mathcal{E}]} \leqslant 2^{-NR_0'}. \quad (6.61b)$$

Substitution of Eq. 6.61b in Eq. 6.47b yields the desired result

$$\overline{\mathrm{P}[\mathcal{E}]} < 2^{-N[R_0' - R_\mathrm{N}]}. \quad (6.62a)$$

By virtue of the symmetry of Eq. 6.61a with respect to the indices l and u the expression for R_0' may also be written

$$R_0' = -\log_2 \sum_{h=1}^{Q}\left[\sum_{l=1}^{A} p_l \sqrt{q_{lh}}\right]^2. \quad (6.62b)$$

Discussion. Equation 6.62 provides a bound on $\overline{\mathrm{P}[\mathcal{E}]}$ that is valid for any set of probabilities $\{p_l\}$. For a given set of transition probabilities $\{q_{lh}\}$, the $\{p_l\}$ may be optimized by use of the formulas of Appendix 5C.

Although Eq. 6.62 has been derived with reference to the quantized additive white Gaussian noise channel, its validity does not depend on the specific mechanism that produces the transition probabilities $\{q_{lh}\}$.† For any discrete channel described by the diagram in Fig. 6.17*a* or the matrix in Fig. 6.17*b* we may communicate one of $M = 2^{NR_\mathrm{N}}$ messages by means of a parity-check-encoded signal set $\{\mathbf{s}_i\}$ with components in $\{a_l\}$. As long as each component of $\mathbf{s}$ is affected independently by the transition probabilities $\{q_{lh}\}$, the ensemble average error probability is bounded by Eq. 6.62.

Increasingly Fine Quantization

We now consider the limiting behavior of R_0' as the quantization grain becomes increasingly fine. By so doing we obtain an exponential bound

† Since the $\{q_{lh}\}$ are probabilities, they must satisfy the conditions $q_{lh} \geqslant 0$ and $\sum_{h=1}^{Q} q_{lh} = 1$.

on $\overline{P[\mathcal{E}]}$ that applies to unquantized-receiver vector channels that are far more general than those disturbed solely by additive Gaussian noise. Indeed, the conditional probability density function of any unquantized received signal component r_j, given the transmitted signal component s_j, may be quite arbitrary. We need only require that this conditional density function is continuous and the same for all components $j = 1, 2, \ldots, N$, and that successive components of **r** are disturbed with statistical independence:

$$p_{\mathbf{r}|\mathbf{s}} = \prod_{j=1}^{N} p_{r_j|s_j} \tag{6.63a}$$

$$p_{r_j|s_j} = p_{r|s}; \qquad j = 1, 2, \ldots, N. \tag{6.63b}$$

If we quantize each component r_j as shown in Fig. 6.15, then in accordance with Fig. 6.16 we have

$$q_{lh} = \int_{\Delta_h} p_r(\gamma \mid s = a_l)\, d\gamma, \tag{6.64a}$$

in which Δ_h is the hth quantization interval. When each Δ_h is sufficiently small, Eq. 6.64a can be written

$$q_{lh} \approx p_r(b_h \mid s = a_l)\, \Delta_h, \tag{6.64b}$$

in which b_h is now taken as the midpoint of the interval Δ_h.

In accordance with Eq. 6.64b the expression for R_0' in Eq. 6.62b may be written

$$R_0' \approx -\log_2 \sum_{\text{all } h} \left[\sum_{l=1}^{A} p_l \sqrt{p_r(b_h \mid s = a_l)\, \Delta_h} \right]^2$$

$$= -\log_2 \sum_{\text{all } h} \Delta_h \left[\sum_{l=1}^{A} p_l \sqrt{p_r(b_h \mid s = a_l)} \right]^2.$$

In the limit as the quantization grid becomes increasingly fine the sum on h becomes an integral and the approximation of Eq. 6.64b is exact. Thus for the unquantized case the conditions of Eq. 6.63 suffice to establish the general result

$$\overline{P[\mathcal{E}]} < 2^{-N[R_0 - R_N]}, \tag{6.65a}$$

with

$$R_0 = -\log_2 \int_{-\infty}^{\infty} \left[\sum_{l=1}^{A} p_l \sqrt{p_r(\gamma \mid s = a_l)} \right]^2 d\gamma. \tag{6.65b}$$

For the particular case in which the disturbance is independent additive noise, $r = s + n$, this becomes

$$R_0 = -\log_2 \int_{-\infty}^{\infty} \left[\sum_{l=1}^{A} p_l \sqrt{p_n(\gamma - a_l)} \right]^2 d\gamma. \tag{6.65c}$$

Equation 6.65c can be used to substantiate our intuitive contention that extremely fine quantization does not introduce degradation in attainable error performance. As an example, we consider a particular system with binary modulation and a quantized receiver operating over an additive white Gaussian noise channel. We compare the value of R_0', approximated by the R_0 of Eq. 6.65c if the receiver is finely quantized, with the exponent obtained under the same conditions except that the receiver is unquantized.

Let

$$\begin{aligned} a_1 &= +\sqrt{E_N} \\ a_2 &= -\sqrt{E_N} \end{aligned} \tag{6.66a}$$

and choose

$$p_l = P[s_{ij} = a_l] = \tfrac{1}{2}; \qquad l = 1, 2. \tag{6.66b}$$

For unquantized Gaussian noise

$$p_n(\gamma) = \frac{1}{\sqrt{\pi \mathcal{N}_0}} e^{-\gamma^2/\mathcal{N}_0}.$$

In accordance with Eq. 6.65c, we have

$$\begin{aligned} R_0 &= -\log_2 \int_{-\infty}^{\infty} \left[\frac{1}{2} \left(\frac{1}{\sqrt{\pi \mathcal{N}_0}} e^{-(\gamma - \sqrt{E_N})^2/\mathcal{N}_0} \right)^{1/2} \right. \\ &\qquad \left. + \frac{1}{2} \left(\frac{1}{\sqrt{\pi \mathcal{N}_0}} e^{-(\gamma + \sqrt{E_N})^2/\mathcal{N}_0} \right)^{1/2} \right]^2 d\gamma \\ &= -\log_2 \frac{1}{4} \int_{-\infty}^{\infty} \frac{1}{\sqrt{\pi \mathcal{N}_0}} \\ &\qquad \times [e^{-(\gamma - \sqrt{E_N})^2/\mathcal{N}_0} + e^{-(\gamma + \sqrt{E_N})^2/\mathcal{N}_0} + 2e^{-(\gamma^2 + E_N)/\mathcal{N}_0}] \, d\gamma \\ &= -\log_2 \tfrac{1}{4}(1 + 1 + 2e^{-E_N/\mathcal{N}_0}) \\ &= 1 - \log_2 (1 + e^{-E_N/\mathcal{N}_0}). \end{aligned} \tag{6.67}$$

This agrees with the unquantized-receiver result of Eq. 6.24b.

The R_0 of Eq. 6.67 has been obtained via a bounding technique—$\overline{f(Z)} \leqslant \overline{e^{\lambda Z}}$—that at first appears quite weak. That this R_0 agrees for $E_N/\mathcal{N}_0 \ll 1$ with Shannon's optimum bound R_0^* may seem surprising. The agreement, however, is consistent with the statement in Chapter 2 that the Chernoff bound is exponentially tight.

Comparison of Quantization Schemes

We now apply the results of the analysis of R_0' to the evaluation of certain interesting quantization schemes. As usual, we assume that the transmission is corrupted by additive white Gaussian noise.

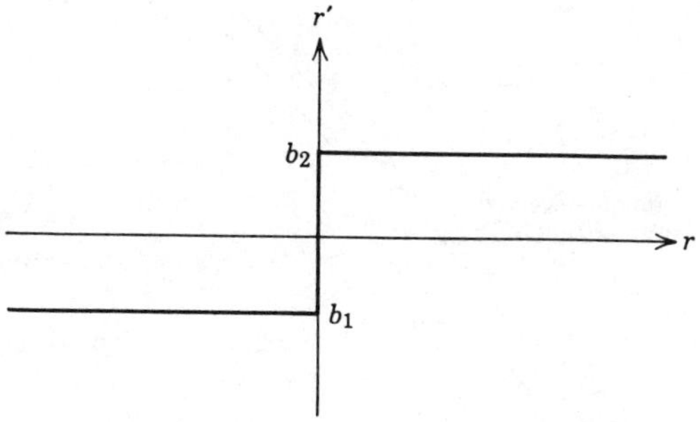

Figure 6.19 Quantizer for binary symmetric channel; $A = 2$, $Q = 2$.

Binary input, binary output. In the first case that we consider the transmitter alphabet consists of only two allowable input amplitudes,

$$a_1 = +\sqrt{E_N}$$
$$a_2 = -\sqrt{E_N}. \tag{6.68}$$

The matched filter output at the receiver is also quantized into two levels, as shown in Fig. 6.19. Thus $A = 2$, $Q = 2$, and the overall channel diagram is that of Fig. 6.20, in which

$$q_{12} = q_{21} \triangleq p \tag{6.69a}$$

$$q_{11} = q_{22} = 1 - p \tag{6.69b}$$

and

$$p = Q(\sqrt{2E_N/\mathcal{N}_0}). \tag{6.69c}$$

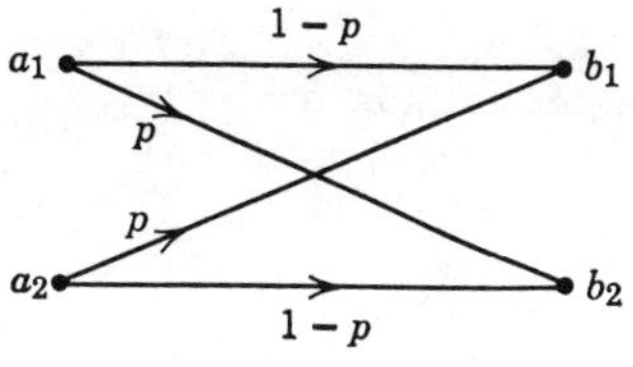

Figure 6.20 Transition diagram for binary symmetric channel.

The transition diagram is that of a *binary symmetric channel* (BSC). Because of the symmetry of this channel, the probability assignment $p_1 = p_2 = \frac{1}{2}$ is optimum. From Eq. 6.62b we then have

$$\begin{aligned} R_0' &= -\log_2 \sum_{h=1}^{2} \left[\sum_{l=1}^{2} p_l \sqrt{q_{lh}} \right]^2 \\ &= -\log_2 [(\tfrac{1}{2}\sqrt{p} + \tfrac{1}{2}\sqrt{1-p})^2 + (\tfrac{1}{2}\sqrt{p} + \tfrac{1}{2}\sqrt{1-p})^2] \\ &= 1 - \log_2 [1 + 2\sqrt{p(1-p)}]. \end{aligned} \tag{6.70}$$

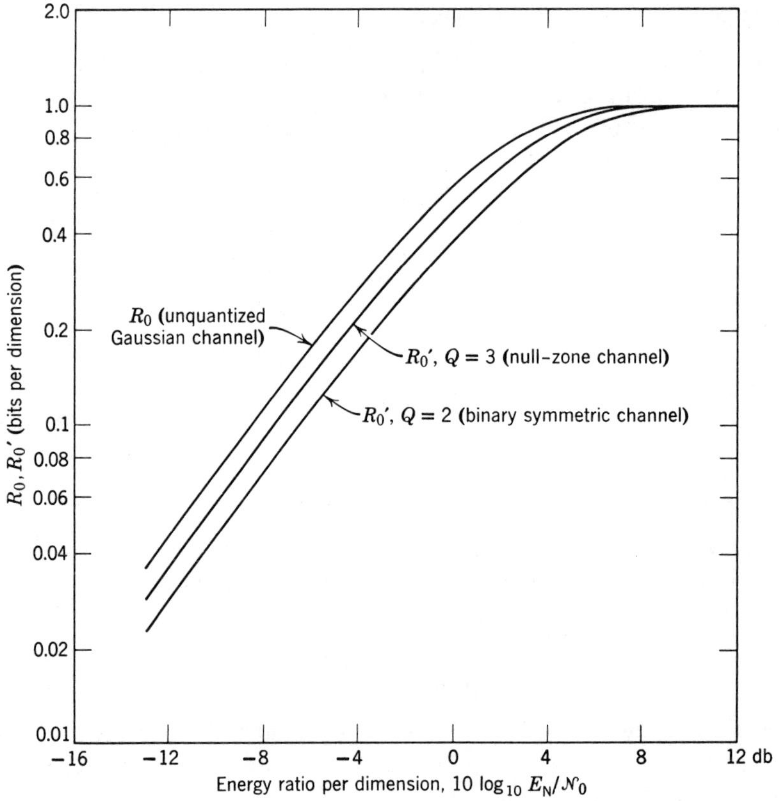

Figure 6.21 R_0 and R_0' for binary antipodal signaling with two- and three-level symmetric quantization.

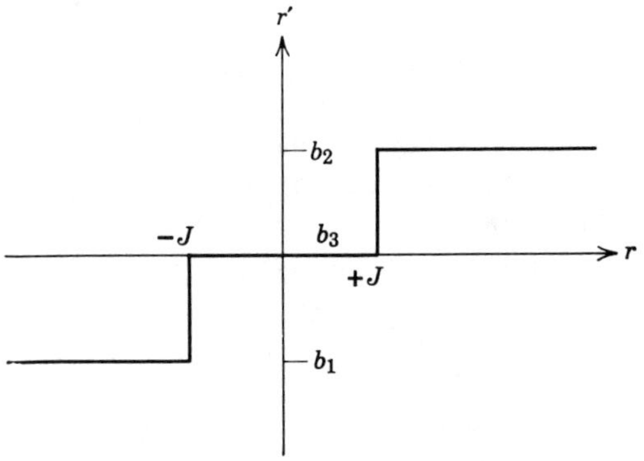

Figure 6.22 Quantizer for null-zone channel, $A = 2$, $Q = 3$.

The value of R_0' from Eq. 6.70 is plotted in Fig. 6.21 as a function of $E_N/\mathcal{N}_0$, together with the unquantized R_0 given by Eq. 6.67. We observe that the quantization loss is approximately -2 db. More precisely, in the limit $E_N/\mathcal{N}_0 \to 0$ (hence $p \to \frac{1}{2}$) it can be shown that the loss in decibels is exactly $10 \log_{10} (2/\pi)$.

Binary input, ternary output. A significant fraction of the degradation in R_0' resulting from binary quantization can be avoided by going to a ternary output. For $A = 2$, $Q = 3$ the appropriate quantizer is that shown in Fig. 6.22 and the resulting over-all channel diagram is that of Fig. 6.23. We have

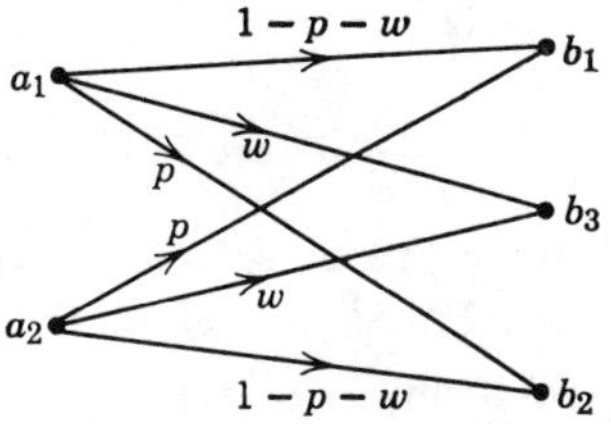

Figure 6.23 Transition probability diagram for null-zone channel.

$$q_{12} = q_{21} \triangleq p \tag{6.71a}$$

$$q_{13} = q_{23} \triangleq w \tag{6.71b}$$

and

$$q_{11} = q_{22} = 1 - p - w, \tag{6.71c}$$

where p and w are given in terms of the quantizer threshold J by the equations

$$p = \int_J^\infty \frac{1}{\sqrt{\pi \mathcal{N}_0}} e^{-(y+\sqrt{E_N})^2/\mathcal{N}_0}\, dy \tag{6.72a}$$

$$w = \int_{-J}^{J} \frac{1}{\sqrt{\pi \mathcal{N}_0}} e^{-(y+\sqrt{E_N})^2/\mathcal{N}_0}\, dy. \tag{6.72b}$$

Such a channel is called either a *null-zone channel* or a *binary symmetric erasure channel* (abbreviated BSEC). By symmetry we again choose $p_1 = p_2 = \frac{1}{2}$. Then, from Eq. 6.62b, we have

$$\begin{aligned} R_0' &= -\log_2 \sum_{h=1}^{3} \left[\sum_{l=1}^{2} p_l \sqrt{q_{lh}} \right]^2 \\ &= -\log_2[(\tfrac{1}{2}\sqrt{1-p-w} + \tfrac{1}{2}\sqrt{p})^2 + (\tfrac{1}{2}\sqrt{w} + \tfrac{1}{2}\sqrt{w})^2 \\ &\qquad + (\tfrac{1}{2}\sqrt{1-p-w} + \tfrac{1}{2}\sqrt{p})]^2 \\ &= 1 - \log_2 [1 + w + 2\sqrt{p(1-p-w)}]. \end{aligned} \tag{6.73}$$

The value of R_0' given by Eq. 6.73 is a function of the quantizer threshold value, J. The optimum value of J (the value that maximizes R_0') can be found as a function of $E_N/\mathcal{N}_0$ by trial and error; it is plotted in Fig. 6.24. The value of R_0' resulting from Eq. 6.73 when J is optimum is plotted as a function of $E_N/\mathcal{N}_0$ in Fig. 6.21. We observe that the degradation from the unquantized case is roughly 1 db and conclude that

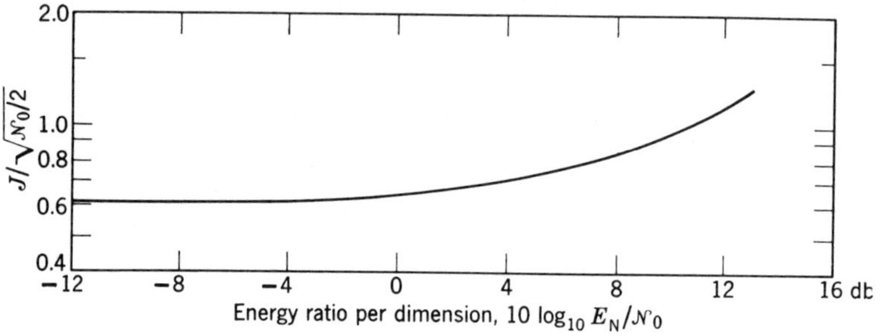

Figure 6.24 Optimum threshold for null-zone channel.

little improvement can be gained by quantizing to more than three levels when $E_N/\mathcal{N}_0$ is sufficiently small that signaling with sequences of binary waveforms is efficient. Note in Fig. 6.24 that $J = 0.65\sqrt{\mathcal{N}_0/2}$ is near optimum over this interesting range of $E_N/\mathcal{N}_0$.

Multiamplitude inputs. Quantization at the receiver also implies a degraded R_0' for systems that employ a multiamplitude modulator to exploit a high energy-to-noise ratio per dimension. For a given input alphabet $\{a_l\}$ and a given quantization grid the first step in evaluating the degradation is to determine the transition probabilities $\{q_{lh}\}$ in accordance with Fig. 6.16. The second step is to substitute these $\{q_{lh}\}$, together with an appropriate choice of letter probabilities $\{p_l\}$, into the expression

$$R_0' = -\log_2 \sum_{h=1}^{Q} \left[\sum_{l=1}^{A} p_l \sqrt{q_{lh}} \right]^2. \tag{6.74}$$

We now apply these results to a particular ensemble of systems operating over an additive white Gaussian noise channel. Each system utilizes a modulator with transmitter letters $\{a_l\}$ equally spaced over the interval $[-\sqrt{E_N}, +\sqrt{E_N}]$ and a receiver with a uniform quantization grid similar to that shown in Fig. 6.25 for $A = 6$; the number, Q, of quantizer output levels is equal to the number, A, of transmitter letters.

Curves of R_0' as a function of $E_N/\mathcal{N}_0$ for $Q = A = 2, 3, 4, 8, 16, 32$, and 64, calculated on a computer, are plotted in Fig. 6.26. In each case the letter probabilities $\{p_l\}$ have been set equal to $1/A$. For reference, the

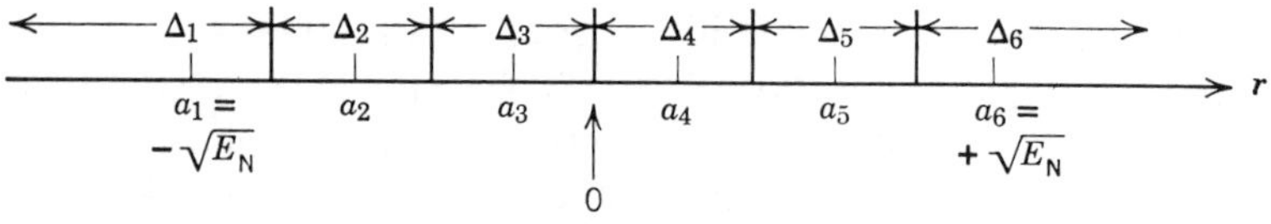

Figure 6.25 Uniform quantization, $Q = A$.

upper envelope of the curves of the unquantized exponent R_0 is replotted from Fig. 5.18. This upper envelope specifies the performance obtainable in the absence of quantization *with A and* $\{p_l\}$ *optimized.*

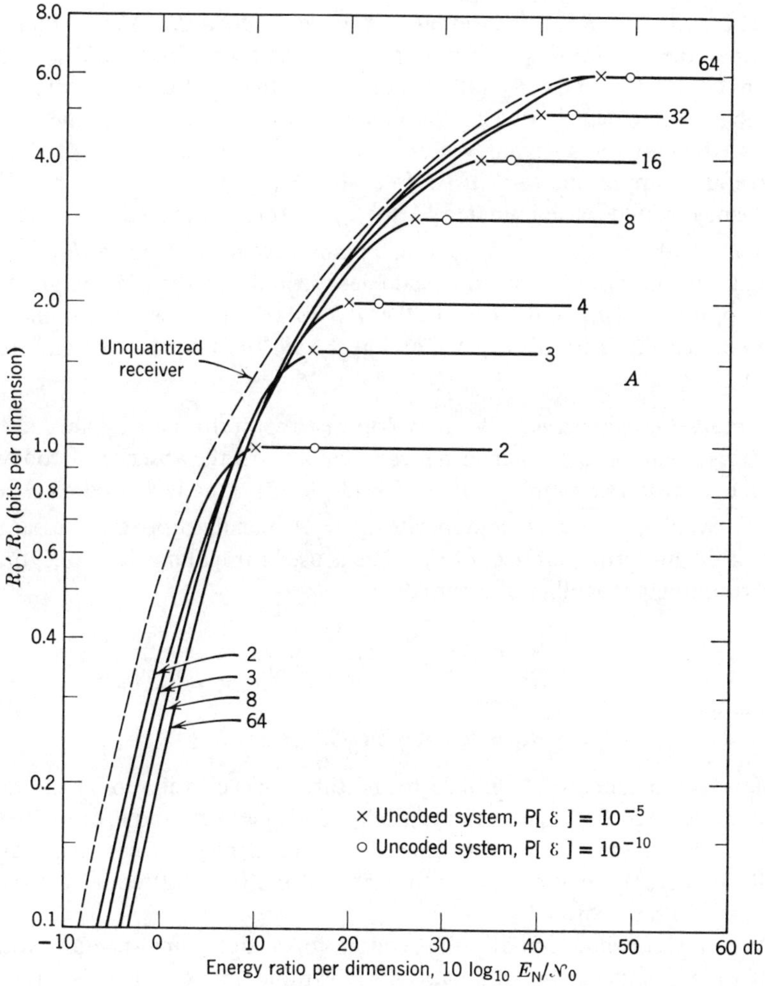

Figure 6.26 R_0' for A-level amplitude modulation, quantized receiver ($Q = A$).

We observe from Fig. 6.26 that the best choice of A depends on the value of $E_N/\mathcal{N}_0$. By choosing A (as a function of $E_N/\mathcal{N}_0$) to maximize R_0', we can operate along the upper envelope of the R_0' curves. It must be recalled, however, that fine quantization increases the cost of the decoder. Thus it is desirable to select A only large enough to yield an efficient set of waveforms; that is, only large enough to prevent R_0' from saturating at $\log_2 A$. When this is done and Q is set equal to A, the resulting degradation due to quantization is approximately 2 db over the full range of $E_N/\mathcal{N}_0$.

The fact that R_0' decreases as A increases when $E_N/\mathcal{N}_0$ is small is attributable to choosing uniform $\{p_l\}$; for example, when $E_N/\mathcal{N}_0$ is less than 5 db and $A = 64$, R_0' falls about 5 db to the right of R_0. Almost all of this discrepancy is due to the fact that with uniform $\{p_l\}$ the mean squared-length of a signal vector, hence the mean energy of a signal waveform, approximates $NE_N/3$ (see also Eq. 5.57 et seq.). This discrepancy would be eliminated if the $\{p_l\}$ were optimized: the letters $+\sqrt{E_N}$ and $-\sqrt{E_N}$ would be used almost exclusively when $E_N/\mathcal{N}_0$ is small and the resulting mean signal energy would be three times greater. For optimum $\{p_l\}$ and $Q = A$, the R_0' curves increase monotonically with increasing A for all $E_N/\mathcal{N}_0$, and approach the unquantized envelope as $A \to \infty$.

Uncoded transmission. We now contrast the performance afforded by coded systems with the performance obtainable in the absence of coding. If the transmitter employs A amplitude levels equally-spaced between $-\sqrt{E_N}$ and $+\sqrt{E_N}$ to communicate $M = A$ equally-probable messages, and if the uniform quantizer of Fig. 6.25 is used for making decisions, then the resulting probability of error is

$$P[\mathcal{E}] = \frac{1}{A}\sum_{l=0}^{A-1}(1 - q_{ll}) = \frac{A-1}{A}\,2Q\left(\frac{1}{A-1}\sqrt{\frac{2E_N}{\mathcal{N}_0}}\right),$$

while the rate is

$$R_N = \log_2 A \quad \text{bits/dimension.}$$

Points are included on Fig. 6.26 to indicate for each value of A the rate and the value of $E_N/\mathcal{N}_0$ necessary to achieve $P[\mathcal{E}] = 10^{-5}$ and $P[\mathcal{E}] = 10^{-10}$. It is observed that for all A coding affords an increase of between 2 and 3 db in the efficiency of energy utilization for $P[\mathcal{E}] = 10^{-5}$ and between 6 and 8 db for $P[\mathcal{E}] = 10^{-10}$.

We may conclude initially that coding for a high signal-to-noise ratio Gaussian channel is not dramatically rewarding. However, it is wise to recall from the central limit theorem discussion that the assumption of Gaussian statistics may be very poor on the tails of the distribution; in particular, the probability of an atypically large noise may be orders of magnitude larger than that predicted by the Gaussian model. Consequently, it is doubtful that the performance of uncoded systems on physical channels will actually approach the performance predicted in Fig. 6.26. Of course, to some extent this same caution also applies to coded systems. With coding, however, a low error probability is attained by observing many noise samples rather than only one. For no single sample must the probability of a large noise be vanishingly small. Thus system performance with coding is less sensitive to the tails of the noise distribution than system performance without coding, and the Gaussian approximation is more tenable.

6.3 BINARY CONVOLUTIONAL CODES

The calculations of the preceding section have shown that it is possible to choose a receiver quantization scheme in such a way that the achievable error exponent R_0' is degraded only slightly from the value it would have without quantization. In making these calculations, we have presumed that the quantizer is followed by an *optimum* decoder—that is, by a computer that determines for which message m_i the a posteriori probability $P[m_i \mid \mathbf{r}']$ is maximum, where $\mathbf{r}'$ denotes the quantizer output vector.

For equally likely messages the a posteriori probability is proportional to $P[\mathbf{r}' \mid \mathbf{s}_i]$. But we have observed before that it is not possible in practice to compute $P[\mathbf{r}' \mid \mathbf{s}_i]$ for every i when K is large and $M = 2^K = 2^{NR_N}$ enormous. *The decoding problem is to avoid exponential growth in decoder complexity as K increases.* Additional degradation in the error exponent results from the necessity of settling for nonoptimum data processing in the box labeled "Decoder" in Fig. 6.14. The remainder of this chapter is devoted to exploring ways in which the degradation in error exponent caused by decoder data processing may be made a small percentage of R_0'.

An ideal decoding scheme would have the following attributes:

1. *The probability of error would decrease exponentially with increasing code constraint length K in agreement with the random coding bound.*
2. *The size of the decoder would be proportional to K.*
3. *The required computational speed of the decoder would be independent of K.*

Unfortunately, so far no scheme exactly satisfying all three conditions has been devised.

In spite of this, diverse approaches[31,57,66,96] to decoding have met with significant success and can provide workable engineering solutions to practical communication problems. We shall focus in particular on one approach, called *sequential decoding*, which evidences operating characteristics that in some regards approximate the ideal.

Sequential decoding procedures are applicable to a subclass of parity-check codes called *convolutional codes* and to a broad class of channels.

It is easiest, however, to convey the central ideas and methodology by concentrating attention on the binary symmetric channel (BSC).

The Binary Symmetric Channel

The BSC has already been encountered in connection with Fig. 6.20; it is obtained from the additive white Gaussian noise channel by restricting the transmitted signal vectors $\{\mathbf{s}_i\}$ to lie on vertices of a hypercube and symmetrically quantizing the components of the relevant received vector into two levels. It is conventional to denote both the input and the output alphabets of the resulting discrete channel by the symbols $\{0, 1\}$. With this notation, the channel transition diagram of the BSC is that of Fig. 6.27, in which p denotes the probability that any particular component of the transmitted vector will be received incorrectly.

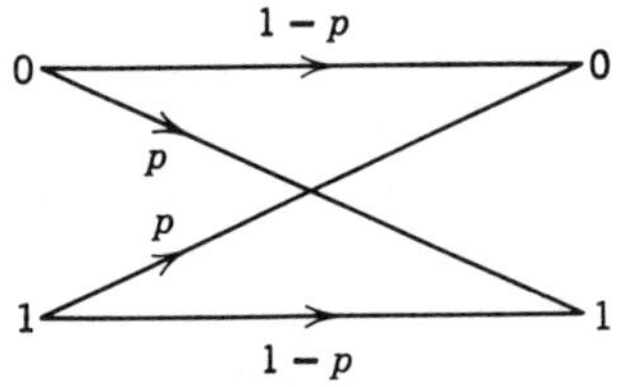

Figure 6.27 Binary symmetric channel.

We may think of communicating over the BSC by feeding the vector $\mathbf{y}$ (with components that are 0, 1) directly from the output of a parity-check coder into the channel, as shown in Fig. 6.28. The channel output vector $\mathbf{r}'$ is fed in turn directly into the decoding computer. The effects of the

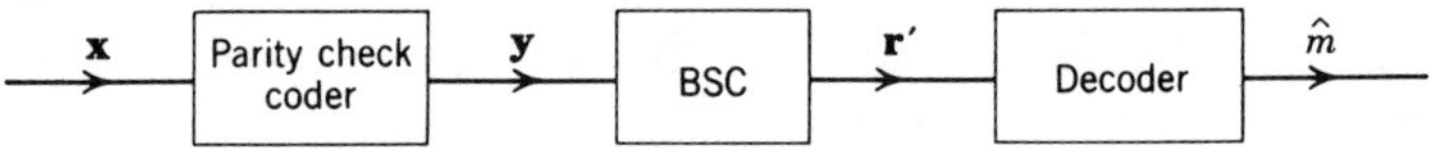

Figure 6.28 Communication over a BSC.

transmitter modulator, the Gaussian channel noise, and the receiver quantizer are all coalesced into the BSC transition probability parameter p.

When one of M equally likely messages is communicated over the BSC by means of a set of N-component binary vectors $\{\mathbf{y}_i\}$, the optimum receiver compares the N-component received vector $\mathbf{r}'$ with each of the $\{\mathbf{y}_i\}$ and determines for which i the probability $P[\mathbf{r}' \mid \mathbf{y}_i]$ is maximum. The probability that a transition occurs with any single use of the BSC is p and successive uses of the channel are statistically independent. Therefore, whenever $\mathbf{r}'$ and $\mathbf{y}_i$ differ in d_i coordinates,

$$
\begin{aligned}
P[\mathbf{r}' \mid \mathbf{y}_i] &= p^{d_i} q^{N-d_i} \\
&= q^N \left(\frac{p}{q}\right)^{d_i}; \qquad q \triangleq 1 - p. \qquad (6.75)
\end{aligned}
$$

The quantity d_i is called the *Hamming*[39] *distance* between $\mathbf{r}'$ and $\mathbf{y}_i$.

The right-hand side of Eq. 6.75 is a monotonically decreasing function of d_i for $p < \frac{1}{2}$. Accordingly, the optimum BSC decoder may determine $\hat{m}$ by computing the set of Hamming distances $\{d_i\}$, $i = 0, 1, \ldots, M - 1$, and setting $\hat{m} = m_k$ whenever d_k is the smallest member of the set.

Since the vector $\mathbf{r}' \oplus \mathbf{y}_i$ contains a "1" only in coordinates in which $\mathbf{y}_i$ differs from $\mathbf{r}'$, the Hamming distance d_i is conveniently obtained by forming $\mathbf{r}' \oplus \mathbf{y}_i$ and counting the resulting number of 1's. By convention, the number of 1's in any binary vector $\mathbf{a}$ is called its *weight*, denoted $w[\mathbf{a}]$. With this notation,

$$d_i \triangleq w[\mathbf{r}' \oplus \mathbf{y}_i]. \tag{6.76}$$

Insight into the problem of communicating over a BSC is gained by formulating the decision problem in geometrical terms analogous to those with which we are already familiar. We begin by reviewing the additive white Gaussian noise channel with binary transmission and *unquantized* reception. In this case the modulator in Fig. 6.1 is capable of generating any one of the 2^N hypercube vertices of an N-dimensional signal space. For rates $R_{\mathsf{N}} = K/N < 1$, the coder specifies a subset of 2^K of these vertices as the signal set $\{\mathbf{s}_i\}$, $i = 0, 1, \ldots, 2^K - 1$. When the input messages are equally likely, the optimum unquantized receiver sets $\hat{m} = m_k$ if the received vector $\mathbf{r}$ lies closer in Euclidean distance to $\mathbf{s}_k$ than to any other signal vector; that is, if $|\mathbf{r} - \mathbf{s}_k|$ is minimum.

When quantization is imposed on the matched filter outputs, the decoder must make the decision $\hat{m}$ on the basis of the quantized output $\mathbf{r}'$, without recourse to $\mathbf{r}$ itself. We interpret this decision geometrically by first observing that the symmetric binary quantization of $\mathbf{r}$ corresponds to a mapping of $\mathbf{r}$ into whichever hypercube vertex, say $\mathbf{v}$, is closest to $\mathbf{r}$. For $R_{\mathsf{N}} = K/N = 1$ and equally likely messages, the vertex $\mathbf{v}$ would itself correspond to the most probable transmission (we first observed that such dimension-by-dimension decisions were optimum for $R_{\mathsf{N}} = 1$ in Section 4.5, Eq. 4.90). For $R_{\mathsf{N}} < 1$, however, the vertex $\mathbf{v}$ may not be a signal vector; when N is large, the fraction $2^{-N(1-R_{\mathsf{N}})}$ of vertices that are signal vectors is very small. The task of the decoder is to map $\mathbf{v}$ onto one of the signal vectors $\{\mathbf{s}_i\}$. If $\mathbf{v}$ differs from a vector $\{\mathbf{s}_i\}$ in h_i coordinates, then

$$|\mathbf{v} - \mathbf{s}_i| = 2h_i\sqrt{E_{\mathsf{N}}}, \tag{6.77}$$

where E_{N} is the energy per component.

In BSC notation (with vector components 0, 1 rather than $+\sqrt{E_{\mathsf{N}}}$, $-\sqrt{E_{\mathsf{N}}}$), the vertex $\mathbf{v}$ corresponds to the BSC output $\mathbf{r}'$, the signal $\mathbf{s}_i$ to the BSC input $\mathbf{y}_i$, and the number of coordinate differences h_i to the Hamming distance d_i. In accordance with Eq. 6.75, the optimum decoder minimizes d_i, hence $|\mathbf{v} - \mathbf{s}_i|$. Symmetric binary quantization followed by optimum decoding thus corresponds to the two-step procedure of first minimizing $|\mathbf{r} - \mathbf{v}|$ and then minimizing $|\mathbf{v} - \mathbf{s}_i|$. That the two-step decision may not be optimum over-all is illustrated by Fig. 6.29, in which a vector $\mathbf{r}$ is mapped onto $\mathbf{v}_5$ by the quantizer and thence onto $\mathbf{s}_1$ by the optimum quantized decoder, even though $|\mathbf{r} - \mathbf{s}_1| > |\mathbf{r} - \mathbf{s}_0|$.

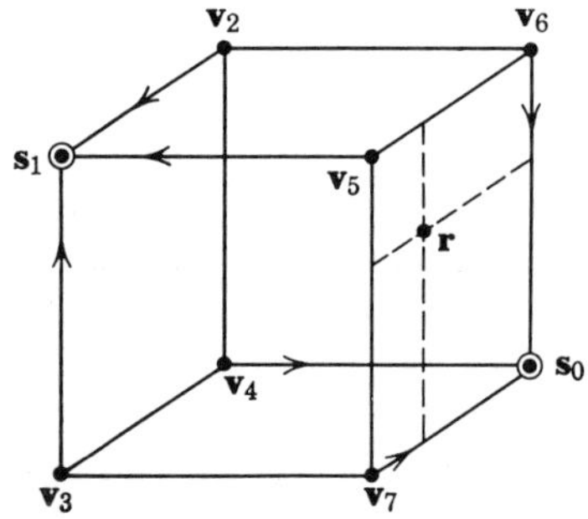

Figure 6.29 Received vector $\mathbf{r}$ for which $Q = 2$ quantization followed by optimum binary decoding does not select signal with minimum Euclidean distance.

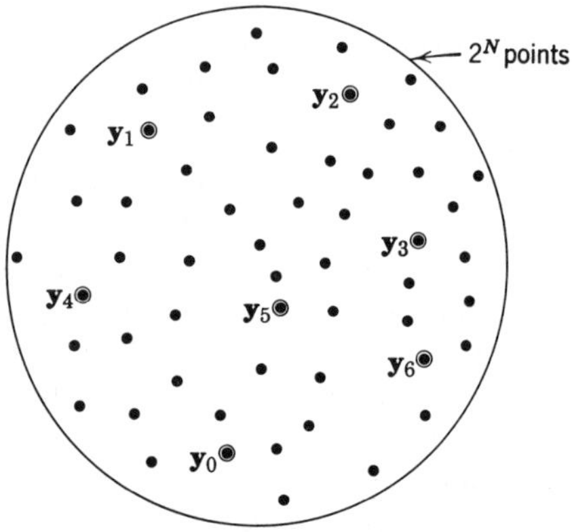

Figure 6.30 An abstract representation of the received signal space for the BSC. Each of the 2^N points represents a distinct N-component binary vector. The circled points correspond to signal vectors.

Of course, a binary symmetric channel may also be derived from quantization of channels that are not Gaussian and is a valid and interesting mathematical abstraction in its own right. It is therefore instructive to introduce a signal space formulation for the BSC that is not tied to Euclidean hypercube geometry. In particular, we can view the set of all possible (N-component) received vectors $\{\mathbf{r}'\}$ with component values 0 or 1 as the 2^N points of a discrete signal space (see Fig. 6.30). The M vectors $\{\mathbf{y}_i\}$ define a subset of these points and form a signal constellation with intersignal Hamming distances $\{d_{ik}\}$ given by

$$d_{ik} \triangleq w[\mathbf{y}_i \oplus \mathbf{y}_k]; \qquad 0 \leqslant i, k \leqslant M - 1. \tag{6.78}$$

The effect of transmitting a signal vector $\mathbf{y}$ over a BSC may be described in terms of a random *noise vector*, $\mathbf{n} = (n_1, n_2, \ldots, n_N)$, defined by

$$\mathbf{n} \triangleq \mathbf{r}' \oplus \mathbf{y}.$$

From the definition, any component n_j of $\mathbf{n}$ is 1 if a transmission error occurs on the jth use of the channel and 0 otherwise. If $m = m_k$, we have

$$\mathbf{r}' = \mathbf{n} \oplus \mathbf{y}_k \tag{6.79a}$$

and

$$d_i = w[(\mathbf{n} \oplus \mathbf{y}_k) \oplus \mathbf{y}_i]. \tag{6.79b}$$

A complete analogy exists between the BSC and the white Gaussian noise decision problems. In both cases we have a constellation of signal vectors and an additive noise vector. The primary distinction is that with the BSC addition is modulo-2 and distance is measured in terms of *weight* rather than *length*. The utility of the analogy rests on the fact that in both cases "probability" is monotonically related to "distance." For example,

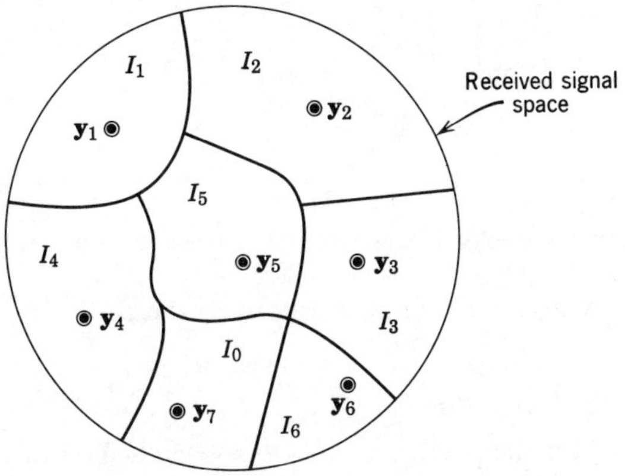

Figure 6.31 Decision regions $\{I_i\}$ for a BSC communication system.

the optimum BSC receiver again partitions the received signal space into M disjoint decision regions $\{I_i\}$, as shown in Fig. 6.31. When every message is equally likely, each region I_k, $k = 0, 1, \ldots, M-1$, contains all points in the received signal space that lie closer in Hamming distance to $\mathbf{y}_k$ than to any other vector in the signal set $\{\mathbf{y}_i\}$.

Convolutional Encoders

Convolutional codes for use over a BSC may be generated by encoding devices, like that diagrammed in Fig. 6.32, which are somewhat simpler than block coders. Just as in the block coder of Fig. 6.6, we have a K-bit x-register. But there is no y-register, and instead of N modulo-2 adders we now have only v of them, where v is typically quite small.

The connection diagram of the encoder is specified by a set of coefficients $\{g_{lj}\}$, $l = 1, 2, \ldots, K$ and $j = 1, 2, \ldots, v$. As with block coders, $g_{lj} = 1$ means that the lth stage of the x-register is connected to the jth adder, whereas $g_{lj} = 0$ means that it is not. We again find it

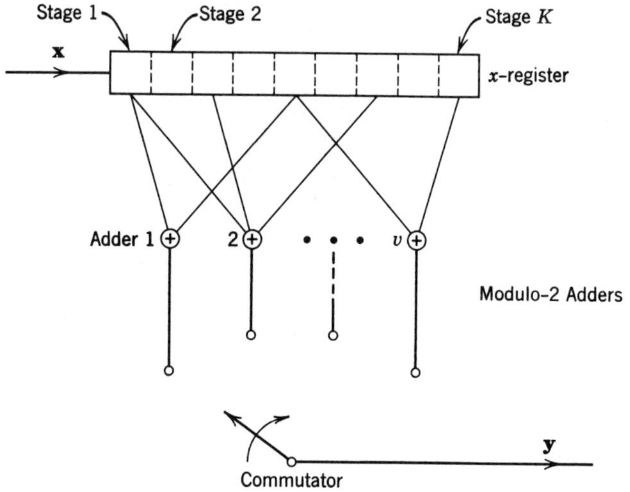

Figure 6.32 Binary convolutional encoder. The x-register is a K-stage shift register.

convenient to write the set of connections to the lth x-register stage as a vector, say $\mathbf{g}_l$:

$$\mathbf{g}_l \triangleq (g_{l1}, g_{l2}, \ldots, g_{lv}); \qquad l = 1, 2, \ldots, K. \tag{6.80}$$

As an example, for the particular $K = 4$, $v = 3$ encoder of Fig. 6.33,

$$\begin{aligned} \mathbf{g}_1 &= (1, \ 1, \ 1) \\ \mathbf{g}_2 &= (0, \ 1, \ 0) \\ \mathbf{g}_3 &= (0, \ 1, \ 1) \\ \mathbf{g}_4 &= (0, \ 1, \ 1). \end{aligned}$$

A convolutional encoder operates as follows: assume that we wish to communicate an L-bit message vector

$$\mathbf{x} = (x_1, x_2, \ldots, x_L), \tag{6.81}$$

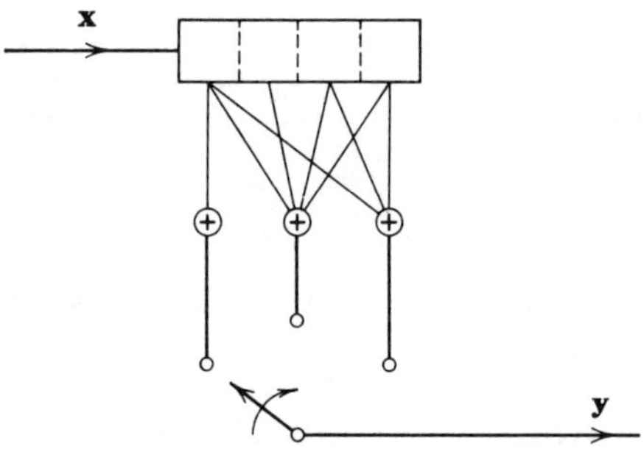

Figure 6.33 A particular $K = 4$, $v = 3$ convolutional encoder.

in which L may be greater than K. First, the contents of all K stages of the x-register are set equal to zero. Next, the first digit, x_1, of $\mathbf{x}$ is shifted into stage 1 of the x-register. The v modulo-2 adders are then sampled one after the other by the commutator shown in Fig. 6.32 and presented to the input of the BSC for transmission. When the vth-adder output has been sampled and transmitted, the second message digit, x_2, is shifted into stage 1 of the x-register, which causes x_1 to shift into stage 2. Each of the v modulo-2 adder outputs is again sampled and transmitted. This procedure continues until the last component, x_L, of $\mathbf{x}$ has been shifted into stage 1 of the x-register. Then, with each adder output still being sampled and transmitted after each shift, K 0's are fed in turn into the x-register, thereby returning it to its initial condition. During each shift the digit forced out of the Kth stage of the x-register is discarded.†

The output sequence produced by an L-component input vector is $(L + K)v$ digits long. We denote this output sequence by a vector $\mathbf{y}$.

As an example of the convolutional encoding procedure, reconsider the $(K = 4, v = 3)$ coder of Fig. 6.33. It may be verified directly that if the message input is the 5-bit sequence

$$\mathbf{x} = (1, 0, 1, 1, 0),$$

the encoder output sequence is

$$\mathbf{y} = (111, 010, 100, 110, 001, 000, 011, 000, 000).$$

(For clarity, commas have been used to indicate the shifting of the x-register and deleted elsewhere.)

In application, one is usually concerned with a message input vector $\mathbf{x}$ that is much longer than the x-register, that is, $L \gg K$. In such a case the tail of zeros added to $\mathbf{x}$ is much shorter than $\mathbf{x}$ itself and the ratio of the number of message digits to the number of transmitted digits is approximately $1/v$. We therefore define the rate R_N of a binary convolutional code of the type described‡ as

$$R_N = \frac{1}{v} \text{ (bits per transmitted symbol).} \tag{6.82}$$

Each message input digit remains within the x-register during K samplings of the modulo-2 adders, hence affects Kv transmitted digits.

† It would suffice to introduce only $(K - 1)$ 0's into the x-register following the last digit of a message, since this last digit is shifted out of the register when the first digit of a new message is shifted in.

‡ It is also possible[90] to generate convolutional codes of rate $R_N = u/v$, where u is any positive integer less than v.

We hereafter refer to K as the *constraint span* (measured in message input bits) of a convolutional code.

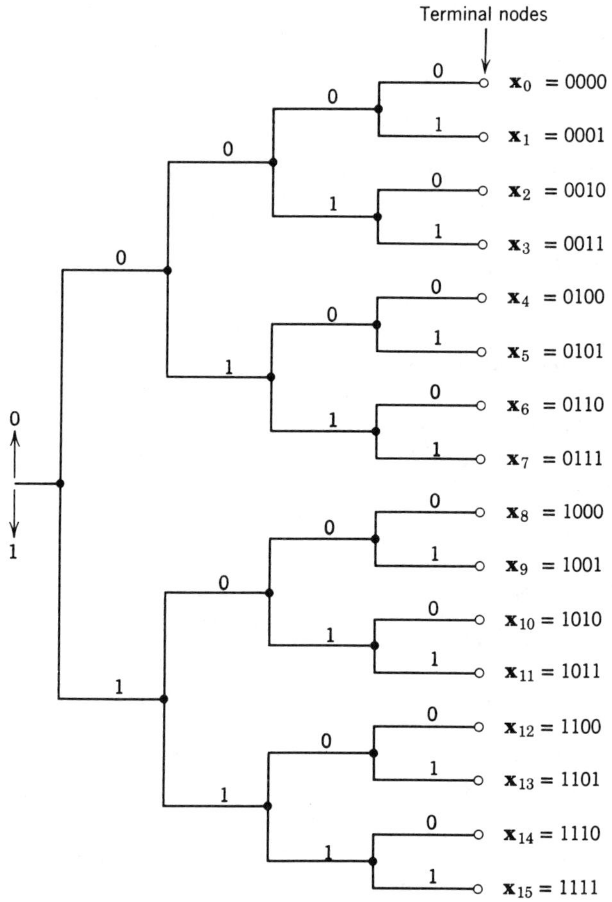

Figure 6.34 A set of $2^L = 16$ input vectors $\{\mathbf{x}_i\}$ diagrammed on an input tree.

Tree structure. We now consider in more detail how a convolutional coder constructs the output codeword $\mathbf{y}$ from the input

$$\mathbf{x} = (x_1, x_2, \ldots, x_L).$$

Since the x-register is initially set to zero, the first v digits of $\mathbf{y}$, obtained by shifting the first component of $\mathbf{x}$ into stage 1 and sampling the v adders, depend only on x_1. Similarly, the second v digits depend only upon x_1 and x_2. In general, the v digits of $\mathbf{y}$ obtained immediately after shifting component x_h into the x-register depend only on x_h and the $(K - 1)$

components of **x** preceding x_h. This implies that if two input vectors agree in their first $(h - 1)$ coordinates the corresponding output vectors agree in their first $(h - 1)v$ coordinates.

The resulting structure of the set of all output code words may be placed in evidence by means of a *code tree*, obtained as follows: first, as shown in Fig. 6.34, the set of all 2^L L-component input vectors $\{\mathbf{x}_i\}$ is diagrammed on an *input tree* by adopting the convention that the upper branch diverging from any node of the tree corresponds to shifting a 0 into the x-register and the lower branch to shifting in a 1. Thus each input vector $\mathbf{x}_i$ designates a distinct path all the way through the input tree to one of 2^L terminal nodes. The association of the $\{\mathbf{x}_i\}$ and the paths is indicated in the figure.

Next consider any intermediate node of the input tree: the path leading up to this node designates the contents of the x-register just before a new input digit is shifted in, and the contents of the x-register immediately thereafter determines the next v digits of **y**. Thus we may associate with the upper branch stemming from each intermediate node of the input tree the v output digits that are generated when this new input digit is a 0 and with the lower branch the v output digits that are generated when the new input digit is a 1. The *code tree* is obtained by writing along each branch of the input tree the v digits of **y** associated therewith. For example, the code tree generated by the particular $K = 4$, $v = 3$ convolutional encoder of Fig. 6.33 is illustrated for input sequences of length $L = 5$ in Fig. 6.35.

We can interpret the message input **x** as a set of L successive instructions that tell the encoder which path of the code tree to follow. The transmitted vector **y** is the sequence of $(L + K)v$ binary digits that lies along the designated path.

Linearity. Additional insight into the structure of the code tree may be gained by exploiting the fact that the convolutional encoder of Fig. 6.32 is a parity-check device; the output of each modulo-2 adder at any instant is 0 if the number of 1's stored in the stages of the x-register to which the adder is connected is even and 1 if the number is odd. Just as for block parity-check coders, a convolutional coder is *linear* in the sense that when $\mathbf{x} = (x_1, x_2, \ldots, x_L)$ is the coder input the output **y** may be written

$$\mathbf{y} = x_1\mathbf{f}_1 \oplus x_2\mathbf{f}_2 \oplus \cdots \oplus x_L\mathbf{f}_L. \tag{6.83}$$

Equation 6.83 is similar in form to the block parity-check code relationship of Eq. 6.28,

$$\mathbf{y} = x_1\mathbf{f}_1 \oplus x_2\mathbf{f}_2 \oplus \cdots \oplus x_K\mathbf{f}_K,$$

in which each $\mathbf{f}_h$, $h = 1, 2, \ldots, K$, is an N-component vector describing the connections between the N modulo-2 adders and the hth stage of the

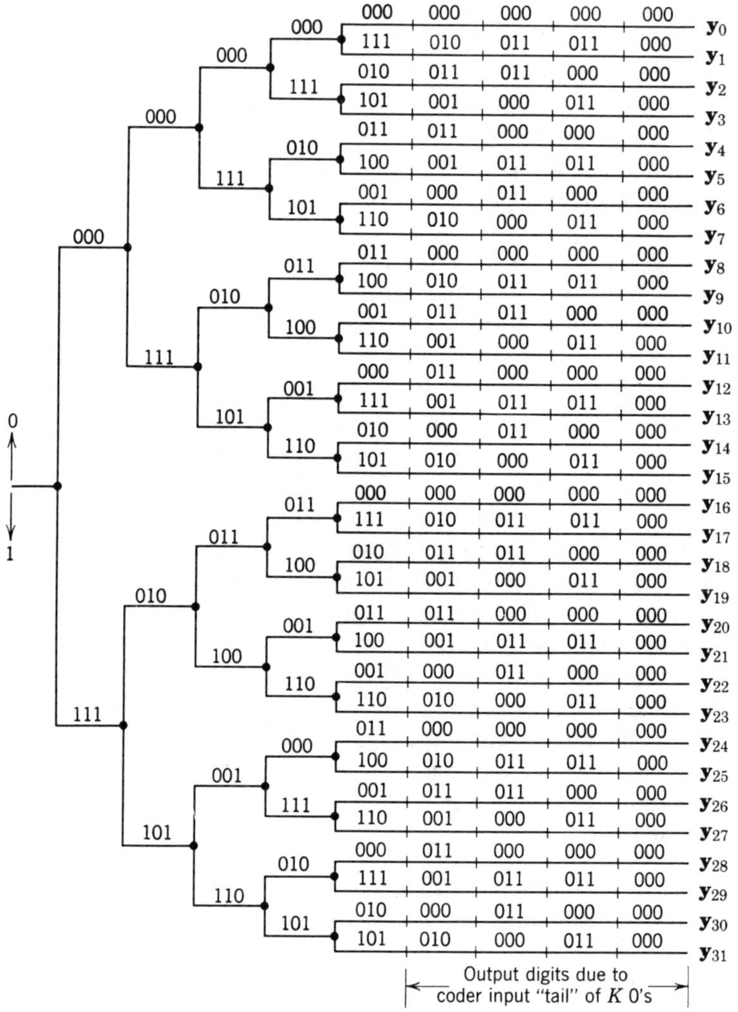

Figure 6.35 Code tree for encoder of Figure 6.33 ($K = 4$, $L = 5$, $v = 3$).

K-bit x-register shown in Fig. 6.6. But for convolutional codes the interpretation of the $\{\mathbf{f}_h\}$ is different; they are *not* connection vectors.

The identity of the convolutional $\{\mathbf{f}_h\}$ is readily established by noting in Eq. 6.83 that when the L-bit input vector $\mathbf{x}$ has $x_h = 1$ and all other components equal to zero the output vector $\mathbf{y}$ is $\mathbf{f}_h$. In particular, by letting

$$\mathbf{x} = (1, 0, 0, \ldots, 0)$$

and recalling from Eq. 6.80 that the vector $\mathbf{g}_l$ designates which of the v modulo-2 adders are connected to the lth stage of the convolutional x-register, we identify $\mathbf{f}_1$ from Fig. 6.32 as the resulting output

$$\mathbf{y} = \mathbf{f}_1 = \big(\mathbf{g}_1, \mathbf{g}_2, \ldots, \mathbf{g}_K, \underbrace{\mathbf{0}, \mathbf{0}, \ldots, \mathbf{0}}_{L\ \mathbf{0}\text{'s}}\big). \tag{6.84a}$$

Here we have used the symbol $\mathbf{0}$ to denote the v-component vector, each component of which is 0. The commas again denote the points at which the x-register shifts right.

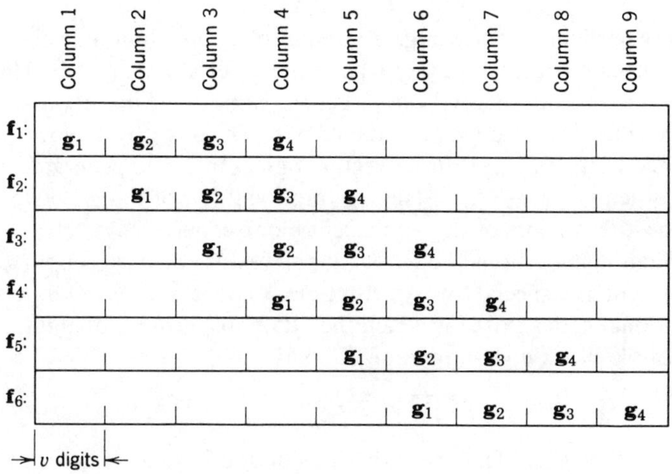

Figure 6.36 Diagram of the $\{\mathbf{f}_h\}$ for a convolutional coder with $K = 4, L = 6$. Empty slots contain v zeros. (A tenth column of all zeros is omitted.)

It is clear from Fig. 6.32 and the description of the convolutional encoding operation that the output $\mathbf{y}$ when only the second digit of $\mathbf{x}$ is 1 is a delayed replica of the output when only $x_1 = 1$. Thus

$$\mathbf{x} = \big(0, 1, 0, \ldots, 0\big)$$

implies

$$\mathbf{y} = \mathbf{f}_2 = \big(\mathbf{0}, \mathbf{g}_1, \mathbf{g}_2, \ldots, \mathbf{g}_K, \underbrace{\mathbf{0}, \ldots, \mathbf{0}}_{(L-1)\ \mathbf{0}\text{'s}}\big). \tag{6.84b}$$

If we delete explicit mention of the vectors $\{\mathbf{0}\}$, the $\{\mathbf{f}_h\}$ may be described pictorially as shown in Fig. 6.36 for the case $K = 4, L = 6$. We note from observation of the hth column of the figure that the v digits of $\mathbf{y}$ produced when x_h is first shifted into the x-register are

$$x_h\mathbf{g}_1 \oplus x_{h-1}\mathbf{g}_2 \oplus \cdots \oplus x_{h-K+1}\mathbf{g}_K, \tag{6.85}$$

which is an expression with indices of convolutional form. (We define $x_{-l} = 0$ for all $l \geqslant 0$.)

It is convenient to refer to the Kv-component vector

$$\mathbf{g} \triangleq (\mathbf{g}_1, \mathbf{g}_2, \ldots, \mathbf{g}_K) \tag{6.86}$$

as the *generator* of the convolutional code; clearly, $\mathbf{g}$ completely specifies the coder connections. The nonzero segments of the $\{\mathbf{f}_h\}$ are just successive v-digit translates of $\mathbf{g}$.

Error Probability

For any particular choice of $\mathbf{g}$, the output of a convolutional coder is the vector $\mathbf{y}$ specified in terms of the $\{\mathbf{f}_h\}$ and the input $\mathbf{x}$ by Eq. 6.83. Thus the set of 2^L possible outputs $\{\mathbf{y}_i\}$ can be generated not only in the way that we have described but also (in accordance with Eq. 6.28) by a block parity-check encoder that accepts input vectors of length L and generates output vectors of length $(K + L)v$. The convolutional $\{\mathbf{f}_h\}$ of Fig. 6.36 would be the connection vectors of this equivalent block coder.

Although convolutional codes for input vectors of fixed length L may be thought of as a special form of L-bit block codes, it does *not* follow that convolutional codes exist for which the attainable error probability obeys the ensemble block-code bound of Eq. 6.62,

$$\overline{P[\mathcal{E}]} < 2^{-N[R_0' - R_N]},$$

with $N = (L + K)v$. The proof that this bound is valid for block parity-check codes depends strongly on freedom to choose the block-coder connection vectors arbitrarily, a freedom of choice that is not available when the $\{\mathbf{f}_h\}$ are constrained to have convolutional form: with unconstrained block codes, each component of the input vector $\mathbf{x}$ can affect any component of the *entire* output vector $\mathbf{y}$, whereas with convolutional codes each component of $\mathbf{x}$ can affect only Kv components of $\mathbf{y}$.

Because of the constraints on the $\{\mathbf{f}_h\}$, we do not anticipate that the error probability with convolutional codes can be forced toward zero with an exponent that is proportional to $(L + K)$. Indeed, intuition correctly informs us that the probability of at least one error in a block of L input digits must tend toward 1, not 0, if L is increased while K is held fixed. On the other hand, it is reasonable to anticipate a bound on error probability that decreases exponentially with an exponent that is linear in the code constraint span K.

With convolutional codes, it is difficult (perhaps impossible) to employ random-coding arguments directly to analyze an optimum decoder; this is because of the way in which successive digits of $\mathbf{x}$ affect overlapping segments of $\mathbf{y}$. Recognizing this, we consider a suboptimum decoder instead. For this decoder, we shall derive an ensemble error probability bound that does decrease exponentially with K. The suboptimum decoding procedure provides preliminary insight into sequential decoding.

Suboptimum decoding. For a convolutional coder used to communicate one of 2^L binary input vectors $\{\mathbf{x}_i\}$ over a BSC, the suboptimum decoding procedure with which we are concerned is described as follows. The decoder decides on each of the L components $x_1, x_2, \ldots, x_L$ of the coder input vector in turn, one after the other, to produce a sequence of decisions $\hat{x}_1, \hat{x}_2, \ldots, \hat{x}_L$. Each decision $\hat{x}_h$, $h = 1, 2, \ldots, L$, is based exclusively on (a) the previous decisions $\hat{x}_1, \hat{x}_2, \ldots, \hat{x}_{h-1}$ and (b) the Kv-digit span of the received vector that is directly affected by x_h. We refer to this span of received digits as the (Kv-component) vector ${}_h\mathbf{r}$, and to the intermediate code-tree node specified by $\hat{x}_1, \hat{x}_2, \ldots, \hat{x}_{h-1}$ as the hth *starting node*. Each x_h is decoded in turn by determining which one of the 2^K K-branch codeword segments that diverge from the hth starting node is the most probable cause of ${}_h\mathbf{r}$. In view of Eq. 6.75, the decoder calculates the Hamming distance between each such Kv-digit codeword segment and ${}_h\mathbf{r}$. If the codeword segment with the smallest distance leaves the hth starting node along the upper branch, the decoder sets $\hat{x}_h = 0$; otherwise it sets $\hat{x}_h = 1$. A typical decoder progression is illustrated in Fig. 6.37 for a convolutional code with $K = 3$.

We first consider any particular convolutional code and devote the next few subsections to bounding the probability, $P[\mathcal{E}]$, that at least one error will be made by the suboptimum decoder in the decision sequence $\hat{x}_1, \hat{x}_2, \ldots, \hat{x}_L$. Denote by $P[\mathcal{E}_h]$ the conditional probability of an error on the hth decision, given that the hth starting node is correct. We bound the (unconditioned) probability $P[\mathcal{E}]$ by deriving the sequence of equations

I. $$P[\mathcal{E}] \leqslant \sum_{h=1}^{L} P[\mathcal{E}_h],$$

II. $$P[\mathcal{E}_h] = P[\mathcal{E}_1],$$

III. $$P[\mathcal{E}_1] = P[\mathcal{E}_1 \mid \mathbf{x}_0],$$

in which the condition on the right-hand side of III indicates that the all-zero message sequence is transmitted. It follows immediately that

$$P[\mathcal{E}] \leqslant L\, P[\mathcal{E}_1 \mid \mathbf{x}_0].$$

Finally, we average both sides of this equation over an ensemble of communication systems, each of which uses a different convolutional code, to establish the bound

IV. $$\overline{P[\mathcal{E}]} < L 2^{-N[R_0' - R_N]}.$$

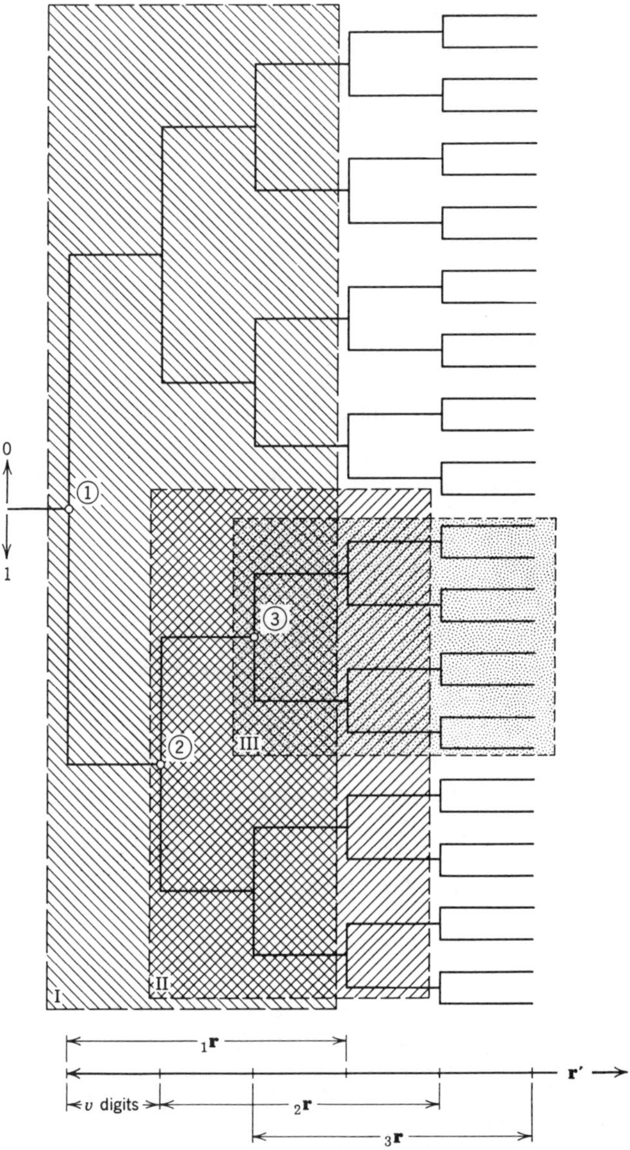

Figure 6.37 Progression of suboptimum decoder for $K = 3$; the segments of the received vector $\mathbf{r}'$ for determining $\hat{x}_1$, $\hat{x}_2$, and $\hat{x}_3$ are $_1\mathbf{r}$, $_2\mathbf{r}$, and $_3\mathbf{r}$. ① is the starting node, and the box labeled *I* encloses the pertinent codeword segments, say $\{_1\mathbf{y}_i\}$, for determining $\hat{x}_1$. If $\hat{x}_1 = 1$, ② is the starting node, and the box labeled II encloses the pertinent codeword segments, say $\{_2\mathbf{y}_i\}$, for determining $\hat{x}_2$. If $\hat{x}_1 = 1$ and $\hat{x}_2 = 0$, ③ is the starting node, and the box labeled III encloses the pertinent codeword segments, say $\{_3\mathbf{y}_i\}$, for determining $\hat{x}_3$.

Equation IV is a bound on the mean probability that one or more errors will be made in decoding an L-bit message input sequence with convolutional coding, a BSC, and the suboptimum decoder that we have described. The code constraint length is $K = NR_{\mathsf{N}} = N/v$, and R_0' is the BSC error exponent of Eq. 6.70,

$$R_0' = 1 - \log_2 [1 + 2\sqrt{p(1-p)}].$$

This performance is comparable to that achievable by block coding with constraint length K and optimum decoding, for which the union bound on the probability of correctly decoding L/K successive blocks is

$$\overline{\mathrm{P}[\mathcal{E}]} < \frac{L}{K} 2^{-N[R_0' - R_{\mathsf{N}}]}. \tag{6.87a}$$

The difference in the tightness of the two bounds is not exponentially significant. This is evident when the convolutional bound, IV, is rewritten in the form

$$\overline{\mathrm{P}[\mathcal{E}]} < \frac{L}{K} 2^{-N[R_0' - R_{\mathsf{N}}] + \log_2 K}$$

$$= \frac{L}{K} 2^{-N[R_0' - R_{\mathsf{N}} - (1/N)\log_2 (N/v)]}. \tag{6.87b}$$

As N gets large, $(1/N) \log_2 N$ approaches zero and the bounds of Eqs. 6.87a and b are substantially equivalent.†

The proofs of Eqs. I, II, III, and IV that follow are somewhat detailed and may be omitted on a first reading.

Proof of I. To prove I, assume initially that a magic genie directs the decoder to the *correct* starting node for determining each $\hat{x}_h$, $h = 1, 2, \ldots, L$. By definition, the probability that $\hat{x}_h$ is then incorrect is $\mathrm{P}[\mathcal{E}_h]$. Employing the familiar union argument, we overbound the probability of one or more errors in L successive decisions of the genie-aided decoder by $\sum_{h=1}^{L} \mathrm{P}[\mathcal{E}_h]$.

Next we observe that in the absence of decoding errors the starting node for each $\hat{x}_h$ is correctly determined by preceding decoder decisions. If no errors are made with the genie, no errors are made without him! Since the converse is also true, the probability of at least one decoding error is unaffected by the presence or absence of the genie and

$$\mathrm{P}[\mathcal{E}] \leqslant \sum_{h=1}^{L} \mathrm{P}[\mathcal{E}_h]. \tag{6.88}$$

† It may be argued that convolutional codes should actually afford error performance superior to that of block codes, but we do not know of any proof that this is so.

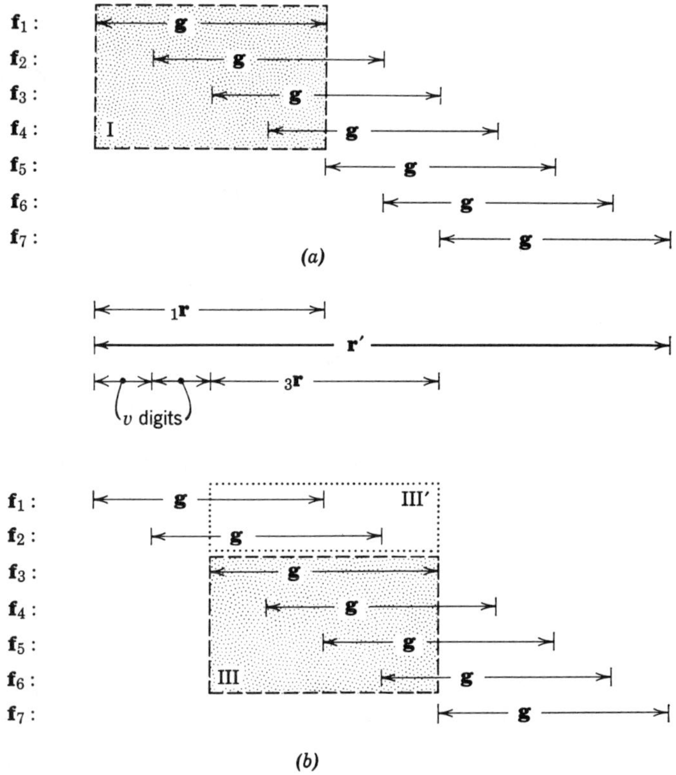

Figure 6.38 Construction of codeword segments; $K = 4$. From Eq. 6.83,

$$\mathbf{y} = x_1\mathbf{f}_1 \oplus x_2\mathbf{f}_2 \oplus \cdots \oplus x_L\mathbf{f}_L.$$

(a) In determining $\hat{x}_1$ we consider only codeword segments having the form

$$\begin{aligned} {}_1\mathbf{y} &= x_1\mathbf{f}_1' \oplus x_2\mathbf{f}_2' \oplus \cdots \oplus x_K\mathbf{f}_K' \\ &= \text{first } Kv \text{ digits of } \mathbf{y}. \end{aligned}$$

The $\{\mathbf{f}_h'\}$ are the portions of the $\{\mathbf{f}_h\}$ enclosed within the box labeled I. (b) Codeword segments pertinent to determining $\hat{x}_3$ depend only on the portions of the $\{\mathbf{f}_h\}$ enclosed in boxes III and III′. The portions of the $\{\mathbf{f}_h\}$ determining ${}_h\mathbf{a}$ are enclosed in box III′.

Proof of II. Proof that the probability of decoding x_h incorrectly is the same for all h, given in each case the correct starting node, hinges on the structure of the code tree. Denote the Kv-digit codeword segments that enter into the decision $\hat{x}_1$ by the special symbols $\{{}_1\mathbf{y}_i\}$, $i = 0, 1, \ldots, 2^K - 1$. The particular codeword segment ${}_1\mathbf{y}_k$ is transmitted when $(x_1, x_2, \ldots, x_K)$ is the binary representation of the number k: we write

$$ {}_1\mathbf{y} = {}_1\mathbf{y}_k \Leftrightarrow (x_1, x_2, \ldots, x_K) = k. \tag{6.89}$$

The construction of the Kv-digit transmitted segment ${}_1\mathbf{y}$ may be identified with the help of Fig. 6.38*a* as

$$ {}_1\mathbf{y} = x_1\mathbf{f}_1' \oplus x_2\mathbf{f}_2' \oplus \cdots \oplus x_K\mathbf{f}_K', \tag{6.90a} $$

in which we have introduced the definition

$$ \mathbf{f}_h' \triangleq \text{the first } Kv \text{ digits of } \mathbf{f}_h; \qquad h = 1, 2, \ldots, K. \tag{6.90b} $$

Equation 6.90a follows from Eq. 6.83 by truncating both sides, hence each $\mathbf{f}_h$, after Kv digits. We observe that $\mathbf{f}_1' = \mathbf{g}$, where $\mathbf{g}$ is the generator sequence of the convolutional coder.

In similar fashion we next denote the set of Kv-digit codeword segments that enter into the determination of $\hat{x}_h$—given the correct starting node—by $\{{}_h\mathbf{y}_i\}$, $i = 0, 1, \ldots, 2^K - 1$. As before, the particular segment ${}_h\mathbf{y}_k$ is transmitted when $(x_h, x_{h+1}, \ldots, x_{h+K-1})$ is the binary representation of the number k:

$$ {}_h\mathbf{y} = {}_h\mathbf{y}_k \Leftrightarrow (x_h, x_{h+1}, \ldots, x_{h+K-1}) = k. \tag{6.91} $$

It is clear from Fig. 6.38*b* that for any h

$$ {}_h\mathbf{y}_i = {}_1\mathbf{y}_i \oplus {}_h\mathbf{a}; \qquad i = 0, 1, \ldots, 2^K - 1, \tag{6.92} $$

in which ${}_h\mathbf{a}$ is a binary vector, independent of i, which is determined by the input bits that precede x_h into the encoder. *Knowledge of the* hth *starting node implies knowledge of* ${}_h\mathbf{a}$.

Now consider the decision $\hat{x}_h$, given that the correct starting node is known. When the kth segment is transmitted, the suboptimum receiver compares the received segment

$$ \begin{aligned} {}_h\mathbf{r} &= {}_h\mathbf{y}_k \oplus {}_h\mathbf{n} \\ &= {}_1\mathbf{y}_k \oplus {}_h\mathbf{a} \oplus {}_h\mathbf{n} \end{aligned} \tag{6.93a} $$

with each of the possible transmitted segments

$$ {}_h\mathbf{y}_i = {}_1\mathbf{y}_i \oplus {}_h\mathbf{a}; \qquad i = 0, 1, \ldots, 2^K - 1. \tag{6.93b} $$

Here, ${}_h\mathbf{n}$ denotes the Kv channel noise digits that are present in ${}_h\mathbf{r}$. But the decision $\hat{x}_h$ is unaltered if the known vector ${}_h\mathbf{a}$ is added modulo-2 (a reversible operation!) both to ${}_h\mathbf{r}$ and to each of the $\{{}_h\mathbf{y}_i\}$. Let this be done. It is clear from Eqs. 6.93a and b that the decision $\hat{x}_h$, now based on comparing $({}_1\mathbf{y}_k \oplus {}_h\mathbf{n})$ with each of the $\{{}_1\mathbf{y}_i\}$, has the same error probability as the decision $\hat{x}_1$ when ${}_1\mathbf{y}_k$ is transmitted. It is only necessary to use the fact that the channel noise is stationary, so that

$$ P[{}_h\mathbf{n} = \boldsymbol{\alpha}] = P[{}_1\mathbf{n} = \boldsymbol{\alpha}]; \qquad \text{for all } Kv\text{-digit binary vectors } \boldsymbol{\alpha}. \tag{6.94} $$

We therefore have

$$P[\mathcal{E}_h \mid (x_h, x_{h+1}, \ldots, x_{h+K-1}) = k]$$
$$= P[\mathcal{E}_1 \mid (x_1, x_2, \ldots, x_K) = k]; \qquad \text{all } h, k. \quad (6.95)$$

If all encoder input vectors are equally likely, then

$$P[(x_h, x_{h+1}, \ldots, x_{h+K-1}) = k]$$
$$= P[(x_1, x_2, \ldots, x_K) = k]; \qquad \text{all } k, \quad (6.96)$$

and both sides of Eq. 6.95 may be averaged to yield

$$P[\mathcal{E}_h] = P[\mathcal{E}_1], \quad (6.97)$$

which is Eq. II. In the next subsection we show that

$$P[\mathcal{E}_1 \mid (x_1, x_2, \ldots, x_K) = k]$$

is independent of k. It follows that both sides of Eq. 6.95 are independent of k, and Eq. 6.97 remains valid even when the $\{\mathbf{x}_i\}$ are not equally likely.

The proof of Eq. 6.97 depends heavily on the fact that the correct starting node for the decision $\hat{x}_h$, hence ${}_h\mathbf{a}$, is known. If the hth starting node is incorrect, ${}_h\mathbf{a}$ cannot be correctly accounted for, and the probability that $\hat{x}_h$ will be incorrect becomes large. We discuss this property at the conclusion of the chapter.

Proof of III. We now show that for our suboptimum receiver,

$$P[\mathcal{E}_1] = P[\mathcal{E}_1 \mid \mathbf{x}_0] = P[\mathcal{E}_1 \mid \mathbf{x}_k]; \qquad \text{all } k. \quad (6.98)$$

Proof depends on a closure property of the truncated codeword segments $\{{}_1\mathbf{y}_i\}$. As with block parity-check codes, the linearity of Eq. 6.90a

$${}_1\mathbf{y} = x_1\mathbf{f}_1' \oplus x_2\mathbf{f}_2' \oplus \cdots \oplus x_K\mathbf{f}_K'$$

ensures that the modulo-2 sum of any two vectors in $\{{}_1\mathbf{y}_i\}$ is also in $\{{}_1\mathbf{y}_i\}$. For convolutional codes we also have the following stronger closure property:

Let S_0 denote the subset of all 2^{K-1} vectors in $\{{}_1\mathbf{y}_i\}$ consistent with $x_1 = 0$, and let S_1 denote the subset consistent with $x_1 = 1$. Thus S_1 encompasses all ${}_1\mathbf{y}_i$ that contain $\mathbf{f}_1'$, and S_0 encompasses all ${}_1\mathbf{y}_i$ that do not. Since $\mathbf{f}_1' \oplus \mathbf{f}_1' = \mathbf{0}$, we have

$$\left.\begin{array}{l} {}_1\mathbf{y}_k \text{ in } S_0 \text{ and } {}_1\mathbf{y}_i \text{ in } S_0 \\ {}_1\mathbf{y}_k \text{ in } S_1 \text{ and } {}_1\mathbf{y}_i \text{ in } S_1 \end{array}\right\} \Rightarrow ({}_1\mathbf{y}_k \oplus {}_1\mathbf{y}_i) \text{ in } S_0, \quad (6.99a)$$

whereas

$$\left.\begin{array}{l} {}_1\mathbf{y}_k \text{ in } S_1 \text{ and } {}_1\mathbf{y}_i \text{ in } S_0 \\ {}_1\mathbf{y}_k \text{ in } S_0 \text{ and } {}_1\mathbf{y}_i \text{ in } S_1 \end{array}\right\} \Rightarrow ({}_1\mathbf{y}_k \oplus {}_1\mathbf{y}_i) \text{ in } S_1. \quad (6.99b)$$

Furthermore, if the vector ${}_1\mathbf{y}_k$ *is in* S_0, *then* $({}_1\mathbf{y}_k \oplus \mathbf{u})$ *ranges through every vector in* S_0 *as* $\mathbf{u}$ *ranges through every vector in* S_0. *On the other hand, if* ${}_1\mathbf{y}_k$ *is in* S_1, *then* $({}_1\mathbf{y}_k \oplus \mathbf{v})$ *ranges through every vector in* S_0 *as* $\mathbf{v}$ *ranges through every vector in* S_1.

The suboptimum decoder determines which vector in $\{{}_1\mathbf{y}_i\}$ is closest in Hamming distance to ${}_1\mathbf{r}$ and sets $\hat{x}_1 = 0$ if this vector is in S_0 and $\hat{x}_1 = 1$ if it is in S_1. Thus, if the signal ${}_1\mathbf{y}_k$ actually transmitted is in S_0, the decision $\hat{x}_1$ is correct unless, *for some vector* $\mathbf{v}$ *in* S_1,

$$w[({}_1\mathbf{n} \oplus {}_1\mathbf{y}_k) \oplus \mathbf{v}] \leqslant w[({}_1\mathbf{n} \oplus {}_1\mathbf{y}_k) \oplus \mathbf{u}]; \qquad \text{all } \mathbf{u} \text{ in } S_0.$$

Here, as in Eq. 6.76, $w[\ \ ]$ denotes Hamming distance. But $({}_1\mathbf{y}_k \oplus \mathbf{v})$ is in S_1 and $({}_1\mathbf{y}_k \oplus \mathbf{u})$ ranges through S_0. Thus an equivalent, but simpler, statement is that $\hat{x}_1$ is correct when any vector in S_0 is transmitted unless, for some vector $\mathbf{v}$ in S_1,

$$w[{}_1\mathbf{n} \oplus \mathbf{v}] \leqslant w[{}_1\mathbf{n} + \mathbf{u}]; \qquad \text{all } \mathbf{u} \text{ in } S_0. \tag{6.100}$$

On the other hand, when the transmitted signal ${}_1\mathbf{y}_k$ is in S_1, the decision $\hat{x}_1$ is correct unless, *for some vector* $\mathbf{u}$ *in* S_0,

$$w[({}_1\mathbf{n} \oplus {}_1\mathbf{y}_k) \oplus \mathbf{u}] \leqslant w[({}_1\mathbf{n} \oplus {}_1\mathbf{y}_k) \oplus \mathbf{v}]; \qquad \text{all } \mathbf{v} \text{ in } S_1.$$

But now $({}_1\mathbf{y}_k \oplus \mathbf{u})$ is in S_1, whereas $({}_1\mathbf{y}_k \oplus \mathbf{v})$ ranges through S_0. Thus Eq. 6.100 again describes the condition for error. The probability that ${}_1\mathbf{n}$ causes Eq. 6.100 to be satisfied, hence $\hat{x}_1$ to be in error, is independent of k, which proves III.

Proof of IV. The derivations of the three preceding subsections establish the bound

$$\mathrm{P}[\mathcal{E}] \leqslant L\, \mathrm{P}[\mathcal{E}_1 \mid \mathbf{x}_0] \tag{6.101}$$

on the over-all error probability for any particular convolutional encoder and our suboptimum decoder. The remaining task is to determine the attainable exponential behavior of $\mathrm{P}[\mathcal{E}_1 \mid \mathbf{x}_0]$.

The number of codeword segments $\{{}_1\mathbf{y}_i\}$ entering into the decision $\hat{x}_1$ is 2^K, which is still enormous when K is large. As usual, we evade the problem of calculating the error probability for any particular convolutional code by resorting to a random-coding argument. We consider an ensemble of communication systems, each of which uses a different convolutional code, and calculate a bound on the mean value of $\mathrm{P}[\mathcal{E}_1 \mid \mathbf{x}_0]$ over the ensemble. Most systems in the ensemble must afford a $\mathrm{P}[\mathcal{E}_1 \mid \mathbf{x}_0]$ not substantially larger than the mean.

We have already noted that a convolutional coder is specified by its generator sequence $\mathbf{g}$. In calculating $\overline{\mathrm{P}[\mathcal{E}_1 \mid \mathbf{x}_0]}$, it is convenient to consider the ensemble in which $\mathbf{g}$ is equally likely to be any one of the 2^N possible binary sequences of length $N \triangleq Kv$. In other words, over the ensemble of communication systems $\mathbf{g}$ is *EL*.

The first step in bounding $\overline{P[\mathcal{E}_1 \mid \mathbf{x}_0]}$ is to show that over the ensemble of generator sequences any codeword in subset S_1 is also *EL*. Proof rests on the observation that when the generator—defined in Eq. 6.86 as

$$\mathbf{g} \triangleq (\mathbf{g}_1, \mathbf{g}_2, \ldots, \mathbf{g}_K)$$

—is *EL*, the v-component connection vectors $\{\mathbf{g}_l\}$ (defined in Eq. 6.80) are necessarily *EL* and *statistically independent*. But any codeword in S_1, say $\mathbf{v}$, corresponds to a coder input vector for which $x_1 = 1$. In accordance with Eq. 6.90a and Fig. 6.36, $\mathbf{v}$ may therefore be written in the form

$$\begin{aligned} \mathbf{v} &= 1 \cdot \mathbf{f}_1' \oplus x_2\mathbf{f}_2' \oplus \cdots \oplus x_K\mathbf{f}_K' \\ &= (\mathbf{g}_1', \mathbf{g}_2', \ldots, \mathbf{g}_K'), \end{aligned} \tag{6.102}$$

in which

$$\begin{aligned} \mathbf{g}_1' &\triangleq \mathbf{g}_1 \\ \mathbf{g}_2' &\triangleq \mathbf{g}_2 \oplus (x_2\mathbf{g}_1) \\ \mathbf{g}_3' &\triangleq \mathbf{g}_3 \oplus (x_2\mathbf{g}_2 \oplus x_3\mathbf{g}_1) \\ &\ \ \vdots \\ \mathbf{g}_K' &\triangleq \mathbf{g}_K \oplus (x_2\mathbf{g}_{K-1} \oplus \cdots \oplus x_K\mathbf{g}_1). \end{aligned}$$

Each $\mathbf{g}_l'$ is the modulo-2 sum of the *EL* vector $\mathbf{g}_l$ and another vector (in parentheses) of which it is statistically independent. Accordingly, the $\{\mathbf{g}_l'\}$ also are both *EL* and statistically independent, which implies that any codeword $\mathbf{v}$ in S_1 is *EL*.

When $\mathbf{x}_0$ is the message, so that ${}_1\mathbf{y} = {}_1\mathbf{y}_0$, a correct decision $\hat{x}_1$ is made by each system in the ensemble for which at least *one* codeword in S_0 is a more probable cause of ${}_1\mathbf{r}$ than is *any* codeword in S_1. In particular, an error does *not* occur in systems such that

$$w[{}_1\mathbf{r} \oplus \mathbf{v}] > w[{}_1\mathbf{r} \oplus {}_1\mathbf{y}_0]; \qquad \text{all } \mathbf{v} \text{ in } S_1. \tag{6.103}$$

We overbound $P[\mathcal{E}_1 \mid \mathbf{x}_0]$ for each system in the ensemble, hence overbound $\overline{P[\mathcal{E}_1 \mid \mathbf{x}_0]}$, by neglecting the fact that x_1 may still be decoded correctly (because of codewords in S_0 other than ${}_1\mathbf{y}_0$) even if Eq. 6.103 is not satisfied. Thus $\overline{P[\mathcal{E}_1 \mid \mathbf{x}_0]}$ is bounded by the probability that at least one of the 2^{K-1} *EL* vectors in S_1 is a more probable cause of ${}_1\mathbf{r}$ than is the transmitted segment ${}_1\mathbf{y}_0$.

The remaining step is to recognize that this last probability is closely related to our mean probability of error bound on $\overline{P[\mathcal{E} \mid m_0]}$ with a BSC and a Kv-digit block parity-check code having 2^K equally likely messages. The only mathematical distinction is that with a convolutional code there are only 2^{K-1} EL vectors that can cause an error, whereas in the block-code case there are $2^K - 1$. Without further ado, we have

$$\overline{P[\mathcal{E}_1 \mid \mathbf{x}_0]} < 2^{K-1}\, \overline{P_2[\mathcal{E}]} < 2^K 2^{-NR_0'}$$

$$= 2^{-N[R_0' - R_N]}, \qquad (6.104a)$$

in which

$$N \triangleq Kv \qquad (6.104b)$$

and, from Eq. 6.70,

$$R_0' = 1 - \log_2 [1 + 2\sqrt{p(1-p)}]. \qquad (6.104c)$$

This completes the proof IV.

6.4 SEQUENTIAL DECODING

Although in principle both block and convolutional codes afford a $\overline{P[\mathcal{E}]}$ that decreases exponentially with K, we have not yet addressed the crucial problem of actually building decoders that achieve such error performance. Specifically, the suboptimum decoder considered thus far is not realizable for large K because its procedure for decoding each successive input bit x_h, $h = 1, 2, \ldots, L$, involves comparison of the received message span ${}_h\mathbf{r}$ with 2^K K-branch codeword segments. The adoption of a "sequential" procedure for determining each $\hat{x}_h$ evades this exponential blow-up and permits us to specify a decoder that achieves an exponentially small error probability while remaining realizable even when K is large.

In this section we introduce sequential decoding by a heuristic discussion of its application to the binary symmetric channel. We then detail a specific decoding algorithm due to Fano.[28] The algorithm is extended to more general channels and analyzed mathematically in Appendix 6A. Engineering applications are discussed in Section 6.5.

In its simplest form a sequential decoder proceeds in much the same way as our suboptimum decoder. Both decide on each successive message input bit in turn, one after the other, as indicated in Fig. 6.37. For both the problem of decoding x_h is equivalent to the problem of decoding x_1, provided that the hth starting node is correct. The two decoders differ distinctly, however, in how the decisions $\{\hat{x}_h\}$ are determined.

Tree Searching

We have already remarked that the convolutional coder input $\mathbf{x}$ may be regarded as a set of instructions that direct the transmitter along some path through the code tree. Let ${}_1\mathbf{y}$ represent the first $N = Kv$ digits encountered along that path and let ${}_1\mathbf{n}$ denote the first N noise digits. If we assume initially that the BSC is noiseless, so that ${}_1\mathbf{n} = \mathbf{0}$, then ${}_1\mathbf{r} = {}_1\mathbf{y} \oplus {}_1\mathbf{n} = {}_1\mathbf{y}$. In this trivial case a decoder provided with a replica of the encoder can easily trace out the first K branches of the path designated by $\mathbf{x}$. The decoder starts at the first node of the code tree, generates both branches diverging therefrom, and follows the one that agrees with the first v digits of ${}_1\mathbf{r}$. Having thus been directed to a particular second-level node of the code tree, the decoder again generates both branches diverging therefrom and follows whichever branch agrees with the second v digits of ${}_1\mathbf{r}$ to a third-level node. Continuing in this way, the decoder rapidly determines the first K digits of $\mathbf{x}$. The procedure works without difficulty as long as the two branches diverging from any node of the code tree differ by at least one digit. It is clear from Fig. 6.32 that such a difference may be guaranteed by connecting the first x-register stage to the first modulo-2 adder, that is, by making $g_{11} = 1$.

When the BSC is noisy, ${}_1\mathbf{n}$ is not in general $\mathbf{0}$ and the procedure just described is not sufficient even to decode the first message digit, x_1. But a simple modification is appealing and may be used to decode x_1 with high reliability. If neither branch stemming from an intermediate node coincides with the corresponding v digits of ${}_1\mathbf{r}$, the decoder first follows whichever branch agrees best. Clearly, when more than $v/2$ transitions occur in the transmission of a branch, such a decoder initially proceeds to an incorrect node. Having once made this mistake, however, in subsequent branch comparisons the decoder is unlikely to find *any* path stemming from this incorrect node which agrees well with the remaining digits of ${}_1\mathbf{r}$. For example, with the truncated $K = 4$, $v = 5$ code tree of Fig. 6.39, assume

$$\mathbf{x} = (1, 1, 0, 1) \tag{6.105a}$$

$${}_1\mathbf{n} = (10010, 00111, 00000, 00100), \tag{6.105b}$$

so that the transmitted vector is

$${}_1\mathbf{y} = (11111, 10101, 01101, 11011) \tag{6.106}$$

and

$${}_1\mathbf{r} = (01101, 10010, 01101, 11111). \tag{6.107}$$

In this case, as shown in the figure, the decoder follows the correct path to node (a), thence the incorrect path to node (b). But none of the paths

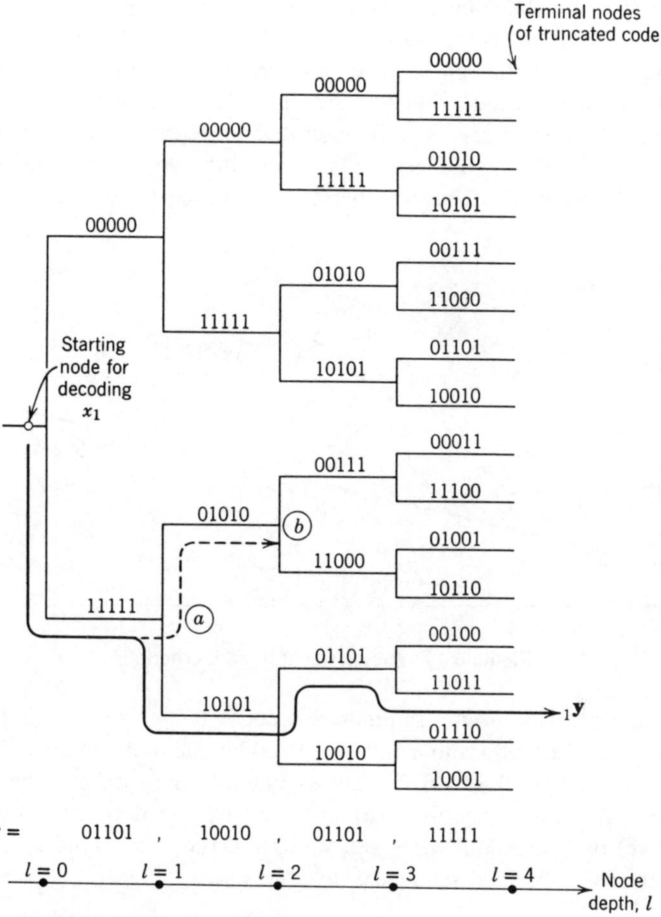

Figure 6.39 The effect of an incorrect turn in penetrating the truncated K-branch code tree pertinent to decoding x_1. For the case shown $K = 4, v = 5$; 2^{K-l} paths to terminal nodes diverge from any intermediate node of depth l.

extending beyond node (b) agrees with $_1\mathbf{r}$ in nearly so many coordinates as does the correct path $_1\mathbf{y}$. When v is properly chosen with regard to the BSC transition probability p, the effect of a wrong turn is likely to be readily noticeable as the decoder attempts to penetrate deeper into the code tree.

The idea of sequential decoding is to program the decoder to act much as a driver who occasionally makes a wrong choice at a fork in the road, but quickly discovers his error, goes back, and tries the other. The decoder's objective is to construct a path K branches long extending all the way through the truncated code in Fig. 6.39 to one of its 2^K terminal nodes. As soon as such a path is found $\hat{x}_1$ is determined in accord with the *first branch* of that path. The observed N-digit span of the received sequence is then shifted v digits to the right, as indicated in Fig. 6.37, and the entire decoding procedure is reiterated to determine $\hat{x}_2$. An error in decoding x_1 results if and only if a wrong turn at the first node is not recognized before the decoder penetrates K branches beyond it.

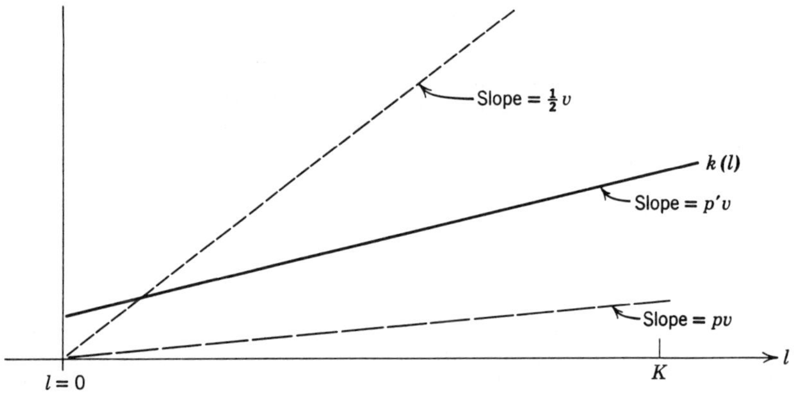

Figure 6.40 A convenient discard criterion.

We now describe how a sequential decoder recognizes wrong turns in decoding x_1. Let us assume that the decoder has penetrated l branches into the code tree, $0 \leqslant l < K$. Let $d(l)$ denote the total number of differences (the Hamming distance) observed by the decoder between the (tentative) path it is following, say $\mathbf{y}^*(l)$, and the corresponding l-branch segment of the received sequence, say $\mathbf{r}(l)$:

$$d(l) \triangleq w[\mathbf{y}^*(l) \oplus \mathbf{r}(l)]. \tag{6.108}$$

As the sequential decoder penetrates branch by branch deeper into the code tree along the tentative path, it maintains a running count of $d(l)$. After each successive penetration the decoder compares $d(l)$ against a *discard criterion function*, $k(l)$. If $d(l)$ ever exceeds $k(l)$, the tentative path is discarded as too improbable. The decoder then backs up to the nearest *unexplored* branch for which $d(l) \leqslant k(l)$ and again starts moving forward as far as the discard criterion function $k(l)$ permits. The decoder keeps track of the branches it has explored and thereby avoids needless retracing of any branch.

From the point of view of decoder implementation, a convenient discard criterion $k(l)$ is a straight line, as shown in Fig. 6.40. The law of large numbers states that the fraction of digit transitions introduced by the BSC will approximate the channel transition probability p when l is large. When $\mathbf{y}^*(l)$ is *correct*, we therefore anticipate that $d(l)$ will oscillate around a straight line of slope pv. On the other hand, when $\mathbf{y}^*(l)$ departs from the starting node ($l = 0$) along the *incorrect* branch, we anticipate that $d(l)$ will oscillate about† a line of slope $\frac{1}{2}v$. We choose $k(l)$ to be a straight line of intermediate slope $p'v$, $p < p' < \frac{1}{2}$. Since it is not unlikely that a burst of noise will cause many of the initial digits of ${}_1\mathbf{r}$ to be in error, $k(l)$ is taken to have a nonzero intercept at $l = 0$.

Basic Concepts

The use of suitable discard criteria in sequential decoding makes it possible for the decoder to recognize quickly that it is following an

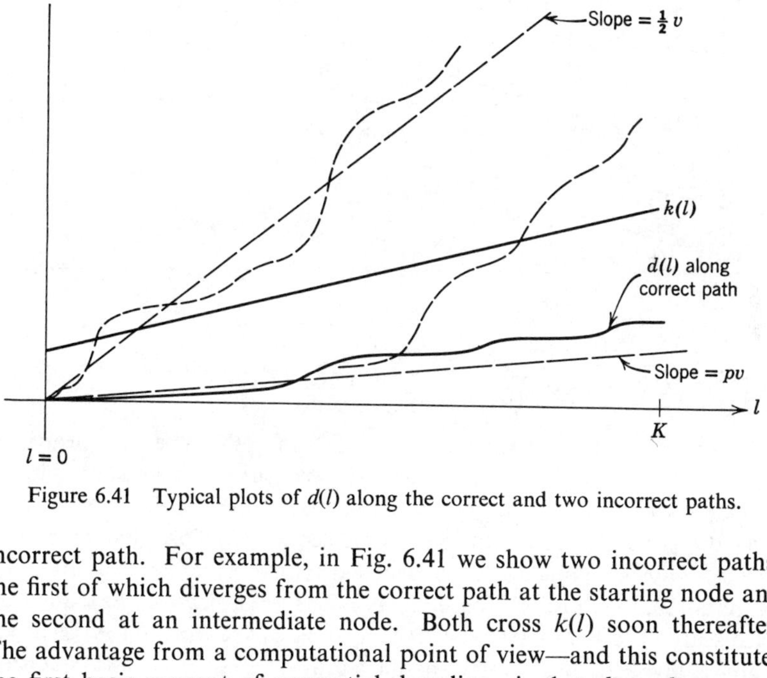

Figure 6.41 Typical plots of $d(l)$ along the correct and two incorrect paths.

incorrect path. For example, in Fig. 6.41 we show two incorrect paths, the first of which diverges from the correct path at the starting node and the second at an intermediate node. Both cross $k(l)$ soon thereafter. The advantage from a computational point of view—and this constitutes the first basic concept of sequential decoding—is that *discarding a path after l branches also effects the discard of the 2^{K-l} other paths in the truncated code tree that diverge therefrom* (see Fig. 6.39). The crucial attribute of convolutional codes is that if wrong turns can be discovered

† The reason is that in good codes the Hamming distance between correct and typical incorrect paths approximates one half the codeword length.

quickly enough the saving in number of computations (measured in terms of the number of branches explored) is exponential.

It is clear that the average number of computations is reduced by making $k(l)$ more stringent, that is, by choosing both its slope and the intercept $k(0)$ to be small. On the other hand, if the discard criterion is too stringent, channel noise may cause *every* sequence in the code tree (including the correct one) to cross $k(l)$ at values of l less than K. In such a case the decoder that we have described is unable to construct a path to any terminal node of Fig. 6.39, hence is unable to decode x_1.

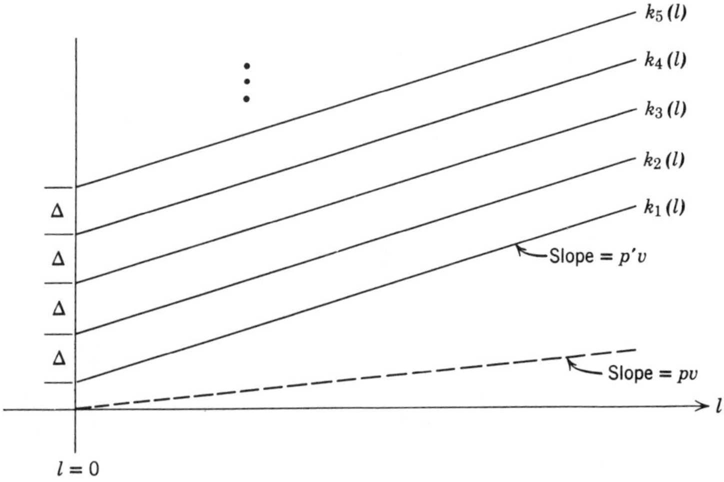

Figure 6.42 A set of equally spaced discard criteria, each with slope $p'v$.

Fortunately, there is a way out of this dilemma; this way out constitutes the second basic concept of sequential decoding. Let us start with a stringent criterion, such as the function $k_1(l)$ shown in Fig. 6.42. Most often the correct path (or at least some sequence whose first branch is correct) will be retained and x_1 decoded with only a small amount of computation. On those less frequent occasions when all code tree sequences are discarded, a less stringent criterion, such as the function $k_2(l)$ in the figure, is invoked. If, as might happen still less frequently, all sequences are discarded with $k_2(l)$, criterion $k_3(l)$ is invoked, and so forth.

By successively relaxing the discard criteria some K-branch path in the code tree will eventually be retained; with high probability the first branch of this retained path will be correct. Of course, the looser criteria require more computation than $k_1(l)$, but since the looser criteria are used less frequently the increased computational load that they imply does not necessarily have a disastrous affect on the *average* computational requirement, again measured in terms of the number of branches explored.

These two basic concepts—early discard of unlikely paths and application of a sequence of criteria—underlie all sequential decoding procedures. A decoding algorithm operating essentially as described above, but modified to curtail vastly the number of computations by exploiting dependencies between successive decisions $\hat{x}_1, \hat{x}_2, \ldots$, has been proposed[90] and tested.[65,54] Although the modifications are not susceptible to mathematical analysis, the experimental results (discussed in Section 6.5) demonstrate that the resulting algorithm is effective. A more sophisticated algorithm, which incorporates the essence of these modifications and extends them in an intuitively satisfying way, has been devised by Fano.[28] The Fano algorithm not only affords more flexible and efficient implementation, but also permits extensive analysis (see Appendix 6A). We consider this algorithm in detail.

The Fano Algorithm

In this discussion of the Fano algorithm we continue to restrict attention to the BSC. An extension to more general channels is provided in Appendix 6A. Explication of the algorithm is simplified by adoption of the "tilted" distance function

$$t(l) \triangleq d(l) - p'vl \tag{6.109}$$

in lieu of the Hamming distance function, $d(l)$, of Eq. 6.108. The corresponding discard criteria, hereafter called *thresholds*, become horizontal lines with spacing Δ, as shown in Fig. 6.43*a*. When $\mathbf{y}^*(l)$ is the correct path, $t(l)$ usually approximates the negative quantity $(p - p')vl$ and tends to decrease as l increases. When $\mathbf{y}^*(l)$ is incorrect, $t(l)$ behaves typically as $(\frac{1}{2} - p')vl$ and tends to increase as l increases.

Before detailing the decoding algorithm, it is helpful to introduce additional terminology. Given the received vector $\mathbf{r}'$, Eqs. 6.108 and 6.109 specify a tilted distance $t(l)$ for each of the 2^l l-branch paths in the code tree, $l = 1, 2, \ldots$. A node of the tree at depth l is assigned a *t-value* equal to the $t(l)$ of the path leading to that node; the node at the origin of the tree is assigned t-value zero. The set of t-values implies a mapping of the code tree into a *received distance tree*, as indicated in Fig. 6.43*b*: the nodes are connected together as in the code tree, but the ordinate of each node is taken to be its t-value.

A node of the received distance tree is said to *satisfy* all thresholds that lie on or above it and to *violate* all thresholds that lie beneath it. The *tightest* threshold satisfied by a node is the one that lies just on or above it. Of the nodes diverging from any given node, the one with smallest t-value

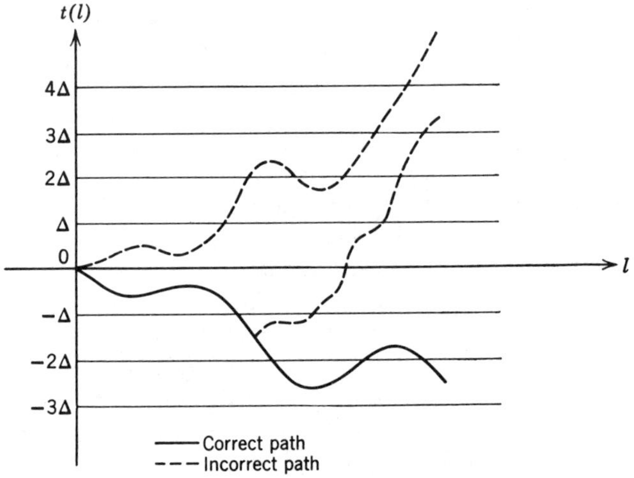

Figure 6.43*a* Thresholds (discard criteria) for use with the Fano algorithm, and typical behavior of $t(l)$ for correct and incorrect paths.

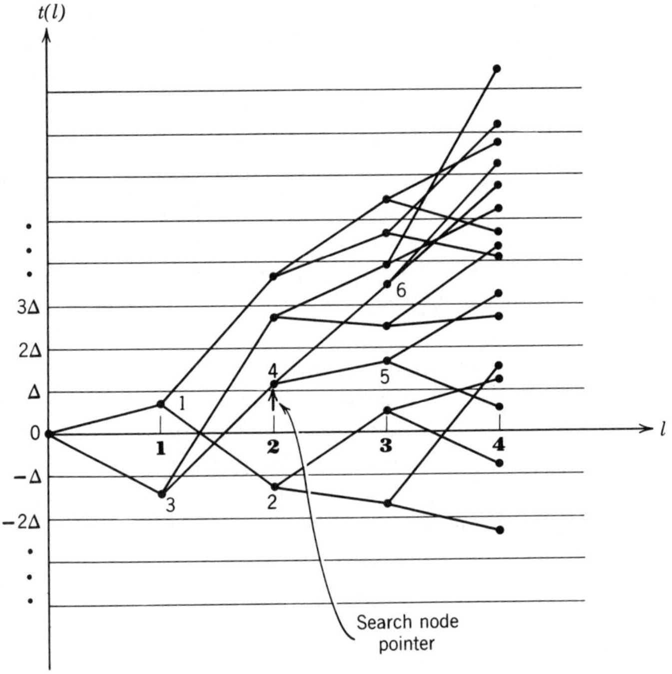

Figure 6.43*b* Received distance tree. The node labeled 4 *satisfies* thresholds $2\Delta, 3\Delta, \ldots,$ and *violates* thresholds $\Delta, 0, -\Delta, \ldots$. The *tightest* threshold satisfied by node 4 is 2Δ. The *best* node diverging from 4 is labeled 5. The *worst* node diverging from 4 is labeled 6.

is called the *best* and the one with largest t-value is called the *worst*. The definitions are exemplified in the figure.

Sequential decoders consider one node of the received distance tree at a time. We may visualize that this node is designated by a (movable) *search node pointer*: the node being considered in Fig. 6.43*b* is the one labeled 4. In addition, the Fano decoder maintains a *running threshold*, denoted T and equal to $k\Delta$, where k is a (variable) integer. We say that the running threshold is *tightened* when k is assigned so that T is the tightest threshold satisfied by the *search node*, that is, by the node then being considered.

Given the received vector $\mathbf{r}'$, the Fano decoder searches for the correct path by moving its search node pointer through the received distance tree. The pointer can move forward or backward, but only to an adjacent node—that is, only to a node connected to the existing search node by a single branch. The pointer movement is controlled by the flow diagram of Fig. 6.44. An essential feature of the algorithm is that the pointer is never moved either forward or backward unless this can be accomplished without violating the running threshold; the running threshold is raised only when necessary to accommodate such a move.

The operation of the decoder is best explained by example. Consider Fig. 6.45. The decoder starts its tree search at the initial node, labeled 0. The initial value of the running threshold T is zero. In accordance with Fig. 6.44 the decoder *looks* forward to the node labeled 1. Since the t-value of this node does not violate T, the search node pointer is then *moved* forward to node 1. By this movement the decoder makes a tentative decision, $\hat{x}_1$; the decision is 0 when the node labeled 1 corresponds to $x_1 = 0$ and 1 when this node corresponds to $x_1 = 1$.

With the search node pointer on node 1, the running threshold $T = 0$ is as tight as possible. The decoder therefore next looks ahead to node 2; it moves the pointer to node 2 after noting that the running threshold is not violated, thereby making a tentative decision $\hat{x}_2$. At node 2 the decoder is able to tighten the running threshold and sets $T = -\Delta$. This procedure of looking, moving the pointer, and tightening T continues until in looking forward from node 4 to node 5 the decoder observes a violation of the running threshold $T = -2\Delta$. The decoder reacts by looking back to node 3. Since the running threshold $T = -2\Delta$ is not violated by node 3, the pointer is moved back. The effect is to *erase* the tentative decision $\hat{x}_4$. On the step forward to node 6 the complementary choice of $\hat{x}_4$ is made. The remainder of Fig. 6.45 is self-explanatory. The search path $\mathbf{y}^*(l)$ is specified at any instant by the tentative decisions $\hat{x}_1, \hat{x}_2, \ldots, \hat{x}_l$, which together determine the position of the search node pointer.

Enough thought will make it clear that the flow diagram of Fig. 6.44 will direct a successful search through any tree and eventually trace out the correct path so long as $t(l)$ for the correct path ultimately decreases, whereas $t(l)$ for every incorrect path ultimately increases. In particular,

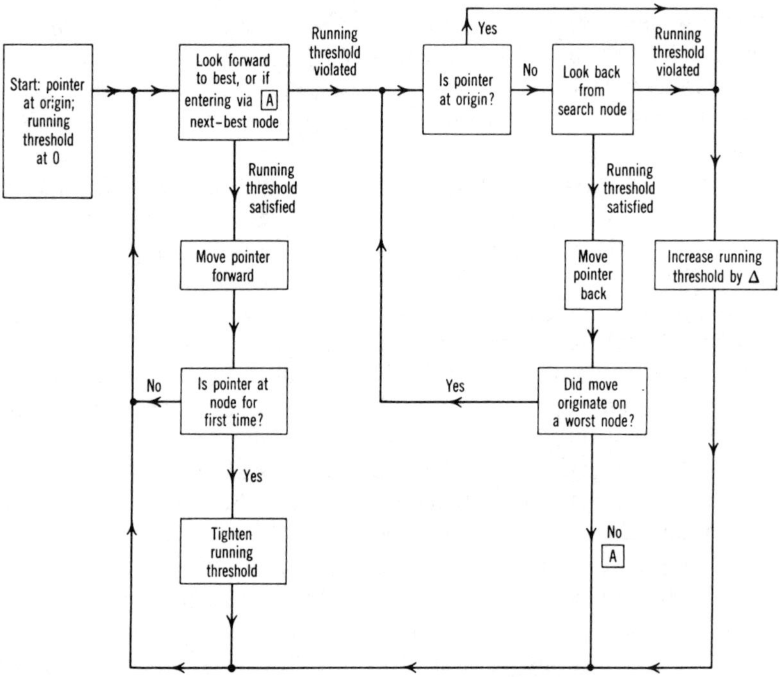

Figure 6.44 Basic flow diagram for the Fano algorithm. In Appendix 6A we consider general convolutional codes with u nodes diverging from each node of the code tree, $u \geqslant 2$. (See Fig. 6A.1.) The flow diagram above is so worded that it pertains to these general codes for which the entire corresponding set of u nodes in the received distance tree is considered to be ordered from *best* to *worst*, according to increasing t-value. Two or more such nodes with equal t-values may be ordered relative to each other in any specific way.

the algorithm cannot become trapped in an endless loop, continually searching the same nodes with the same thresholds.

It is helpful to note that in searching for a path on which $t(l)$ ultimately decreases as l increases the decoder examines *all accessible* nodes lying beneath a given threshold before increasing the running threshold. After an increase no further change in T is permitted until either (i) all accessible paths are found to violate the new running threshold, necessitating another increase of Δ in the value assigned to T or (ii) the search node pointer arrives at a node that it has never reached before. Further properties of

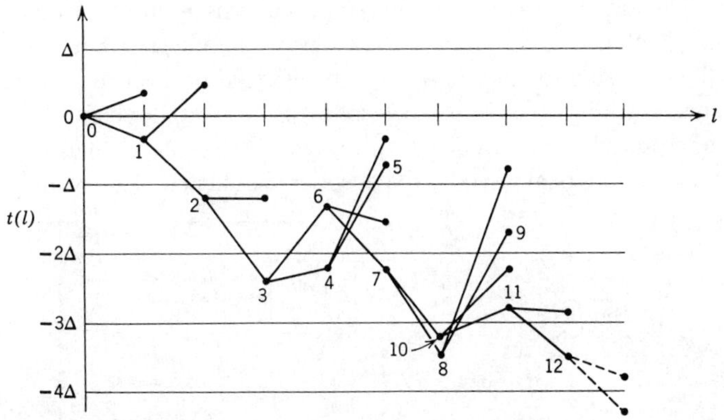

Figure 6.45 Example of tree search with algorithm of Fig. 6.44. For the search detailed below t-values are calculated only for those nodes of the tree actually shown in the figure.

Pointer at Node	Running Threshold	Action (× indicates threshold violation)		
0	0	look at 1	point to 1	
1	0	look at 2	point to 2	set $T = -\Delta$
2	$-\Delta$	look at 3	point to 3	set $T = -2\Delta$
3	-2Δ	look at 4	point to 4	
4	-2Δ	look at 5	× look at 3	point to 3
3	-2Δ	look at 6	× look at 2	× set $T = -\Delta$
3	$-\Delta$	look at 4	point to 4	
4	$-\Delta$	look at 5	× look at 3	point to 3
3	$-\Delta$	look at 6	point to 6	
6	$-\Delta$	look at 7	point to 7	set $T = -2\Delta$
7	-2Δ	look at 8	point to 8	set $T = -3\Delta$
8	-3Δ	look at 9	× look at 7	× set $T = -2\Delta$
8	-2Δ	look at 9	× look at 7	point to 7
7	-2Δ	look at 10	point to 10	set $T = -3\Delta$
10	-3Δ	look at 11	× look at 7	× set $T = -2\Delta$
10	-2Δ	look at 11	point to 11	
11	-2Δ	look at 12	point to 12	set $T = -3\Delta$

the algorithm are stated in Appendix 6A. The analysis performed there permits a sensible choice to be made for the design parameters Δ and p'.

The basic flow diagram of Fig. 6.44 requires one elaboration to permit efficient implementation. The box labeled "Is pointer at node for first time?" can, of course, be realized by providing a sufficiently large memory. But the number of nodes examined by the decoder is in general exceedingly

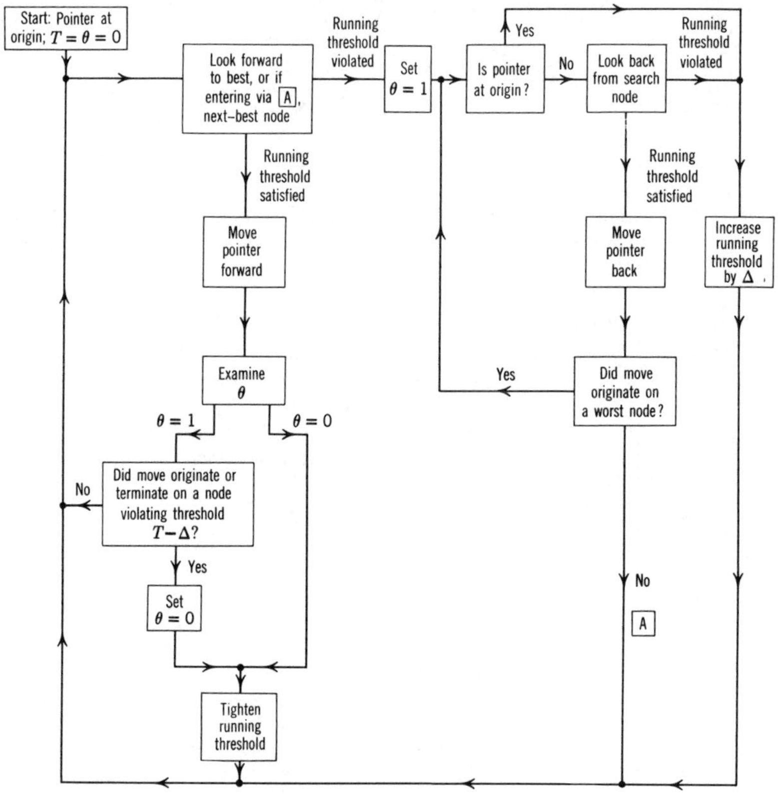

Figure 6.46 Augmented flow diagram for the Fano algorithm.

large, and such a memory is prohibitively costly. An ingenious alternative proposed by Fano uses only a single binary variable, which we designate θ, to determine when to tighten the running threshold. This additional variable and the accompanying logic are included in the augmented flow diagram of Fig. 6.46. The variable θ, initially 0, is set equal to 1 immediately following observation of a running threshold violation on a forward look. As long as θ remains equal to 1 the algorithm prevents tightening of T. As soon as the search node pointer moves to a *new* node (one never reached before) θ is reset to 0 and tightening is again permitted.

A new node can be encountered only on a forward move and is easily recognized. First, a node is new if it violates the threshold, say, $T_0 \triangleq T - \Delta$, just beneath the running threshold T: for example, when node 11 of Fig. 6.45 is reached, it violates the previous value $T_0 = -3\Delta$. Second, a node that satisfies T_0 is new if reached by a forward move from a node that violates T_0: for example, node 10 of Fig. 6.45 satisfies $T_0 = -3\Delta$ but

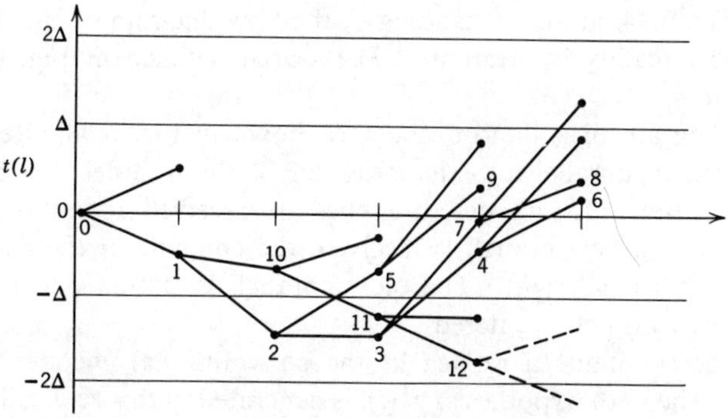

Figure 6.47 Example of tree search with algorithm of Fig. 6.46.

Pointer at Node	Running Threshold	θ	Action ($\times$ indicates "set $\theta = 1$"		
0	0	0	look at 1	point to 1	
1	0	0	look at 2	point to 2	set $T = -\Delta$
2	$-\Delta$	0	look at 3	point to 3	
3	$-\Delta$	0	look at 4	$\times$ look at 2	point to 2
2	$-\Delta$	1	look at 5	$\times$ look at 1	set $T = 0$
2	0	1	look at 3	point to 3	
3	0	1	look at 4	point to 4	set $\theta = 0$
4	0	0	look at 6	$\times$ look at 3	point to 3
3	0	1	look at 7	point to 7	set $\theta = 0$
7	0	0	look at 8	$\times$ look at 3	point to 3
3	0	1	look at 2	point to 2	
2	0	1	look at 5	point to 5	set $\theta = 0$
5	0	0	look at 9	$\times$ look at 2	point to 2
2	0	1	look at 1	point to 1	
1	0	1	look at 10	point to 10	set $\theta = 0$
10	0	0	look at 11	point to 11	set $T = -\Delta$
11	$-\Delta$	0	look at 12	point to 12	

is reached from node 7, which violates this running threshold value. (Running threshold T was increased from -3Δ to -2Δ before the step back from node 8 to node 7.) The search node pointer can arrive at a new node only in one of these two ways; otherwise, the node would have been accessible with running threshold value T_0, hence examined previously. The algorithm of Fig. 6.46 recognizes both possibilities and reacts by setting $\theta = 0$.

As with Fig. 6.44, an understanding of the flow diagram of Fig. 6.46 is obtained most readily by example. The search detailed in Fig. 6.47 is self-explanatory.

A block diagram of a Fano decoder is shown in Fig. 6.48. Received digits are read in parallel into the r-register of the decoder one branch (v digits) at a time. In practice, branches are received at uniform time intervals. As each new branch is received, the contents of the r-register are shifted toward the right. The oldest branch is shifted out and lost whenever a new branch is entered.

The decoder contains a replica of the convolutional encoder at the transmitter. The path hypothesis, $\mathbf{y}^*(l)$, is generated in this replica branch by branch, matched with the corresponding received branch, and $t(l)$ is updated. The penetration index l, represented by the depth of search pointer in Fig. 6.48, is increased (the pointer moved left) or decreased (the pointer moved right) in accordance with the search algorithm. In addition, the pointer and $\hat{x}$-register shift one step to the right each time a new branch is received.

The input bits hypothesized by the encoder replica in generating $\mathbf{y}^*(l)$ are written in the $\hat{x}$-register. Thus the $\hat{x}$-register positions to the right of the pointer are full and those to the left are empty. The decoded output vector $\hat{\mathbf{x}}$ is the sequence of digits shifted out of the rightmost stage of the $\hat{x}$-register. Note that the $\hat{x}$-register is equivalent to the *search node pointer* considered in connection with the flow diagram of Fig. 6.44. In contrast, the *depth of search pointer* of Fig. 6.48 indicates where the received branch being observed by the decoder is located within the r-register.

The ambulations of the pointer in Fig. 6.48 depend on the received data rate, the computational speed of the decoder, and the details of the received noise. When most of the received digits are correct, very little searching is necessary to extend $\mathbf{y}^*(l)$. In this case the pointer usually hovers near the input end of the decoder and waits for new data. On the other hand, if the number of erroneous received digits is too large, a vast amount of searching is involved and the pointer is dragged to the right as new branches are fed into the decoder. The decoder is in trouble if the depth of search pointer is forced to the output end of the decoder. The implications of this event are discussed in Section 6.5.

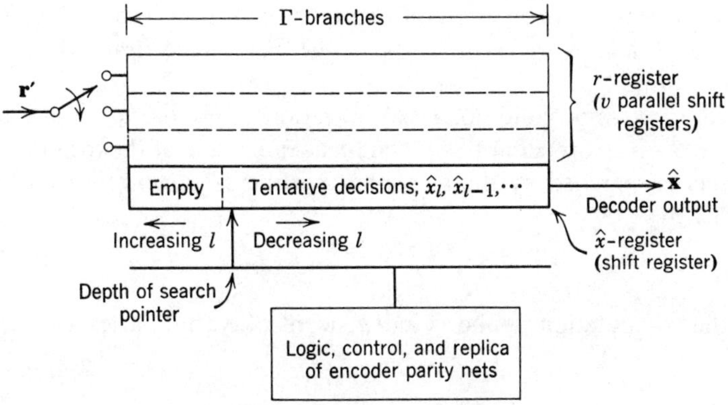

Figure 6.48 Block diagram of Fano decoder for the case $v = 3$.

6.5 SUMMARY OF RESULTS

In this section we summarize certain theoretical analyses of sequential decoding and discuss the major experimental results that have been obtained.

Analytical Results

Precise analysis of an actual Fano decoder is complicated by the fact that the size, Γ, of the r-register in Fig. 6.48 is finite. Meaningful insight into decoder performance, however, is gained by assuming that Γ is so large that the search position pointer is never forced to the output end of the r-register. We use this assumption in Appendix 6A to bound a quantity analogous to the mean probability $\overline{\mathrm{P}[\mathcal{E}_h]}$ considered in connection with the suboptimum decoder of Section 6.3. The overhead bar, as usual, signifies expectation with respect to a suitable ensemble of codes. In particular, for coders like that of Fig. 6.32 operating over a binary symmetric channel, Eq. 6A.18 implies† that

$$\overline{\mathrm{P}[\mathcal{E}_h]} < A_0\, 2^{-\frac{1}{2}K[(R_0'/R_\mathrm{N})-1]}; \qquad R_\mathrm{N} < R_0', \tag{6.110}$$

in which the value of the coefficient A_0 is given by

$$A_0 = \frac{2}{1 - 2^{\frac{1}{2}[(R_0'/R_\mathrm{N})-1]}} \tag{6.111}$$

and R_0' is the exponential bound parameter evaluated for the BSC (see (see Eq. 6.70). As discussed in the appendix, $L\overline{\mathrm{P}[\mathcal{E}_h]}$ may be interpreted

† Equations 6.110 and 6.111 follow from Eqs. 6A.18 and 6A.17b by specializing to the parameter values $u = 2$, $v = 1/R_\mathrm{N}$, $\Delta = 2$.

as indicative of the probability of one or more errors in decoding a long sequence of L message symbols with the Fano algorithm when the r-register is infinite.

Under these same conditions, specialization of Eq. 6A.27 implies that a quantity $\bar{B}$—interpreted in the appendix as indicative of the mean number of branches searched by the algorithm per message symbol decoded—is bounded by

$$\bar{B} < 3A_0^2; \qquad R_N < R_0'. \tag{6.112a}$$

Thus the computation bound is independent of K, but varies as

$$3A_0^2 \approx \frac{100}{[(R_0'/R_N) - 1]^2} \tag{6.112b}$$

for R_N only slightly less than R_0'.

Although the particular bounds presented here have been chosen for ease of derivation and simplicity of form rather than for tightness, they place in evidence three important characteristics of sequential decoding:

1. For $R_N < R_0'$ the code constraint length K can be increased without increasing the bound on $\bar{B}$.
2. For $R_N < R_0'$, $L\overline{P[\mathcal{E}_h]}$ decreases exponentially with an exponent that is linear in K.
3. Although $\bar{B}$ and $\overline{P[\mathcal{E}_h]}$ are well behaved with regard to K, both bounds blow up as R_N approaches R_0'.

Thus by increasing K it is possible to obtain as small an error probability as desired without incurring a concomitant increase in the mean computational speed demanded of the decoder; however, the channel imposes an upper limit, R_0', on the maximum rate at which this kind of performance can be attained.

These three characteristics are believed to be fundamental attributes of all sequential decoding procedures; they are reflected in all bounds obtained and in all experiments reported thus far.[48,78,91]

System Evaluation

Shannon's original and revolutionary proof that channel disturbances fundamentally limit the rate, but not the accuracy, of communication was first published in 1948. Since then a great deal of effort has been devoted to the problem of actually achieving improved communication reliability, and many interesting coding and decoding schemes have been devised. Most of them are well documented,[31,57,66,96] and we shall not discuss them here.

The relative desirability of different solutions to specific communication problems depends critically on the engineering objective. For example, consider a bandlimited Gaussian channel and Shannon's bounding reliability exponent $R_0{}^*$, plotted in Fig. 5.18. If moderate accuracy at low data rates ($R_N/R_0{}^* \ll 1$) suffices, the problem can be resolved by appropriate choice of a modulator and demodulator; coding is not needed. If the objective is to obtain high accuracy at low data rates, easily implemented schemes such as *threshold decoding*[57] are indicated. The most difficult problem arises when we simultaneously require high accuracy and high data rate, $R_N/R_0{}^* \lessapprox 1$. In this case powerful codes ($K \gg 1$) and complex terminal equipment are unavoidable, and the comparison of different coding techniques becomes especially intricate.

A particularly interesting class of codes affording large K is the Bose-Chaudhuri-Hocquenghem[15]—hereafter abbreviated BCH—codes. For any integer m there is a binary BCH code with word length $N = (2^m - 1)$ which contains 2^K codewords and is guaranteed to correct any combination of t or fewer BSC channel transitions, with $K \geqslant N - mt$. Decoding schemes that are applicable to these codes whenever the number of transitions is less than or equal to t have been discovered by Peterson[66] and also by others†; these schemes require a number of computations which grows as a small power of t.

As an example of one way in which different decoding schemes can be compared, we now consider the performances achievable over an additive white Gaussian noise channel with binary BCH codes and with binary convolutional codes and sequential decoding. Antipodal signaling and symmetric two-level receiver quantization are assumed. The resulting BSC transition probability is

$$p = Q\left(\sqrt{\frac{2E_b R_N}{\mathcal{N}_0}}\right), \tag{6.113}$$

in which $E_b/\mathcal{N}_0$ is the energy-to-noise ratio per message input bit and $R_N \triangleq K/N$ is the data rate in bits per transmitted symbol.

With the aid of a digital computer, the minimum value of $E_b/\mathcal{N}_0$ required for any particular BCH code in order to achieve a stated error probability per bit, P_1, can be determined. We define $P_1 \triangleq (1/K)\,\mathrm{P}[\mathcal{E}]$, in

† See, for example, G. D. Forney, Jr., "Concatenated Codes," Sc.D. Thesis, M.I.T., June 1965. See also D. Gorenstein, and N. Zierler, "A Class of Error-Correcting Codes in p^m Symbols," *J. SIAM* **9**, 207–214, June 1961.

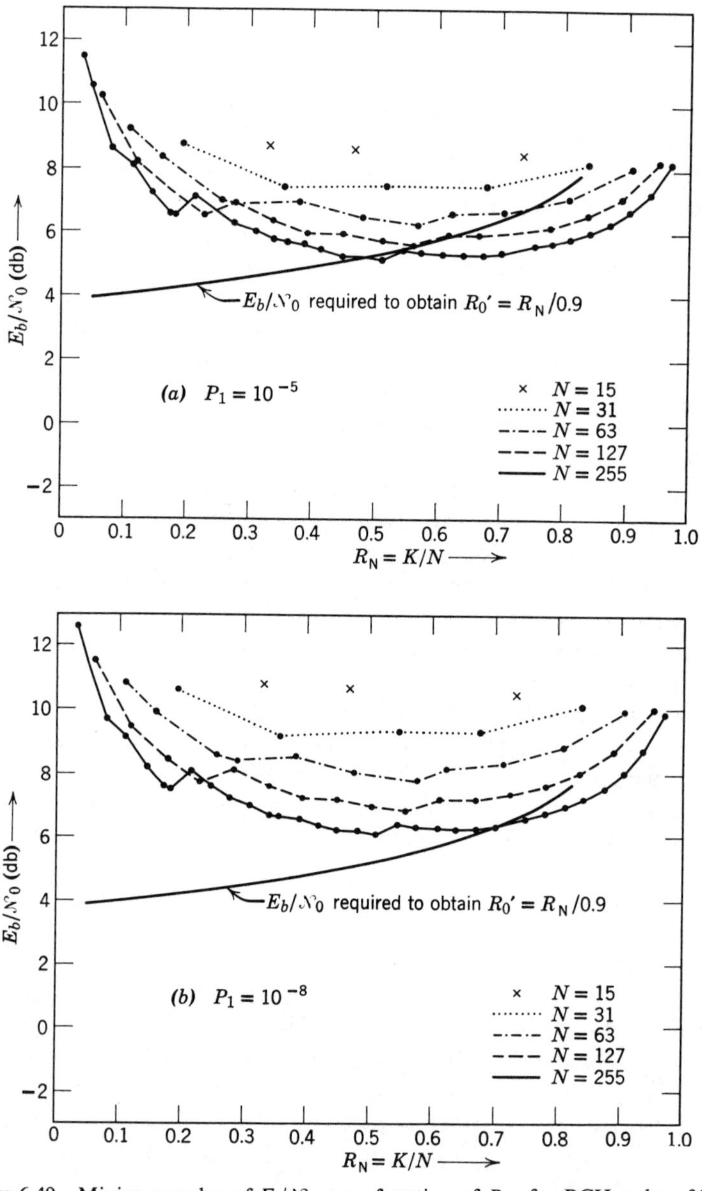

Figure 6.49 Minimum value of $E_b/\mathcal{N}_0$, as a function of R_N, for BCH codes of length $N = 15, 31, 63, 128, 255$. Only the dots represent data points. For small R_N the solid (sequential decoding) curve can be lowered 2 db through use of close-grained, rather than binary, detector quantization (see Eq. 6.114b and Fig. 6.21).

which P[$\mathcal{E}$] is the BCH block error probability. The results† are plotted as a function of R_N for $P_1 = 10^{-5}$ and 10^{-8} in Figs. 6.49*a* and *b*.

For purposes of comparison with sequential decoding we can refer to Eq. 6.70 and determine the value of $E_b/\mathcal{N}_0$ required to obtain $R_N/R_0' = 0.9$. The results are also plotted in Figs. 6.49*a* and *b*. Equations 6.110 and 6.111 state that with these values of $E_b/\mathcal{N}_0$ an arbitrarily small error probability can be obtained by choosing K large enough. We shall soon see that when decoding sequentially it is sensible to choose K so large that the error probability will be truly negligible and to restrict $R_N \leqslant 0.9R_0'$.

From a system-engineering point of view curves such as those in Fig. 6.49, although instructive, are by no means a sufficient basis on which to decide among contrasting design approaches. We must also take into account the fact that different decoding schemes have different operational and implementational advantages and disadvantages. For instance, so far we have considered only the *average* computational demands with sequential decoding; in the next subsection we consider also the *variability* of the number of computations. Although BCH codes in general require a larger average amount of decoding computation than sequential decoding, the computational demand in the BCH case is much less variable, which is a distinct advantage in many applications.

The greatest asset of sequential decoding is the scope of its applicability. We have already mentioned that sequential decoding procedures can be applied to a broad class of communication channels. Specifically, the class includes, but is not restricted to, every constant memoryless discrete channel—that is, every channel for which the statistical connection between input and output symbols on each use of the channel can be modeled adequately by a fixed transition diagram such as that shown in Fig. 6.17. For *any* such channel bounds equivalent to Eqs. 6.110–6.112—but with R_0' given by Eq. 6.62b—are derived in Appendix 6A. Thus great flexibility may be exercised in the design of a modulation and demodulation system to be used in conjunction with sequential decoding.

An immediate implication is that if very close-grained, rather than binary, quantization is used at the matched filter output of an additive white Gaussian noise channel, the limiting value of R_N with binary convolutional coding can be increased from

$$R_0' = 1 - \log_2 [1 + 2\sqrt{p(1 - p)}] \tag{6.114a}$$

† Since no decoding algorithm for BCH codes has been devised for a number of channel transitions greater than t, a block decoding error is presumed whenever this event occurs. In determining the performance of the BCH codes, the values of t and K were taken from Table 9.1 in Peterson[66] and provide stronger results than guaranteed by the bound $K \geqslant N - mt$.

to a value arbitrarily close to the unquantized error exponent

$$R_0 = 1 - \log_2 (1 + e^{-E_N/\mathcal{N}_0}); \qquad E_N = E_b R_N, \qquad (6.114b)$$

with consequent improvement in the efficiency of energy utilization. Also, we need not restrict consideration to binary signaling, but can design a multiamplitude transmitter modulator to yield an R_0' that is nearly optimum for any value of $E_N/\mathcal{N}_0$, as discussed in Chapter 5. A relevant experiment is discussed at the end of this chapter. Calculations of R_0' for certain propagation channels characterized by random phase shift and fading are considered in Chapter 7.

Simulation Results

Analytical difficulties with sequential decoding are such that even the tightest bounds that have been derived are not numerically accurate

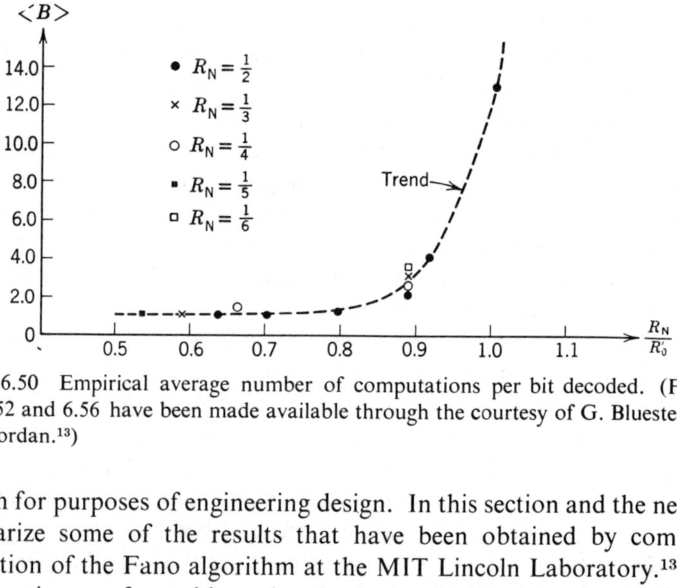

Figure 6.50 Empirical average number of computations per bit decoded. (Figures 6.50–6.52 and 6.56 have been made available through the courtesy of G. Bluestein and K. L. Jordan.[13])

enough for purposes of engineering design. In this section and the next we summarize some of the results that have been obtained by computer simulation of the Fano algorithm at the MIT Lincoln Laboratory.[13]

The actions performed by a decoder in communicating a long sequence $\mathbf{x}$ of L convolutional coder input bits over a BSC has been simulated on a digital computer programed to count the number of code-tree branches actually searched during the entire decoding procedure. We define $\langle B \rangle$ as this total divided by L. Thus $\langle B \rangle$ is the *empirical average number of branches searched per message input bit decoded.*

In Fig. 6.50 we plot the observed values of $\langle B \rangle$ as a function of the ratio R_N/R_0'. The code constraint length K used in the simulation was equal to 60, and was large enough so that no decoding errors occurred. For this value of K the suboptimum decoder considered in Section 6.3 would make approximately $2^{60} \approx 10^{18}$ branch comparisons per decoded digit, and for $R_N = 0.9R_0'$ even the bound of Eq. 6.112 claims only that $\bar{B} < 8100$. In contrast, for the experiments summarized in Fig. 6.50 we observe that $\langle B \rangle < 4$ for all $R_N/R_0' < 0.9$. As $R_N \to R_0'$, the value of

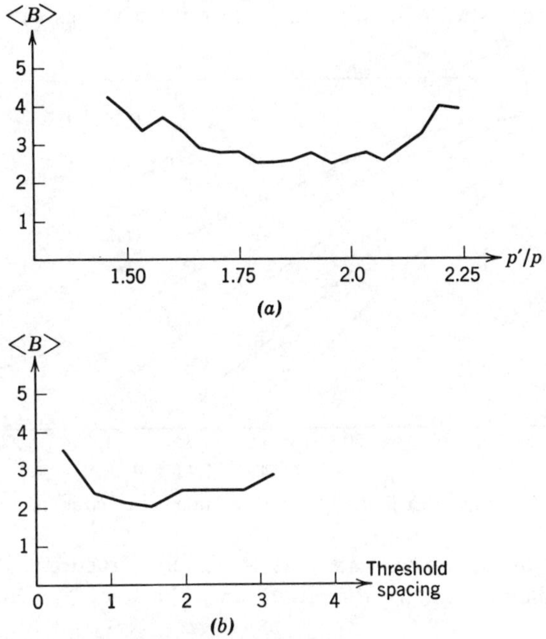

Figure 6.51 Average number of computations in decoding as a function of (*a*) tilt; (*b*) threshold spacing. For both curves, $R_N/R_0' = 0.89$.

$\langle B \rangle$ rapidly becomes large, a behavior that is in accord with the bound of Eq. 6.112. Experimentally, $\langle B \rangle$ is found to depend strongly on the ratio of R_N and R_0' but only weakly on the value of these parameters individually.

The data of Fig. 6.50 were taken with the tilt parameter p' (see Eq. 6.109) and threshold spacing Δ optimized empirically to minimize $\langle B \rangle$. The behavior of $\langle B \rangle$ as a function of tilt and spacing in a typical case is shown in Figs. 6.51*a*, *b*. We observe that precise minimization with regard to these parameters is not necessary. Finally, it should be remarked that the first several digits of the generators $\{\mathbf{g}\}$ used in the experiments reported here were carefully chosen to yield good performance[90]; only the tails of the generators were chosen at random.

Dynamical Decoding Behavior

Although Fig. 6.50 shows that the *average* computational demand $\langle B \rangle$ with sequential decoding is quite small for $R_N/R_0' < 0.9$, the *actual number of branches, say B, searched by the computer in the dynamical process of penetrating from one node to the next in the code tree is extremely variable.* We denote the relative frequency with which B exceeds any number γ by $F[B > \gamma]$. Typical plots of $F[B > \gamma]$, with R_N/R_0' as a parameter, are shown in Fig. 6.52. For large values of γ the relative

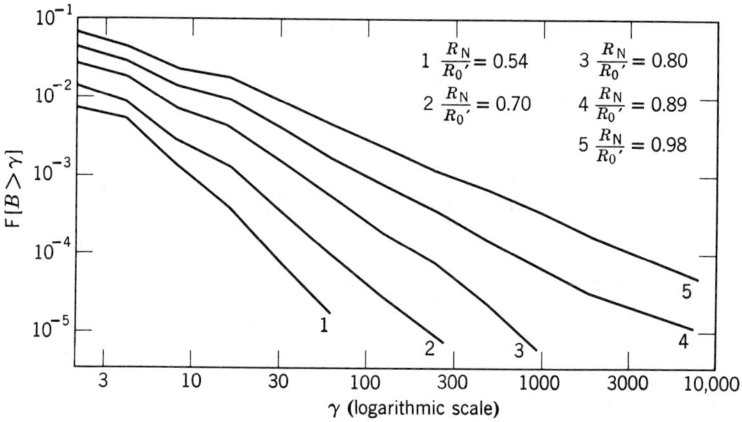

Figure 6.52 Empirical distribution function of number of computations in decoding.

frequency varies approximately as an inverse fractional power† of γ. For these data an empirical relationship, valid for $\gamma \gg 1$ and $R_N < R_0'$, is[13]

$$F[B > \gamma] \approx 3^{-(1-R_N/R_0')}\gamma^{-(2.9-2R_N/R_0')}. \qquad (6.115)$$

For an analytical expression, see Problem 6.17.

The variability of the number of computations has a profound influence on the design and evaluation of a sequential decoding system. For example, with a BSC and an appropriate convolutional code we anticipate that except for short excursions the pattern of channel transitions will usually leave the received sequence much closer in Hamming distance to the sequence actually transmitted than to any of the other possible encoder outputs. Then a Fano decoder typically searches out the correct

† A probability distribution with this type of behavior is called "Paréto." If a Paréto random variable is to have finite mean, the exponent of γ must be no greater than minus one. This condition would be met in Eq. 6.115 for $R_N = R_0'$ if the constant 2.9 were replaced by 3.0. The empirical value 2.9 reflects a small amount of experimental performance degradation.

path through the code tree with great rapidity, which accounts for the small value of $\langle B \rangle$. In such circumstances the pointer designating the depth of search of the decoder in Fig. 6.48 hovers near the input end of the decoder and all is well.

Infrequently, however, the channel transition pattern will cause the tilted distance along the correct path to increase with l over a span of

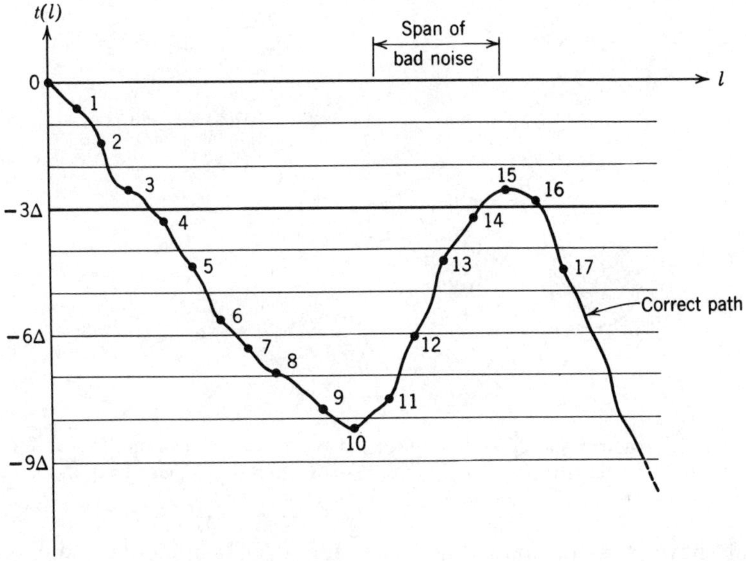

Figure 6.53 A plot of $t(l)$ along the correct path which involves a great amount of computation in decoding. Before reaching node 15 the decoder must examine *each* path diverging from nodes 4 through 14 until the path crosses threshold -3Δ.

considerable length. In this atypical event the decoder must search far back into the code tree, examining an enormous number of branches before it can follow the correct path over the local maximum, as illustrated in Fig. 6.53. The probability of a deep search decreases, but the resulting number of computations increases, rapidly with search depth. The balance between the two effects accounts† for the fact that $\mathrm{F}[B > \gamma]$ is only a slowly decreasing function of γ. In such circumstances the on-pouring stream of received digits may force the depth of search pointer to the output end of the decoder memory, a condition called *overflow*.

† The distribution of computation is analyzed in J. E. Savage, "The Computation Problem with Sequential Decoding," Ph.D. Thesis, M.I.T., February 1965. Additional empirical data is to be found in K. L. Jordan, "The Performance of Sequential Decoding in Conjunction with Efficient Modulation," *IEEE Trans. Comm. Tech.*, COM-**14**, 283–297, June 1966

With surpassing infrequency, the channel transition pattern may create a received sequence that closely approximates one of the possible, but incorrect, coder outputs. As an extreme example, if the channel noise sequence is

$$\mathbf{n} = \mathbf{f}_h, \tag{6.116}$$

where $\mathbf{f}_h$ is the hth translate of the code generator sequence $\mathbf{g}$, it follows from Eq. 6.83 that the received sequence is exactly that code word which

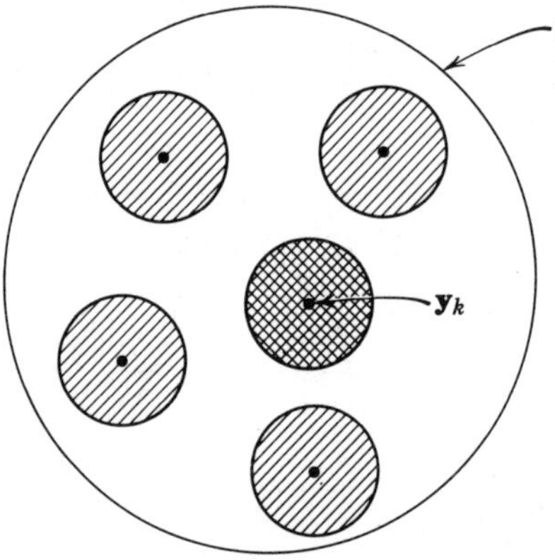
Received signal space. (Points that are close together indicate vectors that are near each other in Hamming distance)
$\mathbf{y}_k$

Figure 6.54 An abstract representation of the events "overflow" and "error" for the BSC. The dots represent the encoder outputs $\{\mathbf{y}_i\}$. Received signals lying in the open region are not decoded because of overflow.

would have been transmitted had the hth digit of $\mathbf{x}$ in fact been different. In this case x_h will with certainty be decoded both easily *and* incorrectly. Even in less extreme cases it is possible for several incorrect digits to be released from the $\hat{x}$-register without a large increase in the number of branches searched and concomitant dragging of the search position pointer to the right. Such events are called *undetectable errors.*

From an operational point of view, we need to distinguish between errors and overflows. For conceptual purposes the distinction may be envisioned geometrically as shown in Fig. 6.54: when the actual encoder input is $\mathbf{x}_k$, channel transition patterns producing received sequences that lie within the crosshatched area correspond to correct operation of the decoder. By symmetry, received sequences lying within the shaded areas must therefore yield undetectable errors. Intermediate transition patterns, producing received sequences lying within the open region, yield overflow.

In order to be practicable, a sequential decoder must be designed and operated so that *both the overflow and error probabilities will be very small.* Obtaining a small overflow probability is the more difficult problem, and we discuss it first.

Probability of overflow. The magnitude of the overflow probability depends primarily on the size of the decoder memory and the computational speed of the decoder. Like $\langle B \rangle$, it is insensitive to the code constraint length but very sensitive to R_0'/R_N.

We gain insight into the probability of overflow with the Fano algorithm by considering the decoding of a new input bit on the assumption that the decoder's depth of search pointer starts out at the extreme left of the memory, as in Fig. 6.55. If Γ is the number of received branches that can

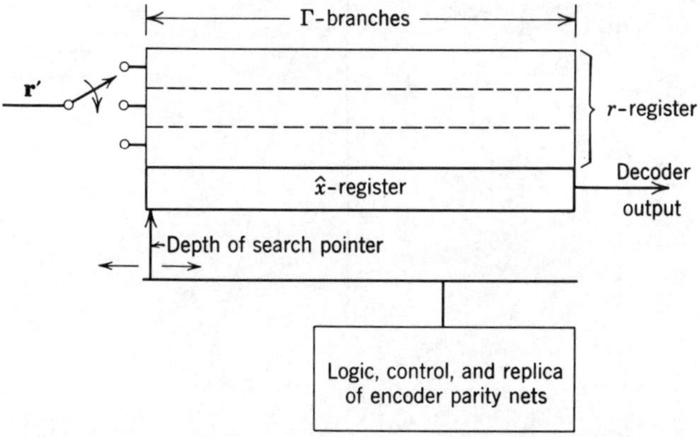

Figure 6.55 Initial condition of decoder for simplified overflow analysis.

be stored in the memory, an overflow is then certain to occur unless the decoder is able to penetrate at least one branch deeper into the code tree before Γ new branches are received. An equivalent statement is that overflow must occur if more than $\lambda\Gamma$ branches are searched before additional penetration, where λ denotes the *number of branches the decoder can search in the time allotted to the transmission of each branch.* From Eq. 6.115 the relative frequency, say F, of this event is

$$F \triangleq \mathrm{F}[B > \lambda\Gamma] \approx 3^{-(1-R_N/R_0')}[\lambda\Gamma]^{-[2.9-2(R_N/R_0')]}. \tag{6.117}$$

In the process of searching the decoder moves back into the code tree, so that an overflow may occur before $\lambda\Gamma$ branches have been searched. As a practical matter, however, whenever $\lambda > \langle B \rangle$ and the right-hand side of Eq. 6.117 is very small, F provides a useful estimate of the probability of overflow.† The validity of this statement rests on the waiting-line behavior observed in the course of the decoder simulation experiments. By *waiting-line* we mean the position of the decoder depth of search pointer, under the assumption that Γ is infinite.

† If λ is less than $\langle B \rangle$, the decoder will not even be able to keep pace with the average computational demands of the received message stream.

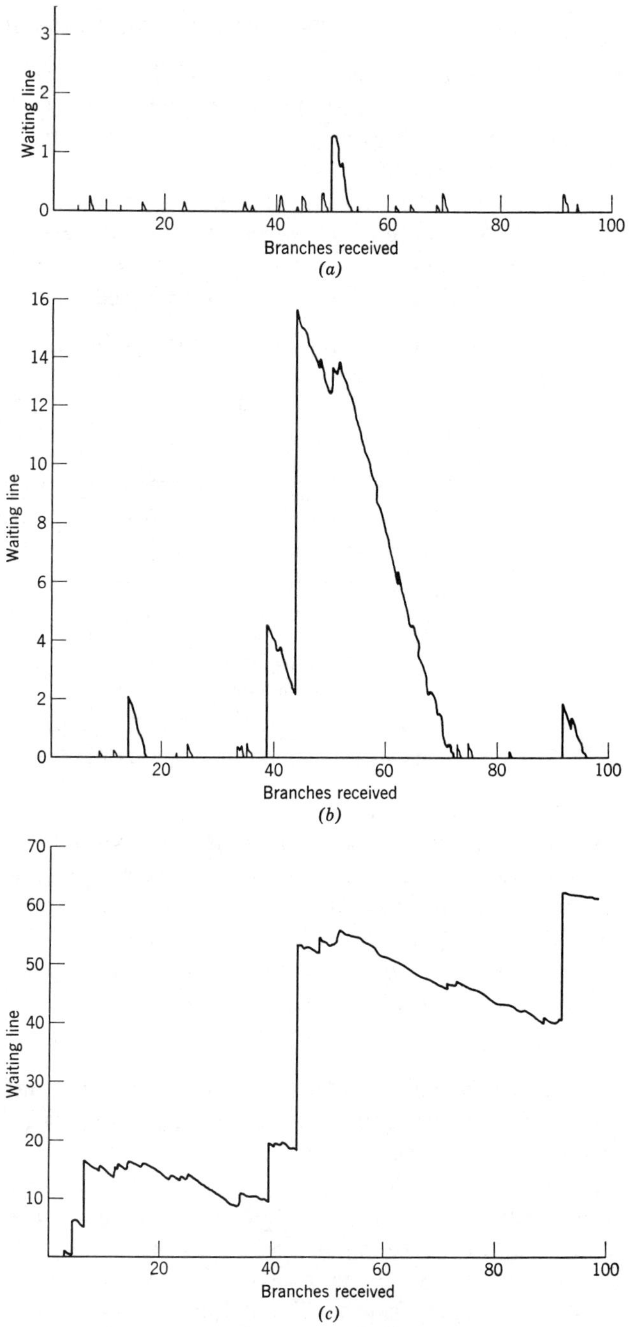

Figure 6.56 Typical waiting line behavior; $\lambda = 3\langle B\rangle$. (All scales are calibrated in thousands of branches.)
(a) $R_N/R_0' = 0.89$ (b) $R_N/R_0' = 0.96$ (c) $R_N/R_0' = 1.06$

In Figs. 6.56*a*, *b*, *c* we show the types of waiting-line behavior that result when λ is held fixed and R_N/R_0' is varied. For $R_N/R_0' = 0.89$ and $\lambda = 3\langle B\rangle$ the waiting line is usually zero, although the channel transition pattern causes an occasional long search and consequent intermittent waiting-line buildup. For $R_N/R_0' = 0.96$ the long searches are more frequent and there is danger that the residuum of one waiting-line buildup is not cleaned out before the next one occurs. For $R_N/R_0' = 1.06$ the long searches coalesce and the waiting line is unbounded.

A small overflow probability with reasonable values of Γ and λ is possible only when the waiting-line behavior is typified by Fig. 6.56*a*. In such cases, overflows are primarily attributable to difficulty in decoding isolated message input digits, and the probability of overflow interpretation of Eq. 6.117 is meaningful. With interesting values of data rate, a value of $\Gamma \gg K$ is then required if F is to be small, and *it is* Γ, *rather than the code constraint length K, that primarily governs the size of the decoder.*

As an example, assume for a BSC that

$$F = 10^{-6}$$

$$R_N = \tfrac{1}{3}$$

$$R_0' = \frac{R_N}{0.85} = 0.392 \qquad (p = 0.074)$$

$$K = 100$$

$$R = 20 \text{ kilobits/sec.}$$

From Eq. 6.117 we require

$$10^{-6} = 3^{-(1-0.85)}(\lambda\Gamma)^{-(2.9-1.7)},$$

or

$$\lambda\Gamma = 8.7 \times 10^4.$$

If it takes 7.5 μsec for a special-purpose decoding computer to search a branch, we have

$$\lambda = \frac{\text{time to receive a branch}}{\text{time to search a branch}} = \frac{0.05 \times 10^{-3}}{7.5 \times 10^{-6}} = 6.7,$$

which, from Fig. 6.50, meets the requirement $\lambda > \langle B\rangle$. Hence we need

$$\Gamma = 1.3 \times 10^4 \gg K.$$

For this example each of the received branches requires 3 bits for storage ($v = 1/R_N = 3$), and the storage of each decoded hypothesis $\hat{x}_h$ requires 1 bit. Thus the total bit storage requirement is approximately

$4\Gamma = 5.2 \times 10^4$. With magnetic-core memories, this is quite feasible. It should be noted, however, that it would be difficult to make the overflow probability very much smaller without sacrificing data rate. For example, fixing $R_N/R_0' = 0.85$ and increasing $\lambda\Gamma$ by a factor of 100 reduces F only from 10^{-6} to $10^{-8.4}$. The overflow probability is *not* an exponentially decreasing function of the decoder memory size or speed.

Probability of error. Since the overflow probability is controlled by the decoder memory size and speed of computation, it is difficult to make it extremely small. This is not true of the probability of undetectable error. Consistent with Eq. 6.110, the undetectable error probability for a Fano decoder decreases exponentially with the convolutional code constraint length K. By choosing K large enough, we can achieve an arbitrarily small error probability, provided that $R_N < R_0'$. Furthermore, in interesting cases it is possible to attain incredibly minute values of error probability—say 10^{-12}—with values of K that are orders of magnitude less than the decoder memory size Γ required to make the overflow probability reasonably small—say 10^{-6}. Thus the incremental cost of undetectable error control is not material.

Insight into the relative insignificance of the undetectable error probability is provided by reconsideration of the geometrical representation of Fig. 6.54. The shaded regions, which correspond to undetectable errors, typically occupy only a small fraction of the total number of points in the received signal space. Moreover, the shaded regions are typically far apart from one another in Hamming distance and surrounded by the open region, which corresponds to overflows. It is therefore reasonable that when the overflow probability is small the probability of undectable error is minute.

This conclusion has been verified analytically[28,78]. Not only does the undetectable error probability decay exponentially with K, but it decays with a considerably larger exponent than that given by the random-coding bound of Eq. 6.110. The reason that the bound is weak is that it neglects the possibility of overflow. The effect is interpreted geometrically in Fig. 6.57.

There is another contributant to the over-all error probability which we have not yet discussed. This contributant is the probability that an incorrect hypothesis $\hat{x}_h$ is forced out of the decoder *just before an overflow occurs*. For the Fano decoder structure considered thus far the probability of such an event is comparable to the overflow probability. Indeed, the code structure of Fig. 6.35 implies that the usual number of computations involved in a search l branches back into the code tree grows exponentially with l. Thus even moderate values of l typically force the depth of search

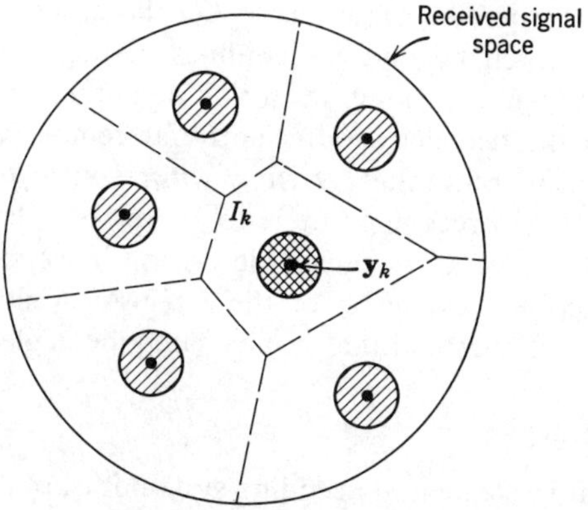

Figure 6.57 Geometrical interpretation of the weakness of the error probability bound. An undetectable error occurs when $\mathbf{y}_k$ is transmitted if $\mathbf{r}'$ lies in one of the shaded regions. On the other hand, the bound on $\overline{P[\mathcal{E}_h]}$ estimates the probability that $\mathbf{r}'$ lies outside the decision region I_k that is applicable in the absence of overflow.

pointer rapidly to the right, so that overflows occur because the decoder is uncertain of the identity of the hypothesized message bits at the extreme right end of the $\hat{x}$-register. Since errors of this type accompany overflows, they are called *detectable*.

Decoder release of detectable errors can be controlled by modifying the decoder in a simple way: we need only extend the $\hat{x}$-register several code constraint lengths—say $3K$ digits—beyond the end of the decoder r-register, as shown in Fig. 6.58. The effectiveness of the procedure rests on the fact that, if the decoder never needs to search back to an $\hat{x}_h$ that passes beyond the end of the r-register, $\hat{x}_h$ must either be correct or

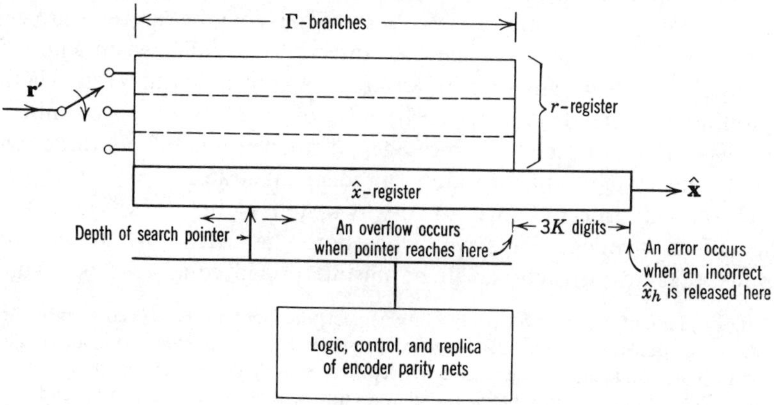

Figure 6.58 Modification of Fano decoder to incorporate error detection.

correspond to an undetectable error. On the other hand, if the decoder does need to search beyond the confines of the r-register, an overflow will occur. When the point at which hypothesized bits are actually released from the decoder is sufficiently far removed from the overflow position, the probability that overflow will result *before* enough time has elapsed for an incorrect hypothesis to be released becomes comparable to the probability of an undetectable error. If we stop decoding at the instant of overflow, extension of the $\hat{x}$-register yields an over-all error probability so infinitesimal that it may safely be neglected.

Two-Way Strategies

In an operative sequential decoding system it is, of course, not sufficient that the error probability be negligibly small; provision must also be made to start decoding again automatically after each overflow. In a one-way communication system this can be arranged by periodically interrupting the message input bit stream to the transmitter's encoder, say after every block of L bits, and arbitrarily inserting K zeros. The decoder can then always resynchronize within L data bits after an overflow and thus continue on with its work by discarding the undecodable block.

On the one hand, for $K = 100$, $F = 10^{-6}$, $\Gamma = 10^4$, and $L = 10^3$ such a one-way strategy implies only a 10% reduction in effective transmitted data rate—that is, reduction by the factor $(L - K)/L$. But on the other hand, from the union bound there is a probability of approximately† $LF = 10^{-3}$ that all or part of each block of $L = 10^3$ message bits will be discarded, hence *not decoded at all*, even though blocks that are decoded are almost certainly correct. In many applications an operating characteristic of this type would not be acceptable.

When communication is *two-way*, a more attractive remedy to the overflow problem is available. A few "service" bits can be inserted into each of the two data streams at specified intervals, as indicated in Fig. 6.59. The service bits originating at terminal A inform terminal B whether decoding at A has been stopped because of overflow. If so, terminal B retransmits the undecodable message. If not, terminal B continues with new traffic. Each terminal follows an identical strategy.

The crucial aspect of such a two-way system is that the service bits are themselves encoded. Thus even when both channels are noisy the probability that an instruction will be misinterpreted equals the probability

† This estimate of the overflow probability neglects the fact that the procedure introduces a statistical dependence between overflows: when resynchronizing after an overflow on one block of L digits, the decoder's depth of search pointer is set initially to the beginning of the succeeding block rather than all the way back to the input end of the decoder memory.

of decoding error and may largely be ignored. There remains, however, the probability that a service bit will not be decoded at all—and since this is related to the overflow probability it may *not* be ignored.

The difficulty is resolved by adopting a fail-safe strategy wherein each terminal when confronted with an undecodable block always acts exactly as if it had in fact decoded a request for retransmission. Matters can be

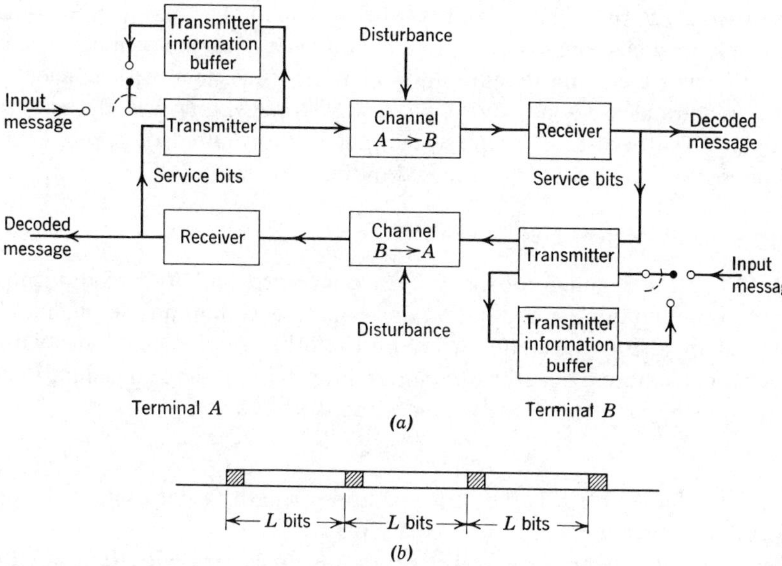

Figure 6.59 (*a*) A two-way communication system. The transmitter buffers store the encoder input data streams for possible retransmission. It is assumed that the input message at each terminal is available on demand. (*b*) Structure of encoder input data stream. The shaded intervals represent service bits; the open intervals represent customer traffic.

arranged[88] so that the entire data stream at each encoder input is decoded in proper sequence and without block elisions, provided that undetectable errors do not occur. Thus the one-way problem of undecodable blocks is circumvented. The major incremental cost incurred is the provision at each transmitter of a slow speed memory in which to store the message input traffic over a time interval equal to the combined round-trip propagation and data-processing time, say T.

Each repeat-request involves the "loss" (for communication purposes) of the combined round-trip time; that is, the transmitter re-encodes all input data that it has transmitted during the preceding T-sec interval. Since the relative frequency of repeat-requests is F, the average fraction of time remaining is $(1 - TF)$. As long as F can be made small enough that $TF < 0.1$, the effective rate at which data is communicated (in bits per second) is not seriously reduced by overflows. A safeguard against undetectable service-bit errors can be provided by periodic resynchronization after every 10^6 or 10^7 transmitted bits.

The need for a two-way system appears to be unavoidable if communication that is both accurate and efficient is to be maintained over actual communication channels. The parameters of most channels are time-variant, so that their reliability functions fluctuate. A system without feedback must be designed to operate reliably at a data rate commensurate with the worst channel condition, which is inconsistent with efficiency when conditions are good. With a two-way strategy, however, the service bits may also be used to request changes in transmitted data rate. An example of such a system is discussed in the next section.

Experimental System Design

In Chapters 5 and 6 we have been concerned with the relationship between modulation-demodulation and coding-decoding on the one hand and system performance/complexity on the other. For block codes with maximum likelihood decoding the interrelations (excluding considerations of equipment complexity) are evidenced in the bound

$$\overline{P[\mathcal{E}]} < 2^{-N[R_0' - R_N]}, \qquad (6.118a)$$

in which $N = K/R_N$, K is the code constraint length in data bits, and R_N is the data rate in bits per transmitted symbol.

With bandlimited channels, we are usually concerned with data rate in bits per second. If D denotes the number of orthogonal building-block signals that can be propagated over the channel per second, Eq. 6.118a can be rewritten in the form

$$\overline{P[\mathcal{E}]} < 2^{-T[DR_0' - R]}, \qquad (6.118b)$$

in which $R = DR_N$ is the data rate in bits per second and $T = K/R$ is the block duration in seconds. Equation 6.118b implies that an arbitrarily small error probability can be obtained by making T large enough, provided, of course, that $R < DR_0'$. In order to communicate at a high data rate, we wish to design the modulation-demodulation system in such a way that DR_0' is large.

When we consider sequential decoding and include decoder complexity in the formulation of a two-way-system design problem, the interrelationships are somewhat modified. By choosing T large enough, we obtain as small a decoded probability of error as desired; it is sensible to choose T large enough so that the probability of error is truly negligible. The primary design problem is to make TF small, where as before T is the combined round-trip propagation and data-processing time and F is the relative frequency of overflows.

In this connection also it is the value of DR_0' that determines the allowable data rate. Since

$$\frac{R_N}{R_0'} = \frac{R}{DR_0'}, \tag{6.119}$$

the frequency of overflow estimate of Eq. 6.117 can be rewritten in the form

$$F \approx 3^{-(1-R/DR_0')}[\lambda\Gamma]^{-[2.9-2(R/DR_0')]}. \tag{6.120}$$

Thus the value of $\lambda\Gamma$ required to obtain a stated value of F decreases as DR_0' is increased with R held fixed.

When sequential decoding is to be used, the value of DR_0' is a fundamental measure of the effectiveness of the modulation-demodulation scheme that produces it. An appropriate design philosophy is to maximize DR_0', subject to constraints on the complexity of instrumentation. For the simple case of a bandlimited additive white Gaussian noise channel we have seen in Chapter 5 that there are unavoidable theoretical limits to the maximum achievable values of both D and R_0'. The complexity of instrumentation will increase if we attempt to push either of these parameters too close to its theoretical limit. One must settle for a design that approaches the limit of diminishing returns.

The maximization of DR_0' with actual communication channels will usually be complicated by the lack of an adequate mathematical model of the channel disturbance. An experimental investigation of how one might proceed has been made in connection with a toll-quality long-distance voice telephone line. The experiment, conducted by the MIT Lincoln Laboratory,[54] provides an instructive example of the interplay between the various design factors introduced in Chapters 5 and 6.

Intersymbol interference. With toll telephone lines, the main disturbance in propagation is not additive Gaussian noise but intersymbol interference: if we try to transmit a narrow pulse such as that shown in Fig. 6.60*a*, we actually receive a smeared pulse of longer duration such as that shown in Fig. 6.60*b*.† The smearing is primarily attributable to the fact that the phase of the telephone-line transfer function is not a linear function of frequency. The result is that different frequency groups in the transmitted spectrum propagate with different velocities and therefore arrive at the receiver with different delays. Although the 3-db amplitude

† In this discussion we presume that the telephone line is terminated in such a way that the input and output signals have low-pass spectra. How this may be accomplished will be studied in Chapter 7.

bandwidth of the telephone channel used in the experiment was 3.4 kc, the unequalized bandwidth affording delay variations of less than $\pm\frac{1}{2}$ msec was only 1.9 kc.

Intersymbol interference may be controlled to some extent by careful phase equalization of the line and careful shaping of the transmitted pulse.

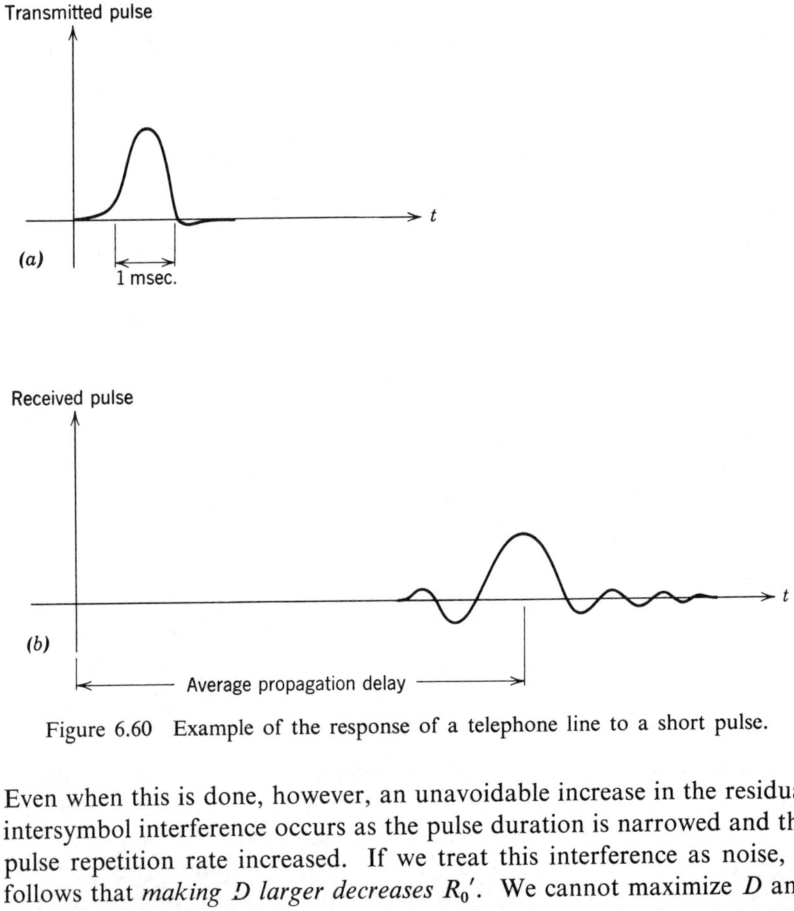

Figure 6.60 Example of the response of a telephone line to a short pulse.

Even when this is done, however, an unavoidable increase in the residual intersymbol interference occurs as the pulse duration is narrowed and the pulse repetition rate increased. If we treat this interference as noise, it follows that *making D larger decreases* R_0'. We cannot maximize D and R_0' separately.

Signaling alphabets. Toll-quality telephone lines are normally characterized by a high signal-to-noise ratio. Given adequate suppression of intersymbol interference, we therefore anticipate (from Fig. 5.17) that the transmitter alphabet should provide many more than two amplitude levels if the bound parameter R_0 afforded by an unquantized receiver is to be maximized. We also anticipate from Fig. 6.26 that the quantized parameter R_0' should be substantially equivalent to R_0 if the receiver output samples are quantized in such a way that the multiamplitude transmitter and decoder alphabets are the same. The problem of alphabet design then reduces to the determination (as a function of D) of how many signal amplitude levels should be used.

For alternative choices of D and number of amplitude levels, A, empirical estimates of the resulting transition probabilities between letters of the input and output alphabets can be made from experimental measurements. An optimal design procedure is then to calculate corresponding values of R_0' from Eq. 6.62 and to choose that A and D for which DR_0' is maximum.

Decoding distance. We now consider the determination of a suitable distance function for the decoder to use in testing possible transmitted signal hypotheses against the received data. For Gaussian noise we would use Euclidean distance and for BSC noise we would use Hamming distance. In each case the choice is dictated first by the optimality of using a distance measure that is monotonically related to a posteriori probability and second by the relative ease of decoder instrumentation.

In our telephone-line experiment a decoder that used the empirical estimates of the transition probabilities to compute the a posteriori probability of the received signal, given any transmitted signal hypothesis, would be most desirable from the point of view of performance. The value of R_0' would then be that given by Eq. 6.62, and in principle we could even contemplate designing the coder to use the transmitter alphabet letters in proportions that maximize R_0'. In practice, however, the implementation of such a coder and decoder would be extremely difficult. We seek an acceptable engineering compromise instead.

Fortunately, it is not necessary to use an optimum system in order to obtain good results; in engineering design one seeks not so much to be optimum as to avoid crippling nonoptimalities. In the particular cascade of modulator/telephone line/demodulator with which we are concerned, the dominant characteristic of the over-all disturbance is that small errors in received amplitude level are much more prevalent than large ones. We therefore anticipate that an appropriate, albeit non-optimum, decoding distance function might be the cumulative sum of the absolute voltage difference between received and hypothesized signals. For example, if the quantized received pulse amplitudes are

$$\mathbf{r}' = (r_1', r_2', \ldots, r_N') \tag{6.121a}$$

and the signal hypothesis is

$$\mathbf{s}_i = (s_{i1}, s_{i2}, \ldots, s_{iN}), \tag{6.121b}$$

for decoding purposes we may define the *distance* between $\mathbf{r}'$ and $\mathbf{s}_i$ as

$$d_i \triangleq \sum_{j=1}^{N} |r_j' - s_{ij}|. \tag{6.121c}$$

The distance function of Eq. 6.121c is monotonically related to the logarithm of the a posteriori probability when all signals are equally likely and the channel disturbance is an additive noise vector $\mathbf{n} = (n_1, n_2, \ldots n_N)$ with statistically independent, exponentially distributed components; that is, when

$$p_{n_j}(\alpha) = \frac{b}{2} e^{-b|\alpha|}; \qquad j = 1, 2, \ldots, N, \quad b > 0, \tag{6.122a}$$

and

$$p_{\mathbf{n}} = \prod_{j=1}^{N} p_{n_j}. \tag{6.122b}$$

Of course, our cascade of modulator/telephone line/demodulator cannot be described precisely in this way. The discrepancy, however, was not too great for the several different choices of multiamplitude signaling alphabets and values of D tested in the experiment. Most important of all, the distance function of Eq. 6.121c has the advantage of being easy to implement in a decoder, and was therefore adopted.

Experimental results. Once a suitable decoding distance function is adopted, a convenient and reasonable compromise method for estimating R_0' is to fit the empirical data to the density function appropriate to that distance function rather than to insert the empirical data directly into Eq. 6.62. (In general, less empirical data is necessary.) In the telephone-line experiment the exponential density function of Eq. 6.122 was used, and the parameter b was adjusted as a function of D and the alphabet size to give the best match to the corresponding experimental data. The resulting set of exponential density functions was then used to calculate an *estimate* of the actual error exponent DR_0' for each choice of D and number of signaling levels. With the pulse waveshape and phase-equalization techniques used in the experiment,† the estimate of DR_0' was found to be maximum for $D = 3000$ pulses/sec and a signaling alphabet comprising 32 different amplitude levels, and these choices were adopted. At this maximum the relative frequency of receiving the same signal level as the

† The pulse waveshape used in the experiment was adjusted to minimize intersymbol interference for each value of D by observation of the received waveform. This was possible because both ends of the telephone line terminated at the same laboratory bench. Other techniques of interference suppression would be necessary in practical applications. See for example F. K. Becker et al., "Automatic Equalization for Digital Communication," *Proc. IEEE*, **53,** No. 1, 96–97, January 1965.

one actually transmitted was only 0.9. A modulation-demodulation system suitable for use in a coded communication system is not necessarily suitable for a system in which coding is not used, and conversely.

The convolutional coder used in the telephone-line experiment had a constraint length of $K = 60$. It could operate at three data rates: $R_N = \frac{1}{5}$,

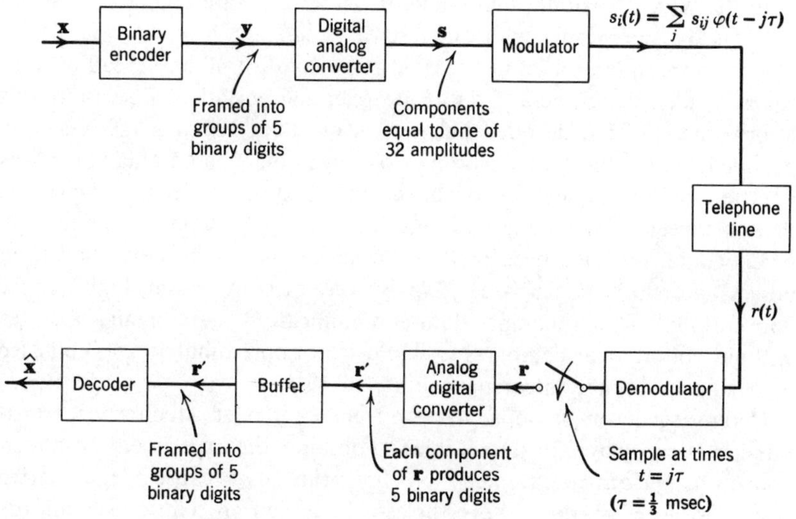

Figure 6.61 Simplified block diagram of telephone line experiment.

$\frac{2}{5}$, and $\frac{3}{5}$. The binary output sequence from the coder was framed into groups of 5 digits, each of which corresponded to 1, 2, or 3 input bits, the number depending on R_N. Each successive group of 5 digits was fed in parallel to a binary-analog converter and specified one of 32 possible amplitudes as output. The resulting sequence of voltage levels was used to modulate successive signal pulses.

At the receiver the procedure was reversed. A block diagram of the over-all system is shown in Fig. 6.61. The received signal $r(t)$ was sampled in synchronism with the transmitted pulses, and the resulting sequence of samples was fed to an analog-binary converter. Each analog sample was quantized into one of 32 levels, and the 5 resulting binary digits were passed in parallel into a storage buffer.

The sequential decoder used in this experiment antedated the Fano search algorithm, and the buffer was separate from the decoder itself. As each successive 5-digit data group was decoded and shifted out of the decoder r-register the oldest data group stored in the buffer was shifted in. The buffer and r-register contained 3000 and 300 bits, respectively.

The data rate R_N at which the equipment operated was controlled by the decoder. Whenever decoding was too difficult or buffer overflows occurred, the decoder automatically sent a service bit to the encoder requesting a decrease in data rate. Conversely, whenever the decoding was too easy, the decoder automatically requested an increase in R_N. The data rate was observed to fluctuate primarily between $R_N = \frac{3}{5}$ and $R_N = \frac{2}{5}$, with occasional reductions to $R_N = \frac{1}{5}$. Rate changes occurred with an average frequency of one in 6 or 7 sec.

The entire apparatus was operated for a total of 40 hr, spread over all times of day. The average data rate over the period of operation was approximately 7500 decoded bits/sec. More than 10^9 message bits were decoded before the first decoding error was made, and this error was detected before the next few decoded digits had been released. Since the delay between bit decoding and bit release was only K bits, this decoding error would not have been made if an additional $2K$-bit delay had been added onto the decoder $\hat{x}$-register. By way of comparison, high quality conventional telephone-line data-communication equipment operates without coding over comparable channels at approximately 2400 bits/sec with an approximate error probability of 10^{-5}.

Coding seems most appropriate on channels over which good transmission is expensive (or impossible) to obtain; the experiment described above was performed on a telephone line primarily because of the relative ease of experimentation. Nevertheless, the design procedure used affords insight into the compromises that arise in the engineering of coded communication systems.

APPENDIX 6A EXTENSION AND ANALYSIS OF THE FANO ALGORITHM

In this appendix we obtain upper bounds on quantities that estimate the average number of computations and the probability of error for the Fano sequential decoding algorithm. Before doing so, it will be useful to observe that the algorithm may be applied with no essential change to tree codes in which u, rather than 2, branches diverge from each node and to channels far more general than the BSC. We limit attention here to discrete memoryless channels (see Fig. 6.17) with A input letters $\{a_i\}$, Q output letters $\{b_j\}$, and transition probabilities $\{q_{ij}\}$ $(i = 1, 2, \ldots, A;\ j = 1, 2, \ldots, Q)$.

We shall consider convolutional codes in which each branch of the code tree encompasses v channel input letters. The rate, R_N, for a tree with u branches per node and v channel symbols per branch is defined as

$$R_N \triangleq \frac{1}{v} \log_2 u \qquad \text{bits per channel symbol,} \tag{6A.1}$$

which is a generalization of Eq. 6.82. The code constraint length, K, is still defined as the span of code tree branches affected by any one coder input symbol. Examples of the type of code tree to be considered are shown in Fig. 6A.1.

To adapt the Fano decoding algorithm to these more general channels and tree codes, it is only necessary to generalize the tilted distance function of Eq. 6.109. Letting $y_k{}^*$ denote the kth symbol of a hypothesized transmitted sequence lv channel input symbols long and letting $r_k{}'$ denote the

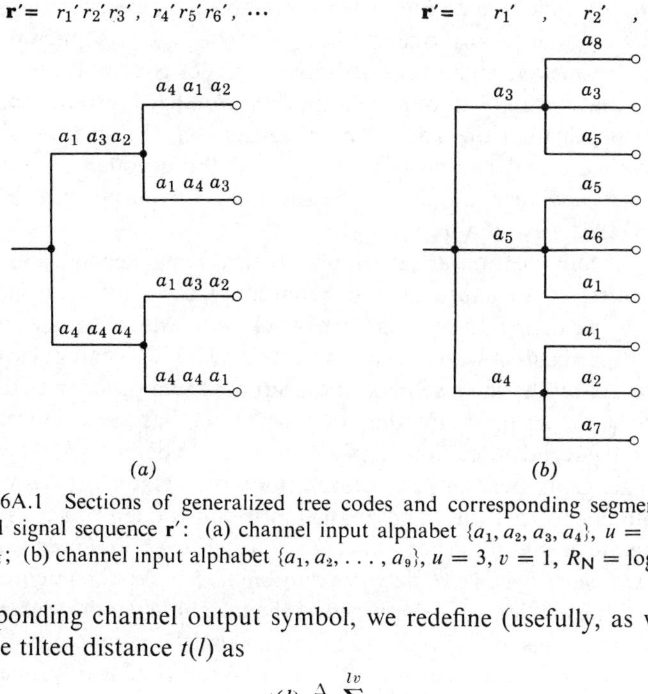

Figure 6A.1 Sections of generalized tree codes and corresponding segment of the received signal sequence $\mathbf{r}'$: (a) channel input alphabet $\{a_1, a_2, a_3, a_4\}$, $u = 2$, $v = 3$, $R_N = \frac{1}{3}$; (b) channel input alphabet $\{a_1, a_2, \ldots, a_9\}$, $u = 3$, $v = 1$, $R_N = \log_2 3$.

corresponding channel output symbol, we redefine (usefully, as we shall see) the tilted distance $t(l)$ as

$$t(l) \triangleq \sum_{k=1}^{lv} z_k, \tag{6A.2}$$

where

$$z_k \triangleq -\log_2\left[\frac{P[r_k' \mid y_k^*]}{f(r_k')}\right] + R_N. \tag{6A.3}$$

Here $f(r_k')$ serves as a scaling factor with value specified when r_k' is b_j by

$$f(b_j) = f_j \triangleq \sum_{i=1}^{A} p_i q_{ij}; \qquad j = 1, 2, \ldots, Q, \tag{6A.4}$$

in which $\{p_i\}$ is a set of non-negative numbers that sum to 1. We shall soon introduce a random coding argument in which $\{p_i\}$ is the set of probabilities with which channel input letters are assigned to codewords.

In this case f_j is identified as the a priori probability of the channel output letter b_j. Note that

$$\sum_{j=1}^{Q} f_j = 1. \tag{6A.5}$$

Error Probability

Extension of the Fano algorithm to the class of situations considered here affects neither the flow diagrams of Figs. 6.44 and 6.46 nor the decoder block diagram structure of Fig. 6.48, although each r-register stage must now be able to store any one of the Q letters $\{b_j\}$. As mentioned in Section 6.5, however, analysis of an actual decoder is complicated by the possibility that the algorithm may require a search back into the code tree of greater depth than the size of the r-register—in conjuncture with the data arrival rate and computational speed of the decoder—can accommodate. We obviate the difficulty by assuming for purposes of analysis that the r-register is infinite.

A second complication arises from statistical dependencies due to the sliding constraint structure of a convolutional code. We obviate this difficulty by resorting to an analytical trick with which we are already familiar. Specifically, we consider an error event $\mathcal{E}_h$ analogous to the event denoted by the same symbol in the suboptimum decoder analysis of Section 6.3. We again define the hth *starting node* as the code-tree node designated by decoder decisions $\hat{x}_1, \hat{x}_2, \ldots, \hat{x}_{h-1}$. In defining $\mathcal{E}_h$ we assume that a magic genie positions the search node pointer on the *correct* hth starting node and that the Fano algorithm is constrained to act as if this node were the origin of the code tree. *Thus the decoder is allowed to search forward, but never backward, from the starting node.* We then define $\mathcal{E}_h$ as the event that decision $\hat{x}_h$, determined at the instant when the search node pointer first reaches any one of the u^K nodes that lie K branches beyond the hth starting node, is incorrect. We shall bound the mean probability, $\overline{P[\mathcal{E}_h]}$, of the event $\mathcal{E}_h$ over an ensemble of convolutional codes. The significance of the bound with respect to an actual decoder is discussed at the end of this section.

Labeling of nodes in the incorrect subset for $\hat{x}_h$. The derivations that follow specialize a method of analysis devised and used by Stiglitz and Yudkin to obtain more general results.† The derivations are simplified by introducing additional notation. We first define the *incorrect subset* for $\hat{x}_h$ as the set of all nodes connected to the *correct* hth starting node via one of the $u - 1$ incorrect branches diverging therefrom, plus

† I. G. Stiglitz, and H. L. Yudkin, *Probabilistic Decoding*, to be published.

the starting node itself. (See Fig. 6A.2.) We say that a node in the incorrect subset for $\hat{x}_h$ is at *depth* ℓ if it is connected to the hth starting node by a path containing ℓ branches. Thus there is 1 node (the starting node) at depth 0; $u - 1$ nodes at depth 1; $(u - 1)u$ at depth 2; and $(u - 1)u^{\ell-1}$ at depth ℓ, all $\ell > 0$. We observe from Eq. 6A.1 that the number of nodes, say N_ℓ, in the incorrect subset at depth ℓ satisfies

$$N_\ell \leqslant 2^{\ell v R_N}; \qquad \ell = 0, 1, \ldots. \tag{6A.6}$$

It will be convenient to label nodes in the incorrect subset for $\hat{x}_h$ by an ordered pair of integers (ℓ, n). The number ℓ indicates the depth of the

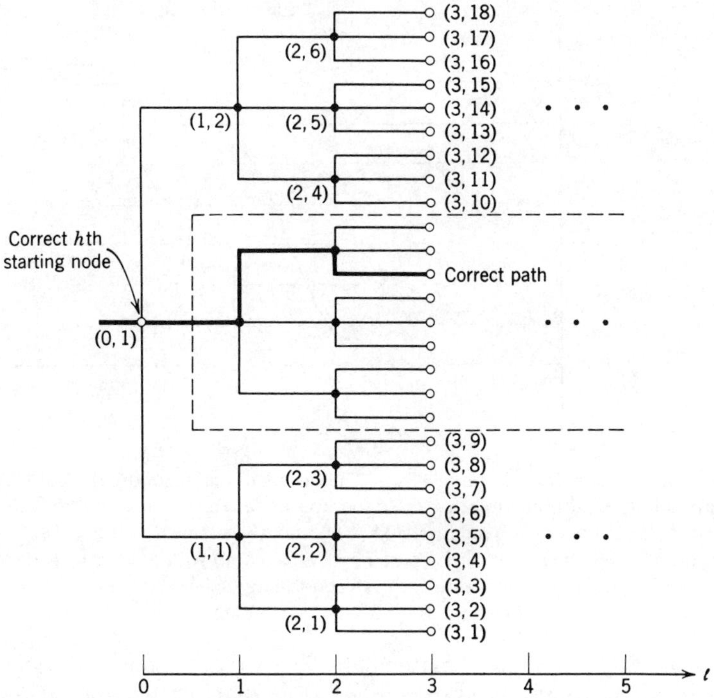

Figure 6A.2 Section of incorrect subset for $\hat{x}_h$. If the heavy line indicates the correct (transmitted) path, the incorrect subset for the decision $\hat{x}_h$ consists of all nodes outside the dashed line. These nodes are labeled as shown.

node; the number n indicates the node's vertical position in the code tree relative to all N_ℓ nodes of depth ℓ. The labeling is illustrated in Fig. 6A.2.

Bound on $\mathrm{P}[\mathcal{E}_h]$. For any particular code and transmitted path we define $\mathrm{P}[\mathcal{E}_h]$ as the conditional probability that $\hat{x}_h$ is incorrect at the instant that the algorithm first reaches a search node K branches beyond the hth starting node, given that the genie initially positions the search node pointer on the correct starting node and that searching behind the starting node is prohibited. We observe from Fig. 6A.3 that the starting conditions—which we always assume hereafter—imply that the event $\mathcal{E}_h$ cannot occur unless some node at depth K in the incorrect subset for $\hat{x}_h$ has t-value satisfying the lowest threshold, say T_c, simultaneously satisfied by all nodes along the segment of the correct path extending K branches beyond the hth starting node. Otherwise, the algorithm requires the decoder to trace out the correct path in preference to any of these incorrect paths.

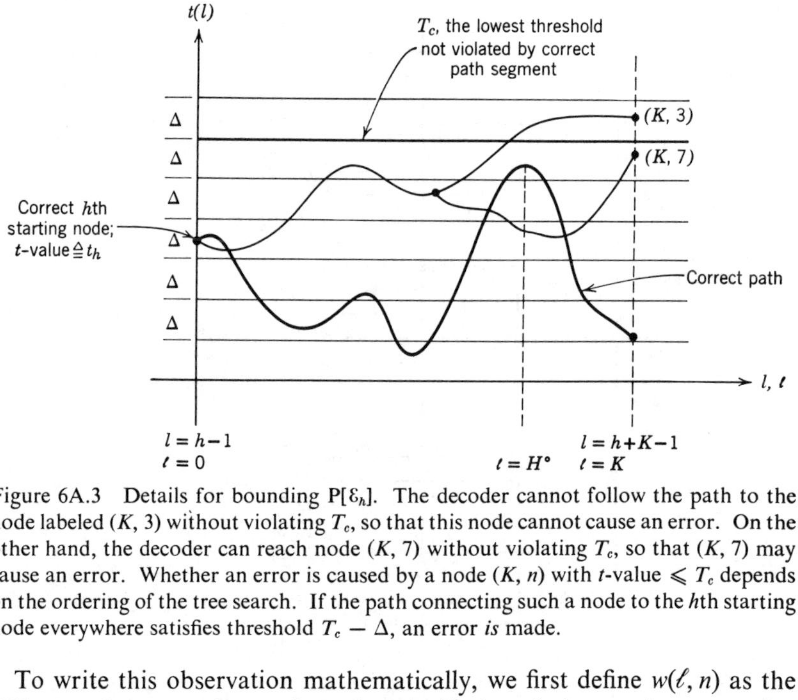

Figure 6A.3 Details for bounding P[$\mathcal{E}_h$]. The decoder cannot follow the path to the node labeled (K, 3) without violating T_c, so that this node cannot cause an error. On the other hand, the decoder can reach node (K, 7) without violating T_c, so that (K, 7) may cause an error. Whether an error is caused by a node (K, n) with t-value $\leqslant T_c$ depends on the ordering of the tree search. If the path connecting such a node to the hth starting node everywhere satisfies threshold $T_c - \Delta$, an error *is* made.

To write this observation mathematically, we first define $w(\ell, n)$ as the difference between the t-value of node (ℓ, n) and the maximum t-value along the K-branch extension of the correct path. Let H° denote the branch depth at which this maximum occurs, let z'_k denote the kth increment to the t-value of node (ℓ, n), and let z°_k denote the kth increment to the t-value along the correct path. From Eq. 6A.2,

$$w(\ell, n) = \left[t_h + \sum_{k=1}^{\ell v} z'_k\right] - \left[t_h + \sum_{k=1}^{H^\circ v} z^\circ_k\right]$$

$$= \sum_{k=1}^{\ell v} z'_k - \sum_{k=1}^{H^\circ v} z^\circ_k, \tag{6A.7}$$

in which t_h is the t-value of the starting node and the index k counts symbols to the right of this node. The range of H° is $0 \leqslant H^\circ \leqslant K$. (If $H^\circ = 0$, the second sum on the right-hand side of Eq. 6A.7 is identically zero.)

It is clear from Fig. 6A.3 that one of the N_K incorrect nodes at depth K, say node (K, n), cannot satisfy T_c unless $w(K, n) < \Delta$. Invoking the familiar union bound, we have

$$\begin{aligned} \mathrm{P}[\mathcal{E}_h] &\leqslant \mathrm{P}[w(K, 1) < \Delta \quad \text{or} \quad w(K, 2) < \Delta \quad \text{or} \cdots \text{or} \quad w(K, N_K) < \Delta] \\ &\leqslant \sum_{n=1}^{N_K} \mathrm{P}[w(K, n) < \Delta]. \end{aligned} \tag{6A.8}$$

Bounding $\mathrm{P}[w(\ell, n) < \Delta]$. As a preliminary to overbounding the right-hand side of Eq. 6A.8, we account for ignorance of the specific value of H° in the definition of $w(\ell, n)$, Eq. 6A.7, by the following argument. Let $w(\ell, n, H)$ be the value of $w(\ell, n)$ in Eq. 6A.7 when H° is replaced by H, $0 \leqslant H \leqslant K$. Then

$$\begin{aligned} \mathrm{P}[w(\ell, n) < \Delta] = \mathrm{P}[w(\ell, n, 0) < \Delta \quad &\text{or} \quad w(\ell, n, 1) < \Delta \quad \text{or} \\ \ldots \quad \text{or} \quad & w(\ell, n, K) < \Delta] \leqslant \sum_{H=0}^{K} P_H, \end{aligned} \tag{6A.9a}$$

in which we define

$$P_H \triangleq \mathrm{P}[w(\ell, n, H) < \Delta]. \tag{6A.9b}$$

An upper bound on P_H can be obtained by using two techniques, Chernoff bounding and random coding, with which we are already familiar. Letting $f(\quad)$ denote the unit step function (as in Eq. 6.55a and sequel), we observe from Eq. 6A.7 (with H° replaced by H) that

$$\begin{aligned} P_H &= \overline{f[\Delta - w(\ell, n, H)]} \\ &\leqslant \overline{\exp\,[\lambda\{\Delta - w(\ell, n, H)\}]} \\ &= e^{\lambda\Delta}\, \overline{\exp\left[-\lambda\left(\sum_{k=1}^{\ell v} z_k' - \sum_{k=1}^{Hv} z_k^\circ\right)\right]}; \qquad \lambda \geqslant 0. \end{aligned} \tag{6A.10}$$

The expectation in Eq. 6A.10 is over the ensemble of channel noise sequences. To simplify the expression further we use random coding and evaluate the mean, $\bar{P}_H$, of P_H over an appropriate ensemble of codes. In particular, we consider generalized convolutional encoders like that in Fig. 6A.4 and the ensemble of codes obtained when each lead of the connection matrix is statistically independent and equally likely to have weight $0, 1, \ldots, u - 1$. We assume that each coder in the ensemble uses

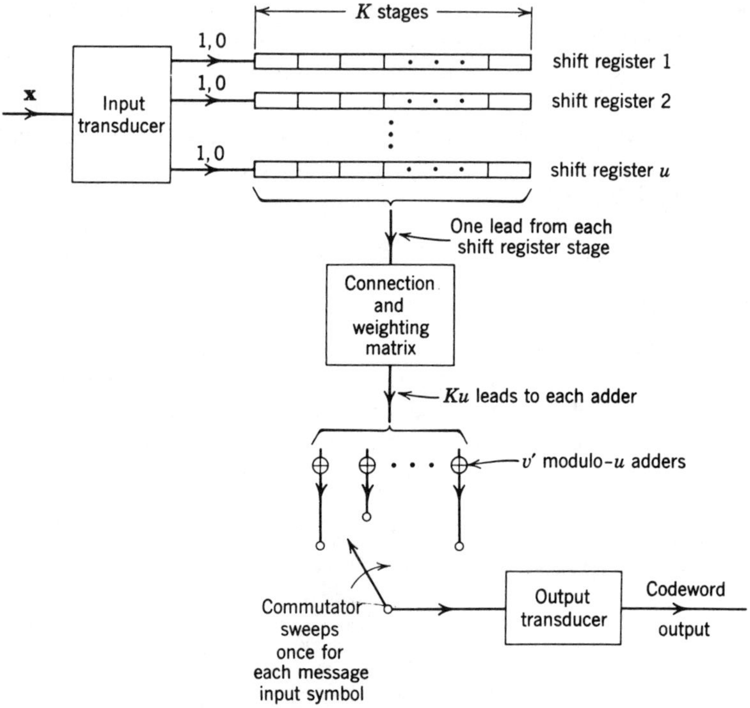

Figure 6A.4 Generalized convolutional coder. The input message **x** has components $\{x_h\}$ which can be any one of a set of u symbols. The input transducer identifies each x_h in turn and applies a 1 to the kth binary shift register if and only if x_h is the kth symbol in the set. Each of the Ku shift-register stages is connected to each of the v' modulo-u adders by a line that multiplies the stage's content by a number which can be preassigned independently as any one of the integers $0, 1, \ldots, u - 1$. Thus each x_h produces a sequence of v' integers at the commutator output. The output transducer breaks the sequence into groups of length v'/v and maps each group into one of the channel input letters $\{a_i\}$, as described in connection with Fig. 6.8. The number of adders, v', is taken to be large enough so that the $\{a_i\}$ can be generated with the desired probabilities $\{p_i\}$. (A more efficient coder design utilizes only μ K-stage shift registers, $\log_2 u < \mu \leqslant 1 + \log_2 u$.)

an identical transducer, so designed that the channel input letters $\{a_i\}$ are assigned with probabilities $\{p_i\}$, $i = 1, 2, \ldots, A$. For this ensemble the correct path and any incorrect subset path to depth $\ell \leqslant K$ are statistically independent. Moreover, by letting y_k° denote the kth symbol along the correct path, r_k denote the kth received symbol and y_k' denote the kth symbol along the (incorrect) path leading to node (ℓ, n), we have

$$P[y_k^\circ = a_i, r_k = b_j, y_k' = a_h] = p_i q_{ij} p_h; \qquad i, h = 1, 2, \ldots, A \quad j = 1, 2, \ldots, Q, \qquad (6A.11)$$

independently for each value of k. Taking an overhead bar (now and hereafter) to mean expectation also with respect to the specified code ensemble yields

$$\bar{P}_H \leqslant e^{\lambda\Delta} \overline{\exp\left[-\lambda\left(\sum_{k=1}^{\ell v} z_k' - \sum_{k=1}^{Hv} z_k^\circ\right)\right]}$$

$$= \begin{cases} e^{\lambda\Delta}\left[\prod_{k=1}^{Hv} \overline{\exp\{\lambda(z_k^\circ - z_k')\}}\right]\left[\prod_{k=Hv+1}^{\ell v} \overline{\exp(-\lambda z_k')}\right]; & H \leqslant \ell \leqslant K \\ e^{\lambda\Delta}\left[\prod_{k=1}^{\ell v} \overline{\exp\{\lambda(z_k^\circ - z_k')\}}\right]\left[\prod_{k=\ell v+1}^{Hv} \overline{\exp(\lambda z_k^\circ)}\right]; & H > \ell. \end{cases} \qquad (6A.12)$$

In writing Eq. 6A.12 in factored form, we have exploited the fact that the probability assignment of Eq. 6A.11 is made with statistical independence for different k.

Evaluation of factors. Evaluation of the individual averages in Eq. 6A.12 is straight-forward. By using Eq. 6A.11 and the generalized tilted distance definition of Eq. 6A.3, we have

$$\overline{\exp[\lambda(z_k^\circ - z_k')]} = \sum_{i=1}^{A}\sum_{j=1}^{Q}\sum_{h=1}^{A} p_i q_{ij} p_h \exp\left[\lambda\left(-\log_2\frac{q_{ij}}{f_j} + \log_2\frac{q_{hj}}{f_j}\right)\right].$$

Setting $\lambda = \frac{1}{2}\log_e 2$ (which is positive), a choice which simplifies the analysis, yields

$$\begin{aligned}\overline{\exp[\lambda(z_k^\circ - z_k')]} &= \sum_i\sum_j\sum_h p_i q_{ij} p_h \left(\frac{q_{hj}}{q_{ij}}\right)^{1/2} \\ &= \sum_{j=1}^{Q}\left[\sum_{i=1}^{A} p_i\sqrt{q_{ij}}\right]^2 \\ &= 2^{-R_0'}; \qquad \lambda = \tfrac{1}{2}\log_e 2,\end{aligned} \qquad (6A.13)$$

where R_0' is the exponential bound parameter defined in Eq. 6.62b.

The remaining factors in Eq. 6A.12 are evaluated in much the same way. First

$$\begin{aligned}\overline{\exp[\lambda z_k^\circ]} &= \sum_{i=1}^{A}\sum_{j=1}^{Q} p_i q_{ij} \exp\left[\lambda\left(-\log_2\frac{q_{ij}}{f_j} + R_N\right)\right] \\ &= 2^{\frac{1}{2}R_N}\sum_i\sum_j p_i\sqrt{q_{ij}}\sqrt{f_j}; \qquad \lambda = \tfrac{1}{2}\log_e 2.\end{aligned}$$

A straightforward extension of the Schwarz inequality, Eq. 4.64, to multidimensional vectors **a** and **b** yields

$$\sum_{j=1}^{Q} a_j b_j \leqslant \left[\sum_{j=1}^{Q} a_j^2\right]^{1/2}\left[\sum_{j=1}^{Q} b_j^2\right]^{1/2}.$$

Thus

$$\begin{aligned}
\overline{\exp[\lambda z_k^\circ]} &= 2^{\frac{1}{2}R_N}\sum_{j=1}^{Q}\sqrt{f_j}\left[\sum_{i=1}^{A}p_i\sqrt{q_{ij}}\right] \\
&\leqslant 2^{\frac{1}{2}R_N}\left[\sum_{j=1}^{Q}f_j\right]^{1/2}\left[\sum_{j=1}^{Q}\left(\sum_{i=1}^{A}p_i\sqrt{q_{ij}}\right)^2\right]^{1/2} \\
&= 2^{\frac{1}{2}[R_N-R_0']},
\end{aligned} \tag{6A.14}$$

in which we have used Eq. 6A.5 to equate $\sum_j f_j = 1$.

The last factors in Eq. 6A.12 are evaluated with the help of Eq. 6A.4. We have

$$\begin{aligned}
\overline{\exp[-\lambda z_k']} &= \sum_{i=1}^{A}\sum_{j=1}^{Q}\sum_{h=1}^{A}p_i q_{ij} p_h \exp\left[\lambda\left(\log_2\frac{q_{hj}}{f_j} - R_N\right)\right] \\
&= 2^{-\frac{1}{2}R_N}\sum_j\sum_h f_j p_h\left(\frac{q_{hj}}{f_j}\right)^{1/2} \\
&= 2^{-\frac{1}{2}R_N}\sum_j\sqrt{f_j}\left[\sum_h p_h\sqrt{q_{hj}}\right]; \qquad \lambda = \tfrac{1}{2}\log_e 2.
\end{aligned}$$

Application of the Schwarz inequality yields

$$\overline{\exp[-\lambda z_k']} \leqslant 2^{-\frac{1}{2}[R_N+R_0']}. \tag{6A.15}$$

Recombination. The desired bound on $\overline{P[\mathcal{E}_h]}$ follows from a series of substitutions. First, substituting Eqs. 6A.13–15 into Eq. 6A.12 (with $\lambda = \frac{1}{2}\log_e 2$), we have

$$\bar{P}_H \leqslant \begin{cases} 2^{\frac{1}{2}\Delta}[2^{-R_0'}]^{Hv}[2^{-\frac{1}{2}(R_N+R_0')}]^{\ell v-Hv}; & H \leqslant \ell \leqslant K \\ 2^{\frac{1}{2}\Delta}[2^{-R_0'}]^{\ell v}[2^{\frac{1}{2}(R_N-R_0')}]^{Hv-\ell v}; & H > \ell. \end{cases}$$

Hence

$$\bar{P}_H \leqslant 2^{\frac{1}{2}\Delta}2^{-\frac{1}{2}\ell v[R_0'+R_N]}2^{-\frac{1}{2}Hv[R_0'-R_N]}; \qquad \text{all } H, \ell \leqslant K \tag{6A.16}$$

By averaging Eq. 6A.9 over the ensemble of codes and substituting Eq. 6A.16 we obtain

$$\overline{P[w(\ell, n) < \Delta]} \leqslant 2^{\frac{1}{2}\Delta}2^{-\frac{1}{2}\ell v[R_0'+R_N]}\sum_{H=0}^{K}2^{-\frac{1}{2}Hv[R_0'-R_N]}.$$

The bound is weakened by extending the sum to infinity. Thus

$$\overline{P[w(\ell, n) < \Delta]} < A_0 2^{-\frac{1}{2}\ell v[R_0'+R_N]}; \qquad R_N < R_0', \tag{6A.17a}$$

in which the coefficient A_0 is defined as

$$A_0 \triangleq \frac{2^{\frac{1}{2}\Delta}}{1 - 2^{-\frac{1}{2}v[R_0'-R_N]}}. \tag{6A.17b}$$

Setting $\ell = K$ and substituting in Eq. 6A.8 yields the final result,

$$\overline{\mathrm{P}[\mathcal{E}_h]} < N_K A_0 2^{-\frac{1}{2}Kv[R_0' + R_\mathrm{N}]}; \qquad R_\mathrm{N} < R_0'.$$

By virtue of Eq. 6A.6 this may be written

$$\overline{\mathrm{P}[\mathcal{E}_h]} < A_0 2^{-\frac{1}{2}Kv[R_0' - R_\mathrm{N}]}; \qquad R_\mathrm{N} < R_0'. \tag{6A.18}$$

We find that the ensemble average probability of the event "$\hat{x}_h$ incorrect when the tree search first penetrates K branches beyond the (correct) starting node" decays exponentially with increasing code constraint length K, provided $R_\mathrm{N} < R_0'$. Stiglitz and Yudkin use more sensitive arguments to derive tighter bounds.

Interpretation. Relating the bound on $\overline{\mathrm{P}[\mathcal{E}_h]}$ to the error probability of an actual Fano decoder involves a series of arguments. As with the suboptimum decoder of Section 6.3, we presume that a long sequence $\mathbf{x} = (x_1, x_2, \ldots, x_L)$ of coder input symbols is to be communicated and count an error unless all L symbols are decoded correctly. Because the bound of Eq. 6A.18 is independent of h and the transmitted path, when the genie-aided decoder is used to decode the entire sequence one symbol after another the mean error probability is overbounded by $L\overline{\mathrm{P}[\mathcal{E}_h]}$. Thus the error probability can be made arbitrarily small by appropriate choice of K and R_N. For ease of reference we call the genie-aided decoder $\mathrm{D_I}$.

Now consider a second decoder, say $\mathrm{D_{II}}$, identical to $\mathrm{D_I}$ except that the hth starting node, $h = 1, 2, \ldots, L$, is determined by the preceding decoder decisions $\hat{x}_1, \hat{x}_2, \ldots, \hat{x}_{h-1}$ rather than by the genie. Because $\mathrm{D_{II}}$ determines $\mathbf{x}$ correctly if and only if $\mathrm{D_I}$ does, $L\overline{\mathrm{P}[\mathcal{E}_h]}$ is an upper bound on the error performance of $\mathrm{D_{II}}$ even though the genie has been dismissed.†

The next argument is more subtle. Consider a third decoder, say $\mathrm{D_{III}}$, which like $\mathrm{D_I}$ and $\mathrm{D_{II}}$ has an infinite r-register but which uses a search algorithm more akin to that of an actual machine. In particular, for $\mathrm{D_{III}}$ the only modification of the Fano algorithm is that we prohibit the change of any decision $\hat{x}_h$, $h = 1, 2, \ldots, L$, once the search node pointer has first penetrated to a node $l = h + K - 1$ branches deep in the code tree. Thus $\mathrm{D_{III}}$ maintains a running record of its path of deepest penetration to date and at any instant treats the node $K - 1$ branches back from the point of deepest penetration as if it were the code origin. Decoders II and III differ in that III does not return to the next starting node after each decision is made. We shall see, however, that these two decoders always make the same decisions, even when they decode incorrectly.

† The role of the genie in the derivation is to avoid the necessity of conditioning the ensemble used in analyzing $\overline{\mathrm{P}[\mathcal{E}_h]}$ on the event "$\hat{x}_1, \hat{x}_2, \ldots, \hat{x}_{h-1}$ correct." Specification of the probability assignment for the conditional ensemble would be difficult, if not impossible.

The equivalence of D_{III} and D_{II} may be demonstrated with the help of Fig. 6A.5. Consider D_{II}; let node 1 be its starting node and let node 3 be its "decision node" for $\hat{x}_h$. By the *decision node* for $\hat{x}_h$ we mean the terminus of the first path constructed by D_{II} extending K branches beyond its hth starting node. We therefore identify node 2 as D_{II}'s starting node for $\hat{x}_{h+1}$. In the process of determining $\hat{x}_h$, D_{II} may need to pass through node 2 many times, with successively higher values of the running threshold T. The important point, however, is that the value of T required to reach node 3 depends *solely* on $t(l)$ along the path from node 2 to node 3 and is independent of the t-value of node 1. Moreover, node 3 is the *first* node reached by D_{II} at depth $l = h + K - 1$.

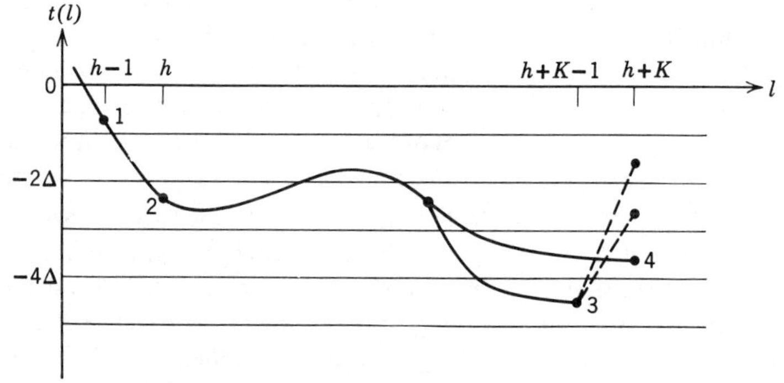

Figure 6A.5 Starting and decision nodes.

In the process of determining the next decision $\hat{x}_{h+1}$, D_{II} first starts at node 2 and again moves forward with running thresholds that are independent of the t-value of node 1. It follows from careful consideration of the Fano algorithm that D_{II} must *again arrive at node* 3 *before reaching any other node at depth* $l = h + K - 1$. In addition, D_{II} arrives at node 3 the second time with T and θ having *the same values they had on the first arrival.* [These facts, of course, do not preclude subsequent retrogression before the decision node for $\hat{x}_{h+1}$, say node 4 in Fig. 6A.5, is finally reached.]

The equivalence of decoders II and III is immediate. Start with the determination of $\hat{x}_1$. Both decoders begin at the code origin and simultaneously reach the same decision node (for $\hat{x}_1$) with the same value of T. Now let D_{II} move back to the starting node for $\hat{x}_2$, holding D_{III} immobile until D_{II} rejoins it. Then release D_{III} and again allow it to move in synchronism with D_{II} to a decision node for $\hat{x}_2$. Since both decoders follow the same rules and depart from the same node with the same initial conditions, this decision node and all movements in reaching it are also common. Continuing in this way, we see that the operations performed by D_{II} and D_{III} are identical, except that D_{II} must redo many operations which D_{III} elides. Thus the mean error probability for D_{III} is also overbounded by $L\overline{P[\mathcal{E}_h]}$ and can be made arbitrarily small.

The remaining task is to relate $\overline{P[\mathcal{E}_h]}$ to an actual decoder. We first note that extension of the $\hat{x}$-register beyond the end of the r-register, as in Fig. 6.58, guarantees that the actual decoder—like D_{III}—will not release any $\hat{x}_h$ until the search node pointer has reached a node (at least) K branches deeper in the code tree. The significance of $\overline{P[\mathcal{E}_h]}$ arises from the fact that an actual decoder exactly duplicates the movements of D_{III} whenever two conditions are met. The first condition is that the actual machine determines all L of the $\hat{x}_h$ without incurring a search $K - 1$ or more branches back from the node of deepest penetration; the second is that the (finite) r-register does not overflow. Since the number of branches typically observed by a decoder in a deep search is enormous, we anticipate that the second condition will dominate in practice. We therefore interpret the bound on $\overline{P[\mathcal{E}_h]}$ as a conservative estimate of the mean probability of undetected error per message symbol decoded. The estimate is conservative because it neglects the likelihood that overflow will occur before an erroneous decision is released at the $\hat{x}$-register output. When the $\hat{x}$-register extension is greater than K, as in Fig. 6.58, we expect the estimate to be exceedingly conservative.

Mean Computation

We now bound the mean number of computations (over the ensemble of convolutional codes) performed by decoder D_I in decoding $x_1, x_2, \ldots x_L$. Since the analysis discounts repetitive computation in retracing from each genie-specified starting node to the first node encountered $K - 1$ branches beyond it, the result estimates computations performed by D_{III} when D_I decodes all L of the $\{x_h\}$ correctly, hence estimates the computations performed by an actual decoder in the absence of overflow.

We define computation by saying that the decoder performs one computation each time it enters either the "look forward" or the "look back" box in the flow diagram of Fig. 6.46. In particular, we define $\bar{B}_h$ as the total mean number of times the decoder enters either box with its search node pointer on nodes in the incorrect subset for $\hat{x}_h$. We observe from Fig. 6A.2 that *every* node in the code tree belongs to the incorrect subset for one and only one $\hat{x}_h$, $h = 1, 2, \ldots, L$. Thus the mean number of computations per decoded symbol, say $\bar{B}$, is given by

$$\bar{B} = \frac{1}{L}\sum_{h=1}^{L} \bar{B}_h. \qquad (6A.19)$$

We overbound the $\{\bar{B}_h\}$, hence $\bar{B}$, by exploiting two basic properties of the search algorithm. (i) At most $u + 1$ computations can be performed with the search node pointer on a given node and with a given threshold in force. (ii) The maximum number of different thresholds ever used with the pointer on a node in the incorrect subset for $\hat{x}_h$ is equal to the number of thresholds lying on or above the t-value of that node but below $T_c + \Delta$, where T_c has been defined in Fig. 6A.3.

Property (i) is true because, with a given threshold in force, only one computation may be performed in looking ahead on each of the u branches diverging from the node and only one computation may be performed in looking back from the node. Indeed, the function of the variable θ in the

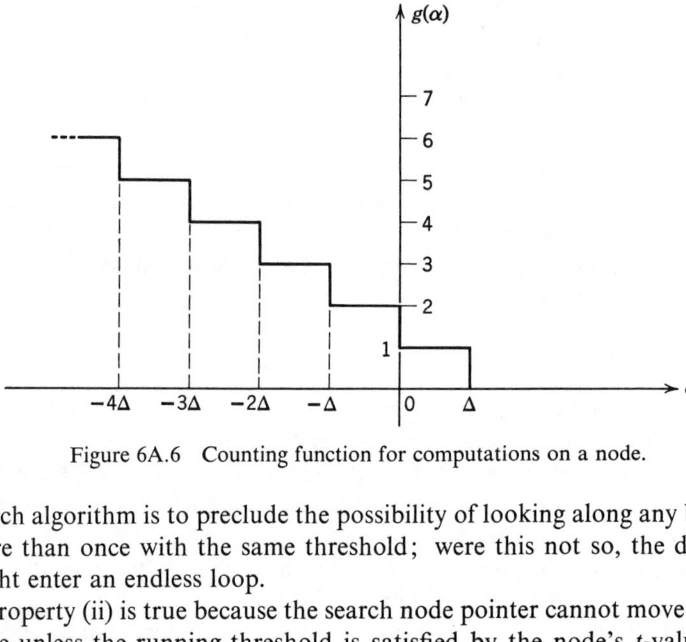

Figure 6A.6 Counting function for computations on a node.

search algorithm is to preclude the possibility of looking along any branch more than once with the same threshold; were this not so, the decoder might enter an endless loop.

Property (ii) is true because the search node pointer cannot move to any node unless the running threshold is satisfied by the node's t-value and because the algorithm never uses a threshold higher than T_c while searching the incorrect subset for $\hat{x}_h$.

In bounding $\bar{B}_h$, we first consider a particular code and transmitted path and use these two properties to note that the number of computations—say $B(\ell, n)$—performed on node (ℓ, n) of the incorrect subset for $\hat{x}_h$ is bounded by

$$B(\ell, n) \leqslant (u + 1)g[w(\ell, n)]. \qquad (6A.20)$$

Here the staircase function $g(\ )$, plotted in Fig. 6A.6, bounds the maximum number of thresholds that can be in force when (l, n) is the search node. Observing that

$$g(\alpha) = \sum_{j=-1}^{\infty} f(-\alpha - j\Delta), \tag{6A.21}$$

where $f(\ )$ is the unit step function used in the derivation of Eq. 6A.10, we have

$$B(\ell, n) \leqslant (u + 1) \sum_{j=-1}^{\infty} f[-w(\ell, n) - j\Delta]. \tag{6A.22}$$

Taking the expectation of both sides of this inequality with respect to the probability assignment of Eq. 6A.11, we obtain

$$\overline{B(\ell, n)} \leqslant (u + 1) \sum_{j=-1}^{\infty} \overline{\mathrm{P}[w(\ell, n) < -j\Delta]}. \tag{6A.23}$$

We now observe from its derivation that the validity of the bound of Eq. 6A.17 does not depend on the specific value assigned to the parameter Δ. Substituting $-j\Delta$ for Δ in Eq. 6A.17 and applying the result to Eq. 6A.23, we obtain for $\ell \leqslant K$

$$\begin{aligned}\overline{B(\ell, n)} &< A_1 2^{-\frac{1}{2}\ell v[R_0' + R_{\mathrm{N}}]} \sum_{j=-1}^{\infty} 2^{-\frac{1}{2}j\Delta} \\ &= A_1 \frac{2^{\frac{1}{2}\Delta}}{1 - 2^{-\frac{1}{2}\Delta}} 2^{-\frac{1}{2}\ell v[R_0' + R_{\mathrm{N}}]}; \qquad R_{\mathrm{N}} < R_0',\end{aligned} \tag{6A.24a}$$

in which the coefficient A_1 is defined as

$$A_1 \triangleq \frac{u + 1}{1 - 2^{-\frac{1}{2}v[R_0' - R_{\mathrm{N}}]}}. \tag{6A.24b}$$

The bound is minimized by choosing Δ, the threshold spacing, equal to 2. With this choice

$$\overline{B(\ell, n)} < 4A_1 2^{-\frac{1}{2}\ell v[R_0' + R_{\mathrm{N}}]}; \qquad R_{\mathrm{N}} < R_0', \tag{6A.25}$$

The mean number of computations $\bar{B}_h$ is, by definition of decoder $\mathrm{D_I}$, the mean of the total nonrepetitive computations performed on nodes of the incorrect subset for $\hat{x}_h$ at depths less than or equal to K. Since the mean of a sum is the sum of the means,

$$\bar{B}_h = \sum_{\ell=0}^{K} \sum_{n=1}^{N_\ell} \overline{B(\ell, n)}. \tag{6A.26}$$

Thus, again by virtue of Eq. 6A.6,

$$\begin{aligned}\bar{B}_h &< 4A_1 \sum_{\ell=0}^{K} N_\ell 2^{-\frac{1}{2}\ell v[R_0' + R_{\mathrm{N}}]} \\ &< 4A_1 \sum_{\ell=0}^{K} 2^{-\frac{1}{2}\ell v[R_0' - R_{\mathrm{N}}]} \\ &< \frac{4(u + 1)}{(1 - 2^{-\frac{1}{2}v[R_0' - R_{\mathrm{N}}]})^2}; \qquad R_{\mathrm{N}} < R_0'.\end{aligned} \tag{6A.27}$$

The bound of Eq. 6A.27 is independent of h. From Eq. 6A.19 the right-hand side of Eq. 6A.27 is therefore also an upper bound on $\bar{B}$. If $R_N < R_0'$, the mean computation per message symbol decoded is bounded by a number that is independent of the code constraint length K.

For data rates $R_N < R_0'$ and decoder D_I we have seen so far that over an ensemble of convolutional codes both $\bar{B}$ and the over-all mean probability of one or more errors, say $\overline{P[\mathcal{E}]}$, are individually bounded, respectively, by a constant and by an exponentially decreasing function of K. (The bound on $\overline{P[\mathcal{E}]}$ follows from Eq. 6A.18 and the inequality $\overline{P[\mathcal{E}]} \leqslant L\overline{P[\mathcal{E}_h]}$.) It remains to be shown that there are convolutional codes for which both bounds are satisfied simultaneously. The argument proving that such codes do exist is a simple extension of one with which we are already familiar; we know that no more than a fraction $1/a$ of the codes in the ensemble can yield

$$P[\mathcal{E}] \geqslant a\overline{P[\mathcal{E}]} \tag{6A.28a}$$

and that no more than a fraction $1/b$ of the codes can require a number of computations

$$B \geqslant b\bar{B}, \tag{6A.28b}$$

where the left-hand sides of Eqs. 6A.28a and b denote quantities averaged only over the channel noise. The worst possible situation would obtain if the set of codes that produces high error probabilities were disjoint from the set that produces high computational requirements. It follows immediately that a fraction of at least $(1 - 1/a - 1/b)$ of the codes in the ensemble simultaneously satisfies inequalities converse to Eqs. 6A.28a and b. Thus at least 80 per cent of the convolutional codes yield

$$P[\mathcal{E}] < 10\overline{P[\mathcal{E}]} \tag{6A.29a}$$

$$B < 10\bar{B}. \tag{6A.29b}$$

PROBLEMS

6.1 Consider the parity check coder in Fig. P6.1.

a. How should the coder be connected in order to produce the following transformations?

x_3	x_2	x_1	y_5	y_4	y_3	y_2	y_1
0	1	1	1	0	1	0	1
1	0	1	0	1	0	1	0
0	1	0	0	0	1	1	0

b. Give a complete listing of the transformation $\mathbf{x} \rightarrow \mathbf{y}$.

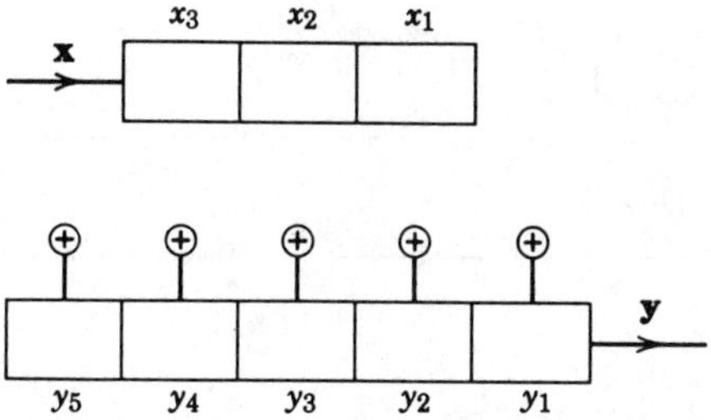

Figure P6.1

6.2 The following code is to be used on a BSC with transition probability p:

$$\begin{array}{llllll} \mathbf{y}_0: & 0 & 0 & 0 & 0 & 0 \\ \mathbf{y}_1: & 0 & 1 & 1 & 1 & 0 \\ \mathbf{y}_2: & 1 & 0 & 1 & 0 & 1 \\ \mathbf{y}_3: & 1 & 1 & 0 & 1 & 1 \end{array}$$

a. Show that the minimum Hamming distance between any two codewords is the weight of the non zero codeword with the smallest number of 1's.

b. Use this number to compute a bound on the probability of error with this code.

c. Generalize the result to any binary code which has the property that the modulo-2 sum of every pair of distinct codewords is a non zero codeword.

6.3 Let x and y be real numbers and define the operation $\circ$ to mean "addition" modulo-(1); that is

$$x \circ y \triangleq (x + y) - [\text{integral part of } (x + y)].$$

Consider $K + 1$ vectors $\{\mathbf{f}_h\}$, each with N components chosen with statistical independence from a density function that is uniform over [0, 1]. Let $\{\mathbf{s}_i\}$ be the set of all 2^K vectors of the form

$$\mathbf{s}_i = \mathbf{f}_0 \circ x_1\mathbf{f}_1 \circ \cdots \circ x_K\mathbf{f}_K,$$

where the $\{x_h\}$ are 0 or 1 and "addition" is component by component.

a. Prove that any two vectors $\mathbf{s}_i$ and $\mathbf{s}_k$ are statistically independent and determine their joint density function.

b. Specify a transformation on the components of the $\{\mathbf{s}_i\}$ which produces a new set $\{\mathbf{s}_i'\}$ such that

$$p_{\mathbf{s}'_i,\mathbf{s}'_j}(\boldsymbol{\alpha}, \boldsymbol{\beta}) = \frac{1}{(2\pi\sigma^2)^N} \exp\left[-\frac{1}{2\sigma^2}(|\boldsymbol{\alpha}|^2 + |\boldsymbol{\beta}|^2)\right]$$

for all $i \neq j$.

6.4 The device shown in the Fig. P6.4 is used as a coder in the following way. A 5-bit block of message bits in inserted in the shift register. The coder is then stepped (shifted right) 31 times to produce an output codeword of length 31,

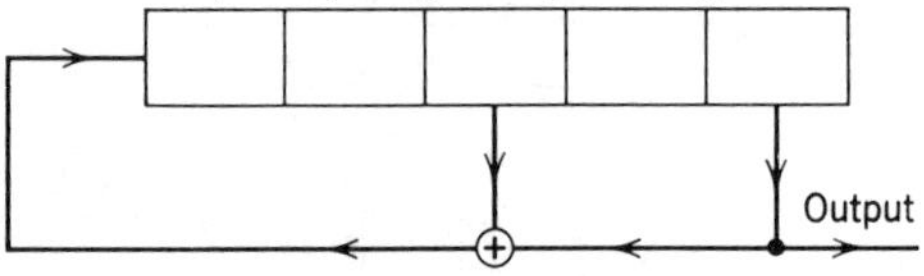

Figure P6.4

the first 5 digits of which are the message block. For example, if 0 0 0 1 0 is inserted, we obtain after each shift

Shift	Contents	Output
	0 0 0 1 0	
1	0 0 0 0 1	0
2	1 0 0 0 0	1
3	0 1 0 0 0	0
4	0 0 1 0 0	0
5	1 0 0 1 0	0
6	0 1 0 0 1	0
7	1 0 1 0 0	1

and so on.

a. Show that the coder is linear; that is, if $\mathbf{x}_i$ and $\mathbf{x}_j$ are two 5-bit message blocks and $\mathbf{y}_i$ and $\mathbf{y}_j$ are the respective coder outputs, then

$$\mathbf{x} = \mathbf{x}_i \oplus \mathbf{x}_j \Rightarrow \mathbf{y} = \mathbf{y}_i \oplus \mathbf{y}_j.$$

b. Demonstrate that if the message block contains at least one 1, the coder returns to its original state on the 32nd shift, but not before. The shift register is said to have a "maximal length" feedback configuration because the maximum number of distinct nonzero shift register states is $2^K - 1$, where K is the length of the shift register. It can be shown[36] that a maximal length feedback configuration exists for all K.

c. Let $\mathbf{z}_i$ be the vector obtained from $\mathbf{y}_i$ by the component transformation $0 \to 1$, $1 \to -1$. Define $\mathbf{s}_i = \sqrt{E_N}\,\mathbf{z}_i$ to be a signal vector, each component of which is $\pm\sqrt{E_N}$. Show that

$$\sum_{j=1}^{N} s_{ij} = \begin{cases} N\sqrt{E_N}; & \text{if } \mathbf{y}_i \text{ is all zeros,} \\ -\sqrt{E_N}; & \text{otherwise.} \end{cases}$$

d. Prove that the set of 32 signals $\{\mathbf{s}_i\}$ forms a simplex.

e. Generalize the proof to maximal length shift register coders for which the number, K, of shift register stages is arbitrary.

6.5 Consider a binary parity-check coder that generates $\mathbf{y}$ by performing one parity check on each distinct non-null subset of the components of the input vector $\mathbf{x} = (x_1, x_2, \ldots, x_K)$.

a. Show that $\mathbf{y}$ has $N = 2^K - 1$ components.

b. The coder output $\mathbf{s} = (s_1, s_2, \ldots, s_N)$ is produced from $\mathbf{y}$ by the component transformation $0 \rightarrow +1$, $1 \rightarrow -1$. Show that if

$$\mathbf{s}_i = (s_{i1}, s_{i2}, \ldots, s_{iN})$$
$$\mathbf{s}_j = (s_{j1}, s_{j2}, \ldots, s_{jN})$$

are codewords, the vector

$$\mathbf{s}_k = (s_{i1}s_{j1}, s_{i2}s_{j2}, \ldots, s_{iN}s_{jN})$$

obtained by multiplying corresponding components is also a codeword.

Hint. Multiplication of the numbers $+1$ and -1 is equivalent to addition modulo-2 of the numbers 0 and 1.

c. Now let $\mathbf{z} \overset{\Delta}{=} (z_1, z_2, \ldots, z_K)$ denote the vector produced from $\mathbf{x}$ by the component transformation $0 \rightarrow +1$, $1 \rightarrow -1$. Show that the arithmetic sum

$$s_1 + s_2 + \cdots + s_N = [(1 + z_1)(1 + z_2) \cdots (1 + z_K)] - 1$$
$$= \begin{cases} 2^K - 1; & \text{all } z_\ell = 1,\ \ell = 1, 2, \ldots, K, \\ -1; & \text{otherwise.} \end{cases}$$

d. Use (b) and (c) to prove that the codewords $\{\mathbf{s}_i\}$ form a simplex.

6.6 a. Calculate the exponential bound parameter R_0' (in bits per channel use) for the two discrete channel models shown in Fig. P6.6.

b. Devise a way to use the channel of (i) at rate $R_N = 1$ with $P[\mathcal{E}] = 0$.

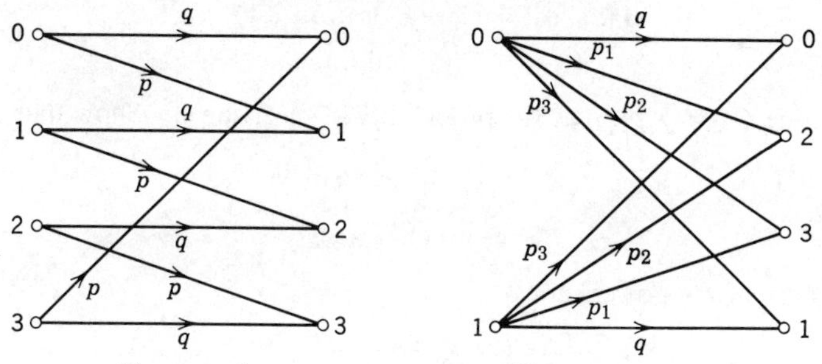

Figure P6.6

6.7 a. Calculate R_0' for the A input letter, $Q = A + 1$ output letter discrete memoryless erasure channel described by the transition probabilities

$$q_{ij} = q\delta_{ij}; \qquad i = 1, 2, \ldots, A; \qquad j = 1, 2, \ldots, A,$$
$$q_{i,A+1} = 1 - q; \qquad i = 1, 2, \ldots, A.$$

b. At what maximum average rate R_N (in bits per channel use) can we communicate over the channel with $P[\mathcal{E}] = 0$ when a noiseless binary channel is available for feedback from receiver to transmitter?

c. The capacity of a memoryless channel is not increased by feedback (see Wolfowitz[86], pp. 48–50). Use this fact to construct a simple argument to prove that the rate of (b) is the erasure channel's capacity, C_N.

d. How do R_0' and C_N vary when q is small and A is increased?

6.8 Determine the value of the unquantized exponential bound parameter R_0 that results when the coder of (b) of Problem 6.3 is used to construct signals of the form

$$s(t) = \sum_{j=1}^{N} s_j \varphi_j(t)$$

for transmission over an additive white Gaussian noise channel with power density $\mathcal{N}_0/2$.

6.9 Consider a discrete communication channel described by the transition probabilities

$$P[b_j \mid a_i] = q_{ij}; \qquad \begin{aligned} i &= 1, 2, \ldots, A \\ j &= 1, 2, \ldots, Q. \end{aligned}$$

We are interested in the calculation of

$$R_0' = -\log_2 \sum_j \left[\sum_i p_i \sqrt{q_{ij}} \right]^2,$$

when the channel is very "noisy," by which we mean that the a posteriori probability of the input letter a_i, given that the output letter b_j is received, differs little (for all i, j) from the a priori probability p_i. We write this condition as

$$P[a_i \mid b_j] = (1 + \epsilon_{ij})p_i; \qquad \text{all } i, j,$$

$$|\epsilon_{ij}| \ll 1; \qquad \text{all } i, j.$$

a. Define $Q_j = \sum_i p_i q_{ij}$ as the probability of receiving b_j. Show that

(i)
$$\sum_i p_i \epsilon_{ij} = \sum_j Q_j \epsilon_{ij} = 0,$$

(ii)
$$q_{ij} = (1 + \epsilon_{ij})Q_j.$$

b. By use of the power series

$$\sqrt{1 + \alpha} = 1 + \frac{\alpha}{2} - \frac{\alpha^2}{8} - \cdots; \qquad |\alpha| < 1,$$

$$\log_e (1 + \alpha) = \alpha - \frac{\alpha^2}{2} + \cdots; \qquad |\alpha| < 1,$$

show that

$$R_0' \approx \frac{\log_2 e}{4} \sum_i \sum_j p_i Q_j \epsilon_{ij}^2.$$

c. Now suppose the channel is a BSC derived from an additive white Gaussian noise channel by antipodal signaling and binary quantization of receiver matched filter outputs. Show that

$$\epsilon_{01} = \epsilon_{10} \approx -2\sqrt{\frac{E_N}{\pi \mathcal{N}_0}},$$

when the energy-to-noise ratio per dimension $E_N/\mathcal{N}_0$ is small. Evaluate R_0' and compare with the value of R_0 obtained by unquantized reception.

6.10 Consider a modulator that transmits one of A orthogonal signals, $\{\sqrt{E_s}\,\varphi_i(t)\}$, $i = 1, 2, \ldots, A$, over an additive white Gaussian noise channel, $\mathcal{S}_n(f) = \mathcal{N}_0/2$. At the receiver the quantities

$$r_i = \int_{-\infty}^{\infty} r(t)\,\varphi_i(t)\,dt; \qquad i = 1, 2, \ldots, A$$

are calculated and listed in order of decreasing numerical value.

a. If $\sqrt{E_s}\,\varphi_k(t)$ is transmitted, show that the probability, say Q_l, that r_k is lth in the list is

$$Q_l = \binom{A-1}{l-1}\,\overline{[Q(y)]^{l-1}[1 - Q(y)]^{A-l}}; \qquad l = 1, 2, \ldots, A,$$

where the average is with respect to the unit-variance Gaussian random variable y with mean $\bar{y} = \sqrt{2E_s/\mathcal{N}_0}$. Prove that

$$\sum_{l=1}^{A} Q_l = 1.$$

b. The receiver is said to use *list of L detection*[89] if its detector output is an ordered list of the subscripts of the L largest r_i's. Thus, if

$$r_{i_1} \geqslant r_{i_2} \geqslant \cdots \geqslant r_{i_L} \geqslant \text{all other } r_i,$$

the detector output is the list $(i_1, i_2, \ldots, i_L)$.

The system from modulator input to detector output can be modeled by a discrete memoryless channel with A input letters and Q output letters, with $Q = A(A-1)\cdots(A-L+1)$. [Each distinct list is an output letter.] Verify

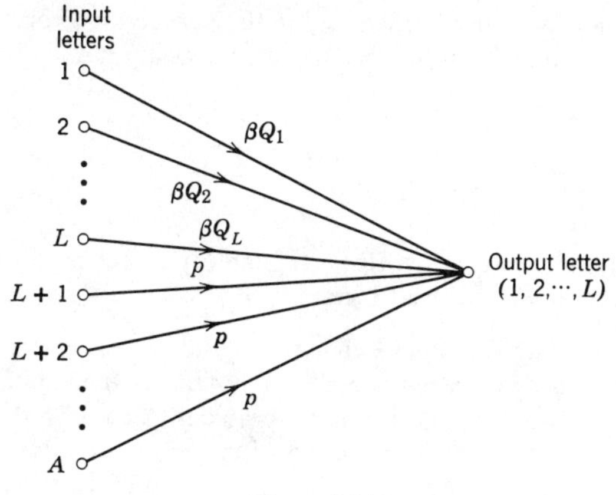

Figure P6.10

that the transition probabilities q_{ij} converging onto the output letter (1, 2, . . . , L) are as shown in Fig. P6.10, with

$$\beta \triangleq \frac{(A-L)!}{(A-1)!}, \qquad p \triangleq [Q_{L+1} + Q_{L+2} + \cdots + Q_A] \frac{(A-L-1)!}{(A-1)!}.$$

Show that a similar fan of probabilities converges onto each output letter.

c. Determine an expression for R_0' in terms of the $\{Q_l\}$, assuming that all input letters are equally likely. (See I. M. Jacobs, "Sequential Decoding with Biorthogonal Alphabet and List Decoding," Jet Propulsion Lab. SPS 37–33, Vol. IV, May–June 1965, for detailed analysis of this modulation/detection system.)

6.11 Two binary parity-check codes are said to be equivalent if one can be converted into the other by coordinate permutations and/or reassignment of the codeword subscripts.

a. Prove that equivalent codes afford the same P[$\mathcal{E}$] when used on a BSC.

b. Show that any binary parity-check code $\{\mathbf{y}_i\}$ in which all codewords are distinct is equivalent to another such code, say $\{\mathbf{y}_i'\}$, in which the first K digits of each codeword are the corresponding coder input vector $\mathbf{x}_i$. The code $\{\mathbf{y}_i'\}$ is said to have "canonic form".

6.12 Apply the Fano search algorithm of Fig. 6.46 to the t-value plot of Fig. 6.45. Detail the successive locations of the search node pointer and the values of T and θ in a fashion similar to that of Fig. 6.47.

6.13 Apply the Fano search algorithm of Fig. 6.46 to a binary tree and a t-value plot of your own devising. Be certain that every box in the search algorithm is entered at least once. Detail the successive locations of the search node pointer and the values of T and θ in a fashion similar to that of Fig. 6.47.

6.14 Consider a system communicating over a BSC at $R_N = 0.9R_0'$. If the transmitter employs a convolutional coder and the receiver a Fano decoder with 5 μsec computation time per branch and a 1000-branch memory, estimate the largest communication rate in bits per second consistent with

(i) P[overflow] $\leqslant 10^{-6}$,

(ii) P[overflow] $\leqslant 10^{-8}$.

Repeat for $R_N = 0.5R_0'$.

6.15 Prove that $t(l)$, as given by Eqs. 6A.2 and 6A.3, reduces for the BSC to a constant times the tilted distance function of Eq. 6.109, with $p < p' < 1/2$.

6.16 a. Consider using the erasure channel of Problem 6.7 with binary ($u = 2$) convolutional coding and without feedback. What is the probability that k successive channel input symbols will be erased? Assuming that this event occurs, lower bound the number of branches that a Fano decoder must examine before it can determine the correct path beyond the end of the erasures. Express your answer as a function of the rate R_N.

b. Let $P_B[\gamma]$ denote the probability that γ or more branches are searched by the decoder before the first encoder input symbol is determined. Use the bound of (a) with an appropriate choice of k to establish a lower bound on $P_B[\gamma]$. At what rate R_N does the bound imply an infinite mean number of computations (branches searched)? Compare this value with R_0'.

6.17 a. Using the results of Appendix 6A, show that the kth moment of the number of branches in the incorrect subset for $\hat{x}_h$ searched by decoder D_I is bounded (when retracing is discounted) by

$$\overline{B_h^{\,k}} \leqslant \overline{\left\{\sum_{\ell=0}^{K} \sum_{n=1}^{N_\ell} \sum_{i=-1}^{\infty} f[-w(\ell, n) - i\Delta]\right\}^k}; \qquad k \geqslant 1,$$

in which the average is over the ensemble of convolutional codes.

b. Minkowski's inequality states that for $k \geqslant 1$ and any set of random variables $\{x_j\}$

$$\left[\overline{\left(\sum_j |x_j|\right)^k}\right]^{1/k} \leqslant \sum_j (\overline{|x_j|^k})^{1/k}.$$

Use this inequality to prove that $\overline{B_h^{\,k}}$ is finite for $R_0'/R_N > 2k - 1$.

c. Generalize Chebyshev's inequality to prove that for any random variable x

$$P[x \geqslant \gamma] \leqslant \overline{x^k}\, \gamma^{-k}.$$

d. From (b) and (c) prove that over the ensemble of codes

$$\overline{P[B_h \geqslant \gamma]} \leqslant C_\epsilon \gamma^{-\frac{1}{2}[1-\epsilon+(R_0'/R_N)]},$$

where C_ϵ is a number independent of γ which tends to ∞ as $\epsilon \to 0$.

6.18 The proof of the negative capacity theorem of Chapter 5 can be applied to a wide variety of channels. Let us consider the binary symmetric channel. The transmitter maps one of M equally likely messages into an N component vector,

$$m_i \to \mathbf{y}_i = (y_{i1}, y_{i2}, \ldots, y_{iN}),$$

where the $\{y_{ij}\}$ are each 0 or 1. The channel output is an N component output vector $\mathbf{r} = \mathbf{y}_i \oplus \mathbf{n}$, where the components of $\mathbf{n}$ are statistically independent binary random variables with probability $p < \frac{1}{2}$ of being 1 and probability $q = 1 - p$ of being 0. Verify the following sequence of steps:

a. Let $\{I_i\}$ denote the decision regions: $\mathbf{r}$ in $I_i \Leftrightarrow \hat{m} = m_i$. As usual, the $\{I_i\}$ are disjoint. The "volume" of I_i, denoted V_i, is defined as the number of binary vectors in I_i. Thus

$$\sum_{i=0}^{M-1} V_i = 2^N \triangleq V.$$

Obviously,

$$P[\mathcal{C}] = \frac{1}{M} \sum_{i=0}^{M-1} P[\mathbf{r} \text{ in } I_i \mid m_i].$$

Verify that

$$P[\mathbf{r} \text{ in } I_i \mid m_i] \leqslant P[\mathbf{r} \text{ in } S_i \mid m_i],$$

in which S_i is a "sphere" around $\mathbf{y}_i$, of "radius" ρ_i, with the same "volume" as I_i. Specifically, S_i contains all vectors whose Hamming distance from $\mathbf{y}_i$ is $\rho_i - 1$ or less plus enough vectors at Hamming distance ρ_i to round out the total to V_i. Thus ρ_i is defined by

$$\sum_{j=0}^{\rho_i - 1} \binom{N}{j} < V_i, \qquad \sum_{j=0}^{\rho_i} \binom{N}{j} \geqslant V_i.$$

b. Verify that

$$P[\mathcal{C}] \leqslant \frac{1}{M} \sum_{i=0}^{M-1} P[\mathbf{r} \text{ in } \tilde{S}_i \mid m_i]$$

$$= P[|\mathbf{n}| \leqslant \tilde{\rho}],$$

where $|\mathbf{n}|^2$ is the number of 1's in $\mathbf{n}$, and $\tilde{S}_i$ is a sphere of volume V/M and radius $\tilde{\rho}$ centered on $\mathbf{y}_i$.

c. Verify that $P[\mathcal{C}] < \epsilon$ for large enough N whenever $\tilde{\rho} < (p - \Delta)N$.

d. Prove that Δ can be taken small enough so that $\tilde{\rho} < (p - \Delta)N$ for large enough N whenever $R_N > C_N$, where

$$M = 2^{NR_N}, \qquad C_N = 1 - H(p).$$

Hint. From Stirling's approximation to the factorial, for large N

$$\sum_{j=0}^{\tilde{\rho}-1} \binom{N}{j} > \binom{N}{\tilde{\rho} - 1} > \frac{1}{N} 2^{NH[(\tilde{\rho} - 1)/N]},$$

in which H is the binary entropy function, defined as

$$H(x) \triangleq -x \log_2 x - (1 - x) \log_2 (1 - x); \qquad 0 \leqslant x \leqslant 1.$$

Show first that $\tilde{\rho}$ satisfies the inequality

$$H\left(\frac{\tilde{\rho} - 1}{N}\right) < 1 - R_N - \frac{1}{N} \log_2 N,$$

which, if $1 - R_N < H(p)$, implies $(\tilde{\rho} - 1)/N < p - \Delta$ for sufficiently large N and small Δ.

e. Evaluate C_N when the BSC is derived from antipodal signaling over an additive white Gaussian noise channel with a quantized receiver. Assume that $E_N/\mathcal{N}_0 \ll 1$ and compare with R_0'.

7

Important Channel Models

In this chapter we extend the results of Chapters 4, 5, and 6 to channel models that more closely approximate certain aspects of actual communication systems. In particular, we consider additive Gaussian noise channels in which the noise is not white and in which the received signal component may have an unknown attenuation or phase or both. The tools used in the study of these channels—the theorem on reversibility, the whitening filter, the representation of narrow-band noise, and the elimination of random parameters by integration—are exceedingly powerful and may be applied to still more general channel models involving time-variant dispersive propagation.[49]

7.1 EFFECTS OF FILTERING

In Chapter 4 we assumed that the signal component of the received waveform was unaffected by transmission except for the addition of white Gaussian noise. Actually, noise is never exactly white, and in some cases a white-noise approximation may be seriously inappropriate. Also, most transmission media alter the waveshapes of the transmitted signals in one way or another.

It is frequently possible to attribute such phenomena to the action of linear filters operating on white noise to "color" it or on the signal to modify it. We deal first with channels containing a filter whose transfer function is known.

Filtered-Signal Channels

The channel pictured in Fig. 7.1 is a simple extension of the additive white Gaussian noise channel of Chapter 4 and requires no new tools for its analysis. The linear filter† is time-invariant, hence is characterized by

† The restrictions of linearity and time-invariance are unnecessary except insofar as they facilitate description of the operation relating $s(t)$ and $s^{\circ}(t)$. The important assumption is that the receiver in Fig. 7.1 must be able to calculate $s^{\circ}(t)$ from knowledge of $s(t)$ and the transmission characteristic of the channel.

its impulse response $h(t)$, which is assumed to be known at the receiver. As a trivial example, we might have

$$h(t) = a\,\delta(t - \tau) \tag{7.1a}$$

so that

$$s^{\circ}(t) = a\,s(t - \tau). \tag{7.1b}$$

Here a is a *known* attenuation and τ is a *known* delay.

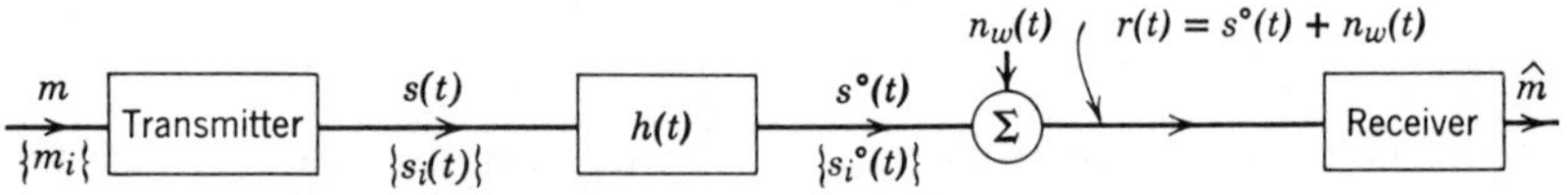

Figure 7.1 The filtered-signal channel with additive white Gaussian noise. Because

$$s_i^{\circ}(t) = \int_{-\infty}^{\infty} s_i(\alpha)h(t - \alpha)\,d\alpha; \qquad i = 0, 1, \ldots, M - 1,$$

the filter input and output processes are related by $s^{\circ}(t) = s(t) * h(t)$.

The derivation of the optimum receiver for the additive white Gaussian channel with filtering is identical to the derivation in Chapter 4 for the channel without filtering. Since the essential condition that the $\{m_i\}$ uniquely specify the $\{s_i^{\circ}(t)\}$ is satisfied, we need only add a superscript "°" to each signal waveform and corresponding vector. Thus the optimum receiver selects $\hat{m} = m_i$ if and only if

$$P[m_i]\, p_{\mathbf{r}}(\boldsymbol{\rho} \mid \mathbf{s}^{\circ} = \mathbf{s}_i^{\circ}) \tag{7.2a}$$

is maximum or (equivalently) if and only if

$$\int_{\infty}^{\infty} r(t)\, s_i^{\circ}(t)\, dt + c_i^{\circ} \tag{7.2b}$$

is maximum, where

$$c_i^{\circ} = \frac{\mathcal{N}_0}{2} \ln P[m_i] - \frac{1}{2}\int_{-\infty}^{\infty} [s_i^{\circ}(t)]^2\, dt. \tag{7.2c}$$

The probability of error depends on the location of the vectors $\{\mathbf{s}_i^{\circ}\}$ rather than directly on the vectors $\{\mathbf{s}_i\}$. In general, the $\{\mathbf{s}_i^{\circ}\}$ must be determined from the filtered waveforms $\{s_i^{\circ}(t)\}$ by means of the Gram-Schmidt procedure of Appendix 4A. It is not usually possible to avoid this step and obtain the $\{\mathbf{s}_i^{\circ}\}$ directly from the $\{\mathbf{s}_i\}$ because the same set of N orthonormal functions $\{\varphi_j(t)\}$ cannot in general be used to represent both the $\{s_i(t)\}$ and the $\{s_i^{\circ}(t)\}$.

One form of optimum receiver is the correlation receiver shown in Fig. 7.2. Since the reference waveforms $\{s_i(t)\}$ are filtered before being correlated with $r(t)$, this implementation is often called a "filtered-reference" receiver.

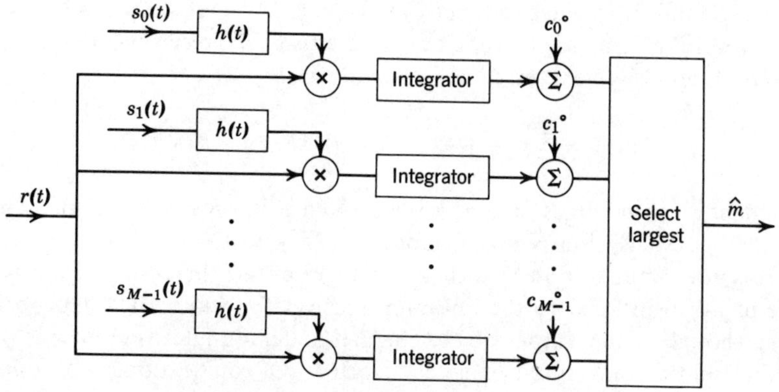

Figure 7.2 Filtered-reference correlation receiver.

The matched-filter version of the optimum receiver is shown in Fig. 7.3. Since the spectrum of $s_i^\circ(t)$ is

$$S_i^\circ(f) = S_i(f)\,H(f), \tag{7.3a}$$

we know from Eq. 4.67 that the transfer function of a filter matched to $s_i^\circ(t)$ with delay T is

$$\begin{aligned} G_i(f) &= [S_i^\circ(f)]^* e^{-j2\pi fT} \\ &= S_i^*(f)\,H^*(f) e^{-j2\pi fT}. \end{aligned} \tag{7.3b}$$

Thus each matched filter, $i = 0, 1, \ldots, M-1$, may be realized as the cascade of a filter $H^*(f)e^{-j2\pi fT_1}$ matched to $h(t)$ and a filter $S_i^*(f)e^{-j2\pi fT_2}$ matched to $s_i(t)$, with $T_1 + T_2 = T$. Since the first filter is common to all i,

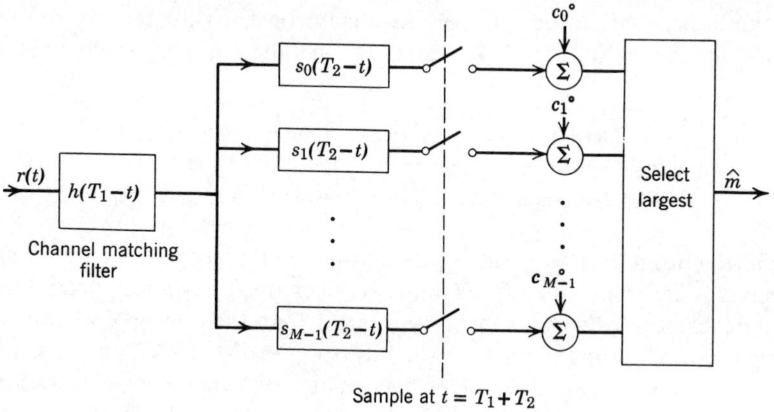

Figure 7.3 Filtered-signal receiver with M signal-matched filters.

it is economical to place it directly after the channel, as shown in Fig. 7.3. The resulting structure is called a "filtered-signal" receiver. If the (unfiltered) signals are expressed as

$$s_i(t) = \sum_{j=1}^{N} s_{ij}\, \varphi_j(t); \qquad i = 0, 1, \ldots, M - 1, \tag{7.4}$$

the final receiver stages may be implemented with only N filters, matched to the $\{\varphi_j(t)\}$, as discussed in Chapter 4.

It is interesting to note that the final stages of the filtered-signal receiver are identical in form to the optimum receiver for white Gaussian noise, even though at the output of the channel-matching filter the noise is not white and the transmitted signal is distorted. Of course it does not follow that the error probability is the same as that obtained with white Gaussian noise and without channel filtering.

If the relationship between the transmitted signal $s(t)$ and the received signal $s^\circ(t)$ is statistical rather than causal (for instance if a in Eq. 7.1b is a random parameter), the unique correspondence between the $\{m_i\}$ and the $\{s_i^\circ(t)\}$ will be broken, and the foregoing analysis will be invalid. Such situations are considered in Section 7.3. As a practical matter, whether we should treat a parameter as random or known depends on whether the vector signal constellation and the decision regions implied thereby are seriously affected when the value of the parameter varies over its probable range (see the discussion of component accuracy, Section 4.4).

Theorem on Reversibility

Analysis is somewhat more complicated when a linear filter colors white Gaussian noise before it is added to the received signal. In this and certain other cases to be considered we may construct the receiver in two steps, as shown in Fig. 7.4. First, an operation is performed on the

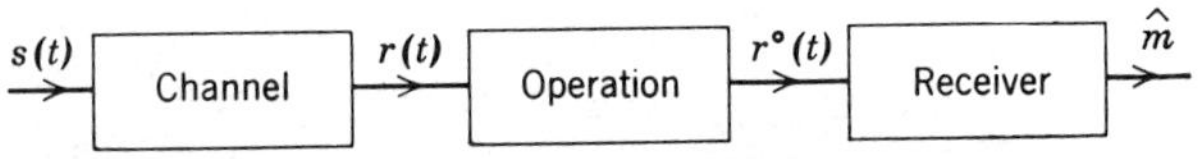

Figure 7.4 Insertion of an operation between channel and receiver.

channel output $r(t)$ to yield a new output, $r^\circ(t)$; second, an optimum receiver is designed with $r^\circ(t)$ as input. Clearly, such a two-step procedure cannot result in a *lower* probability of error than the one-step process of designing an optimum receiver directly for the input $r(t)$; indeed, an *increase* in the probability of error may result. But if an inverse operation exists which permits $r(t)$ to be reconstructed from $r^\circ(t)$ (as discussed in Section 4.2), the theorem on reversibility states that the probability of error need not be increased by the two-step procedure. [The second step may consist of the calculation of $r(t)$ from $r^{\circ}(t)$ followed by the optimum receiver for $r(t)$.] In its most general form the *theorem on reversibility* states:

A reversible operation, transforming $r(t)$ into one or more waveforms, may be inserted between the channel output and the receiver without affecting the minimum attainable probability of error.

Additive Nonwhite Gaussian Noise

The theorem on reversibility may be applied immediately to the design of an optimum receiver for a channel with additive nonwhite Gaussian noise. Suppose that the received signal is

$$r(t) = s(t) + n(t), \tag{7.5}$$

where $n(t)$ is zero-mean Gaussian noise whose power spectrum $\mathcal{S}_n(f)$ is not constant for all frequencies. Under very weak conditions,† which we may always assume to be satisfied in a physical system, there exists a linear filter, with impulse response $g(t)$ and transfer function $G(f)$, which *has a realizable inverse* and for which

$$|G(f)|^2 = \frac{\mathcal{N}_0}{2} \frac{1}{\mathcal{S}_n(f)}. \tag{7.6a}$$

If $n(t)$ is the input to this filter, the output (by Eq. 3.114) is a Gaussian process with power spectrum

$$|G(f)|^2 \mathcal{S}_n(f) = \mathcal{N}_0/2; \tag{7.6b}$$

that is, the output is white noise. The filter $G(f)$ is called a *whitening* filter.

As an example, consider

$$\mathcal{S}_n(f) = \frac{f^2 + 4}{f^2 + 1}. \tag{7.7a}$$

† The condition is that the Paley-Wiener[38] criterion

$$\int_{-\infty}^{\infty} \frac{|\ln \mathcal{S}_n(f)|}{1 + f^2}\, df < \infty$$

be satisfied. If it is not, the noise is singular in the sense that its future values may be predicted exactly from knowledge of any interval of its past. We have already observed one such example in Appendix 5B. For a complete discussion, see W. L. Root, "Singular Gaussian measures in Detection Theory," Chapter 20 of *Time Series Analysis* (M. Rosenblatt, Ed.), John Wiley & Sons, New York, 1963.

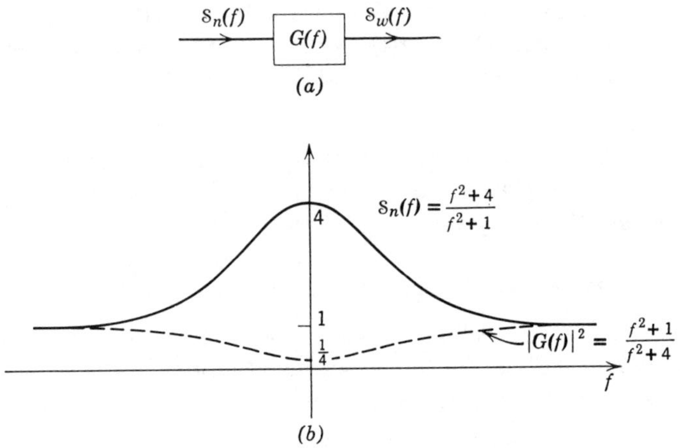

Figure 7.5 Example of power spectrum of noise and whitening filter.

As illustrated in Fig. 7.5, we may set

$$G(f) = \frac{jf + 1}{jf + 2}, \tag{7.7b}$$

which yields at its output the power spectrum $\mathcal{S}_w(f) = \mathcal{N}_0/2 = 1$. A possible implementation is shown in Fig. 7.6*a*, in which $n(t)$ and $n_w(t)$ are assumed to be voltages. Clearly, the filter $G(f)$ has a realizable inverse, to wit, the filter with system function

$$G^{-1}(f) = \frac{jf + 2}{jf + 1}. \tag{7.7c}$$

A realization for the filter $G^{-1}(f)$ is shown in Fig. 7.6*b*.

The filter $G(f)$ in Eq. 7.7 was determined by a general method that is

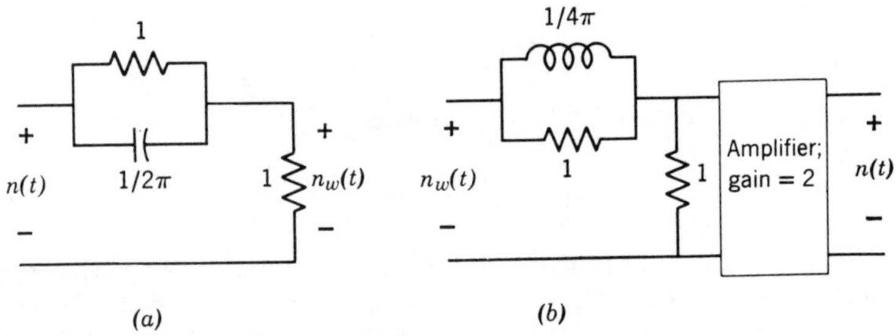

Figure 7.6 Realization of whitening filter and inverse for $\mathcal{S}_n(f) = (f^2 + 4)/(f^2 + 1)$: (*a*) $G(f)$; (*b*) $G^{-1}(f)$.

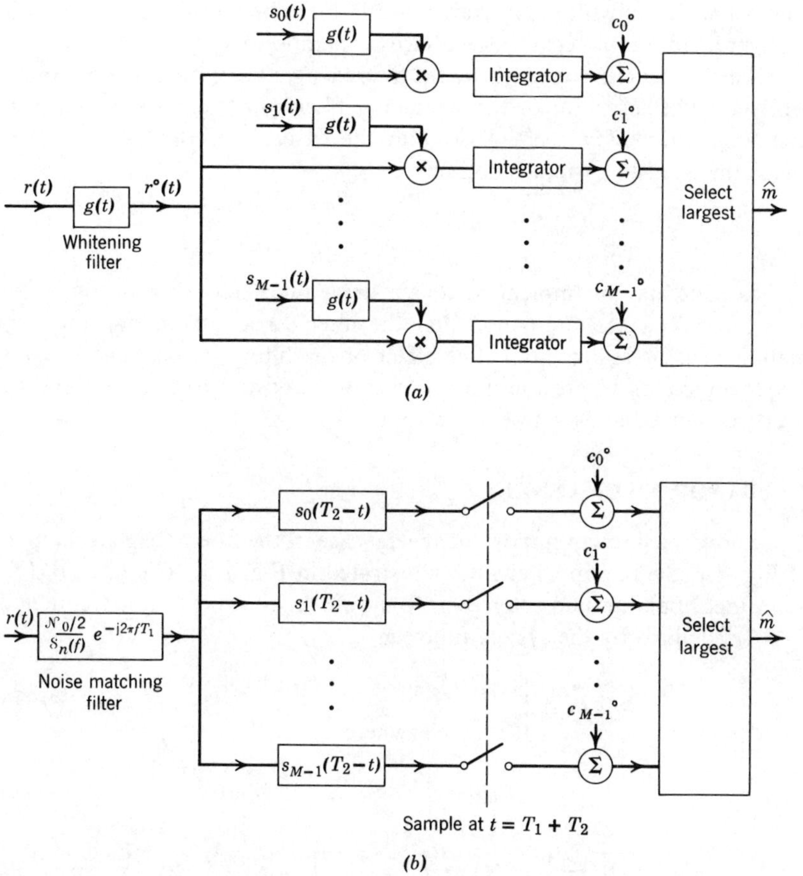

Figure 7.7 Optimum receivers for nonwhite Gaussian noise channel, $r(t) = s(t) + n(t)$: (*a*) filtered-reference receiver; (*b*) filtered-signal receiver.

applicable whenever $\mathcal{S}_n(f)$ can be written as a ratio of two polynomials in f. The method is discussed in Appendix 7A.

Once the (reversible) whitening filter is known, the optimum receiver is easily determined. Place the whitening filter at the channel output. Since the filter input is $r(t) = s(t) + n(t)$, the filter output is

$$r^\circ(t) = s^\circ(t) + n_w(t), \tag{7.8}$$

where $s^\circ(t)$ is the response of the whitening filter to the input $s(t)$. The combination of channel and $G(f)$ in cascade appears as an additive white Gaussian noise, filtered-signal channel. The filtered-reference receiver for $r^\circ(t)$ is that given in Fig. 7.2, hence the entire receiver for an additive channel with nonwhite Gaussian noise is that shown in Fig. 7.7*a*. This receiver is optimum because the filtering operation $G(f)$ is reversible.

It is also instructive to consider the filtered-signal version of the optimum receiver. The insertion of the whitening filter $G(f)$ calls for a channel-matching filter $G^*(f)e^{-j2\pi fT_1}$, so that the cascade of the two together yields the over-all system function

$$G(f)\, G^*(f)e^{-j2\pi fT_1} = \frac{\mathcal{N}_0/2}{\mathcal{S}_n(f)}\, e^{-j2\pi fT_1}. \tag{7.9}$$

The cascade may be implemented as a single filter, as shown in Fig. 7.7*b*; we choose T_1 large enough so that the filter (or a satisfactory approximation of it) is realizable.† The effect of the filter is to pass energy over frequency bands where the noise power is weak and to suppress energy over frequency bands where it is strong.

7.2 BANDPASS CHANNELS

We now consider an important special case of the filtered-signal channel of Fig. 7.1, the bandpass channel illustrated in Fig. 7.8. The filter $W_0(f)$ is an ideal bandlimited filter, with bandwidth $2W$ and center frequency $f_0 > W$, defined by the system function

$$W_0(f) \triangleq \begin{cases} 1; & f_0 - W < |f| < f_0 + W \\ 0; & \text{elsewhere.} \end{cases} \tag{7.10}$$

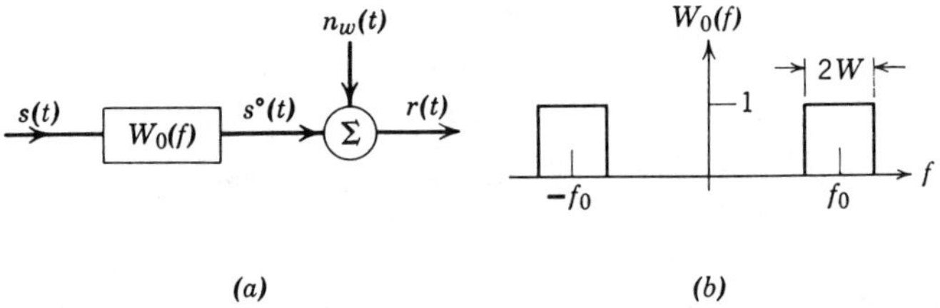

Figure 7.8 Ideal bandpass additive white Gaussian noise channel.

Since this channel is a special case of the general filtered channel, the preceding derivation of the optimum receiver and the implementation diagrammed in Fig. 7.2 remain valid. It is common engineering practice, however, to produce the signal set $\{s_i°(t)\}$ directly at the transmitter by first generating low-frequency (*baseband*) signals $\{s_i(t)\}$ and then translating them in frequency (*heterodyning* them) up into the passband of

† Determination of the best receiver is more involved when a constraint is imposed on the maximum allowable value of the delay T_1.[21]

$W_0(f)$. At the receiver the signals are heterodyned back down from passband to baseband, and the decision about the transmitted message is based on the resulting low-frequency waveforms. The technique is useful even when the channel noise is not white.

DSB-SC Modulation

A possible system of this sort is shown in Fig. 7.9: the frequency translation at the transmitter is called *double-sideband suppressed carrier*

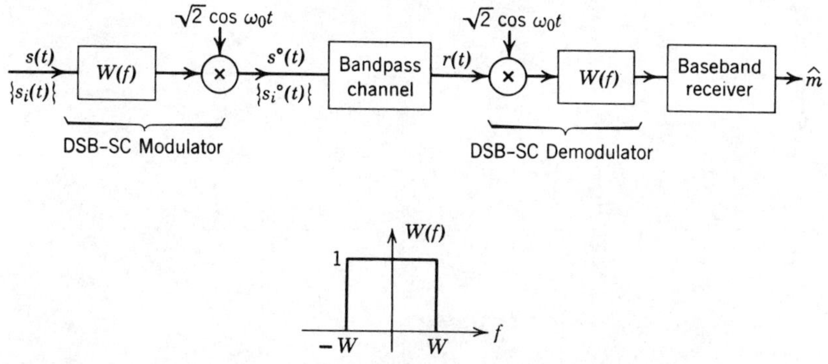

Figure 7.9 System utilizing DSB-SC modulation-demodulation; $\omega_0 \triangleq 2\pi f_0$.

(DSB-SC) amplitude modulation and that at the receiver is called *synchronous demodulation*. We shall consider bandpass channels identical to that of Fig. 7.8, except generalized to situations in which the power spectrum of the noise is not white. The ideal lowpass modulator filter

$$W(f) \triangleq \begin{cases} 1; & |f| < W \\ 0; & \text{elsewhere} \end{cases} \tag{7.11}$$

has been introduced into Fig. 7.9 as an explicit reminder [for all $s_i(t)$] that $S_i(f) \equiv 0$ for $|f| \geqslant W$, where $S_i(f)$ denotes the Fourier transform of $s_i(t)$.

The reason for the nomenclature "double-sideband suppressed carrier" is clarified in Fig. 7.10. Since multiplying two functions in the time domain corresponds to convolving their spectra in the frequency domain, the Fourier spectrum of any transmitted signal $s_i^\circ(t)$ contains two sidebands located symmetrically about $\pm f_0$ and therefore occupies twice the bandwidth occupied by $s_i(t)$. The sinusoid $\sqrt{2}\cos\omega_0 t$ is called the *carrier*; the fact that $s_i^\circ(t)$ does not contain any discrete Fourier component at f_0 accounts for the suppressed-carrier terminology.

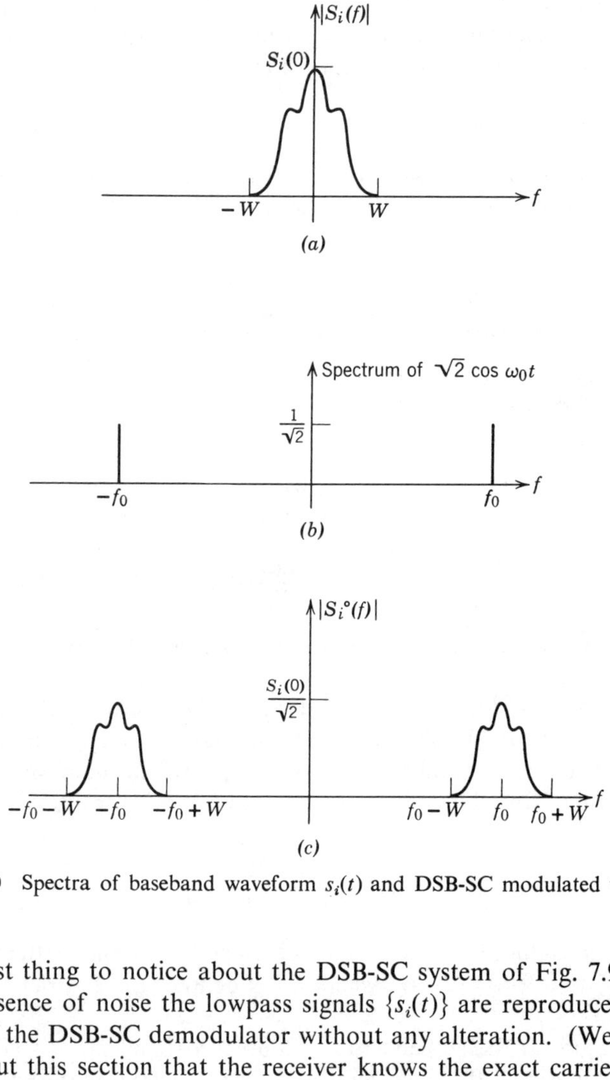

Figure 7.10 Spectra of baseband waveform $s_i(t)$ and DSB-SC modulated waveform $s_i^\circ(t)$.

The first thing to notice about the DSB-SC system of Fig. 7.9 is that in the absence of noise the lowpass signals $\{s_i(t)\}$ are reproduced at the output of the DSB-SC demodulator without any alteration. (We assume throughout this section that the receiver knows the exact carrier phase. The random-phase case is considered in Section 7.3.) Indeed, remultiplying by $\sqrt{2} \cos \omega_0 t$ at the receiver and lowpass filtering with $W(f)$ exactly undoes the modulation performed at the transmitter: using the subscript "lp" to mean "the low-frequency components of," we have

$$\{[s_i(t)\sqrt{2} \cos \omega_0 t]\,[\sqrt{2} \cos \omega_0 t]\}_{lp} = 2s_i(t)[\tfrac{1}{2} + \tfrac{1}{2} \cos 2\omega_0 t]_{lp} = s_i(t). \quad (7.12)$$

The normalizing factors $\sqrt{2}$ maintain the energy of $s_i{}^\circ(t)$ equal to that of $s_i(t)$; by inspection of Fig. 7.10 and use of Parseval's theorem we have

$$\int_{-\infty}^{\infty} [s_i(t)]^2\, dt = \int_{-\infty}^{\infty} |S_i(f)|^2\, df = \int_{-\infty}^{\infty} |S_i{}^\circ(f)|^2\, df = \int_{-\infty}^{\infty} [s_i{}^\circ(t)]^2\, dt. \quad (7.13)$$

The reason for the restriction $f_0 > W$ in Eq. 7.10 is illustrated in Fig. 7.11*a*: if $f_0 < W$, the spectral terms $S_i(f+f_0)$ and $S_i(f-f_0)$ overlap

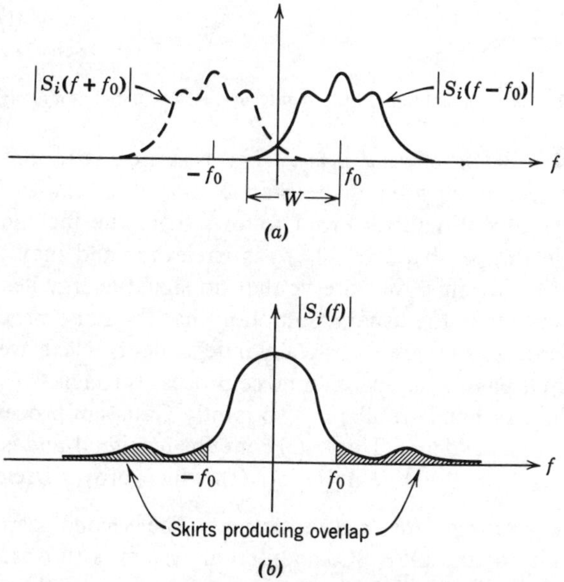

Figure 7.11 Distortion in DSB-SC operation due to aliasing.

around $f = 0$, and $s_i(t)$ is not regained exactly from $s_i{}^\circ(t)$ by DSB-SC demodulation; the resulting distortion is called "aliasing." In engineering practice we deal with actual rather than ideal lowpass signals, which are, of course, unrealizable. Aliasing becomes a problem when the spectrum skirts and frequency f_0 are so related that the spectral overlap is significant, as indicated in Fig. 7.11*b*.

It remains to determine the conditions under which the modulation and demodulation operations, in addition to being convenient from an engineering point of view, do not degrade the error performance that can be achieved when stationary Gaussian noise $n(t)$ (which may or may not be white) is present. The derivation is somewhat long, but it can be broken down into a series of relatively straightforward steps, each of which provides important insight into the problem.

$$W_0(f) = \begin{cases} 1; & f_0 - W < |f| < f_0 + W \\ 0; & \text{elsewhere} \end{cases}$$

$$\widetilde{W}_0(f) = \begin{cases} 0; & f_0 - W < |f| < f_0 + W \\ 1; & \text{elsewhere} \end{cases}$$

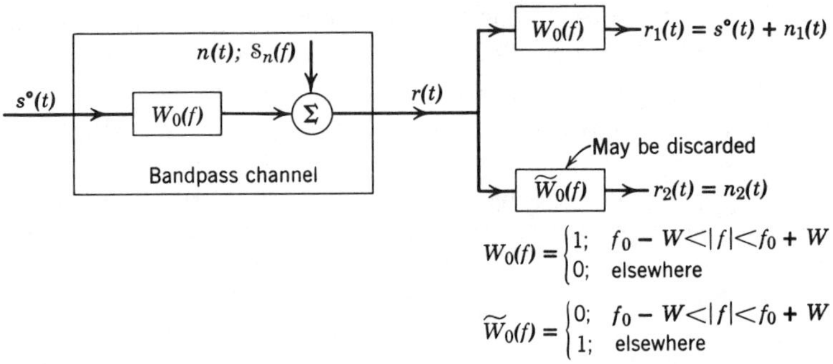

Figure 7.12 Bandpass channel output filtering. It is clear that $r(t) = r_1(t) + r_2(t)$.

Elimination of out-of-band noise. The first step is to observe that a filter $W_0(f)$ can be applied at the channel output, as shown in Fig. 7.12, without loss of optimality. Proof follows from the fact that the noise $r_2(t)$ outside the passband of $W_0(f)$ is irrelevant and may therefore be discarded. To see this, we observe that no signal energy lies outside the passband and make the usual assumption that the noise process $n(t)$ and the signal process $s°(t)$ are statistically independent. Next, we recall from Eq. 3.130 that passing a Gaussian noise process through two linear filters with disjoint passbands results in two jointly Gaussian processes that are statistically independent. Thus $r_2(t)$ contains no signal and is statistically independent of the additive noise in $r_1(t)$, which proves irrelevance.

Bandpass filtering with lowpass filters. The second step in proving the optimality of the DSB-SC modulation system is to observe that the bandpass filter $W_0(f)$ can be implemented by means of the parallel sine-cosine demodulator-modulator cascades shown in Fig. 7.13. Let $h_r(t)$ denote the response of this demodulator-modulator complex to an

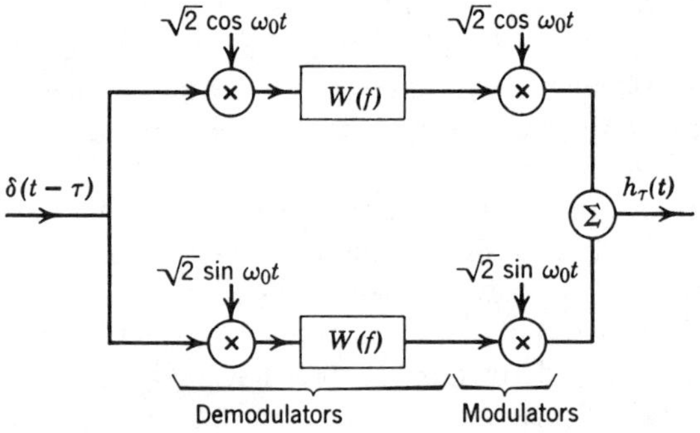

Figure 7.13 Demodulator-modulator cascade with parallel sine and cosine channels.

impulse $\delta(t-\tau)$ applied at time τ and let $w(t)$ denote the impulse response of the lowpass filter $W(f)$. We observe directly from Fig. 7.13 that

$$\begin{aligned} h_\tau(t) &= \sqrt{2}\cos\omega_0 t\int_{-\infty}^{\infty}\delta(\alpha-\tau)\sqrt{2}\cos\omega_0\alpha\, w(t-\alpha)\,d\alpha \\ &\quad + \sqrt{2}\sin\omega_0 t\int_{-\infty}^{\infty}\delta(\beta-\tau)\sqrt{2}\sin\omega_0\beta\, w(t-\beta)\,d\beta \\ &= 2w(t-\tau)[\cos\omega_0 t\cos\omega_0\tau + \sin\omega_0 t\sin\omega_0\tau] \\ &= 2w(t-\tau)\cos\omega_0(t-\tau). \end{aligned} \tag{7.14}$$

On the other hand, since $W_0(f)$ is obtained when $W(f)$ is convolved with $[\delta(f-f_0)+\delta(f+f_0)]$, the impulse response of $W_0(f)$ is the product of $w(t)$ and the inverse Fourier transform of $[\delta(f-f_0)+\delta(f+f_0)]$, namely $2\cos\omega_0 t$. Hence the response of $W_0(f)$ to the delayed impulse $\delta(t-\tau)$ is $2w(t-\tau)\cos\omega_0(t-\tau)$, which is identical to the response of the demodulator-modulator complex given by Eq. 7.14. We conclude that the demodulator-modulator complex is interchangable with the time-invariant filter $W_0(f)$—both produce the same output when driven by a common input.

By combining the results of the first two steps of our analysis, we see that the cascaded receiver arrangement of Fig. 7.14*a* entails no loss of optimality: the demodulator-modulator complex is equivalent to the bandpass filter $W_0(f)$ of Fig. 7.12 and acts only to discard irrelevant noise outside the signal band.

Since the output of the modulator and summing stages in Fig. 7.14*a* is sufficient for making an optimum determination of $\hat{m}$, so also must be the two modulator inputs. Thus we may drop the modulator and summing stages and build an optimum receiver that operates directly on the lowpass signals $r_c(t)$ and $r_s(t)$, as shown in Fig. 7.14*b*.

Demodulated noise. Figure 7.14*b*, except for the sine demodulator, is identical in form to the corresponding stages of Fig. 7.9. Moreover, with reference to these figures we note that

$$[(s_i(t)\sqrt{2}\cos\omega_0 t)(\sqrt{2}\sin\omega_0 t)]_{lp} = [s_i(t)\sin 2\,\omega_0 t]_{lp} \equiv 0 \tag{7.15}$$

for all i, so that no signal term is present in $r_s(t)$. When $m = m_i$, we therefore have

$$r_c(t) \triangleq s_i(t) + n_c(t), \tag{7.16a}$$

$$r_s(t) \triangleq n_s(t). \tag{7.16b}$$

The third step in determining the optimality of our DSB-SC receiver is to ascertain under what conditions the noise $n_s(t)$ is irrelevant and may be discarded. Since $n_c(t)$ and $n_s(t)$ result from linear (albeit time-variant) operations performed on the stationary Gaussian process $n(t)$, they are jointly Gaussian. We assume that $n(t)$, hence $n_c(t)$ and $n_s(t)$, is zero-mean. It follows that $n_s(t)$ is statistically independent of $n_c(t)$ and may be discarded if and only if the crosscorrelation function

$$\mathcal{R}_{cs}(t_1, t_2) \triangleq \overline{n_c(t_1)\, n_s(t_2)} \tag{7.17a}$$

is zero for *all* observation instants t_1 and t_2.

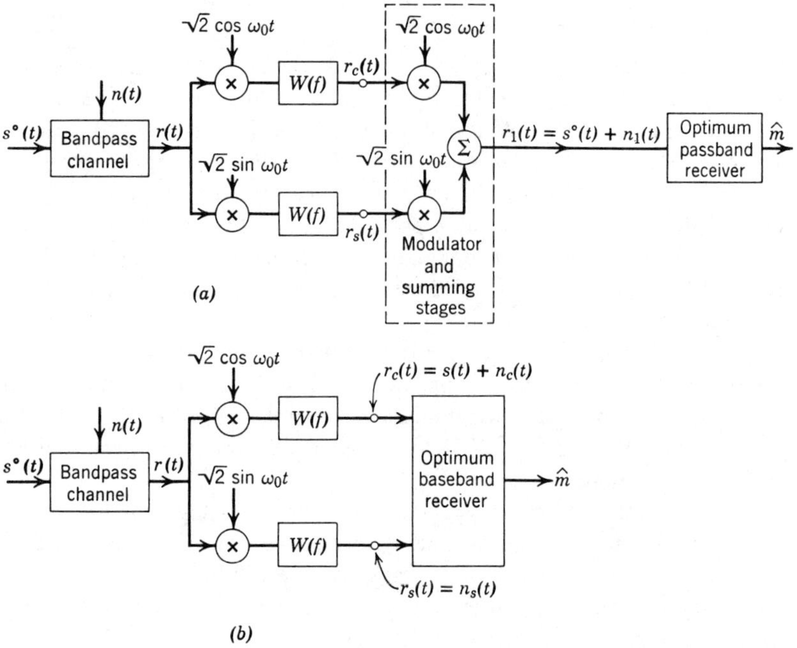

Figure 7.14 Optimum receiver for sine and cosine DSB-SC demodulation; $r(t) = s^\circ(t) + n(t)$.

In this section we determine the crosscorrelation function $\mathcal{R}_{cs}$, as well as the autocorrelation functions

$$\mathcal{R}_c(t_1, t_2) \triangleq \overline{n_c(t_1)\, n_c(t_2)} \tag{7.17b}$$

$$\mathcal{R}_s(t_1, t_2) \triangleq \overline{n_s(t_1)\, n_s(t_2)}. \tag{7.17c}$$

From Fig. 7.14*b*

$$n_c(t) = \sqrt{2}\int_{-\infty}^{\infty} n(\alpha) \cos \omega_0\alpha\, w(t - \alpha)\, d\alpha \tag{7.18a}$$

$$n_s(t) = \sqrt{2}\int_{-\infty}^{\infty} n(\alpha) \sin \omega_0\alpha\, w(t - \alpha)\, d\alpha, \tag{7.18b}$$

where $w(t)$ is the impulse response of the ideal lowpass filter $W(f)$. As a labor-saving device, we introduce the definition

$$\gamma(t) \triangleq n_c(t) + jn_s(t) = \sqrt{2}\int_{-\infty}^{\infty} n(\alpha)e^{j\omega_0\alpha}\, w(t-\alpha)\, d\alpha. \tag{7.19a}$$

Thus

$$\gamma^*(t) = n_c(t) - jn_s(t) = \sqrt{2}\int_{-\infty}^{\infty} n(\beta)e^{-j\omega_0\beta}\, w(t-\beta)\, d\beta. \tag{7.19b}$$

We then have

$$\overline{\gamma(t_1)\,\gamma^*(t_2)} = 2\int_{-\infty}^{\infty}\int_{-\infty}^{\infty} \overline{n(\alpha)\, n(\beta)}e^{j\omega_0(\alpha-\beta)}\, w(t_1-\alpha)\, w(t_2-\beta)\, d\alpha\, d\beta$$

$$= 2\int_{-\infty}^{\infty}\int_{-\infty}^{\infty} \mathcal{R}_n(\alpha-\beta)e^{j2\pi f_0(\alpha-\beta)}\, w(t_1-\alpha)\, w(t_2-\beta)\, d\alpha\, d\beta.$$

Substituting

$$\mathcal{R}_n(\alpha-\beta) = \int_{-\infty}^{\infty} \mathcal{S}_n(f)e^{+j2\pi f(\alpha-\beta)}\, df$$

and separating the integrals yields

$$\overline{\gamma(t_1)\,\gamma^*(t_2)} = 2\int_{-\infty}^{\infty} \mathcal{S}_n(f)\, df \int_{-\infty}^{\infty} w(t_1-\alpha)e^{j2\pi\alpha(f+f_0)}\, d\alpha$$

$$\times \int_{-\infty}^{\infty} w(t_2-\beta)e^{-j2\pi\beta(f+f_0)}\, d\beta. \tag{7.20a}$$

Letting $\mu = t_1 - \alpha$, we observe that

$$\int_{-\infty}^{\infty} w(t_1-\alpha)e^{j2\pi\alpha(f+f_0)}\, d\alpha = \int_{-\infty}^{\infty} w(\mu)e^{j2\pi(t_1-\mu)(f+f_0)}\, d\mu$$

$$= e^{j2\pi t_1(f+f_0)}\, W(f+f_0). \tag{7.20b}$$

Similarly,

$$\int_{-\infty}^{\infty} w(t_2-\beta)e^{-j2\pi\beta(f+f_0)}\, d\beta = e^{-j2\pi t_2(f+f_0)}\, W^*(f+f_0). \tag{7.20c}$$

It follows that

$$\overline{\gamma(t_1)\,\gamma^*(t_2)} = 2\int_{-\infty}^{\infty} \mathcal{S}_n(f)\, |W(f+f_0)|^2\, e^{j2\pi(f+f_0)(t_1-t_2)}\, df$$

$$= 2\int_{-W}^{W} \mathcal{S}_n(\nu - f_0)e^{j2\pi\nu\tau}\, d\nu. \tag{7.21a}$$

in which we have used $\tau \triangleq t_1 - t_2$ and introduced the change of variables $\nu = f + f_0$.

A parallel derivation leads to the result

$$\overline{\gamma(t_1)\,\gamma(t_2)} = 2\int_{-\infty}^{\infty} \mathcal{S}_n(f)\, W(f+f_0)\, W^*(f-f_0) \times \exp\{j2\pi[t_1(f+f_0) - t_2(f-f_0)]\}\, df \equiv 0. \tag{7.21b}$$

Here the identity stems from the fact that

$$W(f+f_0)\, W^*(f-f_0) \equiv 0; \qquad \text{for all } f$$

whenever $f_0 > W$.

We now combine Eqs. 7.21a and b. From Eqs. 7.19

$$\overline{\gamma(t_1)\,\gamma^*(t_2)} = \overline{[n_c(t_1) + jn_s(t_1)][n_c(t_2) - jn_s(t_2)]} \tag{7.22a}$$

and

$$\overline{\gamma(t_1)\,\gamma(t_2)} = \overline{[n_c(t_1) + jn_s(t_1)][n_c(t_2) + jn_s(t_2)]}. \tag{7.22b}$$

Equating the real and imaginary parts in both Eqs. 7.21 and 7.22 and invoking the definitions of Eqs. 7.17, we have

$$\mathcal{R}_c(\tau) = \mathcal{R}_s(\tau) = \operatorname{Re}\int_{-W}^{W} \mathcal{S}_n(f-f_0)e^{j2\pi f\tau}\, df, \tag{7.23a}$$

$$\mathcal{R}_{sc}(\tau) = -\mathcal{R}_{cs}(\tau) = \operatorname{Im}\int_{-W}^{W} \mathcal{S}_n(f-f_0)e^{j2\pi f\tau}\, df. \tag{7.23b}$$

Finally, if we write $\mathcal{S}_n(f-f_0)$, $-W < f < W$, in terms of its *even* and *odd* parts, say $\mathcal{S}_e(f)$ and $\mathcal{S}_o(f)$, respectively, we obtain the important results

$$\mathcal{S}_n(f-f_0) = \mathcal{S}_e(f) + \mathcal{S}_o(f); \qquad -W < f < W, \tag{7.24a}$$

$$\mathcal{R}_c(\tau) = \mathcal{R}_s(\tau) = \int_{-W}^{W} \mathcal{S}_e(f) \cos 2\pi f\tau\, df, \tag{7.24b}$$

$$\mathcal{R}_{sc}(\tau) = -\mathcal{R}_{cs}(\tau) = \int_{-W}^{W} \mathcal{S}_o(f) \sin 2\pi f\tau\, df, \tag{7.24c}$$

where, as before, $\tau \triangleq t_1 - t_2$. The mechanics of Eqs. 7.24 are illustrated in Fig. 7.15.

In interpreting the significance of Eqs. 7.24, it is important to note that the derivation does not require that $n(t)$ be a Gaussian process but only that it be wide-sense stationary. From this attribute alone it follows that the two demodulated processes $n_c(t)$ and $n_s(t)$ are also wide-sense stationary and that each has the same power spectrum, $\mathcal{S}_e(f)$. Remarkably, this is true even though these processes are obtained from $n(t)$ by means of a time-variant operation. We note that samples taken from the two lowpass processes at the same instant (implying $\tau = 0$) are always uncorrelated; $\overline{n_c(t)\, n_s(t)} = 0$. The samples are uncorrelated for *all* observation instants t_1 and t_2 *if and only if* $\mathcal{S}_n(f - f_0)$ *is even over the band* $[-W, W]$.

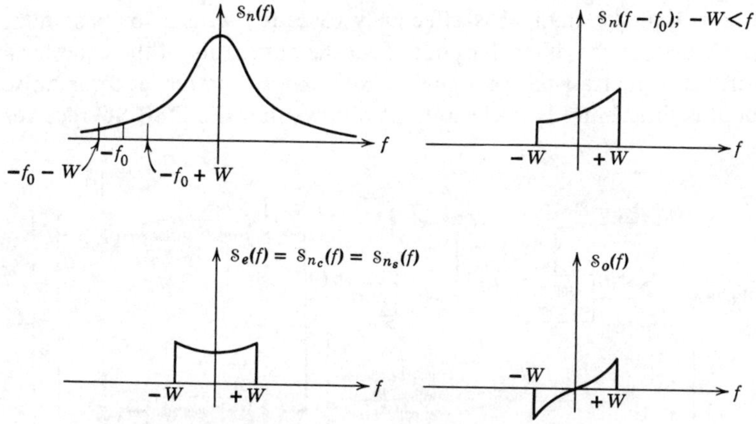

$\mathcal{S}_e(f) = \frac{1}{2}[\mathcal{S}_n(f - f_0) + \mathcal{S}_n(-f - f_0)]; \quad -W < f < W$

$\mathcal{S}_o(f) = \frac{1}{2}[\mathcal{S}_n(f - f_0) - \mathcal{S}_n(-f - f_0)]; \quad -W < f < W$

Figure 7.15 Determination of $\mathcal{S}_e(f)$ and $\mathcal{S}_o(f)$ from $\mathcal{S}_n(f)$.

Optimum receivers. When the stationary noise process $n(t)$ is Gaussian, $n_c(t)$ and $n_s(t)$ are statistically independent as long as they are uncorrelated for all pairs of observation instants. Thus $n_s(t)$ is irrelevant whenever $\mathcal{S}_n(f - f_0)$ is even over $[-W, W]$. It is under this condition that the sine demodulator in Fig. 7.14*b* can be discarded without increasing the minimum attainable probability of error. In particular, the condition is met when $n(t)$ is white Gaussian noise. In this case, to which we now direct our attention,

$$\mathcal{S}_n(f - f_0) = \mathcal{S}_n(-f - f_0) = \frac{\mathcal{N}_0}{2}. \tag{7.25a}$$

Thus

$$\mathcal{S}_e(f) = \mathcal{S}_{n_c}(f) = \begin{cases} \dfrac{\mathcal{N}_0}{2}; & \text{for } |f| < W \\ 0; & \text{elsewhere} \end{cases} \tag{7.25b}$$

and

$$\mathcal{R}_{cs}(\tau) \equiv 0. \tag{7.25c}$$

The fourth and final step in deriving the optimum DSB-SC receiver for white Gaussian noise is to make an optimum decision in regard to the transmitted signal on the basis of the remaining baseband signal

$$r_c(t) = s(t) + n_c(t). \tag{7.26}$$

This problem we have already solved in Chapter 4. If the signals $\{s_i(t)\}$ were to be transmitted directly over a channel corrupted by additive white Gaussian noise, the optimum receiver would crosscorrelate the received signal against each of the $\{s_i(t)\}$. The only difference implied by Eqs. 7.25b and 7.26 is that the channel is effectively cascaded with a lowpass filter $W(f)$. Clearly, such a filter does not affect the optimality of the Chapter 4 receiver, since the transmitted signal is not changed thereby and the noise outside this filter band is irrelevant. It follows that the DSB-SC receiver

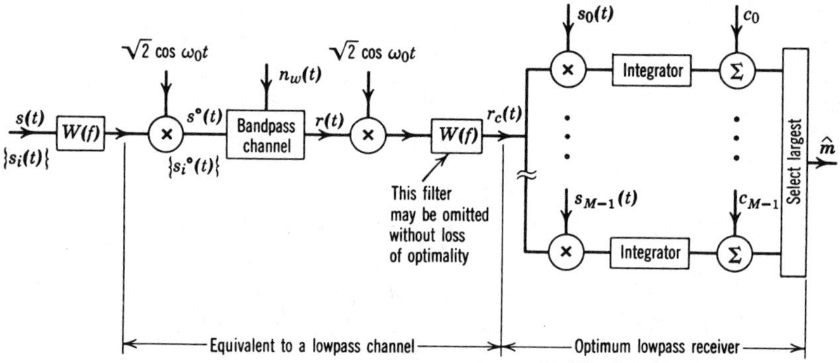

$$c_i = \mathcal{N}_0/2 \ln P[m_i] - \tfrac{1}{2}\int_{-\infty}^{\infty} s_i^2(t)\,dt; \quad i = 0, 1, \ldots, M-1$$

Figure 7.16 Complete DSB-SC system for white Gaussian noise.

shown in Fig. 7.16 is optimum and that the over-all system performance is identical to that which would be obtained if the lowpass signals $\{s_i(t)\}$ were used, without modulation, over a white Gaussian noise channel with the same noise power density $\mathcal{N}_0/2$. The fact that the lowpass filter $W(f)$ may be omitted from the receiver demodulator should be noted: since correlation of $r_c(t)$ with the $\{s_i(t)\}$ can also be performed by matched filtering and each matched filter is itself a lowpass filter, $W(f)$ is redundant.

If $S_n(f-f_0)$ is even but not constant over $[-W, W]$, a realization of the optimum lowpass receiver may be constructed by passing $r_c(t)$ through an invertible filter that effectively "whitens" $n_c(t)$ over the baseband.

Bandpass signal decomposition. The equivalence of the demodulator-modulator complex of Fig. 7.13 to the bandpass filter $W_0(f)$ has other interesting implications, the most immediately obvious being that any Fourier-transformable bandpass signal of bandwidth $2W$ may be written in terms of two lowpass signals, each of bandwidth W, as

$$s(t) = s_c(t)\sqrt{2}\cos 2\pi f_0 t + s_s(t)\sqrt{2}\sin 2\pi f_0 t. \tag{7.27}$$

The notation is that of Fig. 7.17*a*, with $x(t)$ set equal to $s(t)$. Thus the use of two DSB-SC modulators, one with a cosine and one with a sine carrier, permits the generation of completely general bandpass signals. This same observation applies equally to a (wide-sense) stationary bandpass noise process, $n(t)$, the sample functions of which have infinite energy and therefore do *not* possess a Fourier transform. Again from Fig. 7.17*a*, with

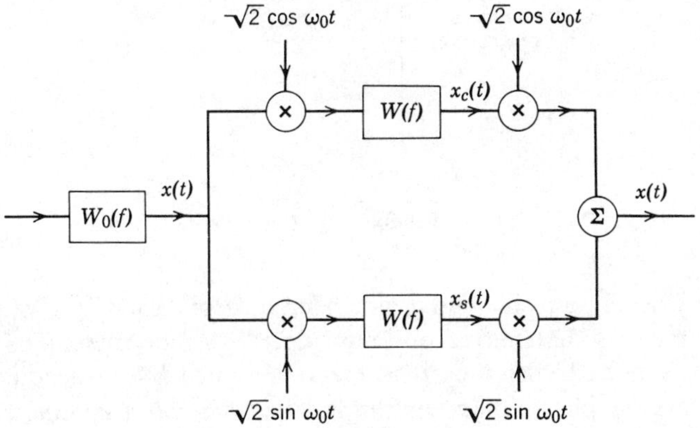

Figure 7.17*a* Decomposition of a bandpass waveform $x(t)$ into two lowpass waveforms.

$x(t) = n(t)$, we have directly

$$n(t) = n_c(t)\sqrt{2}\cos\omega_0 t + n_s(t)\sqrt{2}\sin\omega_0 t. \tag{7.28}$$

Any bandpass noise process, $n(t)$, of bandwidth $2W$ may therefore be decomposed into two lowpass noise processes, $n_c(t)$ and $n_s(t)$, each of bandwidth W.†

Equation 7.28 can be interpreted graphically as shown in Fig. 7.17*b*. We think of $\cos\omega_0 t$ as being a rapidly rotating phasor, with an amplitude $\sqrt{2}n_c(t)$ that varies slowly with respect to the rate of rotation. The term $\sqrt{2}n_s(t)\sin\omega_0 t$ is another such rotating phasor, shifted 90° in phase in relation to the first. The waveform $n(t)$ is the projection of the vector sum of these two phasors on the horizontal axis.

For the Gaussian bandpass channel of Fig. 7.16 the two lowpass noise processes $n_c(t)$ and $n_s(t)$ are statistically independent. If at the transmitter we use both sine and cosine modulators, in accordance with Eq. 7.27 we can simultaneously transmit two waveforms through the bandpass filter $W_0(f)$, each of which is selected under the control of a different, statistically independent transmitter input. In this case the optimum receiver can

† The normalizing factor $\sqrt{2}$ is often dropped. This causes $\mathcal{R}_c(\tau)$, $\mathcal{R}_s(\tau)$, $\mathcal{R}_{cs}(\tau)$, and $\mathcal{R}_{sc}(\tau)$ to have twice the values given by Eqs. 7.24.

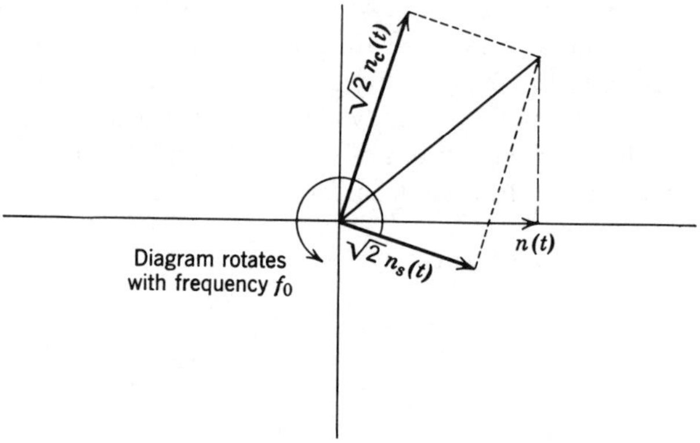

Figure 7.17*b* Phasor bandpass noise representation.

be realized by using both sine and cosine demodulators, each followed by a baseband receiver that makes optimum decisions independent of the other. Since sine and cosine carriers are represented by perpendicular rotating vectors in a phasor diagram, this is called *quadrature multiplexing*.

Single-Sideband Modulation

A second way of performing frequency translation from baseband to passband, called *single-sideband modulation* (SSB), is illustrated in Fig. 7.18. A lowpass waveform $s_i(t)$ is first multiplied by $2 \cos \omega_1 t$, which yields the familiar double-sided frequency spectrum, symmetric about $\pm f_1$. Because of this symmetry it is clear that *both* sidebands are not required to reconstruct the original $s_i(t)$. Accordingly, in an SSB system one of these sidebands is eliminated before transmission, perhaps by means of a sharp cutoff filter which we idealize for analytical purposes by the filter $W_1(f)$ shown in the figure. The transmitted signal $s_i^\circ(t)$ then occupies only a bandwidth W rather than $2W$ as in DSB-SC.

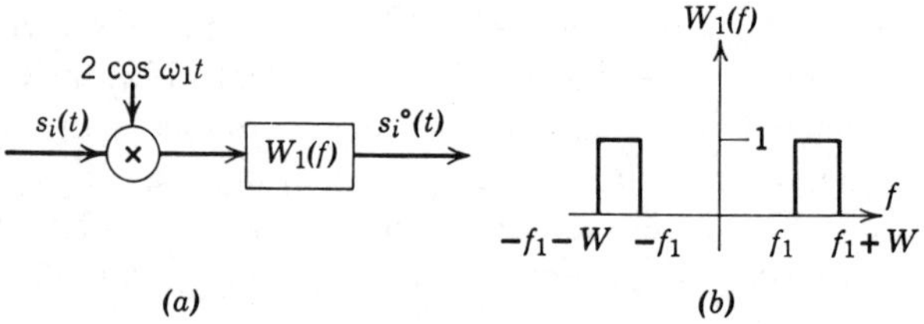

Figure 7.18 Single-sideband modulation; $\omega_1 \triangleq 2\pi f_1$. The baseband signal spectrum $S_i(f)$ is presumed to be identically zero for $|f| \geqslant W$.

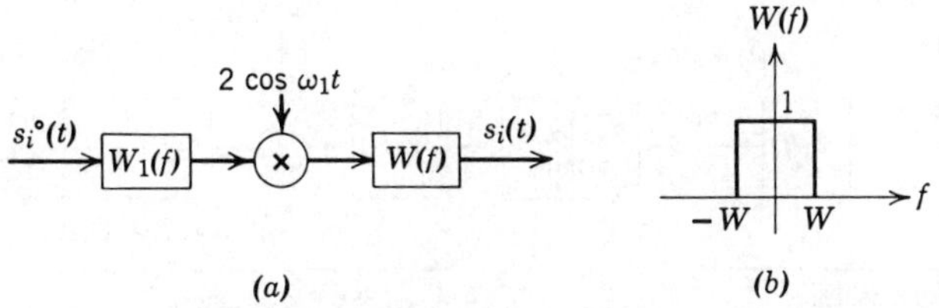

Figure 7.19 Single-sideband demodulator.

An SSB demodulator is shown in Fig. 7.19, and the spectral transformations corresponding to SSB modulation followed by SSB demodulation are illustrated in Fig. 7.20. It is clear that in the absence of noise any Fourier-transformable lowpass signal $s_i(t)$ passing through the SSB modulator-demodulator cascade is reproduced exactly at the output. Conversely, any Fourier-transformable bandpass waveform $s_i^\circ(t)$ applied *first* to the SSB demodulator and *then* to the SSB modulator, as shown in Fig. 7.21, is also reproduced exactly.

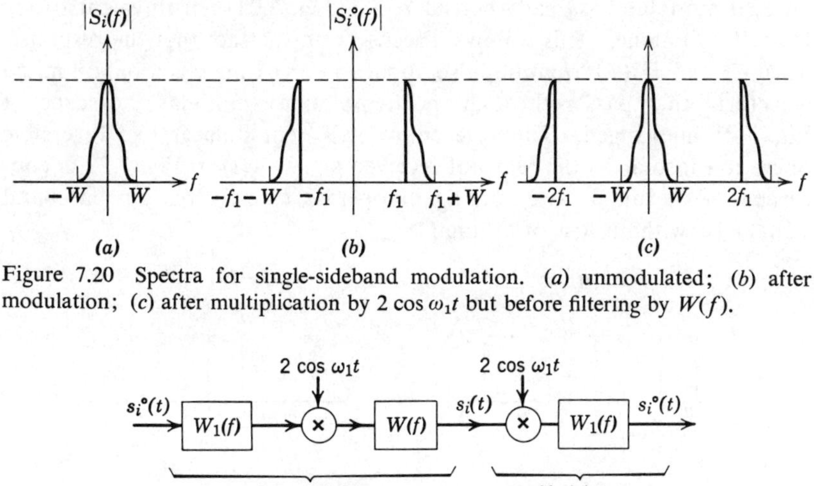

Figure 7.20 Spectra for single-sideband modulation. (*a*) unmodulated; (*b*) after modulation; (*c*) after multiplication by 2 cos $\omega_1 t$ but before filtering by $W(f)$.

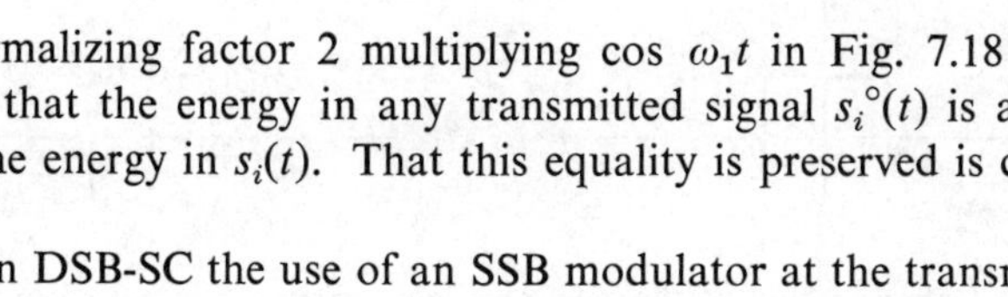

Figure 7.21 SSB demodulator-modulator cascade.

The normalizing factor 2 multiplying cos $\omega_1 t$ in Fig. 7.18 has been chosen so that the energy in any transmitted signal $s_i^\circ(t)$ is again held equal to the energy in $s_i(t)$. That this equality is preserved is clear from Fig. 7.20.

Just as in DSB-SC the use of an SSB modulator at the transmitter and an SSB demodulator at the receiver entails no loss of optimality when

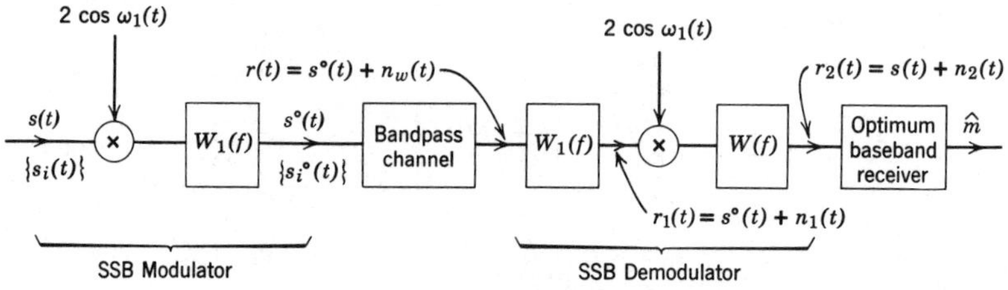

Figure 7.22 Single-sideband system. We assume the channel adds white Gaussian noise but propagates $s°(t)$ without other disturbance.

additive white Gaussian noise is present. Proof is exactly parallel to that for DSB-SC. The notation used in the arguments that follow is defined in the system diagram of Fig. 7.22.

The first step is to note that $s°(t)$ passes through $W_1(f)$ undistorted and that the noise in $r(t)$ outside the passband of $W_1(f)$ is independent of the noise within the band, hence is irrelevant. Thus the insertion of the receiving filter $W_1(f)$ in Fig. 7.22 entails no loss of optimality.

The second step is to note that the cascade of an SSB demodulator and an SSB modulator (already considered in Fig. 7.21) is equivalent to the filter $W_1(f)$ alone. This follows directly from the fact that the response, $w_1(t - \tau)$, of $W_1(f)$ to an impulse applied at any time τ is a band-limited waveform that passes through the demodulator-modulator cascade of Fig. 7.21 unchanged. Thus the entire SSB demodulator is a reversible operation insofar as the relevant received signal $r_1(t)$ in Fig. 7.22 is concerned. Accordingly, we can again operate directly on the baseband signal $r_2(t)$ without loss of optimality.

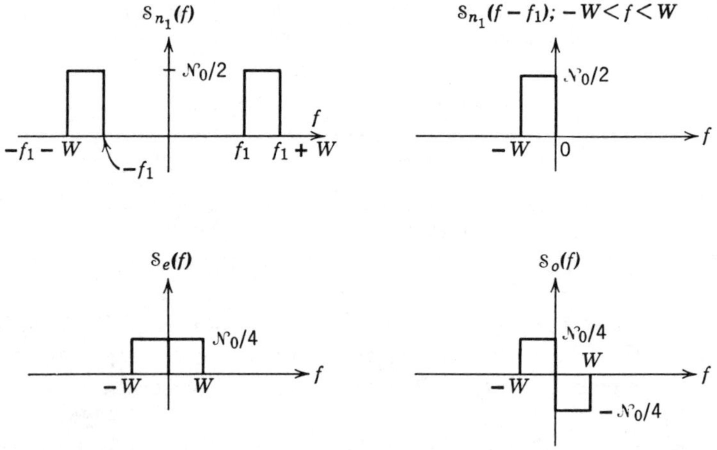

Figure 7.23 Determination of the even and odd parts of $\mathcal{S}_{n_1}(f - f_1)$ over $[-W, W]$. See also Figure 7.15.

[An immediate implication is that we now have a second representation for a bandpass noise process. The process $n_1(t)$, with bandwidth W, completely determines and is determined by a single lowpass process $n_2(t)$, also with bandwidth W. In contradistinction, for DSB-SC we represented a bandpass noise process with bandwidth $2W$ by means of two lowpass processes each with bandwidth W.]

The third step in proving no loss of optimality with SSB requires knowledge of the power spectrum $\mathcal{S}_{n_2}(f)$ of $n_2(t)$, which can be determined immediately by application of Eq. 7.25*b* (see Fig. 7.23). If the normalizing factor multiplying $\cos \omega_1 t$ in the SSB demodulator were $\sqrt{2}$, we would have an output noise-power spectrum of $\mathcal{N}_0/4$ over the band $[-W, W]$. Since the actual factor is 2, however, we multiply $\mathcal{N}_0/4$ by $(2/\sqrt{2})^2$ and obtain

$$\mathcal{S}_{n_2}(f) = \begin{cases} \dfrac{\mathcal{N}_0}{2}, & |f| < W \\ 0, & \text{elsewhere.} \end{cases} \tag{7.29}$$

The final step concerns the optimum reception of lowpass signals in the additive Gaussian noise $n_2(t)$. This noise is flat, with power density $\mathcal{N}_0/2$, over the band occupied by the signals. Thus the receiver of Fig. 7.22 is indeed optimum, and the use of SSB has in no way affected the attainable accuracy of communication. It is important to note that in the SSB receiver the preliminary filter $W_1(f)$ is essential, whereas prefiltering is not essential with DSB-SC. The reason is that $W_1(f)$ prevents noise in the frequency interval $[f_1 - W, f_1]$ from contributing to the demodulator output $r_2(t)$.

Comparison of DSB-SC and SSB

The foregoing analyses have shown that there is no difference for an idealized mathematical model between the best obtainable performance with DSB-SC and SSB, but many engineering subtleties enter into a preference for one or the other.† For example, for any given set $\{s_i(t)\}$ of lowpass modulating waveforms with bandwidth W, SSB requires one half of the bandwidth of DSB-SC, which permits frequency multiplexing and alleviates the frequency assignment problem when the spectrum is crowded. Use of quadrature multiplexing with DSB-SC can balance the accounts; however, departures of a bandpass channel from our idealized model may introduce more cross talk (co-channel interference) with quadrature multiplexing than with frequency multiplexing. In particular, cross talk is

† See the Single Sideband Issue, *Proc. IRE*, **44**, No. 12, December 1956.

introduced with quadrature multiplexing by channels distorted by a *time-invariant* linear filter $H(f)$ whenever $H(f_0 + \Delta f) \neq H^*(f_0 - \Delta f)$ for all $|\Delta f| < W$, whereas cross talk with ideal frequency multiplexing is introduced by a linear filter only if it is *time-variant*. An advantage of DSB-SC is that high power SSB signals are more difficult to generate.

7.3 RANDOM AMPLITUDE AND PHASE

Thus far we have assumed that the signal has been subjected only to transformations whose characteristics are precisely known by the receiver. In particular, we assumed in the bandpass signal case that both the gain and phase of the signal component of the received waveform were known exactly. In practice, this knowledge is not always available. We now consider certain simple mathematical models of filtered-signal channels in which the signal filtering depends on one or more unknown (random) parameters.

Random Amplitude

An elementary random-parameter channel is the pure fading model in which the received signal is

$$r(t) = as(t) + n_w(t), \tag{7.30}$$

where a is a random variable with known probability density function p_a. We assume that a is statistically independent both of the transmitted signal $s(t)$ and the additive white Gaussian noise $n_w(t)$.

In cases such as that of Eq. 7.30 the derivation of the optimum receiver involves only a simple extension of preceding results. We again set $\hat{m} = m_i$ if and only if i maximizes the quantity

$$\mathrm{P}[m_i \mid \mathbf{r} = \boldsymbol{\rho}] = \frac{\mathrm{P}[m_i]\, p_{\mathbf{r}}(\boldsymbol{\rho} \mid m_i)}{p_{\mathbf{r}}(\boldsymbol{\rho})}. \tag{7.31}$$

Here the correspondence between waveforms and vectors is the same as in Chapter 4. For simplicity, we assume throughout the rest of this chapter that the $\{m_i\}$ are equally likely. It follows that the optimum receiver need only determine the i that maximizes $p_{\mathbf{r}}(\boldsymbol{\rho} \mid m_i)$.

A random parameter such as a enters into the optimum receiver formulation by virtue of the fact that

$$p_{\mathbf{r}}(\boldsymbol{\rho} \mid m_i) = \int_{-\infty}^{\infty} p_{\mathbf{r}}(\boldsymbol{\rho} \mid m_i, a = \alpha)\, p_a(\alpha)\, d\alpha. \tag{7.32}$$

It is convenient, now and in the sequel, to introduce the notation

$$\int_{-\infty}^{\infty} p_{\mathbf{r}}(\boldsymbol{\rho} \mid m_i, a = \alpha)\, p_a(\alpha)\, d\alpha \triangleq \overline{p_{\mathbf{r}}(\boldsymbol{\rho} \mid m_i, a)}. \tag{7.33}$$

The interpretation of Eq. 7.33 is as follows: for given values of $\boldsymbol{\rho}$ and i, the entity $p_{\mathbf{r}}(\boldsymbol{\rho} \mid m_i, a = \alpha)$ is a number whose value depends on α. But a is a random variable, and the probability that a will lie in an interval $[\alpha, \alpha + d\alpha]$ is $p_a(\alpha)\, d\alpha$. This probability assignment, together with the collection of numbers $\{p_{\mathbf{r}}(\boldsymbol{\rho} \mid m_i, a = \alpha)\}$ obtained by varying α with $\boldsymbol{\rho}$ and i held fixed, defines another random variable which we denote $p_{\mathbf{r}}(\boldsymbol{\rho} \mid m_i, a)$. (A function of a random variable is a random variable.) From the theorem of expectation (Eq. 2.126) the mean value of this new random variable is

$$\mathrm{E}[p_{\mathbf{r}}(\boldsymbol{\rho} \mid m_i, a)] = \int_{-\infty}^{\infty} p_{\mathbf{r}}(\boldsymbol{\rho} \mid m_i, a = \alpha)\, p_a(\alpha)\, d\alpha,$$

which is Eq. 7.33. Similarly, if $\mathbf{x}$ and $\mathbf{y}$ are random vectors and A is a random event, we write

$$p_{\mathbf{x}}(\boldsymbol{\beta}) = \int_{-\infty}^{\infty} p_{\mathbf{x}}(\boldsymbol{\beta} \mid \mathbf{y} = \boldsymbol{\gamma})\, p_{\mathbf{y}}(\boldsymbol{\gamma})\, d\boldsymbol{\gamma} = \overline{p_{\mathbf{x}}(\boldsymbol{\beta} \mid \mathbf{y})} \tag{7.34a}$$

and

$$\mathrm{P}[A] = \int_{-\infty}^{\infty} \mathrm{P}[A \mid \mathbf{y} = \boldsymbol{\gamma}]\, p_{\mathbf{y}}(\boldsymbol{\gamma})\, d\boldsymbol{\gamma} = \overline{\mathrm{P}[A \mid \mathbf{y}]}. \tag{7.34b}$$

In this abbreviated notation Eq. 7.32 becomes

$$p_{\mathbf{r}}(\boldsymbol{\rho} \mid m_i) = \overline{p_{\mathbf{r}}(\boldsymbol{\rho} \mid m_i, a)}. \tag{7.35}$$

Equation 7.35 provides the key to the analysis of the optimum receiver for the fading case of Eq. 7.30. With white Gaussian noise,

$$p_{\mathbf{r}}(\boldsymbol{\rho} \mid m_i, a) = p_{\mathbf{n}}(\boldsymbol{\rho} - a\mathbf{s}_i) \sim \exp\left(-\frac{1}{\mathcal{N}_0}|\boldsymbol{\rho} - a\mathbf{s}_i|^2\right) \tag{7.36a}$$

and therefore

$$p_{\mathbf{r}}(\boldsymbol{\rho} \mid m_i) \sim \overline{\exp\left(-\frac{1}{\mathcal{N}_0}|\boldsymbol{\rho} - a\mathbf{s}_i|^2\right)}. \tag{7.36b}$$

Whether or not this average can be evaluated (and meaningfully interpreted) depends on both the $\{\mathbf{s}_i\}$ and p_a. From the vector-signal point of view it is clear that the attenuation factor a corresponds to a radial scaling of the received signal constellation $\{a\mathbf{s}_i\}$, as shown in Fig. 7.24. If a were known to the receiver, it would use this knowledge in the

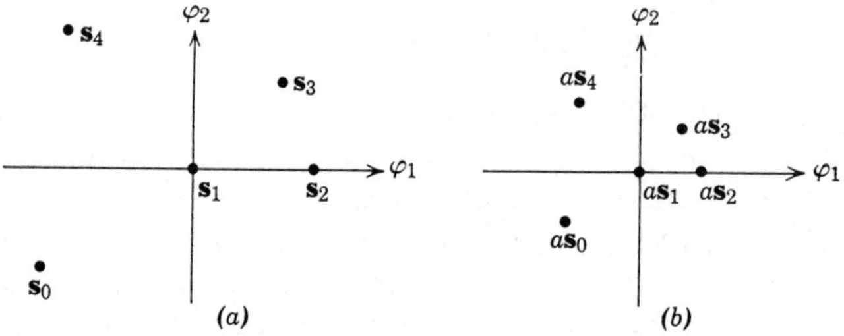

Figure 7.24 Radial scaling of signals; $a = \frac{1}{2}$.

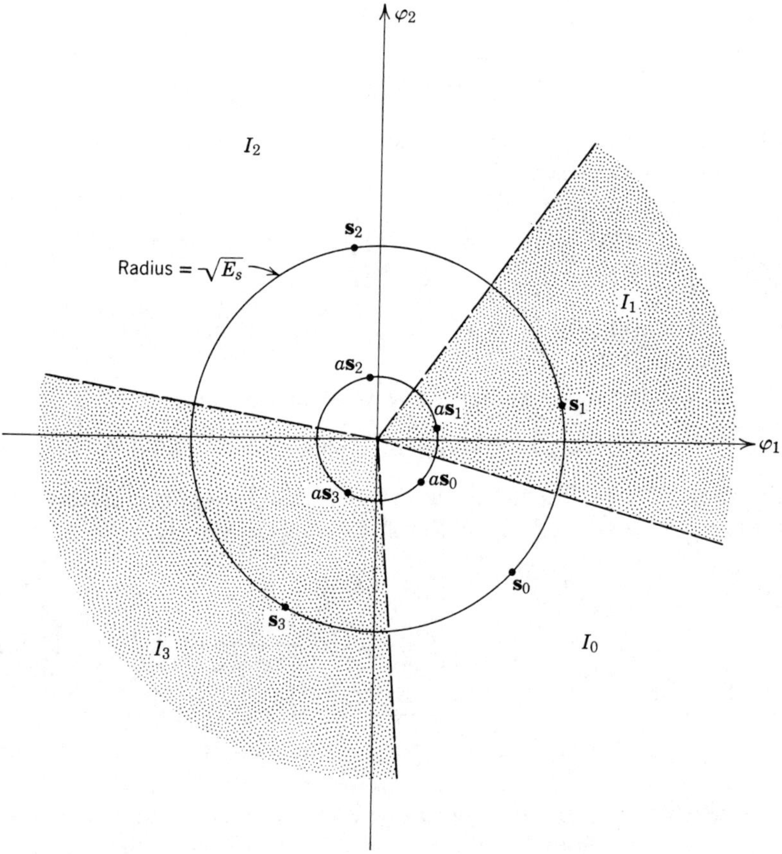

Figure 7.25 Decision regions that are invariant to positive attenuation.

determination of optimum decision regions (see Chapter 4). Accordingly, we may expect that the optimum decision regions when a is *not* known will be some complicated compromise between the different optimum regions implied by the different values that a may assume, weighted in accordance with the probability density with which a assumes such values.

In one instance the situation is uncomplicated. If the attenuation a is always *positive* and if the signals $\{s_i(t)\}$ are all of *equal energy* E_s, then the boundaries of the optimum decision regions are themselves radial, as shown in Fig. 7.25, and thus invariant to radial scaling of the received signals. Under these conditions, it is obvious that a correlation or matched-filter receiver structure is still optimum, completely independent of whether a, or even p_a, is known precisely.

The validity of this argument can be checked formally by eliminating terms that are independent of i in Eq. 7.36b. With equal-energy signals we have

$$p_{\mathbf{r}}(\boldsymbol{\rho} \mid m_i) \sim \int_{-\infty}^{\infty} \exp\left(+\frac{2\alpha}{\mathcal{N}_0}\boldsymbol{\rho}\cdot\mathbf{s}_i\right) e^{-\alpha^2 E_s/\mathcal{N}_0}\, p_a(\alpha)\, d\alpha. \tag{7.37}$$

For *any* p_a such that $p_a(\alpha) \equiv 0$ for $\alpha < 0$, the index i that maximizes this integral is the index i that maximizes $\boldsymbol{\rho}\cdot\mathbf{s}_i$.

On the other hand, it must be emphasized that the error performance provided by the optimum receiver is very much affected by p_a. For example, if equally likely binary signals are used, with

$$\mathbf{s}_0 = -\mathbf{s}_1 = \sqrt{E_s}\,\boldsymbol{\varphi}_1, \tag{7.38a}$$

then the received signal energy when $a = \alpha$ is $\alpha^2 E_s$ and

$$P[\mathcal{E}] = \int_{-\infty}^{\infty} Q\left(\alpha\sqrt{\frac{2E_s}{\mathcal{N}_0}}\right) p_a(\alpha)\, d\alpha = \overline{Q\left(a\sqrt{\frac{2E_s}{\mathcal{N}_0}}\right)}. \tag{7.38b}$$

If a has a high probability of being near zero, the probability of error is large. In any event, it is shown in Appendix 7B that

$$P[\mathcal{E}] \geqslant Q\left(\bar{a}\sqrt{\frac{2E_s}{\mathcal{N}_0}}\right), \tag{7.38c}$$

in which $\bar{a}$ is the mean of a. The equal sign holds if and only if a is not random; that is, if $p_a(\alpha) = \delta(\alpha - \bar{a})$.

Random Phase

Random phase introduces additional complication into the analysis of the optimum receiver for bandpass signals. We now consider the situation in which the transmitted signal is

$$s^\circ(t) = s(t)\sqrt{2}\cos(\omega_0 t - \theta), \tag{7.39a}$$

where $s(t)$ is chosen from a set of equally likely signals $\{s_i(t)\}$ of ideal lowpass bandwidth W and θ is a random variable with a probability density function p_θ that is uniform over the interval $[0, 2\pi]$.

$$p_\theta(\alpha) = \begin{cases} \dfrac{1}{2\pi}, & 0 \leqslant \alpha < 2\pi \\ 0, & \text{elsewhere.} \end{cases} \tag{7.39b}$$

As usual, we shall consider the received signal to be corrupted with additive white Gaussian noise:

$$r(t) = s^\circ(t) + n_w(t). \tag{7.39c}$$

The transmitted signal $s^\circ(t)$ corresponds to the DSB-SC signal in Fig. 7.9, except that θ reflects uncertainty at the receiver about the exact phase of the received signal. This uncertainty may develop in many different ways; for example, by slow oscillator drift or by small random changes (of the order of $1/f_0$) in the propagation time between transmitter and receiver. In spite of the unknown phase, a DSB-SC demodulator with

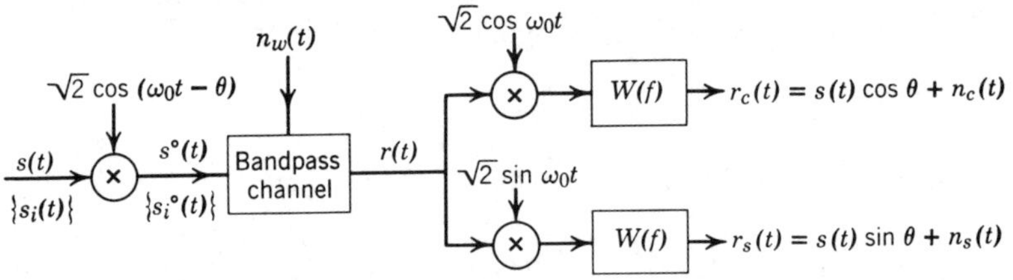

Figure 7.26 DSB-SC demodulation with random phase. It is convenient to ascribe the parameter θ to the transmitter, even through the random phase may actually originate within the channel. With this convention and appropriately band-limited signals, the channel disturbs transmission only by adding white Gaussian noise, so that $r(t) = s(t)\sqrt{2}\cos(\omega_0 t - \theta) + n_w(t)$.

sine and cosine channel outputs may still be used as the first stage of an optimum receiver, as shown in Fig. 7.26: the only irreversible effect is the discarding of noise outside the band occupied by the signals.

Recalling the trigonometric identity

$$\cos(x - y) = \cos x \cos y + \sin x \sin y, \tag{7.40}$$

we can write

$$s^\circ(t) = \sqrt{2}\,[s(t)\cos\theta]\cos\omega_0 t + \sqrt{2}\,[s(t)\sin\theta]\sin\omega_0 t. \tag{7.41}$$

The two demodulated waveforms in Fig. 7.26 are therefore

$$r_c(t) = s(t) \cos \theta + n_c(t) \tag{7.42a}$$

$$r_s(t) = s(t) \sin \theta + n_s(t). \tag{7.42b}$$

The corresponding vector representation is

$$\mathbf{r}_c = \mathbf{s} \cos \theta + \mathbf{n}_c \tag{7.43a}$$

$$\mathbf{r}_s = \mathbf{s} \sin \theta + \mathbf{n}_s, \tag{7.43b}$$

where $\mathbf{s}$, $\mathbf{n}_c$, and $\mathbf{n}_s$ denote the projections of the random processes $s(t)$, $n_c(t)$ and $n_s(t)$ on the set of orthonormal functions $\{\varphi_j(t)\}$ used to describe the lowpass signal set

$$s_i(t) = \sum_{j=1}^{N} s_{ij}\, \varphi_j(t); \qquad i = 0, 1, \ldots, M-1.$$

The first important observation to make about Eqs. 7.43 is that *both* demodulator outputs contain signal components and that the optimum receiver must therefore observe them both. Accordingly, given $\mathbf{r}_c = \boldsymbol{\alpha}$ and $\mathbf{r}_s = \boldsymbol{\beta}$, the optimum receiver sets $\hat{m}$ equal to that m_i for which $P[m_i \mid \mathbf{r}_c = \boldsymbol{\alpha}, \mathbf{r}_s = \boldsymbol{\beta}]$ is maximum. Since we are assuming that all m_i are equally likely, this is equivalent to maximizing

$$p_{\mathbf{r}_c,\mathbf{r}_s}(\boldsymbol{\alpha}, \boldsymbol{\beta} \mid m_i) = \overline{p_{\mathbf{r}_c,\mathbf{r}_s}(\boldsymbol{\alpha}, \boldsymbol{\beta} \mid m_i, \theta)}, \tag{7.44}$$

in which we again use the notation of Eq. 7.33.

The next important observation is that $n_c(t)$ and $n_s(t)$ are (see Eq. 7.25c) *statistically independent* stationary Gaussian processes, each having a power spectrum that is uniform (with density $\mathcal{N}_0/2$) over the rectangular frequency band $[-W, W]$ occupied by $s(t)$. Since noise power outside the band occupied by the signals does not affect the optimum receiver, we may assume $n_c(t)$ and $n_s(t)$ to be white. Projections of these independent processes onto orthonormal functions yield independent Gaussian variables, each of variance $\mathcal{N}_0/2$. Hence

$$p_{\mathbf{n}_c,\mathbf{n}_s}(\boldsymbol{\mu}, \boldsymbol{\nu}) = p_{\mathbf{n}_c}(\boldsymbol{\mu}) p_{\mathbf{n}_s}(\boldsymbol{\nu}) = \frac{1}{(\pi \mathcal{N}_0)^N} \exp\left[-\frac{1}{\mathcal{N}_0}(|\boldsymbol{\mu}|^2 + |\boldsymbol{\nu}|^2)\right], \tag{7.45}$$

in which N is the number of orthonormal functions in the set $\{\varphi_j(t)\}$ used to describe the $\{s_i(t)\}$. Thus

$$p_{\mathbf{r}_c,\mathbf{r}_s}(\boldsymbol{\alpha}, \boldsymbol{\beta} \mid m_i, \theta) = p_{\mathbf{n}_c}(\boldsymbol{\alpha} - \mathbf{s}_i \cos \theta)\, p_{\mathbf{n}_s}(\boldsymbol{\beta} - \mathbf{s}_i \sin \theta)$$

$$\sim \exp\left[-\frac{1}{\mathcal{N}_0}(|\boldsymbol{\alpha} - \mathbf{s}_i \cos \theta|^2 + |\boldsymbol{\beta} - \mathbf{s}_i \sin \theta|^2)\right].$$

Expanding the magnitude-squared terms in the exponent and dropping factors independent of i, we find that the receiver must maximize

$$p_{\mathbf{r}_c,\mathbf{r}_s}(\boldsymbol{\alpha}, \boldsymbol{\beta} \mid m_i) \sim \overline{\exp\left[\frac{2}{\mathcal{N}_0}(\boldsymbol{\alpha} \cdot \mathbf{s}_i \cos\theta + \boldsymbol{\beta} \cdot \mathbf{s}_i \sin\theta)\right]}\, e^{-E_i/\mathcal{N}_0}, \tag{7.46}$$

in which E_i is the energy of $s_i(t)$.

The form of the optimum receiver may be extracted from Eq. 7.46 in a straightforward manner. We define, for $i = 0, 1, \ldots, M - 1$,

$$X_i \triangleq \sqrt{(\mathbf{r}_c \cdot \mathbf{s}_i)^2 + (\mathbf{r}_s \cdot \mathbf{s}_i)^2} \tag{7.47a}$$

and

$$\phi_i \triangleq \tan^{-1} \frac{\mathbf{r}_s \cdot \mathbf{s}_i}{\mathbf{r}_c \cdot \mathbf{s}_i}, \tag{7.47b}$$

where

$$\mathbf{r}_c \cdot \mathbf{s}_i = \int_{-\infty}^{\infty} r_c(t)\, s_i(t)\, dt \tag{7.47c}$$

and

$$\mathbf{r}_s \cdot \mathbf{s}_i = \int_{-\infty}^{\infty} r_s(t)\, s_i(t)\, dt \tag{7.47d}$$

are the correlations of the ith signal with the outputs of the cosine and sine demodulator, respectively. Applying the identity of Eq. 7.40 and invoking the transformation of Fig. 7.27, we have

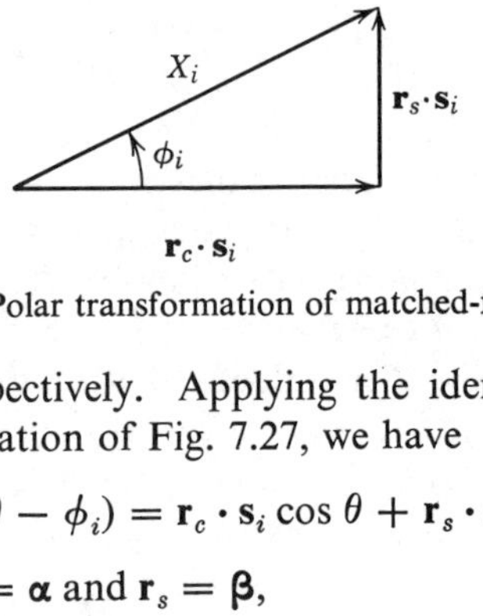

Figure 7.27 Polar transformation of matched-filter outputs.

$$X_i \cos(\theta - \phi_i) = \mathbf{r}_c \cdot \mathbf{s}_i \cos\theta + \mathbf{r}_s \cdot \mathbf{s}_i \sin\theta. \tag{7.47e}$$

In particular, when $\mathbf{r}_c = \boldsymbol{\alpha}$ and $\mathbf{r}_s = \boldsymbol{\beta}$,

$$X_i \cos(\theta - \phi_i) = \boldsymbol{\alpha} \cdot \mathbf{s}_i \cos\theta + \boldsymbol{\beta} \cdot \mathbf{s}_i \sin\theta \tag{7.48a}$$

and the average in Eq. 7.46 may be written

$$\overline{\exp\left[\frac{2X_i}{\mathcal{N}_0}\cos(\theta - \phi_i)\right]} \triangleq \int_{-\infty}^{\infty} \exp\left[\frac{2X_i}{\mathcal{N}_0}\cos(\gamma - \phi_i)\right] p_\theta(\gamma)\, d\gamma$$

$$= \frac{1}{2\pi}\int_0^{2\pi} \exp\left[\frac{2X_i}{\mathcal{N}_0}\cos(\gamma - \phi_i)\right] d\gamma. \tag{7.48b}$$

This integral has been encountered often enough to have been given a name and to have been tabulated. Specifically,

$$I_0(x) \triangleq \frac{1}{2\pi} \int_0^{2\pi} e^{x \cos \alpha} \, d\alpha, \tag{7.49a}$$

where $I_0(x)$ is called the "zero-order modified Bessel function of the first

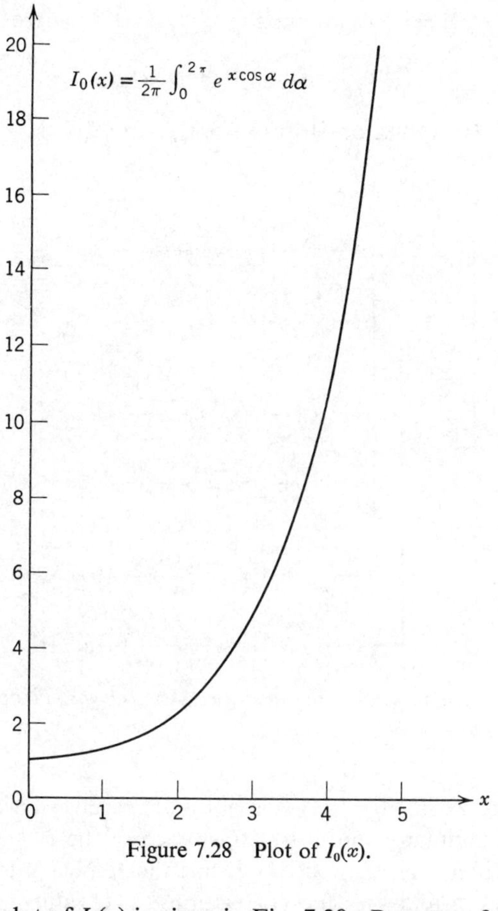

Figure 7.28 Plot of $I_0(x)$.

kind."[46,56] A plot of $I_0(x)$ is given in Fig. 7.28. Because of the periodicity of the cosine, for any ϕ we also have

$$I_0(x) = \frac{1}{2\pi} \int_0^{2\pi} e^{x \cos (\alpha + \phi)} \, d\alpha. \tag{7.49b}$$

Hence, given observed values of the $\{X_i\}$, the optimum decision rule is to set $\hat{m} = m_i$ if and only if

$$I_0\left(\frac{2X_i}{\mathcal{N}_0}\right)e^{-E_i/\mathcal{N}_0} \tag{7.50}$$

is maximum.

Additional simplification is possible when the signals $\{s_i(t)\}$ have equal energy, $E_i = E_s$ for all $i = 0, 1, \ldots, M-1$. Then we need only to maximize $I_0(2X_i/N_0)$; or still more simply, since $I_0(x)$ is a monotone increasing function of x, we need only to maximize X_i or X_i^2, where

$$X_i^2 = (\mathbf{r}_c \cdot \mathbf{s}_i)^2 + (\mathbf{r}_s \cdot \mathbf{s}_i)^2. \tag{7.51}$$

Equation 7.51 specifies one form of optimum receiver for equal-energy

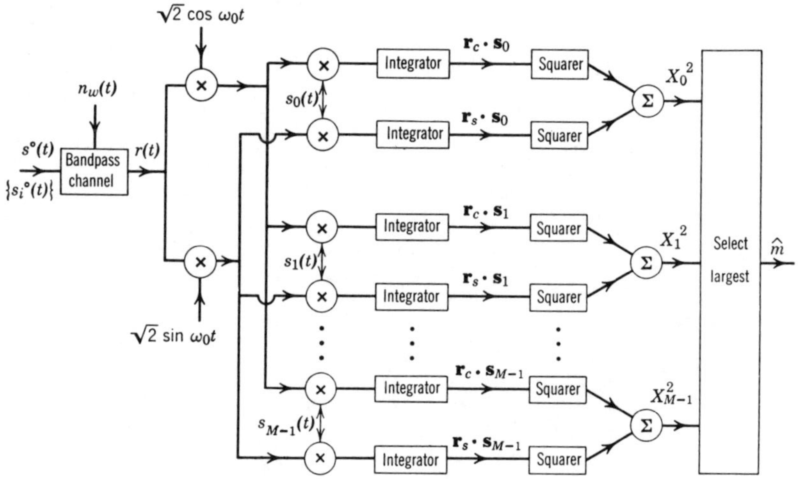

Figure 7.29 Correlation receiver for equal-energy signals with random phase; $r(t) = s(t)\sqrt{2}\cos(\omega_0 t - \theta) + n_w(t)$.

signals. As shown in Fig. 7.29, this optimum receiver correlates the sine and cosine demodulator outputs against each of the M possible lowpass signals. For each $s_i(t)$, the receiver forms the sum of the squares of the cosine correlation and the sine correlation. The values of the $\{X_i^2\}$ so obtained are then fed to a comparison device that determines which X_i^2 is largest, $i = 0, 1, \ldots, M-1$.

Just as with the known-phase receiver of Fig. 7.16, the fact that the demodulator outputs are correlated against the lowpass signals $\{s_i(t)\}$ implies that the lowpass filters $W(f)$ at the demodulator outputs in Fig. 7.26 are redundant; they have been eliminated in Fig. 7.29. It is clear from this figure that Eqs. 7.47c and d may also be written

$$\mathbf{r}_c \cdot \mathbf{s}_i = \int_{-\infty}^{\infty} r(t)\sqrt{2}\, s_i(t) \cos \omega_0 t \, dt \tag{7.52a}$$

$$\mathbf{r}_s \cdot \mathbf{s}_i = \int_{-\infty}^{\infty} r(t)\sqrt{2}\, s_i(t) \sin \omega_0 t \, dt. \tag{7.52b}$$

An alternative form of optimum receiver is shown in Fig. 7.30, in which lowpass matched filters with impulse response

$$g_i(t) = s_i(T - t); \qquad i = 0, 1, \ldots, M - 1 \tag{7.53}$$

are substituted for the correlators. Of course, all ideal lowpass signals

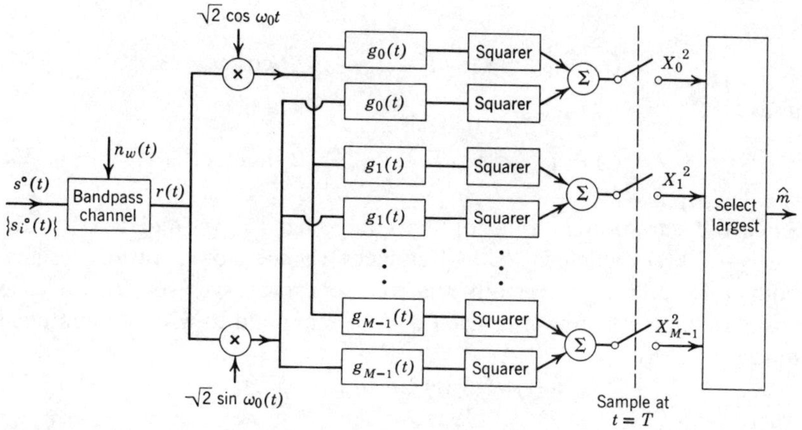

Figure 7.30 Matched-filter receiver for equal-energy signals with random phase.

must have infinite duration and the $\{g_i(t)\}$ are not physically realizable As a practical matter, however, the receiver of Fig. 7.30 becomes both physically realizable and essentially optimum whenever almost all of the energy in each of the $\{s_i(t)\}$ is located within $0 \leqslant t < T$ and $-W < f < W$.

Envelope detection. A substantially different form of optimum detection for equally likely equal-energy signals with random phase may be realized as follows. Let us consider feeding the signal $r(t)$ in Fig. 7.26 directly into a filter bank with impulse responses $\{h_i(t)\}$ matched to the bandpass signals $\{s_i°(t)\}$ except for the discrepancy necessitated by the fact that the phase is unknown. We define

$$h_i(t) \triangleq s_i(T - t)\sqrt{2} \cos \omega_0 t; \qquad i = 0, 1, \ldots, M - 1. \tag{7.54}$$

The output of the ith filter, say $u_i(t)$, is

$$u_i(t) = \int_{-\infty}^{\infty} r(\alpha)\, h_i(t-\alpha)\, d\alpha$$

$$= \sqrt{2}\int_{-\infty}^{\infty} r(\alpha)\, s_i(T-t+\alpha) \cos \omega_0(t-\alpha)\, d\alpha$$

$$= \sqrt{2} \cos \omega_0 t \int_{-\infty}^{\infty} r(\alpha)\, s_i(T-t+\alpha) \cos \omega_0\alpha\, d\alpha$$

$$+ \sqrt{2} \sin \omega_0 t \int_{-\infty}^{\infty} r(\alpha)\, s_i(T-t+\alpha) \sin \omega_0\alpha\, d\alpha$$

$$= u_{ci}(t) \cos \omega_0 t + u_{si}(t) \sin \omega_0 t. \tag{7.55}$$

In the last line we have introduced the definitions

$$u_{ci}(t) \triangleq \int_{-\infty}^{\infty} r(\alpha)\, s_i(T-t+\alpha)\sqrt{2} \cos \omega_0\alpha\, d\alpha, \tag{7.56a}$$

and

$$u_{si}(t) \triangleq \int_{-\infty}^{\infty} r(\alpha)\, s_i(T-t+\alpha)\sqrt{2} \sin \omega_0\alpha\, d\alpha. \tag{7.56b}$$

Since the variation in time of the components $u_{ci}(t)$ and $u_{si}(t)$ is due solely to $s_i(t)$, which is a low-frequency (hence slowly varying) signal, both $u_{ci}(t)$ and $u_{si}(t)$ remain relatively constant over several cycles of $\cos \omega_0 t$. Thus it is useful to use Eq. 7.40 again and to write the matched-filter output as

$$u_i(t) = X_i(t) \cos [\omega_0 t - \phi_i(t)], \tag{7.57a}$$

where

$$X_i(t) \triangleq \sqrt{u_{ci}^2(t) + u_{si}^2(t)} \tag{7.57b}$$

is a slowly varying "envelope" and

$$\phi_i(t) \triangleq \tan^{-1} \frac{u_{si}(t)}{u_{ci}(t)} \tag{7.57c}$$

is a slowly varying phase.

In conclusion, we observe from Eqs. 7.52 and the definitions of Eqs. 7.56 that at the instant $t = T$

$$u_{ci}(T) = \mathbf{r}_c \cdot \mathbf{s}_i, \qquad u_{si}(T) = \mathbf{r}_s \cdot \mathbf{s}_i. \tag{7.58a}$$

Hence

$$X_i(T) = X_i \triangleq [(\mathbf{r}_c \cdot \mathbf{s}_i)^2 + (\mathbf{r}_s \cdot \mathbf{s}_i)^2]^{1/2} \tag{7.58b}$$

$$\phi_i(T) = \phi_i \triangleq \tan^{-1} \frac{\mathbf{r}_s \cdot \mathbf{s}_i}{\mathbf{r}_c \cdot \mathbf{s}_i}. \tag{7.58c}$$

It follows that an optimum receiver can be built by using bandpass filters matched (except for the unknown phase) directly to the $\{s_i^\circ(t)\}$, followed by envelope detectors sampled at time T, as shown in Fig. 7.31.

Figure 7.32 illustrates how the envelope of $u_i(t)$ changes slowly with time, whereas $u_i(t)$ itself varies sinusoidally with frequency f_0 within its envelope. This fact explains why the optimum receiver looks at the envelope, rather than at $u_i(t)$ itself, when the phase of the sinusoidal

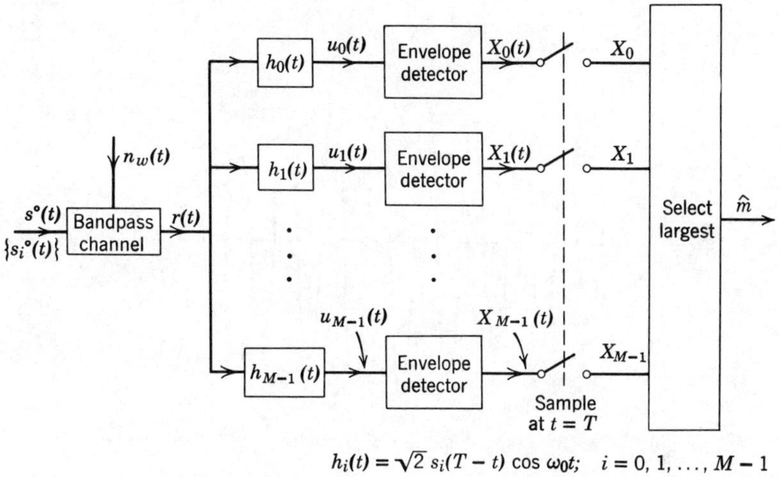

Figure 7.31 Envelope-detector receiver for equal-energy signals with random phase.

variation is unknown. Receivers that examine only the envelope of the matched-filter output, hence do not utilize knowledge of the phase, are termed *incoherent* receivers; receivers that do exploit knowledge of the phase are called *coherent*.

Probability of error. Since an incoherent receiver does not consider phase information, it cannot yield so small an error probability as a coherent receiver. To illustrate this, we now calculate the probability of error for white Gaussian noise when one of two equally likely messages is communicated over a system utilizing an incoherent receiver and the DSB-SC modulated equal-energy orthogonal lowpass signals

$$s_1(t) = \sqrt{E_s}\, \varphi_1(t), \qquad \mathbf{s}_1 = \sqrt{E_s}\, \boldsymbol{\varphi}_1 \tag{7.59a}$$

$$s_2(t) = \sqrt{E_s}\, \varphi_2(t), \qquad \mathbf{s}_2 = \sqrt{E_s}\, \boldsymbol{\varphi}_2. \tag{7.59b}$$

From Eq. 7.51 the optimum incoherent receiver in this case sets $\hat{m} = m_1$ if and only if

$$(\mathbf{r}_c \cdot \mathbf{s}_1)^2 + (\mathbf{r}_s \cdot \mathbf{s}_1)^2 > (\mathbf{r}_c \cdot \mathbf{s}_2)^2 + (\mathbf{r}_s \cdot \mathbf{s}_2)^2. \tag{7.60}$$

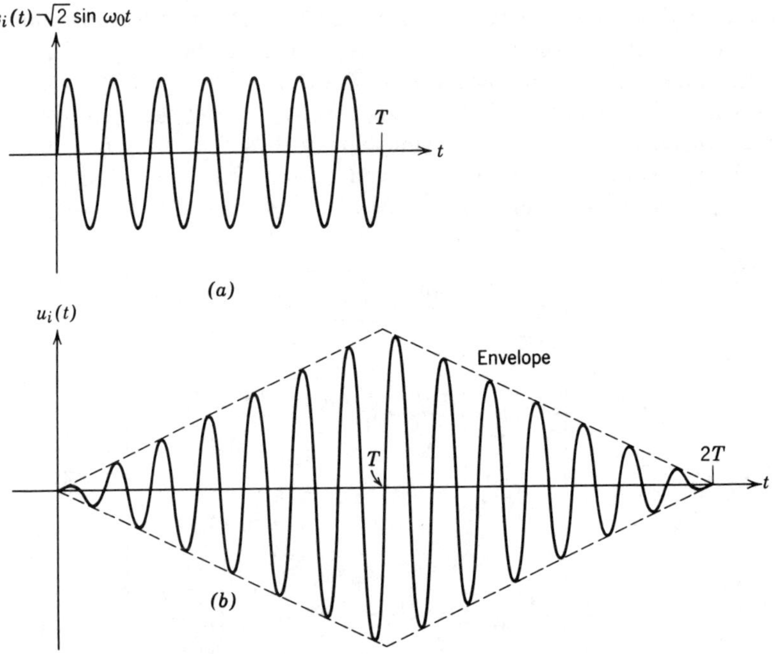

Figure 7.32 Envelope detection of (noiseless) pulsed sine wave.

Each of the vectors in Eq. 7.60 is two-dimensional. In accordance with Eq. 7.43,

$$\mathbf{r}_c = \mathbf{s}\cos\theta + \mathbf{n}_c$$

$$\mathbf{r}_s = \mathbf{s}\sin\theta + \mathbf{n}_s,$$

so that when $m = m_1$ the vector components of $\mathbf{r}_c$ and $\mathbf{r}_s$ are

$$\begin{aligned} r_{c1} &\triangleq \mathbf{r}_c \cdot \boldsymbol{\varphi}_1 = \sqrt{E_s}\cos\theta + n_{c1}, \\ r_{s1} &\triangleq \mathbf{r}_s \cdot \boldsymbol{\varphi}_1 = \sqrt{E_s}\sin\theta + n_{s1}, \\ r_{c2} &\triangleq \mathbf{r}_c \cdot \boldsymbol{\varphi}_2 = n_{c2}, \\ r_{s2} &\triangleq \mathbf{r}_s \cdot \boldsymbol{\varphi}_2 = n_{s2}. \end{aligned} \tag{7.61}$$

In terms of these coefficients, after cancellation of a common factor of $\sqrt{E_s}$ the condition of Eq. 7.60 becomes

$$r_{c1}^2 + r_{s1}^2 > r_{c2}^2 + r_{s2}^2. \tag{7.62}$$

Since $\varphi_1(t)$ and $\varphi_2(t)$ are orthonormal and $n_c(t)$ and $n_s(t)$ are statistically independent Gaussian processes, the random variables n_{c1}, n_{s1}, n_{c2}, n_{s2}

are statistically independent Gaussian variables, each with density function

$$p_n(\alpha) = \frac{1}{\sqrt{\pi \mathcal{N}_0}} e^{-\alpha^2/\mathcal{N}_0}. \tag{7.63}$$

From Eqs. 7.62 and 7.63

$$\begin{aligned}
\mathrm{P}[\mathcal{E} \mid m_1, (r_{c1}^2 + r_{s1}^2) = R^2] &= \mathrm{P}[r_{c2}^2 + r_{s2}^2 \geqslant R^2] \\
&= \iint_{\alpha^2+\beta^2 \geqslant R^2} p_n(\alpha)\, p_n(\beta)\, d\alpha\, d\beta \\
&= \iint_{\alpha^2+\beta^2 \geqslant R^2} \frac{1}{\pi \mathcal{N}_0} e^{-(\alpha^2+\beta^2)/\mathcal{N}_0}\, d\alpha\, d\beta \\
&= \int_R^\infty r\, dr \int_0^{2\pi} d\theta \frac{1}{\pi \mathcal{N}_0} e^{-r^2/\mathcal{N}_0} \\
&= e^{-R^2/\mathcal{N}_0} = e^{-(r_{c1}^2 + r_{s1}^2)/\mathcal{N}_0}.
\end{aligned} \tag{7.64}$$

We calculate $\mathrm{P}[\mathcal{E} \mid m_1]$ by averaging Eq. 7.64 over the random variable $(r_{c1}^2 + r_{s1}^2)$. Thus

$$\begin{aligned}
\mathrm{P}[\mathcal{E} \mid m_1] &= \overline{\mathrm{P}[\mathcal{E} \mid m_1, r_{c1}^2 + r_{s1}^2]} \\
&= \overline{e^{-(r_{c1}^2 + r_{s1}^2)/\mathcal{N}_0}} \\
&= \overline{e^{-r_{c1}^2/\mathcal{N}_0}}\; \overline{e^{-r_{s1}^2/\mathcal{N}_0}}.
\end{aligned} \tag{7.65}$$

The last line exploits the fact that r_{c1} and r_{s1} are statistically independent under the condition that m_1 is transmitted.

The averaging in Eq. 7.65 is most easily carried out in two steps: we first calculate the conditional error probability $\mathrm{P}[\mathcal{E} \mid m_1, \theta = \gamma]$ and then average over the random phase θ. Using the notation $\mathrm{E}[z \mid y = \beta]$ to denote the conditional mean of z, given $y = \beta$, from Eq. 7.65 we have

$$\mathrm{P}[\mathcal{E} \mid m_1, \theta = \gamma] = \mathrm{E}[e^{-r_{c1}^2/\mathcal{N}_0} \mid \theta = \gamma]\, \mathrm{E}[e^{-r_{s1}^2/\mathcal{N}_0} \mid \theta = \gamma]. \tag{7.66a}$$

When $\theta = \gamma$, the random variables r_{c1} and r_{s1} are Gaussian, with variance $\mathcal{N}_0/2$ and means

$$\bar{r}_{c1} = \sqrt{E_s} \cos \gamma, \qquad \bar{r}_{s1} = \sqrt{E_s} \sin \gamma. \tag{7.66b}$$

In Appendix 7C we prove the following extremely useful lemma:

Lemma. *If x is any Gaussian random variable with mean m_x and variance σ_x^2, and w is any complex constant with real part less than $(2\sigma_x^2)^{-1}$, the* *expectation of* e^{wx^2} *is*

$$\overline{e^{wx^2}} = \frac{e^{wm_x^2/(1-2w\sigma_x^2)}}{\sqrt{1 - 2w\sigma_x^2}}\,; \qquad \mathrm{Re}(w) < \frac{1}{2\sigma_x^2}. \tag{7.67}$$

Applying this lemma to Eq. 7.66a, with $w = -1/\mathcal{N}_0$, we have

$$\mathrm{P}[\mathcal{E} \mid m_i, \theta = \gamma] = \frac{\exp\left(-\dfrac{1}{2\mathcal{N}_0} E_s \cos^2 \gamma\right)}{\sqrt{2}} \cdot \frac{\exp\left(-\dfrac{1}{2\mathcal{N}_0} E_s \sin^2 \gamma\right)}{\sqrt{2}}$$

$$= \frac{1}{2} \exp\left[-\frac{1}{2\mathcal{N}_0} E_s(\cos^2 \gamma + \sin^2 \gamma)\right].$$

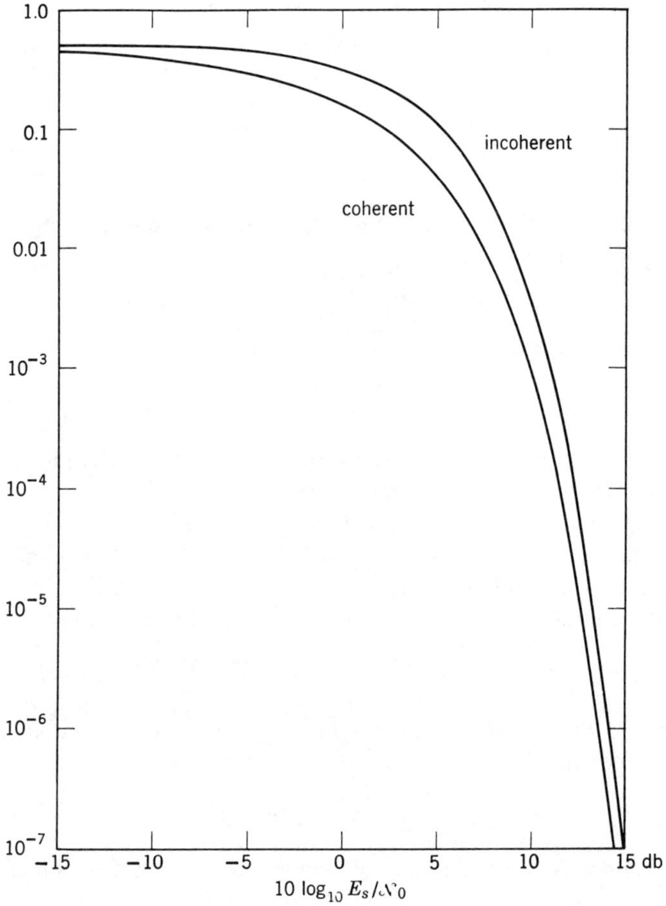

Figure 7.33 Probability of error for coherent and incoherent reception of two equally likely orthogonal signals of energy E_s.

Finally, since the right-hand side is independent of m_1 and γ, averaging over m and θ yields

$$P[\mathcal{E}] = \tfrac{1}{2}e^{-E_s/2\mathcal{N}_0}. \tag{7.68}$$

It is interesting to compare this result for two equally likely orthogonal lowpass signals with *incoherent* reception to the corresponding result for *coherent* reception. In the coherent case we have from Eqs. 4.78 and 2.121

$$P(\mathcal{E}) = Q\left(\sqrt{\frac{E_s}{\mathcal{N}_0}}\right) \leqslant \frac{1}{\sqrt{2\pi E_s/\mathcal{N}_0}}\, e^{-E_s/2\mathcal{N}_0}. \tag{7.69}$$

For large $E_s/\mathcal{N}_0$ the bound of Eq. 7.69 is very tight and the error performances of optimum coherent and incoherent receivers are exponentially equivalent. Plots of the two error behaviors are given in Fig. 7.33.

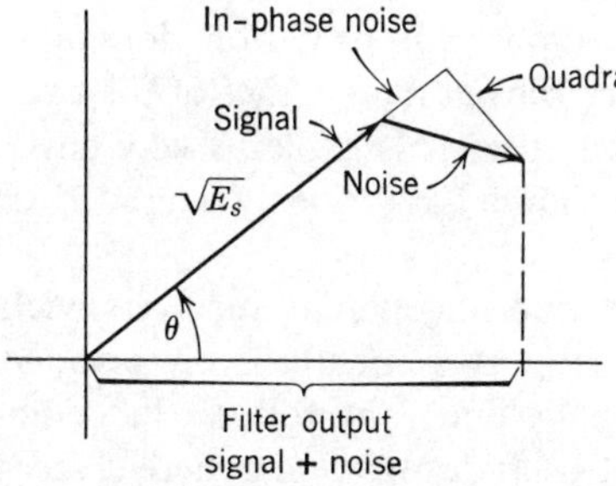

Figure 7.34 Phasor diagram for envelope detection.

Insight into the near equivalence of the coherent and incoherent cases is provided by the phasor diagram in Fig. 7.34. In accordance with Eqs. 7.57, 7.58, and 7.61, we can think of the output of the signal-excited bandpass matched filter in Fig. 7.31 (scaled by the normalizing factor $1/\sqrt{E_s}$) as being represented for $t \approx T$ by a signal phasor of length $\sqrt{E_s}$ and phase θ to which is added vectorially a random noise phasor. The resultant phasor rotates with angular frequency $\omega_0 = 2\pi f_0$, and the normalized filter output is the projection on the horizontal axis.

The noise phasor can be resolved into two components, one in phase with and one in quadrature with the signal phasor. Since the lowpass noise processes $n_c(t)$ and $n_s(t)$ in the bandpass noise representation of Eq. 7.28 are stationary and a change in the signal phase corresponds to a shift in time origin, the statistical properties of the in-phase and quadrature noise components are the same regardless of the value of θ. Thus these narrow-band filtered lowpass noise phasor components vary slowly in length, each having the amplitude of a statistically independent Gaussian process with mean power $\mathcal{N}_0/2$ and rms amplitude $\sqrt{\mathcal{N}_0/2}$.

In the case of coherent reception, the phase θ is known and the optimum receiver observes only in-phase noise components. On the other hand, the incoherent receiver observes the envelope of the filter outputs. For the signal-excited filter, this corresponds to the length of the *total* signal-plus-noise phasor. When $\sqrt{E_s/\mathcal{N}_0} \gg 1$, however, both the in- and out-of-phase noise components are usually much smaller than the signal component. It is clear from the geometry of Fig. 7.34 that the amplitude of the envelope is then affected primarily by the in-phase noise alone.

We may also consider the bandpass matched filter whose output is noise alone in much the same way. The length of the vector sum of two orthogonal Gaussian vectors can be large (in relation to the signal) only if one or both of its components are large. With weak noise, the probability of such an event is not substantially larger than that which would obtain if we observed only a single noise component, as with the coherent receiver. Thus lack of phase information does not seriously affect the statistical nature of the output from either of the two orthogonal matched filters when $E_s/\mathcal{N}_0$ is large. This explains why envelope detection yields an error performance that is not seriously degraded under high energy-to-noise ratio conditions.

Although coherent and incoherent receivers yield comparable error performance when one of two equally likely orthogonal signals is transmitted in weak noise, it does not follow that complete lack of phase knowledge is not costly. Indeed, when coherent reception is possible, the two signals may be chosen to be antipodal rather than orthogonal, which saves 3 db. The 3 db may also be saved when the channel phase varies slowly enough so that phase continuity between successive transmissions can be exploited, even though the absolute phase may be unknown. One way to accomplish this goal is described in the next two sections.

Phase comparison and channel measurement. An interesting strategy for communicating binary data over a random-phase channel is to transmit a *known* reference waveform, say $q(t)\sqrt{2}\cos\omega_0 t$, to measure the phase of the channel, and then to transmit the message by means of antipodal signals $\pm s_o(t)\sqrt{2}\cos\omega_0 t$, corresponding to $m = m_1$ and $m = m_2$, respectively. Note that these message signals are optimum if the phase is known but are indistinguishable if the phase is uniformly distributed over $[0, 2\pi]$, which points out the need for the phase-reference measurement.

We now consider the particular case in which the lowpass waveforms $q(t)$ and $s_o(t)$ are orthogonal, each with energy $\frac{1}{2}E_s$. One possible choice of signals, with corresponding vector representation, is illustrated in Fig. 7.35.

It is immediately apparent from the vector representation that the total transmitted waveform (reference waveform plus signal) may be generated in a single step by appropriately supplying either

$$s_1(t) = q(t) + s_o(t) \tag{7.70a}$$

or

$$s_2(t) = q(t) - s_o(t) \tag{7.70b}$$

to the input of the transmitter modulator. The two signals $s_1(t)$ and $s_2(t)$ are orthogonal and each has energy E_s. Thus there is no distinction (other than point of view) between the signal set here and in the envelope detector analysis encompassing Eq. 7.59.

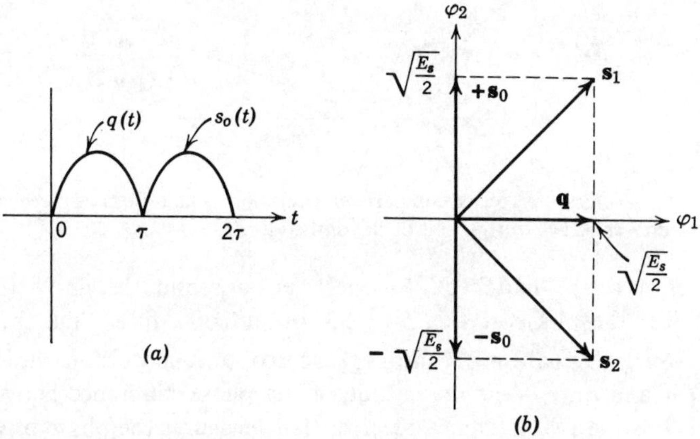

Figure 7.35 Signals for channel measurements and phase-comparison reception.

It remains to be shown how this point of view may be extended to the design of an optimum receiver. We now prove that an appropriate phase-reference and comparison receiver always makes the same decision as the optimum envelope-detector receiver. First, from Eq. 7.60 we note that the latter receiver sets $\hat{m} = m_1$ if and only if

$$(\mathbf{r}_c \cdot \mathbf{s}_1)^2 + (\mathbf{r}_s \cdot \mathbf{s}_1)^2 > (\mathbf{r}_c \cdot \mathbf{s}_2)^2 + (\mathbf{r}_s \cdot \mathbf{s}_2)^2,$$

which may be rewritten as

$$[\mathbf{r}_c \cdot (\mathbf{q} + \mathbf{s}_o)]^2 + [\mathbf{r}_s \cdot (\mathbf{q} + \mathbf{s}_o)]^2 > [\mathbf{r}_c \cdot (\mathbf{q} - \mathbf{s}_o)]^2 + [\mathbf{r}_s \cdot (\mathbf{q} - \mathbf{s}_o)]^2.$$

Simplifying, we observe that the optimum receiver sets $\hat{m} = m_1$ if and only if

$$(\mathbf{r}_c \cdot \mathbf{q})(\mathbf{r}_c \cdot \mathbf{s}_o) + (\mathbf{r}_s \cdot \mathbf{q})(\mathbf{r}_s \cdot \mathbf{s}_o) > 0. \tag{7.71}$$

Finally, if, as illustrated in Fig. 7.36, we define the two new vectors

$$\mathbf{Q} \triangleq (\mathbf{r}_c \cdot \mathbf{q}, \mathbf{r}_s \cdot \mathbf{q}) \tag{7.72a}$$

$$\mathbf{S}_o \triangleq (\mathbf{r}_c \cdot \mathbf{s}_o, \mathbf{r}_s \cdot \mathbf{s}_o), \tag{7.72b}$$

then Eq. 7.71 may be written

$$\mathbf{Q} \cdot \mathbf{S}_o > 0. \tag{7.72c}$$

The interpretation of the optimum decision rule of Eq. 7.72c is clarified in Fig. 7.37. First, from Eq. 7.58c and the discussion leading to Eq. 7.57 we note that the angle (phase) of $\mathbf{Q}$ is just the phase at $t = T$ of the

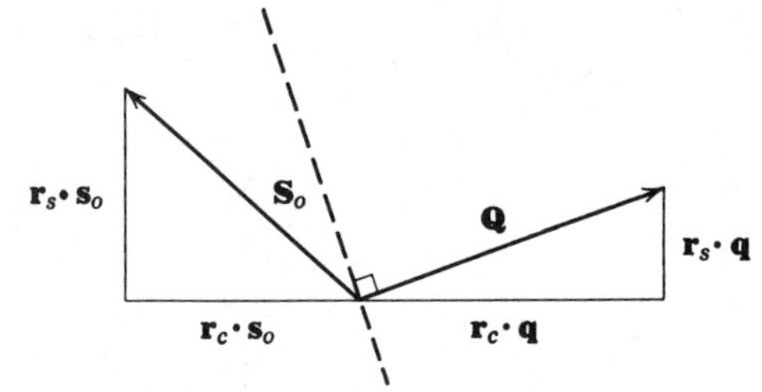

Figure 7.36 Vectors for phase-comparison decision. The optimum receiver sets $\hat{m} = m_1$ whenever $\mathbf{S}_0$ lies to the right of the dashed line.

output of a filter "matched" to $q(t)\sqrt{2}\cos\omega_0 t$ and the angle (phase) of $\mathbf{S}_o$ is just the phase at $t = T$ of the output of a filter "matched" to $s_o(t)\sqrt{2}\cos\omega_0 t$. Equation 7.72 implies that an optimum decision rule is to set $\hat{m} = m_1$ if and only if the magnitude of the phase difference between $\mathbf{Q}$ and $\mathbf{S}_o$ is less than 90°. Thus a receiver that measures the phase of $\mathbf{Q}$ and uses it as a reference for comparison against the phase of $\mathbf{S}_o$ is optimum.

When $E_s/\mathcal{N}_0$ is large, the measured-reference phase is with high probability nearly the same as the actual phase of the channel, which provides another interpretation of the smallness of the degradation of performance sustained by the incoherent receiver under these conditions.

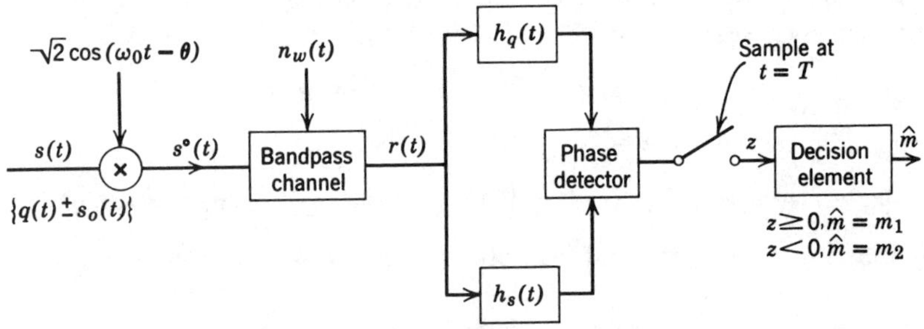

Figure 7.37 Matched-filter and phase-detector receiver. As usual, the random (but time-invariant) channel phase θ has been ascribed to the modulator. The filters are matched, except for phase, to the transmitted signals

$$h_q(t) = q(T - t)\sqrt{2}\cos\omega_0 t,$$
$$h_s(t) = s_o(T - t)\sqrt{2}\cos\omega_0 t.$$

Differential phase-shift keying. A practical system[22] exploits the reference-phase idea in a clever fashion to transmit a sequence of binary messages over a channel whose phase changes very slowly. To transmit the first binary message, a signal is preceded by a reference. For the second binary message, the signal portion of the first transmission is used as reference and only the new signal is sent. This scheme is continued with each signal serving as reference for the next, as illustrated in Fig. 7.38. If at any time m_1 is to be transmitted, the phase is left unchanged from the preceding transmission, whereas if m_2 is to be transmitted the phase is changed by 180°. Decisions are made on the basis of whether the new received phase and the preceding received phase differ in magnitude by more or less than 90°. It follows that as long as negligible channel phase drift occurs between successive transmissions the error probability is the same as that of the incoherent reception of orthogonal signals with energy equal to that of the reference plus signal, say E. From Eq. 7.68

$$P[\mathcal{E}] = \tfrac{1}{2}e^{-E/2\mathcal{N}_0}.$$

But for differential phase-shift keying, the energy actually used in the transmission of each binary message is just that of the signal portion, $E_s = E/2$. Hence

$$P[\mathcal{E}] = \tfrac{1}{2}e^{-E_s/\mathcal{N}_0} \tag{7.73}$$

and a 3-db improvement has been obtained by the double use of energy. For large values of $E_s/\mathcal{N}_0$ and slow phase drift, the degradation in average performance from that obtained with an optimum coherent binary system by using antipodal signals is negligible. The major distinction is that errors tend to occur in pairs, since an error on one message implies a high probability of having received a bad noise, which in turn implies a poor reference for the next decision.

7.4 FADING CHANNELS

We have just treated situations in which either the phase or the amplitude of the received signal is random. We now treat one in which both phase *and* amplitude are random. In particular, we shall investigate the design and performance of optimum receivers for the case in which, if

$$s^{\circ}(t) = s(t)\sqrt{2}\cos\omega_0 t \tag{7.74a}$$

is transmitted, the received signal in the absence of additive noise is

$$r^{\circ}(t) = as(t)\sqrt{2}\cos(\omega_0 t - \theta). \tag{7.74b}$$

In Eq. 7.74b we assume that $s(t)$ is a lowpass modulating signal with

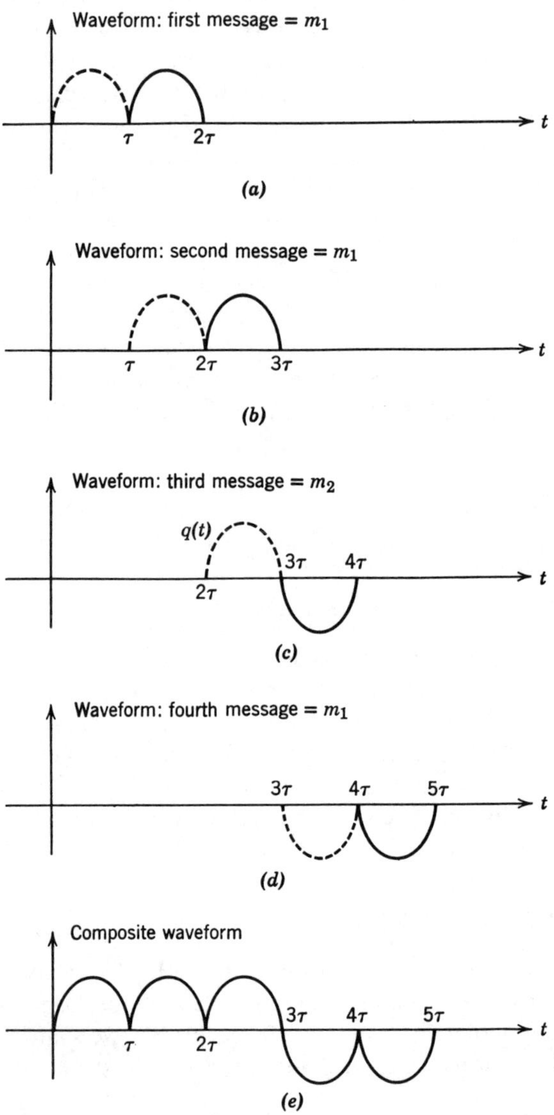

Figure 7.38 Differential-phase-shift-keyed waveforms for message sequence m_1, m_1, m_2, m_1. For each message the reference waveform is the dashed pulse, and the signal waveform is the solid one. The energy of each pulse is E_s.

bandwidth $W \ll \omega_0/2\pi$ and that the joint probability density function of the gain and phase parameters (a, θ) is

$$p_{a,\theta}(\alpha, \phi) = \begin{cases} \dfrac{\alpha}{\pi b} e^{-\alpha^2/b}; & \alpha \geqslant 0, 0 \leqslant \phi < 2\pi \\ 0; & \text{elsewhere.} \end{cases} \tag{7.75a}$$

Thus a and θ are statistically independent, with

$$p_a(\alpha) = \frac{2\alpha}{b} e^{-\alpha^2/b}; \qquad \alpha \geqslant 0, \tag{7.75b}$$

$$p_\theta(\phi) = \frac{1}{2\pi}; \qquad 0 \leqslant \phi < 2\pi. \tag{7.75c}$$

The transmission gain a is Rayleigh distributed with

$$\bar{a} = \tfrac{1}{2}\sqrt{\pi b}, \tag{7.76a}$$

$$\overline{a^2} = b > 0. \tag{7.76b}$$

Thus if the transmitted energy is

$$\int_{-\infty}^{\infty} [s^\circ(t)]^2 \, dt = \int_{-\infty}^{\infty} s^2(t) \, dt \triangleq E_s, \tag{7.77a}$$

the mean received signal energy is

$$\mathrm{E} \int_{-\infty}^{\infty} [r^\circ(t)]^2 \, dt = \mathrm{E}[a^2 E_s] = bE_s \triangleq \overline{E_s}. \tag{7.77b}$$

Scattering Model

It is instructive to investigate the circumstances under which the input-output relation given by Eqs. 7.74a and b is a reasonable model for an actual communication problem. Consider the situation shown in Fig. 7.39, in which there is a large number of "scatterers" located at random points within the propagation path. Let the component received from the jth scatterer be

$$r_j^\circ(t) \triangleq c_j \, s(t - \tau_j)\sqrt{2} \cos \omega_0(t - \tau_j).$$

The total noiseless received signal is then

$$r^\circ(t) = \sum_{\text{all } j} r_j^\circ(t).$$

If the delays $\{\tau_j\}$ are all small in relation to the reciprocal bandwidth of $s(t)$ but comparable to $2\pi/\omega_0$, then we can write

$$r^\circ(t) \approx s(t) \sum_{\text{all } j} c_j \sqrt{2} \cos(\omega_0 t - \phi_j), \tag{7.78}$$

in which $\phi_j \triangleq \omega_0 \tau_j$. Equation 7.78 is predicated on the fact that $s(t)$, being narrow-band, cannot change significantly over the time interval spanned by the $\{\tau_j\}$, so that $s(t - \tau_j) \approx s(t)$ for all j.†

If $r^\circ(t)$ is fed into sine and cosine DSB demodulators such as those in

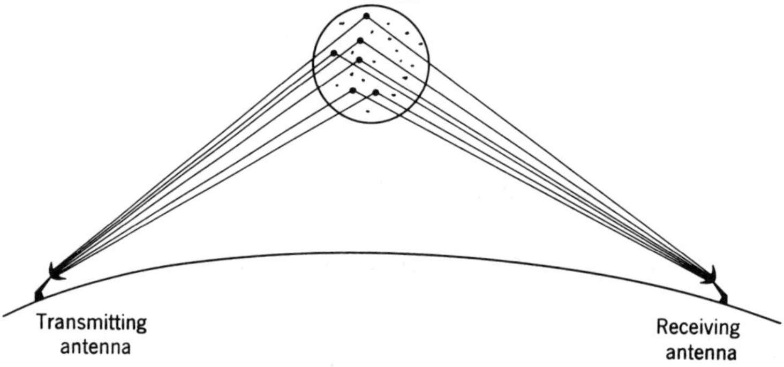

Figure 7.39 Scattering of transmitted signal.

Fig. 7.14*b*, the two outputs are

$$r_c(t) = s(t) \sum_j c_j \cos \phi_j \tag{7.79a}$$

and

$$r_s(t) = s(t) \sum_j c_j \sin \phi_j. \tag{7.79b}$$

We now investigate the statistical properties of the parameters

$$z_c \triangleq \sum_j c_j \cos \phi_j \tag{7.80a}$$

$$z_s \triangleq \sum_j c_j \sin \phi_j. \tag{7.80b}$$

The simplest case—and the only one that we consider—occurs when the $\{\phi_j\}$ are statistically independent and each is uniformly distributed over $[0, 2\pi]$. Assume initially that the $\{c_j\}$ are identically distributed random variables, each of which is statistically independent of the others and of the $\{\phi_j\}$. Then the central limit theorem states that both z_c and z_s are approximately Gaussian whenever the number of scatterers is large. Moreover, by virtue of the statistical independence of the $\{c_j\}$ and the

† In Eq. 7.78 we neglect the gross delay that is due to the average distance over which the signal must propagate. Such delay amounts to a shift in time origin. Only incremental delays are pertinent to the analysis.

$\{\phi_j\}$, we have

$$\begin{aligned}\bar{z}_c &= \sum_j \bar{c}_j\,\overline{\cos\phi_j},\\ \bar{z}_s &= \sum_j \bar{c}_j\,\overline{\sin\phi_j},\\ \overline{z_c^{\,2}} &= \sum_k\sum_j \overline{c_k c_j}\;\overline{\cos\phi_k\cos\phi_j},\\ \overline{z_s^{\,2}} &= \sum_k\sum_j \overline{c_k c_j}\;\overline{\sin\phi_k\sin\phi_j},\\ \overline{z_c z_s} &= \sum_k\sum_j \overline{c_k c_j}\;\overline{\cos\phi_k\sin\phi_j}.\end{aligned} \tag{7.81}$$

But

$$\overline{\sin\phi_j} = \overline{\cos\phi_j} = \int_0^{2\pi} \frac{1}{2\pi}\cos\alpha\,d\alpha = 0,$$

$$\overline{\cos\phi_j\sin\phi_j} = \int_0^{2\pi} \frac{1}{2\pi}\cos\alpha\sin\alpha\,d\alpha = 0,$$

$$\overline{\sin^2\phi_j} = \overline{\cos^2\phi_j} = \int_0^{2\pi} \frac{1}{2\pi}\cos^2\alpha\,d\alpha = \tfrac{1}{2},$$

and

$$\left.\begin{aligned}\overline{\cos\phi_k\sin\phi_j} &= \overline{\cos\phi_k}\;\overline{\sin\phi_j} = 0\\ \overline{\cos\phi_k\cos\phi_j} &= \overline{\cos\phi_k}\;\overline{\cos\phi_j} = 0\\ \overline{\sin\phi_k\sin\phi_j} &= \overline{\sin\phi_k}\;\overline{\sin\phi_j} = 0\end{aligned}\right\}\ k \neq j,$$

in which we have exploited the statistical independence of the $\{\phi_j\}$. Thus Eqs. 7.81 become

$$\bar{z}_c = \bar{z}_s = 0, \tag{7.82a}$$

$$\overline{z_c^{\,2}} = \overline{z_s^{\,2}} = \tfrac{1}{2}\sum_j \overline{c_j^{\,2}}, \tag{7.82b}$$

$$\overline{z_c z_s} = 0. \tag{7.82c}$$

We see that z_c and z_s are not only Gaussian but are also statistically independent of each other and have zero means and equal variances. It follows that

$$p_{z_c,z_s}(\alpha, \beta) = \frac{1}{\pi b}\, e^{-(\alpha^2+\beta^2)/b} \tag{7.83a}$$

with

$$b \triangleq \sum_j \overline{c_j^{\,2}} = 2\overline{z_c^{\,2}} = 2\overline{z_s^{\,2}}. \tag{7.83b}$$

It is interesting to note from Eqs. 7.81 that the central limit theorem implies that the joint density function p_{z_c,z_s} is given by Eqs. 7.83 even if the $\{c_j\}$ are constants, say

$$c_j = c; \qquad \text{for all } j.$$

Thus the critical conditions required to justify modeling z_c and z_s by statistically independent Gaussian random variables are that the $\{\phi_j\}$ be uniformly distributed and statistically independent and that the number of scatterers be very large. The assumption that these conditions are met is valid in many cases of practical interest, in particular with tropospheric- and ionospheric-scattering channels.

It is now easy to see that the density function of Eq. 7.83 leads to the input-output relation given by Eqs. 7.74 and 7.75. We can recompose $r^\circ(t)$ from the quadrature components of Eq. 7.79 and write

$$\begin{aligned} r^\circ(t) &= s(t)[z_c \sqrt{2} \cos \omega_0 t + z_s \sqrt{2} \sin \omega_0 t] \\ &= s(t)\sqrt{2}\, a \cos (\omega_0 t - \theta), \end{aligned} \tag{7.84a}$$

in which

$$a \triangleq \sqrt{z_c^{\,2} + z_s^{\,2}} \tag{7.84b}$$

$$\theta \triangleq \tan^{-1} \frac{z_s}{z_c}. \tag{7.84c}$$

But we have already observed (Eq. 2A.11 with $\rho = 0$) that the density function p_{z_c, z_s} of Eq. 7.83a implies the density function $p_{a,\theta}$ of Eq. 7.75a. Thus our scattering-channel model leads to a received signal with a uniformly distributed phase and a Rayleigh-distributed amplitude.

Single Transmission

We now consider the simplest case involving both fading and the addition of white Gaussian noise, in which $s(t)$ represents the single transmission of one of M equally likely lowpass signals $\{s_i(t)\}$. The total received signal is therefore

$$r(t) = a\, s(t) \sqrt{2} \cos (\omega_0 t - \theta) + n_w(t). \tag{7.85}$$

Determination of the optimum receiver structure is straightforward. We first observe that if a were known, the optimum receiver would simply act as if the modulating signal set had been $\{as_i(t)\}$ and in accordance with Eq. 7.50 would therefore determine that i for which

$$I_0\left(\frac{2aX_i}{\mathcal{N}_0}\right) e^{-a^2 E_i/\mathcal{N}_0} \tag{7.86a}$$

is maximum. Here E_i denotes the energy of $s_i(t)$ and as before the quantity

$$X_i \triangleq \left\{\left[\int_{-\infty}^{\infty} r_c(t)\, s_i(t)\, dt\right]^2 + \left[\int_{-\infty}^{\infty} r_s(t)\, s_i(t)\, dt\right]^2\right\}^{1/2} \tag{7.86b}$$

may be identified as the sampled envelope of a bandpass filter matched to $s_i(t)\sqrt{2}\cos\omega_0 t$. When all E_i are equal, $i = 0, 1, \ldots, M-1$, the decision implied by this rule is the same regardless of the specific (positive) value assumed by a. In this case the envelope detector of Fig. 7.31 is still an optimum receiver, even though a is now a (positive) random variable.

Probability of error. For $M = 2$ and orthogonal signals of energy E_s, the probability of error is also easy to determine. From Eq. 7.68 we have

$$P[\mathcal{E}] = \overline{P[\mathcal{E} \mid a]} = \overline{\tfrac{1}{2}e^{-a^2E_s/2\mathcal{N}_0}}. \tag{7.87}$$

But

$$a^2 = z_c^2 + z_s^2,$$

and z_c and z_s are statistically independent Gaussian random variables with zero mean and variance $b/2$. Accordingly,

$$P[\mathcal{E}] = \tfrac{1}{2}\overline{e^{-z_c^2(E_s/2\mathcal{N}_0)}}\;\overline{e^{-z_s^2(E_s/2\mathcal{N}_0)}}.$$

By invoking the lemma of Eq. 7.67, with $w = -E_s/2\mathcal{N}_0$, $\sigma_x^2 = b/2$, and $m_x = 0$, we have

$$P[\mathcal{E}] = \frac{1}{2}\left(1 + \frac{E_s}{\mathcal{N}_0}\,b/2\right)^{-\frac{1}{2}}\left(1 + \frac{E_s}{\mathcal{N}_0}\,b/2\right)^{-\frac{1}{2}}$$

$$= \frac{1}{2 + \bar{E}_s/\mathcal{N}_0}, \tag{7.88}$$

in which $\bar{E}_s = bE_s$ is the mean value of the received energy.

Discussion. Equation 7.88 states that the minimum attainable error probability in communicating one of two equally likely orthogonal signals over a Rayleigh-fading channel decreases only inversely with the transmitted energy. This behavior is in marked contrast to the nonfading case, in which the error probability decreases exponentially with E_s. The difference in performance is attributable to the fact that even when the *average* received energy on a fading channel is high there is still an appreciable probability that the actual energy received on any given transmission is quite small; that is, there is an appreciable probability of a "deep fade." This is evident in the plot of the Rayleigh density function in Fig. 2.21b.

Diversity Transmission

The only efficient way to reduce the error probability with a Rayleigh-fading channel is to circumvent the high probability of a deep fade on a single transmission. This is accomplished by means of *diversity* transmission. The idea of diversity is simple: scattering channels of practical interest are characterized by the fact that the scattering elements in Fig. 7.39 move randomly with respect to one another as time goes on.

Thus the received signal amplitude and phase are actually random processes, say, $a(t)$ and $\theta(t)$. Of course, at any stated observation instant t_l, the parameters $a(t_l)$ and $\theta(t_l)$ are Rayleigh and uniformly distributed random variables, respectively. The preceding analysis of a single transmission is therefore valid whenever the duration of the signal $s(t)$ is short enough compared with the rate of variation of $a(t)$ and $\theta(t)$ that these processes are relatively constant over the signaling interval. Over an extended period of time, however, we anticipate that the observed values of $a(t)$ will fluctuate, being sometimes large and sometimes small. One form of diversity, called *time diversity*, involves sending the same signal $s(t)$ over and over again, say L times, in the hope that not all of the transmissions will be subjected to deep fades.

The objective of time diversity is to space successive transmissions in time in such a way that the fading experienced by each transmission is statistically independent. Let the instants at which successive transmissions begin be $\{t_l\}$, $l = 1, 2, \ldots, L$. The value of $a(t)$ observed at any instant depends primarily on the phase relationships then existing between the mutually interfering incremental wavelets received from individual scatterers. Accordingly, if the $\{t_l\}$ are spaced far enough apart so that the phase samples

$$\theta(t_1), \theta(t_2), \ldots, \theta(t_L)$$

are statistically independent, so also are the corresponding gain samples

$$a(t_1), a(t_2), \ldots, a(t_L).$$

We therefore assume for purposes of analysis that

$$p_{\mathbf{a},\boldsymbol{\theta}} = \prod_{l=1}^{L} p_{a_l,\theta_l}, \tag{7.89a}$$

where

$$a_l \triangleq a(t_l), \qquad \theta_l \triangleq \theta(t_l), \tag{7.89b}$$

$$\mathbf{a} \triangleq (a_1, a_2, \ldots, a_L), \tag{7.89c}$$

$$\boldsymbol{\theta} \triangleq (\theta_1, \theta_2, \ldots, \theta_L). \tag{7.89d}$$

As in the single-transmission case, we also assume for $l = 1, 2, \ldots, L$ that

$$p_{a_l,\theta_l}(\alpha, \phi) = \begin{cases} \dfrac{\alpha}{\pi b_l} e^{-\alpha^2/b_l}; & \alpha \geqslant 0, 0 \leqslant \phi < 2\pi \\ 0; & \text{elsewhere.} \end{cases} \tag{7.89e}$$

Equation 7.89e makes provision for the fact that the fading parameters $\{b_l\}$ affecting different transmissions may be unequal. The final assumption is that each of the L diversity transmissions is sufficiently short compared to the spacing between the $\{t_l\}$ that the fading during each transmission may be considered constant.

Thus far we have considered only time diversity. Other methods of obtaining L different received signals are frequency and space diversity. These techniques are discussed briefly at the end of this chapter. Since the performance attainable with diversity depends only upon the $2L$-dimensional joint probability density function $p_{\mathbf{a},\boldsymbol{\theta}}$, the analysis that follows is independent of the particular diversity technique from which $p_{\mathbf{a},\boldsymbol{\theta}}$ results.

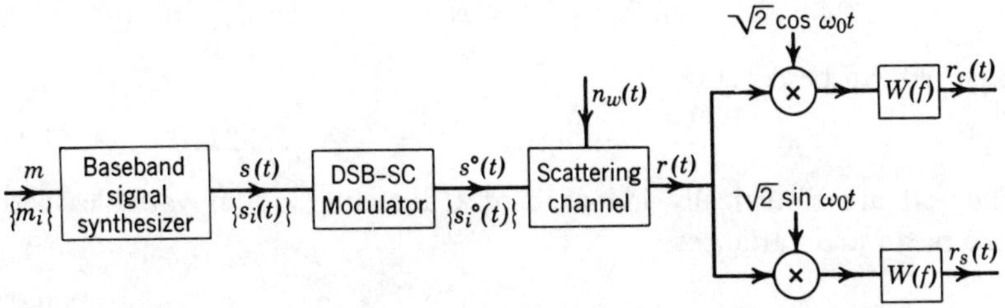

Figure 7.40 DSB demodulation of L-fold time diversity transmission. When $m = m_k$ the baseband signal is

$$s(t) = \sum_{l=1}^{L} s_k(t - t_l).$$

For the scattering channel model under consideration, the resulting demodulator outputs are

$$r_c(t) = \sum_{l=1}^{L} a_l \cos\theta_l \, s_k(t - t_l) + n_c(t),$$

$$r_s(t) = \sum_{l=1}^{L} a_l \sin\theta_l \, s_k(t - t_l) + n_s(t).$$

Optimum diversity receivers. When L-fold time diversity is used in conjunction with DSB demodulation, as in Fig. 7.40, each transmission results in two lowpass output waveforms: one each from the sine and the cosine demodulators. Thus there is a total of $2L$ relevant lowpass waveforms available at the receiver. We now consider the optimum way to use these waveforms in the determination of $\hat{m}$.

Assuming that the input message is m_k and numbering the cosine demodulator outputs consecutively from 1 to L and the sine demodulator outputs consecutively from $(L + 1)$ to $2L$, we may write these $2L$ waveforms as

$$r_l(t) \triangleq \begin{cases} (a_l \cos\theta_l)\, s_k(t) + n_l(t); & l = 1, 2, \ldots, L \\ (a_{l-L} \sin\theta_{l-L})\, s_k(t) + n_l(t); & l = L+1, L+2, \ldots, 2L. \end{cases} \tag{7.90}$$

Here, for notational simplicity, each of the L transmissions has been referred to its own time origin. It is important to remember, however, that successive transmissions actually occur during disjoint time intervals, so that the $\{n_l(t)\}$ represent statistically independent noise processes.

In accordance with Eq. 7.89, the $\{a_l\}$ are statistically independent Rayleigh random variables with $\overline{a_l^2} = b_l$, and the $\{\theta_l\}$ are statistically independent random variables, each of which is uniformly distributed over $[0, 2\pi]$. If we define

$$z_l \triangleq \begin{cases} a_l \cos \theta_l; & l = 1, 2, \ldots, L \\ a_{l-L} \sin \theta_{l-L}; & l = L+1, L+2, \ldots, 2L, \end{cases} \tag{7.91}$$

Eq. 7.90 can be rewritten as

$$r_l(t) = z_l\, s_k(t) + n_l(t); \qquad l = 1, 2, \ldots, 2L. \tag{7.92}$$

The $\{z_l\}$ are statistically independent Gaussian random variables with zero mean and variances

$$\overline{z_l^2} = \frac{b_l}{2}; \qquad l = 1, 2, \ldots, 2L, \tag{7.93a}$$

where we define

$$b_l \triangleq b_{l-L}; \qquad l = L + 1, L + 2, \ldots, 2L. \tag{7.93b}$$

Finally, in terms of an appropriate orthonormal set $\{\varphi_j(t)\}$, we have

$$s_i(t) = \sum_{j=1}^{N} s_{ij}\, \varphi_j(t); \qquad i = 0, 1, \ldots, M - 1, \tag{7.94}$$

so that the vector equivalent to Eq. 7.92 is

$$\mathbf{r}_l = z_l \mathbf{s}_k + \mathbf{n}_l; \qquad l = 1, 2, \ldots, 2L, \tag{7.95}$$

in which each vector has N components.

As usual, the relevant part of the additive noise disturbance is encompassed in the $\{\mathbf{n}_l\}$. Each component of $\mathbf{n}_l$, $l = 1, 2, \ldots, 2L$ is a zero-mean Gaussian random variable with variance $\mathcal{N}_0/2$ and is statistically independent of all other parameters of the problem.

In formulating the optimum receiver, it is convenient to abbreviate notation by defining the $2LN$-component vectors

$$\mathbf{r} \triangleq (\mathbf{r}_1, \mathbf{r}_2, \ldots, \mathbf{r}_{2L}) \tag{7.96a}$$

$$\boldsymbol{\rho} \triangleq (\boldsymbol{\rho}_1, \boldsymbol{\rho}_2, \ldots, \boldsymbol{\rho}_{2L}). \tag{7.96b}$$

When $\mathbf{r} = \boldsymbol{\rho}$, the optimum receiver sets $\hat{m}$ equal to that m_i for which

$P[m_i \mid \mathbf{r} = \boldsymbol{\rho}]$ is maximum. Assuming that all $\{m_i\}$ are equally likely, we have

$$P[m_i \mid \mathbf{r} = \boldsymbol{\rho}] \sim p_{\mathbf{r}}(\boldsymbol{\rho} \mid m_i). \tag{7.97}$$

But the noise vectors $\{\mathbf{n}_l\}$ are statistically independent and

$$p_{\mathbf{n}_l} = p_{\mathbf{n}}; \qquad l = 1, 2, \ldots, 2L, \tag{7.98}$$

with

$$p_{\mathbf{n}}(\boldsymbol{\alpha}) = \frac{1}{(\pi \mathcal{N}_0)^{N/2}} e^{-|\boldsymbol{\alpha}|^2/\mathcal{N}_0}. \tag{7.99}$$

Given the transmission gains $\{z_l\}$, we therefore have

$$p_{\mathbf{r}}(\boldsymbol{\rho} \mid m_i, \{z_l\}) = \prod_{l=1}^{2L} p_{\mathbf{n}}(\boldsymbol{\rho}_l - z_l \mathbf{s}_i). \tag{7.100}$$

Since the $\{z_l\}$ are random variables, we obtain the likelihood $p_{\mathbf{r}}(\boldsymbol{\rho} \mid m_i)$ by averaging Eq. 7.100 over the $\{z_l\}$. Thus the optimum receiver determines that i which maximizes

$$\begin{aligned} p_{\mathbf{r}}(\boldsymbol{\rho} \mid m_i) &= \overline{p_{\mathbf{r}}(\boldsymbol{\rho} \mid m_i, \{z_l\})} \\ &= \frac{1}{(\pi \mathcal{N}_0)^{LN}} \overline{\left[\prod_{l=1}^{2L} \exp\left(-\frac{1}{\mathcal{N}_0} |\boldsymbol{\rho}_l - z_l \mathbf{s}_i|^2\right)\right]} \\ &\sim \prod_{l=1}^{2L} \overline{\exp\left(-\frac{1}{\mathcal{N}_0} |\boldsymbol{\rho}_l - z_l \mathbf{s}_i|^2\right)}. \end{aligned} \tag{7.101}$$

In the last line we have exploited the fact that the $\{z_l\}$ are statistically independent and have discarded factors independent of i.

The exponent in Eq. 7.101 may be expanded as follows, with $E_i \triangleq |\mathbf{s}_i|^2$:

$$|\boldsymbol{\rho}_l - z_l \mathbf{s}_i|^2 = |\boldsymbol{\rho}_l|^2 - 2z_l(\boldsymbol{\rho}_l \cdot \mathbf{s}_i) + z_l^2 E_i \tag{7.102a}$$

$$= |\boldsymbol{\rho}_l|^2 + E_i\left(z_l - \frac{\boldsymbol{\rho}_l \cdot \mathbf{s}_i}{E_i}\right)^2 - \frac{(\boldsymbol{\rho}_l \cdot \mathbf{s}_i)^2}{E_i}. \tag{7.102b}$$

Introducing Eq. 7.102 into Eq. 7.101, discarding terms that are independent of i, and defining $\rho_{li} \triangleq \boldsymbol{\rho}_l \cdot \mathbf{s}_i / E_i$ yields

$$p_{\mathbf{r}}(\boldsymbol{\rho} \mid m_i) \sim \prod_{l=1}^{2L} \overline{\exp\left[-\frac{E_i}{\mathcal{N}_0}(z_l - \rho_{li})^2\right]} \exp\left(\rho_{li}^2 \frac{E_i}{\mathcal{N}_0}\right). \tag{7.103}$$

Each of the $2L$ expectations in Eq. 7.103 may be evaluated by invoking the lemma of Eq. 7.67, with $w = -E_i/\mathcal{N}_0$, $m_x = -\rho_{li}$, and $\sigma_x^2 = b_l/2$:

$$\exp\left[-\frac{E_i}{\mathcal{N}_0}(z_l - \rho_{li})^2\right] = \frac{1}{\sqrt{1 + b_l(E_i/\mathcal{N}_0)}} \exp\left[-\frac{(E_i/\mathcal{N}_0)\rho_{li}^2}{1 + b_l(E_i/\mathcal{N}_0)}\right].$$

But

$$\exp\left[-\frac{(E_i/\mathcal{N}_0)\rho_{li}^2}{1 + b_l(E_i/\mathcal{N}_0)}\right] \exp\left(\rho_{li}^2 \frac{E_i}{\mathcal{N}_0}\right) = \exp\left[\rho_{li}^2 \frac{b_l(E_i/\mathcal{N}_0)^2}{1 + b_l(E_i/\mathcal{N}_0)}\right]$$

$$= \exp\left[(\boldsymbol{\rho}_l \cdot \mathbf{s}_i)^2 \frac{b_l/\mathcal{N}_0^2}{1 + b_l(E_i/\mathcal{N}_0)}\right].$$

Thus

$$p_{\mathbf{r}}(\boldsymbol{\rho} \mid m_i) \sim \prod_{l=1}^{2L} \frac{1}{\sqrt{1 + b_l(E_i/\mathcal{N}_0)}} \exp\left[(\boldsymbol{\rho}_l \cdot \mathbf{s}_i)^2 \frac{b_l/\mathcal{N}_0^2}{1 + b_l(E_i/\mathcal{N}_0)}\right]. \tag{7.104}$$

Defining the weighting factors

$$w_{li} \triangleq \frac{b_l(E_i/\mathcal{N}_0)}{1 + b_l(E_i/\mathcal{N}_0)}; \qquad l = 1, 2, \ldots, 2L; \qquad i = 0, 1, \ldots, M - 1, \tag{7.105a}$$

and the bias constants

$$c_i \triangleq -\frac{\mathcal{N}_0}{2} \sum_{l=1}^{2L} \ln\left[1 + b_l(E_i/\mathcal{N}_0)\right]; \qquad i = 0, 1, \ldots, M - 1, \tag{7.105b}$$

we can write Eq. 7.104 in the simpler form

$$p_{\mathbf{r}}(\boldsymbol{\rho} \mid m_i) \sim \exp\left\{\frac{1}{\mathcal{N}_0}\left[c_i + \frac{1}{E_i} \sum_{l=1}^{2L} w_{li}(\boldsymbol{\rho}_l \cdot \mathbf{s}_i)^2\right]\right\}. \tag{7.105c}$$

The optimum receiver therefore determines the index i for which the decision function

$$c_i + \frac{1}{E_i} \sum_{l=1}^{2L} w_{li}(\boldsymbol{\rho}_l \cdot \mathbf{s}_i)^2 \tag{7.106}$$

is maximum.

If all $\{s_i(t)\}$ have the same energy, $E_i = E_s$, the $\{c_i\}$ are independent of i and may be ignored. If in addition the mean-square gains $\{b_l\}$ are the same for all transmissions, the weighting factors $\{w_{li}\}$ are the same for all l and i and may also be ignored. The optimum decision rule then becomes the following:

Set $\hat{m} = m_i$ when $\mathbf{r}_l = \boldsymbol{\rho}_l$, $l = 1, 2, \ldots, 2L$, if and only if $\sum_{l=1}^{2L} (\boldsymbol{\rho}_l \cdot \mathbf{s}_i)^2$ is maximum.

The quantity $\sum_{l=1}^{2L} (\boldsymbol{\rho}_l \cdot \mathbf{s}_i)^2$ may be computed by correlating the sine and cosine demodulator outputs for each of the L transmissions against the lowpass signal $s_i(t)$, squaring, and summing. Alternatively, we recognize from Eqs. 7.54 and 7.58 that for each transmission $l = 1, 2, \ldots, L$, the quantity $[(\boldsymbol{\rho}_l \cdot \mathbf{s}_i)^2 + (\boldsymbol{\rho}_{l+L} \cdot \mathbf{s}_i)^2]$ is the square of the envelope of the output from a filter matched to $s_i(t)\sqrt{2}\cos \omega_0 t$. Thus an optimum receiver may sum (over the L transmissions) the squared-envelope samples from filters matched to each of the M bandpass signals and determine $\hat{m}$ in accordance with whichever sum is largest. Such a receiver realization is diagrammed in Fig. 7.41.

When the mean energy received on each of the L diversity transmissions is not equal, the squared-envelope samples must be weighted before summation. For any transmission such that the ratio of the average received energy and the noise power density, $b_l E_i/\mathcal{N}_0$, is very small, we see from Eq. 7.105a that the weighting factor w_{li} is proportional thereto; on the other hand, when $b_l E_i/\mathcal{N}_0$ becomes very large, w_{li} approaches 1. If the $\{E_i\}$ are not all equal, the bias constants $\{c_i\}$ are necessary if the receiver decision $\hat{m}$ is to be optimum.

Receiver interpretation.[47] If the $2L$ transmission gains $\{z_l\}$ were not random but instead were known to the receiver in advance, the optimum receiving strategy with equally likely messages would be to determine that i for which $p_{\mathbf{r}}(\boldsymbol{\rho} \mid m_i, \{z_l\})$ is maximum. From Eqs. 7.100 and 7.102a the receiver would therefore maximize

$$\tilde{c}_i + \sum_{l=1}^{2L} z_l(\boldsymbol{\rho}_l \cdot \mathbf{s}_i), \tag{7.107a}$$

where

$$\tilde{c}_i \triangleq -\frac{1}{2}\sum_{l=1}^{2L} z_l^2 E_i. \tag{7.107b}$$

On the other hand, when the $\{z_l\}$ are zero-mean Gaussian random variables, we have seen in Eq. 7.106 that the optimum receiver maximizes

$$c_i + \frac{1}{E_i}\sum_{l=1}^{2L} w_{li}(\boldsymbol{\rho}_l \cdot \mathbf{s}_i)^2. \tag{7.108a}$$

This expression can be written in a form analogous to that of Eq. 7.107a by defining

$$\tilde{z}_{li} \triangleq \frac{w_{li}}{E_i}(\boldsymbol{\rho}_l \cdot \mathbf{s}_i). \tag{7.108b}$$

We then have

$$\frac{1}{E_i}\sum_{l=1}^{2L} w_{li}(\boldsymbol{\rho}_l \cdot \mathbf{s}_i)^2 = \sum_{l=1}^{2L} \tilde{z}_{li}(\boldsymbol{\rho}_l \cdot \mathbf{s}_i). \tag{7.108c}$$

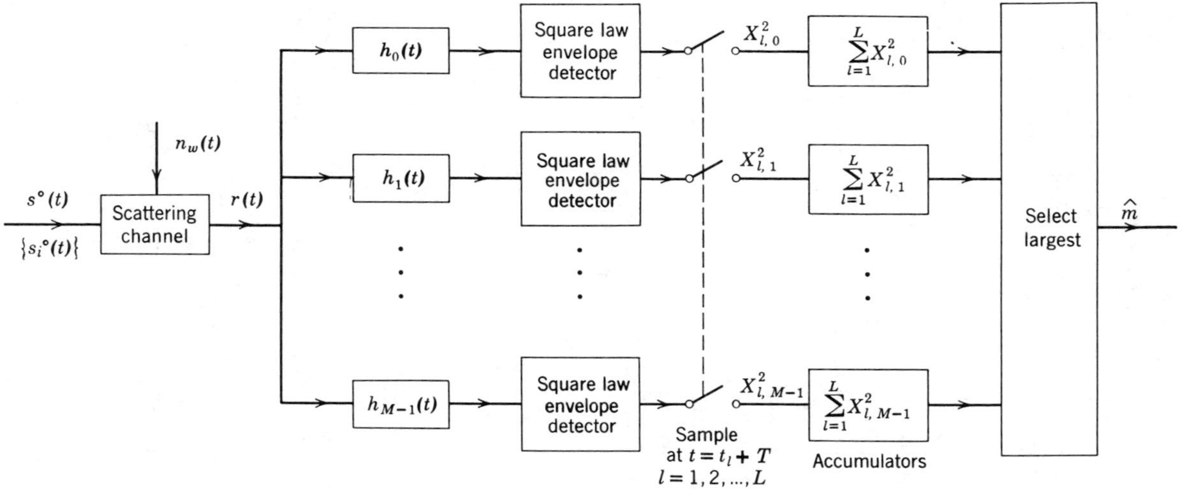

Figure 7.41 Optimum envelope detector receiver for L-fold time diversity transmission. The matched filter impulse responses are $h_i(t) = s_i(T - t)\sqrt{2}\cos\omega_0 t$; $i = 0, 1, \ldots, M - 1$. Each "square law envelope detector" box contains an envelope detector followed by a square-law device.

The interpretation of Eq. 7.108c is of interest. We can think of each $\tilde{z}_{li}$ as an estimate of the transmission gain z_l based on the received signal $\boldsymbol{\rho}_l$ and the hypothesis that $\mathbf{s}_i$ is transmitted. With this interpretation, the optimum receiver can be visualized as first estimating each z_l, $l = 1, 2, \ldots, 2L$, on the basis of hypothesis $\mathbf{s}_i$ and the received signal $\boldsymbol{\rho}_l$ and then testing this hypothesis (aside from the bias term c_i) as if each z_l were actually known to equal the estimated value $\tilde{z}_{li}$. Since the appropriate estimate of each z_l is in general different for each hypothesis $\mathbf{s}_i$, the implementation of a receiver that actually proceeded in this way would be complicated. The visualization, however, provides insight into how a "good" receiver might be constructed for use in certain communication situations wherein the $\{z_l\}$ are not Gaussian.

We now show in what sense the $\{\tilde{z}_{li}\}$ are estimates of the $\{z_l\}$. In particular, we show that

$$\tilde{z}_{li} = \mathrm{E}[z_l \mid m_i, \mathbf{r}_l = \boldsymbol{\rho}_l]; \qquad 1 \leqslant l \leqslant 2L, \quad 0 \leqslant i \leqslant M-1, \quad (7.109)$$

in which the right-hand side means "the conditional mean of z_l, given m_i and $\mathbf{r}_l = \boldsymbol{\rho}_l$."

Proof of Eq. 7.109 is straightforward. We first determine how $p_{z_l}(\beta \mid m_i, \mathbf{r}_l = \boldsymbol{\rho}_l)$ varies as a function of β. Discarding factors that are independent of β, we have

$$\begin{aligned} p_{z_l}(\beta \mid m_i, \mathbf{r}_l = \boldsymbol{\rho}_l) &= \frac{p_{\mathbf{r}_l, z_l}(\boldsymbol{\rho}_l, \beta \mid m_i)}{p_{\mathbf{r}_l}(\boldsymbol{\rho}_l \mid m_i)} \\ &\sim p_{\mathbf{r}_l}(\boldsymbol{\rho}_l \mid m_i, z_l = \beta)\, p_{z_l}(\beta \mid m_i) \\ &\sim e^{-|\boldsymbol{\rho}_l - \beta \mathbf{s}_i|^2/\mathcal{N}_0} e^{-\beta^2/b_l}. \end{aligned} \quad (7.110)$$

The last line follows from Eqs. 7.93, 7.101, and the fact that z_l is statistically independent of the transmitted message. Completing the square in the exponent of Eq. 7.110 and again discarding factors independent of β yields

$$p_{z_l}(\beta \mid m_i, \mathbf{r}_l = \boldsymbol{\rho}_l) \sim \exp\left\{-\frac{1 + b_l(E_i/\mathcal{N}_0)}{b_l}\left[\beta - (\boldsymbol{\rho}_l \cdot \mathbf{s}_i)\frac{b_l/\mathcal{N}_0}{1 + b_l(E_i/\mathcal{N}_0)}\right]^2\right\}.$$

From the definition of w_{li} in Eq. 7.105a an equivalent expression is

$$p_{z_l}(\beta \mid m_i, \mathbf{r}_l = \boldsymbol{\rho}_l) \sim \exp\left\{-\frac{E_i}{\mathcal{N}_0 w_{li}}\left[\beta - (\boldsymbol{\rho}_l \cdot \mathbf{s}_i)\frac{w_{li}}{E_i}\right]^2\right\}. \quad (7.111a)$$

Since the functional dependence on β in Eq. 7.111a is of Gaussian form, $p_{z_l}(\ \mid m_i, \mathbf{r}_l = \boldsymbol{\rho}_l)$ is a Gaussian probability density function. It follows immediately that the conditional mean of z_l is

$$\mathrm{E}[z_l \mid m_i, \mathbf{r}_l = \boldsymbol{\rho}_l] = \frac{w_{li}}{E_i}(\boldsymbol{\rho}_l \cdot \mathbf{s}_i) \triangleq \tilde{z}_{li}, \quad (7.111b)$$

and that the conditional variance is $w_{li}(\mathcal{N}_0/2E_i)$. Thus $\tilde{z}_{li}$ is indeed identifiable as the conditional mean of z_l, given m_i and $\mathbf{r}_l = \boldsymbol{\rho}_l$.

A final point is that $\tilde{z}_{li}$ is also the *minimum mean-square error* estimate of z_l conditioned upon m_i and $\mathbf{r}_l = \boldsymbol{\rho}_l$. This follows immediately from the fact that, if y is any random variable with mean $\bar{y}$ and $\tilde{y}$ is *any* estimate of y, choosing $\tilde{y} = \bar{y}$ minimizes the mean-square error $\overline{(y - \tilde{y})^2}$. Indeed, let $\tilde{y}$ be any other number, say

$$\tilde{y} = \bar{y} + \Delta. \tag{7.112a}$$

Then

$$\begin{aligned}\overline{(y - \tilde{y})^2} &= \overline{(y - \bar{y} - \Delta)^2} \\ &= \overline{(y - \bar{y})^2} - \overline{2\Delta(y - \bar{y})} + \Delta^2 \\ &= \overline{(y - \bar{y})^2} + \Delta^2,\end{aligned} \tag{7.112b}$$

which is minimum when $\Delta = 0$. This is true regardless of the probability system over which the expectation is taken. In particular, when the probability system is specified by a set of conditions, $\bar{y}$ is the *conditional mean* and $\overline{(y - \bar{y})^2}$ is the *conditional variance*. Thus Eqs. 7.111a and 7.112b imply that the mean-square error when z_l is estimated by $\tilde{z}_{li}$, given $m = m_i$ and $\mathbf{r}_l = \boldsymbol{\rho}_l$, is just the conditional variance $w_{li}(\mathcal{N}_0/2E_i)$.

Error probability. Although exact calculation of the minimum attainable error probability for an L-diversity fading channel is quite difficult even when $M = 2$, it is relatively easy to obtain a useful upper bound. This is done in the next section. As a preliminary measure we now determine an exact expression for the $P[\mathcal{E}]$ in the simple case in which the L transmission gains all have the same mean-square value; that is,

$$\overline{a_l^2} = b; \qquad l = 1, 2, \ldots, L. \tag{7.113}$$

We assume that there are two equally likely messages, m_1 and m_2, and that the corresponding lowpass modulator input waveforms at the transmitter, $s_1(t)$ and $s_2(t)$, are orthogonal and have the same energy, E_s. Thus these signals may be represented by vectors

$$\begin{aligned}\mathbf{s}_1 &= \sqrt{E_s}\,\boldsymbol{\varphi}_1 \\ \mathbf{s}_2 &= \sqrt{E_s}\,\boldsymbol{\varphi}_2.\end{aligned} \tag{7.114}$$

In accordance with Eq. 7.106 and its sequel, the optimum decision rule is then to set $\hat{m} = m_1$ if and only if

$$\frac{1}{E_s}\sum_{l=1}^{2L}(\mathbf{r}_l \cdot \mathbf{s}_1)^2 > \frac{1}{E_s}\sum_{l=1}^{2L}(\mathbf{r}_l \cdot \mathbf{s}_2)^2. \tag{7.115a}$$

An equivalent condition is

$$\sum_{l=1}^{2L} r_{l1}^2 > \sum_{l=1}^{2L} r_{l2}^2, \tag{7.115b}$$

where

$$r_{li} \triangleq \mathbf{r}_l \cdot \boldsymbol{\varphi}_i; \qquad i = 1, 2; \qquad l = 1, 2, \ldots, 2L. \tag{7.115c}$$

If $m = m_2$, then $\mathbf{r}_l = z_l \mathbf{s}_2 + \mathbf{n}_l$ and

$$\left.\begin{aligned} r_{l1} &= n_{l1} \\ r_{l2} &= z_l \sqrt{E_s} + n_{l2} \end{aligned}\right\} \quad l = 1, 2, \ldots, 2L. \tag{7.116}$$

Since n_{l1}, n_{l2}, and z_l are statistically independent, zero-mean Gaussian random variables with variances

$$\left.\begin{aligned} \overline{n_{l1}^2} &= \overline{n_{l2}^2} = \frac{\mathcal{N}_0}{2} \\ \overline{z_l^2} &= \tfrac{1}{2}\overline{a_l^2} = \tfrac{1}{2}b \end{aligned}\right\}; \qquad \text{all } l, \tag{7.117a}$$

it follows that the $\{r_{li}\}$ are statistically independent zero-mean Gaussian random variables with variances

$$\left.\begin{aligned} \overline{r_{l1}^2} &= \frac{\mathcal{N}_0}{2} \triangleq \sigma_1^2 \\ \overline{r_{l2}^2} &= \frac{bE_s + \mathcal{N}_0}{2} \triangleq \sigma_2^2 \end{aligned}\right\} \qquad l = 1, 2, \ldots, 2L. \tag{7.117b}$$

Defining

$$\mathbf{R}_1 \triangleq (r_{11}, r_{21}, \ldots, r_{2L,1}) \tag{7.118a}$$

$$\mathbf{R}_2 \triangleq (r_{12}, r_{22}, \ldots, r_{2L,2}), \tag{7.118b}$$

we observe from Eq. 7.115b that an error occurs when $m = m_2$ if and only if

$$|\mathbf{R}_1| > |\mathbf{R}_2|. \tag{7.119}$$

Letting p_1 and p_2 denote, respectively, the conditional density functions of $|\mathbf{R}_1|$ and $|\mathbf{R}_2|$, given $m = m_2$, we therefore have

$$\mathrm{P}[\mathcal{E} \mid m_2] = \int_{-\infty}^{\infty} p_2(\beta)\, d\beta \int_{\beta}^{\infty} p_1(\alpha)\, d\alpha. \tag{7.120}$$

Both $\mathbf{R}_1$ and $\mathbf{R}_2$ are random vectors with $2L$ components, each component being a zero-mean, identically distributed, statistically independent

Gaussian random variable. The component variance for $\mathbf{R}_1$ is σ_1^2, whereas for $\mathbf{R}_2$ it is σ_2^2. In Appendix 5D we determined the density function of the magnitude of a similar N-component vector with unit-variance components: from Eqs. 5D.10a and 5D.14,

$$p_{|\mathbf{n}|}(\rho) = \frac{N\rho^{N-1}B_N}{(2\pi)^{N/2}} e^{-\rho^2/2} \tag{7.121a}$$

with

$$B_N = \frac{\pi^{N/2}}{(N/2)!}; \qquad N \text{ even.} \tag{7.121b}$$

Scaling to variance σ_i^2 and simplifying yields

$$p_i(\alpha) = \frac{1}{(L-1)!}\frac{\alpha}{\sigma_i^2}\left(\frac{\alpha^2}{2\sigma_i^2}\right)^{L-1} e^{-\alpha^2/2\sigma_i^2}; \qquad i = 1, 2. \tag{7.121c}$$

Carrying out the integrations of Eq. 7.120 by parts, we obtain first

$$\int_\beta^\infty p_1(\alpha)\, d\alpha = e^{-\beta^2/2\sigma_1^2}\left[1 + \frac{\beta^2/2\sigma_1^2}{1!} + \frac{(\beta^2/2\sigma_1^2)^2}{2!} + \cdots + \frac{(\beta^2/2\sigma_1^2)^{L-1}}{(L-1)!}\right]$$

and then

$$\mathrm{P}[\mathcal{E} \mid m_2] = \left(\frac{\sigma_1^2}{\sigma_1^2+\sigma_2^2}\right)^L\left[1 + \binom{L}{1}\left(\frac{\sigma_2^2}{\sigma_1^2+\sigma_2^2}\right) + \binom{L+1}{2}\left(\frac{\sigma_2^2}{\sigma_1^2+\sigma_2^2}\right)^2 + \cdots + \binom{2L-2}{L-1}\left(\frac{\sigma_2^2}{\sigma_1^2+\sigma_2^2}\right)^{L-1}\right]. \tag{7.122a}$$

By symmetry,

$$\mathrm{P}[\mathcal{E} \mid m_2] = \mathrm{P}[\mathcal{E} \mid m_1] = \mathrm{P}[\mathcal{E}]. \tag{7.122b}$$

The error probability depends on the average received signal energy $\bar{E}_s = bE_s$ only through the parameters

$$p \triangleq \frac{\sigma_1^2}{\sigma_1^2 + \sigma_2^2} \tag{7.123a}$$

and

$$1 - p = \frac{\sigma_2^2}{\sigma_1^2 + \sigma_2^2}. \tag{7.123b}$$

We identify these parameters by observing in Eqs. 7.122 that $\mathrm{P}[\mathcal{E}] = p$ when $L = 1$. Introducing the values of σ_1^2 and σ_2^2 given by Eq. 7.117b, we have

$$p = \frac{\mathcal{N}_0/2}{(bE_s + \mathcal{N}_0)/2 + \mathcal{N}_0/2} = \frac{1}{2 + \bar{E}_s/\mathcal{N}_0}, \tag{7.124a}$$

which checks with the error probability for $L = 1$ (no diversity) given by

Eq. 7.88. In terms of p, Eq. 7.122 is written concisely as[67]

$$P[\mathcal{E}] = p^L \sum_{j=0}^{L-1} \binom{L+j-1}{j} (1-p)^j. \tag{7.124b}$$

Upper bound on P[$\mathcal{E}$]. Although exact, Eq. 7.124 is cumbrous and inconvenient to use when L is large. We now obtain an exponentially tight upper bound on the attainable error probability with binary orthogonal signals, each having energy E_s, which is useful even when the L-transmission gains $\{a_l\}$ do not all have the same mean-square value. The result is obtained by means of the Chernoff bounding technique.

The weighting factors $\{w_{li}\}$ of Eq. 7.105a must be used by an optimum receiver when the

$$\overline{a_l^2} = b_l; \qquad l = 1, 2, \ldots, L, \tag{7.125}$$

are not all equal. For binary signals with equal energy E_s,

$$w_{li} = w_l \triangleq \frac{b_l(E_s/\mathcal{N}_0)}{1 + b_l(E_s/\mathcal{N}_0)} = \frac{\bar{E}_l/\mathcal{N}_0}{1 + \bar{E}_l/\mathcal{N}_0}; \qquad i = 1, 2; \quad l = 1, 2, \ldots, 2L, \tag{7.126}$$

where $\bar{E}_l \triangleq b_l E_s$ is the average energy received on the lth transmission. Equation 7.106 then states that the optimum receiver sets $\hat{m} = m_1$ if and only if

$$\frac{1}{E_s} \sum_{l=1}^{2L} w_l(\mathbf{r}_l \cdot \mathbf{s}_1)^2 > \frac{1}{E_s} \sum_{l=1}^{2L} w_l(\mathbf{r}_l \cdot \mathbf{s}_2)^2. \tag{7.127a}$$

An equivalent expression, analogous to Eq. 7.115b, is

$$\sum_{l=1}^{2L} r_{l1}^2 > \sum_{l=1}^{2L} r_{l2}^2, \tag{7.127b}$$

in which the $\{r_{li}\}$ are now defined to include the weighting factors $\{w_l\}$:

$$\left.\begin{aligned} r_{l1} &\triangleq \sqrt{w_l}\,(\mathbf{r}_l \cdot \boldsymbol{\varphi}_1) \\ r_{l2} &\triangleq \sqrt{w_l}\,(\mathbf{r}_l \cdot \boldsymbol{\varphi}_2) \end{aligned}\right\}; \qquad l = 1, 2, \ldots, 2L. \tag{7.127c}$$

When $m = m_2$,

$$\mathbf{r}_l \cdot \boldsymbol{\varphi}_1 = n_{l1}$$

$$\mathbf{r}_l \cdot \boldsymbol{\varphi}_2 = z_l\sqrt{E_s} + n_{l2},$$

which implies

$$\sigma_1^2 \triangleq \overline{r_{l1}^2} = \frac{\bar{E}_l/2}{1 + \bar{E}_l/\mathcal{N}_0} \tag{7.128a}$$

$$\sigma_2^2 \triangleq \overline{r_{l2}^2} = \frac{\bar{E}_l/\mathcal{N}_0}{1 + \bar{E}_l/\mathcal{N}_0} \cdot \frac{\bar{E}_l + \mathcal{N}_0}{2} = \frac{\bar{E}_l}{2}. \tag{7.128b}$$

The $\{r_{li}\}$ are again independent zero-mean Gaussian random variables.

In accordance with Eq. 7.127b, an error is made when $m = m_2$ if and only if

$$\sum_{l=1}^{2L} (r_{l1}^2 - r_{l2}^2) > 0.$$

The probability of this event is

$$P[\mathcal{E}] = P[\mathcal{E} \mid m_2] = E\left[f\left(\sum_{l=1}^{2L} (r_{l1}^2 - r_{l2}^2)\right)\right], \tag{7.129}$$

in which $f(\ )$ is the unit-step function of Fig. 7.42 and the expectation over the random variables $\{r_{li}\}$ is conditioned on $m = m_2$.

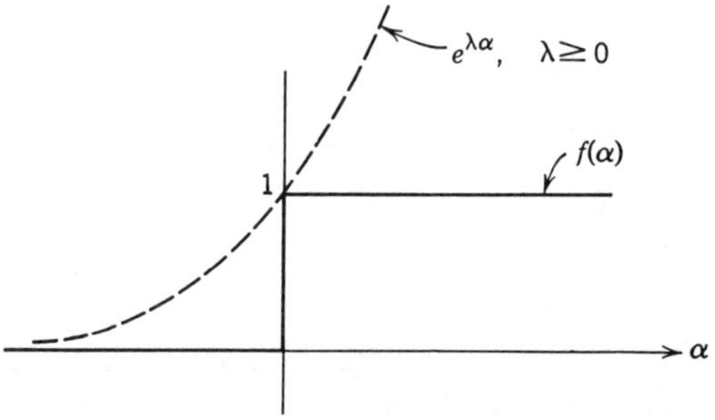

Figure 7.42 Unit-step function and exponential overbound.

We obtain the Chernoff bound on $P[\mathcal{E}]$ by again observing that for any $\lambda \geqslant 0$ the unit step is overbounded by an exponential:

$$f(\alpha) \leqslant e^{\lambda\alpha}; \qquad \lambda \geqslant 0. \tag{7.130}$$

Thus

$$P[\mathcal{E}] \leqslant E\left[\exp \lambda \sum_{l=1}^{2L} (r_{l1}^2 - r_{l2}^2)\right]$$
$$= \prod_{l=1}^{2L} \overline{\exp(\lambda r_{l1}^2)}\ \overline{\exp(-\lambda r_{l2}^2)}; \qquad \lambda > 0. \tag{7.131}$$

In Eq. 7.131 the statistical independence of the $\{r_{li}\}$ has been exploited in writing the mean of the product as the product of the means.

Each of the $4L$ expectations in Eq. 7.131 can be evaluated by means of the lemma of Eq. 7.67, with $w = \pm\lambda$, $m_x = 0$, and $\sigma_x^2 = \sigma_1^2$ or σ_2^2. We then have

$$\overline{\exp(\lambda r_{l1}^2)} = \frac{1}{\sqrt{1 - 2\lambda\sigma_1^2}}; \qquad \lambda < \frac{1}{2\sigma_1^2}$$

$$\overline{\exp(-\lambda r_{l2}^2)} = \frac{1}{\sqrt{1 + 2\lambda\sigma_2^2}}; \qquad \lambda > \frac{-1}{2\sigma_2^2}.$$

Hence for $0 \leqslant \lambda < 1/2\sigma_1^2$

$$\mathrm{P}[\mathcal{E}] \leqslant \prod_{l=1}^{2L} \left[\left(1 - \lambda \frac{\bar{E}_l}{1 + \bar{E}_l/\mathcal{N}_0}\right)^{-1/2} \cdot (1 + \lambda \bar{E}_l)^{-1/2}\right].$$

Since $\bar{E}_l = \bar{E}_{l+L}$, $l = 1, 2, \ldots, L$,

$$\mathrm{P}[\mathcal{E}] \leqslant \prod_{l=1}^{L} \frac{1 + \dfrac{\bar{E}_l}{\mathcal{N}_0}}{\left[1 + \bar{E}_l\left(\dfrac{1}{\mathcal{N}_0} - \lambda\right)\right][1 + \lambda \bar{E}_l]}; \qquad 0 \leqslant \lambda < \frac{1}{\mathcal{N}_0} + \frac{1}{\bar{E}_l}. \tag{7.132}$$

The remaining task is to choose λ in such a way that the bound is as tight as possible. The value of λ that minimizes the lth factor is determined as follows:

$$\frac{d}{d\lambda}\left[1 + \bar{E}_l\left(\frac{1}{\mathcal{N}_0} - \lambda\right)\right](1 + \lambda \bar{E}_l) = 0$$

or

$$-\bar{E}_l(1 + \lambda \bar{E}_l) + \bar{E}_l\left[1 + \bar{E}_l\left(\frac{1}{\mathcal{N}_0} - \lambda\right)\right] = 0$$

or

$$\lambda = \frac{1}{2\mathcal{N}_0}. \tag{7.133}$$

Since this minimizing value is independent of l and falls within the allowable range of λ,

$$\mathrm{P}[\mathcal{E}] \leqslant \prod_{l=1}^{L} \frac{1 + \bar{E}_l/\mathcal{N}_0}{(1 + \bar{E}_l/2\mathcal{N}_0)^2}. \tag{7.134}$$

If we define

$$p_l \triangleq \frac{1}{2 + \bar{E}_l/\mathcal{N}_0}, \tag{7.135a}$$

the result may be written succinctly as

$$\mathrm{P}[\mathcal{E}] \leqslant \prod_{l=1}^{L} 4p_l(1 - p_l). \tag{7.135b}$$

Equation 7.135 is the desired bound. We note that for $L = 1$ it differs from the exact expression of Eq. 7.124, $\mathrm{P}[\mathcal{E}] = p_l$, by the factor $4(1 - p_l)$. When the mean-square transmission gains $\{b_l\}$ are all equal to b, then $\bar{E}_l = bE_s = \bar{E}_s$ for all l and the bound simplifies to

$$\mathrm{P}[\mathcal{E}] \leqslant [4p(1 - p)]^L, \tag{7.136a}$$

$$p \triangleq \frac{1}{2 + \bar{E}_s/\mathcal{N}_0}. \tag{7.136b}$$

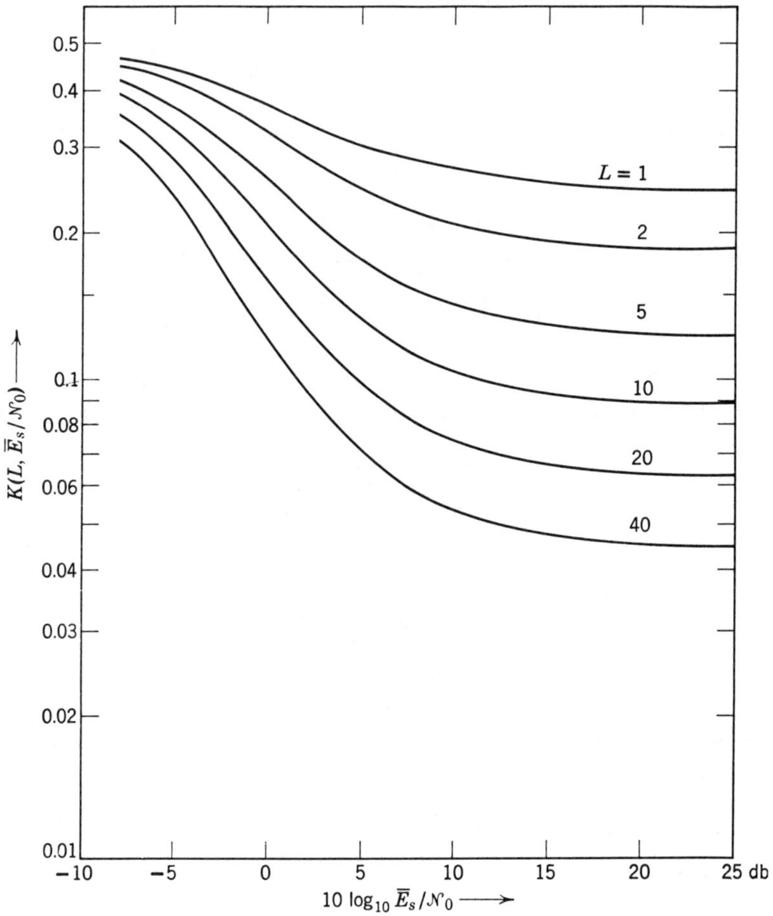

Figure 7.43 Ratio of P[ℰ] to Chernoff bound for equal strength L-fold diversity, $M = 2$.

The exact expression of Eq. 7.124 and the bound of Eq. 7.136 may be readily compared by rewriting the exact expression as

$$\mathrm{P}[\mathcal{E}] = K(L, \bar{E}_s/\mathcal{N}_0)[4p(1 - p)]^L. \tag{7.136c}$$

The parameter K is plotted in Fig. 7.43 as a function of $\bar{E}_s/\mathcal{N}_0$ for several values of L. We observe that K is always less than 0.5 and asymptotically approaches a constant, for each L, as $\bar{E}_s/\mathcal{N}_0$ becomes large. It is not difficult to show that the value of this constant is close to

$$[2\sqrt{\pi L}(1 - 2p)]^{-1}$$

when L is large.

Optimum Diversity

If the most important parameter in the design of a diversity communication system is the probability of error obtainable with a fixed expenditure of energy per message input bit, say E_b, Eq. 7.136 implies that there is an optimum choice for the number of diversity transmissions, L.[50,67] Assume that the $\{b_l\}$ are all equal and E_b is divided equally among the transmissions. For L transmissions, the available energy per transmission is then

$$E_s = \frac{E_b}{L},$$

and the ratio of average received signal energy to noise power density on each transmission is

$$\eta \triangleq \frac{\bar{E}_s}{\mathcal{N}_0} = \frac{bE_b/L}{\mathcal{N}_0} \triangleq \frac{\bar{E}_b/L}{\mathcal{N}_0}. \tag{7.137}$$

We then have

$$p = \frac{1}{2+\eta},$$

so that the bound of Eq. 7.136 becomes

$$\begin{aligned} \mathrm{P}[\mathcal{E}] &\leqslant \left[4\frac{1+\eta}{(2+\eta)^2}\right]^L \\ &= \exp\left[-\frac{\bar{E}_b}{\mathcal{N}_0}(\log_e 2)g(\eta)\right] \end{aligned} \tag{7.138a}$$

where we define

$$g(\eta) \triangleq \frac{1}{\eta}\log_2\frac{(2+\eta)^2}{4(1+\eta)}. \tag{7.138b}$$

The factor $g(\eta)$ is plotted in Fig. 7.44 as a function of η. We observe that the maximum value is approximately 0.215, attained for $\eta \approx 5$ db ≈ 3. It follows that the probability of error may be made to decrease exponentially with $\bar{E}_b/\mathcal{N}_0$ by means of diversity,† even though the channel is subject to fading. The maximum in Fig. 7.44 is quite broad; choosing

$$L \approx \frac{1}{3}\frac{\bar{E}_b}{\mathcal{N}_0} \tag{7.139a}$$

† The decision to use equal energy on each transmission is optimum unless L is so large that the resulting value of η is less than 5 db. Values of L larger than that for which $\eta = 5$ db always reduce the constant in the exponent of the bound on $\mathrm{P}[\mathcal{E}]$ below 0.215. See Example 2, Appendix 7B.

yields the bound

$$P[\mathcal{E}] \lessapprox 2^{-0.215\bar{E}_b/\mathcal{N}_0}. \tag{7.139b}$$

By way of comparison, for a *nonfading* Gaussian channel with unknown phase, we have seen in Eq. 7.68 that the use of two equally likely orthogonal signals each with received energy E_b yields

$$P[\mathcal{E}] = \tfrac{1}{2}e^{-E_b/2\mathcal{N}_0} \approx \tfrac{1}{2}\, 2^{-0.72E_b/\mathcal{N}_0}. \tag{7.140}$$

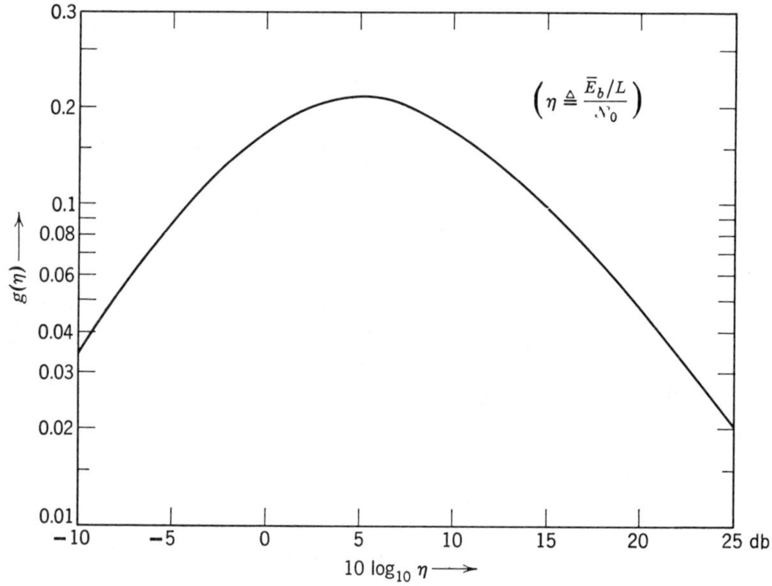

Figure 7.44 The "efficiency factor" $g(\eta)$ for $M = 2$, as a function of diversity order L and energy-to-noise ratio per diversity transmission.

Thus fading costs approximately 5.25 db in signal energy.

The reason why an optimum value of L exists is simple: on the one hand, as L increases with the total energy held fixed, the average signal-to-noise ratio at the output of a bandpass filter matched to $s(t)\sqrt{2}\cos\omega_0 t$ decreases and the loss introduced by incoherent reception becomes larger. On the other hand, increasing L provides additional diversity and decreases the probability that most of the transmissions are badly faded. The optimum value of L reflects the best compromise between these two effects.

7.5 CODING FOR FADING CHANNELS

Although diversity may be used to obtain a probability of error that decreases exponentially as $\bar{E}_b/\mathcal{N}_0$ is increased, an arbitrarily small $P[\mathcal{E}]$

can be obtained in this way only by making $\bar{E}_b/\mathcal{N}_0$ arbitrarily large. Just as in the unfaded case, coding provides a method for making P[$\mathcal{E}$] as small as we please without concomitant increase in transmitted energy per bit, provided that $\bar{E}_b/\mathcal{N}_0$ exceeds a minimum threshold. That this is so follows from random-coding arguments similar to those we have encountered heretofore.

Unquantized Receiver

We begin by considering the use of the two specific lowpass sequences $s_0(t)$ and $s_1(t)$ shown in Fig. 7.45 as the modulator input set in communicating one of two equally likely messages, m_0 and m_1, over a Rayleigh-fading channel. Each sequence comprises N transmissions (or *elements*) and each element consists of a waveform (or *letter*) chosen from an *alphabet* containing A orthogonal lowpass waveforms $\{x_j(t)\}$. We assume that each of the A "building-block" waveforms $\{x_j(t)\}$ has energy E_s.

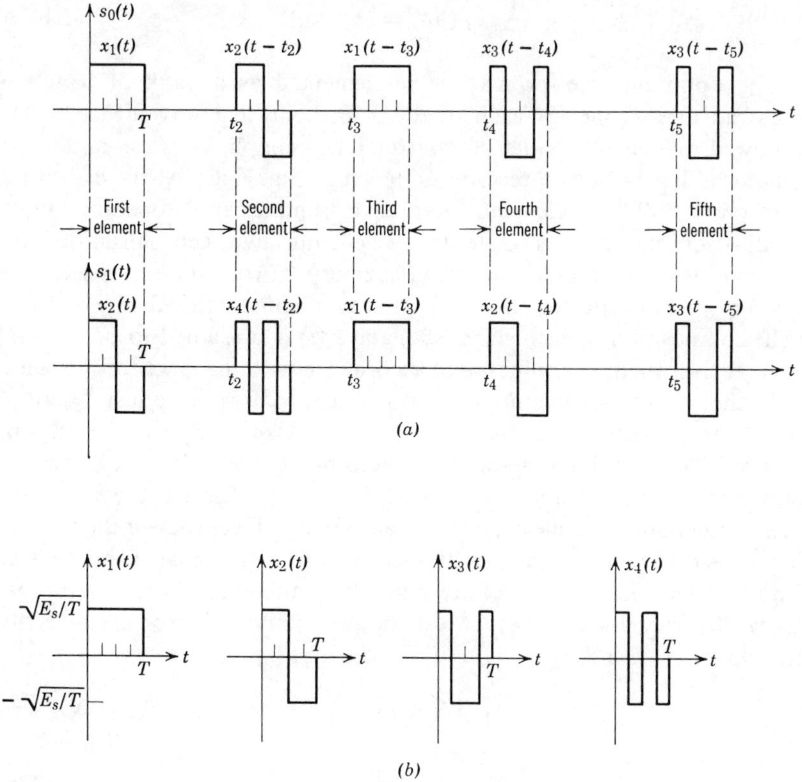

Figure 7.45 Composition of two ($N = 5$)-element signals: (*a*) signals; (*b*) letters.

Thus $x_j(t) = \sqrt{E_s}\,\varphi_j(t)$, $j = 1, 2, \ldots, A$, and the $\{x_j(t)\}$ can be represented by a set of A orthogonal vectors $\{\sqrt{E_s}\boldsymbol{\varphi}_j\}$.

We also assume that the fades affecting successive elements are statistically independent and of equal variance, $\overline{a_l^2} = b$ for $l = 1, 2, \ldots, N$. Thus the receiver for the signaling sequences $s_0(t)$ and $s_1(t)$ is very much like the receiver for an N-diversity system. The difference is that for N-diversity the same letter would be transmitted during each element, whereas now successive elements in general consist of different letters. The receiver must reflect this difference. In particular, setting $E_i = E_s$ in Eq. 7.105 and observing that the $\{c_i\}$ and $\{w_{li}\}$ are independent of i and l, we have

$$p_{\mathbf{r}}(\boldsymbol{\rho} \mid m_i) \sim \sum_{l=1}^{2N} \frac{1}{E_s} (\boldsymbol{\rho}_l \cdot \mathbf{s}_i)^2; \qquad i = 0, 1, \tag{7.141a}$$

in which, if the lth element of $s_i(t)$ is the letter $x_j(t)$,

$$\frac{1}{E_s} (\boldsymbol{\rho}_l \cdot \mathbf{s}_i)^2 = (\boldsymbol{\rho}_l \cdot \boldsymbol{\varphi}_j)^2. \tag{7.141b}$$

The optimum receiver may be implemented as a bank of bandpass matched filters (one for each of the A orthonormal waveforms $\{\varphi_j(t)\}$) followed by envelope detectors, squarers, sampling gates, and combinatorial logic. Such a receiver is shown in Fig. 7.46. At the end of the transmission of each element, the receiver samples and stores the output of all A squaring circuits. After the N elements have been transmitted, the receiver has NA samples stored in memory. From these it selects the $\{(\boldsymbol{\rho}_l \cdot \boldsymbol{\varphi}_j)^2\}$ requisite for calculating the two sums required by Eq. 7.141. (The composition of each signal $s_0(t)$ and $s_1(t)$ is presumed to be known.) The receiver then determines $\hat{m}$ in accordance with the larger of the sums.

In the two-message communication system that we have just described the error probability is easy to calculate. Assume that $s_0(t)$ and $s_1(t)$ involve identical building-block waveforms (letters) in h of their N elements. (For the sequences of Fig. 7.45, $h = 2$.) Clearly, the h overlaps contribute nothing to message distinguishability. Over each of the remaining $N - h$ elements, however, the signals are orthogonal. This follows from the fact that the $\{x_j(t)\}$ are mutually orthogonal. Thus the probability of error, say $P_2[\mathcal{E} \mid h]$, is just the probability of error for diversity transmission with $L = N - h$. From Eq. 7.136,

$$P_2[\mathcal{E} \mid h] \leqslant [4p(1 - p)]^{N-h} \tag{7.142a}$$

with

$$p = \frac{1}{2 + \bar{E}_s/\mathcal{N}_0}. \tag{7.142b}$$

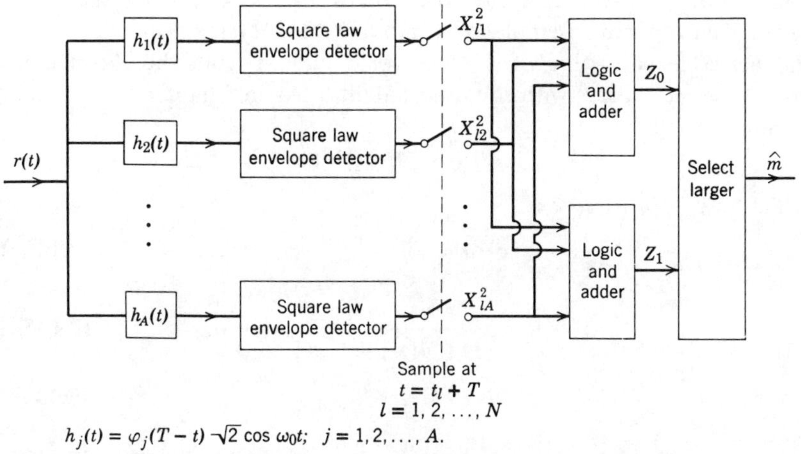

Figure 7.46 Receiver implementation for coded diversity transmission, $M = 2$. For the signals of Fig. 7.45,

$$Z_0 = X_{11}^2 + X_{22}^2 + X_{31}^2 + X_{43}^2 + X_{53}^2$$
$$Z_1 = X_{12}^3 + X_{24}^2 + X_{31}^2 + X_{42}^2 + X_{53}^2$$

The squared envelope samples from elements number 3 and 5 make no contribution to the receiver decision.

Next consider an ensemble of two-message communication systems in which every possible signaling sequence appears with equal probability. There are A^N distinct signaling sequences, or codewords, that can be constructed by using one of A letters in each of N elements. Thus the probability of the subset of systems which use codewords overlapping in h positions is

$$\mathrm{P}[h] = \binom{N}{h}\left(\frac{1}{A}\right)^h\left(1 - \frac{1}{A}\right)^{N-h}. \tag{7.143}$$

Over the ensemble the mean probability of error is therefore

$$\begin{aligned}\overline{\mathrm{P}_2[\mathcal{E}]} &\triangleq \sum_{h=0}^{N} \mathrm{P}[h]\, \mathrm{P}_2[\mathcal{E} \mid h] \\ &\leqslant \sum_{h=0}^{N}\binom{N}{h}\left(\frac{1}{A}\right)^h\left[\left(1 - \frac{1}{A}\right)4p(1-p)\right]^{N-h} \\ &= \left[\frac{1}{A} + \frac{A-1}{A}4p(1-p)\right]^N \\ &= 2^{-N\log_2\{A/[1+4(A-1)p(1-p)]\}}. \end{aligned} \tag{7.144}$$

The final step in a random-coding argument, as usual, is to extend consideration to the case in which there are $M = 2^K$ messages. We again envision an ensemble of communication systems in which each distinct code consisting of M codewords chosen from the A^N-member code-base set appears with equal probability. As in Chapter 5, the union argument yields

$$\overline{\mathrm{P}[\mathcal{E}]} < M\,\overline{\mathrm{P}_2[\mathcal{E}]},$$

which can be written† as

$$\overline{\mathrm{P}[\mathcal{E}]} < 2^{-N[R_0 - R_{\mathrm{N}}]} \tag{7.145a}$$

with

$$R_0 \triangleq \log_2\left[\frac{A}{1 + 4(A-1)p(1-p)}\right], \tag{7.145b}$$

$$M = 2^K \triangleq 2^{NR_{\mathrm{N}}}, \tag{7.145c}$$

$$p = \frac{1}{2 + \bar{E}_s/\mathcal{N}_0}. \tag{7.145d}$$

It is instructive to rewrite Eq. 7.145a in a form that places the dependence of $\overline{\mathrm{P}[\mathcal{E}]}$ on the number of bits coded together, K, and the average received energy per bit, $\bar{E}_b$, directly in evidence. Let

$$L \triangleq \frac{N}{K} = \frac{1}{R_{\mathrm{N}}} \tag{7.146a}$$

denote the number of elements (diversity) per bit, and (as in Eq. 7.137) define

$$\eta \triangleq \frac{\bar{E}_b}{L\mathcal{N}_0} = \frac{\bar{E}_s}{\mathcal{N}_0}. \tag{7.146b}$$

Then we again have

$$p = \frac{1}{2 + \eta} \tag{7.147a}$$

and

$$p(1-p) = \frac{1 + \eta}{(2 + \eta)^2}. \tag{7.147b}$$

With this notation, Eq. 7.145a becomes

$$\overline{\mathrm{P}[\mathcal{E}]} < \exp\left\{-K(\log_e 2)\left[\frac{\bar{E}_b}{\mathcal{N}_0}\, g_A(\eta) - 1\right]\right\}, \tag{7.148a}$$

† Note that in Eq. 7.145a R_{N} has units of bits per element, not bits per dimension; each of the N elements requires A dimensions, since we anticipate that each of the $\{x_j(t)\}$ will appear as the lth element, $l = 1, 2, \ldots, N$, in at least one of the M codewords.

in which

$$g_A(\eta) \triangleq \frac{1}{\eta} \log_2 \frac{A}{1 + 4(A - 1)[(1 + \eta)/(2 + \eta)^2]}. \qquad (7.148b)$$

For any η the function $g_A(\eta)$ increases monotonically with increasing A. (The probability that any two code-word sequences overlap in h positions decreases as the alphabet size A becomes larger.) Furthermore, as $A \to \infty$ the function $g_A(\eta)$ becomes the function $g(\eta)$ plotted in Fig. 7.44. Thus when A can be made arbitrarily large, the optimum choice of L is that value for which $\eta \approx 5$ db. Finally, an easy calculation shows that for this choice of L any value of $A \geqslant 18$ yields an exponent that is at least 0.935 times as large as the exponent for $A = \infty$. Thus for $\eta \approx 5$ db and $A \approx 18$ we have

$$\overline{P[\mathcal{E}]} \leqslant 2^{-K[0.2(\bar{E}_b/\mathcal{N}_0)-1]}. \qquad (7.149)$$

As long as the mean received energy-to-noise ratio per bit $\bar{E}_b/\mathcal{N}_0$ is greater than approximately 7 db, the probability of error decreases exponentially with the code constraint length K. Furthermore, this can be accomplished with a set of building-block signals $\{x_j(t)\}$ comprising only 18 orthogonal waveforms. If we restrict A to 2 (binary orthogonal signaling), the optimum value of η changes only slightly to approximately 2.7. The effect on Eq. 7.148, however, is that $\bar{E}_b/\mathcal{N}_0$ must now be slightly greater than 10 db for the bound to converge to zero with increasing K.

As with the Gaussian channel, the simple union argument used to derive Eq. 7.149 does not lead to the tightest possible bound for all values of $\bar{E}_b/\mathcal{N}_0$. Indeed, it can be shown[49] by more sensitive analytical techniques that the capacity of an infinite-bandwidth Rayleigh-fading channel is the same as that of an infinite-bandwidth Gaussian channel with the same mean energy-to-noise ratio. The bound of Eq. 7.149, however, is exponentially tight for values of $\bar{E}_b/\mathcal{N}_0$ somewhat greater than 7 db. In addition, 7 db approximates the minimum value of $\bar{E}_b/\mathcal{N}_0$ for which the mean number of computations required by the sequential decoding procedures of Chapter 6 converges.

Binary Quantization

With pure additive white Gaussian noise, we found it necessary [see Chapter 6] to quantize the matched-filter outputs to implement a feasible decoder. Similarly, with a Rayleigh-fading channel we must also reduce the decoder input to discrete form. The probability of error bounds of Eq. 7.145 and 7.149 are meaningful in an engineering sense only when the squared-envelope samples resulting from the transmission of each element are quantized with sufficiently fine grain. In this section we illustrate the degradation that results when the quantization grain is coarse. In particular, we consider the case $A = 2$, so that the building-block alphabet consists of only two letters, which we may take to be the orthogonal low-pass waveforms $x_1(t) = \sqrt{E_s}\,\varphi_1(t)$ and $x_2(t) = \sqrt{E_s}\,\varphi_2(t)$.

In the transmission of the lth element the optimum receiver observes the two squared-envelope samples, say X_{l1}^2 and X_{l2}^2, produced at the output of bandpass filters matched to $\varphi_1(t)\sqrt{2}\cos\omega_0 t$ and $\varphi_2(t)\sqrt{2}\cos\omega_0 t$,

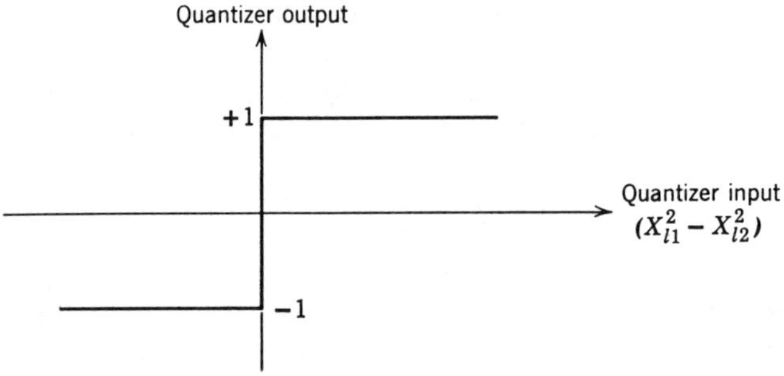

Figure 7.47 Symmetric binary quantization of the difference of squared envelope samples.

respectively. It is clear that symmetric binary quantization (see Fig. 7.47) of the difference of these two samples $X_{l1}^2 - X_{l2}^2$ corresponds to making an optimum binary decision about which letter was actually transmitted as the lth element, under the assumption that both letters are equally likely. If successive received elements are quantized in this same way, $l = 1, 2, \ldots, N$, the channel is converted into a binary symmetric channel with transition probability

$$p = \frac{1}{2 + \bar{E}_s/\mathcal{N}_0} \tag{7.150a}$$

equal to the error probability for a single binary decision (Eq. 7.88).

The transmission of N elements in succession corresponds to N uses of the BSC, so that from Eq. 6.70

$$\overline{P[\mathcal{E}]} < 2^{-N[R_0' - R_N]}, \tag{7.150b}$$

with

$$R_0' = 1 - \log_2 [1 + \sqrt{4p(1-p)}]. \tag{7.150c}$$

The error exponent R_0' is plotted as a function of $\bar{E}_s/\mathcal{N}_0$ in Fig. 7.48, together with the corresponding unquantized exponent

$$R_0 = 1 - \log_2 [1 + 4p(1-p)], \tag{7.151}$$

which results from specializing Eq. 7.145b to $A = 2$.

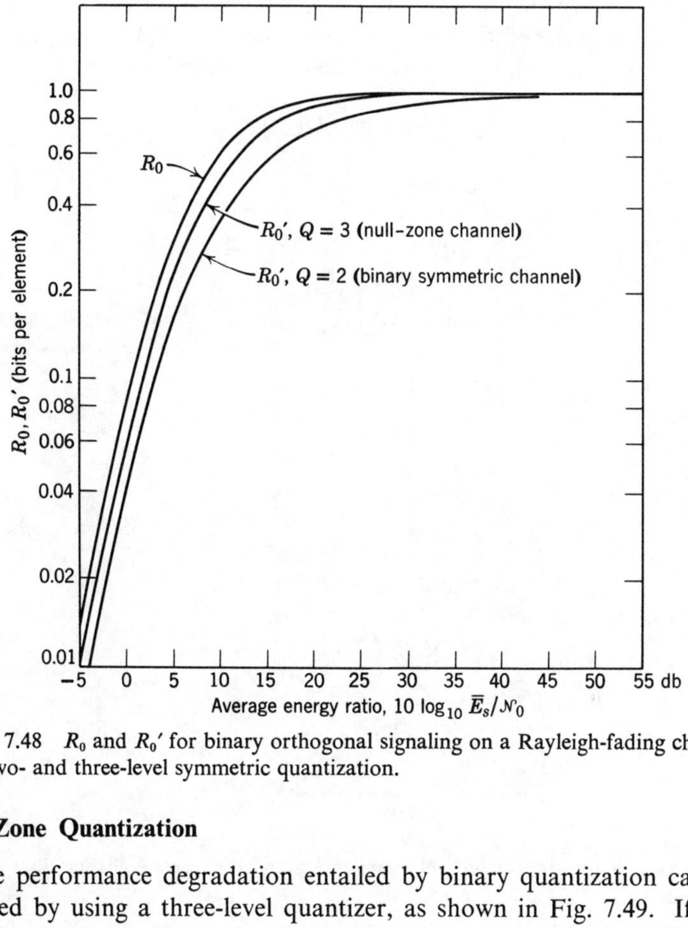

Figure 7.48 R_0 and R_0' for binary orthogonal signaling on a Rayleigh-fading channel with two- and three-level symmetric quantization.

Null-Zone Quantization

The performance degradation entailed by binary quantization can be reduced by using a three-level quantizer, as shown in Fig. 7.49. If, for any element $l = 1, 2, \ldots, N$, the input to the quantizer is the difference

$$y \triangleq (X_{l1}^2 - X_{l2}^2), \tag{7.152a}$$

the output is

$$z = \begin{cases} +1; & y \geqslant J \\ 0; & -J < y < J \\ -1; & y \leqslant -J. \end{cases} \tag{7.152b}$$

Thus the channel is converted into a null-zone channel (cf. Fig. 6.23) with transition probabilities q, w, and $1 - q - w$, which are functions of the threshold J. From Eq. 6.73 the resulting error exponent is

$$R_0' = 1 - \log_2 [1 + w + 2\sqrt{q(1 - q - w)}]. \tag{7.153}$$

We choose J in such a way that R_0' is maximum. The first step is to determine the probability density function, say $p_y(\ \mid \mathbf{x}_2)$, of the quantizer *input* that results when the transmitted letter is $x_2(t)$. Clearly,

$$p_y(\gamma \mid \mathbf{x}_1) = p_y(-\gamma \mid \mathbf{x}_2). \tag{7.154}$$

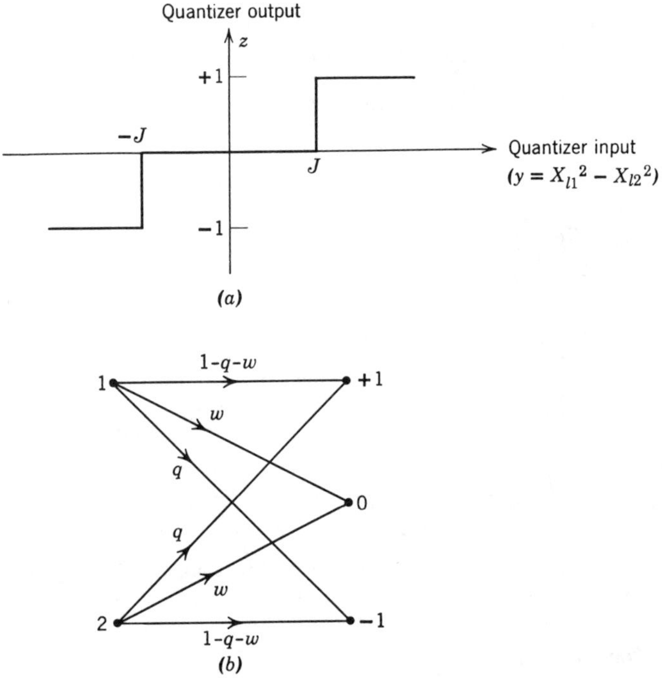

Figure 7.49 Symmetric three-level quantization and the discrete channel that results therefrom.

The density function $p_y(\ \mid \mathbf{x}_2)$ may be found from its characteristic function. For the lth diversity element we have

$$y = (r_{l1}^2 + r_{L+l,1}^2) - (r_{l2}^2 + r_{L+l,2}^2), \tag{7.155a}$$

in which each squared term is a statistically independent zero-mean Gaussian random variable with variance (from Eq. 7.117b)

$$\left.\begin{aligned} \sigma_1^2 &= \overline{r_{l1}^2} = \overline{r_{L+l,1}^2} = \frac{\mathcal{N}_0}{2} \\ \sigma_2^2 &= \overline{r_{l2}^2} = \overline{r_{L+l,2}^2} = \frac{\bar{E}_s + \mathcal{N}_0}{2} \end{aligned}\right\}; \qquad \mathbf{x}_2 \text{ transmitted.} \tag{7.155b}$$

Thus for each l the characteristic function of y conditional on $\mathbf{x}_2$ is

$$M_y(\nu) \triangleq \overline{e^{j\nu y}} = \overline{e^{j\nu r_{l1}^2}}\;\overline{e^{j\nu r_{L+l,1}^2}}\;\overline{e^{-j\nu r_{l2}^2}}\;\overline{e^{-j\nu r_{L+l,2}^2}}$$

$$= \frac{1}{[1 - j\nu\mathcal{N}_0][1 + j\nu(\bar{E}_s + \mathcal{N}_0)]}. \qquad (7.156)$$

In the last line we have again invoked the lemma of Eq. 7.67, this time with $w = \pm j$. Expanding the right-hand side of Eq. 7.156 in a partial fraction yields

$$M_y(\nu) = \frac{p}{1 - j\nu\mathcal{N}_0} + \frac{1 - p}{1 + j\nu\mathcal{N}_0(1 - p)/p}, \qquad (7.157a)$$

where, as usual

$$p = \frac{1}{2 + \bar{E}_s/\mathcal{N}_0}. \qquad (7.157b)$$

The inverse Fourier transform of $M_y(\nu)$ is

$$p_y(\gamma \mid \mathbf{x}_2) = \begin{cases} \dfrac{p}{\mathcal{N}_0} \exp\left(-\dfrac{\gamma}{\mathcal{N}_0}\right); & \gamma \geqslant 0 \\[2ex] \dfrac{p}{\mathcal{N}_0} \exp\left(\dfrac{\gamma}{\mathcal{N}_0}\dfrac{p}{1 - p}\right); & \gamma < 0, \end{cases} \qquad (7.158)$$

a result that may readily be verified by using Eq. 7.158 to recalculate $M_y(\nu)$.

The rest is easy. The transition probabilities for the null-zone channel created by a three-level quantizer with threshold J are

$$q = \int_J^\infty p_y(\gamma \mid \mathbf{x}_2)\, d\gamma = pe^{-J/\mathcal{N}_0}, \qquad (7.159a)$$

$$w = \int_{-J}^{J} p_y(\gamma \mid \mathbf{x}_2)\, d\gamma$$

$$= p(1 - e^{-J/\mathcal{N}_0}) + (1 - p)\left[1 - \exp\left(-\frac{J}{\mathcal{N}_0}\frac{p}{1 - p}\right)\right]$$

$$= 1 - pe^{-J/\mathcal{N}_0} - (1 - p)\exp\left(-\frac{J}{\mathcal{N}_0}\frac{1}{1 - p}\right). \qquad (7.159b)$$

Our objective is to maximize the value assumed by R_0' when q and w are substituted in Eq. 7.153. We therefore wish to minimize the quantity

$$w + 2\sqrt{q(1 - q - w)}.$$

It is readily verified by differentiation that the optimum value of J is given by

$$\frac{J}{\mathcal{N}_0} = \frac{1-p}{1-2p} \ln \frac{1-p}{p}$$
$$= \left(1 + \frac{\mathcal{N}_0}{\bar{E}_s}\right) \ln \left(1 + \frac{\bar{E}_s}{\mathcal{N}_0}\right). \tag{7.160}$$

The error exponent R_0' for the null-zone channel obtained with the optimum threshold setting is also plotted in Fig. 7.48 as a function of $\bar{E}_s/\mathcal{N}_0$. We note that the curve falls between the unquantized and binary-quantized error exponents, as it should. It is also apparent that R_0' cannot be substantially increased by using more than three quantization levels when the alphabet size A is restricted to 2. This does not mean, however, that the problem of effectively reducing the relevant received data to discrete form is always trivial. For alphabet sizes A larger than 2, strategies more subtle than the independent quantization of the squared-envelope sample for each letter are indicated (cf. Problem 6.10).

Discussion

The objective in all types of diversity communication is to obtain L received signals for which the transmission gains $\{a_l\}$ are statistically independent. If this condition is to be met, it is essential that the phase

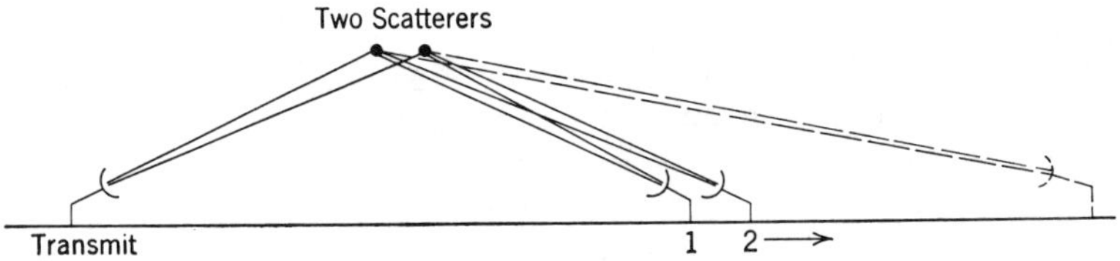

Figure 7.50 Space diversity.

interference pattern of the wavelets from individual scatterers be distinctly different for each of the L received signals.

One way to accomplish this with only a single transmitted signal is called space diversity. Consider the situation illustrated in Fig. 7.50 and assume that the transmitter, the two scatterers, and the first receiver site are held fixed in space. Thus the phase difference between the two received wavelets at site 1 is fixed. Now consider moving site 2 away from site 1. The phase at site 2 depends on its position and rotates through 2π radians as the difference in path length from transmitter to scatterers to site 2 changes by an amount equal to the wavelength of the RF carrier.

When the two sites are far removed from each other, small percentage changes in the geometry introduce radical changes in the difference between the received phase at sites 1 and 2. If myriad scatterers are moving at random through the scattering volume intersected by the antenna beams, it is usually reasonable to assume that the transmission gains to the two sites will be statistically independent whenever the separation between sites is many carrier wavelengths. L-diversity may be obtained by using L dispersed receivers.

A similar rationale justifies an assumption of statistical independence when frequency diversity is used. In this technique there is only one receiver, but the lowpass signal simultaneously modulates L different carriers, each having a different frequency. The difference in path length for two stationary scatterers is now fixed in number of meters but varies in number of wavelengths as a function of carrier frequency. With many moving scatterers, good diversity usually results whenever the greatest difference in path length within the scattering volume implies a phase difference greater than 2π between adjacent received sidebands.

The objective with space diversity but no signal diversity is to provide enough receivers sufficiently separated that a tolerable error probability is obtained for a given mean received energy-to-noise ratio per bit, $\bar{E}_b/\mathcal{N}_0$. Additional design freedom is introduced when signal diversity is considered. This may be accomplished by time or frequency diversity, a combination of the two, or by other means.[49] In accordance with Eq. 7.139a, the objective is to obtain $\bar{E}_b/L\mathcal{N}_0 \approx 3$. The attainable error probability is then bounded by Eq. 7.139b if no coding is used and by Eq. 7.149 if there is orthogonal-letter coding with $A \geqslant 18$.

APPENDIX 7A WHITENING FILTERS

The filter $G(f)$ in Eq. 7.7b was determined by a general method which always guarantees that both $G(f)$ and $G^{-1}(f)$ are physically realizable whenever $\mathcal{S}_n(f)$ can be written as a ratio of two polynomials in f:†

$$\mathcal{S}_n(f) = k\,\frac{N(f)}{D(f)} = k\,\frac{(f-\zeta_1)(f-\zeta_2)\cdots(f-\zeta_n)}{(f-\eta_1)(f-\eta_2)\cdots(f-\eta_d)}. \qquad (7A.1)$$

In Eq. 7A.1 $\{\zeta_i\}$ is the set of complex roots of the numerator polynomial $N(f)$, assumed to have degree n, and $\{\eta_i\}$ is the set for the denominator polynomial $D(f)$, assumed to have degree d. The set $\{\zeta_i\}$ is the zeros, and $\{\eta_i\}$ the poles, of $\mathcal{S}_n(f)$. Since $\mathcal{S}_n(f) = \mathcal{S}_n(-f) = \mathcal{S}_n^*(f)$ (a power

† If $\mathcal{S}_n(f)$ is not rational, it may still be possible to approximate it sufficiently closely by a rational function.

spectrum is real and even), both zeros and poles are symmetrically located about the real and imaginary axis, as shown in Fig. 7A.1. It is convenient to number the roots so that odd-numbered roots have positive imaginary parts and even-numbered roots have negative imaginary parts. For example, in the power spectrum of Eq. 7.7a,

$$N(f) = f^2 + 4 = (f - j2)(f + j2); \qquad \zeta_1 = j2, \zeta_2 = -j2$$
$$D(f) = f^2 + 1 = (f - j1)(f + j1); \qquad \eta_1 = j1, \eta_2 = -j1.$$

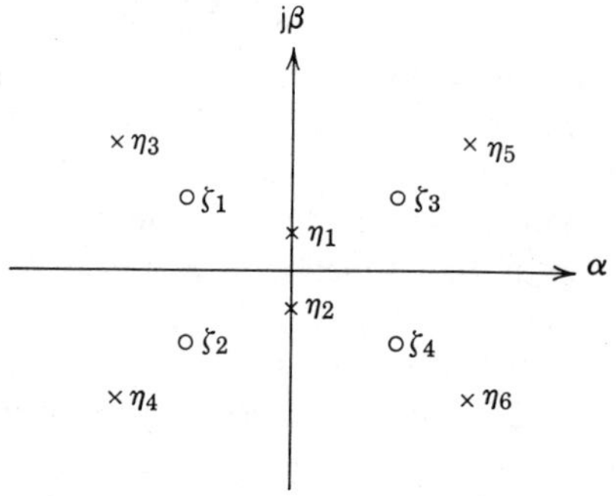

Figure 7A.1 Roots of $\mathcal{S}_n(f) = k\,\dfrac{N(f)}{D(f)}$.

The whitening filter, $G(f)$, may now be easily specified. Define

$$N_U(f) = (f - \zeta_1)(f - \zeta_3)\cdots(f - \zeta_{n-1}), \tag{7A.2}$$
$$N_L(f) = (f - \zeta_2)(f - \zeta_4)\cdots(f - \zeta_n), \tag{7A.3}$$
$$D_U(f) = (f - \eta_1)(f - \eta_3)\cdots(f - \eta_{d-1}), \tag{7A.4}$$
$$D_L(f) = (f - \eta_2)(f - \eta_4)\cdots(f - \eta_d), \tag{7A.5}$$

and set

$$G(f) = \frac{D_U(f)}{N_U(f)}. \tag{7A.6}$$

Thus the numerator of $G(f)$ incorporates the upper half-plane poles of $\mathcal{S}_n(f)$ and the denominator incorporates the upper half-plane zeros of $\mathcal{S}_n(f)$. Clearly,

$$\begin{aligned} |G(f)|^2 &= \frac{D_U(f)\,D_U^*(f)}{N_U(f)\,N_U^*(f)} \\ &= \frac{D_U(f)\,D_L(f)}{N_U(f)\,N_L(f)} \\ &= \frac{D(f)}{N(f)} \\ &= \frac{k}{\mathcal{S}_n(f)}, \end{aligned} \tag{7A.7}$$

so that k is identified as the power density $\mathcal{N}_0/2$ at the output of the whitening filter.

For the spectrum of Eq. 7.7a,

$$G(f) = \frac{f - j1}{f - j2} = \frac{jf + 1}{jf + 2}.$$

It remains to be shown that *both* filters $G(f)$ and $G^{-1}(f) = N_U(f)/D_U(f)$ are realizable. Consider a filter transfer function of the form

$$\frac{\prod_{i=1}^{n/2} (f - \zeta_{2i-1})}{\prod_{i=1}^{d/2} (f - \eta_{2i-1})}.$$

Letting $s = j2\pi f$, we may express the filter characteristic in terms of the complex frequency variable s as

$$\frac{\prod_{i \text{ odd}} (s/j2\pi - \zeta_i)}{\prod_{i \text{ odd}} (s/j2\pi - \eta_i)} = \frac{\prod_{i \text{ odd}} (s - j2\pi\zeta_i)}{\prod_{i \text{ odd}} (s - j2\pi\eta_i)} (j2\pi)^{(d-n)/2}.$$

If $\eta_i = a + jb$ has positive imaginary part, the s-plane pole $j2\pi\eta_i = -2\pi b + j2\pi a$ has negative real part and lies in the left-half s-plane. All denominator roots of both $G(f)$ and $G^{-1}(f)$ satisfy this condition of positive imaginary part. Thus all the poles of both filters fall in the left-half s-plane, hence both are realizable. Filtering with $G(f)$ is therefore a reversible operation.

Roots of $\mathcal{S}_n(f)$ on the real axis are always of even multiplicity; the situation may be handled mathematically by assigning consecutive indices to any such root. Of course, these roots correspond to lossless resonances and do not occur in practice.

A more substantive issue is that any $\mathcal{S}_n(f)$ encountered in practice goes to zero as $f \to \infty$. Because all physical circuits ultimately become capacitive at high frequencies, ideal whitening is impossible. The difficulty is resolved by recognizing that $G(f)$ need only "whiten" the noise over the frequency band containing most of the transmitted signal energy.

APPENDIX 7B CONVEXITY

A function f is said to be "convex" over $[0, \infty]$ if its second derivative satisfies

$$f''(x) \leqslant 0; \qquad \text{all } x > 0. \tag{7B.1a}$$

The function f is "concave" over $[0, \infty]$ if

$$f''(x) \geqslant 0; \qquad \text{all } x > 0. \tag{7B.1b}$$

If the equality sign in Eq. 7B.1a (7B.1b) is not permitted, f is "strictly convex" (or "strictly concave"). A convex function over $[0, \infty]$ is pictured in Fig. 7B.1*a* and a strictly convex function over $[0, \infty]$ in Fig. 7B.1*b*.

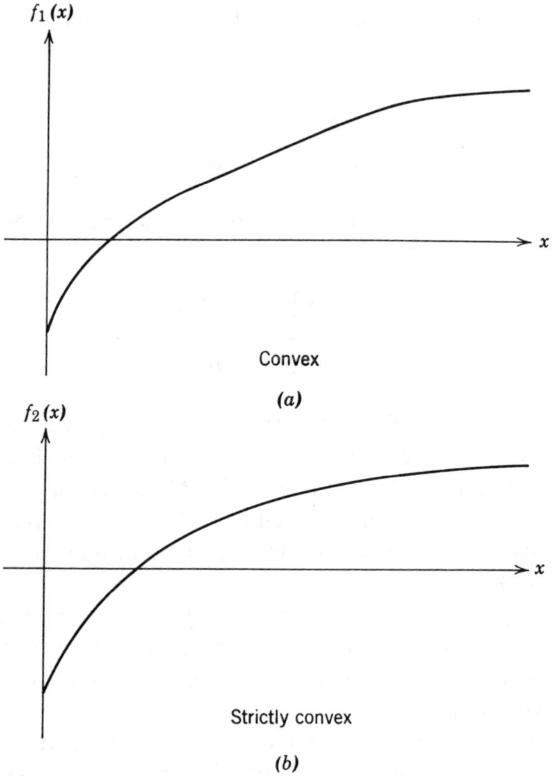

Figure 7B.1 A convex and a strictly convex function over $[0, \infty]$.

Theorem. *Let $\{x_i\}$, $i = 1, 2, \ldots, N$, be a set of real numbers subject to the constraints*

$$x_i \geqslant 0, \qquad i = 1, 2, \ldots, N \tag{7B.2a}$$

and

$$\sum_{i=1}^{N} x_i = K, \tag{7B.2b}$$

and let $\bar{f}$ be defined as

$$\bar{f} = \frac{1}{N}\sum_{i=1}^{N} f(x_i). \tag{7B.3}$$

If f is convex over [0, ∞], then

$$\bar{f} \leqslant \frac{1}{N}\sum_{i=1}^{N} f(\bar{x}) = f(\bar{x}) \quad \text{(7B.4a)}$$

$$\bar{f} \geqslant \frac{1}{N} f(K), \quad \text{(7B.4b)}$$

in which

$$\bar{x} \triangleq \frac{1}{N}\sum_{i=1}^{N} x_i = \frac{K}{N}. \quad \text{(7B.4c)}$$

Whenever f is strictly convex, the equal sign holds in Eq. 7B.4a if and only if $x_i = \bar{x}$, $i = 1, 2, \ldots, N$.

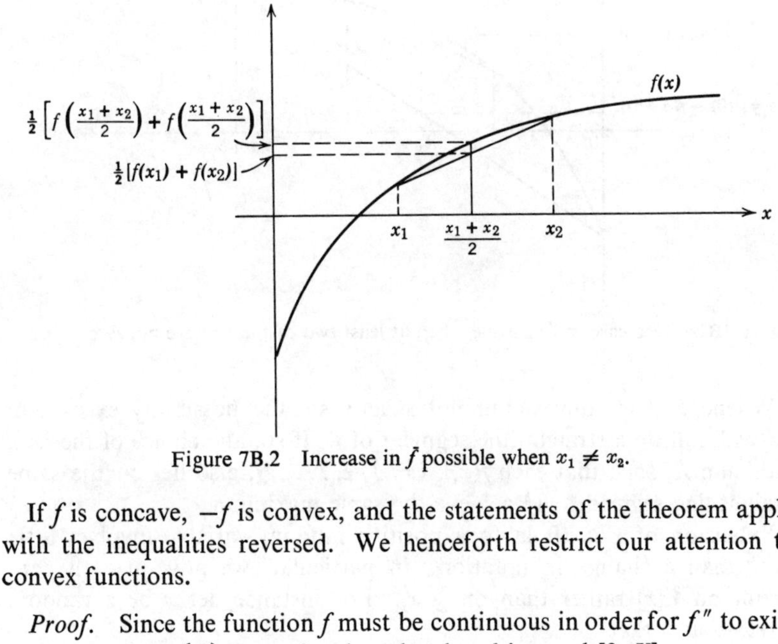

Figure 7B.2 Increase in $\bar{f}$ possible when $x_1 \neq x_2$.

If f is concave, $-f$ is convex, and the statements of the theorem apply with the inequalities reversed. We henceforth restrict our attention to convex functions.

Proof. Since the function f must be continuous in order for f'' to exist and each of the $\{x_i\}$ is restricted to the closed interval $[0, K]$,

$$\bar{f} = \frac{1}{N}\sum_{i=1}^{N} f(x_i)$$

must take on a maximum and a minimum as the $\{x_i\}$ are varied. Let f be strictly convex. We now prove by a geometrical argument that $\bar{f}$ is maximum when $x_i = \bar{x}$ for all i. For assume that some set $\{x_i\}$ not satisfying $x_i = \bar{x}$, all i, produces the maximum. At least one pair of the $\{x_i\}$ must be unequal, say $x_1 \neq x_2$. However, it is clear from Fig. 7B.2 that replacing both x_1 and x_2 by $(x_1 + x_2)/2$ increases $\bar{f}$ without changing $\sum_{i=1}^{N} x_i = K$. Hence the assumption that any set of $\{x_i\}$ not satisfying $x_i = \bar{x}$, all i, produces the maximum leads to a contradiction and the proof of Eq. 7B.4a is complete.

A similar argument proves that the set $\{x_1 = K, x_2 = x_3 = \cdots = x_N = 0\}$ minimizes $\bar{f}$, which verifies Eq. 7B.4b: it is necessary only to observe as in Fig. 7B.3 that if $x_1 = a$, $x_2 = b$, $0 < a \leqslant b$, then $\bar{f}$ is decreased by setting $x_1 = 0$ and $x_2 = a + b$.

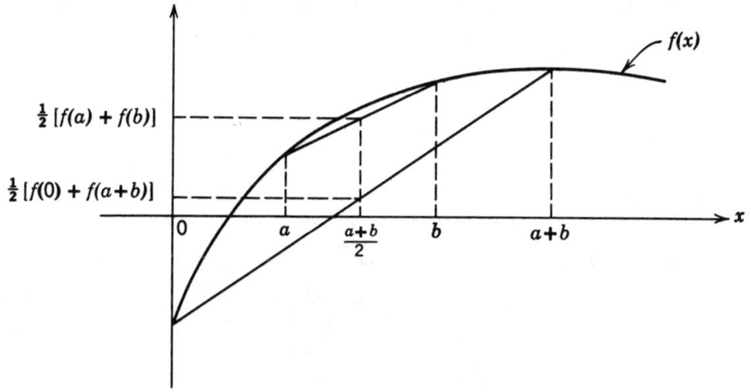

Figure 7B.3 Decrease in $\bar{f}$ possible when at least two of the $\{x_i\}$ are nonzero.

Whenever f is convex, but not strictly so, the possibility exists that $f(\bar{x})$ will fall on a straight-line segment of f. If so, any choice of the $\{x_i\}$, with sum K, such that each $f(x_i)$, $i = 1, 2, \ldots, N$, also lies on the same straight-line segment, will achieve the same maximum.

Extension of Eq. 7B.4a to a positive random variable involves little more than a change in notation: in particular, we now place a constraint on $\mathrm{E}[x]$ rather than on $\sum_i x_i$. For instance, let x be a random variable such that

$$\int_0^\infty p_x(\alpha)\, d\alpha = 1, \tag{7B.5a}$$

$$\int_0^\infty \alpha p_x(\alpha)\, d\alpha = \mathrm{E}[x] = \bar{x}, \tag{7B.5b}$$

in which $\bar{x}$ is a specified positive number. Observe that when f is convex,

$$f(\alpha) \leqslant f(\bar{x}) + (\alpha - \bar{x})f'(\bar{x}); \quad \alpha \geqslant 0.$$

Thus

$$\overline{f(x)} \leqslant \overline{f(\bar{x})} + \overline{(x - \bar{x})} f'(\bar{x}) = f(\bar{x}). \tag{7B.6}$$

If f is strictly convex, the equality will hold if and only if

$$p_x(\alpha) = \delta(\alpha - \bar{x}). \tag{7B.7}$$

Example 1. In Eq. 7.38b,

$$P[\mathcal{E}] = \overline{Q(a\sqrt{2E_s/\mathcal{N}_0})},$$

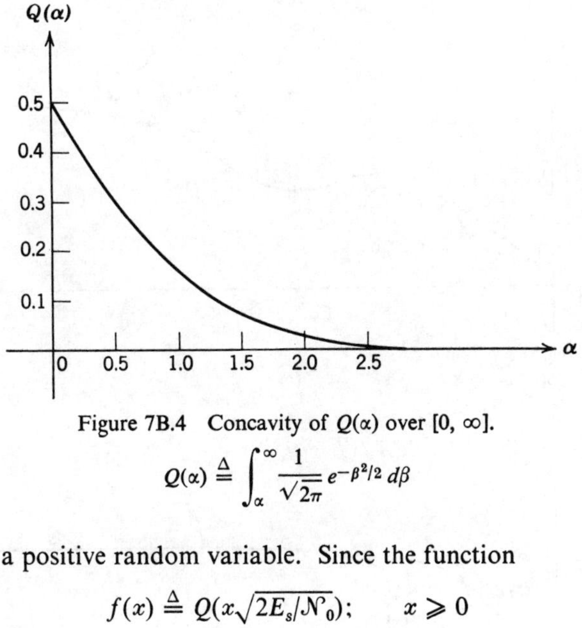

Figure 7B.4 Concavity of $Q(\alpha)$ over $[0, \infty]$.

$$Q(\alpha) \triangleq \int_\alpha^\infty \frac{1}{\sqrt{2\pi}} e^{-\beta^2/2}\, d\beta$$

where a is a positive random variable. Since the function

$$f(x) \triangleq Q(x\sqrt{2E_s/\mathcal{N}_0}); \qquad x \geqslant 0$$

is strictly concave, as shown in Fig. 7B.4, we have

$$P[\mathcal{E}] \geqslant Q(\bar{a}\sqrt{2E_s/\mathcal{N}_0}), \tag{7B.8}$$

with equality if and only if $a = \bar{a}$ with probability one.

Extension to Nonconvex Functions

We now extend Eq. 7B.6 to nonconvex functions. Consider the function f defined in Fig. 7B.5a over $[0, \infty]$. We can construct from f a unique convex function f^* such that $f \leqslant f^*$ for all x in $[0, \infty]$. We do so by starting at the origin and following f to the first point, say a, at which a

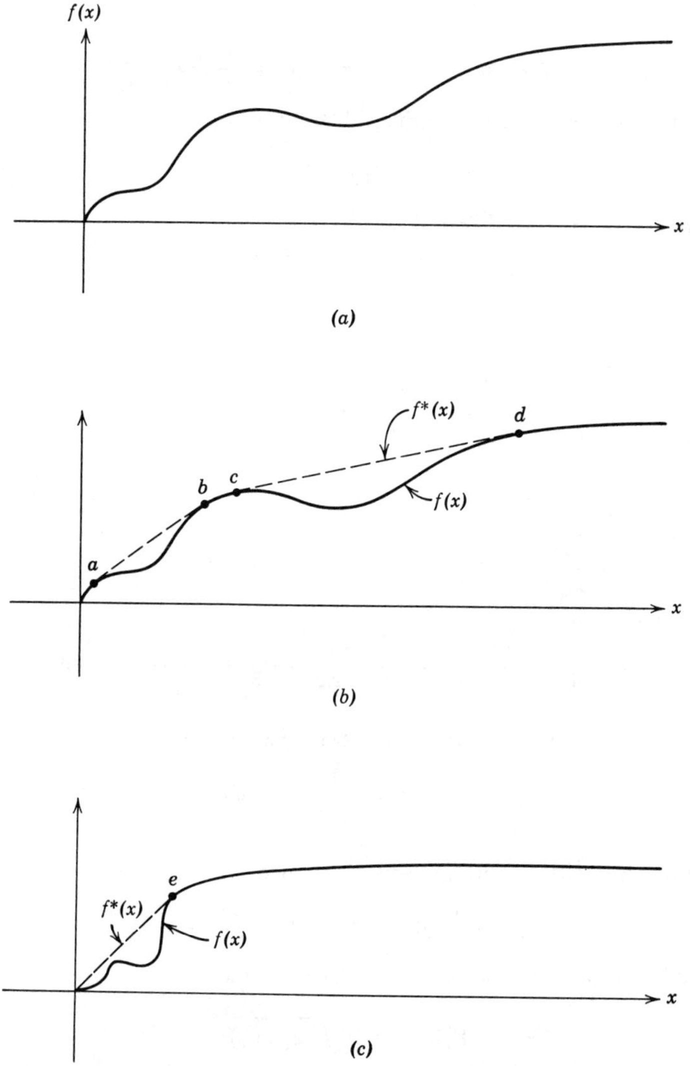

Figure 7B.5 Construction of a convex overbound to $f(x)$.

line tangent to f at a is also tangent to f for some $x > a$, say b. The straight line connecting $f(a)$ and $f(b)$ is made part of f^* and the process is continued. This process is made clear in Fig. 7B.5*b*.

The only exception to this construction of f^* occurs when a line tangent to f at the origin falls below f at some positive argument. In this case the first segment of f^* is a straight line passing through the origin and tangent to f at some point, say e. If several points of tangency are possible, the one yielding maximum slope is chosen, as shown in Fig. 7B.5c.

Since $f \leqslant f^*$, and f^* is convex, we have

$$\overline{f(x)} \leqslant \overline{f^*(x)} \leqslant f^*(\bar{x}); \tag{7B.9}$$

the second inequality follows from Eq. 7B.6.

We often wish to find a p_x, with specified mean $\bar{x}$, such that $\overline{f(x)}$ is maximized. We now show that there is always a density p_x with mean $\bar{x}$ such that $\overline{f(x)}$ actually equals $f^*(\bar{x})$. There are two situations. First, if $\bar{x}$ is such that $f(\bar{x}) = f^*(\bar{x})$, the choice $p_x(\alpha) = \delta(\alpha - \bar{x})$ produces the desired maximum. Second, if $\bar{x}$ is such that $f(\bar{x}) \neq f^*(\bar{x})$, then $\bar{x}$ lies in an interval over which f^* is a straight-line segment. As noted earlier, we can distribute x over the straight-line segment without changing the value of $\overline{f^*(x)}$. In particular, we can place the probability in two impulses, one at each of the end points, say a and b, of the straight line. In this case

$$p_x(\beta) = \alpha\delta(\beta - a) + (1 - \alpha)\delta(\beta - b)$$

and

$$\begin{aligned} f^*(\bar{x}) &= \alpha f^*(a) + (1 - \alpha) f^*(b) \\ &= \alpha f(a) + (1 - \alpha) f(b) \\ &= \overline{f(x)}, \end{aligned}$$

where α is chosen to satisfy the constraint equation

$$\bar{x} = \alpha a + (1 - \alpha) b.$$

Example 2. In Eq. 7.134 we have

$$\mathrm{P}[\mathcal{E}] \leqslant \prod_{l=1}^{L} \left[4 \frac{1 + \bar{E}_l/\mathcal{N}_0}{(2 + \bar{E}_l/\mathcal{N}_0)^2} \right], \tag{7B.10a}$$

where

$$\sum_{l=1}^{L} \frac{\bar{E}_l}{\mathcal{N}_0} = \frac{\bar{E}_b}{\mathcal{N}_0}. \tag{7B.10b}$$

By varying the $\{\bar{E}_l\}$ subject to Eq. 7B.10b, we wish to minimize the bound of Eq. 7B.10a or, equivalently, to maximize

$$\sum_{l=1}^{L} f(x_l) \tag{7B.11a}$$

in which

$$f(x) \triangleq \ln \frac{(2 + x)^2}{4(1 + x)} \tag{7B.11b}$$

and

$$x_l \triangleq \frac{\bar{E}_l}{\mathcal{N}_0}. \tag{7B.11c}$$

The function $f(x)$ is plotted in Fig. 7B.6, together with the convex function $f^*(x)$. If $\bar{x}$ (which corresponds to the over-all average received energy-to-noise ratio per diversity path, $\bar{E}_b/L\mathcal{N}_0$, is greater than ≈ 3, the minimum bound occurs when all $x_l = \bar{x}$. If $\bar{x}$ is less than ≈ 3, the minimum occurs when several of the x_l are set equal to zero and the remainder are set approximately equal to 3. In the latter case several of the available diversity paths are not used.

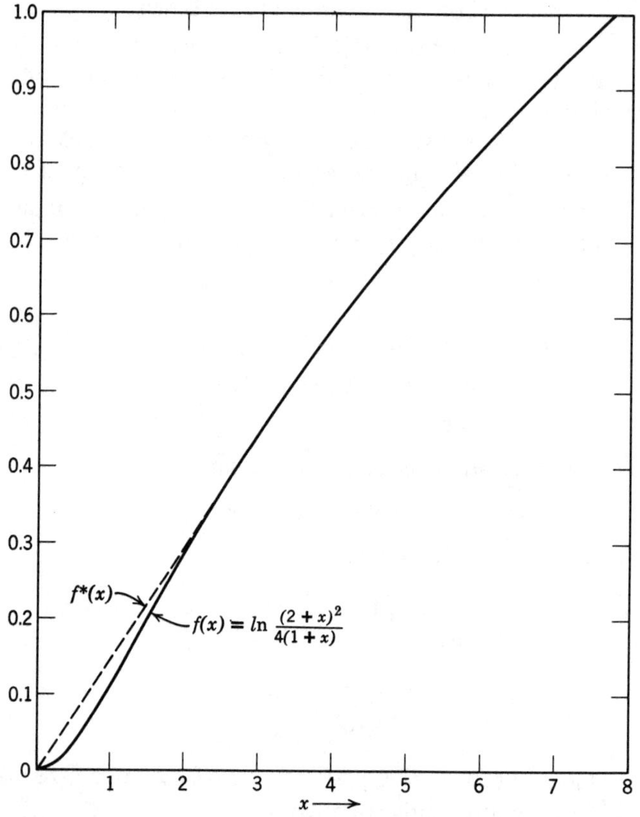

Figure 7B.6 Graph for minimizing P[ℰ] in L-diversity signaling.

APPENDIX 7C LEMMA

In this appendix we prove the following lemma:

Lemma. *If x is a Gaussian random variable with mean m and variance σ^2 and w is any complex constant with real part less than $(2\sigma^2)^{-1}$, then*

$$\overline{e^{wx^2}} = \frac{1}{\sqrt{1 - 2w\sigma^2}} e^{wm^2/(1-2w\sigma^2)}; \qquad \operatorname{Re}(w) < \frac{1}{2\sigma^2}. \tag{7C.1}$$

Proof. By definition,

$$\overline{e^{wx^2}} \triangleq \frac{1}{\sqrt{2\pi}\,\sigma}\int_{-\infty}^{\infty} e^{w\alpha^2-(\alpha-m)^2/2\sigma^2}\,d\alpha. \tag{7C.2}$$

After completing the square in the exponent, this equation becomes

$$\overline{e^{wx^2}} = e^{wm^2/(1-2w\sigma^2)}\int_{-\infty}^{\infty}\frac{1}{\sqrt{2\pi}\,\sigma}\exp\left[-\frac{1-2w\sigma^2}{2\sigma^2}\left(\alpha-\frac{m}{1-2w\sigma^2}\right)^2\right]d\alpha. \tag{7C.3}$$

Defining

$$\beta \triangleq \left(\alpha-\frac{m}{1-2w\sigma^2}\right)\frac{\sqrt{1-2w\sigma^2}}{\sigma}, \tag{7C.4}$$

we have

$$\overline{e^{wx^2}} = \frac{1}{\sqrt{1-2w\sigma^2}}\,e^{wm^2/(1-2w\sigma^2)}\int_{\Gamma}\frac{1}{\sqrt{2\pi}}\,e^{-\beta^2/2}\,d\beta, \tag{7C.5}$$

in which Γ is the path traversed by the complex variable β as the real variable α varies from $-\infty$ to $+\infty$.

The lemma is proved by showing that the integral in Eq. 7C.5 is unity whenever $\text{Re}(w) < (2\sigma^2)^{-1}$. The first step is to determine Γ. Let

$$w = u + \text{j}v \tag{7C.6}$$

and define

$$ce^{-\text{j}\phi} \triangleq 1 - 2w\sigma^2 = (1-2\sigma^2u) - \text{j}2\sigma^2v. \tag{7C.7}$$

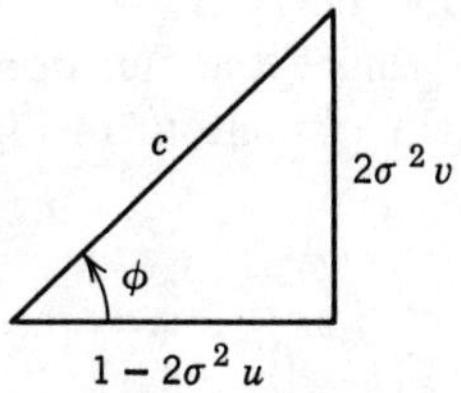

Figure 7C.1 Polar transformation for evaluating integral.

Thus c and ϕ are given by the polar transformation of Fig. 7C.1. From Eqs. 7C.4 and 7C.7

$$\begin{aligned}\beta &= \left[\alpha - \frac{m}{c}\,e^{\text{j}\phi}\right]\frac{\sqrt{c}}{\sigma}\,e^{-\text{j}\phi/2}\\ &= \frac{\sqrt{c}}{\sigma}\left[\alpha e^{-\text{j}\phi/2} - \frac{m}{c}\,e^{+\text{j}\phi/2}\right]\\ &= \frac{\sqrt{c}}{\sigma}\left[\left(\alpha-\frac{m}{c}\right)\cos\frac{\phi}{2} - \text{j}\left(\alpha+\frac{m}{c}\right)\sin\frac{\phi}{2}\right].\end{aligned} \tag{7C.8}$$

It follows that

$$\text{Re}(\beta) = 0 \quad \text{for} \quad \alpha = +\frac{m}{c},$$

$$\text{Im}(\beta) = 0 \quad \text{for} \quad \alpha = -\frac{m}{c}.$$

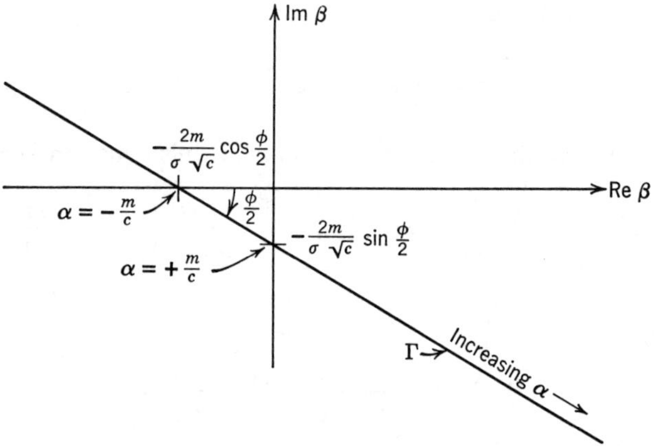

Figure 7C.2 Path of integration.

The locus Γ is therefore the infinite straight line of slope $-\tan \frac{1}{2}\phi$ shown in Fig. 7C.2.

Since the function $e^{-\beta^2/2}$ has no finite poles, the integral around the closed contour in Fig. 7C.3 is zero and

$$\int_{\Gamma} = \lim_{A\to\infty}\left[\int_{\Gamma_1} + \int_{\Gamma_2} + \int_{\Gamma_3}\right]. \tag{7C.9}$$

We assume first that A is finite and then take the limit as $A \to \infty$. Since

$$\lim_{A\to\infty}\int_{\Gamma_2}\frac{1}{\sqrt{2\pi}}\,e^{-\beta^2/2}\,d\beta = \int_{-\infty}^{\infty}\frac{1}{\sqrt{2\pi}}\,e^{-\beta^2/2}\,d\beta = 1, \tag{7C.10}$$

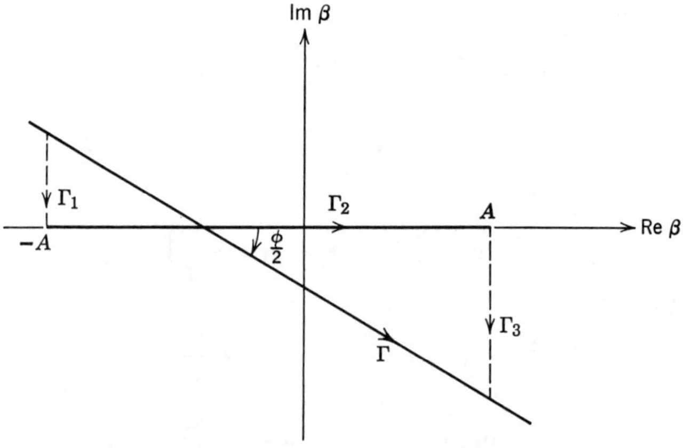

Figure 7C.3 Change in path of integration.

it follows that the integral of Eq. 7C.5 is also equal to one whenever

$$\lim_{A\to\infty}\left|\int_{\Gamma_1}+\int_{\Gamma_3}\right| = 0.$$

Now consider Γ_3. For all points along this path $\beta = A - \mathrm{j}\gamma$, $0 \leqslant \gamma \leqslant A \tan \frac{1}{2}\phi$. Thus

$$\int_{\Gamma_3} = \frac{1}{\sqrt{2\pi}}\int_0^{A\tan\phi/2} e^{-(A-\mathrm{j}\gamma)^2/2}(-\mathrm{j}\, d\gamma). \tag{7C.11}$$

Taking the absolute value of both sides of Eq. 7C.11 yields

$$\begin{aligned}\left|\int_{\Gamma_3}\right| &= \frac{1}{\sqrt{2\pi}}\left|\int_0^{A\tan\phi/2} e^{-(A^2-\gamma^2-\mathrm{j}2A\gamma)/2}(-\mathrm{j})\, d\gamma\right| \\ &\leqslant \int_0^{A\tan\phi/2} |-\mathrm{j}e^{-(A^2-\gamma^2-\mathrm{j}2A\gamma)/2}|\, d\gamma \\ &= e^{-A^2/2}\int_0^{A\tan\phi/2} e^{+\gamma^2/2}\, d\gamma \\ &< \left(A\tan\frac{\phi}{2}\right)\exp\left[-\frac{A^2}{2}\left(1-\tan^2\frac{\phi}{2}\right)\right].\end{aligned} \tag{7C.12}$$

It is clear that

$$\lim_{A\to\infty}\left|\int_{\Gamma_3}\right| = 0; \qquad \text{for } \tan^2\frac{\phi}{2} < 1. \tag{7C.13}$$

An equivalent condition for the vanishing of $\int_{\Gamma_3}$ is that

$$\left|\frac{\phi}{2}\right| < \frac{\pi}{4} \quad \text{or} \quad |\phi| < \frac{\pi}{2}. \tag{7C.14}$$

We see from Fig. 7C.1 that the condition is met whenever $1 - 2\sigma^2 u > 0$ or

$$u = \mathrm{Re}(w) < \frac{1}{2\sigma^2}. \tag{7C.15}$$

An identical argument applied to $\int_{\Gamma_1}$ shows that this integral also vanishes in the limit $A \to \infty$ whenever Eq. 7C.15 is satisfied, which completes the proof of the lemma.

PROBLEMS

7.1 A communication system uses the $\{\varphi_j(t)\}$ shown in Fig. P7.1(i) to transmit one of two equally likely messages by means of the signals $s_1(t) = \sqrt{E_s}\,\varphi_1(t)$, $s_2(t) = \sqrt{E_s}\,\varphi_2(t)$. The channel is illustrated in Fig. P7.1(ii).

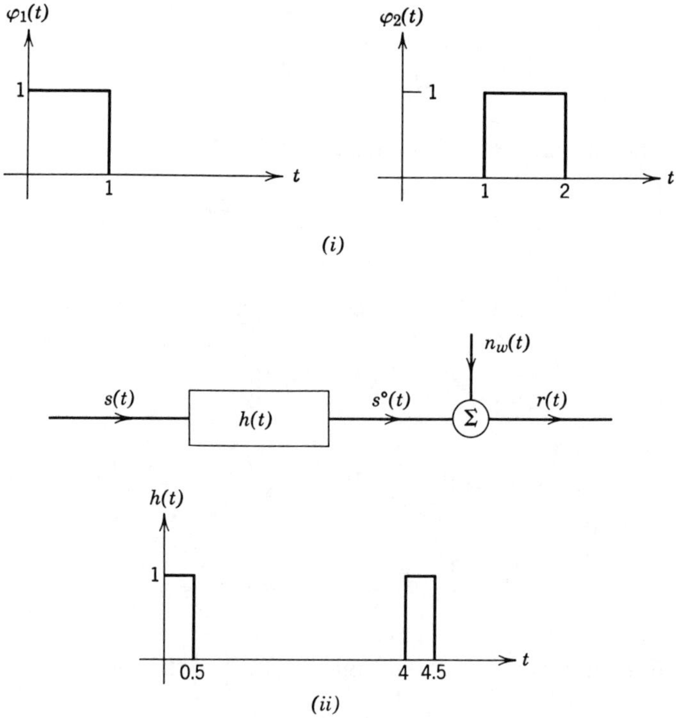

Figure P7.1

a. What is the probability of error for an optimum receiver when $E_s/\mathcal{N}_0 = 5$?
b. Give a detailed block diagram, including waveshapes in the absence of noise, of the optimum filtered-signal receiver.

7.2 Let white noise with $\mathcal{S}_w(f) = 1$ be passed through a filter with transfer function

$$H(s) = \frac{s^3 - 5s^2 + 11s - 15}{s^4 + 5s^3 + 8s^2 + 6s}; \qquad s = \sigma + j2\pi f.$$

a. Determine the power density function $\mathcal{S}_n(f)$ of the noise $n(t)$ at the filter output.
b. Determine the transfer function $G(f)$ and the impulse response $g(t)$ of the whitening filter with realizable inverse.

c. Discuss how $G(f)$ might be modified in the design of a receiver for signals, with lowpass bandwidth $W = 1$, corrupted by the addition of $n(t)$.

7.3 Consider an additive Gaussian noise channel, that is $r(t) = s(t) + n(t)$, where $\mathcal{S}_n(f)$ is not white. Assume the transmission of one of M equally likely signals, each of which is identically zero for $|t| > T/2$.

a. Show that the optimum receiver must observe the entire received waveform $r(t)$, $-\infty < t < \infty$.

b. Let

$$\mathcal{S}_n(f) = \frac{\mathcal{N}_0}{2}\frac{f^2+1}{f^2+4},$$

and let $M = 2$, with

$$s(t) = \begin{cases} \pm\sqrt{E_s}; & |t| \leqslant \frac{1}{2}, \\ 0; & \text{elsewhere.} \end{cases}$$

Exercise engineering judgment to determine a small finite interval to which observation of $r(t)$ may be restricted without incurring substantial performance degradation.

7.4 A random process $n(t)$ is defined as

$$n(t) = n_c(t)\sqrt{2}\cos\omega_0 t + n_s(t)\sqrt{2}\sin\omega_0 t,$$

in which $n_c(t)$ and $n_s(t)$ are zero-mean, jointly wide-sense stationary random processes. In terms of

$$\mathcal{R}_c(\tau) = \overline{n_c(t)n_c(t-\tau)},$$
$$\mathcal{R}_s(\tau) = \overline{n_s(t)n_s(t-\tau)},$$
$$\mathcal{R}_{cs}(\tau) = \overline{n_c(t)n_s(t-\tau)},$$
$$\mathcal{R}_{sc}(\tau) = \overline{n_s(t)n_c(t-\tau)},$$

determine sufficient conditions for $n(t)$ to be wide-sense stationary.

7.5 Two lowpass signals $s_1(t)$ and $s_2(t)$ of bandwidth W are DSB-SC modulated on quadrature high-frequency carriers, and the modulated carriers are added before transmission. Thus the transmitted signal is

$$s^\circ(t) = s_1(t)\sqrt{2}\cos 2\pi f_0 t + s_2(t)\sqrt{2}\sin 2\pi f_0 t.$$

The channel is shown in Fig. P7.5, where $h(t)$ is the impulse response of a linear time-invariant filter with transfer function $H(f)$. Prove that the condition

$$H(f_0+f) = H^*(f_0-f); \qquad 0 \leqslant f \leqslant W$$

ensures that the lowpass signals regained by quadrature DSB-SC demodulation do not contain crosstalk (i.e., energy from one signal in the output of the demodulator for the other).

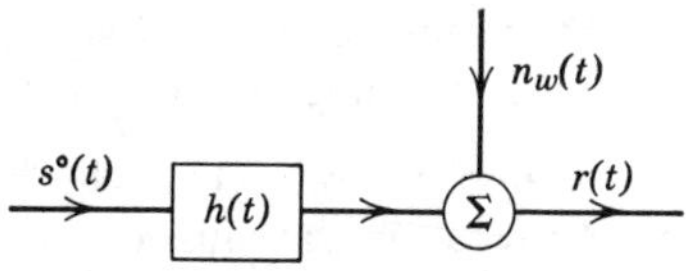

Figure P7.5

7.6 Because ideal rectangular filters are unrealizable, SSB is not possible in practice when the baseband signals (of bandwidth W) contain significant energy in the immediate vicinity of $f = 0$. The difficulty is often evaded by use of "vestigial sideband" modulation. Show that the idealized vestigial sideband system diagrammed in the Fig. P7.6 also yields error performance equal to that of DSB-SC when $H(f)$ is appropriately chosen and $n_w(t)$ is Gaussian. What conditions must $H(f)$ satisfy over $[f_0 - \Delta, f_0 + \Delta]$?

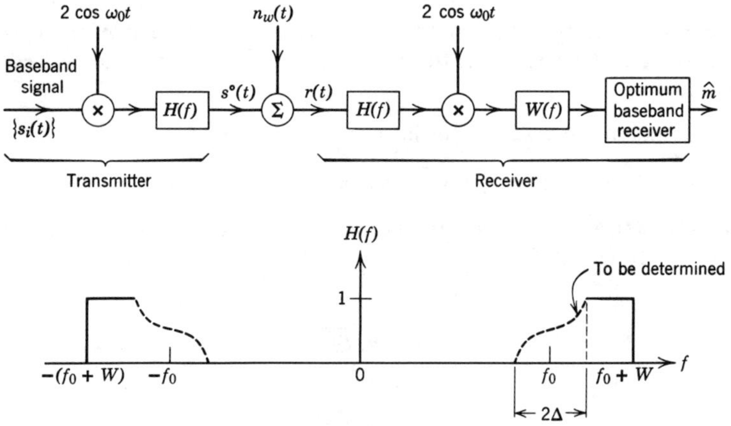

Figure P7.6

7.7 When $s(t)$ is transmitted over a particular fading channel, the received signal is

$$r(t) = as(t) + n_w(t),$$

where

$$p_a(\alpha) = .01\ \delta(\alpha) + 0.09\ \delta(\alpha - 1) + 0.9\ \delta(\alpha - 2)$$

and $n_w(t)$ is white Gaussian noise with mean power density $\mathcal{N}_0/2$. One of two equally likely messages is transmitted by means of antipodal signals of energy E_s.

a. What is the average energy of the signal component of $r(t)$?
b. Determine P[$\mathcal{E}$] as a function of $E_s/\mathcal{N}_0$.
c. What value does P[$\mathcal{E}$] approach as $E_s/\mathcal{N}_0$ becomes very large?

7.8 After observing the received waveform, the optimum receiver for a binary communication system calculates a decision variable, say y, and sets $\hat{m} = m_0$ if

$y > 0$ and $\hat{m} = m_1$ if $y \leqslant 0$. Assume that the signaling is symmetric in the sense that

$$p_y(\alpha \mid m_0) = p_y(-\alpha \mid m_1); \qquad \text{all } \alpha.$$

Show in consequence that

$$\mathrm{P}[\mathcal{E}] = \overline{f(y)} \leqslant \tfrac{1}{2}\overline{e^{\lambda y}}; \qquad \text{for all } \lambda, \; -\infty < \lambda < \infty,$$

where f is the unit step function and the expectation is conditioned on m_1. *Hints.* Consider the necessity of the condition

$$p_y(-\alpha \mid m_1) \geqslant p_y(\alpha \mid m_1); \qquad \text{for all } \alpha \geqslant 0,$$

and note that for any probability density function $p(\alpha)$

$$\int_{-\infty}^{\infty} p(\alpha)e^{\lambda\alpha}\, d\alpha = \int_0^{\infty} [p(-\alpha) - p(\alpha)]e^{-\lambda\alpha}\, d\alpha + \int_0^{\infty} p(\alpha)[e^{\lambda\alpha} + e^{-\lambda\alpha}]\, d\alpha.$$

7.9 One of M equally likely messages is communicated over a random-phase, additive white Gaussian noise channel by means of M orthogonal signals, each of energy E_s. The noise power density is $\mathcal{N}_0/2$.

a. Draw a block diagram of the optimum receiver.

b. Show that when the channel phase θ is equal to γ the conditional error probability may be written as

$$\mathrm{P}[\mathcal{E} \mid \theta = \gamma] = 1 - \overline{[1 - e^{-(x^2+y^2)/2}]^{M-1}}.$$

Here x and y are statistically independent Gaussian random variables with unit variance and means equal to $\sqrt{2E_s/\mathcal{N}_0}\cos\gamma$ and $\sqrt{2E_s/\mathcal{N}_0}\sin\gamma$, respectively; the expectation is with respect to x and y, conditioned on $\theta = \gamma$.

c. Using the lemma of Eq. 7.67, show that

$$\mathrm{P}[\mathcal{E}] = \sum_{i=1}^{M-1} \binom{M-1}{i} (-1)^{i+1} \frac{\exp\left[-\dfrac{E_s}{\mathcal{N}_0}\dfrac{i}{i+1}\right]}{i+1},$$

which is a generalization of the result of Eq. 7.68 for the case $M = 2$.

7.10 Consider signaling over a bandpass, known-phase, additive white Gaussian noise channel with codewords that are sequences chosen from an A-letter alphabet of orthogonal waveforms with equal energy. Assume that the letters are chosen with equal probability and statistical independence. Show that the resulting value of the (unquantized) exponential bound parameter R_0 is the same for either a coherent or an incoherent receiver. Would this be true if the letters formed an A-waveform simplex? (Assume that the channel phase is constant.)

7.11 A random phase, nonfading, additive white Gaussian noise channel is converted to a discrete channel by the following modulation/demodulation scheme. Each use of the discrete channel corresponds to the transmission of a waveform chosen from a four-letter alphabet of orthogonal waveforms, each with energy E_s. The channel phase is constant over each use of the channel, uniformly distributed, and statistically independent from use to use. At the receiver maximum-likelihood (incoherent) detection is performed on each letter. The detector outputs are then passed through a "quantizer" whose output is an ordered pair of integers, the first indicating the letter whose detector output (likelihood) is largest and the second indicating the letter whose detector output is second largest. (See also Problem 6.10.)

a. Verify that the following transition probability matrix describes the discrete channel.

OUTPUT

INPUT		1, 2	1, 3	1, 4	2, 1	2, 3	2, 4	3, 1	3, 2	3, 4	4, 1	4, 2	4, 3
	1	q	q	q	w	p	p	w	p	p	w	p	p
	2	w	p	p	q	q	q	p	w	p	p	w	p
	3	p	w	p	p	w	p	q	q	q	p	p	w
	4	p	p	w	p	p	w	p	p	w	q	q	q

b. Express R_0' for the discrete channel in terms of q, w, and p.

c. Show that

$$q = \tfrac{1}{3}\overline{[1 - e^{-(x^2+y^2)/2}]^3}$$
$$w = \overline{[1 - e^{-(x^2+y^2)/2}]^2[e^{-(x^2+y^2)/2}]}$$
$$p = (1 - 3q - 3w)/6,$$

where x and y are statistically independent unit-variance Gaussian random variables with $\bar{x} = \sqrt{2E_s/\mathcal{N}_0}$, $\bar{y} = 0$.

d. Use the lemma of Eq. 7.67 to evaluate q and w in terms of $E_s/\mathcal{N}_0$.

7.12 A communication system operating on the random phase, additive white Gaussian noise channel of Problem 7.11 uses codewords constructed from the two orthogonal waveforms $\sqrt{E_s}\,\varphi_0(t)$, $\sqrt{E_s}\,\varphi_1(t)$. The receiver utilizes a maximum-likelihood detector followed by a three-level quantizer. Whenever both

$$(\mathbf{r}_c \cdot \boldsymbol{\varphi}_0)^2 + (\mathbf{r}_s \cdot \boldsymbol{\varphi}_0)^2 \leqslant T^2 \frac{\mathcal{N}_0}{2}$$

and

$$(\mathbf{r}_c \cdot \boldsymbol{\varphi}_1)^2 + (\mathbf{r}_s \cdot \boldsymbol{\varphi}_1)^2 \leqslant T^2 \frac{\mathcal{N}_0}{2},$$

in which T is a preset threshold, the quantizer output is the erasure symbol "?." Otherwise the quantizer output is the letter with largest likelihood.

a. Show that the system can be modeled by the discrete channel illustrated in Fig. P7.12.

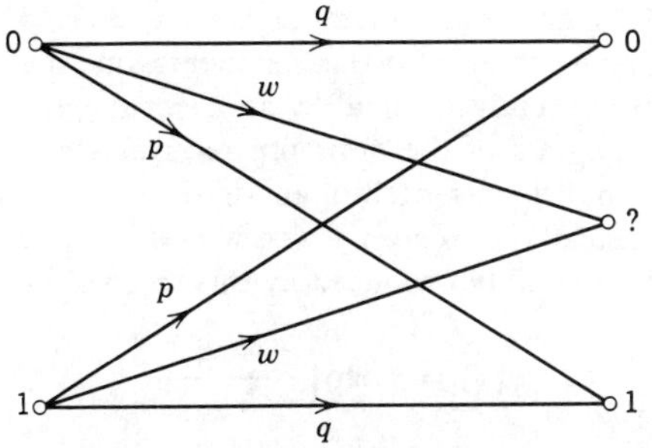

Figure P7.12

b. Show that

$$w = (1 - e^{-T^2/2})(1 - \mathrm{P}[x_1^2 + x_2^2 > T^2]),$$
$$q = \mathrm{P}[(x_1^2 + x_2^2 > T^2) \cap (x_1^2 + x_2^2 > x_3^2 + x_4^2)]$$
$$p = 1 - q - w,$$

in which x_1, x_2, x_3, x_4 are statistically independent unit-variance Gaussian random variables and

$$\bar{x}_1^2 + \bar{x}_2^2 = 2E_s/\mathcal{N}_0, \qquad \bar{x}_3 = \bar{x}_4 = 0.$$

c. Express $\mathrm{P}[x_1^2 + x_2^2 > T^2]$ in terms of the Marcum Q-function,† defined as

$$Q(m, T) \triangleq \int_T^\infty re^{-\frac{1}{2}(r^2+m^2)}\, I_0(mr)\, dr.$$

[$I_0(\;)$ is the zero-order modified Bessel function of Eq. 7.49a.]

d. Similarly, express q as a single integral involving $I_0(\;)$.

e. Express R_0' for the discrete channel in terms of p, q, and w.

7.13 Consider a bandpass fading channel and DSB-SC sine-and-cosine demodulation. If a lowpass signal $s(t)$ is transmitted, the two demodulator outputs are

$$r_c(t) = z_c s(t) + n_c(t),$$
$$r_s(t) = z_s s(t) + n_s(t),$$

in which $n_c(t)$ and $n_s(t)$ are statistically independent zero-mean Gaussian noise processes with power spectrum $\mathcal{N}_0/2$ over the frequency band $|f| < W$ occupied by $s(t)$.

Heretofore we have considered only the case in which z_c and z_s are zero-mean Gaussian random variables, each with variance $b/2$. If the channel model is modified so that

$$\bar{z}_c = a \cos\theta, \qquad \bar{z}_s = a \sin\theta,$$

the fading is called "Rician." Here a and θ are known constants.

† J. I. Marcum, "A Statistical Theory of Target Detection by Pulsed Radar," *IRE Trans. Inform. Theory*, **IT-6,** 159, April 1960.

a. Show that the Rician model corresponds to a received signal that (in the absence of noise) is the resultant of two components, one specular and the other Rayleigh. Represent the received signal by a phasor diagram.

b. Derive a block diagram of the optimum receiver when $s(t)$ is one of two equally likely orthogonal signals, each of energy E_s.

c. Now consider instead the receiver which would be optimum if a were zero. Show that the error probability produced by this receiver is

$$P[\mathcal{E}] = p \exp\left(\frac{-pa^2E_s}{\mathcal{N}_0}\right),$$

in which

$$p = \left(2 + \frac{bE_s}{\mathcal{N}_0}\right)^{-1}.$$

7.14 One of two equally likely binary messages is communicated over a random-phase, additive white Gaussian noise channel by means of the signals

$$s_1(t) = q(t) + s_o(t),$$
$$s_2(t) = q(t) - s_o(t).$$

The waveforms $q(t)$ and $s_o(t)$ are orthogonal, with energy E_q and E_o, respectively ($E_o \neq E_q$). The channel phase is uniformly distributed and the noise power density is $\mathcal{N}_0/2$.

a. Is the receiver optimum which estimates channel phase from $q(t)$ and uses this estimate to make a "coherent" decision between $\pm s_o(t)$?

b. Specify the error probability of the optimum receiver in terms of the Marcum Q-function (see Problem 7.12, part c.) You will also need to use the following result: if x_1, x_2, x_3, x_4 are statistically independent unit-variance Gaussian random variables,† then

$$P[x_1^2 + x_2^2 \geqslant x_3^2 + x_4^2] = \tfrac{1}{2}[1 - Q(b, a) + Q(a, b)],$$

in which

$$a^2 = \frac{\bar{x}_1^2 + \bar{x}_2^2}{2}; \qquad b^2 = \frac{\bar{x}_3^2 + \bar{x}_4^2}{2}.$$

† S. Stein, "Unified Analysis of Certain Coherent and Non-Coherent Binary Communications Systems," *IEEE Trans. Inform. Theory*, **IT-10,** 43–51, January 1964.

8

Waveform Communication

In the preceding chapters we have considered discrete communication systems, in which the transmitter input is chosen from a finite set of possible messages. The communication problem is somewhat different when the set of possible input messages is defined on a continuum. For example, consider the system shown in Fig. 8.1. A random variable, m, is

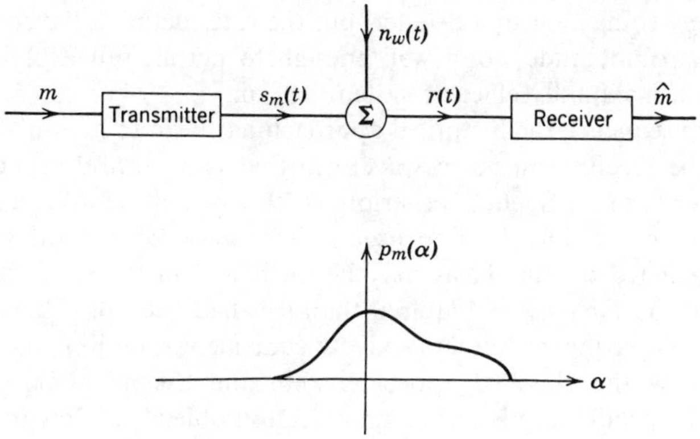

Figure 8.1 Communication of a continuous random variable.

presented to the transmitter and a waveform $s_m(t)$—some attribute of which depends on m—is transmitted over the noisy channel. After observing the received signal, $r(t)$, the receiver must deliver at its output an estimate, $\hat{m}$, of m. The essential difference between this system and those already considered is that m is now assumed to be a *continuous* rather than a *discrete* random variable. For example, we might assume that m can take on any value between -1 and 1, whereas in the corresponding discrete case m might be restricted to the values

$$\{\pm 2i/M\}, \quad i = 0, 1, \ldots, M/2.$$

In an operable discrete communication system the probability that the receiver output $\hat{m}$ will equal the transmitter input m is close to unity, and it is meaningful to measure the system performance in terms of the probability of error. In the continuum case, however, the probability that $\hat{m} = m$ is, in general, zero; small noise perturbations produce changes in the received signal which are indistinguishable from those produced by small variations in the input m itself. When m is a continuous random variable, it is not meaningful to judge the performance of a communication system on the basis of probability of error. Some other criterion of goodness is required.

In engineering practice the main attributes of a desirable criterion of goodness are that it should be mathematically tractable, that it should point the way to efficient system designs, and that it should accurately reflect the degree of user satisfaction with the system. In actual problems of continuum communication, however, such as the transmission of speech, it is exceedingly difficult to devise a performance criterion that simultaneously satisfies all three of the desirable attributes listed. The essential difficulty is that entirely different speech waveforms may be subjectively equivalent to a listener, but the rules defining the equivalence relations are not understood well enough to permit full exploitation in achieving a maximally efficient system design.

As a consequence the historical approach has been to attempt to reproduce at the receiver output a waveform that is a faithful replica of the transmitter input. Such a criterion is clearly sufficient, since a high fidelity obviously does lead to user satisfaction. On the other hand, a system designed on this basis may be inefficient in the sense that more transmitter power may be required than if it had been possible to design around a less stringent but subjectively equivalent criterion.

We follow the classical approach here and assume that fidelity of waveform reproduction is our communication objective. How to measure "fidelity" is then the problem. The requirement of mathematical tractability has been of paramount importance historically and for systems disturbed by additive white Gaussian noise has led to the acceptance of the mean-square error between input and output waveforms as the criterion of goodness. We shall see that this criterion also meets the objective of leading to useful design procedures. For the single random variable communication system of Fig. 8.1 the mean-square error is defined by the equation

$$\overline{\epsilon^2} \triangleq \mathrm{E}[(m - \hat{m})^2] = \overline{(m - \hat{m})^2}. \tag{8.1}$$

The expectation is taken over the joint ensemble of all allowable inputs and all allowable noise disturbances.

We begin by analyzing certain continuum communication schemes to determine the mean-square error when the channel is perturbed with additive white Gaussian noise. The analysis procedure is first to consider a single random variable input and then to apply the results to a random waveform input. After illustrating how continuum (as well as discrete) communication is constrained by channel capacity, we return to discrete systems in the consideration of pulse-code modulation, abbreviated PCM.

8.1 LINEAR MODULATION

Various devices are used in practice to generate transmitted waveforms. An important class, called linear modulators, generates waveforms that vary linearly with the transmitter input. This class includes double-sideband (DSB), double-sideband-suppressed carrier (DSB-SC), and single-sideband (SSB) systems.

Single-Parameter Input

Consider the communication system illustrated in Fig. 8.2. The transmitted waveform is given by

$$s_m(t) = mA\,\varphi_1(t), \tag{8.2}$$

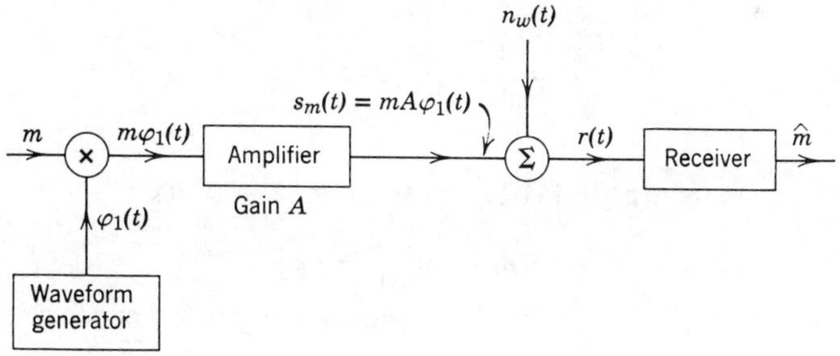

Figure 8.2 System using a linear modulator to communicate the random variable m.

in which A is the voltage gain of the transmitter amplifier and $\varphi_1(t)$ is some waveform with unit energy,

$$\int_{-\infty}^{\infty} \varphi_1^2(t)\,dt = 1. \tag{8.3}$$

The transmission is disturbed by an additive white Gaussian noise process $n_w(t)$ with power density $\mathcal{N}_0/2$. Thus the received signal is

$$r(t) = s_m(t) + n_w(t). \tag{8.4}$$

Our first task is to determine the structure of the least mean-square error receiver and evaluate its performance.

Mean-square error. In formulating the receiver design problem we assume that the received random process $r(t)$ is represented by some vector $\mathbf{r}$. In order that the over-all mean-square error (averaged over all possible pairs of transmitted and received vectors) may be minimum, it is clearly necessary and sufficient that the conditional mean-square error, $\overline{\epsilon^2}(\boldsymbol{\rho})$, given each possible value $\boldsymbol{\rho}$ of the received vector $\mathbf{r}$, should be minimum.

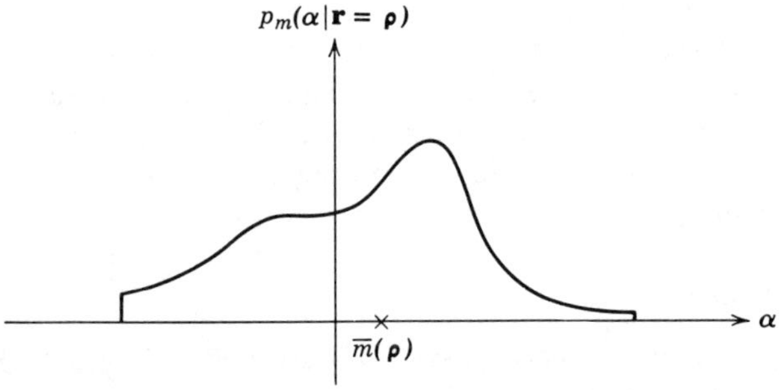

Figure 8.3 Possible a posteriori density function with conditional mean $\overline{m}(\boldsymbol{\rho})$.

This follows from the fact that the over-all mean-square error can be written

$$\overline{\epsilon^2} = \int_{-\infty}^{\infty} \overline{\epsilon^2}(\boldsymbol{\rho}) p_{\mathbf{r}}(\boldsymbol{\rho})\, d\boldsymbol{\rho} \tag{8.5}$$

with

$$\begin{aligned} \overline{\epsilon^2}(\boldsymbol{\rho}) &\triangleq \int_{-\infty}^{\infty} (\alpha - \hat{m})^2\, p_m(\alpha \mid \mathbf{r} = \boldsymbol{\rho})\, d\alpha \\ &\triangleq \mathrm{E}[(m - \hat{m})^2 \mid \mathbf{r} = \boldsymbol{\rho}]. \end{aligned} \tag{8.6}$$

As in Chapter 7, E[|] is used to denote a conditional expectation.

Equations 8.5 and 8.6 give an analytic expression for $\overline{\epsilon^2}$ in terms of $\hat{m}$; the remaining problem is to find a rule for determining the receiver estimate $\hat{m}$ in such a way that $\overline{\epsilon^2}$ will be minimized. Figure 8.3 illustrates a typical a posteriori density function, $p_{m \mid \mathbf{r}}$, with conditional mean

$$\overline{m}(\boldsymbol{\rho}) \triangleq \mathrm{E}[m \mid \mathbf{r} = \boldsymbol{\rho}]. \tag{8.7}$$

We now show that the assignment $\hat{m} = \overline{m}(\boldsymbol{\rho})$ minimizes $\overline{\epsilon^2}(\boldsymbol{\rho})$. The argument is identical to one already encountered in Section 7.4, *Receiver Interpretation*. Assume that the receiver assigns any other number to $\hat{m}$, say

$$\hat{m} = \overline{m}(\boldsymbol{\rho}) + \Delta.$$

Taking the expectation over the ensemble of all possible values of m, we have (as in Eq. 7.112)

$$\begin{aligned}\overline{\epsilon^2}(\boldsymbol{\rho}) &= \mathrm{E}[(m - \bar{m}(\boldsymbol{\rho}) - \Delta)^2 \mid \mathbf{r} = \boldsymbol{\rho}] \\ &= \mathrm{E}[(m - \bar{m}(\boldsymbol{\rho}))^2 \mid \mathbf{r} = \boldsymbol{\rho}] - 2\Delta\, \mathrm{E}[m - \bar{m}(\boldsymbol{\rho}) \mid \mathbf{r} = \boldsymbol{\rho}] + \Delta^2 \\ &= \mathrm{E}[(m - \bar{m}(\boldsymbol{\rho}))^2 \mid \mathbf{r} = \boldsymbol{\rho}] + \Delta^2.\end{aligned}$$

Clearly, $\overline{\epsilon^2}(\boldsymbol{\rho})$ is minimized by choosing $\Delta = 0$, that is, by assigning

$$\hat{m} = \bar{m}(\boldsymbol{\rho}). \tag{8.8a}$$

Thus the least mean-square-error estimate of m (given $\mathbf{r} = \boldsymbol{\rho}$) is the *conditional mean* and the resulting mean-square error is the *conditional variance*

$$\overline{\epsilon^2}(\boldsymbol{\rho}) = \mathrm{E}[(m - \bar{m}(\boldsymbol{\rho}))^2 \mid \mathbf{r} = \boldsymbol{\rho}]. \tag{8.8b}$$

Since the derivation of Eqs. 8.8a and b involves neither the assumption that the modulation is linear nor that the channel is Gaussian, Eqs. 8.8 have unrestricted validity.

In the particular case of linear modulation and additive white Gaussian noise let $\varphi_1(t)$ define one axis of the signal space; the transmitted signal is then represented by the vector $mA\boldsymbol{\varphi}_1$:

$$s_m(t) = mA\,\varphi_1(t) \leftrightarrow \mathbf{s}_m = mA\boldsymbol{\varphi}_1. \tag{8.9a}$$

If we now let $n_1(t)$ denote the component of $n_w(t)$ along $\varphi_1(t)$, then $n_1(t)$ is also represented by a one-dimensional vector,

$$n_1(t) = n_1\,\varphi_1(t) \leftrightarrow \mathbf{n}_1 = n_1\boldsymbol{\varphi}_1, \tag{8.9b}$$

where

$$n_1 \triangleq \int_{-\infty}^{\infty} n_w(t)\,\varphi_1(t)\,dt. \tag{8.9c}$$

Finally, if we let $n^*(t)$ denote the rest of the noise,

$$n^*(t) \triangleq n_w(t) - n_1(t) = r(t) - [s_m(t) + n_1(t)],$$

it follows from Eqs. 4.45b, 4.46 and 4.25b that any vector $\mathbf{n}^*$ formed from $n^*(t)$ is statistically independent of both $\mathbf{s}_m$ and $\mathbf{n}_1$ and is therefore irrelevant; we have

$$p_{m \mid \mathbf{r}} = p_{m \mid r_1}, \tag{8.10a}$$

in which

$$r_1 \triangleq \mathbf{r} \cdot \boldsymbol{\varphi}_1 = \int_{-\infty}^{\infty} r(t)\varphi_1(t)\,dt = mA + n_1. \tag{8.10b}$$

Hence the vector notation of Eqs. 8.8a and b is superfluous: the least mean-square-error estimate of m may be written as

$$\hat{m} = \bar{m}(\rho) \triangleq \int_{-\infty}^{\infty} \alpha p_m(\alpha \mid r_1 = \rho)\, d\alpha \tag{8.11a}$$

and the resulting mean-square error as

$$\overline{\epsilon^2}(\rho) = \mathrm{E}[(m - \bar{m}(\rho))^2 \mid r_1 = \rho]. \tag{8.11b}$$

The conditional density function $p_{m \mid r_1}$ is given by Bayes rule: for all α and ρ

$$p_m(\alpha \mid r_1 = \rho) = \frac{p_m(\alpha)}{p_{r_1}(\rho)} p_{r_1}(\rho \mid m = \alpha). \tag{8.12}$$

But $r_1 = mA + n_1$, and n_1 is a zero-mean Gaussian random variable (with variance $\mathcal{N}_0/2$) that is statistically independent of m. Hence

$$\begin{aligned} p_{r_1}(\rho \mid m = \alpha) &= p_{n_1}(\rho - \alpha A) \\ &= \frac{1}{\sqrt{\pi \mathcal{N}_0}} e^{-(\rho - \alpha A)^2/\mathcal{N}_0}. \end{aligned}$$

Substituting in Eq. 8.12, we have

$$p_m(\alpha \mid r_1 = \rho) = B_1\, p_m(\alpha) e^{-(\rho - \alpha A)^2/\mathcal{N}_0}. \tag{8.13}$$

Here B_1 is a constant that normalizes the integral of $p_{m \mid r_1}$ to unity.

Further analysis depends critically on the a priori probability density function p_m. The simplest situation occurs when m is also a Gaussian random variable, say with zero mean and variance σ^2.

$$p_m(\alpha) = \frac{1}{\sqrt{2\pi}\,\sigma} e^{-\alpha^2/2\sigma^2}. \tag{8.14}$$

Then

$$p_m(\alpha \mid r_1 = \rho) = \frac{B_1}{\sqrt{2\pi}\,\sigma} \exp\left[-\frac{\alpha^2}{2\sigma^2} - \frac{1}{\mathcal{N}_0}(\rho - \alpha A)^2\right].$$

After completing the square in the exponent, we obtain

$$p_m(\alpha \mid r_1 = \rho) = B_2 \exp\left[-\frac{1}{2}\,\frac{A^2\sigma^2 + \mathcal{N}_0/2}{\sigma^2 \mathcal{N}_0/2}\left(\alpha - \rho\,\frac{\sigma^2 A}{\sigma^2 A^2 + \mathcal{N}_0/2}\right)^2\right]. \tag{8.15}$$

Since the functional dependence on α is of Gaussian form, the a posteriori density function $p_{m \mid r_1}$ (as well as the a priori density p_m) is Gaussian. It follows that the normalizing constant B_2 is

$$B_2 = \frac{1}{\sqrt{2\pi}}\left(\frac{\sigma^2 \mathcal{N}_0/2}{A^2\sigma^2 + \mathcal{N}_0/2}\right)^{1/2}.$$

The conditional mean is identified as

$$\bar{m}(\rho) = \frac{\rho}{A} \frac{1}{1 + \dfrac{\mathcal{N}_0/2}{\sigma^2 A^2}}, \tag{8.16a}$$

and the mean-square error when $m = \bar{m}(\rho)$ is

$$\overline{\epsilon^2}(\rho) = \frac{\sigma^2 \mathcal{N}_0/2}{A^2\sigma^2 + \mathcal{N}_0/2}$$

$$= \sigma^2 \frac{1}{1 + \dfrac{\sigma^2 A^2}{\mathcal{N}_0/2}}. \tag{8.16b}$$

We note from Eq. 8.16b that the transmission of $s_m(t)$ yields an a posteriori variance of m that is reduced from the a priori value, σ^2, by the factor $(1 + 2\bar{E}_m/\mathcal{N}_0)^{-1}$, where

$$\bar{E}_m \triangleq \mathrm{E}\left[\int_{-\infty}^{\infty} s_m{}^2(t)\,dt\right] = A^2\overline{m^2} = \sigma^2 A^2 \tag{8.17}$$

is the mean signal energy. Perfect communication is obtained only in the limit as $\bar{E}_m/\mathcal{N}_0 \to \infty$. Since $\overline{\epsilon^2}(\rho)$ is independent of ρ, it follows from Eq. 8.5 that the right-hand side of Eq. 8.16b is also the over-all mean-square error. We therefore have

$$\overline{\epsilon^2} = \overline{m^2} \frac{1}{1 + 2\bar{E}_m/\mathcal{N}_0}. \tag{8.18}$$

Minimax reception. We recognize from Eq. 8.16a that $\bar{m}(\rho)$ is a linear function of the relevant received signal component ρ. Thus the minimum mean-square error receiver when p_m is Gaussian is a *linear* receiver. A receiver realization is shown in Fig. 8.4. It consists of a filter matched to $\varphi_1(t)$, followed by an attenuator with gain

$$G = \frac{1}{A} \frac{2\bar{E}_m/\mathcal{N}_0}{1 + 2\bar{E}_m/\mathcal{N}_0}. \tag{8.19}$$

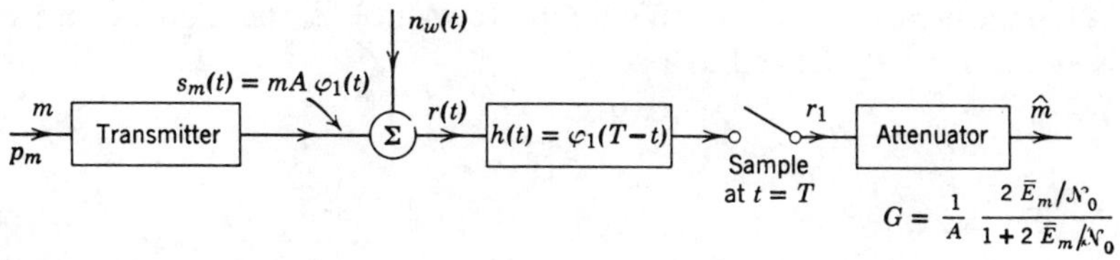

Figure 8.4 Minimum mean-square-error receiver when p_m is Gaussian. This receiver is also minimax.

Of course, the minimum mean-square error receiver is not linear when p_m is not Gaussian, even though the transmitted signal $s_m(t)$ depends linearly on m. This follows from the fact that $p_{m|r_1}$ in Eq. 8.12 involves p_m, as well as $p_{r_1|m}$. But it is easy to show that the linear receiver of Fig. 8.4 is *minimax* in the sense that no other receiver yields a smaller mean-square error when the modulation is linear and p_m is most adverse. In particular, we have already observed that no other receiver performs as well when p_m is Gaussian. The minimax claim may therefore be proved by showing that the receiver of Fig. 8.4 produces the *same* mean-square error for every p_m with second moment $\overline{m^2}$.

Proof follows directly from Eq. 8.10b and Fig. 8.4. We have

$$\hat{m} = (mA + n_1)G$$

$$(m - \hat{m}) = m(1 - AG) - n_1G. \tag{8.20a}$$

Averaging over the joint ensemble of m and n_1 yields

$$\overline{\epsilon^2} \triangleq \overline{(m - \hat{m})^2} = \overline{m^2}(1 - AG)^2 + \overline{n_1^2}G^2, \tag{8.20b}$$

in which the second equality follows from the statistical independence of m and n_1. But

$$\bar{E}_m = \overline{m^2}A^2, \qquad \overline{n_1^2} = \frac{\mathcal{N}_0}{2},$$

$$G = \frac{1}{A}\frac{2\bar{E}_m/\mathcal{N}_0}{1 + 2\bar{E}_m/\mathcal{N}_0},$$

and

$$1 - AG = \frac{1}{1 + 2\bar{E}_m/\mathcal{N}_0}.$$

Substituting in Eq. 8.20b and simplifying again yields

$$\overline{\epsilon^2} = \overline{m^2}\frac{1}{1 + 2\bar{E}_m/\mathcal{N}_0},$$

which agrees with the Gaussian result of Eq. 8.18 and is independent of the functional form of p_m.

A convenient measure of system performance is the signal-to-noise power ratio, $\mathcal{S}/\mathcal{N}$, defined as

$$\frac{\mathcal{S}}{\mathcal{N}} \triangleq \frac{\overline{m^2}}{\overline{\epsilon^2}}. \tag{8.21a}$$

From Eq. 8.18,

$$\frac{\mathcal{S}}{\mathcal{N}} = 1 + \frac{2\bar{E}_m}{\mathcal{N}_0}. \tag{8.21b}$$

Acceptable communication is possible with minimax reception if and only if the available mean energy-to-noise ratio can be made relatively large, say $\bar{E}_m/\mathcal{N}_0 > 5$.

Maximum-likelihood reception. A receiver that considers all allowable values of m and assigns $\hat{m}$ from among them in such a way that

$$p_{\mathbf{r}}(\boldsymbol{\rho} \mid m = \hat{m}) \geqslant p_{\mathbf{r}}(\boldsymbol{\rho} \mid m = \alpha); \qquad \text{all allowable } \alpha \tag{8.22}$$

is called a *maximum-likelihood* receiver. For linear modulation we have seen that

$$p_{\mathbf{r}}(\boldsymbol{\rho} \mid m = \alpha) \sim p_{r_1}(\rho \mid m = \alpha) = \frac{1}{\sqrt{\pi\mathcal{N}_0}}\, e^{-(\rho-\alpha A)^2/\mathcal{N}_0}, \tag{8.23}$$

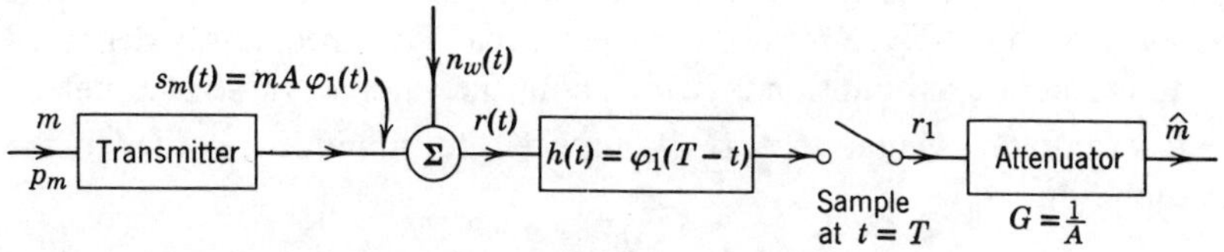

Figure 8.5 Maximum-likelihood receiver when $p_m(\alpha) > 0$ for $-\infty < \alpha < \infty$.

so that the value of α for which the right-hand side of Eq. 8.23 is maximum is ρ/A. Thus a maximum-likelihood receiver sets

$$\hat{m} = \frac{\rho}{A} \tag{8.24}$$

when $r_1 = \rho$ and when the allowable range of m is unrestricted.† The resulting receiver structure, shown in Fig. 8.5, is identical to that of Fig. 8.4 except that the gain G is now chosen to be $1/A$ regardless of the value of $\mathcal{N}_0/2$.

The mean-square error for the receiver of Fig. 8.5 is readily determined. We have

$$\hat{m} = (mA + n_1)\frac{1}{A} = m + \frac{n_1}{A}$$

$$\overline{\epsilon^2} = \overline{(m - \hat{m})^2} = \frac{\mathcal{N}_0}{2A^2}. \tag{8.25a}$$

Because $A^2 = \bar{E}_m/\overline{m^2}$,

$$\frac{\mathcal{S}}{\mathcal{N}} = \frac{2\bar{E}_m}{\mathcal{N}_0}. \tag{8.25b}$$

† A priori density functions p_m that restrict the range of m to a finite interval of the real line are considered in the next section.

These results are similar to those of Eqs. 8.18 and 8.21 for the minimax receiver; both are independent of the form of p_m.

We conclude from Eq. 8.25 that maximum-likelihood reception is essentially minimax for large values of mean energy-to-noise ratio, $\bar{E}_m/\mathcal{N}_0$, a condition that we have already noted is necessary for good communication. The conclusion follows from observing that the minimax mean-square error of Eq. 8.18 is obtained by multiplying the maximum-likelihood mean-square error of Eq. 8.25a by the factor

$$\frac{1}{1 + \mathcal{N}_0/2\bar{E}_m}, \tag{8.25c}$$

which approaches unity as $\bar{E}_m/\mathcal{N}_0$ becomes large.

An advantage of maximum-likelihood reception is that the attenuator gain, $G = 1/A$, does not involve knowledge of $\overline{m^2}$ and $\mathcal{N}_0/2$. With the receiver of Fig. 8.4, the mean-square error may be unnecessarily degraded if an inaccurate assumption is made about the value of these parameters. For example, assume that G is adjusted to minimize $\overline{\epsilon^2}$ under the assumption

$$\mathcal{S}_w(f) = \frac{\mathcal{N}_0}{2}; \qquad \text{all } f. \tag{8.26}$$

From Eq. 8.20, the receiver output error is then

$$\overline{\epsilon^2} = \overline{(m - \hat{m})^2} = \overline{m^2}(1 - AG)^2 + \overline{n_1^2}G^2$$
$$= \overline{m^2}\left(\frac{1}{1 + 2\bar{E}_m/\mathcal{N}_0}\right)^2 + \overline{n_1^2}G^2.$$

If the true noise power density on the channel is zero, so that $\overline{n_1^2} = 0$, there is a mean-square erro

$$\overline{\epsilon^2} = \overline{m^2}\left(\frac{1}{1 + 2\bar{E}_m/\mathcal{N}_0}\right)^2 \tag{8.27}$$

which is not equal to zero even though the channel is noiseless. On the other hand, with maximum-likelihood reception $\overline{\epsilon^2}$ approaches zero as the channel becomes noiseless even when this occurs unbeknown to the receiver.

Bounded inputs. The receiver of Fig. 8.5 is not strictly maximum-likelihood when m is restricted to lie within a finite interval of the real line. An example is any a priori density function such that

$$p_m(\alpha)\begin{cases} > 0; & -a \leqslant \alpha \leqslant a \\ = 0; & \text{elsewhere.} \end{cases} \tag{8.28a}$$

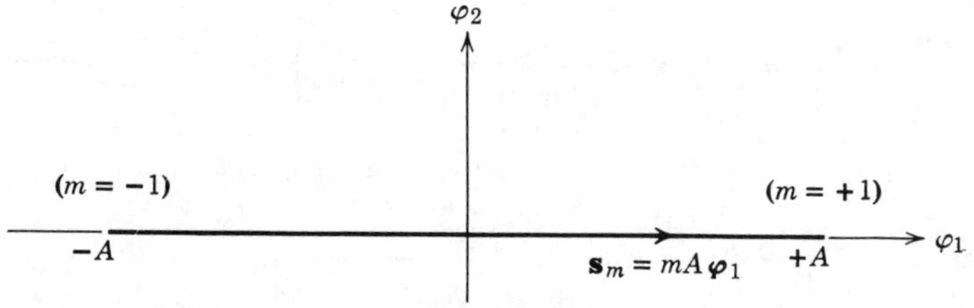

Figure 8.6 Locus of transmitted signal vector, $\mathbf{s}_m = mA\boldsymbol{\varphi}_1$, when m is bounded.

Without loss of generality, we hereafter normalize the (positive) constant a to 1, so that

$$-1 \leqslant m \leqslant 1. \tag{8.28b}$$

Bounding m constrains the locus of the transmitted signal vector $\mathbf{s}_m = mA\boldsymbol{\varphi}_1$ as shown in Fig. 8.6. As m ranges over the interval $[-1, +1]$, the tip of the vector $\mathbf{s}_m$ moves along the φ_1-axis from $-A$ to $+A$.

The dependence of the likelihood function $p_{r_1|m}$ of Eq. 8.23 on the value of m is plotted in Fig. 8.7 for several values of ρ. If $|\rho| \leqslant A$, the value of m that maximizes $p_{r_1|m}$ is ρ/A. On the other hand, ρ/A is not an allowable value of m if $|\rho| > A$. It is apparent from Fig. 8.7 that when $|m|$ is bounded by 1 the maximum-likelihood receiver sets

$$\hat{m} = \begin{cases} +1; & \rho > A \\ \dfrac{\rho}{A}; & -A \leqslant \rho \leqslant A \\ -1; & \rho < -A. \end{cases} \tag{8.29}$$

Such a receiver is diagrammed in Fig. 8.8a; it differs from the unbounded receiver of Fig. 8.5 only by the inclusion of a saturating transducer.

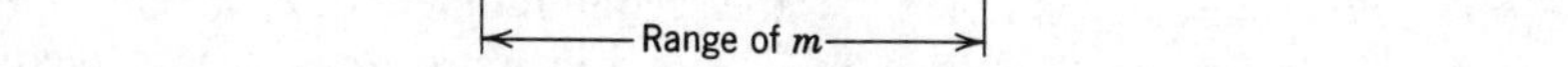

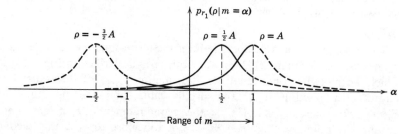

Figure 8.7 Dependence of the likelihood function on the value of m, for several values of ρ.

$$p_{r_1}(\rho \mid m = \alpha) = \frac{1}{\sqrt{\pi \mathcal{N}_0}} \exp\left[-\frac{(\rho - \alpha A)^2}{\mathcal{N}_0}\right].$$

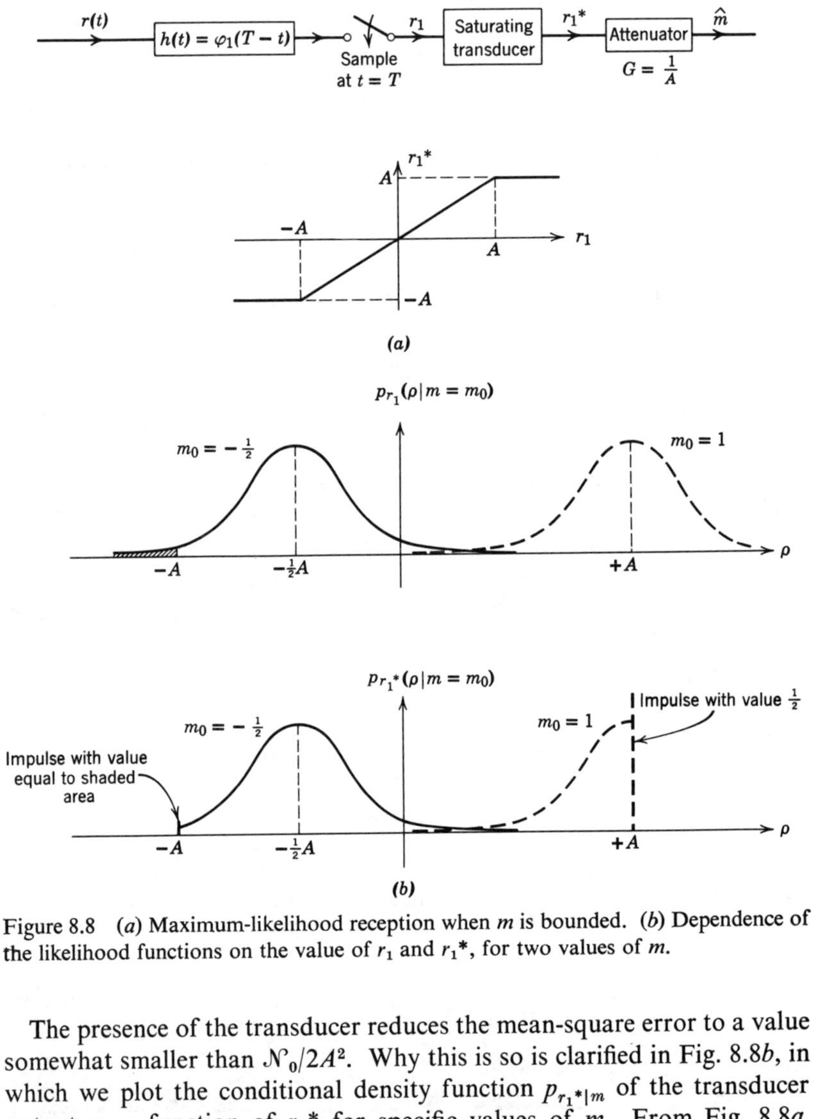

Figure 8.8 (*a*) Maximum-likelihood reception when m is bounded. (*b*) Dependence of the likelihood functions on the value of r_1 and $r_1{}^*$, for two values of m.

The presence of the transducer reduces the mean-square error to a value somewhat smaller than $\mathcal{N}_0/2A^2$. Why this is so is clarified in Fig. 8.8*b*, in which we plot the conditional density function $p_{r_1{}^*|m}$ of the transducer output as a function of $r_1{}^*$ for specific values of m. From Fig. 8.8*a*, $\mathrm{E}[(m - \hat{m})^2 \mid m = m_0]$ is $1/A^2$ times the second moment of $p_{r_1{}^*}(\ \mid m = m_0)$ around the point m_0A. When m_0 is not too close to ± 1, this second moment is substantially equal to $\mathcal{N}_0/2$, the variance of $p_{r_1|m}$. As m_0 approaches ± 1, however, the second moment of $p_{r_1{}^*}(\ \mid m = m_0)$ around m_0A decreases: when $m_0 = +1$, only negative values of the relevant noise component n_1 contribute any error at all. The conditional mean-square error is then approximately

$$\mathrm{E}[(m - \hat{m})^2 \mid m = 1] \approx \frac{1}{2}\left(\frac{1}{A^2}\right)\left(\frac{\mathcal{N}_0}{2}\right).$$

Because the over-all mean-square error

$$\mathrm{E}[(m - \hat{m})^2]$$

is obtained by averaging $\mathrm{E}[(m - \hat{m})^2 \mid m = m_0]$ with respect to p_m, one implication is that maximum-likelihood reception always produces

$$\overline{\epsilon^2} \leqslant \frac{\mathcal{N}_0}{2A^2}, \tag{8.30}$$

in which the equality holds if and only if m is unbounded. A second implication, however, is that bounding m does not reduce $\overline{\epsilon^2}$ materially unless p_m concentrates nearly unit probability within intervals of length $(1/A)\sqrt{\mathcal{N}_0/2}$ or so adjacent to the end points $m = \pm 1$. Unless this condition on p_m is met, we have

$$\overline{\epsilon^2} \approx \frac{\mathcal{N}_0}{2A^2} \tag{8.31a}$$

$$\frac{\mathcal{S}}{\mathcal{N}} \approx \frac{2\bar{E}_m}{\mathcal{N}_0}, \tag{8.31b}$$

and the effect of the transducer on $\overline{\epsilon^2}$ is negligible.

In most cases knowledge that $|m| < 1$ may safely be ignored; that is, the saturating transducer may be omitted from the receiver without substantially degrading system performance. On the other hand, a priori knowledge that p_m approximates the degenerate form

$$p_m(\alpha) = \tfrac{1}{2}[\delta(\alpha - 1) + \delta(\alpha + 1)]$$

should *not* be ignored. In this extreme case, for example, it is clear from Fig. 8.9 that the attainable mean-square error is $4Q(A\sqrt{2/\mathcal{N}_0})$, which is very much less than $\mathcal{N}_0/2A^2$ when $2A^2/\mathcal{N}_0$ is large. We do not treat degenerate p_m henceforth and therefore consider only those receivers that do not incorporate a saturating transducer. It is convenient to refer to these receivers as "maximum-likelihood" even when p_m is bounded. For such receivers Eqs. 8.31 are exact rather than approximate.

Bounded density functions are important in systems having linear modulation because they permit a bound to be placed on the peak signal energy. Since $s_m(t) = mA\,\varphi_1(t)$, the restriction $|m| \leqslant 1$ guarantees that the actual signal energy $E_m = m^2A^2$ is less than or equal to A^2 for all m.

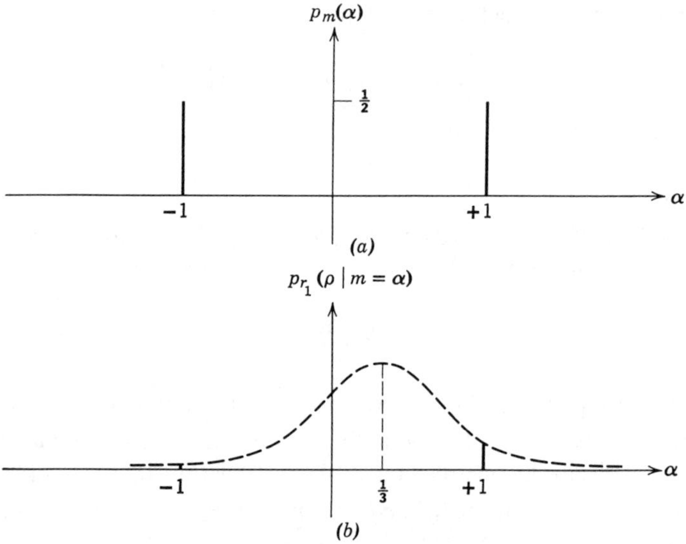

Figure 8.9 A degenerate case. As shown in (b) for the case $\rho = \frac{1}{3}A$, the likelihood function is larger for $\alpha = +1$ than for $\alpha = -1$ unless $\rho \leqslant 0$. The conditional probability of this event when $m = +1$ is $Q(A\sqrt{2/\mathcal{N}_0})$ and the resulting error is $(m - \hat{m})^2 = [1 - (-1)]^2 = 4$.

We hereafter denote the *maximum signal energy* by E_s. For linear modulation with $|m| \leqslant 1$ and maximum-likelihood (but transducerless) receivers, we have

$$E_s = A^2$$

and

$$\overline{\epsilon^2} = \frac{\mathcal{N}_0}{2A^2} = \frac{\mathcal{N}_0}{2E_s}. \tag{8.32}$$

If p_m is uniform over $[-1, 1]$, then $\overline{m^2} = \frac{1}{3}$ and

$$\bar{E}_m = \overline{m^2}A^2 = \frac{E_s}{3}. \tag{8.33}$$

The average signal energy then differs from the peak signal energy by approximately 4.8 db.

Sequences of Input Parameters

The single-input parameter analysis and the mean-square-error result of Eq. 8.32 both extend trivially to the communication of a sequence (vector) of continuous random parameters, say

$$\mathbf{m} = (m_1, m_2, \ldots, m_K), \tag{8.34}$$

provided that successive components of **m** modulate orthogonal waveforms. Consider, for example, the communication system illustrated in Fig. 8.10*a*: the transmitted signal is given by

$$s_{\mathbf{m}}(t) = A \sum_{k=1}^{K} m_k\, \varphi_k(t), \tag{8.35}$$

in which the $\{\varphi_k(t)\}$ are assumed to be orthonormal. The communication objective is to produce at the receiver output an appropriate estimate, $\hat{\mathbf{m}}$,

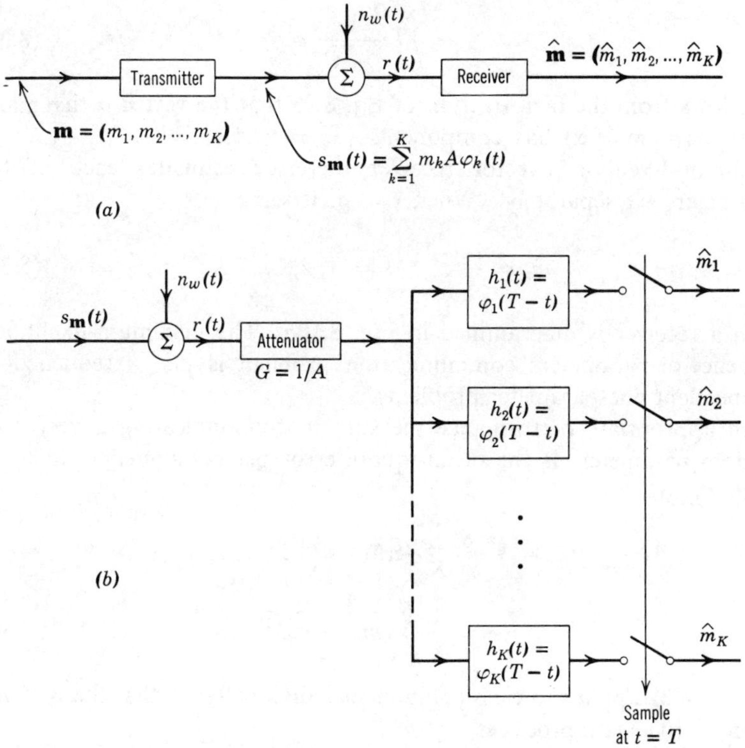

Figure 8.10 Communication of a random vector by means of linear modulation and maximum-likelihood reception.

of the transmitter input vector, in which

$$\hat{\mathbf{m}} \triangleq (\hat{m}_1, \hat{m}_2, \ldots, \hat{m}_K). \tag{8.36}$$

As usual, the relevant part of the received signal $r(t) = s_{\mathbf{m}}(t) + n_w(t)$ is incorporated in the vector

$$\mathbf{r} = (r_1, r_2, \ldots, r_K), \tag{8.37a}$$

with components

$$r_k \triangleq \int_{-\infty}^{\infty} r(t)\, \varphi_k(t)\, dt$$

$$= m_k A + n_k; \qquad k = 1, 2, \ldots, K. \tag{8.37b}$$

Since $n_w(t)$ is white Gaussian noise, the likelihood function is

$$p_{\mathbf{r}}(\boldsymbol{\rho} \mid \mathbf{m} = \boldsymbol{\alpha}) = \frac{1}{(\pi \mathcal{N}_0)^{K/2}}\, e^{-|\boldsymbol{\rho} - \boldsymbol{\alpha} A|^2/\mathcal{N}_0}$$

$$= \prod_{k=1}^{K} \frac{1}{\sqrt{\pi \mathcal{N}_0}}\, e^{-(\rho_k - \alpha_k A)^2/\mathcal{N}_0}. \tag{8.38}$$

It follows from the factorization of Eq. 8.38 that the vector $\boldsymbol{\alpha}$ that maximizes $p_{\mathbf{r}}(\boldsymbol{\rho} \mid \mathbf{m} = \boldsymbol{\alpha})$ has components $\{\alpha_k = \rho_k/A\}$, $k = 1, 2, \ldots, K$. A maximum-likelihood vector receiver therefore estimates each of the parameters m_k separately. When $\mathbf{r} = \boldsymbol{\rho}$, it sets

$$\hat{m}_k = \frac{\rho_k}{A}; \qquad k = 1, 2, \ldots, K. \tag{8.39}$$

Such a receiver is diagrammed in Fig. 8.10*b*. The maximum-likelihood sequence-of-parameters communication problem is just a sequence of independent one-parameter problems.

An appropriate performance measure in communicating a vector of random parameters is the mean-square error per component, which we again denote $\overline{\epsilon^2}$:

$$\overline{\epsilon^2} \triangleq \frac{1}{K}\, \mathrm{E}[|\mathbf{m} - \hat{\mathbf{m}}|^2]$$

$$= \frac{1}{K} \sum_{k=1}^{K} \overline{(m_k - \hat{m}_k)^2}. \tag{8.40a}$$

But Eq. 8.32 applies to each component individually, so that the receiver of Fig. 8.10*b* again produces

$$\overline{\epsilon^2} = \frac{\mathcal{N}_0}{2A^2}. \tag{8.40b}$$

As before, the noise performance is essentially minimax when the energy-to-noise ratio is high.

It is apparent from Eq. 8.39 that the maximum-likelihood receiver always acts as if the $\{m_k\}$ were statistically independent, since then only r_k is relevant to the estimation of m_k. On the other hand, significantly improved noise performance can be obtained if it is known in advance that the $\{m_k\}$ are tightly dependent. For example, if it is known that $m_k = m_1$,

$k = 2, 3, \ldots, K$, a nonmaximum-likelihood receiver can be designed to exploit this knowledge.

Sequence-of-parameter communication systems, such as the pulse amplitude modulation (abbreviated PAM) system of Fig. 8.10, are frequently encountered in practice. When the $\{\varphi_k(t)\}$ are given by

$$\varphi_k(t) = \begin{cases} \sqrt{\dfrac{2}{T}} \cos 2\pi\left(f_0 + \dfrac{k}{T}\right)t; & 0 \leqslant t \leqslant T, \quad f_0T = \text{an integer} \\ 0; & \text{elsewhere} \end{cases}$$

and the $\{m_k\}$ are provided by different input sources, the system is called *frequency-multiplexed*. If the inputs $\{m_k\}$ are chosen by sequencing

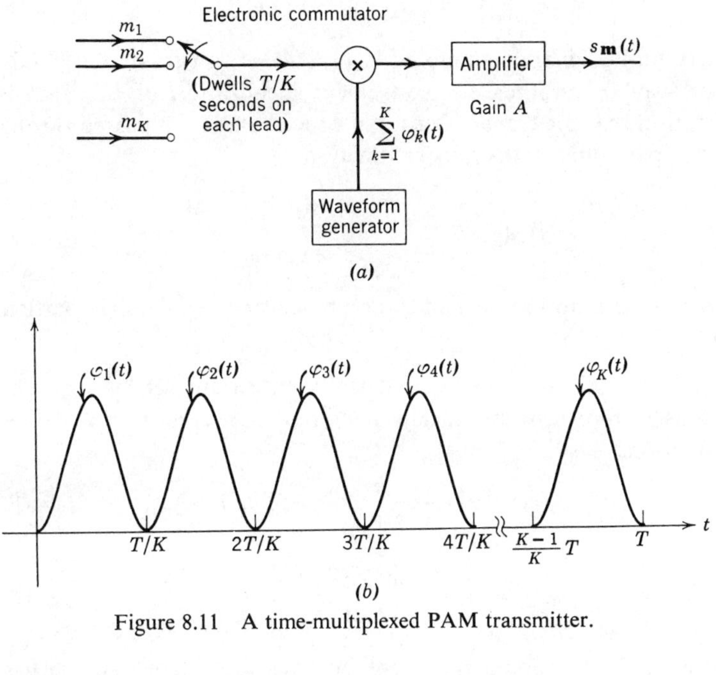

Figure 8.11 A time-multiplexed PAM transmitter.

through the different input sources, as shown in Fig. 8.11, and the orthogonal waveforms $\{\varphi_k(t)\}$ are translated pulses of duration T/K,

$$\varphi_k(t) = \varphi\left(t - \frac{k}{T}\right),$$

the system is called *time-multiplexed*. The receivers used in conjunction with these systems are usually close approximations to the maximum-likelihood receiver.

Waveform Inputs

The problem of communicating a random waveform is intimately related to the sequence-of-parameters problem. That such a relation should exist is immediately apparent whenever the transmitter input process, say $m(t)$, can be adequately described by an equation of the form

$$m(t) = \sum_{k=1}^{K} m_k\, \psi_k(t), \tag{8.41a}$$

in which $\{\psi_k(t)\}$ is an appropriate set of orthonormal functions.† Then $m(t)$ is specified by the random vector

$$\mathbf{m} = (m_1, m_2, \ldots, m_K). \tag{8.41b}$$

Every input signal encountered in practice is constrained in bandwidth in one way or another. A convenient idealization of this fact is the assumption that the transmitter input process has been passed through an ideal lowpass filter with transfer function

$$W_m(f) \triangleq \begin{cases} 1; & -W_m < f < W_m \\ 0; & \text{elsewhere.} \end{cases} \tag{8.42}$$

When this assumption is made, the choice of the $\{\psi_k(t)\}$ is particularly simple.

Sampling. We now show that an appropriate set of orthonormal functions to represent any ideally bandlimited process $m(t)$ is defined by the equations

$$\psi_k(t) \triangleq \psi\left(t - \frac{k}{2W_m}\right); \qquad k \text{ an integer}, \tag{8.43a}$$

$$\psi(t) \triangleq \sqrt{2W_m}\, \frac{\sin 2\pi W_m t}{2\pi W_m t}. \tag{8.43b}$$

Proof of the foregoing statement involves four steps. In the first we observe that

$$\psi(t) = \frac{1}{\sqrt{2W_m}}\, w_m(t), \tag{8.44a}$$

† It can be shown[21] by methods beyond the scope of this text that any random process can be satisfactorily represented over a finite time interval $[0, T]$ by means of Eq. 8.41a with $\{m_k\}$ that are uncorrelated. We need only take K/T to be large enough and choose an appropriate set $\{\psi_k(t)\}$. The resulting representation is referred to as a Karhunen-Loeve expansion.

where $w_m(t)$ is the impulse response of $W_m(f)$:

$$w_m(t) = \int_{-\infty}^{\infty} W_m(f) e^{j2\pi ft}\, df$$
$$= \int_{-W_m}^{W_m} \cos 2\pi ft\, df = 2W_m \frac{\sin 2\pi W_m t}{2\pi W_m t}. \tag{8.44b}$$

Thus $\psi(t)$, hence each of the $\{\psi_k(t)\}$, is an ideally bandlimited waveform. Several of the $\{\psi_k(t)\}$ are sketched in Fig. 8.12.

In the second step we observe that the $\{\psi_k(t)\}$ are in fact orthonormal: the Fourier transform of $\psi_k(t)$ is

$$\Psi_k(f) = e^{-j2\pi fk/(2W_m)} \frac{1}{\sqrt{2W_m}} W_m(f),$$

from which it follows by Parseval's theorem that

$$\int_{-\infty}^{\infty} \psi_l(t)\, \psi_k(t)\, dt = \int_{-\infty}^{\infty} \Psi_l(f)\, \Psi_k^*(f)\, df$$
$$= \frac{1}{2W_m} \int_{-W_m}^{W_m} e^{j\pi f(k-l)/W_m}\, df = \delta_{lk}. \tag{8.45}$$

In the third step, we invoke the *sampling theorem*, which is proved in Appendix 8A. The theorem may be stated:

Theorem. If $z(t)$ is any finite energy waveform whose Fourier transform is identically zero for $|f| \geqslant W_m$, then

$$z(t) = \sum_{k=-\infty}^{\infty} z_k\, \psi_k(t), \tag{8.46a}$$

in which, of course,

$$z_k = \int_{-\infty}^{\infty} z(t)\, \psi_k(t)\, dt; \qquad \textit{for all } k. \tag{8.46b}$$

A remarkable property of the $\{\psi_k(t)\}$ is that each z_k may also be evaluated simply by observing $z(t)$ at the instant $t = k/2W_m$: letting $Z(f)$ denote the Fourier transform of $z(t)$, we have

$$\int_{-\infty}^{\infty} z(t)\, \psi(t-\tau)\, dt = \int_{-\infty}^{\infty} Z(f) \left[\frac{1}{\sqrt{2W_m}} W_m(f) e^{-j2\pi f\tau}\right]^* df$$
$$= \frac{1}{\sqrt{2W_m}} \int_{-W_m}^{W_m} Z(f) e^{+j2\pi f\tau}\, df = \frac{1}{\sqrt{2W_m}} z(\tau),$$

so that setting $\tau = k/2W_m$ yields

$$z_k = \frac{1}{\sqrt{2W_m}} z\left(\frac{k}{2W_m}\right), \qquad \text{for all } k. \tag{8.47}$$

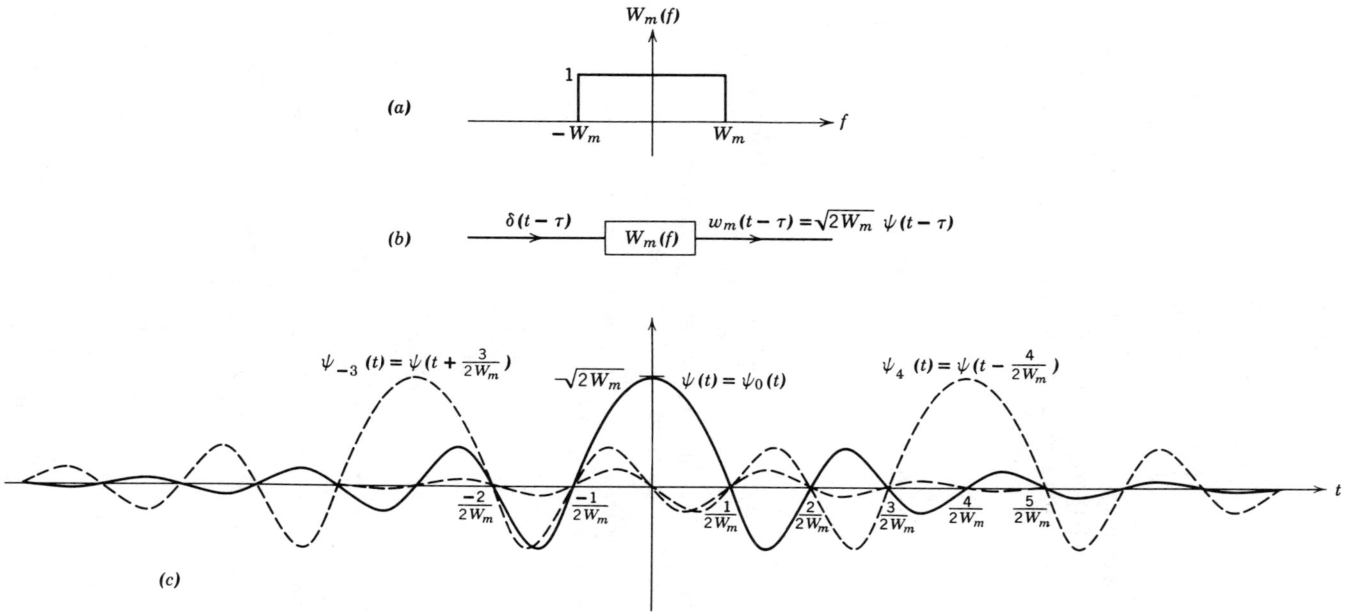

Figure 8.12 Impulse response of an ideal band-limited filter.

Because of this unique characteristic, the $\{\psi_k(t)\}$ of Eq. 8.43 are called *sampling functions*. Equations 8.44 and 8.47 imply that the sampling theorem may also be written in the form

$$z(t) = \sum_{k=-\infty}^{\infty} z\left(\frac{k}{2W_m}\right)\frac{\sin 2\pi W_m(t - k/2W_m)}{2\pi W_m(t - k/2W_m)}. \tag{8.48}$$

(A check on Eq. 8.48 may be obtained by setting $t = i/2W_m$.)

The fourth step in verifying the appropriateness of adopting the sampling functions for the $\{\psi_k(t)\}$ involves extending the sampling theorem to ideally bandlimited random processes. Since the sample functions of such

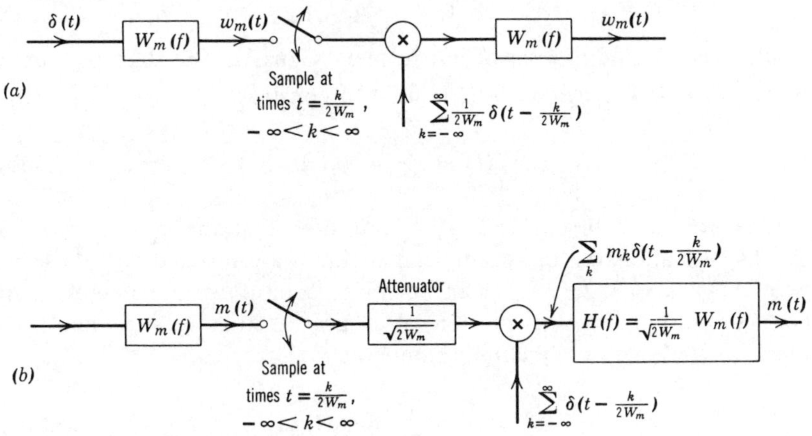

Figure 8.13 Implementation of the sampling theorem. From Eq. 8.44, the impulse response of the filter $H(f)$ is $h(t) = \psi(t)$.

a process do not in general contain finite energy, the sampling theorem as originally stated does not apply to them.

The key to the extension is to note that the theorem *does* apply to the impulse response of the first filter in Fig. 8.13*a*. But the following cascade of sampler, impulse-train modulator, and second filter is simply a realization of the mathematical construct of Eq. 8.48. Thus the over-all circuit of Fig. 8.13*a* is equivalent to just the first filter $W_m(f)$ alone.

It is clear that passing a random process $m(t)$ through a second filter $W_m(f)$ does not affect the sample functions when $m(t)$ has already been passed once through such a filter. Thus Eq. 8.46a applies also to any random process $m(t)$ that is already bandlimited to $[-W_m, W_m]$. From Fig. 8.13*b*, it is evident that

$$m(t) = \sum_{k=-\infty}^{\infty} m_k\, \psi_k(t), \tag{8.49a}$$

in which each random variable m_k is given by

$$m_k = \int_{-\infty}^{\infty} m(t)\, \psi_k(t)\, dt = \frac{1}{\sqrt{2W_m}}\, m\left(\frac{k}{2W_m}\right). \tag{8.49b}$$

For the special case in which $m(t)$ is filtered white Gaussian noise with power density $\mathcal{M}_0/2$, the $\{m_k\}$ are statistically independent zero-mean Gaussian random variables with variance $\mathcal{M}_0/2$. Conversely, a stationary Gaussian process, say $n(t)$, with

$$\mathcal{S}_n(f) = \begin{cases} \dfrac{\mathcal{N}_0}{2}; & |f| < W_m \\ 0; & \text{elsewhere}, \end{cases} \tag{8.50a}$$

results when an infinite set of independent Gaussian variables $\{n_k\}$, each having $\overline{n_k} = 0$ and $\overline{n_k^2} = \mathcal{N}_0/2$, is used to construct

$$n(t) = \sum_{k=-\infty}^{\infty} n_k\, \psi_k(t). \tag{8.50b}$$

It is not, of course, necessary to presume that the process $m(t)$ in Eq. 8.49 is stationary. For example, if we know a priori that only those m_k with index $k = 1, 2, \ldots, K$ can be nonzero or if we are interested in communicating only the portion of a process that is attributable to these $\{m_k\}$, we may use the finite summation

$$m(t) = \sum_{k=1}^{K} m_k\, \psi_k(t) \tag{8.51a}$$

to represent the transmitter input. Alternatively, with a shift of time origin, we would have

$$m(t) = \sum_{k=-(K-1)/2}^{(K-1)/2} m_k\, \psi_k(t); \qquad K \text{ an odd integer.} \tag{8.51b}$$

Such nonstationary processes are completely defined once the joint probability density function of the coefficients, $p_{\mathbf{m}}$, is specified. It is convenient to view the infinite summation of Eq. 8.49a as the limit of Eq. 8.51b as K becomes infinite.

The assumption that a process $m(t)$ is ideally bandlimited is not completely realistic. We have already noted in Chapter 7 that the filter $W_m(f)$ is physically unrealizable. On the other hand, as discussed in Appendix 8A, the approximation entailed in such an assumption is a good one in most cases of engineering interest and, of course, for any given process becomes increasingly accurate as W_m is increased. We therefore assume that $m(t)$ can be adequately represented by means of Eq. 8.51 and the sampling functions of Eq. 8.43. The issues of maximum-likelihood reception remain unchanged, however, if the orthonormal set $\{\psi_k(t)\}$ is defined in some other suitable way.

Performance measure. A convenient performance measure to use in the communication of nonstationary random processes having the form of Eq. 8.51a is the mean-integral-square error between $m(t)$ and the receiver output process, say $\hat{m}(t)$, normalized by the number of samples, K. We define

$$\overline{\epsilon^2} = \frac{1}{K}\,\mathrm{E}\left[\int_{-\infty}^{\infty} [m(t) - \hat{m}(t)]^2\, dt\right]. \tag{8.52}$$

We now show that the adoption of this performance criterion implies equivalence between the problems of random waveform and random vector communication.

When the receiver knows a priori that $m(t)$ is bandlimited to $[-W_m, W_m]$, it is clear that $\hat{m}(t)$ should also be bandlimited. Indeed, if $m_0(t) = \sum_{k=1}^{K} m_{0k}\, \psi_k(t)$ denotes the particular sample function of $m(t)$ that is actually transmitted and $\hat{m}_0(t)$ denotes the resulting receiver estimate when any particular noise disturbance occurs, the integrated square error is

$$\begin{aligned}\epsilon_0^{\,2} &\triangleq \int_{-\infty}^{\infty} [m_0(t) - \hat{m}_0(t)]^2\, dt \\ &= \int_{-\infty}^{\infty} |M_0(f) - \hat{M}_0(f)|^2\, df.\end{aligned} \tag{8.53}$$

Here $M_0(f)$ and $\hat{M}_0(f)$ are the Fourier transforms of $m_0(t)$ and $\hat{m}_0(t)$, respectively. Evidently, $\epsilon_0^{\,2}$ must be increased if $\hat{M}_0(f)$ is nonzero outside $[-W_m, W_m]$, so that no loss in performance is entailed if the receiver estimate $\hat{m}_0(t)$ is also represented by the sampling theorem:

$$\hat{m}_0(t) = \sum_{k=-\infty}^{\infty} \hat{m}_{0k}\, \psi_k(t), \tag{8.54a}$$

$$\hat{m}_{0k} = \frac{1}{\sqrt{2W_m}}\, \hat{m}_0\!\left(\frac{k}{2W_m}\right). \tag{8.54b}$$

Next, using Eq. 4.58b to write

$$\epsilon_0^{\,2} = \sum_{k=-\infty}^{\infty} (m_{0k} - \hat{m}_{0k})^2,$$

we observe that $\epsilon_0^{\,2}$ is further reduced by setting to zero all $\hat{m}_{0k}$ outside the range $1 \leqslant k \leqslant K$ spanned by $m_0(t)$. The result is

$$\epsilon_0^{\,2} = \sum_{k=1}^{K} (m_{0k} - \hat{m}_{0k})^2. \tag{8.55}$$

Since Eq. 8.55 is valid for any $m_0(t)$ and any particular noise disturbance, the receiver output process can always be written

$$\hat{m}(t) = \sum_{k=1}^{K} \hat{m}_k \, \psi_k(t). \tag{8.56}$$

Averaging Eq. 8.55 over the message and noise processes yields

$$\overline{\epsilon^2} = \frac{1}{K} \sum_{k=1}^{K} \overline{(m_k - \hat{m}_k)^2}. \tag{8.57}$$

Equation 8.57 implies that the problem of communicating $m(t)$ is indeed equivalent to the problem of communicating $\mathbf{m} = (m_1, m_2, \ldots, m_K)$. We may use any convenient set of orthonormal functions $\{\varphi_k(t)\}$ and transmit

$$s_{\mathbf{m}}(t) = \sum_{k=1}^{K} m_k A \varphi_k(t). \tag{8.58}$$

The receiver then estimates $\mathbf{m}$ by a vector $\hat{\mathbf{m}} = (\hat{m}_1, \hat{m}_2, \ldots, \hat{m}_K)$, and constructs $\hat{m}(t)$ in accordance with Eq. 8.56.

Receiver implementation. The structure of the maximum-likelihood receiver follows directly from Eq. 8.56 and Fig. 8.10. An over-all system is illustrated in Fig. 8.14. From Eqs. 8.40 and 8.57 the mean-square error per component at the receiver output is

$$\overline{\epsilon^2} = \frac{1}{K} \sum_{k=1}^{K} \frac{\mathcal{N}_0}{2A^2} = \frac{\mathcal{N}_0}{2A^2}. \tag{8.59}$$

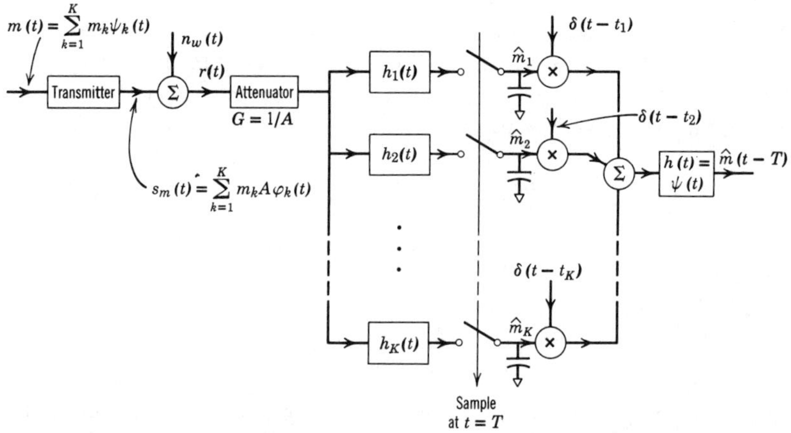

Figure 8.14 Maximum-likelihood receiver for linearly modulated waveform communication (K finite). The capacitors "hold" the output $\hat{m}_k$ from each matched filter, $h_k(t) = \varphi_k(T - t)$, until time $t_k = T + k/2W_m$, $k = 1, 2, \ldots, K$.

In accordance with Eq. 8.58, the average energy transmitted per sample is

$$\bar{E}_m \triangleq \mathrm{E}\left[\frac{1}{K}\int_{-\infty}^{\infty} [s_{\mathrm{m}}(t)]^2\, dt\right]$$

$$= A^2 \frac{1}{K}\sum_{k=1}^{K} \overline{m_k^{\,2}}. \tag{8.60a}$$

Whenever

$$\overline{m_k^{\,2}} = \overline{m^2}; \quad \text{all } k,$$

we have

$$\bar{E}_m = \overline{m^2} A^2. \tag{8.60b}$$

The signal-to-noise ratio per component then also agrees with the single-input-variable result of Eq. 8.25b,

$$\frac{\mathcal{S}}{\mathcal{N}} = \frac{2\bar{E}_m}{\mathcal{N}_0}. \tag{8.60c}$$

Similarly, if $|m_k| \leqslant 1$, all k, then $A^2 = E_s$, the peak transmitted energy per sample, and Eq. 8.59 becomes

$$\overline{\epsilon^2} = \frac{\mathcal{N}_0}{2E_s}. \tag{8.60d}$$

The special case in which the $\{\varphi_k(t)\}$ of Eq. 8.58 are chosen to be just the sampling functions $\{\psi_k(t)\}$ themselves is shown in Fig. 8.15*a*. If we assume that

$$m(t) = \sum_{k=-K/2}^{K/2} m_k\, \psi_k(t), \tag{8.61a}$$

then

$$s_{\mathrm{m}}(t) = A\, m(t). \tag{8.61b}$$

In accordance with Fig. 8.13, in the limit $K \to \infty$ the maximum-likelihood receiver becomes just an attenuator followed by an ideal filter. The resulting system is illustrated in Fig. 8.15*b*; it is apparent that the receiver-output noise is stationary, with

$$\overline{n^2(t)} = \overline{[m(t) - \hat{m}(t)]^2} = \frac{\mathcal{N}_0 W_m}{A^2}. \tag{8.61c}$$

Note that in the stationary case the mean-square error per sample and $\overline{n^2(t)}$ are related by

$$\overline{\epsilon^2} = \frac{\overline{n^2(t)}}{2W_m}. \tag{8.61d}$$

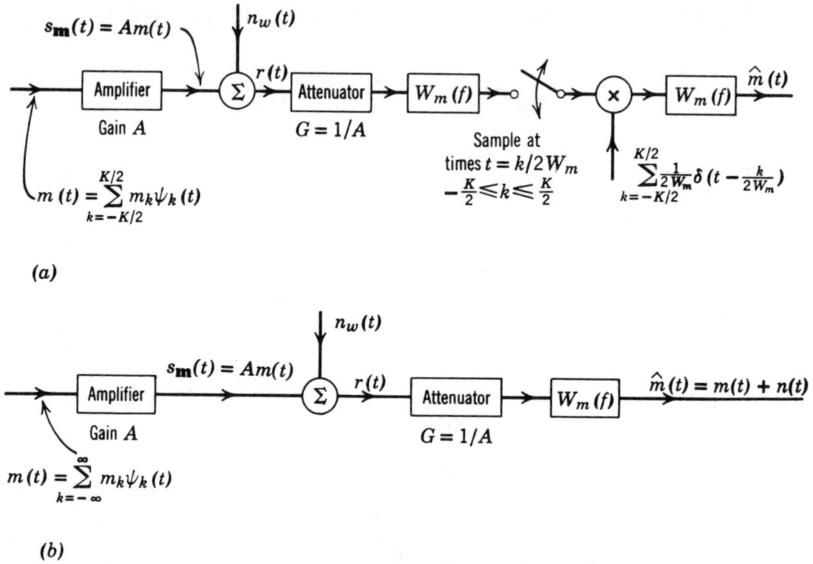

Figure 8.15 Maximum likelihood receiver when the transmitter is an amplifier: (*a*) K finite; (*b*) K infinite.

The minimum mean-square error receiver when $m(t)$ is a stationary Gaussian process with power density function

$$\mathcal{S}_m(f) = \begin{cases} \dfrac{\mathcal{M}_0}{2}; & -W_m < f < W_m \\ 0; & \text{elsewhere} \end{cases} \tag{8.62a}$$

is very similar to the maximum-likelihood receiver. Since

$$\mathcal{R}_m(\tau) = \mathcal{M}_0 W_m \frac{\sin 2\pi W_m \tau}{2\pi W_m \tau}, \tag{8.62b}$$

each of the normalized samples $\{(2W_m)^{-1/2} m(k/2W_m)\}$, k an integer, has variance $\sigma^2 = \mathcal{M}_0/2$, and all such samples are statistically independent. The receiver may therefore estimate each sample independently and recombine the sample estimates in accordance with Eq. 8.56. It follows from Eq. 8.19 that the minimum mean-square error receiver consists of an ideal filter $W_m(f)$ and an attenuator with gain

$$G = \frac{1/A}{1 + \mathcal{N}_0/2\bar{E}_m}, \tag{8.63a}$$

in which

$$\bar{E}_m = \frac{A^2}{2W_m}\overline{m^2(t)} = \frac{\mathcal{M}_0}{2}A^2 \tag{8.63b}$$

is the mean transmitted energy per sample. Such a receiver is shown in Fig. 8.16. It may be verified directly that the resulting mean-square error is

$$\overline{[m(t) - \hat{m}(t)]^2} = \frac{\mathcal{N}_0 W_m}{A^2} \frac{1}{1 + \mathcal{N}_0/2\bar{E}_m}, \tag{8.63c}$$

which differs from Eq. 8.61c only by the factor $(1 + \mathcal{N}_0/2\bar{E}_m)^{-1}$. In Eq. 8.63c we have chosen not to denote $[m(t) - \hat{m}(t)]$ by $n(t)$ because the error is not a message-independent additive term; as observed in connection with Eq. 8.27, the fact that the gain, G, in Eq. 8.63a is not $1/A$ implies an error that depends on $m(t)$ as well as on the actual receiver input noise.

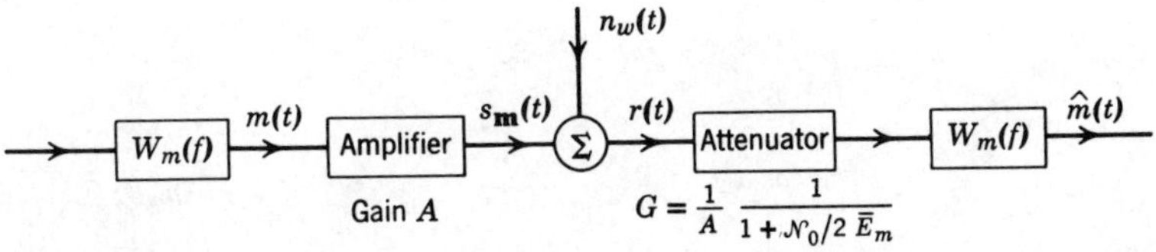

Figure 8.16 Minimum mean-square-error receiver when $m(t)$ is a stationary band-limited Gaussian process.

The receiver of Fig. 8.16 is minimax and yields the same mean-square error for any $m(t)$ having the power density function of Eq. 8.62a, regardless of whether or not $m(t)$ is Gaussian. An alternate derivation of the structure of this receiver, using minimum mean-square-error linear filter theory, is provided in Appendix 8B.

Although the instrumentation of the transmitter and receiver is simplified for $K \to \infty$ by using the sampling functions for the $\{\varphi_k(t)\}$ in communicating $m(t)$, there is often good reason not to do so. For example, a PAM time-multiplexed voice communication system is built by choosing the $\{\varphi_k(t)\}$ to be evenly spaced pulses whose duration is much less than the sampling interval $1/2W_m$. Several voice channels can then be interleaved in time onto a single transmission facility. A PAM system may also be frequency-multiplexed.

Frequency translation. Another reason for using a different set of orthonormal functions than the $\{\psi_k(t)\}$ for transmission purposes concerns the propagation of electromagnetic energy: an audio-frequency process $m(t)$ must be converted into a radio-frequency (RF) process if radio transmission is to be used. Functions $\{\varphi_k(t)\}$ can be chosen whose spectra lie in a convenient frequency range.

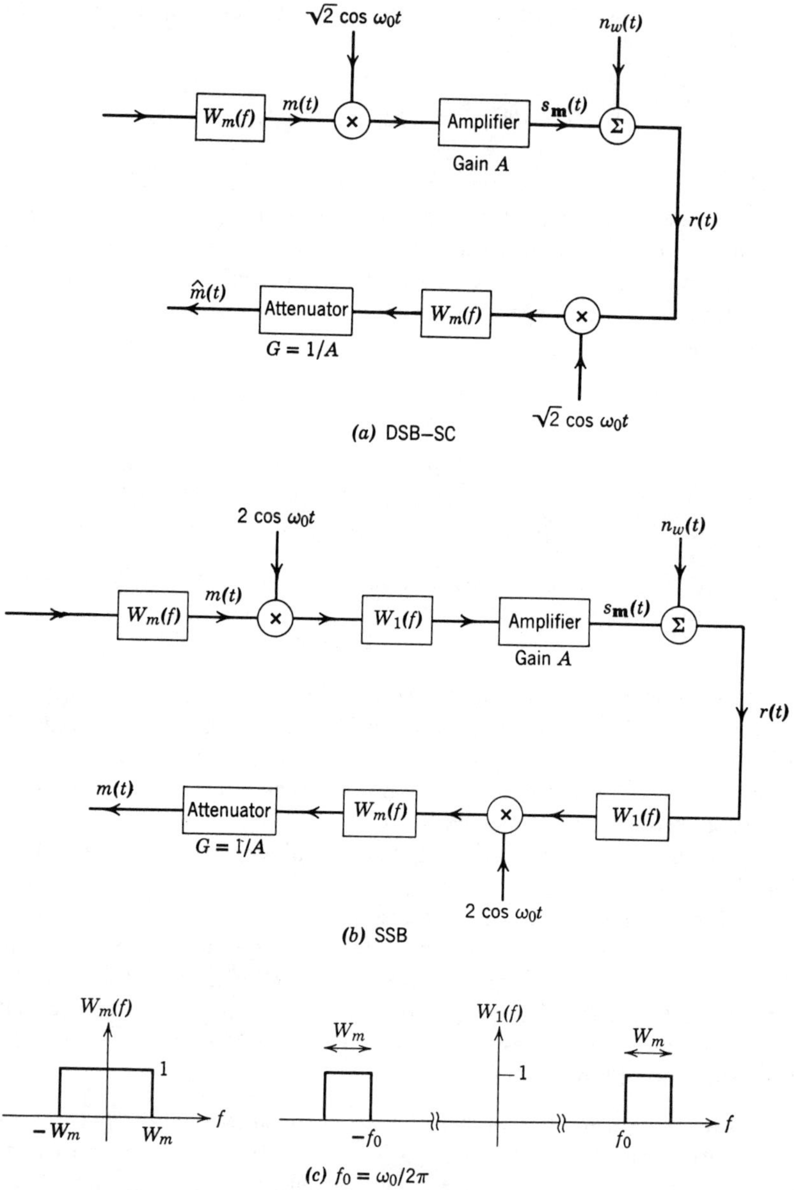

Figure 8.17 Frequency translation and maximum-likelihood reception ($K \to \infty$).

Just as in the discrete communication discussion in Section 7.2, a more usual way to achieve this same objective is to multiply $m(t)$ against a sine-wave carrier, say $\sqrt{2}\cos 2\pi f_0 t$, in which $f_0 > W_m$ is the desired radio frequency. The signal is then heterodyned back down to baseband at the receiver. As in Chapter 7, either DSB-SC or SSB transmission may be used. The corresponding maximum likelihood receivers are illustrated in Figs. 8.17*a* and *b* for the limiting case $K \to \infty$. Both receivers produce stationary output noise with variance

$$\overline{n^2(t)} = \frac{\mathcal{N}_0 W_m}{A^2}.$$

With waveform-input communication, a third common type of linear modulation is standard double sideband (DSB), in which the transmitted signal process is

$$s_m(t) = A[1 + a\, m(t)]\sqrt{2}\cos \omega_0 t. \tag{8.64a}$$

Thus an additive carrier term $A\sqrt{2}\cos \omega_0 t$ is transmitted in addition to the input-signal-dependent term. A typical sample function of $s_m(t)$ is shown in Fig. 8.18*a*. We require that the parameter a, called the "modulation index," be chosen so that

$$1 + a\, m(t) > 0; \qquad \text{for all } t. \tag{8.64b}$$

Thus the envelope of $s_m(t)$ is a replica of $m(t)$, which is the reason for using DSB.

As shown in Fig. 8.18*b* the maximum-likelihood receiver in this case again multiplies the received signal by $\sqrt{2}\cos \omega_0 t$ and passes the product through a lowpass filter $W_m(f)$. The output is

$$r_1(t) = A + aA\, m(t) + n_1(t), \tag{8.64c}$$

in which $n_1(t)$ is lowpass Gaussian with power density $\mathcal{N}_0/2$ over the band $[-W_m, W_m]$. The dc component of $r_1(t)$, caused by the carrier, is removed by a blocking capacitor. After scaling, the output waveform is

$$\hat{m}(t) \approx m(t) + \frac{n_1(t)}{aA}, \tag{8.64d}$$

in which equality is not exact because the blocking capacitor also effects $n_1(t)$ and (possibly) $m(t)$. The output noise, $n(t) \approx n_1(t)/aA$, is stationary, but now has variance

$$\overline{n^2(t)} \approx \frac{\mathcal{N}_0 W_m}{a^2 A^2}. \tag{8.64e}$$

From the point of view of the energy transmitted in the modulation sidebands, DSB, SSB, and DSB-SC all yield equivalent noise performance; but the carrier $\sqrt{2}\, A \cos \omega_0 t$ in DSB consumes transmitted energy which does not contribute to improving the estimate $\hat{m}(t)$. It follows that DSB suffers at least a 3-db†, and usually a 6-db or greater, disadvantage over DSB-SC and SSB, the value depending on the modulation index and the waveshape of the modulating signal.

In spite of this disadvantage, DSB is in common use. The primary reason is that with DSB an inexpensive receiver which utilizes an envelope

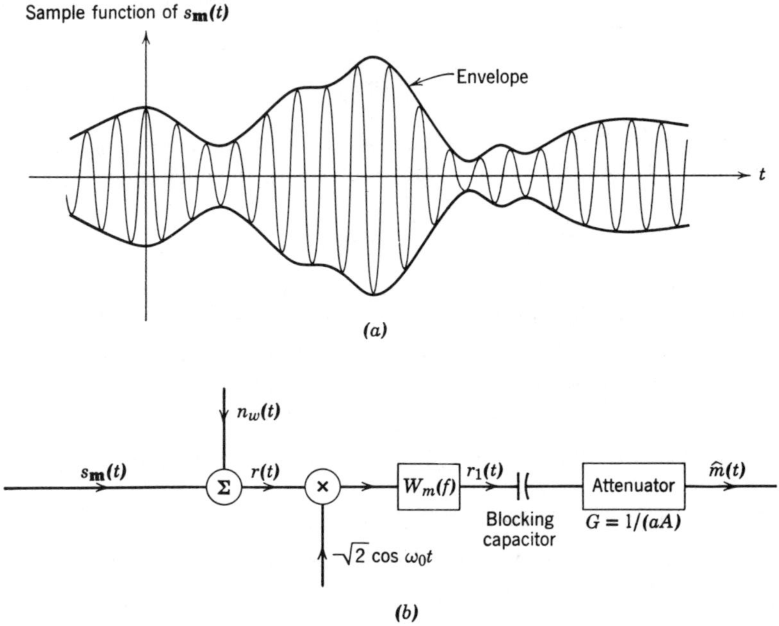

Figure 8.18 DSB modulation and maximum-likelihood reception ($K \to \infty$); $s_{\mathbf{m}}(t) = A[1 + am(t)]\sqrt{2}\cos\omega_0 t$.

detector can be used for demodulation. Such an incoherent receiver is nonideal when the phase is known, but, as in the discrete case, the performance loss is small when $\mathcal{N}_0 W_m$ is much less than A^2. Also, the DSB signal is the easiest to generate at high power levels.

As discussed in Chapter 7, SSB has the advantage over DSB-SC or DSB of reduced bandwidth. Moreover, if the phase relations between the two sidebands in DSB-SC or DSB are disturbed during propagation, interference effects result in the demodulator output. Finally, the apparent requirement for phase-lock between the SSB modulator and demodulator oscillators is not essential in voice communication systems: the human ear is relatively insensitive to received phase and even a few cycles of

† We assume, as usual, that $m(t)$ itself contains no dc component.

slowly drifting frequency offset is tolerable. As a result of these considerations, SSB finds frequent application in systems for operation over long-range, high-frequency channels, whereas DSB is used extensively in medium-frequency broadcast transmission. DSB-SC has found little application in audio communication.

8.2 TWISTED MODULATION

Linear modulation and maximum-likelihood reception produce a mean-square error that can be reduced in general only by increasing the transmitted energy. For white Gaussian noise with power density $\mathcal{N}_0/2$ we have seen that

$$\overline{\epsilon^2} = \frac{\mathcal{N}_0}{2A^2} = \frac{\overline{m^2}}{2\bar{E}_m/\mathcal{N}_0}.$$

If we no longer require that the modulation be linear, it is sometimes possible to decrease $\overline{\epsilon^2}$ for a given $\overline{m^2}$ without increasing the transmitted energy. In particular, various *twisted modulation* schemes such as pulse-position modulation (PPM) and frequency modulation (FM) can yield an $\overline{\epsilon^2}$ smaller than that afforded by linear modulation.

Geometrical Considerations

Insight into the advantages and limitations of twisted modulation can be gained by investigating the geometrical relations between the channel noise and $\overline{\epsilon^2}$. Let us begin by reconsidering the locus of the transmitted vector,

$$\mathbf{s}_m = mA\boldsymbol{\varphi}_1, \tag{8.65}$$

when a single bounded random variable is communicated by means of linear modulation. As illustrated in Fig. 8.19, we may think of the transmitter amplifier as "stretching" the interval $[-1, +1]$ over which p_m is nonzero onto the larger interval $[-A, +A]$ in the signal space. The stretching is uniform in the sense that

$$\left|\frac{d\mathbf{s}_m}{dm}\right| = A; \qquad \text{for all } m. \tag{8.66}$$

The effect of maximum-likelihood reception is to undo the stretching performed by the transmitter. The receiver's attenuator in Fig. 8.19 compresses the message component Am from the interval $[-A, +A]$ back onto the interval $[-1, +1]$. If $m = m_0$ and $r_1 = \rho$, the relevant error in transmission is

$$n_1 = \rho - m_0A. \tag{8.67a}$$

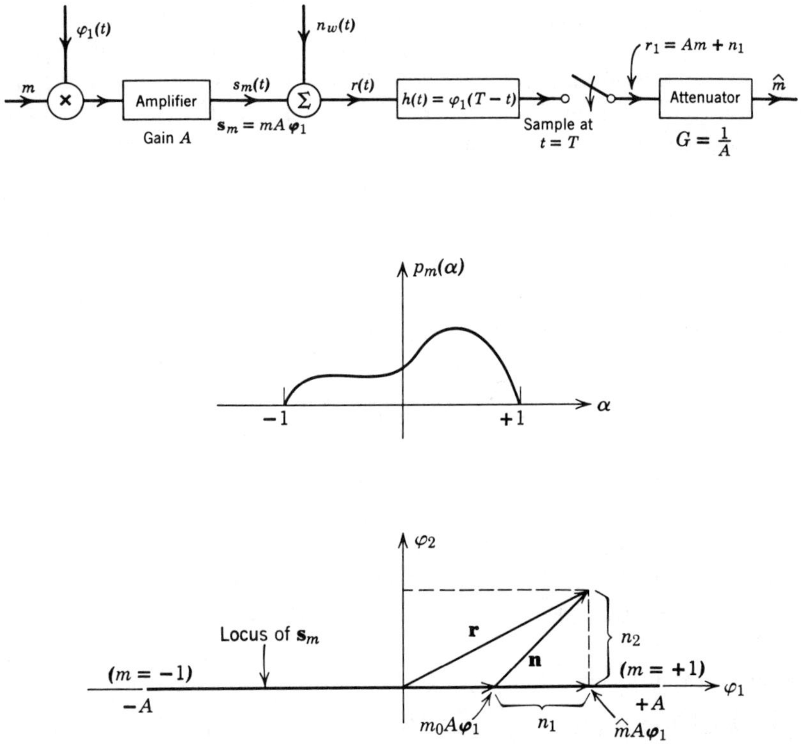

Figure 8.19 Geometrical relations with linear modulation and a single random variable input. The maximum-likelihood receiver chooses $\hat{m}$ to minimize $|\mathbf{r} - \mathbf{s}_m|$.

With no saturating transducer in the receiver, undoing the stretch compresses the transmission error by the inverse factor $1/A$ and again yields

$$\overline{\epsilon^2} = \overline{\left(\frac{n_1}{A}\right)^2} = \frac{\mathcal{N}_0}{2A^2}. \tag{8.67b}$$

The dependence of $\overline{\epsilon^2}$ on the amount of stretching at the transmitter can be made explicit by defining

$$S \triangleq \left|\frac{d\mathbf{s}_m}{dm}\right|, \tag{8.68}$$

where S is independent of m by virtue of Eq. 8.66. We call S the *stretch factor*. In terms of S, Eq. 8.67b is written

$$\overline{\epsilon^2} = \frac{\mathcal{N}_0/2}{S^2}. \tag{8.69}$$

Twisted loci. The stretch factor plays a fundamental role in determining the mean-square error for twisted as well as for linear modulation schemes. Before considering specific systems, it is convenient to illustrate the basic concept of twisted modulation in a simple situation. Consider again the single-input-parameter communication system of Fig. 8.1 and for simplicity assume that the transmitter signal space is a two-dimensional plane with Euclidean axes φ_1 and φ_2. This implies that the transmitted signal vector, as a function of the input parameter m, has the form

$$\mathbf{s}_m = a_1(m)\boldsymbol{\varphi}_1 + a_2(m)\boldsymbol{\varphi}_2, \tag{8.70a}$$

where the $\{\boldsymbol{\varphi}_i\}$ are orthonormal vectors. The corresponding signal waveform is

$$s_m(t) = a_1(m)\,\varphi_1(t) + a_2(m)\,\varphi_2(t), \tag{8.70b}$$

with

$$\int_{-\infty}^{\infty} \varphi_i(t)\,\varphi_j(t)\,dt = \delta_{ij}. \tag{8.70c}$$

If the modulation system is to be linear, the coefficients $\{a_i(m)\}$ must be linear functions of m. But let us now broaden the class of systems under consideration and allow the $\{a_i(m)\}$ to be arbitrary differentiable functions. In general, these functions may be complicated, as in the case of the example shown in Fig. 8.20: the curved (twisted) line represents the locus—described parametrically by the $\{a_i(m)\}$—of the tip of the vector $\mathbf{s}_m$ as a function of m. We again assume that m is constrained to the

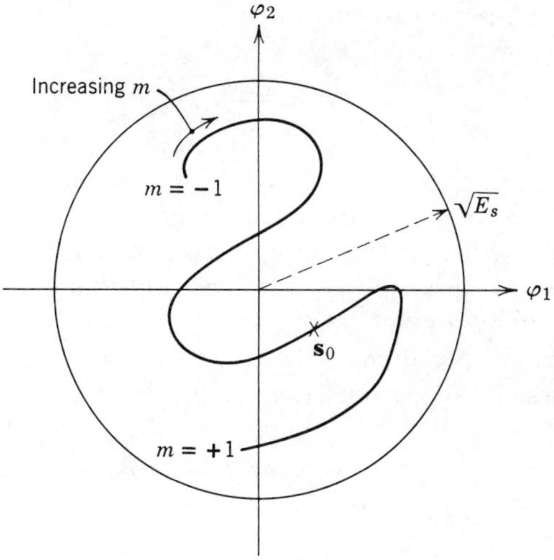

Figure 8.20 A twisted signal locus.

interval $[-1, +1]$. If we impose a constraint on the maximum transmitted energy such that $|\mathbf{s}_m|^2 \leqslant E_s$, the locus (called the "signal curve") must be contained within a circle of radius $\sqrt{E_s}$.

The signal curve by itself is not a complete description of the mapping $m \to \mathbf{s}_m$; we must also specify how the tip of $\mathbf{s}_m$ moves along the locus as a function of m. It is convenient to assume that equal increments in m correspond to equal increments in distance measured along the signal curve; that is,

$$\left|\frac{d\mathbf{s}_m}{dm}\right| = \frac{L}{2}; \qquad \text{for all } m, \tag{8.71a}$$

where L is the total length of the locus traversed by $\mathbf{s}_m$ as m increases from -1 to $+1$. Then we can again define a stretch factor S that is independent of m:

$$S \triangleq \left|\frac{d\mathbf{s}_m}{dm}\right| = \frac{L}{2}. \tag{8.71b}$$

It is apparent that this definition is consistent with that given previously in the case of linear modulation. We shall see later that the *uniform stretch* assumption of Eq. 8.71a is justified by minimax considerations, as well as by considerations of mathematical simplicity.

Weak noise suppression. We now show that the mean-square error for a maximum-likelihood receiver, given the signaling scheme of Fig. 8.20 and an additive white Gaussian noise disturbance whose power density is sufficiently weak, is approximated by

$$\overline{\epsilon^2} = \frac{\mathcal{N}_0/2}{S^2}. \tag{8.72}$$

Why this is so is clarified in Fig. 8.21, which represents an enlargement of a small section of Fig. 8.20 around some point $\mathbf{s}_0$. We assume that the input parameter m has the value m_0 corresponding to $\mathbf{s}_m = \mathbf{s}_0$ and that the noise density is so small that with high probability the received point $\mathbf{r}$ will lie close to $\mathbf{s}_0$. By this we mean that within a circle of radius equal to several standard deviations of the noise, centered on $\mathbf{r}$, the signal curve may be accurately approximated by a single straight line tangent to $\mathbf{s}_m$ at $\mathbf{s}_0$:

$$\mathbf{s}_m \approx \mathbf{s}_0 + (m - m_0)\,\dot{\mathbf{s}}_0 \tag{8.73a}$$

with

$$\dot{\mathbf{s}}_0 \triangleq \left.\frac{d\mathbf{s}_m}{dm}\right|_{m=m_0} \tag{8.73b}$$

Under these conditions the "local" reception problem is geometrically the same as the problem with linear modulation. With white Gaussian noise the maximum likelihood receiver chooses $\hat{m}$ as that value of m for which $|\mathbf{r} - \mathbf{s}_m|$ is minimum. Given sufficiently weak noise, we may neglect the probability that $\mathbf{r}$ will lie closer to some other fold of the signal curve than to the section approximated by Eq. 8.73. In the vicinity

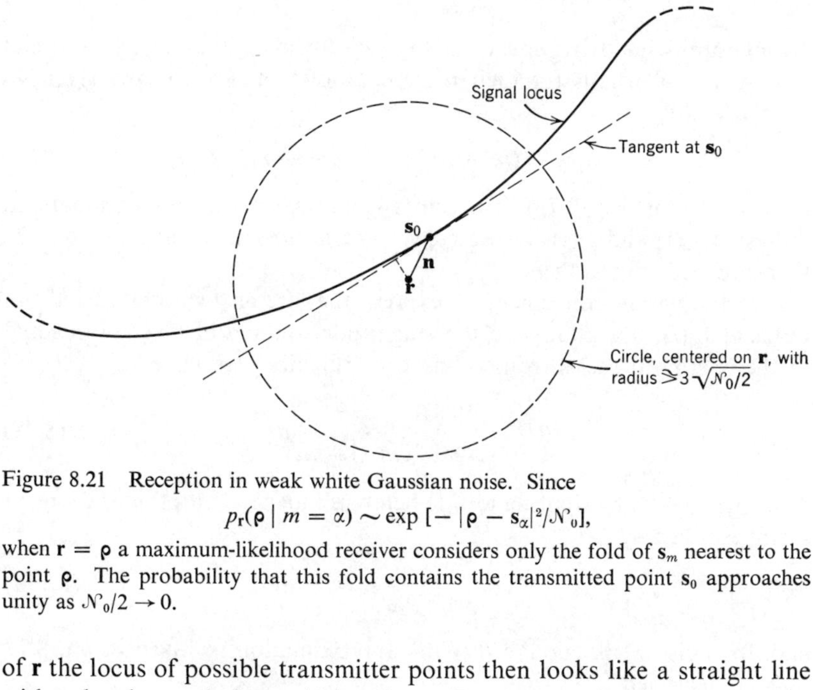

Figure 8.21 Reception in weak white Gaussian noise. Since

$$p_{\mathbf{r}}(\boldsymbol{\rho} \mid m = \alpha) \sim \exp[-|\boldsymbol{\rho} - \mathbf{s}_\alpha|^2/\mathcal{N}_0],$$

when $\mathbf{r} = \boldsymbol{\rho}$ a maximum-likelihood receiver considers only the fold of $\mathbf{s}_m$ nearest to the point $\boldsymbol{\rho}$. The probability that this fold contains the transmitted point $\mathbf{s}_0$ approaches unity as $\mathcal{N}_0/2 \to 0$.

of $\mathbf{r}$ the locus of possible transmitter points then looks like a straight line with a local stretch factor $|\dot{\mathbf{s}}_0|$. Hence Eq. 8.69 applies locally, and the conditional mean-square error is

$$E[(m - \hat{m})^2 \mid m = m_0] \approx \frac{\mathcal{N}_0/2}{|\dot{\mathbf{s}}_0|^2}. \tag{8.74}$$

Invoking the condition

$$|\dot{\mathbf{s}}_0| = S; \qquad \text{for all } m_0 \tag{8.75}$$

and averaging with respect to p_m yields Eq. 8.72. (We again neglect end truncation effects that reduce the error in the vicinity of $m = \pm 1$.)

Next, we show that the validity of Eq. 8.72 for weak noise is *not* restricted to transmitted waveforms $s_m(t)$ defined (as in Eq. 8.70) on only two $\{\varphi_i(t)\}$; $s_m(t)$ may involve any number of orthonormal functions. For noise that is weak enough the conditional mean-square error when $m = m_0$ depends *only* on the behavior of $s_m(t)$ in the neighborhood of m_0.

In this vicinity it is true for any differentiable $s_m(t)$ that

$$s_m(t) \approx s_0(t) + (m - m_0)\dot{s}_0(t); \qquad |m - m_0| \ll 1, \tag{8.76a}$$

with

$$s_0(t) \triangleq s_m(t)\big|_{m=m_0}, \tag{8.76b}$$

$$\dot{s}_0(t) \triangleq \frac{\partial}{\partial m} s_m(t)\bigg|_{m=m_0} \tag{8.76c}$$

By a Gram-Schmidt argument the two waveforms $s_0(t)$ and $\dot{s}_0(t)$ require at most two dimensions for their representation. Hence, for any given m_0 we can write

$$\mathbf{s}_m \approx \mathbf{s}_0 + (m - m_0)\dot{\mathbf{s}}_0; \qquad |m - m_0\,| \ll 1, \tag{8.77}$$

in which (as in Eq. 8.73) the vectors $\mathbf{s}_0$ and $\dot{\mathbf{s}}_0$ are two-dimensional and represent $s_0(t)$ and $\dot{s}_0(t)$, respectively. The argument leading to Eq. 8.72 then proceeds unchanged.

It is frequently convenient to express the stretch factor S directly in terms of $s_m(t)$. Recalling that the magnitude squared of a vector is equal to the energy in the corresponding time function, we have

$$|\dot{\mathbf{s}}_0|^2 = \int_{-\infty}^{\infty} \left[\frac{\partial s_m(t)}{\partial m}\right]^2_{m=m_0} dt. \tag{8.78}$$

Thus, whenever the right-hand side below is independent of m, the stretch factor is given by

$$S^2 = \int_{-\infty}^{\infty} \left[\frac{\partial}{\partial m} s_m(t)\right]^2 dt \tag{8.79a}$$

and, for noise weak enough that the approximation involved in Eq. 8.77 may be neglected,

$$\overline{\epsilon^2} = \frac{\mathcal{N}_0/2}{S^2}. \tag{8.79b}$$

Threshold. For any given differentiable signal curve such as that of Fig. 8.20 it is always possible to take the noise density $\mathcal{N}_0/2$ small enough that the linearized analysis leading to Eq. 8.79 will be valid. For a given signal space with $\mathcal{N}_0/2$ and E_s fixed, however, it is definitely *not* true that the mean-square error can be made as small as we like by making the length of the signal curve, hence the stretch factor S, larger and larger.

The nature of the fallacy is clarified in Fig. 8.22. If we confine the signal curve to a sphere of fixed dimensionality and of radius $\sqrt{E_s}$, the length of the curve cannot be increased indefinitely without folds of the curve necessarily lying closer and closer together. On the other hand, as indicated by the dotted circles, the conditional probability density function of the received vector **r**, given $\mathbf{s} = \mathbf{s}_0$, is spherically symmetric about the transmitted point $\mathbf{s}_0$, with contours of equal probability density that depend only on the noise density $\mathcal{N}_0/2$. It follows that when L is increased indefinitely while E_s and $\mathcal{N}_0/2$ are held constant a situation must ultimately be reached in which several different folds of the signal curve will pass through regions in which $p_{\mathbf{r}|\mathbf{s}}$ is significantly large. When this happens, the signal curve in the vicinity of the

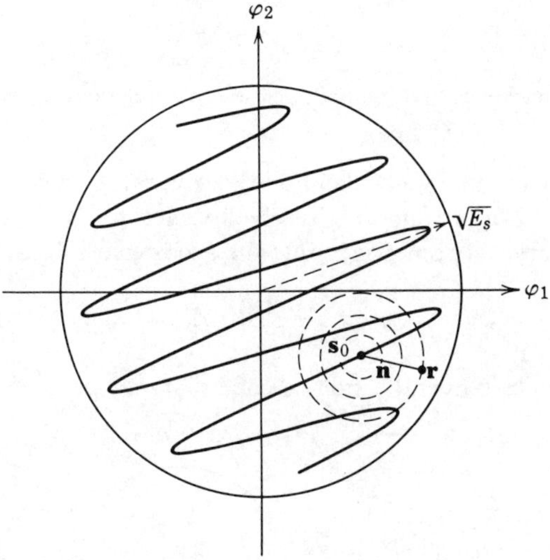

Figure 8.22 A signal locus for which the linearized analysis is invalid. The radii of the dotted circles are $\sqrt{\mathcal{N}_0/2}$, $2\sqrt{\mathcal{N}_0/2}$, $3\sqrt{\mathcal{N}_0/2}$. Because

$$p_{\mathbf{r}}(\boldsymbol{\rho} \mid m = m_0) = p_{\mathbf{n}}(\boldsymbol{\rho} - \mathbf{s}_0) \sim \exp\left[-|\boldsymbol{\rho} - \mathbf{s}_0|^2/\mathcal{N}_0\right],$$

the probability is high that **r** will lie closer to some other fold of $\mathbf{s}_m$ than to $\mathbf{s}_0$.

set of vectors that is likely to be received when $\mathbf{s}_0$ is transmitted can no longer be well approximated by the single straight line of Eq. 8.77, and the linearized analysis leading to Eq. 8.79 becomes invalid.

Actually, we can see that not only the linearized analysis but also the entire communication system will break down under these conditions. For example, the output $\hat{m}$ from a maximum-likelihood receiver jumps discontinuously as the received vector **r** moves continuously across the boundary separating the points $\boldsymbol{\rho}_1$ and $\boldsymbol{\rho}_2$ in Fig. 8.23. Crossing such a boundary essentially "disconnects" $\hat{m}$ from the actual transmitter input, $m = m_0$.

Furthermore, the breakdown of the communication system under these conditions is *fundamentally unavoidable* and cannot be ascribed merely to

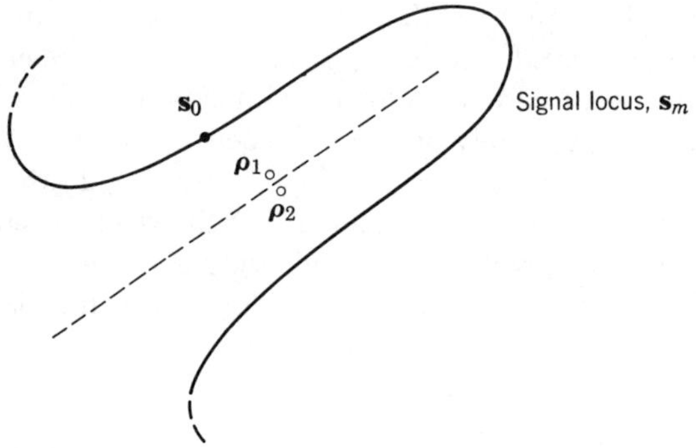

Figure 8.23 When $\mathbf{r} = \boldsymbol{\rho}_1$, the point of $\mathbf{s}_m$ closest to $\mathbf{r}$ is close to $\mathbf{s}_0$, hence $\hat{m}$ is close to m_0. This is not true when $\mathbf{r} = \boldsymbol{\rho}_2$.

some deficiency in maximum-likelihood reception. Consider the situation shown in Fig. 8.24*a* in which the received vector $\boldsymbol{\rho}$ lies close to two folds of the signal curve. From Bayes rule the a posteriori density function of m is

$$p_m(\alpha \mid \mathbf{r} = \boldsymbol{\rho}) = \frac{p_m(\alpha)}{p_{\mathbf{r}}(\boldsymbol{\rho})}\, p_{\mathbf{r}}(\boldsymbol{\rho} \mid m = \alpha). \tag{8.80}$$

As long as $p_m(\alpha) > 0$ over the intervals of α that map onto these folds of $\mathbf{s}_m$,

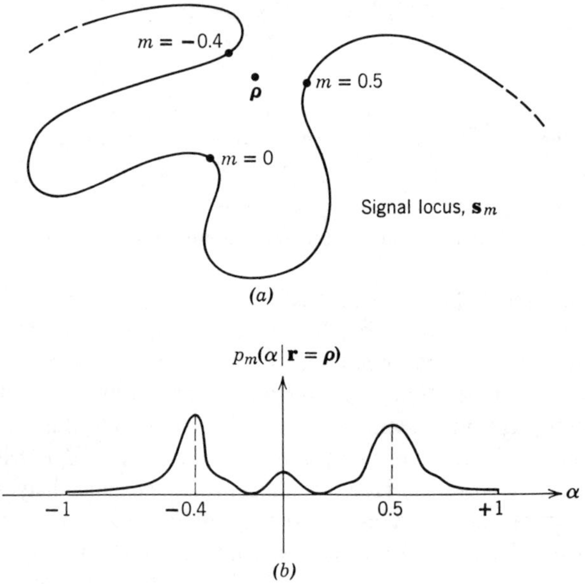

Figure 8.24 A received vector leading to a multimodal a posteriori density function. Setting $\hat{m}$ equal to either -0.4 or $+0.5$ is likely to incur a large error. Moreover, the conditional mean in (*b*) lies in a region of low probability density, so that the minimum mean-square estimate of m is even less credible.

some region of $\boldsymbol{\rho}$ must exist between the folds for which $p_m(\alpha \mid \mathbf{r} = \boldsymbol{\rho})$ is violently multimodal—that is, $p_m(\alpha \mid \mathbf{r} = \boldsymbol{\rho})$ contains two or more disconnected local maxima of substantially the same magnitude, as shown in Fig. 8.24*b*.

When $p_{m|\mathbf{r}}$ is violently multimodal (or, even worse, unimodal around some value of m disconnected from the transmitted value), we say that the received signal is *anomalous*. In an anomalous situation it is not possible for *any* receiver to make a meaningful estimate of m; this follows from the fact that the a posteriori density function $p_{m|\mathbf{r}}$, which contains all data relevant to any estimate of m, is either fundamentally ambiguous or is misleading. The objective of minimizing the mean-square error, for example, is clearly inappropriate.

With maximum-likelihood reception, the received signal is anomalous whenever $\mathbf{r}$ lies closer to a different fold of the signal curve than it does to the one containing the transmitted point $\mathbf{s}_0$. It is evident geometrically that for a signal space of fixed dimensionality anomalous receptions are bound to occur with increasing probability in either of two circumstances:

1. When $\mathcal{N}_0/2$ and E_s are fixed and the stretch factor S is increased.
2. When the twisted signal curve (hence E_s and S) is fixed and $\mathcal{N}_0/2$ is increased.

When the conditions are such that the probability of an anomaly exceeds some tolerable level, say 10^{-4} or less (determined by the application), we say that *threshold* is exceeded and do not expect communication to be acceptable. Unfortunately, although the mean-square error provided by a twisted and uniformly stretched modulation system is reduced by the factor $1/S^2$ when the noise density $\mathcal{N}_0/2$ is small enough, the noise density at which threshold is exceeded (for fixed E_s and fixed signal-space dimensionality) is in general small when S is large. In practice, it is necessary to design a twisted-modulation system to achieve a satisfactory compromise between these two effects.

The arguments and concepts we have discussed have been illustrated for convenience in a two-dimensional signal space. The same considerations and conclusions apply to signal curves defined on any finite dimensional space. In the sequel, we also apply these ideas to signal loci that require an infinite number of dimensions for a complete description. (The observation in Chapter 4 that a finite number of dimensions is always sufficient for describing a signal set applies only to discrete systems with a finite number of messages.) It is shown in Section 8.4 that the probability of anomaly must increase as the length L of the signal locus increases whenever $E_s/\mathcal{N}_0$ is held fixed, even though the dimensionality of the locus is increased simultaneously

Minimax considerations. We now show that the uniform-stretch assumption of Eq. 8.71b leads to a maximum-likelihood receiver that is "weak-noise minimax." By this we mean that uniform stretch minimizes the mean-square error produced by maximum-likelihood reception when p_m is chosen most adversely and $\mathcal{N}_0/2$ is very small.

Let us assume that a particular twisted signal locus of length L (such as that shown in Fig. 8.20) is given but that we are free to specify the "velocity" with which $\mathbf{s}_m$ moves along this locus as a function of m; that is to say, assume that we can vary $S(m) \triangleq |d\mathbf{s}_m/dm|$, subject to the constraint that $\mathbf{s}_m$ moves from one end of the locus to the other as m ranges over $[-1, +1]$:

$$\int_{-1}^{1} S(m)\, dm = L. \tag{8.81}$$

Our problem is to assign $S(m)$, as a function of m, in such a way that $\overline{\epsilon^2}$ is minimax when $\mathcal{N}_0/2$ is small.

The case in which $S(m) = L/2$ for all $|m| \leqslant 1$ has already been investigated. From Eq. 8.79 we have

$$\overline{\epsilon^2} = \frac{\mathcal{N}_0/2}{(L/2)^2}, \tag{8.82}$$

a result that is valid for *any* bounded p_m as long as the error-truncation effects near $m = \pm 1$ are negligible. Thus the weak-noise minimax assertion may be proved by considering every other assignment of $S(m)$ and showing that the resulting value of $\overline{\epsilon^2}$ is larger than $2\mathcal{N}_0/L^2$ when p_m is chosen to be as disadvantageous as possible.

If the stretch is not uniform, there is some region along the locus over which $S(m)$ is minimum. The constraint of Eq. 8.81 implies that this minimum value, say S_{min}, must be less than $L/2$. If p_m is chosen so that almost unit probability is concentrated in the region corresponding to minimum $S(m)$, it follows from Eq. 8.74 that

$$\begin{aligned} \overline{\epsilon^2} &= \int_{-1}^{1} \mathrm{E}[(m - \hat{m})^2 \mid m = \alpha]\, p_m(\alpha)\, d\alpha \\ &\approx \frac{\mathcal{N}_0/2}{S_{\text{min}}^2} \\ &> \frac{\mathcal{N}_0/2}{(L/2)^2}, \end{aligned} \tag{8.83}$$

which completes the proof. An illustrative example is shown in Fig. 8.25.

The significance of this result is that, with weak enough noise, the minimax mean-square error when m is mapped onto any given signal locus is independent of the *shape* of that locus under the assumption of maximum-likelihood reception. It is only the *length* of the signal curve that counts. Hence, a preference for one locus of a given length over another of the same length must depend entirely on other factors; for example, on which curve has the larger threshold or on which curve is easier to generate and receive.

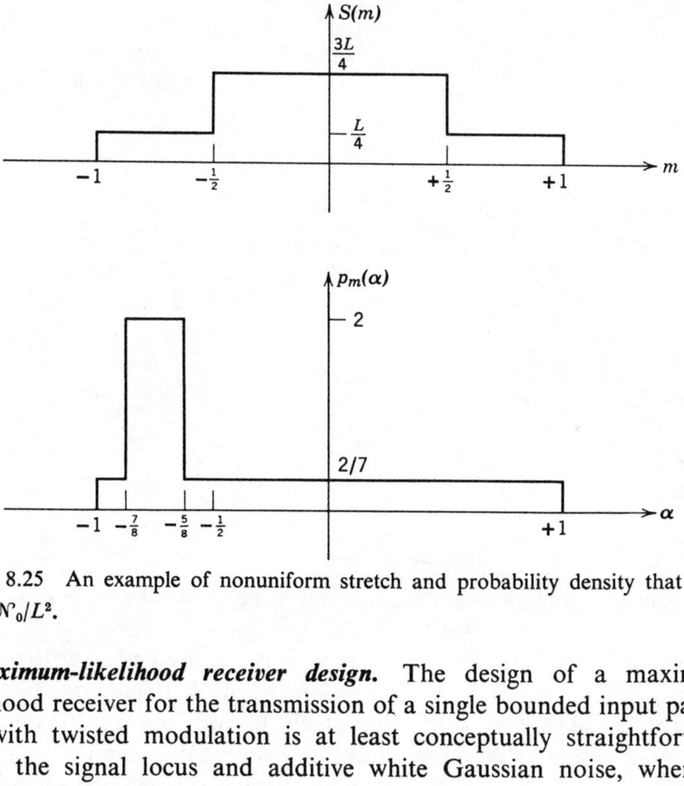

Figure 8.25 An example of nonuniform stretch and probability density that yields $\overline{\epsilon^2} > 2\mathcal{N}_0/L^2$.

Maximum-likelihood receiver design. The design of a maximum-likelihood receiver for the transmission of a single bounded input parameter with twisted modulation is at least conceptually straightforward. Given the signal locus and additive white Gaussian noise, when the received signal is $\rho(t)$ we have

$$
\begin{aligned}
p_{\mathbf{r}}(\boldsymbol{\rho} \mid m = \alpha) &\sim e^{-|\boldsymbol{\rho}-\mathbf{s}_\alpha|^2/\mathcal{N}_0} \\
&\sim \boldsymbol{\rho} \cdot \mathbf{s}_\alpha - \tfrac{1}{2}E_\alpha \\
&= \int_{-\infty}^{\infty} \rho(t)\, s_\alpha(t)\, dt - \tfrac{1}{2}E_\alpha,
\end{aligned} \tag{8.84}
$$

in which $\mathbf{s}_\alpha$—representing $s_\alpha(t)$—is the transmitted signal and $E_\alpha \triangleq |\mathbf{s}_\alpha|^2$ is the transmitted energy when $m = \alpha$. For a maximum likelihood decision

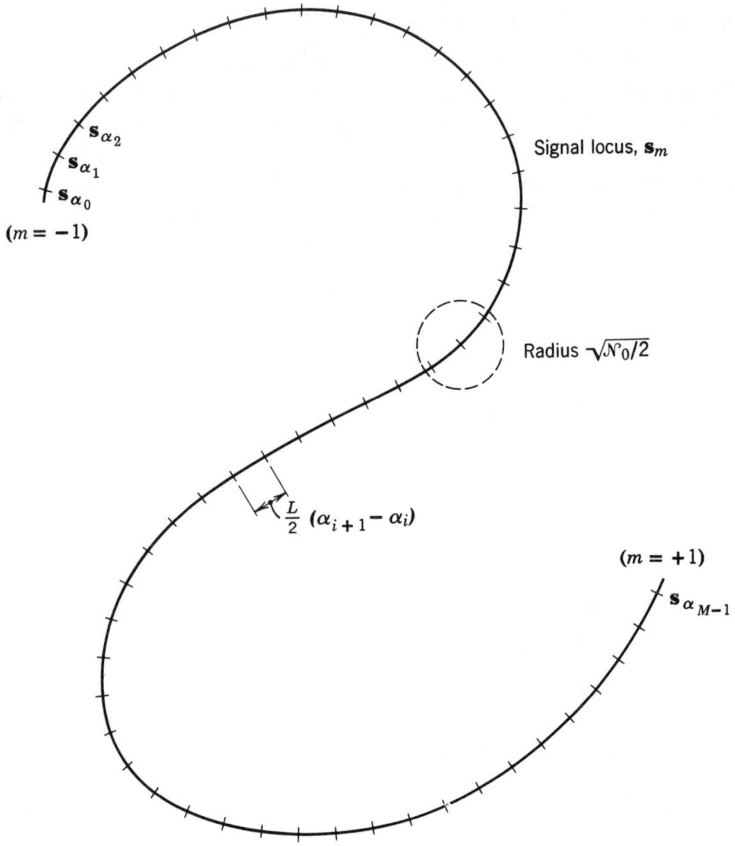

Figure 8.26 A discrete set of vectors $\{\mathbf{s}_{\alpha_i}\}$ that approximates the locus $\mathbf{s}_m$.

the received signal must be correlated against each member of the entire set of transmitter signals $\{s_\alpha(t)\}$, $-1 \leqslant \alpha \leqslant 1$; if E_α is independent of α, $\hat{m}$ is set equal to that value of α for which the correlation is maximum.

The maximum-likelihood receiver for *linear* modulation is a special case of the receiver implied by Eq. 8.84. With linear modulation $s_\alpha(t) = \alpha A\, \varphi(t)$, so that

$$\int_{-\infty}^{\infty} \rho(t)\, s_\alpha(t)\, dt - \tfrac{1}{2}E_\alpha = \alpha A \rho - \tfrac{1}{2}\alpha^2 A^2, \tag{8.85a}$$

in which

$$\rho \triangleq \int_{-\infty}^{\infty} \rho(t)\, \varphi(t)\, dt. \tag{8.85b}$$

As we have already noted, only a single correlator is needed. The receiver sets $\hat{m}$ equal to that value of α for which the right-hand side of Eq. 8.85a is maximum. Differentiating, we have

$$0 = A\rho - \alpha A^2\big|_{\alpha=\hat{m}},$$

hence

$$\hat{m} = \frac{\rho}{A}, \tag{8.85c}$$

as expected.

The implementation of a maximum-likelihood receiver for an *arbitrary* signal locus would involve an infinitum of correlators (or calculations), one for each value of α in the interval $[-1, +1]$. In general, of course, such a receiver cannot be built. One realizable approximation results from specifying a finite set of M points $\{\alpha_i\}$ equally spaced over $[-1, +1]$ and correlating the received signal against each of the corresponding M signals $\{s_{\alpha_i}(t)\}$. It is evident from Fig. 8.26 that the resulting performance degradation is negligible when M is chosen large enough that neighboring $\mathbf{s}_{\alpha_i}$ are approximately colinear and

$$\alpha_{i+1} - \alpha_i \lesssim \tfrac{1}{2}\sqrt{\overline{\epsilon^2}}; \qquad i = 0, 1, \ldots, M-2, \tag{8.86}$$

in which $\overline{\epsilon^2}$ is the mean-square error with true maximum likelihood reception.

In the next section we examine pulse-position modulation and observe, as in linear modulation, that the exact maximum-likelihood receiver can be realized by means of a single matched filter.

Pulse-Position Modulation

A common example of a noise-suppressing twisted modulation scheme is pulse-position modulation (abbreviated PPM). We first treat an idealized single-parameter communication system. As shown in Fig. 8.27, the bounded random input m causes an impulse of value $1/\sqrt{2W}$ to be generated at time mT_0. This impulse excites the ideal lowpass filter $W(f)$ of bandwidth W. The filter output is amplified and transmitted, so that

$$s_m(t) = \sqrt{E_s}\,\varphi(t - mT_0); \qquad -1 \leqslant m \leqslant +1. \tag{8.87a}$$

Here

$$\varphi(t) \triangleq \sqrt{2W}\,\frac{\sin 2\pi Wt}{2\pi Wt} \tag{8.87b}$$

is a unit-energy waveform similar to those encountered in the sampling theorem, except that the bandwidth is now W rather than W_m.

The form of the maximum-likelihood PPM receiver follows immediately from Eq. 8.84: since the transmitted energy is E_s, independent of the value

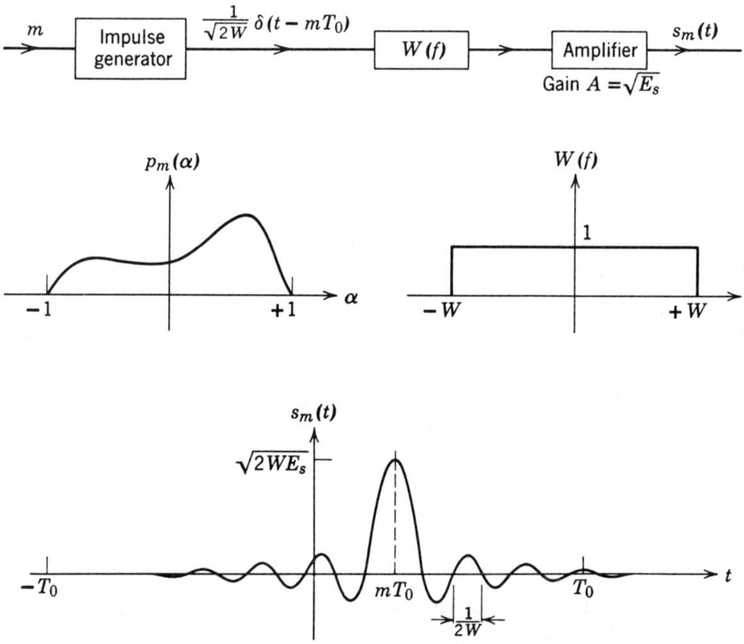

Figure 8.27 Idealized PPM transmitter; $T_0 \gg \frac{1}{2W}$.

of m, we have

$$p_{\mathbf{r}}(\boldsymbol{\rho} \mid m = \alpha) \sim \int_{-\infty}^{\infty} \rho(\gamma)\, \varphi(\gamma - \alpha T_0)\, d\gamma. \tag{8.88}$$

But the right-hand side of Eq. 8.88 is just the output at time $t = \alpha T_0$ of a matched filter, with impulse response

$$h(t) = \varphi(-t), \tag{8.89}$$

whose input is the received signal $\rho(t)$. Since $\varphi(-t) = \varphi(t)$, a maximum-likelihood receiver need only pass the received signal through another ideal bandlimiting filter $W(f)$, determine the time instant $\hat{t}$, $-T_0 \leqslant \hat{t} \leqslant T_0$,

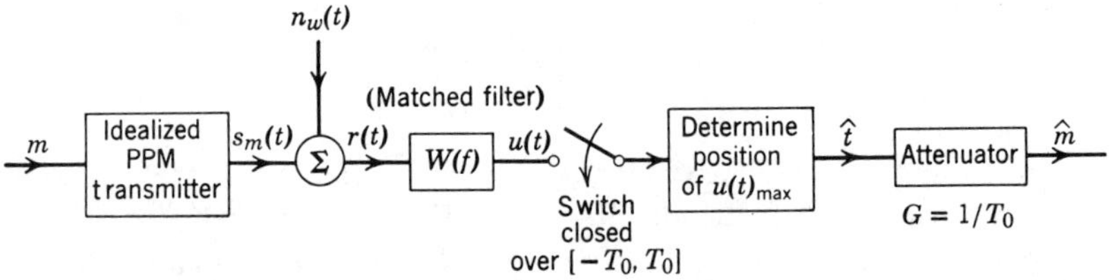

Figure 8.28 Idealized maximum-likelihood PPM receiver.

at which the filter output is maximum, and set $\hat{m} = \hat{t}/T_0$. Such a receiver is illustrated in Fig. 8.28.

Weak-noise suppression. Even though the set of all $\{s_m(t)\}$, $-1 \leqslant m \leqslant 1$, cannot be described in a finite-dimensional signal space, the arguments leading to Eqs. 8.79 remain valid. The mean-square error produced by maximum-likelihood reception in weak noise may therefore be determined by evaluating

$$S^2 \triangleq \int_{-\infty}^{\infty} \left| \frac{\partial}{\partial m} s_m(t) \right|^2 dt$$

$$= E_s T_0^2 \int_{-\infty}^{\infty} [\varphi'(t - mT_0)]^2 \, dt \tag{8.90}$$

and showing that the right-hand side is independent of m. The prime notation in Eq. 8.90 means differentiation with respect to the argument.

To evaluate S^2 in the time domain would be difficult, but it is easy to do so in the frequency domain. Since $\varphi(t)$ is the response of the ideal filter $W(f)$ to an impulse of value $1/\sqrt{2W}$, the spectrum of $\varphi(t)$ is

$$\Phi(f) = \begin{cases} \dfrac{1}{\sqrt{2W}}; & |f| < W \\ 0; & \text{elsewhere.} \end{cases} \tag{8.91}$$

Differentiation in time corresponds to multiplication by $j2\pi f$ in frequency. The spectrum of $\varphi'(t)$ is therefore $j2\pi f \Phi(f)$. From Parseval's theorem,

$$\int_{-\infty}^{\infty} [\varphi'(t - mT_0)]^2 \, dt = \int_{-\infty}^{\infty} [\varphi'(t)]^2 \, dt$$

$$= \frac{1}{2W} \int_{-W}^{W} |j2\pi f|^2 \, df = \frac{(2\pi W)^2}{3}. \tag{8.92}$$

Substitution in Eq. 8.90 yields

$$S^2 = \frac{E_s}{3} (2\pi T_0 W)^2, \tag{8.93}$$

which is independent of m. It follows from Eq. 8.79b that

$$\overline{\epsilon^2} = \frac{12}{\pi^2} \left(\frac{1}{4T_0 W} \right)^2 \frac{\mathcal{N}_0}{2E_s}, \tag{8.94}$$

when the noise is sufficiently weak that the probability of anomalous reception is negligible. For somewhat stronger noise, Eq. 8.94 can be interpreted as the conditional mean-square error, given that an anomaly does not occur.

The significance of the quantity $4T_0W$ is important. Recall that the signal bandwidth is W and that the maximum of the (infinite-duration) signal $s_m(t)$ is positioned over an interval whose total width is $2T_0$. Thus the quantity $4T_0W$ is twice the product of the signal bandwidth and the "signaling interval." In view of Appendices 5A and 8A, the quantity $4T_0W$ in some sense represents the dimensionality of the signaling set, even though an infinite number of dimensions is required to represent the infinite set of signals $\{s_m(t)\}$ exactly. We shall henceforth refer to twice the product of the signaling bandwidth and signaling interval as

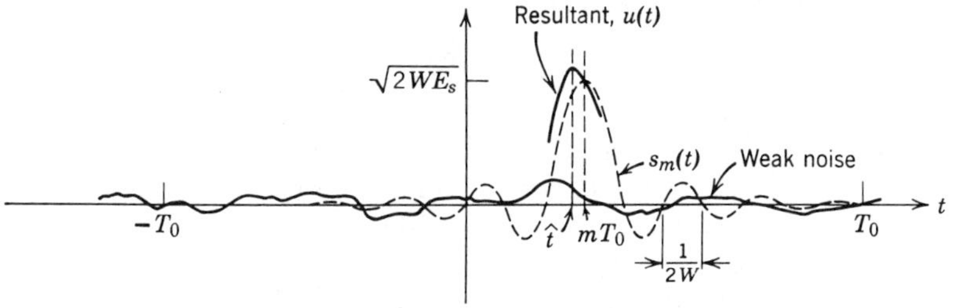

Figure 8.29 Suppression of weak noise. The output, $u(t)$, of the receiver's matched filter is the sum of $s_m(t)$ and band-limited Gaussian noise. It is clear from the geometry that steepening the skirts of $s_m(t)$ reduces the displacement of $\hat{t}$.

the *effective dimensionality* of the signal set and denote it β. For the PPM signals under consideration

$$\beta = 4T_0W. \tag{8.95a}$$

Equation 8.94 may then be rewritten in terms of β as

$$\overline{\epsilon^2} = \frac{12}{\pi^2}\frac{1}{\beta^2}\frac{\mathcal{N}_0}{2E_s}. \tag{8.95b}$$

With linear modulation, the mean-square error is $\mathcal{N}_0/2E_s$. Thus PPM achieves a weak-noise advantage over linear modulation† which increases as the square of the effective dimensionality. The larger the product $4T_0W$, the greater the improvement, as long as an anomaly does not occur.

Insight into the physical phenomena by means of which weak noise is suppressed can be gained from Fig. 8.29. When the bandwidth W of $\varphi(t)$ is much greater than $1/2T_0$, the effective duration of $\varphi(t)$ is short compared with $2T_0$ and the signal pulse at the matched-filter output has steep skirts. Weak noise at the output of the matched filter adds to the

† The advantage enjoyed by PPM over linear modulation is decreased if the comparison is made on the basis of average rather than peak energy: for PPM $\bar{E}_m = E_s$, whereas for linear modulation, with m uniformly distributed over $[-1, 1]$, $\bar{E}_m = E_s/3$.

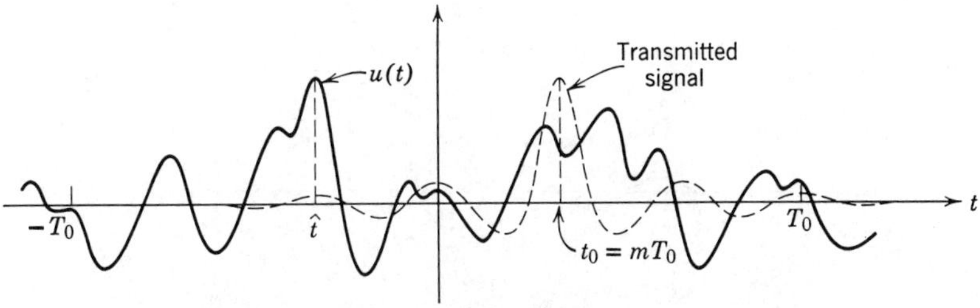

Figure 8.30 Anomalous reception in strong noise.

signal output and causes the location of the maximum of the sum to be displaced slightly from the signal maximum. The greater the signal bandwidth, the steeper the skirts of the signal pulse and the smaller the mean-square value of the displacement.

Threshold. Exact analysis of the threshold behavior with maximum-likelihood reception of PPM appears to be both difficult and unrewarding. It is possible, however, to make an approximate analysis that places the fundamental phenomenon clearly in evidence and agrees remarkably well with experimental measurements. In the arguments that follow we use m_0 to denote the actual value assumed by the transmitter input variable m.

Consider Fig. 8.30, which depicts the output $u(t)$ of the matched filter $W(f)$ when the input is $\sqrt{E_s}\,\varphi(t - t_0) + n_w(t)$. The signal component of $u(t)$ attains its maximum at time $t_0 \triangleq m_0 T_0$ and weak noise usually causes the observed maximum to be shifted from t_0 by only a small amount. But strong noise may cause the maximum to occur far from t_0 and thereby introduce an anomalous error, as shown in the illustration.

To calculate an approximation to the probability of an anomalous error, let us focus attention on the finite set of instants $\{t_i\}$, i an integer, defined by

$$t_i = t_0 + \frac{i}{2W}; \qquad -T_0 \leqslant t_i \leqslant T_0. \tag{8.96a}$$

It is clear from Fig. 8.31 that for any t_0 in $[-T_0, T_0]$, hence for any m_0 in the allowable range $-1 \leqslant m \leqslant 1$, there are substantially

$$\beta = 4T_0W \tag{8.96b}$$

such instants, in which β is the effective dimensionality of the signaling set.

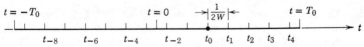

Figure 8.31 The $\{t_i\}$ are constructed by marking off increments of length $1/2W$ on both sides of t_0.

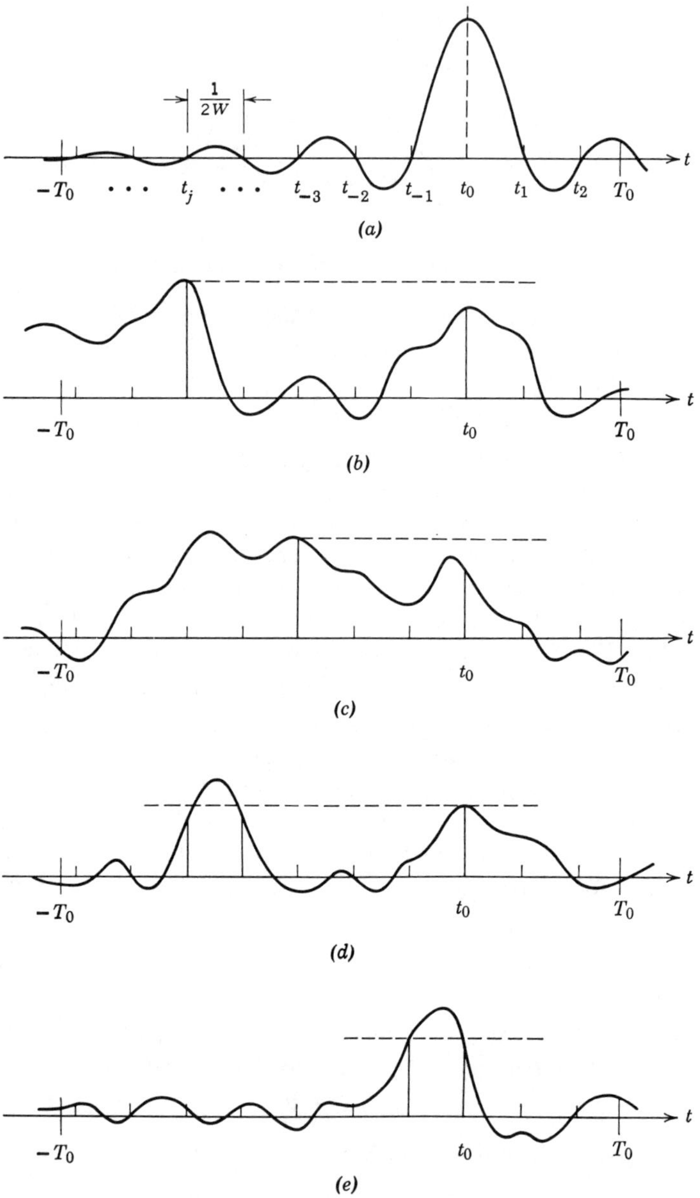

Figure 8.32 Possible waveforms at the matched filter output of an idealized PPM receiver: (*a*) signal component at matched filter output; (*b*), (*c*) anomalous outputs included in the event B; (*d*) anomalous output excluded from B; (*e*) nonanomalous output in B.

Equation 8.96a and the properties of the sampling function $\varphi(t)$ guarantee that

$$\int_{-\infty}^{\infty} \varphi(t - t_i)\, \varphi(t - t_j)\, dt = \delta_{ij}$$

for any pair of instants (t_i, t_j) in the set $\{t_i\}$. Since the signals $\{\varphi(t - t_i)\}$ are orthogonal, the probability that $u(t)$ will be larger at one of the incorrect time instants in the set $\{t_i\}$ than at t_0 is close to the probability of error in the communication of one of β equally likely messages when using equal-energy orthogonal signals. Letting B denote the event

$$B \triangleq [u(t_j) > u(t_0) \text{ for at least one } t_j \text{ in } \{t_i\}],$$

we have from Eqs. 4.96a, 4.111, and 2.121

$$\begin{aligned} \mathrm{P}[B] &\approx 1 - \int_{-\infty}^{\infty} \frac{1}{\sqrt{\pi \mathcal{N}_0}}\, e^{-(\gamma - \sqrt{E_s})^2/\mathcal{N}_0} \left[1 - Q\left(\frac{\gamma}{\sqrt{\mathcal{N}_0/2}}\right)\right]^{\beta-1} d\gamma \\ &\lessapprox \frac{\beta - 1}{\sqrt{2\pi E_s/\mathcal{N}_0}}\, e^{-E_s/2\mathcal{N}_0}. \end{aligned} \qquad (8.97)$$

The bound is very tight under usual conditions of operation.

It appears that the probability of error for the orthogonal signals $\{\sqrt{E_s}\, \varphi(t - t_j)\}$ provides a reasonable approximation to what one wishes to mean by the probability of anomaly, say $\mathrm{P}[\mathcal{A}]$, in our idealized PPM system. There are two difficulties in making the statement more precise. By far the most important is the logical impossibility of dichotomizing the infinitum of all possible waveforms $u(t)$ at the filter output in Fig. 8.28 into disjoint subsets labeled "anomalous" and "nonanomalous." As shown in Fig. 8.32, however, the event B does include most cases that we would reasonably call anomalous, although it also excludes some that obviously are anomalous and includes others that obviously are not.

The second difficulty is illustrated in Fig. 8.33: it is evident that the Euclidean distance between $\sqrt{E_s}\, \varphi(t - mT_0)$ and $\sqrt{E_s}\, \varphi(t - t_0)$ is less than $\sqrt{2E_s}$ for certain values of mT_0 between the $\{t_i\}$. These intermediate values could conceivably contribute more to the probability of anomaly than do the orthogonal points. But this possibility evanesces when we consider actual PPM signals in which filter ringing is carefully minimized by design. For example, measurements have been performed[1] on a laboratory model of a maximum-likelihood PPM receiver which uses the approximately Gaussian pulse shown in Fig. 8.34. The effective dimensionality β was defined as $4T_0\Delta$, with Δ taken as one half the width of the pulse between the -10 db points, and an anomaly was said to occur whenever

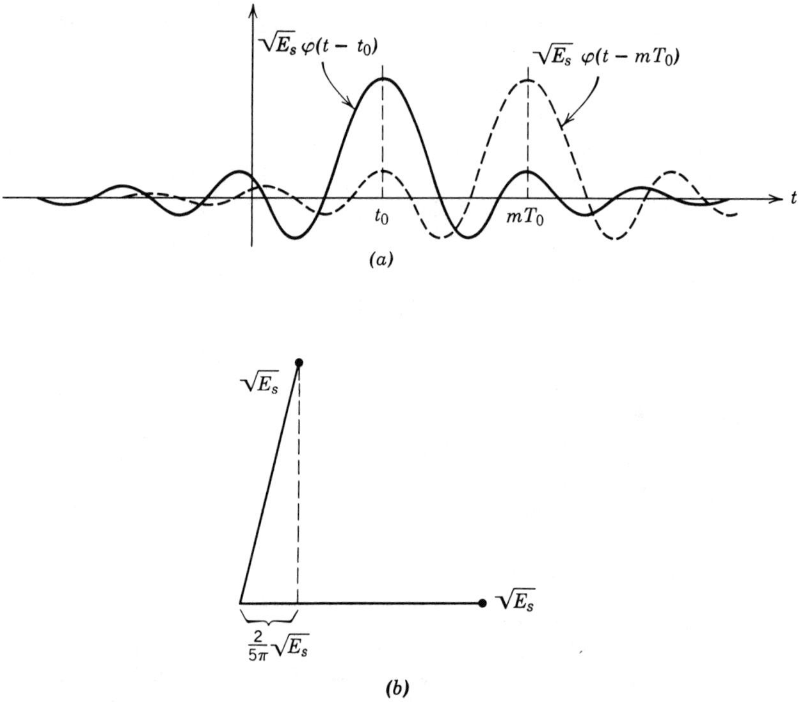

Figure 8.33 The signals $\varphi(t - t_0)$ and $\varphi(t - mT_0)$ are not orthogonal for all m in $[-1, 1]$. It is easy to prove that

$$\int_{-\infty}^{\infty} \varphi(t)\,\varphi(t - \tau)\,dt = \frac{1}{\sqrt{2W}}\,\varphi(\tau),$$

so that the worst case, illustrated in (*a*), occurs when $mT_0 \approx t_0 + \dfrac{5}{4W}$. The geometrical relation of the two signals in (*a*) is illustrated in (*b*).

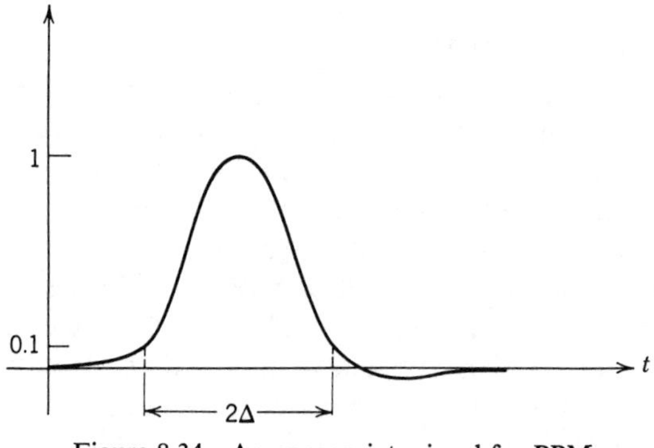

Figure 8.34 An appropriate signal for PPM.

the receiver output $\hat{m}$ differed by more than $\pm\Delta$ from the transmitted message m. The close experimental agreement between the relative frequency of anomalies and the equation

$$P[\mathcal{A}] \approx P[B] \approx (\beta - 1)\frac{e^{-E_s/2\mathcal{N}_0}}{\sqrt{2\pi E_s/\mathcal{N}_0}} \tag{8.98}$$

is evident from Fig. 8.35. We conclude that Eq. 8.98 provides a good estimate of the anomalous behavior in white Gaussian noise of a maximum-likelihood PPM system using well-designed signals.

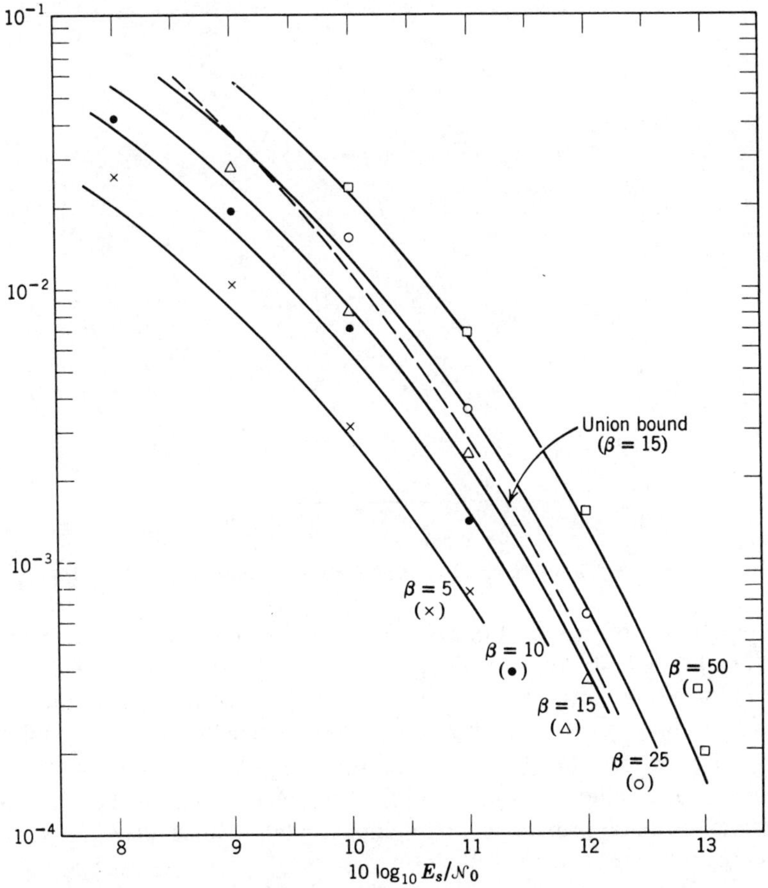

Figure 8.35 The experimental points are the relative frequency of anomaly with PPM; the solid curves are the true P[$\mathcal{E}$] for β equally likely orthogonal signals. Equation 8.98 results when the true P[$\mathcal{E}$] is approximated by the union bound; the approximation improves as P[$\mathcal{E}$] decreases, as indicated by the dashed line for $\beta = 15$.

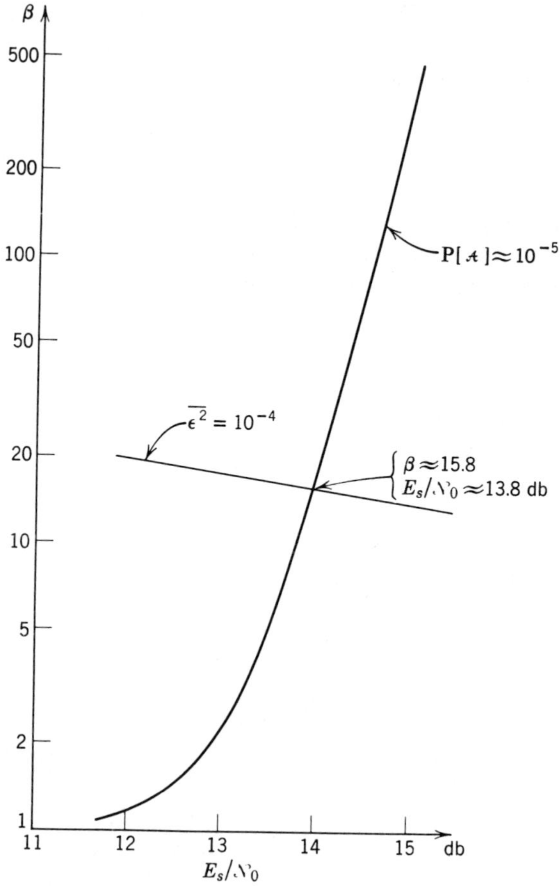

Figure 8.36 Graphical solution for $E_s/\mathcal{N}_0$ and β for PPM.

The estimate of $\mathrm{P}[\mathcal{A}]$ in Eq. 8.98, together with the mean-square error result of Eq. 8.95, permits the design of efficient PPM systems. Once the maximum tolerable (threshold) value of $\mathrm{P}[\mathcal{A}]$ is specified, the value of $E_s/\mathcal{N}_0$ required by Eq. 8.98 may be plotted as a function of β. A similar plot can be made from Eq. 8.95b for the maximum tolerable $\overline{\epsilon^2}$ in the absence of anomalies. As shown in Fig. 8.36, the intersection of these two plots yields the approximate minimum-acceptable value of $E_s/\mathcal{N}_0$ and the corresponding required value of β.

A one-parameter characterization of the performance of continuous PPM may be obtained by combining the mean-square error in the absence of anomalous errors with the mean-square error contributed by the anomalies themselves. When an anomaly occurs, $\hat{m}$ is substantially equally likely to be anywhere in the interval $[-1, 1]$, regardless of the value of m. (β mutually orthogonal signals are completely symmetric.) Furthermore, the event "anomaly" is independent of m. Thus

$$\begin{aligned} \mathrm{E}_{\mathcal{A}}[(m - \hat{m})^2] &= \mathrm{E}_{\mathcal{A}}[m^2] + \mathrm{E}_{\mathcal{A}}[\hat{m}^2] \\ &= \overline{m^2} + \left(\frac{1}{2}\int_{-1}^{1} \alpha^2\, d\alpha\right) = \overline{m^2} + \frac{1}{3}, \end{aligned} \tag{8.99}$$

in which $\mathrm{E}_{\mathcal{A}}[\ \ ]$ denotes expectation conditioned on the occurrence of an anomaly. If we asume that m is uniformly distributed over $[-1, 1]$ and denote the combined mean-square error by $\overline{\epsilon_T^2}$, Eqs. 8.95 and 8.98 yield†

$$\begin{aligned} \overline{\epsilon_T^2} &\approx \overline{\epsilon^2}\,(1 - \mathrm{P}[\mathcal{A}]) + \tfrac{2}{3}\,\mathrm{P}[\mathcal{A}] \\ &\approx \frac{12}{\pi^2}\left(\frac{1}{\beta}\right)^2 \frac{\mathcal{N}_0}{2E_s} + \frac{2}{3}\,\frac{\beta - 1}{\sqrt{2\pi E_s/\mathcal{N}_0}}\, e^{-E_s/2\mathcal{N}_0}. \end{aligned} \tag{8.100}$$

Equation 8.100 may be plotted in terms of the output signal-to-noise ratio, defined in accordance with Eq. 8.21a as $\overline{m^2}/\overline{\epsilon_T^2}$. Typical plots are given in Fig. 8.37. The knee of the output signal-to-noise ratio curve is referred to as the "threshold region."

The use of $\overline{\epsilon_T^2}$ as a single-parameter characterization of performance requires a certain amount of caution: the statistical properties and the effect of anomalies and of additive Gaussian noise are very different. In particular, if $\overline{\epsilon_T^2}$ truly measured user satisfaction, it would be good engineering practice to minimize $\overline{\epsilon_T^2}$ for a fixed value of $E_s/\mathcal{N}_0$ by proper choice of β. Such a choice leads to a value of $\mathrm{P}[\mathcal{A}]$ which is too large to be tolerable in most applications (such as speech). Thus a design procedure utilizing $\overline{\epsilon^2}$ and $\mathrm{P}[\mathcal{A}]$ separately seems preferable.

Discussion. With idealized PPM, the increased stretch necessary for weak-noise suppression is obtained by twisting the signal locus more or less onto a β-dimensional sphere with fixed radius $\sqrt{E_s}$. The resulting locus may be visualized roughly as indicated in Fig. 8.38: the signal curve is wound onto the sphere very loosely, with "coils" looping from one orthogonal axis to the next without ever coming into proximity. It is because of this that the probability of anomaly can be estimated by examining only β orthogonal points along the locus.

Of course, it is not true that $\mathrm{P}[\mathcal{A}]$ can be approximated in this way when the signal locus is arbitrary. Indeed, the approximation is not even valid for PPM when the transmitting waveshape is not judiciously designed.

† Equation 8.100 is written as an approximation primarily because it neglects the effect of higher order terms in the Taylor series approximation of Eq. 8.76. See Problem 8-15.

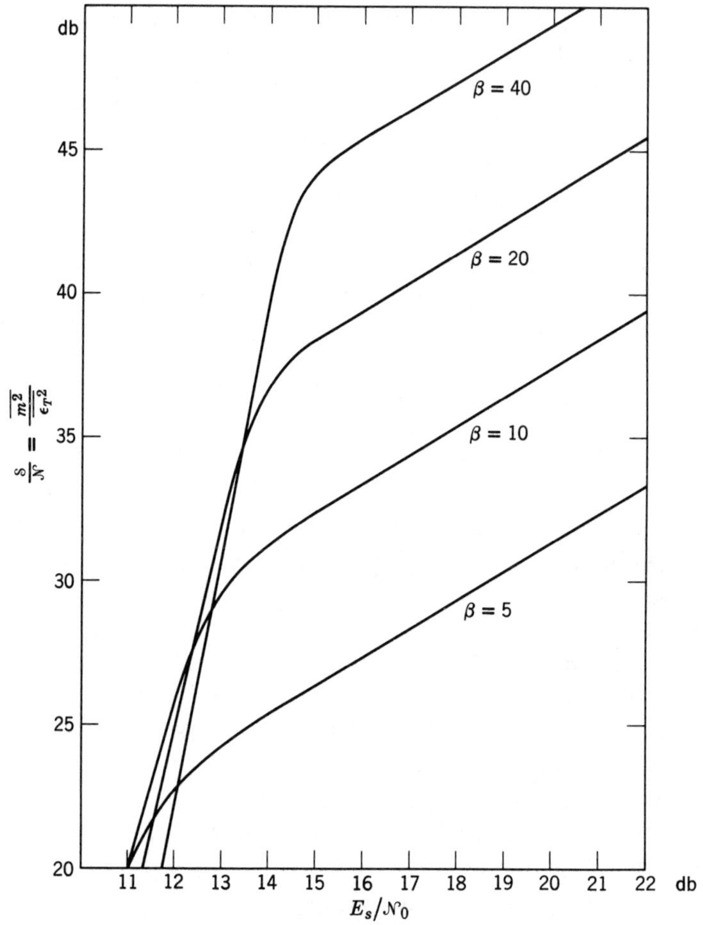

Figure 8.37 Signal-to-noise ratio of ordinary PPM when m is uniformly distributed.

As an example, consider position modulating an arbitrary unit-energy pulse, say $x(t)$, so that

$$s_m(t) = \sqrt{E_s}\, x(t - mT_0). \tag{8.101a}$$

The weak-noise performance is again determined by the stretch

$$\begin{aligned} S^2 &= \int_{-\infty}^{\infty} \left| \frac{\partial s_m(t)}{\partial m} \right|^2 dt \\ &= E_s T_0^{\,2} \int_{-\infty}^{\infty} [x'(t - mT_0)]^2\, dt \\ &= E_s T_0^{\,2} \int_{-\infty}^{\infty} [x'(t)]^2\, dt, \end{aligned}$$

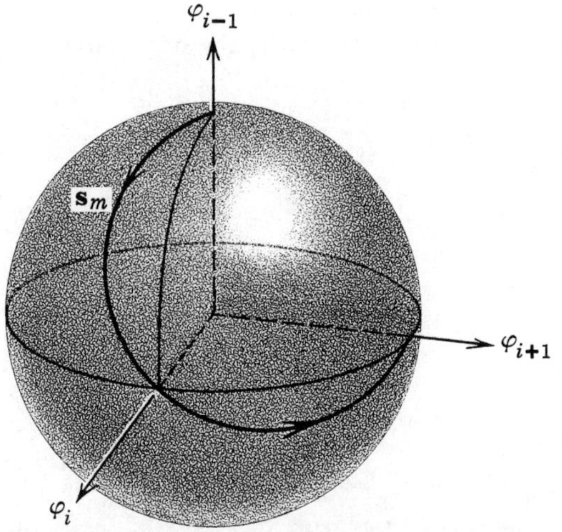

Figure 8.38 Approximate projection of a portion of the idealized PPM locus onto a three-dimensional sphere of radius $\sqrt{E_s}$. For $mT_0 = j/2W$, we have $\mathbf{s}_m = \sqrt{E_s}\,\boldsymbol{\varphi}_j$, $j = i-1,\ i,\ i+1$. The looping of the locus for intermediate values of m reflects the nonorthogonality evidenced in Fig. 8.33.

in which the prime denotes differentiation with respect to the argument. If $X(f)$ is the Fourier transform of $x(t)$, then $j2\pi f\, X(f)$ is the transform of $x'(t)$. It follows from Parseval's theorem that

$$\begin{aligned} S^2 &= E_s T_0^{\,2} \int_{-\infty}^{\infty} |j2\pi f\, X(f)|^2\, df \\ &= \frac{E_s}{3}(2\pi W_x T_0)^2, \end{aligned} \tag{8.101b}$$

in which we have introduced the definition

$$W_x^{\,2} \triangleq 3\int_{-\infty}^{\infty} f^2\, |X(f)|^2\, df. \tag{8.101c}$$

The factor 3 in Eq. 8.101c normalizes the definition so that $W_x = W$ when $X(f)$ is the ideal normalized rectangular filter function $(1/\sqrt{2W})W(f)$. In terms of W_x, the mean-square error in the absence of anomaly is

$$\overline{\epsilon^2} = \frac{12}{\pi^2}\left(\frac{1}{4W_x T_0}\right)^2 \frac{\mathcal{N}_0}{2E_s}. \tag{8.102}$$

Thus the weak-noise performances afforded by any two PPM systems for which W_x is the same are equivalent.

In order to see that this equivalence does not extend to the probability of anomaly, we need consider only the situation in which $x(t)$ is specialized to

$$x(t) = \begin{cases} \dfrac{1}{\sqrt{\Delta}} \sin 2\pi f_0 t; & -\Delta \leqslant t \leqslant \Delta, \quad f_0\Delta \text{ an integer} \\ 0; & \text{elsewhere.} \end{cases} \tag{8.103a}$$

It can be verified that $\int_{-\infty}^{\infty} [x'(t)]^2\, dt = (2\pi f_0)^2$, so that

$$W_x = \sqrt{3}\, f_0. \tag{8.103b}$$

When f_0 is chosen as $(1/\sqrt{3})W$ the mean-square error in weak noise afforded by $x(t)$ is therefore the same as that afforded by position-modulating $\varphi(t)$, the impulse response of an ideal normalized rectangular filter of bandwidth W. This is true regardless of the duration, Δ, of $x(t)$.

On the other hand, the probability of anomaly with $x(t)$ depends critically on Δ, a fact that is clarified by Fig. 8.39, in which we plot the output of the filter matched to $x(t)$: when Δ is large compared with $1/f_0$, this output, which is just the correlation function of $x(t)$, has many local maxima of slowly decreasing amplitude. It is evident that these local

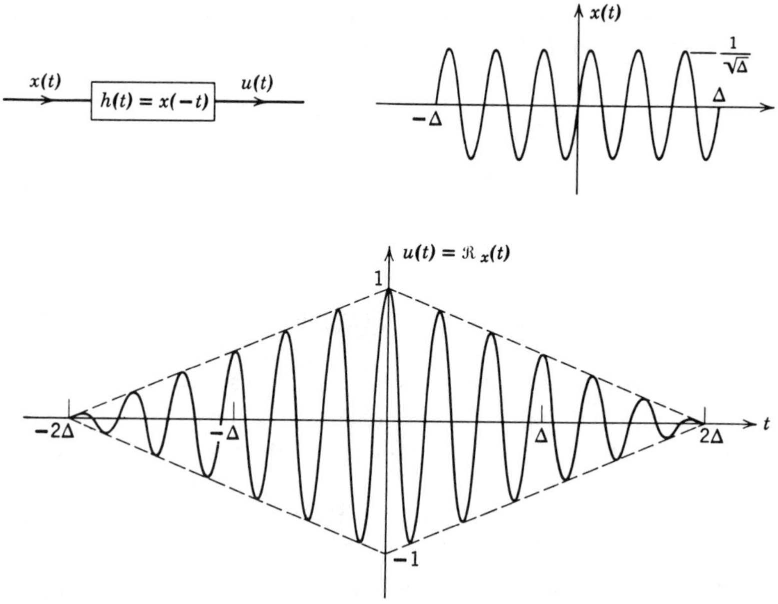

Figure 8.39 A signal whose correlation function is sensitive to anomalies.

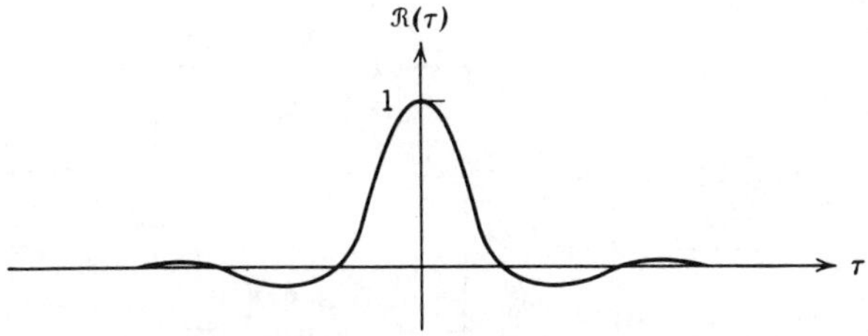

Figure 8.40 A signal correlation function for which the probability of anomaly may be estimated by means of Eq. 8.98.

maxima imply an inordinately high probability of anomaly when noise is present. Moreover, if we attempt to decrease $\overline{\epsilon^2}$ by choosing $f_0 > (1/\sqrt{3})W$, the number of local maxima, hence $P[\mathcal{A}]$, becomes even larger.

Estimating $P[\mathcal{A}]$ by counting the number of essentially orthogonal pulse positions at the output of the receiver's matched filter is valid if and only if the correlation function of $x(t)$ is relatively "compact," as in Fig. 8.40. The equivalent geometrical requirement is that the signal locus be loosely coiled. This condition must be satisfied if an unwarranted susceptibility to anomalies is to be avoided.

Antipodal PPM. It is possible to increase stretch without changing the effective number of dimensions occupied by a PPM signal—and without violating the loosely coiled condition—by adopting the antipodal signaling set

$$s_m(t) = \begin{cases} -\sqrt{E_s}\,\varphi(t - 2\,|m|\,T_0); & -1 \leqslant m < 0 \\ +\sqrt{E_s}\,\varphi(t - 2\,|m|\,T_0); & 0 \leqslant m \leqslant 1. \end{cases} \tag{8.104}$$

The effect of dividing the range of m into two parts is to increase the stretch by 2, which reduces $\overline{\epsilon^2}$ by the factor $\frac{1}{4}$. We have

$$\overline{\epsilon^2} = \frac{12}{\pi^2}\left(\frac{1}{2\beta}\right)^2 \frac{\mathcal{N}_0}{2E_s}; \qquad \text{for antipodal PPM,} \tag{8.105a}$$

where

$$\beta \triangleq 4T_0W \tag{8.105b}$$

is again the effective dimensionality of the signal space.

The effect of antipodal PPM on the probability of anomaly is evident from the structure of the maximum-likelihood receiver. As illustrated in Fig. 8.41, such a receiver first determines the instant $\hat{t}$ within the interval

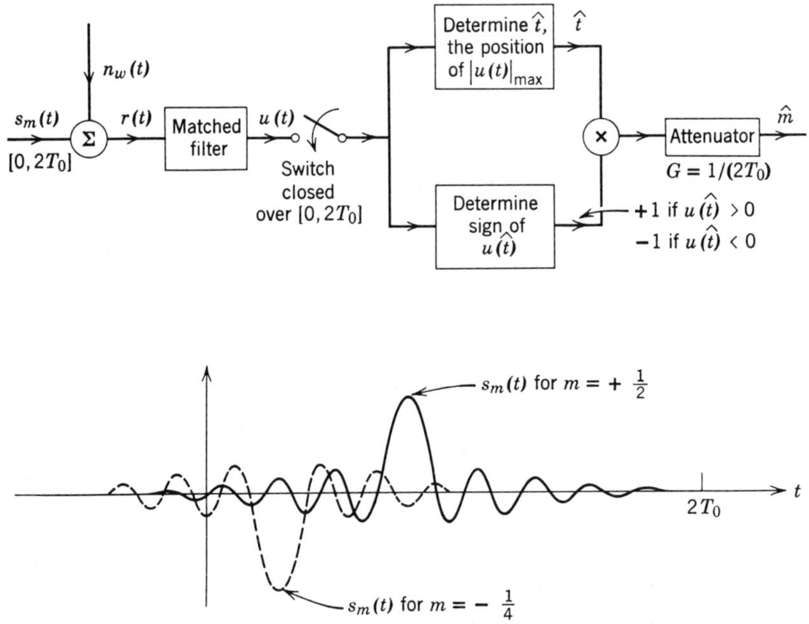

Figure 8.41 Maximum likelihood receiver for antipodal PPM. (The matched filter is assumed to have zero delay.)

$[0, 2T_0]$ for which the *magnitude* of the matched-filter output is greatest and then sets

$$\hat{m} = \pm \frac{\hat{t}}{2T_0}$$

in accordance with a positive or negative filter output at $t = \hat{t}$.

The considerations that led us to estimate the probability of anomaly in terms of the probability of error for β discrete orthogonal signals are still germane. Now, however, it is apparent from Fig. 8.41 that these same arguments lead us to estimate $P[\mathcal{A}]$ in terms of the probability of error for 2β equally likely *biorthogonal signals*, each with energy E_s. From Eqs. 4.112 and 2.121 we have

$$P[\mathcal{A}] \approx (2\beta - 1)\frac{e^{-E_s/2\mathcal{N}_0}}{\sqrt{2\pi E_s/\mathcal{N}_0}}; \qquad \text{for antipodal PPM.} \qquad (8.105c)$$

We note from Eqs. 8.105a and c that antipodal PPM with effective dimensionality β is equivalent, both with regard to $\overline{\epsilon^2}$ and $P[\mathcal{A}]$, to ordinary PPM with effective dimensionality 2β.

Although the weak-noise performance of antipodal PPM is 6 db superior to that of ordinary PPM for the same value of β, it is not necessarily easy to attain this improvement in practice. The reason, of course, is that actual systems use bandpass rather than lowpass signals. The usual technique is to use DSB-SC to heterodyne from baseband to RF and then back down again. Antipodal PPM then requires an accurate receiver phase reference, whereas ordinary PPM is not particularly sensitive to RF phase. Indeed, an ordinary PPM receiver may consist of a bandpass matched filter, followed by an envelope detector, without material degradation of performance when $E_s/\mathcal{N}_0 \gg 1$.

Waveform communication with PPM. We next consider the efficiency of PPM in communicating an ideally band-limited random process

$$m(t) = \sum_{k=-\infty}^{\infty} m_k\, \psi_k(t) \tag{8.106}$$

with lowpass bandwidth W_m. For convenience, we assume that the process has been so normalized that $|m_k| \leqslant 1$ for all k.

With PPM each m_k is transmitted and estimated by a (maximum-likelihood) receiver in succession. The receiver then constructs

$$\hat{m}(t) = \sum_{k=-\infty}^{\infty} \hat{m}_k\, \psi_k(t). \tag{8.107}$$

In the absence of anomaly, we have

$$\hat{m}_k = m_k + n_k; \qquad \text{for all } k, \tag{8.108}$$

in which each n_k is a statistically independent zero-mean Gaussian random variable with variance $\overline{\epsilon^2}$ given by Eq. 8.95b. It follows from Eq. 8.50 that

$$\hat{m}(t) = m(t) + n(t), \tag{8.109a}$$

in which

$$n(t) \triangleq \sum_{k=-\infty}^{\infty} n_k\, \psi_k(t) \tag{8.109b}$$

is a stationary Gaussian process with power density

$$\mathcal{S}_n(f) = \begin{cases} \overline{\epsilon^2}; & |f| < W_m \\ 0; & \text{elsewhere.} \end{cases} \tag{8.109c}$$

The average power of the additive noise for ordinary PPM in weak noise is therefore

$$\overline{n^2(t)} = 2\overline{\epsilon^2}W_m. \tag{8.109d}$$

Substitution of Eq. 8.95b yields

$$\overline{n^2(t)} = \frac{12}{\pi^2}\left(\frac{1}{\beta^2}\right)\frac{\mathcal{N}_0 W_m}{E_s}; \qquad \text{for ordinary PPM,} \tag{8.110}$$

whereas with linear modulation we found $\overline{n^2(t)} = \mathcal{N}_0 W_m / E_s$. Increasing the effective dimensionality, β, yields weak-noise suppression without an increase in the peak transmitted energy per sample.

The value of β in Eq. 8.110 is related to the transmission bandwidth W and the modulating bandwidth W_m: the time available for the transmission of each m_k is the sampling interval, $1/2W_m$. The maximum allowable position deviation for each transmission is therefore constrained by

$$2T_0 \leqslant \frac{1}{2W_m}. \tag{8.111}$$

If, as shown in Fig. 8.42, a nominal interval of $1/2W$ sec is included at both ends of every sampling interval to guard against overlap of transmitted pulses into adjacent intervals, we have

$$\frac{1}{2W_m} = 2\left(\frac{1}{2W}\right) + 2T_0$$

or

$$\beta \triangleq 4T_0 W = \frac{W}{W_m} - 2.$$

We see that the effective dimensionality is related to the *bandwidth expansion ratio*, W/W_m, by

$$\frac{W}{W_m} = \beta + 2. \tag{8.112}$$

When PPM is used in conjunction with DSB-SC modulation, W is identified as one half the RF bandwidth.

As already noted, it is possible by means of antipodal PPM to retain a fixed bandwidth expansion ratio W/W_m while achieving the performance that ordinary PPM achieves only when the effective dimensionality is $2\beta = 2(W/W_m - 2)$. The resulting increase in the efficiency of channel spectrum utilization may be desirable when $E_s \gg \mathcal{N}_0$ if the allowable bandwidth is limited and an RF phase reference can be made available. It may even be desirable to compound antipodal signaling with quadrature DSB-SC multiplexing; that is, to transmit

$$s_m(t) = \begin{cases} +\sqrt{2E_s}\,\varphi(t - 4\,|m + \tfrac{1}{2}|\,T_0)\cos\omega_0 t; & -1 \leqslant m < -\tfrac{1}{2} \\ -\sqrt{2E_s}\,\varphi(t - 4\,|m|\,T_0)\cos\omega_0 t; & -\tfrac{1}{2} \leqslant m < 0 \\ +\sqrt{2E_s}\,\varphi(t - 4\,|m|\,T_0)\sin\omega_0 t; & 0 \leqslant m < \tfrac{1}{2} \\ -\sqrt{2E_s}\,\varphi(t - 4\,|m - \tfrac{1}{2}|\,T_0)\sin\omega_0 t; & \tfrac{1}{2} \leqslant m \leqslant 1. \end{cases} \tag{8.113a}$$

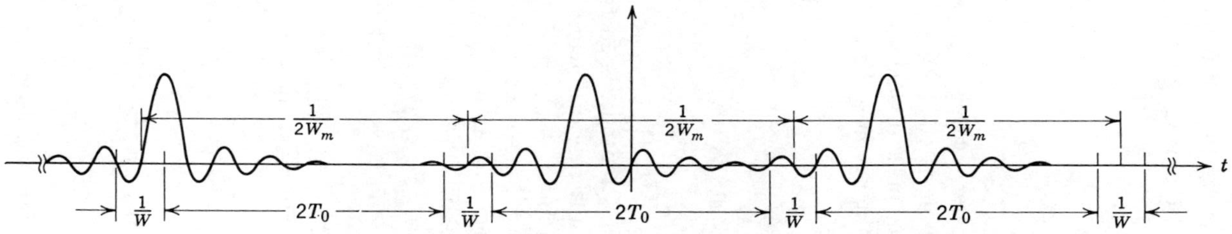

Figure 8.42 Time interval allocation for a sequence of PPM transmissions.

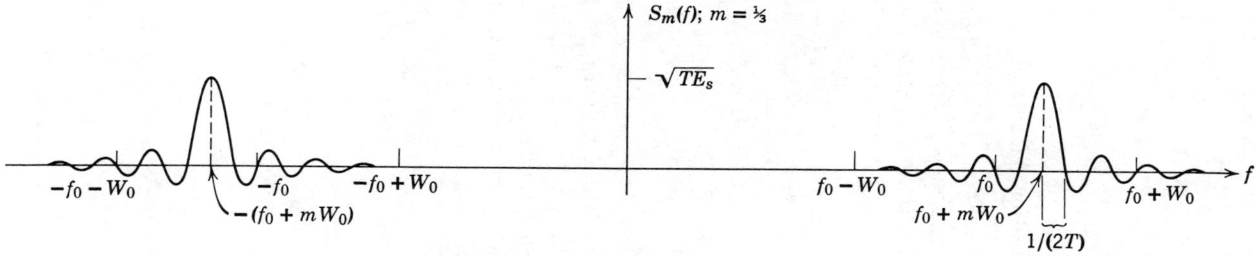

Figure 8.43 Spectrum of idealized FPM signal:

$$s_m(t) = \begin{cases} \sqrt{E_s/T}\cos 2\pi(f_0 + mW_0)t; & -T \leqslant t \leqslant T \\ 0; & \text{elsewhere.} \end{cases}$$

Such a quadrature-antipodal system multiplies the effective dimensionality of ordinary PPM by 4, still without increasing the RF bandwidth required for transmission. The values of $\overline{\epsilon^2}$ and P[$\mathcal{A}$] are then given by Eqs. 8.95b and 8.98 with

$$\beta = 4\left(\frac{W}{W_m} - 2\right). \tag{8.113b}$$

Frequency-Position Modulation

A second example of a single-input-parameter twisted modulation scheme is frequency-position modulation (abbreviated FPM). With ordinary FPM, the transmitted signal is a $2T$-sec pulse of sine wave, the frequency of which is determined by the transmitter input. We take

$$s_m(t) = \sqrt{E_s}\,\varphi_m(t) \tag{8.114a}$$

with

$$\varphi_m(t) \triangleq \begin{cases} \dfrac{1}{\sqrt{T}} \cos 2\pi(f_0 + mW_0)t; & -T \leqslant t \leqslant T \\ 0; & \text{elsewhere.} \end{cases} \tag{8.114b}$$

The factor $1/\sqrt{T}$ normalizes $\varphi_m(t)$ so that the transmitted energy is essentially equal to E_s when $f_0 \gg W_0$, which is the case of interest. We assume that the random variable m is confined to $[-1, +1]$.

As the name implies, FPM is the frequency-domain equivalent of idealized PPM. The equivalence is obvious when Fig. 8.43 is compared with Fig. 8.27. It follows that the stretch factor for FPM is

$$S^2 = \frac{E_s}{3}(2\pi T W_0)^2, \tag{8.115}$$

a conclusion that may be readily verified† from Eqs. 8.79a and 8.114. In the absence of anomaly, the mean-square error with maximum-likelihood reception is therefore again

$$\overline{\epsilon^2} = \frac{12}{\pi^2}\left(\frac{1}{\beta^2}\right)\frac{\mathcal{N}_0}{2E_s}, \tag{8.116a}$$

in which the effective dimensionality of the signal set is‡

$$\beta \triangleq 4TW_0; \qquad \text{for FPM.} \tag{8.116b}$$

† In Eq. 8.115 we neglect the double-frequency term in evaluating the integral of Eq. 8.79a.

‡ The effective dimensionality is the product of effective bandwidth $2W_0$ and the signal duration $2T$. The usual factor 2 multiplying the time-bandwidth product is omitted, since the quadrature components are not used.

The probability of anomaly estimate is

$$P[\mathcal{A}] \approx (\beta - 1)\frac{e^{-E_s/2\mathcal{N}_0}}{\sqrt{2\pi E_s/\mathcal{N}_0}}. \tag{8.116c}$$

Just as with idealized PPM, the $(\sin x)/x$ shape of the transmitted pulse spectrum introduces some error into this estimate of $P[\mathcal{A}]$, but the error can be substantially eliminated by appropriate pulse-envelope wave-shaping.

When FPM is used to communicate a bandlimited process $m(t)$, we can allow only a time

$$2T = \frac{1}{2W_m} \tag{8.117a}$$

for each transmission, which implies

$$\beta = \frac{W_0}{W_m}. \tag{8.117b}$$

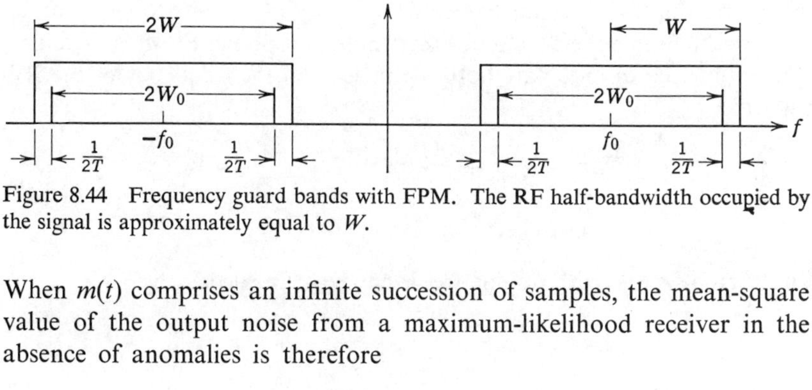

Figure 8.44 Frequency guard bands with FPM. The RF half-bandwidth occupied by the signal is approximately equal to W.

When $m(t)$ comprises an infinite succession of samples, the mean-square value of the output noise from a maximum-likelihood receiver in the absence of anomalies is therefore

$$\overline{n^2(t)} = \frac{12}{\pi^2}\left(\frac{W_m}{W_0}\right)^2\frac{\mathcal{N}_0 W_m}{E_s}; \qquad \text{for FPM.} \tag{8.118}$$

The modulating bandwidth and the transmission bandwidth are related to the effective dimensionality with FPM in the same way as with PPM. The zero crossings of the $(\sin x)/x$ spectrum of each FPM pulse are spaced $1/2T = 2W_m$ cps apart. If we allow a nominal guard band of $2W_m$ cps on each side of the frequency interval $[f_0 - W_0, f_0 + W_0]$, as indicated in Fig. 8.44, the half-bandwidth required for transmission is

$$W = W_0 + 2W_m = W_m(\beta + 2). \tag{8.119}$$

Thus the bandwidth expansion factor W/W_m again equals $(\beta + 2)$.

A major distinction between FPM and PPM is the difference in ease of maximum-likelihood receiver instrumentation. The frequency-domain equivalent of the PPM receiver of Fig. 8.28 is a device that takes the Fourier cosine transform of the relevant received signal over the time interval $[-T, T]$, determines the frequency $\hat{f}$ in the range $[f_0 - W_0, f_0 + W_0]$ for which the transform is maximum, and sets

$$\hat{m} = \frac{\hat{f} - f_0}{W_0}. \tag{8.120}$$

Clearly, such a device is more difficult to build than the PPM receiver. An approximation to the FPM maximum-likelihood receiver, can, of course, be constructed as indicated in Fig. 8.26.†

The equivalence of FPM and PPM—including the phase reference problem—extends also to the possibility of using antipodal FPM signals: the resulting performance is equivalent to that of ordinary FPM with the effective dimensionality doubled. Furthermore, quadrature multiplexing may be used to redouble the effective dimensionality, again without increasing the transmission bandwidth.

A modulation scheme closely related to antipodal FPM is obtained when m is used to modulate both the phase and the frequency of the RF carrier:

$$s_m(t) = \begin{cases} \sqrt{\dfrac{E_s}{T}} \cos 2\pi[f_0 t + m W_0 (t + T)]; & -T \leqslant t \leqslant T \\ 0; & \text{elsewhere.} \end{cases} \tag{8.121}$$

The stretch factor (with double-frequency terms neglected) is

$$S^2 = \frac{E_s}{T}(2\pi W_0)^2 \frac{1}{2} \int_{-T}^{T} (t + T)^2 \, dt$$

$$= \frac{E_s}{3}(4\pi T W_0)^2, \tag{8.122a}$$

so that, with β equal to $4TW_0$ as before,

$$\overline{n^2(t)} = \frac{12}{\pi^2}\left(\frac{1}{2\beta}\right)^2 \frac{\mathcal{N}_0 W_m}{E_s}$$

$$= \frac{3}{\pi^2}\left(\frac{W_m}{W_0}\right)^2 \frac{\mathcal{N}_0 W_m}{E_s}. \tag{8.122b}$$

† Darlington[20] has proposed that radar pulse-compression techniques may be useful in converting the received FPM signal into PPM format.

For the waveforms of Eq. 8.121, orthogonal signals result when m increases by $1/\beta = 1/4TW_0$, so that 2β values of m within the interval $[-1, +1]$ lead to mutually orthogonal signals. It follows that we again have

$$\mathrm{P}[\mathcal{E}] \approx (2\beta - 1)\frac{e^{-E_s/2\mathcal{N}_0}}{\sqrt{2\pi E_s/\mathcal{N}_0}}. \tag{8.122c}$$

With maximum-likelihood reception, both $\overline{\epsilon^2}$ and $\mathrm{P}[\mathcal{E}]$ are equivalent to the performance obtained with antipodal FPM.

When a sequence of signals, each having the form of Eq. 8.121, is used to communicate a modulating process $m(t)$, the terminal phase of each transmission in turn can be chosen as the initial phase of the succeeding one. Frequency modulation (abbreviated FM), to which we next direct our attention, is a scheme closely akin to this. In particular, the phase continuity of an FM signal enables FM receivers to combat slow drifts in phase.

8.3 FREQUENCY MODULATION

With PPM and FPM, the modulating process $m(t)$ is sampled once each $1/2W_m$ sec, and the transmitter and receiver must operate synchronously in time. On the other hand, with FM the input waveform modulates the transmitted signal continuously and timing problems do not exist.

An FM signal may be written in the form

$$s_{\mathrm{m}}(t) = A\sqrt{2}\cos 2\pi\left[f_0 t + W_1 \int m(t)\,dt\right]. \tag{8.123}$$

Here the factor $\sqrt{2}$ is chosen to normalize the transmitted *power* to A^2. In contradistinction, for PPM and FPM we normalized the signals so that E_s was the transmitted *energy* per input sample. For modulating processes with rectangular bandwidth W_m the two normalizations are equivalent when

$$A^2 = 2W_m E_s. \tag{8.124}$$

The argument $\theta(t)$ in any signal having the form $\cos\theta(t)$ is called the *instantaneous phase*, and $(1/2\pi)\dfrac{d}{dt}\theta(t)$ is called the *instantaneous frequency*, denoted f_I. Frequency modulation takes its name from the fact that f_I depends linearly on $m(t)$. From Eq. 8.123 we have

$$f_I = \frac{d}{dt}\left[f_0 t + W_1 \int m(t)\,dt\right]$$

$$= f_0 + W_1\, m(t). \tag{8.125a}$$

If we normalize $m(t)$ so that

$$|m(t)| \leqslant 1; \quad \text{for all } t, \tag{8.125b}$$

then

$$f_0 - W_1 \leqslant f_I \leqslant f_0 + W_1, \tag{8.125c}$$

and W_1 is the *maximum instantaneous-frequency deviation*..

The *modulation index* of an FM signal is defined as the ratio of the maximum instantaneous-frequency deviation to the bandwidth of $m(t)$. The modulation index plays the same role in FM as effective dimensionality in PPM and FPM. For this reason we also denote it β:

$$\beta \triangleq \frac{W_1}{W_m}; \qquad \text{for FM,} \tag{8.126}$$

when $|m(t)| \leqslant 1$.

Signal Bandwidth

We now show that the half-bandwidth, again denoted W, required to pass most of the energy of an FM signal is approximately related to W_m and β by the familiar equation

$$\frac{W}{W_m} = (\beta + 2). \tag{8.127}$$

An instructive, albeit imprecise, justification for the relationship follows from quasi-static extension of arguments already encountered in connection with FPM. The rate of change of f_I in an FM signal is essentially controlled by the bandwidth of $m(t)$; over any interval that is short compared with $1/2W_m$, f_I will be more or less constant. But we have observed in Fig. 8.43 that the spectrum of a $1/2W_m$-sec pulse of sinusoid varies as $(\sin x)/x$, with zero crossings $2W_m$ cps apart. When $\beta \gg 1$, we may visualize the spectrum requirements for FM in terms of a similar $(\sin x)/x$ pulse that moves quasi-statically within the band $[f_0 - W_1, f_0 + W_1]$ under the control of $m(t)$. Allowing a nominal guard band of $2W_m$ cps on either side of the range of f_I leads to Eq. 8.127.

An exact expression for the spectrum of an FM signal can be obtained when $m(t)$ is a sinusoid. Letting $m(t) = \cos 2\pi W_m t$, $\omega_0 = 2\pi f_0$, and $\omega_m = 2\pi W_m$, we have

$$\begin{aligned} s_m(t) &= A\sqrt{2} \cos\left(\omega_0 t + \frac{W_1}{W_m} \sin \omega_m t\right) \\ &= A\sqrt{2}[\cos(\beta \sin \omega_m t) \cos \omega_0 t - \sin(\beta \sin \omega_m t) \sin \omega_0 t]. \end{aligned} \tag{8.128}$$

But for any integer k

$$\frac{1}{2\pi}\int_{-\pi}^{\pi} e^{j[\beta \sin\alpha - k\alpha]}\, d\alpha \triangleq J_k(\beta), \tag{8.129}$$

in which $J_k(\beta)$ is the kth-order Bessel function† of the first kind.[83] It may be verified from Eq. 8.129 that

$$\frac{1}{2\pi}\int_{-\pi}^{\pi} \cos(\beta\sin\alpha)\cos k\alpha\, d\alpha = \begin{cases} J_k(\beta), & k \text{ even} \\ 0, & k \text{ odd}, \end{cases}$$

$$\frac{1}{2\pi}\int_{-\pi}^{\pi} \sin(\beta\sin\alpha)\sin k\alpha\, d\alpha = \begin{cases} 0, & k \text{ even} \\ J_k(\beta), & k \text{ odd}. \end{cases}$$

Thus the Fourier series expansion of $s_{\mathrm{m}}(t)$ is

$$s_{\mathrm{m}}(t) = A\sqrt{2}\cos\omega_0 t\Big[J_0(\beta) + 2\sum_{k\text{ even}} J_k(\beta)\cos k\omega_m t\Big]$$
$$-A\sqrt{2}\sin\omega_0 t\Big[2\sum_{k\text{odd}} J_k(\beta)\sin k\omega_m t\Big]; \qquad k \geqslant 0. \tag{8.130}$$

With cosinusoidal modulation at frequency W_m, the spectrum of $s_{\mathrm{m}}(t)$ contains an infinite number of discrete terms at frequencies $f_0 \pm kW_m$, $k = 0, 1, 2, \ldots$.

Bessel functions appear frequently in mathematical physics and have been extensively tabulated.[46] Representative examples are plotted against β in Fig. 8.45. For $k > \beta > 2$ it can be shown from the series expansion[56] of $J_k(\beta)$ that

$$|J_k(\beta)| < \frac{1}{k!}\left(\frac{\beta}{2}\right)^{k+(\beta/2)}. \tag{8.131a}$$

Introducing Stirling's approximation to the factorial into Eq. 8.131a, we note in particular that

$$|J_k(\beta)| < \frac{(\beta/2)^{\beta/2}}{\sqrt{2\pi k}}\left(\frac{e\beta}{2k}\right)^k, \tag{8.131b}$$

which goes rapidly to zero as k increases beyond $(e\beta/2)$.

We conclude from Eq. 8.131b that only a finite number of terms in Eq. 8.130 actually contribute significantly to $s_{\mathrm{m}}(t)$ and that this number *grows linearly with* β. But we must also conclude that the first sideband components at $f_0 \pm W_m$ are significant even when $\beta \ll 1$; neglecting them would mean approximating $s_{\mathrm{m}}(t)$ by a pure sinusoid, without any modulation at all! Both conclusions are consistent with Eq. 8.127 and are

† The function $I_0(x)$ encountered in Eq. 7.49 is equal to $J_0(jx)$.

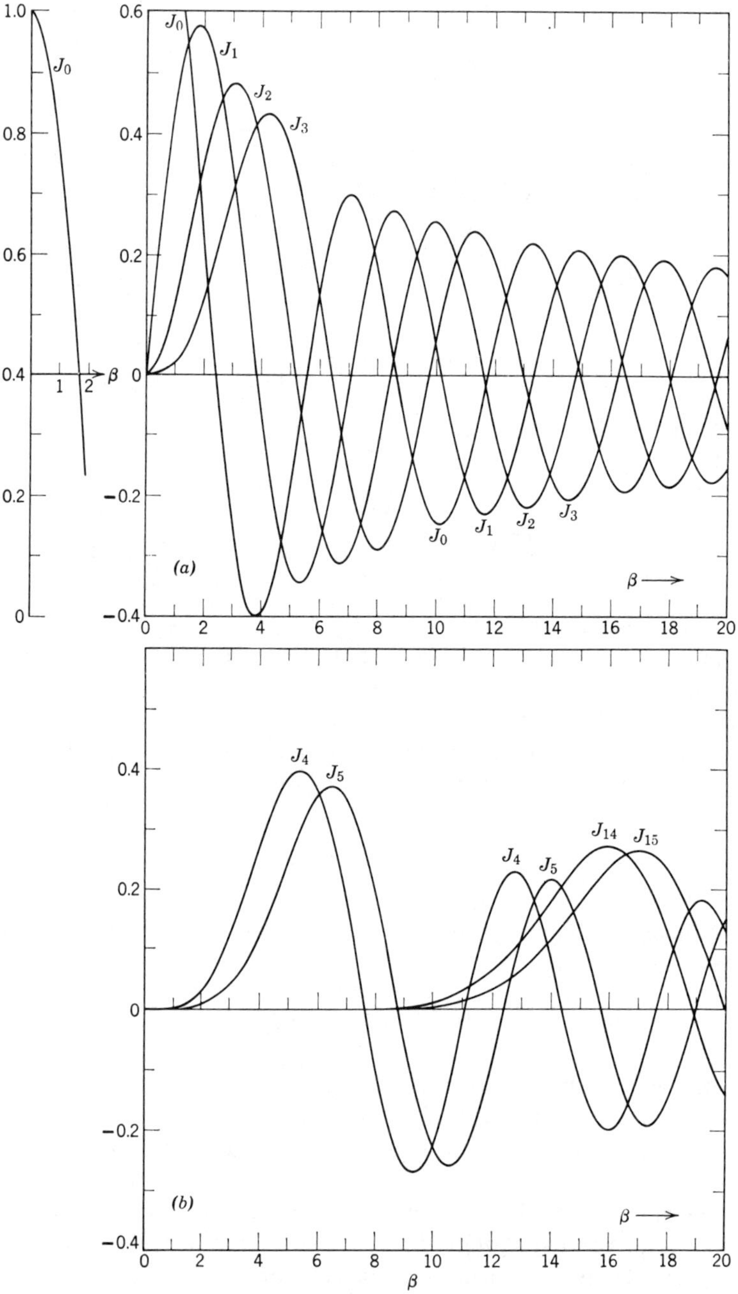

Figure 8.45 Bessel functions.

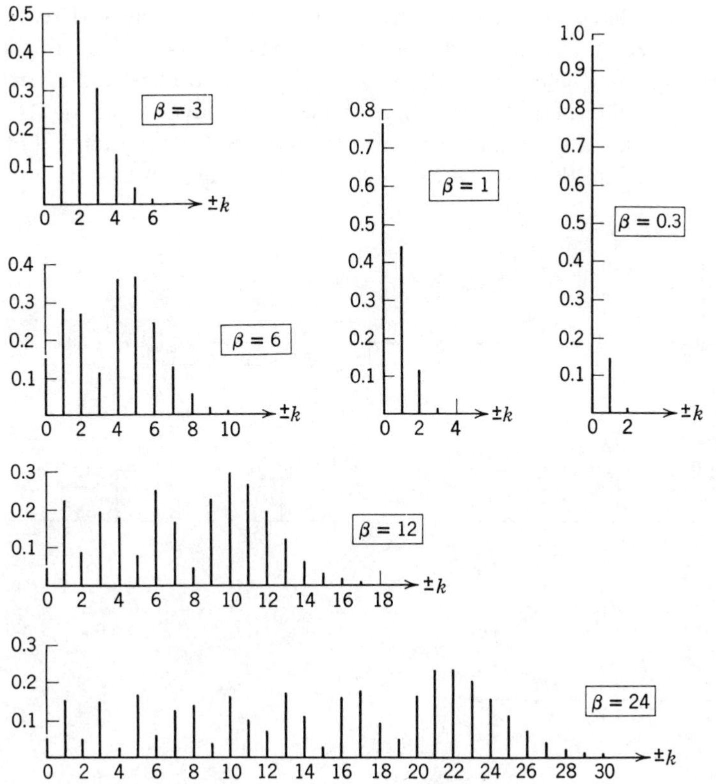

Figure 8.46 Relative magnitude of spectral components at $f_0 \pm kW_m$ as a function of k for FM with cosinusoidal modulation.

further substantiated by Fig. 8.46, in which we plot the spectrum of $s_m(t)$ for cosinusoidal modulation with various values of modulation index. Equation 8.127 is especially accurate when $\beta \gg 1$. For $\beta \ll 1$ a half-bandwidth of W_m cps would suffice.

Weak-Noise Suppression

We now consider the weak-noise suppression afforded by frequency modulation. Our first step is to analyze the mean-square noise produced at the output of an idealized conventional FM receiver. We then investigate pre-emphasis FM, which is also called phase modulation or PM, and show that conventional receivers perform as well as maximum-likelihood receivers when the noise is sufficiently weak. We conclude by comparing the weak-noise performance of FM and PM with that of FPM and PPM. The probability of anomaly is studied in the next subsection.

Conventional FM receivers. An idealized conventional FM receiver is diagrammed in Fig. 8.47. The received signal is first passed through a rectangular unit-gain filter $H_1(f)$ centered on the transmitted carrier frequency f_0. The output from $H_1(f)$ is then heterodyned into the IF filter $H_2(f)$, which is also rectangular with unit gain. Both $H_1(f)$ and $H_2(f)$ have half-bandwidth $W = W_1 + 2W_m$, so that we may presume the input to

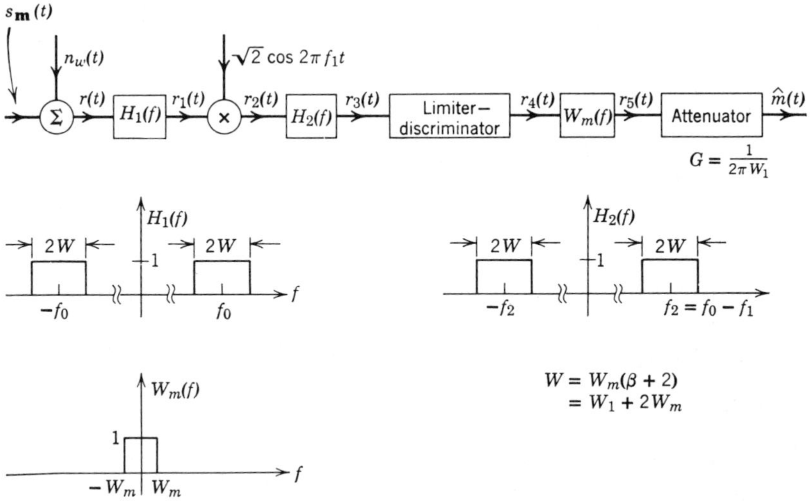

Figure 8.47 Idealized conventional FM receiver:

$$s_{\mathbf{m}}(t) = A\sqrt{2}\cos 2\pi[f_0 t + W_1 \textstyle\int m(t)\,dt].$$

the limiter-discriminator in the absence of noise to be a relatively undistorted replica of the transmitted signal, except for amplitude scaling and frequency translation. In the noiseless case we therefore assume

$$r_3(t) = A\cos 2\pi\left[f_2 t + W_1 \int m(t)\,dt\right]. \tag{8.132}$$

Frequency demodulation is accomplished in the limiter-discriminator, which is a nonlinear device that responds only to variations in instantaneous frequency.[2,71] We model the device mathematically by saying that whenever the input to the device is

$$r_3(t) = a(t)\cos[\omega_2 t + \phi(t)], \tag{8.133a}$$

the output is

$$r_4(t) = \frac{d\phi(t)}{dt}. \tag{8.133b}$$

But we have seen that the spectrum of the derivative of a signal with Fourier transform $X(f)$ is $j2\pi f\, X(f)$. For purposes of analysis we may therefore replace the limiter-discriminator by a box that extracts $\phi(t)$ from $r_3(t)$, followed by a "differentiating filter" with transfer function

$$H'(f) \triangleq j2\pi f, \tag{8.134}$$

as shown in Fig. 8.48.

The final stages of an idealized conventional FM receiver comprise an ideal unit-gain filter $W_m(f)$ that eliminates noise outside the band

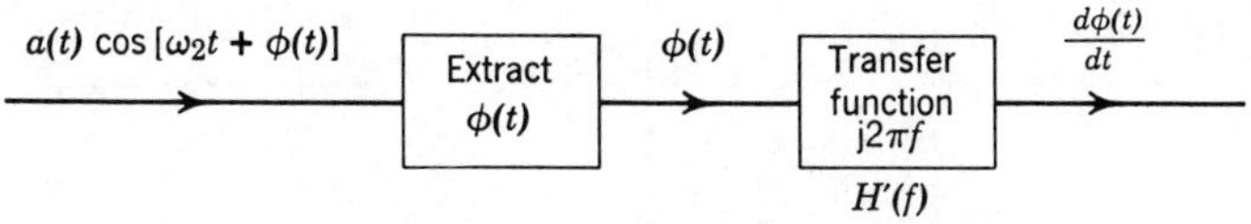

Figure 8.48 Idealized functional representation of limiter-discriminator.

$[-W_m, W_m]$ occupied by $m(t)$ and an attenuator with gain G. In the noiseless case

$$r_4(t) = \frac{d}{dt}\left[2\pi W_1 \int m(t)\,dt\right] = 2\pi W_1\, m(t), \tag{8.135a}$$

so that we obtain $\hat{m}(t) = m(t)$ by setting

$$G = \frac{1}{2\pi W_1}. \tag{8.135b}$$

Weak-noise effects with conventional receivers. We now make a quasi-static analysis of the mean-square output noise, $\overline{n^2(t)}$, obtained with conventional FM reception in weak additive white Gaussian noise. We begin by assuming that the modulating signal is some constant, say

$$m(t) = m_I; \qquad -1 \leqslant m_I \leqslant 1, \tag{8.136a}$$

so that the RF filter output in Fig. 8.47 is

$$r_1(t) = A\sqrt{2}\cos 2\pi(f_0 + W_1 m_I)t + n_1(t). \tag{8.136b}$$

Here $n_1(t)$ is a bandpass Gaussian process with power density

$$\mathcal{S}_{n_1}(f) = \begin{cases} \dfrac{\mathcal{N}_0}{2}; & f_0 - W < |f| < f_0 + W \\ 0; & \text{elsewhere.} \end{cases} \tag{8.137}$$

We next resolve $n_1(t)$ into two components, one in and one out of phase with $\cos \omega_I t$, where

$$\omega_I \triangleq 2\pi f_I = 2\pi(f_0 + W_1 m_I). \tag{8.138}$$

We have

$$n_1(t) = n_c(t)\sqrt{2}\cos\omega_I t + n_s(t)\sqrt{2}\sin\omega_I t. \qquad (8.139)$$

In accordance with Eq. 7.24b, $n_c(t)$ and $n_s(t)$ are stationary lowpass Gaussian processes with power spectra given by the even part of $\mathcal{S}_{n_1}(f-f_I)$. The power density spectra $\mathcal{S}_{n_c}(f)$ and $\mathcal{S}_{n_s}(f)$ are therefore as plotted in Fig. 8.49. Note that the restriction $|m_I| \leqslant 1$ guarantees that $\mathcal{S}_{n_c}(f)$ and $\mathcal{S}_{n_s}(f)$ equal $\mathcal{N}_0/2$ for all f within the restricted interval $[-2W_m, 2W_m]$.

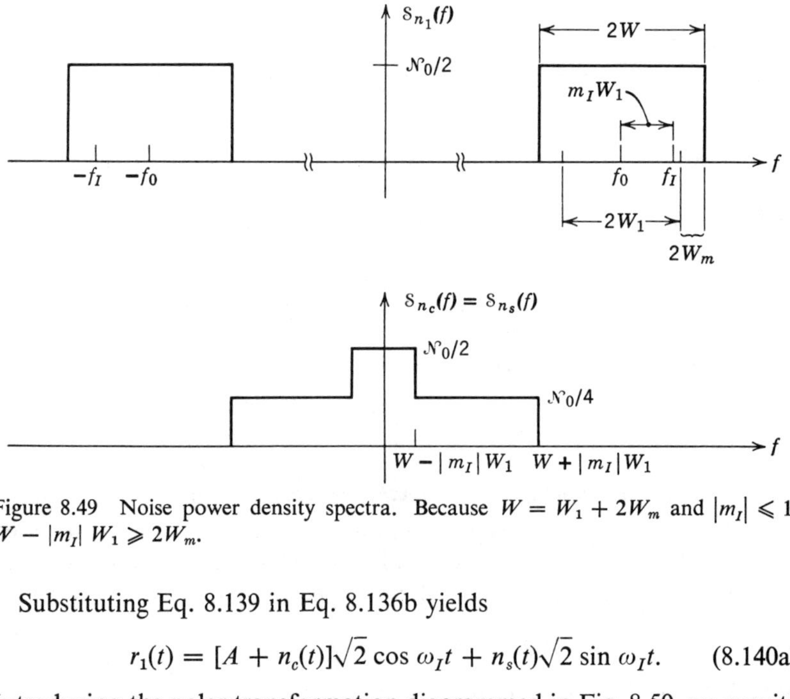

Figure 8.49 Noise power density spectra. Because $W = W_1 + 2W_m$ and $|m_I| \leqslant 1$, $W - |m_I|\, W_1 \geqslant 2W_m$.

Substituting Eq. 8.139 in Eq. 8.136b yields

$$r_1(t) = [A + n_c(t)]\sqrt{2}\cos\omega_I t + n_s(t)\sqrt{2}\sin\omega_I t. \qquad (8.140a)$$

Introducing the polar transformation diagrammed in Fig. 8.50, we rewrite this equation as

$$r_1(t) = a(t)\sqrt{2}\cos[\omega_I t + \phi(t)], \qquad (8.140b)$$

in which

$$a(t) \triangleq \sqrt{[A + n_c(t)]^2 + n_s^2(t)} \qquad (8.140c)$$

$$\phi(t) \triangleq \tan^{-1}\frac{-n_s(t)}{A + n_c(t)}. \qquad (8.140d)$$

It follows that the input to the limiter-discriminator in Fig. 8.47 is

$$r_3(t) = a(t)\cos[2\pi(f_2 + W_1 m_I)t + \phi(t)]. \qquad (8.141)$$

Next, we introduce the weak-noise assumption that the total noise power in the over-all signal bandwidth is much less than the signal power:

$$2\mathcal{N}_0 W \ll A^2. \tag{8.142}$$

Under this condition, the approximation

$$\phi(t) = \tan^{-1}\frac{-n_s(t)}{A + n_c(t)} \approx \frac{-n_s(t)}{A + n_c(t)} \approx \frac{-n_s(t)}{A} \tag{8.143}$$

is valid except for certain improbable (hence infrequent) time intervals during which $|n_s(t)|$ and/or $|n_c(t)|$ assume values much larger than usual.

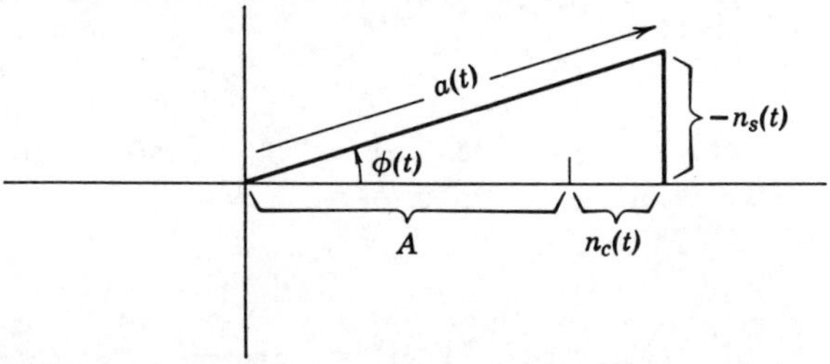

Figure 8.50 Polar transformation for substitution in the trigonometric identity $\cos(\alpha + \beta) = \cos\alpha\cos\beta - \sin\alpha\sin\beta$.

Excluding such intervals from consideration, we have

$$r_3(t) \approx a(t)\cos\left[\omega_2 t + 2\pi W_1 m_I t - \frac{n_s(t)}{A}\right]. \tag{8.144}$$

The final step in our analysis is to recall that the output of the limiter-discriminator, $r_4(t)$, may be identified with the output of a differentiating filter $H'(f) = j2\pi f$ whose input is $[2\pi W_1 m_I t - n_s(t)/A]$. Since the receiver output is obtained from $r_4(t)$ by attenuation and lowpass filtering, neglecting the approximation involved in Eq. 8.144 yields

$$\hat{m}(t) \approx m_I + n(t), \tag{8.145a}$$

in which $n(t)$ is a stationary Gaussian noise whose power density function,

$$\mathcal{S}_n(f) = \left(\frac{-G}{A}\right)^2 \mathcal{S}_{n_s}(f)\,|H'(f)|^2\,|W_m(f)|^2, \tag{8.145b}$$

is plotted in Fig. 8.51. From Eqs. 8.134 and 8.135b

$$\begin{aligned}
\overline{n^2(t)} &= \int_{-\infty}^{\infty} \mathcal{S}_n(f)\,df \\
&= \left(\frac{1}{2\pi W_1 A}\right)^2 \int_{-W_m}^{W_m} (2\pi f)^2 \frac{\mathcal{N}_0}{2}\,df \\
&= \left(\frac{1}{W_1 A}\right)^2 \frac{\mathcal{N}_0}{2}\frac{2}{3} W_m^{\,3}.
\end{aligned}$$

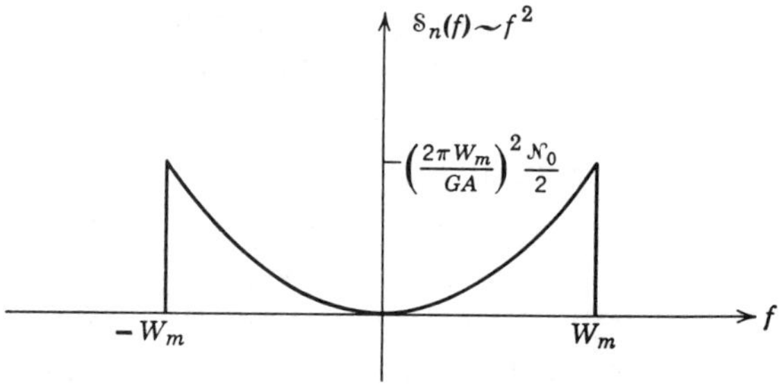

Figure 8.51 Noise power density spectrum at output of FM receiver with weak noise and constant modulation.

In terms of the energy transmitted per sample of $m(t)$, it follows from Eq. 8.124 that the mean-square effect of weak white noise on the output of a conventional FM receiver is

$$\overline{n^2(t)} = \frac{1}{3}\left(\frac{W_m}{W_1}\right)^2 \frac{\mathcal{N}_0}{2E_s} = \frac{1}{3}\frac{1}{\beta^2}\frac{\mathcal{N}_0}{2E_s}. \tag{8.146}$$

Thus far we have considered $m(t)$ to be a constant, much as in the FPM case. The analysis can be extended to situations in which $m(t)$ is not a constant, provided that $\beta \gg 1$. As shown in Fig. 8.52, we can then approximate $m(t)$ by a succession of rectangular pulses of duration Δ, where Δ can be chosen short compared with $1/2W_m$ and long compared with $1/2W_1$. Thus it is possible to make the approximation to $m(t)$ a good one and simultaneously to retain the essential validity of the foregoing (static) weak-noise analysis. Within this quasi-static approximation, the output noise is therefore given by Eq. 8.146 for large β and arbitrary (bounded) $m(t)$. It is found experimentally that Eq. 8.146 remains approximately correct even for moderate values of β.

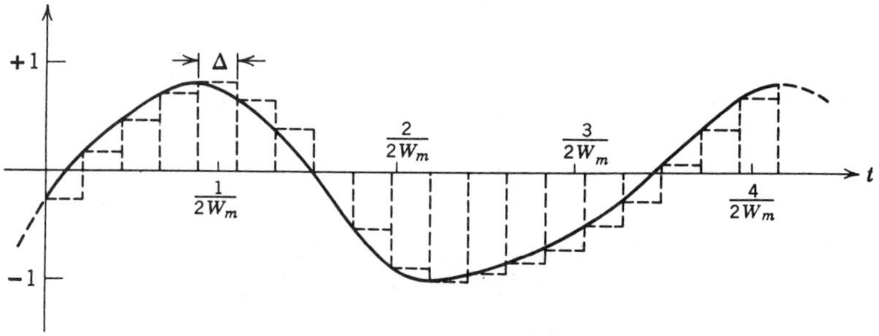

Figure 8.52 Pulse approximation to $m(t)$.

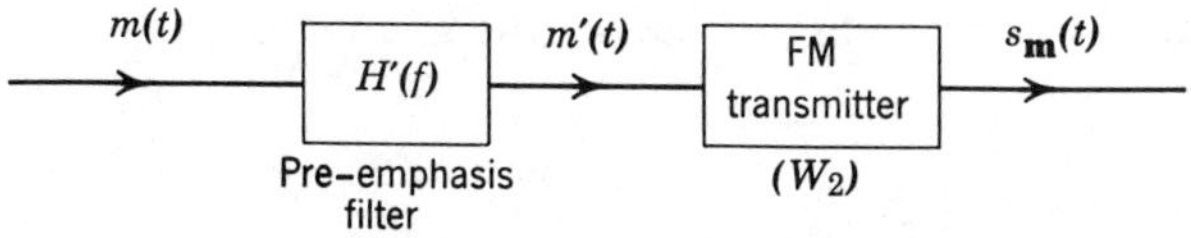

Figure 8.53 Pre-emphasis FM, or PM, transmitter.

Phase modulation. Until now we have been concerned only with the total mean-square noise as a criterion of communication system performance in the absence of anomaly. As a practical matter, however, the distribution of noise power as a function of frequency may also be important. For example, a difficulty with FM is that the noise power density at the receiver output is not uniform; we have seen in Fig. 8.51 that $\mathcal{S}_n(f)$ varies as f^2 for $-W_m < f < W_m$. Thus the high-frequency components of $m(t)$, which are particularly important to articulation when $m(t)$ represents a voice signal, are received with less fidelity than the low-frequency components.

This difficulty is overcome in practice by passing $m(t)$ through a linear filter that pre-emphasizes high frequencies before modulation. Such a transmitter is shown in Fig. 8.53, in which the pre-emphasis is accomplished by means of a differentiating filter $H'(f)$. In this case the transmitted process is

$$s_m(t) = A\sqrt{2}\cos 2\pi\left[f_0 t + W_2\int m'(t)\,dt\right]$$

$$= A\sqrt{2}\cos 2\pi[f_0 t + W_2\, m(t)]. \tag{8.147}$$

In Eq. 8.147 it is the instantaneous phase $2\pi W_2\, m(t)$ of $s_m(t)$ that is linearly related to $m(t)$; as a consequence such a signal is called *phase modulated* (PM).

A PM signal can be received by means of a conventional FM receiver and a de-emphasizing filter, as indicated in Fig. 8.54. Consider the FM

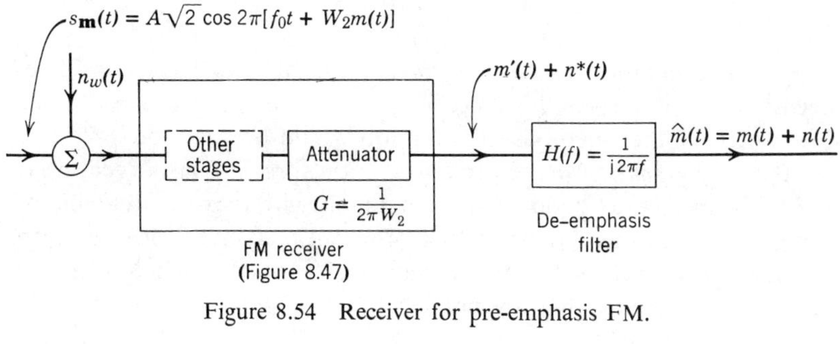

Figure 8.54 Receiver for pre-emphasis FM.

receiver embedded in the figure and set the attenuator gain to

$$G = \frac{1}{2\pi W_2}. \tag{8.148}$$

When the RF and IF bandwidths are large enough to pass $s_m(t)$ with negligible distortion, the FM receiver output in the absence of anomaly is $m'(t) + n^*(t)$, where $n^*(t)$ is a Gaussian noise process and (in accordance with Eq. 8.145b)

$$\mathcal{S}_{n^*}(f) = \begin{cases} \left(\dfrac{2\pi f}{2\pi A W_2}\right)^2 \dfrac{\mathcal{N}_0}{2}; & -W_m < f < W_m \\ 0; & \text{elsewhere.} \end{cases} \tag{8.149}$$

The output of the de-emphasis (or integrating) filter in Fig. 8.54 is therefore

$$\hat{m}(t) = m(t) + n(t), \tag{8.150a}$$

in which

$$\begin{aligned} \mathcal{S}_n(f) &= \left|\frac{1}{j2\pi f}\right|^2 \mathcal{S}_{n^*}(f) \\ &= \begin{cases} \left(\dfrac{1}{2\pi A W_2}\right)^2 \dfrac{\mathcal{N}_0}{2}; & -W_m < f < W_m \\ 0; & \text{elsewhere.} \end{cases} \end{aligned} \tag{8.150b}$$

We note that $n(t)$ has uniform power density over the modulation bandwidth, as was desired. The mean-square value of the final noise output (with weak noise input) is

$$\overline{n^2(t)} = \frac{\mathcal{N}_0 W_m}{(2\pi A W_2)^2}. \tag{8.151a}$$

In terms of the energy transmitted per sample of $m(t)$, Eq. 8.151a is

$$\overline{n^2(t)} = \left(\frac{1}{2\pi W_2}\right)^2 \frac{\mathcal{N}_0}{2E_s}. \tag{8.151b}$$

Maximum-likelihood reception. Thus far we have considered conventional examples of FM receiving techniques but have not determined whether other methods of reception would be superior. We now show that the *weak-noise* performance of the pre-emphasis receiver of Fig. 8.54 is, in fact, as good as that obtainable with maximum-likelihood reception. On the other hand, it does *not* follow that conventional receivers are equally ideal in regard to the incidence of anomalies. Indeed, in the sequel we shall see that they are not.

The weak-noise performance of a maximum-likelihood receiver when

$$s_{\mathbf{m}}(t) = A\sqrt{2}\cos 2\pi[f_0 t + W_2\, m(t)] \tag{8.152a}$$

may be determined by again representing $m(t)$ by a vector,

$$\mathbf{m} = (m_{-K/2}, \ldots, m_{K/2}).$$

For $m(t)$ bandlimited to $[-W_m, W_m]$, we have

$$s_{\mathbf{m}}(t) = A\sqrt{2}\cos 2\pi\left[f_0 t + W_2 \sum_{k=-K/2}^{K/2} m_k\, \psi_k(t)\right], \tag{8.152b}$$

where the $\{\psi_k(t)\}$ are the sampling functions of Eq. 8.43. [We assume initially that only $K + 1$ samples of $m(t)$ can be nonzero.] We then have

$$\frac{\partial s_{\mathbf{m}}(t)}{\partial m_j} = [-2\pi A W_2\, \psi_j(t)]\sqrt{2}\sin 2\pi\left[f_0 t + W_2 \sum_k m_k\, \psi_k(t)\right];$$

$$j = -\frac{K}{2}, \ldots, +\frac{K}{2}. \tag{8.153a}$$

Hence

$$\int_{-\infty}^{\infty} \frac{\partial s_{\mathbf{m}}(t)}{\partial m_j}\frac{\partial s_{\mathbf{m}}(t)}{\partial m_l}\, dt =$$

$$\int_{-\infty}^{\infty} (2\pi A W_2)^2\, \psi_j(t)\, \psi_l(t)\left[1 - \cos 4\pi\left(f_0 t + W_2 \sum_k m_k\, \psi_k(t)\right)\right] dt. \tag{8.153b}$$

Since the $\{\psi_k(t)\}$ are orthonormal, neglecting the high-frequency term yields

$$\int_{-\infty}^{\infty} \frac{\partial s_{\mathbf{m}}(t)}{\partial m_j}\frac{\partial s_{\mathbf{m}}(t)}{\partial m_l}\, dt = (2\pi A W_2)^2\, \delta_{jl}, \qquad \text{for all } j \text{ and } l. \tag{8.153c}$$

Equation 8.153c may be interpreted geometrically as indicated in Fig. 8.55. In the vicinity of any particular signal vector, say $\mathbf{s_m} = \mathbf{s}_0$, small changes in m_j and m_l cause $\mathbf{s_m}$ to move in *orthogonal directions* when $j \neq l$. But with weak enough noise it is only the signal locus, in this case a $(K + 1)$-dimensional surface, in the immediate vicinity of the transmitted signal that enters into the determination of a maximum-likelihood receiver's estimate of $\mathbf{m}$. Furthermore, with white Gaussian noise, only the noise projection onto the signal locus is relevant and noise projections along orthonormal axes are statistically independent zero-mean Gaussian random variables with variance $\mathcal{N}_0/2$. Thus in weak noise the geometrical relations are locally equivalent to those previously encountered in the sequence-of-parameters communication problem of Section 8.1: only

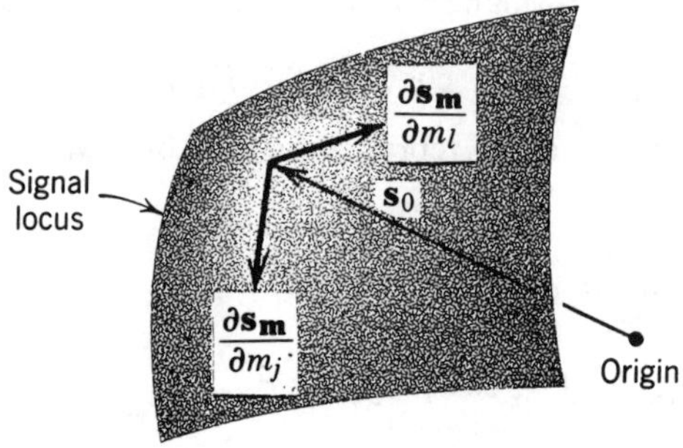

Figure 8.55 Geometrical interpretation of Eq. 8.153c.

the set of orthonormal functions, which are obtained by normalizing the right-hand side of Eq. 8.153a to unit energy, is different. The identity of these orthonormal functions depends on **m**; their orthogonality does not.

It follows immediately from Fig. 8.55 that the weak-noise mean-square error in a maximum-likelihood estimate of each of the $\{m_k\}$ is $\mathcal{N}_0/2$ divided by the square of the stretch factor in the direction specified by $\partial s_{\mathbf{m}}(t)/\partial m_k$. But the stretch is the same for all k: from Eq. 8.153c

$$S^2 = (2\pi A W_2)^2. \tag{8.154}$$

Thus a maximum-likelihood receiver in weak noise produces

$$\hat{m}(t) = m(t) + \sum_{k=-K/2}^{K/2} n_k \, \psi_k(t), \tag{8.155a}$$

in which the $\{n_k\}$ are zero-mean Gaussian random variables with

$$\overline{n_k^{\,2}} = \frac{\mathcal{N}_0/2}{(2\pi A W_2)^2}. \tag{8.155b}$$

Letting K go to infinity and invoking Eq. 8.50 yields

$$\hat{m}(t) = m(t) + n(t) \tag{8.156a}$$

with

$$\overline{n^2(t)} = \frac{\mathcal{N}_0 W_m}{(2\pi A W_2)^2}. \tag{8.156b}$$

Comparison of Eqs. 8.156b and 8.151a verifies the fact that the performance of conventional pre-emphasis FM receivers in weak noise is identical to that obtainable with maximum-likelihood reception.

System comparison. It is interesting to contrast the weak-noise performance of FM, PM, and ordinary FPM when the signals are simultaneously normalized to the same transmitted energy per sample of $m(t)$

and the same transmission bandwidth. For convenience of reference we summarize the weak-noise performances of these systems.

FPM.

$$s_m(t) = \begin{cases} A\sqrt{2}\cos 2\pi(f_0 + mW_0)t; & -\dfrac{1}{4W_m} \leqslant t \leqslant \dfrac{1}{4W_m}, \\ 0; \quad \text{elsewhere,} & \end{cases} \tag{8.157a}$$

$$\overline{n^2(t)} = \frac{12}{\pi^2}\left(\frac{W_m}{W_0}\right)^2 \frac{\mathcal{N}_0 W_m}{E_s}.$$

FM.

$$s_m(t) = A\sqrt{2}\cos 2\pi\left[f_0 t + W_1 \int m(t)\, dt\right],$$

$$\overline{n^2(t)} = \frac{1}{3}\left(\frac{W_m}{W_1}\right)^2 \frac{\mathcal{N}_0}{2E_s}. \tag{8.157b}$$

PM.

$$s_m(t) = A\sqrt{2}\cos 2\pi[f_0 t + W_2\, m(t)],$$

$$\overline{n^2(t)} = \left(\frac{1}{2\pi W_2}\right)^2 \frac{\mathcal{N}_0}{2E_s}. \tag{8.157c}$$

For each system the signal power has been normalized to A^2, so that the energy transmitted per sample is

$$E_s = \frac{A^2}{2W_m}. \tag{8.158}$$

The question of bandwidth normalization remains. For all three signals the RF half-bandwidth W may be taken as the maximum instantaneous-frequency deviation, plus a guard band of $2W_m$ cps.

$$W = |\Delta f|_{\max} + 2W_m, \tag{8.159a}$$

$$\Delta f \triangleq f_I - f_0. \tag{8.159b}$$

At any sampling instant t_k, we have the following relations.

FPM.

$$\Delta f = W_0 \frac{1}{\sqrt{2W_m}}\, m(t_k). \tag{8.160a}$$

FM.

$$\Delta f = W_1\, m(t_k). \tag{8.160b}$$

PM.

$$\Delta f = W_2\, m'(t_k). \tag{8.160c}$$

Equation 8.160a follows from Eq. 8.49b. It would be desirable to scale the parameters W_0, W_1, and W_2 in such a way that the maximum instantaneous-frequency deviations are the same. Difficulty arises, however, because there is no general way of specifying the relationship between $m(t)|_{\max}$ and $m'(t)|_{\max}$.

This difficulty may be partly resolved by assuming that $m(t)$ is the result of passing a white Gaussian process of spectral density $\mathcal{N}_0/2$, $-\infty < f < \infty$, through an ideal filter $W_m(f)$, as shown in Fig. 8.56. Each of the instantaneous-frequency deviations in Eqs. 8.160 is then a zero-mean Gaussian random variable and is, of course, unbounded. The residual difficulty entailed by the assumption that $m(t)$ is Gaussian is that it is not meaningful to normalize the maximum value of the Δf.

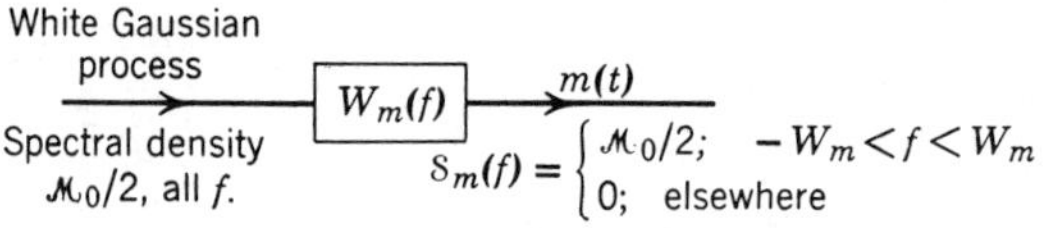

Figure 8.56 An ideal bandlimited Gaussian message process.

On the other hand, it is meaningful—although less satisfying—to normalize W_0, W_1, and W_2 in such a way that the probability that Δf exceeds any stated value, say, W_I, is the same for all three systems. Then W_I can be chosen so that the probability $P[\Delta f > W_I]$ is acceptably small, say comparable to the probability of anomaly, and the transmission half-bandwidth can be taken as

$$W = W_I + 2W_m. \tag{8.161}$$

The advantage of the assumption that $m(t)$ is a Gaussian process is that it simplifies equating the probabilities $P[\Delta f > W_I]$. From Fig. 8.56 we have

$$\overline{m^2(t)} = \mathcal{N}_0 W_m \tag{8.162a}$$

and

$$\overline{[m'(t)]^2} = \int_{-W_m}^{W_m} (2\pi f)^2 \frac{\mathcal{N}_0}{2}\, df = \tfrac{1}{3}(2\pi W_m)^2 \mathcal{N}_0 W_m. \tag{8.162b}$$

From Eqs. 8.160, the variances of Δf are therefore as follows:

FPM.

$$\overline{\Delta^2 f} = \frac{W_0^{\,2}}{2W_m}(\mathcal{N}_0 W_m). \tag{8.163a}$$

FM.

$$\overline{\Delta^2 f} = W_1^{\,2}(\mathcal{N}_0 W_m). \tag{8.163b}$$

PM.

$$\overline{\Delta^2 f} = \tfrac{1}{3} W_2^{\,2}(2\pi W_m)^2(\mathcal{N}_0 W_m). \tag{8.163c}$$

Clearly, the three P[$\Delta f > W_I$] are equal for any W_I if we scale the parameters W_0, W_1, and W_2 so that

$$\frac{W_0}{\sqrt{2W_m}} = W_1 = (2\pi W_m)\frac{W_2}{\sqrt{3}}. \tag{8.164}$$

If we adopt W_1 as the basic parameter, the normalization of Eq. 8.164 implies that the mean-square noise values of Eqs. 8.157 are the following.

FPM.

$$\overline{n^2(t)} = \frac{12}{\pi^2}\left(\frac{W_m}{W_1}\right)^2 \frac{\mathcal{N}_0}{2E_s}. \tag{8.165a}$$

FM.

$$\overline{n^2(t)} = \frac{1}{3}\left(\frac{W_m}{W_1}\right)^2 \frac{\mathcal{N}_0}{2E_s}. \tag{8.165b}$$

PM.

$$\overline{n^2(t)} = \frac{1}{3}\left(\frac{W_m}{W_1}\right)^2 \frac{\mathcal{N}_0}{2E_s}. \tag{8.165c}$$

We see that PM and FM yield equal noise-output power, whereas ordinary FPM is approximately 6 db inferior. This difference in weak-noise performance reflects the fact that FM and PM are analogous to the FPM scheme of Eq. 8.121 in which m modulates both the RF *phase and frequency*. Given an adequate phase reference and maximum-likelihood reception, either phase-and-frequency or antipodal FPM would afford a weak-noise mean-square error essentially equal to that provided by FM or PM. Perhaps even more significant, however, is the fact that the availability of a phase reference would permit the use of quadrature multiplexed antipodal FPM (or PPM). With bandwidth normalization, the $\overline{n^2(t)}$ afforded by this technique in the absence of anomaly would be 6 db superior to that afforded by FM or PM.

Probability of Anomaly

Although the mean-square noise produced by conventional FM receivers in the absence of anomaly is equivalent to that afforded by antipodal FPM, the equivalence does *not* extend to the probability of anomaly. We now show that conventional FM receivers yield a P[$\mathcal{A}$] that is substantially inferior.

The mechanism leading to anomalies with conventional FM receivers is inherent in the behavior of the signal phase at the limiter-discriminator input. In the absence of modulation, we have used (Eq. 8.143) the approximation

$$\phi(t) \triangleq \tan^{-1}\frac{-n_s(t)}{A + n_c(t)} \approx -\frac{n_s(t)}{A}.$$

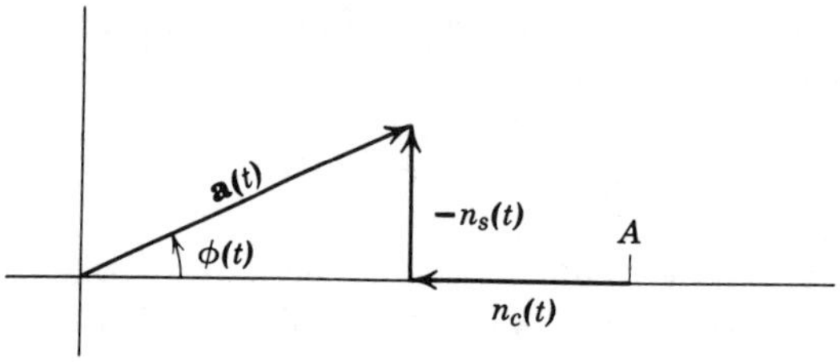

(a) Phasor diagram

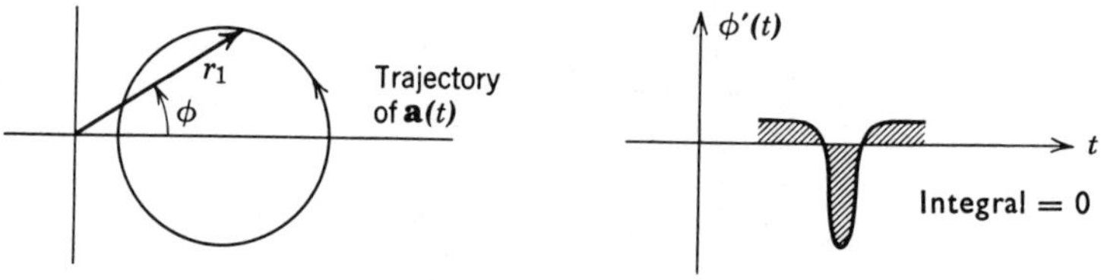

(b) No encirclement of origin

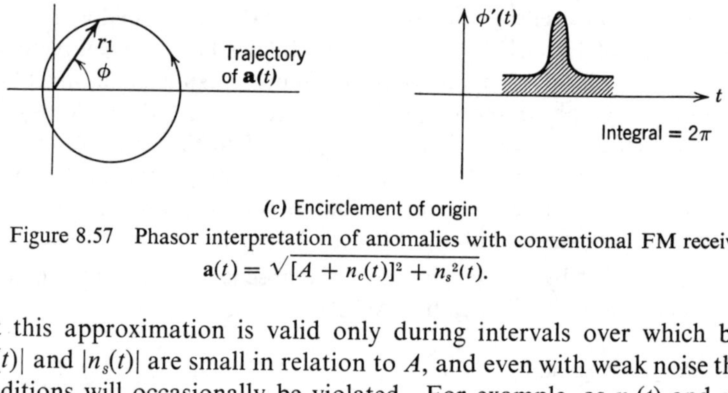

(c) Encirclement of origin

Figure 8.57 Phasor interpretation of anomalies with conventional FM receivers: $\mathbf{a}(t) = \sqrt{[A + n_c(t)]^2 + n_s^2(t)}$.

But this approximation is valid only during intervals over which both $|n_c(t)|$ and $|n_s(t)|$ are small in relation to A, and even with weak noise these conditions will occasionally be violated. For example, as $n_c(t)$ and $n_s(t)$ change randomly with time there is a certain probability that the tip of the phasor $\mathbf{a}(t)$ of Fig. 8.57*a* will swing close to the origin, as shown in Fig. 8.57*b*.

As long as the resultant phasor does not encircle the origin, the effect of such a swing on the receiver is not particularly disastrous: for instance, if we assume that $\mathbf{a}(t)$ moves with uniform velocity along the trajectory of Fig. 8.57*b*, the accompanying plot of $d\phi/dt$ shows a small positive value during most of the time of traverse, with a sharp negative spike in the center. The net change in ϕ is zero, which implies that most of the energy content of $d\phi/dt$ is in high frequencies that are eliminated by the output filter $W_m(f)$.

On the other hand, if the tip of $\mathbf{a}(t)$ does encircle the origin, as shown in Fig. 8.57*c*, the effect is very different. The limiter-discriminator output, $d\phi/dt$, now exhibits a sharp *positive* pulse and the net change in ϕ is 2π rather than zero. Since $n_c(t)$ and $n_s(t)$ are lowpass noise processes with bandwidth $W = W_1 + 2W_m$, to the narrow-bandwidth filter $W_m(f)$ such a pulse typically will look like an impulse of value 2π. It follows that there is now substantial low-frequency energy in the disturbance, which effectively overrides any substantial dependence of the receiver output on the transmitted signal. Thus $\hat{m}(t)$ is "disconnected" from $m(t)$, and we say that an anomaly has occurred.

Following arguments that are due to Rice,[70] we can estimate the probability, again denoted $\mathrm{P}[\mathcal{A}]$, that at least one origin encirclement occurs during the interval $[0, 1/2W_m]$. As shown in Fig. 8.57*c*, a necessary condition for origin encirclement is that $n_c(t)$ must be less than $-A$ during some included subinterval during which $n_s(t)$ changes sign. Following such a crossing of the negative real axis, $\mathbf{a}(t)$ will proceed to encircle the origin during the interval $[0, 1/2W_m]$ with a probability that (conservatively) will be greater than $\frac{1}{2}$. It follows that $\mathrm{P}[\mathcal{A}]$ may be estimated by dividing $[0, 1/2W_m]$ into a large number of small intervals of duration $\Delta \ll 1/2W_m$ (as shown in Fig. 8.52) and calculating the probability that $\mathbf{a}(t)$ will cross the negative real axis during at least one of these $1/(2W_m\Delta)$ subintervals.

Now let us focus upon the particular subinterval $[0, \Delta]$ and consider the two events

$$B_1 \triangleq \{n_c(t) < -A \text{ during } [0, \Delta]\}$$

$$B_2 \triangleq \{n_s(t) \text{ crosses through zero during } [0, \Delta]\}.$$

The intersection $B_1 \cap B_2$ is just the event that $\mathbf{a}(t)$ does cross the negative real axis during $[0, \Delta]$. Furthermore, $n_c(t)$ and $n_s(t)$ are statistically independent when the modulating signal $m(t)$ is identically zero, which implies that in this case

$$\mathrm{P}[B_1 \cap B_2] = \mathrm{P}[B_1]\,\mathrm{P}[B_2]. \tag{8.166}$$

In the absence of modulation both $n_c(t)$ and $n_s(t)$ are lowpass Gaussian processes with bandwidth W and mean power density $\mathcal{N}_0/2$. Thus

$$\overline{n_c^2(t)} = \overline{n_s^2(t)} = \mathcal{N}_0 W. \tag{8.167}$$

If we choose $\Delta \ll 1/2W$—which guarantees $\Delta \ll 1/2W_m$—the small variation of $n_c(t)$ with time over the interval $[0, \Delta]$ may be neglected. It follows immediately that

$$\mathrm{P}[B_1] \approx \mathrm{P}\left[n_c\left(\frac{\Delta}{2}\right) < -A\right] = Q\left(\frac{A}{\sqrt{\mathcal{N}_0 W}}\right). \tag{8.168a}$$

The determination of $P[B_2]$ is somewhat more complicated. Obviously it is not reasonable to neglect the variation with time of $n_s(t)$ over $[0, \Delta]$ when the question of interest is whether $n_s(t)$ will change from + to − (or conversely) over this interval. It is shown in Appendix 8C that

$$P[B_2] \approx \frac{2W\Delta}{\sqrt{3}}. \tag{8.168b}$$

Thus we have

$$P[B_1 \cap B_2] \approx \frac{2W\Delta}{\sqrt{3}} Q\left(\frac{A}{\sqrt{\mathcal{N}_0 W}}\right). \tag{8.169}$$

Since we have chosen $\Delta \ll 1/2W$, it is apparent that the behavior of the phasor $\mathbf{a}(t)$ is statistically dependent from one interval to the next. But the probability of a union is bounded by the sum of the probabilities of its constituent events—whether or not they are statistically independent. Since $n_c(t)$ and $n_s(t)$ are stationary, each constituent of the union has probability $P[B_1 \cap B_2]$. Neglecting the possibility that the axis may be crossed without the origin being encircled, we estimate $P[\mathcal{A}]$ for the unmodulated case by the bound

$$\begin{aligned} P[\mathcal{A}] &\leqslant \frac{1}{2W_m\Delta} P[B_1 \cap B_2] \\ &\approx \frac{1}{\sqrt{3}} \frac{W}{W_m} Q\left(\frac{A}{\sqrt{\mathcal{N}_0 W}}\right) \\ &\approx \frac{1}{\sqrt{3}} \frac{W}{W_m} \frac{e^{-A^2/2\mathcal{N}_0 W}}{\sqrt{2\pi A^2/\mathcal{N}_0 W}}. \end{aligned} \tag{8.170}$$

When $m(t)$ is a nonzero constant, the preceding analysis is affected in two ways. First, $n_c(t)$ and $n_s(t)$ are no longer statistically independent. Second, as we have seen in Fig. 8.49, the bandwidth of $n_s(t)$ increases, thereby causing the average number of zero crossings per unit time produced by $n_s(t)$ to increase. Thus $P[B_2]$ increases somewhat when modulation is present. A corresponding small increase in $P[\mathcal{A}]$ is observed experimentally, but Eq. 8.170 remains a good estimate of the probability of anomaly with conventional FM receivers under the usual operating conditions of $P[\mathcal{A}] \ll 1$.

Comparison with FPM. For purpose of comparison with FPM, it is convenient to rewrite Eq. 8.170 in terms of the energy $E_s = A^2/2W_m$ transmitted during each modulation sampling interval. We then have

$$P[\mathcal{A}] \leqslant \frac{1}{\sqrt{6}}\left(\frac{W}{W_m}\right)^{3/2} \frac{e^{-(E_s/2\mathcal{N}_0)(2W_m/W)}}{\sqrt{2\pi(E_s/\mathcal{N}_0)}}; \qquad \text{for conventional FM.} \tag{8.171}$$

We have already observed (Eq. 8.165 and its sequel) that antipodal FPM affords a mean-square output noise level that is essentially equal to that of FM when both are assigned the same signal energy and are adjusted to utilize equal RF bandwidth. But from Eqs. 8.122c and 8.119 the probability of anomaly for antipodal (or phase-and-frequency) FPM is

$$P[\mathcal{A}] \approx \left(2\frac{W}{W_m} - 5\right)\frac{e^{-E_s/2\mathcal{N}_0}}{\sqrt{2\pi(E_s/\mathcal{N}_0)}}. \tag{8.172}$$

It is apparent from Eqs. 8.171 and 8.172 that antipodal FPM affords a very much smaller probability of anomaly than conventional FM reception when both systems are providing the same mean-square noise output in the absence of anomaly.

FM feedback receivers. From the foregoing analysis it is evident that the major cause of the poor anomalous performance of conventional FM receivers is the large bandwidth required at the limiter-discriminator input. This requirement can be ameliorated by the use of a "frequency-compressive feedback" [FMFB] receiver.[26] A block diagram is illustrated in Fig. 8.58.

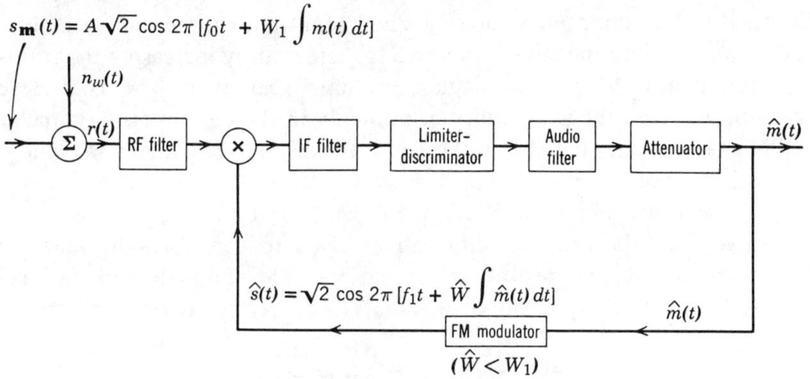

Figure 8.58 FMFB receiver.

An analysis of the mean-square output noise afforded by idealized FMFB in the absence of anomaly is presented in Appendix 8D. In particular, for noise sufficiently weak that $\mathcal{N}_0(W_1 + 2W_m) \ll A^2$, it is shown that

$$\hat{m}(t) = m(t) + n(t), \tag{8.173a}$$

with

$$\overline{n^2(t)} = \frac{1}{3}\left(\frac{W_m}{W_1}\right)^2\frac{\mathcal{N}_0}{2E_s}. \tag{8.173b}$$

Thus the weak-noise performances of FMFB and conventional FM (Eq. 8.146) are identical.

The strong connection between FM and phase-and-frequency FPM leads us to believe that the probability of anomaly—in addition to the mean-square output noise in the absence of anomaly—of these two systems would be equivalent if *maximum-likelihood* reception were used. If this conjecture is true, the bandwidth-normalized phase-and-frequency (or antipodal) FPM result of Eq. 8.172,

$$P[\mathcal{A}] \approx \left(2\frac{W}{W_m} - 5\right)\frac{e^{-E_s/2\mathcal{N}_0}}{\sqrt{2\pi(E_s/\mathcal{N}_0)}},$$

represents an approximate lower bound to the probability of anomaly afforded by FMFB receivers.

8.4 CHANNEL CAPACITY

We have seen that twisted modulation schemes can be used to decrease mean-square error at the cost of introducing a threshold phenomenon. For maximum-likelihood FPM (or PPM) receivers, it was possible to use the union bound to establish relatively simple quantitative measures of the trade-off between these two effects when the maximum energy E_s allotted to the communication of a single (continuous) random variable is held constant and the stretch factor S is increased by increasing the transmission bandwidth. In particular, we have seen that there is a close relation between the probability of anomaly in the continuous-parameter FPM case and the probability of error in the discrete-parameter M-orthogonal-signal case.

On the other hand, in Section 5.6 we found that arguments more sensitive than the union bound can be used to derive results that are stronger over certain regions of operation. The union bound on $P[\mathcal{E}]$ with M equally likely orthogonal signals each having energy E_s is

$$P[\mathcal{E}] < (M-1)\frac{e^{-E_s/2\mathcal{N}_0}}{\sqrt{2\pi(E_s/\mathcal{N}_0)}}. \tag{8.174}$$

But Eq. 5.106 states also that

$$P[\mathcal{E}] < 2 \cdot 2^{-T_m E^*(R)}, \tag{8.175a}$$

where T_m denotes the total signaling interval and

$$M = 2^{T_m R}, \tag{8.175b}$$

$$E^*(R) \triangleq \begin{cases} \dfrac{C_\infty}{2} - R; & 0 < R \leqslant \dfrac{C_\infty}{4} \\[2ex] (\sqrt{C_\infty} - \sqrt{R})^2; & \dfrac{C_\infty}{4} \leqslant R < C_\infty. \end{cases} \tag{8.175c}$$

Here, C_∞ is the infinite-bandwidth Gaussian channel capacity,

$$C_\infty = \frac{P_s}{\mathcal{N}_0} \log_2 e, \tag{8.175d}$$

and $P_s = E_s/T_m$ is the signal power. Equations 8.174 and 8.175 are exponentially equivalent for $R \leqslant C_\infty/4$, but Eq. 8.175 is both stronger and *exponentially tight* for values of R larger than this. The reliability function $E^*(R)$ of Eq. 8.175c is replotted for convenience in Fig. 8.59.

The identification of the probability of anomaly with the M-orthogonal probability of error permits us to use Eq. 8.175, as well as Eq. 8.174, in

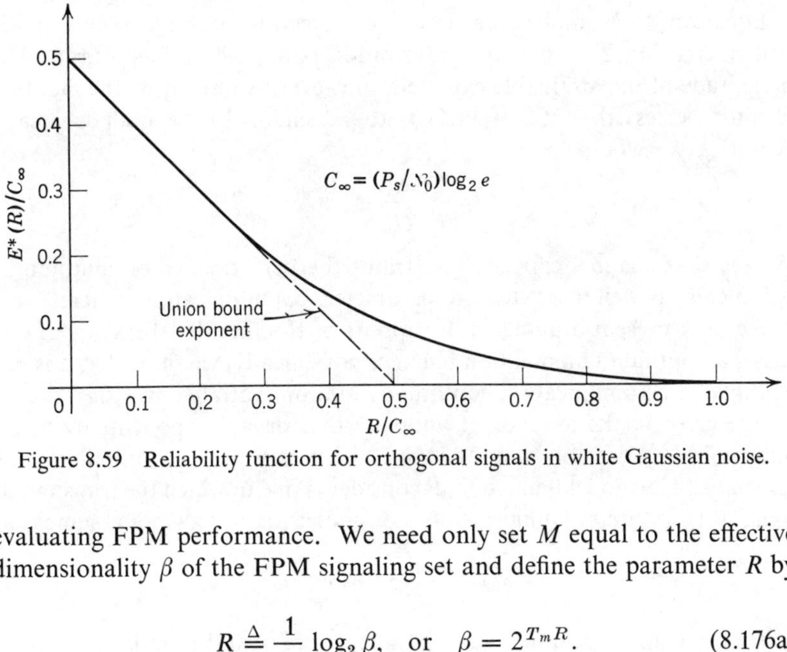

Figure 8.59 Reliability function for orthogonal signals in white Gaussian noise.

evaluating FPM performance. We need only set M equal to the effective dimensionality β of the FPM signaling set and define the parameter R by

$$R \triangleq \frac{1}{T_m} \log_2 \beta, \quad \text{or} \quad \beta = 2^{T_m R}. \tag{8.176a}$$

In the notation of Eq. 8.95a $\beta = 4TW_0$, in which W_0 is the maximum instantaneous frequency deviation when $|m| \leqslant 1$. Since the total signaling interval is $T_m = 2T$, we now have

$$\beta = 2T_m W_0. \tag{8.176b}$$

It follows from Eq. 8.95b,

$$\overline{\epsilon^2} = \frac{12}{\pi^2} \frac{1}{\beta^2} \frac{\mathcal{N}_0}{2E_s},$$

that the weak noise performance of a maximum-likelihood receiver for ordinary FPM is governed by the parametric relations

$$\left.\begin{aligned} \overline{\epsilon^2} &= \frac{12}{\pi^2}\frac{\mathcal{N}_0}{2E_s}\,2^{-2T_mR} \\ \mathrm{P}[\mathcal{A}] &\lessapprox 2\cdot 2^{-T_mE^*(R)} \end{aligned}\right\}; \qquad 0 < R < \frac{P_s}{\mathcal{N}_0}\log_2 e. \tag{8.177}$$

In principle, R may be chosen anywhere within the allowable range and a desirable balance between $\overline{\epsilon^2}$ and $\mathrm{P}[\mathcal{A}]$ obtained. As a practical matter, however, the effective dimensionality of the signal space, $\beta = 2^{T_mR}$, grows exponentially with R so that the largest applicable value of R may be constrained by the available channel bandwidth.

Equation 8.177 implies that $\overline{\epsilon^2}$ can be forced to decrease exponentially with increasing T_m when the transmitter power is held constant. The magnitude of the attainable exponent, however, is limited by the fact that R must be less than C_∞ if $\mathrm{P}[\mathcal{A}]$ is to be small. In the boundary case, $R = C_\infty$, we would have

$$\overline{\epsilon^2} = \frac{12}{\pi^2}\frac{\mathcal{N}_0}{2E_s}\,e^{-2E_s/\mathcal{N}_0}. \tag{8.178}$$

We see that channel capacity constrains the performance of continuous-parameter, as well as of discrete-parameter, communication systems.

We now present arguments in support of the fact that FPM is, in one sense, an optimum modulation scheme. Specifically, we show that it is not possible to communicate a continuous random variable m with a mean-square error in the absence of anomaly that decays exponentially faster than $e^{-2E_s/\mathcal{N}_0}$ without simultaneously incurring a large probability of anomaly. The model that we shall consider is one in which the transmitted signal $s_m(t)$ occupies a finite number of dimensions. Thus we assume that

$$s_m(t) = \sum_{j=1}^{N} s_j(m)\,\varphi_j(t), \tag{8.179}$$

where the $\{s_j(m)\}$ are differentiable functions of m and $\{\varphi_j(t)\}$ is a set of N orthonormal functions. We shall also assume that the a priori probability density p_m is uniform over the interval $[-1, 1]$ and zero elsewhere.

The question that we seek to answer is how fast the mean-square error $\overline{\epsilon^2}$ can be forced to zero as N is increased, when the maximum allowable transmitted energy per dimension, E_N, is held constant and we require simultaneously that the probability of anomaly approach zero.

When transmission is disturbed by additive white Gaussian noise, so that the received signal is

$$r(t) = s_m(t) + n_w(t), \tag{8.180a}$$

the relevant received signal can be represented by the N-dimensional vector

$$\mathbf{r} = \mathbf{s}_m + \mathbf{n}. \tag{8.180b}$$

The vector components are the projection of $s_m(t)$ and $n_w(t)$ on the orthonormal functions $\{\varphi_j(t)\}$. The energy constraint implies that

$$\int_{-\infty}^{\infty} s_m^2(t)\, dt \leqslant NE_{\mathrm{N}}. \tag{8.181}$$

Since N is to be a variable, it is convenient (as in the channel-capacity arguments of Section 5.5) to normalize the vector representation by the factor $1/\sqrt{N}$. We define

$$\underline{\mathbf{s}}_m \triangleq \frac{1}{\sqrt{N}}\, \mathbf{s}_m \tag{8.182a}$$

$$\underline{\mathbf{n}} \triangleq \frac{1}{\sqrt{N}}\, \mathbf{n} \tag{8.182b}$$

$$\underline{\mathbf{r}} \triangleq \frac{1}{\sqrt{N}}\, \mathbf{r} = \underline{\mathbf{s}}_m + \underline{\mathbf{n}}. \tag{8.182c}$$

With this convention, we have

$$|\underline{\mathbf{s}}_m|^2 = \frac{1}{N}\int_{-\infty}^{\infty} s_m^2(t)\, dt \leqslant E_{\mathrm{N}}, \tag{8.183a}$$

and

$$\mathrm{E}[|\underline{\mathbf{n}}|^2] = \sum_{j=1}^{N} \frac{1}{N}\, \overline{n_k^2} = \frac{\mathcal{N}_0}{2}. \tag{8.183b}$$

The geometric picture of the resulting communication problem is illustrated in Fig. 8.60. For every N, the twisted locus $\underline{\mathbf{s}}_m$ is constrained to lie on or within an N-dimensional sphere of radius $\sqrt{E_{\mathrm{N}}}$. As N approaches infinity, the probability that the squared length of the noise vector $|\underline{\mathbf{n}}|^2$ exceeds $\mathcal{N}_0/2$ by any amount Δ goes to zero. Just as in the discrete comunication case (Eq. 5.69), it follows that the received vector $\underline{\mathbf{r}}$ will lie on or within a sphere of radius

$$\sqrt{E_{\mathrm{N}} + \mathcal{N}_0/2 + \Delta}, \tag{8.184}$$

with probability one in the limit $N \to \infty$.

We have already observed in the discussion encompassing Eq. 8.82 that the maximum weak-noise suppression attainable with a signal trace of total length L occurs when $|d\underline{\mathbf{s}}_m/dm| = L/2$ for all m. If we assume that this condition is met, the only remaining task is to determine how large L can be made as N increases while still requiring the probability of anomaly to approach zero.

Given any signal locus, the maximum-likelihood receiving strategy is to assign the received vector $\underline{\mathbf{r}}$ to that point $\underline{\mathbf{s}}_m$ for which $|\underline{\mathbf{r}} - \underline{\mathbf{s}}_m|^2$ is minimum. The effect of this decision rule is to assign each volume element dv of the received signal space to a corresponding lineal element dl along the signal curve. By implication, to any given twisted signal curve there must correspond a set of boundaries in the received space such that a *small* (continuous) dislocation of $\underline{\mathbf{r}}$ across a boundary implies a *large* (discontinuous)

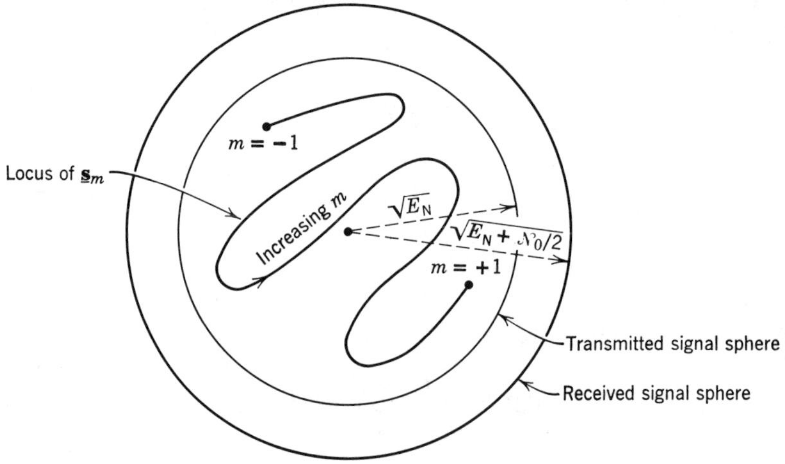

Figure 8.60 Normalized N-dimensional signal spheres.

dislocation in the receiver's estimate of the transmitted vector. We say that an anomaly occurs whenever the noise vector $\underline{\mathbf{n}}$ crosses such a boundary, as shown in Fig. 8.61.

The problem of optimum signal design is to coil a signal locus of the greatest possible length into an N-dimensional sphere of radius $\sqrt{E_N}$ in such a way that the probability of transcending any threshold boundary is minimum. Instead of trying to find such a locus explicitly, we proceed as with discrete signals and seek to establish a bound on how good a noise performance can possibly be achieved.

In particular, let us consider first a signal locus that is a straight line of length L. If we were to enclose this straight line in an N-dimensional tube of total volume V, it would be clear how this volume should be distributed spatially to minimize the probability of a noise vector crossing the tube boundary: aside from end effects, at every point of the line the intersection of the tube with the plane perpendicular to the signal locus should be a circle of fixed radius centered on the locus. In other words, the cross section of the tube at every point $\underline{s}$ should be an $(N-1)$-dimensional sphere. This follows from the fact that if this condition were not met it would be possible to move distant volume elements to locations that are closer to the signal locus, as shown in Fig. 8.62*a* for the three-dimensional case.

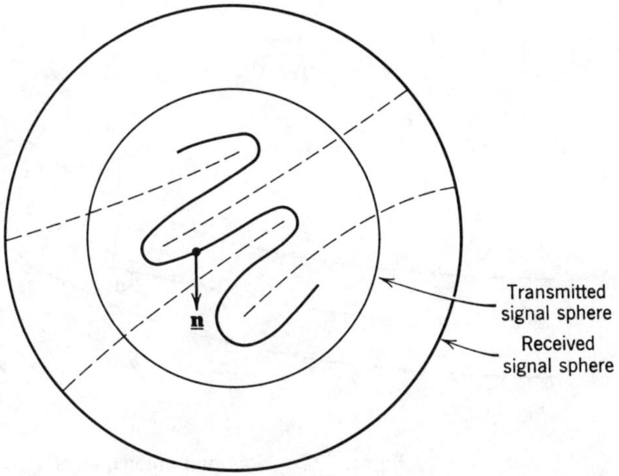

Figure 8.61 Anomalous error due to boundary crossing. (The dashed lines represent the boundaries.)

Moreover, it is clear from Fig. 8.62*b* that bending the N-dimensional right circular cylinder recommended by the preceding argument increases the probability of a noise vector $\underline{\mathbf{n}}$ crossing a boundary. This follows from the fact that, given $m = m_0$, $\underline{\mathbf{n}}$ can be decomposed into two statistically independent components, a one-dimensional component $\underline{\mathbf{n}}_1$ in the direction of

$$\left.\frac{d\underline{\mathbf{s}}_m}{dm}\right|_{m=m_0},$$

and an $(N-1)$-dimensional component $\underline{\mathbf{n}}_2$ that is perpendicular to $\underline{\mathbf{n}}_1$. When the tube is bent, the tubular cross section erected perpendicular to $\underline{\mathbf{n}}_1$ at the point $\underline{\mathbf{n}}_1 + \underline{\mathbf{s}}_{m_0}$ is no longer spherically symmetric about that point, and the probability of $\underline{\mathbf{n}}_2$ escaping from the tube is therefore increased. We conclude that for a given length L and a constrained volume V a straight line that is the axis of an N-dimensional right circular cylinder would be an optimum signal-space geometry.

The rest is easy. The normalized perpendicular noise component $\underline{\mathbf{n}}_2$ contains $N-1$ statistically independent components, each with variance

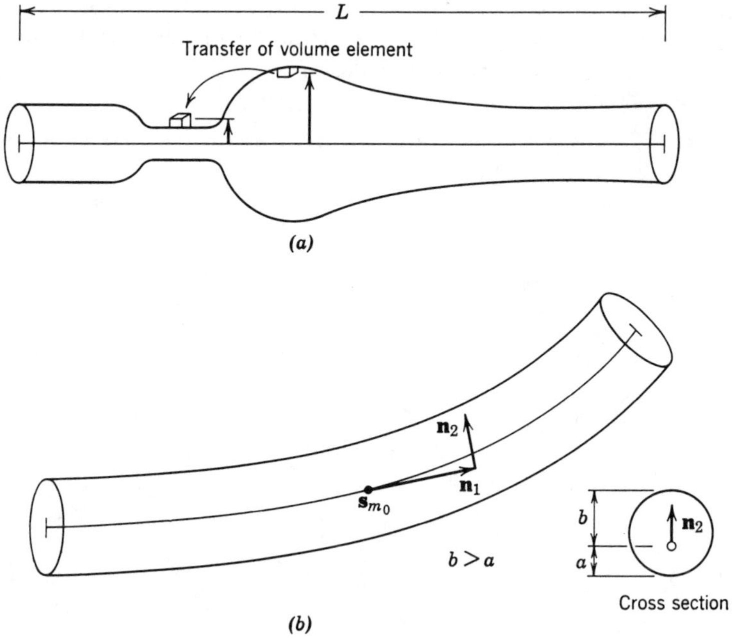

Figure 8.62 Nonoptimum cylinders.

$(1/N)(\mathcal{N}_0/2)$. With probability one, the length of $\underline{\mathbf{n}}_2$ therefore approaches $\sqrt{(\mathcal{N}_0/2)(N-1)/N}$ as N approaches infinity. Thus the radius of our right circular cylinder must be at least $\sqrt{(\mathcal{N}_0/2)(N-1)/N}$ if the probability of an anomaly is to be forced to zero. Also, the total volume at our disposal, from Eqs. 8.184 and 5D.5, approaches

$$V = B_N\left(E_{\mathrm{N}} + \frac{\mathcal{N}_0}{2}\right)^{N/2}. \tag{8.185}$$

Since we cannot coil a signal locus of length L into the signal sphere in any way that uses the available volume more effectively than a right circular cylinder, it follows that L cannot be so long that the volume of the cylinder would exceed V. Thus, for large enough N, we must have

$$LB_{N-1}\left(\frac{N-1}{N}\frac{\mathcal{N}_0}{2}\right)^{(N-1)/2} \leqslant B_N\left(E_{\mathrm{N}} + \frac{\mathcal{N}_0}{2}\right)^{N/2} \tag{8.186}$$

if anomalies are to be avoided. Accordingly,

$$L \leqslant \frac{B_N}{B_{N-1}}\sqrt{\mathcal{N}_0/2}\left(\frac{1}{1-1/N}\right)^{(N-1)/2}\left[1 + \frac{2E_{\mathrm{N}}}{\mathcal{N}_0}\right]^{N/2}. \tag{8.187}$$

We have noted in Appendix 5D that the ratio of the constants B_N and B_{N-1} approaches $\sqrt{2\pi/N}$ when N is large. Moreover,

$$\lim_{N\to\infty}\left(\frac{1}{1-1/N}\right)^{(N-1)/2} = \sqrt{e}.$$

It follows that for large N,

$$L \leqslant \sqrt{\frac{2\pi e}{N}}\sqrt{\frac{\mathcal{N}_0}{2}}\,2^{NC_{\mathrm{N}}}, \tag{8.188a}$$

in which

$$C_{\mathrm{N}} \triangleq \tfrac{1}{2}\log_2\left(1+\frac{2E_{\mathrm{N}}}{\mathcal{N}_0}\right) \quad \text{bits/dimension} \tag{8.188b}$$

is the Gaussian channel capacity per dimension previously encountered in Eq. 5.59.

Equations 8.188 place an upper bound on the allowable length of the signal locus when we hold E_{N} and $\mathcal{N}_0/2$ constant and increase N while simultaneously requiring the probability of anomaly to approach zero. The mean-square error in the absence of anomaly is approximated by

$$\overline{\epsilon^2} = \frac{\mathrm{E}[|\underline{\mathbf{n}}_1|^2]}{S^2}\;; \qquad S = \frac{L}{2}.$$

For our scaled geometry the mean-squared length of the one-dimensional vector $\underline{\mathbf{n}}_1$ is

$$\mathrm{E}[|\underline{\mathbf{n}}_1|^2] = \frac{1}{N}\frac{\mathcal{N}_0}{2}.$$

It follows that we must have

$$\overline{\epsilon^2} = \frac{\mathcal{N}_0/2}{NL^2/4} \gtrsim \frac{2}{\pi e}\,2^{-2NC_{\mathrm{N}}} \tag{8.189}$$

when N is large.

Equation 8.189 can be rewritten in terms of the transmitted power per second, P_s, and the signal's bandwidth W and total duration T_m by identifying

$$N = 2T_mW \tag{8.190a}$$

and

$$P_s = \frac{NE_{\mathrm{N}}}{T_m} = 2WE_{\mathrm{N}}. \tag{8.190b}$$

We then have

$$\overline{\epsilon^2} \gtrsim \frac{2}{\pi e}\,2^{-2T_mC}, \tag{8.191a}$$

in which C is the Gaussian channel capacity in bits per second:

$$C = W \log_2 \left(1 + \frac{P_s}{\mathcal{N}_0 W}\right). \tag{8.191b}$$

Equation 8.191 is our desired result, and its interpretation is important. We have seen that twisted modulation schemes can suppress "weak" noise at the cost of introducing a threshold phenomenon. Equation 8.191 places an asymptotic bound on how much noise can be considered "weak." If we attempt to increase the length of the signal curve (as a function of T_m) so rapidly that $\overline{\epsilon^2}$ decreases exponentially with an exponent more negative than $-2T_mC$, the noise perforce becomes "strong" in the sense that threshold considerations become dominant and the probability of anomaly approaches unity. This occurs even when the available number of dimensions is unbounded. Since C is greatest when W becomes infinite and $C_\infty = (P_s/\mathcal{N}_0) \log_2 e$, we see that $\overline{\epsilon^2}$ cannot be made to approach zero exponentially faster than

$$2^{-2C_\infty T_m} = e^{-2E_s/\mathcal{N}_0}, \tag{8.192}$$

which is the same as the strongest exponent afforded by FPM.†

8.5 PULSE-CODE MODULATION

Thus far in this chapter we have been concerned with communicating a continuous random variable m by means of a waveform $s_m(t)$, some attribute of which varies continuously with m. An alternative procedure called pulse-code modulation (PCM) involves passing m through a quantizer before modulation, as shown in Fig. 8.63, and then utilizing a discrete communication system.

Let us denote the set of values at the quantizer output by $\{m_i\}$, $i = 0, 1, \ldots, M - 1$. With PCM, the index i is communicated by transmitting one of a corresponding set of waveforms, $\{s_i(t)\}$. The receiver decides which waveform was actually transmitted and sets $\hat{m}$ equal to the center value of the quantizer interval corresponding thereto.

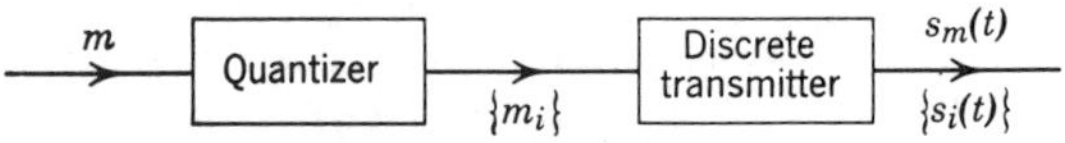

Figure 8.63 PCM transmission.

† The expression for $\overline{\epsilon^2}$ with FPM (Eq. 8.178) includes a factor $\mathcal{N}_0/2E_s$ that does not appear in Eq. 8.191. This discrepancy is attributable to the fact that the P[$\mathcal{A}$] with FPM is slightly larger than the P[$\mathcal{E}$] for β orthogonal signals. The discrepancy is not exponentially significant.

Conventional PCM

In conventional PCM it is customary to choose the number of quantization intervals to be a power of 2 and to employ a binary antipodal signaling alphabet. The transmitted signal may then be written

$$s_i(t) = \sum_{j=1}^{K} s_{ij}\, \varphi_j(t); \qquad i = 0, 1, \ldots, M-1, \tag{8.193a}$$

in which the $\{\varphi_j(t)\}$ are an appropriate set of orthonormal functions, $K = \log_2 M$, and the vector

$$\mathbf{s}_i = (s_{i1}, s_{i2}, \ldots, s_{iK}) \tag{8.193b}$$

represents the number i written in binary form. For example, if we adopt the mapping $(0 \to -\sqrt{E_N}, 1 \to +\sqrt{E_N})$ and let $j = 1$ correspond to the

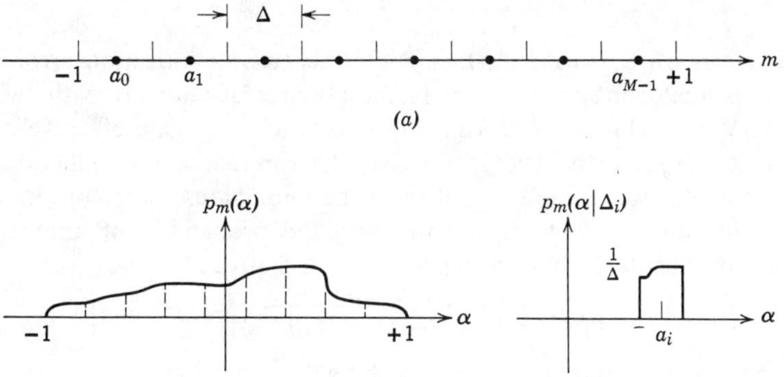

Figure 8.64 Uniform quantization: (*a*) quantization interval; (*b*) a priori and conditional probability densities.

most significant digit, then, with $M = 32$,

$$\mathbf{s}_{20} = (+\sqrt{E_N}, -\sqrt{E_N}, +\sqrt{E_N}, -\sqrt{E_N}, -\sqrt{E_N}).$$

Provided that the receiver determines the transmitted index i correctly, the error $(m - \hat{m})$ is due solely to the effect of quantization. The mean-square quantization error is easily determined whenever the quantization grain is uniform and sufficiently fine that p_m is essentially constant over each individual quantization interval. Letting Δ_i denote the ith quantization interval in Fig. 8.64*a* and a_i the interval's midpoint, we have

$$\mathrm{E}[(m - \hat{m})^2 \mid m \text{ in } \Delta_i] = \int_{-\infty}^{\infty} (\alpha - a_i)^2\, p_m(\alpha \mid \Delta_i)\, d\alpha. \tag{8.194a}$$

But, as shown in Fig. 8.64*b*, the conditional density function of m, given that m falls in Δ_i, is essentially a rectangle of unit area and width Δ centered on a_i. Thus

$$\mathrm{E}[(m - \hat{m})^2 \mid m \text{ in } \Delta_i] \approx \frac{1}{\Delta} \int_{-\Delta/2}^{\Delta/2} \beta^2 \, d\beta = \frac{\Delta^2}{12}. \tag{8.194b}$$

Since the right-hand side is independent of i, the over-all mean-square quantization error is also given approximately by

$$\overline{\epsilon^2} = \frac{\Delta^2}{12}. \tag{8.195a}$$

When m is constrained to $[-1, +1]$, the number of quantization intervals is $M = 2/\Delta$. In terms of M, we have

$$\overline{\epsilon^2} = \frac{1}{3}\left(\frac{1}{M}\right)^2. \tag{8.195b}$$

The symbol $\overline{\epsilon^2}$ is used in Eqs. 8.195 because quantization error with PCM is analogous to the error in the absence of anomaly with twisted modulation. This follows from the fact that $\hat{m}$ is again effectively disconnected from m whenever the receiver determines the index i incorrectly, an event that we define by analogy to be anomalous. For conventional PCM in additive white Gaussian noise the probability of anomaly is therefore identified (in accordance with Eq. 5.10) as

$$\begin{aligned} \mathrm{P}[\mathcal{A}] &= 1 - [1 - Q(\sqrt{2E_N/\mathcal{N}_0})]^{\log_2 M} \\ &\lessapprox (\log_2 M) \frac{e^{-E_N/\mathcal{N}_0}}{\sqrt{4\pi E_N/\mathcal{N}_0}}. \end{aligned} \tag{8.196}$$

Conventional PCM is particularly useful when the communication channel is a series of cable links connected in tandem; regenerative repeaters can then be installed at each node. As long as the product of the probability of error per bit on each link times the number of links is negligibly small, cumulative noise and distortion effects are effectively circumvented and $\overline{\epsilon^2}$ represents the only significant degradation effect.

PCM with Error Correction

The specific relationships among $\overline{\epsilon^2}$, $\mathrm{P}[\mathcal{A}]$, M, and $E_N/\mathcal{N}_0$ stated in Eqs. 8.195 and 8.196 reflect the nature of the particular (conventional) transmission scheme to which they apply. These relationships, however, are in no sense fundamental attributes of PCM. Indeed, a most intriguing aspect of PCM is that it permits us to break the constraint that causes P[$\mathcal{A}$] and $\overline{\epsilon^2}$ to be so tightly interrelated in FPM and equivalent modulation systems.

The essence of this constraint is that an FPM signal depends at any time instant on only a single sample of the modulator input process. The import is that the *same* time parameter, T_m, enters into *both* of the parametric relations

$$\overline{\epsilon^2} = \frac{12}{\pi^2}\frac{\mathcal{N}_0}{2E_s}\, 2^{-2T_mR'}$$
$$\mathrm{P}[\mathcal{A}] \lessapprox 2 \cdot 2^{-T_mE^*(R)} \tag{8.197}$$

[c.f. Eqs. 8.177].

In contradistinction, quantization of the modulator input frees us from this constraint and reduces the PCM communication problem to one in which the techniques of coding can be exploited. Let us assume that the message process $m(t)$ has bandwidth W_m, so that, in the notation of Eq. 8.49a,

$$m(t) = \sum_{k=-\infty}^{\infty} m_k\, \psi_k(t). \tag{8.198}$$

If each sample of $m(t)$ is quantized into one of M different levels, in time T there will be M^{T/T_m} different possible messages, in which we have identified T_m as the sampling interval,

$$T_m = \frac{1}{2W_m}. \tag{8.199}$$

In accordance with Eq. 5.2, the communication rate when each message is equally likely is then

$$R = \frac{1}{T}\log_2 (M^{T/T_m})$$
$$= \frac{1}{T_m}\log_2 M \text{ bits/sec}, \tag{8.200a}$$

whence

$$M = 2^{T_mR}. \tag{8.200b}$$

In coding, the mean-square error (when the decoder output is correct) is again due solely to the effect of quantization. In terms of the parameter R, it follows from Eqs. 8.195b and 8.200b that

$$\overline{\epsilon^2} = \tfrac{1}{3}\, 2^{-2T_mR}. \tag{8.201a}$$

On the other hand, the probability of a decoding error (anomaly) depends not on T_m but on the code-constraint length, say T. Equation 5.106 implies that the probability of anomaly with block orthogonal coding is

$$\mathrm{P}[\mathcal{A}] \lessapprox 2 \cdot 2^{-TE^*(R)}. \tag{8.201b}$$

Here $E^*(R)$ is the same reliability function, plotted in Fig. 8.59, that enters into Eq. 8.197.

The crucial distinction between the parametric relations of Eqs. 8.197 for FPM and Eqs. 8.201 for PCM lies in our ability to choose $T \gg T_m$. Thus $\mathrm{P}[\mathcal{E}]$ can be made arbitrarily small for any $R < C_\infty = (P_s/\mathcal{N}_0)\log_2 e$. We observe, however, that the constraint on R again implies that $\overline{\epsilon^2}$ can be forced to zero no faster than $e^{-2E_s/\mathcal{N}_0}$, where $E_s = P_s T_m$ is the energy transmitted per sample of $m(t)$.

The difficulty of unbounded bandwidth implied by block orthogonal coding can be avoided by using convolutional coding and sequential decoding, or any other suitable coding-decoding technique. With sequential decoding, the constraint on R becomes

$$R < R_0, \tag{8.202a}$$

where R_0 is the two-message error parameter plotted in Fig. 6.21. For sufficiently large (but finite) channel bandwidths the corresponding constraint on $\overline{\epsilon^2}$ is

$$\overline{\epsilon^2} \gtrsim \tfrac{1}{3}e^{-E_s/\mathcal{N}_0}. \tag{8.202b}$$

We conclude that a continuous source may be converted to an equivalent discrete source and communicated over a digital system without sacrifice in performance potential. For many systems the availability of digital techniques for achieving operation close to the theoretical limits will make this conversion attractive. Moreover, conversion to a standard digital form serves to focus attention on the problem of reducing the rate of the equivalent digital source without impairing fidelity (for example, by speech and television bandwidth compression). Such matters will be the subject of research for many years to come.

APPENDIX 8A THE SAMPLING THEOREM

One statement of the sampling theorem is that any waveform, $x(t)$, whose Fourier transform $X(f)$ exists and is identically zero outside the range $-W < f < W$, can be represented by the equation

$$x(t) = \sum_{k=-\infty}^{\infty} x\left(\frac{k}{2W}\right) v\left(t - \frac{k}{2W}\right). \tag{8A.1}$$

Here the "interpolation function"

$$v(t) \triangleq \frac{\sin 2\pi Wt}{2\pi Wt} \tag{8A.2a}$$

is the impulse response of an ideal rectangular filter with transfer function

$$V(f) \triangleq \begin{cases} 1/2W; & -W < f < W \\ 0; & \text{elsewhere.} \end{cases} \tag{8A.2b}$$

Proof of this theorem is an interesting exercise in Fourier analysis. Following Woodward,[85] we first observe that the periodic time-domain

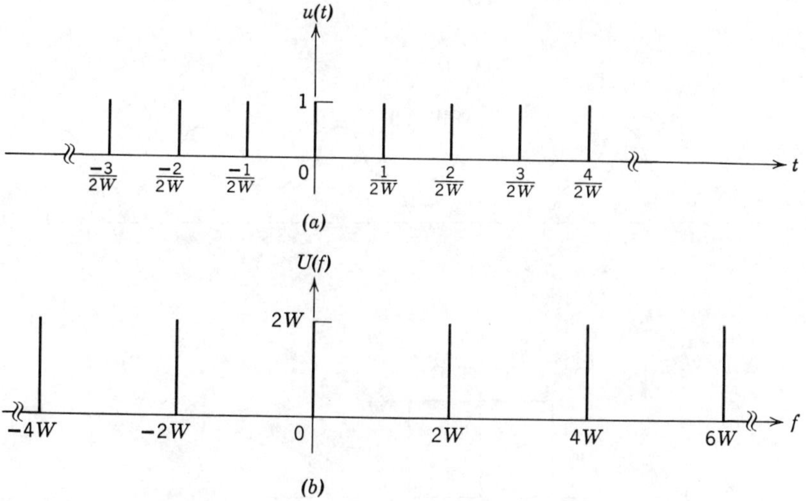

Figure 8A.1 The unit impulse train and its Fourier transform.

unit impulse train shown in Fig. 8A.1*a* can be written as

$$u(t) \triangleq \sum_{k=-\infty}^{\infty} \delta\left(t - \frac{k}{2W}\right) = \int_{-\infty}^{\infty} U(f) e^{j2\pi ft}\, df, \tag{8A.3a}$$

in which

$$U(f) \triangleq \sum_{k=-\infty}^{\infty} 2W\,\delta(f - 2kW) \tag{8A.3b}$$

is the periodic frequency-domain impulse train shown in Fig. 8A.1*b*. Equations 8A.3 follow from the fact that the bilateral Fourier series expansion of $u(t)$ is

$$u(t) = \sum_{k=-\infty}^{\infty} c_k e^{j2\pi(k/T)t}, \tag{8A.4a}$$

where $T \triangleq 1/2W$ is the period of $u(t)$ and, for all k,

$$c_k \triangleq \frac{1}{T}\int_{-T/2}^{T/2} u(t) e^{-j2\pi(k/T)t}\, dt = \frac{1}{T}. \tag{8A.4b}$$

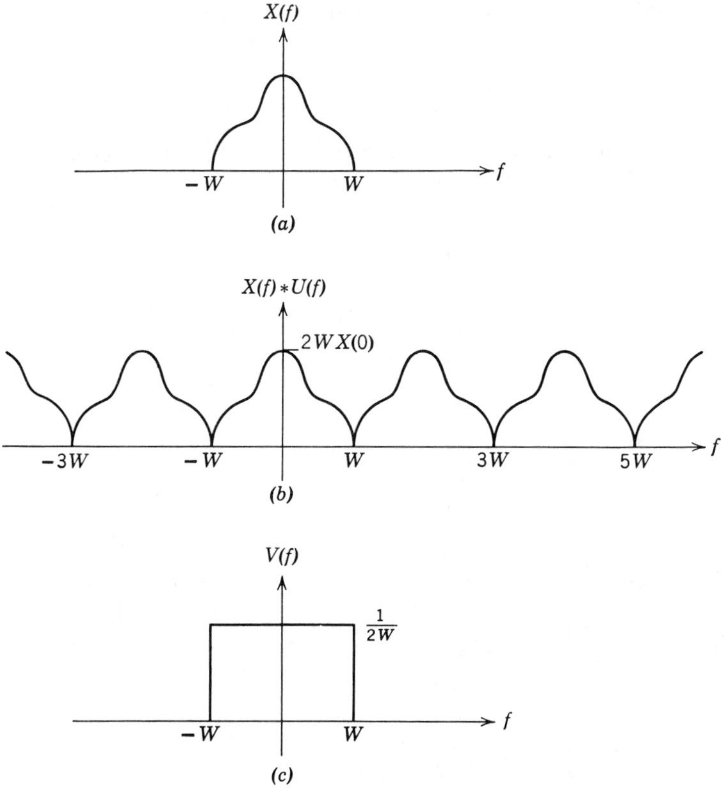

Figure 8A.2 Convolution of $X(f)$ with $U(f)$, followed by multiplication by $V(f)$, regains $X(f)$.

Since the integration in Eq. 8A.3a yields the right-hand side of Eq. 8A.4a, we treat $U(f)$ and $u(t)$ as a Fourier transform pair.

Next, we observe from Fig. 8A.2 that $X(f)$ is regained if we first convolve $X(f)$ with $U(f)$ and then multiply by $V(f)$:

$$X(f) = [X(f) * U(f)]V(f). \tag{8A.5}$$

Since convolution in time corresponds to multiplication in frequency and conversely, taking the inverse Fourier transform of both sides of Eq. 8A.5 yields

$$\begin{aligned} x(t) &= [x(t)\, u(t)] * v(t) \\ &= v(t) * \sum_{k=-\infty}^{\infty} x(t)\, \delta\left(t - \frac{k}{2W}\right). \end{aligned}$$

By interchanging the order of integration and summation, we have

$$x(t) = \sum_{k=-\infty}^{\infty} \int_{-\infty}^{\infty} x(\alpha)\, \delta\left(\alpha - \frac{k}{2W}\right) v(t - \alpha)\, d\alpha$$

$$= \sum_{k=-\infty}^{\infty} x\left(\frac{k}{2W}\right) v\left(t - \frac{k}{2W}\right), \tag{8A.6}$$

which completes the proof.

In terms of the unit-energy interpolation function

$$\psi(t) = \sqrt{2W}\, \frac{\sin 2\pi W t}{2\pi W t}, \tag{8A.7a}$$

Eq. 8A.1 is written

$$x(t) = \sum_{k=-\infty}^{\infty} x_k\, \psi\left(t - \frac{k}{2W}\right), \tag{8A.7b}$$

$$x_k = \frac{1}{\sqrt{2W}}\, x\left(\frac{k}{2W}\right). \tag{8A.7c}$$

We recall from Section 8.1 that the $\{\psi(t - k/2W)\}$ are orthonormal.

Discussion. The condition that $X(f)$ vanish outside $[-W, W]$ is critical in the proof of the sampling theorem. Otherwise, convolution of $X(f)$ and $(1/2W)U(f)$ causes spectral overlap from one frequency band of width $2W$ to the next, as indicated in Fig. 8A.3. The resulting distortion is called "aliasing."

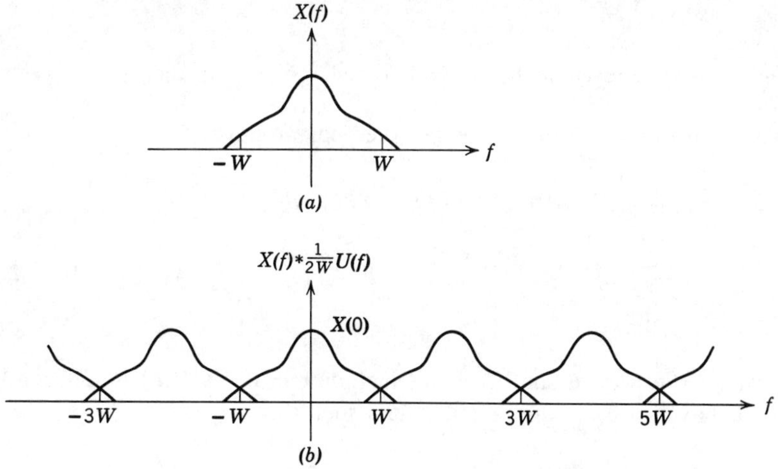

Figure 8A.3 Aliasing.

Since ideally bandlimited waveforms are physically unrealizable, sampling, in principle, always introduces a certain amount of aliasing. As a practical matter, however, this distortion becomes negligible when $x(t)$ is effectively bandlimited and the sampling period is selected judiciously. Consider, for example, the waveform $x(t)$ and spectrum $|X(f)|$ shown in Fig. 8A.4. If we define

$$y(t) \triangleq \sum_{k=-\infty}^{\infty} x_k \, \psi\left(t - \frac{k}{2W}\right), \tag{8A.8a}$$

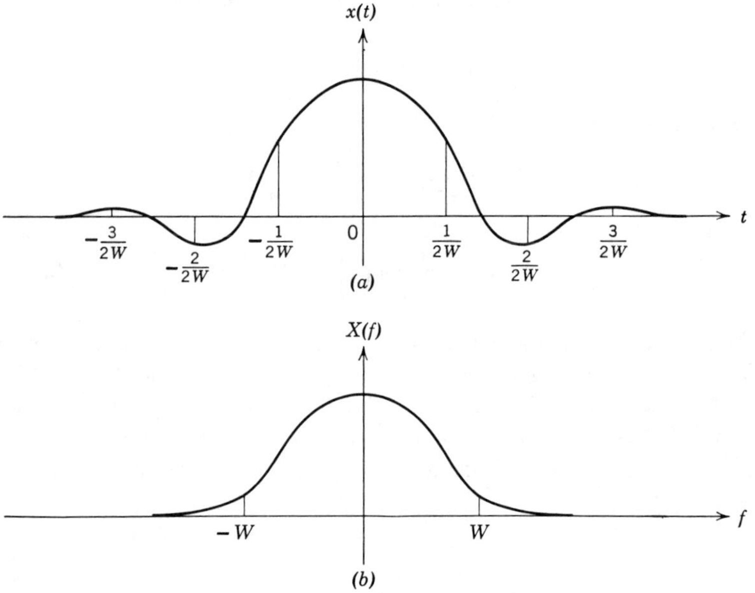

Figure 8A.4 A waveform that is effectively limited both in duration and bandwith.

then from Fig. 8A.3 and Parseval's theorem we have

$$\int_{-\infty}^{\infty} [x(t) - y(t)]^2 \, dt = \int_{-\infty}^{\infty} |X(f) - Y(f)|^2 \, df$$
$$= 2\int_{W}^{\infty} |X(f)|^2 \, df + \int_{-W}^{W} \left| \sum_{k=-\infty}^{\infty}{}' X(f - 2kW) \right|^2 df, \tag{8A.8B}$$

in which the primed sum does not include $k = 0$. If $X(f)$ is sufficiently well-behaved, we can find a constant B such that

$$\left| \sum_{k=-\infty}^{\infty}{}' X(f - 2kW) \right| \leqslant B \max_{k \neq 0} |X(f - 2kW)| \;; \qquad \text{all } |f| < W.$$

Thus $y(t)$ is a good approximation to $x(t)$ whenever the sampling interval $1/2W$ is chosen small enough that

$$(2 + B^2)\int_W^{\infty} |X(f)|^2\, df \ll \int_{-\infty}^{\infty} |X(f)|^2\, df = \int_{-\infty}^{\infty} x^2(t)\, dt. \tag{8A.9}$$

A further approximation to $x(t)$, say $z(t)$, results if we discard all terms in Eq. 8A.8a for which $|k|$ is greater than some integer $K/2$:

$$z(t) = \sum_{k=-K/2}^{K/2} x_k\, \psi\left(t - \frac{k}{2W}\right). \tag{8A.10}$$

By virtue of the orthonormality of the $\{\psi(t - k/2W)\}$, we then have

$$\int_{-\infty}^{\infty} [y(t) - z(t)]^2\, dt = \sum_{k=-\infty}^{-(1+K/2)} x_k^{\,2} + \sum_{k=1+(K/2)}^{\infty} x_k^{\,2}. \tag{8A.11a}$$

Thus $z(t)$ is a good $(K + 1)$-dimensional approximation to $y(t)$, hence to the original waveform $x(t)$, as long as K is chosen to be sufficiently great that the sums on the right-hand side of Eq. 8A.11 are also much less than the energy of $x(t)$:

$$\int_{-\infty}^{\infty} [y(t) - z(t)]^2\, dt \ll \int_{-\infty}^{\infty} x^2(t)\, dt. \tag{8A.11b}$$

For any lowpass waveform $x(t)$ encountered in engineering practice, minimum values can be chosen for K and W such that Eqs. 8A.9 and 8A.11b are both satisfied. In common parlance, $x(t)$ is then said to have effective bandwidth W and effective duration $T = K/2W$. Sampling techniques are useful in obtaining a finite-dimensional approximation to such a waveform. For precise relations governing the minimum dimensionality of classes of time- and bandwidth-limited waveforms refer to Appendix 5A.

APPENDIX 8B OPTIMUM MEAN-SQUARE LINEAR FILTERING

The problem of optimum (i.e., minimum mean-square error) receiver design when linearly modulated signals are corrupted by additive white Gaussian noise $n_w(t)$ was considered from a sampling theorem point of view in Section 8.1. In particular, when $m(t)$ is a stationary Gaussian process with mean power density function

$$\mathcal{S}_m(f) = \begin{cases} \dfrac{\mathcal{M}_0}{2}; & -W_m < f < W_m \\ 0; & \text{elsewhere,} \end{cases} \tag{8B.1}$$

we found (Eq. 8.63) that the optimum receiver for

$$r(t) = A\,m(t) + n_w(t) \tag{8B.2}$$

consists of an ideal linear filter with transfer function

$$H(f) = \begin{cases} \dfrac{1/A}{1 + \mathcal{N}_0/2\bar{E}_m}; & |f| < W_m \\ 0; & \text{elsewhere.} \end{cases} \tag{8B.3a}$$

Here $\mathcal{N}_0/2$ is the mean power density of $n_w(t)$, and

$$\bar{E}_m \triangleq \frac{A^2}{2W_m}\,\overline{m^2(t)} \tag{8B.3b}$$

is the mean energy transmitted during a sampling interval.

We now use the techniques of optimum mean-square linear filter theory[14,55] to obtain Eq. 8B.3 in a different way. Although the fact that the optimum receiver in this case is indeed a *linear* filter cannot be established by these techniques, the theory does show that the transfer function of Eq. 8B.3 is best within the class of all linear receivers. In addition, the theory may be used to investigate the performance degradation that ensues when $H(f)$ is required to be physically realizable; that is, when we impose the additional constraint that the impulse response of $H(f)$ must satisfy

$$h(t) = 0; \text{ all } t < 0. \tag{8B.4}$$

It is convenient to formulate the minimum mean-square error linear filtering problem in a quite general way. Let $z(t)$ be the *desired* signal and let $x(t)$ be the input to a linear filter with impulse response $h(t)$. We wish to design $h(t)$ in such a way that the filter output, say $\hat{z}(t)$, will minimize the mean-square error

$$\overline{\epsilon^2(t)} \triangleq \overline{[z(t) - \hat{z}(t)]^2}. \tag{8B.5}$$

The constraint of Eq. 8B.4 is introduced by writing

$$\hat{z}(t) = \int_I x(t - \alpha)\,h(\alpha)\,d\alpha, \tag{8B.6}$$

in which the domain of integration I is taken to be $[0, \infty]$ if the filter must be physically realizable. Otherwise, we take I to be $[-\infty, \infty]$.

In determining the best linear filter, we need not require that $x(t)$ and $z(t)$ be Gaussian processes. We do assume that both processes are wide-sense stationary, with known correlation functions $\mathcal{R}_x(\tau)$ and $\mathcal{R}_z(\tau)$, and that the crosscorrelation function of z and x is wide-sense stationary and known:

$$\overline{z(t)\,x(s)} \triangleq \mathcal{R}_{zx}(t - s). \tag{8B.7}$$

As an example, in the communication problem of Fig. 8B.1 the desired output might be a delayed replica of $m(t)$:

$$z(t) = m(t - T). \tag{8B.8}$$

Then

$$\begin{aligned}\mathcal{R}_{zx}(\tau) &= \overline{z(t)\,x(t-\tau)} \\ &= \overline{m(t-T)[A\,m(t-\tau) + n_w(t-\tau)]} \\ &= A\,\overline{m(t-T)\,m(t-\tau)} \\ &= A\,\mathcal{R}_m(\tau - T),\end{aligned} \tag{8B.9}$$

in which we have used the fact that $n_w(t)$ is a zero-mean noise process that is independent of $m(t)$. Negative values of T correspond to prediction of $m(t)$.

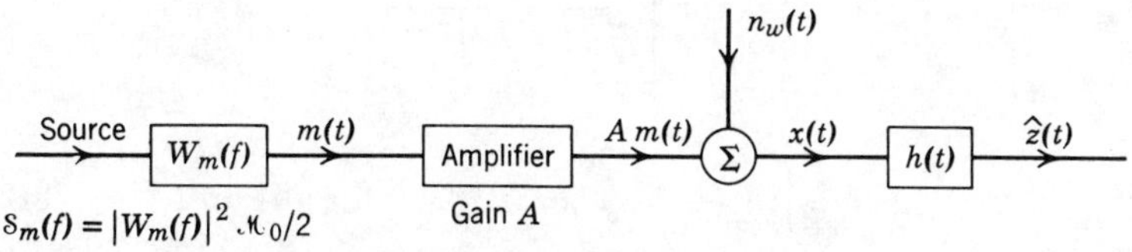

Figure 8B.1 A communication problem in which optimum mean-square linear filter theory may be used to design the receiving filter $h(t)$.

We first prove that h is optimum if and only if the resulting error, $\epsilon(t) \triangleq z(t) - \hat{z}(t)$, is uncorrelated with the filter input $x(t)$ for all time displacements within the domain I; that is, if and only if

$$\overline{\epsilon(t)\,x(t-\tau)} = 0; \qquad \text{for all } \tau \text{ in } I. \tag{8B.10}$$

Proof is immediate. Let h be the filter that satisfies Eq. 8B.10 and let g be any other linear filter. We use $\hat{z}(t)$ to denote the output of h and $\tilde{z}(t)$ to denote the output of g. Then

$$\begin{aligned}\overline{[z(t)-\tilde{z}(t)]^2} &= \overline{[z(t)-\hat{z}(t)+\hat{z}(t)-\tilde{z}(t)]^2} \\ &= \overline{[z(t)-\hat{z}(t)]^2} + \overline{[\hat{z}(t)-\tilde{z}(t)]^2} + \overline{2[z(t)-\hat{z}(t)][\hat{z}(t)-\tilde{z}(t)]}.\end{aligned}$$

But $[z(t) - \hat{z}(t)] = \epsilon(t)$, and $\epsilon(t)$ satisfies Eq. 8B.10. Thus

$$\begin{aligned}\overline{[z(t)-\hat{z}(t)][\hat{z}(t)-\tilde{z}(t)]} &= \overline{\epsilon(t)\int_I x(t-\tau)[h(\tau)-g(\tau)]\,d\tau} \\ &= \int_I \overline{\epsilon(t)\,x(t-\tau)}[h(\tau)-g(\tau)]\,d\tau = 0.\end{aligned}$$

It follows that

$$\overline{[z(t) - \tilde{z}(t)]^2} = \overline{\epsilon^2(t)} + \overline{[\hat{z}(t) - \tilde{z}(t)]^2},$$

which is clearly minimum when

$$\tilde{z}(t) = \hat{z}(t).$$

Equation 8B.10 is called the Wiener-Hopf condition. The remaining problem is to solve this equation for the function h that satisfies the condition. The first step is to rewrite Eq. 8B.10 in the form

$$\overline{[z(t) - \hat{z}(t)]\, x(t - \tau)} = 0; \qquad \text{for all } \tau \text{ in } I,$$

which yields

$$\begin{aligned}\overline{z(t)\, x(t - \tau)} &= \overline{\hat{z}(t)\, x(t - \tau)} \\ &= \int_I \overline{x(t - \tau)\, x(t - \alpha)}\, h(\alpha)\, d\alpha,\end{aligned}$$

or

$$\mathcal{R}_{zx}(\tau) = \int_I \mathcal{R}_x(\alpha - \tau)\, h(\alpha)\, d\alpha; \qquad \text{for all } \tau \text{ in } I. \qquad (8B.11)$$

Unrealizable Filters

Solving Eq. 8B.11 for the optimum filter is simple when $I = [-\infty, \infty]$, that is, when h is permitted to be unrealizable. Taking the Fourier transform of both sides, we then have

$$\mathcal{S}_{zx}(f) = \mathcal{S}_x(f)\, H(f),$$

in which $\mathcal{S}_{zx}(f)$, the transform of $\mathcal{R}_{zx}(\tau)$, is the *cross power density function* of $z(t)$ and $x(t)$. Thus the transfer function of the optimum linear filter is

$$H(f) = \frac{\mathcal{S}_{zx}(f)}{\mathcal{S}_x(f)}; \qquad \text{for } I = [-\infty, \infty]. \qquad (8B.12)$$

Equation 8B.12 is a general result applicable to any case for which $\mathcal{S}_{zx}(f)$ and $\mathcal{S}_x(f)$ are known.

It is easy to show that Eq. 8B.12 reduces to Eq. 8B.3 in the special case in which we identify $x(t)$ with the received signal in Eq. 8B.2 and $z(t)$ with $m(t)$. We then have

$$\begin{aligned}\mathcal{R}_{zx}(\tau) &= \overline{m(t)\, [A\, m(t - \tau) + n_w(t - \tau)]} \\ &= A\, \mathcal{R}_m(\tau) \qquad (8B.13a)\end{aligned}$$

and

$$\mathcal{R}_x(\tau) = \overline{[A\, m(t) + n_w(t)][A\, m(t-\tau) + n_w(t-\tau)]}$$
$$= A^2\, \mathcal{R}_m(\tau) + \frac{\mathcal{N}_0}{2}\, \delta(\tau). \tag{8B.13b}$$

It follows that

$$\mathcal{S}_{zx}(f) = A\, \mathcal{S}_m(f) \tag{8B.14a}$$

and

$$\mathcal{S}_x(f) = A^2\, \mathcal{S}_m(f) + \frac{\mathcal{N}_0}{2}. \tag{8B.14b}$$

Hence

$$H(f) = \frac{A\, \mathcal{S}_m(f)}{A^2\, \mathcal{S}_m(f) + \mathcal{N}_0/2},$$

or

$$H(f) = \begin{cases} \dfrac{A(\mathcal{M}_0/2)}{A^2(\mathcal{M}_0/2) + \mathcal{N}_0/2}; & |f| < W_m \\ 0; & \text{elsewhere.} \end{cases}$$

Recognizing that $\bar{E}_m = (A^2/2W_m)\,(\mathcal{M}_0 W_m)$, we have

$$H(f) = \begin{cases} \dfrac{1/A}{1 + \mathcal{N}_0/2\bar{E}_m}; & |f| < W_m \\ 0, & \text{elsewhere,} \end{cases} \tag{8B.15}$$

which agrees with Eq. 8B.3.

Realizable Filters, White Input

Solving Eq. 8B.11 for the optimum filter is more difficult when $I = [0, \infty]$; that is, when $H(f)$ is required to be realizable. The simplest case occurs when $x(t)$ is white, say with power density $X_0/2$, so that

$$\mathcal{R}_x(\tau) = \frac{X_0}{2}\, \delta(\tau). \tag{8B.16}$$

Then Eq. 8B.11 becomes

$$\mathcal{R}_{zx}(\tau) = \int_0^\infty \mathcal{R}_x(\alpha - \tau)\, h(\alpha)\, d\alpha$$
$$= \frac{X_0}{2}\, h(\tau); \qquad 0 \leqslant \tau \leqslant \infty,$$

which implies

$$h(t) = \begin{cases} \dfrac{2}{X_0}\, \mathcal{R}_{zx}(t); & 0 \leqslant t \leqslant \infty \\ 0, & \text{elsewhere.} \end{cases} \tag{8B.17}$$

A simple—although at first glance artificial—application occurs when $\mathcal{S}_m(f)$ is given by Eq. 8B.1 and

$$x(t) = A\, m(t) + n(t), \tag{8B.18a}$$

where $n(t)$ is stationary and

$$\mathcal{S}_n(f) = \begin{cases} \dfrac{\mathcal{N}_0}{2}; & |f| < W_m \\ \dfrac{\mathcal{N}_0 + A^2\mathcal{M}_0}{2}; & |f| \geqslant W_m. \end{cases} \tag{8B.18b}$$

Assuming that $n(t)$ and $m(t)$ are statistically independent, we then have

$$\begin{aligned} \mathcal{S}_x(f) &= A^2\, \mathcal{S}_m(f) + \mathcal{S}_n(f) \\ &= \frac{\mathcal{N}_0 + A^2\mathcal{M}_0}{2}; \qquad \text{for all } f. \end{aligned} \tag{8B.19}$$

If we further assume that the desired receiver output is a delayed replica

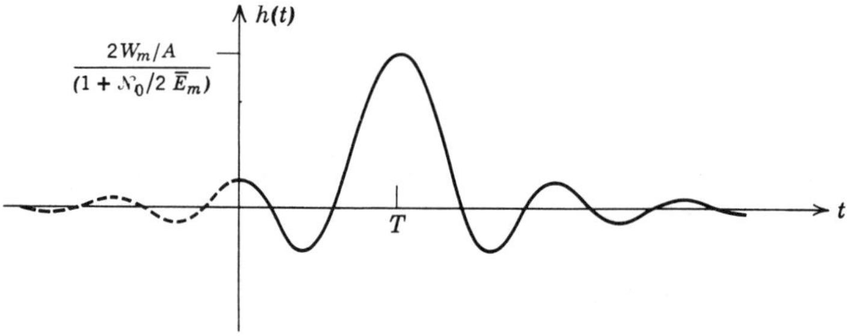

Figure 8B.2 Delayed impulse response of an ideal lowpass filter; the optimum realizable approximation is obtained by deleting the (dashed) section to the left of $t = 0$.

of $m(t)$, as in Eq. 8B.8, then $\mathcal{R}_{zx}(\tau)$ is given by Eq. 8B.9 even though $n(t)$ is not white. Identifying X_0 with $\mathcal{N}_0 + A^2\,\mathcal{M}_0$, we have

$$h(t) = \begin{cases} \dfrac{2A}{\mathcal{N}_0 + A^2\mathcal{M}_0}\, \mathcal{R}_m(t - T); & t \geqslant 0 \\ 0, \quad \text{elsewhere.} \end{cases} \tag{8B.20a}$$

Since $\mathcal{R}_m(\tau) = \mathcal{M}_0 W_m(\sin 2\pi W_m\tau)/2\pi W_m\tau$ and $\bar{E}_m = A^2\mathcal{M}_0/2$, Eq. 8B.20a can also be written as

$$h(t) = \begin{cases} \dfrac{1/A}{1 + \mathcal{N}_0/2\bar{E}_m}\, 2W_m\, \dfrac{\sin 2\pi W_m(t - T)}{2\pi W_m(t - T)}; & t \geqslant 0 \\ 0; \quad t < 0. \end{cases} \tag{8B.20b}$$

As shown in Fig. 8B.2, as T becomes large $h(t)$ approaches the (delayed) impulse response of a rectangular lowpass filter with gain

$$[A(1 + \mathcal{N}_0/2\bar{E}_m)]^{-1},$$

which again agrees with Eq. 8B.3. The agreement reflects the fact that the noise outside the band $[-W_m, W_m]$ is irrelevant in the limit $T \to \infty$. The delay T is introduced by the requirement for physical realizability. If the value of T is negative, the output from the filter of Eq. 8B.20 is the optimum mean-square linear prediction of the value that $m(t)$ will assume T seconds later.

Mean-Square Error

The mean-square error for the optimum linear filter of Eq. 8B.17 is obtained as follows: we first write

$$\overline{\epsilon^2(t)} = \overline{\epsilon(t)[z(t) - \hat{z}(t)]} = \overline{\epsilon(t)\, z(t)},$$

in which the second equality follows from the Wiener-Hopf condition:

$$\begin{aligned}\overline{\epsilon(t)\, \hat{z}(t)} &= \overline{\epsilon(t) \int_I x(t-\tau)\, h(\tau)\, d\tau} \\ &= \int_I \overline{\epsilon(t)\, x(t-\tau)}\, h(\tau)\, d\tau = 0.\end{aligned}$$

Thus

$$\begin{aligned}\overline{\epsilon^2(t)} &= \overline{[z(t) - \hat{z}(t)]\, z(t)} \\ &= \overline{z^2(t)} - \int_I \overline{z(t)\, x(t-\tau)}\, h(\tau)\, d\tau \\ &= \mathcal{R}_z(0) - \int_I \mathcal{R}_{zx}(\tau)\, h(\tau)\, d\tau. \qquad (8B.21a)\end{aligned}$$

Invoking Eq. 8B.17, we have

$$\overline{\epsilon^2(t)} = \mathcal{R}_z(0) - \frac{2}{X_0} \int_I \mathcal{R}_{zx}^{\,2}(\tau)\, d\tau; \qquad \text{for } x(t) \text{ white.} \qquad (8B.21b)$$

As an example, for the case leading to Eq. 8B.20b we have

$$\begin{aligned} I &= [0, \infty] \\ \mathcal{R}_z(0) &= \overline{m(t-T)^2} = \overline{m^2(t)} = \mathcal{M}_0 W_m, \\ X_0 &= \mathcal{N}_0 + A^2 \mathcal{M}_0 \\ \mathcal{R}_{zx}(\tau) &= A\, \mathcal{R}_m(\tau - T) = A \mathcal{M}_0 W_m \frac{\sin 2\pi W_m(\tau - T)}{2\pi W_m(\tau - T)}.\end{aligned}$$

Thus

$$\overline{\epsilon^2(t)} = \mathcal{M}_0 W_m\left\{1 - (1 + \mathcal{N}_0/2\bar{E}_m)^{-1}\int_0^\infty 2W_m\left[\frac{\sin 2\pi W_m(\tau - T)}{2\pi W_m(\tau - T)}\right]^2 d\tau\right\}. \tag{8B.22}$$

The integral in Eq. 8B.22 is plotted in Fig. 8B.3 as a function of the normalized delay $2W_mT$. As T becomes large, the integral approaches unity. Thus the signal-to-noise ratio,

$$\frac{\mathcal{S}}{\mathcal{N}} \triangleq \frac{\overline{m^2(t)}}{\overline{\epsilon^2(t)}} = \frac{\mathcal{M}_0 W_m}{\overline{\epsilon^2(t)}}, \tag{8B.23a}$$

approaches the value obtained with the unrealizable filter of Eq. 8B.15:

$$\frac{\mathcal{S}}{\mathcal{N}} \to 1 + 2\bar{E}_m/\mathcal{N}_0, \qquad \text{as } T \to \infty. \tag{8B.23b}$$

We observe that $2W_mT$ need not be greater than unity in order to obtain

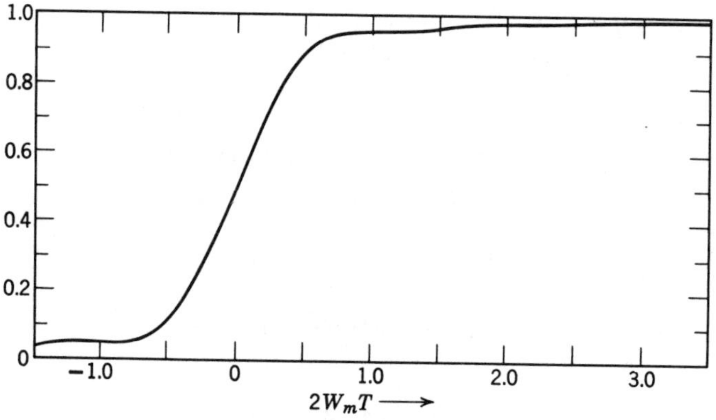

Figure 8B.3 The value of the integral

$$\int_0^\infty 2W_m\left[\frac{\sin 2\pi W_m(\tau - T)}{2\pi W_m(\tau - T)}\right]^2 d\tau = \frac{1}{\pi}\int_{-2\pi W_mT}^\infty \left(\frac{\sin \alpha}{\alpha}\right)^2 d\alpha.$$

an $\mathcal{S}/\mathcal{N}$ that is very nearly equal to this limiting value. The utility of the somewhat artificial noise power density function specified in Eq. 8B.18b lies in the fact that Fig. 8B.3 implies a lower bound on the value of $\mathcal{S}/\mathcal{N}$ attainable with realizable filters when $\mathcal{S}_n(f) = \mathcal{N}_0/2$ for all f: clearly, increasing $\mathcal{S}_n(f)$ outside $[-W_m, W_m]$ can only reduce $\mathcal{S}/\mathcal{N}$. On the other hand, the $\mathcal{S}/\mathcal{N}$ when the noise is white cannot exceed the limiting value of Eq. 8B.23b. Thus we have tight upper and lower bounds on $\mathcal{S}/\mathcal{N}$ for white additive noise and $T \geqslant 1/2W_m$.

The residual error when $T \to \infty$ is called "irreducible." Setting $I = [-\infty, \infty]$ in Eq. 8B.21a, and introducing $h(t)$ from Eq. 8B.12, we observe that the irreducible error is equal to

$$\overline{\epsilon_{\text{irr}}^2} = \mathcal{R}_z(0) - \int_{-\infty}^{\infty} \mathcal{R}_{zx}(\tau)\, d\tau \int_{-\infty}^{\infty} H(f) e^{j2\pi f\tau}\, df$$

$$= \mathcal{R}_z(0) - \int_{-\infty}^{\infty} H(f) \mathcal{S}_{zx}{}^*(f)\, df$$

$$= \int_{-\infty}^{\infty} \mathcal{S}_z(f) \left[1 - \frac{|\mathcal{S}_{zx}(f)|^2}{\mathcal{S}_z(f)\, \mathcal{S}_x(f)}\right] df. \tag{8B.24}$$

Equation 8B.24 is valid whether or not the process $x(t)$ is white.

Nonwhite $x(t)$

When $x(t)$ is nonwhite and $I = [0, \infty]$, a reversible whitening filter (cf. Appendix 7A) may be used to whiten $x(t)$ as a first step in optimum linear filtering without degradation of the attainable performance. Let $x_w(t)$ denote the output of the whitening filter. As shown in Fig. 8B.4, we

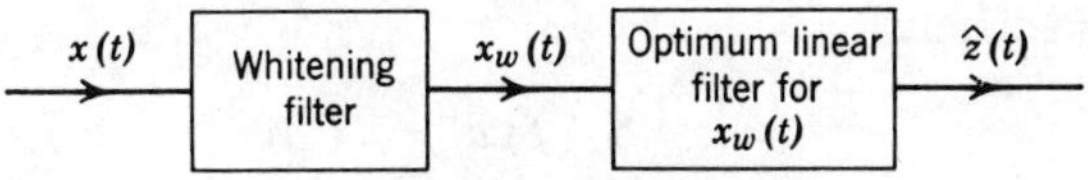

Figure 8B.4 Prewhitening.

may then complete the optimum filtering job by concatenating the optimum filter for estimating $z(t)$ from $x_w(t)$. This filter is again specified by Eq. 8B.17, with $\mathcal{R}_{zx_w}(\tau)$ substituted for $\mathcal{R}_{zx}(\tau)$. The same substitution enables us to use Eq. 8B.21b to evaluate the resulting mean-square error.

APPENDIX 8C DETERMINATION OF THE PROBABILITY THAT $n_s(t)$ CROSSES ZERO DURING A SHORT INTERVAL

Let x denote $n_s(t)\,|_{t=0}$ and let y denote $dn_s(t)/dt|_{t=0}$. Now, as shown in Fig. 8C.1, $n_s(t)$ passes through zero from $-$ to $+$ during the interval $[0, \Delta]$, where $\Delta \ll 1/2W$, if and only if $x < 0$ and $x + y\Delta > 0$. Thus the probability of a ($-$ to $+$) zero-crossing over $[0, \Delta]$, say P, is

$$P = \int_0^{\infty} d\beta \int_{-\beta\Delta}^{0} p_{x,y}(\alpha, \beta)\, d\alpha. \tag{8C.1}$$

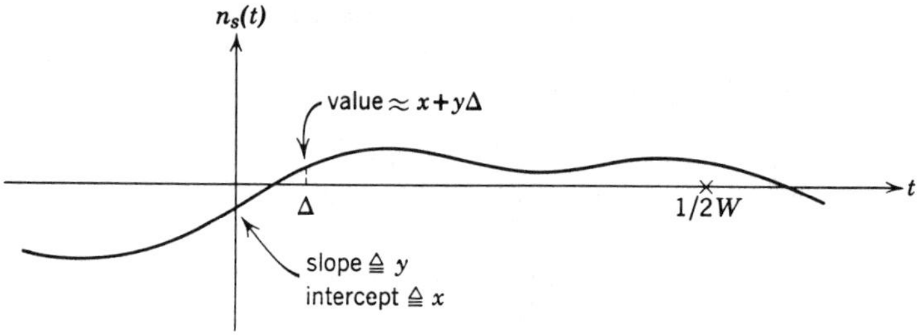

Figure 8C.1 Conditions for positive-going zero-crossing. Since $n_s(t)$ has bandwidth W, neither $n_s(t)$ nor $n_s'(t)$ can change appreciably over the interval $[0, \Delta]$.

Since $dn_s(t)/dt = n_s'(t)$ is obtainable by passing $n_s(t)$ through a filter with transfer function

$$H'(f) = \mathrm{j}2\pi f, \tag{8C.2}$$

both x and y are Gaussian random variables. To determine $p_{x,y}$, it is therefore only necessary to calculate $\overline{x^2}$, $\overline{y^2}$, and $\overline{xy}$. Since

$$\mathcal{S}_{n_s}(f) = \begin{cases} \dfrac{\mathcal{N}_0}{2}, & \text{for } |f| < W \\ 0, & \text{elsewhere,} \end{cases} \tag{8C.3}$$

we have immediately

$$\overline{x^2} = \int_{-\infty}^{\infty} \mathcal{S}_{n_s}(f)\, df = \mathcal{N}_0 W \tag{8C.4}$$

and

$$\overline{y^2} = (2\pi)^2 \int_{-\infty}^{\infty} f^2\, \mathcal{S}_{n_s}(f)\, df = \tfrac{1}{3}(2\pi W)^2(\mathcal{N}_0 W). \tag{8C.5}$$

Thus

$$\frac{\overline{y^2}}{\overline{x^2}} = \tfrac{1}{3}(2\pi W)^2, \tag{8C.6}$$

a result that we shall invoke later. [In the general (nonrectangular) case we would have

$$\frac{\overline{y^2}}{\overline{x^2}} = \frac{(2\pi)^2 \displaystyle\int_{-\infty}^{\infty} f^2\, \mathcal{S}_{n_s}(f)\, df}{\displaystyle\int_{-\infty}^{\infty} \mathcal{S}_{n_s}(f)\, df}, \tag{8C.7}$$

provided that the integral in the numerator converges.]

In order to determine $\overline{xy}$ we first note that

$$n_s'(t) = \int_{-\infty}^{\infty} n_s(t-\gamma)\, h'(\gamma)\, d\gamma, \tag{8C.8}$$

in which $h'(t)$ denotes the impulse response of the differentiating filter $H'(f)$. Defining $\tau \triangleq t_2 - t_1$, we have

$$\overline{n_s(t_1)\, n_s'(t_2)} = \int_{-\infty}^{\infty} \overline{n_s(t_1)\, n_s(t_2 - \gamma)}\, h'(\gamma)\, d\gamma$$

$$= \int_{-\infty}^{\infty} \mathcal{R}_{n_s}(\tau - \gamma)\, h'(\gamma)\, d\gamma$$

$$= \frac{d\mathcal{R}_{n_s}(\tau)}{d\tau}. \tag{8C.9}$$

But

$$\mathcal{R}_{n_s}(\tau) = \int_{-\infty}^{\infty} \mathcal{S}_{n_s}(f) e^{i2\pi f\tau}\, df$$

$$= \frac{\mathcal{N}_0}{2} \int_{-W}^{W} \cos 2\pi f\tau\, df$$

$$= \mathcal{N}_0 W \frac{\sin 2\pi W\tau}{2\pi W\tau}, \tag{8C.10}$$

from which it is clear that

$$\left.\frac{d\mathcal{R}_{n_s}(\tau)}{d\tau}\right|_{\tau=0} = 0. \tag{8C.11}$$

Thus $\overline{xy} = 0$, hence

$$p_{x,y} = p_x p_y, \tag{8C.12}$$

where p_x and p_y are zero-mean Gaussian density functions with variances given by Eqs. 8C.4 and 8C.5, respectively.

The integration of Eq. 8C.1 is straightforward when Δ is small. Since $p_y(\beta)$ goes rapidly to zero as β becomes large, for small enough Δ we have

$$P = \int_0^{\infty} d\beta \int_{-\beta\Delta}^{0} p_{x,y}(\alpha, \beta)\, d\alpha = \int_0^{\infty} p_y(\beta)\, d\beta \int_{-\beta\Delta}^{0} p_x(\alpha)\, d\alpha$$

$$\approx \int_0^{\infty} p_y(\beta)\, d\beta [\beta\, \Delta p_x(0)]$$

$$= \frac{\Delta}{\sqrt{2\pi \overline{x^2}}} \int_0^{\infty} \beta\, p_y(\beta)\, d\beta$$

$$= \frac{\Delta}{\sqrt{2\pi \overline{x^2}}} \int_0^{\infty} \frac{\beta}{\sqrt{2\pi \overline{y^2}}} e^{-\beta^2/2\overline{y^2}}\, d\beta.$$

Letting $\gamma = \beta^2/2\overline{y^2}$ yields

$$P \approx \frac{\Delta}{2\pi\sqrt{\overline{x^2}\,\overline{y^2}}}\int_0^\infty \overline{y^2} e^{-\gamma}\, d\gamma$$

$$= \frac{\Delta}{2\pi}\sqrt{\overline{y^2}/\overline{x^2}}. \tag{8C.13}$$

By symmetry, the probability of a zero crossing from + to − is also equal to P. Thus the total probability that $n_s(t)$ will cross zero in any direction in a small time interval $[0, \Delta]$ is approximately

$$2P \approx \frac{\Delta}{\pi}\sqrt{\overline{y^2}/\overline{x^2}} = \frac{\Delta}{\pi}\frac{2\pi W}{\sqrt{3}} = \frac{2W\Delta}{\sqrt{3}}. \tag{8C.14}$$

In the case of arbitrary (nonrectangular) $\mathcal{S}_{n_s}(f)$, $2P$ can be evaluated by substituting Eq. 8C.7 in Eq. 8C.13.

APPENDIX 8D WEAK-NOISE PERFORMANCE OF FM FEEDBACK RECEIVERS

Consider the idealized FMFB receiver diagrammed in Fig. 8D.1. We assume that $|m(t)| \leqslant 1$ and

$$s_m(t) = A\sqrt{2}\cos 2\pi\left[f_0 t + W_1 \int m(t)\, dt\right], \tag{8D.1a}$$

$$\hat{s}(t) = \sqrt{2}\cos 2\pi\left[f_1 t + \hat{W}\int \hat{m}(t)\, dt\right]; \quad \hat{W} < W_1. \tag{8D.1b}$$

Our first task is to determine the setting of the attenuator G which leads to perfect reception in the absence of noise. The conditions are that the

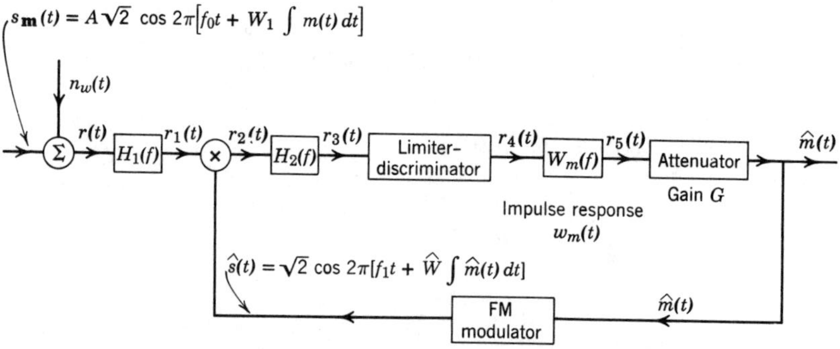

Figure 8D.1 Idealized FMFB receiver.

modulating process $m(t)$ has ideal bandwidth W_m; the RF half-bandwidth of $s_m(t)$ and $H_1(f)$ is $W = W_1 + 2W_m$; and the center frequency of $H_2(f)$ is $f_2 = f_0 - f_1$.

When $\overline{n_w^2(t)} = 0$, the difference-frequency (DF) component of the IF filter input is

$$r_2(t)\big|_{\mathrm{DF}} = A \cos [2\pi f_2(t) + \theta(t) - \hat{\theta}(t)] \tag{8D.2a}$$

in which

$$\theta(t) \triangleq 2\pi W_1 \int m(t)\, dt, \tag{8D.2b}$$

$$\hat{\theta}(t) \triangleq 2\pi \hat{W} \int \hat{m}(t)\, dt. \tag{8D.2c}$$

It is convenient to assume initially that the bandwidth of $H_2(f)$ is large enough that

$$r_3(t) = r_2(t)\big|_{\mathrm{DF}}.$$

By convention, the output of the limiter-discriminator is then

$$r_4(t) = \frac{d}{dt}[\theta(t) - \hat{\theta}(t)] = \theta'(t) - \hat{\theta}'(t).$$

Since $m(t)$ and $\hat{m}(t)$ both have bandwidth W_m,

$$\begin{aligned}\hat{m}(t) &= G[\theta'(t) - \hat{\theta}'(t)] * w_m(t)\\ &= G[\theta'(t) - \hat{\theta}'(t)]\\ &= 2\pi G[W_1\, m(t) - \hat{W}\, \hat{m}(t)].\end{aligned}$$

Thus

$$\hat{m}(t)[1 + 2\pi \hat{W} G] = 2\pi G W_1\, m(t).$$

It follows that $\hat{m}(t) = m(t)$ when

$$G = \frac{1}{2\pi(W_1 - \hat{W})}. \tag{8D.3}$$

We next determine the minimum allowable bandwidth of $H_2(f)$. When $\hat{m}(t) = m(t)$, we have

$$\theta(t) - \hat{\theta}(t) = 2\pi(W_1 - \hat{W}) \int m(t)\, dt.$$

Thus the difference-frequency component at the input to the IF filter is an FM signal whose maximum instantaneous frequency deviation is

$$\Delta f_{\max} = 2\pi(W_1 - \hat{W})\, m(t)_{\max}.$$

The objective of FMFB is to reduce the probability of anomaly by reducing the IF bandwidth. We therefore assume that the feedback is sufficiently strong—that is, $\hat{W}$ is sufficiently large—that $\Delta f_{\max} \ll W_m$. In this case $r_2(t)\big|_{\mathrm{DF}}$ is a narrow-band FM signal which we may assume passes through $H_2(f)$ with negligible distortion as long as the filter half-bandwidth is at least W_m cps. Accordingly, we take

$$H_2(f) = \begin{cases} 1; & f_2 - W_m < |f| < f_2 + W_m \\ 0; & \text{elsewhere.} \end{cases} \tag{8D.4}$$

The final step in our analysis is to investigate the effects of weak noise when G and $H_2(f)$ are given by Eqs. 8D.3 and 8D.4. We consider the case in which there is no modulation, that is, $m(t) \equiv 0$. We then have

$$\begin{aligned} r_1(t) &= A\sqrt{2}\cos\omega_0 t + \text{bandpass noise} \\ &= [A + n_c(t)]\sqrt{2}\cos\omega_0 t + n_s(t)\sqrt{2}\sin\omega_0 t, \end{aligned} \tag{8D.5}$$

where $n_c(t)$ and $n_s(t)$ are statistically independent lowpass Gaussian processes, each with power density spectrum equal to $\mathcal{N}_0/2$ over $[-W, W]$. Introducing the polar transformation of Fig. 8.50 yields

$$r_1(t) = a(t)\sqrt{2}\cos[2\pi f_0 + \phi(t)], \tag{8D.6a}$$

in which

$$\phi(t) \triangleq \tan^{-1}\frac{-n_s(t)}{A + n_c(t)}, \tag{8D.6b}$$

$$a^2(t) \triangleq [A + n_c(t)]^2 + n_s^2(t). \tag{8D.6c}$$

Just as in the noiseless case, it is convenient to assume initially that the bandwidth of $H_2(f)$ is large enough to pass

$$r_2(t)|_{\mathrm{DF}} = a(t)[\cos 2\pi f_2 t + \phi(t) - \hat{\theta}(t)] \tag{8D.7}$$

without distortion. This definitely does *not* occur when $H_2(f)$ is given by Eq. 8D.4, but the effect of narrowing the IF half-bandwidth to W_m cps is most easily determined by first establishing the nature of $\hat{m}(t)$ when $H_2(f)$ is broadband.

When $H_2(f)$ is so wide that

$$r_3(t) = r_2(t)\big|_{\mathrm{DF}},$$

we have

$$r_4(t) = \phi'(t) - \hat{\theta}'(t)$$

and

$$\begin{aligned} \hat{m}(t) &= G[\phi'(t) - \hat{\theta}'(t)] * w_m(t) \\ &= G[\phi'(t) - 2\pi\hat{W}\,\hat{m}(t)] * w_m(t). \end{aligned}$$

But $\hat{m}(t) * w_m(t) = \hat{m}(t)$, so that the equation above becomes

$$\hat{m}(t)(1 + 2\pi G\hat{W}) = G[\phi'(t) * w_m(t)].$$

Substituting $G = [2\pi(W_1 - \hat{W})]^{-1}$ yields

$$\hat{m}(t) = \frac{1}{2\pi W_1}[\phi'(t) * w_m(t)]. \tag{8D.8}$$

We now introduce the weak-noise assumption

$$\mathcal{N}_0 W \ll A^2. \tag{8D.9}$$

It follows that, with high probability,

$$\phi(t) \approx \frac{-n_s(t)}{A}.$$

In the absence of anomaly we therefore have

$$\hat{m}(t) \approx \frac{-1}{2\pi W_1 A}[n_s'(t) * w_m(t)] \triangleq n(t). \tag{8D.10}$$

Integrating the power density function of $n(t)$ yields

$$\overline{n^2(t)} = \left(\frac{1}{2\pi W_1 A}\right)^2 \frac{\mathcal{N}_0}{2}\int_{-W_m}^{W_m}(2\pi f)^2\, df$$

$$= \frac{1}{3}\left(\frac{W_m}{W_1}\right)^2 \frac{\mathcal{N}_0 W_m}{A^2}, \tag{8D.11a}$$

or, in terms of the energy $E_s = A^2/2W_m$ transmitted during a sampling interval of $m(t)$,

$$\overline{n^2(t)} = \frac{1}{3}\left(\frac{W_m}{W_1}\right)^2 \frac{\mathcal{N}_0}{2E_s}. \tag{8D.11b}$$

We see that the assumption that $H_2(f)$ is broadband leads to the same weak-noise suppression provided by conventional FM (Eq. 8.146).

The remaining task is to investigate the weak-noise behavior when $H_2(f)$ is given by Eq. 8D.4. Only the part of $n_s'(t)$ that passes through $W_m(f)$ affects $\hat{m}(t)$. But with weak noise the effect of narrowing $H_2(f)$ is simply to eliminate those spectral components of $n_s'(t)$ that $W_m(f)$ would discard anyway. It follows that $\overline{n^2(t)}$ is unchanged from the value given by Eq. 8D.11 even when $H_2(f)$ is narrow-band.

Just as with conventional FM receivers, the foregoing analysis can be extended to the quasi-static situation in which $m(t)$ is a slowly varying function of time. The value of $\overline{n^2(t)}$ remains the same as long as the probability of anomaly is negligible.

It appears from a first perusal of the weak-noise behavior in the absence of modulation that only the noise in a bandwidth of $\pm W_m$ cps around the signal contributes to the probability of anomaly. On the other hand, the requirement that the receiver be able to respond to all possible amplitude-bounded input messages $m(t)$ of bandwidth W_m, including those that cause $s_m(t)$ to sweep over the full bandwidth $f_0 \pm W$ during a single sampling interval, implies that the full input bandwidth must enter into the determination of $\hat{m}(t)$ when the noise is not weak. We feel that this requirement prevents $P[\mathcal{A}]$ from being smaller than that afforded by FPM with comparable stretch. As mentioned previously, however, we have not been able to construct convincing mathematical arguments that this is so for idealized FMFB receivers with rectangular filters. The practical case where the filters within the closed loop have broad nonzero skirts has been considered on a partly empirical basis and with a somewhat different definition of anomaly in the literature.[26]

PROBLEMS

8.1 We wish to communicate a random variable m with probability density

$$p_m(\alpha) = \frac{1}{2\sqrt{2\pi}} \left[e^{-(\alpha-4)^2/2} + e^{-(\alpha+4)^2/2} \right]$$

over an additive white Gaussian noise channel by means of the linearly modulated signal

$$s_m(t) = mA\,\varphi(t); \qquad \int_{-\infty}^{\infty} \varphi^2(t)\,dt = 1.$$

a. Estimate the minimum attainable mean-square error when $\mathcal{N}_0/(2A^2) \ll 4$.

b. Sketch $p_m(\alpha \mid r = \rho)$ for several typical values of ρ when $\mathcal{N}_0/(2A^2) = 16$. Discuss the validity of mean-square error as a performance criterion in this case; suggest and discuss alternative criteria.

8.2 Consider a communication channel with $r = mA + n$, in which r, m, and n are random voltages and

$$p_m(\alpha) = \tfrac{1}{2}\, e^{-|\alpha|}, \qquad p_n(\beta) = \frac{1}{2b}\, e^{-|\beta|/b}.$$

Assume m and n are statistically independent.

a. Determine as a function of A/b the mean-square error of a maximum liklihood receiver; a maximum a posteriori probability density receiver; and a receiver which ignores the channel output and sets $\hat{m} = 0$.

b. What is the minimum mean-square error decision rule when the maximum-likelihood rule is indeterminate?

8.3 Consider communicating two correlated Gaussian random variables, $\mathbf{m} = (m_1, m_2)$, with

$$p_{\mathbf{m}}(\boldsymbol{\alpha}) = \frac{1}{2\pi\sqrt{1-\rho^2}} \exp\left[-\frac{\alpha_1^2 - 2\rho\alpha_1\alpha_2 + \alpha_2^2}{2(1-\rho^2)}\right],$$

over an additive white Gaussian noise channel by means of two different systems. System A transmits

$$s_{\mathbf{m}}(t) = m_1 A\, \varphi_1(t) + m_2 A\, \varphi_2(t)$$

where $\varphi_1(t)$ and $\varphi_2(t)$ are orthonormal, and estimates each m_i *independently* by means of two uncoupled one-dimensional minimum mean-square error receivers.

System B transforms $\mathbf{m}$ into two uncorrelated random variables, say $\tilde{\mathbf{m}} = (\tilde{m}_1, \tilde{m}_2)$, and transmits

$$s_{\tilde{\mathbf{m}}}(t) = \tilde{m}_1 A\, \varphi_1(t) + \tilde{m}_2 A\, \varphi_2(t).$$

The receiver of system B determines $\hat{m}$ by first making a minimum mean-square error estimate of the vector $\tilde{\mathbf{m}}$ and then applying thereto the transformation inverse to that of the transmitter.

Evaluate and compare the total mean-square error produced by each system as a function of the total mean energy transmitted.

8.4 Consider the waveform

$$s(t) = \sum_{j=1}^{N} s_j\, \psi_j(t),$$

in which

$$\psi_j(t) \triangleq \psi\left(t - \frac{j}{2W}\right), \qquad \psi(t) \triangleq \frac{\sin 2\pi W t}{2\pi W t}.$$

a. Prove that, for any τ, we also have

$$s(t) = \sum_{j=-\infty}^{\infty} s\left(\frac{j}{2W} + \tau\right) \psi_j(t + \tau).$$

b. What assignment of the $\{s_j\}$ approximately maximizes $s(0)$ when $\tau = 1/4W$ and we require $|s_j| \leqslant 1$ for all j?

8.5 Consider the random process

$$n(t) \triangleq \lim_{K\to\infty} \sum_{j=-K/2}^{K/2} n_j\, \psi_j(t),$$

in which the $\{n_j\}$ are statistically independent, zero-mean Gaussian random variables and the $\{\psi_j(t)\}$ are as defined in Problem 8.4. Prove that $n(t)$ is a stationary Gaussian process with power density function

$$S_n(f) = \begin{cases} \mathcal{N}_0/2; & |f| < W, \\ 0; & \text{elsewhere,} \end{cases}$$

as claimed in Eq. 8.50.

8.6 The envelope detector illustrated in Fig. P8.6 is to be used to demodulate the DSB (voltage) signal

$$s(t) = A[1 + \cos 2\pi Wt] \cos 2\pi f_0 t; \qquad f_0 \gg W.$$

a. Sketch the waveshape of the current through the diode.
b. Determine the largest permissible value of the time-constant, RC.
c. Consider the detector output when RC is adjusted in accord with (b), and estimate the ratio of the Fourier components at the frequencies W and f_0 as a function of f_0/W.

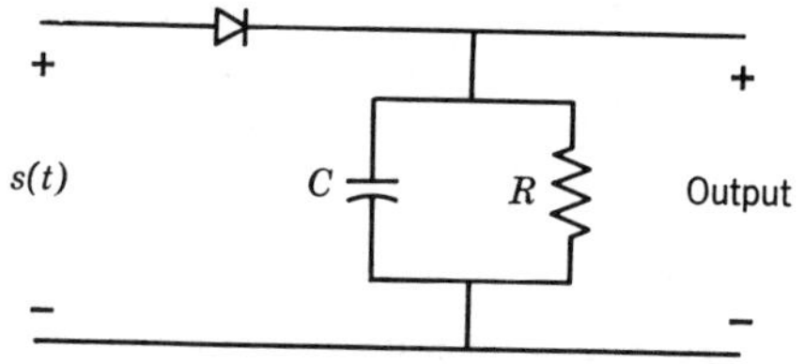

Figure P8.6

8.7 Appendix 8B contains a proof that the least mean-square linear filter produces an output error, $\epsilon(t)$, that is uncorrelated with the input. This does not imply that some nonlinear operation might not afford a smaller value of $\overline{\epsilon^2}$; in general, it will. When the input $x(t)$ is a zero-mean Gaussian process, however, linear filtering is best. Prove that this is true. *Hint.* Let $\mathbf{x}$ represent any set of observations of $x(t)$, let the desired output be $z(t)$, and let $f(\mathbf{x})$ denote an arbitrary nonlinear estimate of $z(t)$. Expand $\overline{[z(t) - f(\mathbf{x})]^2}$ in terms of the optimum linear estimate $\hat{z}(t)$, as in the proof of Eq. 8B.10, and show that the crossterms vanish.

8.8 Let x, y, and z be three zero-mean random variables with known variances and covariances.

a. Specify the constants a and b for which

$$\hat{z} \overset{\Delta}{=} ax + by$$

is the least mean-square error linear estimate of z, based on x and y.

b. Let $\tilde{x}$ and $\tilde{z}$ be the least mean-square error linear estimates, based only on y, of x and z. Without using the explicit parameter values specified in (a), show that

$$\tilde{z} = a\tilde{x} + by.$$

c. We may generalize (b) to the case in which $x(t)$, $y(t)$, and $z(t)$ are zero-mean, jointly wide-sense stationary random processes. Let

$$\hat{z}(t) = \int_{I_x} x(\alpha)\, h(t - \alpha)\, d\alpha + \int_{I_y} y(\alpha)\, g(t - \alpha)\, d\alpha,$$

$$\tilde{x}(t) = \int_{I_y} y(\alpha) f(t, t - \alpha)\, d\alpha; \qquad t \text{ in } I_x,$$

denote optimum linear estimates of $z(t)$ and $x(t)$. Without solving for the functions h, g, or f, prove that

$$\tilde{z}(t) = \int_{I_x} \tilde{x}(\alpha)\, h(t-\alpha)\, d\alpha + \int_{I_y} y(\alpha)\, g(t-\alpha)\, d\alpha$$

is the optimum estimate of $z(t)$ based only on knowledge of $y(t)$ within the interval I_y.

8.9 A Poisson impulse train $x(t)$ (see Problem 3.15), consisting of impulses occurring at an average of m per second, is the input to a realizable linear filter with impulse response $g(t)$ and output $y(t)$. The area of the ith impulse is a zero-mean, unit variance random variable and is statistically independent of the areas and times of occurrence of all other impulses. Determine the optimum realizable linear filter for predicting $y(T)$, $T > 0$, from $y(t)$, $t \leqslant 0$, when the criterion is to minimize the mean-square error $\overline{\epsilon^2} = \overline{[z(0) - \hat{z}(0)]^2}$. Here $z(0) = y(T)$ is the desired output, and $\hat{z}(0)$ is the output of the predictor at the time $t = 0$. Assume that the filter $g(t)$ possesses a realizable inverse, $g^{-1}(t)$. Discuss the optimum solution. In particular, consider the contribution of an impulse in $x(t)$ to both $y(T)$ and $\hat{z}(0)$ if

(i) the impulse occurs prior to $t = 0$,
(ii) the impulse occurs after $t = 0$.

(Bode and Shannon[14] treat problems of this sort in detail.)

8.10 A random variable m, with density function

$$p_m(\alpha) = \begin{cases} \frac{1}{2}; & |m| \leqslant 1, \\ 0; & \text{elsewhere}, \end{cases}$$

is communicated over an additive white Gaussian noise channel by means of the signal

$$s_m(t) = a(m)\, \varphi_1(t) + b(m)\, \varphi_2(t).$$

in which

$$\sqrt{a^2(m) + b^2(m)} \triangleq \rho(m) = 10m + 11,$$

$$\tan^{-1} \frac{b(m)}{a(m)} \triangleq \theta(m) = 5\pi(m+1).$$

a. Sketch the locus of the signal vector $\mathbf{s}_m$.
b. For weak noise, sketch the approximate behavior of the conditional mean-square error as a function of m when a maximum-likelihood receiver is used.
c. Estimate the probability of anomaly that results when $m = 0$ and the noise power density is $\mathcal{N}_0/2 = 2$.

8.11 Consider an FPM system with

$$s_m(t) = \begin{cases} A\sqrt{2} \sin 2\pi(f_0 + mW_0)t; & -T \leqslant t \leqslant T, \\ 0; & \text{elsewhere}, \end{cases}$$

operating over an additive white Gaussian noise channel with power density $\mathcal{N}_0/2$. Assume $T = \frac{1}{2}10^{-3}, A = 200\sqrt{2}, \mathcal{N}_0/2 = 1, |m| \leqslant 1$, and maximum-likelihood reception.

a. Estimate $\overline{\epsilon^2}$ if we require $P[\mathcal{A}] \approx 10^{-3};\ 10^{-4}$.
b. Estimate $P[\mathcal{A}]$ if we require $\overline{\epsilon^2} \approx 10^{-4};\ 10^{-5}$.
c. Determine (approximately) the minimum value of A such that by appropriate choice of W_0 we can simultaneously achieve $\overline{\epsilon^2} \approx 10^{-4}$ and $P[\mathcal{A}] \approx 10^{-4}$. What is the corresponding value of W_0?

8.12 A random variable m with p_m uniform over $[-1, 1]$ is communicated over an additive white Gaussian noise channel by means of the following signal scheme, which uses $M + 1$ orthonormal functions $\{\varphi_j(t)\}, j = 0, 1, \ldots, M$. The transmitter first determines the unique integer i and continuous variable $\tilde{m}$, $-1 \leqslant \tilde{m} < 1$, which satisfy the equation

$$m = -1 + \frac{2i + 1 + \tilde{m}}{M}; \qquad i = 0, 1, \ldots, M - 1.$$

The signal

$$s_m(t) = \sqrt{E_s - \tilde{E}}\ \varphi_i(t) + \tilde{m}\ \sqrt{\tilde{E}}\ \varphi_M(t)$$

is then transmitted. The receiver reconstructs the value of m from maximum-likelihood estimates of i and $\tilde{m}$.

a. Describe the signal locus. What is its total length? What is the value of the stretch factor?
b. Define the event "anomaly" and determine an upper bound on its probability.
c. Upper bound the mean-square error in the absence of anomaly.
d. Compare the system's performance with that of ordinary PPM. In particular, comment on the significance of freedom to choose the energy $\tilde{E}$ anywhere in the interval $[0, E_s]$.

8.13 Assume that the phase-and-frequency FPM signal $s_m(t)$ of Eq. 8.121 is used to transmit the value $m = \frac{1}{4}$ over an additive white Gaussian noise channel. Determine all other values of m in the interval $-1 \leqslant m \leqslant 1$ which produce a signal $s_m(t)$ orthogonal to the one actually transmitted. Consider intermediate values of m and justify estimating $P[\mathcal{A}]$ by Eq. 8.122c.

8.14 An antipodal FPM system is used to communicate a stationary lowpass Gaussian process with power density $\mathcal{M}_0/2 = \frac{1}{3}$ and bandwidth W_m. Assume that the available energy-to-noise ratio per sample is $E_s/\mathcal{N}_0 = 15$ and that we require a receiver output signal-to-noise ratio (in the absence of anomaly) equal to 10^4. What is the minimum transmission half-bandwidth such that the probability of generating a signal falling outside the transmission band is less than the probability of anomaly? *Hint.* Determine how $P[\mathcal{A}]$ is affected by relaxation of the constraint $|m| \leqslant 1$.

8.15 For ordinary PPM in weak additive white Gaussian noise we have approximated the mean-square error in the absence of anomaly by a linearized analysis involving the first two terms in the power series expansion of the signal

$$s_m(t) = \sqrt{E_s}\,\psi(t - mT_0); \qquad \psi(t) \triangleq \sqrt{2W}\,\frac{\sin 2\pi Wt}{2\pi Wt}.$$

The effect of slightly stronger noise can be estimated by considering three terms of the power series expansion. Because $|\mathbf{s}_m|$ and $|d\mathbf{s}_m/dm| \triangleq S$ are constant, the

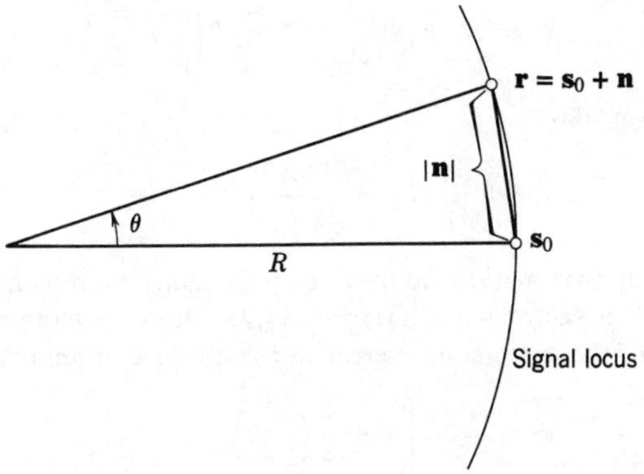

Figure P8.15

vector locus in the vicinity of $m = 0$ is identified as the arc of a circle, say in polar coordinates

$$\mathbf{s}_m \approx (R(m), \theta(m)) \qquad m \approx 0,$$

with

$$R(m) = R = \sqrt{E_s},$$

$$\frac{d\theta(m)}{dm} = \frac{1}{R}\left|\frac{d\mathbf{s}_m}{dm}\right| = \frac{S}{R}.$$

$\left[\text{From Eq. 8.93, } S^2 = \frac{E_s}{3}(2\pi T_0 W)^2.\right]$

a. Show that the coefficients in the truncated power series expansion

$$\mathbf{s}_m \approx \mathbf{s}_0 + m\dot{\mathbf{s}}_0 + \tfrac{1}{2}m^2\ddot{\mathbf{s}}_0; \qquad m \approx 0$$

are

$$\mathbf{s}_0 = \sqrt{E_s}\,\mathbf{i}_r$$

$$\dot{\mathbf{s}}_0 \triangleq \left.\frac{d\mathbf{s}_m}{dm}\right|_{m=0} = S\,\mathbf{i}_\theta$$

$$\ddot{\mathbf{s}}_0 \triangleq \left.\frac{d\mathbf{s}_m{}^2}{dm^2}\right|_{m=0} = -\frac{S^2}{\sqrt{E_s}}\,\mathbf{i}_r.$$

b. Because of the curvature of the signal locus, a noise vector of length $|\mathbf{n}|$ may introduce an error in the maximum-likelihood estimation of m that is greater than is accounted for by the linearized analysis. Show that the error in the situation illustrated in Fig. P8.15 is

$$(m - \hat{m}) = \frac{\sqrt{E_s}}{S}\,\theta,$$

in which θ is the solution to the equation

$$|\mathbf{n}| = 2\sqrt{E_s}\sin\frac{\theta}{2} \approx \sqrt{E_s}\,\theta\left(1 - \frac{\theta^2}{24}\right).$$

For small θ show that

$$\theta \approx \frac{|\mathbf{n}|}{\sqrt{E_s}}\left(1 + \frac{1}{24}\frac{|\mathbf{n}|^2}{E_s}\right).$$

c. To a first approximation we may consider the relevant component of $\mathbf{n}$ as a one-dimensional vector with variance $\mathcal{N}_0/2$. Show that the resulting weak-noise estimate of the mean-square error in the absence of anomaly is

$$\overline{\epsilon^2} \approx \frac{\mathcal{N}_0/2}{S^2}\left[1 + \frac{1}{4}\left(\frac{\mathcal{N}_0}{2E_s}\right)\right].$$

The output noise increment attributable to the local curvature of $\mathbf{s}_m$ is called "quasi-Gaussian."

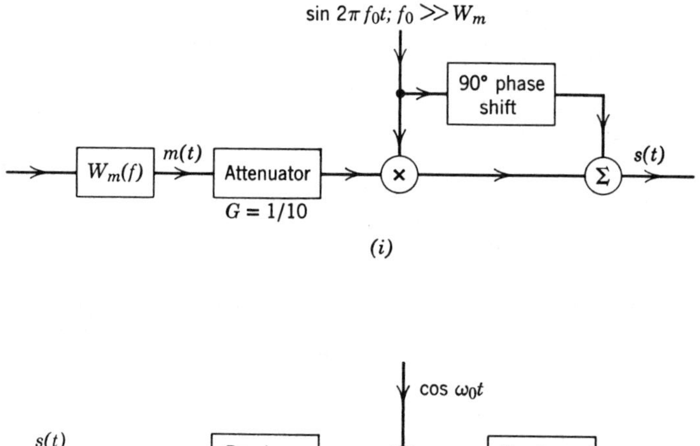

(i)

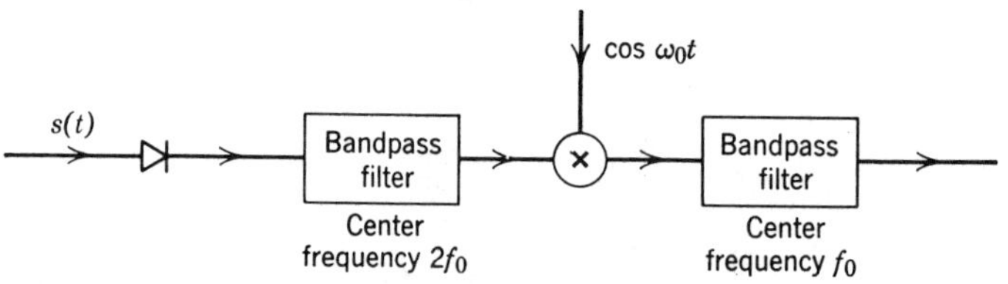

(ii)

Figure P8.16

8.16 The DSB-SC modulator/phase shift combination shown in Fig. P8.16(i) produces an output signal $s(t)$ called "quadrature modulated."

a. Show that $s(t)$ closely approximates a PM signal when G is $\frac{1}{10}$ or less and $|m(t)| \leqslant 1$.
b. The modulation index of the PM signal $\cos 2\pi[f_0 t + W_2 m(t)]$ is defined as $\beta \triangleq 2\pi W_2$. Why? What is the value of β for $s(t)$?
c. What does the modulation index become if $s(t)$ is first applied to a frequency doubler and then heterodyned back to center frequency f_0, as shown in Fig. P8.16(ii)? (The half-bandwidth of each filter is much greater than W_m but less than f_0.)
d. Assume that there are k stages of doubling and frequency translation and that the resulting signal is amplified and transmitted over an additive white Gaussian noise channel with $\mathcal{N}_0/2 = 10^{-11}$ joule. What value of k is required if we use maximum-likelihood reception and require $\overline{n^2(t)} = 10^{-4}$ (in the absence of anomaly); assume that $W_m = 3$ kc and the received power is $P_s = 10^{-6}$ watt.
e. Show how the system analyzed can be modified to provide a broad-band FM signal. (Armstrong[3] generated signals this way.)

8.17 Consider a lowpass modulating signal $m(t)$ of T-sec duration. Show that FM and PM yield equivalent total mean-square error (in the absence of anomaly) when maximum-likelihood receivers are used and the transmitted bandwidth is normalized in accordance with Eq. 8.164. *Hint.* Expand the FM modulating signal (approximately) in an N-term orthonormal Fourier series analogous to Eq. 8.152b and use the fact that

$$\sum_{k=1}^{N} k^2 = \frac{N(N+1)(2N+1)}{6}.$$

8.18 Assume that the weak-noise FMFB analysis of Appendix 8B remains valid as the modulation index W_1/W_m is increased indefinitely, with signal power A^2 and noise power density $\mathcal{N}_0/2$ held constant. Show that such an assumption violates the channel-capacity constraint of Eq. 8.191.

8.19 An idealized phase-lock PM receiver is illustrated in Fig. P8.19. The bandpass filter $H_1(f)$ is broad enough to pass $s_{\mathbf{m}}(t)$ with negligible distortion.

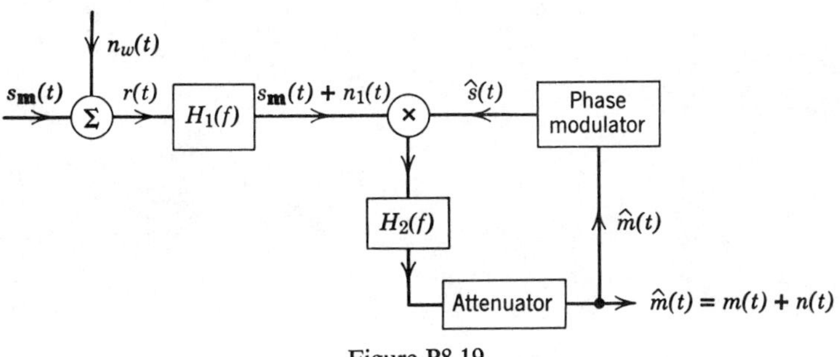

Figure P8.19

Assume that the modulating signal $m(t)$ is the output from an ideal lowpass filter of bandwidth W_m and that

$$s_m(t) = A\sqrt{2}\cos 2\pi[f_0t + W_2m(t)],$$

$$\hat{s}(t) = \sqrt{2}\cos 2\pi[f_0t + \hat{W}\hat{m}(t)]; \qquad \hat{W} < W_2.$$

a. $H_2(f)$ represents another ideal (rectangular passband) filter. Determine the smallest bandwidth for $H_2(f)$, and the value of the attenuator gain, such that $\hat{m}(t) = m(t)$ in the absence of noise.

b. Determine the mean-square value of the output noise $\overline{n^2(t)}$ when the multiplier input noise is weak; that is, when $\overline{n_1^2(t)} \ll A^2$.

8.20 A conventional PCM system, with binary antipodal signaling and without error-correcting coding, is used to communicate an ideally band-limited 3-kc voice signal, $m(t)$, over a system that incorporates 20 repeaters. At each repeater a decision is made on each bit and the PCM wave is reconstructed before retransmission. Each link is disturbed (independently) by additive white Gaussian noise with $\mathcal{N}_0/2 = 10^{-10}$ and the maximum allowable transmission level produces 10^{-4} watt of received signal power. Assume that the largest tolerable probability of anomaly (per speech sample) is 10^{-4} and that $|m(t)| \leqslant 1$. What is the smallest attainable value of mean-square error per sample?

8.21 The voice signal of Problem 8.20 is now to be communicated over a single infinite-bandwidth, additive white Gaussian noise channel with $\mathcal{N}_0/2 = 10^{-3}$ joule.

a. Determine the minimum value of peak transmitter power (in watts) required to obtain

$$\overline{[m(t) - \hat{m}(t)]^2} \approx 10^{-5}$$

when PCM is used in conjunction with block coding and maximum-likelihood decoding.

b. Repeat (a) for convolutional coding and sequential decoding.

References and Selected Reading

1. Adcock, T. G. "Error Statistics with Optimum Pulse Position Modulation," S. M. Thesis, MIT, Department of Electrical Engineering, June 1963.
2. Arguimbau, L. B. *Vacuum-Tube Circuits and Transistors*, Wiley, New York, 1956.
3. Armstrong, E. H. "A Method of Reducing Disturbances in Radio Signaling by a System of Frequency Modulation," *Proc. IRE*, **24**, 689–740, May 1936.
4. Arthurs, E., and H. Dym. "On the Optimum Detection of Digital Signals in the Presence of White Gaussian Noise—A Geometric Interpretation and a Study of Three Basic Data Transmission Systems," *IRE Trans. Commun. Systems*, **CS-10,** 336–372, December 1962.
5. Baghdady, E. J. (Ed.) *Lectures on Communication System Theory*, McGraw-Hill, New York, 1961.
6. Berlekamp, E. R. "Block Coding with Noiseless Feedback," PhD Thesis, MIT, Department of Electrical Engineering, June, 1964.
7. Bartee, T. C., and D. I. Schneider. "An Electronic Decoder for Bose-Chaudhuri-Hocquenghem Error-Correcting Codes," *IRE Trans. Inform. Theory*, **IT-8,** S17–S24, September 1962.
8. Bendat, J. S. *Principles and Applications of Random Noise Theory*, Wiley, New York, 1958.
9. Bennett, W. R. *Electrical Noise*, McGraw-Hill, New York, 1960.
10. Birkhoff, G., and S. Mac Lane. *A Survey of Modern Algebra*, Macmillan, New York, 1953.
11. Black, H. S. *Modulation Theory*, Van Nostrand, Princeton, N.J., 1953.
12. Bloom, F. J., et al. "Improvement of Binary Transmission by Null-Zone Reception," *Proc. IRE*, **45,** 963–975, July 1957.
13. Bluestein, G., and K. L. Jordan, Jr. "An Investigation of the Fano Sequential Decoding Algorithm by Computer Simulation," *MIT Lincoln Laboratory Report 62 G-5*, July 1963.
14. Bode, H. W., and C. E. Shannon. "A Simplified Derivation of Linear Least-square Smoothing and Prediction Theory," *Proc. IRE*, **38,** 417–425, April 1950.
15. Bose, R. C., and D. K. Ray-Chaudhuri. "On a Class of Error-Correcting Binary Group Codes," *Inform. and Control*, **3,** 68–79, March 1960.
16. Campbell, G. A. U.S. Patent 1,227,113, May 22, 1917, "Basic Types of Electric Wave Filters."
17. Carson, J. R. "Notes on the Theory of Modulation," *Proc. IEEE*, **51,** No. 6, 893–896, June 1963. (Reprint from *Proc. IRE*, **10,** 57–64, February 1922.)
18. Chernoff, H. "A Measure of Asymptotic Efficiency for Tests of a Hypothesis Based on a Sum of Observations," *Ann. Math. Stat.* **23,** 493–507, 1952.

19. Cramer, H. *Mathematical Methods of Statistics*, Princeton University Press, Princeton, N.J., 1946.

20. Darlington, S. "Demodulation of Wideband, Low-Power FM Signals," *Bell System Tech. J.*, **43,** No. 1, Part 2, 339–374, January 1964.

21. Davenport, W. B., Jr., and W. L. Root. *An Introduction to the Theory of Random Signals and Noise*, McGraw-Hill, New York, 1958.

22. Doelz, M.,E. Heald, and D. Martin. "Binary Data Transmission Techniques for Linear Systems," *Proc. IRE,* **45,** 656–661, May 1957.

23. Dollard, P. M. "On the Time-Bandwidth Concentration of Signal Functions Forming Given Geometric Vector Configurations," *IEEE Trans. Inform. Theory,* **IT-10,** 328–338, Oct. 1964.

24. Dugundji, J. "Envelopes and Pre-envelopes of Real Waveforms," *IRE Trans. Inform. Theory*, **IT-4,** 53–57, March 1958.

25. Electrical Engineering Staff, MIT. *Applied Electronics*, 2nd ed., Technology Press and Wiley, New York, 1954.

26. Enloe, L. H. "Decreasing the Threshold in FM by Frequency Feedback," *Proc. IRE,* **50,** 18–30, January 1962.

27. Fano, R. M. *The Transmission of Information*, The MIT Press and Wiley, New York, 1961.

28. Fano, R. M. "A Heuristic Discussion of Probabilistic Decoding," *IEEE Trans. Inform. Theory*, **IT-9,** 64–74, April 1963.

29. Feller, W. *An Introduction to Probability Theory and Its Applications*, 2nd ed., Wiley, New York, 1957.

30. Fisz, M. *Probability Theory and Mathematical Statistics*, 3rd ed., Wiley, New York, 1963.

31. Gallager, R. G. *Low-Density Parity-Check Codes*, MIT Press, Cambridge, Mass., 1963.

32. Gallager, R. G. "A Simple Derivation of the Coding Theorem and Some Applications," *IEEE Trans. Inform. Theory*, **IT-11,** 3–18, January 1965.

33. Gallager, R. G. "Information Theory," Chapter 4 of *The Mathematics of Physics and Chemistry*, H. Margenau and G. M. Murphy (Eds.), Van Nostrand, Princeton, N.J., vol. 2, 1964.

34. Gallager, R. G. "Lower Bounds on the Tails of Probability Distributions," *MIT Research Lab. of Electronics, Quarterly Progress Report*, No. 77, 277–291, April 1965.

35. Gnedenko, B. V., and A. N. Kolmogorov. *Limit Distributions for Sums of Independent Random Variables*, Addison-Wesley, Cambridge, Mass., 1954.

36. Golomb, S. W. (Ed.) *Digital Communications with Space Applications*, Prentice-Hall, Englewood Cliffs, N.J., 1964.

37. Guillemin, E. A. *The Mathematics of Circuit Analysis*, Technology Press and Wiley, New York, 1949.

38. Guillemin, E. A. *Theory of Linear Physical Systems*, Wiley, New York, 1963.

39. Hamming, R. W. "Error Detecting and Error Correcting Codes," *Bell System Tech. J.*, **29,** No. 2, 147–160, April 1950.

40. Harman, W. W. *Principles of the Statistical Theory of Communication*, McGraw-Hill, New York, 1963.

41. Hartley, R. V. L. "Transmission of Information," *Bell System Tech. J.*, **7,** No. 3, 535–563, July 1928.

42. Helstrom, C. W. "*Statistical Theory of Signal Detection*," Pergamon, New York, 1960.

43. Hildebrand, F. B. *Methods of Applied Mathematics*, Prentice-Hall, New York, 1952.

44. Huffman, D. A. "The Generation of Impulse-Equivalent Pulse Trains," *IRE Trans. Inform. Theory*, **IT-8,** S10-S16, September 1962.

45. Jacobs, I. M. "Method and Merit of Binary Coding for Analog Channels," *Proc. Nat'l Electronics Conf.*, **18,** 765–773, 1962.

46. Jahnke, E., and F. Emde, *Tables of Functions*, 4th ed., Dover, New York, 1945.

47. Kailath, T. "Optimum Receivers for Randomly Varying Channels," *Proc. 4th London Symp. Inform. Theory*, 109–122, C. Cherry (Ed.), Butterworths, Washington, 1961.

48. Kennedy, R. S. "Finite State Binary Symmetric Channels," Sc.D. Thesis, Department of Electrical Engineering, MIT, January 1963.

49. Kennedy, R. S. *Performance Limitations of Fading Dispersive Channels.* (To be published.)

50. Kennedy, R. S., and I. L. Lebow. "Signal Design for Dispersive Channels," *IEEE Spectrum*, **1,** No. 3, 231–237, March 1964.

51. Kotel'nikov, V. A. *The Theory of Optimum Noise Immunity*, McGraw-Hill, New York, 1959. (Doctoral dissertation presented in January 1947 before the academic council of the Molotov Energy Institute in Moscow.)

52. Landau, H. J. and D. Slepian. "On the Optimality of the Regular Simplex Code," to be published in Bell System Tech. J.

53. Landau, H. J., and H. O. Pollak. "Prolate Spheroidal Wave Functions, Fourier Analysis and Uncertainty-III: The Dimension of the Space of Essentially Time- and Band-Limited Signals," *Bell System Tech. J.*, **41,** 1295–1336, July 1962.

54. Lebow, I., et al. "Application of Sequential Decoding to High-Rate Data Communication on a Telephone Line," *IRE Trans. Inform. Theory*, **IT-9,** 124–126, April 1963.

55. Lee, Y. W. *Statistical Theory of Communication*, Wiley, New York, 1960.

56. Magnus, W., and F. Oberhettinger. *Special Functions of Mathematical Physics*, Chelsea, New York, 1949.

57. Massey, J. L. *Threshold Decoding*, MIT Press, Cambridge, Mass., 1963.

58. Middleton, D. *An Introduction to Statistical Communication Theory*, McGraw-Hill, New York, 1960.

59. National Bureau of Standards. *Handbook of Mathematical Functions*, Applied Math. Series 55, U.S. Government Printing Off., Washington, 1964.

60. Nyquist, H. "Certain Factors Affecting Telegraph Speed," *Bell System Tech. J.*, **3,** No. 2, 324–346, April 1924.

61. Oliver, B. M., J. R. Pierce, and C. E. Shannon. "The Philosophy of PCM," *Proc. IRE*, **36,** 1324–1331, November 1948.

62. Papoulis, A. *The Fourier Integral and Its Applications*, McGraw-Hill, New York, 1962.

63. Parzen, E. *Stochastic Processes*, Holden-Day, San Francisco, 1962.

64. Parzen, E. *Modern Probability Theory and Its Applications*, Wiley, New York, 1960.

65. Perry, K. E., and J. M. Wozencraft. "SECO: A Self-Regulating Error Correcting Coder-Decoder," *IRE Trans. Inform. Theory*, **IT-8,** S128–S135, September 1962.

66. Peterson, W. W. *Error-Correcting Codes*, Wiley, New York, 1961.

67. Pierce, J. N. "Theoretical Diversity Improvement in Frequency-shift-keying," *Proc. IRE*, **46,** 903–910, May 1958.

68. Reiffen, B. "Sequential Decoding for Discrete Input Memoryless Channels," *IRE Trans. Inform. Theory*, **IT-8,** 208–220, April 1962.

69. Rice, S. O. "Mathematical Analysis of Random Noise," *Bell System Tech. J.*, **23,** 283–332, July 1944; **24,** 46–156, January 1945.

70. Rice, S. O. "Noise in FM Receivers," Chapter 25 of *Proceedings of the Symposium on Time Series Analysis*, M. Rosenblatt (Ed.), Wiley, New York, 1963.

71. Schwartz, M. *Information Transmission, Modulation, and Noise*, McGraw-Hill, New York, 1959.

72. Shannon, C. E. "Communication in the Presence of Noise," *Proc. IRE*, **37,** No. **1,** 10–21, January 1949.

73. Shannon, C. E. Unpublished Seminar Notes, Department of Electrical Engineering, MIT, Spring 1956.

74. Shannon, C. E. "Probability of Error for Optimal Codes in a Gaussian Channel," *Bell System Tech, J.*, **38,** 611–656, May 1959.

75. Shannon, C. E., and W. Weaver. *The Mathematical Theory of Communication*, University of Illinois Press, Urbana, 1949.

76. Slepian, D. "A Class of Binary Signaling Alphabets," *Bell System Tech. J.*, **35,** 203–234, 1956.

77. Slepian, D. "The Threshold Effect in Modulation Systems that Expand Bandwidth," *IRE Trans. Inform. Theory*, **IT-8,** S122–S127, September 1962.

78. Stiglitz, I. G. "Sequential Decoding with Feedback," Sc.D. Thesis, Department of Electrical Engineering, MIT, August 1963.

79. Thompson, B. J., D. O. North, and W. A. Harris. "Fluctuations in Space-charge-limited Currents at Moderately High Frequencies," *RCA Review*, January 1940 et seq.

80. Turin, G. L. "An Introduction to Matched Filters," *IRE Trans. Inform. Theory*, **IT-6,** 311–329, June 1960.

81. Turin, G. L. "On Optimal Diversity Reception, II," *IRE Trans. Commun. Systems*, **CS-10,** 22–31, March 1962.

82. Van der Ziel, A. *Noise*, Prentice-Hall, Englewood Cliffs, N.J., 1954.

83. Watson, G. H. *A Treatise on the Theory of Bessel Functions*, The University Press, Cambridge, 1944; Macmillan, New York, 1944.

84. Wiener, N., *The Extrapolation, Interpolation, and Smoothing of Stationary Time Series with Engineering Applications*, Wiley, New York, 1949. (Original work appeared as an MIT Radiation Laboratory Report in 1942.)

85. Woodward, P. M. *Probability and Information Theory, with Applications to Radar*, McGraw-Hill, New York, 1955; Pergamon, London, 1953.

86. Wolfowitz, J. *Coding Theorems of Information Theory*, Prentice-Hall, Englewood Cliffs, N.J., 1961.

87. Wozencraft, J. M. "Active Filters," U.S. Patent No. 2,880,316, March 31, 1959.

88. Wozencraft, J. M., and M. Horstein. "Coding for Two-Way Channels," *Proc. 4th London Symp. Inform. Theory*, 11–23, C. Cherry (Ed.), Butterworths, Washington, 1961.

89. Wozencraft, J. M., and R. S. Kennedy. "Modulation and Demodulation for Probabilistic Coding," *IEEE Trans. Inform. Theory*, **IT-12,** 291–297, July 1966.

90. Wozencraft, J. M., and B. Reiffen. "Sequential Decoding," Technology Press and Wiley, New York, 1961.

91. Yudkin, H. L. "Channel State Testing in Information Decoding," Sc.D. Thesis, Department of Electrical Engineering, MIT, September 1964.

92. Zadeh, L., and C. Desoer *Linear System Theory*, McGraw-Hill, New York, 1963.

93. Zetterburg, L. H. "Data Transmission over a Noisy Gaussian Channel," *Trans. Roy. Inst. Technol.*, Stockholm, No. 184, 1961.

94. Ziv, J. "Coding and Decoding for Time-Discrete Amplitude-Continuous Memoryless Channels," *IRE Trans. Inform. Theory,* **IT-8,** S199–S205, September 1962.

95. Ziv, J. "Further results on the Asymptotic Complexity of an Iterative Coding Scheme," *IEEE Trans. Inform. Theory*, **IT-12,** 168–171.

96. Ziv, J. "A New Efficient Coding and Decoding Scheme for Memoryless Channels," *IEEE Trans. Inform. Theory.* (To be published.)

Index